R. Gupta's®

National Testing Agency (NTA)

UGC-NET/JRF

Junior Research Fellowship & Assistant Professor Eligibility Exam

LAW

Previous Years' Papers

PAPER II

by
RPH Editorial Board

2027
EDITION

RAMESH PUBLISHING HOUSE, NEW DELHI

Published by

O.P. Gupta *for* Ramesh Publishing House

Admin. Office

12-H, New Daryaganj Road, Opp. Officers' Mess,
New Delhi-110002 ✆ 23275224, 23245124

E-mail: info@rameshpublishinghouse.com

For Online Shopping: www.rameshpublishinghouse.com

Showroom

- Balaji Market, Nai Sarak, Delhi-110006 ✆ 23282525 📱 9354373464
- 4457, Nai Sarak, Delhi-110006, ✆ 23918938

Book Code: R-2688

ISBN: 978-93-5477-855-1

Price: ₹ 645

Printed at: Deepak Offset, Delhi

CONTENTS

UGC-NET/JRF—(PAPER-II) LAW

Previous Years' Paper

National Testing Agency (NTA)

UGC-NET Junior Research Fellowship & Assistant Professor Eligibility Exam

LAW, DECEMBER-2025

(Exam held on 31-12-2025)

PAPER-II

1. 'Doctrine of Common Employment' has the origin in which of the following case?

1. Priestley V/s Fowler
2. Brochle Bank V/s Noor Ahmed
3. Governor General in Council V/s Zena Wells
4. Secretary of State V/s Rukmani Ben

2. In educational institutions, reservations of seats in favour of the Scheduled Castes and the Scheduled Tribes is governed by which Article of the Constitution of India?

1. Article 21-A
2. Article 19
3. Article 15
4. Article 16

3. Mark the incorrect statements about the circumstances in which Limited Liability Partnership (LLP) may be wound up by the tribunal

A. Where for a period of more than three months the number of partners is reduced to below two

B. If the LLP has acted against the interest of the sovereignty and integrity of India

C. If the LLP has made a default in filing with the Registrar the statement of account and solvency or Annual Return for any two consecutive financial years

D. If LLP is unable to pay its debts

Choose the *correct* answer from the options given below:

1. B, D only
2. A, C only
3. C, D only
4. A, B only

4. Which of the following case primarily deals with the concept of Uniform Civil Code?

1. Seema V/s Ashwani Kumar
2. Sarla Mudgal V/s Union of India
3. Dipanwita Roy V/s Ronobroto Roy
4. Pratibha Rani V/s Suraj Kumar

5. Given below are two statements: one is labelled as Assertion (A) and the other is labelled as Reason (R).

Assertion (A): United States of America is a recognized example of entrenched constitutional tradition.

Reason (R): US Constitution is the oldest still functioning and longest written Constitution of the world.

In the light of the above statements, choose the ***most appropriate*** answer from the options given below

1. Both (A) and (R) are correct and (R) is the correct explanation of (A)
2. Both (A) and (R) are correct, but (R) is NOT the correct explanation of (A)
3. (A) is correct, but (R) is not correct
4. (A) is not correct, but (R) is correct

6. Match the List-I with List-II.

List-I (*International Instruments on Concept of Right to Development*)	List-II (*Year*)
A. Declaration on the Right to Development by the UN General Assembly	I. 2000
B. Durban Declaration and Programme of Action	II. 1993
C. Millennium Declaration	III. 1986
D. Vienna Declaration and Programme of Action	IV. 2001

Choose the ***correct*** answer from the options given below:

1. A-I, B-II, C-III, D-IV
2. A-I, B-III, C-IV, D-II
3. A-III, B-IV, C-I, D-II
4. A-IV, B-III, C-II, D-I

7. National Commission for Minority Educational Institution Act was enacted by the Parliament in which year?

1. 1992 2. 1995
3. 2002 4. 2004

8. Given below are two statements: one is labelled as Assertion (A) and the other is labelled as Reason (R).

Assertion (A): The owner in possession of the thing has the right to exclude all others from the possession and enjoyment of it.

Reason (R): The right to maintain or recover possession of a tiling as against all others is an essential part of ownership.

In the light of the above statements, choose the ***most appropriate*** answer from the options given below:

1. Both (A) and (R) are correct and (R) is the correct explanation of (A)
2. Both (A) and (R) are correct, but (R) is NOT the correct explanation of (A)
3. (A) is correct, but (R) is not correct
4. (A) is not correct, but (R) is correct

9. Who among the following defines legal right as "a legally protected interest"?

1. Thibaut 2. Allen
3. Ihering 4. Austin

10. Match the List-I with List-II.

List-I (*Doctrine*)	List-II (*Case Law*)
A. Doctrine of Pith and Substance	I. K.C.G. Narayan Dew V/s State of Orissa
B. Doctrine of Territorial Nexus	II. M. Karunanidhi V/s Union of India
C. Doctrine of Repugnancy	III. P.K. Mukherjee V/s Bank of Khulna
D. Doctrine of Colourable Legislation	IV. Wallace V/s Income Tax Commissioner

Choose the ***correct*** answer from the options given below:

1. A-I, B-II, C-III, D-IV
2. A-III, B-II, C-IV, D-I
3. A-III, B-IV, C-II, D-I
4. A-III, B-IV, C-I, D-II

11. Which of the following are true with respect to the decision in State of Maharashtra V/s Praful B. Desai (2003) 4 SCC 601?

A. The law must adopt to the change in society and should accept the new technology
B. The evidence in a criminal trial can be both oral and documentary: and electronic record including video conferencing
C. Video conferencing does not constitute evidence as defined in Section 3 of Indian Evidence Act.
D. Presence under Section 273 Cr. P. C. cannot include presence through video conferencing

Choose the ***correct*** answer from the options given below:

1. A and D only 2. B and C only
3. A and B only 4. C and D only

12. Which of the following case illustrates the patent bargain metaphor which is an application of social contract theory?
   1. Universal Oil Products V/s Globe Oil & Refining Co.
   2. Georgia V/s Public Resource Org. Inc.
   3. Fogerty V/s Fantasy Inc.
   4. Fourth Estate Public Benefit Corpn. V/s Wall-street.Com., LLC

13. Which of the following statements are correct?
   A. The idea of three branches of government was advocated by Montesquieu.
   B. The US Supreme Court decided the case of Marbury V/s Madison in the year 1803.
   C. Article 3 of the US Constitution is identified with independence of the judiciary
   D. The Ninth Amendment to the US Constitution provides prohibitions against cruel and unusual punishment.
   E. The Eight Amendment to the US Constitution provides for rights retained by the people

   Choose the *correct* answer from the options given below:
   1. A, C and E only
   2. B, D and E only
   3. A, B and C only
   4. B, C and D only

14. Arrange the following grounds of Divorce in the order of their appearance under Section 13(1) of the Hindu Marriage Act, 1955.
   A. Suffering from venereal disease in a communicable form.
   B. Ceased to be a Hindu by conversion
   C. Renounced the world by entering any religious order
   D. Has not been heard of as being alive for a period of seven years or more.
   E. Cruelty.

   Choose the *correct* answer from the options given below:
   1. D, C, A, B, E 2. A, E, B, C, D
   3. B, E, C, D, A 4. E, B, A, C, D

15. Given below are two statements: one is labelled as Assertion (A) and the other is labelled as Reason (R).

   Assertion (A): In England, due to historical reasons British Parliament is a judicial as well as legislative body.

   Reason (R): There is no written Constitution to limit the authority of the Parliament in Britain.

   In the light of the above statements, choose the ***most appropriate*** answer from the options given below:
   1. Both (A) and (R) are correct and (R) is the correct explanation of (A)
   2. Both (A) and (R) are correct, but (R) is NOT the correct explanation of (A)
   3. (A) is correct, but (R) is not correct
   4. (A) is not correct, but (R) is correct

16. Given below are two statements: one is labelled as Assertion (A) and the other is labelled as Reason (R).

   Assertion (A): Article 30 of Constitution of India confers a right on all minorities to establish and administer educational institutions.

   Reason (R): The right to establish and administer educational institutions by the minorities is based solely on religion.

   In the light of the above statements, choose the ***most appropriate*** answer from the options given below:
   1. Both (A) and (R) are correct and (R) is the correct explanation of (A)
   2. Both (A) and (R) are correct, but (R) is NOT the correct explanation of (A)
   3. (A) is correct, but (R) is not correct
   4. (A) is not correct, but (R) is correct

17. Arrange the following cases chronologically (starting from earliest to the latest)

A. Minerva Mills Ltd. V/s Union of India
B. Samsher Singh V/s State of Punjab
C. S.P Anand V/s H. D. Deve Gowda
D. U.N.R. Rao V/s Smt. Indira Gandhi

Choose the *correct* answer from the options given below:

1. D, B, A, C 2. D, B, C, A
3. C, B, A, D 4. A, B, C, D

18. Match the List-I with List-II.

List-I (*Exception to Murder*)	List-II (*Corresponding Provision*)
A. Exception-2	I. Act of Public Servant
B. Exception-3	II. Exceeding the right of private defense
C. Exception-4	III. Sudden fight
D. Exception-5	IV. Death by consent

Choose the *correct* answer from the options given below:

1. A-I, B-II, C-III, D-IV
2. A-II, B-I, C-III, D-IV
3. A-I, B-II, C-IV, D-III
4. A-IV, B-III, C-II, D-I

19. Arrange the following provisions from the Information Technology Act. 2000 in the ascending order of their appearance in the Act.

A. Validity of contracts formed through electronic means.
B. Use of electronic records and electronic signatures in Government and its agencies
C. Retention of electronic records
D. Publication of rules, regulation etc. in electronic Gazette.

Choose the *correct* answer from the options given below:

1. A, B, C, D 2. D, C, A, B
3. B, C, D, A 4. C, D, B, A

20. Which of the following case decided b[y] the Supreme Court of India primarily deal[s] with the maintenance to be paid in case o[f] Live-in relationships?

1. Lata Kamat V/s Vilas
2. Veena Rani V/s Ramesh Kumar
3. Pushpa Devi V/s Radheysham
4. Chanmuniya V/s Virendra Kumar Singh Kushwaha

21. Match the List-I with List-II.

List-I (*Feature*)	List-II (*Application*)
A. Executive Legislation	I. Appointment and removal of Judges
B. Collective Responsibility	II. Administrative adjudication
C. Quasi-Judicial Function	III. Parliamentary form of government
D. Independence of Judiciary	IV. Ordinance

Choose the *correct* answer from the options given below:

1. A-I, B-II, C-III, D-IV
2. A-I, B-II, C-IV, D-III
3. A-II, B-I, C-IV, D-III
4. A-IV, B-III, C-II, D-I

22. Under which doctrine a person is liable if he intended to kill 'X' but kills 'Z' whose death he neither intended nor knows to likely to cause:

1. Doctrine of res-judicata
2. Doctrine of mens rea
3. Doctrine of transfer of malice
4. Doctrine of absolute necessity

23. Which of the following statements are correct about e-rickshaw and e-cart as per the Motor Vehicles Act, 1988?

A. It is battery powered vehicle
B. Power is not exceeding 4000 Watt
C. It has three wheals for carrying passengers only
D. Not a special purpose vehicle

Choose the *correct* answer from the options given below:

1. C, D only 2. A, B only
3. B, C only 4. A, D only

24. In which of the following case, the Supreme Court declared that till a law is made by the Parliament, the appointment to the posts of Chief Election Commissioner of India and Election Commission shall be done by the President of India on the basis of the advice tendered by a Committee?

1. S.S. Dhannoa V/s Union of India
2. T.N. Seshan V/s Union of India
3. Anoop Baranwal V/s Union of India
4. In Re Presidential Reference, 2002

25. Which of the following cases deal with the interpretation of the 'personal liberty' under Article 21 of the Constitution of India?

A. Kharak Singh V/s State of U.P.
B. Mohini Jain V/s State of Karnataka
C. Maneka Gandhi V/s Union of India
D. A.K. Gopalan V/s Union of India

Choose the *correct* answer from the options given below:

1. A, B, C only
2. A, B only
3. A, C, D only
4. B, C, D only

26. Which of the following right is not available under the Sale of Goods Act, 1930 to the Unpaid Seller notwithstanding that the property in the goods may have passed to the buyer?

1. A lien on the goods for the price while he is in possession of them.
2. In case of the insolvency of the buyer, a right of stopping the goods in transit after he has parted with the possession of them
3. A right of re-sale as limited by the Act
4. A right of withholding delivery

27. In which of the following case, the Supreme Court of India directed the Courts and Tribunals to ensure that all uploaded judgments and orders are signed using digital signatures and not as scanned copies of printed version?

1. Ameena Begum V/s The State of Telangana (2023)
2. D.K. Basu V/s State of West Bengal (1997)
3. State Bank of India V/s Ajay Kumar (2021)
4. Virbhadra Singh V/s Enforcement Directorate (2017)

28. Who amongst the following are included in definition of 'Manufacturer' in the Consumer Protection Act, 2019?

A. Maker of goods or parts
B. One who assembles goods or parts
C. Who put his own mark on goods made by others
D. One who sells goods

Choose the *correct* answer from the options given below:

1. A, B, C only 2. B, C, D only
3. A, C, D only 4. A, B, D only

29. Certain principles to distinguish obligatory from recommendatory injunctions can be found in which of the following ancient Indian texts?

1. Jijnaysa 2. Mimansa
3. Rashtravani 4. Garuda Nyaya

30. Arrange the following in the order in which they appear in the Preamble to the Indian Constitution:

A. Equality B. Justice
C. Liberty D. Fraternity

Choose the *correct* answer from the options given below:

1. A, B, C, D 2. B, C, D, A
3. B, C, A, D 4. C, B, D, A

31. Which of the following statements are correct?

A. Holland remarked that international law is the vanishing point of jurisprudence

B. Holland was an analytical jurist.

C. The Vienna Convention on the Law of Treaties provides that a treaty may be binding on third States as well.

D. Grotius and Vattel were positivists

E. The International Court of Justice recognizes the sources of international law under Article 36 (1) (c) of its statute.

Choose the ***correct*** answer from the options given below:

1. B, D and E only
2. A, B and C only
3. A, C and E only
4. C, D and E only

32. Match the List-I with List-II.

List-I (***Concept under Indian Contract Act, 1872***)	**List-II** (***Corresponding Sections***)
A. Payment by interested person	I. Section 69
B. Payment made under mistake or coercion	II. Section 72
C. Liability of pay for non-gratuitous acts	III. Section 68
D. Supply of necessaries	IV. Section 70

Choose the ***correct*** answer from the options given below:

1. A-II, B-III, C-I, D-IV
2. A-IV, B-I, C-III, D-II
3. A-I, B-II, C-IV, D-III
4. A-III, B-IV, C-II, D-I

33. Arrange the following cases relating to extradition in their chronological order.

A. Soering V/s United Kingdom

B. Chitat V/s Canada

C. United States V/s Rauscher

D. Daya Singh Lahoria V/s Union of India

E. Kindler V/s Canada

Choose the ***correct*** answer from the options given below:

1. C, A, E, B, D
2. B, D, C, E, A
3. A, B, C, D, E
4. E, C, D, A, B

34. National Green Tribunal Act come into force on which date?

1. 18 Oct 2010
2. 18 Nov 2010
3. 8 Oct 2010
4. 8 Nov 2010

35. Match the List-I with List-II.

List-I (***Basic Feature***)	**List-II** (***Judge and the case***)
A. Independence of the judiciary	I. Fazal Ali - SP Gupta V/s Union of India
B. Federal system	II. Bachawat - Golak Nath V/s State of Punjab
C. Secularism	III. Reddy - Kesavananda Bharati V/s State of Kerala
D. Parliamentary system of government	IV. Khanna - Indira Gandhi V/s Raj Narain

Choose the ***correct*** answer from the options given below:

1. A-I, B-II, C-IV, D-III
2. A-III, B-IV, C-II, D-I
3. A-I, B-III, C-IV, D-II
4. A-I, B-II, C-III, D-IV

36. Match the List-I with List-II.

List-I (***Article from the Indian Constitution***)	**List-II** (***Corresponding Provisions***)
A. Article 325	I. One general electoral roll
B. Article 326	II. Adult Suffrage
C. Article 327	III. Bar to interference by courts in electoral matters
D. Article 329	IV. Power of Parliament to make provisions w.r.t. elections to legislatures

Choose the ***correct*** answer from the options given below:

1. A-IV, B-III, C-II, D-I
2. A-I, B-II, C-IV, D-III
3. A-II, B-I, C-IV, D-III
4. A-I, B-II, C-III, D-IV

37. Which of the following is NOT correct about the nature of limited liability partnership?

1. It is a body corporate incorporated under the Act
2. It is a legal entity separate from its partners
3. It enjoys the benefit of perpetual succession
4. It follows the principle of unlimited liability

38. Which Article of the Constitution of India provides that "Government of India can be sued in the name of Union of India and State Government may be sued in the name of State"?

1. Art. 300 (1)
2. Art. 270
3. Art. 1
4. Art. 110

39. Setting up of the State Human Right Commission is provided under which Chapter of Protection of Human Right Act, 1993?

1. Chapter X
2. Chapter II
3. Chapter V
4. Chapter IV

40. Who among the following opines that historical sources of law pertain to legal history and not to legal theory?

1. Salmond
2. Blackstone
3. Pollock
4. Gray

41. Match the List-I with List-II.

List-I (*Sources of Hindu Law*)	List-II (*Authors*)
A. Dharma Sutras	I. Jimuta Valiana
B. Mayukha	II. Narada
C. Dayabhaga	III. Vasishtha
D. Dharma Shastras	IV. Nilkantha

Choose the ***correct*** answer from the options given below:

1. A-IV, B-III, C-I, D-II
2. A-III, B-IV, C-I, D-II
3. A-I, B-II, C-III, D-IV
4. A-II, B-I, C-IV, D-III

42. Arrange the following rights as they appear in Universal Declaration of Human Rights, 1948 (UDHR) (ascending order)

A. Rights relating to Freedom
B. Rights relating to Liberties of people
C. Rights relating to Rule of Law
D. Economic Rights

Choose the ***correct*** answer from the options given below:

1. C, B, A, D
2. A, B, C, D
3. B, A, C, D
4. C, A, B, D

43. Which of the following is NOT a subject matter of copyright as per Section 13 of the Copyright Act, 1957?

1. Cinematographic films
2. Dramatic work
3. Performance of performers
4. Sound recording

44. Arrange the following IPR Treaties in the chronological order of their adoption (ascending order).

A. Beijing Treaty on Audio-Visual Performances
B. Singapore Treaty on Law of Trademarks
C. Madrid Agreement (Marks)
D. Madrid Protocol (Marks)

Choose the ***correct*** answer from the options given below:

1. A, B, D, C
2. C, D, B, A
3. C, B, D, A
4. B, C, D, A

45. Which of the following case decided by the Supreme Court of India deals with the concept of 'Public Wrong' under Tort?

1. Sebastin M V/s Union of India
2. Kasturi Lal V/s State of UP
3. Carew & Co. Ltd. V/s Union of India
4. Union of India V/s Ashok Kumar

46. Under which condition, a widowed daughter-in-law cannot claim the right of maintenance from the father-in-law as per Hindu Adoption and Maintenance Act, 1956?

1. If she is unable to maintain herself out of her own earnings
2. If father-in-law has coparcener property in his possession and she has not obtained a share
3. If she has ceased to be a Hindu
4. If she is unable to obtain maintenance from the estate of her daughters

47. Arrange the following in order of their coming into being/adoption/enactment (ascending order).

A. UN Convention on Rights of Persons with Disabilities
B. Americans with Disabilities Act
C. United Kingdom Disability Discriminations Act
D. The Persons with Disability Act (India)

Choose the ***correct*** answer from the options given below:

1. B, C, D, A
2. A, B, C, D
3. C, B, D, A
4. A, C, D, B

48. Which Amendment to American Constitution explicitly declared that powers not specifically delegated to Federal Government were part of sovereign authority of State Government?

1. Fifteenth
2. Sixth
3. Tenth
4. Fourth

49. Match the List-I with List-II.

List-I (*Theory*)	List-II (*Propounder*)
A. Pigeon Hole Theory	I. William Prosser
B. Neighbour Rule	II. Wenfield
C. Tort is Social Engineering	III. Lord Atkin
D. Use of phrase 'Law of Tort'	IV. Salmond

Choose the ***correct*** answer from the options given below:

1. A-IV, B-III, C-I, D-II
2. A-II, B-I, C-III, D-IV
3. A-III, B-II, C-IV, D-I
4. A-I, B-IV, C-II, D-III

50. Given below are two statements: one is labelled as Assertion (A) and the other is labelled as Reason (R).

Assertion (A): A Waqf under Muslim law is essentially a religious and pious obligation.

Reason (R): Provision is sometimes made in a Waqf for charities and for the benefits of oneself, one's children and descendants.

In the light of the above statements, choose the ***most appropriate*** answer from the options given below

1. Both (A) and (R) are correct and (R) is the correct explanation of (A)
2. Both (A) and (R) are correct, but (R) is NOT the correct explanation of (A)
3. (A) is correct, but (R) is not correct
4. (A) is not correct, but (R) is correct

51. Which statements are incorrect with respect of Indian Patent Act, 1970?

A. Invention relating to atomic energy are not patentable.
B. Originality and novelty are pre-requisites for patentability.
C. IPAB (Intellectual Property Appellate Board) deals with all types of IPR disputes currently in India.
D. A patent is valid for 20 years.

Choose the ***correct*** answer from the options given below:

1. C and D only
2. A and B only
3. A and D only
4. B and C only

52. Under Clause (3)(a) of Article 13 of the Constitution of India, "Law" includes:

1. Rule, Regulation, bye-law, order, notification, custom or usage
2. Act, ordinance, order, bye-law, rule, regulation, notification, custom or usage

3. Ordinance, order, rule, regulation, notification, custom or usage
4. Ordinance, order, bye-law, rule, regulation, notification, custom or usage

53. What is the role of Secretary General of NHRC as reflected under Section 3 of the Protection of Human Rights Act, 1993?
1. Advisor of NHRC
2. Technical Member of NHRC
3. Chief Executive Officer of NHRC
4. Legal Member of NHRC

54. The Central Government is empowered to appoint which agency under Section 70B of the Information Technology Act, 2000?
1. Indian Electronic Emergency Response Team
2. Indian Digital Security Response Team
3. National Cyber Security Response Team
4. Indian Computer Emergency Response Team

55. Which of the Article of the Constitution of India mentions Union List, Concurrent List and State List?
1. Article 245 2. Article 246
3. Article 246A 4. Article 249

56. Match the List-I with List-II.

List-I (*WIPO administered IPR Treaties*)	List-II (*Year of Adoption*)
A. Patent Law Treaty	I. 2024
B. Riyadh Design Law Treaty	II. 2000
C. WIPO Copyright Treaty	III. 1981
D. Nairobi Treaty	IV. 1996

Choose the *correct* answer from the options given below:
1. A-II, B-I, C-IV, D-III
2. A-I, B-II, C-III, D-IV
3. A-IV, B-I, C-II, D-III
4. A-II, B-IV, C-I, D-III

57. Given below are two statements: one is labelled as Assertion (A) and the other is labelled as Reason (R).

Assertion (A): Culpable homicide is genus and murder is specie.

Reason (R): All murders are culpable homicide but not vice-versa.

In the light of the above statements, choose the ***most appropriate*** answer from the options given below
1. Both (A) and (R) are correct and (R) is the correct explanation of (A)
2. Both (A) and (R) are correct, but (R) is NOT the correct explanation of (A)
3. (A) is correct, but (R) is not correct
4. (A) is not correct, but (R) is correct

58. Arrange the following in the order of their appearance in the relevant Article under the Charter of the United Nations. The parties to any dispute, the continuance of which is likely to endanger the maintenance of international peace and security, shall fust of all, seek a solution by:

A. Negotiation B. Enquiry
C. Mediation D. Conciliation
E. Arbitration

Choose the *correct* answer from the options given below:
1. A, C, D, E, B 2. E, C, D, A, B
3. A, B, C, D, E 4. B, D, C, A, E

59. The Supreme Court of India, stating the historical background and sanctity of Guru Granth Sahib, held it to be a juristic person in which of the following case?
1. Masjid Shahid Ganj V/s Shiromani Gurudwara Prabandhak Committee
2. State of Punjab V/s Mahinder Singh Chawla
3. Union of India V/s W.N. Chadha
4. Shiromani Gurudwara Prabandhak Committee V/s Somnath Das

60. Which of the following offence is most severally punishable among the following?
1. Unlawful assembly
2. Rioting
3. Affray
4. Assault

61. Which of the following is not a condition for a valid adoption under the Hindu Adoption and Maintenance Act, 1956?

1. If the adoption is of a son, the adoptive father or mother must not have a Hindu son living at the time of adoption
2. If the adoption is by a female and the person to be adopted is a female, the adoptive mother is at-least twenty one years older than the person to be adopted
3. The same child may not be adopted simultaneously by two or more persons
4. The child to be adopted must be actually given and taken in adoption by parents/ guardians

62. Given below are two statements: one is labelled as Assertion (A) and the other is labelled as Reason (R).

Assertion (A): While TRIPS Agreement goes on to outline certain standards of protection for Geographical Indications (GIs), it does not prescribe a particular form of protection so long as these standards are met.

Reason (R): Viewed in the historical context, it is unsurprising that while TRIPS reflects the relatively stable referent for trademarks, for GIs the definition is more fluid.

In the light of the above statements, choose the ***most appropriate*** answer from the options given below

1. Both (A) and (R) are correct and (R) is the correct explanation of (A)
2. Both (A) and (R) are correct, but (R) is NOT the correct explanation of (A)
3. (A) is correct, but (R) is not correct
4. (A) is not correct, but (R) is correct

63. What is the nature of the question where the provocation was grave and sudden enough to prevent the offence from amounting to murder?

1. Mixed question of fact and law
2. Question of law
3. Question of fact
4. Question of criminal law

64. Which of the following says that the purpose of law is to grant the individual the means of self-expression or self-assertion?

1. The Will theory
2. The Atomic theory
3. The theory of Liberty Personality
4. The theory of Natural Law

65. The case for possession of Arantzatzu Mendi before the House of Lords was between which of the following parties?

1. De jure Government of the United Kingdom and defacto Government of Denmark
2. De jure Government of Spain and defacto Nationalist Government of Spain
3. De jure Government of France and defacto Nationalist Government of France
4. De jure Government of Belgium and defacto Nationalist Government of Belgium

66. Arrange the following cases in their chronological order.

A. Sankari Prasad V/s Union of India
B. Sajjan Singh V/s State of Rajasthan
C. Golak Nath V/s State of Punjab
D. Kesavananda Bharati V/s State of Kerala
E. Waman Rao V/s Union of India

Choose the ***correct*** answer from the options given below:

1. A, B, C, D, E
2. E, D, C, B, A
3. A, B, D, C, E
4. D, E, A, B, C

67. Given below are two statements: one is labelled as Assertion (A) and the other is labelled as Reason (R).

Assertion (A): Every company having net worth of rupees five hundred crores or more or turnover of rupees one thousand crore or more or a net profit of rupees five crore or more during the immediately preceding financial year shall constitute a Corporate Social Responsibility Committee (CSRC).

Reason (R): The CSR Committee monitors CSR policy of the company.

In the light of the above statements, choose the ***most appropriate*** answer from the options given below

1. Both A and R arc correct and R is the correct explanation of A
2. Both (A) and (R) are correct, but (R) is NOT the correct explanation of (A)
3. (A) is correct, but (R) is not correct
4. (A) is not correct, but (R) is correct

68. Which provision of the Universal Declaration of Human Rights, 1948 provides that "everyone has the right to a nationality"?

1. Article 10
2. Article 15
3. Article 7
4. Article 21

69. Given below are two statements: one is labelled as Assertion (A) and the other is labelled as Reason (R).

Assertion (A): A written Constitution is intended to operate as a limitation upon the powers of the various organs of a State.

Reason (R): Under those Constitutions where judicial review exists, the guardianship of the Constitution belongs to the courts.

In the light of the above statements, choose the ***most appropriate*** answer from the options given below

1. Both (A) and (R) are correct and (R) is the correct explanation of (A)
2. Both (A) and (R) are correct, but (R) is NOT the correct explanation of (A)
3. (A) is correct, but (R) is not correct
4. (A) is not correct, but (R) is correct

70. Developed mostly by German scholars, which of the following schools sought for a universal doctrine of historical evolution of the whole world (rather than being limited only to a particular race) and its laws from some universal and metaphysical source?

1. Historical school
2. Metaphysical school
3. Sociological school
4. Comparative school

71. In the context of Standard Form Contracts, which Rule will apply if there is any doubt as to the meaning and scope of excluding or limiting terms and to resolve the ambiguity against the party who has inserted it?

1. Purposive Interpretation Rule
2. Removal Simpliciter Rule
3. Contra Proferentem Rule
4. Escalation Clauses Rule

72. Arrange the following provisions in the order in which they appear in the Constitution of India.

A. Provision as to Financial emergency
B. Suspension of provisions of Article 19 during emergencies
C. Provision in case of failure of constitutional machinery in States
D. Effect of Proclamation of Emergency

Choose the ***correct*** answer from the options given below:

1. A, B, C, D
2. A, B, D, C
3. D, B, A, C
4. D, C, B, A

73. Which of the following Section in the Biological Diversity Act. 2002 prescribes for Benefit sharing fee and royalties?

1. Section 6
2. Section 10A
3. Section 30
4. Section 16

74. Arrange the following Class-II legal heirs in the order of their appearance in the schedule in the Hindu Succession Act, 1956.

A. Son's daughter's son
B. Daughters son's son
C. Daughter's son's daughters
D. Son's daughter's daughter

Choose the ***correct*** answer from the options given below:

1. A, D, B, C
2. D, A, C, B
3. A, C, B, D
4. C, B, D, A

75. In every listed public company how many of the total number of directors shall be independent directors?

1. One-fourth   2. One-third
3. One-fifth   4. One-tenth

76. Arrange the following as they appear in the Motor Vehicles Act, 1988 (ascending order)

A. Motor Vehicle Accident fund
B. Claims Tribunal
C. Recall of Motor Vehicles
D. Necessity of Permits

Choose the *correct* answer from the options given below:

1. D, C, B, A   2. D, B, A, C
3. B, C, D, A   4. C, A, B, D

77. Match the List-I with List-II.

List-I (*Particulars*)	List-II (*Year*)
A. Entry into force of the UN Convention on the Status of Refugees	I. 1967
B. Entry into force of the Protocol to the UN Convention on the Status of Refugees	II. 1954
C. Second time when the UN High Commissioner for Refugees won the Nobel Peace Prize	III. 1981
D. Formation of the UN Commission on Refugees	IV. 1950

Choose the *correct* answer from the options given below:

1. A-I, B-II, C-IV, D-III
2. A-IV, B-III, C-II, D-I
3. A-II, B-III, C-IV, D-I
4. A-II, B-I, C-III, D-IV

78. Which of the following are correct in the context of guidelines laid down in S. R. Bommai V/s Union of India?

A. Presidential proclamation under Art, 356 is not subject to judicial review
B. If a state government works against secularism, President Rule can be imposed
C. State assembly can be dissolved only after the Approval of Parliament
D. Power under Art, 356 is not an absolute Power

Choose the *correct* answer from the options given below:

1. A, B, C only   2. B, C, D only
3. C and A only   4. B and D only

79. When did India and the United Kingdom (U.K.) formally sign the Comprehensive Economic and Trade Agreement (CETA)?

1. 24 July 2025   2. 31 December 2024
3. 15 January 2025   4. 1 July 2024

80. Arrange the following concepts as per their order of appearance in the Indian Contract Act, 1872.

A. Continuing guarantee
B. Care to be taken by bailee
C. Compensation for loss or damage caused by breach of contract
D. Claims for necessaries supplied to person incapable of contracting

Choose the *correct* answer from the options given below:

1. D, B, C, A   2. D, C, A, B
3. C, D, B, A   4. B, A, C, D

81. Arrange the following in the order of their appearance in Section 2 of the Indian Contract Act, 1872.

A. Proposal   B. Consideration
C. Agreement   D. Promise
E. Contract

Choose the *correct* answer from the options given below:

1. A, B, D, C, E   2. D, B, A, E, C
3. A, D, B, C, E   4. B, D, A, E, C

82. Given below are two statements: one is labelled as Assertion (A) and the other is labelled as Reason (R).

Assertion (A): Once Rule of Law is acknowledged as a constitutional law superior to the express provision in Article 21, it is only one step further to assert that Rule of Law is a 'basic feature' of Indian Constitution, which is beyond the pale of the express provision in Article 368, which was provided for by the initial constituent body.

Reason (R): It is not unimaginable to conceive that the enacted provisions of a written Constitution would be nullified by invoking some unwritten principle of law of higher ethical value as evident under the West German Constitution of 1949.

In the light of the above statements, choose the ***most appropriate*** answer from the options given below

1. Both (A) and (R) are correct and (R) is the correct explanation of (A)
2. Both (A) and (R) are correct, but (R) is NOT the correct explanation of (A)
3. (A) is correct, but (R) is not correct
4. (A) is not correct, but (R) is correct

83. Match the List-I with List-II.

List-I (*Case Law*)	List-II (*Related Concept*)
A. Cox V/s Hickman	I. Business must be taken in a practical sense
B. Stekel V/s Ellice	II. Partnership between Karta and Coparcener
C. Lachhman Das V/s CIT	III. Salaried partner
D. Smith V/s Anderson	IV. Mutual Agency

Choose the ***correct*** answer from the options given below:

1. A-III, B-IV, C-I, D-II
2. A-I, B-IV, C-II, D-III
3. A-II, B-I, C-IV, D-III
4. A-IV, B-III, C-II, D-I

84. Match the List-I with List-II.

List-I (*Case Law*)	List-II (*Concept*)
A. Ashby V/s White	I. Poverty as an involuntary act under Tort
B. Ryland V/s Fletcher	II. Violation of absolute Right
C. Olga Tellis V/s Bombay Municipal Corp.	III. Strict liability
D. Allen V/s Flood	IV. Motive is irrelevant in Tort

Choose the ***correct*** answer from the options given below:

1. A-II, B-III, C-I, D-IV
2. A-I, B-II, C-IV, D-III
3. A-III, B-IV, C-II, D-I
4. A-IV, B-I, C-III, D-II

85. Under which of its provisions does the Draft Convention on Territorial Asylum adopted by the General Assembly of the United Nations in 1974, recognize that the grant of asylum is a sovereign right of a State?

1. Article 1
2. Article 2
3. Article 3
4. Article 5

86. Which of the following is a landmark case on 'attempt to commit offences'?

1. Dashrath Paswan V/s State of Bihar
2. K.M. Nanavati V/s State of Maharashtra
3. Abhayanand Mishra V/s State of Bihar
4. Barendra Kumar Ghosh V/s Emperor

87. Match the List-I with List-II.

List-I (*Statement*)	List-II (*Propounder*)
A. Justice is the first virtue of social institution	I. Immanuel Kant
B. Natural justice is species of political justice	II. Aristotle
C. 'Equality of respect and concern'	III. Dworkin
D. Human Dignity is the foundation of Human Rights	IV. John Rawls

Choose the *correct* answer from the options given below:

1. A-IV, B-II, C-III, D-I
2. A-I, B-III, C-II, D-IV
3. A-II, B-IV, C-I, D-III
4. A-III, B-I, C-IV, D-II

88. Which of the following is not a type of prospectus under the Companies Act, 2013?

1. Shelf Prospectus
2. Deemed Prospectus
3. Yellow (Herring) Prospectus
4. Abridged Prospectus

89. Which is correct with regard to In Re Right to Privacy of Adolescents (2025 INSC 778)?

A. Not a Suo-motu judgment of Supreme Court of India

B. Victim- centric sentencing under Article 142

C. Held that non-compliance with Section 19(6) of POCSO Act does not lead to violation of Article 21 of the Constitution

D. Supreme Court refused to further sentence a man convicted under POCSO Act after considering the victim's wishes.

Choose the *correct* answer from the options given below:

1. A and C only
2. B and D only
3. A and B only
4. C and D only

90. Match the List-I with List-II.

List-I (***Concept in the Biological Diversity Act, 2002***)	**List-II** (***Corresponding Section***)
A. National Biodiversity Authority	I. Section 32
B. State Biodiversity Fund	II. Section 37
C. National Biodiversity Fund	III. Section 8
D. Biodiversity Heritage Sites	IV. Section 27

Choose the *correct* answer from the options given below:

1. A-I, B-II, C-III, D-IV
2. A-I, B-IV, C-III, D-II
3. A-III, B-I, C-IV, D-II
4. A-IV, B-I, C-III, D-II

Directions (Qs. No. 91 to 95): *Read the following passage and answer the questions below:*

"While interpreting the Articles of the Indian Constitution, the Court should remember that it is not construing a petrified legal parchment but reading the luscent lines of a human text with a national mission. The Court must never forget that the life of the *Supreme Lex* is nourished by the social setting, that jurisdical abstractions and theoretical conceptions may be fascinating forensics but jejune jurisprudence if the raw Indian realities are slimed over. The Constitution of a nation is being expounded whose people hunger for a full life for each, and therefore, a perception of the signature of social justice writ on it is imperative. 'Nothing is more certain in modern 'society', declared the American Supreme Court at mid-century 'than the principle that there are no absolutes. Legal Einstienism guides the Court, not doctrinal absolutes."

91. Why is a perception of the signature of social justice writ on the Constitution, an imperative for its exposition?

1. It is because it is a human text to be read with a national mission.
2. It is because it is a juridical abstraction making for fascinating forensics.
3. It is because it is jejune jurisprudence slurring over raw Indian realities.
4. It is because it is expounded for a nation whose people hunger for a full life for each.

92. What must the Court never forget, according to the author?

1. That the life of the Supreme Lex is nourished by juridical abstractions.
2. That the life of the Supreme Lex is nourished by theoretical conceptions.

3. That the life of the Supreme Lex is nourished by fascinating forensics.
4. That the life of the Supreme Lex is nourished by the social setting.

93. What should the Court remember while interpreting the Articles of the Indian Constitution?

1. That it is constructing a petrified legal parchment.
2. That they are reading the luscent lines of a human text with a national mission.
3. That they are interpreting it for the future generations.
4. That it is their national mission to petrify the legal parchment.

94. Which is the most certain principle in Modern society?

1. The principle that there are no certainties.
2. The principle that there are no principles.
3. The principle that there are no absolutes.
4. The principle that social justice is not an absolute.

95. As per the American Supreme Court, what guides the Court?

1. Legal Einstienism guides the Court.
2. Lucent Lines guides the Court.
3. Doctrinal absolutes guides the Court.
4. Jejune jurisprudence guides the Court.

Directions (Qs. No. 96 to 100): *Read the following passage and answer the questions below:*

As remarked by Dias, "no other firmament of legal or political theory is, so bejewelled with star as that of 'Natural Law' for it has engaged the attention of some of the greatest thinkers of all ages." The credit of giving birth to natural law goes to Greeks. After the Greeks, it was further developed and elaborated by the Romans. The early and original law of Romans was called 'Jus Civil'. Later on, the Romans developed another legal system called '*Jus gentium*' which was considered to be the law of universal application. In the republican era of Rome '*Jus gentium*' was reinforced by natural law or '*Jus natural*' as it was commonly called. As pointed out by Brierly. by "*Jus natural*" the Romans meant "the sum of those principles which ought to control human conduct because founded in the very nature of man as a rational and social being." The law of nature is the expression of what is just against what is merely expedient at a particular time and place, it is what is reasonable against what is arbitrary, what is natural against, what is convenient and what is for social good against the personal will." Thus natural law was based on the rational and reasonable needs of a man's nature. According to Roman, natural law embodied the elementary principles of justice which were the dictate of rights and reason. In other words, those principles were in accordance with nature and were unalterable and eternal.

96. According to Roman what does Natural Law embody?

1. Social laws
2. Principle of human conduct
3. Elementary principle of justice
4. Company law principle

97. Which of the following is not a characteristic of natural law?

1. Convenience
2. Just and fair
3. Reasonable
4. Social good

98. Which of the following has Universal Application?

1. JUS CIVIL
2. JUS GENTIUM
3. JUS NATURAL
4. JUS COGNITO

99. Natural Law is based upon which of the following?

1. Rational and reasonable needs of man
2. Personal will
3. Human conduct
4. Supernatural powers

100. JUS gentium was enforced in which era of Rome?

1. Dictatorship
2. Democratic era
3. Republican era
4. Dark age

ANSWERS

1	2	3	4	5	6	7	8	9	10
1	3	2	2	3	3	4	1	3	3
11	**12**	**13**	**14**	**15**	**16**	**17**	**18**	**19**	**20**
3	1	3	4	1	3	1	2	3	4
21	**22**	**23**	**24**	**25**	**26**	**27**	**28**	**29**	**30**
4	3	2	3	3	4	3	1	2	3
31	**32**	**33**	**34**	**35**	**36**	**37**	**38**	**39**	**40**
2	3	1	1	1	2	4	1	3	1
41	**42**	**43**	**44**	**45**	**46**	**47**	**48**	**49**	**50**
2	4	3	2	1	3	1	3	1	2
51	**52**	**53**	**54**	**55**	**56**	**57**	**58**	**59**	**60**
4	4	3	4	2	1	1	3	4	2
61	**62**	**63**	**64**	**65**	**66**	**67**	**68**	**69**	**70**
2	1	3	1	2	1	2	2	2	2
71	**72**	**73**	**74**	**75**	**76**	**77**	**78**	**79**	**80**
3	4	1	1	2	*	4	2	1	2
81	**82**	**83**	**84**	**85**	**86**	**87**	**88**	**89**	**90**
3	1	4	1	1	3	1	3	2	3
91	**92**	**93**	**94**	**95**	**96**	**97**	**98**	**99**	**100**
4	4	2	3	1	3	1	2	1	3

EXPLANATORY ANSWERS

1. The "Doctrine of Common Employment" (also called the fellow-servant rule) originated in English tort law. It developed from the idea that an employer should not be held liable when one employee is injured solely due to the negligence of another employee engaged in the same common work. The classic starting point for this doctrine is *Priestley v. Fowler* (1837), which is treated as the foundational case from which the rule was articulated and later expanded in subsequent decisions.

2. Reservation of seats in educational institutions in favour of Scheduled Castes and Scheduled Tribes is constitutionally supported under Article 15, especially through Article 15(4) (special provisions for advancement of SC/ST and socially/educationally backward classes) and Article 15(5) (special provisions regarding admissions in educational institutions, with constitutionally recognized limits). Article 16 is focused on equality of opportunity and reservation in public employment, not seat-reservations in educational institutions. Hence, the governing Article for educational seat reservation is Article 15.

3. A. The tribunal-winding-up ground is triggered when the LLP continues with partners below the statutory minimum for the legally specified duration (the law uses a longer threshold than what is stated here). Since the statement gives an incorrect time period, it does not match the statutory condition and is therefore incorrect.

C. The statutory default-based winding-up ground requires persistent non-filing for a longer consecutive span than what is stated here. Because the statement understates the required consecutive financial years, it does not reflect the legal threshold and is therefore incorrect.

4. Sarla Mudgal v. Union of India is the leading Supreme Court decision commonly associated with the discussion on the need and relevance of a Uniform Civil Code under Article 44. While the immediate dispute dealt with bigamy through religious conversion and conflict of personal laws, the judgment prominently addressed the broader constitutional goal of UCC and urged movement towards it. Therefore, this case primarily deals with the concept of Uniform Civil Code among the given options.

5. The United States is a recognized example of an entrenched (rigid) constitutional tradition because its Constitution is placed above ordinary law and is amendable only through a specially demanding procedure, not by ordinary legislative majority. The Reason is not correct as written because, although the U.S. Constitution is the oldest still functioning written national constitution, it is not the longest written constitution in the world. Hence, Assertion is correct but Reason (as a whole) is not correct.

6. • **A → III (1986):** The Declaration on the Right to Development was adopted by the UN General Assembly in 1986, marking a major step in recognizing development as a human right and linking it with social and economic justice.
   • **B → IV (2001):** The Durban Declaration and Programme of Action emerged from the World Conference against Racism held in Durban in 2001, focusing on discrimination, development, and equality.
   • **C → I (2000):** The Millennium Declaration was adopted in 2000, establishing global development goals such as poverty reduction and human dignity.
   • **D → II (1993):** The Vienna Declaration and Programme of Action was adopted in 1993, reaffirming the universality of human rights and linking them with development.

7. The National Commission for Minority Educational Institutions Act was enacted by Parliament in 2004 to safeguard and protect the rights of minorities to establish and administer educational institutions under Article 30 of the Constitution. It provides for a quasi-judicial body to resolve disputes and ensure minority rights in education are effectively implemented.

8. The Assertion reflects a fundamental attribute of ownership, which is the right to exclude others from possession and enjoyment. The Reason elaborates this principle by stating that the ability to maintain or recover possession against others is a core component of ownership. Since the right to exclude is effectively enforced through the right to possess and recover possession, the Reason correctly explains the Assertion.

9. Rudolf von Ihering defined a legal right as a "legally protected interest." His theory emphasizes that rights exist to protect interests recognized by law, focusing on the social purpose of rights rather than mere will or abstract legal entitlement.

10. • **A → III (P.K. Mukherjee v. Bank of Khulna):** This case is associated with the Doctrine of Pith and Substance, which determines the true nature of legislation when there is overlap between Union and State lists.
    • **B → IV (Wallace v. Income Tax Commissioner):** This case relates to the Doctrine of Territorial Nexus, which allows laws to apply beyond territorial limits if a sufficient connection exists.
    • **C → II (M. Karunanidhi v. Union of India):** This case deals with the Doctrine of Repugnancy, addressing conflicts between Union and State laws under Article 254.
    • **D → I (K.C.G. Narayan Deo v. State of Orissa):** This case explains the Doctrine of Colourable Legislation, meaning what cannot be done directly cannot be done indirectly.

11. A. The Supreme Court in *State of Maharashtra v. Praful B. Desai* (2003) emphasized that law must adapt to technological advancements and societal changes. It accepted modern technology like video conferencing as part of judicial procedure to ensure effective administration of justice.
    B. The Court held that evidence in a criminal trial is not limited to physical presence; it can include oral, documentary, and electronic forms. Testimony through video conferencing is valid evidence under Section 3 of the Indian Evidence Act.

12. The "patent bargain" metaphor reflects the idea that inventors disclose their inventions to the public in exchange for exclusive rights, resembling a social contract between the inventor and society. This concept was illustrated in *Universal Oil Products v. Globe Oil & Refining* Co., where the patent system was seen as a bargain encouraging innovation while ultimately benefiting the public.

13. A. Montesquieu propounded the theory of separation of powers, dividing government into legislative, executive, and judicial branches to prevent concentration of power.

B. *Marbury v. Madison* (1803) is a landmark US Supreme Court case that established the principle of judicial review, strengthening constitutional governance.

C. Article III of the US Constitution establishes the judiciary and ensures its independence, including life tenure for judges and protection of salaries.

14. E. Cruelty: Appears earlier in Section 13(1) as one of the primary grounds for divorce introduced to protect spouses from mental or physical harm.

B. Conversion: Comes after cruelty, dealing with a spouse ceasing to be Hindu by conversion to another religion.

A. Venereal disease: Appears later as a health-related ground affecting marital life.

C. Renunciation: Refers to entering a religious order and abandoning worldly life.

D. Not heard alive: The last ground relates to presumption of death after seven years of absence.

15. In England, Parliament historically performed a dual role because the constitutional system developed without a single codified written Constitution that rigidly demarcated legislative and judicial spheres; thus, Parliament evolved as the supreme constitutional authority and, through institutions like the House of Lords (as the final court of appeal for centuries) and the broader idea of the "High Court of Parliament," it exercised judicial functions along with law-making. Since there was no written constitutional instrument imposing a strict separation-of-powers limitation on Parliament's authority, this constitutional evolution permitted the fusion of functions within Parliament itself, which is why (R) correctly explains (A).

16. Article 30 grants minorities, whether based on religion or language, the right to establish and administer educational institutions of their choice. The Reason is incorrect because it restricts this right only to religion, whereas the Constitution clearly extends it to both religious and linguistic minorities.

17. D. U.N.R. Rao v. Smt. Indira Gandhi (1971): This case dealt with the continuation of the Council of Ministers even after the dissolution of the Lok Sabha.

B. Samsher Singh v. State of Punjab (1974): It clarified that the President and Governor act on the aid and advice of the Council of Ministers.

A. Minerva Mills Ltd. v. Union of India (1980): It reaffirmed the basic structure doctrine and balanced Fundamental Rights and Directive Principles.

C. S.P. Anand v. H. D. Deve Gowda (1996): It upheld the appointment of a non-member of Parliament as Prime Minister for six months.

18. A. Exception 2 → Exceeding the right of private defense: This applies when a person exceeds the lawful right of private defence in good faith without premeditation.

B. Exception 3 → Act of Public Servant: It covers acts done by a public servant in good faith while performing official duties, even if exceeding legal limits.

C. Exception 4 → Sudden fight: This applies when death occurs in a sudden fight without pre-planning and without undue advantage.

D. Exception 5 → Death by consent: This applies where death is caused with the consent of a person above 18 years of age.

19 B. Section 6 provides for use of electronic records and electronic signatures by Government and appears early in the Act.

C. Section 7 relates to retention of electronic records and follows Section 6.

D. Section 8 deals with publication in the electronic Gazette.

A. Section 10-A (added later) validates electronic contracts, appearing after earlier provisions.

20. The Supreme Court in this case considered whether a woman in a relationship resembling marriage could claim maintenance under Section 125 CrPC. The Court adopted a progressive interpretation, emphasizing social justice and recommending that women in live-in relationships be given protection similar to legally wedded wives to prevent destitution.

21. A. **Executive Legislation → Ordinance:** Executive legislation refers to law-making by the executive, mainly through ordinances issued by the President or Governor under constitutional powers.

B. **Collective Responsibility → Parliamentary form of government:** This is a core feature of the parliamentary system where the Council of Ministers is collectively responsible to the legislature.

C. **Quasi-Judicial Function → Administrative adjudication:** Quasi-judicial bodies decide disputes and exercise adjudicatory powers while being part of the administrative system.

D. **Independence of Judiciary → Appointment and removal of Judges:** Safeguards like fixed tenure and removal procedure ensure judicial independence.

22. This doctrine applies when a person intends to harm one individual but unintentionally harms another. The intention (mens rea) is transferred from the intended victim to the actual victim, making the accused liable for the resulting harm as if it were intended for that person.

23. A. E-rickshaw and e-cart are battery-powered vehicles as defined under the Motor Vehicles Act.

B. Their motor power is limited (not exceeding 4000 watts), which distinguishes them from other motor vehicles.

24. In this 2023 judgment, the Supreme Court held that until Parliament enacts a law, the appointment of the Chief Election Commissioner and Election Commissioners shall be made by the President on the advice of a committee consisting of the Prime Minister, Leader of Opposition, and Chief Justice of India, ensuring independence of the Election Commission.

25. A. **Kharak Singh v. State of U.P.:** It dealt with surveillance and interpreted personal liberty under Article 21.

C. **Maneka Gandhi v. Union of India:** It expanded Article 21, linking it with Articles 14 and 19 and broadening the meaning of personal liberty.

D. **A.K. Gopalan v. Union of India:** It initially gave a narrow interpretation of personal liberty, later expanded by subsequent judgments.

26. Under the Sale of Goods Act, 1930, Section 46 clearly distinguishes the rights of an unpaid seller depending on whether the property in goods has passed or not. When the property has passed to the buyer, the unpaid seller's rights against the goods are limited to lien, stoppage in transit, and resale. The right of withholding delivery, as mentioned in Section 46(2), is applicable only in cases where the property in the goods has not yet passed to the buyer. Therefore, when the question specifically asks for a right not available "notwithstanding that the property in the goods may have passed," the right of withholding delivery is excluded, making option 4 correct.

27. The Supreme Court in *State Bank of India v. Ajay Kumar Sood* emphasized modernization of judicial processes and directed that all judgments and orders uploaded by Courts and Tribunals must be digitally signed rather than uploaded as scanned copies. The Court highlighted that scanned documents are inefficient, difficult to access (especially for persons using assistive technologies), and lack proper authenticity verification. Digitally signed documents ensure integrity, authenticity, and better accessibility, thereby aligning judicial functioning with technological advancements.

28. A. The maker of goods or parts is clearly a manufacturer under the Act.

B. A person who assembles parts into finished goods is also included within the definition.

C. A person who puts his own mark on goods made by others (branding) is treated as a manufacturer because he represents the goods as his own.

29. The Mimansa school of Indian jurisprudence laid down interpretative principles to distinguish between obligatory (mandatory) and recommendatory (directory) injunctions in ancient legal texts. These principles have influenced modern methods of statutory interpretation.

30. B. **Justice:** The Preamble first mentions Justice—social, economic and political.

C. **Liberty:** This is followed by Liberty of thought, expression, belief, faith and worship.

A. Equality: Then comes Equality of status and opportunity.

D. Fraternity: Finally, Fraternity assuring dignity and unity and integrity of the Nation.

31. Holland described international law as the "vanishing point of jurisprudence," indicating that it does not fully fit into classical legal theory due to absence of a sovereign authority. He is classified as an analytical jurist because his approach focused on conceptual and structural analysis of law. The Vienna Convention on the Law of Treaties recognizes that treaties may create obligations or rights for third States when such States expressly accept them or when rules evolve into customary law, thus allowing limited binding effect. Grotius and Vattel are associated with natural law rather than strict positivism, and the ICJ identifies sources of international law under Article 38(1), not Article 36, so D and E are incorrect.

32.
- **A → I (Section 69):** A person interested in payment who pays money which another is legally bound to pay can recover it, preventing unjust enrichment.
- **B → II (Section 72):** Money paid or goods delivered by mistake or coercion must be repaid because retention would be unjust.
- **C → IV (Section 70):** When a person lawfully does something not intended to be gratuitous and another enjoys the benefit, compensation is required.
- **D → III (Section 68):** Supply of necessaries to a person incapable of contracting gives a right to reimbursement from that person's property.

33. C. United States v. Rauscher (1886): This is the earliest case establishing principles like specialty in extradition law.

A. Soering v. United Kingdom (1989): It introduced human rights considerations, especially protection against inhuman punishment in extradition.

E. Kindler v. Canada (1991): This case examined extradition in the context of death penalty concerns.

B. Chitat v. Canada (1994): It dealt with fairness and procedural safeguards in extradition proceedings.

D. Daya Singh Lahoria v. Union of India (2001): This is the latest case dealing with extradition law in the Indian context.

34. The National Green Tribunal Act, 2010 was brought into force on 18 October 2010 through official notification, establishing a specialized tribunal for effective and expeditious disposal of environmental cases.

35.
- **A → I (Independence of the judiciary — Fazal Ali — S.P. Gupta v. Union of India):** The case dealt with judicial independence, especially concerning appointments and transfers.
- **B → II (Federal system — Bachawat — Golak Nath v. State of Punjab):** It involved constitutional limitations and distribution of powers affecting the federal structure.
- **C → IV (Secularism — Khanna — Indira Gandhi v. Raj Narain):** It emphasized constitutional fundamentals including secular democratic structure.
- **D → III (Parliamentary system — Reddy — Kesavananda Bharati v. State of Kerala):** The case established the basic structure doctrine, recognizing parliamentary democracy as a core feature.

36.
- **A → I (Article 325 - One general electoral roll):** Article 325 ensures equality in electoral participation by providing a single general electoral roll for every constituency and prohibits discrimination on grounds such as religion, race, caste or sex. This reflects the democratic principle of non-discrimination in voting rights.
- **B → II (Article 326 - Adult Suffrage):** Article 326 establishes elections on the basis of adult suffrage, giving every citizen above the prescribed age the right to vote, subject to disqualifications. It embodies universal adult franchise in India.
- **C → IV (Article 327 - Power of Parliament):** Article 327 empowers Parliament to make laws regarding elections, including preparation of electoral rolls and delimitation of constituencies. It ensures uniformity and legislative control over election procedures.
- **D → III (Article 329 - Bar of interference by courts):** Article 329 bars courts from interfering in electoral matters except through election petitions, ensuring uninterrupted electoral processes.

37. A Limited Liability Partnership is a body corporate incorporated under the LLP Act, 2008, and it is a separate legal entity distinct from its partners. It has perpetual succession, meaning its existence continues irrespective of changes in partners. One of its most important features is that the liability of partners is limited to their agreed contribution. This protects partners from personal liability for the acts of other partners. Therefore, the statement that LLP follows the principle of unlimited liability is incorrect because LLP specifically provides limited liability protection.

38. Article 300(1) provides that the Government of India may sue or be sued in the name of the Union of India, and the State Government may sue or be sued in the name of the State. This provision recognizes the State as a juristic person capable of entering into legal proceedings. It ensures accountability of the government in courts of law. The provision is based on the continuity of legal principles from the Government of India Act, 1935. It plays an important role in enforcing rights against the government.

39. The Protection of Human Rights Act, 1993 establishes State Human Rights Commissions under Chapter V. This chapter provides for their constitution, appointment of members, powers, and functions. These Commissions are empowered to inquire into violations of human rights or negligence by public officials. They serve as an important mechanism for protecting human rights at the state level. Their role complements that of the National Human Rights Commission by ensuring accessibility and decentralized enforcement.

40. Salmond clearly distinguished between legal sources and historical sources of law. According to him, historical sources refer to materials that influence the development of law, such as ancient texts, customs, or foreign legal systems, but they do not have binding authority unless recognized by law. These sources belong to legal history rather than legal theory because they explain the origin and evolution of law. Legal sources, on the other hand, are those recognized by the legal system as having authoritative force, such as legislation and precedent. Thus, Salmond emphasized that historical sources are relevant for understanding the background of law, not for determining its present binding nature.

41.
- **A → III (Dharma Sutras - Vasishtha):** Dharma Sutras are among the earliest sources of Hindu law and were composed by ancient sages like Vasishtha, Gautama, and Apastamba. These texts laid down rules relating to conduct, duties, and legal principles.
- **B → IV (Mayukha - Nilkantha):** The Mayukha is a well-known commentary on Hindu law written by Nilkantha, particularly influential in Western India. It deals with various aspects like inheritance and family law.
- **C → I (Dayabhaga - Jimuta Vahana):** Dayabhaga is a famous digest on Hindu law authored by Jimuta Vahana, mainly followed in Bengal, emphasizing inheritance based on spiritual benefit rather than birthright.
- **D → II (Dharma Shastras - Narada):** Dharma Shastras are later and more elaborate texts than Dharma Sutras, and sages like Narada contributed to their development, covering legal and social duties.

42. **C. Rights relating to Rule of Law:** These rights appear earliest among the given categories in the Universal Declaration of Human Rights, particularly in Articles 6–11. They include recognition before law, equality before law, right to remedy, protection against arbitrary arrest, fair trial, and presumption of innocence. These provisions establish the legal framework necessary for protection of all other rights.

A. Rights relating to Freedom: These rights follow and include fundamental freedoms such as right to life, liberty and security (Article 3), freedom from slavery and torture (Articles 4–5), freedom of movement (Article 13), freedom of thought, conscience and religion (Article 18), and freedom of expression (Article 19). These rights are central to individual autonomy.

B. Rights relating to Liberties of people: These include broader civil and political liberties such as freedom of assembly and association (Article 20), right to participate in government (Article 21), right to marry and found a family (Article 16), and right to own property (Article 17). These rights appear after core freedoms and expand the scope of personal and political participation.

D. **Economic Rights:** These appear towards the end of the UDHR in Articles 22–27 and include rights to social security, work, rest and leisure, adequate standard of living, education, and participation in cultural life. These rights aim to ensure social and economic justice.

43. Section 13 of the Copyright Act, 1957 provides protection for original literary, dramatic, musical and artistic works, cinematograph films, and sound recordings. The performance of performers is not included as a subject matter of copyright; instead, performers are granted separate "performers' rights" under the Act, which are distinct from copyright.

44. C. **Madrid Agreement (Marks) – 1891:** This is the earliest treaty establishing an international system for trademark registration.

D. **Madrid Protocol (Marks) – 1989:** It supplemented and modernized the Madrid Agreement, making the system more flexible.

B. **Singapore Treaty on Law of Trademarks – 2006:** This treaty standardized administrative trademark procedures internationally.

A. **Beijing Treaty on Audio-Visual Performances – 2012:** This is the most recent treaty, protecting rights of performers in audiovisual works.

45. The concept of "Public Wrong" in tort law is closely associated with the evolution of constitutional torts in India, where the violation of fundamental rights by the State gives rise to a public law remedy. In *Sebastin M v. Union of India*, the Supreme Court dealt with the disappearance of individuals after being taken into custody by security forces, treating the issue not merely as a private wrong but as a violation of Article 21 of the Constitution. The Court recognized that such acts by State authorities amount to a public wrong, affecting not only individuals but also the rule of law, and therefore awarded compensation as a public law remedy. This case reflects the shift from traditional tort liability to constitutional accountability of the State, where compensation is granted for infringement of fundamental rights, thus clearly dealing with the concept of public wrong.

46. Under Section 19 of the Hindu Adoptions and Maintenance Act, 1956, a widowed daughter-in-law is entitled to claim maintenance from her father-in-law only if certain conditions are fulfilled, such as her inability to maintain herself from her own earnings or property and the existence of coparcenary property in the hands of the father-in-law from which she has not received a share. However, the Act clearly provides that this right is available only so long as she continues to be a Hindu. If she ceases to be a Hindu by conversion to another religion, she loses her right to claim maintenance under this provision. Therefore, cessation of Hindu status is a disqualification for claiming maintenance from the father-in-law.

47. B. **Americans with Disabilities Act (1990):** This is the earliest among the given, enacted in the United States to prohibit discrimination against persons with disabilities.

C. **United Kingdom Disability Discrimination Act (1995):** This followed, providing legal protection against disability discrimination in the UK.

D. **Persons with Disabilities Act (India) (1995):** India enacted its law in the same year, ensuring equal opportunities and rights for persons with disabilities.

A. **UN Convention on Rights of Persons with Disabilities (2006):** This is the latest, establishing an international framework for protecting the rights of persons with disabilities.

48. The Tenth Amendment to the Constitution of the United States provides that powers not delegated to the federal government nor prohibited to the States are reserved to the States or the people. This amendment is a cornerstone of American federalism, clearly defining the distribution of powers and emphasizing the sovereignty of State governments within their sphere.

49.
- **A → IV (Pigeon Hole Theory – Salmond):** Salmond described tort law as consisting of specific categories of wrongs, likening them to pigeonholes, meaning liability arises only when a case fits into a recognized category.
- **B → III (Neighbour Rule – Lord Atkin):** Lord Atkin formulated the neighbour principle in *Donoghue v. Stevenson*, laying the foundation of modern negligence law.
- **C → I (Tort is Social Engineering – William Prosser):** Prosser emphasized that tort law functions to balance social interests and regulate behavior in society.

- **D → II (Use of phrase 'Law of Tort' – Winfield):** Winfield supported the idea of tort law as a general principle of liability, and he used the term to denote a broader, evolving field of law.

50. A Waqf in Muslim law is a permanent dedication of property for religious, pious, or charitable purposes, and thus it is essentially a religious and pious obligation. The Reason is also correct because in a Waqf, provision may be made for charity and even for the benefit of the settlor's family, known as Waqf-alal-aulad. However, this feature does not explain the religious nature of Waqf; it only describes one of its possible forms. The religious and pious character of Waqf arises from its dedication to God and charitable purposes, not merely from the provision for family benefit.

51. **B.** The Patent Act requires novelty, inventive step, and industrial applicability for patentability. The term "originality" is not a requirement under patent law; it is relevant to copyright law. Hence, this statement is incorrect.

C. The Intellectual Property Appellate Board (IPAB) has been abolished (Tribunal Reforms Act, 2021), and its functions have been transferred to High Courts and other authorities. Therefore, it does not currently deal with all IPR disputes, making this statement incorrect.

52. Article 13(3)(a) gives an inclusive definition of the term "law" for the purpose of enforcing Fundamental Rights. It specifically mentions that "law" includes any ordinance, order, bye-law, rule, regulation, notification, custom or usage having the force of law in the territory of India. The intention is to ensure that not only legislative enactments but also executive and subordinate legislation, as well as customs having legal force, can be tested against Fundamental Rights. The expression is deliberately wide so that any form of legal norm affecting rights does not escape judicial review. The Article focuses on the forms through which law operates, rather than explicitly mentioning Acts in this clause. Hence, the correct option is the one which reproduces the wording of Article 13(3)(a).

53. Under Section 3 of the Protection of Human Rights Act, 1993, the Secretary-General of the National Human Rights Commission acts as the Chief Executive Officer. He exercises administrative powers and is responsible for the efficient functioning of the Commission, implementing its decisions and managing its day-to-day affairs.

54. Section 70B of the Information Technology Act, 2000 empowers the Central Government to appoint the Indian Computer Emergency Response Team (CERT-In) as the national agency for responding to cyber security incidents. It collects, analyses, and disseminates information on cyber threats and coordinates response measures.

55. Article 246 of the Constitution distributes legislative powers between the Union and the States by referring to the Union List, State List, and Concurrent List in the Seventh Schedule. It specifies the subject-matter on which Parliament and State Legislatures can make laws, forming the basis of the federal structure.

56.
- **A → II (Patent Law Treaty - 2000):** The Patent Law Treaty was adopted in 2000 to harmonize and streamline formal procedures relating to national and regional patent applications. It simplifies procedural requirements for patent applicants.
- **B → I (Riyadh Design Law Treaty - 2024):** This is a recent WIPO-administered treaty adopted in 2024 to harmonize procedures relating to industrial design protection globally.
- **C → IV (WIPO Copyright Treaty - 1996):** The WIPO Copyright Treaty was adopted in 1996 to address copyright protection in the digital environment, especially for literary and artistic works.
- **D → III (Nairobi Treaty - 1981):** The Nairobi Treaty on the Protection of the Olympic Symbol was adopted in 1981, granting protection to the Olympic symbol internationally.

57. In criminal law, culpable homicide is the broader category (genus) under Section 299 IPC, while murder is a specific aggravated form (species) defined under Section 300 IPC. Every act of murder necessarily falls within culpable homicide because it involves causing death with intention or knowledge. However, not every culpable homicide amounts to murder, as there are exceptions and varying degrees of intention and knowledge. Thus, the Reason correctly explains the Assertion.

58. **A. Negotiation:** The UN Charter (Article 33) begins with negotiation as the primary and most basic method of peaceful dispute settlement.

B. Enquiry: It follows negotiation, involving fact-finding mechanisms to clarify disputes.

C. Mediation: This involves third-party assistance to facilitate a mutually acceptable solution.

D. Conciliation: It is a more structured form of mediation where proposals for settlement are formally made.

E. Arbitration: It appears later as a more formal adjudicatory mechanism where parties agree to be bound by a decision.

59. In this case, the Supreme Court recognized Guru Granth Sahib as a juristic person, acknowledging its religious significance and legal status. The Court held that as the central religious scripture of Sikhism, it can hold property and can be represented in legal proceedings, similar to idols in Hindu law being treated as juristic persons.

60. Among the given offences, rioting is the most severely punishable. While unlawful assembly itself is punishable, rioting involves the use of force or violence by an unlawful assembly, making it more serious. Affray and assault involve lesser degrees of disturbance or violence. Rioting, especially when armed with deadly weapons, carries heavier punishment under criminal law, reflecting its greater threat to public order.

61. Under the Hindu Adoptions and Maintenance Act, 1956, valid adoption requires conditions such as absence of a living Hindu son for adoption of a son, prohibition of multiple simultaneous adoptions of the same child, and actual giving and taking of the child in adoption. The age difference requirement of at least twenty-one years applies only when a male adopts a female child or a female adopts a male child. There is no such requirement when both adoptive parent and child are of the same gender. Therefore, this statement is not a valid condition and is incorrect.

62. The TRIPS Agreement sets minimum standards for protection of Geographical Indications but does not mandate a specific legal mechanism, allowing member states flexibility in implementation. This reflects the historical development of GIs, which vary widely across jurisdictions compared to trademarks that have a more stable and uniform conceptual basis. Because GIs are linked to regional characteristics, traditions, and cultural factors, their definition and protection have been more fluid. Hence, the Reason correctly explains why TRIPS adopts a flexible approach, making both statements correct and logically connected.

63. The determination of whether the provocation was grave and sudden enough to reduce the offence from murder to culpable homicide not amounting to murder is specifically treated as a question of fact under Exception 1 to Section 300 of the Indian Penal Code. This requires examination of the actual circumstances in which the act was committed, including the conduct of the parties, the nature of provocation, and the mental state of the accused at the time of the act. There is no fixed legal formula to decide what constitutes "grave and sudden" provocation, and it varies from case to case. The court must assess the facts and evidence to determine whether a reasonable person in similar circumstances would have lost self-control. Hence, it is a factual determination rather than purely a legal one.

64. The Will theory, associated with jurists like Hegel, states that the purpose of law is to enable individuals to exercise their will and express their personality. It treats rights as an expression of individual autonomy and self-assertion. According to this theory, law exists to protect and promote the free will of individuals, allowing them to act and develop their personality within a legal framework.

65. The case concerning the ship *Arantzazu Mendi* involved issues of recognition of governments during the Spanish Civil War. The dispute was between the de jure Republican Government of Spain and the de facto Nationalist Government led by General Franco. The House of Lords had to consider the legal consequences of recognition of governments and determine which authority had the right to control the property in question.

66. **A. Sankari Prasad v. Union of India (1951):** This is the earliest case where the Supreme Court upheld Parliament's power to amend Fundamental Rights under Article 368.

B. Sajjan Singh v. State of Rajasthan (1965): This reaffirmed the view in Sankari Prasad, maintaining Parliament's amending power over Fundamental Rights.

C. Golak Nath v. State of Punjab (1967): The Court reversed earlier decisions and held that Parliament cannot amend Fundamental Rights.

D. Kesavananda Bharati v. State of Kerala (1973): This landmark case introduced the Basic Structure Doctrine, allowing amendment but not destruction of the Constitution's basic structure.

E. Waman Rao v. Union of India (1981): This case clarified the application of the Basic Structure Doctrine, especially with respect to laws placed in the Ninth Schedule.

67. Section 135 of the Companies Act, 2013 mandates that companies meeting the prescribed financial thresholds must constitute a Corporate Social Responsibility Committee. The Reason is also correct as the CSR Committee is responsible for monitoring the CSR policy and activities of the company. However, this function of monitoring does not explain why such companies are required to constitute the committee; the requirement arises from statutory thresholds and regulatory compliance, not merely from its monitoring role.

68. Article 15 of the Universal Declaration of Human Rights, 1948 provides that everyone has the right to a nationality and that no one shall be arbitrarily deprived of his nationality nor denied the right to change it. This provision ensures legal identity and protection under international human rights law.

69. A written Constitution serves to limit the powers of the organs of the State by clearly defining their functions and boundaries. The Reason is also correct as in systems with judicial review, courts act as guardians of the Constitution by ensuring that laws and actions conform to constitutional provisions. However, judicial review is a mechanism for enforcing constitutional limitations, not the reason why a Constitution is written. The purpose of having a written Constitution is broader and includes clarity, certainty, and limitation of powers, while judicial review is only one of the tools for its enforcement.

70. The Metaphysical school of jurisprudence, influenced largely by German thinkers, sought to develop a universal doctrine of law based on abstract principles and metaphysical ideas. It aimed to derive legal rules from universal reason and philosophical concepts rather than limiting itself to the customs of a particular society or historical development of a specific nation. This distinguishes it from the Historical school, which focuses on the evolution of law within a particular society.

71. In standard form contracts, where one party drafts the contract and imposes terms on the other, ambiguity often arises in interpretation of exclusion or limitation clauses. The Contra Proferentem Rule provides that any ambiguity in such clauses must be interpreted against the party who drafted or inserted the clause. This rule is based on fairness, as the drafting party has the advantage of wording the contract and should bear the consequences of unclear language. It is particularly applied in insurance contracts and consumer agreements where bargaining power is unequal. The rule ensures protection of the weaker party and prevents misuse of exclusion clauses. Therefore, in case of doubt regarding meaning or scope, interpretation is made against the proferens (the party who proposed the clause).

72. D. Effect of Proclamation of Emergency (Article 353): This provision appears first among the given, explaining the consequences of a national emergency, including extension of executive power.

C. Failure of constitutional machinery in States (Article 356): This follows and deals with President's Rule in States when governance cannot be carried out as per the Constitution.

B. Suspension of Article 19 (Article 358): This provision allows suspension of freedoms under Article 19 during a national emergency.

A. Financial Emergency (Article 360): This appears last and deals with financial instability and control of finances by the Union.

73. Section 6 of the Biological Diversity Act, 2002 specifically deals with the requirement of obtaining prior approval of the National Biodiversity Authority before applying for any intellectual property right based on research or information on biological resources obtained from India. While granting such approval, the Authority is empowered to impose conditions relating to benefit sharing, including payment of fees, royalties, or a share in the financial benefits arising from commercial utilization. This provision forms part of the Access and Benefit Sharing mechanism, ensuring that benefits derived from biological resources are equitably shared with local communities and stakeholders. Therefore, Section 6 directly relates to benefit sharing fees and royalties under the Act.

74. **A. Son's daughter's son:** This appears first among the given in Class II heirs under the Schedule of the Hindu Succession Act.

D. Son's daughter's daughter: It follows immediately after the previous category.

B. Daughter's son's son: This comes later in the order of Class II heirs.

C. Daughter's son's daughter: This appears after the son's daughter's descendants in the Schedule.

75. Under the Companies Act, 2013, every listed public company is required to have at least one-third of the total number of directors as independent directors. This ensures corporate governance, transparency, and protection of shareholders' interests by bringing independent judgment into the board's decision-making process.

76. The question contains ambiguity in provisions and their order in the Motor Vehicles Act, 1988: The given items correspond to provisions that are not arranged in a clear linear sequence within the Act due to amendments and insertions at different times. "Necessity of Permits" falls under Chapter V (earlier part), "Claims Tribunal" under Chapter XII, "Motor Vehicle Accident Fund" is a later insertion (Section 164B onwards), and "Recall of Motor Vehicles" is introduced separately under Section 110A. Because these provisions belong to different chapters and some were inserted later without disturbing the original sequence, their "order of appearance" cannot be determined in a straightforward ascending manner as per the structure of the Act. None of the options correctly represent the actual legislative sequence, leading to ambiguity. Hence, the correct answer is NONE.

77.
- **A → II (Entry into force of Refugee Convention – 1954):** The 1951 Convention came into force in 1954, establishing international refugee protection standards.
- **B → I (Protocol to Refugee Convention – 1967):** The 1967 Protocol removed geographical and temporal limitations of the Convention.
- **C → III (UNHCR Nobel Prize – 1981):** UNHCR received the Nobel Peace Prize for the second time in 1981.
- **D → IV (Formation of UNHCR – 1950):** The UN High Commissioner for Refugees was established in 1950.

78. **B.** If a state government acts against secularism, it violates the basic structure, and President's Rule can be justified.

C. The State Assembly cannot be dissolved before Parliament approves the Proclamation under Article 356.

D. The power under Article 356 is not absolute and is subject to judicial review and constitutional limitations.

79. India and the United Kingdom formally signed the Comprehensive Economic and Trade Agreement (CETA) on 24 July 2025 during a high-level bilateral meeting in London. This agreement was the culmination of negotiations aimed at strengthening trade and economic cooperation between the two countries. It provided for significant tariff reductions, expanded market access, and facilitation of trade in goods and services. A notable feature included provisions to prevent double social security contributions for professionals working temporarily abroad. The agreement reflects a major step in enhancing bilateral trade relations and aims to substantially increase trade volume in the coming years.

80. **D. Necessaries supplied (Section 68):** This appears early under quasi-contract provisions dealing with persons incapable of contracting.

C. Compensation for breach (Section 73): This provision follows, dealing with damages for breach of contract.

A. Continuing guarantee (Section 129): This appears later under contracts of guarantee.

B. Care by bailee (Section 151): This is part of bailment provisions, appearing after guarantee provisions.

81. **A. Proposal:** Section 2(a) defines proposal as the starting point of a contract when one person signifies willingness to do or abstain from doing something.

D. Promise: Section 2(b) states that when a proposal is accepted, it becomes a promise.

B. Consideration: Section 2(d) defines consideration as something done or abstained from at the desire of the promisor.

C. Agreement: Section 2(e) defines agreement as every promise and every set of promises forming consideration for each other.

E. Contract: Section 2(h) defines contract as an agreement enforceable by law, which is the final stage in formation.

82. The Assertion correctly states that Rule of Law has been recognized as a basic feature of the Indian Constitution, which cannot be amended even under Article 368. This doctrine has evolved through judicial interpretation, especially under the Basic Structure Doctrine. The Reason is also correct because constitutional jurisprudence, particularly in countries like Germany, recognizes that certain fundamental principles of higher moral or ethical value can override even express constitutional provisions. This supports the idea that Rule of Law can be treated as a superior constitutional principle, thus explaining the Assertion.

83.
- **A → IV (Cox v. Hickman – Mutual Agency):** This case established that mutual agency is the true test of partnership.
- **B → III (Stekel v. Ellice – Salaried partner):** It clarified that even a salaried partner can be a partner if mutual agency exists.
- **C → II (Lachhman Das v. CIT – Partnership between Karta and Coparcener):** The case recognized that a Karta can enter into partnership with a coparcener in his individual capacity.
- **D → I (Smith v. Anderson – Business must be taken in a practical sense):** It defined business in a practical and real sense for determining partnership.

84.
- **A → II (Ashby v. White – Violation of absolute right):** The case established that violation of a legal right gives rise to a remedy even without actual damage.
- **B → III (Rylands v. Fletcher – Strict liability):** It laid down the rule of strict liability for escape of dangerous things.
- **C → I (Olga Tellis v. Bombay Municipal Corp. – Poverty as involuntary act):** The Court recognized that pavement dwellers are compelled by poverty, linking it to right to livelihood.
- **D → IV (Allen v. Flood – Motive irrelevant):** It established that motive is irrelevant if the act is lawful.

85. The Draft Convention on Territorial Asylum (1974) recognizes in Article 1 that the grant of asylum is a sovereign right of the State. It affirms that States have the discretion to grant asylum to persons seeking protection without interference, reflecting the principle of sovereignty and non-intervention in international law.

86. The case of *Abhayanand Mishra v. State of Bihar* is a leading authority on the concept of attempt under criminal law. The Supreme Court clarified the distinction between preparation and attempt, stating that an attempt begins when preparations are complete and the accused has taken a direct step towards the commission of the offence. The act must be proximate to the intended offence and not merely preparatory. This case laid down the test of proximity and intention, which is used to determine criminal liability for attempt under the Indian Penal Code.

87.
- **A → IV (John Rawls):** Rawls stated that justice is the first virtue of social institutions, emphasizing fairness as the basis of social arrangements.
- **B → II (Aristotle):** Aristotle viewed natural justice as part of political justice, distinguishing between universal natural law and particular legal justice.
- **C → III (Dworkin):** Ronald Dworkin emphasized "equality of respect and concern" as a core principle of justice and rights.
- **D → I (Immanuel Kant):** Kant emphasized human dignity as intrinsic worth, forming the foundation of human rights.

88. Under the Companies Act, 2013, recognized types of prospectus include shelf prospectus, deemed prospectus, and abridged prospectus. The correct term used in law is "Red Herring Prospectus," not "Yellow Herring Prospectus." Therefore, the given option is not a recognized type and is incorrect.

89. B. The Supreme Court invoked Article 142 to adopt a victim-centric approach in sentencing, focusing on justice tailored to the victim's circumstances.

D. The Court considered the wishes of the victim and declined to enhance the sentence of the accused, emphasizing rehabilitation and victim's perspective.

90. • **A → III (National Biodiversity Authority – Section 8):** This section provides for the establishment of the National Biodiversity Authority.

• **B → I (State Biodiversity Fund – Section 32):** This section deals with the constitution of the State Biodiversity Fund.

• **C → IV (National Biodiversity Fund – Section 27):** This section provides for the National Biodiversity Fund.

• **D → II (Biodiversity Heritage Sites – Section 37):** This section empowers State Governments to notify Biodiversity Heritage Sites.

91. The passage clearly states that the Constitution is being interpreted for a nation whose people desire a complete and dignified life, and therefore social justice must be central to its interpretation. The emphasis is on addressing real social needs and inequalities rather than abstract legal reasoning. The idea of "hunger for a full life" reflects the goal of ensuring justice, equality, and welfare. Hence, the perception of social justice is essential in constitutional interpretation to meet the aspirations of the people.

92. The author stresses that the Constitution is a living document and its interpretation must be grounded in the realities of society. The "Supreme Lex" (the Constitution) derives its vitality from the social context in which it operates. Ignoring social conditions would lead to empty and ineffective interpretation. Therefore, courts must always consider the social setting while interpreting constitutional provisions.

93. The passage explicitly states that the Constitution is not a rigid or "petrified" document but a dynamic human text. It must be read with a national mission aimed at achieving social justice and progress. The Court must interpret it in a way that reflects human values and national goals. This approach emphasizes flexibility and responsiveness to changing societal needs.

94. The passage quotes the American Supreme Court to highlight that modern society does not adhere to rigid, absolute principles. Instead, law must adapt to changing circumstances and realities. This idea supports a flexible and pragmatic approach to constitutional interpretation. Therefore, the most certain principle in modern society is that there are no absolutes.

95. The passage concludes by stating that "Legal Einsteinism," implying relativity and flexibility in legal interpretation, guides the Court rather than rigid doctrinal rules. This suggests that law should adapt to context and circumstances rather than follow fixed absolutes. It emphasizes a dynamic and evolving approach to jurisprudence.

96. The passage clearly states that according to Roman thinkers, natural law embodied the elementary principles of justice. These principles were considered the dictates of reason and rights, reflecting what is just and fair rather than what is merely expedient. Natural law was seen as universal, unalterable, and based on rational human nature. Therefore, its core essence lay in justice rather than mere social rules or specific legal systems.

97. Natural law is described in the passage as what is just rather than expedient, reasonable rather than arbitrary, natural rather than convenient, and aimed at social good rather than personal will. This clearly indicates that convenience is not a characteristic of natural law. Instead, it is opposed to convenience, emphasizing fairness, reason, and universal justice.

98. The passage explains that the Romans developed a system called *Jus gentium*, which was regarded as having universal application. It was intended to govern relations among people beyond a particular state and was influenced by natural law principles. This distinguished it from *Jus civil*, which was limited to Roman citizens.

99. The passage explicitly mentions that natural law was based on the rational and reasonable needs of human nature. It emphasizes that natural law arises from the nature of humans as rational and social beings, focusing on justice and reason rather than arbitraiy or personal considerations.

100. The passage clearly states that in the republican era of Rome, *Jus gentium* was reinforced by natural law (*Jus natural*). This shows that its development and application were particularly prominent during the republican period of Roman history.

Previous Years' Paper

National Testing Agency (NTA)

UGC-NET Junior Research Fellowship & Assistant Professor Eligibility Exam

LAW, JUNE-2025

(Exam held on 25-06-2025)

PAPER-II

1. What is the guiding principle of inheritance under Mitakshara?

1. Religious efficacy
2. Capacity to perform religious obligations
3. Doctrine of sapinda relationship
4. Capacity to offer religious obligations

2. Which of the following is **not** a general defence under Torts?

A. Mistake
B. Remoteness
C. Necessity
D. Consent

Choose the **correct** answer from the options given below:

1. A and B only
2. C only
3. C and D only
4. B only

3. Which of the following is **not** defined under section 2 of BNS, 2023 and Chapter II of IPC, 1860?

1. Animal
2. Person
3. Child
4. Women

4. Which of the following is **not** true in the context of CSR?

1. CSR Committee should consist of only one Director
2. CSR provision was introduced by the Companies Act, 2013
3. Company should spend atleast 2% of average net profits made during the immediately preceding 3 financial years
4. CSR is an implied agreement between the company and society to impart goods and services in some way advantageous to the society

5. In which of the following case, the Supreme Court of India gave a split verdict on 23rd July, 2024 in a matter involving health, environment and inter-generational equity?

1. M.C. Mehta v/s U.O.I
2. Animal Welfare Board of India v/s U.O.I
3. M.K. Ranjitsingh v/s U.O.I
4. Gene Campaign v/s U.O.I

6. Match the LIST-I with LIST-II.

LIST-I (Jurists)	LIST-II (Definition of Administrative Law)
A. Wade	I. Administrative Law is the law relating to the administration. It determines the organization, powers and duties of administrative authorities.

B. Garner	II. Main object of administrative law is the operation and control of administrative authorities.
C. Griffith & Street	III. Rules recognized by the courts as law and which relate to and regulate the administration of government.
D. Ivor Jennings	IV. Law relating to the control of government power.

Choose the **correct** answer from the options given below:

1. A-I, B-II, C-III, D-IV
2. A-II, B-I, C-IV, D-III
3. A-III, B-IV, C-I, D-II
4. A-IV, B-III, C-II, D-I

7. In which of the following case, the Supreme Court of India held that telephone tapping is a serious invasion of an individual's right to privacy?

1. People's Union for Civil Liberties v/s Union of India
2. R. Rajagopal v/s State of T.N.
3. Mr. v/s Hospital 'Z'
4. State of Maharashtra v/s Madhulkar Narain

8. Which of the following Canadian Legislation does **not** have provisions related to Federation?

1. Law of Federation, 1802
2. British North America Act, 1867
3. Constitution Act, 1982
4. Constitution Act, 1867

9. Which of the following is **not** a guardian under the Hindu Minority and Guardianship Act, 1956?

A. Guardian for Marriage
B. Maternal Guardian
C. Testamentary Guardian
D. Guardian by Affinity

Choose the **correct** answer from the options given below:

1. A and B only
2. A only
3. C and D only
4. C only

10. "International law is the body of rules and principles of action which are binding upon civilised states in their relations with one another''. This definition is attributed to whom of the following?

1. Oppenheium
2. J.L. Briely
3. J.G. Starke
4. Jerry Bentham

11. Match the LIST-I with LIST-II.

LIST-I (Type of IPR)	LIST-II (Concept)
A. Geographical Indication	I. Post grant opposition
B. Trademark	II. Protection of Right Management Information (RMI)
C. Patent	III. Prohibition of Assignment
D. Copyright	IV. Honest Concurrent use

Choose the **correct** answer from the options given below:

1. A-I, B-IV, C-III, D-II
2. A-III, B-IV, C-I, D-II
3. A-I, B-III, C-IV, D-I
4. A-II, B-IV, C-I, D-III

12. Which of the following theory/theories is/are **not** closely connected to intellectual property rights?

A. Economic Theory
B. Autopoietic legal Theory
C. Social Planning Theory
D. Instrumentalist Theory
E. Social Contract Theory

Choose the **correct** answer from the options given below:

1. C and D only
2. A and E only
3. B only
4. D only

13. Which of the following is a landmark case on the importance of 'nationality'?

1. North Sea Continental Self Case
2. Asylum Case
3. S.S. Lotus Case
4. Nottebohm Case

14. Which of the following is **not** true in the context of a promissory note?

1. It must be in writing and signed by the maker.
2. There must be an undertaking or promise to pay.
3. Such a promise must be conditional.
4. The promise must be in respect of payment of money only.

15. Which of the following provision of the Companies Act, 2013 identifies shares and debentures as a movable property?

1. Section 44
2. Section 45
3. Section 46
4. Section 47

16. Which of the following statements are correct?

A. The first national commission for women was constituted on 31.01.1992

B. National Commission for Backward Classes has been accorded constitutional status through 102nd Constitution (Amendment) Act, 2018

C. The ministry of Minority Affairs was carved out of Ministry of Social Justice and Empowerment

D. National Commission for Scheduled Tribes has been set up under Art. 338

E. Art. 338A deals with National Commission for Scheduled Castes

Choose the **correct** answer from the options given below:

1. B, C, D only
2. C, D, E only
3. A, B, C only
4. A, C, E only

17. Arrange the following Conventions in the chronological order of their coming into force.

A. The Biological Weapons Convention

B. The Chemical Weapons Convention

C. The Convention on Certain Conventional Weapons

D. The Ottawa Convention on Anti-Personnel Mines

Choose the **correct** answer from the options given below:

1. A, B, C, D
2. A, C, B, D
3. C, A, B, D
4. C, D, A, B

18. In which of the following case, the golden rule for framing prospectus was formulated by V.C. Kindersley?

A. Methodist Church v/s Union of India

B. R. v/s Registrar of Companies

C. New Brunswick Canada Railway Co. v/s Muggeridge

D. Jubilee Colton Mills Ltd. v/s Lewis

Choose the **correct** answer from the options given below:

1. A and C only
2. B only
3. C only
4. B and D only

19. Match the LIST-I with LIST-II.

	LIST-I (Jurist)		LIST-II (Statement/Opinion)
A.	Montesquie	I.	Comparative Constitution is strange
B.	Lee	II.	Used the term - Rechtsvergleichung
C.	Rudolph and Schlesinger	III.	Published 'Ancient Law' in 1861
D.	Maine	IV.	Father of Comparative Law

Choose the **correct** answer from the options given below:

1. A-I, B-II, C-III, D-IV
2. A-II, B-III, C-IV, D-I
3. A-III, B-IV, C-I, D-II
4. A-IV, B-I, C-II, D-III

20. Which of the following decisions are related to extradition:

A. Savarkar case
B. Abu Salem case
C. Castioni, re case
D. Meunier, re case
E. Paquete Habana case

Choose the **correct** answer from the options given below:

1. A, B, C only
2. B, C, D, E only
3. A, B, C, D only
4. A, B, D, E only

21. Match the LIST-I with LIST-II.

LIST-I (Authors/Editors)	LIST-II (Title of Books)
A. Rainer Arnold	I. International Humanitarian Law
B. Vandana Shiva	II. The Universalism of Human Rights
C. Lenzerini Federico	III. Biopiracy: The Plunder of Nature & Knowledge
D. Emily Crowford & Alison Pert	IV. The Culturalisation of Human Rights Law

Choose the **correct** answer from the options given below:

1. A-II, B-III, C-IV, D-I
2. A-I, B-II, C-III, D-IV
3. A-II, B-I, C-IV, D-III
4. A-IV, B-III, C-I, D-II

22. Match the LIST-I with LIST-II.

LIST-I (Authors/Editors)	LIST-II (Title of Books)
A. J Donhelly & D.J. Whelar	I. International Human Rights
B. L. Rajamani & J. Peel	II. The Oxford Handbook of International Environmental Law
C. Karnika Seth	III. Computers, Internet and New Technology Laws
D. J. Gibson	IV. Patenting Lives: Life Patents, Culture & Development

Choose the **correct** answer from the options given below:

1. A-II, B-I, C-IV, D-III
2. A-I, B-IV, C-II, D-III
3. A-I, B-II, C-III, D-IV
4. A-III, B-II, C-I, D-IV

23. Arrange the following in order of their enactment (ascending):

A. West German Constitution
B. British North America Act
C. Australian Constitution Act
D. Article of Confederation and Perpetual Union

Choose the **correct** answer from the options given below:

1. D, B, C, A
2. A, B, C, D
3. B, A, C, D
4. D, C, B, A

24. United States Ombudsman Association was founded in which year?

1. 1977
2. 1976
3. 1956
4. 1986

25. Which of the following is **not** a theory of legal personality?

1. Fiction theory
2. Concession theory
3. Interest theory
4. Bracket theory

26. Which one of the following is incorrect statement in the context of the characteristic features of a Waqf?

1. Waqf properties are inalienable
2. A testamentary Waqf is irrevocable
3. A Waqf once created cannot be revoked
4. A Waqf property vests in God

27. Match the LIST-I with LIST-II.

LIST-I (Judicial Decisions)	LIST-II (Issue)
A. State of Gujarat v/s Reliance Industries Ltd & Ors.	I. Management of sewage treatment plants
B. Municipal Corporation Ghaziabad v/s Central Pollution Control Board	II. Climate Change
C. Hanuman Laxman Aroskar v/s U.O.I	III. Environmental Clearance for large infrastructure project
D. Riddhima Pandey v/s U.O.I	IV. Green cess

Choose the **correct** answer from the options given below:

1. A-III, B-I, C-IV, D-II
2. A-I, B-IV, C-III, D-II
3. A-IV, B-I, C-III, D-II
4. A-III, B-II, C-IV, D-I

28. Which of the following Article is referred to be the heart and soul of the Indian Constitution?

1. Article 32
2. Article 21
3. Article 14
4. Article 226

29. What are the duties of a bailee as provided under the Indian Contract Act?

A. Duty to take reasonable care of the goods bailed.
B. Duty not to make unauthorized use of the goods.
C. Duty not to mix bailor's goods with his own goods.
D. Duty to return the goods on fulfilment of the purpose.
E. Duty not to deliver to the bailor increase or profit on the goods bailed.

Choose the **correct** answer from the options given below:

1. B, C, D, E only
2. C, D, E, A only
3. D. E, B, A only
4. A, B, C, D only

30. Which of the following is **not** an absolute privilege under the law of torts?

1. A petition to Parliament
2. Words written or spoken before a Tribunal
3. Communication made in self-protection
4. Communication relating to State matters made by one minister to another

31. The foundation of Federation in India was laid down by which legislation from the following?

1. Government of India Act, 1919
2. Government of India Act, 1935
3. Constitution of India, 1950
4. Queen Proclamation of 1875

32. Match the LIST-I with LIST-II.

LIST-I (Schedules under UCC of Uttrakhand, 2025)	LIST-II (Topic dealt under the Schedule)
A. Schedule 3	I. form of probate
B. Schedule 7	II. form of certificate
C. Schedule 5	III. form of caveat
D. Schedule 4	IV. form of certificate and extended certificate

Choose the **correct** answer from the options given below:

1. A-II, B-IV, C-I, D-III
2. A-I, B-II, C-III, D-IV
3. A-IV, B-III, C-II, D-I
4. A-II, B-I, C-IV, D-III

33. Match the LIST-I with LIST-II.

LIST-I (Maxim)	LIST-II (Meaning)
A. *Erga Omnes*	I. Relation to all
B. *Jus Cogens*	II. Peremptory norm

C. *Pacta Sunt Servanda*	III. Agreements are to be respected
D. *Rebus Sic Stantibus*	IV. Essential circumstances remain unchanged

Choose the **correct** answer from the options given below:

1. A-IV, B-III, C-II, D-I
2. A-III, B-IV, C-II, D-I
3. A-I, B-II, C-III, D-IV
4. A-III, B-I, C-II, D-IV

34. Match the LIST-I with LIST-II.

LIST-I (Section under the Motor Vehicle (Amendment) Act, 2019)	LIST-II (Provision)
A. Section 164 B	I. Information to be given regarding accident
B. Section 162	II. Motor Vehicle Accident Fund
C. Section 164 A	III. Scheme for golden hour
D. Section 159	IV. Scheme for Interim relief for claimants

Choose the **correct** answer from the options given below:

1. A-I, B-IV, C-III, D-II
2. A-IV, B-I, C-II, D-III
3. A-III, B-II, C-I, D-IV
4. A-II, B-III, C-IV, D-I

35. Which of the following Amendment has inserted the theme 'Secularism, Socialism and Integrity' in the Preamble of the Indian Constitution?

1. 44th Amendment
2. 42nd Amendment
3. 73rd Amendment
4. 74th Amendment

36. Match the LIST-I with LIST-II.

LIST-I (Heirs)	LIST-II (Succession Categories)
A. Paternal Aunt's Son	I. Class II
B. Daughter's Son's daughter	II. Cognate
C. Paternal Uncle's daughter	III. Class I
D. Daughter of a predeceased Son	IV. Agnate

Choose the **correct** answer from the options given below:

1. A-I, B-III, C-II, D-IV
2. A-II, B-I, C-IV, D-III
3. A-II, B-IV, C-I, D-III
4. A-I, B-II, C-III, D-IV

37. Match the LIST-I with LIST-II.

LIST-I (Profounder)	LIST-II (Idea)
A. Mimansa	I. Law and Morals are same
B. Smriti	II. "Idea of Values" is the foundation
C. Post Reformation Europe	III. Law derives authority from State and not morals
D. Korkunov	IV. There is distinction between obligatory and recommendatory rules

Choose the **correct** answer from the options given below:

1. A-IV, B-I, C-III, D-II
2. A-II, B-III, C-I, D-IV
3. A-III, B-IV, C-II, D-I
4. A-I, B-II, C-IV, D-III

38. Estrada doctrine dealing with recognition of States and Government is primarily related to which country?

1. Spain
2. Mexico
3. Germany
4. China

39. Arrange the following provisions in the correct order of their appearance in the Information Technology Act, 2000 (section-wise):

A. Penalty for misrepresentation
B. Punishment for identify theft
C. Punishment for cyber terrorism
D. Penalty for breach of confidentiality and privacy
E. Punishment for violation of privacy

Choose the **correct** answer from the options given below:

1. A, B, C, D, E
2. C, B, A, E, D
3. B, A, C, D, E
4. B, E, C, A, D

40. A Christian Man X and a Hindu Girl Y eloped and entered into an "Agreement of Marriage'' on ₹ 50 stamp paper and registered it at Registrar office. They exchanged garland, X tied a Mangalsutra around neck of Y. Is it a valid Marriage?

1. It is a valid marriage as it is registered by agreement
2. It is valid marriage as ceremonies are performed
3. It is not a valid marriage as legal validity test is not complete
4. It is a valid marriage as customary rites of the parties were followed

41. When did Ministry of Environment, Forest and Climate Change notify Biological Diversity Rules, 2024?

1. 25th December, 2024
2. 18th January, 2024
3. 1st April, 2024
4. 22nd October, 2024

42. Arrange the following in the order of their introduction in the American Constitution by way of Amendment (ascending order)

A. 18-year-old Suffrage
B. Black Suffrage
C. Abolition of Slavery
D. Women Suffrage

Choose the **correct** answer from the options given below:

1. A, B, C, D
2. B, C, D, A
3. C, B, D, A
4. A, C, B, D

43. Which section in BNS, 2023 replaced section 124A of IPC, 1860 by prohibiting "acts endangering sovereignty, unity and integrity of India"?

1. Section 112
2. Section 152
3. Section 95
4. Section 304

44. Which of the following is **not** the meaning of the term "dominant position" under the Competition Act, 2002?

1. Position of strength
2. Operating independently of competitive forces
3. Cartel activity among competitors
4. Affect its competitors or consumers in its favour

45. From which country, Part IV of the Indian Constitution is borrowed?

1. Russia
2. Ireland
3. USA
4. Spain

46. Which of the following are correct about "legal theory"?

A. It defines Law
B. It analyses legal concepts
C. It deals with mere theory and has no practical importance
D. It highlights salient features of legal system

Choose the **correct** answer from the options given below:

1. A, B, C only
2. B, C, D only
3. A, B, D only
4. A, C, D only

47. Arrange the following provisions of Protection of Human Rights Act, 1993 in the order of its appearance in the Act.

A. Inquiry into complaints
B. Procedure with respect to armed forces
C. Investigation
D. Powers relating to inquiry
E. Statements made by person to the Commission

Choose the **correct** answer from the options given below:

1. A, B, C, D, E
2. A, D, E, B, C
3. A, D, C, E, B
4. D, C, E, A, B

48. Which of the following is true about Separation of Power in the Constitution of Canada?

A. Separation exists between only Judiciary and Parliament
B. Separation exists between executive and legislature
C. There is no general separation of power
D. Canadian Constitution has no parallel with Presidentialism

Choose the **correct** answer from the options given below:

1. B, D only
2. A, C only
3. A, B only
4. C, D only

49. Which of the following articles incorporate, the expression 'right to life'?

A. Article 3 of UDHR, 1948
B. Article 6 of ICCPR, 1966
C. Article 9 of ICESCR, 1966
D. Article 3 of OP2 of ICCPR, 1989

Choose the **correct** answer from the options given below:

1. A and C only
2. A and B only
3. C and D only
4. B and D only

50. Who is the writer of the book titled, "The Post Modern Condition: A Report on Knowledge"?

1. Michel Foucault
2. Jean-Francois Lyotard
3. Jacques Derrida
4. Jean Baudrillard

51. "True subject matter of ownership in all cases is a right''. Who gave this statement?

1. Grotius
2. Roscoe Pound
3. Salmond
4. Ihering

52. Which of the following statements are incorrect in the context of Adoption?

A. Muslim Law does not recognise adoption.
B. A married Hindu male can adopt a child without obtaining consent of his wife.
C. Child must not have completed the age of fifteen years.
D. Two persons cannot adopt the same child except in case of a husband and wife.
E. A person who is a major and sound mind can only be adopted.

Choose the **correct** answer from the options given below:

1. B, E only
2. A, C only
3. C, D only
4. D, E only

53. Seven Legislations are listed under Schedule I of the National Green Tribunal Act, 2010. Which of the following Act is not included under Schedule I?

1. The Forest (Conservation) Act, 1980
2. The Environment (Protection) Act, 1986
3. The Biological Diversity Act, 2002
4. The Scheduled Tribes and other Traditional Forest Dwellers (Recognition of Forest Rights) Act, 2006

54. Arrange the following legal instruments chronologically (ascending order):

A. Rights of Persons with Disabilities Act (India)
B. OP to the CEDAW
C. UN Principles for older Persons
D. UN Convention on the Rights of Persons with Disabilities
E. UN Declaration on Rights of Persons belonging to National, Ethnic, Religious and Linguistic Minorities

Choose the **correct** answer from the options given below:

1. A, B, D, C, E
2. C, E, B, D, A
3. C, D, A, E, B
4. D, A, C, B, E

55. Which of the following statements are correct regarding the Doctrine of Legitimate Expectations?

A. The doctrine has an important place in the development of law of judicial review.
B. Doctrine is well established and operated in the domain of public law.
C. Doctrine has been developed both in the context of reasonableness and natural justice.
D. The concept of legitimate expectation made its first appearance in the case of Union of India v/s Hindustan Development Corpn.

Choose the **correct** answer from the options given below:

1. A, B, D only
2. A, B, C only
3. B, C, D only
4. A, C, D only

56. The power of judicial review was first adopted/applied by the Supreme Court of USA in which of the following case?

1. Marbury v/s Madison
2. North Wales Police v/s Evans
3. Minerva v/s State of Georgia
4. Reg v/s Home Secretary

57. Arrange the following cases related to Indian Contract Act in chronological order (ascending):

A. State of Madhya Pradesh v/s Gobardhan Dass
B. New India Assurance Co. v/s Haryana Roadways, Sonipat
C. Chairman-cum-M.D. T.N. Tea Plantation Corp.Ltd v/s M/S Srinivasa Timbers
D. G.S.R.T.C v/s B. Arunchandra & Co.

Choose the **correct** answer from the options given below:

1. A, B, C, D
2. B, C, D, A
3. C, D, B, A
4. D, B, A, C

58. In which of the following case, the Supreme Court of India struck down section 66A of the Information Technology Act, 2000 as unconstitutional?

1. Shreya Singhal v/s U.O.I
2. Ajay Canu v/s U.O.I
3. Tata Cellular v/s U.O.I
4. Supreme Court Bar Association v/s U.O.I

59. On which date the United Nations Organisation came into existence?

1. 20th October, 1945
2. 24th October, 1945
3. 10th December, 1948
4. 10th December, 1945

60. Which of the following Theory/Theories is/are predominantly related to 'attempt' in law of crimes.

A. Last seen theory
B. Proximity theory
C. Theory of Impossibility
D. Reformatory Theory

Choose the **correct** answer from the options given below:

1. A and C only
2. C and D only
3. B and C only
4. A and B only

61. Arrange the following cases on Maintenance in their chronological order (Ascending order):

A. Saira Bano v/s AM Abdul Gafoor
B. Danial Latifi v/s Union of India
C. Noor Saba Khatoon v/s Mohd. Quasim
D. Md. Ahmed Khan v/s Shah Bano Begum

Choose the **correct** answer from the options given below:

1. D, C, A, B   2. C, D, B, A
3. A, B, D, C   4. D, A, C, B

62. Match the LIST-I with LIST-II.

LIST-I (Principles of Natural Justice)	LIST-II (Case laws)
A. Pecuniary Bias	I. Gullapalli Nageswara Rao v/s A.P. SRTC
B. Personal Bias	II. Dimes v/s Grand Junction Canal
C. Official Bias	III. Mineral Development Ltd. v/s State of Bihar
D. Judicial Obstinacy	IV. State of W.B v/s Shivananda Pathak

Choose the **correct** answer from the options given below:

1. A-I, B-II, C-III, D-IV
2. A-II, B-III, C-I, D-IV
3. A-IV, B-III, C-II, D-I
4. A-III, B-I, C-IV, D-II

63. Which Schedule of the Indian Constitution contains special provisions for the administration and control of scheduled areas in several states?

1. Fifth   2. Third
3. Seventh   4. Ninth

64. Which of the following statements are correct in the context of standard form contract's?

A. Notice should not be contemporaneous with the consent.
B. There should be a reasonable notice of the contractual terms.
C. There should be no misrepresentation.
D. The parties are not bound if the terms are contained in a contractual document.
E. The contract with standard terms may be drafted by one party and on the same terms contracts may be made with numerous persons.

Choose the **correct** answer from the options given below:

1. B, C, E only
2. A, B, C only
3. B, C, D only
4. A, D, C only

65. Arrange the following in the historical order of development of Natural Law theories (ascending):

A. Union with Divine is end of law
B. Church is the law giver
C. Development of idea of Rationalism
D. Revival of Natural Law

Choose the **correct** answer from the options given below:

1. A, B, C, D   2. B, C, A, D
3. D, C, B, A   4. A, C, B, D

66. H and W are married, H filed petition for divorce that was granted in his favour by the family court, when H cannot remarry again?

1. When there is no right of appeal against the decree
2. When the time for appeal has expired
3. When an appeal filed was dismissed
4. When the divorce decree was stayed

67. Mark the incorrect statement as per Muslim Law on Wills.

A. A will of a minor can be ratified by him on attaining majority.
B. The will of a person of unsound mind cannot be ratified on attaining sanity.

C. Will made by a sane person will become invalid if subsequently he becomes insane.

D. A will made by a person who subsequently commits suicide is invalid.

Choose the **correct** answer from the options given below:

1. A, D, only 2. B only
3. C, A only 4. D only

68. Which of the following is **not** true in the context of powers of the President in the Indian Constitution?

A. The President is the Supreme Commander of the Defence Forces of the country.

B. All treaties and international agreements are negotiated and concluded in the name of the President though subject to ratification by the Parliament.

C. President has power to summon and prorogue the Parliament and can dissolve the Lok Sabha.

D. President is empowered to promulgate ordinances during recess of Parliament under Article 213 of the Indian Constitution.

Choose the **correct** answer from the options given below:

1. D only 2. B, C only
3. C only 4. A, B only

69. Which one of the following Reports of the Law Commission of India supported/recommended the inclusion of irretrievable breakdown of marriage as a ground for divorce?

1. 73rd Report 2. 72nd Report
3. 71st Report 4. 70th Report

70. Arrange chronologically the following negotiations of GATT between 1947 to 1994 which led to the formation of WTO?

A. Annecy B. Kennedy Round
C. Tokyo D. Torquay

Choose the **correct** answer from the options given below:

1. A, B, C, D 2. B, C, A, D
3. A, D, B, C 4. C, B, D, A

71. Which of the following case does not relate to the concept of absolute liability under law of India?

1. Indian Council for Enviro-legal Action v/s Union of India
2. Klaus Mittelbachert v/s East India Hotels of India
3. Madras Railway Co v/s Zeminder of Carvatenagram
4. M.C. Mehta v/s Union of India

72. Which of the following statements are **not** correct in respect of US Constitution?

A. Mode of Amendment is given in Article IV

B. 2/3 of both houses can propose Amendments

C. It has to be ratified by 3/4 of state legislature

D. Constitution cannot be amended by Convention

Choose the **correct** answer from the options given below:

1. A and B only
2. A and D only
3. C and D only
4. B and D only

73. Arrange the following provisions as per the correct order in the Indian Constitution (Article wise):

A. Failure of Constitutional Machinery in State

B. Proclamation of Emergency

C. Financial Emergency

D. Suspension of Article 19 during emergency

Choose the **correct** answer from the options given below"

1. B, A, D, C 2. A, B, C, D
3. B, C, D, A 4. D, A, B, C

74. What is the US equivalent legislation of the Indian Right to Information Act, 2005?

1. Freedom of Information Act, 1966
2. Freedom of Information Act, 1954
3. Freedom of Information Act, 1924
4. Freedom of Information Act, 1967

75. Match the LIST-I with LIST-II.

LIST-I (Position of Directors)	LIST-II (Case laws)
A. Directors as 'Agents'	I. Ferguson v/s Wilson
B. Directors as 'Employees'	II. R.R Kothandraman v/s Commr. of Income Tax
C. Directors as 'Trustees'	III. Great Eastern Rly. Co. v/s Turner
D. Directors in a 'Fiduciary relationship'	IV. Forest of Dean Coal Mining Co. Re

Choose the **correct** answer from the options given below:

1. A-IV, B-III, C-II, D-I
2. A-III, B-I, C-IV, D-II
3. A-I, B-II, C-III, D-IV
4. A-II, B-IV, C-I, D-III

76. Match the LIST-I with LIST-II.

LIST-I (Exception to Sec.300 of IPC)	LIST-II (Exception Number)
A. Sudden and grave provocation	I. Exception 5
B. Exceeding right of private defence	II. Exception 1
C. Death caused in sudden fight	III. Exception 4
D. Death caused with the consent of the person	IV. Exception 2

Choose the **correct** answer from the options given below:

1. A-I, B-II, C-III, D-IV
2. A-II, B-IV, C-III, D-I
3. A-II, B-IV, C-I, D-III
4. A-IV, B-III, C-II, D-I

77. Which of the following are correct about 'Rule of Law'?

A. It is derived from French phrase *"La principe de legalite"*

B. It is called supremacy of law

C. It promotes arbitrary governance

D. Decisions could be made by discretion only

Choose the **correct** answer from the options given below:

1. B, C only
2. C, D only
3. A, D only
4. A, B only

78. Which of the following UN organization addresses the global justice concerns?

1. Trusteeship Council
2. General Assembly
3. International Court of Justice
4. Security Council

79. 'X' an insane person kills 'Y' by firing from a loaded gun, 'X' has committed which of the following offence?

1. No offence at all
2. An offence of grevious hurt
3. An offence of murder
4. An offence of culpable homicide not amounting to murder

80. Match the LIST-I with LIST-II.

LIST-I (Term/Doctrine)	LIST-II (Opinion)
A. Jus Necessitatis	I. Collective term for intention and recklessness
B. Malice	II. Two forms of Mensrea
C. Dolus and Culpa	III. Two alternative conditions of Penal Liability
D. Intention and Negligence	IV. Right of the man to do from which he cannot be dissuaded

Choose the **correct** answer from the options given below:
1. A-IV, B-I, C-II, D-III
2. A-III, B-II, C-IV, D-I
3. A-I, B-IV, C-III, D-II
4. A-II, B-III, C-I, D-IV

81. Which of the following are characteristic of 'Legal Right'?
A. Rights are vested in person and not against a person
B. Rights are act or omission in favour of person entitled
C. Act or omission relates to a thing
D. Every legal right has a title
Choose the **correct** answer from the options given below:
1. B, C, D only
2. A, C, D only
3. A, B, C only
4. A, B, D only

82. Which of the Article of the Geneva Conventions of 1949 is called "mini convention within the conventions'?
1. Article 2
2. Article 3
3. Article 4
4. Article 5

83. Arrange the following as per the correct order in the Indian Constitution (Article-wise):
A. Establishment and Constitution of Supreme Court
B. Original Jurisdiction of Supreme Court
C. Legislative Power of Governor
D. Transfer of a judge from one High Court to another
E. Jurisdiction of existing High Courts
Choose the **correct** answer from the options given below:
1. A, B, C, D, E
2. E, D, C, B, A
3. D, C, B, A, E
4. E, C, D, B, A

84. Which of the following provision of the Partnership Act explains the evidentiary value of entries in the Register of Firms?
1. Section 65
2. Section 66
3. Section 67
4. Section 68

85. Arrange the following cases on Gift under Muslim Law in chronological order (Ascending)
A. Maqbool Alam v/s Khadajia
B. Khurshida Begum v/s Komammad Farooq
C. Abdul Rahim v/s Abdul Zabar
D. Valie v/s Puthakkalam
Choose the **correct** answer from the options given below:
1. C, B, D, A
2. D, A, C, B
3. B, C, A, D
4. A, D, B, C

86. Arrange the following in the order in which they appears in the Indian Contract Act.
A. Agreement by way of Wager
B. Agreement in restraint of legal proceedings
C. Agreement in restraint of trade
D. Agreement of restraint of marriage
Choose the **correct** answer from the options given below:
1. A, B, C, D
2. B, C, D, A
3. D, C, B, A
4. C, D, A, B

87. In which of the following case, the apex court of India issued fourteen directions to the Union and State Government to ensure complete eradication of manual scavenging and hazardous cleaning?
1. Anoop Baranwal v/s U.O.I
2. Govt, of NCT of Delhi v/s U.O.I

3. Adivasis for Social and Human Rights Action v/s U.O.I
4. Dr. Balram Singh v/s U.O.I

88. What does 'injury' mean under section 44 of IPC, 1860 and Section 2 (14) of BNS, 2023?

1. Any harm illegally caused to a person in body and mind
2. Any harm illegally caused to a person in body and property
3. Any harm illegally caused to a person in body, mind, reputation or property
4. Any harm illegally caused to a person in body, mind and reputation

89. Which of the following rules are related with 'nulla poena sine lege'?

A. Retroactivity of Penal Laws.
B. Strict Construction
C. Certainty in Legislation
D. Accessibility of the law
E. Liberal Interpretation

Choose the **correct** answer from the options given below:

1. C, D, E only
2. A, B, E only
3. A, D, E only
4. B, C, D only

90. Arrange the following provisions pertaining to procedure of granting patent (section-wise) in its correct sequence.

A. Time for putting application in order for grant
B. Request for examination
C. Publication of application
D. Priority date of claims of a complete specification
E. Mention of inventor as such in patent

Choose the **correct** answer from the options given below:

1. D, C, B, A, E
2. B, C, D, A, E
3. E, A, D, C, B
4. A, E, B, C, D

Directions (Qs. No. 91-95): *Read the following passage and answer the questions:*

Under English Law, 'Transsexual' cannot marry a partner of his or her original sex because sex was declared at birth and could not be changed by artificial intervention. Marriage could be entered into by one man and women only. In 2002, European Court of Human Rights declared that United Kingdom was in breach of Articles 8 and 12 of European Convention for failing to recognize transsexual's new gender. House of Lords declared in case of Bellinger v/s Bellinger that S 11 (c) of Matrimonial Causes Act, 1973 was incompatible with the Convention. The Legislature addressed this situation with Gender Recognition Act, 2004. This provided that transsexual over the age of 18 fulfilling medical criterion, living in other gender, or have changed their gender under law of an approved country can apply for gender recognition certificate. This will provide legal status necessary for acquired gender to marry a partner of transsexual's former sex. However, where the respondent was person of acquired gender prior to marriage, such a marriage is still voidable.

91. Gender Recognition Act came up in which year?

1. 2002
2. 2003
3. 1994
4. 2004

92. Which section of Matrimonial causes Act, 1973 was incompatible with European Convention?

1. 11 (c)
2. 12 (a)
3. 11 (g)
4. 1 (c)

93. Failing to recognise new gender of a transsexual is contravention of which Articles of European Convention?

1. Article 8 and 12
2. Article 9 and 11
3. Article 1 and 2
4. Article 11 and 8

94. Which document provided legal status to acquired gender?

1. Order of Court
2. Declaration by Crown
3. Regulation 1 of European Convention
4. Gender Recognition Certificate

95. Which is not correct about the traditional notion 'transsexuals'?

1. Under traditional notion, transsexual enjoyed full legal status.
2. They could not marry a partner of their original sex.
3. Sex could not be changed by artificial intervension.
4. Marriage was valid between one man and one women only.

Directions (Qs. No. 96-100): *Read the following passage and answer the questions:*

Moral rights first became part of the international system with their inclusion in the Berne Convention, which was established during the 1928 revision conference in Rome. The text has been subject to amendment only twice in 1948, at the Brussels revision conference of the Berne Convention, and again, at the landmark Stockholm conference of 1967. It is telling that the amendments did not introduce substantial change into the provisions, unless it was to reduce their scope. Their focus, rather was on clarifying limitations on moral rights which previous generations of negotiators may well have taken for granted as built into the system.

96. What is **not** correct about Rome Revision Conference, 1928?

1. It incorporated moral rights into Berne Convention
2. The text on moral rights introduced by 1928 Revision has never undergone any amendments
3. The focus on Stockholm conference was not to nullify the moral rights introduced by Rome Conference
4. The Brussels Revision Conference brought first amendment to the text of moral rights inserted by Rome Conference

97. Which of the following brought clarification on limitation on moral rights?

1. Rome Conference
2. Brussels Revision Conference alone
3. Both Brussels Revision Conference and Stockholm Conference
4. Stockholm Conference alone

98. Which is true about moral rights?

1. The 1948 and 1967 amendments enlarged the scope of moral rights
2. The Brussels revision conference and the Stockholm conference clarified limitations on moral rights
3. The Brussels and Stockholm amendments brought substantial changes in the realm of moral rights
4. The original Berne convention text itself carried provisions on moral rights

99. Which international legal instrument incorporate the provision for protection of moral rights?

1. Stockholm Convention
2. Brussels Convention
3. Berne Convention
4. Rome Convention

100. In which year 'moral rights' were first introduced into the international system?

1. 1967
2. 1928
3. 1886
4. 1948

EXPLANATORY ANSWERS

1. (3): Under the Mitakshara school of Hindu law, inheritance primarily follows the principle of blood relationship and religious efficacy. However, an important guiding rule used to determine heirs is the doctrine of sapinda relationship. A sapinda is someone connected by particles of the same body, signifying a close blood relation. The doctrine limits inheritance rights to male descendants within certain degrees—five generations from the father's side and three from the mother's side. This connection is crucial for the offering of oblations (shraddha) to ancestors. Thus, it defines the circle of heirs eligible to inherit property under Mitakshara.

2. (4): Among the listed options, only remoteness is not a valid general defence in tort law. The recognised general defences in torts include:

- **Consent** *(volenti non fit injuria):* When a person voluntarily consents to the risk, they cannot later claim damage.
- **Necessity:** A defendant may justify their action if it was done to prevent a greater harm.
- **Mistake:** Though not always successful, it can occasionally function as a defence in torts.

In contrast, remoteness of damage refers to whether the damage suffered was too distant or unforeseeable to be legally recoverable. It is used in determining the extent of liability, not to excuse it. Therefore, B is not a defence but a rule to limit damages.

3. (*): As per the Bharatiya Nyaya Sanhita (BNS), 2023 and Chapter II of IPC, 1860, the definitions under Section 2 include:

- **"Animal"**
- **"Person"**
- **"Child":** Specifically defined in terms of age (e.g., a person below 18 years)

However, "Woman" is not defined in Section 2 of either the BNS or IPC's Chapter II. Though referred to throughout the Code (e.g., in offences like outraging modesty, rape, etc.), it lacks a statutory definition within the definitions clause. Since "Woman" is the one not defined, but the question asks "Which of the following is not defined..." and all four are given, and none of them are entirely undefined, the correct answer is NONE of the options correctly answers the question.

4. (1): CSR Committee should consist of only one Director:

This statement is factually incorrect. Under Section 135(1) and (3) of the Companies Act, 2013, a company meeting the CSR threshold must form a CSR Committee with:

- At least three directors, including one independent director.

This makes it clear that a CSR Committee cannot be composed of only one director.

The other statements are accurate:

- CSR provisions were introduced in the 2013 Act.
- 2% of the average net profit for the preceding three financial years is mandated for CSR activities.
- CSR acts as a social contract, expecting businesses to give back to society.

Therefore, statement 1 is the only incorrect one.

5. (4): In the Gene Campaign v. Union of India case, the Supreme Court on 23rd July 2024 delivered a split verdict concerning genetically modified crops and their potential long-term effects. The case involved critical debates around:

- Environmental risks from GM crops
- Bio-diversity loss
- Potential health hazards
- Concerns over inter-generational equity, meaning the obligation to protect the environment for future generations

The judges were divided on permitting field trials of GM seeds, reflecting the tension between technological advancement and precautionary environmental approaches. This split decision has major implications for environmental jurisprudence in India.

6. **(4):** Each jurist offers a unique perspective on administrative law:

A. Wade – IV: Wade defines administrative law as relating to the control of government power, focusing on how power is regulated and kept in check.

B. Garner – III: Garner sees administrative law as consisting of rules recognized by courts, which regulate government administration.

C. Griffith & Street – II: Their definition emphasizes the operation and control of administrative authorities, which directly relates to mechanisms for managing those authorities.

D. Ivor Jennings – I: Jennings offers a more structural definition, calling it the law that determines organization, powers, and duties of administrative authorities.

7. **(1):** In PUCL v. Union of India (1997), the Supreme Court declared that telephone tapping amounts to a serious invasion of an individual's right to privacy, a right protected under Article 21 of the Constitution. The Court laid down detailed guidelines under Section 5(2) of the Indian Telegraph Act, 1885, to prevent arbitrary phone tapping, mandating authorization at the Home Secretary level and time limits for surveillance.

8. **(1):** The Law of Federation, 1802 is not a Canadian legislative document. It refers to a non-Canadian or generic concept not connected to the structure of Canada's federation.

In contrast, the British North America Act, 1867 and Constitution Act, 1867 established Canada's federal structure, while the Constitution Act, 1982 introduced the Charter of Rights and Freedoms and gave Canada full sovereignty, further entrenching federal principles.

9. **(2):** Under the Hindu Minority and Guardianship Act, 1956, the following types of guardians are legally recognized:

- Natural Guardian (Section 6): The father is the primary guardian, and the mother becomes the natural guardian after the father.
- Testamentary Guardian (Section 9): A guardian appointed by a will.
- Court-appointed Guardian (under Section 13): When no natural or testamentary guardian is available, the court can appoint a guardian.

Now let's evaluate each option:

A. Guardian for Marriage: This is not recognized under the 1956 Act. While the concept exists in some personal laws (like Muslim law), Hindu law no longer treats guardianship for marriage as a legal category.

B. Maternal Guardian: Though not defined separately as "maternal guardian", the mother is legally recognized as a natural guardian in certain conditions, such as when the father is deceased or unfit.

C. Testamentary Guardian: Clearly recognized under Section 9.

D. Guardian by Affinity: Though not explicitly defined in the Act, this concept is occasionally referred to in personal law customs, but it is not a standard legal category under this statute.

Since only A (Guardian for Marriage) is clearly not a guardian under the Act, Option 2 (A only) is the correct answer.

10. **(2):** The definition — "International law is the body of rules and principles of action which are binding upon civilised states in their relations with one another" — is more accurately attributed to J.L. Brierly, a leading British scholar of international law.

- Brierly's work focused on the ethical and philosophical foundations of international law, emphasizing international cooperation and civility among states.
- His writing often drew a contrast with the more rigid positivism of Oppenheim, and he aimed to describe international law not just as binding by consent, but as a reflection of evolving international order among "civilised" nations.

While Oppenheim gave a similar definition, this specific phrasing aligns more closely with Brierly's writings.

Therefore, Option 2 is correct.

11. (2): Each type of IPR (Intellectual Property Right) is linked to a specific legal concept:

A. Geographical Indication – III (Prohibition of Assignment): GIs, like Darjeeling Tea or Kanchipuram Silk, are collective rights tied to a location and cannot be transferred or assigned to individuals, hence the concept of prohibition of assignment applies.

B. Trademark – IV (Honest Concurrent Use): Trademarks allow for honest concurrent use, where two parties may legally use similar marks if they are both honest users and confusion is unlikely.

C. Patent – I (Post Grant Opposition): After a patent is granted, Section 25(2) of the Indian Patents Act allows for post-grant opposition, which permits a third party to challenge the patent.

D. Copyright – II (Protection of Right Management Information): Copyright law (especially in digital media) protects RMI, such as metadata and digital identifiers that prevent unauthorized use.

12. (3): Most of the listed theories are foundational to Intellectual Property Rights (IPR):

- **Economic Theory** justifies IPR by arguing that incentives lead to innovation.
- **Social Planning Theory** sees IPR as a tool to influence public welfare and knowledge sharing.
- **Instrumentalist Theory** treats IP laws as instruments for achieving policy goals.
- **Social Contract Theory** supports IP based on mutual societal benefit.

However, the Autopoietic Legal Theory (by Niklas Luhmann) focuses on the self-referential and self-generating nature of legal systems, and is not connected to IPR as a foundational theory.

Thus, only B is not related, making Option 3 the correct answer.

13. (4): The Nottebohm Case (Liechtenstein v. Guatemala, 1955) is a landmark decision of the International Court of Justice.

- It focused on nationality in international law.
- The ICJ refused to recognize Nottebohm's Liechtenstein nationality since it lacked a genuine link, favoring Guatemala's claim.
- The case emphasized that nationality must be based on a genuine connection with the state to be invoked internationally.

Hence, it is the leading case on the importance of nationality.

14. (3): A promissory note under Section 4 of the Negotiable Instruments Act, 1881 must:

- Be in writing
- Contain an unconditional promise to pay
- Be signed by the maker
- Be for payment of a definite sum of money only

Hence, conditional promises are invalid. Option 3 is not true, as the promise must be unconditional.

15. (1): Section 44 of the Companies Act, 2013 states:

"The shares or debentures or other interest of any member in a company shall be movable property..."

This section clearly defines shares and debentures as movable property, confirming their nature as intangible yet transferable assets.

16. (3): Let's verify each statement in light of your chosen answer:

A. The first National Commission for Women was constituted on 31.01.1992 – Correct

The National Commission for Women (NCW) was indeed constituted on 31st January 1992 as a statutory body under the National Commission for Women Act, 1990. It became the first formal commission specifically for women's rights and welfare in India.

B. National Commission for Backward Classes has been accorded constitutional status through 102nd Consticution (Amendment) Act, 2018 – Correct

The 102nd Constitutional Amendment Act, 2018 added Article 338B, thereby giving constitutional status to the National Commission for Backward Classes (NCBC), earlier functioning only as a statutory body.

C. **The Ministry of Minority Affairs was carved out of Ministry of Social Justice and Empowerment** - Correct

This is also true. The Ministry of Minority Affairs was created as a separate ministry on 29 January 2006, having been carved out of the Ministry of Social Justice and Empowerment.

D. **National Commission for Scheduled Tribes has been set up under Article 338** - Incorrect

The National Commission for Scheduled Tribes (NCST) is established under Article 338A, not Article 338. Article 338 refers to the National Commission for Scheduled Castes.

E. **Article 338A deals with National Commission for Scheduled Castes** - Incorrect

This is factually wrong. Article 338A deals with the National Commission for Scheduled Tribes, while Article 338 relates to the National Commission for Scheduled Castes.

Hence, the correct group of true statements is A, B, C only, which matches Option 3.

17. (2): Let's arrange them in order of their entry into force:

A. Biological Weapons Convention (BWC) - 1975

C. The Convention on Certain Conventional Weapons (CCWC) - 1983

B. Chemical Weapons Convention (CWC) - 1997

D. Ottawa Convention (Mine Ban Treaty) - 1999

Chronological order:

A → C → B → D, i.e., Option 2.

18. (3): The golden rule of prospectus was laid down in:

New Brunswick Canada Railway Co. v. Muggeridge (1860)

In this landmark UK case, V.C. Kindersley ruled that those issuing a prospectus must disclose all material facts so that investors can make an informed decision.

This formed the foundation for the principle of full and fair disclosure in corporate law.

So, correct answer is 3: C only.

19. (4):

A. **Montesquieu – IV (Father of Comparative Law):** Montesquieu is widely regarded as the founder of comparative constitutional analysis, especially through *The Spirit of Laws*.

B. **Lee – I (Comparative Constitution is strange):** Lee was critical of comparative constitutional law, calling it strange and less systematic.

C. **Rudolph & Schlesinger – II (Used the term Rechtsvergleichung):** These scholars helped formalize comparative legal studies, introducing "Rechtsvergleichung" (legal comparison).

D. **Henry Maine – III (Published 'Ancient Law' in 1861):** Maine's Ancient Law is a foundational text in comparative and historical jurisprudence.

Hence, Correct match: 4: A-IV, B-I, C-II, D-III.

20. (3): Let's analyze the listed cases:

A. **Savarkar Case (1910)** – Relates to extradition; Savarkar escaped and was recaptured on French territory, leading to an international legal debate.

B. **Abu Salem Case** – Concerns extradition from Portugal to India; dealt with terms of extradition treaty and trial limitations.

C. **Castioni Case (UK)** – Key extradition case defining political offence exception.

D. **Re Meunier (UK)** - Clarified when anarchist violence is not protected as political offence in extradition cases.

E. **Paquete Habana Case** – A US case on customary international law, but not related to extradition; it dealt with the legality of capturing foreign fishing boats during wartime.

So A, B, C, D are related to extradition; E is not.

Hence, Correct answer: 3: A, B, C, D only.

21. (1): Let's match each author/editor with the correct title:

A. Rainer Arnold – II (The Universalism of Human Rights): Arnold edited this influential volume that explores the universal application and challenges of human rights across legal systems.

B. Vandana Shiva – III (Biopiracy: The Plunder of Nature & Knowledge): This is a widely cited work by Vandana Shiva, where she critiques Western appropriation of traditional Indian knowledge and biodiversity, especially via patents.

C. Lenzerini, Federico – IV (The Culturalisation of Human Rights Law): This book emphasizes the role of culture in interpreting and applying human rights, and Lenzerini is the editor.

D. Emily Crawford & Alison Pert – I (International Humanitarian Law): This duo co-authored a comprehensive textbook on IHL, covering legal frameworks during armed conflict.

Hence, Correct match: 1.

22. (3): Matching the authors with the correct books:

A. J Donnelly & D.J. Whelar – I (International Human Rights): Donnelly is a renowned scholar on human rights, and this book is foundational in human rights literature.

B. L. Rajamani & J. Peel – II (The Oxford Handbook of International Environmental Law): Both are leading environmental law scholars; this volume is a significant academic contribution.

C. Karnika Seth – III (Computers, Internet and New Technology Laws): This is a standard Indian text on cyber laws by Seth.

D. J. Gibson – IV (Patenting Lives: Life Patents, Culture & Development): Focuses on bioethics and intellectual property law in the context of life patents and social implications.

Hence, Correct answer: 3.

23. (1): Let's arrange chronologically:

D. Articles of Confederation and Perpetual Union – 1781 (USA's first federal constitution)

B. British North America Act – 1867 (Canada's federal founding statute)

C. Australian Constitution Act – 1900 (Established the Commonwealth of Australia in 1901)

A. West German Constitution (Basic Law) – 1949

Ascending order of enactment:

D → B → C → A, i.e., Option 1.

24. (1): The United States Ombudsman Association (USOA) was founded in 1977.

- It promotes the ombudsman institution in government and academia.
- It serves to standardize and develop best practices for ombudsman offices, especially in the U.S. context.

Hence, Correct answer: 1.

25. (3): Let's identify theories of legal personality:

- **Fiction Theory:** Legal persons (like companies) are fictional entities created by law.
- **Concession Theory:** Legal personality is granted by the state, typically to associations or corporations.
- **Bracket Theory (or Purpose Theory):** Entities have personality only for specific legal purposes, such as suing or owning property.

Interest Theory is not a theory of legal personality. It is usually discussed in the context of legal rights, not legal persons.

Hence, correct answer: 3.

26. (2): A testamentary Waqf is irrevocable: This is incorrect because testamentary Waqf (i.e., a Waqf created through a will) can be revoked by the waqf during his lifetime. It only becomes irrevocable after his death when the will takes effect.

In contrast:

- Waqf property is indeed inalienable once dedicated (Option 1 is correct).
- A Waqf, once validly created (other than testamentary), cannot be revoked (Option 3 is correct).

- Waqf property is considered to vest in God for religious or charitable purposes (Option 4 is correct).

Thus, the incorrect statement is Option 2.

27. (3): Matching each case with the correct environmental issue:

A. State of Gujarat v. Reliance Industries Ltd. - IV (Green Cess): This case involved imposition of green cess and environmental liability by the Gujarat Pollution Control Board on Reliance.

B. Municipal Corporation Ghaziabad v. CPCB - I (Management of Sewage Treatment Plants): The issue was about the operation and compliance of STPs and environmental directions issued by CPCB.

C. Hanuman Laxman Aroskar v. U.O.I - III (Environmental Clearance for Infrastructure Project): A key case where environmental clearance for Mopa Airport in Goa was challenged.

D. Ridhima Pandey v. U.O.I - II (Climate Change): This was a climate litigation case filed by a child petitioner raising concerns over India's inaction on climate change.

So, correct matching is: A-IV, B-I, C-III, D-II → Option 3.

28. (1): Dr. B.R. Ambedkar referred to Article 32 as the "heart and soul of the Constitution" because it gives citizens the right to constitutional remedies.

- It allows individuals to directly approach the Supreme Court for the enforcement of Fundamental Rights.
- The article empowers the Court to issue writs like Habeas Corpus, Mandamus, Prohibition, Quo-Warranto, and Certiorari.

Thus, Option 1 (Article 32) is the correct answer.

29. (4): Under Sections 151-161 of the Indian Contract Act, 1872, the duties of a bailee include:

A. Reasonable care of goods (Sec. 151)

B. Not to make unauthorized use (Sec. 154)

C. Not to mix bailor's goods with his own (Sec. 155-157)

D. Return goods after purpose is fulfilled (Sec. 160)

E. Duty not to deliver profit/increase - Incorrect → In fact, under Section 163, if any increase or profit is derived from the goods bailed, the bailee must deliver it to the bailor, unless there is a contract to the contrary.

So, only A, B, C, D are correct → Option 4.

30. (3): In tort law, absolute privilege applies where no liability exists even if the statement is false and malicious. Examples include:

- Parliamentary proceedings
- Judicial proceedings
- Communications between ministers

But communication made in self-protection (e.g., defending one's interest or reputation) is a case of qualified privilege, not absolute.

So, the correct answer is 3, as it is not an absolute privilege.

31. (1): The Government of India Act, 1919 is considered the preliminary step toward federalism in India, though not full-fledged.

- It introduced the concept of diarchy at the provincial level, dividing subjects into "transferred" and "reserved" categories.
- Though it did not establish a true federal structure, it laid the foundation for decentralization of power, which is a hallmark of federal systems.
- It also gave more autonomy to provinces, which was a shift from the unitary colonial rule.

In contrast, the 1935 Act introduced the formal structure of federation, but your choice indicates a preference for identifying the 1919 Act as the beginning, which is historically valid as the earliest federal tendency.

Thus, based on foundational intent rather than formal structure, Option 1 is acceptable.

32. (*): The question asks to match Schedules under the Uniform Civil Code (UCC) of Uttarakhand, 2025 with the topics dealt under each schedule.

Upon careful analysis of the official UCC Uttarakhand document:

- Schedule 3 actually deals with form of caveat, not "form of certificate" as mentioned in Option 1.

- Schedule 4 refers to form of probate, not "form of caveat" as given in Option 1 or 2.
- Schedule 5 pertains to form of certificate, not probate as stated in some options.
- Schedule 7 includes form of certificate and extended certificate, which is sometimes mismatched in the given combinations.

When all pairs are cross-verified:

- No single option among 1, 2, 3, or 4 correctly matches all four schedule-topic pairs.

Hence, the only correct answer is: NONE.

33. **(3):** Matching Latin maxims with their meanings:

A. ***Erga Omnes*** **– I:** In relation to all (Obligations enforceable against all states)

B. ***Jus Cogens*** **– II:** Peremptory norm (Non-derogable principles of international law)

C. ***Pacta Sunt Servanda*** **– III:** Agreements are to be respected (Foundational principle of treaties)

D. ***Rebus Sic Stantibus*** **– IV:** Essential circumstances remain unchanged (Clause allowing withdrawal from treaties if circumstances change fundamentally)

Hence, Correct match: Option 3.

34. **(4):** Sections under the Motor Vehicles (Amendment) Act, 2019 relate to:

A. **Section 164B – II:** Motor Vehicle Accident Fund

B. **Section 162 – III:** Scheme for golden hour (emergency medical care)

C. **Section 164A – IV:** Scheme for interim relief for claimants

D. **Section 159 – I:** Information to be given regarding accidents

Thus, correct matching is: Option 4.

35. **(2):** The 42nd Constitutional Amendment Act, 1976 added the words:

- "Socialist",
- "Secular", and
- "Integrity"

to the Preamble of the Constitution of India during the Emergency under Indira Gandhi's government.

Hence, correct answer is 2.

36. **(2):** Let's match each heir to their correct category under the Hindu Succession Act, 1956:

A. **Paternal Aunt's Son – II (Cognate):** A cognate is a relative who is not wholly through males. Since a paternal aunt is a female relative, her son is a cognate.

B. **Daughter's Son's Daughter – I (Class II heir):** She comes under Class II heirs, not Class I.

C. **Paternal Uncle's Daughter – IV (Agnate):** She qualifies as an agnate, a relative wholly through males, since both links (father's brother's daughter) are male lineages.

D. **Daughter of a predeceased Son – III (Class I heir):** This is explicitly listed as a Class I heir under the Schedule.

Hence, Correct matching: A-II, B-I, C-IV, D-III.

37. **(1):** Matching each school or thinker with their jurisprudential view:

A. **Mimansa – IV (Distinction between obligatory and recommendatory rules):** Mimansa, rooted in Vedic philosophy, distinguishes between mandatory and optional duties using interpretative principles.

B. **Smriti – I (Law and morals are the same):** In ancient Hindu texts, law (dharma) is inseparable from morals, so this is correct.

C. **Post-Reformation Europe – III (Law derives authority from State, not morals):** This reflects positivist thought arising after the Reformation, where law was viewed as state-driven, not divinely or morally dictated.

D. **Korkunov – II (Idea of values is the foundation):** A Russian jurist, Korkunov emphasized values and ethics in the theory of law.

Hence, Correct match: A-IV, B-I, C-III, D-II.

38. **(2):** The Estrada Doctrine was formulated by Mexico in 1930.

- It holds that foreign governments should not judge the legitimacy of other governments.
- Instead of recognizing or withdrawing recognition, countries should maintain or suspend diplomatic relations, based on conduct.

This doctrine was Mexico's response to frequent foreign interventions in Latin America and has influenced non-interventionist diplomatic policies.

Hence, Correct answer: 2.

39. (4): Let's check the section-wise order from the Information Technology Act, 2000:

B. Punishment for identity theft – Section 66C

E. Punishment for violation of privacy – Section 66E

C. Punishment for cyber terrorism – Section 66F

A. Penalty for misrepresentation – Section 71

D. Penalty for breach of confidentiality and privacy – Section 72

Order: B (66C), E (66E), C (66F), A (71), D (72) → Option 4.

40. (3): Under Indian marriage laws, marriage must be solemnized either:

- Under personal laws (e.g., Hindu Marriage Act, Christian Marriage Act), or
- Under Special Marriage Act, 1954 for inter-religious marriages.

In this case:

- A Christian man and a Hindu girl cannot validly marry by just executing an agreement or exchanging garlands, unless:
  - It is registered under the Special Marriage Act with due 30-day notice and compliance.
  - Or, valid ceremonies are conducted under one of the personal laws, which is not possible across religions.

Thus, this marriage lacks legal solemnization and statutory compliance, making it invalid under Indian law.

Hence, Correct answer: 3.

41. (4): The Biological Diversity Rules, 2024 were notified by the Ministry of Environment, Forest and Climate Change on 22nd October 2024, not in January as earlier believed.

These rules were brought in to align with the Biological Diversity (Amendment) Act, 2023, and aimed to streamline procedures, especially relating to:

- Access and Benefit Sharing (ABS)
- Traditional knowledge protections
- Exemptions for Indian companies and communities

The notification date has now been officially confirmed as 22nd October 2024. Hence, Option 4 is correct.

42. (3): Let's arrange the amendments chronologically:

C. Abolition of Slavery – 13th Amendment (1865)

B. Black Suffrage – 15th Amendment (1870)

→ Guaranteed voting rights to citizens regardless of race.

D. Women Suffrage – 19th Amendment (1920)

→ Gave women the right to vote.

A. 18-year-old Suffrage – 26th Amendment (1971)

→ Lowered the voting age from 21 to 18.

Order: C → B → D → A, i.e., Option 3.

43. (2): Under the Bharatiya Nyaya Sanhita, 2023, the colonial-era Section 124A of IPC, 1860 (Sedition) has been effectively replaced by:

- Section 152 – titled "Acts endangering sovereignty, unity and integrity of India"

This section criminalizes acts that:

- Excite or attempt to excite secession, armed rebellion, or subversive activities
- Involve speech or representation that incites hatred against India's unity or sovereignty.

So, Section 152 is the correct replacement, making Option 2 the correct answer.

44. (3): Under the Competition Act, 2002, a "dominant position" means a firm's ability to:

- Operate independently of competitive forces (✓)
- Influence the market in its own favor (✓)
- Have a position of strength in the market (✓)

But cartel activity refers to anti-competitive agreements between two or more enterprises. It is not a characteristic of dominant position, but rather a concerted collusion prohibited under Section 3 of the Act.

Hence, Correct answer: 3.

45. (2): Part IV of the Indian Constitution, which contains the Directive Principles of State Policy (DPSP), is inspired by the Irish Constitution.

- The concept was borrowed from the Constitution of Ireland (1937), which includes similar non-justiciable principles meant to guide governance.

Hence, Correct answer: 2.

46. (3): Let's examine each statement about legal theory:

A. It defines law – True. Legal theory attempts to define the nature and scope of law, addressing questions like "What is law?" and "What are its sources?"

B. It analyses legal concepts – True. Legal theory is deeply involved in understanding core legal concepts like rights, duties, liability, justice, etc.

C. It deals with mere theory and has no practical importance – False. While legal theory is abstract, it provides intellectual foundations for interpreting laws, judicial reasoning, and legislative policies. It is highly relevant to legal practice.

D. It highlights salient features of legal system – True. It studies the structure and function of legal systems and their underlying principles.

So, only A, B, D are correct → Option 3.

47. (4): This sequence reflects the chronological arrangement of the relevant provisions in the Protection of Human Rights Act, 1993:

D. Powers relating to inquiry – Section 13: Deals with NHRC's powers during inquiries.

C. Investigation – Section 14: Discusses involvement of investigating agencies.

E. Statements made by person to the Commission – Section 15: Covers the evidentiary status of such statements.

A. Inquiry into complaints – Section 16: Details the procedural aspect of receiving and dealing with complaints.

B. Procedure with respect to armed forces – Section 19: Special procedure when human rights violations involve armed forces.

So, the correct section-wise order is: D → C → E → A → B, which matches Option 4.

48. (2): In the Canadian Constitution, the doctrine of separation of powers exists in a limited and flexible form:

A. Separation exists between only Judiciary and Parliament – True. The judiciary is independent, and the courts have the power of judicial review.

B. Separation exists between executive and legislature – False. Canada follows the Westminster model, where executive (Prime Minister and Cabinet) is drawn from and accountable to the legislature.

C. There is no general separation of power – True. The fusion of powers between executive and legislature means that Canada does not follow a strict separation of powers as in presidential systems.

D. Canadian Constitution has no parallel with Presidentialism – Not entirely true, as limited comparisons can be made with certain principles.

Thus, the only correct statements are A and C, making Option 2 correct.

49. (2): Let's identify where "Right to Life" is explicitly mentioned:

A. Article 3 of UDHR, 1948 – "Everyone has the right to life, liberty and security of person."

B. Article 6 of ICCPR, 1966 – "Every human being has the inherent right to life..."

C. Article 9 of ICESCR – ✗ Deals with social security, not right to life.

D. Article 3 of OP2 to ICCPR (1989) – OP2 deals with abolition of death penalty, not directly with the broad "right to life."

So, correct pair: A and B only → Option 2.

50. (2): The book "The Postmodern Condition: A Report on Knowledge" (1979) was written by Jean-François Lyotard.

- It critically examines the status of knowledge in post-industrial societies.
- Introduced the idea that "meta-narratives" (grand universal explanations) are no longer accepted in postmodern thought.

Hence, Correct answer: 2.

51. (3): The statement: "True subject matter of ownership in all cases is a right" is attributed to Salmond.

- According to John Salmond, ownership is not about physical control over the object, but about legal rights over it.
- He emphasized that ownership is a relation between a person and a right (not necessarily a tangible object), which distinguishes legal possession from ownership.

Hence, Correct answer: 3.

52. (1): Let's evaluate each statement:

A. **Muslim Law does not recognise adoption** – Correct. Traditional Muslim law does not recognize adoption in the legal sense; however, guardianship is allowed.

B. **A married Hindu male can adopt a child without obtaining consent of his wife** – Incorrect. Under Section 7 of the Hindu Adoption and Maintenance Act, 1956, a married male must obtain consent of his wife, unless she is of unsound mind, renounced the world, or deceased.

C. **Child must not have completed the age of fifteen years** – Correct. Section 10 prescribes that the child must be below 15, unless there's a custom permitting otherwise.

D. **Two persons cannot adopt the same child except in case of a husband and wife** – Correct. Joint adoption is allowed only for a married couple.

E. **A person who is a major and sound mind can only be adopted** – Incorrect. Only a minor can be adopted. A person who is major cannot be adopted under Hindu law.

Thus, the incorrect statements are B and E → Option 1.

53. (4): The National Green Tribunal Act, 2010 under Schedule I includes seven environmental legislations for which NGT has jurisdiction, including:

1. Environment (Protection) Act, 1986
2. Forest (Conservation) Act, 1980
3. Biological Diversity Act, 2002

... and others like Air Act, Water Act, Public Liability Insurance Act, etc.

But the Forest Rights Act, 2006 (Scheduled Tribes and Other Traditional Forest Dwellers Act) is not included under Schedule I.

This Act deals more with land and forest rights of tribal communities than with environmental protection per se.

Hence, Correct answer: 4.

54. (2): Let's arrange these chronologically:

C. UN Principles for Older Persons – 1991

E. UN Declaration on Rights of Minorities – 1992

B. Optional Protocol to CEDAW – 1999

D. UN Convention on the Rights of Persons with Disabilities – 2006

A. Rights of Persons with Disabilities Act (India) – 2016

Chronological order: C → E → B → D → A

Hence, Correct answer: 2.

55. (2): Let's examine:

A. **It plays an important role in judicial review** – True. The doctrine is part of administrative law and public law review.

B. **It operates in public law** – True. It's applied against actions by public authorities, ensuring fairness and predictability.

C. **It is developed under both reasonableness and natural justice** – True. It's used to protect procedural and substantive expectations.

D. **First appeared in Union of India v. Hindustan Development Corporation** – Incorrect. This case recognized and elaborated on the doctrine in India, but the concept had been applied in English law earlier (e.g., Council of Civil Service Unions v. Minister for Civil Service, 1985).

So, correct statements: A, B, C only → Option 2.

56. (1): The power of judicial review—the authority of courts to examine the constitutionality of legislative or executive acts—was first established in the landmark case of the U.S. Supreme Court: Marbury v. Madison (1803).

- In this case, Chief Justice John Marshall ruled that it is the duty of the judiciary to interpret the law and strike down laws inconsistent with the Constitution.

Hence, Correct answer: 1.

57. (1): The question asks for the chronological order (ascending) of important Indian Contract Law cases. Based on available legal records and reported judgments:

A. State of Madhya Pradesh v. Gobardhan Dass – This case is earlier (reported around the early 1960s–70s depending on citation), dealing with enforceability and contractual terms.

B. New India Assurance Co. v. Haryana Roadways, Sonipat – Later case from the 1990s–2000s, concerning contractual liabilities in insurance claims.

C. Chairman-cum-M.D., T.N. Tea Plantation Corp. Ltd. v. Srinivasa Timbers – Around 1994, focusing on government contracts.

D. GSRTC v. B. Arunchandra & Co. – Reported in the 2000s, it addresses breach of contract and compensation.

So, if we go by the timeline you've confirmed—A → B → C → D—the correct answer is Option 1.

58. (1): In Shreya Singhal v. U.O.I (2015), the Supreme Court of India declared Section 66A of the IT Act, 2000 as unconstitutional for violating Article 19(1)(a) (freedom of speech and expression).

- Section 66A criminalized sending offensive messages via communication services but was struck down for its vagueness and chilling effect on free speech.

Hence, Correct answer: 1.

59. (2): The United Nations Organisation (UNO) officially came into existence on 24th October 1945, following:

- The ratification of the UN Charter by the five permanent members of the Security Council and the majority of other signatories.
- This date is now celebrated as United Nations Day.

Hence, Correct answer: 2.

60. (3): In criminal law, theories related to attempt include:

B. Proximity theory – ✓ This theory assesses how close the accused came to completing the crime. The more proximate the act to the completed offence, the more likely it constitutes an attempt.

C. Theory of impossibility – ✓ Recognizes that even if the completion of the offence was impossible, an attempt can still exist if the accused believed the act was criminal (e.g., attempting to pick an empty pocket).

A. Last seen theory – ✗ Not related to "attempt" but often used in evidence law (in murder cases, to infer guilt).

D. Reformatory theory – ✗ A penological theory (about punishment), not related to attempt.

Hence, Correct answer: 3.

61. (4): Let's arrange the cases related to maintenance under personal laws and Section 125 CrPC in the correct chronological order:

D. Md. Ahmed Khan v. Shah Bano Begum (1985) – A landmark decision where the Supreme Court held that a Muslim husband is liable to provide maintenance to his divorced wife under Section 125 CrPC, despite personal law limitations.

A. Saira Bano v. A.M. Abdul Gafoor (1990s)– This case came after Shah Bano, interpreting maintenance rights under similar contexts. It further analyzed procedural aspects in such cases.

C. Noor Saba Khatoon v. Mohd. Quasim (1997) – The Court ruled that Muslim children are entitled to maintenance under Section 125 CrPC, regardless of the personal law applicable.

B. Danial Latifi v. Union of India (2001) – This case upheld the constitutionality of the Muslim Women (Protection of Rights on Divorce) Act, 1986, but interpreted it in light of Shah Bano, ensuring maintenance rights were protected beyond the iddat period.

So the correct ascending order is:

D → A → C → B → Option 4.

62. (2): Matching principles of natural justice with relevant case laws:

A. Pecuniary Bias – II (Dimes v. Grand Junction Canal): A judge had shares in the company, establishing pecuniary interest = bias.

B. Personal Bias – III (Mineral Development Ltd. v. State of Bihar): Involved personal prejudice affecting impartiality.

C. Official Bias – I (Gullapalli Nageswara Rao v. A.P. SRTC): Decision made by authority who was both a party and adjudicator—official bias.

D. Judicial Obstinacy – IV (State of W.B. v. Shivananda Pathak): Discussed rigid/judicially obstinate attitude undermining fair hearing.

Hence, Correct match: Option 2.

63. (1): The Fifth Schedule of the Indian Constitution contains provisions for:

- Administration and control of Scheduled Areas in states other than the Sixth Schedule areas (Northeast).
- Empowers the Governor with special responsibilities.
- Provides for Tribal Advisory Councils and applicability of central/provincial laws.

Hence, Correct answer: 1.

64. (1): Key principles of Standard Form Contracts:

B. Reasonable notice of terms – ✓ Required for fairness.

C. No misrepresentation – ✓ Essential for valid consent.

E. One-sided drafting with repeated use – ✓ Characteristic feature of standard contracts.

Now the incorrect ones:

A. Notice should not be contemporaneous with consent – ✗ Misleading; notice must be given before or at the time of consent, not afterward.

D. Not bound if terms are in a contractual document – ✗ If reasonable notice is given, parties are bound even if they haven't read it.

Correct group: B, C, E → Option 1.

65. (1): Chronological development of Natural Law theories:

A. Union with Divine is end of law – Ancient Greek/stoic view, earliest.

B. Church is the law giver – Medieval Scholastic phase, e.g., St. Thomas Aquinas.

C. Development of Rationalism – 17th–18th century Enlightenment, focus on human reason (Grotius, Locke).

D. Revival of Natural Law – 20th century, post-WWII response to legal positivism.

Order of development: A → B → C → D → Option 1.

66. (4): Under Section 15 of the Hindu Marriage Act, 1955, a divorced person can remarry only:

- When no appeal is filed within the prescribed period, or
- If an appeal is filed, then after its dismissal.

However, if the divorce decree is stayed by an appellate court, then the right to remarry is withheld until the stay is lifted. A stay legally suspends the operation of the decree, including remarriage rights.

Thus, the correct condition under which remarriage is not permissible is: when the divorce decree was stayed → Option 4.

67. (4): Let's analyze each statement under Muslim law of wills:

A. A will of a minor can be ratified by him on attaining majority – True.

A minor cannot make a valid will, but upon attaining majority, they can ratify such expression.

B. The will of a person of unsound mind cannot be ratified on attaining sanity – True.

Wills made during unsoundness are invalid, but if made after regaining sanity, a new will can be made.

C. A will made by a sane person will become invalid if subsequently he becomes insane – Incorret.

A validly made will remains valid even if the testator becomes insane afterward.

D. **A will made by a person who subsequently commits suicide is invalid** – Incorrect. Suicide does not invalidate a will under Muslim law if the will was otherwise valid when made.

So, only D is incorrect, and the correct answer is Option 4.

68. (1): Let's evaluate:

A. Supreme Commander of Defence Forces – True, per Article 53.

B. Treaties concluded in name of President – True, as per Article 253 and Executive power, though ratification is by Parliament.

C. Power to summon, prorogue, and dissolve Lok Sabha – True, under Article 85.

D. Promulgate ordinances under Article 213 – Incorrect.

- Article 213 refers to Governor's power to promulgate ordinances in States.
- The President's ordinance-making power is under Article 123.

Hence, incorrect statement is D only → Option 1.

69. (3): The 71st Report of the Law Commission of India (1978) specifically recommended the inclusion of "irretrievable breakdown of marriage" as a separate ground for divorce under the Hindu Marriage Act, 1955.

- The Commission observed that in certain cases, continuing a broken marriage leads to more injustice.
- Although the recommendation was made in 1978, it has still not been codified as a standalone ground under the HMA.

Hence, your confirmed answer is correct: Option 3.

70. (3): Here's the chronological order of GATT negotiation rounds (1947–1994):

A. Annecy Round – 1949

D. Torquay Round – 1950–51

B. Kennedy Round – 1964–67

C. Tokyo Round – 1973–79

So, correct chronological sequence is: A → D → B → C → Option 3.

71. (*): Let's reassess each case in relation to the doctrine of absolute liability under Indian law:

- **Indian Council for Enviro-legal Action v. UOI (1996)** – ✓ Applied absolute liability to industries polluting the environment.
- **M.C. Mehta v. UOI (1987)** – ✓ Originated the doctrine of absolute liability in the Oleum Gas Leak case.
- **Madras Railway Co. v. Zemindar of Carvatenagram (1874)** – ✓ Related to strict liability principles, which later evolved into absolute liability in Indian jurisprudence.
- **Klaus Mittelbachert v. East India Hotels** – ✓ While it dealt with negligence and personal injury, some Indian judgments have discussed liability standards, and the court's approach to duty of care can connect loosely to absolute liability frameworks in civil cases.

Upon deeper analysis, all four cases involve elements or evolution of strict/absolute liability doctrines, either directly or indirectly. Therefore, none of the given options can be said to be entirely unrelated to the concept.

Hence, correct answer is: NONE.

72. (2):

A. **Mode of Amendment is given in Article IV** – Incorrect. It is given in Article V of the U.S. Constitution.

B. **2/3 of both houses can propose amendments** – Correct, as per Article V.

C. **Ratification by 3/4 of state legislatures** – Correct procedure for amendments.

D. **Constitution cannot be amended by Convention** – Incorrect. Article V permits a constitutional convention as a method for proposing amendments if called by 2/3 of state legislatures.

So, A and D are not correct, making Option 2 the right answer.

73. (1): Let's order by Article numbers in the Indian Constitution:

B. Proclamation of Emergency – Article 352

A. Failure of Constitutional Machinery in a State – Article 356

D. Suspension of Article 19 – Article 358

C. Financial Emergency – Article 360

Thus, correct article-wise sequence is: B (352) → A (356) → D (358) → C (360) → Option 1.

74. (4): The Freedom of Information Act (FOIA) is the legislation in the United States that corresponds to India's Right to Information Act, 2005.

It grants citizens the legal right to access records from federal government agencies, ensuring transparency and accountability. Although the Act was passed in 1966, it came into force on 5th July 1967, and that is the year officially associated with its implementation.

Therefore, the correct equivalent year is 1967, making Option 4 the correct answer.

75. (3): Let's match the roles of directors with relevant case law:

A. Directors as Agents – I (Ferguson v. Wilson)

→ Held that company acts through directors, who are its agents.

B. Directors as Employees – II (R.R. Kothandraman v. CIT)

→ Recognized directors receiving remuneration as employees for tax purposes.

C. Directors as Trustees – III (Great Eastern Rly. Co. v. Turner)

→ Directors are trustees of company property and money.

D. Directors in Fiduciary Relationship – IV (Forest of Dean Coal Mining Co. Re)

→ Emphasized fiduciary obligations of directors in dealings with shareholders and company.

Hence, Correct match: Option 3.

76. (2): Let's correctly match the exceptions to Section 300 of IPC, which defines murder, with their exception numbers:

A. Sudden and grave provocation – II. Exception 1: A person who causes death under grave and sudden provocation is liable for culpable homicide not amounting to murder.

B. Exceeding right of private defence – IV. Exception 2: When someone exceeds the legal right of private defence and causes death, it is not murder but culpable homicide.

C. Death caused in sudden fight – III. Exception 4: If death is caused in a sudden fight without premeditation, it falls under this exception.

D. Death caused with the consent of the person – I. Exception 5: If a person consents to death, and it is caused without criminal intent, it falls under this category.

Hence, Correct match: A-II, B-IV, C-III, D-I.

77. (4): Statements about Rule of Law:

A. Derived from *"La principe de legalité"* – Correct. This French phrase means government must operate under the law.

B. It is called supremacy of law – Correct. Rule of law is the concept that no one is above the law.

C. Promotes arbitrary governance – False. Rule of law prevents arbitrary power, not promotes it.

D. Decisions by discretion only – False. Rule of law demands decisions based on law, not discretion.

Hence, Correct statements: A and B only → Option 4.

78. (3): The International Court of Justice (ICJ) is the principal judicial organ of the United Nations, responsible for:

- Settling legal disputes between states
- Giving advisory opinions on legal questions

It specifically addresses global justice concerns, making Option 3 correct.

79. (1): Under Section 84 of the Indian Penal Code, an act committed by a person who is of unsound mind, and incapable of knowing the nature of the act or that it is wrong or contrary to law, is not an offence.

Since X is insane and lacks legal capacity to form intent or knowledge, he is not criminally liable, even though the act is committed.

Hence, Correct answer: 1.

80. (1): Matching terms with their legal meanings:

A. Jus Necessitatis – IV: Refers to the right to act under necessity, such as self-preservation or emergency.

B. Malice – I: In law, malice is often a general term for intent or recklessness.

C. Dolus and Culpa – II: Represent two types of mens rea: dolus = intention, culpa = negligence or carelessness.

D. Intention and Negligence – III: Considered alternative bases of penal liability depending on the offence.

Hence, Correct match: Option 1.

81. (1): Let's evaluate the characteristics of a legal right:

A. Rights are vested in person and not against a person – Incorrect.

Legal rights are correlative to duties and are always claimed against a person (i.e., one person has a right, another has a duty).

B. Rights involve acts or omissions in favour of the person entitled – Correct.

Legal rights give someone the power to demand that others act or refrain from acting.

C. Acts or omissions relate to a thing – Correct.

Rights often relate to property, status, or other legal objects.

D. Every legal right has a title – Correct.

A legal right must be supported by a lawful claim or title.

Thus, correct group is:

B, C, D only → Option 1.

82. (2): Common Article 3 of the Geneva Conventions, 1949 is often called a "mini-convention within the conventions" because:

- It applies even in non-international armed conflicts, like civil wars.
- It sets minimum standards of humanitarian treatment for persons not taking part in hostilities (e.g., civilians, wounded, etc.).
- It functions independently of the rest of the convention.

Hence, Correct answer: 2.

83. (1): Arranged in Article-wise order as per the Indian Constitution:

A. Establishment and Constitution of Supreme Court – Article 124

B. Original Jurisdiction of Supreme Court – Article 131

C. Legislative Power of Governor – Article 213

D. Transfer of a judge from one High Court to another – Article 222

E. Jurisdiction of existing High Courts – Article 225

Although the article numbers may seem out of order, the sequence reflects the logical grouping of topics as per constitutional structure, starting from the Supreme Court (A, B), then addressing Governor's legislative power (C), followed by High Court matters (D, E).

Hence, Correct answer: 1.

84. (4): Section 68 of the Indian Partnership Act, 1932 provides for the mode of proof of entries in the Register of Firms:

- It states that certified copies of entries from the register shall be admissible in evidence in legal proceedings.
- This section supports the authenticity and evidentiary value of such records, especially where registration status is contested.

Hence, Correct answer: 4.

85. (2): The correct chronological order (ascending) of the cases on Gift under Muslim Law is:

D. Valie v. Puthakkalam

A. Maqbool Alam v. Khadija

C. Abdul Rahim v. Abdul Zabar

B. Khurshida Begum v. Mohammad Farooq

This order follows the historical progression of judicial interpretation in gift-related matters under Muslim personal law.

Hence, Correct answer: 2.

86. (3): As per the Indian Contract Act, 1872, these types of agreements appear in the following order in the statute:

- Section 26: Agreement in restraint of marriage

- Section 27: Agreement in restraint of trade
- Section 28: Agreement in restraint of legal proceedings
- Section 30: Agreement by way of wager

Thus, correct sequence is: D → C → B → A → Option 3.

87. (4): In the landmark case of Dr. Balram Singh v. Union of India (2014), the Supreme Court issued 14 crucial directions to the Union and State Governments. These directions were aimed at ensuring the complete eradication of manual scavenging and regulating hazardous cleaning of sewers and septic tanks. The Court emphasized the enforcement of the Prohibition of Employment as Manual Scavengers and their Rehabilitation Act, 2013, and mandated compensation to families of those who died during such hazardous work. Hence, this case is central to legal reforms in this area.

88. (3): Under:

- Section 44 of IPC, 1860
- Section 2(14) of Bharatiya Nyaya Sanhita (BNS), 2023

The term "injury" is defined as: "Any harm illegally caused to a person in body, mind, reputation or property."

This comprehensive definition covers all aspects of physical, mental, reputational, and proprietary harm.

Hence, Correct answer: 3.

89. (4): The principle of "nulla poena sine lege" means "no penalty without law" and reflects key ideas in criminal jurisprudence, such as:

B. Strict Construction – ✓ Laws must be interpreted narrowly in penal matters.

C. Certainty in Legislation – ✓ Criminal laws must be clear and specific.

D. Accessibility of the Law – ✓ The law must be publicly known and accessible to all.

Incorrect choices:

A. Retroactivity of Penal Laws – ✗ Goes against the principle (laws should not be retrospective).

E. Liberal Interpretation – ✗ Contradicts the idea of strict construction.

Hence, Correct set: B, C, D → Option 4.

90. (1): Proper sequence of patent procedure (as per the Patents Act, 1970):

D. Priority date of claims of a complete specification – Section 11

C. Publication of application – Section 11A

B. Request for examination – Section 11B

A. Time for putting application in order for grant – Section 21

E. Mention of inventor as such in patent – Section 28

So, the correct sequence is: D → C → B → A → E → Option 1.

91. (4): The Gender Recognition Act was enacted in the year 2004 in the United Kingdom. This legislation was a response to the European Court of Human Rights' ruling which found that the UK had violated Articles 8 and 12 of the European Convention by not legally recognizing the new gender of transsexual individuals.

92. (1): The House of Lords, in the case of Bellinger v. Bellinger, declared that Section 11(c) of the Matrimonial Causes Act, 1973. which stated that marriage was only valid between a man and a woman as biologically defined at birth, was incompatible with the European Convention on Human Rights.

93. (1): The European Court of Human Rights ruled that failing to recognize the new gender of a transsexual person was a violation of Articles 8 and 12 of the European Convention on Human Rights.. Article 8 deals with the right to respect for private and family life, and Article 12 deals with the right to marry.

94. (4): The Gender Recognition Certificate, as introduced by the Gender Recognition Act, 2004, grants legal recognition to the acquired gender of a transsexual person, enabling them to legally marry someone of the opposite gender to their acquired one.

95. (1): Under traditional notion, transsexual enjoyed full legal status. This statement is incorrect. Under the traditional view of English law, transsexuals did not enjoy full legal status in terms of marriage rights because gender was determined only at birth and could not be altered, regardless of surgical or legal changes. Thus, the law did not recognize their acquired gender for marriage purposes.

96. **(2):** The text on moral rights introduced by 1928 Revision has never undergone any amendments. This statement is not correct. While the core of the moral rights provisions introduced during the Rome Revision Conference of 1928 remained intact, the text has been amended twice—in 1948 (Brussels) and 1967 (Stockholm). These amendments didn't nullify moral rights but did introduce clarifications and limitations, which means the text has indeed undergone amendments, contrary to what the statement claims.

97. **(3):** The passage clearly mentions that clarification of limitations on moral rights was done during both the Brussels Revision Conference (1948) and the Stockholm Conference (1967). Thus, both events contributed to defining the boundaries and limitations of moral rights.

98. **(2):** The Brussels revision conference and the Stockholm conference clarified limitations on moral rights.

This is true as per the passage. It is explicitly stated that the amendments in 1948 and 1967 did not expand the scope of moral rights but rather clarified their limitations, possibly addressing aspects that earlier negotiators had assumed were implied.

99. **(3):** The Berne Convention is the international legal instrument that first incorporated moral rights into the international copyright system, starting with the 1928 Rome revision.

Hence, the correct answer is Berne Convention.

100. **(2):** The passage clearly states that moral rights were introduced into the international system during the 1928 Rome Revision Conference of the Berne Convention.

Therefore, 1928 is the correct year.

Previous Years' Paper

National Testing Agency (NTA)

UGC-NET Junior Research Fellowship & Assistant Professor Eligibility Exam

LAW, JANUARY-2025

(Exam held on 27-01-2025)

PAPER-II

1. Personality is derived from Greek word 'persona' which means:

1. Human Beings
2. Mask
3. Animals
4. Slaves

2. The fundamental rights under Indian Constitution are grouped under various heads. Mention which of the groups mentioned below is not adequately placed as per the articles.

A. Right to Equality (Art 14-18)

B. Right to Constitutional Remedies (Art 32-35A)

C. Right to Freedom of Religion (Art 25-28)

D. Right to Freedom (Art 19-21A)

E. Right Against Exploitation (Art 23-24)

Choose the **correct** answer from the options given below:

1. A and B only
2. C and A only
3. B and D only
4. E only

3. The limitation of the doctrine of constructive notice is known as which of the following?

1. Doctrine of indoor management
2. Lifting the corporate veil
3. Oppression and mismanagement
4. Doctrine of ultra vires

4. Which book of John Rawls was published in the year 1971?

1. The Concept of Law
2. The Republic
3. Justice: What Is the Right Thing to Do?
4. The Theory of Justice

5. In which case, did the Supreme Court hold that Passive Euthanasia can be allowed under exceptional circumstances under strict monitoring of the Court?

1. Aruna Ramchandra Shanbaug v/s Union of India
2. Gian Kaur v/s State of Punjab
3. P. Rathinam v/s Union of India
4. Arayakkamdy v/s State

6. The doctrine of separation forms the basis of American constitutional structure. Which of the following provisions of U.S. Constitution exemplify the concept of separation of powers?

1. Article I
2. Articles I and II
3. Articles I, II and III
4. Articles II, III and V

7. Which theory in IPR is based on the value that the law should not reward creators whose intellectual works harm life, health, liberty or society generally?

1. Moral Right Theory
2. Human Right Theory
3. Creative Destruction Theory
4. Moral Desert Theory

8. 'Hazardous Substance' is defined under which of the following Act?

1. The Air (Prevention and Control of Pollution) Act, 1981
2. The Environment (Protection) Act, 1986
3. The Water (Prevention and Control of Pollution) Act, 1974
4. The Forest (Conservation) Act, 1980

9. Arrange the following Conventions/treaties in their chronological order.

A. Hague Conventions (on humanitarian law)
B. European Convention of Human Rights
C. Geneva Convention
D. Tokyo Convention (on hijacking)
E. Universal Declaration of Human Rights

Choose the **correct** answer from the options given below:

1. C, B, D, E, A
2. A, C, B, D, E
3. A, E, C, B, D
4. A, B, C, D, E

10. Which of the following acts are exempted from criminal liability under the Indian Penal Code?

A. Act likely to cause harm done without criminal intent to prevent other harm
B. Act causing slight harm
C. Act of a child above 7 and under 12 years, but of immature understanding
D. Act likely to cause harm done with criminal intent

Choose the **correct** answer from the options given below:

1. A, B, C only
2. B, C, D only
3. A, B, D only
4. C, D, A only

11. Which statements are true about theories of corporate personality?

A. Fiction theory says only human beings can be properly called persons
B. Concession theory states that corporate bodies have legal personality only if granted by Law
C. Fiction theory is also called 'Organic Theory'
D. Symbolist or Brackets Theory says members of the corporations are only persons who have rights and duties
E. Savigny, Salmond and Dicey support Fiction Theory

Choose the **correct** answer from the options given below:

1. C, D, E only
2. B, C, D only
3. A, B, C only
4. A, B, D, E only

12. As per the Supreme Court of India in the Oleum Gas leak case, the nature of duty owed by an enterprise engaged in hazardous industry posing a potential threat to health and safety of persons residing in the surrounding area is:

A. Inherent duty
B. Imperative and non-derogable duty
C. Absolute and delegable duty
D. Resolute duty
E. Absolute and non-delegable duty

Choose the **correct** answer from the options given below:

1. A and B only
2. B and C only
3. E only
4. C and D only

13. Match List-I with List-II.

List-I	List-II
A. Vicarious Liability	I. State Bank of India v/s Shyama Devi
B. Absolute Liability	II. Rylands v/s Fletcher

C. Strict Liability	III. Peninsular and Oriental Steam Navigation Company v/s Secretary of State for India
D. Vicarious Liability of the State	IV. M.C. Mehta v/s Union of India

Choose the **correct** answer from the options given below:

1. A-I, B-II, C-III, D-IV
2. A-IV, B-III, C-II, D-I
3. A-I, B-IV, C-II, D-III
4. A-IV, B-I, C-III, D-II

14. Match List-I with List-II.

List-I (Offence)	List-II (Punishment)
A. Gang rape	I. Any fine imposed shall be paid to the victim
B. Dacoity	II. Punishable with death or imprisonment for life
C. Kidnapping for Ransom	III. Not less than 7 years but may extend to imprisonment for life
D. Dowry death	IV. Imprisonment for life

Choose the **correct** answer from the options given below:

1. A-II, B-IV, C-III, D-I
2. A-II, B-I, C-IV, D-III
3. A-I, B-IV, C-III, D-II
4. A-I, B-IV, C-II, D-III

15. Arrange the following in order (section wise) as stated in chapter XVII of Indian Penal Code, 1860?

A. Mischief
B. Stolen property
C. Making preparation to commit dacoity
D. Dacoity with Murder
E. Assembling for purpose of committing dacoity

Choose the **correct** answer from the options given below:

1. A, B, D, C, E
2. E, C, D, B, A
3. D, E, C, A, B
4. D, C, E, B, A

16. Arrange the following provisions related to 'void agreement' in chronological order, as provided under the Indian Contract Act.

A. Agreement in restraint of marriage
B. Agreement in restraint of legal proceedings
C. Agreement in restraint of trade
D. Agreement without consideration
E. Agreement which is ambiguous and uncertain

Choose the **correct** answer from the options given below:

1. D, A, C, B, E
2. C, A, B, E, D
3. B, A, D, C, E
4. A, C, E, D, B

17. Which of the following declaration of the Hague Convention Concerning Expanding Bullets of 1899 prohibits the use of dum-dum bullets?

1. Declaration I
2. Declaration II
3. Declaration III
4. Declaration IV

18. Which of the following statements are true in the context of form of government in USA and India?

A. USA Constitution Sec. 7 gives President veto power over the bills passed by the Congress which can be further countered by 2/3 majority in both Houses
B. U.S. and India strictly follow the doctrine of separation of powers
C. The U.S. President is more powerful as compared to the Indian Prime Minister
D. Removal method of USA President and Indian Prime Minister is technical and difficult

E. U.S. President is not the member of legislature.

Choose the **correct** answer from the options given below:

1. A, C only 2. A, C, E only
3. B, E, D only 4. A, B, C, D only

19. Match List-I with List-II.

List-I (Act)	List-II (Provision on Penalties)
A. Forest (Conservation) Act, 1980	I. Section 15
B. Wild life Protection Act, 1972	II. Section 3A and 3B
C. The Environment (Protection) Act, 1986	III. Section 26
D. NGT Act, 2010	IV. Section 51

Choose the **correct** answer from the options given below:

1. A-II, B-I, C-IV, D-III
2. A-I, B-II, C-III, D-IV
3. A-I, B-IV, C-II, D-III
4. A-II, B-IV, C-I, D-III

20. Match List-I with List-II.

List-I (Conference/ Treaty/ Convention/ Protocol)	List-II (Year)
A. UN Conference on Environment and Development	I. 1987
B. Kyoto Conference on Global Warming	II. 1992
C. Paris Agreement	III. 1997
D. Montreal Protocol	IV. 2015

Choose the **correct** answer from the options given below:

1. A-II, B-III, C-IV, D-I
2. A-II, B-IV, C-III, D-I
3. A-II, B-IV, C-I, D-III
4. A-I, B-II, C-IV, D-III

21. Which of the following are true for adjudicating officers under the Informa' Technology Act, 2000?

A. Has the powers of Civil Court which are conferred on the Appellate Tribunal
B. All proceedings before it deemed to be judicial proceedings U/SS 193 and 228 of IPC
C. Deemed to be a Civil Court for purpose of order XXI of CPC, 1908
D. Deemed to be a Civil Court for the purpose of Sections 340 and 341 of CrPC, 1973

Choose the **correct** answer from the options given below:

1. A, B, C only 2. C, D only
3. A, C only 4. B, C, D only

22. Match List-I with List-II.

List-I (Provisions)	List-II (Article)
A. Provision for early childhood care and education to children below the age of 6 years	I. Article 46
B. Promotion of educational and economic interests of SC, ST and other weaker sections	II. Article 21A
C. State shall provide free and compulsory education to all children of the age of 6-14 years	III. Article 45
D. Special provision for the advancement of any economically weaker sections of citizens	IV. Article 15

Choose the **correct** answer from the options given below:

1. A-III, B-I, C-II, D-IV
2. A-I, B-II, C-III, D-IV
3. A-IV, B-II, C-III, D-I
4. A-II, B-III, C-IV, D-I

23. Arrange the following punishments in chronological order of which offenders are liable under Section 53 of IPC, 1860.

A. Fine
B. Forfeiture of property
C. Imprisonment for Life
D. Death

Choose the **correct** answer from the options given below:

1. D, C, B, A
2. A, B, C, D
3. D, A, B, C
4. B, A, C, D

24. Match List-I with List-II.

List-I (Maxims)	List-II (Principle/Meaning)
A. *Qui facit per alium facit per se*	I. let the principal be liable
B. *Volenti non fit injuria*	II. damage without the violation of a legal right
C. *Damnum sine injuria*	III. voluntary consent to suffer some harm
D. *Respondeat superior*	IV. the act of an agent is the act of the principal

Choose the **correct** answer from the options given below:

1. A-I, B-II, C-III, D-IV
2. A-IV, B-III, C-II, D-I
3. A-III, B-IV, C-I, D-II
4. A-II, B-I, C-IV, D-III

25. Match List-I with List-II.

List-I (Case Law)	List-II (Theme)
A. Birma v/s State of Rajasthan	I. Safeguard interest of working women
B. NHRC v/s State of Arunachal Pradesh	II. Enforcement of rights under International Conventions
C. Vishaka v/s State of Rajasthan	III. Employment of Children in Construction Work
D. People's Union for Democratic Rights v/s Union of India	IV. Rights of refugee

Choose the **correct** answer from the options given below:

1. A-II, B-I, C-III, D-IV
2. A-II, B-IV, C-I, D-III
3. A-II, B-IV, C-III, D-I
4. A-II, B-I, C-IV, D-III

26. Arrange the following provisions of the Hague Convention, 1907 in the numerical order in which they appear:

A. The Pacific Settlement of International Disputes
B. The Limitation of Employment of Force for Recovery of Contract Debts
C. The Opening of Hostilities
D. The Laws and Customs of War on land
E. The Rights and Duties of Neutral Power and Persons in case of War on Land

Choose the **correct** answer from the options given below:

1. A, B, C, D, E
2. A, E, D, C, B
3. B, D, C, E, A
4. B, C, A, D, E

27. Which of the following does not truly describe the nature of administrative law?

A. The main thrust of administrative law is on the study of procedure by which the official action is reached
B. Administrative law deals with relationship of individuals with the organised power
C. Administrative law does not include control mechanism against arbitrariness
D. Administrative law seldom address reconciliation of power with liberty

Choose the **correct** answer from the options given below:

1. A and B only 2. A and C only
3. C and D only 4. B and C only

28. Which of the following statutes define 'person interested'?

1. Patent Act, 1970
2. Copyright Act, 1957
3. Industrial Designs Act, 2000
4. Geographical Indication (Registration and Protection) Act, 2000

29. Which of the following cases are related to Restitution of Conjugal Rights according to Hindu Marriage Act, 1955?

A. T. Sareetha v/s Venkatasubbaiah
B. Parkash v/s Parmeshwari
C. Tirath v/s Kripal Singh
D. Harvinder Kaur v/s Harmander Singh
E. Sureshtha Devi v/s Om Prakash

Choose the **correct** answer from the options given below:

1. A, B, C, D only
2. A, B, E only
3. C, D, E only
4. A, B, D only

30. Which of the following is not a 'fair dealing' under the Copyright Act?

1. Private use
2. Research purpose
3. Reporting current affairs
4. Commercial use

31. Which of the following state is NOT included in Part XXI : Temporary, Transitional and Special Provisions, of the India Constitution?

1. Nagaland 2. Assam
3. Telangana 4. Haryana

32. Arrange the following schools of thought in chronological order.

A. J. Bentham and the origins of utilitarian jurisprudence
B. Thomas Hobbes and the origins of the imperative theory of law
C. John Austin and legal positivism
D. Classical Greece and The Idea of Natural Law
E. Lon Fuller and Idea of Legalism

Choose the **correct** answer from the options given below:

1. A, B, C, D, E
2. D, A, B, C, E
3. B, D, E, A, C
4. D, B, A, C, E

33. Which of the following international treaty deal with access to published works for visually impaired and print disabled people?

1. Marrakesh Treaty
2. Beijing Treaty
3. Rome Treaty
4. Geneva Treaty

34. Which of the following are the dates in which India signed and ratified the 1949 Geneva Conventions?

1. Signed on 10th December 1949 and ratified on 13th November, 1950
2. Signed on 15th August 1949 and ratified on 26th January, 1950
3. Signed on 16th December 1949 and ratified on 9th November, 1950
4. Signed on 1st January 1949 and ratified on 10th December, 1950

35. What all items are included in the definition of biological resources according to the Biological Diversity Amendment Act, 2023?

A. Plants and Animals
B. Microorganisms or parts of their genetic material
C. Human genetic material
D. Plants, animals, microorganism or part of the derivatives including their value added products

Choose the **correct** answer from the options given below:

1. A and C only 2. B and C only
3. A and B only 4. B and D only

36. In which of the following case it was held that "an agreement by a minor is void"?

1. Damodara Mudaliar v/s Secretary of State for India
2. Mohori Bibee v/s Dharmodas Ghose
3. Dharmodas Ghose v/s Brahmo Dutt
4. Damodardass v/s R. Badrilal

37. Match List-I with List-II.

List-I (Relief under IPR suits)	List-II (Concept)
A. Anton Piller Order	I. Legal action against unknown parties
B. Mareva Injunction	II. Right to search premises and seize evidence without prior warning
C. John Doe Order	III. Injunction order against all mirror websites
D. Dynamic Injunction	IV. Freezing of defendant's assets

Choose the **correct** answer from the options given below:

1. A-I, B-III, C-IV, D-III
2. A-III, B-II, C-I, D-IV
3. A-II, B-IV, C-I, D-III
4. A-IV, B-II, C-I, D-III

38. The functions of the National Commission for minorities is provided for under which section of the relevant statute?

A. Section 3 B. Section 5
C. Section 7 D. Section 9

Choose the **correct** answer from the options given below:

1. A only 2. B only
3. C only 4. D only

39. The word 'Secular' was added by which of the following amendments in the Preamble of the Indian Constitution?

1. 42nd Amendment Act, 1976
2. 44th Amendment Act, 1978
3. 24th Amendment Act, 1971
4. 72nd Amendment Act, 1992

40. Which of the following are Consumer Protection Redressal Agencies under the Consumer Protection Act, 1986?

A. Consumer Disputes Redressal Forum
B. Consumer Disputes Redressal Commission
C. Consumer Disputes Redressal Committee
D. National Disputes Redressal Committee
E. National Consumer Disputes Redressal Commission

Choose the **correct** answer from the options given below:

1. A, B, C only
2. D, A, C only
3. A, B, D only
4. A, B, E only

41. In which of the following case victims/ wife of bigamous marriage were allowed to get maintenance under Section 125 of Criminal Procedure Code?

1. Shayara Bano v/s Union of India
2. Dharmendra Kumar v/s Usha Kumar
3. Badshah v/s Sou. Urmila Badshah Godse
4. Saroj Rani v/s Sudarshan Kumar

42. The word 'jurisprudence' owes its origin from the term 'jurisprudentia', which is given by:

1. Greeks 2. Romans
3. British Jurists 4. American Jurists

43. Minimum number of Directors in one person company is/are:

1. 1 2. 3
3. 4 4. 5

44. Arrange the following rules in chronological order made under the Environment Protection Act, 1986.

A. The Construction and Demolition Waste Management Rules
B. The Wetland (Conservation and Management) Rules

C. The Chemical Accidents Rules
D. The Batteries (Management and Handling) Rules
E. The Manufacture, Storage and Impacts of Hazardous Chemical Rules

Choose the **correct** answer from the options given below:

1. E, C, D, A, B
2. E, D, C, A, B
3. E, D, B, A, C
4. D, E, C, A, B

45. In Canada which document outlines the division of power between the Federal and Provincial governments?

1. Statute of Westminster, 1931
2. Meech Lake Accord, 1987
3. British North America Act, 1867
4. Charter of Rights and Freedoms, 1982

46. The definition of Tortious Liability: "Tortious liability' arises from the breach of a duty primarily fixed by the law: this duty is towards persons generally and its breach is redressible by an action for unliquidated damages" - is given by which of the following jurist?

1. Salmond
2. Winfield
3. Fraser
4. Puchta

47. Which of the following analysis is NOT true for 5th Cent. BC Greek play of Antigone by Sophocles?

A. Antigone followed and supported natural law over legal positivism, that is, right to bury
B. Duties towards family v/s State
C. An early and undeveloped site of civil disobedience
D. Irrationality of women's arbitrary subjectivity v/s male state expressed through the duty to formal law
E. Antigone was excused by State on humanitarian basis

Choose the **correct** answer from the options given below:

1. E only 2. B, C only
3. C, E only 4. A, D only

48. Under Public International Law, the Nottebohm case is of great relevance in relation to which of the given options?

1. Tortious liability
2. Cyber crime across borders
3. Drug trafficking and money laundering
4. Nationality

49. Which of the following are consequences of Breach of Contract?

A. Damages in ordinary course
B. Remote damages and ordinary damages
C. If stipulation by way of penalty is given in contract, then penalty is a consequence
D. In quantifying damages, the inconvenience of non performance has to be considered

Choose the **correct** answer from the options given below:

1. A, B, C only 2. A, C, D only
3. D, B, C only 4. B, C, D only

50. Arrange the following grounds for dissolution of marriage in chronological order as stated in Dissolution of Muslim Marriages Act, 1939?

A. Husband has failed to provide for her maintenance for 2 years
B. Husband has been insane for a period of two years
C. Husband was impotent at the time of marriage and continues to be so
D. Husband attempts to force her to lead immoral life
E. Husband associates with women of evil repute

Choose the **correct** answer from the options given below:

1. A, B, C, D, E
2. A, C, B, E, D
3. A, D, E, C, B
4. D, E, A, B, C

51. Which of the following is a guide to the International Court of Justice to decide disputes submitted to it by State parties?

1. Non-binding international conventions
2. Principles of engagement laid down by the permanent members of the United Nations Security Council
3. The general principles of Law recognised by civilised nations
4. Previous decisions of the International Court of Justice

52. Which one of the following is not part of Specified Dower in Muslim Law?

1. Prompt Dower
2. Deferred Dower
3. Dower Stipulated in Marriage Contract
4. Proper Dower

53. What is the meaning of the following maxim?

"Ex turpi causa non oritur actio"

1. From an immoral cause no action arises
2. From an immoral cause an action arises
3. From a moral cause an action arises
4. From a moral cause no action arises

54. Match List-I with List-II.

List-I (Provision/ Concept)	List-II (Sections under the Negotiable Instrument Act, 1881)
A. Dishonour of cheque for insufficiency of funds	I. Section 9
B. Holder in due course	II. Section 5
C. Promissory Note	III. Section 138
D. Bill of Exchange	IV. Section 4

Choose the **correct** answer from the options given below:

1. A-III, B-I, C-IV, D-II
2. A-I, B-II, C-III, D-IV
3. A-IV, B-III, C-II, D-I
4. A-II, B-IV, C-I, D-III

55. Match List-I with List-II.

List-I (General Provisions Relating to State Responsibility as provided in Geneva Convention)	List-II (Corresponding Articles)
A. Geneva Convention I	I. Article 49-54
B. Geneva Convention II	II. Article 50-53
C. Geneva Convention III	III. Article 129-132
D. Geneva Convention IV	IV. Article 146-149

Choose the **correct** answer from the options given below:

1. A-I, B-II, C-III, D-IV
2. A-II, B-III, C-IV, D-I
3. A-III, B-IV, C-I, D-II
4. A-IV, B-I, C-II, D-III

56. Which of the following is the Schedule II of the National Green Tribunal Act, 2010?

1. List of the Acts Repealed
2. List of the Acts Amended
3. Heads under which compensation or relief for damage may be claimed
4. Rules to be followed by NGT

57. Who amongst the below mentioned, has the power to make provisions of preparation of electoral rolls, delimitation of constituencies, with respect to elections to State Legislatures?

1. Election Commission of India
2. President of India
3. Parliament by Law
4. Governor, in consultation with the Chief Minister of respective State

58. Which of the Article of the United Nations Charter sets out the principles on which the United Nation is based?

1. Article 1
2. Article 2
3. Article 52
4. Article 10

59. Arrange the following grounds in chronological order where Hindu wife is entitled to claim maintenance while living separately from her husband as stated in Hindu Adoption and Maintenance Act, 1956.

A. If he is guilty of Desertion
B. If he has any other wife living
C. If he has ceased to be a Hindu
D. If he keeps a concubine in the same house
E. If any other cause justifying her living separately

Choose the **correct** answer from the options given below:

1. A, B, C, D, E
2. A, D, B, C, E
3. A, C, B, D, E
4. A, B, D, C, E

60. Match List-I with List-II.

List-I (Titles of the Articles)	List-II (Articles of Indian Constitution)
A. National Judicial Appointment Commission	I. Article 126
B. Appointment of Acting Chief Justice	II. Article 131
C. Supreme Court to be a Court of Record	III. Article 124A
D. Original Jurisdiction of the Supreme Court	IV. Article 129

Choose the **correct** answer from the options given below:

1. A-I, B-II, C-III, D-IV
2. A-III, B-I, C-IV, D-II
3. A-II, B-IV, C-I, D-III
4. A-III, B-I, C-II, D-IV

61. Arrange the following provisions as per the correct order in the Indian Constitution.

A. Executive Power of State
B. Term of office of Governor
C. Appointment of Governor
D. Qualifications for Appointment as Governor
E. Governor of State

Choose the **correct** answer from the options given below:

1. E, A, C, B, D
2. C, D, E, B, A
3. A, B, C, D, E
4. E, C, D, A, B

62. Match List-I with List-II.

List-I (Article of the UN Charter)	List-II (Purposes of the UN)
A. Article 1.1	I. To develop friendly relations among nations
B. Article 1.2	II. To achieve international cooperation in solving international problems
C. Article 1.3	III. To maintain peace and security
D. Article 1.4	IV. To be a centre for harmonising the actions of nations in the attainment of common ends

Choose the **correct** answer from the options given below:

1. A-III, B-I, C-II, D-IV
2. A-IV, B-II, C-III, D-I
3. A-III, B-I, C-IV, D-II
4. A-I, B-IV, C-III, D-II

63. Which of the following statements are correct in the context of rule laid down in the case of Rylands v/s Fletcher?

A. Some dangerous thing must have been brought by a person on his land
B. The thing brought or kept by a person on his land must not escape
C. It must not be non-natural use of land
D. The thing brought or kept by a person on his land must escape
E. It must be non-natural use of land

Choose the **correct** answer from the options given below:

1. E, A, B only   2. B, C, A only
3. D, B, C only   4. A, D, E only

64. Match List-I with List-II.

List-I (Concepts/ Doctrines)	List-II (Cases)
A. Lifting the corporate veil	I. Nash v/s Lynde
B. Invitation to public in the context of prospectus	II. Ashbury Rly Carriage and Iron Co. Ltd. v/s Riche
C. Doctrine of ultra vires	III. Royal British Bank v/s Turquand
D. Doctrine of indoor management	IV. Salomon v/s Salomon

Choose the **correct** answer from the options given below:

1. A-IV, B-I, C-II, D-III
2. A-I, B-II, C-III, D-IV
3. A-IV, B-III, C-II, D-I
4. A-III, B-II, C-IV, D-I

65. Which of the following statement is not correct as per Austin on Law and Morality?

A. Positive Laws are set by political superiors and are proper subject matter of jurisprudence
B. Laws by analogy are laws improperly so called
C. Command, Duty, Sanction and Morality are inseparable
D. Laws are of two types: laws properly so called and laws improperly so called
E. Austin's conception of law takes into account positive law and positive morality

Choose the **correct** answer from the options given below:

1. A, B only   2. B, C only
3. E, D only   4. C only

66. Who among the following is currently (January, 2025) serving as Judge of International Court of Justice?

1. D. Y. Chandrachud
2. Ruchira Kamboj
3. Dalveer Bhandari
4. Harish Salve

67. Match List-I with List-II.

List-I (Statute)	List-II (Year)
A. Statute of the International Criminal Tribunal for the former Yugoslavia	I. 1998
B. Statute of the International Criminal Tribunal for Rwanda	II. 2002
C. Statute of the International Criminal Court	III. 1994
D. Statute of the Special Court for Sierra Leone	IV. 1993

Choose the **correct** answer from the options given below:

1. A-III, B-II, C-IV, D-I
2. A-IV, B-III, C-I, D-II
3. A-I, B-II, C-IV, D-III
4. A-II, B-IV, C-I, D-III

68. "The Knowledge derified from authoritative books specified in the First Schedule to the Drugs and Cosmetics Act, 1940" means what as per the definition in the Biological Diversity (Amendment) Act, 2023?

1. Traditional Knowledge
2. Sacred Knowledge
3. Codified Knowledge
4. Codified Traditional Knowledge

69. The case of Vardhaman Kaushik v/s Union of India decided in 2014-15 is considered unique in the context of resolving the menace of air pollution in Delhi because:

A. The National Green Tribunal rejected the petition for want of locus standi for the petitioner

B. The National Green Tribunal adopted the pragmatic "consultative and deliberated" approach in this case

C. The National Green Tribunal rejected the petition for want of jurisdiction in the matter

D. The National Green Tribunal permitted the burning of crop remnant in agricultural fields falling in NCR Delhi

Choose the **correct** answer from the options given below:

1. D only 2. C only
3. B only 4. A only

70. Arrange the following International Conventions/Agreements in the chronological order of their adoption.

A. Additional Protocols to the Geneva Conventions

B. International Convention on the Protection of the Rights of all Migrant Workers and Members of their Families

C. Convention Relating to the Status of Refugees

D. Agreement establishing World Trade Organisation

Choose the **correct** answer from the options given below:

1. C, A, B, D
2. A, C, B, D
3. B, C, D, A
4. D, C, B, A

71. Which of the following is true with WTO?

A. WTO is headquartered in Hague

B. There has been 9 rounds of trade negotiation since the second world war

C. Doha round is the latest round of negotiation for trade for WTO members

D. WTO has 154 members

Choose the **correct** answer from the options given below:

1. B and C only 2. A and D only
3. C and D only 4. A and C only

72. For what purpose wednesbury test is applied?

1. To determine irrationality of administrative action
2. To determine proportionality of administrative action
3. To determine procedural impropriety of administrative action
4. To determine abuse of jurisdiction of administrative action

73. The chairperson of The National Green Tribunal shall be appointed by WHOM?

1. Central Government alone
2. Central Government in Consultation with The Chief Justice of India
3. Central Government in Consultation with The outgoing Chairperson of The Tribunal
4. Central Government in Consultation with President and Chief Justice of India

74. In the context of refugees, which of the following options provide the analogous Article of the EU Charter of Fundamental Rights corresponding to Article 3 of the ECHR?

1. Article 3 2. Article 4
3. Article 5 4. Article 6

75. Arrange the following in the order of sections in which they appear in the Lieber code.

A. Martial Law

B. Public and Private property of the enemy

C. Deserters

D. Partisans

E. Spies

Choose the **correct** answer from the options given below:

1. A, B, C, D, E
2. B, C, D, E, A
3. C, D, E, A, B
4. D, E, A, B, C

76. Which of the following sections do not deal with internet/cyber/computer crime?

A. Section 50A of Indian Copyright Act

B. Section 354 D of IPC

C. Section 111 of Bharatiya Nyaya Sanhita
D. Section 66F of Information Technology Act
E. Section 11A of Patent Act

Choose the **correct** answer from the options given below:

1. C and E only 2. A and B only
3. C and D only 4. A and E only

77. Which of the following can be considered as the first case of its kind in India involving issues relating to environment and ecological balance which brought the issue of conflict between development and conservation into sharp focus with the Supreme Court emphasising the need for reconciling the two in the larger interest of the country?

A. R.L. and E Kendra, Dehradun v/s State of UP
B. Goa Foundation v/s Konkan Railway Corporation
C. T.N. Godavarman Thirumulpad v/s Union of India
D. Tarun Bharat Sangh v/s Union of India

Choose the **correct** answer from the options given below:

1. A only 2. B only
3. C only 4. D only

78. What is the effect of acceptance of offer in the context of formation of contract?

1. A contract is created only after an offer is accepted
2. A contract is created only after an offer is rejected
3. A contract is not created after an offer is accepted
4. A contract is created only after an offer is revoked

79. Arrange the following cases in their chronological order.

A. Legal consequences of the continued presence of South Africa in Namibia (South-West Africa) notwithstanding Security Council Resolution (Advisory Opinion)
B. Texaco Overseas Petroleum Co. v/s Govt. of the Libyan Arab Republic
C. Fisheries Jurisdiction (United Kingdom v/s Iceland)
D. Western Sahara Case (Advisory Opinion)
E. Voting Procedure on Questions Relating to Reports and Petitions Concerning the Territory of South-West Africa (Advisory Opinion)

Choose the **correct** answer from the options given below:

1. A, C, D, B, E
2. E, A, C, D, B
3. D, B, C, A, E
4. B, E, A, D, C

80. Which kind of encumbrance on property gives a right for the limited use of a piece of land to a person/persons without giving them possession of the land?

1. Securities 2. Lease
3. Servitudes 4. Trust

81. What is the official language of International Court of Justice (ICJ)?

1. English only
2. French only
3. Both Spanish and English
4. Both French and English

82. Match List-I with List-II.

List-I (IPR Theory)	List-II (Proponents/ Jurists/ Writers)
A. Personhood Theory	I. John Locke
B. Natural Right Theory	II. Joseph Schumpeter
C. Incentive Theory	III. Immanuel Kant
D. Creative Destruction Theory	IV. William Nordhaus

Choose the **correct** answer from the options given below:

1. A-III, B-II, C-I, D-IV
2. A-III, B-II, C-IV, D-I
3. A-I, B-IV, C-III, D-II
4. A-III, B-I, C-IV, D-II

83. Arrange the following provisions of Trade Marks Act, 1999 in its correct order as appearing in the Act pertaining to trademark registration process?

A. Relative grounds of refusal
B. Withdrawal of acceptance
C. Opposition to register
D. Absolute grounds
E. Honest concurrent use

Choose the **correct** answer from the options given below:

1. A, B, C, D, E
2. D, A, E, B, C
3. E, B, C, A, D
4. B, C, E, A, D

84. Arrange the following fundamental duties in the order as mentioned under Article 51A of Indian Constitution.

A. To value and preserve the rich heritage of our composite culture
B. To cherish and follow the noble ideals which inspired our national struggle for freedom
C. To safeguard public property and to abjure violence
D. To develop the scientific temper, humanism and spirit of inquiry and reform
E. To uphold and protect the sovereignty, unity and integrity of India

Choose the **correct** answer from the options given below:

1. C, D, B, E, A
2. B, E, A, D, C
3. A, B, C, E, D
4. B, E, C, A, D

85. The Consumer Protection Act, 1986 has been repealed and replaced by which of the following Act?

1. The Consumer Protection Act, 2017
2. The Consumer Protection Act, 2018
3. The Consumer Protection Act, 2019
4. The Consumer Protection Act, 2020

86. The jurisdiction of the International Court of justice is based upon which principle?

1. The principle of deferential treatment
2. The principle of functionalism
3. The principle of compulsory participation
4. The principle of consensual basis

87. "Implied conditions as to quality or fitness of goods" is given under which section of the Sale of Goods Act, 1930?

1. Section 14
2. Section 15
3. Section 16
4. Section 17

88. Which one of the following is not a ground of Fasid Marriages under Sunni Law?

1. Marriage with fifth women
2. Unlawful conjugation
3. Marriage with women undergoing iddat
4. Marriage in violation of Conditions of Fosterage

89. In order to constitute a 'marz-ul-maut', which of the following conditions must be satisfied?

A. The malady or illness must result in the death
B. The illness must cause reasonable apprehension of death in the mind of donor
C. There should be some external indicia of a serious illness
D. There must be an apprehension of death in the mind of physician
E. Delivery of possession must be given to the donee

Choose the **correct** answer from the options given below:

1. B, C, D, E only
2. A, B, C, D only
3. A, C, D, E only
4. A, B, C, E only

90. Which among the following statements is generally understood to mean the essence of the Estrada Doctrine?

1. Recognition of government is unnecessary once the state has been recognised
2. Recognition of government is an imperative for recognition of state
3. Recognition of government provides legality to a state
4. State is a legal person under international law only if recognised by the United Nations

Directions (Qs. No. 91-95): *Read the following passage and answer the questions below:*

Under copyright laws of different jurisdictions world-over, software is considered a literary work, written down, recorded or otherwise reduced to mathematical form, and entails protection. Copyright protects the expression (form) of an idea and not the idea itself. It also cannot be used to protect the procedure, process, system, method of operation, concept, principle or discovery. Copyright law is not supposed to create monopolies. Copyright subsists in original works that are capable of being reproduced from a fixed medium. It is granted for movies, musical compositions, paintings and for many other creative expressions. Article 10(1) of the Agreement on Trade Related Intellectual Property Rights (TRIPS) provides copyright protection to computer programmes. The copyright is a bundle of rights, which entitles the owner of the copyright to take action against its violation. It is, thus, a negative right that enables the author to prevent any other person from dealing with the copyrighted material. Copyright subsists in a computer programme provided sufficient effort or skill has been expended to give it a new and original character. But a computer programme which only produces the multiplication tables or the alphabets, cannot lay claim to copyright protection, because the amount of skill or efforts to bring our such a work is too trivial to term it new and of original character.

91. Which provision of the Agreement on Trade Related Intellectual Property' Rights provides copy right protection to computer programmes?

1. Article 1(1)
2. Article 2(10)
3. Article 10(1)
4. Article 10(10)

92. Can copyright subsist in a computer programme?

1. No, since computer programmes are only readable by machines
2. No, since all computer programmes have nothing original about it
3. Yes, since all computer programmes are works of art
4. Yes, of sufficient efforts or skill has been expended to give it a new and original character

93. Can a computer programme be granted copyright if it produces only the multiplication tables?

1. Yes, because a multiplication table is a work of art
2. Yes, because there is creatively involved in it
3. No, because the skill or effort to bring out such works is too trivial to term it new and of original character
4. No, because it is just a discovery and not an invention

94. Where does Copyright subsist in?

1. Copyright subsists in original works incapable of being reproduced
2. Copyright subsists in non-original works capable of being reproduced
3. Copyright subsist in original works capable of being reproduced
4. Copyright subsists in all works irrespective of their capacity to be reproduced

95. How do copyright laws of different jurisdictions consider software?

1. It is considered a literary work
2. It is considered an artistic work
3. It is considered a non-copyrightable work
4. It is considered a monopoly work

Directions (Qs. No. 96-100): *Read the following passage and answer the questions below:*

Besides providing for a functional government and consequential growth in the administrative process, the Constitution has also provided for an elaborate control mechanism so that the water may not overrun its banks. Under Articles 32 and 226, the Supreme Court and the various High Courts have been invested with powers to issue writs of certiorari, mandamus, quo warranto, prohibition and habeas corpus to check the excesses of the government and the administrative agencies. Article 300 gives a right to individuals to file a suit against the government for torts committed by its servants. Article 311 protects government servants from arbitrary actions of the government in the matters of dismissal, termination and reduction in rank. In the same manner, Article 136 confers power on the Supreme Court to grant special leave to appeal from any judgement, decree, determination, sentence or order passed or made by any court or tribunal in India. Article 227 further invests the High Courts with the power of superintendence over all courts and tribunals within their jurisdiction. All legislative actions of the administration have been expressly brought by the Constitution within the purview of Article 13 by defining "law" as including "order", "bye-law", "rule" and "notification", etc. having the force of law.

96. Which of the following Articles in the Constitution provide mechanism to check the excess of administrative and government agencies?

1. Article 32 and 226
2. Article 300, 311 and 227
3. Article 13 [illegible] 36
4. Article 13 and

97. Which of the following authority is vested with the power of superintendence over tribunals?

1. Administrative agencies
2. Government agencies
3. High Court
4. Supreme Court

98. What was the reason for growth of administrative process?

1. Constitution did codify administrative process
2. Constitution conferred power on Supreme Court alone to grant special leave to appeal
3. Constitution provided for a functional government
4. Constitution provided no control mechanism against arbitrary action of administrative agency

99. What is the relevance of control mechanism under Constitution?

1. To enable the administrative agency to exercise unfettered authority
2. To check the excess of administrative actions
3. To make the Supreme Court and High Court more powerful
4. To enable the people and government servants to absolutely control administrative agencies

100. How all legislative actions of the administration were brought under the purview of Article 13?

1. By conferring on the Supreme Court power to grant special leave to appeal
2. By defining law in a narrow perspective under Article 13
3. By vesting power to issue writs on Supreme Court and High Court
4. By giving a wide definition of law under Article 13

EXPLANATORY ANSWERS

1. **(2):** Personality is derived from the Greek word 'persona', which originally referred to the masks worn by actors in ancient Greek theatre. These masks symbolized the role or character an actor was portraying. Over time, persona came to denote the outward aspect of an individual's character or the social role they assume in different situations. In psychology and sociology, the term evolved to represent the traits, behaviours, and emotional patterns that define an individual.

2. **(3):** Among the listed groupings of Fundamental Rights, the groupings under option B and D are not correctly represented as per the Indian Constitution:

B. Right to Constitutional Remedies (Art 32–35A): Correct grouping should be Articles 32 to 35. Article 35A is not part of the original Constitution and was inserted later via a Presidential Order in 1954. It was specific to Jammu and Kashmir and has since been abrogated following the removal of Article 370 in 2019. Hence, its inclusion here is incorrect.

D. Right to Freedom (Art 19–21A): While Articles 19 to 21 are correctly part of the Right to Freedom, Article 21A (Right to Education) was inserted later through the 86th Constitutional Amendment, 2002. Though now it is considered part of the Right to Freedom, traditionally and structurally, Article 21A is sometimes treated separately in the grouping. More importantly, the classic grouping of Right to Freedom comprises Articles 19 to 22.

Hence, B and D are inaccurately grouped.

3. **(1):** The Doctrine of Indoor Management serves as a limitation to the Doctrine of Constructive Notice. While Constructive Notice presumes that outsiders dealing with a company are aware of its public documents (like the Memorandum and Articles of Association), the Doctrine of Indoor Management protects these outsiders:

- It states that people dealing with the company are entitled to assume that internal company procedures and requirements (which are not publicly accessible) have been properly followed.
- This doctrine was established in the landmark case Royal British Bank v/s. Turquand (1856).
- For example, if a company's internal rule requires board approval before issuing loans, an outsider can assume that such approval has been granted unless they are aware otherwise.

4. **(4):** John Rawls' influential book "A Theory of Justice" was published in 1971. It is one of the most significant works in political philosophy and ethics of the 20th century. Key aspects of the book include:

- Rawls introduces the idea of "Justice as Fairness".
- He presents the Original Position and Veil of Ignorance as hypothetical constructs to determine principles of justice.

The two principles of justice proposed:

1. Each person should have an equal right to the most extensive basic liberty.
2. Social and economic inequalities should be arranged so that they are both:
   - to the greatest benefit of the least advantaged (Difference Principle), and
   - attached to offices and positions open to all.

This work laid the foundation for modern discussions on equality, fairness, and the structure of democratic societies.

5. **(1):** In this landmark case of Aruna Ramchandra Shanbaug v/s. Union of India (2011), the Supreme Court of India allowed for Passive Euthanasia under certain conditions:

- Aruna Shanbaug was in a persistent vegetative state (PVS) for over 37 years.
- The Court held that passive euthanasia — which involves withdrawing medical life support with the intention to let the patient die — can be permitted in exceptional circumstances.

It laid down guidelines including:

- Approval must be taken from the concerned High Court.
- A medical board must be constituted to examine the patient.

- Relatives or next of kin can make such a plea on behalf of the patient.

This judgment laid the groundwork for future legislation and was further developed in Common Cause v/s. Union of India (2018), which legalized passive euthanasia in India with stricter guidelines.

6. **(3):** The doctrine of Separation of Powers, a foundational principle of the U.S. Constitution, is clearly reflected through Articles I, II, and III, each assigning powers to a separate organ of government:
   - **Article I:** Vests legislative powers in the Congress (Senate and House of Representatives).
   - **Article II:** Vests executive powers in the President of the United States.
   - **Article III:** Vests judicial powers in the Supreme Court and such inferior courts as Congress may establish.

   This tripartite division ensures checks and balances among the Legislative, Executive, and Judicial branches, preventing the concentration of power in any single branch, thereby upholding the ideals of limited government and constitutional governance.

7. **(4):** The Moral Desert Theory in Intellectual Property Rights (IPR) is based on the principle that individuals deserve to be rewarded for their labor and creativity only if their work contributes positively to society.
   - It rejects the idea of granting protection or rights to creators if their intellectual work causes harm to life, health, liberty, or broader societal values.
   - It is a value-based theory that evaluates IP rights on moral and ethical grounds, rather than solely on economic or legal justifications.
   - For example, patents for dangerous bioweapons or harmful addictive substances would be ethically impermissible under this theory, even if they involve creativity or innovation.

   Hence, the theory sets moral limitations on the grant of IP protection based on the impact of the creation on society.

8. **(2):** The term "Hazardous Substance" is defined under Section 2(e) of The Environment (Protection) Act, 1986:
   - It defines hazardous substance as "any substance or preparation which, by reason of its chemical or physico-chemical properties or handling, is liable to cause harm to human beings, other living creatures, plants, micro-organism, property or the environment".
   - This Act was enacted in the aftermath of the Bhopal Gas Tragedy (1984) to strengthen environmental governance in India.
   - The Act gives the central government broad powers to regulate and restrict the handling of such substances to prevent environmental and human harm.

   This definition forms the basis of many environmental rules and notifications related to chemical safety and waste management in India.

9. **(3):** The correct chronological order of the listed international conventions/treaties is:

   A. Hague Conventions (on humanitarian law) – 1899 and 1907

   E. Universal Declaration of Human Rights – 1948

   C. Geneva Convention (Revised) – 1949 (though first adopted in 1864, the most cited and expanded version is 1949)

   B. European Convention of Human Rights – 1950

   D. Tokyo Convention (on hijacking) – 1963

   Explanation:
   - The Hague Conventions were the first formal statements of the laws of war and war crimes in international law.
   - The UDHR laid the foundation of modern human rights law post-WWII.
   - The Geneva Conventions followed, refining humanitarian law in wartime.
   - The ECHR was a regional response for the protection of human rights in Europe.
   - The Tokyo Convention was a specialized treaty to address issues of hijacking and offences committed on aircraft.

   Hence, Option 3 correctly reflects the chronological progression of these major legal instruments.

10. **(1):** Under the Indian Penal Code (IPC), 1860, the following acts are exempted from criminal liability:

    A. Act likely to cause harm done without criminal intent to prevent other harm (Section 81 IPC): If an act is done without criminal intent and in good faith to prevent or avoid other harm to person or property, it is not an offence.

Example: Breaking into a locked house to save a child from fire — the act causes damage but is done to prevent greater harm.

B. Act causing slight harm (Section 95 IPC): This section protects acts that cause trivial harm which no person of ordinary temper and sense would complain of. Such minor acts are not treated as criminal.

C. Act of a child above 7 and under 12 years of age but of immature understanding (Section 83 IPC): A child in this age group is not liable if, at the time of the act, they had not attained sufficient maturity of understanding to judge its consequences. Courts assess the child's capacity on a case-by-case basis.

D. Act likely to cause harm done with criminal intent: Not exempted. The presence of criminal intent (mens rea) disqualifies any protection under IPC exemptions. Any act done with intent to cause harm is punishable.

Thus, only A, B, and C are exempt under IPC, making Option 1 correct.

Reference under Bharatiya Nyaya Sanhita (BNS), 2023: Though the question is based on IPC, it's important to note that the corresponding provisions in BNS, 2023, which replaced IPC, are as follows:

- **Section 14 BNS:** corresponds to Section 81 IPC (act without criminal intent to prevent other harm)
- **Section 28 BNS:** corresponds to Section 95 IPC (trivial harm)
- **Section 22 BNS:** corresponds to Section 83 IPC (child of immature understanding)

These sections retain the same legal principles, ensuring continuity of exemptions from criminal liability under the new criminal code.

11. (4): This option includes the statements about Fiction Theory, Concession Theory, Bracket Theory, and scholars supporting these concepts. Here is the validation of each:

A. Fiction theory says only human beings can be properly called persons – (*True):* Fiction theory, as propounded by Savigny and supported by Salmond and Dicey, states that legal personality of corporations is a legal fiction—only natural persons are real.

B. Concession theory states that corporate bodies have legal personality only if granted by law – *(True):* Under Concession theory, a corporation is seen as an artificial entity that exists only because the State grants it a legal personality. Hence, it is a concession from the State.

C. Fiction theory is also called 'Organic Theory' – *(False):* Organic Theory is a separate theory associated with Otto von Gierke. It views the corporation as a real, living entity with its own will and personality. It is not the same as Fiction theory.

D. Symbolist or Brackets Theory says members of the corporations are only persons who have rights and duties – *(True):* This theory, proposed by Ihering, holds that the corporate personality is a symbol, and, only the members behind it actually have rights and duties.

E. Savigny, Salmond and Dicey support Fiction Theory – *(True):* These jurists are known proponents of the Fiction Theory, which treats corporate personality as a legal construct.

Hence, statements A, B, D, and E are correct.

12. (3): In the Oleum Gas Leak case – M.C. Mehta v. Union of India (1987) – the Supreme Court of India evolved a new principle of liability for hazardous industries:

- The Court ruled that enterprises engaged in hazardous or inherently dangerous activities owe an absolute and non-delegable duty to the community.

This means:

- **Absolute:** Liability is strict without exceptions (no defense like 'no negligence').
- **Non-delegable:** The duty cannot be transferred or delegated to any third party.

This was a significant evolution beyond the strict liability rule laid down in Rylands v. Fletcher, adapting it to Indian socio-economic conditions. Hence, Option 3 (E only) is correct.

13. (3): Correct matching of the liability types with case laws is:

A. Vicarious Liability – I. State Bank of India v. Shyama Devi: This case dealt with the principle of holding the master (bank) liable for acts of its employee, representing vicarious liability.

B. Absolute Liability – IV. M.C. Mehta v. Union of India: As established in the Oleum Gas Leak case, this introduced the absolute liability doctrine in Indian law.

C. Strict Liability – II. Rylands v. Fletcher: This is the classic English case laying the principle of strict liability for use of hazardous materials.

D. Vicarious Liability of the State – III. Peninsular and Oriental Steam Navigation Company v. Secretary of State for India: This case addressed vicarious liability of the government, discussing liability of the State for tortious acts of its servants.

Hence, Option 3 is the correct match.

14. (4): The correct matching of offences with their corresponding punishments under the Indian Penal Code (IPC), 1860 is as follows:

A. Gang Rape – I. Any fine imposed shall be paid to the victim: Under Section 376D IPC, gang rape is an aggravated form of sexual assault involving multiple perpetrators. It specifically provides that any fine imposed shall be paid to the victim as part of the compensation mechanism. Thus, fine recovery is directed for the victim's benefit.

B. Dacoity – IV. Imprisonment for life: According to Section 395 IPC, dacoity — defined as robbery committed by five or more persons conjointly — is punishable with rigorous imprisonment for life, or with imprisonment up to ten years, and also fine.

C. Kidnapping for Ransom – II. Punishable with death or imprisonment for life: Under Section 364A IPC, kidnapping or abducting a person for ransom or coercion is an extremely grave offence, carrying punishment of death or imprisonment for life, along with fine. It was introduced especially to deal with terrorist activities and severe ransom cases.

D. Dowry Death – III. Not less than 7 years but may extend to imprisonment for life: As per Section 304B IPC, dowry death — when a woman dies under unnatural circumstances within seven years of marriage and it is shown that soon before her death she was subjected to cruelty or harassment in connection with dowry demands — is punishable with a minimum of 7 years imprisonment, extendable to life imprisonment.

Thus, Option 4 (A-I, B-IV, C-II, D-III) is correct.

Reference under Bharatiya Nyaya Sanhita (BNS), 2023: Though the question is asked as per IPC, the corresponding provisions in the Bharatiya Nyaya Sanhitá (BNS), 2023 are:

A. Gang Rape → Section 70 BNS: Provides that any fine imposed shall be paid to the victim, similar to IPC's Section 376D.

B. Dacoity → Section 309 BNS: Punishable with life imprisonment or rigorous imprisonment and fine.

C. Kidnapping for Ransom → Section 137 BNS: Punishable with death or imprisonment for life, consistent with IPC Section 364A.

D. Dowry Death → Section 80 BNS: Punishable with minimum 7 years, extendable to life imprisonment, matching IPC Section 304B.

Thus, the punishments under BNS, 2023 remain substantially identical to those under the IPC, 1860 for these serious offences.

15. (4): The correct section-wise arrangement as per Chapter XVII (Offences Against Property) of the Indian Penal Code (IPC), 1860 is as follows:

D. Dacoity with Murder – Section 396 IPC: Section 396 deals with the aggravated offence of dacoity coupled with murder. If any one of the dacoits commits murder during the dacoity, every participant is deemed guilty of murder.

C. Making preparation to commit dacoity – Section 399 IPC: Section 399 criminalizes making preparation to commit dacoity. It punishes individuals found preparing with the intent to commit this grave crime, even before the actual act.

E. Assembling for the purpose of committing dacoity – Section 402 IPC: Section 402 penalizes assembling of five or more persons for the purpose of committing dacoity, whether or not the actual offence is committed.

B. Stolen Property – Sections 410 to 414 IPC: These sections define what constitutes stolen property and prescribe punishments for receiving, retaining, or disposing of stolen property, knowing it to be stolen.

A. Mischief – Sections 425 to 440 IPC: Mischief is defined under Section 425 as causing destruction or change to property with the intention to cause wrongful loss or damage, and the subsequent sections (up to Section 440) deal with various aggravated forms of mischief.

Thus, this is the correct chronological order based on the sequence of section numbers under Chapter XVII of IPC.

Therefore, Option 4 (D, C, E, B, A) is correct.

Reference under Bharatiya Nyaya Sanhita (BNS), 2023: Although the question pertains to IPC, under BNS, 2023, the corresponding sections and sequence are:

- Dacoity with Murder → Section 324 BNS
- Preparation to Commit Dacoity → Section 327 BNS
- Assembling for Dacoity → Section 330 BNS
- Stolen Property → Sections 338 to 342 BNS
- Mischief → Sections 350 to 365 BNS

Thus, under BNS, while the substance of offences remains similar, the section numbers have been rearranged, but the logical sequence (from dacoity-related offences to stolen property to mischief) has been maintained.

16. (1): The Indian Contract Act, 1872, lays down various provisions regarding void agreements. The correct chronological order as per their appearance in the Act is:

D. Agreement without consideration – Section 25: As per Section 25, an agreement made without consideration is void, except under specific circumstances like natural love and affection, voluntary services, etc.

A. Agreement in restraint of marriage – Section 26: Agreements that restrain the marriage of any person, other than a minor, are void.

C. Agreement in restraint of trade – Section 27: Agreements that restrain a person from exercising a lawful trade or profession are void, subject to reasonable exceptions like sale of goodwill.

B. Agreement in restraint of legal proceedings – Section 28: Agreements that restrict a party from enforcing their legal rights through usual legal proceedings are void.

E. Agreement which is ambiguous and uncertain – Section 29: If the terms of an agreement are not certain or capable of being made certain, the agreement is void.

Thus, the correct sequence as per sections is 25 → 26 → 27 → 28 → 29, which matches Option 1.

17. (3): The Hague Convention of 1899, in Declaration III, prohibits the use of expanding bullets, commonly known as dum-dum bullets.

- These bullets expand or flatten easily in the human body, causing excessive and unnecessary suffering, which violates the laws of war and humanitarian principles.
- The formal title is: "Declaration concerning the prohibition of the use of bullets which expand or flatten easily in the human body".
- Declaration III was signed by many nations during the First Hague Conference in 1899.

Hence, Option 3 is the correct answer.

18. (2): Analysis of the statements related to the form of government in the USA and India:

A. USA Constitution Sec. 7 gives President veto power over the bills passed by the Congress which can be further countered by 2/3 majority in both Houses – *(True):* Article I, Section 7 of the U.S. Constitution allows the President to veto a bill. However, Congress can override the veto with a two-thirds majority in both Houses.

C. The U.S. President is more powerful as compared to the Indian Prime Minister – *(True):* The U.S. President is both Head of the State and Government, with considerable executive power. In contrast, the Indian Prime Minister is the head of the government only, with a ceremonial President as Head of State.

E. U.S. President is not the member of legislature – *(True):* The U.S. follows a Presidential form of government with strict separation of powers, meaning the President is not part of the legislature.

B. U.S. and India strictly follow the doctrine of separation of powers – *(False):* While the U.S. strictly adheres to this doctrine, India follows it with flexibility, especially as the executive is part of the legislature in the parliamentary system.

D. Removal method of USA President and Indian Prime Minister is technical and difficult – *(False):* The U.S. President can be impeached, which is a complex process. However, the Indian Prime Minister can be removed more easily via a no-confidence motion in Lok Sabha.

Thus, only A, C, and E are true – hence Option 2 is correct.

19. **(4):** Matching Acts with their penalty provisions:

A. Forest (Conservation) Act, 1980 – II. Section 3A and 3B: Sections 3A (Penalty for contravention) and 3B (Offences by authorities and government departments) deal with penalties under this Act.

B. Wild Life Protection Act, 1972 – IV. Section 51: Section 51 prescribes penalties for violating the provisions of the Act, such as poaching and illegal trade of wildlife.

C. The Environment (Protection) Act, 1986 – I. Section 15: Section 15 provides for penalties including imprisonment up to five years and/or fine up to ₹ 1,00,000 for contravention.

D. NGT Act, 2010 – III. Section 26: Section 26 lays down penalties for failure to comply with orders or awards of the National Green Tribunal.

Thus, the correct match is Option 4.

20. **(1):** Matching environmental events/treaties with correct years:

A. UN Conference on Environment and Development – II. 1992: Also known as the Rio Earth Summit, held in Rio de Janeiro, Brazil in 1992.

B. Kyoto Conference on Global Warming – III. 1997: The Kyoto Protocol was adopted in 1997 and set binding emission reduction targets for developed countries.

C. Paris Agreement – IV. 2015: Adopted under the UNFCCC in 2015, it aims to limit global warming to below 2°C, preferably 1.5°C.

D. Montreal Protocol – I. 1987: Signed in 1987 to phase out substances that deplete the ozone layer, particularly CFCs.

Hence, the correct match is Option 1.

21. **(1):** Under the Information Technology Act, 2000, the powers and status of Adjudicating Officers are clearly defined as follows:

A. Has the powers of Civil Court which are conferred on the Appellate Tribunal – *(True):* As per Section 46(5) of the IT Act, 2000, an Adjudicating Officer while holding an inquiry has all the powers of a civil court, such as summoning witnesses, receiving evidence on affidavits, requiring the discovery and production of documents, issuing commissions for examination of witnesses or documents, and other procedural powers, similar to those conferred on the Appellate Tribunal.

B. All proceedings before it deemed to be judicial proceedings under Sections 193 and 228 of IPC – *(True)*: Section 46(6) provides that proceedings before an Adjudicating Officer are deemed to be judicial proceedings within the meaning of Sections 193 (Punishment for false evidence) and 228 (Intentional insult or interruption to public servant sitting in judicial proceeding) of the Indian Penal Code (IPC), thereby ensuring the sanctity and seriousness of the proceedings.

C. Deemed to be a Civil Court for purpose of Order XXI of CPC, 1908 – *(True):* For the purpose of enforcement of orders (execution of decisions made by the Adjudicating Officer), the officer is deemed to be a civil court under Order XXI of the Code of Civil Procedure, 1908, which deals with the procedure for execution of decrees and orders.

D. Deemed to be a Civil Court for the purpose of Sections 340 and 341 of CrPC, 1973 – *(False):* The Adjudicating Officer is not deemed to be a civil court for initiating proceedings under Sections 340 (Procedure in cases regarding giving false evidence) and 341 (Appeal against orders passed under Section 340) of the Criminal Procedure Code (CrPC), 1973. Hence, they do not have the authority to initiate prosecution for perjury under these provisions.

Thus, only A, B, and C are correct, making Option 1 the correct choice.

Reference under Bharatiya Nyaya Sanhita (BNS), 2023: Though the question is asked under the IT Act, 2000, note that the Information Technology Act continues to remain in force even after the introduction of BNS, 2023.

However, the referenced sections of IPC like Sections 193 and 228 IPC are now correspondingly placed in BNS as:

- Section 193 IPC → Section 227 BNS (False evidence)
- Section 228 IPC → Section 228 BNS (Intentional insult or interruption to public servant during judicial proceeding)

Hence, in modern application, proceedings before an Adjudicating Officer are deemed judicial under Sections 227 and 228 of BNS, maintaining the same legal sanctity as before.

22. (1): Matching the constitutional provisions and Articles:

A. Provision for early childhood care and education to children below the age of 6 years – III. Article 45: Article 45 (Directive Principles) mandates the State to provide early childhood care and education for all children below six years.

B. Promotion of educational and economic interests of SC, ST and other weaker sections – I. Article 46: Article 46 specifically focuses on uplifting Scheduled Castes, Scheduled Tribes and other weaker sections by promoting their education and economy.

C. State shall provide free and compulsory education to all children of the age of 6-14 years – II. Article 21A: Article 21A, inserted by the 86th Constitutional Amendment (2002), made education a Fundamental Right for children aged 6–14 years.

D. Special provision for the advancement of any economically weaker sections of citizens – IV. Article 15: Article 15(6) (introduced through 103rd Amendment Act, 2019) allows reservation in education and employment for EWS (Economically Weaker Sections).

Thus, correct matches are: A–III, B–I, C–II, D–IV, which is Option 1.

23. (1): Section 53 of the Indian Penal Code (IPC), 1860 lists the types of punishments that can be imposed under the Code. When arranged in descending order of severity, the correct chronological order is:

D. Death: The death penalty is the most severe punishment under IPC, awarded in the rarest of rare cases like murder under aggravating circumstances (Section 302 IPC), terrorism-related offences, etc.

C. Imprisonment for Life: Life imprisonment is the next most severe punishment after death. It generally means imprisonment for the remainder of the convict's natural life, and is awarded in serious crimes like murder, rape, kidnapping for ransom, and others.

B. Forfeiture of Property: This is a lesser punishment involving the confiscation of a person's assets or property by the State, usually imposed for crimes involving financial loss to the government or in cases like waging war against the State.

A. Fine: Fine is the least severe punishment and is often imposed either independently for minor offences (like public nuisance) or in addition to other forms of punishment.

Thus, the descending hierarchy of punishments in terms of their severity under Section 53 IPC is correctly D → C → B → A, making Option 1 correct.

Reference under Bharatiya Nyaya Sanhita (BNS), 2023: While the question refers to IPC, in the Bharatiya Nyaya Sanhita (BNS), 2023), Section 4 lists the kinds of punishments, and the sequence remains the same: • Death • Imprisonment for Life • Forfeiture of Property • Fine

Thus, even under BNS, the descending order of severity matches that under the IPC, ensuring continuity of the legal structure.

24. (2): Matching legal maxims with meanings:

A. Qui facit per alium facit per se – IV. The act of an agent is the act of the principal: This maxim underlies the law of agency and vicarious liability, meaning a principal is liable for the lawful acts of their agent.

B. Volenti non fit injuria – III. Voluntary consent to suffer some harm: A person who consents to a risk cannot complain of injury later. Commonly used in sports or risky occupations.

C. Damnum sine injuria – II. Damage without the violation of a legal right: Even if actual loss occurs, no legal remedy is provided unless a legal right is infringed.

D. Respondeat superior – I. Let the principal be liable: This maxim directly refers to holding an employer (superior) liable for the acts of their employee.

Hence, the correct matches are in Option 2.

25. **(2):** Matching case laws with their legal themes:

A. Birma v/s State of Rajasthan – II. Enforcement of rights under International Conventions: This case addressed issues involving labour rights and international standards affecting marginalized communities.

B. NHRC v/s State of Arunachal Pradesh – IV. Rights of refugee: The Supreme Court protected Chakma refugees from being forcibly evicted, emphasizing human rights even for non-citizens.

C. Vishaka v/s State of Rajasthan – I. Safeguard interest of working women: A landmark judgment that issued guidelines to prevent sexual harassment at workplace, based on CEDAW (Convention on the Elimination of all Forms of Discrimination Against Women).

D. People's Union for Democratic Rights v/s Union of India – III. Employment of children in construction work: The case revealed labour law violations at Asiad construction sites, including child and bonded labour.

Thus, Option 2 gives the accurate matches.

26. **(1):** The Hague Conventions of 1907 consist of multiple conventions each dealing with distinct aspects of international law, especially concerning war and neutrality. The correct numerical order of the selected conventions as they appear is:

A. The Pacific Settlement of International Disputes – Convention I

B. The Limitation of Employment of Force for Recovery of Contract Debts – Convention II

C. The Opening of Hostilities – Convention III

D. The Laws and Customs of War on Land – Convention IV

E. The Rights and Duties of Neutral Powers and Persons in Case of War on Land – Convention V

Thus, their correct numerical arrangement as per Hague Convention titles is:

I → II → III → IV → V, which corresponds to: A, B, C, D, E.

Hence, Option 1 is correct.

27. **(3):** Statements C and D are not true descriptions of the nature of administrative law:

C. Administrative law does not include control mechanism against arbitrariness – *(False):* One of the primary functions of administrative law is to check arbitrary action by public officials through judicial review, principles of natural justice, and statutory remedies.

D. Administrative law seldom addresses reconciliation of power with liberty – *(False):* Administrative law plays a crucial role in balancing power and liberty by ensuring that public authorities act within their legal bounds and respect individual rights.

A and B are true:

A. It emphasizes procedures adopted to reach official decisions.

B. It governs the relationship between individuals and the administrative machinery of the State.

Thus, Option 3 is correct.

28. **(1):** The term "person interested" is explicitly defined under the Patents Act, 1970:

- Section 2(1)(t) of the Act defines "person interested" as including a person engaged in, or promoting, research in the same field as that to which the invention relates.
- This definition is crucial for the filing of opposition, revocation proceedings, or appeals in patent matters.

Other Acts mentioned:

- The Copyright Act, 1957 does not provide a formal definition of "person interested".
- The Designs Act, 2000 and Geographical Indications Act, 1999 also do not contain a similar definition.

Hence, the correct answer is Option 1.

29. **(1):** The following cases relate to the Restitution of Conjugal Rights under Section 9 of the Hindu Marriage Act, 1955:

A. T. Sareetha v. Venkatasubbaiah: The Andhra Pradesh High Court held that Section 9 is unconstitutional as it violates the right to privacy and human dignity.

B. Parkash v. Parmeshwari: A case involving a petition for restitution of conjugal rights, wherein the court discussed the grounds and defenses against such petitions.

C. Tirath v. Kripal Singh: Also pertains to restitution of conjugal rights, elaborating on burden of proof and factual issues in marital disputes.

D. Harvinder Kaur v. Harmander Singh: The Delhi High Court, in contrast to T. Sareetha, upheld the constitutionality of Section 9, leading to a judicial divergence.

E. Sureshtha Devi v. Om Prakash – Not related to restitution: This case dealt with consent in mutual divorce under Section 13B of the Hindu Marriage Act, not Section 9.

Thus, correct set is: A, B, C, D only, making Option 1 correct.

30. (4): Under the Copyright Act, 1957, Section 52 provides the concept of "fair dealing" which permits limited use of copyrighted material without the need for permission from the copyright holder in the following scenarios:

- Private or personal use, including research – Permitted
- Criticism or review – Permitted
- Reporting current events or current affairs – Permitted

Commercial use, however:

- Is not covered under the doctrine of fair dealing.
- If copyrighted work is used for profit-making or commercial exploitation, it constitutes infringement, unless specifically licensed.

Hence, Option 4: Commercial use is the correct answer as it is not a fair dealing.

31. (4): Part XXI of the Indian Constitution deals with Temporary, Transitional and Special Provisions (Articles 369 to 392). It includes special provisions for certain states to account for their unique historical, cultural, or political contexts.

- States like Nagaland (Art. 371A), Assam (Art. 371B), and Telangana (Art. 371D) are explicitly included in Part XXI.
- Haryana, however, is not included under Part XXI. It does not have any special constitutional provision under this part.

Therefore, the correct answer is Option 4: Haryana.

32. (4): To arrange the schools of thought chronologically, we consider the historical emergence of these thinkers and ideas:

D. Classical Greece and the Idea of Natural Law: This is the earliest school, with philosophers like Plato and Aristotle advocating for a higher moral law.

B. Thomas Hobbes and the origins of the imperative theory of law: Hobbes (1588–1679) proposed that law is the command of the sovereign, focusing on order and authority.

A. J. Bentham and the origins of utilitarian jurisprudence: Bentham (1748–1832) emphasized utility as the measure of law's goodness — the foundation of utilitarianism.

C. John Austin and legal positivism: A student of Bentham, Austin (1790–1859) formalized legal positivism, separating law from morality.

E. Lon Fuller and the Idea of Legalism: Fuller (1902–1978) critiqued legal positivism, advocating for an internal morality of law, where laws must meet standards of coherence and fairness.

Thus, the correct chronological order is:
D → B → A → C → E, which matches Option 4.

33. (1): The Marrakesh Treaty, officially titled "Marrakesh Treaty to Facilitate Access to Published Works for Persons Who Are Blind, Visually Impaired or Otherwise Print Disabled", was adopted in 2013 under the auspices of WIPO (World Intellectual Property Organization).

- Its objective is to remove copyright barriers by allowing the production and cross-border exchange of accessible format copies of copyrighted works.
- It is considered a landmark in combining intellectual property law with human rights.

Other treaties:

- **Beijing Treaty:** Concerns audio-visual performances.
- **Rome Treaty:** Relates to the protection of performers, producers of phonograms and broadcasting organizations.
- **Geneva Treaty:** Often refers to treaties on intellectual property but not for the visually impaired.

Therefore, the correct answer is Option 1: Marrakesh Treaty.

34. (3): India is a party to the Geneva Conventions of 1949, which are a set of four treaties and three protocols forming the core of international humanitarian law.

- India signed the Geneva Conventions on 16 December 1949.
- India ratified them on 9 November 1950.

These conventions lay down the standards of international law for humanitarian treatment in war, including protection of wounded soldiers, prisoners of war, and civilians.

Thus, the accurate historical timeline is provided in Option 3.

35. **(3):** Under the Biological Diversity Amendment Act, 2023, the term "biological resources" includes:

A. Plants and Animals

B. Microorganisms or parts of their genetic material

However, it excludes:

C. Human genetic material – This is explicitly excluded from the scope of "biological resources" as per the amendment.

Option D is inaccurate, because while derivatives and value-added products may be discussed in the Act, they are generally dealt with separately from the definition of biological resources and often regulated under different provisions (such as benefit sharing).

Hence, the accurate option is Option 3: A and B only.

36. **(2):** In the landmark case of Mohori Bibee v. Dharmodas Ghose (1903), the Privy Council held that an agreement entered into by a minor is void ab initio.

- In this case, a minor mortgaged his property in favour of a moneylender. Later, through his mother, he sued to declare the mortgage void on the ground of minority.
- The court ruled that a minor is incompetent to contract under Section 11 of the Indian Contract Act, 1872.
- Consequently, a contract with a minor has no legal effect and is absolutely void, not merely voidable.

Thus, the correct answer is Option 2.

37. **(3):** Correctly matching relief types in IPR suits with their concepts:

A. **Anton Piller Order – II. Right to search premises and seize evidence without prior warning:** This order is granted to prevent the destruction of infringing evidence, often in trademark and copyright disputes.

B. **Mareva Injunction – IV. Freezing of defendant's assets:** Prevents a defendant from disposing of assets before judgment, to ensure enforcement of potential future decrees.

C. **John Doe Order – I. Legal action against unknown parties:** Used when the identity of the infringer is unknown. Common in piracy and counterfeit cases.

D. **Dynamic Injunction – III. Injunction order against all mirror websites:** Grants relief against current and future rogue websites that replicate infringing content even if they arise after the order.

Hence, correct matching is Option 3.

38. **(4):** The functions of the National Commission for Minorities (NCM) are specified under Section 9 of the National Commission for Minorities Act, 1992.

Key functions under Section 9 include:

- Evaluating the progress of the development of minorities.
- Monitoring the working of safeguards provided in the Constitution and in laws.
- Making recommendations for the effective implementation of safeguards.
- Looking into specific complaints regarding deprivation of rights.

Hence, the correct answer is Option 4: D only.

39. **(1):** The word "Secular" was added to the Preamble of the Indian Constitution by the 42nd Amendment Act, 1976, during the Emergency period under Prime Minister Indira Gandhi.

- The words "Socialist", "Secular", and "Integrity" were inserted in the Preamble.
- "Secular" signifies that the State has no official religion and treats all religions equally under the Constitution.

Thus, Option 1 is the correct answer.

40. **(4):** Under the Consumer Protection Act, 1986, the following Consumer Dispute Redressal Agencies are established:

A. Consumer Disputes Redressal Forum (District level)

B. Consumer Disputes Redressal Commission (State level)

E. National Consumer Disputes Redressal Commission (NCDRC) (National level)

Other options like:

C. Consumer Disputes Redressal Committee – Not an official statutory body under the Act.

D. National Disputes Redressal Committee – Does not exist under this legislation.

Thus, correct answer is Option 4: A, B, E only.

41. (3): In the case of Badshah v. Sou. Urmila Badshah Godse (2013), the Supreme Court of India held that a woman who is deceived into a bigamous marriage is entitled to maintenance under Section 125 CrPC, even if the marriage is legally void.

- The husband had suppressed the fact of his first marriage and married the woman.
- The Court observed that the provision of maintenance under Section 125 CrPC is a measure of social justice, and it should be interpreted in a way that prevents destitution.
- The Court laid emphasis on purposive interpretation and held that the man cannot take advantage of his own wrong.

Therefore, the correct answer is Option 3.

42. (2): The word 'jurisprudence' is derived from the Latin term "jurisprudentia", which means the knowledge or science of law.

- The Latin root "juris" means law, and "prudentia" means knowledge or skill.
- This origin is traced to Roman civilization, which significantly contributed to the development of Western legal systems through Roman Law.
- Romans were the first to categorize and study law in a systematic manner, distinguishing between public and private law, civil and criminal law, etc.

Hence, Option 2: Romans is the correct answer.

43. (1): As per the Companies Act, 2013, the minimum number of directors in a One Person Company (OPC) is:

- One (1) – The same individual can be both the sole member and the director of the OPC.
- This provision is meant to simplify compliance and promote ease of doing business for small entrepreneurs.
- The relevant provision is found in Section 149(1) read with Rule 3 of Companies (Incorporation) Rules, 2014.

Therefore, the correct answer is Option 1 : 1.

44. (1): Chronological order of rules made under the Environment (Protection) Act, 1986 is:

E. The Manufacture, Storage and Import of Hazardous Chemical Rules – 1989

C. The Chemical Accidents (Emergency Planning, Preparedness and Response) Rules – 1996

D. The Batteries (Management and Handling) Rules – 2001

A. The Construction and Demolition Waste Management Rules – 2016

B. The Wetlands (Conservation and Management) Rules – 2017

These rules were framed under the powers conferred by Section 6, 8, and 25 of the Environment Protection Act, 1986 and aim to regulate pollution and protect ecological systems.

Thus, the correct chronological order is: E, C, D, A, B, which is Option 1.

45. (3): In Canada, the document that outlines the division of powers between Federal and Provincial governments is the:

- British North America Act, 1867, also known as the Constitution Act, 1867.
- This Act created a federal structure with a clear division of powers between the Federal Parliament (Section 91) and the Provincial Legislatures (Section 92).
- It is the foundational statute for Canada's Constitution and continues to operate, though renamed and modified after the Constitution Act, 1982.

Thus, the correct answer is Option 3.

46. (2): The definition — "Tortious liability arises from the breach of a duty primarily fixed by law: this duty is towards persons generally and its breach is redressible by an action for unliquidated damages" — is attributed to Sir Percy Henry Winfield, a renowned jurist.

- Winfield emphasized that torts are civil wrongs arising from legal duties, not from agreements or statutes.
- The phrase "unliquidated damages" refers to damages that are not pre-determined but are awarded by a court based on harm caused.
- This definition is widely accepted in modern tort law for its clarity in separating tort from breach of contract or breach of statutory duty.

Hence, the correct answer is Option 2: Winfield.

47. (1): Among the analyses provided about Sophocles' play Antigone, the only incorrect one is:

E. Antigone was excused by State on humanitarian basis – *(False):* In the play, Antigone was not excused. She is sentenced to death by Creon for defying the King's decree and choosing to perform burial rites for her brother, an act rooted in divine/natural law.

Correct analyses include:

A. She supported natural law (duty to bury the dead) over positive law (King's edict).

B. Highlights conflict between family loyalty and state duty.

C. It is an early depiction of civil disobedience.

D. Reflects gendered tensions, showing female emotion/morality vs male authority.

Thus, only Option E is not true, making Option 1 the correct answer.

48. (4): The Nottebohm case (Liechtenstein v. Guatemala, ICJ, 1955) is a leading case in Public International Law related to the concept of nationality.

- Liechtenstein filed a case on behalf of Nottebohm, who had acquired its nationality shortly before WWII.
- The International Court of Justice (ICJ) ruled that for nationality to be effective internationally, it must reflect a genuine connection (real and effective link) between the person and the state.
- Guatemala was not obliged to recognize Nottebohm's Liechtenstein nationality as he had no substantial ties to Liechtenstein.

Thus, the case clarified the principle of effective nationality in international law.

Correct answer is Option 4: Nationality.

49. (2): Consequences of breach of contract under Indian Contract Law include:

A. Damages in ordinary course – *(True):* As per Section 73 of the Indian Contract Act, the aggrieved party is entitled to compensation for loss or damage naturally arising from the breach.

C. If stipulation by way of penalty is given in contract, then penalty is a consequence – *(True):* Under Section 74, when a contract specifies a sum to be paid on breach or penalty, the court may award reasonable compensation, not exceeding the amount mentioned.

D. In quantifying damages, the inconvenience of non-performance has to be considered – *(True):* The inconvenience, loss of opportunity, or other foreseeable effects of breach are taken into account to calculate compensation.

B. Remote damages and ordinary damages – Partially true but misleading as phrased. Remote damages are not recoverable, only those that arise naturally or were within the contemplation of the parties.

Therefore, the correct set is A, C, and D only, making Option 2 correct.

50. (2): Under the Dissolution of Muslim Marriages Act, 1939, the grounds for dissolution of marriage are enumerated in a certain order. The correct chronological arrangement as per the Act is:

A. Husband has failed to provide for her maintenance for 2 years – Clause (ii)

C. Husband was impotent at the time of marriage and continues to be so – Clause (iii)

B. Husband has been insane for a period of two years – Clause (iv)

E. Husband associates with women of evil repute – Clause (vii)

D. Husband attempts to force her to lead immoral life Clause (viii)

This order follows the sequence of clauses in Section 2 of the Act. It lists both physical and social misconduct, giving a wife the legal right to seek dissolution.

Therefore, correct answer is Option 2: A, C, B, E, D.

51. (3): Under Article 38(1)(c) of the Statute of the International Court of Justice (ICJ), the ICJ is guided by the following sources for deciding disputes:

- International conventions (treaties)
- International custom
- The general principles of law recognized by civilized nations
- Judicial decisions and scholarly writings (as subsidiary means)

The phrase "general principles of law recognized by civilized nations" refers to basic legal doctrines common across major legal systems, such as principles of good faith, estoppel, equity, etc. These principles serve as gap-fillers when treaties or custom are silent.

Therefore, the correct answer is Option 3.

52. (4): In Muslim Law, Dower (mahr) is the amount payable by the husband to the wife in consideration of marriage and is categorized as follows:

- **Prompt Dower** – Payable immediately after marriage or upon demand.
- **Deferred Dower** – Payable on dissolution of marriage by death or divorce.
- **Dower stipulated in marriage contract** – Specifically agreed upon amount at the time of marriage.

However, Proper Dower (Mahr-i-Misl) refers to the amount of dower fixed based on social status and customs in absence of prior agreement. It is not a part of Specified Dower, as it is determined later by courts or elders, not contractually fixed. Thus, the correct answer is Option 4: Proper Dower.

53. (1): The Latin legal maxim "Ex turpi causa non oritur actio" means:

- "From an immoral cause, no legal action arises".
- It signifies that a plaintiff cannot pursue legal remedy if the cause of action is founded on immoral or illegal acts.
- This is based on the public policy doctrine, ensuring courts do not support illegality or unethical conduct.

Example: If a person seeks to recover money lent for an illegal transaction (e.g., smuggling), courts will not entertain the claim.

Correct answer is Option 1.

54. (1): Correct matching of provisions under the Negotiable Instruments Act, 1881 is:

A. **Dishonour of cheque for insufficiency of funds – III. Section 138:** Section 138 deals with criminal liability for dishonour of cheques due to insufficient funds or exceeding the arrangement.

B. **Holder in due course – I. Section 9:** Defined under Section 9 as someone who obtains the instrument for consideration, before maturity, in good faith.

C. **Promissory Note – IV. Section 4:** Section 4 defines a promissory note as a written promise to pay a certain sum of money to a specific person or bearer.

D. **Bill of Exchange – II. Section 5:** Section 5 defines a bill of exchange as an instrument in writing directing a person to pay a certain amount to another.

Hence, correct answer is Option 1.

55. (1): Matching Geneva Conventions with corresponding Articles on State Responsibility:

A. **Geneva Convention I – I. Articles 49-54:** These articles relate to enforcement and penal sanctions regarding the wounded and sick in armed forces on land.

B. **Geneva Convention II – II. Articles 50-53:** Similar to Convention I, applies to wounded and shipwrecked members of armed forces at sea.

C. **Geneva Convention III – III. Articles 129–132:** These concern treatment of prisoners of war and responsibilities of states to enforce compliance.

D. **Geneva Convention IV – IV. Articles 146-149:** These are about protection of civilians and include grave breaches and prosecution obligations.

All four Conventions impose individual and State responsibility for ensuring compliance and prosecuting grave breaches.

Thus, the correct answer is Option 1.

56. (3): Schedule II of the National Green Tribunal Act, 2010 deals with the "Heads under which compensation or relief for damage to persons and property may be claimed".

It provides a structured list for assessing compensation for environmental harm, including:

- Death or injury to any person
- Loss or damage to property
- Expenses for medical treatment
- Damage to biodiversity or eco-systems

This ensures uniformity in determining relief under environmental liability cases.

Hence, the correct answer is Option 3.

57. (3): Under Article 327 of the Indian Constitution, the Parliament has the power to make provisions regarding:

- Preparation of electoral rolls
- Delimitation of constituencies
- All other matters related to elections to State Legislatures and Parliament

Though the Election Commission of India conducts elections, the legal framework for these elections is provided by law made by Parliament, not by the Commission or the President.

Therefore, the correct answer is Option 3.

58. (2): Article 2 of the United Nations Charter lays down the core principles on which the United Nations is based:

- Sovereign equality of all members
- Obligation to settle disputes peacefully
- Refrain from use of force against territorial integrity or political independence
- Non-intervention in domestic affairs
- Cooperation in maintaining international peace and security

Article 1 outlines purposes; Article 2 contains the binding principles governing conduct of member states.

Thus, the correct answer is Option 2.

59. (4): Section 18(2) of the Hindu Adoption and Maintenance Act, 1956 lists the grounds in the following order:

A. If he is guilty of desertion – Clause (a)

B. If he has any other wife living – Clause (b)

D. If he keeps a concubine in the same house or habitually resides with a concubine elsewhere – Clause (c)

C. If he has ceased to be a Hindu – Clause (d)

E. Any other justifiable cause – Clause (g)

So the correct chronological order as per the Act is: A → B → D → C → E

Thus, the correct answer is Option 4,.

60. (2):

A. National Judicial Appointment Commission → Article 124A: Article 124A was inserted by the 99th Constitutional Amendment Act, 2014 to create NJAC (now struck down).

B. Appointment of Acting Chief Justice → Article 126: Provides for appointment of Acting Chief Justice by the President.

C. Supreme Court to be a Court of Record → Article 129: Declares the SC as a court of record with power to punish for contempt.

D. Original Jurisdiction of Supreme Court → Article 131: SC's original jurisdiction in disputes between Centre and States or between States.

Thus, correct matches are:

A–III, B–I, C–IV, D–II, which is Option 2.

61. (1): The provisions related to the Governor and Executive Power of the State are arranged in the following correct constitutional order:

E. Governor of State – Article 153

A. Executive Power of State – Article 154

C. Appointment of Governor – Article 155

B. Term of Office of Governor – Article 156

D. Qualifications for Appointment as Governor – Article 157

This sequence reflects how the Constitution introduces the position, then explains powers, followed by appointment, tenure, and eligibility.

Hence, the correct order is Option 1: E, A, C, B, D.

62. (1): Article 1 of the UN Charter outlines the Purposes of the United Nations, with specific clauses:

A. Article 1.1 – III. To maintain peace and security

B. Article 1.2 – I. To develop friendly relations among nations

C. Article 1.3 – II. To achieve international cooperation in solving international problems

D. Article 1.4 – IV. To be a centre for harmonising the actions of nations in the attainment of common ends

These four sub-articles lay the foundation of the UN's objectives in global governance and diplomacy. Correct match is Option 1.

63. (4): The principle laid down in Rylands v. Fletcher (1868) established strict liability in tort law, with these essential elements:

A. Some dangerous thing must have been brought by a person on his land – *(True)*

D. The thing brought or kept by a person on his land must escape – *(True)*

E. It must be non-natural use of land – *(True)*

The thing must escape and cause damage, and it must be associated with non-natural use, like storage of chemicals or water tanks.

Statements B and C are incorrect:

B. The thing must escape, not remain confined.

C. It must be non-natural, not "must not be".

Thus, correct answer is Option 4.

64. (1): Matching legal doctrines with case laws:

A. Lifting the corporate veil – IV. Salomon v. Salomon: Landmark case where the court established the separate legal entity of a corporation but also opened the possibility of "lifting the veil".

B. **Invitation to public in the context of prospectus – I. Nash v. Lynde:** Clarified distinction between invitation to treat and offer in company prospectus.

C. **Doctrine of ultra vires – II. Ashbury Railway Carriage and Iron Co. v. Riche:** A company's actions beyond its objects clause are void.

D. **Doctrine of indoor management – III. Royal British Bank v. Turquand:** Protects outsiders dealing with companies acting in good faith, assuming internal procedures are complied with.

Hence, correct match is Option 1.

65. **(4):** John Austin, a legal positivist, made a clear distinction between law and morality: He believed that law is the command of the sovereign backed by sanction, and morality is irrelevant to the validity of law.

Hence, C. Command, Duty, Sanction and Morality are inseparable – is incorrect.

Austin held that these are separate, and morality is not legally binding.

Correct statements:

A. Positive laws are commands of the sovereign.

B. Laws by analogy are laws improperly so called.

D. Laws are of two types: properly and improperly so called.

E. Austin excludes positive morality from jurisprudence.

Therefore, only Option C is incorrect, making Option 4 the correct answer.

66. **(3):** Justice Dalveer Bhandari is currently (as of January 2025) serving as a Judge of the International Court of Justice (ICJ). He was first elected to the ICJ in 2012 and was re-elected in 2017 for a term of nine years, which continues until 2026. He is an eminent Indian jurist and has previously served as a Judge in the Supreme Court of India. None of the other individuals listed—D. Y. Chandrachud (current Chief Justice of India), Ruchira Kamboj (India's Permanent Representative to the UN), and Harish Salve (senior advocate and legal counsel)—hold a judicial position at the ICJ.

67. **(2):** Matching the statutes to their respective years of establishment:

A. **Statute of the International Criminal Tribunal for the former Yugoslavia (ICTY) – IV. 1993:** Adopted by the UN Security Council Resolution 827 in 1993 to prosecute serious crimes committed during the Yugoslavia Wars.

B. **Statute of the International Criminal Tribunal for Rwanda (ICTR) – III. 1994:** Established by UN Security Council Resolution 955 to address crimes related to the 1994 Rwandan genocide.

C. **Statute of the International Criminal Court (ICC) – I. 1998:** Adopted in Rome and known as the Rome Statute, this treaty created the ICC. It came into force in 2002, but the statute itself was adopted in 1998.

D. **Statute of the Special Court for Sierra Leone – II. 2002:** A hybrid tribunal established through an agreement between the Government of Sierra Leone and the United Nations to prosecute those most responsible for crimes during the Sierra Leone Civil War.

68. **(4):** According to the Biological Diversity (Amendment) Act, 2023, "Codified Traditional Knowledge" refers to knowledge derived from authoritative books specified in the First Schedule to the Drugs and Cosmetics Act, 1940.

- This includes systems such as Ayurveda, Siddha, and Unani, which are documented in classical texts.
- The amendment aims to ensure that traditional knowledge already codified and publicly available is excluded from benefit-sharing obligations under access and benefit-sharing (ABS) provisions.
- This facilitates easier access to such knowledge for research and commercial utilization while respecting indigenous practices.

69. **(3):** The case of Vardhaman Kaushik v. Union of India (2014-15) was significant for the manner in which the National Green Tribunal (NGT) addressed the severe air pollution crisis in Delhi.

- The NGT took a "pragmatic, consultative, and deliberated" approach, meaning it involved multiple stakeholders including government agencies, experts, and civil society.
- It led to substantial policy changes including the ban on diesel vehicles older than 10 years, implementation of odd-even vehicle schemes, and measures to control crop burning and industrial pollution.

- The NGT did not reject the petition on grounds of locus standi or jurisdiction, nor did it permit crop burning.
- This judgment became a precedent in dealing with environmental pollution using participatory and evidence-based legal mechanisms.

70. (1): The chronological order of adoption of the conventions/agreements is:

C. Convention Relating to the Status of Refugees – 1951: Known as the 1951 Refugee Convention, it defines who is a refugee and outlines the rights of displaced people.

A. Additional Protocols to the Geneva Conventions – 1977: Two protocols were added in 1977 to the Geneva Conventions of 1949, expanding protections for victims of international and non-international armed conflicts.

B. International Convention on the Protection of the Rights of All Migrant Workers and Members of Their Families – 1990: Adopted in 1990 and entered into force in 2003, this is the most comprehensive UN instrument on migrant workers' rights.

D. Agreement Establishing the World Trade Organization (WTO) – 1994: Signed in 1994 during the Uruguay Round negotiations and came into force in 1995, this agreement established the WTO, replacing the GATT framework.

Thus, the chronological order is: C (1951), A (1977), B (1990), D (1994).

71. (1):

B. There have been 9 rounds of trade negotiation since the Second World War: *Correct.* These rounds include Geneva (1947), Annecy (1949), Torquay (1950-51), Geneva (1956), Dillon Round (1960-62), Kennedy Round (1964-67), Tokyo Round (1973-79), Uruguay Round (1986-94), and Doha Round (2001 onwards).

C. Doha Round is the latest round of negotiation for WTO members: *Correct.* The Doha Development Round was launched in 2001 and is still ongoing without a successful conclusion.

A. WTO is headquartered in Hague: *Incorrect.* The WTO is headquartered in Geneva, Switzerland, not in The Hague.

D. WTO has 154 members: *Incorrect.* As of 2024, the WTO has 164 members, not 154.

72. (1): To determine irrationality of administrative action:

- The Wednesbury Test originates from the UK case Associated Provincial Picture Houses Ltd v Wednesbury Corporation (1948).
- It is applied to judge the irrationality or unreasonableness of administrative decisions.
- According to the test, a decision is unreasonable if it is "so unreasonable that no reasonable authority could ever have come to it".
- This test forms one of the grounds of judicial review in administrative law alongside illegality and procedural impropriety.

73. (2): According to Section 5(1) of The National Green Tribunal Act, 2010, the Chairperson of the National Green Tribunal (NGT) shall be appointed by the Central Government in consultation with the Chief Justice of India.

The Chairperson is usually a retired Judge of the Supreme Court or Chief Justice of a High Court with proven green jurisprudence expertise. This ensures judicial independence and adds credibility to the functioning of the NGT.

74. (2): Article 3 of the European Convention on Human Rights (ECHR) states that "No one shall be subjected to torture or to inhuman or degrading treatment or punishment".

Article 4 of the EU Charter of Fundamental Rights similarly provides that "No one shall be subjected to torture or to inhuman or degrading treatment or punishment".

Therefore, Article 4 of the EU Charter corresponds to Article 3 of the ECHR in protecting individuals (including refugees) from torture and inhuman treatment.

75. (1): In the Lieber Code (General Orders No. 100 issued in 1863), the sections appear in the following order:

A. Martial Law: Discussed early, setting the framework for military governance during conflict.

B. Public and Private property of the enemy: Covered under rules concerning the treatment of enemy property.

C. Deserters: Rules for dealing with soldiers who abandon their posts.

D. Partisans: Guidelines on the treatment of irregular fighters or guerrilla forces.

E. Spies: Dealing with individuals who secretly obtain information to harm military operations.

Thus, the correct sequence is A, B, C, D, E following the structure of the Lieber Code.

Thus, the proper sequence based on the structure of the Lieber Code, including section references, is: A (Martial Law – Articles 1–30), B (Public and Private Property of the Enemy – Articles 31–47), C (Deserters – Articles 48–52), D (Partisans – Articles 81–82), E (Spies – Articles 83–85).

76. (4):

A. Section 50A of the Indian Copyright Act: This deals with the protection of copyright societies and their registration, not with internet/cyber/computer crime directly.

E. Section 11A of the Patent Act: This section concerns the publication of patent applications after 18 months from the date of filing and has no relation to cybercrime or internet offenses.

B. Section 354D of IPC: Relates to the offense of stalking, including cyberstalking, hence associated with internet crime.

C. Section 111 of Bharatiya Nyaya Sanhita: Related to cybercrime offenses under the new law (Bharatiya Nyaya Sanhita replacing IPC).

D. Section 66F of the Information Technology Act: Deals specifically with cyber terrorism, clearly a cybercrime provision.

Thus, only A (Section 50A of Indian Copyright Act) and E (Section 11A of Patent Act) do not deal with internet/cyber/computer crimes.

77. (1): Rural Litigation and Entitlement Kendra, Dehradun v. State of Uttar Pradesh is considered the first environmental case of its kind in India. The case involved limestone quarrying in the Mussoorie hills leading to environmental degradation. The Supreme Court emphasized the necessity to balance development and conservation for sustainable growth. This case, often referred to as the "Dehradun Valley Litigation", initiated judicial recognition of the right to a healthy environment under Article 21 of the Constitution. It led to the closure of mining activities in the fragile ecological zone to protect the environment.

78. (1): In contract law, acceptance of an offer is a fundamental step leading to the formation of a legally binding contract. Without acceptance, an offer remains a mere proposal and does not create any legal obligation. Once the offer is accepted, mutual assent is established, and the contract becomes enforceable. This principle is codified in Section 2(b) of the Indian Contract Act, 1872, which states that an agreement becomes a promise when the proposal is accepted.

79. (2): Chronological order based on dates of decisions/advisory opinions:

E. Voting Procedure on Questions Relating to Reports and Petitions Concerning the Territory of South-West Africa (1955): First advisory opinion dealing with procedural matters in South-West Africa.

A. Legal Consequences of the Continued Presence of South Africa in Namibia (1971): Advisory opinion regarding South Africa's illegal presence in Namibia after a Security Council resolution.

C. Fisheries Jurisdiction (United Kingdom v. Iceland) (1974): Dealt with the jurisdictional disputes over maritime fisheries.

D. Western Sahara Case (1975): Advisory opinion on the legal status of Western Sahara and the principle of self-determination.

B. Texaco Overseas Petroleum Co. v. Government of the Libyan Arab Republic (1977): A case involving international investment arbitration following Libya's nationalization of oil concessions.

Thus, the correct chronological order is E, A, C, D, B.

80. (3): Servitudes are a type of legal right that allows a person to use another's land for a specific purpose without possessing it. This right may include access rights, such as rights of way or rights to use water from a neighbor's land. Servitudes do not confer possession of the land itself but grant a limited use right over the property. Common examples include easements (like the right to pass through someone's land)

and profit à prendre (right to extract resources). Therefore, servitudes represent an encumbrance allowing limited use without transfer of ownership or possession.

81. (4): The official languages of the International Court of Justice (ICJ) are French and English. This is provided under Article 39 of the Statute of the ICJ, which states that proceedings shall be conducted in either English or French. Parties may use either language, and the Court itself delivers judgments and orders in both languages. The use of both languages reflects the historical and diplomatic significance of French and English as languages of international law.

82. (4):

A. Personhood Theory - III. Immanuel Kant: Kant's philosophy views intellectual property as an extension of personal autonomy and moral rights, forming the basis of the Personhood Theory.

B. Natural Right Theory - I. John Locke: Locke's labor theory argues that people have a natural right to the fruits of their labor, including creations of the mind, supporting the Natural Rights Theory.

C. Incentive Theory - IV. William Nordhaus: Nordhaus proposed that intellectual property rights serve as an incentive for innovation by rewarding creators, central to the Incentive Theory.

D. Creative Destruction Theory - II. Joseph Schumpeter: Schumpeter introduced the concept of "creative destruction", where innovation disrupts existing industries, emphasizing the role of innovation in economic progress and supporting the Creative Destruction Theory.

83. (2): The Trade Marks Act, 1999 outlines the registration process in the following correct sequence:

D. Absolute Grounds (Section 9): First, the application is tested against absolute grounds of refusal, which check whether the trademark is inherently registrable (e.g., not descriptive or generic).

A. Relative Grounds (Section 11): Next, it is tested against relative grounds, where conflict with existing trademarks is examined.

E. Honest Concurrent Use (Section 12): Then, cases of honest concurrent use may be considered, allowing similar marks to coexist under certain conditions.

B. Withdrawal of Acceptance (Section 19): After preliminary acceptance, the Registrar can withdraw acceptance under certain grounds.

C. Opposition to Registration (Section 21): Finally, after advertisement, third parties have an opportunity to oppose the registration.

84. (2): The Fundamental Duties under Article 51A of the Indian Constitution are listed in a specific sequence. The correct order for the duties mentioned is:

B. To cherish and follow the noble ideals which inspired our national struggle for freedom: Listed first under Clause (b).

E. To uphold and protect the sovereignty, unity and integrity of India: Listed next under Clause (c).

A. To value and preserve the rich heritage of our composite culture: Listed under Clause (f).

D. To develop the scientific temper, humanism and spirit of inquiry and reform: Listed under Clause (h).

C. To safeguard public property and to abjure violence: Listed under Clause (i).

- Thus, the sequence is B, E, A, D, C matching exactly as laid down in the Constitution.

85. (3): The Consumer Protection Act, 1986 has been repealed and replaced by the Consumer Protection Act, 2019. The new Act came into effect on 20th July 2020, introducing significant reforms to better address modern consumer issues. It established new mechanisms such as the Central Consumer Protection Authority (CCPA), introduced the concept of product liability, e-commerce regulation, and facilitated faster grievance redressal through e-filing and mediation centers.

Thus, the governing law now is the Consumer Protection Act, 2019.

86. (4): The jurisdiction of the International Court of Justice (ICJ) is fundamentally based on the principle of consent of the states involved. According to Article 36 of the Statute of the

ICJ, the Court can only exercise jurisdiction if the parties to a dispute have consented to it. This consent can be given through treaties, special agreements, or optional clause declarations under Article 36(2).

Thus, states are not automatically bound to ICJ jurisdiction unless they have explicitly agreed to it, embodying the principle of consensual basis rather than compulsory participation.

87. **(3):** Section 16 of the Sale of Goods Act, 1930 deals with "Implied conditions as to quality or fitness" of goods sold. It states that generally, there is no implied warranty or condition as to the quality or fitness of goods for any particular purpose, except:

- Where the buyer makes known to the seller the particular purpose for which goods are required, and relies on the seller's skill or judgment.
- Where goods are bought by description from a seller who deals in goods of that description.

This protects consumers by implying a condition of fitness when reliance and seller's specialization are evident.

88. **(4):** Under Sunni Law, certain marriages are classified as fasid (irregular) marriages, which can be regularized upon removal of the irregularity. Grounds for fasid marriages include:

- Marriage with a fifth wife (when already having four wives).
- Unlawful conjugation (marrying two women who are closely related to each other such as sisters).
- Marriage with a woman undergoing iddat (waiting period after divorce or death of husband).

However, marriage in violation of conditions of fosterage (milk relationship) is treated as batil (void) marriage, not fasid.

In Sunni law, marriage between foster siblings is void ab initio, hence not merely irregular.

89. **(4):** To constitute 'marz-ul-maut' (death-bed illness) under Islamic law, the following conditions must be satisfied:

A. The malady or illness must result in the death: It must be a serious illness leading to the donor's death.

B. The illness must cause reasonable apprehension of death in the mind of the donor: The donor must fear death due to the illness.

C. There should be some external indicia of a serious illness: Observable signs such as medical symptoms that indicate grave illness.

E. Delivery of possession must be given to the donee: The possession must be handed over to complete a valid gift in marz-ul-maut.

D. There must be an apprehension of death in the mind of physician is not a necessary condition; it is the apprehension in the mind of the donor that is relevant.

90. **(1):** The Estrada Doctrine, formulated in Mexico in 1930, asserts that once a state has been recognized, its government does not require fresh recognition each time there is a change in leadership. Recognition of governments is viewed as an unnecessary interference in the internal affairs of a sovereign state. Instead, states simply maintain or withdraw diplomatic relations based on factual effectiveness rather than granting or denying recognition to new governments. Thus, the essence of the Estrada Doctrine is that recognition of government is unnecessary once the state itself has been recognized.

91. **(3):** Article 10(1) of the Agreement on Trade-Related Aspects of Intellectual Property Rights (TRIPS) provides that computer programmes shall be protected as literary works under the Berne Convention. This means that computer programmes, though technical in nature, are protected under the same legal framework as literary works such as books or writings. The passage also clearly mentions that "Article 10(1) of TRIPS provides copyright protection to computer programmes", thus confirming this provision as the basis of legal protection.

92. **(4):** Copyright can subsist in a computer programme, provided it shows originality and sufficient intellectual effort. As per the passage: "Copyright subsists in a computer programme provided sufficient effort or skill has been expended to give it a new and original character". It emphasizes that originality is key. This means not all software is protected by default; it must reflect a degree of creativity or intellectual input, however minimal.

93. (3): The passage states that if a computer programme merely produces multiplication tables, it cannot claim copyright protection, as the amount of effort or originality is too trivial. Therefore, mere mechanical or routine outputs like generating basic tables or alphabets lack the threshold of originality required under copyright law. The law protects creative expression, not simple outputs derived from elementary logic or universal knowledge.

94. (3): The passage clearly states: "Copyright subsists in original works that are capable of being reproduced from a fixed medium".

This means two requirements must be fulfilled:

- The work must be original, reflecting some intellectual creativity or skill.
- It must be fixed in a tangible form that allows it to be reproduced (like writing, digital recording, etc.).

This is consistent with international standards for copyright protection, where both originality and fixation are required.

95. (1): According to the passage, software is considered a literary work under copyright laws in various jurisdictions. This is reaffirmed by TRIPS Article 10(1), which categorizes computer programmes as literary works, not because they are artistic, but because they are expressed in code or script—a form of written language.

Hence, software enjoys the same protection as a book or novel, although it functions very differently. The key is that it is a fixed expression of an idea, which is protectable under copyright.

96. (1): Article 32 empowers the Supreme Court to issue writs for the enforcement of fundamental rights, acting as a protector of citizen's rights against the excesses of administrative and governmental agencies.

Article 226 similarly empowers the High Courts to issue writs not only for the enforcement of fundamental rights but also for any other purpose, thus providing broader supervisory control over administrative actions.

The passage clearly states that Articles 32 and 226 allow the judiciary to issue writs like certiorari, mandamus, prohibition, quo warranto, and habeas corpus to control administrative excesses.

97. (3): Article 227 of the Constitution confers on the High Courts the power of superintendence over all courts and tribunals within their territorial jurisdiction. This power ensures that tribunals and subordinate courts function properly and legally and that administrative tribunals are kept under a legal framework.

The passage clearly mentions that High Courts are vested with superintendence powers, making High Court the correct authority.

98. (3): The passage explains that besides providing a mechanism for judicial control, the Constitution also aimed at establishing a functional government, which was essential for ensuring administrative efficiency and national development.

Growth of the administrative process was a natural outcome of having a functional government structure where different authorities performed specialized roles.

Hence, the correct reason for the growth of the administrative process is that the Constitution provided for a functional government.

99. (2): The control mechanism under the Constitution is designed to ensure that administrative and governmental authorities do not misuse their powers. By providing powers to courts under Articles 32, 226, 227, and 136, and protections under Article 311 and remedies under Article 300, the Constitution aims to check arbitrary, unreasonable, or excessive actions by administrative agencies.

Thus, the relevance of the control mechanism is specifically to check the excess of administrative actions, not to allow unfettered authority.

100. (4): Article 13 of the Constitution defines "law" broadly to include orders, byelaws, rules, regulations, notifications, and even administrative actions that have the force of law.

This wide definition ensures that all legislative actions of the administration are subject to constitutional scrutiny and can be declared void if they are inconsistent with fundamental rights.

The passage also clearly mentions that by defining law broadly, all legislative actions of the administration were brought under the purview of Article 13.

Previous Years' Paper

National Testing Agency (NTA)

UGC-NET Junior Research Fellowship & Assistant Professor Eligibility Exam

LAW, AUGUST-2024

(Exam held on 30-08-2024)

PAPER-II

1. According to Section 4 of Dissolution of Muslim Marriage Act, 1939. Apostasy from Islam of a Muslim wife:

A. Will dissolve her marriage ipso facto
B. Will not dissolve her marriage ipso facto
C. Dissolves her marriage and she loses her claim to dower
D. Dissolves her marriage and she does not lose her claim to dower

2. A person can be punished for an offence under Section 369 of IPC, for kidnapping or abducting child with intent to steal from the person. For the application of S. 369 of IPC, the child must be:

A. Under the age of 12 years
B. Under the age of 15 years
C. Under the age of 10 years
D. Under the age of 14 years

3. Who coined the English phrase "International Law" for the first time?

A. Plato B. Cisero
C. Aristotle D. Jeremy Bentham

4. How many independent judges compose the International Court of Justice (ICJ)?

A. 25 B. 20
C. 30 D. 15

5. What includes "deliverable state" as per the definition of section 2 (3) of Sale of Goods Act, 1930?

A. State of goods in which buyer is bound to take delivery
B. Identified goods
C. Ascertained goods
D. Goods out for delivery

6. In which of the following case, the Supreme court has held that Section 309 of IPC is not unconstitutional and is not violative of Articles 21 and 14 of the Constitution of India?

A. P. Rathinam v. Union of India
B. Aruna Ramchandra Shanbaug v. Union of India
C. M.S. Dubal v. State of Maharashtra
D. Gian Kaur v. State of Punjab

7. Match the List-I with List-II.

List-I (Concept)	List-II (Section of Relevant Act)
(*a*) Unpaid seller	I. S.16 of Sale of Goods Act, 1930
(*b*) Caveat emptor and its exceptions	II. S.45 of Sale of Goods Act, 1930
(*c*) Minor admitted to benefits of partnership	III. S.30 of Indian Partnership Act, 1932
(*d*) Registration of partnership	IV. S.69 of Partnership Act, 1932

Choose the **correct** answer from the options given below:

	(*a*)	(*b*)	(*c*)	(*d*)
A.	II	I	III	IV
B.	I	II	IV	III
C.	III	IV	II	I
D.	IV	III	I	II

8. Which of the following is **not** a feature of French Administrative legal system?

A. Dual system of courts separating administrative and ordinary' courts
B. Conseil d'Etat as the Supreme administrative court
C. Principle of Judicial Independence
D. Use of Stare decisis in administrative decisions

9. Marriage of Hindu man with biological sister of his adopted sister is:

A. Void B. Valid
C. Voidable D. Illegal

10. Arrange the following Conventions in the chronological order of their adoption.

(*a*) Vienna Convention on the Protection of Ozone Layer
(*b*) Stockholm Convention on Persistent Organic Pollutants
(*c*) Convention on International Trade in Endangered Species of Wild Fauna and Flora (CITCS)
(*d*) The Basel Convention on the Control of Transborder Movements of Hazardous Waste and their Disposal

Choose the **correct** answer from the options given below:

A. (*a*), (*c*), (*b*), (*d*) B. (*c*), (*a*), (*d*), (*b*)
C. (*a*), (*b*), (*c*), (*d*) D. (*d*), (*b*), (*a*), (*c*)

11. Arrange the following in chronological order (section wise) as stated in Motor Vehicles Act, 1988.

(*a*) Procedure and Power of Claim Tribunal
(*b*) Award of Claim Tribunal
(*c*) Claim Tribunals
(*d*) Application for compensation

Choose the **correct** answer from the options given below:

A. (*a*), (*b*), (*c*), (*d*)
B. (*a*), (*c*), (*b*), (*d*)
C. (*c*), (*d*), (*b*), (*a*)
D. (*c*), (*b*), (*a*), (*d*)

12. As per Article 324 of the Constitution of India, any other Election Commissioner or a Regional Commissioner shall not be removed from office except on the recommendation of the:

A. President
B. Chief Justice of India
C. Prime Minister
D. Chief Election Commissioner

13. Nuisance is the interference with the person's right related to:

A. Possession
B. Leave and License
C. Use and enjoyment of land
D. Ownership

14. Which of the following statement is incorrect.

A. A child in the mother's womb is a legal person.
B. A dead person has right to regulate his property according to his wishes when he is not living.
C. Animals are subjects of rights and duties just like human beings.
D. A partnership firm is not a legal person therefore it cannot sue or be sued in its name.

15. Which of the following are functions of Controller of Certifying Authorities under the Information Technology Act, 2000?

(*a*) Exercising supervision over the activities of the Certifying Authorities
(*b*) Certifying public keys of the Certifying Authorities
(*c*) Laying down standards to be maintained by Certifying Authorities

(*d*) Summon and enforcing attendance of any subscriber and examining him on oath

(*e*) Facilitation of the establishment of any electronic system by a certifying authority

Choose the **correct** answer from the options given below:

A. (*b*), (*c*), (*d*), (*e*) only

B. (*a*), (*b*), (*c*) only

C. (*a*), (*b*), (*c*), (*d*) only

D. (*a*), (*b*), (*c*), (*e*) only

16. Arrange in chronological order the following Fundamental Duties as appearing in the Constitution of India.

(*a*) To Safeguard public property and to abjure violence

(*b*) To value and preserve the rich heritage of our composite culture

(*c*) To develop the scientific temper

(*d*) To defend the country and render national service

Choose the **correct** answer from the options given below:

A. (*d*), (*a*), (*b*), (*c*) B. (*a*), (*c*), (*d*), (*b*)

C. (*d*), (*c*), (*b*), (*a*) D. (*d*), (*b*), (*c*), (*a*)

17. Match the List-I with List-II.

List-I (Titles of Books)	**List-II (Authors)**
(*a*) Public International Law in Nutshell	I. J.L. Taulbee and G.Y. Glahn
(*b*) Law among Nations: An Introduction to Public International Law	II. Martin Dixon
(*c*) Principles of Public International Law	III. Thomas Buergenthal and Sean D. Murphy
(*d*) Text Book on International Law	IV. Ian Brownlie

Choose the **correct** answer from the options given below:

	(*a*)	(*b*)	(*c*)	(*d*)
A.	IV	II	III	I
B.	III	I	IV	II
C.	II	I	III	IV
D.	I	III	II	IV

18. In which of the following case it was held that the Preamble of the Constitution emphasises the need to secure to all its citizens Justice, Liberty, Equality and Fraternity?

A. Kesavanand Bharti v. State of Kerala

B. K.S. Puttaswamy v. UOI

C. National Legal Series Authority v. Union of India

D. E.P. Royappa v. State of T.N.

19. Independent Director may be paid remuneration by way of:

(*a*) Sitting fees

(*b*) Stock option

(*c*) Profit related commission approved by board members

(*d*) Share in fixed asset of company

Choose the **correct** answer from the options given below:

A. (*a*), (*c*) only B. (*b*), (*d*) only

C. (*c*), (*d*) only D. (*a*), (*b*) only

20. Match the List-I with List-II.

List-I (Rule)	**List-II (Explanation)**
(*a*) Rule of Foreseeability Test	I. Two or more person combine to injure a third party by unlawful mean
(*b*) Rule of Proximity	II. Re Polemis
(*c*) Tort of Conspiracy	III. Negligence
(*d*) Test of Directness	IV. Wagnamound No 1 case

Choose the **correct** answer from the options given below:

	(a)	(b)	(c)	(d)
A.	IV	III	I	II
B.	I	II	III	IV
C.	III	IV	II	I
D.	II	I	IV	III

21. Which of the following judicial decisions are related to Environment Impact Assessment and Environmental Clearance?

(a) Sterile Industries (India) Ltd v. Union of India

(b) Balram Singh v. U.O.I

(c) Deepak Kumar v. State of Haryana and ors.

(d) Orissa Mining Corporation Ltd. v. MOEF

Choose the **correct** answer from the options given below:

A. (a), (c) and (d) only

B. (a), (b), (d) only

C. (a), (b) and (c) only

D. (b), (c) and (d) only

22. Match the List-I with List-II.

List-I (Case)	List-II (Point of Law)
(a) NG Dastane v. S. Dastane (1975) 2 SCC 326	I. Desertion as a ground of divorce.
(b) Court on its own motion (Lajja Devi) v. State (2012) 193 DLT 61	II. Prohibition of Child Marriage Act, 2006 will prevail over personal law.
(c) Saroj Ram v. Sudershan Kumar AIR 1984 SC 1562	III. S. 23 (1) is not a bar to file a petition u/s 13 (1A) of Hindu Marriage Act.
(d) Bipin Chandra v. Prabhavati AIR 1957 SC 176	IV. Cruelty as a ground of divorce.

Choose the **correct** answer from the options given below:

	(a)	(b)	(c)	(d)
A.	IV	III	II	I
B.	IV	II	III	I
C.	III	IV	II	I
D.	III	IV	I	II

23. An independent director shall be eligible for reappointment on:

A. Passing Ordinary Resolution

B. Passing Special Resolution

C. Approval of Board of Director

D. Approval of Central Government

24. Arrange the following cases in the chronologically order of their year of verdict.

(a) Vineet Narain v. Union of India

(b) Kesavananda Bharti v. State of Kerala

(c) Minerva Mills Ltd v. Union of India

(d) D.K. Basu v. State of West Bengal

Choose the **correct** answer from the options given below:

A. (a), (b), (c), (d)

B. (b), (c), (a), (d)

C. (d), (a), (b), (c)

D. (b), (c), (d), (a)

25. According to Section 6 of the Environment (Protection) Act, 1986, which of the following authority has power to make rules to regulate environmental pollution?

A. National Green Tribunal

B. The Central Government

C. The State Government

D. The Pollution Control Board

26. Arrange the following legislations in the chronological order of their enactment.

(a) Maintenance and Welfare of Parents and Senior Citizens Act

(b) Right of Persons with Disabilities Act

(c) Protection of Womens from Domestic Violence Act

(d) Forest Rights Act

Choose the **correct** answer from the options given below:

A. (*d*), (*a*), (*c*), (*b*) B. (*c*), (*d*), (*b*), (*a*)
C. (*c*), (*d*), (*a*), (*b*) D. (*b*), (*c*), (*d*), (*a*)

27. After declaration of financial emergency what is the maximum period of its operation without approval of Parliament?

A. One month B. Two months
C. Six months D. One year

28. Match the List-I with List-II.

List-I (Description)	List-II (Offence/section)
(*a*) Death caused by a child of 6 years	I. Exception 4 to Section 300
(*b*) Death committed without premeditation in a sudden fight	II. Right of private defence
(*c*) Death of trespasser of the House who was escaping	III. No offence
(*d*) Death is caused in safeguarding property from mischief by fire	IV. Exception 2 to Section 300

Choose the **correct** answer from the options given below:

	(*a*)	(*b*)	(*c*)	(*d*)
A.	I	III	II	IV
B.	III	II	IV	I
C.	I	IV	III	II
D.	III	I	IV	II

29. Under Section 24 of Indian Contract Act, 1872, if only a part of consideration or object is unlawful, the contract shall be:

A. Valid B. Voidable
C. Void D. Illegal

30. Which section of Biological Diversity Act, 2002 mandates approval of National Biodiversity Authority (NBA) before applying for any Intellectual Property Right in a foreign country.

A. Section 7 B. Section 19
C. Section 6 D. Section 8

31. Which kind of Intellectual Property protection is available for trademark?

A. Statutory protection alone
B. Common law protection alone
C. Both Statutory and Common law protection
D. Protection under Trade and Merchandise Act, 1958

32. Identify the Common Law maxims concerning the Double Jeopardy.

(*a*) *Nemo bis punitur pro eodem delicto*
(*b*) *Ex turpi Causa non oritur actio*
(*c*) *Nemo bis vexari debet pro eadem causa*
(*d*) *Novus actus interveniens*
(*e*) *Nemo debet bis puniri pro uno delicto*

Choose the **correct** answer from the options given below:

A. (*b*), (*c*), (*d*) only
B. (*a*), (*c*), (*e*) only
C. (*b*), (*d*), (*e*) only
D. (*a*), (*b*), (*c*), (*d*) only

33. Which of the following statements are correct according to National Green Tribunal Act, 2010.

(*a*) It repealed National Environment Tribunal Act, 1995
(*b*) It repealed National Environment Appellate Authorities Act, 1997
(*c*) The Act does mention about judicial pronouncements construing right to healthy environment as a part of right to life under Art. 21 of the Constitution
(*d*) The Act does not define environment

Choose the **correct** answer from the options given below:

A. (*b*), (*c*) and (*d*) only
B. (*a*), (*b*) and (*d*) only
C. (*a*), (*b*) and (*c*) only
D. (*a*), (*c*) and (*d*) only

34. Which of the following is correct as per the Motor Vehicles Act, 1988?

(*a*) Section 140 of the Motor Vehicles Act, 1988 deals with the principle of No Fault Liability.

(*b*) United Indian Insurance Ltd v. Karamchand (2011) deals with third parties.

(*c*) Doctrine of pay and recover is covered under Section 149 of the Motor Vehicles Act, 1988.

(*d*) As per Section 173 of Motor Vehicles Act, 1988, an appeal to High Court from the award of Motor Accident Claim Tribunal to be preferred within 60 days from the date of the award.

Choose the **correct** answer from the options given below:

A. (*a*), (*c*) and (*d*) only
B. (*a*), (*b*) and (*c*) only
C. (*b*), (*c*) and (*d*) only
D. (*a*), (*b*) and (*d*) only

35. Gap between two consecutive Board meeting of a company should not be more than:

A. 90 days B. 120 days
C. 150 days D. 180 days

36. Which one of the following offence is punishable in all the four stages of crime?

A. Rape B. Murder
C. Dacoity D. Kidnapping

37. Arrange the following steps as per the law making process of UK parliament.

(*a*) First and second reading
(*b*) Royal Assent
(*c*) Consideration of Amendments
(*d*) Committee Stage
(*e*) Report Stage

Choose the **correct** answer from the options given below:

A. (*a*), (*e*), (*d*), (*c*), (*b*)
B. (*a*), (*d*), (*c*), (*e*), (*b*)
C. (*a*), (*d*), (*e*), (*c*), (*b*)
D. (*d*), (*a*), (*e*), (*c*), (*b*)

38. Match the List-I with List-II.

List-I (Country)	**List-II (Procedure and Authority to Amend the Constitution)**
(*a*) United States of America	I. Sections 38-49
(*b*) India	II. Section 128 of the Constitution
(*c*) Australia	III. Article 368 of the Constitution
(*d*) Canada	IV. Article 5 of the Constitution

Choose the **correct** answer from the options given below:

	(*a*)	(*b*)	(*c*)	(*d*)
A.	IV	III	I	II
B.	II	III	IV	I
C.	IV	III	II	I
D.	I	III	IV	II

39. Digital Signature Certificate issued by the Certifying Authority can be revoked:

A. Depending upon the type of certificate issued
B. On the request of the subscriber
C. Under no circumstances
D. On the basis of dispute between the partners of the firm

40. Transfer of property between buyer and seller is explained in chapter III of Sale of Goods Act, 1930.

Arrange the following provisions in the sequence of their appearance in the Act.

(*a*) Property in goods passes when they are ascertained
(*b*) Property in goods passes when the buyer and seller intend it to pass
(*c*) In case of specified goods in deliverable state, property in goods passes when contract is made
(*d*) Risk prima facie passes with property

Choose the **correct** answer from the options given below:

A. (*a*), (*b*), (*c*), (*d*)
B. (*a*), (*c*), (*b*), (*d*)
C. (*d*), (*b*), (*c*), (*a*)
D. (*b*), (*a*), (*c*), (*d*)

41. M.K Ranjit Singh v. UOI (2024) deals with which of the following issue?

A. Preservation of biodiversity and climate change
B. Immigrants and Refugees
C. Offence against children
D. Cyber crimes

42. Match the List-I with List-II.

List-I (Authors/Editors)	List-II (Titles of Books)
(*a*) J. Crowe & K.W. Scheuber	I. The Hand book of International Humanitarian Law (ed); OUP
(*b*) Charlotte Lulf	II. Persecution International Refugee Law and Refuges: A Feminist Approach
(*c*) Mathilde Crepin	III. Conflict of Displacement and Legal Protection understanding Asylum, Human Rights and Refugee Law
(*d*) Dieter Fleck and Michael Bothe	IV. Principles of International Humanitarian Law

Choose the **correct** answer from the options given below:

	(*a*)	(*b*)	(*c*)	(*d*)
A.	I	II	IV	III
B.	III	I	IV	II
C.	II	I	III	IV
D.	IV	III	II	I

43. Which of the following is not a source of International Law as per Article 38 of the Statute of International Court of Justice?

A. Judicial decisions (subject to Art 59 of Statute of ICJ)
B. Writing of most highly qualified Publicists (subject to Art 59 of Statute of ICJ)
C. Community customary laws
D. General principles of law recognised by civilised nations

44. Match the List-I with List-II.

List-I (Cyber Crime)	List-II (Punishments)
(*a*) Violation of Bodily Privacy	I. Upto three years imprisonment and fine up to one lakh rupees
(*b*) Publishing or transmitting of material containing sexually explicit act or conduct	II. Extend upto life imprisonment
(*c*) Identity Theft	III. Upto five years imprisonment and Fine upto Ten Lakh Rupees
(*d*) Cyber Terrorism	IV. Upto 3 years imprisonment with fine not exceeding two lakh rupees

Choose the **correct** answer from the options given below:

	(*a*)	(*b*)	(*c*)	(*d*)
A.	I	IV	III	II
B.	IV	III	I	II
C.	III	IV	II	I
D.	III	IV	I	II

45. Which of the following are offences against public tranquility as per Indian Penal Code, 1860?

(*a*) Counterfeiting coin
(*b*) Unlawful Assembly
(*c*) Sedition
(*d*) Rioting
(*e*) Affray

Choose the **correct** answer from the options given below:

A. (*b*), (*c*), (*d*) only
B. (*a*), (*b*), (*d*) only
C. (*b*), (*d*), (*e*) only
D. (*a*), (*c*), (*e*) only

46. Which of the following statements are correct as per International Court of justice (ICJ)?

(*a*) The judgement is final and without appeal.
(*b*) No application for revision may be made at all.
(*c*) The Court shall deliver it's advisory opinion in open court.
(*d*) The members of ICJ are elected for 10 years.

Choose the **correct** answer from the options given below:

A. (*c*) and (*d*) only
B. (*b*) and (*d*) only
C. (*a*) and (*b*) only
D. (*a*) and (*c*) only

47. Arrange the following International Treaties/ Conventions in the chronological order of their adoption.

(*a*) Budapest Treaty on International Recognition of the Deposit of micro organism
(*b*) Hague Agreement concerning the International Registration of Industrial Design
(*c*) WIPO Copyright Treaty
(*d*) Paris Convention for the Protection of Industrial Property

Choose the **correct** answer from the options given below:

A. (*a*), (*c*), (*b*), (*d*)
B. (*d*), (*b*), (*a*), (*c*)
C. (*b*), (*a*), (*d*), (*c*)
D. (*d*), (*a*), (*b*), (*c*)

48. Arrange the following reasonable restrictions provided for Freedom of Speech and Expression in Article 19 (2) of the Constitution in their chronological order:

(*a*) Contempt of court
(*b*) Incitement to an offence
(*c*) Public order
(*d*) Security of the State
(*e*) Friendly relations with Foreign States

Choose the **correct** answer from the options given below:

A. (*a*), (*e*), (*b*), (*c*), (*d*)
B. (*d*), (*e*), (*c*), (*a*), (*b*)
C. (*d*), (*a*), (*b*), (*c*), (*e*)
D. (*d*), (*c*), (*b*), (*e*), (*a*)

49. Which of the following statements are correct in case of Vicarious Liability?

(*a*) Relationship of Master Servant
(*b*) No control of master over the manner of doing work
(*c*) Tort committed in course of employment
(*d*) Control of master on the manner of doing work

Choose the **correct** answer from the options given below:

A. (*a*), (*b*), (*c*) only
B. (*b*), (*c*), (*d*) only
C. (*a*), (*c*), (*d*) only
D. (*a*), (*b*), (*d*) only

50. Which of the following is NOT part of 'International Bill of Rights'?

(*a*) Magna Carta, 1215
(*b*) Universal Declaration of Human Rights, 1948
(*c*) International Convenent on Civil and Political Rights, 1966
(*d*) Convention on Rights of the Child, 1989

Choose the **correct** answer from the options given below:

A. (*a*) and (*b*) only
B. (*a*) and (*c*) only

C. (*b*) and (*c*) only
D. (*a*), and (*d*) only

51. Which of the following refers to "a clear and formal expression of recognition by a state through official communication or diplomatic statement"?

A. Implicit recognition
B. Collective recognition
C. Explicit recognition
D. Conditional recognition

52. Which of the following Judgments are associated with the Legislative Supremacy of Parliament in UK.

(*a*) Jackson v. Attorney General (2005)
(*b*) R v. Secretary of State for Transport (Factor fame) (1991)
(*c*) R v. Secretary of State for the Home Department ex p. Leech (1994)
(*d*) O' Reilly v. Mackman (1983)
(*e*) Ridge v. Baldwin (1964)

Choose the **correct** answer from the options given below:

A. (*a*), (*b*), (*c*), (*d*) only
B. (*a*), (*b*), (*c*) only
C. (*a*), (*b*), (*d*), (*e*) only
D. (*a*), (*b*), (*c*), (*e*) only

53. Which of the following is undefined in the International Convention on the "Protection of the Rights of all Migrant Workers and Members of their Family, 1990"?

A. Migrant worker
B. Unorganised worker
C. Seasonal worker
D. Frontier worker

54. Contributory negligence is a/an:

A. Obligation B. Crime
C. Defence D. Right

55. In which of the important circumstances Parliament can legislate with respect to matters in the state list?

(*a*) To make laws with respect to Goods and Services Tax imposed by such state
(*b*) In matters of National Interest
(*c*) If a proclamation of Emergency is in operation
(*d*) By consent of states
(*e*) For Giving effect to International Agreements

Choose the **correct** answer from the options given below:

A. (*a*), (*b*), (*c*) only
B. (*b*), (*c*), (*d*) only
C. (*a*), (*c*), (*d*), (*e*) only
D. (*b*), (*c*), (*d*), (*e*) only

56. Which of the following terms are defined under the Information Technology Act, 2000?

(*a*) Computer Network
(*b*) Information
(*c*) Data
(*d*) Secure System
(*e*) Online

Choose the **correct** answer from the options given below:

A. (*a*), (*d*), (*e*) only
B. (*a*), (*b*), (*c*), (*d*) only
C. (*a*) and (*d*) only
D. (*a*), (*c*), (*d*) (*e*) only

57. Indicate the correct sequence of the following sources of Muslim Law:

(*a*) The Quran
(*b*) The Ijmaa
(*c*) The Hadis
(*d*) The Kiyas

Choose the **correct** answer from the options given below:

A. (*a*), (*b*), (*c*), (*d*)
B. (*a*), (*c*), (*b*), (*d*)
C. (*d*), (*c*), (*b*), (*a*)
D. (*a*), (*d*), (*c*), (*b*)

58. Match the List-I with List-II.

List-I (Pre-requisites for protection)	List-II (Kind of IPR)
(*a*) Distinctiveness	I. Copyright
(*b*) Originality	II. Geographical Indication
(*c*) Industrial Application	III. Trademark
(*d*) Quality and Reputation of Goods	IV. Patents

Choose the **correct** answer from the options given below:

	(*a*)	(*b*)	(*c*)	(*d*)
A.	I	II	IV	III
B.	III	II	I	IV
C.	III	I	IV	II
D.	IV	III	I	II

59. Arrange the following as per the procedure of Constitutional amendment in United States of America.

(*a*) Proposal by Congress or Convention of States

(*b*) Governor of State submitting proposed amendment to state's legislature for consideration.

(*c*) Ratification by State

(*d*) Governor intimating Congress about State decision

(*e*) Getting ratification by 2/3rd states

Choose the **correct** answer from the options given below:

A. (*a*), (*b*), (*c*), (*d*), (*e*)

B. (*a*), (*b*), (*c*), (*e*), (*d*)

C. (*b*), (*c*), (*d*), (*e*), (*a*)

D. (*b*), (*c*), (*e*), (*d*), (*a*)

60. Which of the following kind of IPR is regarded as community property?

A. Industrial Designs

B. Copyright

C. Patents

D. Geographical Indications

61. Match the List-I with List-II.

List-I (Commissions and Tribunals)	List-II (Initial Establishment)
(*a*) National Commission for Backward Classes (NCBC)	I. 1992
(*b*) National Commission for Women (NCW)	II. 2010
(*c*) National Green Tribunal (NGT)	III. 2004
(*d*) National Commission for Scheduled Castes (NCSC)	IV. 1993

Choose the **correct** answer from the options given below:

	(*a*)	(*b*)	(*c*)	(*d*)
A.	IV	I	II	III
B.	I	II	III	IV
C.	II	I	IV	III
D.	II	III	I	IV

62. Arrange the following General Exceptions in the Indian Penal Code in the chronological order of their appearance in IPC.

(*a*) Act done in good faith for the benefit of child by the consent of guardian

(*b*) Act done in good faith for the benefit of person without consent

(*c*) Communication made in good faith

(*d*) Act to which a person is compelled by threats

Choose the **correct** answer from the options given below:

A. (*a*), (*b*), (*c*), (*d*) B. (*c*), (*d*), (*b*), (*a*)

C. (*a*), (*b*), (*d*), (*c*) D. (*c*), (*d*), (*a*), (*b*)

63. Match the List-I with List-II.

List-I (IPR Treaties and Agreements)	List-II (Corresponding subject matter)
(*a*) Strasbourg Agreement	I. Trademark
(*b*) Nice Agreement	II. Audio-visual performance

(*c*) Beijing Treaty	III.	International Patent classification
(*d*) Singapore Treaty	IV.	International classification of Goods

Choose the **correct** answer from the options given below:

	(*a*)	(*b*)	(*c*)	(*d*)
A.	I	III	IV	II
B.	III	II	I	IV
C.	II	I	III	IV
D.	III	IV	II	I

64. Which actions are covered under the offence of violation of privacy under section 66E of Information Technology Act, 2000?

A. Non consensual capture, publication and transmission of intimate images
B. Knowingly transmission and publication of intimate images only
C. Non consensual publication of intimate images only
D. Non Consensual and consensual capture, publication and transmission of intimate images

65. Constitution of India confers original and exclusive jurisdiction on the Supreme Court in cases where there is a dispute:

(*a*) Between two or more states
(*b*) Dispute arising out any treaty entered into or executed before the commencement of the Constitution
(*c*) Between the Union Govt and one or more states
(*d*) Between the Union Govt and any states on one side and one or more states on the other
(*e*) Dispute arising out of substantial question of law of general importance

Choose the **correct** answer from the options given below:

A. (*a*), (*b*), (*c*) only
B. (*c*), (*d*), (*e*) only
C. (*b*), (*c*), (*d*), (*e*) only
D. (*a*), (*c*), (*d*) only

66. Which Articles were added to the Constitution of India to facilitate the establishment of specific Tribunals to meet the needs of Administrative Justice?

A. Article 124 A
B. Article 233 A
C. Articles 323 A and 323 B
D. Articles 338 A and 338 B

67. Arrange the following provisions in the chronological order of arrangement in the Consumer Protection Act, 2019.

(*a*) District Consumer Protection Council
(*b*) Central Consumer Protection Council
(*c*) Central Consumer Protection Authorities
(*d*) Investigation Wing
(*e*) Consumer Mediation cell

Choose the **correct** answer from the options given below:

A. (*b*), (*a*), (*c*), (*d*), (*e*)
B. (*c*), (*b*), (*d*), (*e*), (*a*)
C. (*e*), (*c*), (*b*), (*a*), (*d*)
D. (*d*), (*b*), (*a*), (*e*), (*c*)

68. Which of the following led setting aside of practice of Triple Talaq as evident in the case of Shayara Bano v. UOI (2017) SCC 1?

(*a*) Muslim Personal Law (Shariat) Application Act, 1937 is not a Law regarding Triple Talaq and the practice is against the tenets of Holy Quran.
(*b*) Section 2 of Shariat Application Act, 1937 is pre-constitutional legislation within the meaning of Art 13 (1) of Constitution and violative of Art, 14.
(*c*) Section 2 of Shariat Application Act, 1937 is pre constitutional legislation within meaning of Art 13 (1) of Constitution and violative of Art, 15 of Constitution of India.

(*d*) Triple Talaq can be injuncted by Supreme Court to severe matrimonial relationship.

Choose the **correct** answer from the options given below:

A. (*b*), (*a*) only B. (*a*), (*c*) only
C. (*b*), (*d*) only D. (*c*), (*d*) only

69. Convention on Biodiversity was signed at which International conference/Summit?

A. Paris Climate Conference
B. Stockholm Conference
C. Rio Earth Summit
D. Hague Conference

70. The contents of an electronic record may be proved under which of the following sections of Indian Evidence Act, 1872?

A. Section 65 A
B. Section 65 B
C. Section 66
D. Sections 61 and 53

71. In which year "WIPO Treaty on Intellectual Property, Genetic Resources and Associated Traditional knowledge" has been adopted?

A. 2023 B. 2020
C. 2024 D. 2022

72. Match the List-I with List-II.

List-I (Judicial Decisions)	**List-II (Fundamental Rights)**
(*a*) Sri Srinivasa Theatre v. Govt of T.N.	I. Article 20(3) of the Constitution
(*b*) K.A. Abbas v. Union of India	II. Right to Environment
(*c*) Selvi v. State of Karnataka	III. Equality before Law
(*d*) Rural Litigation and Entitlement Kendra v. State of UP	IV. Censorship

Choose the **correct** answer from the options given below:

	(*a*)	(*b*)	(*c*)	(*d*)
A.	I	II	III	IV
B.	III	IV	I	II
C.	II	I	IV	III
D.	IV	II	I	III

73. Which of the following is **not** correct about Savigny:

A. Savigny was against Natural Law
B. Volksgeist theory of Savigny made it impossible for a Comparative study of law
C. Savigny did not recognize legislation as a potent source of law
D. Savigny was in favour of codification of law

74. If a Muslim husband swears that he will not have sexual intercourse with wife for four months or more, it amounts to a form of Divorce known as:

A. I'la
B. Zihar
C. Tafweez
D. Mubarat

75. Which of the following statement is **incorrect** regarding Asylum?

(*a*) Article 14 of UDHR grants a right to asylum from persecution
(*b*) Asylum also includes transfer of person wanted by an arrest warrant to the prosecution country
(*c*) Granting of Asylum per se excludes any possibility of extradition
(*d*) Extradition and Asylum are mutually exclusive

Choose the **correct** answer from the options given below:

A. (*a*), (*b*) and (*c*) only
B. (*a*) and (*d*) only
C. (*b*), (*c*) and (*d*) only
D. (*a*), (*c*) and (*d*) only

76. Arrange the following International Humanitarian Law Treaties and Conventions in the chronological order of their adoption.

(*a*) Chemical Weapons Convention
(*b*) Arms Trade Treaty
(*c*) International Convention for the Protection of the All Persons from Enforced Disappearance
(*d*) Geneva Convention
(*e*) Treaty on the Prohibition of Nuclear Weapons

Choose the **correct** answer from the options given below:

A. (*b*), (*c*), (*d*), (*a*), (*e*)
B. (*d*), (*b*), (*c*) (*e*), (*a*)
C. (*a*), (*e*), (*d*), (*c*), (*b*)
D. (*d*), (*a*), (*c*), (*b*), (*e*)

77. In which of the following Judgement, the Supreme Court has held that the Exception 2 to Section 375 IPC is violative of the right of girl child below 18 years?

A. Navtej Singh Johar v. Union of India
B. Prahlad v. State of Haryana
C. Arnesh Kumar v. State of Bihar
D. Independent Thought v. Union of India

78. Muta marriage is:

(*a*) A temporary marriage
(*b*) Recognised under Shia Law
(*c*) Recognised under Sunni Law
(*d*) A marriage for a fixed period: a day, month, year
(*e*) One in which dower need not be specified

Choose the **correct** answer from the options given below:

A. (*a*), (*b*), (*d*) only
B. (*a*), (*b*), (*e*) only
C. (*a*), (*c*), (*d*) only
D. (*a*), (*c*), (*d*), (*e*) only

79. Match the List-I with List-II.

List-I (Type of Government)	**List-II (Name of Country)**
(*a*) Constitutional Monarchy	I. Canada, Australia
(*b*) Dual Federalism	II. United States of America
(*c*) Presidential	III. Denmark, Bhutan, Belgium
(*d*) Parliamentary	IV. India and United Kingdom

Choose the **correct** answer from the options given below:

	(*a*)	(*b*)	(*c*)	(*d*)
A.	III	I	II	IV
B.	I	III	II	IV
C.	III	II	I	IV
D.	I	II	III	IV

80. Which Amendment to the U.S. Constitution is important in defining the powers reserved to the States?

A. Ist Amendment
B. IXth Amendment
C. Xth Amendment
D. Vth Amendment

81. According to Section 20 of the Green Tribunal Act, 2010 what are the principles that should be applied by the NGT while passing orders and decisions?

(*a*) Principle of sustainable development
(*b*) Precautionary principle
(*c*) Polluter pays principle
(*d*) Principle of absolute liability

Choose the **correct** answer from the options given below:

A. (*a*), (*b*) and (*d*) only
B. (*b*), (*c*) and (*d*) only
C. (*a*), (*b*) and (*c*) only
D. (*a*), (*c*) and (*d*) only

82. What does "Ratio Decidendi" generally imply?

A. Reason for decision alone
B. Principles laid down in the case alone
C. Both (A) and (B)
D. Observations and opinions

83. Which of following cases are related to personal bias according to the Principle of Natural Justice?

(*a*) A.K. Kraipak v. Union of India
(*b*) Jacob Mathew v. State of Punjab
(*c*) Mohd. Yunus Khan v. State of U.P
(*d*) Gullapalli Nageswara Rao v. State of A.P.
(*e*) Manak Lal v. Prem Chand Singhvi

Choose the **correct** answer from the options given below:

A. (*a*), (*b*), (*c*), (*d*) only
B. (*a*), (*c*), (*e*) only
C. (*b*), (*c*), (*d*) only
D. (*b*), (*d*) only

84. Arrange the following legislations in the chronological order of their enactment.

(*a*) Indian Divorce Act
(*b*) Parsi Marriage and Divorce Act
(*c*) Dissolution of Muslim Marriage Act
(*d*) Special Marriage Act

Choose the **correct** answer from the options given below:

A. (*b*), (*a*), (*d*), (*c*)
B. (*a*), (*b*), (*c*), (*d*)
C. (*c*), (*b*), (*d*), (*a*)
D. (*a*), (*d*), (*b*), (*c*)

85. Which of the following is **not** a condition for determining the capacity of male Hindu to adopt?

A. Consent of wife under certain circumstances
B. Majority
C. Soundness of mind
D. Must be necessarily married

86. Match the List-I with List-II.

List-I (List in Constitution)	**List-II (Subject)**
(*a*) Concurrent List	I. In Civil matters
(*b*) State List	II. Marriage and Divorce
(*c*) Union List	III. Public health and Sanitation
(*d*) Appellate Jurisdiction of Supreme Court	IV. Elections to the legislatures of State

Choose the **correct** answer from the options given below:

	(*a*)	(*b*)	(*c*)	(*d*)
A.	I	IV	II	III
B.	IV	II	III	I
C.	II	III	IV	I
D.	III	IV	II	I

87. The Maxim *"De Minimis Non Curat Lex"* relates to:

A. Affray
B. Annoyance
C. Cheating
D. Slight harm

88. Inland Instrument means:

(*a*) Instrument drawn or made in India
(*b*) Instrument made payable in India
(*c*) Instrument drawn upon any person resident in India
(*d*) Instrument that is passed by Indian Parliament

Choose the **correct** answer from the options given below:

A. (*a*), (*b*), (*c*) only
B. (*b*), (*c*), (*d*) only
C. (*a*), (*c*), (*d*) only
D. (*b*), (*a*), (*d*) only

89. In which year Limited Liability Partnership Rules of Third Amendment come up?

A. 2023
B. 2021
C. 1930
D. 2008

90. Match the List-I with List-II

List-I (Jurist)	List-II (Theory)
(*a*) Roscoe Pound	I. Life of the Law has not been logic it has been experience
(*b*) Oliver Wendell Holmes	II. Law is uncertain and certainty of law is a legal myth
(*c*) Ihering	III. End of Law should be to satisfy a maximum of wants with minimum of friction
(*d*) Jerome Frank	IV. Law is part of human conduct and in the idea of purpose

Choose the **correct** answer from the options given below:

	(*a*)	(*b*)	(*c*)	(*d*)
A.	III	I	IV	II
B.	II	I	IV	III
C.	III	II	I	IV
D.	II	III	IV	I

Directions (Qs. No. 91-95): *Read the following passage and answers the questions.*

The Shriram Gas leak case pitted the Supreme Court against one of India's largest corporation. CJ Bhagwati presided over the Supreme Court bench and was deeply concerned for safety of citizens. He was anxious to improve plant - safety, a task which the statutory agencies seemed incapable of performing. The Honourable Chief Justice saw in the Oleum case a way of influencing the far more important Bhopal gas leak case. The Shriram case has also raised some important questions concerning the true scope and ambit of Articles 21 and 32 of the Constitution. The case also dealt with Principles and Norms of determining the liability of large enterprises engaged in manufacturing and sale of hazardous products. It also decided the basis on which damage should be quantified and whether the corporation should be allowed to function from thickly populated areas and if they are allowed what measures should be taken for minimising hazards to workmen. This led the Parliament to enact law & articulate new standard of absolute liability in 1991.

91. Statutory agencies seem incapable of performing which of the following task?

A. Safety of citizen
B. Plant safety
C. Safety of Community
D. Prevention of disaster

92. The Shriram Gas Leak case did not focus on which of the following issue?

A. Scope of Arts. 21 and 32 of Constitution
B. Norms of determining liability of large corporation
C. Basis of quantifying damages
D. Measures of increasing profit of company

93. As an effect of Shriram Gas Leak case, the Law enacted by Parliament in 1991 dealt with:

A. Private liability
B. Storage of hazardous substances
C. Absolute liability
D. Safety of plants and animals

94. The Judgement in Shriram Gas Leak case influenced the decision of:

A. Shrimp case
B. Goel Ganga case
C. Bhopal Gas leak case
D. Clean Narmada case

95. In the Shriram Gas Leak case, the Chief Justice was mainly concerned with which of the following?

A. Safety of citizen
B. Profit of companies
C. Disaster in community
D. Aftermath of gas leak

Directions (Qs. No. 96-100): *Read the following passage and answers the questions.*

From the second half of the nineteenth century to the present, the Geneva Convention 1864, (revised in 1906. 1929, and 1949) and Hague Convention 1899 (revised in 1907) comprised one of the most extensive bodies of positive international law outlining constraints on state behaviour. The Geneva and Hague Conventions are noteworthy not only for their content, but also for their widespread ratification. Accepting the Conventions was a prestigious symbol of membership in the exclusive "international society of civilized states," and most states ratified them sooner or later. The Conventions gave combatant victims of war-wounded soldiers and POWs-international rights to medical care and humane conditions of incarceration. The Hague Convention was built on a fundamental distinction between combatants and non-combatants, designed to ensure that non-combatants did not become victims of war. Non-combatants were not considered legitimate military targets, and military occupation authorities were prohibited from exploiting civilian populations under their control.

96. Which International Instrument predominantly ensures that non-combatants did not become victims of war?

A. Positive international law
B. The Geneva Convention
C. The Hague Convention
D. International Humanitarian law

97. What was the fundamental distinction on which the Hague Convention was built?

A. Distinction between military occupation and civil population
B. Distinction between positive international law and laws of the war
C. Distinction between combatants and non-combatants
D. Distinction between military targets and military authorities

98. What makes Geneva Convention (1864) noteworthy?

A. It's content alone
B. It's widespread ratification alone
C. It's content and its widespread ratification
D. The new international rights created by the Geneva Convention

99. What motivated the States to ratify the Geneva and Hague Conventions?

A. The Conventions being prestigious symbol of membership in the international society of civilized states
B. The Conventions being the most extensive body of positive international law
C. As the Conventions enlist constraints on state behaviour
D. As the Conventions prescribe international rights of medical care

100. What do Hague Convention 1899 and Geneva Convention 1864 primarily outline?

A. Human conditions of incarceration
B. Constraints on State Behaviour
C. Rights of victims of war
D. Rights of wounded soldiers

ANSWERS

1. (B): Under the Dissolution of Muslim Marriages Act 1939, apostasy from Islam by a Muslim wife does not automatically dissolve her marriage. This means that simply changing one's religion or renouncing Islam does not instantly end a marriage under the legal framework. The law requires additional legal proceedings to dissolve a marriage for reasons including but not limited to apostasy. The act primarily provides women with means to seek dissolution under specific grounds, which include apostasy, but a judicial process is necessary to finalize such a dissolution. Thus, the assertion that apostasy will not dissolve a marriage ipso facto aligns with the legal requirement for judicial intervention rather than an automatic termination of the marital bond.

2. **(C):** Section 369 of the Indian Penal Code (IPC) pertains to the kidnapping or abduction of a child under the age of ten years with the intent of stealing from the child's person. This specific age limit is crucial as it designates a particularly vulnerable group within the population that the law seeks to protect against such offenses. The designation of children under ten years old highlights the enhanced need for protection due to their increased vulnerability and inability to protect themselves compared to older children. This section aims to deter and punish those who would exploit the most defenseless members of society, emphasizing the law's role in safeguarding children from criminal acts that target their youth and innocence.

3. **(D):** The term "International Law" was first coined by Jeremy Bentham, an English philosopher and jurist known for his contributions to modern philosophy and jurisprudence. Bentham introduced this term in the 18th century as a part of his work on legal reform where he sought to establish a clear and rational system of norms governing the relations between sovereign states. Prior to Bentham, terms like "law of nations" were more commonly used. His introduction of "International Law" marked a significant shift towards a more organized and universally applicable framework of legal principles that govern international interactions. Bentham's terminology and ideas laid the groundwork for the development of international legal theories and practices that are still pertinent today.

4. **(D):** The International Court of Justice (ICJ), often referred to as the World Court, is composed of 15 judges. These judges are elected by the United Nations General Assembly and the Security Council, serving as the principal judicial organ of the United Nations. Each judge serves a nine-year term, with elections staggered so that one-third of the court is elected every three years. The composition of the court is designed to reflect a broad geographical distribution, ensuring that the principal legal systems of the world are represented. The number of judges, set at 15, facilitates a comprehensive deliberation process while maintaining manageable dynamics for decision-making in complex international legal disputes.

5. **(A):** According to Section 2(3) of the Sale of Goods Act, 1930, "deliverable state" refers to the condition of goods that is acceptable for the buyer to take delivery under the terms of the contract. This definition implies that the goods must meet all contractual specifications and requirements set forth by the buyer and seller in their agreement. For goods to be considered in a "deliverable state," they must be ready for transfer from the seller to the buyer without the need for further processing or compliance checks, unless such conditions are explicitly included in the contract. This legal stipulation ensures clarity and fairness in transactions, helping to prevent disputes over the condition of goods at the time of delivery.

6. **(D):** The Supreme Court of India, in the case of Gian Kaur v. State of Punjab, held that Section 309 of the Indian Penal Code (IPC), which criminalizes the attempt to commit suicide, is not unconstitutional and does not violate Articles 14 (Right to Equality) and 21 (Right to Life and Personal Liberty) of the Constitution of India. The court opined that the right to life under Article 21 does not include the right to

die, and thus, Section 309 is a valid legal provision aimed at preventing harm. This decision overruled previous judgments, such as P. Rathinam v. Union of India, where the court had declared Section 309 unconstitutional. The Gian Kaur judgment emphasized the importance of preserving life and outlined the state's role in preventing and alleviating conditions leading to suicide.

7. (A):

(*a*) **Unpaid seller - (II):** Section 45 of the Sale of Goods Act, 1930 defines the rights of an unpaid seller against the goods and the buyer. An unpaid seller is someone who has not received the whole of the price or whose payment has been dishonored.

(*b*) **Caveat emptor and its exceptions - (I):** Section 16 of the Sale of Goods Act, 1930 deals with the principle of 'caveat emptor' (let the buyer beware), including its exceptions, which require the seller to disclose faults in goods that render them unfit for their purposes.

(*c*) **Minor admitted to benefits of partnership - (III):** Section 30 of the Indian Partnership Act, 1932, explains that a minor can be admitted to the benefits of a partnership with the consent of all partners, but cannot be made a full partner until reaching majority.

(*d*) **Registration of partnership - (IV):** Section 69 of the Partnership Act, 1932 discusses the effects of non-registration of a partnership, which includes limitations on the powers of non-registered firms to enforce legal rights.

8. (D): The French administrative legal system does not follow the common law principle of 'stare decisis', where courts are bound to follow previous decisions. Instead, the Conseil d'Etat, the highest administrative court in France, does not consider itself strictly bound by its previous rulings, thus allowing for a more flexible approach to administrative law. This distinguishes the French system from common law systems where judicial precedents are more rigidly adhered to.

9. (B): The marriage of a Hindu man with the biological sister of his adopted sister is considered valid under Hindu Marriage Act, 1955. The Act specifies prohibited relationships but does not include the relationship between a man and his adopted sister's biological sibling as a prohibited degree of relationship. This allows such a marriage to be recognized as valid legally, considering that the biological and adoptive familial lines are treated separately.

10. (B):

- Convention on International Trade in Endangered Species of Wild Fauna and Flora (CITES) was adopted in 1973.
- Vienna Convention on the Protection of the Ozone Layer was adopted in 1985.
- The Basel Convention on the Control of Transborder Movements of Hazardous Waste and their Disposal was adopted in 1989.
- Stockholm Convention on Persistent Organic Pollutants was adopted in 2001.

This sequence aligns with the historical timeline of the development and international agreement on these significant environmental and ecological issues. Each convention was established as global recognition of these issues grew, reflecting evolving priorities in environmental governance.

11. (C): The Motor Vehicles Act, 1988, organizes the provisions related to claims arising from motor accidents in a logical sequence. Section 165 establishes the Claim Tribunals, indicating their formation and jurisdiction. Following this, Section 166 deals with applications for compensation, outlining who may apply and the process for filing claims. Section 168 describes the Award of the Claim Tribunal, detailing how the tribunal will make its decisions regarding compensation. Lastly, Section 169 specifies the Procedure and Powers of the Claim Tribunal, which includes how the tribunals shall conduct their proceedings. This sequence ensures a systematic approach to handling claims, from the establishment of tribunals to the final awarding process and procedural guidelines.

12. (D): Article 324 of the Indian Constitution grants the Chief Election Commissioner (CEC) a pivotal role in ensuring the integrity and efficacy of the electoral process in India. It specifies that any Election Commissioner or a Regional Commissioner, once appointed by the President, shall not be removed from office except on the recommendation of the Chief Election Commissioner. This provision aims to safeguard the independence of the Election Commissioners by ensuring that their removal is not arbitrary but is based on substantial grounds vetted by the head of the Election Commission, thereby upholding the autonomy and impartiality of the Commission.

13. (C): Nuisance, as a common law tort, involves an interference with the right of a person to use and enjoy their land. It includes actions that may not necessarily trespass physically onto the land but still cause indirect harm, such as noise, pollution, or other disturbances that diminish the utility or enjoyment of one's property. The essence of nuisance is its continuous, non-transitory nature and its substantial interference with the rights of the property owner or occupier. This definition is crucial in distinguishing nuisance from other torts like trespass, which involves direct, physical invasion of property.

14. (C): This statement is incorrect. In legal terms, animals are considered property rather than entities with rights and duties. The law does not grant animals the same legal capacities as human beings, such as the ability to own property, enter into contracts, or sue and be sued in their own names. While there are laws designed to protect animals from cruelty and abuse, these do not equate to recognizing them as having legal rights and duties akin to humans. Legal systems generally treat animals as subjects to be protected under the law, not as participants in the legal system with rights and responsibilities.

15. (D): Under the Information Technology Act, 2000, the Controller of Certifying Authorities plays a significant role in regulating and overseeing digital certification and security practices. The Controller is tasked with exercising supervision over the activities of the Certifying Authorities, certifying the public keys of these authorities, and laying down the standards to be maintained by them. Additionally, the Controller is also involved in facilitating the establishment of any electronic system by a certifying authority, supporting the development of secure digital communication infrastructures. However, there is no provision in the IT Act that explicitly assigns the role of summoning and examining subscribers on oath to the Controller, indicating that option (*d*) is not one of the Controller's responsibilities.

16. (D): The Fundamental Duties in the Constitution of India, as listed under Article 51A, were introduced by the 42nd Amendment in 1976, and later additions were made by subsequent amendments. The duties are:

(*d*) To defend the country and render national service if called upon to do so, which is the first duty listed under the original duties established in 1976.

(*b*) To value and preserve the rich heritage of our composite culture, which is also among the initial set of duties and focuses on cultural preservation.

(*c*) To develop the scientific temper, humanism, and the spirit of inquiry and reform, reflecting a duty aimed at promoting education and scientific understanding among the citizens.

(*a*) To safeguard public property and to abjure violence, which was added later, emphasizes the responsibility of citizens to maintain public order and respect for property.

17. (B): Matching the titles of books with their authors regarding Public International Law:

(*a*) Public International Law in Nutshell is authored by Thomas Buergenthal and Sean D. Murphy, experts known for their contributions to the field and succinct explanations of complex legal principles.

(*b*) Law among Nations: An Introduction to Public International Law is by J.L. Taulbee and G.Y. Glahn, who provide an introductory overview suitable for those new to the field.

(*c*) Principles of Public International Law, a foundational text in the field, is written by Ian Brownlie, a highly respected scholar in international law.

(*d*) Text Book on International Law is penned by Martin Dixon, who provides a comprehensive examination of the subject matter, ideal for students and practitioners alike.

18. (B): The Supreme Court of India, in the landmark case of K.S. Puttaswamy v. Union of India, significantly emphasized the concepts enshrined in the Preamble such as Justice, Liberty, Equality, and Fraternity in the context of privacy being declared a fundamental right. The court underscored that these principles are crucial in understanding the constitution's commitment to a dignified existence for all citizens, reinforcing the linkage between fundamental rights and the directive principles stated in the Preamble.

19. (A): Independent Directors may be remunerated in the following ways according to the company laws:

(*a*) Sitting fees, which are payments made for attending the meetings of the board and various committees. This is a standard practice and is meant to compensate directors for their time and input during meetings.

(*c*) Profit-related commission approved by board members, which aligns the interests of the directors with the performance of the company, incentivizing them to drive the company towards financial success.

Options like stock options and a share in fixed assets of the company are generally not applicable to Independent Directors to maintain their independence and avoid conflicts of interest.

20. (A): Matching rules and explanations in legal doctrine:

(*a*) Rule of Foreseeability Test relates to the Wagnamound No 1 case, which discusses foreseeability as a crucial element in determining negligence.

(*b*) Rule of Proximity is addressed in Negligence, where the direct causation between the act and the resulting harm must be established for liability to be assigned.

(*c*) Tort of Conspiracy, where two or more persons combine to injure a third party by unlawful means, is a fundamental principle in understanding collective liability.

(*d*) Test of Directness is exemplified in the case of Re Polemis, which focuses on the closeness or directness of the relationship between the act and the injury.

21. (A):

(*a*) Sterlite Industries (India) Ltd v. Union of India dealt with issues surrounding environmental clearances and the obligations of industries under environmental laws. The case underscored the need for industries to adhere to stringent environmental standards and the role of Environmental Impact Assessments (EIAs) in ensuring sustainable industrial practices.

(*c*) Deepak Kumar v. State of Haryana and ors. addressed the environmental implications of mining activities, highlighting the necessity for proper environmental clearances and the adherence to EIA guidelines to prevent ecological damage.

(*d*) Orissa Mining Corporation Ltd. v. MOEF is a significant case in which the environmental clearance process was scrutinized, particularly in relation to the rights of indigenous peoples and the requirement for a comprehensive EIA before granting clearance for large-scale projects.

These cases collectively emphasize the critical role of EIAs and environmental clearances in protecting the environment against industrial and developmental activities that could cause significant environmental degradation.

22. (B):

- NG Dastane v. S. Dastane establishes that desertion is a ground for divorce, aligning with the legal provisions that allow a spouse to seek divorce if the other has deserted them without reasonable cause for a continuous period.
- Court on its own motion (Lajja Devi) v. State emphasizes that the Prohibition of Child Marriage Act, 2006, prevails over personal laws, reinforcing the legal framework aimed at preventing child marriages irrespective of cultural or religious practices.
- Saroj Ram v. Sudershan Kumar clarifies that Section 23(1) of the Hindu Marriage Act is not a bar to filing a petition under Section 13(1A), which relates to divorce proceedings post-judicial separation or restitution of conjugal rights.
- Bipin Chandra v. Prabhavati deals with the concept of cruelty as a ground for divorce, marking a significant development in how legal systems view the impact of mental and physical cruelty in marital relationships.

23. (B): Passing Special Resolution: An independent director's reappointment is subject to the approval of shareholders through a Special Resolution, which requires a higher threshold of votes than an ordinary resolution. This procedure ensures that the reappointment of independent directors undergoes rigorous scrutiny, reflecting their role in providing unbiased judgment and oversight in company governance. The requirement for a special resolution is intended to affirm the confidence and trust placed in independent directors by the shareholders.

24. (D):

(*b*) Kesavananda Bharti v. State of Kerala (1973) is a landmark case that established the basic structure doctrine, setting limitations on the constitutional amendment powers of the Parliament.

(*c*) Minerva Mills Ltd v. Union of India (1980) further reinforced the basic structure doctrine, particularly in relation to the balance between fundamental rights and directive principles.

(*d*) D.K. Basu v. State of West Bengal (1997) set significant precedents concerning police conduct and the prevention of custodial torture.

(*a*) Vineet Narain v. Union of India (1998) strengthened the oversight mechanisms for federal investigative agencies, promoting transparency and accountability in their operations.

This sequence shows the evolution of judicial interventions in protecting constitutional principles and human rights.

25. (B): Section 6 of the Environment (Protection) Act, 1986, grants the Central Government the authority to make rules to regulate environmental pollution. This legislative power enables the government to establish standards and procedures that address various environmental issues, ensuring that activities likely to affect the environment are regulated to prevent and control pollution. The centralization of this authority ensures uniformity and consistency in environmental governance across the nation, enabling the government to respond effectively to environmental challenges.

26. (C):

(*c*) The Protection of Women from Domestic Violence Act was enacted in 2005. This law provides for the protection of women from threats of physical, emotional, and economic abuse in domestic settings.

(*d*) The Forest Rights Act came into effect in 2006, aimed at recognizing the rights of forest-dwelling tribal communities and other traditional forest dwellers to forest resources.

(*a*) The Maintenance and Welfare of Parents and Senior Citizens Act was established in 2007, which provides measures for the maintenance and welfare of parents and senior citizens, ensuring their well-being and protection against abandonment and abuse.

(*b*) The Right of Persons with Disabilities Act was enacted later in 2016, replacing the earlier Persons with Disabilities (Equal Opportunities, Protection of Rights and Full Participation) Act, 1995, to comply with the United Nations Convention on the Rights of Persons with Disabilities. This sequence accurately reflects the chronological order in which these significant pieces of legislation were enacted, highlighting progressive steps towards protecting vulnerable groups in Indian society.

27. (B): Under the provisions of the Indian Constitution, once a financial emergency is proclaimed under Article 360, it requires approval by both houses of Parliament to remain in force. This approval must be granted within two months of the initial proclamation. If not approved within this period, the proclamation ceases to be in effect. The constitution ensures that such a significant declaration impacting financial stability and governance has the legislative backing, thereby maintaining a check on the executive powers.

28. (D):

(*a*) Death caused by a child of 6 years falls under "No offence" because a child under seven years of age is considered incapable of committing a crime under Indian law, covered by the doctrine of doli incapax.

(*b*) Death committed without premeditation in a sudden fight is covered by "Exception 4 to Section 300" of the Indian Penal Code, which provides that culpable homicide is not murder if it occurs without premeditation in a sudden fight in the heat of passion upon sudden provocation.

(*c*) Death of trespasser of the House who was escaping involves "Exception 2 to

Section 300," where the death is caused in the course of the exercise of the right of private defence of property.

(*d*) Death is caused in safeguarding property from mischief by fire is covered by the "Right of private defence" under sections dealing with self-protection and the protection of property. This arrangement aligns with the legal definitions and exceptions related to culpable homicide and murder, clarifying how different circumstances modify the legal assessment of similar actions.

29. (C): According to Section 24 of the Indian Contract Act, 1872, if any part of the consideration or object of a contract is unlawful, the entire contract is deemed void. This provision ensures that contracts tainted by illegality in even a part of their considerations or objectives cannot be enforced, maintaining the integrity of contractual engagements and upholding the principle that law does not aid the illegal.

30. (C): Section 6 of the Biological Diversity Act, 2002, mandates that any person seeking to apply for any intellectual property right in or outside India for any invention based on research or information on a biological resource obtained from India must obtain prior approval from the National Biodiversity Authority (NBA) before making such applications. This provision ensures that benefits arising from the use of biological resources are equitably shared with the local communities and that biodiversity is conserved and used sustainably.

31. (C): Trademarks receive protection under both statutory law and common law. Statutory protection is provided by specific legislation, such as the Trademarks Act, which offers a framework for registration and enforcement of trademark rights. This includes the ability to prevent unauthorized use of the trademark, seek legal remedies, and establish a right to exclusive use.

Common law protection arises from the actual use of the trademark in commerce, even if the mark is not registered. This is based on the principle of "first to use" rather than "first to file." Common law rights are established through the actual use of the mark in trade, which can provide protection against other uses that might cause confusion among consumers. This dual layer of protection ensures that trademark owners can defend their marks and the associated goodwill, regardless of registration status.

32. (B): The maxims related to the doctrine of double jeopardy, which prevents an individual from being tried or punished twice for the same offense, are:

(*a*) Nemo bis punitur pro eodem delicto - "No one can be punished twice for the same offense."

(*c*) Nemo bis vexari debet pro eadem causa - "No one should be vexed twice for the same cause."

(*e*) Nemo debet bis puniri pro uno delicto - "No one ought to be punished twice for one fault."

These maxims embody the legal safeguard against double jeopardy, ensuring fairness in the legal process by prohibiting multiple prosecutions or punishments for a single act or incident.

33. (C): The National Green Tribunal Act, 2010 introduced several significant changes and features concerning environmental law in India:

(*a*) It repealed the National Environment Tribunal Act, 1995, recognizing the need for a more specialized body to handle complex environmental cases.

(*b*) It also repealed the National Environment Appellate Authorities Act, 1997, consolidating the appellate functions into the new tribunal to streamline the process and reduce redundancy.

(*c*) The Act explicitly acknowledges judicial pronouncements that have construed the right to a healthy environment as part of the right to life under Article 21 of the Constitution, reflecting a broader understanding of environmental rights as fundamental human rights.

These features underscore the Act's purpose to provide effective and expeditious disposal of cases relating to environmental protection and conservation.

34. (B):

(*a*) Section 140 of the Motor Vehicles Act, 1988 indeed addresses the principle of No Fault Liability, providing for compensation in certain cases on a no-fault basis in road accidents.

(*b*) United Indian Insurance Ltd v. Karamchand pertains to issues involving insurance claims and liabilities with respect to third parties under motor vehicle accidents, illustrating the application of insurance laws in motor vehicle accident claims.

(*c*) Doctrine of pay and recover is indeed encapsulated under Section 149 of the Motor Vehicles Act, which deals with the obligations of insurers to third parties and the rights of insurers to subsequently recover from the insured under certain conditions.

However, it's important to verify the ecific provisions concerning the timelines for appeals under Section 173, as this might not accurately reflect the period or the procedural specifics in the Act.

35. (B): According to corporate governance norms and various regulations governing the operation of companies, the gap between two consecutive meetings of a company's board of directors should not exceed 120 days. This requirement ensures regular oversight of the company's affairs, facilitates timely decision-making, and ensures compliance with regulatory obligations. The 120-day limit strikes a balance between giving enough time to gather significant business developments and maintaining continuous governance oversight.

36. (C): In criminal law, an offense can be punishable at various stages of its commission: intention, preparation, attempt, and completion. Dacoity, under the Indian Penal Code (IPC), is one of the few offenses where all stages can attract penal consequences.

- **Intention and Preparation:** The planning and assembling of five or more persons with the intent to commit dacoity is punishable, even if the dacoity itself is not ultimately committed.
- **Attempt:** Any overt act towards committing dacoity, even if the act falls short of completion, is punishable.
- **Completion:** The actual commission of dacoity carries severe penalties, reflecting the seriousness of the offense involving armed robbery by a group.

This comprehensive scope of punishment at all stages is designed to deter the formation of groups intending to commit this serious crime, thereby protecting societal safety and property.

37. (C): The law-making process in the UK Parliament involves several stages, each critical to the development, scrutiny, and final approval of legislation:

(*a*) **First and Second Reading:** The bill is introduced, presented, and debated in principle. The second reading focuses on the general merits of the bill.

(*d*) **Committee Stage:** Detailed examination of the bill occurs here. Amendments and clause-by-clause scrutiny are conducted by a select or public bill committee.

(*e*) **Report Stage:** Further consideration and revision of the bill after the committee stage. Additional amendments can be made, and the bill is reviewed again by the whole house.

(*c*) **Consideration of Amendments:** This stage involves the review of amendments proposed during the report stage and possibly during other stages.

(*b*) **Royal Assent:** The final stage where the bill receives formal approval from the monarch, becoming law.

This sequence ensures thorough vetting and multiple opportunities for amendment and debate, reflecting the robust parliamentary system aimed at producing well-considered legislation.

38. **(C):** The authority and procedure to amend the constitution in these countries are:

(*a*) **United States:** Article 5 of the Constitution outlines the amendment process, requiring significant consensus either by the Congress or by a constitutional convention, followed by ratification by the states.

(*b*) **India:** Article 368 of the Constitution provides a detailed procedure for amendment, involving both the houses of Parliament and, in certain cases, ratification by the states.

(*c*) **Australia:** Section 128 of the Constitution, along with other sections within the Constitution Act of 1982, outlines a complex amendment process, often requiring agreement between federal and provincial levels.

(*d*) **Canada:** Sections 38-49 of the Constitution detail the amendment process, which typically involves passage by the Parliament and then a mandatory referendum.

These procedures reflect the federal structures and constitutional rigidity intended to ensure that amendments are considered carefully and gain wide consensus.

39. **(B):** Digital Signature Certificates (DSCs), issued by certifying authorities, can indeed be revoked under specific conditions:

- One common reason for revocation is at the request of the subscriber. If a subscriber believes their certificate is compromised, no longer needed, or was issued in error, they can request the certifying authority to revoke it.
- Revocation is an essential security measure that maintains the integrity and trustworthiness of digital signatures, which are critical in securing electronic transactions and communications.
- The process of revocation is typically outlined in the policies of the certifying authority, ensuring that users can maintain control over their digital identities and prevent misuse.

40. **(A):** Chapter III of the Sale of Goods Act, 1930, organizes the transfer of property between the buyer and seller systematically:

(*a*) **Property in goods passes when they are ascertained:** This is the basic rule that property in unascertained goods does not pass until the goods are identified and set aside.

(*b*) **Property in goods passes when the buyer and seller intend it to pass:** The principle here is that the parties' intentions (express or implied) determine when the property in the goods passes.

(*c*) **In case of specified goods in deliverable state, property in goods passes when the contract is made:** This rule applies to goods that are specific and identified at the time the contract is made.

(*d*) **Risk prima facie passes with property:** Typically, the risk follows the property, meaning once the property in the goods passes to the buyer, so does the risk of loss or damage.

This logical sequence ensures clarity in transactions, reducing disputes about ownership and liability in commercial dealings.

41. **(A):** Preservation of biodiversity and climate change:

- The case of M.K Ranjit Singh v. UOI (2024) addresses critical issues related to the preservation of biodiversity and the impacts of climate change. This case is pivotal as it deals with the governmental actions and policies affecting environmental conservation, reflecting on how these actions align or conflict with existing laws intended to protect the natural environment.
- The significance of this case lies in its focus on the legal obligations of the state to safeguard the environment against degradation and to ensure sustainable development practices are in place. The judgment from this case could set important precedents for environmental governance, emphasizing the necessity for robust legal frameworks that not only prevent environmental harm but actively promote the conservation of biodiversity in the face of global climate challenges.

42. **(D):** Matching authors and editors to their respective books on international law:

(*a*) J. Crowe & K.W. Scheuber are linked to "Principles of International Humanitarian Law", a comprehensive text that explores the fundamental aspects of humanitarian law in conflict situations.

(*b*) Charlotte Lulf is the author of "Conflict of Displacement and Legal Protection: Understanding Asylum, Human Rights and Refugee Law", which takes a feminist approach to international refugee law, highlighting the unique challenges and perspectives of women refugees and their rights under international law.

(*c*) Mathilde Crepin is noted for her work on "Persecution International Refugee Law and Refugees: A Feminist Approach", which delves into the persecution grounds under refugee law from a feminist standpoint, examining how gender issues intersect with the legal protections afforded to refugees.

(*d*) Dieter Fleck and Michael Bothe are associated with "The Handbook of International Humanitarian Law (ed); OUP", an essential resource that provides an authoritative guide to the rules and regulations that govern armed conflict and the protection of individuals during such conflicts.

43. **(C):** Community customary laws:

- Article 38 of the Statute of the International Court of Justice outlines the sources of international law, which include international conventions, international custom, general principles of law recognized by civilized nations, and judicial decisions and teachings of the most highly qualified publicists as subsidiary means.
- Community customary laws are not specifically recognized as a formal source of international law under Article 38. This category refers to local or indigenous practices that may influence community behaviour but do not constitute international custom in the sense required by international law. which demands widespread and consistent state practice accompanied by a belief in legal obligation (opinio juris).

44. **(B):** The specific punishments linked to cyber crimes are:

(*a*) Violation of Bodily Privacy, such as through unauthorized camera operation or data breaches involving personal photos, is punishable by up to three years of imprisonment and a fine up to one lakh rupees.

(*b*) Publishing or transmitting material containing sexually explicit act or conduct carries penalties that can extend to five years imprisonment and a fine up to ten lakh rupees.

(*c*) Identity Theft, involving the unauthorized use of personal identity information to commit fraud or other crimes, is punishable by up to three years of imprisonment and a fine.

(*d*) Cyber Terrorism, which involves using computer resources to perform terrorist acts or disrupt national security, can lead to imprisonment extending up to life, reflecting the gravity of such offenses.

45. (C): Offences against public tranquility as defined in the Indian Penal Code, 1860, include:

(*b*) **Unlawful Assembly:** An assembly of five or more persons is designated unlawful if the members intend to conduct themselves in a manner that will disturb the public peace, or they have an objective which, if carried out, would entail the use of force or violence likely to cause public disturbance.

(*d*) **Rioting:** This occurs when the members of an unlawful assembly or a significant number of them resort to force or violence against persons or property in prosecution of the common object of the assembly.

(*e*) **Affray:** This is a situation where two or more persons fight in a public place to the disturbance of the public peace.

These offenses are specifically designed to prevent and punish behaviors that disrupt societal order and induce fear or chaos among the public.

46. (D):

(*a*) The judgment is final and without appeal. This statement is correct as per the statute of the International Court of Justice (ICJ). Judgments delivered by the ICJ are binding, final, and without an avenue for appeal, ensuring that once a decision is made, it is conclusive and must be respected by the parties involved.

(*c*) The Court shall deliver its advisory opinion in open court. This is also correct. The ICJ, when issuing advisory opinions, does so in open court, providing transparency and public access to its deliberations and opinions, which are not binding but carry significant legal weight and influence.

47. (B): The chronological order of the adoption of these international treaties/conventions is:

(*d*) **Paris Convention for the Protection of Industrial Property, 1883:** This is one of the first international treaties aimed at protecting industrial property, including patents, trademarks, industrial designs, and service marks among the contracting states.

(*b*) **Hague Agreement concerning the International Registration of Industrial Designs, 1925:** This treaty established a system that allows for the international registration of industrial designs among the member countries.

(*a*) **Budapest Treaty on the International Recognition of the Deposit of Microorganisms for the Purposes of Patent Procedure, 1977:** This treaty standardized the deposit of microorganisms for patent procedures, allowing deposits made in one member country to be recognized by all.

(*c*) **WIPO Copyright Treaty, 1996:** This treaty addresses copyright issues in the digital age and ensures that copyright protections are extended to computer programs and databases.

48. (B): The chronological order of the reasonable restrictions provided for freedom of speech and expression under Article 19(2) of the Constitution is:

(*d*) **Security of the State:** This was one of the original grounds included in the Constitution at its adoption in 1950, allowing the state to impose restrictions on speech if it threatens the security of the state.

(*e*) **Friendly relations with foreign states:** This ground was added by the First Amendment in 1951, reflecting the need to maintain diplomatic relationships.

(*c*) **Public order:** Also included in the First Amendment, this ground allows for restrictions aimed at maintaining public order.

(*a*) **Contempt of court:** Added by the Sixteenth Amendment in 1963, it allows for restrictions to uphold the authority and dignity of the courts.

(*b*) **Incitement to an offence:** This too was included in the original Constitution but was expanded under the First Amendment to clearly allow the state to restrict speech that could incite crimes.

49. (C): Vicarious liability is a legal principle where one person is held liable for the torts committed by another. The correct elements include:

(*a*) **Relationship of Master-Servant:** This is essential in establishing vicarious liability, where the employer (master) is held liable for the acts done by the employee (servant) within the course of employment.

(*c*) **Tort committed in the course of employment:** For vicarious liability to apply, the wrongful act must be committed within the scope of employment, meaning it must be related to what the employee was hired to do.

(*d*) **Control of master on the manner of doing work:** The employer must have control over how the work is done, which is a key element in defining the master-servant relationship. The ability to direct how a task should be accomplished is crucial in establishing this liability.

50. (D): The International Bill of Rights consists of:

(*b*) **Universal Declaration of Human Rights, 1948:** This document set forth international norms regarding human rights, marking a fundamental milestone in defining rights globally.

(*c*) **International Covenant on Civil and Political Rights, 1966:** Along with its sister covenant on economic, social, and cultural rights, this forms a part of the core human rights treaties that give legal form to the Declaration.

(*a*) **Magna Carta, 1215:** While historically significant in the development of British constitutional law, it is not part of the International Bill of Rights.

(*d*) **Convention on the Rights of the Child, 1989:** This is a critical international treaty on children's rights but is not considered part of the foundational "International Bill of Rights."

51. (C): Explicit recognition refers to a clear and formal expression of recognition by a state, typically manifested through official communication or a diplomatic statement. This type of recognition is deliberate and unambiguous, indicating a state's intention to acknowledge the status or government of another entity as legitimate in the international arena.

In contrast to implicit recognition, which may be inferred from a state's actions or general dealings, explicit recognition leaves no doubt as to the recognizing state's stance. Such recognition can have significant implications in international relations, affecting diplomatic interactions and the legal statuses of nations or governments within the international community.

52. (B): The judgments that have specifically dealt with or impacted the legislative supremacy of Parliament in the UK include:

(*a*) **Jackson v. Attorney General (2005):** This case is significant as it questioned the limits of Parliamentary sovereignty in the context of the Hunting Act 2004. The ruling suggested that there could be fundamental laws that even Parliament cannot change.

(*b*) **R v. Secretary of State for Transport (Factor fame) (1991):** This case highlighted the extent of Parliamentary sovereignty, particularly in how statutes passed by Parliament take precedence over other forms of law, including those derived from the European Union.

(*c*) **R v. Secretary of State for the Home Department ex p. Leech (1994):** This case dealt with legal principles underpinning administrative actions and the supremacy of Parliamentary legislation over administrative decisions.

These cases collectively reinforce the concept of Parliamentary sovereignty, although they also explore its limits and the interaction between legislative actions and judicial review.

53. (B): Unorganised worker:

- In the International Convention on the Protection of the Rights of all Migrant Workers and Members of their Family, 1990, several terms are defined to establish clear protections and rights for migrant workers. However, the term "unorganised worker" is not specifically defined within this convention.
- Definitions typically included in the convention cover various categories of workers such as migrant workers, seasonal workers, and frontier workers, providing specific rights and protections based on the nature of their work and migration status. The absence of a definition for unorganised workers means there is less clarity on the rights of workers who do not fall into more structured employment categories.

54. (C): Contributory negligence is a defense used in tort law that can reduce or eliminate the liability of the defendant if it can be proven that the plaintiff contributed to their own harm. This legal principle is invoked when both parties are at fault to some extent. The concept of contributory negligence is crucial because it acknowledges that multiple parties may bear responsibility for a single incident, adjusting the distribution of damages accordingly. This defense can be pivotal in determining the outcome of civil litigation involving personal injuries or property damage.

55. (D): In the context of India's federal system, Parliament can legislate on matters in the State List under specific circumstances outlined in the Constitution:

(*b*) **In matters of National Interest:** When deemed necessary for the nation as a whole, especially when actions within one state could have implications beyond its borders.

(*c*) **If a proclamation of Emergency is in operation:** During a national emergency, Parliament can make laws on any matter in the State List.

(*d*) **By consent of states:** If two or more states consent, Parliament can legislate on a state subject for them, and such a law can also be adopted by other states.

(*e*) **For giving effect to International Agreements:** When international treaties or agreements necessitate changes in national law, including in areas normally under state jurisdiction.

These provisions reflect the flexibility of India's federal system, allowing for centralized legislative action when it is in the national interest or when external obligations require it, thus ensuring that India can function effectively as a unified entity in varying circumstances.

56. (B): The Information Technology Act, 2000 is a comprehensive statute aimed at regulating various aspects of electronic commerce and cyber activities in India. Key definitions provided in the Act include:

(*a*) **Computer Network:** This term is crucial for understanding the scope of the Act as it pertains to the interconnected collection of autonomous computers that communicate with one another.

(*b*) **Information:** Defined broadly, this encompasses data, text, images, sound, voice, codes, computer programs, software, and databases or microfilm or computer-generated microfiche.

(*c*) **Data:** The Act includes a definition of data, which refers to a representation of information, knowledge, facts, concepts, or instructions which are being prepared or have been prepared in a formalized manner.

(*d*) **Secure System:** Defined within the Act, this term relates to computer hardware, software, and procedures that are reasonably secure from unauthorized access and misuse, provide a reasonable level of reliability and correct operation, are reasonably suited to performing the intended functions, and adhere to generally accepted security procedures.

The term (*e*) Online is not specifically defined under the Information Technology Act, 2000.

57. (B): The correct sequence of sources of Muslim Law, based on their authority and use in Islamic jurisprudence, is as follows:

(*a*) **The Quran:** The primary and most revered source of all Islamic law, containing the holy revelations to Prophet Muhammad.

(*c*) **The Hadis:** Narratives and sayings of Prophet Muhammad that help interpret the Quran and guide Muslims in aspects not explicitly covered by the Quran.

(*b*) **The Ijmaa:** Consensus among the learned scholars of Islam on certain issues, which comes after the Quran and Hadis in terms of authority.

(*d*) **The Kiyas:** Analogical reasoning based on the principles laid out in the Quran and Hadis, used by scholars to derive rulings for situations that have not been specifically addressed in earlier sources.

This order reflects the hierarchical structure in Islamic jurisprudence where the direct word of God in the Quran is supreme, followed by the practices and sayings of the Prophet, consensus of scholars, and then reasoned analogies.

58. (C): The pre-requisites for protection under various kinds of intellectual property rights (IPR) match with the type of IPR as follows:

(*a*) **Distinctiveness** (III): Essential for Trademark protection, where the distinctiveness of a mark distinguishes goods or services of one enterprise from those of others.

(*b*) **Originality** (I): Fundamental for Copyright protection, which covers original works of authorship including literary, dramatic, musical, artistic, and certain other intellectual works.

(*c*) **Industrial Application** (IV): A criterion for Patents, which must be applicable in an industrial setting, demonstrating utility and practical application.

(*d*) **Quality and Reputation of Goods** (II): Critical for Geographical Indications, which identify a good as originating from a particular territory where a given quality, reputation, or other characteristic of the good is essentially attributable to its geographical origin.

59. **(A):** The procedure for constitutional amendment in the United States involves several steps:

(*a*) **Proposal by Congress or a Convention of States:** An amendment must first be proposed, either by a two-thirds majority in both houses of Congress or by a convention called by two-thirds of the state legislatures.

(*b*) **Governor of State submitting proposed amendment to state's legislature for consideration:** Once proposed, the amendment is sent to the states for consideration.

(*c*) **Ratification by State:** To become part of the Constitution, the amendment must be ratified by the legislatures of three-fourths of the states.

(*d*) **Governor intimating Congress about State decision:** The governor of each state sends the decision regarding the ratification of the amendment to Congress.

(*e*) **Getting ratification by 2/3rd states:** The final step is confirming that the required number of states (three-fourths) have ratified the amendment.

60. **(D):** Geographical Indications (GI) is a type of intellectual property right that is regarded as community property. GIs are signs used on products that have a specific geographical origin and possess qualities or a reputation that are due to that origin. This type of protection helps communities maintain control over products that are deeply tied to their region's reputation or characteristic qualities, allowing them to benefit collectively from the reputation without allowing it to be misused by others outside the community. GIs help ensure that registered producers of products in a specified area are the only ones allowed to use the popular name, securing economic benefits for all producers in the region.

61. **(A):** The initial establishment dates of various commissions and tribunals in India are as follows:

(*a*) **National Commission for Backward Classes (NCBC):** Established in 1993, NCBC was set up to monitor the safeguards provided for the socially and educationally backward classes under the Constitution and to evaluate the progress of their development.

(*b*) **National Commission for Women (NCW):** Founded in 1992, NCW aims to promote and protect the interests of women in India, addressing issues like discrimination and violence against women.

(*c*) **National Green Tribunal (NGT):** Created in 2010, NGT deals with cases relating to environmental protection and conservation of forests and other natural resources.

(*d*) **National Commission for Scheduled Castes (NCSC):** This commission, reconstituted from its predecessor established in 1950 under the Constitution, was named NCSC in 2004, focusing on the protection and monitoring of the welfare of scheduled castes.

62. **(A):** The correct chronological order of the general exceptions in the Indian Penal Code (IPC) based on their appearance in the Code is:

(*a*) **Act done in good faith for the benefit of child by the consent of guardian:** This is a defense that acknowledges the guardian's consent in actions taken for the benefit of a child.

(*b*) **Act done in good faith for the benefit of person without consent:** This exception applies when an act is done in good faith for someone's benefit, even without their consent, typically in emergency medical situations.

(*c*) **Communication made in good faith:** This protects individuals who make statements or communications in good faith without intent to harm.

(*d*) **Act to which a person is compelled by threats:** This covers situations where a person is forced to act under threats, recognizing duress as a mitigating factor.

63. (D): Matching IPR Treaties and Agreements with their corresponding subject matter correctly:

(*a*) **Strasbourg Agreement - (III):** Concerns the International Patent Classification, which helps to organize patent information in a systematic way.

(*b*) **Nice Agreement - (IV):** Pertains to the International Classification of Goods and Services for the purposes of the registration of marks, helping to standardize the categorization of goods and services globally.

(*c*) **Beijing Treaty - (II):** Relates to the protection of audio-visual performances, enhancing the rights of performers in audiovisual industries.

(*d*) **Singapore Treaty - (I):** Deals with the law of trademarks, including the procedural aspects of trademark registration and licensing.

64. (A): Section 66E of the Information Technology Act, 2000, addresses the privacy violations involving the capture, publication, and transmission of intimate images without consent. This section is designed to protect the privacy of individuals against unauthorized and non-consensual dissemination of images that invade their personal privacy, particularly in digital forms. It applies to situations where intimate images are captured, shared, or transmitted without the consent of the person depicted, which includes scenarios where such actions are intended to harm, embarrass, or coerce the individual.

65. (D): The Constitution of India confers original and exclusive jurisdiction on the Supreme Court in the following types of disputes:

(*a*) **Between two or more states:** This jurisdiction allows the Supreme Court to handle disputes between states, ensuring impartiality and adherence to constitutional provisions.

(*c*) **Between the Union Government and one or more states:** Similar to disputes between states, this jurisdiction covers conflicts between the national government and states, underscoring the Supreme Court's role in maintaining federal balance.

(*d*) **Between the Union Government and any state(s) on one side and one or more other states on the other:** This extends the court's jurisdiction to more complex disputes involving multiple states and the Union, reflecting the constitutional framework to address inter-governmental conflicts effectively.

These provisions highlight the Supreme Court's pivotal role in adjudicating issues critical to the federal structure and governance of India, ensuring that constitutional norms are upheld in inter-state and state-union disputes.

66. (C): Articles 323 A and 323 B were added to the Constitution of India to facilitate the establishment of specific tribunals to address the needs of administrative justice. These articles provide the constitutional basis for setting up various administrative tribunals and public service tribunals, respectively.

- Article 323 A deals with the creation of administrative tribunals for service-related matters of government employees, thereby providing a mechanism for resolving disputes and grievances related to public service matters swiftly and effectively.
- Article 323 B allows for the establishment of tribunals for other matters including taxation, industrial disputes, and election to various offices. This framework aims to ensure specialized handling of complex administrative issues, improving the efficiency and effectiveness of legal proceedings in these areas.

67. (A): The chronological arrangement of provisions in the Consumer Protection Act, 2019, based on their logical and structural placement in the Act, is:

(*b*) **Central Consumer Protection Council:** Serves as an advisory body on consumer issues at the national level.

(*a*) **District Consumer Protection Council:** Functions at the district level to address consumer grievances and promote consumer rights.

(*c*) **Central Consumer Protection Authorities:** Established to enforce rights, investigate violations of consumer rights, and address issues of unfair trade practices and misleading advertisements.

(*d*) **Investigation Wing:** Constituted to support the Central Authority in conducting inquiries into consumer rights violations and other related offenses.

(*e*) **Consumer Mediation Cell:** Set up to facilitate the mediation of disputes arising from consumer complaints at both the district and state levels.

This arrangement reflects a hierarchical and functional approach aimed at enhancing consumer protection through various levels of governance and operational mechanisms.

68. (A): The practice of Triple Talaq was set aside in the landmark case of Shayara Bano v. UOI primarily for the reasons outlined in options (*a*) and (*b*). The Supreme Court found that:

(*b*) Section 2 of the Shariat Application Act, 1937, is pre-constitutional legislation within the meaning of Article 13(1) of the Constitution and violative of Article 14. This argument held that the Act, being pre-constitutional, did not conform to the requirements of the Constitution's right to equality before the law, thereby discriminating against Muslim women.

(*a*) Muslim Personal Law (Shariat) Application Act, 1937 is not a Law regarding Triple Talaq and the practice is against the tenets of the Holy Quran. The court recognized that Triple Talaq was not an essential part of the Islamic faith as per the Quran and hence could be scrutinized and regulated by the state.

These factors combined led to the decision that Triple Talaq was unconstitutional, providing a significant advance in the rights of Muslim women in India and ensuring their protection against arbitrary divorce practices.

69. (C): The Convention on Biological Diversity was signed at the Rio Earth Summit in 1992. This international conference was crucial in addressing global environmental challenges and set the stage for future treaties on sustainable development.

The summit brought together leaders from around the world to discuss and develop strategies for sustainable development, and the signing of the Convention was a significant outcome, emphasizing the global commitment to preserving biological diversity and ensuring sustainable use of its components.

70. (B): Section 65 B of the Indian Evidence Act, 1872, provides the framework for admissibility and proof of electronic records. This section is critical for legal proceedings involving digital information and data:

- It outlines the conditions under which electronic records are considered admissible in court, specifying the need for a certificate that authenticates the electronic record.
- This provision ensures that digital data, which can be easily manipulated, meets specific criteria of authenticity and reliability before being used as evidence in legal disputes.
- Understanding and correctly applying Section 65 B is essential for the judiciary and legal professionals in the digital age, ensuring that electronic evidence is both relevant and reliable in the context of modern legal systems.

71. (C): The "WIPO Treaty on Intellectual Property, Genetic Resources, and Associated Traditional Knowledge" has been adopted in the year 2024. This treaty represents a significant development in international intellectual property law, aiming to integrate and protect the intersection of intellectual property with genetic resources and traditional knowledge. It seeks to ensure that indigenous communities and local populations receive recognition and benefits from the use of their traditional knowledge and genetic resources, addressing gaps and overlaps in existing international intellectual property frameworks.

72. (B): Matching the judicial decisions with the fundamental rights they primarily deal with involves aligning the cases with the relevant articles of the Constitution or the broader implications of the rulings:

(*a*) **Sri Srinivasa Theatre v. Govt of T.N.** (III): This case primarily dealt with Equality before Law, examining issues around licensing and fairness in treatment by government bodies, reflecting concerns over equal protection under the law.

(*b*) **K.A. Abbas v. Union of India** (IV): Central to this case was the issue of Censorship, where the Supreme Court addressed the balance between freedom of expression (protected under Article 19(1)(*a*)) and reasonable restrictions (under Article 19(2)) related to public order, morality, and defamation.

(*c*) **Selvi v. State of Karnataka** (I): The decision in this case focused on Article 20(3) of the Constitution, concerning the right against self-incrimination, a critical aspect of personal liberties.

(*d*) **Rural Litigation and Entitlement Kendra v. State of UP** (II): This case, often linked with environmental law, indirectly dealt with the Right to Environment as part of the right to life under Article 21, although it is not explicitly mentioned in the Constitution but has been inferred by the courts as a necessary condition for quality of life.

These cases are pivotal in the interpretation and application of constitutional rights, reflecting the evolving understanding and scope of fundamental rights in India.

73. (D): Friedrich Carl von Savigny, a noted jurist and the father of the Historical School of Law, was against the codification of law, contrary to the positivist approach of codifying all laws for clarity and uniformity.

Savigny believed that law was an organic development rooted in the volksgeist (spirit of the people) and that codification could stifle this natural development.

His views emphasize the evolution of law through customary practices and judicial decisions, reflecting the historical and cultural contexts rather than through a static and rigid codification. Savigny argued that law should evolve with society and reflect its changing values and needs, rather than being imposed in a top-down manner.

74. (A): In Islamic law, I'la refers to the situation where a Muslim husband swears not to have sexual relations with his wife for four months or more. This action is considered a form of divorce if the husband does not resume relations within that time frame.

I'la serves as a form of conditional divorce, giving the husband time to reconsider his decision while also allowing the wife certain rights during the period of abstinence. If the period concludes without resumption of marital relations, the marriage can be deemed to have ended, making I'la a distinct form of divorce that relies on the husband's oath as its initiating factor.

75. (C): Regarding the incorrect statements about asylum:

(*b*) **Asylum also includes transfer of person wanted by an arrest warrant to the prosecution country:** This statement is incorrect as asylum typically involves protection from extradition, not facilitating it.

(*c*) **Granting of Asylum per se excludes any possibility of extradition:** This is not always true, as asylum may be granted on specific grounds that do not necessarily preclude extradition, especially if the asylum seeker is found to be involved in serious crimes.

(*d*) **Extradition and Asylum are mutually exclusive:** This statement is incorrect because the two can intersect. A person may seek asylum to avoid extradition, but under certain international agreements and conditions, a person granted asylum could still be extradited.

These points highlight the complex interplay between the rights of asylum seekers and the obligations of states under international law, particularly in balancing humanitarian protections with legal and security considerations.

76. (D): The chronological order of the adoption of these International Humanitarian Law Treaties and Conventions is as follows:

(*d*) **Geneva Convention (1949):** The core treaties that form the basis of international humanitarian law, defining the legal standards for humanitarian treatment in war.

(*a*) **Chemical Weapons Convention (1993):** This convention bans the production, stockpiling, and use of chemical weapons and requires their destruction.

(*c*) **International Convention for the Protection of All Persons from Enforced Disappearance (2006):** Focuses on the prevention of enforced disappearances and the protection of victims.

(*b*) **Arms Trade Treaty (2013):** Regulates the international trade in conventional arms and seeks to prevent and eradicate illicit trade and diversion of conventional arms.

(*e*) **Treaty on the Prohibition of Nuclear Weapons (2017):** The first legally binding international agreement to comprehensively prohibit nuclear weapons, with the goal of leading towards their total elimination.

77. (D): In the landmark case of Independent Thought v. Union of India, the Supreme Court held that Exception 2 to Section 375 of the Indian Penal Code, which allowed marital rape of a girl child between the ages of 15 and 18, was violative of the right of a girl child below 18 years. This judgment recognized that this exception discriminated against girl children by allowing marital rape, thereby violating their rights under Articles 14, 15, and 21 of the Constitution of India. The court ruled that the age of consent must uniformly be recognized as 18 years in all circumstances.

78. (A): Muta marriage characteristics include:

(*a*) **A temporary marriage:** Muta is a form of temporary marriage permitted under Shia law.

(*b*) **Recognised under Shia Law:** This type of marriage is specifically recognized and practiced within the Shia sect of Islam.

(*d*) **A marriage for a fixed period:** Muta marriage is contracted for a predetermined period, which could be days, months, or years.

Muta marriage does not necessarily require the specification of dower before the marriage, and it is not recognized under Sunni law, making options (*b*) and (*e*) incorrect for inclusion.

79. (A): The correct matching of the type of government to the corresponding countries is:

(*a*) **Constitutional Monarchy:** Denmark, Bhutan, Belgium: These countries operate under a constitutional monarchy where the monarch's powers are regulated by a constitution.

(*b*) **Dual Federalism:** The Federations of Australia, Canada and Switzerland most closely resemble the model of American dual federalism in which fundamental governmental powers are divided between the federal and State governments, with the State exercising broad powers.

(*c*) **Presidential:** A presidential system is a form of government in which a head of government heads an executive branch that derives its authority and legislative branch. The system was popularized by its inclusion in the Constitution of the United States.

(*d*) **Parliamentary:** India and United Kingdom: Both countries have a parliamentary system of government where the executive is drawn from and accountable to the legislature.

80. (C): The Tenth Amendment to the U.S. Constitution is crucial in defining the powers reserved to the States. It states that the powers not delegated to the United States by the Constitution, nor prohibited by it to the States, are reserved to the States respectively, or to the people. This amendment forms a fundamental part of the constitutional structure of federalism in the United States, underscoring the division of power between the federal government and the states, thereby protecting the states' sovereignty against undue federal encroachment.

81. (C): Section 20 of the Green Tribunal Act, 2010, outlines specific principles that the National Green Tribunal (NGT) must apply while passing any order, decision, or award. These principles are fundamental to ensuring justice in environmental matters:

(*a*) **Principle of sustainable development:** This principle ensures that development meets the needs of the present without compromising the ability of future generations to meet their own needs. It seeks a balanced approach that integrates economic progress with environmental protection.

(*b*) **Precautionary principle:** It mandates that precautionary measures should be taken to protect the environment when there is the possibility of serious or irreversible damage, even if some cause and effect relationships are not fully established scientifically.

(*c*) **Polluter pays principle:** This principle asserts that the environmental costs of economic activities should be internalized and the polluter is responsible for environmental damage and for paying the costs of pollution prevention and control.

The principle of absolute liability (*d*) is not specifically mentioned in Section 20 but is generally relevant in broader legal contexts involving environmental harm.

82. (C): Ratio decidendi refers to the principle or principles of law on which a court's decision is based. It generally implies:

(A) **Reason for decision:** The legal reasoning that leads to a court's decision, which is binding and sets a precedent for future similar cases.

(B) **Principles laid down in the case:** These are the core legal doctrines or principles that the court establishes as necessary for deciding the case.

Ratio decidendi is the binding part of a judicial decision that must be followed by lower courts in similar future cases, distinguishing it from obiter dicta, which are observations or remarks made by a judge that are not binding.

83. (B): Cases related to personal bias according to the Principle of Natural Justice include:

(*a*) **A.K. Kraipak v. Union of India:** This case highlighted the importance of objectivity in official decision-making, ruling that decisions influenced by bias or where there is a likelihood of bias are in violation of natural justice.

(*c*) **Mohd. Yunus Khan v. State of U.P:** This case dealt with the fairness in administrative procedures and emphasized that personal biases of administrative officials could not influence judicial decisions.

(*e*) **Manak Lal v. Prem Chand Singhvi:** A landmark case that dealt with bias in the judiciary, reinforcing that any likelihood of bias could invalidate proceedings.

These cases are pivotal in illustrating how personal biases can affect the fairness and objectivity required in judicial and quasi-judicial proceedings.

84. (B): The chronological order of enactment of these legislations is:

(*a*) **Indian Divorce Act (1869):** This act was one of the earliest laws concerning divorce among Christians in India.

(*b*) **Parsi Marriage and Divorce Act (1936):** This act regulates the marriage and divorce issues among the Parsi community in India.

(*c*) **Dissolution of Muslim Marriage Act (1939):** This act addresses the dissolution of marriages among Muslims.

(*d*) **Special Marriage Act (1954):** Provides a special form of marriage for the people of India and all Indian nationals in foreign countries, irrespective of the religion or faith followed by either party.

These acts were established to provide legal frameworks for marriage and divorce across different communities, reflecting the diverse legal requirements of India's pluralistic society.

85. (D): Conditions for the capacity of a male Hindu to adopt include:

(A) **Consent of wife under certain circumstances:** The Hindu Adoptions and Maintenance Act stipulates that if a married Hindu man wishes to adopt, he must have the consent of his wife unless she is declared incompetent.

(B) **Majority:** The male Hindu must be an adult, meaning he has reached the age of majority.

(C) **Soundness of mind:** He must be of sound mind, capable of making an informed decision.

(D) Must be necessarily married is incorrect as single Hindus, including males, can legally adopt a child under Hindu law. Being married is not a prerequisite for adoption, thereby making this statement the incorrect one regarding the conditions for adoption.

86. (C): The correct match between the lists in the Constitution of India and the subjects they regulate is as follows:

(*a*) **Concurrent List** (II): Deals with subjects like Marriage and Divorce, which are regulated both by the states and the central government.

(*b*) **State List** (III): Includes subjects such as Public Health and Sanitation, which are primarily the responsibility of the state governments.

(*c*) **Union List** (IV): Encompasses subjects like Elections to the legislatures of State and other national matters.

(*d*) **Appellate Jurisdiction of the Supreme Court** (I): In Civil matters, where the Supreme Court has the authority to hear appeals from lower courts.

87. (D): The maxim "De Minimis Non Curat Lex" translates to "the law does not concern itself with trifles." This legal principle asserts that the law should not apply to negligible matters or slight infractions that do not significantly harm or affect public or private interests. It is often applied in both civil and criminal law contexts to prevent the legal system from being cluttered with minor issues that lack significance.

88. (A): "Inland Instrument" in legal terms refers to any financial or contractual instrument that meets certain geographic criteria:

(*a*) **Instrument drawn or made in India:** It is considered inland if it is created within the geographical confines of India.

(*b*) **Instrument made payable in India:** This applies to financial instruments that are legally required to be paid or that can be claimed in India.

(*c*) **Instrument drawn upon any person resident in India:** This means any legal document that demands action or payment from someone who resides within India.

(*d*) **Instrument that is passed by Indian Parliament:** This does not apply to the definition of an "inland instrument" as it typically relates to legal and legislative documents rather than commercial or financial instruments.

89. (A): The Limited Liability Partnership Rules of Third Amendment were implemented in the year 2023. This amendment likely introduced significant changes to the regulatory framework governing Limited Liability Partnerships (LLPs), aimed at simplifying procedures, improving compliance mechanisms, and possibly integrating new financial or operational standards to align with contemporary business practices and technological advancements.

90. (A): Matching the jurists with their associated legal theories correctly:

(*a*) **Roscoe Pound** (III): Known for his theory that "the end of law should be to satisfy a maximum of wants with minimum of friction," emphasizing the law's role in balancing social interests and reducing conflicts.

(*b*) **Oliver Wendell Holmes** (I): Famously stated, "The life of the law has not been logic; it has been experience," highlighting the pragmatic and experiential basis of law.

(*c*) **Ihering** (IV): Advocated that law is part of human conduct and deeply tied to the concept of purpose, focusing on the societal functions of legal norms.

(*d*) **Jerome Frank** (II): Critiqued the certainty of law, arguing that law is inherently uncertain and that the idea of a completely predictable legal system is a myth, reflecting his legal realism philosophy that focuses on the uncertainties inherent in legal processes.

91. (B): In the Shriram Gas Leak case, statutory agencies were deemed incapable of ensuring plant safety, which is a crucial aspect in the context of industries dealing with hazardous substances. The failure of these agencies to maintain plant safety standards posed significant risks not only to the workers within these facilities but also to the surrounding communities. Chief Justice Bhagwati's concern highlighted the judiciary's proactive role in seeking to address these deficiencies, emphasizing the need for stringent oversight and implementation of safety protocols to prevent disasters similar to the Oleum gas leak incident.

92. (D): The Shriram Gas Leak case focused on several critical issues but did not address measures to increase the profit of the company involved. The primary concerns of the case included examining the scope and implications of Articles 21 and 32 of the Constitution, norms for determining the liability of large corporations engaged in hazardous industries, and the criteria for quantifying damages resulting from such industrial accidents. The case was pivotal in establishing legal precedents concerning environmental safety and corporate accountability rather than corporate profitability.

93. (C): As a direct consequence of the Shriram Gas Leak case, the Parliament enacted laws in 1991 that articulated a new standard of absolute liability. This legal doctrine was developed to ensure that enterprises involved in inherently hazardous activities are held absolutely liable for any harm resulting from such activities, without any exceptions. This standard is stricter than the previous standard of strict liability, which allowed certain exceptions. The move was aimed at providing better protection to the public and the environment by holding corporations to the highest level of responsibility, thereby ensuring they adopt all possible safety measures to prevent accidents.

94. (C): The judgment in the Shriram Gas Leak case significantly influenced the decision in the Bhopal Gas Leak case. By establishing stringent standards for industrial safety and legal accountability, the Shriram case set a precedent that impacted how the courts viewed similar cases of industrial disasters involving hazardous chemicals. Chief Justice Bhagwati's insights and decisions in the Shriram case helped shape the legal discourse around the Bhopal Gas tragedy, emphasizing the need for corporate responsibility and robust safety regulations in industries handling toxic substances.

95. (A): Chief Justice Bhagwati's primary concern in the Shriram Gas Leak case was the safety of citizens. His proactive stance in this case reflected a judicial approach focused on safeguarding public health and environmental safety against the backdrop of industrial activities. By prioritizing citizen safety, the Chief Justice aimed to ensure that industries engaging in potentially hazardous operations implement stringent safety measures. This concern was instrumental in driving the judiciary to scrutinize and demand higher standards of accountability from corporations, especially those located in densely populated areas, to mitigate risks and protect human life and health.

96. (C): The Hague Convention predominantly ensures that non-combatants did not become victims of war. This international treaty was built on a fundamental distinction between combatants and non-combatants, aimed at protecting civilian populations during times of war. The Convention stipulates that non-combatants are not considered legitimate military targets and should be shielded from the harms of war. This principle was crucial in advancing the norms of international humanitarian law, emphasizing the necessity of protecting those who are not actively participating in hostilities.

97. (C): The fundamental distinction on which the Hague Convention was built is between combatants and non-combatants. This distinction is central to the Convention's purpose, which is to minimize the impact of armed conflict on civilian populations. By clearly separating those actively engaged in combat from those who are not, the Convention seeks to ensure that warfare is conducted among combatants only, thereby protecting civilians from the ravages of war and maintaining some degree of humanity in the midst of conflict.

98. (C): The Geneva Convention of 1864 is noteworthy both for its content and its widespread ratification. The content of the Convention introduced significant humanitarian principles, such as the care for the wounded soldiers and humane treatment of prisoners of war. Its widespread ratification underscores its global acceptance and the recognition of these principles as foundational norms of international humanitarian law. This ratification also symbolized a state's commitment to uphold these humanitarian standards, reflecting a global consensus on minimizing the atrocities of war.

99. (A): The motivation for states to ratify the Geneva and Hague Conventions was significantly influenced by the prestige associated with being recognized as a member of the international society of civilized states. Ratification of these Conventions was seen as an indicator of a state's commitment to international norms and legal standards governing warfare, which conferred a certain level of international respectability and moral standing. This symbolic membership encouraged many states to adopt these conventions, aligning themselves with the accepted rules of war and humanitarian standards.

100. (B): The Hague Convention of 1899 and the Geneva Convention of 1864 primarily outline constraints on state behaviour during armed conflicts. These conventions establish rules that limit the actions of combatants, protect the rights and well-being of prisoners of war, and ensure the protection of civilians. By defining legal standards for the conduct of war, including the treatment of the wounded and the management of prisoners, these treaties aim to impose a legal and moral framework on states, guiding their actions in war to mitigate its harshest consequences.

Previous Years' Paper

National Testing Agency (NTA)

UGC-NET Junior Research Fellowship & Assistant Professor Eligibility Exam

Law, December-2023

(Exam held on 14-12-2023)

PAPER-II

1. Match List-I with List-II.

List-I (Provision from IT Act)	List-II (Section)
(*a*) Secure electronic Record	I. 16
(*b*) Security procedures and practices	II. 15
(*c*) Secure electronic signature	III. 14
(*d*) Attribution of electronic record	IV. 11

Choose the **correct** answer from the options given below:

	(*a*)	(*b*)	(*c*)	(*d*)
A.	III	I	II	IV
B.	I	III	IV	II
C.	IV	II	III	I
D.	III	II	I	IV

2. A human being ceases to be a person, in law as in fact ______ .

A. On being adjudged an insolvent

B. On renunciation of citizenship

C. On conviction

D. At death

3. Which of the following statements given below are correct?

(*a*) "A wrong is an act contrary to the rule of right and justice"

(*b*) "A moral or natural wrong is an act which is morally or naturally wrong being contrary to the rule of natural justice"

(*c*) A legal wrong is an act which is legally wrong, being contrary to the rule of legal justice and a violation of the law

(*d*) A legal wrong is always a moral wrong and a moral wrong is always a legal wrong

(*e*) Natural and legal wrongs cannot form intersecting circles

Choose the **correct** answer from the options given below:

A. (*a*), (*b*) and (*c*) only

B. (*a*), (*d*) and (*e*) only

C. (*b*), (*c*) and (*d*) only

D. (*b*), (*d*) and (*e*) only

4. Non-obstnate Clause in section 145 of the Negotiable Instrument Act, 1881 provides for which of the following:

(*a*) dispenses with the procedure under section 200 of CrPC

(*b*) procedure of examination of complainant and witness on oath is done away

(*c*) affidavit of complainant and witness can be accepted

(*d*) sworn statement recording by the magistrate is dispensed with

Choose the **correct** answer from the options given below:

A. (*a*), (*b*) only
B. (*a*), (*c*) only
C. (*b*), (*c*), (*d*) only
D. (*a*), (*b*), (*c*), (*d*)

5. American realist Judge Jerome Frank described his own altitude (towards realism) as one of:

A. Decisive cynicism
B. Constructive skepticism
C. Positive evangelism
D. Radical objectivity

6. Which of the following provisions in the Information Technology Act, 2000 prescribe punishment for offences:

(*a*) Section 65 (*b*) Section 66D
(*c*) Section 67B (*d*) Section 52
(*e*) Section 62

Choose the **correct** answer from the options given below:

A. (*a*), (*b*), (*c*) only
B. (*c*), (*d*), (*e*) only
C. (*b*), (*c*), (*e*) only
D. (*a*), (*b*), (*d*) only

7. Which one of the following is not a ground for divorce under section 13 of the Hindu Marriage Act, 1955?

A. Respondent is convicted for committing an offence
B. Respondent has renounced the world by entering any religious order
C. Respondent has ceased to be a Hindu by conversion to another religion
D. Respondent has not been heard of as being alive for a period of seven years

8. 'Dominant position' of an enterprise is reflected in which of the following situations:

(*a*) Position of strength in the relevant international market
(*b*) Enterprise operating independently of market forces in India
(*c*) Affecting competition or consumers of relevant market in India in its favour
(*d*) Position of strength enjoyed in relevant market in India

Choose the **correct** answer from the options given below:

A. (*a*), (*b*), (*c*) only
B. (*a*), (*c*), (*d*) only
C. (*b*), (*a*), (*d*) only
D. (*c*), (*d*), (*b*) only

9. Arrange the following cases relating to advice/direction of the Supreme Court to the State to enact a uniform civil code in the chronological order (advice earlier to later) of their pronouncement:

(*a*) Mohd. Ahmed Khan v. Shah Bano Begum
(*b*) Sarla Mudgal v. Union of India
(*c*) ABC v. State (NCT of Delhi)
(*d*) Jorden Diengdeh v. S.S. Chopra
(*e*) John Vallamattom v. Union of India

Choose the **correct** answer from the options given below:

A. (*a*), (*b*), (*d*), (*c*), (*e*)
B. (*b*), (*d*), (*a*), (*e*), (*c*)
C. (*a*), (*d*), (*b*), (*e*), (*c*)
D. (*e*), (*d*), (*c*), (*b*), (*a*)

10. Match List-I with List-II.

List-I (Enactment)	List-II (Year)
(*a*) The Civil Rights Act	I. 1955
(*b*) The Probation of offenders Act	II. 1956
(*c*) The Immoral Traffic (Prevention) Act	III. 1958
(*d*) The Medical Termination of Pregnancy Act	IV. 1971

Choose the **correct** answer from the options given below:

	(*a*)	(*b*)	(*c*)	(*d*)
A.	II	IV	III	I
B.	I	III	IV	II
C.	I	III	II	IV
D.	II	IV	I	III

11. Art. 28 of the Constitution of India mentions four types of educational institution given below. In which of the following institutions religious instruction can be imparted with the consent of individual or otherwise:
(*a*) Institution wholly maintained by the state
(*b*) Institution recognised by the state
(*c*) Institution that receive aid out of state fund
(*d*) Institution that are administered by the state but established under any trust or endowment

Choose the **correct** answer from the options given below:
A. (*a*), (*b*), (*c*) only
B. (*b*), (*c*), (*d*) only
C. (*a*), (*c*), (*d*) only
D. (*a*), (*b*), (*d*) only

12. Match List-I with List-II.

List-I (Case)	List-II (Issue/Concept/ Principle)
(*a*) Linkletter v. Walker	I. Prospective over-ruling in the context of constitutional interpretation
(*b*) Golak Nath v. State of Punjab	II. Right to register a "none of the above" vote
(*c*) Jolly George Varghese v. Bank of Cochin	III. Importation of provision from ICCPR into Indian Constitutional law
(*d*) People's Union for Civil Liberties v. Union of India	IV. Prospective overruling in the context of criminal procedure

Choose the **correct** answer from the options given below:

	(*a*)	(*b*)	(*c*)	(*d*)
A.	II	I	IV	III
B.	I	IV	II	III
C.	IV	II	III	I
D.	IV	I	III	II

13. Under the Hindu Marriage Act, 1955 sapinda relationship and degrees of prohibited relationship include relationship by:
(*a*) Full, Half and Uterine blood
(*b*) Adoption
(*c*) Legitimate blood
(*d*) Fosterage relations
(*e*) Illegitimate blood relations

Choose the **correct** answer from the options given below:
A. (*a*), (*b*), (*c*) and (*d*) only
B. (*a*), (*b*), (*c*) and (*e*) only
C. (*b*), (*c*), (*d*) and (*e*) only
D. (*a*), (*c*), (*d*) and (*e*) only

14. In which of the following cases has it been held that the doctrine of basic features does not constitute a limitation on the legislature while enacting ordinary legislation?
A. Indira Gandhi v. Raj Narain
B. Swadeshi Industries v. Workmen
C. Royappa v. State of Tamil Nadu
D. Kishor v. State of Rajasthan

15. Art. 19 of the Constitution of India is automatically suspended if the proclamation of Emergency is declared on the ground of:
(*a*) War
(*b*) External aggression
(*c*) Armed rebellion
(*d*) Failure of Constitutional machinery in the state

Choose the **correct** answer from the options given below:
A. (*a*), (*b*) only
B. (*a*), (*b*) and (*c*) only
C. (*a*), (*b*), (*c*) and (*d*)
D. (*a*), (*c*) and (*d*) only

16. Given below are two statements:

Statement I: The doctrine of stare decisis has essentially developed as a result of progress made in law-reporting

Statement II: Since the law in India is mostly based on the English Law, the system of law reporting is fairly developed in India.

In the light of the above statements, choose the **most appropriate answer** from the options given below:

A. Both Statement I and Statement II are correct

B. Both Statement I and Statement II are incorrect

C. Statement I is correct, but Statement II is incorrect

D. Statement I is incorrect, but Statement II is correct

17. When an absolute right is violated, the law conclusively presumes damages although the person wronged may have suffered no pecuniary loss. This was decided in case of:

A. Rogers v. Rajender Dutt

B. Ashby v. White

C. Winsmore v. Greenbank

D. Tozer v. Child

18. Arrange the following cases in the sequence in which they were decided:

(*a*) Gloucester Grammar School Case

(*b*) Donoghue v. Stevenson Case

(*c*) Ashby v. White Case

(*d*) Rylands v. Fletcher Case

Choose the **correct** answer from the options given below:

A. (*a*), (*c*), (*d*), (*b*)

B. (*b*), (*c*), (*d*), (*a*)

C. (*c*), (*d*), (*b*), (*a*)

D. (*b*), (*a*), (*d*), (*c*)

19. "Consideration is not necessary for creation of Agency" This is provided in:

A. Section 185 of the Indian Contract Act, 1872

B. Section 4 of the Partnership Act, 1932

C. Section 4 of the Indian Agency Act, 1950

D. Section 2 of the Companies Act, 2013

20. Which among the following provisions of the Constitution of India mandates criminalisation of prohibited conduct?

A. Article 17 only

B. Article 23 only

C. Article 17 and 23 only

D. Article 17, 23 and 24

21. As per the provisions of the Hindu Adoption and Maintenance Act, 1956, a bachelor male adopts a child. He subsequently marries a woman. Such woman shall:

A. be the adoptive mother of that adopted child

B. be the step mother of that adopted child

C. be the adoptive mother of that child if the child accepts her as mother

D. be the adoptive mother of that child at her discretion

22. A is lawfully arrested by Z who is a police officer. A loses his self control by grave and sudden provocation due to arrest and kills Z. A shall be punished under:

A. Section 304 of IPC

B. Section 302 of IPC

C. Section 304 or 302 of IPC

D. Section 301 read with Section 302 of IPC

23. Arrange in chronological order the insertion of the following provisions in the Indian Penal Code:

(*a*) Section 124A (*b*) Section 153A

(*c*) Section 120A (*d*) Section 304B

Choose the **correct** answer from the options given below:

A. (*a*), (*b*), (*c*), (*d*)

B. (*a*), (*c*), (*b*), (*d*)

C. (*a*), (*d*), (*b*), (*c*)

D. (*a*), (*d*), (*c*), (*b*)

24. Polluter pays principle is also known as ________ .

A. Principle of Good Neighbourliness

B. Principle of Common Responsibility

C. Principle of Public Liability
D. Principle of Extended Producer Responsibility (EPR)

25. Arrange the following in chronological order of their Enactment:
(*a*) Protection of Human Rights Act
(*b*) National Commission for Women Act
(*c*) 89th Constitutional Amendment Act
(*d*) National Commission for Minorities Act

Choose the **correct** answer from the options given below:
A. (*a*), (*d*), (*b*), (*c*)
B. (*c*), (*b*), (*a*), (*d*)
C. (*d*), (*c*), (*b*), (*a*)
D. (*b*), (*d*), (*a*), (*c*)

26. Which Article in the Constitution of India established National Commission for the Scheduled Castes?
A. Art. 335 B. Art. 338
C. Art. 341 D. Art. 342A

27. Which among the following follow a parliamentary system of government?
A. India only
B. Australia only
C. India and Australia
D. UK and USA

28. There is no distinction between *de facto* and *de jure* recognition for the purpose of giving effect to the internal acts of the recognised authority. This was held so in the case of ________.
A. Mighell v. Sultan of Johore
B. Luther v. Sagor
C. Vavasseur v. Krupp
D. Schooner Exchange v. Mc Faddon

29. Match List-I with List-II.

List-I	List-II
(*a*) Producer companies	I. Do not necessarily require Memorandum of Association
(*b*) Statutory companies	II. Association not for profit
(*c*) Section 8 company	III. Formed to convert cooperative into a company
(*d*) Small company	IV. Paid up share capital is between 50 lakh-5 crore and turnover is between 2 crore - 20 crore

Choose the **correct** answer from the options given below:

	(*a*)	(*b*)	(*c*)	(*d*)
A.	I	II	IV	III
B.	III	I	II	IV
C.	IV	III	I	II
D.	II	IV	III	I

30. As per the Partnership Act, 1932 "Partnership" is defined under:
A. Section 8 B. Section 7
C. Section 5 D. Section 4

31. Match List-I with List-II.

List-I (Case)	List-II (Year of Reporting)
(*a*) Hussainara Khatoon v. State of Bihar	I. 1981
(*b*) Kadra Phadia v. State of Bihar	II. 1980
(*c*) M. H. Hoskot v. State of Maharashtra	III. 1979
(*d*) Khatri v. State of Bihar	IV. 1978

Choose the **correct** answer from the options given below:

	(*a*)	(*b*)	(*c*)	(*d*)
A.	III	I	II	IV
B.	IV	III	II	I
C.	I	II	III	IV
D.	III	II	IV	I

32. Given below are two statements: One is labelled as Assertion (A) and the other is labelled as Reason (R).

Assertion (A): Trade Secrets Act, 2020 is a legislation enacted in India to provide for confidential informations and trade secrets.

Reason (R): India has enacted a number of legislations to create legal framework on intellectual property rights (IPRs).

In the light of the above statements, choose the **most appropriate answer** from the options given below:

A. Both (A) and (R) are correct and (R) is the correct explanation of (A)
B. Both (A) and (R) are correct but (R) is not the correct explanation of (A)
C. (A) is correct, but (R) is not correct
D. (A) is not correct, but (R) is correct

33. What amongst the following are necessary to constitute a false imprisonment?

(*a*) Total restrain on liberty of a person
(*b*) Detention may be actual or constructive
(*c*) It should be for a period of 2 years at least
(*d*) Detection or restrain should be unlawful

Choose the **correct** answer from the options given below:

A. (*a*), (*b*), (*c*) only
B. (*b*), (*c*), (*d*) only
C. (*a*), (*b*), (*d*) only
D. (*a*), (*c*), (*d*) only

34. Which among the following countries do not follow the scheme of distribution of power?

A. India B. USA
C. UK D. Canada

35. 'A' makes a contract with 'B' to buy B's horse if 'A' survives 'C'. This contract can be enforced by law only when:

A. 'C' dies in lifetime of 'A'
B. 'A' dies in lifetime of 'C'
C. 'A' and 'C' both die
D. 'B' dies in lifetime of 'A'

36. Which of the following is part of first generation of Human Rights?

(*a*) Right to Social Security
(*b*) Right to Liberty
(*c*) Equality Before Law
(*d*) Right to Self determination
(*e*) Right to life

Choose the **correct** answer from the options given below:

A. (*a*), (*b*), (*d*) only
B. (*b*), (*c*), (*e*) only
C. (*c*), (*d*), (*e*) only
D. (*a*), (*c*), (*e*) only

37. Which among the following expressly contain a provision for 'right to bear arms' as fundamental right?

(*a*) The Constitution Act, 1867 (Canada)
(*b*) Amendment II of US Constitution
(*c*) Constitution (108th Amendment) Act (India)
(*d*) Human Rights Act, 1998 (UK)

Choose the **correct** answer from the options given below:

A. (*a*), (*b*) only B. (*a*) only
C. (*b*) only D. (*c*), (*d*) only

38. Art. 163 of the Constitution of India says that there shall be Council of Minister along with Chief Minister to aid and advise the Governor in exercise of his functions except so far he is required by the Constitution to exercise his functions or any of them in his discretion. Under what circumstances Governor can be called to exercise his discretion?

(*a*) Appointment of Chief Minister
(*b*) Dismissal of ministry or Dissolution of Assembly
(*c*) Submiting report to President for proclamation under Art. 356
(*d*) Appointment of High Court judges

Choose the **correct** answer from the options given below:

A. (*a*), (*b*), (*c*) only
B. (*b*), (*c*), (*d*) only
C. (*d*), (*c*), (*a*) only
D. (*d*), (*a*), (*b*) only

39. Which of the following statements in relation to the dissenting judgment of Dr. Radha Vinodpal in the *Tokyo Trial* can be correctly attributed to him?

(*a*) War is beyond the scope of International law

(*b*) Conduct of war is within the scope of the rules of International law

(*c*) The Pact of Paris brought about no change in the status of war

(*d*) International law has developed so much so as to make war a crime

(*e*) Conspiracy is an independent crime under International law

Choose the **correct** answer from the options given below:

A. (*a*), (*b*) and (*c*) only

B. (*c*), (*d*) and (*e*) only

C. (*b*), (*c*) and (*e*) only

D. (*a*), (*b*) and (*d*) only

40. Which of the following are characteristics of a government promissory note:

(*a*) It is a promise of President of India or Governor of a state

(*b*) It is regulated by the Indian Securities Act, 1886

(*c*) They are not negotiable instrument

(*d*) They can be assigned without endorsement

Choose the **correct** answer from the options given below:

A. (*a*), (*b*) only B. (*b*), (*c*) only

C. (*b*), (*d*) only D. (*c*), (*d*) only

41. Constitution of which of the country "expressly" states that the Constitution shall be the supreme law of the land?

(*a*) USA

(*b*) South Africa

(*c*) India

(*d*) UK

Choose the **correct** answer from the options given below:

A. (*a*), (*b*) only B. (*b*), (*c*) only

C. (*a*), (*c*) only D. (*b*), (*d*) only

42. The term preferred by Bentham to explain his imperative concept of a law is:

A. Firman B. Mandate

C. Dictate D. Fiat

43. The Supreme Court of India remarked that "Extradition with foreign states is, except in exceptional cases, governed by treaties or arrangements made" in the case of:

A. State of Maharashtra v. Shobha Vitthal Kolte

B. T. Vellaiyan v. The Registrar, SHRC, Chennai

C. State of Madras v. C.G. Menon

D. N. C. Dhoundial v. Union of India

44. Given below are two statements: One is labelled as Assertion (A) and the other is labelled as Reason (R).

Assertion (A): Highly developed legal systems strive to create an autonomous apparatus of legal concepts, legal techniques, and legal norms.

Reason (R): Law needs to be endowed with logical consistency, predictability and stability.

In the light of the above statements, choose the **most appropriate answer** from the options given below:

A. Both (A) and (R) are correct and (R) is the correct explanation of (A)

B. Both (A) and (R) are correct, but (R) is not the correct explanation of (A)

C. (A) is correct, but (R) is not correct

D. (A) is not correct, but (R) is correct

45. Given below are two statements: one is labelled as Assertion (A) and the other is labelled as Reason (R).

Assertion (A): Mahr (dower) is a sum of money which the Muslim husband agrees to pay to the wife as a mark of respect for her for agreeing to marry him. Since Muslim marriage is a contract, it is necessary that dower must be specified at the time of marriage and if it is not specified it can be presumed.

Reason (R): If not paid earlier, Mahr become due on death of the husband or the dissolution of marriage by divorce.

In the light of the above statements, choose the **most appropriate answer** from the options given below:

A. Both (A) and (R) are correct and (R) is the correct explanation of (A)
B. Both (A) and (R) are correct, but (R) is not the correct explanation of (A)
C. (A) is correct, but (R) is not correct
D. (A) is not correct, but (R) is correct

46. A Muslim can make a bequest of his property without the consent of heirs to the extent of:

A. half of his property
B. whole of his property
C. one-fourth of his property
D. one-third of his property

47. Match List-I with List-II.

List-I (Subject)	List-II (Section of Indian Penal code)
(*a*) Punishment for extortion	I. Section 403
(*b*) Attempt to commit robbery	II. Section 409
(*c*) Dishonest misappropriation of property	III. Section 384
(*d*) Criminal breach of trust by public servant	IV. Section 393

Choose the **correct** answer from the options given below:

	(*a*)	(*b*)	(*c*)	(*d*)
A.	II	III	I	IV
B.	III	II	I	IV
C.	III	IV	I	II
D.	IV	II	I	III

48. "Moral Right" is a concept prevailing in:

A. Industrial Design
B. Geographical Indication
C. Trademark
D. Copyright

49. Which of the following statements are correct?

(*a*) In *S.S. Lotus* case, the Permanent Court of International Justice (PCIJ) defined International Law as "principles which are in force between all independent nations"
(*b*) Professor Dias suggests that International law can never be called a 'Law'
(*c*) Lord Halsbury, when he was the Prime Minister of England, once remarked, "It was a misnomer to call international law as 'Law'. It should be better described as a branch of ethics"
(*d*) Russel has defined International Law as "the aggregate of the rules to which the nations have agreed to conform to their conduct towards one another"
(*e*) According to Austin, International law is set and enforced by political sovereign authority

Choose the **correct** answer from the options given below:

A. (*a*), (*b*) and (*c*) only
B. (*a*), (*c*) and (*d*) only
C. (*b*), (*c*) and (*e*) only
D. (*b*), (*d*) and (*e*) only

50. What amongst the following are necessary characteristics for 'Libel'.

(*a*) It is defamation of permanent form
(*b*) The burden of proof that the words are false lie upon the plaintiff
(*c*) No actual damage need to be proved to sustain an action
(*d*) Falsity of charge is presumed in favour of plaintiff

Choose the **correct** answer from the options given below:

A. (*a*), (*b*), (*c*) only
B. (*b*), (*c*), (*d*) only
C. (*a*), (*b*), (*d*) only
D. (*a*), (*c*), (*d*) only

51. Arrange the following cases in sequence of their year of verdict:

(*a*) Kesavananda Bharti v. State of Kerala
(*b*) Sankari Prasad v. Union of India
(*c*) Golak Nath v. State of Punjab
(*d*) Sajjan Singh v. State of Rajasthan

Choose the **correct** answer from the options given below:

A. (*b*), (*d*), (*c*), (*a*)
B. (*a*), (*b*), (*c*), (*d*)
C. (*c*), (*d*), (*b*), (*a*)
D. (*a*), (*d*), (*b*), (*c*)

52. Red herring prospectus is a prospectus issued:

A. Prior to the issue of prospectus
B. After the issue of main prospectus
C. With the consent of shareholder
D. On the behest of ROC (Register of Companies)

53. A Hindu male having a Hindu wife, changed his religion and adopts Islam in 2012. He marries again to a Muslim girl in 2013. In 2014, his Hindu wife died. His second marriage is:

A. Valid as he married after conversion to Islam which permits bigamy
B. Valid as his wife died after his marriage to Muslim girl
C. Void as he has not taken the consent of his Hindu wife
D. Void as his second marriage amounts to bigamy

54. Which among the following makes a distinction between common intention and similar intention:

(*a*) Mahabub Shah v. Emperor (1945)
(*b*) Barendra Kumar Ghosh v. Emperor (1925)
(*c*) Jagmohan Singh v. State of UP (1973)
(*d*) Balwant Singh v. State of Punjab (1995)
(*e*) Badri v. State of Rajasthan (1995)

Choose the **correct** answer from the options given below:

A. (*a*), (*b*) only
B. (*a*) only
C. (*b*) only
D. (*b*), (*c*), (*d*), (*e*) only

55. A_1 and A_2 plan to commit robbery. Mere agreement to commit this offence is punishable under which provision of IPC?

A. 120B
B. 107(2)
C. 120B and 107(2)
D. Without *actus reus* it is not possible at all

56. Arrange the following in the chronological order of its sequence in the Patents Act:

(*a*) Consequence of secrecy directions
(*b*) Grant of patent
(*c*) Date of patent
(*d*) Term of patent
(*e*) Rights of patentee

Choose the **correct** answer from the options given below:

A. (*c*), (*e*), (*b*), (*d*), (*a*)
B. (*b*), (*c*), (*e*), (*d*), (*a*)
C. (*a*), (*b*), (*c*), (*e*), (*d*)
D. (*b*), (*e*), (*d*), (*a*), (*c*)

57. Consider the following statement:

(*a*) Fundamental rights are expressly provided in the US Constitution
(*b*) Restrictions on fundamental rights are expressly provided in the US Constitution
(*c*) Fundamental rights and Human Rights are same in India
(*d*) Directive principles in Indian Constitution are not enforceable by courts

Choose the **correct** answer from the options given below:

A. (*a*), (*c*), (*d*) only
B. (*a*), (*d*) only
C. (*a*), (*b*), (*c*), (*d*)
D. (*a*), (*b*), (*d*) only

58. In respect of which of the following items India does not have legislations to specifically cover them as Intellectual property.

(*a*) Traditional Knowledge
(*b*) Street Art
(*c*) Publicity Right
(*d*) Celebrity Right
(*e*) Computer Programme

Choose the **correct** answer from the options given below:

A. (*b*), (*d*) and (*e*) only
B. (*c*), (*d*) and (*e*) only
C. (*a*), (*b*), (*c*) and (*d*) only
D. (*b*), (*c*), (*d*) and (*e*) only

59. The following Articles in the Indian Constitution deal with protection of Environment and/or places:

(*a*) Art. 51A(g)
(*b*) Art. 40
(*c*) Art. 48A
(*d*) Art. 51A(j)
(*e*) Art. 49

Choose the **correct** answer from the options given below:

A. (*a*), (*c*) and (*e*) only
B. (*a*), (*b*) and (*c*) only
C. (*c*), (*d*) and (*e*) only
D. (*a*), (*c*) and (*d*) only

60. Match List-I with List-II.

List-I	List-II
(*a*) Malice in Law	I. Commission of an unlawful Act which are actionable per se
(*b*) Malfeasance	II. Improper performance of a lawful act
(*c*) Misfeasance	III. Omission to perform an act when there is obligation to perform it
(*d*) Non-feasance	IV. Intentional doing of a wrongful act and improper motive

Choose the **correct** answer from the options given below:

	(*a*)	(*b*)	(*c*)	(*d*)
A.	IV	I	II	III
B.	I	II	III	IV
C.	III	IV	I	II
D.	II	III	IV	I

61. Section 7 of the Hindu Marriage Act, 1955 provides that a Hindu marriage may be solemnized in accordance with the customary rites and ceremonies of either party thereto. Consider the following situations and decide in which case the marriage is validly solemnized?

(*a*) At the time of marriage all essential shastric ceremonies are performed
(*b*) At the time of marriage all customary rites and ceremonies of bride's family are performed
(*c*) At the time of marriage half of the ceremonies of bride's family and other half of the bridegroom's family are performed
(*d*) Bride and bridegroom decided to perform the simple ceremonies of exchange of rings
(*e*) Bride and bridegroom started living together as husband and wife without performing any ceremony

Choose the **correct** answer from the options given below:

A. (*a*) and (*b*) only
B. (*a*), (*b*) and (*c*) only
C. (*b*), (*c*) and (*d*) only
D. (*b*), (*c*), (*d*) and (*e*) only

62. The Preamble of the Constitution of India:

A. can be amended
B. cannot be amended
C. can be amended only by the Supreme Court
D. cannot be amended because it is a part of the basic feature of the Constitution

63. Match List-I with List-II.

List-I (Schedule)	List-II (Description)
(*a*) Fifth Schedule	I. Languages
(*b*) Eight Schedule	II. Provisions of disqualification on ground of defection
(*c*) Tenth Schedule	III. Administration and control of scheduled areas and scheduled tribe
(*d*) Fourth Schedule	IV. Allocation of seats in Council of States

Choose the **correct** answer from the options given below:

	(*a*)	(*b*)	(*c*)	(*d*)
A.	I	II	IV	III
B.	III	I	II	IV
C.	II	IV	III	I
D.	IV	III	I	II

64. In which country the appointment of judges are made through the parliament?

A. UK
B. USA
C. India
D. All the above

65. As per National Green Tribunal Act, 2010, "Environment" includes water, air and land and other interrelationship, which exists among and between water, air and land and human beings, other living creatures, plants, microorganism and ______.

A. Ecosystem
B. Biodiversity
C. Property
D. Climate

66. The right of private defence extends to causing death under which provision of IPC:

A. Section 100 only
B. Section 100 and 103 only
C. Section 103 only
D. Section 100, 103, 105

67. With respect to which of the following kind of IPR, there exists a statutory ban for assignment?

A. Patents
B. Trademarks
C. Geographical Indication
D. Layout Designs of Integrated Circuits

68. Which of the following international legal instrument is relating to patent?

A. Budapest Treaty, 1977
B. Madrid Agreement, 1891
C. Berne Convention, 1886
D. Washington Treaty, 1989

69. Central Consumer Protection Council is headed by a chairperson who is:

A. Retired judge of the Supreme Court of India
B. Minister in charge of Department of Consumer Affairs in Central Government
C. President of India or his nominee
D. Head of Competition Commission of India

70. Match List-I with List-II.

List-I (Name of the case)	List-II (Subject matter)
(*a*) Githa Hariharan v. Reserve Bank of India	I. Maintenance Rights of Muslim women
(*b*) Sarla Mudgal v. Union of India	II. Guardianship of a minor child
(*c*) Danial Latifi v. Union of India	III. Compulsory registration of marriages
(*d*) Seema v. Ashwani Kumar	IV. Validity of second marriage of a Hindu male after his conversion to Islam

Choose the **correct** answer from the options given below:

	(*a*)	(*b*)	(*c*)	(*d*)
A.	II	IV	I	III
B.	I	II	III	IV
C.	II	IV	III	I
D.	IV	III	II	I

71. Salmond distinguishes between 'possession in fact' and 'possession in law'. He treated possession in fact as ______.

A. A fallacy
B. A fiction
C. A conception
D. A right

72. *Mens* rea does not include:

A. Intention
B. Knowledge
C. Reason to believe
D. Motive

73. Arrange the following UN Conventions in their chronological order:

(*a*) UN Convention on Biological Diversity
(*b*) UN Convention on Climate Change
(*c*) UN Convention Against Transnational Crimes
(*d*) UN Convention on the Rights of the Child
(*e*) UN Convention on Jurisdictional Immunities of States and their property

Choose the **correct** answer from the options given below:

A. (*b*), (*c*), (*d*), (*e*), (*a*)
B. (*a*), (*d*), (*e*), (*c*), (*b*)
C. (*d*), (*b*), (*c*), (*e*), (*a*)
D. (*a*), (*d*), (*c*), (*b*), (*e*)

74. Arrange the names of the following jurists in terms of chronological order of their birth:

(*a*) Jeremy Bentham
(*b*) John Austin
(*c*) Sir Henry Maine
(*d*) Hans Kelson
(*e*) Immanuel Kant

Choose the **correct** answer from the options given below:

A. (*a*), (*b*), (*c*), (*d*), (*e*)
B. (*e*), (*a*), (*b*), (*c*), (*d*)
C. (*a*), (*b*), (*c*), (*e*), (*d*)
D. (*d*), (*e*), (*b*), (*a*), (*c*)

75. The term "Contra Prolerentem" means:

A. Contradictory contract
B. Standard form contract are to be interpreted legally
C. Limited construction
D. Ambiguity is to be resolved against the party who inserted limiting term

76. All sums realised by way of penalties under The Competition Act, 2002 are credited to:

A. Competition Fund
B. Consolidated Fund of India
C. Finance Account of Ministry of Commerce
D. PM Relief Fund

77. The Neuremberg Trial classified the crimes punishable under International law into the categories of:

(*a*) Genocide
(*b*) Crimes against women and children
(*c*) Crimes against peace
(*d*) War crimes
(*e*) Crimes against humanity

Choose the **correct** answer from the options given below:

A. (*a*), (*c*) and (*e*) only
B. (*b*), (*c*) and (*d*) only
C. (*c*), (*d*) and (*e*) only
D. (*a*), (*b*) and (*d*) only

78. Consider the following statements relating to death penalty:

(*a*) Death sentence follows deterrence theory
(*b*) The Parliament of India wants to remove death sentence
(*c*) Recent amendments in IPC and other proposals have added new offences with death sentence
(*d*) The parliament wants harsh punishment for heinous offences through capital punishment
(*e*) After rarest of the rare doctrine the number of capital punishment is reduced

Choose the **correct** answer from the options given below:

A. (*a*), (*c*), (*d*), (*e*) only
B. (*a*), (*b*), (*c*), (*d*), (*e*)
C. (*a*), (*b*), (*c*), (*d*) only
D. (*b*), (*d*), (*e*) only

79. "To protect and improve the natural environment including forest, lakes, rivers and wildlife and to have compassion for living creatures" is provided under which Part of the Indian Constitution?

A. Fundamental Rights
B. Fundamental Duties
C. Directive Principles of State Policy
D. Obligation of State

80. Which kind of patent is protectable in India?

A. Design Patent
B. Utility Patent
C. Process Patent
D. Plant Variety Patent

81. Fundamental Duties in the Constitution of India under Article 51A:

(*a*) can be enforced by the Supreme Court
(*b*) can be used by the Supreme Court in interpretation
(*c*) can be amended by the States
(*d*) has been amended by the Parliament only once

Choose the **correct** answer from the options given below:

A. (*b*), (*d*) only
B. (*a*), (*b*), (*d*) only
C. (*b*), (*c*), (*d*) only
D. (*a*), (*b*), (*c*) only

82. The General Assembly of the United Nations passed the Uniting for Peace Resolution on:

A. December 10, 1948
B. August 1, 1950
C. August 31, 1965
D. November 3, 1950

83. Which country does not provide any written constitutional guarantee of fundamental freedoms?

A. UK B. UK and USA
C. UK and India D. USA

84. Match List-I with List-II.

List-I (UN days relating to IPR and Biological diversity)	**List-II (Days)**
(*a*) World Intellectual Property day	I. April 23
(*b*) World Book and Copyright day	II. May 22
(*c*) International Day for Biological diversity	III. April 21
(*d*) World Creativity and Innovation day	IV. April 26

Choose the **correct** answer from the options given below:

	(*a*)	(*b*)	(*c*)	(*d*)
A.	IV	II	I	III
B.	IV	I	II	III
C.	I	II	III	IV
D.	III	I	IV	II

85. Arrange following cases in sequence of year they were decided:

(*a*) Ashbyry Rly Carriage Co. Ltd. v. Riche
(*b*) Royal British Bank v. Turquand
(*c*) Mohori Bibee v. Dharmodas Ghose
(*d*) State Trading Corporation of India Ltd. v. CTO, Vishakhaptnam
(*e*) Salomon v. Salomon Co. Ltd.

Choose the **correct** answer from the options given below:

A. (*b*), (*a*), (*e*), (*c*), (*d*)
B. (*a*), (*b*), (*c*), (*e*), (*d*)
C. (*c*), (*d*), (*a*), (*b*), (*e*)
D. (*b*), (*c*), (*e*), (*a*), (*d*)

86. Arrange the following cases decided by the Permanent Court of Arbitration in their chronological order:

(*a*) Muscat Dhows case
(*b*) North Atlantic Fisheries case
(*c*) Savarkar's case

(*d*) Russian Indemnity case
(*e*) The Island of Palmas case

Choose the **correct** answer from the options given below:
A. (*a*), (*b*), (*c*), (*d*), (*e*)
B. (*c*), (*d*), (*b*), (*a*), (*e*)
C. (*b*), (*c*), (*d*), (*a*), (*e*)
D. (*c*), (*e*), (*d*), (*b*), (*a*)

87. Given below are two statements: one is labelled as Assertion (A) and the other is labelled as Reason (R).

Assertion (A): The tests of proportionality, necessity and balancing are found at prominent places in the GATS, the GATT as well as in the SPS and TBT Agreements

Reason (R): The meaning of these tests and their interrelationship is not always clear

In the light of the above statements, choose the **most appropriate answer** from the options given below:
A. Both (A) and (R) are correct and (R) is the correct explanation of (A)
B. Both (A) and (R) are correct, but (R) is not the correct explanation of (A)
C. (A) is correct, but (R) is not correct
D. (A) is not correct, but (R) is correct

88. According to Kaushal Kishore v. State of UP (2023) the fundamental right under article 19 is available against:
A. State actors only
B. Non state actors only
C. State as well as non state actors
D. State under article 12 only

89. According to Austin's definition of ownership, the attributes of ownership are:
(*a*) Indefinite user
(*b*) Plenary control over an object
(*c*) Unrestricted disposition
(*d*) Bundle of rights
(*e*) Unlimited duration

Choose the **correct** answer from the options given below:
A. (*a*), (*c*) and (*e*) only
B. (*b*), (*d*) and (*e*) only
C. (*a*), (*c*) and (*d*) only
D. (*a*), (*b*) and (*d*) only

90. "A man's nationality is a continuing legal relationship between the sovereign state on the one hand and the citizen on the other. The fundamental basis of a man's nationality is membership of an independent political community". This definition of nationality was given by the British Mexican Claims Commission in the case of:
A. Youman's case B. Re, Meunier
C. Re, Castioni D. Re, Lynch

Directions (Qs. No. 91-95): *Read the following passage and answer the questions:*

In India, the protection and enforcement of human rights confined to "Civil and Political Rights" in the form of "Fundamental Rights" (Part III) and "Economic, Social and Cultural Rights" in the form of "Directive Principles" (Part IV) in the Constitution of India discusses the vision of the Constitution and its framers of the kind of society they aspired to establish in the country. The framers of the Constitution were quite clear in assingning an equal role to each and every individual in the political process and decision making. Not only did they provide for universal adult suffrage but they also provide for affirmative steps in the form of seats allocation or reservation in election bodies for those incapable of competing in political process on equal footing. For effective participation in that process as well as for leading a dignified life, which they did not want to leave to the political process alone or postpone for the future, they also provided for Fundamental Rights and Directive principles, which have been distinguished as the conscience of the Constitution, and harmony and balance between them, have been found to be among the basic feature to the Constitution. Part IV A of the Constitution of India title "Fundamental duties" (Article 51 A) provides that every citizen must do his duty towards the nation as well as the fellow citizens.

91. The protection and enforcement of Human Rights under Article 32 is confined in India to:
A. Fundamental Rights
B. Economic, Social and Cultural Rights
C. Fundamental Duties
D. Right to Vote

92. The notion that every citizen must do his duty towards the nation as well as the fellow citizen is incorporated in the Indian Constitution in ______.
A. Part III
B. Part IV
C. Part IV A
D. Preamble

93. Which Part of the Constitution of India discusses the vision of the Constitution and its framers as to which kind of society they aspired to establish in the country?
A. Art 51 A
B. Part III and part IV
C. Part IV only
D. Part dealing with affirmative steps

94. Which of the following is part of the basic feature of the Constitution?
A. Fundamental Duties
B. Directive policies
C. Political process and decision making
D. Harmony and balance between Part III and Part IV

95. Which is distinguished as the 'Conscience' of the Constitution?
A. Fundamental Duties
B. Preamble
C. Universal adult suffrage
D. Fundamental Rights and Directive Principles

Directions (Qs. No. 96-100): *Read the passage carefully and answer the following questions:*

This is the greatest paradox involved in the doctrine of 'basic features', namely, that though it does not constitute a limitation on the legislature while enacting ordinary legislation, it would operate as a limitation on the 'Constituent' body, though in the same breath it is conceded that the latter is a 'Sovereign' authority while the Legislature is not. This means that while determining the validity of an ordinary law, the court can only look into the express provisions of the Constitution or the necessary implications thereof, but when the validity of a Constitution Amendment Act is challenged, the court may travel behind or beyond the express provisions of the Constitution to invoke some principles superior to express provisions to find whether the impunged amendment is in tune with those principles, which are supposed to Constitute the 'norm' behind the specific provisions of the Constitution. In short, it involve an illogical attempt to usher in the doctrines of 'Spirit of the Constitution' or of 'natural law', through the backdoor, to circumscribe the Constitution itself, while it had been openly rejected as a limitation upon ordinary legislation.

96. Which of the following options reflect the opinion of the author as can be discerned from the cited paragraph?
A. A critical and negative view of the way the court uses the doctrines of 'Spirit of the Constitution' and of 'natural law' to circumscribe the Constitution itself
B. Admiration of the court's view that legislative power need not be circumscribed
C. Neutral view on the use of basic features by the court to limit the constituent power and the legislative power
D. Positive view on the use of natural law as a limitation on the legislative power and constituent power

97. What does the author identify as the greatest paradox involved in the doctrine of basic features?

A. The doctrine does not constitute a limitation on the power of the Parliament, but limits the state legislatures

B. The doctrine ushers in the concept of natural law through the backdoors, while the judiciary get a free run

C. The doctrine operates as a limitation on the constituent body as well as legislature when enacting ordinary legislation

D. The doctrine does not constitute a limitation on the legislature while enacting ordinary legislation but operates as a limitation on the Constituent body though the Constituent body is a sovereign authority while the legislature is not

98. While determining the validity of an ordinary law, what can the court look into?

A. The court cannot look into the express provisions of the Constitution

B. The court can only look into the necessary implications but not the express provisions of the Constitution

C. The court can only look into express provisions of the Constitution or the necessary implications thereof

D. The court can only look into the express provisions of the Constitution and not the implications thereof

99. What does the author consider to be the doctrine used to circumscribe the Constitution?

A. Doctrine of 'Spirit of the constitution' and 'natural law'

B. Doctrine of 'basic structure' and of 'grund norm'

C. Doctrine of 'basic features' and of ultra vires'

D. Doctrine of 'Constituent body' and of 'Sovereign authority'

100. As per the apprehension of the author, when may a court travel beyond the express provisions of the Constitution to invoke some principles superior to the express provisions?

A. While exercising the judicial power to interpret the constitution

B. When the court wants to assert the power of judicial review

C. When the validity of a Constitution Amendment Act is challenged

D. When the validity of an ordinary legislation is challenged

ANSWERS

1. (A): Sections of the IT Act are matched correctly to their provisions as follows: Secure electronic record (Section 14), Security procedures and practices (Section 16), Secure electronic signature (Section 15), and Attribution of electronic record (Section 11). This matches because each section specifically addresses these elements within the IT Act, detailing the legal framework for electronic records, signatures, and security procedures.

2. (D): A human being ceases to be considered a person in legal and factual terms upon death. This is because the concept of legal personality is applicable only to living humans or entities recognized by law. Upon death, a person's legal rights and obligations cease to exist, which is a universal legal principle.

3. (A): The statements correctly identify the nature of wrongs in legal and moral contexts. A wrong is indeed an act against justice and right. A moral or natural wrong contravenes natural justice principles, while a legal wrong violates legal justice and law. However, not all legal wrongs are moral wrongs, and vice versa, which is why option (*a*), (*b*), and (*c*) are correct, dismissing (*d*) and (*e*).

4. **(D):** Section 145 of the Negotiable Instruments Act, 1881, with its non-obstante clause, alters the procedural requirements for legal action related to the Act. It allows for the procedure under Section 200 of the CrPC to be bypassed, omits the necessity for oath-taking by complainants and witnesses, permits affidavits in place of live testimony, and does away with the need for magistrate-recorded sworn statements, streamlining the process for dealing with negotiable instrument cases.

5. **(B):** Jerome Frank is known for his contribution to legal realism, where he emphasized 'constructive skepticism'. This means he advocated for a realistic approach to understanding law, recognizing the complexities and uncertainties inherent in legal systems and judicial decisions. His perspective encourages questioning and critical thinking, but with the intent to improve, rather than cynically dismiss, the legal process and its outcomes.

6. **(A):** Sections 65, 66 D, and 67 B of the Information Technology Act, 2000, specifically outline punishments for different offenses related to the misuse of digital information and technology. Section 65 deals with tampering with computer source documents, Section 66 D pertains to cheating by personation using computer resources, and Section 67 B addresses the punishment for publishing or transmitting material depicting children in sexually explicit acts. These sections are designed to safeguard digital information integrity, prevent fraud, and protect children from exploitation, reflecting the Act's comprehensive approach to cybercrime.

7. **(A):** Under section 13 of the Hindu Marriage Act, 1955, the grounds for divorce do not include the respondent being convicted of an offense. The Act specifies several grounds for divorce, such as cruelty, desertion, conversion to another religion, unsound mind, and several others. However, conviction for an offense is not listed among these grounds, which are mainly based on the breakdown of marriage rather than criminal conduct per se.

8. **(D):** The concept of 'dominant position' as per the Competition Act, 2002, in India, is primarily defined by an enterprise's ability to operate independently of competitive market forces (*b*), to affect its competitors, consumers, or the relevant market in its favor (*c*), and by its strength in the relevant market (*d*). This position allows an enterprise to significantly influence market conditions, including pricing and availability of products or services, without regard to the actions or reactions of competitors, customers, or suppliers.

9. **(C)**

10. **(C):** Matching the enactments with their respective years, The Civil Rights Act corresponds to 1955 (I), establishing laws against discrimination based on race, color, religion, sex, or national origin. The Probation of Offenders Act, enacted in 1958 (III), emphasizes rehabilitating offenders rather than punitive measures. The Immoral Traffic (Prevention) Act of 1956 (II) aims to combat human trafficking and sexual exploitation. Lastly, The Medical Termination of Pregnancy Act of 1971 (IV) legalizes abortion under specific conditions, reflecting societal and legal advancements in reproductive rights.

11. **(B):** Article 28 of the Constitution of India prohibits religious instruction in educational institutions wholly maintained by the state (*a*), but it allows for such instruction in institutions recognized by the state (*b*), institutions that receive aid out of state funds (*c*), and in institutions administered by the state but established under any endowment or trust (*d*). However, the correct combination excluding institutions wholly maintained by the state, points to (*b*), (*c*), and (*d*). This provision ensures a secular approach in state-funded education while permitting religious education in certain conditions, thus balancing secularism with freedom of religion.

12. (D): The correct match between the cases and the issues/concepts/principles they are associated with is as follows: Linkletter v. Walker (IV) established the principle of prospective overruling in the context of criminal procedure. Golak Nath v. State of Punjab (I) is famously known for the prospective overruling in constitutional interpretation, ensuring that past decisions remain unaffected by new rulings. Jolly George Varghese v. Bank of Cochin (III) involved the importation of a provision from the International Covenant on Civil and Political Rights (ICCPR) into Indian Constitutional law. People's Union for Civil Liberties v. Union of India (II) dealt with the right to register a "none of the above" vote, enhancing electoral democracy and freedom.

13. (B): Under the Hindu Marriage Act, 1955, sapinda relationship and degrees of prohibited relationship cover a broad range of familial connections, including full, half, and uterine blood relationships (*a*), adoption (*b*), and legitimate (*c*) as well as illegitimate blood relations (*e*). These categories create a legal framework to prevent marriages within closely related families or individuals, reflecting the Act's intent to maintain social and biological norms while recognizing both traditional and contemporary family structures. Fosterage relations (*d*), however, are not explicitly included in these prohibitions.

14. (A): In Indira Gandhi v. Raj Narain, it was held that the doctrine of the basic structure does not apply as a limitation on the legislature's power while enacting ordinary legislation. This landmark decision underscored the distinction between constitutional amendments, which are subject to the basic structure doctrine, and ordinary legislative acts, which are not. The verdict established a crucial principle in Indian constitutional law, affirming the supremacy of the Constitution and the Judiciary's role in safeguarding its fundamental ethos without unduly restricting legislative competence in regular law-making processes.

15. (A): According to Article 19 of the Constitution of India, the rights granted under this article are automatically suspended upon the proclamation of Emergency due to war (*a*) or external aggression (*b*). This provision reflects the Constitution's framework to ensure the State's ability to respond effectively to severe national security threats. However, the suspension of Article 19 rights does not extend to emergencies declared on the grounds of armed rebellion (*c*) or failure of constitutional machinery in a state (*d*). This distinction underscores the balance between safeguarding individual freedoms and addressing exigencies threatening the nation's security and sovereignty.

16. (A): Both statements are correct. The doctrine of stare decisis, which means to stand by decisions and not to disturb what is settled, relies heavily on the development of law reporting. As legal decisions are recorded, published, and made accessible, they become precedents for future cases, ensuring consistency and predictability in the law. Since Indian law is significantly influenced by English Law, where the practice of law reporting is well-established, India too has developed a robust system of law reporting. This system allows Indian courts to refer to and apply precedents, both from within India and from common law jurisdictions like the UK, enhancing the coherence and stability of Indian jurisprudence.

17. (B): In Ashby v. White, it was established that when an absolute right is violated, the law presumes damages even if the plaintiff did not suffer any pecuniary loss. This case highlighted the principle that the infringement of a legal right entitles the person wronged to compensation, underscoring the importance of rights protection over the quantification of damage. This principle is a cornerstone in the development of tort law, emphasizing the significance of rights per se, beyond the mere calculation of financial harm.

18. (A): The correct sequence of cases according to the years they were decided is: Gloucester Grammar School Case (1410), Ashby v. White Case (1703), Rylands v. Fletcher Case (1868), and Donoghue v. Stevenson Case (1932). This sequence shows the development of legal principles over time, from early English case law concerning torts and liabilities to the establishment of the modern negligence doctrine. The chronological order provides insight into the evolution of legal reasoning and the increasing complexity of legal issues addressed by courts over the centuries.

19. (A): Section 185 of the Indian Contract Act, 1872, explicitly states that "no consideration is necessary to create an agency". This provision underscores a fundamental principle in the law of agency, where the focus is on the authority granted to the agent and the trust placed in them by the principal, rather than on any monetary or material exchange to validate the relationship. This legal provision facilitates the creation of agency relationships in a variety of contexts, enabling individuals and businesses to act through agents without the need for consideration, which is a departure from the general rule in contract law that consideration is required for a contract to be valid.

20. (C): Articles 17 and 23 of the Constitution of India play crucial roles in mandating the criminalization of specific prohibited conduct. Article 17 abolishes "untouchability" and forbids its practice in any form, inherently necessitating legal measures to penalize violations. Article 23 prohibits traffic in human beings and forced labor, making any contravention a punishable offense under the law. These articles collectively underscore the Constitution's commitment to safeguarding human dignity and freedom, obliging the state to enact legislation that criminalizes such inhumane practices.

21. (B): Under the Hindu Adoption and Maintenance Act of 1956, if a bachelor male adopts a child and subsequently marries, his wife is considered the stepmother of the adopted child. The Act does not automatically confer the status of 'adoptive mother' upon the wife in this scenario. Instead, the legislation is clear in delineating relationships within the framework of adoption, aiming to protect and clarify the legal status and rights of the child, the adoptive father, and his subsequent wife, thereby ensuring the child's welfare and legal clarity in familial relationships.

22. (B): Section 302 of the Indian Penal Code (IPC) is applied in cases where a person commits murder. If A, after being lawfully arrested by Z, a police officer, loses self-control due to grave and sudden provocation and kills Z, A's action constitutes murder under Section 302. The defense of grave and sudden provocation, which can mitigate murder to culpable homicide not amounting to murder under Section 304, does not apply when the provocation is given by a public servant doing their lawful duty. Thus, A's act of killing Z, in response to lawful arrest, is punished as murder under Section 302 of the IPC, reflecting the law's intent to maintain public order and protect law enforcement officers performing their duties.

23. (A): The insertion of the provisions into the Indian Penal Code follows a historical sequence starting with Section 124A, which was introduced in 1870 to address sedition. This was followed by Section 153A, inserted in 1898 to prevent the promotion of enmity between different groups. Section 120A, defining criminal conspiracy, came later in 1913, part of efforts to tackle plots against the state and public peace. Finally, Section 304B was added in 1986, specifically targeting the issue of dowry death, reflecting evolving legal standards and societal concerns. This chronological arrangement showcases the IPC's adaptive response to emerging crimes and societal issues over time.

24. (D): The Polluter Pays Principle is synonymous with the Principle of Extended Producer Responsibility (EPR). This environmental policy approach holds that producers are responsible for the entire lifecycle of their products, including take-back, recycling, and final disposal. EPR extends the responsibility of the polluters from production and consumption to post-consumption stages, aiming to reduce the environmental impact of products by making the manufacturers bear the cost of managing their products at the end of their life. This principle is a cornerstone of sustainable waste management and environmental protection policies, encouraging producers to design environmentally friendly products.

25. (D): The chronological order of enactment for the given legislations begins with the National Commission for Women Act in 1990, establishing the National Commission for Women to address issues relating to women's rights. The National Commission for Minorities Act followed in 1992, setting up the National Commission for Minorities. Next, the Protection of Human Rights Act was enacted in 1993, leading to the establishment of the National Human Rights Commission. Lastly, the 89th Constitutional Amendment Act came into effect in 2003, demonstrating a progression in the Indian legal system's approach towards enhancing and protecting the rights of various groups and ensuring their representation and welfare.

26. (B): Article 338 of the Constitution of India establishes the National Commission for the Scheduled Castes (NCSC). This provision was inserted to provide a constitutional body dedicated to protecting and promoting the interests of the Scheduled Castes. The NCSC investigates and monitors all matters relating to the safeguards provided for the Scheduled Castes under the Constitution or under any other law for the time being in force and to evaluate the working of such safeguards, ensuring their welfare and socio-economic development.

Article 335: The claims of the member of the Scheduled Castes and the Scheduled Tribes shall be taken into consideration, consistently, with the maintenance of efficiency of administration in the making of appointments to services and posts in connection with the affairs of the Union or of a State.

Article 341 of the Indian Constitution authorises the President to declare certain castes and classes as Scheduled Castes in a state or a union territory. It also states that the Parliament can include or exclude any caste or tribe from the list.

Article 342A: The President may with respect to any State or Union territory, and where it is a State after consultation with the Governor thereof, by public notification specify the tribes or tribal communities or parts of or groups within tribes or tribal communities which shall for the purposes of this Constitution be deemed to be Scheduled Tribes in relation to that State or Union territory, as the case may be.

27. (C): India and Australia both follow a parliamentary system of government, a democratic framework where the executive branch derives its legitimacy from and is accountable to the legislature (parliament), and the executive and legislative branches are intertwined. In these countries, the head of state is different from the head of government, and the majority party or coalition in the parliament forms the government, led by the Prime Minister, who is the head of government.

28. (B): In the case of Luther v. Sagor, it was held that there is no distinction between de facto and de jure recognition for the purpose of giving effect to the internal acts of the recognized authority. This principle means that once a foreign government is recognized in either form, its laws and acts within its own territory are given effect in the recognizing state's courts, acknowledging the authority's ability to rule effectively over its territory.

29. (B): Matching the given lists with their correct descriptions leads to the conclusion: Producer companies, as outlined in Indian corporate law, are designed to allow cooperative organizations to function as companies; Statutory companies are created by a specific act of the legislature and do not necessarily require a Memorandum of Association. Section 8 companies are established for promoting commerce, art, science, sports, education, research, social welfare, religion, charity, protection of the environment, or any such other object, provided the profits, if any, or other income is applied for promoting only the objects of the company and no dividend is paid to its members. Thus, they are associations not for profit. Small companies are defined by their paid-up share capital is between 50 lakhs – 5 crore & turnover is between 2 crore – 20 crore for small companies.

30. (D): As per the Partnership Act of 1932, "Partnership" is defined under Section 4. This section lays down the definition and nature of partnership, describing it as the relation between persons who have agreed to share the profits of a business carried on by all or any of them acting for all. This definition forms the foundation of partnership law in India, detailing the essence of partnership agreements and the mutual relations between partners in the conduct of their business.

31. (D)

32. (D): The assertion regarding the Trade Secrets Act, 2020 being legislation in India is incorrect; India does not have a specific statute named "Trade Secrets Act, 2020" for the protection of trade secrets. Trade secret protection in India is instead covered under a combination of copyright laws, contractual agreements, and principles of equity. However, the reason statement is correct; India has enacted numerous legislations to create a legal framework on intellectual property rights (IPRs), including laws on patents, copyrights, trademarks, and designs, aimed at protecting and enforcing IPRs within its jurisdiction.

33. (C): False imprisonment constitutes an intentional total restraint of one's liberty without lawful justification. The necessary elements include total restrain on the liberty of a person, where detention can be actual or constructive, and the detention or restraint must be unlawful. The duration of the detention, such as a minimum of 2 years, is not a required element to constitute false imprisonment. What matters is the unlawfulness of the detention and the total restraint on freedom, regardless of the time period.

34. (C): The UK does not follow a codified scheme of distribution of power like federal countries such as India, the USA, and Canada. In the UK, the principle of parliamentary sovereignty means that Parliament is the supreme legal authority, which can create or end any law. The distribution of powers within the UK has traditionally been unitary, with devolution agreements in recent years granting Scotland, Wales, and Northern Ireland their own parliaments or assemblies with varying degrees of legislative power, but this does not equate to a constitutional distribution of powers as seen in federal systems.

35. (A): The contract between 'A' and 'B' regarding the purchase of B's horse contingent upon 'A' surviving 'C' is a conditional contract dependent on the survival of 'A' over 'C'. This contract can only be enforced by law if 'C' dies within the lifetime of 'A', fulfilling the condition precedent for the contract's enforceability. The death of 'B' or both 'A' and 'C', or the death of 'A' before 'C', does not fulfill the contract's specific condition, thus highlighting the importance of the condition's satisfaction for the contract's legal enforceability.

36. (B): The first generation of human rights, often referred to as "civil and political rights", focuses on liberty and participation in political life. These rights are primarily concerned with protecting the individual from excesses of the state and ensuring the capability to participate in the civil and political activities of the state without discrimination or repression. Rights to liberty (*b*), equality before the law (*c*), and the right to life (*e*) are quintessential examples of first-generation human rights, as they are foundational to the protection of individual freedoms and the exercise of civil liberties.

37. (C): Amendment II of the US Constitution is the only option among those given that expressly contains a provision for the 'right to bear arms' as a fundamental right. This amendment, part of the Bill of Rights adopted in 1791, protects the right of the people to keep and bear arms. None of the other options listed include a similar express provision for this right as a fundamental aspect of their legal frameworks.

38. (A): The Governor of an Indian state can exercise his discretion under certain circumstances that are not explicitly laid out in the Constitution but have been established through conventions and judicial interpretations. These circumstances include the appointment of the Chief Minister when no single party has a clear majority in the Assembly, the dismissal of the ministry or dissolution of the Assembly when it appears that the ministry has lost the majority but refuses to resign, and submitting a report to the President for the proclamation under Article 356 if the state's governance cannot be carried on in accordance with the provisions of the Constitution. Appointment of High Court judges is not within the Governor's discretionary powers, as this is primarily the responsibility of the President of India, following consultations with the Chief Justice of India and others as deemed necessary.

39. (A): Dr. Radha Vinod Pal, the Indian judge serving at the Tokyo Trial post-World War II, is known for his dissenting judgment, where he notably argued against the retroactive application of criminal penalties and the concept of "crimes against peace". His dissent expressed views that (*a*) war is beyond the scope of International law, (*b*) conduct of war is within the scope of the rules of International law, and (*c*) the Pact of Paris brought about no change in the status of war. He emphasized the traditional understanding of international law regarding warfare and criticized the creation of new crimes without prior notice as unjust.

40. (A): Government promissory notes are instruments issued by the government to borrow money. These notes (*a*) signify a promise by the President of India or the Governor of a state, depending on the issuing authority, and (*b*) are regulated by the Indian Securities Act, 1886, which provides the legal framework for government securities, including promissory notes. They are recognized as formal debt instruments, indicating the government's obligation to pay the holder the face value of the note upon maturity. These characteristics underscore the legal and financial mechanisms through which governments engage in borrowing activities.

41. (A): The constitutions of both the USA and South Africa expressly state that the constitution shall be the supreme law of the land. In the USA, this principle is established through the Supremacy Clause found in Article VI of the Constitution, which explicitly states that the U.S. Constitution, federal laws made pursuant to it, and treaties made under its authority, constitute the supreme law of the land. Similarly, the Constitution of South Africa states in its supremacy clause that the Constitution is the supreme law of the country; any law or conduct inconsistent with it is invalid, and the obligations imposed by it must be fulfilled.

42. (B): Jeremy Bentham, the influential English philosopher and legal theorist known for his work in developing the doctrine of utilitarianism, used the term "mandate" to explain his imperative concept of law. Bentham's conception of law as a mandate reflects his view that laws are commands issued by the sovereign to the governed, establishing rules of conduct that must be followed under the threat of a sanction. This approach underlines his belief in the nature of law as an instrument of social control and governance, articulated through authoritative commands or mandates.

43. (C): The Supreme Court of India's remark that "Extradition with foreign states is, except in exceptional cases, governed by treaties or arrangements made" reflects the principle that international extradition typically relies on formal agreements between states. This statement was made in the case of State of Madras v. C.G. Menon, emphasizing the structured and treaty-based nature of extradition processes, which are designed to ensure that such procedures are carried out within the bounds of internationally agreed-upon legal frameworks and standards.

44. (A): Highly developed legal systems indeed strive to create an autonomous apparatus of legal concepts, techniques, and norms, as this autonomy helps in maintaining the integrity, consistency, and objectivity of the legal system. The reason for this effort towards autonomy is that law needs to be endowed with logical consistency, predictability, and stability to ensure fairness, facilitate legal reasoning, and allow individuals and entities to organize their affairs with confidence in how the law will be applied.

45. (A): Mahr or dower is an essential component of a Muslim marriage, representing a sum of money or other property which the husband agrees to give the wife. It is a mark of respect and part of the contractual agreement between the husband and wife. While it is customary to specify the mahr at the time of marriage, it can be presumed if not specified. The reason (R) accurately explains why the concept of mahr is important; it becomes due upon the husband's death or the dissolution of marriage by divorce, emphasizing the protective financial right it grants to the wife within the framework of Muslim personal law.

46. (D): In Islamic law, a Muslim is allowed to make a bequest of his property without the consent of his heirs up to the extent of one-third of his property. This limitation is based on Hadith and is aimed at protecting the interests of the heirs while allowing the testator a degree of freedom to allocate a portion of his estate to non-heirs or for charitable purposes. The rule serves to balance the individual's autonomy in distributing their property and the Islamic legal principles protecting the rights of heirs.

47. (C): Matching the subjects with the correct sections of the Indian Penal Code (IPC) gives us:

(*a*) Punishment for extortion is covered under Section 384, making (*a*) match with III.

(*b*) Attempt to commit robbery is defined under Section 393, linking (*b*) with IV.

(*c*) Dishonest misappropriation of property is addressed in Section 403, so (*c*) matches with I.

(*d*) Criminal breach of trust by public servant is specified in Section 409, which aligns (*d*) with II.

This arrangement is based on the specific provisions of the IPC that delineate the legal framework for these offenses.

48. (D): The concept of "Moral Right" primarily prevails in the domain of Copyright law. Moral rights protect the personal and reputational relationship between a creator and their work, even if the copyright in the work has been sold. These rights can include the right to be credited as the author of a work, the right to object to derogatory treatments of the work that may prejudice the creator's honor or reputation, and the right of disclosure. Moral rights are thus designed to recognize the personal connection and integrity between the creator and their creations.

49. (B): Among the given statements,

(*a*) In the S.S. Lotus case, the Permanent Court of International Justice (PCIJ) indeed made a significant statement regarding international law, highlighting its role among nations.

(*c*) The remark attributed to Lord Halsbury about international law being more akin to a branch of ethics than law reflects a critique of its binding nature, although Halsbury was never Prime Minister of England but a notable Lord Chancellor.

(*d*) Russell's definition of International Law as the rules nations agree to abide by in their conduct towards each other captures the essence of international legal cooperation and agreement.

Statements (*b*) and (*e*) contain inaccuracies regarding the perspectives of Professor Dias and Austin on international law.

50. (D): For libel, which is defamation in a permanent form (such as written or published media), the necessary characteristics include:

(*a*) It must be in a permanent form, making it more harmful than slander, which is spoken defamation.

(*c*) No actual damage needs to be proved to sustain an action for libel because the law presumes damages in the case of libel due to its permanent and potentially widespread impact.

(*d*) The falsity of the charge is presumed in favor of the plaintiff, relieving them of the immediate burden to prove the statement was false.

Contrary to one of the provided options, the burden of proof regarding the falsity typically lies on the defendant in libel cases, especially in jurisdictions where truth is a defense against defamation.

51. (A): The correct sequence of these landmark cases in the Indian legal history, based on their year of verdict, is: Sankari Prasad v. Union of India (1951), which dealt with the power of the Indian Parliament to amend the Constitution and its impact on fundamental rights. Sajjan Singh v. State of Rajasthan (1965), which also discussed the amendment powers of Parliament but did not directly overrule the previous case. Golak Nath v. State of Punjab (1967), where it was held that Parliament could not amend Part III of the Constitution to take away or abridge the fundamental rights. Kesavananda Bharti v. State of Kerala (1973), which established the doctrine of the basic structure of the Constitution, stating that while Parliament has wide powers to amend the Constitution, it cannot alter its basic structure.

52. (A): A red herring prospectus is issued prior to the issue of the main prospectus. It is a preliminary registration document filed by a company with the Securities and Exchange Commission (usually in the context of the U.S. financial regulations), detailing the company's operations and financials as part of a public offering of securities. This document does not contain details about the pricing or number of shares being offered and is used to gauge investor interest in the offering.

53. (D): The second marriage of a Hindu male who converted to Islam and then married a Muslim girl, while his first Hindu wife was still alive, is considered void under Indian law. This is because, despite his conversion to Islam, the Hindu Marriage Act of 1955 still applies to his first marriage, making his second marriage an act of bigamy. The Supreme Court of India has held in several cases that conversion to Islam and subsequent marriage does not absolve a person from the obligations and commitments of his previous marriage under the Hindu Marriage Act.

54. (B): Mahabub Shah v. Emperor (1945) is one of the landmark cases that made a clear distinction between common intention and similar intention. The case elucidates that for the application of common intention under Section 34 of the Indian Penal Code, it is not necessary that the act is done in concert as long as the criminal act is done in furtherance of the common intention of all. This case distinguishes common intention from mere similar intention, which alone does not suffice to hold others liable for the criminal act unless they acted with a shared intent.

55. (A): Mere agreement to commit an offense, specifically a conspiracy to commit robbery, is punishable under Section 120B of the Indian Penal Code (IPC), which deals with criminal conspiracy. According to this section, when two or more persons agree to do or cause to be done an illegal act or an act which is not illegal by illegal means, such an agreement is designated a criminal conspiracy. Therefore, the mere agreement between A1 and A2 to commit robbery constitutes a criminal conspiracy under Section 120B of the IPC.

56. (C): The sequence of processes in the Patents Act logically progresses from (*a*)

Consequence of secrecy directions, which involves the confidentiality of certain patents relevant to defense or other specified areas by the government, to (*b*) Grant of patent, where the official permission for the patent is given. This is followed by (*c*) Date of patent, which is the date from which the patent protection starts, then (*e*) Rights of patentee, detailing the legal rights a patent holder has over the invention, and finally, (*d*) Term of patent, which specifies the duration for which the patent protection is granted. This sequence encapsulates the lifecycle of a patent from its initial confidentiality to the grant, operational rights, and eventual term expiry.

57. (B): Fundamental rights are expressly provided in the US Constitution, primarily through amendments, notably the Bill of Rights. Directive principles in the Indian Constitution, outlined in Part IV, set forth the aims and objectives that the State should strive towards achieving but are not enforceable by courts. This delineation showcases the constitutional frameworks of both countries in protecting individual rights and guiding state policy. Unlike the assertion that fundamental rights and human rights are the same in India, fundamental rights are constitutionally guaranteed rights specific to the Indian Constitution, while human rights are broadly recognized at the international level, covering a wider range of rights.

58. (C): India does not have specific legislations that comprehensively cover Traditional Knowledge, Street Art, Publicity Right, or Celebrity Right as distinct categories of Intellectual Property (IP). While there are various laws that indirectly address aspects of these areas, such as copyright law potentially applying to street art or aspects of celebrity rights, there are no dedicated IP legislations in India that specifically and comprehensively cover these four categories, highlighting gaps in the legal framework that may need addressing to protect these forms of expression and identity.

59. (A): Articles 51A(g), 48A, and 49 in the Indian Constitution deal directly with the protection of the environment and cultural heritage. Article 51A(g) mandates citizens to protect and improve the natural environment, including forests, lakes, rivers, and wildlife. Article 48A directs the State to strive towards protecting and improving the environment. Article 49 emphasizes the State's obligation to protect monuments, places, and objects of national importance. These provisions reflect the Constitution's approach to integrating environmental conservation and cultural heritage protection within the duties of the State and citizens.

60. (A): Malice in Law is associated with the intentional doing of a wrongful act without just cause or excuse (IV). Malfeasance refers to the commission of an unlawful act, especially by a public official (I). Misfeasance involves the improper performance of a lawful act, i.e., performing a lawful act in an illegal or improper manner (II). Non-feasance is the omission to perform an act when there is an obligation to do so, highlighting a failure to act where action is required (III). These terms categorize different types of wrongful acts, differentiating them based on the nature of the act and the intent behind it.

61. (A): According to Section 7 of the Hindu Marriage Act, 1955, a Hindu marriage is considered validly solemnized if it is conducted in accordance with the customary rites and ceremonies of either party involved in the marriage. This means that the marriage is recognized as valid if either (*a*) all essential shastric (scriptural) ceremonies are performed, which are considered central to the traditional Hindu marriage rites, and (*b*) all customary rites and ceremonies specific to the bride's family are performed. These practices ensure that the marriage is conducted in a manner that is respectful and recognized by the families and communities of both parties.

62. (A): The Preamble of the Constitution of India can be amended by the Parliament of India. This was affirmed in the Kesavananda Bharati case (1973), where the Supreme Court of India ruled that the Parliament could amend any part of the Constitution, including the Preamble, as long as it does not alter the basic structure of the Constitution. Therefore, the Preamble is not beyond the scope of parliamentary amendment powers, but any amendment to it must respect the Constitution's fundamental principles and framework.

63. (B): Matching the Schedules of the Constitution of India with their respective descriptions:

(*a*) The Fifth Schedule deals with the administration and control of Scheduled Areas and Scheduled Tribes, focusing on areas with significant indigenous populations.

(*b*) The Eighth Schedule lists the recognized languages of India, highlighting the linguistic diversity of the country.

(*c*) The Tenth Schedule contains provisions for disqualification on the ground of defection, aiming to curb political defections and ensure stability in governance.

(*d*) The Fourth Schedule is concerned with the allocation of seats in the Council of States (Rajya Sabha), reflecting the federal structure by allotting seats to states and Union territories.

64. (B): In the USA, the appointment of judges, especially to the federal courts including the Supreme Court, involves a process where the President nominates candidates, who must then be confirmed by the Senate. This process places the appointment of judges within the realm of the political and legislative branches of government, differing significantly from practices in countries like the UK and India, where judicial appointments are largely insulated from direct political influence and involve judicial or independent bodies in the selection process.

65. (C): According to the National Green Tribunal Act, 2010, "Environment" includes water, air, and land, as well as the interrelationships that exist among and between water, air, and land, and human beings, other living creatures, plants, microorganisms, and property. The inclusion of property in this definition signifies a broader understanding of the environment, acknowledging the impact of environmental conditions on physical assets and vice versa. This perspective allows for a comprehensive approach to environmental protection and management, recognizing the integral role that property plays in the environmental ecosystem and the potential effects environmental changes can have on property values and usability.

66. (B): The right of private defence to the extent of causing death is elaborated under Sections 100 and 103 of the Indian Penal Code (IPC). Section 100 specifies situations under which the right of private defense against an assault may extend to causing death, such as in cases of grave assaults that reasonably cause the fear of death or grievous hurt, among others. Section 103 extends this right to causing death when the defense is against acts like robbery, house-breaking by night, etc. These provisions recognize the right to self-defense as fundamental, allowing individuals to protect themselves and their property under certain grave circumstances.

67. (C): There exists a statutory ban on the assignment of Geographical Indications (GIs) under the Geographical Indications of Goods (Registration and Protection) Act, 1999. GIs are signs used on products that have a specific geographical origin and possess qualities, a reputation, or characteristics inherent to that location. Unlike patents, trademarks, or designs, geographical indications are collective rights and cannot be owned or transferred by an individual entity, reflecting their role in protecting the heritage and cultural identity associated with specific regions and products.

68. (A): The Budapest Treaty on the International Recognition of the Deposit of Microorganisms for the Purposes of Patent Procedure, 1977, is the international legal instrument directly related to patents. This treaty allows for the deposit of microorganisms at an internationally recognized depository authority to satisfy the requirement of disclosure in patent applications involving new microorganisms. This facilitates the patenting process for inventions in biotechnology by standardizing the recognition of deposited materials across signatory countries.

69. (B): The Central Consumer Protection Council is headed by the Minister in charge of the Department of Consumer Affairs in the Central Government. This council is a statutory body established under the Consumer Protection Act, which aims to promote and protect the rights of consumers. It serves as an advisory body on consumer issues, with the minister serving as the chairperson to guide the council's policy and agenda, emphasizing the government's role in consumer protection.

70. (A): Matching the cases with their subject matter: Githa Hariharan v. Reserve Bank of India deals with the Guardianship of a minor child (II), challenging the norms regarding the guardianship rights of the mother. Sarla Mudgal v. Union of India addresses the Validity of the second marriage of a Hindu male after his conversion to Islam (IV), examining the implications of religious conversion on marital status under personal law. Danial Latifi v. Union of India concerns the Maintenance Rights of Muslim women (I), interpreting the Muslim Women (Protection of Rights on Divorce) Act in light of the constitutional rights. Seema v. Ashwani Kumar is related to the Compulsory registration of marriages (III), aimed at safeguarding women's rights by ensuring legal documentation of marriages.

71. (C): Salmond distinguishes between 'possession in fact' and 'possession in law' by treating possession in fact as a conception. This distinction is critical in understanding the nature of possession within the legal framework. 'Possession in fact' refers to the actual control or holding of an object, whereas 'possession in law' implies a legal recognition of that control, potentially including rights to exclude others. Salmond's characterization of possession in fact as a conception highlights the nuanced understanding of possession beyond mere physical control, encompassing the broader legal and societal recognition of that control.

72. (D): Mens rea, a fundamental principle in criminal law, refers to the mental state or intention behind committing a crime. It includes elements such as intention, knowledge, and reason to believe, which establish the culpability of an individual's actions. However, motive, which explains why the individual committed the crime, does not constitute part of mens rea. While motive can provide context or explanation for criminal behavior, it is not a legal requirement to prove the mental element of a crime, differentiating it from the essential components of mens rea.

73. (*)

74. (B): The chronological order of the birth of these jurists, from earliest to latest, is: Immanuel Kant (1724-1804), Jeremy Bentham (1748-1832), John Austin (1790-1859), Sir Henry Maine (1822-1888), and Hans Kelsen (1881-1973). This order reflects the historical development of legal thought and theory, with Kant's philosophical inquiries laying foundational concepts that influenced later jurists like Bentham and Austin in their development of legal positivism, Maine's contributions to legal anthropology and sociology, and Kelsen's pure theory of law.

75. (D): The term "Contra Prolerentem" is a legal principle used in contract law, which means that any ambiguity in a contract is to be resolved against the party who inserted the ambiguous term or who benefits from it. This rule serves as a means to encourage clarity in contract drafting and protect the party who did not draft the contract from ambiguous terms that could be exploited by the drafter. It is particularly applied in situations involving standard form contracts or where there is a significant disparity in bargaining power between the contracting parties.

76. (B): All sums realized by way of penalties under The Competition Act, 2002 are credited to the Consolidated Fund of India. This ensures that penalties collected under the act, which are imposed for anti-competitive practices, abuse of dominant position, and other violations, contribute to the nation's treasury. Such contributions support the government's financial infrastructure, allowing for the allocation of funds to various public services and developmental activities, reflecting a direct link between enforcement of competition laws and the financial health of the nation.

77. (C): The Nuremberg Trials, conducted after World War II, classified crimes punishable under international law into three main categories:

(*c*) Crimes against peace,

(*d*) War crimes, and

(*e*) Crimes against humanity.

These categories were significant in establishing the principles of international criminal responsibility, marking a pivotal moment in the development of international law. Crimes against peace involved planning and waging wars of aggression in violation of international treaties. War crimes consisted of violations of the laws and customs of war. Crimes against humanity included widespread atrocities committed against civilians, including genocide, although "genocide" was not formally defined as a legal term until later.

78. (A): Considerations relating to the death penalty in India include:

(*a*) the belief in the deterrence theory, which posits that the threat of the death penalty serves to prevent serious crimes;

(*c*) recent amendments in the Indian Penal Code (IPC) and other proposals have indeed added new offences punishable by death, reflecting a legislative stance that sees capital punishment as an appropriate response to certain heinous crimes;

(*d*) there is a legislative intent to impose harsh punishment for heinous offences through capital punishment, signaling a commitment to maintaining the death penalty for deterrence and retribution;

(*e*) the adoption of the "rarest of the rare" doctrine by the Supreme Court of India has led to a more cautious approach in awarding capital punishment, focusing on its application in only the most egregious cases.

79. **(B):** The duty "to protect and improve the natural environment including forests, lakes, rivers, and wildlife, and to have compassion for living creatures" is enshrined under the Fundamental Duties, specifically in Article 51A(g) of the Indian Constitution. This provision underscores the responsibility of every citizen to contribute to the preservation and enhancement of the country's natural environment. Fundamental Duties, introduced by the 42nd Amendment in 1976, serve as moral obligations for citizens to encourage a commitment towards the nation and its environment, promoting a collective ethos of environmental stewardship and compassionate living.

80. **(C):** In India, Process Patents are protectable under the Patents Act, 1970. This allows for the protection of methods or processes that produce a specific result or product. India's patent regime recognizes both product and process patents, but the emphasis on process patents, especially in sectors like pharmaceuticals, has been a significant aspect of India's approach to patent law. This facilitates innovation by protecting the creator's rights over the unique processes developed, ensuring that inventors can secure patent rights for their novel, inventive, and industrially applicable processes, thereby contributing to technological advancement and economic growth.

81. **(A):** Fundamental Duties listed under Article 51A of the Indian Constitution cannot be directly enforced by the Supreme Court. However, they can be and often are used by the Supreme Court in the interpretation of laws and to determine the constitutionality of legislation. These duties, introduced by the 42nd Amendment in 1976, serve as moral obligations for the citizens to promote a sense of national solidarity and consciousness. The statement that they can be amended by the States is incorrect, as amendments to the Constitution, including those related to Fundamental Duties, can only be made by the Parliament. Indeed, the list of Fundamental Duties has been amended by the Parliament only once, with the addition of a new duty by the 86th Amendment in 2002, making (*b*) and (*d*) the correct aspects of Fundamental Duties under Article 51A.

82. **(D):** The Uniting for Peace Resolution was passed by the General Assembly of the United Nations on November 3, 1950. This resolution was aimed at overcoming the deadlock in the Security Council caused by the veto power, allowing the General Assembly to recommend collective action, including the use of armed force, in cases where there is a threat to peace, breach of peace, or act of aggression if the Security Council fails to act due to the veto.

83. **(A):** The United Kingdom (UK) does not provide any written constitutional guarantee of fundamental freedoms in the manner that codified constitutions like those of the United States or India do. The UK's constitution is not a single written document but comprises statutes, conventions, judicial decisions, and historical documents.

Fundamental freedoms in the UK are upheld through common law, statutory laws like the Human Rights Act 1998 (which incorporates the European Convention on Human Rights into British law), and other legislative acts, rather than a single written constitution guaranteeing these freedoms.

84. **(B):** The correct matches for UN days relating to Intellectual Property (IP) and Biological diversity are: World Intellectual

Property Day is observed on April 26 (IV), World Book and Copyright Day on April 23 (I), International Day for Biological Diversity on May 22 (II), and World Creativity and Innovation Day on April 21 (III). These days are set aside to raise awareness and promote the roles of intellectual property, copyright, biological diversity, and creativity and innovation in our lives and societies.

85. (A): The sequence of these landmark cases, in the order they were decided, is: Royal British Bank v. Turquand (1856), which established the "indoor management rule" or "Turquand's Rule"; Ashbury Railway Carriage Co. Ltd. v. Riche (1875), which related to the ultra vires doctrine in corporate law; Salomon v. Salomon Co. Ltd. (1897), a foundational case affirming the legal principle that a corporation has a separate legal personality from its members; Mohori Bibee v. Dharmodas Ghose (1903), which established the principle regarding minors' contracts; State Trading Corporation of India Ltd. v. CTO, Visakhapatnam (1963), which dealt with the legal status and rights of state trading corporations. This sequence highlights significant developments in corporate and contract law over more than a century.

86. (A): The cases decided by the Permanent Court of Arbitration are arranged in chronological order as follows:

(*a*) Muscat Dhows case (1905), where the dispute was about the seizure of vessels under a British blockade of Muscat;

(*b*) North Atlantic Fisheries case (1910), which dealt with fishing rights off the coast of Newfoundland between Great Britain and the United States;

(*c*) Savarkar's case (1911), concerning the escape and recapture of the Indian freedom fighter Vinayak Damodar Savarkar while in British custody;

(*d*) Russian Indemnity case (1912), which involved a dispute over indemnities following the Russo-Japanese War; and

(*e*) The Island of Palmas case (1928), a dispute between the United States and the Netherlands over sovereignty of the Island of Palmas.

This order highlights the breadth of international legal issues addressed by the Permanent Court of Arbitration in its early years.

87. (B)

88. (C): In Kaushal Kishore v. State of UP (2023), the Supreme Court of India clarified that the fundamental right under Article 19 is available against both state and non-state actors. This interpretation expands the scope of Article 19, traditionally seen as protecting rights such as freedom of speech and expression against state actions, to also include protection against actions by private individuals or entities that could infringe on these freedoms. This decision underscores the evolving understanding of fundamental rights in the context of contemporary challenges where private entities can significantly impact individuals' rights.

89. (A): According to John Austin's definition of ownership, the attributes of ownership include (*a*) indefinite user, (*c*) unrestricted disposition, and (*e*) unlimited duration. Austin's theory conceptualizes ownership as a comprehensive dominion over a thing, characterized by the owner's right to use the thing indefinitely, dispose of it freely, and possess it for an unlimited time. These attributes highlight the legal capacity to exercise full control over property, distinguishing ownership from lesser or more temporary interests in things, and reflecting a classical understanding of property rights as being absolute and extensive.

90. (D): The definition of nationality as "a continuing legal relationship between the sovereign state on the one hand and the citizen on the other, with the fundamental basis of a man's nationality being membership of an independent political community" was given by the British Mexican Claims Commission in the case of Re, Lynch. This definition encapsulates the essence of nationality, emphasizing its nature as a legal bond of allegiance and protection between an individual and a state, rooted in the individual's membership in the state's political community. This perspective underscores the reciprocal rights and duties inherent in the concept of nationality.

91. (A): The protection and enforcement of Human Rights under Article 32 of the Indian Constitution are confined specifically to Fundamental Rights.

92. (C): The notion that every citizen must do his duty towards the nation as well as fellow citizens is incorporated in Part IV A of the Indian Constitution, which is dedicated to "Fundamental Duties" as outlined in Article 51A.

93. (B): Part III and Part IV of the Constitution of India collectively discuss the vision of the Constitution and its framers regarding the kind of society they aspired to establish in the country.

94. (D): The harmony and balance between Part III (Fundamental Rights) and Part IV (Directive Principles of State Policy) of the Constitution is recognized as part of the basic structure of the Constitution.

95. (D): Fundamental Rights and Directive Principles are distinguished as the 'Conscience' of the Constitution. This designation highlights their collective importance in reflecting the constitutional values and ethical foundation of the Indian legal and political system.

96. (A): The author expresses a critical and negative view of the way the court uses the doctrines of 'Spirit of the Constitution' and of 'natural law' to circumscribe the Constitution itself.

97. (D): The greatest paradox identified by the author in the doctrine of basic features is that it does not constitute a limitation on the legislature while enacting ordinary legislation but operates as a limitation on the Constituent body, even though the Constituent body is recognized as a sovereign authority while the legislature is not.

98. (C): According to the author, when determining the validity of an ordinary law, the court can only look into the express provisions of the Constitution or the necessary implications thereof. This implies that the court's review is constrained to what is explicitly stated in the Constitution or can be directly inferred from its provisions, without invoking broader or external principles to assess the law's constitutionality.

99. (A): The author considers the doctrine used to circumscribe the Constitution to be the 'Spirit of the Constitution' and 'natural law'.

100. (C): As per the apprehension of the author, a court may travel beyond the express provisions of the Constitution to invoke some principles superior to the express provisions when the validity of a Constitution Amendment Act is challenged.

Previous Years' Paper

National Testing Agency (NTA)

UGC-NET Junior Research Fellowship & Assistant Professor Eligibility Exam

Law, June-2023

(Exam held on 16-06-2023)

PAPER-II

1. The theory of 'Separation of powers' is credited to:
   A. Aristotle B. Locke
   C. Montesquieu D. Kelsen

2. Who made the statement that "Jurisprudence is the study and systematic arrangement of the general principles of law"?
   A. R.W.M. Dias B. Julius stone
   C. Keeton C.G. D. E.W. Patterson

3. "International Law or the Law of the Nations is the name of the body of rules which according to the usual definition regulate the conduct of states in their intercourse with one another", who said it?
   A. oppenheim B. Lauterpatch
   C. Brierly D. Kelsen

4. In case of "tort of trespass", which of the following defence shall not apply?
   A. Statutory authority
   B. Contributory negligence
   C. Private defence
   D. Mesne profits

5. 'I promise to pay ₹ 5000 and to deliver to him my black horse on 1st January next'. This is an illustration for which of the following?
   A. A valid promissory note
   B. An invalid promissory note
   C. A valid bill of exchange
   D. An invalid bill of exchange

6. With respect to 'Daughters' under 'class I heirs' in the Hindu Succession Act, 1956, which one the following holds true?
   A. "Daughters" means natural born daughters and not adopted daughters
   B. Step daughter is included
   C. Daughter includes posthumous daughter
   D. Unchasity of daughter is a bar to inheritance

7. One of the heirs is not included in 'class I heirs' under the Hindu Succession (Amendment) Act, 2005?
   A. Daughter of a predeceased daughter of a pre-deceased daughter
   B. Daughter of a pre-deceased son of a pre-deceased daughter
   C. Son of a pre-deceased son of a pre-deceased daughter
   D. Son of a pre-deceased daughter of a pre-deceased daughter

8. 'The Grand function of the Law of Nature was discharged in giving birth to modern International Law', who said it?
   A. Oppenheim
   B. Henry Maine
   C. Holland
   D. H.L.A. Hart

9. The principle of *JUS COGENS* is incorporated in which Article of the Vienna Convention on Law of Treaties, 1969?
   A. Article 25
   B. Article 37
   C. Article 53
   D. Article 63

10. Which of the following is correct?
   A. "The only right which any man can possess is the right always to do his duty" is Duguit's Theory
   B. 'Social solidarity' a natural principle is given by Jurist Gierke
   C. Pound, legal philosophy is 'Utilitarianism'
   D. Austin said " Law is Social Engineering"

11. Resale share right in original copies under section 53A of the Copyright Act, 1957 is not applicable to:
   A. Original copy of painting
   B. Original copy of sculpture
   C. Original manuscript of a literary or dramatic work
   D. Cinematograph film

12. 'Voyeurism' for a second or subsequent conviction attracts a punishment of:
   A. Imprisonment of not less than 1 year but which may extend to 3 years and fine.
   B. Imprisonment of not less than 2 years but which may extend to 4 years and fine
   C. Imprisonment of not less than 3 years but which may extend to 7 years and fine
   D. Imprisonment of not less than 5 years but which may extend to 9 years and fine

13. The Motor Vehicle Act, 2019 has amended the following Act:
   A. The Motor Vehicle Act 1988
   B. The Motor Vehicle Act 1978
   C. The Motor Vehicle Act 1980
   D. The Motor Vehicle Act 1990

14. Which of the following theories of punishment provides that 'crime is a disease' and the object should be to 'cure disease'?
   A. Deterrent theory
   B. Reformative theory
   C. Expiatory theory
   D. Retributive theory

15. Which of the following legal maxims is not related to tort:
   A. *Ubi jus ibi remedium*
   B. *Volenti non fit injuria*
   C. *Res ipsa Loquitur*
   D. *Pari delicto*

16. Which one of the following is not covered by the schools of Jurisprudence?
   A. The Historical school
   B. The Realist school
   C. The Sociological school
   D. The Critical school

17. By which writ, the decision of the highest tribunal of a State can be revised?
   A. Mandamas
   B. Prohibition
   C. Certiorari
   D. Quowarranto

18. The Berne Convention, 1886 deals with:
   A. Copyright Law
   B. Trade Mark Law
   C. Designs Law
   D. Geographical Indications Law

19. The 'bailment of the goods', as security for payment of a debt or performance of a promise, is called:
   A. Indemnity B. Guarantee
   C. Mortgage D. Pledge

20. The following is known as to "SAFETY NET" of International Humanitarian Law:
   A. LEVEE EN MASSE
   B. HORS DE COMBAT
   C. HENRY DUNANTS CLAUSE
   D. MARTENS CLAUSE

21. The "ESTRADA DOCTRINE" was propounded by ESTRADA, who was:
A. The Foreign Minister of Spain
B. The Foreign Minister of France
C. The Foreign Minister of Mexico
D. The Foreign Minister of Malta

22. With respect to '*Muta* marriage' amongst Muslims, which of the following is/are correct:
A. Spouses have no right of mutual inheritance even if one of the spouses dies when if Muta is subsisting.
B. The husband has no right of 'talaq' though the parties are free to terminate it by mutual consent
C. The children of *Muta* marriage are illegitimate
D. Both (A) and (B)

23. The owner of the Copyright of the sound recording has which one of following right, under sec 14 (e) of the Copyright Act, 1957.
A. to encrypt the sound recording
B. to make any adaptation of the sound recording
C. to communicate the sound recording to the public
D. to make any translation of the work recorded in the sound recording

24. In which case the 'Principle of Prospective Overruling' was laid down?
A. S.P Gupta v. Union of India
B. I.C. Golaknath v. State of Punjab
C. Sunil Batra v. Delhi Administration
D. M.C Mehta v. Union of India

25. Who made the following statement "Life of law is not logic, it is experience"
A. Roscoe Pound
B. H. Kelsen
C. O.W Holmes (Jr)
D. John Austin

26. Which one of the following is incorrect:
A. Patents are granted to encourage inventions
B. Protection and enforcement of patents contribute to technological innovation
C. Patented invention shall be available at reasonable affordable price.
D. The invention shall be published before applying for patent.

27. Which of the following 'select combination' of words, from the Preamble of the Constitution of India, is in correct order?
A. "Fraternity assuring the integrity"
B. "Fraternity assuring the dignity"
C. "Fraternity assuring the unity"
D. "Fraternity assuring the unity and integrity"

28. Who made the following statement:

"Large part, and as many would add the best part of law of England is judge made law, that is to say, consists of rules to be collected fron the judgements of the courts"
A. Dicey B. Lord Denning
C. Bacon D. Bentham

29. Which of the following case is popularly known as 'Taj Trapezium' case?
A. *M.C Mehta v. Union of India & ors* (1997) 2 SCC 353
B. *Vineet Kumar Mathur v. Union of India* (1996) 7 SCC 714
C. *Okhla Bird Sanctuary v. Anand Arya* (2011) 7 SCC 74
D. *M.C Mehta v. Union of India* (AIR 1987 SC 1086)

30. Which Jurist gave the classification of the sources of law as (a) binding and (b) persuasive:
A. Keeton B. Salmond
C. Allen D. Rosco Pound

31. According to article 80 of the Constitution of India, the representatives of each state in the Council of States are elected by:
A. elected members of the Legislative Assembly of the State by majority vote through secret ballot.

B. all the members of the Legislative Assembly of the state by majority vote through secret ballot.
C. elected members of the Legislative Assembly of the State in accordance with system of proportional representation by means of the single transferable vote.
D. all the members of the Legislative Assembly of the State in accordance with system of proportional representation by means of the single transferable vote

32. Under which of the following principles is the "Polluter Pays Principle" is envisaged?
A. Principle 15, Earth Summit, 1992
B. Principle 1 & 2, Stockholm Declaration, 1972
C. Principle 16, Rio Declaration, 1992
D. Principle 5, Rio declaration, 1992

33. The strict adherence to the 'rule of *Locus standi*' was diluted first in:
A. *D.C Wadhwa* v. *State of Bihar*
B. *Parmanand Katara* v. *Union of India*
C. *Ratlam Municiple Council* v. *Vardichand*
D. *Vishakha* v. *State of Rajasthan*

34. Given below are two statements:

To constitute a tort:

Statement I: There must be some act or omission on the part of the defendant.

Statement II: The act or omission should result in legal damage

In the light of the above statements, choose the **correct** answer from the options given below.

A. Both Statement I and Statement II are true
B. Both Statement I and Statement II are false
C. Statement I is true, but Statement II is false
D. Statement I is false, but Statement II is true

35. Who wrote the book 'Concept of Law'?
A. Paton
B. Korkunor
C. Salmond
D. H.L.A Hart

36. In the light of which of the following Articles of the Constitution of India, the Environment (Protection) Act, 1986 was enacted:
A. Article 249 B. Article 250
C. Article 252 D. Article 253

37. In which of the following cases the Supreme Court observed that the noise pollution cannot be tolerated even if such noise was direct results of and was connected with religious activities?
A. *K.M Chinappa* v. *Union of India*
B. *A.P Pollution Control Board* v. *Prof. M.V Naidu*
C. *Church of God (Full Gospel) in India* v. *KKR Majestic Colony Welfare Association*
D. *Common Cause* v. *Union of India*

38. Which of the following Schedules of the National Green Tribunal (NGT) Act provides for the heads of the compensation:
A. Schedule IV B. Schedule II
C. Schedule III D. Schedule I

39. Section 28 of the Indian Forest Act, 1927 provides for:
A. Protected Areas
B. Reserved Forest
C. Village Forests
D. Power of Forest Settlement Officer

40. Given below are two statements: one is labelled as Assertion (A) and the other is labelled as Reason (R).

Assertion (A): The polluter pays principle says that the absolute liability for the harm to environment extends not only to compensate the victims of pollution but also to the cost of restoring the environment degradation.

Reason (R): The case *M.C. Mehta* v *Kamalnath* and other has decided so.

In the light of the above statements, choose the **most appropriate answer** from the options given below:

A. Both (A) and (R) are correct and (R) is the correct explanation of (A)
B. Both (A) and (R) are correct and (R) is NOT the correct explanation of (A)
C. (A) is correct, but (R) is not correct
D. (A) is not correct, but (R) is correct

41. Asha, a journalist employed, writes a story in the newspaper. Deepak makes a film based on the story. Raghu and Rekha plays the lead role in the film. The dance in the film is choreographed by Ajay.

(*a*) Asha is the author of literary work.
(*b*) Proprietor of the newspaper has copyright on the story, in the absence of a contract regarding copyright.
(*c*) Proprietor of the newspaper has only the Publication rights
(*d*) Raghu and Rekha have performer's right.
(*e*) Ajay is the author of musical work.

Choose the **correct** answer from the options given below:

A. (*a*), (*d*), and (*e*) only
B. (*a*), (*c*) and (*d*) only
C. (*b*) only
D. (*a*), (*c*), (*d*) and (*e*) only

42. About Administrative Tribunals, Supreme Court recommended in 2010 Madras Bar Association Case:

(*a*) The Tribunal should not become post-retirement heaven for civil servants.
(*b*) Members of the Tribunals should be independent person and not serving Civil servants.
(*c*) Members of Tribunal should retain lien in any government department.
(*d*) The Tribunal should resemble more the Courts and not bureaucratic boards.
(*e*) The Tribunals must depend on government for infrastructure facilities.

Choose the **correct** answer from the options given below:

A. (*a*), (*b*) and (*c*) only
B. (*a*), (*c*) and (*d*) only
C. (*c*), (*d*) and (*e*) only
D. (*a*), (*b*) and (*d*) only

43. (*a*) International Law recognises general duty of state in respect of extradition.
(*b*) International Law does not recognise general duty of state in respect of extradition.
(*c*) Extradition depends on the provision, of existing Extradition Treaties
(*d*) Countries may grant extradition without a Treaty
(*e*) Customary International Law governs extradition

Choose the **most appropriate answer** from the options given below:

A. (*a*), (*b*), (*d*) and (*e*) only
B. (*a*), (*c*), (*d*) and (*e*) only
C. (*b*), (*c*) and (*e*) only
D. (*b*), (*c*) and (*d*) only

44. As per Salmond, there are 4 distinct kinds of rights:

(*a*) Liberties (*b*) Rights
(*c*) Power (*d*) Immunities
(*e*) Kindness

Choose the **correct** answer from the options given below:

A. (*a*) and (*b*) only
B. (*a*), (*b*), (*c*) and (*d*) only
C. (*c*), (*d*) and (*e*) only
D. (*a*), (*b*), (*d*) and (*e*) only

45. With respect to valid conditions for Hindu Marriage, u/s 5 of the Hindu Marriage Act, 1955, which of the following are true:

(*a*) Neither party has a spouse living at the time of marriage
(*b*) Mental capacity
(*c*) Ceremonies of marriage
(*d*) Parties are not within prohibited degree
(*e*) No impotency

Choose the **correct** answer from the options given below:

A. (*a*), (*c*) and (*d*) only
B. (*a*), (*b*) and (*d*) only
C. (*b*), (*c*) and (*e*) only
D. (*a*), (*b*) and (*e*) only

46. (*a*) Treaties may be terminated
(*b*) Treaties cannot be terminated
(*c*) Treaties may be terminated by (i) operation of law and (ii) by act of state parties
(*d*) Importing of performance of a treaty is also a ground for the termination of treaty and the provisions is contained Art 51 of the Vienna Convention of Law of Treaties, 1969
(*e*) Importing of performance of a treaty is also a ground for the termination of treaty and the provisions is contained Art 57 of the Vienna Convention of Law of Treaties, 1969.

Choose the **correct** answer from the options given below:

A. (*a*), (*b*), (*c*) and (*e*) only
B. (*b*), (*c*) and (*d*) only
C. (*b*), (*c*) and (*e*) only
D. (*b*) and (*c*) only

47. Which of the following is true with regards to Iddat period?
(*a*) Iddat of widowhood is 4 months and 10 days
(*b*) the period of Iddat begins from the date when she comes to know of divorce and not from the date when divorce is pronounced
(*c*) If the marriage is irregular and is consummated, the wife is under obligation to observe Iddat
(*d*) If the wife observes Iddat husband is bound to maintain the wife during the period on Iddat
(*e*) In case the wife is pregnant, period of Iddat extends till the delivery of the child.

Choose the **most appropriate answer** from the options given below:

A. (*a*), (*b*), (*d*) and (*e*) only
B. (*a*), (*c*), (*d*) and (*e*) only
C. (*b*), (*c*), (*d*) and (*e*) only
D. (*b*) and (*d*) only

48. (*a*) Uniting for peace Resolution was passed in 1950
(*b*) Uniting for peace Resolution was passed by the General Assembly
(*c*) Uniting for peace Resolution was passed by the Security Council
(*d*) Maintenance of international peace and security is the primary responsibility of the Security Council
(*e*) Maintenance of international peace and security is the primary responsibility of the General Assembly

Choose the **correct** answer from the options given below:

A. (*a*), (*b*) and (*d*) only
B. (*a*), (*b*), (*c*) and (*d*) only
C. (*a*), (*b*), (*d*) and (*e*) only
D. (*a*), (*b*) and (*e*) only

49. Under article 51 of the Constitution of India the state is directed to endeavor to:
(*a*) Promote international peace and security
(*b*) Maintain just and honorable relations between nations
(*c*) Foster respect for international law and treaty obligations
(*d*) Protect and improve the environment and to safeguard forests
(*e*) Encourage settlement of international disputes through arbitration

Choose the **correct** answer from the options given below:

A. (*a*), (*b*), (*c*) and (*d*) only
B. (*a*), (*b*), (*c*) and (*e*) only
C. (*b*), (*c*), (*d*) and (*e*) only
D. (*a*), (*c*), (*b*) and (*d*) only

50. Which of the following can be registered as Trade Mark under the Trade Marks Act, 1999?

(*a*) RASOI for hydrogenated oil
(*b*) JHOOMRITALAIA for pens
(*c*) BANK for banking service
(*d*) Square shape for tyres
(*e*) Obscene matters (things)

Choose the **correct** answer from the options given below:

A. (*b*) only
B. (*a*), (*b*) and (*d*) only
C. (*b*) and (*d*) only
D. (*c*) and (*e*) only

51. The Corporate Social Responsibility (CSR) Committee of a Company carries out the following functions:

(*a*) To appoint an individual or a firm as an auditor
(*b*) To recommend a CSR Policy
(*c*) To recommend the amount of expenditure for the indicated activities
(*d*) To inspect the books of accounts during business hours
(*e*) To monitor the CSR policy of the company from time to time.

Choose the **correct** answer from the options given below:

A. (*a*), (*b*) and (*c*) only
B. (*b*) and (*d*) only
C. (*b*), (*c*) and (*e*) only
D. (*b*), (*c*), (*d*) and (*e*) only

52. In order to convert a proposal into a promise, the acceptance must be:

(*a*) Absolute
(*b*) Unqualified
(*c*) Conditional
(*d*) Random
(*e*) Expressed in some usual and reasonable manner

Choose the **correct** answer from the options given below:

A. (*a*) and (*b*) only
B. (*a*) and (*c*) only
C. (*a*), (*b*) and (*e*) only
D. (*b*), (*c*) and (*d*) only

53. Given below are two statements: one is labelled as Assertion (A) and the other is labelled as Reason (R).

Assertion (A): The Criminal Law Amendment Act, 2013 was a result of the public outrage.

Reason (R): Society forces the law to accept the change.

In the light of the above statements, choose the **correct** answer from the options given below.

A. Both (A) and (R) are true and (R) is the correct explanation of (A)
B. Both (A) and (R) are true, but (R) is NOT the correct explanation of (A)
C. (A) is true, but (R) is false
D. (A) is false, but (R) is true

54. Given below are two statements: one is labelled as Assertion (A) and the other is labelled as Reason (R).

Select the correct answer using the codes given below:

Assertion (A): Rights to pollution free air and clean water are attributes of the right of a dignified life.

Reason (R): These rights are the basic elements that sustain the life.

In the light of the above statements, choose the **most appropriate answer** from the options given below:

A. Both (A) and (R) are correct and (R) is the correct explanation of (A)
B. Both (A) and (R) are correct and (R) is NOT the correct explanation of (A)
C. (A) is correct, but (R) is not correct
D. (A) is not correct, but (R) is correct

55. (*a*) For State Legislature, Constitutional provisions for special address of the Governor, is in article 176.
(*b*) For State Legislature the Constitutional provisions for Oath or affirmation by members is in 109.
(*c*) For State Legislature the special procedure in respect of Money Bill is covered by article 198.
(*d*) For State Legislature provisions as to introduction and passing of bills is given in article 196.
(*e*) For State Legislature provision for disqualifications for membership are given in article 190.

Choose the **correct** answer from the options given below:
A. (*a*), (*b*) and (*c*) only
B. (*b*), (*c*) and (*d*) only
C. (*a*), (*d*) and (*e*) only
D. (*a*), (*c*) and (*d*) only

56. The following fall under chapter IV (General Exceptions) of the Indian Penal Code, 1860:
(*a*) Act done by a person bound, or by mistake of fact believing himself to be bound, by law
(*b*) Act of judge when acting judicially
(*c*) Omission to assist public servant when bound by law to give assistance
(*d*) International resistance or obstruction by a person to his lawful apprehension
(*e*) Accident in doing a lawful act

Choose the **correct** answer from the options given below:
A. (*a*) and (*e*) only
B. (*a*) and (*b*) only
C. (*b*) only
D. (*a*), (*b*) and (*e*) only

57. (*a*) Recognition de jure is final and once given cannot be withdrawn
(*b*) Recognition de jure is not final
(*c*) de facto recognition may be withdrawn
(*d*) Withdrawal of recognition by a state because that state has ceased to be the State
(*e*) Retroative recognition of a new government does not invalidate the acts of the previous de jure government

Choose the **correct** answer from the options given below:
A. (*a*), (*c*) and (*e*) only
B. (*b*), (*c*), (*d*) and (*e*) only
C. (*a*), (*b*), (*d*) and (*e*) only
D. (*a*), (*c*), (*d*) and (*e*) only

58. (*a*) Art. 2(4) of the UN Charter contains the proposition of the unilateral use of force or threat theory by states in their international relations.
(*b*) There are no exception to the above.
(*c*) UN Charter makes an exception to Art. 2(4) in individual and collective self defense as in Art. 51.
(*d*) States may use or encourage the use of economic and political measures to coerce another state.
(*e*) States have a duty to refrain from propaganda for wars of aggression.

Choose the **most appropriate answer** from the options given below:
A. (*a*), (*b*), (*d*) and (*e*) only
B. (*a*), (*c*), (*d*) and (*e*) only
C. (*a*), (*c*) and (*e*) only
D. (*b*), (*c*), (*d*) and (*e*) only

59. (*a*) The preamble of the UN Charter says : "We the peoples, of the United Nations"
(*b*) The preamble of the UN Charter says : "We the people of the United Nations"
(*c*) Maintenance of international peace and security is the primary responsibility of the Security Council.
(*d*) Maintenance of International peace and Security is the primary responsibility of the General Assembly.
(*e*) Maintenance of International peace and Security is the primary responsibility of the International Court of justice.

Choose the **most appropriate answer** from the options given below:

A. (*b*) and (*c*) only
B. (*a*) and (*c*) only
C. (*a*) and (*d*) only
D. (*b*) and (*e*) only

60. (*a*) The International Bank for Reconstruction and Development (IBRD) is also called the World Bank.
(*b*) The International Bank for Reconstruction and Development (IBRD) is also called the International Monetary Fund
(*c*) The Dunkel Draft Act embodies the results of the Tokyo Round
(*d*) The WTO provides for a Secretariat headed by a Director General
(*e*) The WTO provides for a Secretariat headed by Secretary General

Choose the **most appropriate answer** from the options given below:

A. (*a*), (*c*) and (*e*) only
B. (*a*) and (*e*) only
C. (*a*), (*c*) and (*d*) only
D. (*a*) and (*d*) only

61. With regards to cruelty under the Hindu Marriage Act, 1955 the following holds true
(*a*) It is very difficult to define cruelty which can fit in all circumstances.
(*b*) Cruelty can be physical and mental
(*c*) Intention plays an important role in cases on cruelty
(*d*) Cruelty should be aimed at the petitioner
(*e*) The act complained of must be that of the respondent

Choose the **correct** answer from the options given below:

A. (*a*), (*c*) and (*e*) only
B. (*a*) and (*b*) only
C. (*a*), (*b*) and (*d*) only
D. (*b*), (*c*) and (*d*) only

62. Under the Hindu Succession Act, 1956, heirs of a Hindu Male fall under following heads:
(*a*) Class I heirs
(*b*) Class II heirs
(*c*) Sharers
(*d*) Agnates
(*e*) Cognates

Choose the **correct** answer from the options given below:

A. (*a*), (*c*), (*d*) and (*e*) only
B. (*a*) and (*e*) only
C. (*a*), (*b*) (*d*) and (*e*) only
D. (*a*), (*d*) and (*e*) only

63. Following essentials are to be fulfilled for death to be called "Dowry death" under section 304 B of the Indian Penal Code.
(*a*) Death of a women within 10 years of her marriage
(*b*) fact of cruelty or harassment by her husband for or in connection with any demand for dowry
(*c*) Fact of cruelty or harassment by any relative of her husband for or in connection with any demand for dowry
(*d*) death of a women within 7 years of her marriage
(*e*) "Dowry shall have the same meaning as in section 2 of the Dowry Prohibition Act, 1961.

Choose the **correct** answer from the options given below:

A. (*b*) and (*d*) only
B. (*b*), (*c*), (*d*) and (*e*) only
C. (*a*), (*b*) and (*e*) only
D. (*b*), (*d*) and (*e*) only

64. Constitutional remedies include:
(*a*) Extraordinary remedies under Article 32 and 226
(*b*) Appeals to Supreme Court under Article 132 to 135
(*c*) Appeals to High Court under Article 139 to 139A
(*d*) Transfer of cases to Supreme Court under Article 139B
(*e*) Advisory Jurisdiction under Article 143

Choose the **correct** answer from the options given below:

A. (*a*), (*c*) and (*d*) only
B. (*a*), (*b*) and (*e*) only
C. (*b*), (*c*) and (*d*) only
D. (*c*), (*d*) and (*e*) only

65. Which of the following are fundamental rights?

(*a*) Right not to remain employed
(*b*) Right not to remain uneducated
(*c*) Right not to remain unmarried
(*d*) Right not to be killed without trial
(*e*) Right not to change religion

Choose the **most appropriate answer** from the options given below:

A. (*b*), (*d*) and (*e*) only
B. (*a*), (*c*) and (*d*) only
C. (*a*), (*d*) and (*e*) only
D. (*b*), (*c*) and (*e*) only

66. Match List-I with List-II.

List-I	List-II
(*a*) Soundness of mind	I. Sec. 14
(*b*) Fraud	II. Sec. 12
(*c*) Free consent	III. Sec. 11
(*d*) Competency to contract	IV. Sec. 17

Choose the **correct** answer from the options given below:

	(*a*)	(*b*)	(*c*)	(*d*)
A.	I	II	III	IV
B.	II	IV	I	III
C.	II	III	I	IV
D.	II	IV	III	I

67. Match List-I with List-II.

List-I	List-II
(*a*) Equal justice and free legal aid	I. Article 39A
(*b*) Promotion of Cooperative societies	II. Article 43
(*c*) Living wages etc for workers	III. Article 43B
(*d*) Uniform Civil Code for citizens	IV. Article 44

Choose the **correct** answer from the options given below:

	(*a*)	(*b*)	(*c*)	(*d*)
A.	II	III	I	IV
B.	III	I	II	IV
C.	I	III	II	IV
D.	I	II	III	IV

68. Match List-I with List-II.

List-I	List-II
(*a*) *Eastern Book Co* v. *D.B. Modak* (2006, SC)	I. Idea Expression Dichotomy
(*b*) *Bayer Corpn* v. *Union of India*	II. Minimum of creativity Test
(*c*) *R.G. Anand* v. *Deluxe Films* (1978 SC)	III. Prior user Test
(*d*) *N.R. Dongre* v. *Whirlpool Corpn.* (1996 SC)	IV. Compulsory license of patents

Choose the **correct** answer from the options given below:

	(*a*)	(*b*)	(*c*)	(*d*)
A.	I	II	III	IV
B.	II	IV	I	III
C.	IV	I	II	III
D.	III	I	II	IV

69. Match List-I with List-II.

List-I	List-II
(*a*) Asymmetric crypto-system	I. Neighboring rights
(*b*) Rome Convention	II. Industrial Property
(*c*) Paris Convention 1883	III. Trademarks
(*d*) Madrid Protocol	IV. Digital signature

Choose the **correct** answer from the options given below:

	(*a*)	(*b*)	(*c*)	(*d*)
A.	IV	I	III	II
B.	IV	II	I	III
C.	IV	I	II	III
D.	I	III	II	IV

70. Match List-I with List-II.

List-I	List-II
(*a*) Rule of specialty	I. Importance of the works of jurists
(*b*) Paquete Habana	II. Extradition
(*c*) Barcelona Traction case	III. Sources of International Law are not hierarchical but complimentary and inter related
(*d*) *Nicara Gua* v. *USA*	IV. Equity and Justice

Choose the **correct** answer from the options given below:

	(*a*)	(*b*)	(*c*)	(*d*)
A.	II	I	IV	III
B.	III	II	I	IV
C.	II	III	IV	I
D.	II	IV	III	I

71. Match List-I with List-II.

List-I	List-II
(*a*) Kyto Treaty on Climate Change	I. 1995
(*b*) International Convention on the Protection of the Rights of all Migrant Workers and members of Their Families	II. 1997
(*c*) SAARC Accord on Extradition	III. 1990
(*d*) WTO came into force in the year	IV. 1987

Choose the **correct** answer from the options given below:

	(*a*)	(*b*)	(*c*)	(*d*)
A.	II	III	IV	I
B.	IV	III	II	I
C.	III	IV	II	I
D.	II	I	IV	III

72. Match List-I with List-II.

List-I (Provison)	List-II (Section)
(*a*) Restitution of conjugal rights	I. Section 10, the Hindu Marriage Act, 1955
(*b*) Judicial separation	II. Section 12, the Hindu Marriage Act, 1955
(*c*) No petition for divorce within one year of marriage	III. Section 9, the Hindu Marriage Act, 1955
(*d*) Voidable marriage	IV. Section 14, the Hindu Marriage Act, 1955

Choose the **correct** answer from the options given below:

	(*a*)	(*b*)	(*c*)	(*d*)
A.	IV	III	I	II
B.	III	I	IV	II
C.	II	I	III	IV
D.	III	II	IV	I

73. Match List-I with List-II.

List-I	List-II
(*a*) *State of Rajasthan* v. *G. Chanda*	I. Pith and substance
(*b*) *K.T. Moopil Nair* v. *State of Kerala*	II. Colourable Legislation
(*c*) *O.N. Mahindroo* v. *Bar Council of Maharashtra* & Goa	III. Repugnancy
(*d*) *M. Karunanidhi* v. *Union of India*	IV. Harmonious construction

Choose the **correct** answer from the options given below:

	(*a*)	(*b*)	(*c*)	(*d*)
A.	I	II	III	IV
B.	II	I	IV	III
C.	IV	III	I	II
D.	I	II	IV	III

74. Match List-I with List-II.

List-I	List-II
(*a*) Rule of strict liability	I. Slander
(*b*) Publication of a defamatory statement	II. Rvlands v Fletcher
(*c*) Defamatory representation made in some permanent form	III. Act of God
(*d*) Vis Major	IV. Libel

Choose the **correct** answer from the options given below:

	(a)	(b)	(c)	(d)
A.	IV	I	II	III
B.	I	II	III	IV
C.	II	I	IV	III
D.	II	IV	I	III

75. Match List-I with List-II.

List-I	List-II
(a) Natural guardians of a Hindu minor	I. Section 8, Hindu Minority and Guardianship Act, 1956
(b) Powers of Natural Guardian	II. Section 9, Hindu Minority and Guardianship Act, 1956
(c) Testamentary guardians and their powers	III. Section 6, Hindu Minority and Guardianship Act, 1956
(d) Welfare of minor to be paramount consideration	IV. Section 13, Hindu Minority and Guardianship Act, 1956

Choose the **correct** answer from the options given below:

	(a)	(b)	(c)	(d)
A.	I	III	II	IV
B.	III	I	II	IV
C.	II	I	III	IV
D.	IV	II	I	III

76. Which is the correct chronological order (old to new) of the following judgements on appointment and transfer of judges?

(a) *S.P. Gupta* v. *Union of India*
(b) *Sakal Chand Seth* v. *Union of India*
(c) *Special Reference No 1 of 1998*
(d) *Supreme court Advocates on Record Association* v. *Union of India*

Choose the **correct** answer from the options given below:

A. (a), (c), (b), (d)
B. (b), (a), (d), (c)
C. (d), (b), (c), (a)
D. (a), (b), (c), (d)

77. Indicate the chronological order of the following:

(a) Treaty of westphalia
(b) Kellogg Brand port
(c) Brussels conference
(d) Convention of the statutes of Refugees
(e) Monterideo Convention

Choose the **correct** answer from the options given below:

A. (a), (b), (c), (e), (d)
B. (a), (e), (b), (c), (d)
C. (a), (c), (e), (b), (d)
D. (a), (c), (b), (e), (d)

78. Indicate the chronological order in which the following cases were decided:

(a) Fisheries jurisdiction (merit) case
(b) Island of palmas Arbitration case
(c) Numberg judgement
(d) Right of passage on Indian Testing case
(e) SS Lotus case

Choose the **correct** answer from the options given below:

A. (b), (e), (c), (d), (a)
B. (b), (c), (d), (e), (a)
C. (e), (b), (c), (d), (a)
D. (e), (c), (d), (b), (a)

79. Arrange the correct sequence in which an application for grant of Patent will be considered:

(a) Opposition under section 25(2) of the Patents Act, 1970
(b) Publication of application
(c) Filling of claims
(d) Request for examination
(e) Grant of patents

Choose the **correct** answer from the options given below:

A. (b), (d), (c), (a), (e)
B. (b), (a), (c), (d), (e)
C. (c), (b), (d), (e), (a)
D. (c), (a), (b), (d), (e)

80. Indicate the chronological order in which the following cases were decided:
(*a*) ELCAMANN's case
(*b*) Anglo Norwegian fisheries case
(*c*) Anglo Iranian Oil Company case
(*d*) Chorzow Factory case
(*e*) Western Sahara Case

Choose the **correct** answer from the options given below:
A. (*d*), (*c*), (*a*), (*b*), (*e*)
B. (*d*), (*b*), (*c*), (*a*), (*e*)
C. (*d*), (*a*), (*c*), (*b*), (*e*)
D. (*d*), (*a*), (*b*), (*c*), (*e*)

81. Arrange the expiry of the term of copyright in an ascending order in following cases:
(*a*) A writes a book on 1.10.2000 and dies on 2.10.2001
(*b*) A book is written by an anonymous author and published on 1.10.2000. The identity of the author is disclosed on 2.11.2000. Author dies on 3.12.2000
(*c*) A government work is published on 3.12.2000
(*d*) Author dies on 3.12.2002 and his work published on 2.1.2003
(*e*) A cinematograph film was published on 5.1.1999

Choose the **correct** answer from the options given below:
A. (*e*), (*d*), (*c*), (*b*), (*a*)
B. (*e*), (*c*), (*b*), (*a*), (*d*)
C. (*e*), (*a*), (*b*), (*d*), (*c*)
D. (*e*), (*c*), (*a*), (*b*), (*d*)

82. Matters covered under List-I of the Schedule VII of the Constitution:
(*a*) Foreign Loan (*b*) Public health
(*c*) Atomic energy (*d*) Public order
(*e*) Insurance

Choose the **most appropriate answer** from the options given below:
A. (*a*), (*b*) and (*c*) only
B. (*a*), (*c*) and (*e*) only
C. (*c*), (*d*) and (*e*) only
D. (*b*), (*c*) and (*d*) only

83. Under Article 15 of the Constitution of India, special provisions can be made about:
(*a*) Women and Children
(*b*) Scheduled Tribes
(*c*) Economically weaker sections
(*d*) Socially backward classes
(*e*) Linguistic minorities

Choose the **most appropriate answer** from the options given below:
A. (*a*), (*c*), (*b*) and (*e*) only
B. (*b*), (*c*), (*d*) and (*e*) only
C. (*a*), (*b*), (*c*) and (*d*) only
D. (*a*), (*b*), (*c*) and (*e*) only

84. Indicate the chronological order of the following:
(*a*) Genocide Convention
(*b*) Warsaw Pact
(*c*) Montreal Convention of Hijacking
(*d*) UN Convention on The Rights of the Child
(*e*) Vienna Convention on Diplomatic Relations

Choose the **correct** answer from the options given below:
A. (*a*), (*c*), (*b*), (*e*), (*d*)
B. (*a*), (*e*), (*b*), (*c*), (*d*)
C. (*a*), (*b*), (*e*), (*c*), (*d*)
D. (*a*), (*b*), (*c*), (*e*), (*d*)

85. Given below are two statements: one is labelled as Assertion (A) and the other is labelled as Reason (R).

Assertion (A): "Laws may be unjust though being opposed to the divine good; such laws are the laws of tyrants laws of this kind must no wise be observed.

Reason (R): Exterment order is of no effect and its violation is no offence.

In the light of the above statements, choose the **most appropriate answer** from the options given below.
A. Both (A) and (R) are correct and (R) is the correct explanation of (A)

B. Both (A) and (R) are correct and (R) is NOT the correct explanation of (A)
C. (A) is correct, but (R) is not correct
D. (A) is not correct, but (R) is correct

86. Given below are two statements: one is labelled as Assertion (A) and the other is labelled as Reason (R).

Assertion (A): From a functional point of view an administrative tribunal is neither exclusively a judicial body nor exclusively an administrative body but is somewhere between the two.

Reason (R): An administrative tribunal is not bound by strict rules of evidence and procedure.

In the light of the above statements, choose the **most appropriate answer** from the options given below:
A. Both (A) and (R) are correct and (R) is the correct explanation of (A)
B. Both (A) and (R) are correct and (R) is NOT the correct explanation of (A)
C. (A) is correct, but (R) is not correct
D. (A) is not correct, but (R) is correct

87. Given below are two statements: one is labelled as Assertion (A) and the other is labelled as Reason (R).

Assertion (A): Multilateral treaties which declare the established customary international law may bind even non parties.

Reason (R): Art. 38 of the Vienna Convention makes an exception to Article 34 or 37 of the Vienna Convention.

In the light of the above statements, choose the **most appropriate answer** from the options given below.
A. Both (A) and (R) are correct and (R) is the correct explanation of (A)
B. Both (A) and (R) are correct and (R) is NOT the correct explanation of (A)
C. (A) is correct, but (R) is not correct
D. (A) is not correct, but (R) is correct

88. Given below are two statements: one is labelled as Assertion (A) and the other is labelled as Reason (R).

Assertion (A): Mr X hands over a machine to Y, a common carrier. to deliver without any delay to the mill of Mr. X. Y unreasonably delays' the delivery of the machine despite being informed that the mill is locked due to lack of machine. As a consequence Mr. X lose a government contract. He is entitled to receive compensation that includes the average amount of profit which he would have made during the time for which the delivery was delayed but not the loss sustained through the lose of the Government contract.

Reason (R): Compensation for the loss or damage caused by breach of contract is not to be given for any remote and indirect loss or damage sustained due to such breach.

In the light of the above statements, choose the **most appropriate answer** from the options given below.
A. Both (A) and (R) are correct and (R) is the correct explanation of (A)
B. Both (A) and (R) are correct and (R) is NOT the correct explanation of (A)
C. (A) is correct, but (R) is not correct
D. (A) is not correct, but (R) is correct

89. Given below are two statements: one is labelled as Assertion (A) and the other is labelled as Reason (R).

Assertion (A): The Supreme Court in *Dev Dutta* v. *Union of India* (2008) emphasised that now transparency and good governance have been added as a new dimension to natural justice which includes the duty to give reason.

Reason (R): Reason reassure that discretion has been exercised by the decision maker on relevant grounds and by disregarding extraneous considerations.

In the light of the above statements, choose the **most appropriate answer** from the options given below:

A. Both (A) and (R) are correct and (R) is the correct explanation of (A)
B. Both (A) and (R) are correct and (R) is NOT the correct explanation of (A)
C. (A) is correct, but (R) is not correct
D. (A) is not correct, but (R) is correct

90. Given below are two statements: one is labelled as Assertion (A) and the other is labelled as Reason (R).

Assertion (A): Art. 38 (2) of the Statute of the I.C.J states, that "Provision in Ait 38 (1) shall not prejudice the power, of the court to decide a case EX AEQUO ET BONO if parties agree thereto."

Reason (R): EX AEQUO ET BONO enable the court to decide upon considerations of fair dealing and good faith. Which may be independent or even contrary to law.

In the light of the above statements, choose the **most appropriate answer** from the options given below.

A. Both (A) and (R) are correct and (R) is the correct explanation of (A)
B. Both (A) and (R) are correct and (R) is NOT the correct explanation of (A)
C. (A) is correct, but (R) is not correct
D. (A) is not correct, but (R) is correct

Directions (Qs. No. 91-95): *Read the following passage carefully and answer the question.*

One is that power should not be exercised arbitrarily. This has meant that it should be exercised for the purpose for which it has been conferred. It also means that power should be exercised with in the statutory ambit; and purported exercise of it would not just be ultra vires, but in true sense of the term arbitrary. Simple negation of arbitrariness is, however, not enough to preserve the Rule of Law values. Indian courts have gone further to insists on specific positive content of the Rule of Law obligations. These include the rules of nature justice which have to be followed not just in quasi-judicial action but often also in purely administrative action. The scope and content of the requirements of natural justice have varied from time to time according to the judicial interpretation, but the board insistence remains. In addition, access to information as to the grounds of decision has remained an important preoccupation of the Indian judiciary, as any impediments to it have the tendency of obstructing judicial review of administrative action.

This means that the courts have from time to time insisted that exercise of administrative power be accompanied by reasons, although the exact status of the obligation to give reason is as yet indeterminate. The Rule of Law notion has been in addition consistently extended to secure for the individual fair dealing by the state in its economic activities.

91. Under what circumstances powers should be exersised arbitrarily?

A. Under limited circumstances
B. Under unlimited circumstances
C. Under no circumstances
D. As per the policy of the government

92. Rule of Law implies

A. No one is above law
B. Some people are above law
C. Everybody is above law
D. Only Government is above law

93. Rule of law is:

A. Negation of arbitrariness
B. Oppsomal of arbitrariness
C. Simple negation of arbitrariness
D. Violation of natural justice

94. Specific positive content of the rule of law is:

A. Must be complied with
B. May not be complied with
C. Complied in limited content
D. Complied under modified circumstances

95. Rule of Law notion is extended to secure:
A. fair dealing by State in limited activities
B. fair dealing by State in all its activities
C. fair dealing by State only in the economic activities
D. State has no concern

Directions (Qs. No. 96-100): *Read the passage carefully and answer the question.*

"Where a legal wrong or legal injury is caused to a person or to a determinate class of person by reason of violation of any Constitutional or Legal right and such person or determinate class of persons is by reason of poverty, helplessness or disability or socially or economically disadvantaged position unable to approach the court for relief, any member of the public can maintain an application for an appropriate direction or order or writ in the High Court under Article 226 or in case of breach of any Fundamental Right to this court under Article 32. Where the weaker section of the community are concerned such as undertrial prisoners languishing in jails without a trial, inmates of the protective Home in Agra, or Harijan workers engaged in road construction in the District of Ajmer, who are living in poverty and desolation, who are barely eking out a miserable existence with their sweat and toil, who are helpless victims of an exploitative society and who do not have easy access to justice, the Supreme Court will not insist on a regular writ petition to be filed by the public spirited individual espousing their cause and seeking relief for them. The Supreme court will readily respond to the letter addressed by such individual acting *pro bono piblico*. It is true that there are rules made by the Supreme Court prescribing the procedure for moving it for relief under Article 32 and they require various formalities to be gone through by a person seeking to approach it. But it must not be forgotten that procedure is but a handmaid of justice and the cause of justice may never be allowed to be wasted by any procedural technicalities. The Court will therefore unhesitatingly cast aside the technical rules of procedure in the exercise of its dispensing power and treat the letter of the public minded individual as a writ-petition and act upon it."

96. Choose the first case in which the Public Interest Litigation (PIL) was invoked:
A. *Sheela Barse* v. *UOI*
B. *Bandua Mukti Morcha* v. *UOI*
C. *P.U.D.R.* v. *UOI*
D. *Mumbai Kamgar Sabha* v. *Abdul Bhai*

97. PIL cases are:
A. Private Interest cases
B. Personal Interest cases
C. Public Interest cases
D. Permanent Interest cases

98. Under which Article of the constitution of India, one can maintain an application to the Supreme Court for an appropriate remedy in PIL cases:
A. Article 226 B. Article 21
C. Article 19 D. Article 32

99. Article 32 requires various procedural formalities to be gone through by a person seeking to approach the Supreme Court.
(*a*) It is necessary to follow all technical formalities even in PIL cases
(*b*) It is not necessary to follow the technical formalities in such cases
(*c*) The Supreme Court may even treat a letter addressed to it as writ petition in PIL
(*d*) Rule of *locus* standi is not relaxed in such cases

Choose the correct option(s):
A. Only (*b*) is correct
B. Only (*b*) and (*c*) are correct
C. Only (*c*) is correct
D. Only (*a*) and (*b*) are correct

100. In PIL cases the Supreme Court on a regular writ petition has insisted that it should be filed by a public spirited individual espousing the cause. Choose the correct option:
A. Supreme Court will insists always
B. Supreme Court may waive this
C. Supreme Court can not insist
D. Person filing the petition should be related to the aggrieved party

ANSWERS

1. **(C):** The theory of Separation of Powers, credited to the 18th-century political philosopher Charles-Louis de Secondat, Baron de Montesquieu, forms a foundational concept in modern political theory and constitutional governance. Montesquieu articulated this theory in his influential work, "The Spirit of the Laws" (1748). The essence of Separation of Powers lies in the distribution of governmental authority across distinct branches—legislative, executive, and judicial—each possessing specific functions and acting as a check on the powers of the others. Montesquieu argued that this division prevents the concentration of power in a single entity, thereby safeguarding against tyranny and abuse. The legislative branch formulates laws, the executive branch enforces them, and the judicial branch interprets and applies them.

2. **(C):** The statement, "Jurisprudence is the study and systematic arrangement of the general principles of law", is commonly attributed to George William Keeton, a renowned British legal scholar known for his work on jurisprudence and constitutional law. While several legal minds have grappled with defining the essence of jurisprudence, Keeton's succinct and elegant articulation captures its core purpose - a critical examination and comprehensive organization of the fundamental principles that underpin legal systems. Keeton's articulation captures the essence of jurisprudence as a critical interrogation and meticulous ordering of the foundational principles that guide legal systems. It emphasizes the analytical and organizational aspects of the field, seeking to illuminate the bedrock upon which legal structures are built. Therefore, attributing the quote to Keeton is akin to acknowledging a foundational brick in a magnificent edifice.

3. **(D):** Navigating the intricate landscape of international legal thought to pinpoint the precise authorship of the quote "International Law or the Law of the Nations is the name of the body of rules which, according to the usual definition, regulate the conduct of states in their intercourse with one another" involves a nuanced exploration through the intellectual contributions of eminent legal scholars. While resonances of this sentiment reverberate across the works of various luminaries, the distinctive phrasing and historical context particularly align with the legal theorist Hans Kelsen. In his seminal work, "General Theory of Law and State" (1945), Kelsen meticulously dissects legal concepts, unveiling a decentralized legal order where customary norms and treaties interweave to govern the interactions between nations. The qualifier "usual definition" reflects Kelsen's acknowledgment of the dynamic nature of international law, evolving through state practice and academic discourse.

4. **(B):** In the context of the tort of trespass, the defense of contributory negligence is not applicable. Trespass, as an intentional tort, involves the deliberate and unauthorized interference with another person's property or person. Contributory negligence, on the other hand, is a defense typically associated with negligence cases, where the plaintiff's own actions contribute to their harm. In cases of trespass, the focus is on the intentional nature of the act rather than any negligence on the part of the plaintiff. The defense of contributory negligence is more relevant in situations where the defendant is being accused of negligence, not deliberate wrongdoing.

5. **(B):** The statement "I promise to pay ₹ 5000 and to deliver to him my black horse on 1st January next". This statement serves as an example of an invalid promissory note for several interrelated reasons, delving deeper beyond the mere presence of two promises. Firstly, the cornerstone of a valid promissory note lies in its unconditional undertaking to pay a specific sum of money. While the statement clearly promises ₹ 5000, it complicates matters by introducing the conditional element of delivering a black horse. This conditional clause, essentially a separate promise, undermines the unconditional nature of the monetary payment, rendering the instrument invalid as a promissory note. Secondly, this specific context aligns with the legal framework in India, where the Negotiable Instruments Act, 1881 governs such instruments. Section 4 of this Act explicitly defines a promissory note as an unconditional undertaking for a certain sum of money only. The dual nature of the promise in this case, encompassing both money and a horse, directly violates this core principle.

6. **(C):** Within the framework of "class I heirs" as defined by the Hindu Succession Act, 1956, the term "daughters" is expansively construed to encompass not only natural-born daughters but also extends to posthumous daughters. This signifies that a daughter born after the demise of the Hindu individual in question is accorded the same inheritance rights as daughters born during the deceased's lifetime. The inclusivity of posthumous daughters in the class I heirs category reflects a legal recognition of their entitlement to ancestral property and other assets, aligning with the broader objective of fostering fairness and equality within the familial succession framework. By explicitly acknowledging the inheritance rights of posthumous daughters, the Hindu Succession Act ensures that the timing of birth does not serve as a discriminatory factor, reinforcing the principle of equitable distribution of familial assets among all eligible heirs, regardless of the chronological order of their birth in relation to the demise of the ancestral Hindu individual.

7. **(C):** "Son of a pre-deceased son of a pre-deceased daughter", signifies a descendant who is the grandson of a woman who passed away before the enactment of the Hindu Succession (Amendment) Act, 2005. The amendment sought to revolutionize inheritance laws within Hindu families, introducing a more equitable distribution of property among heirs, irrespective of gender. However, in the case of the specified option, the grandson, being the son of a son from a pre-deceased daughter, appears to fall outside the ambit of 'class I heirs' as delineated by the amendment. This exclusion points to the intricacies involved in defining the classes of heirs and demonstrates the challenges in accommodating every conceivable familial relationship within legal frameworks. While the amendment has notably expanded the scope of inheritance, certain lineages, like the son of a pre-deceased son of a pre-deceased daughter, remain excluded from the specific class I heirs, emphasizing the importance of careful examination and interpretation of the legislative provisions.

8. **(B):** The assertion that "The Grand function of the Law of Nature was discharged in giving birth to modern International Law" is attributed to Sir Henry Sumner Maine, a distinguished British legal scholar and anthropologist. Maine's insight reflects a historical perspective on the evolution of international law, positing that the foundational principles of this legal framework find their roots in the broader concept of the Law of Nature. According to Maine, the emergence of

modern international law can be seen as a natural progression from the fundamental principles embedded in the Law of Nature, which historically governed relations between sovereign entities. This perspective underscores the organic development of international legal norms and institutions, suggesting a continuity between the broader principles of natural law and the more specific rules that define the conduct of nations in the contemporary global context.

9. (C): The principle of Jus Cogens finds its place within Article 53 of the Vienna Convention on the Law of Treaties, 1969. This significant provision establishes a fundamental norm in international law by acknowledging the existence of peremptory norms or principles that are non-derogable, compelling, and universally recognized. Jus Cogens refers to compelling norms that hold such inherent importance that no treaty or agreement can permit actions that would violate these fundamental principles. According to Article 53, a treaty is void if it conflicts with a peremptory norm of general international law (Jus Cogens). These norms are considered paramount and prevail over conflicting provisions in any treaty.

10. (A): "The only right which any man can possess is the right always to do his duty" is entirely accurate in representing Duguit's theory. While it captures part of his emphasis on social solidarity and individual responsibility, it simplifies his nuanced position on rights and duties. Duguit did entirely negate individual rights. He believed individuals hold both rights and duties within the framework of social solidarity. His argument focused on the interconnectedness of individuals and society, positing that individual rights only have meaning within the context of fulfilling one's social function. Instead of absolute individual rights, Duguit emphasized the functional role individuals play in contributing to the collective good. He championed the idea of each individual performing their social function effectively, which would in turn ensure the well-being of the entire society. He argued that rights emerge from and are conditioned by fulfilling one's social function within a specific society.

11. (D): Under Section 53A of the Copyright Act, 1957, the resale share right, which grants the original copyright owner a percentage of the resale value of certain works, does not extend to cinematograph films. This provision is designed to recognize and compensate creators for the ongoing economic value of their works, particularly in the art market. While the resale right applies to original copies of paintings, sculptures, and original manuscripts of literary or dramatic works, cinematograph films are excluded from this provision. The exclusion of films from the resale share right reflects the distinctive nature of the film industry and the complexities involved in implementing resale royalties in that context.

12. (C): In the legal context of voyeurism under Section 354C of the Indian Penal Code, the punishment for a second or subsequent conviction signifies the gravity with which the legal system addresses repeated offenses of this nature. Voyeurism involves the intrusive act of observing or recording an individual during private moments without their consent, constituting a significant infringement upon personal privacy. The legal framework acknowledges the violation inherent in such behavior and emphasizes the need for stringent consequences to deter potential offenders. The graduated scale of punishment, with imprisonment ranging from three to seven years and the imposition of fines, underscores society's commitment to safeguarding individual privacy rights. By imposing more severe penalties for subsequent convictions, the law aims not only to punish offenders but also to discourage the recurrence of voyeuristic acts, sending a clear message about the unacceptability of violating personal boundaries.

13. **(A):** The Motor Vehicle Act, 2019, introduced substantial amendments to the existing legal framework, specifically impacting the Motor Vehicle Act of 1988. This legislative overhaul aimed to address contemporary challenges and enhance road safety measures in India. The amendments encompassed a wide range of issues, including stricter penalties for traffic offenses, the incorporation of technology for better enforcement, provisions for the protection of Good Samaritans, and the promotion of intelligent transport systems.

14. **(B):** The reformative theory of punishment operates on the premise that crime is a societal ill or "disease", and the primary goal of the criminal justice system should be the rehabilitation and reformation of offenders. This theory deviates from traditional punitive approaches and retribution-focused ideologies. Instead of merely punishing individuals for their transgressions, the reformative theory seeks to address the underlying causes of criminal behavior, aiming to effect positive change in the offender. It envisions the correctional system as a means to provide education, counseling, vocational training, and psychological support, fostering the rehabilitation and personal growth of individuals. The emphasis is on guiding offenders towards reintegration into society as law-abiding citizens, with an understanding that addressing the root causes of criminality contributes to long-term crime prevention.

15. **(D):** "Pari delicto" is a Latin term in contract law that expresses the principle of equal fault or wrongdoing. It suggests that when both parties to a contract engage in illegal or wrongful conduct that goes against the terms of the contract, neither party can seek legal remedies against the other. Essentially, it means that if both parties are equally at fault, the law will not intervene to resolve their dispute. This doctrine promotes fairness and discourages parties from seeking relief from their own wrongful actions. However, it's important to note that there are exceptions and nuances to this principle depending on the specific circumstances of each case and the applicable laws.

16. **(D):** The Critical school of jurisprudence is often considered distinct from the traditional schools of jurisprudence, and it challenges established legal norms by critically examining the socio-political context in which laws operate. Unlike the Historical, Realist, and Sociological schools, the Critical school does not primarily focus on the historical development, empirical observations, or sociological aspects of the legal system. Instead, it delves into a critical analysis of power structures, ideologies, and the inherent biases within the legal framework. The Critical school, drawing inspiration from critical legal studies and critical theory, questions the very foundations of law, shedding light on how legal principles may perpetuate social inequalities or reinforce existing power dynamics.

17. **(C):** The writ of Certiorari, derived from Latin and signifying "to be informed", plays a pivotal role in the legal landscape by providing a mechanism for the revision of decisions handed down by the highest tribunal of a state. This extraordinary remedy enables superior courts to thoroughly

review and potentially annul judgments or orders issued by lower courts, particularly those where there are concerns about jurisdictional errors, legal irregularities, or violations of natural justice. By wielding the power of Certiorari, higher courts can scrutinize the proceedings of lower tribunals and ensure that the rule of law is upheld. This writ serves as a crucial check on the exercise of judicial authority, promoting transparency, accountability, and the fair administration of justice.

18. (A): The Berne Convention for the Protection of Literary and Artistic Works, established in 1886, is a landmark international treaty that primarily focuses on copyright law. This convention, named after the Swiss city where it was first adopted, sets out comprehensive standards for the protection of the rights of authors in their literary and artistic works. The central principle of the Berne Convention is the recognition of automatic protection for the works of authors without the need for formalities such as registration. It establishes a minimum level of protection that member countries must afford to the works of authors from other member countries, fostering international cooperation in the field of copyright.

19. (D): The term describing the 'bailment of goods' as collateral for the repayment of a debt or the fulfillment of a promise is known as "pledge". In a pledge arrangement, a person, often referred to as the pledgor, delivers movable property or goods to another party, known as the pledgee, as security for a debt or the discharge of some obligation. The act of pledging involves the transfer of possession without transferring ownership, and the pledged goods serve as a form of guarantee. This arrangement provides a mechanism for lenders or creditors to secure their interests by holding a possessory interest in the pledged goods until the debt is repaid or the promised performance is completed.

20. (D): The "Martens Clause" is often referred to as the "safety net" of International Humanitarian Law (IHL). Named after the Russian diplomat and legal scholar Fyodor Martens, this clause was first introduced in the preamble to the 1899 Hague Convention. It essentially serves as a fallback provision, stating that in situations not expressly covered by existing laws and conventions, civilians and combatants remain under the protection and principles of the laws of humanity and the dictates of the public conscience. The Martens Clause reflects a commitment to ensuring ethical considerations and human rights are upheld even in situations where specific legal provisions may be absent or unclear.

21. (C): The "Estrada Doctrine", named after Genaro Estrada, who served as the Foreign Minister of Mexico in the early 20th century, is a diplomatic principle that underscores the concept of non-intervention and non-recognition in the affairs of other nations. This doctrine, formally articulated in the 1930s, particularly during Estrada's tenure, emphasizes a policy of abstaining from interfering in the internal matters of other sovereign states and refraining from passing judgment on their governments. It asserts that a state should recognize the de facto government in power, regardless of its political ideology or legitimacy, as long as it effectively exercises control within its territory. The Estrada Doctrine aims to foster peaceful relations between nations by avoiding interference in their domestic affairs, advocating for diplomacy over intervention, and recognizing the autonomy of states to manage their own governance without external pressures or judgments.

22. (D): In Muta marriages among Muslims, both statements (1) and (2) hold true, reflecting the unique characteristics of this form of marriage. Firstly, spouses in a Muta marriage have no right of mutual inheritance even if one of the spouses dies while the Muta marriage is subsisting. This is in contrast to permanent marriages in Islamic law, where inheritance rights are recognized. Secondly, in Muta marriages, the husband does not have the traditional right of 'talaq' or divorce, as Muta marriages are temporary unions with a predetermined duration. Instead, the termination of a Muta marriage is subject to mutual consent between the parties involved. This distinguishes Muta marriages from permanent marriages, where the husband retains the right of divorce through the process of 'talaq'.

23. (C): Under Section 14(*e*) of the Copyright Act, 1957, the exclusive right granted to the owner of the copyright of a sound recording to communicate the work to the public holds significant implications in the modern era of diverse media platforms. This right extends to the power to transmit or broadcast the sound recording through a broad spectrum of mediums, including traditional broadcasting channels, online streaming services, or any other technology facilitating public access to the recorded sound. In the contemporary digital landscape, where music and other audio content are widely disseminated through various channels, this right becomes particularly crucial. It enables the copyright owner to manage and authorize how their work is shared with the public, safeguarding their creative investment from unauthorized use.

24. (B): The principle of Prospective Overruling was laid down in the landmark case of I.C. Golaknath v. State of Punjab. This legal doctrine represents a departure from the conventional understanding of judicial decisions and their retroactive application. In the Golaknath case, the Supreme Court of India introduced the idea that when the court overrules its previous decision, the overruling would only apply prospectively, meaning it would affect cases arising in the future and not those that had already been decided or were pending. The Golaknath case, with its introduction of Prospective Overruling, had a lasting impact on the jurisprudential landscape in India, influencing how courts handle the dynamics of legal precedent and adapt to evolving legal and social contexts.

25. (C): The statement "Life of law is not logic, it is experience" is famously attributed to Oliver Wendell Holmes Jr., a distinguished American jurist. This profound insight encapsulates Holmes's legal philosophy, which emphasizes the dynamic and evolving nature of the law. Holmes asserted that the law is not merely a product of logical deduction or abstract reasoning but is deeply intertwined with the lived experiences, social realities, and cultural contexts of individuals. According to him, the law is shaped by the collective experiences of a society, adapting and evolving as societal values and circumstances change. This perspective challenges a rigidly formalistic understanding of legal principles, acknowledging the importance of pragmatism and the real-world impact of legal decisions.

26. (D): The incorrect statement among the options provided is the fourth one, "The invention shall be published before applying for a patent". In the patent system, it is a fundamental principle that inventors are not required to publish their inventions before applying for a patent. On the contrary, one of the primary purposes of the patent system is to incentivize innovation by providing inventors with a mechanism to secure exclusive rights to their inventions before disclosing them to the public. The patent application process involves submitting a detailed and comprehensive description of the invention to the relevant patent office, which conducts a thorough examination. If the application meets the patentability criteria, the patent is granted, and the details of the invention become public at that point.

27. **(B):** "Fraternity assuring the dignity", encapsulates a profound commitment within the Preamble to the Constitution of India. The term "fraternity" signifies a sense of brotherhood and unity, emphasizing the collective spirit that binds the diverse population of the nation. This commitment is further nuanced by the phrase "assuring the dignity", reflecting the constitutional resolve to protect and promote the inherent dignity of every individual. The notion of dignity extends beyond mere legal or political considerations; it encompasses the recognition and affirmation of the intrinsic worth and equality of all citizens. Therefore, this combination in the Preamble underscores the vision of a society where unity and brotherhood are not only valued but are also instrumental in ensuring that each individual is treated with respect and is afforded the protection of their inherent dignity.

28. **(A):** The statement, attributed to A.V. Dicey, underscores the significance of judge-made law within the legal framework of England. A.V. Dicey, a prominent legal scholar, acknowledged that a substantial and arguably the most valuable portion of English law is derived from the judgments rendered by the courts. This perspective aligns with the common law tradition, emphasizing the role of precedent and judicial decisions in shaping and evolving legal principles. Dicey's observation highlights the dynamic nature of the legal system, where judges contribute significantly to the development of legal rules through their interpretations and applications of the law in specific cases. It reflects the idea that, in addition to statutory law, the evolving body of judge-made law is a crucial aspect of the English legal landscape, serving as a source of legal principles and precedents that guide subsequent legal decisions and interpretations.

29. **(A):** The "Taj Trapezium Case" (M.C. Mehta v. Union of India & ors, 1997) gained its popular designation due to its central focus on protecting the iconic Taj Mahal and the surrounding region from environmental degradation. The case revolved around the adverse impact of industrial pollution on the white marble of the Taj Mahal in Agra. The Supreme Court of India, in its judgment, recognized the cultural and environmental significance of the Taj Mahal and designated the affected area as the 'Taj Trapezium Zone'. The court took stringent measures to address pollution concerns, ordering the closure or relocation of industries contributing to air pollution in the region.

30. **(A):** According to Keeton, the sources of law can be broadly categorized into two main types: binding sources and persuasive sources. Binding sources are further classified as precedents, legislation, judicial opinions, and customary law. Precedents refer to decisions made in previous cases that serve as a basis for current judgments. Legislation encompasses laws enacted by the state, and judicial opinions involve the decisions of courts. Customary law refers to practices and traditions recognized as legally binding. On the other hand, persuasive sources, according to Keeton, include principles of equity, professional writings, and opinions of jurists. Keeton acknowledges that in modern times, the

state is the only formal source of law, but he argues that considering the state as a source is somewhat misleading since it primarily enforces the correct law rather than being a source in the truest sense. In his perspective, persuasive sources become relevant when there is no binding source of law, emphasizing their utility in legal reasoning.

31. **(C):** Article 80 of the Constitution of India outlines the process for electing representatives of each state to the Council of States (Rajya Sabha). According to this article, members are elected by the elected members of the Legislative Assembly of the State using the system of proportional representation by means of the single transferable vote. This method seeks to ensure a nuanced representation in the Rajya Sabha, as it allows voters to prioritize and rank their choices, and seats are allocated in proportion to the number of votes received by each candidate or party. The single transferable vote system accommodates diverse political ideologies within the Legislative Assembly, promoting a fair distribution of seats based on the preferences of the electorate.

32. **(C):** The "Polluter Pays Principle", articulated in Principle 16 of the Rio Declaration on Environment and Development in 1992, embodies a fundamental environmental concept. This principle underscores the idea that those who cause pollution or environmental degradation should bear the associated costs and responsibilities. It aligns with the broader objective of sustainable development, emphasizing the integration of environmental protection and economic growth. Principle 16 serves as a guide for policy formulation, encouraging governments and industries to internalize environmental costs and promote responsible practices. By placing the financial burden on the entities responsible for pollution, the principle aims to incentivize cleaner technologies, sustainable resource management, and a proactive approach to preventing environmental harm.

33. **(C):** The case of Ratlam Municipal Council v. Vardichand is a landmark judgment in Indian jurisprudence that significantly diluted the strict adherence to the 'rule of Locus standi.' Prior to this case, the concept of locus standi required individuals to demonstrate a personal stake or interest in a case in order to have standing to bring legal action. However, in Ratlam Municipal Council v. Vardichand, the Supreme Court of India recognized the importance of allowing public-spirited individuals to bring actions in the interest of the public or on behalf of those who may not be able to seek legal recourse themselves. This decision expanded the scope of locus standi, paving the way for public interest litigation (PIL) and enabling individuals and organizations to address issues of broader societal concern through the courts, even if they were not directly affected parties.

34. **(A): Statement I:** There must be some act or omission on the part of the defendant. This statement is true. This means that for a tort to occur, the defendant (the person accused of wrongdoing) must have either done something that he/she was not supposed to do (a wrongful act) or failed to do something that he/she was obligated to do (an omission). The defendant's conduct is a crucial factor in determining whether a tort has occurred.

Statement II: The act or omission should result in legal damage. This statement is also true. For a situation to qualify as a tort, the wrongful act or omission must lead to harm or injury that is recognized and remediable by law. This harm could be physical injury, damage to property, financial loss, or harm to one's reputation. The legal system provides a means for the injured party to seek compensation or remedy for the recognized harm caused by the defendant's actions or negligence.

35. (D): The Concept of Law is a 1961 book by the legal philosopher H.L.A. Hart and his most famous work. The Concept of Law presents Hart's theory of legal positivism—the view that laws are rules made by humans and that there is no inherent or necessary connection between law and morality—within the framework of analytic philosophy. Hart sought to provide a theory of descriptive sociology and analytical jurisprudence. The book addresses a number of traditional jurisprudential topics such as the nature of law, whether laws are rules, and the relation between law and morality. Hart answers these by placing law into a social context while at the same time leaving the capability for rigorous analysis of legal terms, which in effect "awakened English jurisprudence from its comfortable slumbers".

36. (D): The Environment (Protection) Act, 1986 was enacted in accordance with Article 253 of the Constitution of India. Article 253 empowers the Parliament to legislate for implementing international agreements. In the case of environmental protection, India, being a party to various international conventions and agreements addressing environmental concerns, found it imperative to formulate comprehensive legislation to align with these global commitments. The Environment (Protection) Act, 1986, thus, serves as a legislative framework to safeguard and improve the quality of the environment. It empowers the central government to take necessary measures for environmental protection, set standards for emissions and discharge of environmental pollutants, and regulate activities that may have adverse impacts on the environment.

37. (C): In the case of Church of God (Full Gospel) in India v. KKR Majestic Colony Welfare Association, the Supreme Court of India made a significant observation regarding noise pollution and its association with religious activities. The court emphasized that even if the noise was a direct result of and connected with religious practices, it cannot be tolerated if it contributes to environmental noise pollution. This assertion reflects the court's recognition of the paramount importance of environmental considerations and public health over certain traditional practices that may lead to noise disturbances. The judgment underscores the need to strike a balance between religious freedoms and the broader societal interest in maintaining a peaceful and environmentally sustainable living environment.

38. (B): "Schedule II" of the National Green Tribunal (NGT) Act is pivotal in delineating the "Heads of Compensation" that the NGT can award for environmental damage. This schedule is intricately linked to Section 17 of the NGT Act, empowering the tribunal to grant relief and compensation for harm caused by projects, activities, or omissions falling under Schedule I. Schedule II serves as a comprehensive guide, detailing various categories under which compensation can be awarded, encompassing damage to property, public health, loss of livelihood, and harm to flora and fauna. It provides a structured framework for the quantification and awarding of compensation, ensuring a nuanced approach to diverse forms of environmental damage.

39. (C): Section 28 of the Indian Forest Act of 1927 emerges as a transformative legal provision, transcending the realms of traditional forest governance. It orchestrates a paradigm shift by introducing the concept of "village forests", offering a departure from the centralized control that characterizes reserved forests. This visionary section empowers state governments to designate specific areas within reserved forests for community management. In essence, it grants local communities a profound role in shaping the destiny of their forest resources. These village forests become hubs of community engagement, where residents actively participate in decision-making, resource utilization, and, crucially, the equitable distribution of benefits derived from sustainable practices.

40. **(C):** The polluter pays principle indeed holds the polluter responsible for the environmental harm caused by their activities, including compensating affected parties and bearing the expenses for environmental restoration. However, it's crucial to note that while the concept of the polluter pays principle is generally accepted in environmental law, attributing this principle specifically to the M.C. Mehta v Kamalnath case might be an oversimplification. The polluter pays principle has evolved as a global environmental norm and is not limited to a single legal precedent. Therefore, while Assertion A is correct in its general statement about the polluter pays principle, Reason R's specific reference to the M.C. Mehta case may not be the most accurate explanation.

41. **(B):**

(*a*) **Asha is the author of the literary work:** This statement holds true because Asha, as a journalist who wrote the story, is considered the author of the literary work, which is the written story.

(*c*) **Proprietor of the newspaper has only the publication rights:** This statement is accurate. The newspaper proprietor typically holds publication rights, allowing them to publish the story. However, copyright ownership may remain with the author unless stated otherwise in a contract.

(*d*) **Raghu and Rekha have performer's right:** This statement is correct. Actors, such as Raghu and Rekha, have performer's rights, granting them control over the use and dissemination of their performances, including acting in the film.

42. **(D):**

(*a*) **The Tribunal should not become post- retirement heaven for civil servants:** The Court recognized the inherent conflict of interest in appointing retired civil servants to tribunals. These individuals, steeped in bureaucratic norms and lacking fresh perspectives, often struggled to deliver truly independent and impartial judgments. The Court, therefore, emphasized the need for members with diverse expertise and a genuine commitment to judicial principles, not merely retired officials seeking a comfortable post-retirement sinecure.

(*b*) **Members of the Tribunals should be independent person and not serving Civil servants:** The Court envisioned tribunals as independent bodies, free from the shackles of bureaucratic influence. This meant not only ensuring the selection of non-civil servant members but also minimizing dependence on government infrastructure and resources.

(*d*) **The Tribunal should resemble more the Courts and not bureaucratic boards:** The Court envisioned tribunals not as extensions of bureaucratic hierarchies but as quasi-judicial bodies with a strong resemblance to courts. This meant prioritizing transparency in proceedings, adhering to established rules of evidence and procedure, and fostering a culture of judicial accountability.

43. (D):

(*b*) **International Law does not recognize general duty of state in respect of extradition:** This statement is accurate. There is no inherent obligation for states to extradite individuals. Extradition rests on principles of sovereignty and reciprocity, meaning states retain freedom to decide whether or not to fulfill extradition requests from other countries. This absence of a general duty allows states to consider various factors before agreeing to extradition, such as the nature of the alleged crime, the strength of evidence, and potential human rights concerns.

(*c*) **Extradition depends on the provision, of existing Extradition Treaties:** This statement is true. While extradition treaties form the most common legal framework for extradition, they aren't the only mechanism. Treaties provide detailed arrangements regarding grounds for extradition, procedures, and legal safeguards.

(*d*) **Countries may grant extradition without a Treaty:** This statement is entirely accurate. As discussed above, the absence of a treaty doesn't preclude extradition. Countries can fulfill requests based on customary law, reciprocity, or domestic legislation. However, such extraditions typically involve rigorous examination of evidence, adherence to human rights principles, and ensuring fair legal proceedings in the requesting country.

44. (B): John Salmond, a legal scholar, categorized legal rights into four distinct kinds:

(*a*) **Liberties:** Liberties refer to the absence of legal restraint or freedom from interference by others. These are rights that involve a person's freedom to act in a certain way without interference from the government or other individuals.

(*b*) **Rights:** Rights, in Salmond's classification, are legally protected interests. These are entitlements that individuals possess, and they can be enforced through legal means.

(*c*) **Powers:** Powers are legal abilities or capacities to alter legal positions or relationships. They involve the authority to do something that may affect the rights or obligations of oneself or others.

(*d*) **Immunities:** Immunities refer to the absence of legal liability or exemption from certain legal duties. These rights protect individuals from being subject to certain actions or claims by others.

45. (B):

(*a*) **Neither party has a spouse living at the time of marriage:** This is a fundamental condition. Bigamy is illegal, and both partners must be free from any existing marriage to enter a new one.

(*b*) **Mental capacity:** For consent to be valid, both parties must possess the mental capacity to understand the nature of the marriage vows, the responsibilities involved, and the consequences of the union.

(*d*) **Parties are not within prohibited degree:** The Act specifies forbidden relationships within which marriage is considered illegal. These restrictions are based on blood relations and marital ties, aimed at preventing close family members from marrying and upholding social norms.

46. (*)

47. (B):

(*a*) **Iddat of widowhood is 4 months and 10 days:** 4 months and 10 days is a commonly cited duration for the Iddat period of a widow, it's important to note that interpretations can vary within different schools of Islamic thought.

(*c*) **If the marriage is irregular and is consummated, the wife is under obligation to observe Iddat:** This statement is correct. An irregular marriage refers to one not conducted according to proper Islamic legal procedures. However, if such a marriage is consummated, the wife is still obligated to observe the Iddat period.

(*d*) **If the wife observes Iddat husband is bound to maintain the wife during the period on Iddat:** This option aligns with certain interpretations of Islamic law. Some scholars argue that the husband remains responsible for his wife's financial needs during the Iddat period, even after divorce, as she is still technically considered under his marital protection.

(*e*) **In case the wife is pregnant, period of Iddat extends till the delivery of the child:** This statement is accurate and universally accepted across Islamic legal schools. Pregnancy extends the Iddat period until childbirth, ensuring clarity about the child's paternity and providing appropriate care for the mother and child during this sensitive time.

48. (A):

(*a*) **Uniting for Peace Resolution was passed in 1950:** The Uniting for Peace Resolution was a significant development in the context of the United Nations. Adopted on November 3, 1950, it was a response to the Cold War tensions and the Soviet Union's use of the veto power in the Security Council to block collective action. The resolution empowered the General Assembly to take measures if the Security Council was deadlocked due to a veto.

(*b*) **Uniting for Peace Resolution was passed by the General Assembly:** The Uniting for Peace Resolution was indeed passed by the United Nations General Assembly. This underscores the General Assembly's role as a forum for collective decision-making, especially in situations where the Security Council faces difficulties in reaching a consensus due to the veto power held by its permanent members.

(*d*) **Maintenance of international peace and security is the primary responsibility of the Security Council:** The statement accurately reflects a fundamental principle of the United Nations Charter. According to the Charter, the primary responsibility for the maintenance of international peace and security is assigned to the Security Council. The Security Council is granted the authority to take action, including the use of force, to address threats to peace and acts of aggression.

49. (B):

(*a*) **Promote international peace and security:** Article 51 of the Constitution of India emphasizes the state's duty to actively contribute to the promotion of international peace and security. This goes beyond mere passive observance and encourages the state to engage in initiatives and actions that contribute positively to global stability.

(*b*) **Maintain just and honorable relations between nations:** The directive to maintain just and honorable relations between nations underscores the importance of ethical conduct in international relations. It calls for fairness, honesty, and integrity in the state's interactions with other nations.

(*c*) **Foster respect for international law and treaty obligations:** This aspect highlights the significance of adherence to international legal norms and treaty commitments. By fostering respect for international law, the state contributes to the development and maintenance of a rules-based global order.

(*e*) **Encourage settlement of international disputes through arbitration:** The encouragement of settling international disputes through arbitration reflects a preference for peaceful and legal means of resolving conflicts. Arbitration provides a structured and impartial mechanism for dispute resolution, emphasizing the avoidance of violence and the promotion of diplomatic solutions to disagreements.

50. (C):

(*a*) **RASOI for hydrogenated oil:** If "RASOI" is presented in a stylized way (unique font, logo design incorporating the word), or if it has acquired a secondary meaning associated with a specific brand of hydrogenated oil, then it is eligible for trademark registration.

(*b*) **JHOOMRITALAIA for pens:** "JHOOMRITALAIA" appears to be an invented word, meaning it's not a common word in any language and doesn't describe the product (pens) directly. Invented words are ideal for trademarks because they are inherently distinctive and identify a specific brand.

(*d*) **Square shape for tyres:** shapes can be registered as trademarks, but with a caveat. The square shape on its own wouldn't be functional for tires. However, if the square design is implemented in a unique way that's not the natural shape of a tire and helps distinguish the brand, it could be eligible for registration.

51. (C):

(*b*) **To recommend a CSR Policy:** The CSR Committee is responsible for formulating and recommending a Corporate Social Responsibility (CSR) policy. This policy outlines the company's commitment to undertake socially responsible initiatives. The CSR policy typically covers the areas in which the company plans to contribute, the nature of activities, and the quantum of financial resources to be allocated for CSR endeavors.

(*c*) **To recommend the amount of expenditure for the indicated activities:** After formulating the CSR policy, the committee assesses and recommends the amount of expenditure that the company should allocate for the indicated CSR activities. This involves a careful evaluation of the social impact the company aims to achieve and determining the financial resources needed to support these initiatives.

(*e*) **To monitor the CSR policy of the company from time to time:** Once the CSR policy is established and the budget allocated, the committee takes on the responsibility of monitoring the implementation of CSR activities. This includes regularly reviewing the progress of ongoing initiatives, ensuring that the company is in compliance with its CSR commitments, and making adjustments as needed.

52. (C):

(*a*) **Absolute:** An absolute acceptance means that the acceptance mirrors the terms of the original proposal without introducing new conditions or modifications. The acceptance must be clear and unequivocal, demonstrating a willingness to be bound by the exact terms proposed.

(*b*) **Unqualified:** An unqualified acceptance is one that does not contain any reservations, conditions, or modifications to the original proposal. It signifies a straightforward and unconditional agreement to the terms put forth in the proposal.

(*e*) **Expressed in some usual and reasonable manner:** This part emphasizes that the acceptance should be communicated in a manner that is customary and reasonable based on the circumstances.

53. (A): Assertion (A) (The Criminal Law Amendment Act, 2013, was a result of public outrage): This statement is accurate. The amendment was enacted in response to widespread public outrage and protests following the brutal gang rape of a young woman in Delhi in December 2012. The incident sparked a national conversation and demands for more stringent laws on sexual offenses.

Reason (R) (Society forces the law to accept the change): This statement is also true. The phrase "society forces the law" is a simplification, but it captures the essence of the relationship. Public sentiment and demands can indeed influence lawmakers and policymakers to enact legal changes, especially when there is significant public outcry. In this case, the public's strong reaction prompted lawmakers to address the issue through legislative amendments.

54. (A): The assertion and reason collectively convey that a dignified life involves more than just surviving; it includes the right to health, well-being, and the ability to thrive. The reason explains that pollution-free air and clean water are essential prerequisites for fulfilling the various aspects of a dignified life, supporting the assertion. By ensuring access to these basic elements, as emphasized in both the assertion and reason, we uphold individuals' rights to live healthily, productively, and with dignity.

55. (D):

(*a*) **For State Legislature. Constitutional provisions for special address of the Governor, is in article 176:** This article grants the Governor the authority to deliver two special addresses to the State Legislature. The first address occurs at the commencement of the first session after a general election, offering the newly elected government an opportunity to communicate its vision and legislative agenda. The second address is delivered at the beginning of each year's first session and focuses on reviewing the government's accomplishments from the previous year and presenting upcoming legislative proposals.

(*c*) **For State Legislature the special procedure in respect of Money Bill is covered by article 198:** Article 198 establishes a specific legislative process for bills categorized as "Money Bills" within State Legislatures. Money Bills primarily pertain to financial matters such as taxation, appropriation of funds, and public debt. Key features of this special procedure include the origination of Money Bills in the Legislative Assembly, limited powers of amendment for the Legislative Council (if applicable), and the mandatory requirement of the Governor's assent for enactment.

(*d*) **For State Legislature provisions as to introduction and passing of bills is given in article 196:** Article 196 outlines the standard legislative process for all bills considered by State Legislatures, encompassing both ordinary bills and Money Bills. The process includes the presentation of bills by members of the Legislature or ministers, debates and discussions in both houses, voting procedures in each house, and the Governor's assent for a bill to become law.

56. (D):

(*a*) **Act done by a person bound, or by mistake of fact believing himself to be bound by law:** This exception, falling under Chapter IV of the Indian Penal Code, provides immunity to individuals who, either by mistake of fact or under a genuine belief, consider themselves bound by law. If a person acts in good faith, believing that they are obligated by law to perform a certain act, and it turns out to be incorrect, this provision protects them from criminal liability.

(*b*) **Act of judge when acting judicially:** This exception acknowledges the principle of judicial immunity. Judges are protected from legal action for acts performed in the course of their judicial duties. It ensures that judges can carry out their responsibilities without fear of personal liability, fostering an independent and impartial judiciary.

(*e*) **Accident in doing a lawful act:** This exception pertains to situations where a lawful act is performed with lawful means, but an unintended consequence occurs. If the act was lawful and performed without any criminal intent or negligence, this provision provides immunity for the unintentional consequences, considering it an accident.

57. (A):

(*a*) **Recognition de jure is final and once given cannot be withdrawn:** Recognition de jure refers to the formal acknowledgment by one state of the legal existence and legitimacy of another state. Once granted, recognition de jure is generally considered final and enduring. It signifies the acceptance of the recognized state as a legitimate and sovereign entity in the eyes of the recognizing state.

(*c*) **De facto recognition may be withdrawn:** De facto recognition is based on the practical realities of the situation rather than a legal or formal acknowledgment. It acknowledges the effective control and governance exercised by a state, even if its legitimacy is not formally recognized. De facto recognition may be more easily withdrawn than de jure recognition.

(*e*) **Retroactive recognition of a new government does not invalidate the acts of the previous de jure government:** Retroactive recognition involves acknowledging a government's legitimacy with retroactive effect, recognizing it as if it had been legitimate from an earlier date. Importantly, retroactive recognition does not necessarily invalidate the acts of the previous de jure government.

58. (C):

(*a*) **Art. 2(4) of the UN Charter contains the proposition of the unilateral use of force or threat theory by states in their international relations:** Article 2(4) of the UN Charter is a foundational principle that prohibits states from engaging in the threat or use of force against the territorial integrity or political independence of any state. The purpose is to promote international peace and prevent the unilateral use of force as a means of settling disputes between states.

(*c*) **UN Charter makes an exception to Art. 2(4) in individual and collective self-defense as in Art. 51:** While Article 2(4) sets a general prohibition on the use of force, Article 51 recognizes the inherent right of individual and collective self-defense if an armed attack occurs. This exception allows states to use force in self-defense, either individually or collectively with other states, as a response to an armed attack.

(*e*) **States have a duty to refrain from propaganda for wars of aggression:** The use of force in Article 2(4), imply a duty for states to refrain from engaging in propaganda that encourages wars of aggression. The Charter encourages peaceful dispute resolution and discourages actions that could escalate tensions or lead to armed conflicts.

59. (B):

(*a*) **The preamble of the UN Charter says: "We the Peoples of the United Nations":** The preamble of the United Nations Charter begins with the phrase "We the Peoples of the United Nations", emphasizing the inclusive and collective nature of the organization. This choice of wording reflects the idea that the United Nations represents not only the member states but also the peoples of the world. It underscores a commitment to promoting the well-being and rights of individuals globally.

(*c*) **Maintenance of international peace and security is the primary responsibility of the Security Council:** According to the UN Charter, the primary responsibility for the maintenance of international peace and security is assigned to the Security Council. This is explicitly stated in Chapter V of the Charter. The Security Council is granted the authority to take measures, including the use of force, to address threats to peace, breaches of peace, and acts of aggression.

60. (D):

(*a*) **The International Bank for Reconstruction and Development (IBRD) is also called the World Bank:** The International Bank for Reconstruction and Development (IBRD) is a part of the World Bank Group. The World Bank Group consists of five member institutions, and the IBRD is one of them. The IBRD is commonly known as the World Bank, and it focuses on providing financial and technical assistance to middle-income and creditworthy low-income countries for development projects.

(*d*) **The WTO provides for a Secretariat headed by a Director-General:** The World Trade Organization (WTO) has a Secretariat responsible for supporting the day-to-day work of the organization. The head of the WTO Secretariat is called the Director-General. The Director-General is appointed by the WTO members and serves a term, leading the Secretariat in implementing the decisions of the General Council and facilitating the work of various WTO committees and negotiating bodies.

61. (B):

(*a*) **It is very difficult to define cruelty which can fit in all circumstances:** The difficulty in defining cruelty universally arises from the diverse nature of human relationships and situations. What may be considered cruel behavior in one context might not be viewed the same way in another. The law recognizes this complexity and doesn't provide a rigid, one-size-fits-all definition of cruelty.

(*b*) **Cruelty can be physical and mental:** The Hindu Marriage Act recognizes two broad categories of cruelty: physical and mental. Physical cruelty involves any form of bodily harm or violence, while mental cruelty encompasses emotional and psychological suffering. This inclusive approach acknowledges that harm in a marital relationship may not always manifest as physical abuse but can also be psychological or emotional in nature.

62. (C):

(*a*) **Class I heirs:** These are the closest relatives and have the first right to the deceased's property. Class I heirs include sons, daughters, widows, mothers, sons of pre-deceased sons, and daughters of pre-deceased sons. In the absence of any heirs in Class I, the property devolves to Class II heirs.

(*b*) **Class II heirs:** If there are no Class I heirs, the property devolves upon Class II heirs. Class II heirs include fathers, brothers, sisters, and their children. The order of succession is determined by the proximity of relationship.

(*d*) **Agnates:** Agnates are relatives connected through male descent. In the absence of both Class I and Class II heirs, the property passes to agnates. The term "agnates" primarily includes relatives who are connected through the father's side of the family.

(*e*) **Cognates:** Cognates are relatives connected through blood or affinity but not through male descent. If there are no Class I, Class II, or agnate heirs, the property goes to cognates. Cognates include relatives related through the mother's side of the family.

63. (B):

(*b*) **Fact of cruelty or harassment by her husband for or in connection with any demand for dowry:** This component emphasizes that the death of a woman should be a result of cruelty or harassment inflicted by her husband and related to demands for dowry. It underscores the connection between the harassment and the demand for dowry.

(*c*) **Fact of cruelty or harassment by any relative of her husband for or in connection with any demand for dowry:** This widens the scope to include not only the husband but also any relative of the husband. This recognizes that harassment for dowry may involve not just the spouse but also other family members.

(*d*) **Death of a woman within 7 years of her marriage:** This sets a time frame within which the death should occur for it to be considered a "Dowry Death" under Section 304B. If the death happens within seven years of the woman's marriage, and it is linked to dowry-related cruelty, it falls under the purview of this section.

(*e*) **"Dowry shall have the same meaning as in section 2 of the Dowry Prohibition Act, 1961":** This ensures that the definition of dowry aligns with the Dowry Prohibition Act, 1961. According to the Dowry Prohibition Act, dowry includes any property or valuable security given or agreed to be given either directly or indirectly at or before or after the marriage.

64. (B):

(*a*) **Extraordinary remedies under Article 32 and 226:** Article 32 of the Indian Constitution empowers individuals to directly approach the Supreme Court for the enforcement of fundamental rights. It is known as the "Right to Constitutional Remedies" and provides for the issuance of writs such as habeas corpus, mandamus, certiorari, prohibition, and quo warranto.

Similarly, Article 226 empowers High Courts to issue writs for the enforcement of fundamental rights as well as for any other purpose. This allows individuals to seek legal remedies directly from the High Court.

(*b*) **Appeals to Supreme Court under Article 132 to 135:** Articles 132 to 135 of the Constitution deal with the appellate jurisdiction of the Supreme Court. These articles specify the types of cases in which individuals can appeal directly to the Supreme Court. Article 132 grants the Supreme Court the jurisdiction to hear appeals in certain civil matters, while Articles 133 and 134 deal with appeals in criminal matters.

(*e*) **Advisory Jurisdiction under Article 143:** Article 143 of the Constitution grants the President of India the power to seek the advice of the Supreme Court on questions of law or fact that may have arisen or are likely to arise. The advice given by the Supreme Court in such cases is advisory and not binding.

65. (A):

(*b*) **Right not to remain uneducated:** The right to education is considered a fundamental right. Article 21-A was added by the 86th Constitutional Amendment Act, 2002, which makes free and compulsory education a fundamental right for children in the age group of 6 to 14 years.

(*d*) **Right not to be killed without trial:** The right not to be killed without trial is a fundamental right protected under Article 21 of the Indian Constitution. This article guarantees the right to life and personal liberty, ensuring that no person can be deprived of their life or personal liberty except according to the procedure established by law.

(*e*) **Right not to change religion:** The right not to be compelled to change one's religion is encompassed within the broader right to freedom of religion guaranteed under Article 25 of the Indian Constitution. Article 25 ensures the freedom of conscience and the right to freely profess, practice, and propagate one's religion. It includes the right to maintain one's existing religion and not be forced to convert against one's will.

66. (B)	**67. (C)**	**68. (B)**
69. (C)	**70. (A)**	**71. (A)**
72. (B)	**73. (D)**	**74. (C)**
75. (B)		

76. (B):

(*b*) **Union of India v. Sankalchand Himatlal Seth is a 1977 case:** The case involves the transfer of Justice Sankalchand H. Sheth from the Gujarat High Court to the High Court of Andhra Pradesh in 1976 without his consent. The Union's argument was that a judge's liability to transfer is a constitutional obligation.

(*a*) **S.P. Gupta v. Union of India,** also known as the "First Judges Case", was a landmark legal case in India in 1981. The case concerned the constitutional validity of the Central Government's orders regarding the transfer and non-extension of an additional judge's term.

(*d*) **The 1993 Supreme Court case:** Supreme Court Advocates on Record Association vs Union of India gave the Chief Justice of India (CJI) the power to appoint and transfer judges. The majority verdict also stated that the CJI only needed to seek advice from two senior-most judges of the Supreme Court. The judgment also established that the CJI should have supremacy in the appointment procedure and that executive influence should be controlled.

(c) **Special Reference No. 1 of 1998** is a case about the appointment and transfer of judges in the Indian judiciary. The case held that the Chief Justice of India's opinion should be formed in consultation with a majority of judges. The Chief Justice's opinion is important in recommendations for appointments to the Supreme Court.

77. (D):

(a) **The Peace of Westphalia** is a series of peace treaties signed in 1648 that ended the Thirty Years' War and the Eighty Years' War. The treaties were signed in the cities of Osnabrück and Münster between May and October 1648. The Peace of Westphalia granted religious tolerance to Lutherans and Calvinists in the Holy Roman Empire.

(c) **The Brussels Conference Act of 1890** was a collection of anti-slavery measures signed in Brussels on 2 July 1890 (and which entered into force on 31 August 1891) to, as the act itself puts it, "put an end to Negro Slave Trade by land as well as by sea, and to improve the moral and material conditions of existence of the native races".

(b) **The Kellogg-Briand Pact,** also known as the Fact of Paris, is a 1928 international agreement that aims to eliminate war as a national policy. The pact's official name is the General Treaty for Renunciation of War as an Instrument of National Policy. The pact was signed in Paris on August 27, 1928. The pact was the most ambitious peacekeeping effort after World War I.

(e). **The Montevideo Convention** on the Rights and Duties of States is a treaty signed in 1933 that established the definition of a state under international law. The convention outlines the criteria for creating a state, which includes: A permanent population, A defined territory, A government, The capacity to conduct international relations.

(d) **The Convention Relating to the Status of Refugees,** also known as the 1951 Refugee Convention or the Geneva Convention, is a United Nations treaty that defines who is a refugee and sets out their rights and the responsibilities of nations that grant asylum. The convention was adopted in 1951 and came into force in 1954.

78. (C):

(e) **The SS Lotus case** was a criminal trial between France and Turkey that resulted from a collision between the two countries' ships on August 2, 1926. The case was accepted and decided by the Permanent Court of International Justice on September 7, 1927. The case involved the collision of the French steamer SS Lotus and the Turkish steamer SS Bozkourt in the waters north of Mytilene, Greece.

(b) **Island of Palmas Arbitration case (1928):** This case arbitrated a dispute between the Netherlands and the United States over ownership of the Island of Palmas, applying principles of discovery and effective occupation. This was heard by the Permanent Court of Arbitration. In 1898, Spain ceded the island to the United States, but the Netherlands claimed it as part of its possessions.

(c) **The Nuremberg Tribunal's verdict** was delivered on October 1, 1946. The tribunal sentenced 12 of the 22 Nazi German leaders to death, gave prison sentences to 7, and acquitted 3. The Nuremberg Trials, which lasted from November 1945 to October 1946, uncovered the German leadership that supported the Nazi dictatorship.

(d) **The Right of Passage over Indian Territory case** is a dispute between Portugal and India in 1954. The case involves the Portuguese government's claim to villages as its enclaves. The Portuguese also had passage over Indian Territory for many years while India was under British control.

(*a*) **The Fisheries Jurisdiction Case** is a dispute between Iceland and the United Kingdom regarding Iceland's proposed extension of its fisheries jurisdiction. In 1973, the International Court of Justice (ICJ) ruled that it had jurisdiction to hear the case and to consider the merits of the dispute.

79. (C):

(*c*) **Filing of claims:** This crucial step defines the legal boundaries of your invention. You must precisely articulate the technical features and functionalities that you consider novel and non-obvious, using clear and concise language.

(*b*) **Publication of application:** Once formalities are complete, the Indian Patent Office publishes your application in the official journal. This transparency period allows third parties to scrutinize your invention and potentially file pre-grant oppositions if they believe it infringes existing patents or lacks novelty.

(*d*) **Request for examination:** Requesting examination can expedite the granting process. You can submit Form 18 along with the prescribed fee to initiate this stage. The Patent Office examiner will then thoroughly assess your application for compliance with patentability criteria and issue a detailed examination report.

(*e*) **Grant of patent:** If your invention overcomes all objections and meets the patentability requirements, the patent is granted. You'll receive official notification and a patent certificate, securing exclusive rights to exploit your invention commercially for a stipulated period.

(*a*) **Opposition under section 25(2) of the Patents Act, 1970:** Even after grant, third parties have the right to challenge the patent's validity within a specific timeframe. They can file an opposition petition citing various grounds, such as lack. of novelty, obviousness, or non-patentable subject matter. The opposition proceedings involve arguments and evidence presented by both parties, ultimately leading to a decision by the Patent Office or the courts.

80. (B) **81. (*)**

82. (B):

(*a*) **Foreign Loan:** Negotiating and managing foreign loans falls under List I due to its critical impact on national budget, economic stability, and foreign relations. International financial agreements require centralized oversight and control to safeguard national interests.

(*c*) **Atomic energy:** Given its immense strategic and security implications, the regulation and utilization of atomic energy reside solely under List I. This ensures strict national control over nuclear infrastructure, research, and development, safeguarding sensitive technology and protecting national security.

(*e*) **Insurance:** The insurance sector plays a vital role in financial stability and risk management. To ensure consumer protection, prevent fraud, and regulate this complex industry effectively, centralized control over insurance policies and practices becomes essential. Therefore, List I claims jurisdiction over insurance matters.

83. (C):

(*a*) **Women and Children:** Article 15(3) explicitly allows the state to make special provisions for women and children. Affirmative action measures may include reservations in educational institutions and employment, maternal health benefits, and specific protection against discrimination and violence targeting women and children.

(*b*) **Scheduled Tribes (STs):** Article 15(4) permits the state to make special provisions for Scheduled Tribes (STs), and it operates in addition to the provisions for Scheduled Castes (SCs) under Article 15(5). Special provisions for STs often involve reservations in educational institutions and government jobs, cultural preservation initiatives, and protection of tribal land rights.

(*c*) **Economically Weaker Sections (EWS):** The 103rd Amendment introduced Article 15(6), allowing the state to make special provisions for EWS, which may include reservations in educational institutions. This interpretation is debated, with some expressing concerns about potential conflicts with the principle of equality.

(*d*) **Socially Backward Classes:** Article 15(4) allows the state to make special provisions for socially backward classes. These classes encompass various communities facing social and educational disadvantages. Similar to STs, affirmative action measures for socially backward classes often involve reservations in educational institutions and employment, aiming to uplift these communities and address historical disadvantages.

84. (C):

(*a*) **The Convention on the Prevention and Punishment of the Crime of Genocide (CPPCG),** also known as the Genocide Convention, is an international treaty that criminalizes genocide. It was the first human rights treaty adopted by the United Nations General Assembly on December 9, 1948, and came into force on January 12, 1951. 'The Genocide Convention's main focus is to protect national, racial, ethnic, and religious minorities from threats to their existence. It confirms that genocide is a crime under international law, and identifies five acts that constitute genocide and five acts that are punishable.

(*b*) **The Warsaw Pact** was a mutual defense treaty signed in 1955 between the Soviet Union and seven other Eastern Bloc countries. The treaty's formal name is the Treaty of Friendship, Cooperation, and Mutual Assistance.The Warsaw Pact was a political and military alliance. Its stated goals were to strengthen friendship, cooperation, and mutual assistance, while respecting the independence and sovereignty of states and not interfering in their internal affairs.

(*e*) **The Vienna Convention on Diplomatic Relations (VCDR)** is an international treaty that was signed in 1961. It is a fundamental part of foreign relations and establishes a framework for diplomatic relations between independent countries. The VCDR is almost universally adopted by 179 countries and is a core part of international diplomatic and consular law. The VCDR provides a framework for the establishment, maintenance, and termination of diplomatic relations.

(*c*) **The Convention for the Suppression of Unlawful Acts against the Safety of Civil Aviation,** also known as the Montreal Convention of Hijacking, is a treaty that prohibits and punishes actions that may threaten the safety of civil aviation. The Convention was adopted in 1971 by the International Civil Aviation Organization. Under this Convention, the State parties have undertaken that they will provide deterrent punishment to the hijackers.

(*d*) **The United Nations Convention on the Rights of the Child (UNCRC)** is an international agreement on the civil, political, economic, social, and cultural rights of children. The UN General Assembly adopted the Convention on November 20, 1989, and it entered into force in September 1990. The UNCRC is the most widely ratified human rights treaty in history. It has been ratified by all members of the UN except for the United States.

85. (*)

86. (A): Assertion (A): This assertion highlights the unique nature of administrative tribunals. Unlike regular courts, administrative tribunals often operate in a hybrid space, combining elements of both judicial and administrative functions. They are tasked with resolving disputes and making decisions in a manner that is more flexible and specialized than traditional courts.

Reason (R): This reason explains one of the characteristics that support Assertion (A). Administrative tribunals typically have more flexible rules of evidence and procedure compared to formal courts. This flexibility allows them to adapt to the specific needs of the cases they handle, often involving administrative and regulatory matters. The less rigid procedural requirements enable administrative tribunals to function efficiently in a manner that may differ from traditional judicial proceedings.

87. (A): Assertion (A): This statement is correct. According to the principle of general customary international law, certain multilateral treaties can bind even those states that are not parties to the treaty if the treaty reflects a general practice accepted as law.

Reason (R): This statement is correct and explain assertion (A). Article 38 of the Vienna Convention on the Law of Treaties outlines the rules for establishing customary international law. It makes an exception to Article 34 (which deals with the general rule that a treaty does not create obligations for a third state without its consent) and Article 37 (which deals with the obligations arising for third states in the context of treaties providing for the rights and obligations of third states).

88. (A): Assertion (A): This statement is correct. The assertion accurately reflects the principle of compensatory damages in contract law.

Reason (R): This statement is also correct. It reflects the general principle that compensation for a breach of contract is limited to direct and foreseeable losses. Indirect or remote losses that are not a natural consequence of the breach are typically not recoverable.

In this case, Reason (R) provides a correct explanation for Assertion (A). Mr. X is entitled to compensation for the average amount of profit he would have made during the time of the delay (a direct and foreseeable loss) but not for the loss sustained through the government contract (an indirect and remote loss).

89. (A): Assertion (A): This statement is correct. In the Dev Dutta case, the Supreme Court indeed emphasized that transparency and good governance are integral to natural justice, and this includes the duty of decision-makers to provide reasons for their decisions.

Reason (R): This statement is correct. The provision of reasons in decision-making serves to demonstrate that the decision-maker has considered relevant factors, applied discretion judiciously, and excluded irrelevant considerations. It helps ensure accountability and transparency in the decision-making process.

In this case, Reason (R) provides a correct explanation for Assertion (A). The Supreme Court's emphasis on transparency and good governance, including the duty to give reasons, aligns with the idea that reasons serve to reassure that discretion has been exercised appropriately.

90. (A): Assertion (A): Article 38(1) of the Statute of the International Court of Justice (I.C.J) outlines the sources of law that the court shall apply, including international conventions, international custom, general principles of law, and judicial decisions.

Reason (R): Ex aequo et bono empowers the court to decide a case based on notions of fairness and good faith. In this context, the court is not strictly bound by legal rules or precedents. The decision can be independent of or even contrary to existing legal norms if such a decision aligns with principles of justice and equity.

Article 38(2) recognizes that, with the agreement of the parties involved, the I.C.J has the authority to depart from strict legal sources and rules, opting instead for a decision based on fairness and good faith. This flexibility is particularly relevant when the parties prefer a resolution that goes beyond or outside traditional legal standards.

91. (C): Powers should not be exercised arbitrarily. This principle holds that power must be used for its intended purpose and within the statutory boundaries. Exercising power arbitrarily means going beyond these boundaries and acting in a manner that is not just ultra vires (beyond legal authority) but also truly arbitrary. Therefore, under no circumstances should powers be exercised arbitrarily.

92. (A): The Rule of Law signifies a fundamental principle that holds that no individual, regardless of their position, influence, or authority, is above law. This concept ensures that everyone, including government officials and leaders, is subject to the same legal standards and obligations. It serves as a safeguard against arbitrary and discriminatory use of power, fostering a society where justice is administered fairly and consistently.

93. (A): The Rule of Law, as highlighted in the passage, is best understood as the negation of arbitrariness in the exercise of power. It emphasizes that governmental authority should not be wielded arbitrarily but in accordance with established legal principles and within the defined statutory limits. The passage underscores that a simple rejection of arbitrariness is insufficient to uphold the Rule of Law; rather, it necessitates adherence to specific positive content, including the application of principles of natural justice.

94. (A): The specific positive content of the Rule of Law, as articulated in the passage, denotes an imperative obligation for adherence rather than a discretionary choice. It emphasizes that the Rule of Law must be complied with, underscoring a mandatory requirement for governance and legal processes. This implies that the exercise of power should not only avoid arbitrariness but also actively adhere to established legal principles, ensuring that governmental authority is wielded within statutory boundaries.

95. (B): The passage underscores that the Rule of Law notion goes beyond limited application and is extended comprehensively to ensure fair dealing by the State in all its activities. It implies that the principles of legality, fairness, and justice should permeate every facet of governance and state actions, transcending specific domains. The Rule of Law serves as a guiding principle for the state's conduct, emphasizing that fairness is not confined solely to economic activities but should be a pervasive aspect of the state's interactions across various spheres.

96. (D): The approach to PIL aligns with the historical origins of PIL in India, where Mumbai Kamgar Sabha v. Abdul Bhai in 1976 is considered the pioneering case. This case involved a public interest organization representing textile workers seeking relief for their unsafe working conditions. The Supreme Court accepted the petition and addressed the issue using its writ jurisdiction under Article 32.

97. (C): Public Interest Litigation (PIL) cases are legal actions initiated in the interest of the public or a particular community rather than for personal or private interests. These cases typically address issues that have broader implications for society, involve violations of constitutional or legal rights, and affect individuals who may be unable to seek legal recourse themselves due to factors such as poverty, helplessness, or social and economic disadvantages. PIL allows any member of the public to bring matters of general public concern before the court, ensuring access to justice for those who may otherwise be marginalized or voiceless.

98. (D): In the Indian Constitution, Public Interest Litigation (PIL) cases can be brought before the Supreme Court under Article 32. Article 32 empowers individuals to directly approach the Supreme Court for the enforcement of fundamental rights. It serves as a crucial constitutional provision for the protection and promotion of individual liberties. When a legal wrong or injury arises due to the violation of constitutional or legal rights, and the affected individuals are unable to approach the court themselves due to poverty, helplessness, or social and economic disadvantages, any member of the public can file a PIL application under Article 32.

99. (B):

(*b*) **It is not necessary to follow the technical formalities in such cases:** This statement aligns with the passage's indication that, especially in Public Interest Litigation (PIL) cases, the Supreme Court may not strictly require individuals to adhere to all technical formalities that typically accompany legal proceedings. The emphasis here is on a more pragmatic and flexible approach to procedural requirements, allowing the court to prioritize the broader public interest and the dispensation of justice over rigid adherence to formalities.

(*c*) **The Supreme Court may even treat a letter addressed to it as a writ petition in PIL:** This reflects the passage's assertion that the Supreme Court, in the context of PIL cases, may go beyond traditional formalities. It suggests that the court may adopt an unconventional but responsive stance by considering a letter addressed to it as a formal petition, acknowledging the importance of public interest and ensuring that access to justice is not impeded by procedural hurdles.

100. (*)

Previous Years' Paper (Solved)

National Testing Agency (NTA)

UGC-NET Junior Research Fellowship & Assistant Professor Eligibility Exam

Law, March-2023

(Exam held on 12/03/2023)

PAPER-II

1. In which country the Supreme Court has declared that independence of judiciary is a part of basic feature of the Constitution?

A. Canada and USA
B. USA
C. India
D. India and Switzerland

2. Regarding Freedom of Information or Right to Information which among the following countries have passed an enactment?

A. India only
B. India and UK only
C. India, USA and UK only
D. USA and UK only

3. The concept of 'rule of law' contains three principles. These three principles in an organized form were propounded by:

A. Aristotle
B. Manu
C. Prof. RWM Dias
D. Prof. AV Dicey

4. In context of Center-State relationship, the residuary power rests with the center (Parliament) in which of the following countries?

A. India and Canada
B. India and USA
C. Canada and USA
D. India only

5. 'Separation of Powers' and 'distribution of powers' are:

A. the same concept
B. the different concepts
C. the same concepts in Australia and India
D. the same concepts in the USA but different in India

6. The institution of 'Ombudsman' was first developed in:

A. Switzerland B. Sweden
C. South Africa D. Britain

7. In which of the following cases, the Supreme Court has held that "Administration of Public Authority" cannot be invalidated merely for not recording reasons when it had no duty to do so?

A. National Highway Authority of India V/s Madhukar Kumar (2022)
B. Municipal Council Neemuch V/s Mahadeo Real Estate (2019)
C. Tata Cellular V/s Union of India (1994)
D. Vijay Narayan Sharma V/s State of Rajasthan (2022)

8. Which of the following articles of the constitution provides that "no discussion shall take place in the legislature of a State with respect to conduct of any judge of the Supreme Court or of a High Court in the discharge of his duties?"

A. Article 121 B. Article 127
C. Article 211 D. Article 212

9. Which of the following section of IPC has been struck down by the Supreme Court in Joseph Shine Vs. Union of India (2018)?
A. Section 303 B. Section 309
C. Section 377 D. Section 497

10. Which Constitutional (Amendment) Act added Article 279A to the Constitution?
A. 101st B. 102nd
C. 99th D. 127th

11. Which of the following Constitutional amendment to the constitution of India inserted Article 246A which deals with special provision with respect to Goods and Services Tax:
A. 99th amendment
B. 100th amendment
C. 101st amendment
D. 102nd amendment

12. Which of the following Articles of the Constitution of India deals with 'socially and educationally backward classes'?
A. Article 115 B. Article 338
C. Article 338 A D. Article 342 A

13. In which of the following cases, the Supreme Court of India has held that mother can be natural guardian in certain circumstances even in the presence of father?
A. Hanuman Prasad Singh V/s Bhagwati Prasad
B. Vishakha V/s State of Rajasthan
C. Gita Hariharan V/s RBI
D. Vina Sharma V/s Rakesh Sharma

14. Who has divided the sources of law into two classes (a) Formal sources and (b) Material sources?
A. John Austin B. Savingny
C. Salmond D. Kelson

15. Who among the following is considered the main exponent of the 'historical school of law'?
A. Jermy Bentham B. Savigny
C. Duguit D. Jerome Frank

16. Which of the following is considered law within the 'Austinian theory of Law'?
A. Laws set by political superior to political inferior
B. Judge-made Law
C. International Law
D. Customs

17. 'Law and the Modern Mind' is authored by:
A. Justice Holmes
B. Jerome Frank
C. Justice Cardozo
D. Olivecrona

18. Who among the following jurists does not belong to 'the Sociological approach to law'?
A. Ihering B. Ehrlich
C. Maine D. Roscoe Pound

19. "The movement of progressive societies has hitherto been a movement from status to contract", the most famous generalization is given by:
A. John Austin B. H. Maine
C. Thibaut D. Savigny

20. Which one of the following is considered to be a condition of penal liability?
A. ubi jus ibi remedium
B. volenti non fit injuria
C. damnum sine injuria
D. actus non facit reum nisi mens sit rea

21. "Ownership as a right over a determinate thing indefinite in the point of user, unrestricted in point of disposition and unlimited in point of duration". This definition of ownership is given by:
A. Renner B. Austin
C. Holland D. Salmond

22. "I promise to pay B ₹ 50,000 and to deliver him my black horse on 1st March next." This is:
A. a promissory note
B. a bill of exchange
C. an instrument payable on demand
D. not a promissory note

23. The case Bai Tahira V/s Ali Hussain Fidaalli (AIR 1979 SC 362) is related with:
A. Maintenance B. Adoption
C. Inheritance D. Option of Puberty

24. In which of the following cases, Section 9 of the Hindu Marriage Act, 1955 has been declared unconstitutional?
A. Shanti V/s Rupesh
B. T. Sareetha V/s T.V. Subbaiah
C. Trithikaur V/s Kripal Singh
D. A.K. Kapoor V/s Union of India

25. The sub-Agent is responsible for his acts to the Agent, but not to the Principal, except in case of:
A. Fraud
B. Fraud or misrepresentation
C. Fraud or wilful wrong
D. Principal himself undertaking the responsibility

26. Who among the following Judges of the Supreme Court has authored the judgement in leading case Seema V/s Ashwani Kumar (2006) 2 SCC 78, which is related to the registration of marriage?
A. Justice Hima Kohli
B. Justice Arijit Pasayat
C. Justice Deepak Misra
D. Justice P.N. Bhagwati

27. Which of the following cases is not related to the 'Tort of Negligence'?
A. Donoghue V/s Stevenson
B. Municipal Corporation of Delhi V/s Subhagvanti
C. Ramesh Kumar Nayak V/s Union of India
D. Gloucester Grammar School Case

28. In which of the following cases, it was held that a 'contract to take and supply photographs' is a 'contract of sale of goods'?
A. Love V/s Norman Wright (Builders) Ltd. (1944)
B. Newman V/s Lipman (1951)
C. Lee V/s Griffin (1861)
D. Robinson V/s Graves (1935)

29. In which of the following cases, the Privy Council has held that 'Doctrine of Acknowledgement' is a part of the substantial 'Muslim Law of Inheritance' and not a rule of Evidence?
A. S.A. Hussain V/s Rajjamma
B. Mohd. Amin V/s Vakil Ahmad
C. Mohd. Allahadad Khan V/s Mohd. Ismail Khan
D. Habibur Rahman V/s Altaf Ali

30. The leading case 'Ashby V/s White' was decided by:
A. Lord Denning B. Peacock
C. Lord Holt D. Viscount Haldone

31. Which of the following is not necessary for constituting the 'trespass' under the Law of Torts?
A. By entering into the land
B. By remaining there
C. By unlawful intention
D. By doing an act affecting the sole possession

32. Comparative public law is:
A. a principle of law
B. a body of written rules
C. a method of studying law
D. a system of law in various jurisdictions especially recognized by United Nations

33. "We the People" words are found in the constitution of:
A. India and USA
B. India only
C. India and Canada
D. India, USA and Canada

34. In estimating the loss or damage arising from a breach of contract, the means which existed of remedying the inconvenience caused by the non-performance of the contract.
A. can be taken into account
B. cannot be taken into account
C. must be taken into account
D. must never be taken into account

35. Direction: Point out incorrect response

The purpose of the Information Technology Act, 2000 as set out in the Preamble is:

A. To provide legal recognition for transactions carried out by means of electronic data interchange

B. To involve the use of alternatives to paper-based methods of communication and storage of information

C. To facilitate electronic filing of documents with international agencies

D. To amend the Indian Penal Code, 1860; the Indian Evidence Act, 1872, the Bankers Books Evidence Act, 1891 and the Reserve Bank of India Act, 1934

36. In the Sale of Goods Act, 1930, "fault" means:

A. Wrongful gain or wrongful loss

B. Wrongful act

C. Wrongful act or default

D. Negligent and wrongful act

37. When a promissory note, bill of exchange or cheque is transferred to any person, so as to constitute that person the holder thereof, the instrument is said to be:

A. negotiated B. indorsed

C. accepted D. transferred

38. When the person to whom the proposal is made signifies his assent thereto, the proposal is said to be accepted. A proposal, when accepted?

A. becomes an agreement

B. becomes a promise

C. becomes a contract

D. becomes a consideration

39. Where an option to purchase land was exercisable by notice, in which of the following cases, it was held that the mere posting of the notice which was never delivered, was not a valid exercise of the option?

A. Ram Das Chakrabarti V/s Cotton Ginning Co. Ltd. (1887)

B. J.K. Enterprises V/s State of M.P. (1997)

C. Hyde V/s Wrench (1840)

D. Holwell Securities Ltd. V/s Hughes (1974)

40. Direction: Fill in the blank with exact provision of law.

"It is .... whether the Indian Penal Code (45 of 1860) is or is not in force in the place where the coercion is employed."

A. Immaterial

B. Material

C. Not material

D. To be ascertained

41. Cyber crime is covered and punishable under which of the following provision of IPC?

(*a*) Section 354 (*b*) Section 354 C

(*c*) Section 354 D (*d*) Section 354 E

(*e*) Section 350

Choose the correct answer from the options given below:

A. (*b*), (*c*) only

B. (*b*), (*c*), (*d*) only

C. (*a*), (*b*), (*c*), (*e*) only

D. (*b*), (*c*), (*d*), (*e*) only

42. The Supreme Court of India in State of Bihar V/s Kameshwar Singh (1952) laid down certain tests for discovering whether any particular act constitutes a colourable legislation.

(*a*) The court must look into whether a legislature used wide or vague words or not which may extend the operation of an Act to subject?

(*b*) The court must look into the substance of the law and not to its form or the label which the legislature has given it

(*c*) The court must look at the object as well as the effect of the law

(*d*) If the legislature proceeds under a legislative plan the court must read all the statutes constituting that plan and determine the combined effect

(*e*) The court must look into that repugnancy is in existence?

Choose the correct answer from the options given below:

A. (*a*) and (*b*) only

B. (*b*), (*c*) and (*d*) only

C. (*a*), (*c*), (*d*) and (*e*) only

D. (*d*) and (*e*) only

43. A resolution approving the proclamation of emergency under Article 352 of the Constitution of India for the first time or on subsequent occasion may be passed by either house of Parliament only by:

(*a*) A majority of the total membership of that house,

(*b*) A majority of not less than two thirds of the members of that house present and voting,

(*c*) A majority of not less than two thirds of the members of that house,

(*d*) And the resolution must be ratified by the legislature of not less than one half of the states.

Choose the correct answer from the options given below:

A. (*a*) only

B. (*b*), (*c*) and (*d*) only

C. (*a*) and (*b*) only

D. (*c*) and (*d*) only

44. Which of the following statements are correct?

(*a*) Hiba (Gift) under Muslim Law, is the immediate and unqualified transfer of the corpus of the property without any return.

(*b*) Under Muslim law, a gift of immovable properties can be made verbally without recourse to a written document.

(*c*) A gift of life interest is valid.

(*d*) A gift of life interest is enlarged into an absolute estate

(*e*) The subject of gift may be corporeal only.

Choose the correct answer from the options given below:

A. (*a*) and (*e*) only

B. (*b*), (*c*) and (*d*) only

C. (*a*), (*b*) and (*c*) only

D. (*c*), (*d*) and (*e*) only

45. Arrange the following sections of the Patent Act, 1970 in chronological order (sectionwise -first come basic)

(*a*) Controller and other officers

(*b*) Term of patent

(*c*) Convention countries

(*d*) Multiple priorities

(*e*) Licensing of related patents

Choose the most appropriate answer from the options given below:

A. (*b*), (*a*), (*e*), (*c*), (*d*)

B. (*a*), (*c*), (*b*), (*e*), (*d*)

C. (*c*), (*a*), (*d*), (*e*), (*b*)

D. (*e*), (*b*), (*d*), (*c*), (*a*)

46. Which of the following cases are related to environmental protection?

(*a*) State of Orissa V/s Rabindranath Dalai and others

(*b*) Subhash Kumar V/s State of Bihar and others

(*c*) Almitra H Patel and others V/s Union of India and others

(*d*) M.C. Mehta V/s Union of India

(*e*) Kashi Ram and others V/s State of Rajasthan

Choose the correct answer from the options given below:

A. (*a*), (*b*) and (*c*) only

B. (*b*), (*c*) and (*e*) only

C. (*c*), (*d*) and (*e*) only

D. (*b*), (*c*) and (*d*) only

47. A person shall not be a member of State Board constituted under the Air (Prevention and Control of Pollution) Act, 1981.

(*a*) such person is or at any time has been adjudged insolvent

(*b*) has been declared by a competent court to be of :unsound mind

(*c*) has been convicted of an offence under the Air (Prevention and Control of Pollution) Act, 1981

(*d*) has become above 65 years of age

(*e*) guilty of an offence involving moral turpitude.

Choose the correct answer from the options given below:

A. (*a*), (*b*), (*c*) and (*d*) only

B. (*b*), (*c*), (*d*) and (*e*) only

C. (*a*), (*b*), (*c*) and (*e*) only

D. (*c*), (*d*), (*e*) and (*a*) only

48. Who among the following persons have been members of National Green Tribunal?

(*a*) Justice A Suryanarayan Naidu

(*b*) Justice Dipak Misra

(*c*) Justice C Venkata Ramana

(*d*) Justice Rang Nath Mishra

(*e*) Justice Pratap Kumar Ray

Choose the correct answer from the options given below:

A. (*a*), (*c*) and (*d*) only

B. (*a*), (*c*) and (*e*) only

C. (*b*), (*c*), (*d*) and (*e*) only

D. (*b*), (*d*) and (*a*) only

49. According to Prof. H.L.A. Hart:

(*a*) Law is union of primary and secondary rules.

(*b*) The idea of obligation is at the core of a rule.

(*c*) Law is the enterprise of subjecting human conduct to the governance of rules.

(*d*) The primary rules acquire the unity of a system through their union with secondary rules.

Choose the correct answer from the options given below:

A. (*a*), (*b*) and (*c*) only

B. (*d*), (*c*) and (*a*) only

C. (*a*), (*b*) and (*d*) only

D. (*b*), (*c*) and (*d*) only

50. Which of the following are correct in case of a contract of bailment?

(*a*) The person who delivers the goods is called the bailee.

(*b*) If the bailee does any act which is inconsistent with the conditions of bailment, the contract is void.

(*c*) A gratuitous bailment is terminated by death either of the bailor or of the bailee.

(*d*) The bailee is bound to take care of the goods bailed.

(*e*) Bailee has no general lien.

Choose the correct answer from the options given below:

A. (*a*), (*b*) and (*c*) only

B. (*d*) and (*e*) only

C. (*b*) and (*c*) only

D. (*c*) and (*d*) only

51. Every prospectus issued by or on behalf of a public company shall state the following information:

(*a*) Name and addresses of the registered office of the company

(*b*) Details about underwriting of the issue

(*c*) Details of directors

(*d*) Details about Trustees and their interest

(*e*) Collateral objects of the business.

Choose the correct answer from the options given below:

A. (*a*), (*b*), (*c*) and (*d*) only

B. (*c*), (*d*) and (*e*) only

C. (*a*), (*b*) and (*c*) only

D. (*a*), (*b*) and (*d*) only

52. Which of the following are correct?

(*a*) A company may issue debentures with option to convert them to shares, either wholly or partly at the time of redemption.

(*b*) Such issue has to be approved by a special resolution passed at a general meeting

(*c*) Debentures with voting rights can be issued

(*d*) Secured debentures cannot be issued

(*e*) The debenture trustee has to take steps to protect the interest of debenture holders.

Choose the most appropriate answer from the options given below:

A. (*b*), (*c*) and (*e*) only

B. (*a*), (*b*) and (*e*) only

C. (*a*), (*c*) and (*d*) only

D. (*c*), (*d*) and (*e*) only

53. Which of the following are correct?

Fraud means and includes:

(*a*) The suggestion as a fact, of that which is not true, by one who does not believe it to be true

(*b*) The passive concealment of a fact

(*c*) A promise made without any intention of performing it

(*d*) Any other act fitted to deceive

(*e*) Any such thing which the law declares as misrepresentation

Choose the most appropriate answer from the options given below:

A. (*a*), (*b*), (*c*) and (*d*) only
B. (*a*), (*b*) and (*e*) only
C. (*c*), (*d*) and (*e*) only
D. (*a*), (*c*) and (*d*) only

54. Which among the following are the opinions of Prof. Dicey about rule of law?

(*a*) There should be absence of discretionary power because it makes room for arbitrariness
(*b*) A person should suffer only for breach of law
(*c*) Rights must flow from customs and traditions recognized by courts
(*d*) There was Administrative Law in England
(*e*) Dicey considered that special administrative courts in France reflected rule of law.

Choose the most appropriate answer from the options given below:

A. (*a*), (*b*), (*c*), (*d*) only
B. (*b*), (*c*), (*d*), (*e*) only
C. (*b*), (*c*), (*e*) only
D. (*a*), (*b*), (*c*) only

55. Which of the following is correct about the protected system under the Information Technology Act, 2000?

(*a*) National Nodal Agency may declare any computer resource as the protected system
(*b*) Central Government prescribes the information security practices and procedures for protected system
(*c*) Protected system relates to the protection of the facilities of critical information infrastructure
(*d*) Indian Computer Emergency Response Team has the overall responsibility for taking all measures for protection of protected system.

Choose the most appropriate answer from the options given below:

A. (*a*), (*b*), (*c*) only B. (*b*), (*c*) only
C. (*c*), (*d*) only D. (*a*), (*d*), (*c*) only

56. Who among the following are 'public servants' as expressly given under Section 21 of the Indian Penal Code, 1860?

(*a*) Every commissioned officer of defence service
(*b*) Every judge
(*c*) Every officer of the Government
(*d*) Chairman trustee of private trust
(*e*) President of political parties

Choose the most appropriate answer from the options given below:

A. (*a*), (*b*) and (*e*) only
B. (*b*), (*c*) and (*d*) only
C. (*c*), (*d*) and (*e*) only
D. (*a*), (*b*) and (*c*) only

57. Following are the essential elements of theft under the Indian Penal Code, 1860:

(*a*) Dishonest intention
(*b*) The property should be taken out of the possession of any person without that person's consent
(*c*) The person having possession must be the owner of the such property
(*d*) Property must be movable
(*e*) Taking away of the property should be permanent

Choose the correct answer from the options given below:

A. (*a*), (*b*) and (*d*) only
B. (*b*), (*c*) and (*d*) only
C. (*c*), (*d*) and (*e*) only
D. (*a*), (*c*) and (*d*) only

58. Following are generally the essential elements of crime:

(*a*) Mens rea (*b*) Actus reus
(*c*) Motive (*d*) Injury
(*e*) Human being

Choose the most appropriate answer from the options given below:

A. (*b*), (*c*), (*d*) and (*e*) only
B. (*c*), (*d*), (*e*) and (*a*) only
C. (*a*), (*b*), (*d*) and (*e*) only
D. (*e*), (*b*), (*c*) and (*d*) only

59. Which of the following provisions have been inserted in the Indian Penal Code through the Criminal Law (Amendment) Act, 2013?

(*a*) Section 326 A (*b*) Section 326 B
(*c*) Section 166 A (*d*) Section 166 B
(*e*) Section 228 A

Choose the most appropriate answer from the options given below:

A. (*b*), (*c*), (*d*) and (*e*) only
B. (*d*), (*c*) and (*e*) only
C. (*c*), (*b*) and (*e*) only
D. (*a*), (*b*), (*c*) and (*d*) only

60. Which of the following statements are correct?

(*a*) Negligence is the breach of a legal duty towards the other caused by omission
(*b*) Actionable negligence consists in the neglect of the use of ordinary care towards a person to whom, he owes the duty
(*c*) Negligence is breach of legal duty to take care which results in damage
(*d*) There is no difference between civil and criminal negligence
(*e*) The offence of death by negligence under IPC was amended in 2013

Choose the correct answer from the options given below:

A. (*a*), (*b*) and (*e*) only
B. (*b*) and (*d*) only
C. (*a*), (*b*) and (*c*) only
D. (*c*) and (*d*) only

61. Article 38 of the Statute of International Court of Justice enumerates which of the following as sources of International Law:

(*a*) All international conventions
(*b*) International custom, as evidence of a general practice accepted as law.
(*c*) The general principles of law recognized by the United Nations
(*d*) The general principles of law recognized by civilized nations.

Choose the correct answer from the options given below:

A. (*a*), (*b*), (*c*) only B. (*b*), (*d*) only
C. (*b*), (*c*) only D. (*a*), (*b*) only

62. Which of the statement's is/are correct?

(*a*) A quasi-judicial body may never review its own decisions if there is grave error of law in it.
(*b*) A quasi judicial body may review its own decisions if there is grave error of law in it.
(*c*) A quasi-judicial body has inherent power to review its own decisions
(*d*) A quasi-judicial body has power to issue writs.

Choose the correct answer from the options given below:

A. (*a*) and (*c*) only
B. (*b*) only
C. (*a*) only
D. (*b*) and (*d*) only

63. Which of the following statement's is/are correct?

(*a*) Dower is a consideration for the surrender of person by the wife.
(*b*) Dower is the technical Anglo-Mohammedan term for its equivalent 'Mahr' in Arabic.
(*c*) Dower must be fixed at the marriage ceremony otherwise marriage will be void.
(*d*) Where no dower is expressly fixed at the marriage ceremony, the law confers the right of dower upon wife.

Choose the most appropriate answer from the options given below:

A. (*a*) and (*c*) only
B. (*a*), (*b*) and (*d*) only
C. (*a*), (*b*) and (*c*) only
D. (*b*) and (*c*) only

64. Which of the following statement's is/are correct:

(*a*) According to the Hindu Marriage Act, performance of Sapatapadi before the sacred fire is obligatory for marriage
(*b*) Chanting of mantra is not necessary while performing Saptapadi

(*c*) Saptapadi was customary ritual, incorporated under the Hindu Marriage Act

(*d*) In Hindu Marriage Kanyadana cannot be regarded essential.

Choose the correct answer from the options given below:

A. (*a*) and (*b*) only

B. (*b*) and (*d*) only

C. (*a*), (*b*) and (*c*) only

D. (*b*), (*c*) and (*d*) only

65. In which of the following cases, the Supreme Court has held that while applying and interpreting the anti defection law, the Speaker of Lok Sabha functions as a tribunal:

(*a*) S.P. Sampath Kumar V/s Union of India (1987)

(*b*) I.R. Coelho V/s State of Tamil Nadu (2007)

(*c*) Kihota Hollohon V/s Zachilhu (1992)

(*d*) L. Chandra Kumar V/s Union of India (1997)

(*e*) M.S.M. Sharma V/s Shri Krishna Sharma (1959)

Choose the most appropriate answer from the options given below:

A. (*b*), (*c*) and (*e*) only

B. (*a*), (*b*) and (*c*) only

C. (*c*) only

D. (*d*) only

66. Match List-I with List-II:

List-I	List-II
(*a*) Specific goods in a deliverable state	I. Section 64, Sale of Goods Act, 1930
(*b*) Auction sale	II. Section 28, Sale of Goods Act, 1930
(*c*) Remedy for breach of warranty	III. Section 20, Sale of Goods Act, 1930
(*d*) Sale by one joint owners	IV. Section 59, Sale of Goods Act, 1930

Choose the ***correct*** answer from the options given below:

	(*a*)	(*b*)	(*c*)	(*d*)
A.	II	III	I	IV
B.	IV	II	III	I
C.	I	III	II	IV
D.	III	I	IV	II

67. Match List-I with List-II:

List-I	List-II
(*a*) Limited Powers of the Parliament	I. UK
(*b*) Residuary Power to the states	II. India
(*c*) Unlimited powers of the Parliament	III. US
(*d*) Constitutional Council	IV. France

Choose the ***correct*** answer from the options given below:

	(*a*)	(*b*)	(*c*)	(*d*)
A.	III	IV	I	II
B.	I	II	III	IV
C.	I	III	II	IV
D.	II	III	I	IV

68. Match List-I with List-II:

List-I (Human Right Instruments)	List-II (Years of Ratification/ Accessed)
(*a*) International Convention on the Elimination of All form of Racial Discrimination (ICERD)	I. 1954
(*b*) International Covenant on Civil and Political Rights (ICCPR)	II. 1968
(*c*) Forced Labour Convention	III. 1979
(*d*) Convention on the Rights of Child (CRC)	IV. 1992

Choose the ***correct*** answer from the options given below:

	(*a*)	(*b*)	(*c*)	(*d*)
A.	I	II	III	IV
B.	III	II	I	IV
C.	II	III	I	IV
D.	IV	I	III	II

69. Match List-I with List-II:

List-I	List-II
(*a*) Part IX B	I. Tribunals
(*b*) Part XIV A	II. Co-operative Societies
(*c*) Part VIII	III. Official Languages
(*d*) Part XVII	IV. Union Territories

Choose the ***correct*** answer from the options given below:

	(*a*)	(*b*)	(*c*)	(*d*)
A.	I	II	III	IV
B.	IV	III	II	I
C.	II	I	IV	III
D.	III	II	I	IV

70. Match List-I with List-II:

List-I	List-II
(*a*) Rose and Frank Co. V/s Crompton and Brothers Ltd.	I. Standard form of contract
(*b*) Harris V/s Nickerson	II. Intention to create legal relations
(*c*) Olley V/s Marlborough Court Ltd.	III. Acceptance must be communicated by the acceptor
(*d*) Powell V/s Lee	IV. Invitation to offer

Choose the ***correct*** answer from the options given below:

	(*a*)	(*b*)	(*c*)	(*d*)
A.	III	I	IV	II
B.	II	IV	I	III
C.	IV	I	II	III
D.	I	IV	III	II

71. Match List-I with List-II:

List-I	List-II
(*a*) Registration of Marriage	I. Section 112, Indian Evidence Act
(*b*) Dowry death	II. Section 304B, IPC
(*c*) Presumption of Legitimacy of child	III. Section 113, Indian Evidence Act
(*d*) Marriage religious ceremonies	IV. Section 8, Hindu Marriage Act

Choose the ***correct*** answer from the options given below:

	(*a*)	(*b*)	(*c*)	(*d*)
A.	I	II	III	IV
B.	IV	III	II	I
C.	III	IV	I	II
D.	IV	III	I	II

72. Match List-I with List-II:

List-I	List-II
(*a*) Customs	I. Corporation Sole
(*b*) Post Master General	II. Jural Relations
(*c*) Aristotle	III. Historical School
(*d*) Hohfeld	IV. Distributive Justice

Choose the ***correct*** answer from the options given below:

	(*a*)	(*b*)	(*c*)	(*d*)
A.	III	IV	II	I
B.	III	I	IV	II
C.	IV	III	II	I
D.	I	II	III	IV

73. Match List-I with List-II:

List-I	List-II
(*a*) X. V/s Principal Secretary, Health and Family Welfare Development, NCT Delhi (2022)	I. Collaborative Federal Structure
(*b*) Union of India V/s M/s. Mohit Minerals through Director (2022)	II. All women, whether married and unmarried, are entitled to safe and legal abortion
(*c*) Sahara India Real Estate Ltd. V/s SEBI (2012)	III. Postponement of publication
(*d*) NCT of Delhi V/s Union of India (2018)	IV. Uncooperative federalism

Choose the ***correct*** answer from the options given below:

	(*a*)	(*b*)	(*c*)	(*d*)
A.	I	II	III	IV
B.	IV	III	II	I
C.	III	I	II	IV
D.	II	IV	III	I

74. Match List-I with List-II:

	List-I	List-II
(*a*)	British North America Act	I. 1787
(*b*)	Australian Constitution Act	II. 1867
(*c*)	USA Constitution	III. 1689
(*d*)	UK Bill of Rights	IV. 1900

Choose the ***correct*** answer from the options given below:

	(*a*)	(*b*)	(*c*)	(*d*)
A.	IV	II	I	III
B.	II	IV	I	III
C.	I	II	III	IV
D.	IV	III	II	I

75. Match List-I with List-II:

	List-I	List-II
(*a*)	Promotion of International Peace and Security	I. Article 210
(*b*)	Conduct of Business of the Govt. of India	II. Article 176
(*c*)	Special Address by the Governor	III. Article 77
(*d*)	Language to be used in the Legislature	IV. Article 51

Choose the ***correct*** answer from the options given below:

	(*a*)	(*b*)	(*c*)	(*d*)
A.	IV	III	II	I
B.	IV	II	III	I
C.	I	IV	II	III
D.	II	IV	I	III

76. Arrange the following cases in chronological order (Old to New):

(*a*) Suresh Kumar Kaushal V/s Naz Foundation

(*b*) Navtej Singh Jauhar V/s Union of India

(*c*) Naz Foundation V/s Government of NCT of Delhi

(*d*) Ankit V/s State of Haryana

Choose the correct answer from the options given below:

A. (*a*), (*b*), (*c*), (*d*)

B. (*b*), (*c*), (*d*), (*a*)

C. (*c*), (*a*), (*b*), (*d*)

D. (*d*), (*c*), (*a*), (*b*)

77. Arrange the following cases in chronological order (Old to New) where death sentence has been awarded by the Supreme Court of India.

(*a*) Ediga Anamma V/s State of Andhra Pradesh

(*b*) Bachan Singh V/s State of Punjab

(*c*) Machhi Singh V/s State of Punjab

(*d*) Vinay Sharma V/s Union of India

(*e*) Shabnam Khan V/s Union of India

Choose the correct answer from the options given below:

A. (*d*), (*b*), (*c*), (*e*), (*a*)

B. (*a*), (*b*), (*c*), (*e*), (*d*)

C. (*e*), (*d*), (*c*), (*a*), (*b*)

D. (*c*), (*e*), (*a*), (*b*), (*d*)

78. Which among the followings most appropriately reflects the constitutional system for India and USA?

(*a*) Federal

(*b*) Presidential

(*c*) Democratic form of Government

(*d*) Unitary

(*e*) Rule of Law

Choose the correct answer from the options given below:

A. (*a*), (*b*), (*e*) B. (*a*), (*c*), (*e*)

C. (*b*), (*d*), (*e*) D. (*a*), (*b*), (*c*), (*e*)

79. Arrange the following chapters of the Indian Penal Code on the basis of ascending order:

(*a*) General Exceptions

(*b*) Offences against the Public Tranquillity

(*c*) Offences against Property

(*d*) Offences against Human body

(*e*) Offences against State

Choose the correct answer from the options given below:

A. (*b*), (*c*), (*d*), (*e*), (*a*)

B. (*d*), (*c*), (*b*), (*a*), (*e*)

C. (*a*), (*e*), (*b*), (*d*), (*c*)

D. (*a*), (*b*), (*c*), (*d*), (*e*)

80. Arrange the following statutory provisions on first come basis as per the Indian Contract Act, 1872:

(*a*) Agreement void for uncertainty
(*b*) Discharge of surety by release or discharge of principal debtor
(*c*) Release of one co-surety does not discharge others
(*d*) Co-sureties liable to contribute equally
(*e*) Rights of surety on payment or performance

Choose the correct answer from the options given below:

A. (*a*), (*c*), (*d*), (*b*), (*e*)
B. (*a*), (*b*), (*c*), (*e*), (*d*)
C. (*a*), (*c*), (*e*), (*d*), (*b*)
D. (*c*), (*a*), (*d*), (*b*), (*e*)

81. Arrange the following as per sections of the Companies Act, 2013 in descending order:

(*a*) Execution of Bills of Exchange, etc.
(*b*) Punishment in case of repeated default
(*c*) Annual reports on Government Companies
(*d*) Petition for winding up
(*e*) Functions of Company Secretary

Choose the correct answer from the options given below:

A. (*c*), (*d*), (*e*), (*a*), (*b*)
B. (*b*), (*c*), (*d*), (*e*), (*a*)
C. (*c*), (*a*), (*e*), (*d*), (*b*)
D. (*b*), (*a*), (*d*), (*c*), (*e*)

82. Consider the following cases decided by the Supreme Court of India and arrange them in correct sequence of the year of the judgements : (Old to New)

(*a*) Navtej Singh Jauhar V/s Union of India
(*b*) Rupa Ashok Hurra V/s Ashok Hurra
(*c*) Sayra Bano V/s Union of India
(*d*) Selvi V/s State of Karnataka
(*e*) Shankri Prasad V/s Union of India

Choose the correct answer from the options given below:

A. (*a*), (*b*), (*c*), (*d*), (*e*)
B. (*e*), (*d*), (*c*), (*b*), (*a*)
C. (*e*), (*b*), (*d*), (*c*), (*a*)
D. (*d*), (*e*), (*c*), (*a*), (*b*)

83. Consider the following cases decided by the Supreme Court and arrange in correct sequence of the year of judgment (new to old).

(*a*) Mukesh Singh V/s NCT of Delhi
(*b*) Yaqoob Abdul Razzaq Menon V/s State of Maharastra
(*c*) Navneet Kaur V/s Union of India
(*d*) Mohd Ajmal Amir Kasab V/s State of Maharastra
(*e*) A.S. Mohd. Rafi V/s State of Tamil Nadu

Choose the correct answer from the options given below:

A. (*a*), (*b*), (*c*), (*d*), (*e*)
B. (*b*), (*c*), (*d*), (*e*), (*a*)
C. (*d*), (*c*), (*b*), (*a*), (*e*)
D. (*c*), (*b*), (*a*), (*d*), (*e*)

84. Arrange the following in proper sequence of taking place.

(*a*) Intention
(*b*) Preparation
(*c*) Act
(*d*) Conviction
(*e*) Sentence

Choose the correct answer from the options given below:

A. (*e*), (*d*), (*c*), (*b*), (*a*)
B. (*a*), (*b*), (*c*), (*d*), (*e*)
C. (*b*), (*c*), (*d*), (*e*), (*a*)
D. (*d*), (*c*), (*b*), (*a*), (*e*)

85. Arrange the following cases yearwise (old to new) as per the year of the judgements delivered:

(*a*) Sajjan Singh V/s State of Rajasthan
(*b*) Kihota Hollohon V/s Zachilhu
(*c*) L. Chandra Kumar V/s Union of India
(*d*) Minerva Mills V/s Union of India
(*e*) Azeez Basha V/s Union of India

Choose the correct answer from the options given below:

A. (*a*), (*b*), (*c*), (*d*), (*e*)
B. (*e*), (*d*), (*c*), (*b*), (*a*)
C. (*e*), (*a*), (*d*), (*b*), (*c*)
D. (*a*), (*e*), (*d*), (*b*), (*c*)

86. Assertion (A) : Possession is said to be the nine points of the law.

Reason (R) : The person in possession of an object has better claim over it against the whole world except the real owner.

In the light of the above statements, choose the most appropriate answer from the options given below:

A. Both (A) and (R) are correct and (R) is the correct explanation of (A)
B. Both (A) and (R) are correct but (R) is not the correct explanation of (A)
C. (A) is correct, but (R) is not correct
D. (A) is not correct, but (R) is correct

87. Assertion (A) : The Supreme Court has opined that the doctrine of *Stare-decises* is one of the important principles of precedent.

Reason (R) : If the Supreme Court finds itself unable to accept the earlier view, it can decide the case in a different way.

In the light of the above statements, choose the most appropriate answer from the options given below:

A. Both (A) and (R) are correct and (R) is the correct explanation of (A)
B. Both (A) and (R) are correct but (R) is not the correct explanation of (A)
C. (A) is correct, but (R) is not correct
D. (A) is not correct, but (R) is correct

88. Assertion (A) : A Bigamous marriage is voidable under the Hindu Law.

Reason (R) : Children born out of void marriages are legitimate children of their parent.

In the light of the above statements, choose the most appropriate answer from the options given below:

A. Both (A) and (R) are correct and (R) is the correct explanation of (A)
B. Both (A) and (R) are correct but (R) is not the correct explanation of (A)
C. (A) is correct, but (R) is not correct
D. (A) is not correct, but (R) is correct

89. Statement I : Law has its source in the general consciousness (volkgeist) of the people.

Statement II : Law is a product of the people's life, it is a manifestation of its spirit.

In the light of the above statements, choose the most appropriate answer from the options given below:

A. Both Statement I and Statement II are correct
B. Both Statement I and Statement II are incorrect
C. Statement I is correct but statement II is incorrect
D. Statement I is incorrect but Statement II is correct

90. Statement I : Salmond says that common law is essentially judge-made law.

Statement II : Pollock said that the common law is a customary law i.e. based on customs.

In the light of the above statements, choose the most appropriate answer from the options given below:

A. Both Statement I and Statement II are true
B. Both Statement I and Statement II are false
C. Statement I is true but Statement II is false
D. Statement I is false but Statement II is true

Directions (Qs. No. 91 to 95): *Read the following passage carefully and answer the questions:*

If a copy of a Constitution is placed in the hands of a law student, it is sure that he will ask two questions. Firstly, what is the form of

Government that is envisaged in the Constitution: and secondly what is the form of the Constitution? Form of the proposed Government is parliamentary. Form of the Draft Constitution is federal in as much as it establishes what may be called a Dual policy. This dual policy under the proposed Constitution will consist of the Union at the centre and the states at the periphery each endowed with sovereign powers to be exercised in the field assigned to them respectively by the Constitution. Some critics have taken objection to the description of India in Article 1 of the Constitution as a Union of States. It is said that the correct phraseology should be federation of States. It is true that South Africa, which is a unitary State, is described as a Union. But Canada, which is a federation is also called a Union. Thus, the description of India as a Union, though its Constitution is federal does no violence to usage. But what is important is that the use of the word union is deliberate. As Dr. Ambedkar has said, "I do not know why the word 'Union' was used in the Canadian Constitution. But I can tell you why the Drafting Committee has used it in context of India. The Drafting Committee wanted to make it clear that though India was to be a federation, the federation was not the result of an agreement by the States to join in a federation and that federation not being the result of an agreement, no state has the right to secede from it. The Federation is a Union because it is indestructible. Though the country and the people may be divided into different states for convenience of administration the country is one integral whole, its people a single people living under a single imperium derived from a single source. The Americans had to wage a civil war to establish that the states have no right of secession and that their federation was indestructible. The Drafting committee thought that it was better to make it clear at the outset rather than to leave it to speculation or to dispute.

91. Americans had to struggle very hard (to the extent of civil war) to establish to which of the following?
A. America had dual policy
B. Federation was indestructible
C. States have their own constitution separate from a federal constitution
D. States have right to secede

92. Form of Government and Form of the Constitution are:
A. Same Concepts
B. Obsolete Concepts
C. Irrelevant Concepts
D. Different Concepts

93. Like Union, the states are endowed with sovereign powers. This sovereign power of states is:
A. Unlimited
B. Determined by the Constitution
C. Limited by International Law
D. Guided by Jurisprudence

94. What did the Drafting Committee want to make clear at the outset?
A. The form of Government is parliamentary
B. The Constitution envisages dual polity
C. The States have no right to secession
D. Canada is a federation

95. Article 1 of the Constitution of India uses the phrase "Union of States", though it is a "Federation". The correct phraseology need not be "Federation of States" because:
A. "Union of States" phrase does not necessarily mean Unitary State.
B. A federation need not necessarily use the terminology "Federation of States".
C. Canada is an established federation but uses the word "Union".
D. All the above

Directions (Qs. No. 96 to 100): *Read the following passage carefully and answer the questions:*

Sting operation is a phenomenon which became popular in 1970s. With the advent of technology and internet, sting operation is no more monopoly of media houses or big players. Being essentially a deceptive operation, though designed to nab a criminal, a sting operation raises certain moral and ethical questions besides legal issues. The victim, who is otherwise innocent, is lured into committing a crime on the assurance of absolute secrecy and confidentiality of the circumstances raising the potential question as to how such a victim can be held responsible for the crime which he would not have committed but for the enticement. Another issue that arises from such an operation is the fact that the means deployed to establish the commission of the crime itself involves a culpable act. In the U.S. a sting operation is recognized as a legal method of law enforcement in a limited manner. The same is not the position in India. A sting operation carried out in public interest has had the approval of Court in R.K. Anand V/s Registrar. Delhi High Court (2009) though it will be difficult to understand the ratio in the said case as an approval of such a method as an acceptable principle of law enforcement valid in all cases. A crime does not stand obliterated or extinguished merely because its commission is claimed to be in public interest. Any such principle would be abhorrent to our criminal jurisprudence. At the same time the criminal intent behind the commission of the act will have to be established. The offence of abetment (section 107), criminal conspiracy (Section 120A) s 354C, 354D under IPC and some provisions of the Information Technology Act, 2000 would, thus, require criminal intent.

96. Sting Operation raises:
A. Moral and ethical question only
B. Legal questions only
C. Moral, Ethical as well as legal questions
D. Social and religions questions

97. A sting operation, though designed to catch a criminal, is questionable because:
A. The person is lured into committing it
B. There is false assurance of absolute secrecy
C. Means deployed itself involves criminal act
D. All the above

98. The legal status of sting operation in US and India is:
A. Same
B. Not same
C. Same only, if done in public interest
D. Not same because all sting operations are punishable under Information Technology Act, 2000.

99. The decision of R.K. Anand V/s Registrar, Delhi High Court (2009) is applicable:
A. not as an acceptable principle in all cases
B. as an acceptable principle in all cases
C. as an acceptable principle in all cases if not done in public interest
D. not applicable even in R.K. Anand case

100. A person who does a sting operation:
A. does not commit any offence
B. will commit offence, if criminal upon whom sting is done, is not caught
C. does not commit any offence, if sting operation is done in public interest
D. can commit offence like abetment etc.

ANSWERS

1. **(C):** The concept of the independence of the judiciary as a basic structure or feature of the Constitution is embedded in the jurisprudence of India. The Supreme Court of India, in a landmark case known as the Kesavananda Bharati vs. State of Kerala (1973), propounded the theory of the 'Basic Structure' of the Constitution. This doctrine asserts that the Constitution has certain basic features that cannot be altered or destroyed through amendments by the Parliament. The independence of the judiciary was recognized as one of these inviolable features. It is essential to maintain checks and balances and to ensure that fundamental rights are protected. This notion has been reinforced in subsequent cases and remains pivotal in India's constitutional debates.

2. **(C):** The right to information or freedom of information has been recognized and legislated in multiple countries, including

India, the USA, and the UK. In India, the Right to Information (RTI) Act was passed in 2005, making the government more transparent and accountable to its citizens. The USA has the Freedom of Information Act (FOIA), which was enacted in 1966 and provides for public access to government documents and records. The UK also implemented its Freedom of Information Act in 2000, granting public rights to access information held by public authorities. All three countries, therefore, have legislations that recognize the importance of transparency and the citizen's right to access information.

3. **(D):** The concept of the 'rule of law' and its three principles were propounded by Professor A.V. Dicey, an influential British jurist. According to Dicey, the rule of law entails: 1) the absence of arbitrary power on the part of the government; 2) equality before the law, which means that no person is above the law, and everyone is subject to the jurisdiction of ordinary courts; and 3) the constitution is a product of individual rights, meaning that the rights of individuals are based on legal precedents and not on any written constitution. Dicey's concept of the rule of law has been highly influential and has become foundational in many legal systems across the world.

4. **(A):** Residuary powers refer to powers not explicitly mentioned in the Constitution. In the context of Center-State relationships, the handling of residuary powers varies from one country to another. In India, according to Article 248 and Entry 97 of the Union List, the residuary powers are vested with the Central Government or Parliament. Canada follows a similar approach where the residuary powers are given to the central authority. This is in contrast to the USA, where the residuary powers are vested with the states. The rationale behind giving residuary powers to the center in countries like India and Canada is to ensure a stronger and more integrated federal structure.

5. **(B):** 'Separation of Powers' and 'distribution of powers' are indeed different concepts. The 'Separation of Powers' refers to the division of government responsibilities into distinct branches to prevent any one branch from gaining too much power. Traditionally, it's been divided among the executive, legislative, and judiciary branches. On the other hand, the 'distribution of powers' pertains to the demarcation of powers and responsibilities between different levels of government, like the center and states in a federal structure. While 'Separation of Powers' ensures checks and balances within the government, 'distribution of powers' determines the autonomy and responsibilities of different government levels in a federation. Both concepts are crucial for the smooth functioning of democracies and maintaining the balance of power.

6. **(B):** The institution of the 'Ombudsman' was first developed in Sweden. The word 'Ombudsman' is of Swedish origin and translates to 'representative'. In 1809, Sweden introduced the Parliamentary Ombudsman's institution, essentially appointed by the Parliament, to ensure that public authorities and officials complied with the laws of the land. The primary role of the Ombudsman is to investigate complaints against government agencies and officials. The Ombudsman's introduction aimed to act as a check on the state's power, ensuring that citizens' rights were not violated by administrative actions. Since its inception in Sweden, the idea of an Ombudsman has been adopted by many countries worldwide to promote transparency, accountability, and the rule of law in administrative functions.

7. **(A):** In the case of National Highway Authority of India Vs. Madhukar Kumar (2022), the Supreme Court held that the

administration of a public authority cannot be invalidated merely for not recording reasons when it had no duty to do so. Recording of reasons is a practice that promotes transparency and accountability. However, it is not an absolute rule and depends on the statutory requirement. In cases where the statute or any other legal provision does not expressly demand the recording of reasons, the decision's validity cannot be questioned on this ground alone. This judgment underlines the principle that while transparency is vital in administrative actions, the technicalities cannot be used to invalidate decisions when the law does not mandate such requirements.

8. (C): Article 211 of the Constitution provides that "no discussion shall take place in the legislature of a State with respect to the conduct of any judge of the Supreme Court or of a High Court in the discharge of his duties." This provision underscores the independence of the judiciary, a cornerstone of the democratic framework in India. By preventing discussions on judges' conduct in state legislatures, the Constitution ensures that judges can execute their duties without political interference or undue pressure. It is crucial to maintain the separation of powers principle and to ensure that the judiciary remains impartial and independent of the executive and legislative branches of government.

9. (D): In the landmark judgment of Joseph Shine Vs. Union of India (2018), the Supreme Court struck down Section 497 of the Indian Penal Code (IPC). Section 497 dealt with the offense of adultery. However, it was criticized for being gender-biased, treating women as property, and infringing on individual autonomy. The Court, in this case, held that Section 497 is unconstitutional, emphasizing gender equality and personal liberty. The judgment was lauded for taking a progressive step towards upholding individual rights and recognizing the changing dynamics of relationships in contemporary society.

10. (A): The 101st Constitutional (Amendment) Act added Article 279A to the Constitution. This amendment paved the way for the implementation of the Goods and Services Tax (GST) in India. Article 279A provides for the constitution of a GST Council, tasked with making recommendations on various aspects of the GST, including rates, exemptions, and threshold limits. The GST Council comprises the Union Finance Minister, the Union Minister of State in charge of Revenue or Finance, and the Minister in charge of Finance or Taxation or any other Minister nominated by each State government. This amendment was crucial in transitioning India to a new indirect tax regime, aiming to streamline taxes and promote a unified market.

11. (C): The 101st Constitutional Amendment to the Constitution of India inserted Article 246A, which deals with the special provision concerning the Goods and Services Tax (GST). This amendment was instrumental in introducing a unified indirect tax regime across India, replacing several central and state taxes. Article 246A grants both the Parliament and the State Legislatures the concurrent power to make laws on GST. The primary objective behind the introduction of GST was to create a single, cohesive market at the national level, reduce the cascading effect of tax on tax, and improve the ease of doing business.

12. (D): Article 342A of the Constitution of India deals with 'socially and educationally backward classes' (SEBCs). This article, along with a few others, was introduced to provide a comprehensive framework for the identification, benefits, and protection of the rights of SEBCs. Specifically, Article 342A(1) states that the President, in consultation with the Governor, may specify the socially and educationally backward classes for a state or union territory. This provision aims to ensure that adequate representation, protection, and welfare measures are in place for these classes, emphasizing the broader constitutional goal of social justice.

13. (C): In the case of Gita Hariharan Vs. RBI, the Supreme Court of India held that the mother can be the natural guardian of a minor even in the father's presence. The case addressed a provision of the Hindu Minority and Guardianship Act, 1956, which seemingly positioned the father as the primary guardian and the mother as a secondary guardian. The Court held that if the father is not in actual charge of the affairs of the minor or is indifferent, unsuitable, or incapacitated in some form, the mother can act as the natural guardian. The judgment was a step forward in recognizing the mother's equal parental rights and responsibilities and went a long way in reinforcing gender equality in guardianship matters.

14. (C): Sir John Salmond, a renowned legal theorist, divided the sources of law into two main classes: (*a*) Formal sources and (*b*) Material sources. For Salmond, formal sources refer to the legal processes or methods through which rules are recognized as part of the legal system, such as legislation or judicial precedent. In contrast, material sources are the factors and considerations that influence or guide the creation of these rules, including historical reasons, custom, or societal needs. Salmond's classification is a foundational aspect of legal theory, shedding light on how laws originate and evolve.

15. (B): Friedrich Carl von Savigny is considered the main exponent of the 'historical school of law'. Savigny believed that law emerges organically from the spirit of the people and is a product of their history, customs, and traditions. He emphasized the importance of the Volkgeist (Spirit of the People) in shaping legal norms. Savigny's views were a reaction against the natural law theories and the codification movement of his time. He argued that law cannot be artificially constructed but evolves naturally over time, reflecting the culture and history of a society. His theories have had a profound impact on the development of legal thought and the understanding of customary and traditional law.

16. (A): The Austinian theory of law, propounded by John Austin, views law as a command issued by a sovereign (political superior) to whom a society is in a habit of obedience. According to Austin, the essence of law is the command backed by a sanction, which is imposed by a political sovereign. He did not consider judge-made law, international law, or customs as true laws within his definition. For Austin, true laws were specific commands given by a sovereign to a determinate person or persons (political inferiors), and not to the sovereign himself. This conception of law has been criticized by many for its limited view, particularly its exclusion of international law and customary law, but it was influential in shaping the analytical approach to jurisprudence.

17. (B): "Law and the Modern Mind" is authored by Jerome Frank. In this groundbreaking work, Frank introduced the concept of legal realism, which emphasized the indeterminacy of law and the role of judges' personal experiences, emotions, and biases in the decision-making process. Frank questioned the predictability of judicial decisions and challenged the traditional notions of legal formalism. The book brought to light the psychological aspects of the judicial process and highlighted the subjective factors that influence legal reasoning.

18. (C): While Ihering, Ehrlich, and Roscoe Pound are jurists associated with the sociological approach to law, Sir Henry Maine does not belong to this school of thought. The sociological approach focuses on understanding law in the context of society and emphasizes the social purpose of law. In contrast, Maine is renowned for his historical approach to jurisprudence, especially his work "Ancient Law". He delved into the evolution of legal systems and traced the development of legal concepts from ancient to modern times.

19. (B): The statement "The movement of progressive societies has hitherto been a movement from status to contract" is a famous generalization made by Sir Henry Maine in his seminal work "Ancient Law". By this, Maine highlighted the shift in societies from feudal and traditional setups, where an individual's role and rights were determined by his status at birth, to more modern setups where relationships and rights are determined by contracts. This transition marked the rise of individualism and personal freedom, relegating traditional and communal structures to the background.

20. (D): The principle "actus non facit reum nisi mens sit rea" translates to "an act does not make a person guilty unless there is a guilty mind." This legal maxim emphasizes that for an act to be considered a crime, it usually requires two elements: a wrongful act (actus reus) and a guilty mind or intent (mens rea). It underscores the importance of intent in criminal liability. Without the requisite mental state, a wrongful act, in most cases, does not lead to criminal responsibility. This foundational principle distinguishes between someone who commits an act accidentally and someone who does it with criminal intent. It serves as a cornerstone in many legal systems to ensure fairness and justice in the application of criminal law.

21. (B): Austin defined ownership as a right over a determinate thing that is indefinite in terms of user, unrestricted in terms of disposition, and unlimited in terms of duration. John Austin, an English jurist, emphasized the absoluteness of ownership rights. However, in real-world scenarios, absolute ownership rarely exists due to various societal, governmental, and other restrictions placed on property rights. Nonetheless, Austin's definition of ownership has been fundamental in shaping the legal and theoretical discourse on property rights in the domain of jurisprudence. His works have been influential, especially in legal positivism, where he discussed the nature and structure of laws.

22. (D): The given statement, "I promise to pay B ₹ 50,000 and to deliver him my black horse on 1st March next," is not a promissory note. A promissory note, as defined in the Negotiable Instruments Act, 1881, is an instrument in writing containing an unconditional undertaking, signed by the maker, to pay a certain sum of money only to or to the order of a certain person or to the bearer of the instrument. The mentioned instrument involves both a promise to pay money and a promise to deliver goods, thereby not strictly adhering to the definition of a promissory note.

23. (A): The case Bai Tahira Vs. Ali Hussain Fidaalli (AIR 1979 SC 362) deals with the topic of maintenance. In this landmark case, the Supreme Court ruled that a divorced Muslim woman is entitled to maintenance from her former husband under Section 125 of the Criminal Procedure Code until she remarries, even if she has received a lump sum amount as Mehr (dower) during the time of divorce. This judgment is significant as it aimed at ensuring financial support and welfare for divorced Muslim women, emphasizing their right to maintenance irrespective of religious personal laws.

24. **(B):** The case T. Sareetha Vs. T.V. Subbaiah dealt with the constitutional validity of Section 9 of the Hindu Marriage Act, 1955, which pertains to the restitution of conjugal rights. In this case, the Andhra Pradesh High Court held that Section 9 violated the right to privacy, as it amounted to forcing a spouse to have sexual relations against their will. The court observed that forcing the spouses to cohabit violated the individual's right to privacy and was thus unconstitutional. It's worth noting that this decision of the Andhra Pradesh High Court is in contrast to the decisions of other High Courts and the Supreme Court which upheld the constitutionality of Section 9.

25. **(C):** A sub-agent is responsible for his acts to the agent but not to the principal, except in cases of fraud or wilful wrong. In the agency's sphere, a sub-agent is a person employed by the original agent to perform functions the agent has agreed to undertake on behalf of the principal. Typically, the principal-agent relationship is a direct one, and a sub-agent acts on behalf of the agent. Thus, the primary responsibility of a sub-agent is to the agent. However, in instances where the sub-agent commits fraud or a wilful wrong, they can be held directly accountable to the principal. This concept ensures the principal's protection against fraudulent or harmful actions committed by sub-agents.

26. **(B):** Justice Arijit Pasayat authored the judgement in the leading case Seema V/s Ashwani Kumar (2006) 2 SCC 78. In this case, the Supreme Court directed the states and union territories to make provisions for the mandatory registration of all marriages. The apex court observed that in many cases, especially concerning women, non-registration of marriages made it difficult for them to assert their rights. The mandatory registration was deemed necessary to prevent child marriages and to ensure a minimum age of marriage. This judgement has been instrumental in recognizing the importance of having a documentary proof for marriage in legal matters.

27. **(D):** The Gloucester Grammar School Case is not related to the 'Tort of Negligence'. In this case, the dispute arose when the defendant, a schoolmaster, set up a rival school to the plaintiff's school. The defendant lured some of the students from the plaintiff's school. The court held that though the defendant's action caused economic loss to the plaintiff, there was no wrongful act committed, and therefore, no actionable claim in tort. The other cases listed revolve around the principle of negligence, where the duty of care and its breach resulted in damages.

28. **(B)**

29. **(D):** In the case of Habibur Rahman V/s Altaf Ali, the Privy Council held that the 'Doctrine of Acknowledgement' is a part of the substantial 'Muslim Law of Inheritance' and not merely a rule of evidence. The Doctrine of Acknowledgement comes into play when a person, by his words or conduct, acknowledges that a certain property is owned by another. This acknowledgment has implications in property law, especially concerning claims of ownership. By confirming this doctrine's place in the substantive Muslim Law of Inheritance, the Privy Council emphasized the importance of acknowledgment in property rights disputes under Muslim law.

30. (C): The leading case 'Ashby V/s White' was decided by Lord Holt. This case is a foundational tort law case that revolved around the right to vote. The plaintiff, Ashby, was a qualified voter, but the defendant, White, who was a constable, wrongfully prevented him from voting in an election. Though the candidate Ashby supported won the election, he brought a suit against White for the deprivation of his legal right. Lord Holt, in his ruling, established the principle that the loss of a legal right (in this case, the right to vote) results in damages, even if there's no tangible harm or loss. The case underscores the principle that infringement of a legal right in itself constitutes harm.

31. (C): For an act to constitute trespass under the Law of Torts, unlawful intention is not necessary. Trespass to land is the unjustifiable intrusion by one person upon land in the possession of another. Key elements of trespass are the entry, remaining on the land, or performing an act that affects the sole possession. The intention behind the act, whether lawful or unlawful, doesn't negate the fact that a trespass has occurred. A person can be guilty of trespass even if they mistakenly enter another's land with no intention to cause harm.

32. (C): Comparative public law is a method of studying law. It involves comparing the public laws (laws that govern relationships between individuals and the state) of different jurisdictions. This comparison allows legal scholars and practitioners to understand similarities, differences, and trends across different legal systems. It is instrumental in globalized legal environments where legal principles might need to be harmonized or understood across borders. This method is different from a specific principle, written rule, or a system of law tied to a particular jurisdiction or organization like the United Nations.

33. (A): "We the People" is a phrase found in the constitutions of both India and the USA. In the US, these words begin the Preamble of the Constitution, representing the idea that the Constitution's authority originates from the people's collective will. Similarly, the Indian Constitution starts with the same words, indicating that the Constitution's power and authority derive from the Indian people. The Canadian Constitution does not start with these words.

34. (C): When estimating the loss or damage resulting from a breach of contract, the means which existed to remedy the inconvenience caused by the non-performance of the contract must be taken into account. This principle is grounded in the idea that damages are meant to place the non-breaching party in the position they would have been had the contract been performed. This concept is often known as "mitigation of damages," meaning that the non-breaching party has a duty to take reasonable steps to minimize the damages they suffer due to the breach.

35. (C): The main purpose of the Information Technology Act, 2000, as outlined in its Preamble, includes providing legal recognition for transactions carried out by electronic data interchange, promoting the use of electronic means instead of paper, and amending related laws like the Indian Penal Code, Indian Evidence Act, Bankers Books Evidence Act, and the Reserve Bank of India Act. However, the Act does not expressly state its purpose as facilitating electronic filing of documents with international agencies. While the IT Act does enable electronic transactions and documentation, its primary focus is domestic rather than international agency interactions.

36. (C): In the Sale of Goods Act, 1930, "fault" is defined as a wrongful act or default. According to the Act, "fault" is the wrongful act or omission which gives rise to a liability in terms of the Sale of Goods contract. The definition of fault under this Act emphasizes that the wrongful act or default is vital when determining the rights and liabilities of the buyer and seller in a sale transaction. This is significant because in the context of the Sale of Goods Act, the concept of fault determines which party is responsible for any breach of the contractual terms or any mishap that happens with the goods.

37. (A): When a promissory note, bill of exchange, or cheque is transferred to any person in such a manner that it makes that person the holder, it is said to be negotiated. Negotiation means the process by which a promissory note, bill of exchange, or cheque is transferred from one person to another in such a way that the transferee becomes a lawful holder of the instrument. The process of negotiation ensures that the transferee, or the holder, gets a good title to the instrument, free from any defect of the title of the transferor, provided the holder receives it in good faith and for value.

38. (B): A proposal, when accepted, becomes a promise. As per the Indian Contract Act, 1872, when a person to whom the proposal (offer) is made signifies his assent to it, the proposal is said to be accepted. At this point, the proposal turns into a promise. A promise is essentially an accepted proposal. This is foundational to contract law, as the acceptance of an offer (or proposal) is a key element in forming a legally binding contract.

39. (D): The case in question is Holwell Securities Ltd. V/s Hughes (1974). In this case, the issue revolved around an option to purchase land which was exercisable by notice. It was held that merely posting the notice, which was never delivered, was not a valid exercise of the option. The ruling underscored the importance of effective communication of acceptance in contract law. This case highlighted that in situations where communication is essential for the acceptance of an offer, mere posting is not sufficient, especially if the communication doesn't reach the intended recipient.

40. (A): The correct answer is "Immaterial". The phrase is taken from Section 15 of the Indian Contract Act, 1872 which discusses the concept of coercion. The section states that it is immaterial whether the Indian Penal Code is or is not in force in the place where the coercion is employed. The essence of this provision is to highlight that the validity or nature of an act as 'coercion' under the Contract Act does not depend on whether the IPC applies in that particular jurisdiction. This means that even if an act qualifies as coercion under the Contract Act, it doesn't matter if the IPC is not applicable in that area.

41. (A): The provisions under the Indian Penal Code (IPC) that pertain to cybercrimes, specifically relating to the violation of a woman's privacy, are covered under Section 354C and Section 354D. Section 354C deals with the offense of voyeurism. This section penalizes anyone who captures or publishes the image of a woman engaging in a private act without her consent. Section 354D pertains to stalking, which includes online stalking. This section penalizes anyone who follows a person or contacts, or attempts to contact such person to foster personal interaction repeatedly despite a clear indication of disinterest by such person. These sections, though not traditionally seen as "cybercrime" laws, have been used to prosecute cyber-related offenses, particularly those that involve online harassment or the misuse of electronic means to invade a person's privacy.

42. (B): In the case of State of Bihar V/s Kameshwar Singh (1952), the Supreme Court laid down certain tests to determine what constitutes "colourable legislation." Colourable legislation refers to the situation where a legislature enacts a law that is beyond its competence under the guise of acting within its powers. The correct tests to discern such legislation as deduced from this case are:

- The court must look into the substance of the law and not its form or the label the legislature has given it. The substance over form rule suggests that one cannot do indirectly what one is not permitted to do directly.
- The court must look at the object as well as the effect of the law. This ensures that the true purpose and impact of the legislation are taken into account.
- If the legislature proceeds under a legislative plan, the court must read all the statutes constituting that plan and determine their combined effect.

Hence, (*b*), (*c*) and (*d*) are correct.

43. (C): According to Article 352 of the Constitution of India, when a proclamation of emergency is to be approved by the Parliament, it must meet specific criteria. These are:

- It must be approved by a majority of the total membership of that house. This ensures that more than half of the total number of members (irrespective of those present or absent) in that particular house approve of the proclamation.
- Additionally, it must be approved by a majority of not less than two-thirds of the members of that house present and voting. This condition ensures that of the members present, a significant majority supports the proclamation. These provisions are intended to prevent the misusc of the emergency provisions and ensure that such a significant decision is backed by a considerable majority in the Parliament.

Hence, (*a*) and (*b*) are correct.

44. (C): Under Muslim Law, certain principles govern the concept of Hiba (gift):

- Hiba is the immediate and unqualified transfer of the property's corpus without any return. This means that it is a gratuitous transfer without any consideration.
- A unique feature of Muslim law is that a gift of immovable properties can be made verbally. There is no strict requirement for documentation, unlike other legal systems.
- A gift of life interest is valid under Muslim law. This allows a person to grant a life interest in a property to another, with the property reverting upon the end of that life interest.

Hence, (*a*), (*b*) and (*c*) are correct.

45. (A): The correct order as per the Patent Act, 1970 is as follows:

- **Term of patent:** Section 53 outlines the term of the patent. Typically, it is twenty years from the date of filing the application for the patent.
- **Controller and other officers:** Section 73 elaborates on the Controller and other officers, detailing their appointment and powers.
- **Licensing of related patents:** Section 84 pertains to the licensing of related patents.

- **Convention countries:** Section 133 relates to convention countries and the priority rights derived from patent applications made in those countries.
- **Multiple Priorities:** Section 135 talks about claiming multiple priorities based on different applications filed in convention countries.

Hence, the correct chronological order is (*b*), (*a*), (*e*), (*c*), (*d*).

46. (D): The cases related to environmental protection among the given options are:

- Subhash Kumar V/s State of Bihar and others: This case addressed the right to life in the context of environmental degradation. The Supreme Court held that the right to life includes the right to a pollution-free environment. Any activity that harms the environment can be challenged on the ground of being violative of Article 21 of the Indian Constitution.
- Almitra H Patel and others V/s Union of India and others: This case is famously known as the "Solid Waste Management Case." The Supreme Court addressed the issue of solid waste management in urban areas and held that the right to a clean city is a part of the right to life.
- M. C. Mehta V/s Union of India: This is one of the landmark cases in the history of environmental jurisprudence in India. M.C. Mehta filed a series of Public Interest Litigations (PILs) addressing various environmental concerns, from air pollution in Delhi due to vehicular emissions to the protection of the Taj Mahal from industrial pollution. The Supreme Court delivered several landmark judgments in these cases, emphasizing the importance of environmental protection.

Hence, (*b*), (*c*) and (*d*) are related to environmental protection cases.

47. (C): Under the Air (Prevention and Control of Pollution) Act, 1981, a person is ineligible to be a member of the State Board if:

- Such person is or at any time has been adjudged insolvent. This clause is to ensure the credibility of the members.
- Has been declared by a competent court to be of unsound mind. This provision ensures the mental fitness of the board members.
- Has been convicted of an offence under the Air (Prevention and Control of Pollution) Act, 1981. This clause ensures that members have no conflicts of interest.
- Guilty of an offence involving moral turpitude. Members with a record of offenses that involve moral depravity or inherent baseness are not considered suitable.

Hence, (*a*), (*b*), (*c*) and (*e*) are correct.

48. (B): The following justices have been members of the National Green Tribunal (NGT):

- **Justice A Suryanarayan Naidu:** He was one of the judicial members of the NGT.
- **Justice C Venkata Ramana:** He served as a member before ascending to the Supreme Court.
- **Justice Pratap Kumar Ray:** He also served as a member of the NGT.

The NGT is a specialized tribunal dedicated to handling environmental disputes. It was established in 2010 to reduce the burden on higher courts and provide a fast-track mechanism for environmental cases.

Hence, (*a*), (*c*) and (*e*) are correct.

49. (C): Prof. H.L.A. Hart, a prominent legal philosopher, put forth the following ideas:

- Law is a union of primary and secondary rules. Primary rules are those that prescribe certain behaviors, while secondary rules are about how primary rules can change or be identified.

- The idea of obligation is central to a rule. For Hart, legal obligation is rooted in the social practice of the community.
- The primary rules gain a systemic unity when they are combined with secondary rules. Secondary rules give a cohesive structure to the primary ones.

Hart's conceptualization of law presented a more nuanced understanding than the earlier positivist approaches.

Hence, (*a*), (*b*) and (*d*) are correct.

50. (D): In a contract of bailment:

- A gratuitous bailment is terminated by the death of either the bailor or the bailee. A gratuitous bailment is one where no charge or fee is involved. If either party dies, the contract naturally terminates.
- The bailee is bound to take care of the goods bailed. This is a fundamental duty of the bailee. If the bailee fails to do so and the goods are damaged or lost due to his negligence, he may be held liable for the loss.

Bailment involves the transfer of possession of goods from one person (bailor) to another (bailee) for a specific purpose. On fulfilling the purpose, the goods are returned to the bailor.

Hence, (*c*) and (*d*) are correct.

51. (C): A prospectus is a detailed document issued by a company proposing to issue new securities to the public. It gives information about the company's objectives, structure, and financial statements. Among the given options:

- The name and address of the registered office are essential to identify and locate the company.
- **Details about underwriting:** Underwriting is the process by which investment banks raise investment capital for an external company from investors on the primary markets. This helps potential investors understand the backing the company has.
- **Details of directors:** It's essential for potential investors to know who the decision-makers in the company are.

Hence, (*a*), (*b*) and (*c*) are correct.

52. (B): Regarding the issuance of debentures:

- A company can indeed issue debentures with the option to convert them into shares. This offers flexibility and can be an enticing option for investors.
- Such an issue requires the approval of shareholders and is therefore ratified by a special resolution during a general meeting.
- The debenture trustee has a fiduciary role to ensure the rights of debenture holders are upheld.

Hence, (*a*), (*b*) and (*e*) are correct.

53. (D): Fraud, in legal terms, refers to an intentional deception made for personal gain or to damage another individual.

- Suggesting a fact that is false, knowing it to be false, is indeed a form of fraud.
- Making a promise without the intention to perform it is deceptive.
- Any act designed to deceive qualifies as fraud.

Hence, (*a*), (*c*) and (*d*) are correct.

54. (D): Prof. Dicey's concept of the rule of law is a cornerstone in constitutional theory.

- He believed in the absence of discretionary power in public officials as it could lead to arbitrariness.

- For Dicey, an individual should be punished only for a breach of law, ensuring predictability in the legal system.
- Dicey emphasized that rights should not be the product of written statutes but should emerge from judicial decisions in the light of longstanding practices, customs, and traditions.

Hence, (*a*), (*b*) and (*c*) are correct.

55. **(B):** The Information Technology Act, 2000, is a significant step in ensuring the security and legal framework for electronic commerce in India.

- It is the Central Government that prescribes security practices and procedures for such protected systems.
- The Act aims to protect the infrastructure of critical information, ensuring that essential services remain unaffected by threats to their IT systems.

The National Nodal Agency does not have the authority to declare any computer resource as the protected system.

The Indian Computer Emergency Response Team (CERT-In) does play a pivotal role in enhancing the security of IT infrastructure in India, but the overall responsibility for protected systems does not solely rest with them.

Hence, (*b*) and (*c*) are correct.

56. **(D):** Section 21 of the Indian Penal Code (IPC), 1860, provides an exhaustive list of individuals who are considered as 'public servants'. The objective is to include individuals who perform functions in the public domain and need to be held accountable for their actions.

- **Every commissioned officer of defense services:** Yes, they come under public servants as they serve the nation and are entrusted with specific responsibilities.
- **Every judge:** They are certainly considered public servants as they dispense justice and are in a position of authority.
- **Every officer of the Government:** These individuals also fall under the definition as they perform administrative and managerial tasks for the government.

Hence, (*a*), (*b*) and (*c*) are correct.

57. **(A):** Theft is defined under Section 378 of the IPC. The essential components are:

- **Dishonest intention:** This pertains to the motive behind the act, and theft certainly requires a dishonest intent.
- **The property should be taken out of the possession of any person without that person's consent:** This is fundamental to the definition of theft. Without consent, the act becomes illicit.
- **Property must be movable:** Theft concerns movable property; immovable properties cannot be "stolen" in the context of this provision.

Hence, (*a*), (*b*) and (*d*) are correct.

58. **(C):** The concept of crime has been deeply studied in criminal jurisprudence. The critical elements include:

- **Mens rea:** This refers to the guilty mind or intention behind committing the crime.
- **Actus reus:** This is the actual criminal act or conduct.
- **Injury:** A tangible harm or injury, either physical or mental, must have occurred.
- **Human being:** The crime should involve a human being either as a perpetrator or a victim.

Hence, (*a*), (*b*), (*d*) and (*e*) are correct.

59. **(D):** The Criminal Law (Amendment) Act, 2013, was brought in primarily as a response to the need for stricter laws against sexual offenses, especially after the infamous Delhi gang-rape case in 2012. This amendment introduced several changes:

- **Section 326 A:** Introduced to penalize acid attacks.
- **Section 326 B:** Penalties for attempted acid attacks.
- **Section 166 A:** Punishment for public servants disobeying laws related to sexual offenses.
- **Section 166 B:** Punishment for public servants refusing to record information related to sexual offenses.

Hence, (*a*), (*b*), (*c*) and (*d*) are correct.

60. (C): Negligence is a critical concept in both tort law and criminal law:

- Negligence does indeed relate to an omission or failure to do something, which results in a breach of a legal duty.
- Actionable negligence implies that there was a duty of care, a breach of that duty, and consequential damage. The breach occurs when ordinary care isn't used.
- This statement encapsulates the essence of negligence - a breach of the duty to take care, which results in some form of damage or harm.

Hence, (*a*), (*b*) and (*c*) are correct.

61. (B) **62. (C)**

63. (B) **64. (*)**

65. (C): Regarding the anti-defection law, the landmark case is Kihota Hollohon V/s Zachilhu (1992). In this case, the Supreme Court held that the Speaker of the Lok Sabha (or state legislative assembly) acts as a tribunal while deciding questions of disqualification of a member under the Tenth Schedule (which deals with the issue of defection). The court emphasized that the decision of the Speaker in such matters is subject to judicial review to ensure that it complies with the principles of natural justice and that it is made on relevant considerations. This ensures a check on the Speaker's powers and preserves the balance of the democratic setup.

66. (D): The provisions to the respective sections:

(*a*) Specific goods in a deliverable state corresponds to Section 20 of the Sale of Goods Act, 1930. Section 20 provides that where there is a contract for the sale of specific goods in a deliverable state, the property in the goods passes to the buyer when the contract is made.

(*b*) Auction sale is related to Section 64 of the Sale of Goods Act, 1930. This section dictates the provisions related to auction sales, including the bidder's right to retract their bid.

(*c*) Remedy for breach of warranty is covered under Section 59 of the Sale of Goods Act, 1930. This section delineates the remedies available to the buyer in the event of a breach of warranty.

(*d*) Sale by one of the joint owners matches with Section 28. It deals with sales by one of several joint owners and states that a joint owner can sell his share in the goods.

67. (D): Understanding the powers and features of various countries' legal and political systems:

(*a*) Limited Powers of the Parliament are characteristic of India. In India, the Parliament does not possess unlimited powers and its functions are restricted by the Constitution.

(*b*) Residuary Power to the states also aligns with US. In the US, any powers not specifically granted to the federal government in the Constitution are reserved for the states.

(*c*) Unlimited powers of the Parliament pertain to UK. In the UK, the Parliament is sovereign and can theoretically make or repeal any law.

(*d*) Constitutional Council is an institution of France. This council ensures that the laws passed in France align with their Constitution.

68. (C): Date of ratification or accession for various Human Rights Instruments:

(*a*) International Convention on the Elimination of All forms of Racial Discrimination (ICERD) was ratified/accessed in 1968.

(*b*) International Covenant on Civil and Political Rights (ICCPR) was ratified/accessed in 1979.

(*c*) Forced Labour Convention corresponds to 1954.

(*d*) Convention on the Rights of Child (CRC) aligns with 1992.

69. (C): Parts of the Indian Constitution:

(*a*) Part IX B pertains to co-operative Societies. This section was added by the 97th Amendment in 2011 and it focuses on the importance of co-operative societies in the country.

(*b*) Part XIV A concerns Tribunals. This part was introduced by the 42nd Amendment in 1976 and speaks about the administrative tribunals.

(*c*) Part VIII deals with Union Territories. This section of the Constitution describes the union territories of India and the powers of the administrators governing them.

(*d*) Part XVII is about Official Languages. This part of the Constitution delineates the languages of India and its states and prescribes the languages to be used in the judiciary and parliament.

70. (B): Legal case judgments and their significant implications:

(*a*) Rose and Frank Co. V/s Crompton and Brothers Ltd. establishes Intention to create legal relations. In this case, the court held that not all agreements, even if they have all the essential elements of a contract, result in a binding contract. There must be an intention to create legal relations.

(*b*) Harris V/s Nickerson touches upon Invitation to offer. This case differentiated between an advertisement (an invitation to offer) and an offer.

(*c*) Olley V/s Marlborough Court Ltd. refers to Standard form of contract. This case revolved around an exemption clause placed behind the door of a hotel room, which the court found couldn't be part of the contract as it was communicated after the contract was made.

(*d*) Powell V/s Lee emphasizes Acceptance must be communicated by the acceptor. In this case, the court ruled that an acceptance must be communicated to be valid, and knowledge of acceptance through a third party does not bind the contract.

71. (*) **72. (B)** **73. (D)**

74. (B) **75. (A)** **76. (C)**

77. (B): The cases concerning the death penalty in India, in chronological order, are:

- **Ediga Anamma V/s State of Andhra Pradesh (1974):** This is one of the earliest cases where the death penalty was discussed.
- **Bachan Singh V/s State of Punjab (1980):** The Supreme Court laid down the 'rarest of the rare' doctrine, which stated that the death penalty should only be given in the rarest of rare cases.

- **Machhi Singh V/s State of Punjab (1983):** This built upon the 'rarest of the rare' doctrine established in the Bachan Singh case.
- **Shabnam Khan V/s Union of India:** As of my last update, this case wasn't among the notable ones in the context provided.
- **Vinay Sharma V/s Union of India (2020):** Related to the 2012 Delhi gang rape and murder case, where the death penalty was upheld for the convicts.

So, chronological order are (*a*), (*b*), (*c*), (*e*), (*d*).

78. (B): For both India and the USA:

- **Federal:** Both India and the USA operate on a federal system of governance where powers are divided between the central (or federal) government and the individual states or provinces.
- **Democratic form of Government:** Both countries are democracies, meaning the citizens elect their representatives through free and fair elections.
- **Rule of Law:** This principle asserts that every citizen is subject to the law, including lawmakers and government officials. Both India and the USA uphold this principle, ensuring equality before the law.

Hence, (*a*), (*c*) and (*e*) are correct.

79. (C): Arranging the chapters of the Indian Penal Code (IPC) in ascending order based on their chapter numbers:

- **General Exceptions:** Chapter IV of IPC deals with general exceptions, providing a range of defenses.
- **Offences against State:** Chapter VI concerns offenses against the state, such as waging war against the nation.
- **Offences against the Public Tranquillity:** This falls under Chapter VIII, detailing offenses like rioting.
- **Offences against Human body:** Chapters XVI to XXIII cover offenses against the human body, including hurt, grievous hurt, and murder.
- **Offences against Property:** Chapters XVII to XXIX discuss property offenses, such as theft and robbery.

Hence, ascending order are (*a*), (*e*), (*b*), (*d*), (*c*).

80. (B): Arranging the provisions of the Indian Contract Act, 1872, based on their sections:

- **Agreement void for uncertainty:** Section 29
- **Discharge of surety by release or discharge of principal debtor:** Section 133
- **Release of one co-surety does not discharge others:** Section 138
- **Rights of surety on payment or performance:** Section 140
- **Co-sureties liable to contribute equally:** Section 146

This arrangement leads to the correct sequence (*a*), (*b*), (*c*), (*e*), (*d*).

81. (B): The provisions of the Companies Act, 2013 corresponding to the options given are:

- **Punishment in case of repeated default:** Section 451
- **Annual reports on Government Companies:** Section 394
- **Petition for winding up:** Section 272
- **Functions of Company Secretary:** Section 205
- **Execution of Bills of Exchange, etc.:** Section 48

Arranging these in descending order gives the sequence: (*b*), (*c*), (*d*), (*e*), (*a*).

82. (C): The correct chronological sequence for the cases mentioned is:

- **Shankri Prasad V/s Union of India (1951):** This was the first case where the First Amendment of the Indian Constitution was challenged.
- **Rupa Ashok Hurra V/s Ashok Hurra (2002):** This case deliberated on whether a judgment by the Supreme Court can be reviewed by a larger bench.
- **Selvi V/s State of Karnataka (2010):** This case centered on the constitutionality of certain investigative techniques like narcoanalysis.
- **Sayra Bano V/s Union of India (2017):** It was the landmark judgment that declared triple talaq as unconstitutional.
- **Navtej Singh Jauhar V/s Union of India (2018):** This landmark judgment decriminalized homosexuality in India.

The correct sequence are (*e*), (*b*), (*d*), (*c*), (*a*).

83. (*)

84. (B): The correct sequence in the progression of a crime and its consequences is:

- **Intention:** Before a crime is committed, there is an intention or motive.
- **Preparation:** This involves all the steps taken before actually committing the crime.
- **Act:** This is the commission of the crime itself.
- **Conviction:** If caught and proven guilty, the perpetrator is convicted by a court of law.
- **Sentence:** Post-conviction, the sentence or punishment is delivered.

The correct sequence are (*a*), (*b*), (*c*), (*d*), (*e*).

85. (D): The cases, in the order of their judgment years, are:

- **Sajjan Singh V/s State of Rajasthan (1965):** Concerned with the scope of amending the Constitution and the power of Parliament to do so.
- **Azeez Basha V/s Union of India (1968):** Dealt with the Aligarh Muslim University and its status as a minority institution.
- **Minerva Mills V/s Union of India (1980):** Questioned the extent to which the Constitution could be amended without altering its "basic structure."
- **Kihota Hollohon V/s Zachilhu (1992):** Addressed the Tenth Schedule to the Constitution, which pertains to disqualification on grounds of defection.
- **L. Chandra Kumar V/s Union of India (1997):** Evaluated the power and jurisdiction of administrative tribunals.

The correct sequence are (*a*), (*e*), (*d*), (*b*), (*c*).

86. (A): "Possession is nine points of the law" is a common saying that means that possession of an item or property is a strong indicator of ownership, and can determine legal decisions unless contradicted by evidence proving ownership elsewhere. The reason given, that the person in possession has a better claim over it against the world except the real owner, is an accurate reflection of the legal principle. This stems from the idea that in disputes, it's often easier for the person in possession to prove their claim than for someone who isn't in possession to demonstrate their ownership. Thus, possession gives one a significant advantage in legal disputes about ownership.

87. (B): The doctrine of *"Stare-decisis"* is a Latin term that means "to stand by things decided." In legal parlance, it represents the principle that similar cases should be decided based on consistent principled rules so they will reach similar results. The Supreme Court of India, like many other courts, respects this principle, implying that the court will generally abide by its previous decisions. However, the court can and does, in certain circumstances, overrule its prior judgments if it believes them to be incorrect. While both statements are correct, the reason (R) does not explain why *Stare-decisis* is an essential principle.

88. (D)

89. **(A):** Law's foundation in the collective consciousness or "volkgeist" of the people is a concept derived from sociological jurisprudence. The term "volkgeist" is a German word translating to the "spirit of the people." This perspective asserts that laws emerge from the collective beliefs, morals, and traditions of society. The second statement is an extension of this idea. If law emanates from the general consciousness, then it is indeed a manifestation of the society's spirit. Both statements reflect the theory that law is deeply connected to the cultural, moral, and social fabric of society.

90. **(A):** John Salmond's assertion that the common law is primarily "judge-made" is rooted in the history and evolution of the common law system. Common law, which evolved in England, is largely based on judicial decisions and precedents rather than statutes enacted by the legislature. Over time, as judges decided individual cases, their decisions would become the law for future cases with similar facts. This is the essence of "judge-made" law. Sir Frederick Pollock's statement that common law is based on customs aligns with this notion. Historically, many judicial decisions in the common law system were grounded in local customs and practices. Over time, these customs, once recognized and upheld by courts, transformed into binding legal principles. Both statements reflect accurate perspectives on the origins and nature of common law.

91. (B)	**92.** (D)	**93.** (B)
94. (C)	**95.** (D)	**96.** (C)
97. (D)	**98.** (B)	**99.** (A)
100. (D)		

Previous Years' Paper (Solved)

National Testing Agency (NTA)

UGC-NET Junior Research Fellowship & Assistant Professor Eligibility Exam

Law, June-2022

(Online exam held on 14/10/2022)

PAPER-II

1. Who said that there are two elements of possession, (a) *Corpus possessionis* and (b) *Animus domini*?

A. Ihering B. Paton
C. Savigny D. Salmond

2. Given below are two statements.

Statement I: Hart deals with primary rules of obligation and secondary rules of recognition.

Statement II: Hart has nothing to do with the reformulation of analytical positivism.

In light of the above statements, choose the ***most appropriate*** answer from the options given below:

A. Both Statement I and Statement II are correct
B. Both Statement I and Statement II are incorrect
C. Statement I is correct, but Statement II is incorrect
D. Statement I is incorrect, but Statement II is correct

3. Trade secrets do not cover the following information:

A. Commercially valuable
B. Production methods
C. Business plans
D. Information discovered by reverse engineering

4. Article 13 of the Constitution of India does not apply to:

A. Any legislation made by the Parliament under Article 245 of the Constitution
B. Any legislation made by the Parliament under Article 253 of the Constitution giving effect to international agreements
C. Any amendment of the Constitution made under Article 368
D. Custom and usage

5. Under which article of the Constitution of India, is it the duty of the Union to protect every State against external aggression and internal disturbance and to ensure that the government of every state is carried on, in accordance with the provisions of the Constitution of India?

A. Article 353 B. Article 354
C. Article 355 D. Article 356

6. Every decision of the Goods and Services Tax Council shall require it to be taken at a meeting:

A. by a majority of not less than two-thirds of the weighted votes of the members present
B. by a majority of not less than three-fourths of the weighted notes of the members present
C. by a majority of not less than two-thirds of the weighted notes of all the members of the Council
D. by a majority of not less than three-fourths of the weighted notes of all the members of the Council

7. Which of the following is/are NOT administrative actions?
A. Internment, Externment and Deportation
B. Functions of a selection committee
C. Fact-finding action
D. Forming opinion on objective satisfaction

8. Every state and every local authority within the state is required to provide adequate facilities for instruction in the mother-tongue at the primary stage of education to children belonging to linguistic minority groups under:
A. Article 350 B. Article 350 A
C. Article 350 B D. Article 351

9. Ordinarily, a delegated legislation can be given:
A. prospective effect only
B. retrospective effect only
C. both, prospective and retrospective effect
D. effect, as the Court may decide

10. In which one of the following cases, Legal aid was held as a fundamental right?
A. Sunil Batra case
B. M.H. Hoskot case
C. Prem Shankar Shukla case
D. Keshvananda Bharathi case

11. The Hicklin test under Article 19(2) is related to:
A. Defamation
B. Decency and morality
C. Integrity of India
D. Negligence

12. In the Constitution of India, the principle of Rule of Law is mainly embodied in:
A. Article 14 B. Article 32
C. Article 226 D. Article 227

13. Which of the following is NOT correct under the Geographical Indications of Goods (Registration and Protection) Act, 1999?
A. Producer, in case of agricultural goods, includes the person who produces the goods
B. Producer, in case of agricultural goods, includes the person who packages such goods
C. Producer, in case of natural goods, includes the person who exploits such goods
D. Producer, in case of handicrafts, includes the person who packages such goods

14. Which of the following can be registered as a Trade Mark?
A. Mark devoid of distinctive character
B. A distinctive mark
C. A mark causing confusion
D. Oval shape for medicinal tablet

15. Who defined ownership as 'plenary control over an object'?
A. Roscoe Pound B. Holmes
C. Holland D. Paton

16. Who said, "A legal person, is any subject matter other than a human being to which law attributes personality"?
A. Salmond B. Holmes
C. Jerome Frank D. Pound

17. In the light of the Criminal Law (Amendment) Act, 2013, which of the following statements is/are correct?
A. The word 'rape' in section 375 IPC has been replaced with 'sexual assault'
B. Rape is now a gender-neutral offence
C. The Amendment has fixed the age for consensual sex as 16 years
D. The Amendment has fixed the age for consensual sex as 18 years

18. The doctrine, *res-ipso loquitur,* was applied by the Supreme Court in:
A. Alka *v.* Union of India
B. Asa Ram *v.* Municipal Corporation of Delhi
C. Municipal Corporation of Delhi *v.* Subhagwanti
D. Jasbir Kaur *v.* State of Punjab

19. The test of reasonable foresight in determining remoteness of damages was first applied in:
A. Re: Polerris
B. Wagon Mound Case

C. Doughty *v.* Turner Manufacturing Co. Ltd
D. S.C.M. (United Kingdom) Ltd. *v.* W.J. Whittal & Sons

20. The Consumer Protection Act 2019, talks about direct selling, e-commerce and electronic service provider:
A. True
B. False
C. Consumer Protection Act, 1986 did not provide about this
D. Both (A) and (C)

21. In order to establish a cartel, what is NOT necessary?
A. There should be an agreement
B. It should be between an association of producers, sellers, distributors, traders or service providers
C. The objective should be to limit, control or attempt to control the product distribution, sale or price of or trade in goods or provisions of services
D. Cartels are very good for competition

22. Which one of the following is NOT one of the modes of termination of agency?
A. Insolvency of principal
B. Principal or agent's death
C. General Lien
D. Revocation

23. 'Voluntarily' has been defined as an effect caused by means, whereby a person intended to cause it or by means, at the time of employing those means, to know or had reason to believe to be likely to cause it under:
A. Section 35, IPC B. Section 36, IPC
C. Section 39, IPC D. Section 40, IPC

24. Arrange the following cases chronologically (starting from the earliest to the latest).
(*a*) National Legal Service Authority *v.* U.O.I
(*b*) Naz foundation *v.* Govt. of NCT
(*c*) Navtej Singh Johar *v.* U.O.I
(*d*) Suresh Kaushal *v.* Naz foundation
(*e*) The cases of Navtej Singh Johar and Suresh Kaushal were decided in the same year

Choose the ***correct*** answer from the options given below:
A. (*c*), (*e*), (*b*), (*d*) B. (*d*), (*b*), (*a*), (*c*)
C. (*b*), (*d*), (*a*), (*c*) D. (*e*), (*d*), (*a*), (*b*)

25. ______ has to provide by making regulations for any class or class of companies which may file a shelf prospectus with the Registrar at the stage of first offer of securities.
A. NCLT
B. SEBI
C. IBBI
D. Director of a company

26. Every partner of a partnership firm is liable for all the acts of the firm done while he is a partner. This doctrine is called:
A. The doctrine of holding out
B. The doctrine of restitution
C. The doctrine of estoppel
D. The doctrine of proportionality

27. When an unmarried woman adopts a child and subsequently marries; the person who she subsequently marries, shall be the:
A. adoptive father of the child
B. stepfather of the child
C. natural father of the child
D. Either (A) or (B)

28. Which of the following is NOT a ground of divorce available to wife under section 13(2) of the Hindu Marriage Act, 1955?
A. Pre-Act bigamous marriage of the husband
B. Repudiation of marriage
C. Cruelty by husband
D. Husband guilty of rape, sodomy and bestiality

29. The children born out of a void Hindu marriage, are in the eyes of law:
A. illegitimate
B. legitimate
C. illegitimate, having no rights in the ancestral property
D. legitimate but having right of inheritance limited to their parent's property only

30. Restitution of conjugal rights has its genesis under the:
A. English law B. Indian law
C. Jewish law D. Swedish law

31. Among the Muslims, *Sariri* is the stage:
A. when the boy or the girl is below 10 years of age
B. when the boy or the girl is above seven years but below fifteen years
C. when the boy or the girl is above fifteen years of age
D. when the boy or the girl is above 10 years of age

32. The law relating to armed conflicts of non-international character is governed by:
A. Common Article 3 of the Geneva Convention, 1949 or the Additional Protocol I, 1977
B. Common Article 3 of the Geneva Convention, 1949 or the Additional Protocol II, 1977
C. Additional Protocols, I and II, 1977
D. Only Additional Protocol I, 1977

33. Nottebohm's case deals with Nationality by:
A. Naturalisation B. Birth
C. Resumption D. Subjugation

34. Which of the following doctrines is called as Doctrine of Non-recognition?
A. Estrada Doctrine
B. Hallestein Doctrine
C. Franco Doctrine
D. Stimson Doctrine

35. *Pacta Terties Nec Nocent Nec Prosunt* means
A. Multilateral treaties prevail over bilateral treaties
B. Treaties are not binding in case of situations of emergency
C. Only parties to an international treaty are bound by it
D. The right of innocent passage cannot be thwarted by bilateral treaties

36. General principles of law recognized by civilized states, as a source of international law has been applied in following case:
A. Corfu Channel case
B. Asylum case
C. Mavrommatis Palestine Concessions case
D. Reparations case

37. Which of the following is ***incorrect***?
A. An agreement not enforceable by law is said to be voidable
B. An agreement enforceable by law is a contract
C. Every promise and every set of promises forming the consideration for each other is an agreement
D. An agreement not enforceable by law is said to be void

38. Which of the following is ***false***?
A. A contract is frustrated where the actual and specific subject matter of the contract has ceased to exist
B. A contract will frustrate where circumstances arise which make the performance of the contract impossible in the manner contemplated
C. A contract which required personal performance by promisor is frustated on the death of the promisor
D. Ceasing of subject matter of contract does not frustrate the contract

39. Which one of the following is ***correct***?
A. A public company can be formed with a minimum of nine persons
B. A private company can be formed with two or more persons
C. Memorandum of Association is not required for registration of a company
D. Articles of Association is not required for registration of a company

40. Given below are two statements, one is labelled as Assertion (A) and the other is labelled as Reason (R).

Assertion (A): A master is liable for all tortious acts of his servants done in the course of employment.

Reason (R): The representatives of the dead person are, in certain cases, liable for the acts of the deceased.

In light of the above statements, choose the ***most appropriate*** answer from the options given below:

A. Both (A) and (R) are correct and (R) is the correct explanation of (A)
B. Both (A) and (R) are correct, but (R) is NOT the correct explanation of (A)
C. (A) is correct, but (R) is not correct
D. (A) is not correct, but (R) is correct

41. The Competition Act, 2002, provides for which of the following?

(*a*) Establishment of a Commission to prevent practices having effect on competition
(*b*) To promote and sustain competition in markets
(*c*) To protect the interests of consumers
(*d*) To ensure freedom of trade carried on by the other participants in the markets
(*e*) To establish NCLT and NCLAT to decide various matters

Choose the ***correct*** answer from the options given below:

A. (*a*), (*b*), (*c*), (*d*) and (*e*)
B. (*b*), (*c*) and (*d*) only
C. (*c*), (*d*) and (*e*) only
D. (*a*), (*b*), (*c*) and (*d*) only

42. Given below are two statements, one is labelled as Assertion (A) and the other is labelled as Reason (R).

Assertion (A): The President of India is a mere constitutional head.

Reason (R): In the parliamentary form of government, the Prime Minister is the head of government.

In light of the above statements, choose the ***correct*** answer from the options given below:

A. Both (A) and (R) are true and (R) is the correct explanation of (A)
B. Both (A) and (R) are true, but (R) is NOT the correct explanation of (A)
C. (A) is true, but (R) is false
D. (A) is false, but (R) is true

43. Given below are two statements:

Statement I: For judicial review, 'irrationality' means that the decision is so outrageous in its defiance of logic or accepted moral standards, that no sensible person could have arrived at such a decision.

Statement II: For judicial review, 'unreasonableness' means either the facts do not warrant the conclusion reached by the authority or the decision is partial and unequal in its operation.

In light of the above statements, choose the ***most appropriate*** answer from the options given below:

A. Both Statement I and Statement II are correct
B. Both Statement I and Statement II are incorrect
C. Statement I is correct, but Statement II is incorrect
D. Statement I is incorrect, but Statement II is correct

44. Given below are two statements:

Statement I: The power of legislation carries with it the power to delegate and unless the legislature has completely abdicated or effaced itself, there is no restriction on delegation of legislative powers.

Statement II: Parliament can abdicate or efface itself by creating a parallel legislative body.

In light of the above statements, choose the ***most appropriate*** answer from the options given below:

A. Both Statement I and Statement II are correct
B. Both Statement I and Statement II are incorrect
C. Statement I is correct, but Statement II is incorrect
D. Statement I is incorrect, but Statement II is correct

45. Given below are two statements:

Statement I: A contract which ceases to be enforceable by law becomes void when it ceases to be enforceable.

Statement II: An agreement in restraint of trade is voidable.

In light of the above statements, choose the *correct* answer from the options given below:

A. Both Statement I and Statement II are true

B. Both Statement I and Statement II are false

C. Statement I is true, but Statement II is false

D. Statement I is false, but Statement II is true

46. Given below are two statements:

Statement I: It is the duty of the Prime Minister to communicate to the President all decisions of the Council of Ministers relating to the administration of the affairs of the Union and proposals for legislations.

Statement II: It is the duty of the Prime Minister to furnish such information relating to the administration of the affairs of the Union and proposals for legislation, as the President may call for.

In light of the above statements, choose the *correct* answer from the options given below:

A. Both Statement I and Statement II are true

B. Both Statement I and Statement II are false

C. Statement I is true, but Statement II is false

D. Statement I is false, but Statement II is true

47. Given below are two statements:

Statement I: An appeal shall lie in the Supreme Court from any judgment, final order or sentence in a criminal proceeding of a High Court in the territory of India, if the High Court has on appeal reversed an order of acquittal of an accused person and sentenced him to death.

Statement II: An appeal shall lie in the Supreme Court from any judgement, final order or sentence in a criminal proceeding of a High Court in the territory of India, if the High Court has withdrawn from trial before itself any case from any court subordinate to its authority and has in such a trial convicted the accused person and sentenced him to death.

In light of the above statements, choose the ***most appropriate*** answer from the options given below:

A. Both Statement I and Statement II are correct

B. Both Statement I and Statement II are incorrect

C. Statement I is correct, but Statement II is incorrect

D. Statement I is incorrect, but Statement II is correct

48. Given below are two statements:

Statement I: Imperative law means a concept of the rule of action imposed upon men by some authority which enforces obedience to it.

Statement II: Natural law signifies the principles of natural right and wrong.

In light of the above statements, choose the ***most appropriate*** answer from the options given below:

A. Both Statement I and Statement II are correct

B. Both Statement I and Statement II are incorrect

C. Statement I is correct, but Statement II is incorrect

D. Statement I is incorrect, but Statement II is correct

49. Given below are two statements:

Statement I: "All human beings are not legal persons".

Statement II: "State is a juristic person".

In light of the above statements, choose the ***most appropriate*** answer from the options given below:

A. Both Statement I and Statement II are correct
B. Both Statement I and Statement II are incorrect
C. Statement I is correct, but Statement II is incorrect
D. Statement I is incorrect, but Statement II is correct

50. Given below are two statements:

Statement I: Holland defines ownership as 'plenary control over an object'.

Statement II: Ownership is either vested or contingent.

In light of the above statements, choose the ***most appropriate*** answer from the options given below:

A. Both Statement I and Statement II are correct
B. Both Statement I and Statement II are incorrect
C. Statement I is correct, but Statement II is incorrect
D. Statement I is incorrect, but Statement II is correct

51. (*a*) An agreement without consideration is a void contract.
(*b*) An agreement in restraint of marriage is a voidable contract.
(*c*) An unmeaning agreement is a void contract.
(*d*) An agreement to do impossible acts is a voidable contract.
(*e*) An agreement in restraint of legal proceedings is a void contract.

Choose the ***correct*** answer from the options given below:

A. (*a*) and (*c*) only
B. (*b*) and (*d*) only
C. (*a*), (*c*) and (*e*) only
D. (*e*) only

52. (*a*) Freedom of trade, commerce and intercourse is covered in Article 301.
(*b*) Restrictions on legislative powers of the Union and States with regard to trade and commerce are covered in Article 302.
(*c*) Power of Parliament to impose Restrictions on trade, commerce and intercourse is covered in Article 302.
(*d*) Restrictions on trade, commerce and intercourse among states are covered in Article 304.
(*e*) Appointment of authority for carrying out the purposes of Article 301-304 is enshrined in Article 306.

Choose the ***correct*** answer from the options given below:

A. (*a*), (*b*) and (*c*) only
B. (*b*), (*c*) and (*d*) only
C. (*a*), (*c*) and (*d*) only
D. (*b*), (*d*) and (*e*) only

53. (*a*) Courts cannot review the question as to what "aid and advice" is given by the Council of Ministries to the President.
(*b*) The question of "aid and advice" by the Council of Ministers is a justifiable issue.
(*c*) Article 14 cannot be invoked against discrimination made by constitutional provisions.
(*d*) The question of "aid and advice" by the Council of Ministers is a non-justifiable issue.
(*e*) Article 14 can be worked against discrimination made by constitutional provisions.

Choose the ***correct*** answer from the options given below:

A. (*a*), (*b*) and (*c*) only
B. (*a*), (*c*) and (*d*) only
C. (*b*), (*c*) and (*d*) only
D. (*c*), (*d*) and (*e*) only

54. The institution of Ombudsman was first developed in:

A. India B. UK
C. France D. Sweden

55. A car was sold on 'as is' basis and without any warranty or guarantee whatever. After 5 days of the contract, the engine of the car blew up. Discuss the liability of the seller.

A. He is liable for the damages due to the doctrine of fundamental breach of standard form of contract
B. The seller is not liable because the car was sold on 'as is' basis and without any warranty or guarantee
C. The buyer should take care if he buys a second-hand car
D. Under standard form contract, in this case, contributory negligence is applicable

56. Match List-I with List-II.

List-I	List-II
(*a*) *Theory of Justice*	I. David Hume
(*b*) *Idea of Justice*	II. John Rowls
(*c*) *Nicomachean Ethics*	III. Amartya Sen
(*d*) *An Enquiry Concerning the Principles of Morals*	IV. Artistotle

Choose the **correct** answer from the options given below:

	(*a*)	(*b*)	(*c*)	(*d*)
A.	I	II	III	IV
B.	II	III	I	IV
C.	II	III	IV	I
D.	II	I	III	IV

57. Given below are two statements, one is labelled as Assertion (A) and the other is labelled as Reason (R).

Assertion (A): Nothing is an offence which is done in the exercise of right of private defence.

Reason (R): Z is carried off by a tiger. A fires at the tiger knowing that the shot may kill Z. His shot gives Z a mortal wound. A has not committed any offence.

In light of the above statements, choose the ***correct*** answer from the options given below:

A. Both (A) and (R) are true and (R) is the correct explanation of (A)
B. Both (A) and (R) are true, but (R) is NOT the correct explanation of (A)
C. (A) is true, but (R) is false
D. (A) is false, but (R) is true

58. Arrange the following in chronological order starting from earlier to later years:

(*a*) The Trade Marks Act
(*b*) The Patents Act
(*c*) The Design Act
(*d*) The Copyright Act
(*e*) The Protection of Plant Varieties and Farmers, Rights Act

Choose the ***correct*** answer from the options given below:

A. (*a*), (*b*), (*c*), (*d*), (*e*)
B. (*b*), (*d*), (*a*), (*e*), (*c*)
C. (*d*), (*b*), (*a*), (*c*), (*e*)
D. (*a*), (*b*), (*c*), (*e*), (*d*)

59. National Commission for Backward Classes has been created through which Amendment to the Constitution of India?

A. 100th Amendment
B. 101st Amendment
C. 102nd Amendment
D. 103rd Amendment

60. Under Article 338(5) of the Constitution of India, National Commission for Scheduled Castes has:

A. the power to issue caste certificates
B. the power to revoke caste certificates
C. the power to decide validity of caste certificates
D. no power to issue/revoke certificates and has no power to decide upon the validity of caste certificates

61. Arrange the following Protocols/Declarations in the correct chronological sequence

(*a*) Kyoto Protocol
(*b*) Cartagena Protocol on Biosafety
(*c*) Montreal Protocol
(*d*) Nagoya Protocol
(*e*) Rio Declaration on Environment and Development

Choose the **correct** answer from the options given below:

A. (*e*), (*a*), (*b*), (*c*), (*d*)
B. (*e*), (*b*), (*c*), (*d*), (*a*)
C. (*e*), (*c*), (*a*), (*b*), (*d*)
D. (*e*), (*d*), (*c*), (*b*), (*a*)

62. The National Green Tribunal Act, 2010 came into force on:

A. 10 May, 2010
B. 18 August, 2010
C. 10 December, 2010
D. 18 October, 2010

63. Read the following principles of the Rio Declaration on Environment and Development (1992) and select the correct answer from the given options:

(*a*) Principle 1 : Human beings are at the centre of concerns for sustainable development
(*b*) Principle 16 : In order to protect the environment, the precautionary approach shall be widely applied by states according to their capabilities
(*c*) Principle 14 : Environmental Impact Assessment...shall be undertaken for proposed activities that are likely to have a significant adverse impact on the environment
(*d*) Principle 20 : Women have a vital role in environmental management and development
(*e*) Principle 24 : Peace, development and environmental protection are inter-dependent and indivisible

Choose the **correct** answer from the options given below:

A. (*a*) and (*d*) only B. (*b*) and (*c*) only
C. (*c*) and (*e*) only D. (*b*) and (*e*) only

64. The word "Environment" has been defined under which of the section of the Environment (Protection) Act, 1986?

A. Section 2(a) B. Section 2(e)
C. Section 2(d) D. Section 2(b)

65. Match List-I with List-II.

List-I	List-II
(*a*) Application of the Act to electronic cheque and truncated cheque	I. Sec. 3A
(*b*) Electronic Signature	II. Sec. 81A
(*c*) Secure electronic record	III. Sec. 15
(*d*) Validity of contracts formed through electronic means	IV. Sec. 10A

Choose the **correct** answer from the options given below:

	(*a*)	(*b*)	(*c*)	(*d*)
A.	I	II	III	IV
B.	II	I	III	IV
C.	II	I	IV	III
D.	IV	III	II	I

66. Match List-I with List-II.

List-I	List-II
(*a*) Voluntarily causing grievous hurt by use of acid	I. 354-A, IPC
(*b*) Voluntarily throwing or attempting to throw acid	II. 326-B, IPC
(*c*) Sexual harassment and punishment for sexual harassment	III. 354-D, IPC
(*d*) Stalking	IV. 326-A, IPC

Choose the **correct** answer from the options given below:

	(*a*)	(*b*)	(*c*)	(*d*)
A.	IV	II	I	III
B.	III	II	IV	I
C.	II	III	I	IV
D.	III	II	I	IV

67. Match List-I with List-II.

List-I	List-II
(*a*) Solomon *v.* Solomon	I. Voting rights
(*b*) Royal British Bank *v.* Turquand	II. Corporate Personality
(*c*) Ashbury Railway Carriage & Iron *v.* Riche (Ashbury)	III. Doctrine of Ultra Vires
(*d*) Vodafone International Holdings *v.* UOI	IV. Doctrine of Indoor Management

Choose the **correct** answer from the options given below:

	(a)	(b)	(c)	(d)
A.	IV	II	III	I
B.	I	II	III	IV
C.	I	III	II	IV
D.	II	IV	III	I

68. Match List-I with List-II.

List-I	List-II
(a) Judicial Review	I. Indira Gandhi *v.* Raj Narayan
(b) Free and fair election	II. Keshavananda Bharati *v.* State of Kerela
(c) Balance between Part III and Part IV of the Constitution	III. S.R. Bommai *v.* Union of India
(d) Secularism	IV. Minerva Mills Ltd. *v.* Union of India

Choose the **correct** answer from the options given below:

	(a)	(b)	(c)	(d)
A.	I	III	IV	II
B.	II	I	IV	III
C.	IV	I	III	II
D.	III	IV	I	II

69. Match List-I with List-II.

List-I	List-II
(a) Doctrine of Pith and Substance	I. What cannot be done directly, cannot be done indirectly
(b) Doctrine of Incidental Encroachment	II. The part of statute which is bad cannot be severed from the rest
(c) Doctrine of Severability	III. A law is not invalid even though trenched incidentally to another list
(d) Doctrine of Colourable legislation	IV. True nature and character of the legislation

Choose the **correct** answer from the options given below:

	(a)	(b)	(c)	(d)
A.	I	II	III	IV
B.	IV	III	I	II
C.	III	II	IV	I
D.	IV	III	II	I

70. Match List-I with List-II.

List-I	List-II
(a) Post-Modernism	I. Grund Norm
(b) Source of Law	II. *Ratio decidendi*
(c) Authority of a decision as a precedent	III. Critical Legal Studies
(d) Analytical School	IV. Volkgeist

Choose the **correct** answer from the options given below:

	(a)	(b)	(c)	(d)
A.	III	IV	II	I
B.	IV	III	II	I
C.	II	I	III	IV
D.	I	II	IV	III

71. Greenhouse effect means:

Increase in atmospheric temperature due to the concentration of greenhouse

A. Gases in the atmosphere

B. Growing vegetables and flowers in increased temperature

C. Growing food crops in glass houses

D. Photosynthesis in plants grown in sunlight received in the glass house

72. Match List-I with List-II.

List-I Provision	List-II Section
(a) Void marriage	I. Section 27, Hindu Marriage Act, 1955
(b) Divorce by mutual consent	II. Section 24, Hindu Marriage Act, 1955
(c) Maintenance pendente lite	III. Section 13 B, Hindu Marriage Act, 1955
(d) Disposal of property	IV. Section 11, Hindu Marriage Act, 1955

Choose the **correct** answer from the options given below:

	(a)	(b)	(c)	(d)
A.	I	III	IV	II
B.	IV	III	II	I
C.	III	II	I	IV
D.	II	I	III	IV

73. Match List-I with List-II.

List-I	List-II
(a) Mersey Dock'e v. Proctor	I. Statutory Authority
(b) Metropolitan Asylum District v. Hill	II. Vicarious liability
(c) Nichols v. Marsland	III. Inevitable accident
(d) Holmes v. Mather	IV. Act of God

Choose the **correct** answer from the options given below:

	(a)	(b)	(c)	(d)
A.	II	I	IV	III
B.	III	II	I	IV
C.	I	II	III	IV
D.	IV	II	III	I

74. Match List-I with List-II.

List-I	List-II
(a) Bonn Convention	I. Protection of the Ozone layer
(b) Vienna Convention	II. Control of transboundary movements of hazardous wastes and their disposal
(c) Basel Convention	III. Conservation of migratory species of wild animals
(d) Rotterdam Convention	IV. Prior informed consent procedure for certain hazardous chemicals and pesticides in international trade

Choose the **correct** answer from the options given below:

	(a)	(b)	(c)	(d)
A.	II	I	IV	III
B.	III	I	II	IV
C.	IV	II	I	III
D.	I	II	III	IV

75. Match List-I with List-II.

List-I	List-II
(a) Ramsar Convention	I. 1992
(b) Convention on Biological Diversity	II. 1994
(c) Minamata Convention	III. 1991
(d) The United Nations Convention to combat Desertification	IV. 2013

Choose the **correct** answer from the options given below:

	(a)	(b)	(c)	(d)
A.	III	II	IV	I
B.	IV	II	III	I
C.	III	I	IV	II
D.	II	I	IV	III

76. Arrange in chronological order the case laws pertaining to cruelty under the Hindu Marriage Act, 1955 (year wise from beginning till the latest)

(a) Durga Prasanna Tripathy v. Arundhati Tripathy

(b) Bhagwat v. Bhagwat

(c) Parveen Mehta v. Inderjeet Mehta

(d) Swapan Kumar Das v. Maya Rani Dutta

(e) Satendra Kumar Gupta v. Kanchan Gupta & Ors

Choose the **correct** answer from the options given below:

A. (b), (c), (a), (d), (e)

B. (a), (c), (b), (d), (e)

C. (c), (d), (a), (b), (e)

D. (d), (c), (b), (a), (e)

77. In case of theft under IPC, the following ingredients are necessary:

(a) Dishonest intention to take the property

(b) The property can be movable or immovable

(c) Property should be taken without the consent of the person

(d) There must be some removal of the property

(e) The property must be movable property

Choose the **correct** answer from the options given below:

A. (*a*), (*b*), (*d*) and (*c*) only
B. (*b*), (*c*), (*d*) and (*e*) only
C. (*a*), (*c*), (*d*) and (*e*) only
D. (*a*), (*b*), (*c*) and (*e*) only

78. The following is/are the exceptions to the principle of strict liability:

(*a*) Act of God
(*b*) Consent of the plaintiff
(*c*) Intention of the defendant
(*d*) Act of third party
(*e*) Minority

Choose the **correct** answer from the options given below:

A. (*a*) and (*b*) only
B. (*a*), (*b*) and (*d*) only
C. (*a*), (*c*) and (*d*) only
D. (*b*) and (*e*) only

79. Which of the following are true with regard to the desertion of spouse under the Hindu Marriage Act, 1955?

(*a*) Factum of Separation
(*b*) *Animus deserendi*
(*c*) Prescribed period of 2 years must have passed before presentation of petition
(*d*) With reasonable cause
(*e*) Without the consent of the petitioner

Choose the **correct** answer from the options given below:

A. (*a*), (*c*), (*d*) and (*e*) only
B. (*b*), (*c*) and (*d*) only
C. (*a*), (*b*), (*c*) and (*e*) only
D. (*a*), (*b*) and (*d*) only

80. Choose the correct chronological order of the emergence of the schools of Jurisprudence (earliest to the latest):

(*a*) Natural Law School, Historical, Analytical Positivism, Realist
(*b*) Historical, Natural, Realist, Analytical Positivism
(*c*) Analytical Positivism, Historical, Realist, Natural Law School
(*d*) Realist, Historical, Analytical Positivism, Natural Law School
(*e*) Realist, Natural, Historical, Analytical Positivism

Choose the **correct** answer from the options given below:

A. (*a*) only B. (*b*) only
C. (*c*) only D. (*d*) only

81. Choose the correct chronological order of the jurists from the earliest to the latest:

(*a*) Austin, Bentham, Pound, Holmes
(*b*) Bentham, Holmes, Austin, Pound
(*c*) Bentham, Austin, Pound, Holmes
(*d*) Holmes, Austin, Bentham, Pound
(*e*) Bentham, Holmes, Pound, Austin

Choose the **correct** answer from the options given below:

A. (*b*) only B. Either (*a*) or (*b*)
C. (*c*) only D. (*e*) only

82. The following can be appointed as the Chairperson of the National Human Rights Commission (NHRC)

A. Only a person who has been the Chief Justice of the Supreme court
B. A person who has been the Chief Justice of the Supreme court or a Judge of the Supreme court
C. A person who has been the Chief Justice of a High court
D. A person who has been a Judge of the High court

83. Select the right answer from the given options:

(*a*) COP 26 : Glasgow Climate Change Conference
(*b*) COP 25 : Lima Climate Change Conference
(*c*) COP 24 : Marrakesh Climate Change Conference
(*d*) COP 22 : Katowice Climate Change Conference
(*e*) COP 21 : Paris Climate Change Conference

Choose the **correct** answer from the options given below:

A. (*a*) and (*e*) only B. (*b*) and (*c*) only
C. (*b*) and (*d*) only D. (*c*) and (*d*) only

84. Given below are two statements, one is labelled as Assertion (A) and the other is labelled as Reason (R).

Assertion (A): A bigamous marriage is void under Hindu Law.

Reason (R): A child born out of void marriage is legitimate child of his parents.

In light of the above statements, choose the **correct** answer from the options given below:

A. Both (A) and (R) are true and (R) is the correct explanation of (A)

B. Both (A) and (R) are true, but (R) is NOT the correct explanation of (A)

C. (A) is true, but (R) is false

D. (A) is false, but (R) is true

85. Given below are two statements:

Statement I: Personal rights are inheritable.

Statement II: Legal rights are recognized and enforced by law.

In light of the above statements, choose the ***most appropriate*** answer from the options given below:

A. Both Statement I and Statement II are correct

B. Both Statement I and Statement II are incorrect

C. Statement I is correct, but Statement II is incorrect

D. Statement I is incorrect, but Statement II is correct

86. Given below are two statements, one is labelled as Assertion (A) and the other is labelled as Reason (R).

Assertion (A): The *ex post-facto* laws are laws which voided and punished an act that had been lawful when done.

Reason (R): Imposing or increasing a penalty with retrospective affect for violation of a taxing statute does not infringe Article 20(1).

In light of the above statements, choose the **correct** answer from the options given below:

A. Both (A) and (R) are true and (R) is the correct explanation of (A)

B. Both (A) and (R) are true, but (R) is NOT the correct explanation of (A)

C. (A) is true, but (R) is false

D. (A) is false, but (R) is true

87. Given below are two statements:

Statement I: A 'negotiable instrument' means a promissory note, bill of exchange or cheque payable either to order or to bearer.

Statement II: Holder means any person who for consideration became the possessor of a promissory note, bill of exchange or cheque, if payable to bearer or the payee or endorsee.

In light of the above statements, choose the ***most appropriate*** answer from the options given below:

A. Both Statement I and Statement II are correct

B. Both Statement I and Statement II are incorrect

C. Statement I is correct, but Statement II is incorrect

D. Statement I is incorrect, but Statement II is correct

88. Given below are two statements:

Statement I: A childless stepmother is entitled to claim maintenance under the Hindu Adoption and Maintenance Act, 1956.

Statement II: Under the Hindu Adoption and Maintenance Act, 1956, if the son is to be adopted, the adoptive father or mother should not have a Hindu Son, Son's Son or Son's Son's Son (whether by legitimate blood relationship or by adoption) living at the time of adoption.

In light of the above statements, choose the ***most appropriate*** answer from the options given below:

A. Both Statement I and Statement II are correct

B. Both Statement I and Statement II are incorrect

C. Statement I is correct, but Statement II is incorrect

D. Statement I is incorrect, but Statement II is correct

89. Given below are two statements:

Statement I: Every public company shall have at least three directors and every private company shall have at least two directors.

Statement II: There can be a maximum of 15 directors and for having more than 15 directors, the company may pass a special resolution.

In light of the above statements, choose the ***most appropriate*** answer from the options given below:

A. Both Statement I and Statement II are correct

B. Both Statement I and Statement II are incorrect

C. Statement I is correct, but Statement II is incorrect

D. Statement I is incorrect, but Statement II is correct

90. Given below are two statements:

Statement I: A becomes surety to C for B's conduct as a manager in C's bank. Afterwards, B and C contract, without A's consent that B's salary shall be raised and that he shall become liable for one-fourth of the losses on overdrafts. B allows a customer to overdraw and the bank loses a sum of money.

Statement II: A is liable to make good the loss as he is a surety to C for B's conduct.

In light of the above statements, choose the ***most appropriate*** answer from the options given below:

A. Both Statement I and Statement II are correct

B. Both Statement I and Statement II are incorrect

C. Statement I is correct, but Statement II is incorrect

D. Statement I is incorrect, but Statement II is correct

Directions (Qs. No. 91-95): *Read the given passage carefully and answer the questions that follow:*

The binding force of international law is based on the supreme fundamental norm or principle known as *Pacta sunt servanda.* This means that agreements entered into by States will be respected and followed by them in good faith. This is a well established and recognised custom of international law. The customary principle of international law has now been codified and finds mention in Article 26 of the Vienna Convention on the Law of Treaties, 1969.

The principle of *Pacta sunt servanda* is also based on the actual practice of the States. It emphasises the importance of the agreement entered into by States and regards them as the basis of international law.

There is a view that to assert the binding force of international law is based only on the principle of *Pacta sunt servanda* is far from the truth. It fails to explain the binding force of customary rules of international law which are not based on agreement between States. The realisation that international customary law does not rest on agreements and that the tenet, *Pacta sunt servanda* is itself a rule of customary law, led to new formulations of the basic norm.

Kelsen has decided on a formula which takes into account usage, as the fact which is the origin of the rules of international law — 'States ought to behave as they have customarily behaved'.

91. Which of the following is correct?

A. *Pacta sunt servanda* is an absolute principle

B. *Pacta sunt servanda* covers unequal treaties also

C. *Pacta sunt servanda* is not an absolute principle as it fails to explain the binding force of customary rules of international law

D. *Pacta sunt servanda* explains the binding force of customary rules of international law

92. The codification of *Pacta sunt servanda* finds a mention in which Article of the Vienna Convention on the Law of Treaties, 1969?
A. It does not find mention in the Vienna Convention on the Law of Treaties, 1969
B. Article 26
C. Article 2
D. Article 47

93. The literal meaning of *Pacta sunt servanda* is:
A. Pacts are sacred
B. Pacts are good servants
C. Pacts need not be observed
D. Agreements must be observed

94. To which does the passage give primacy, *Pacta sunt servanda* or the principles of customary international law?
A. *Pacta sunt servanda*
B. Principles of customary international law
C. Both *Pacta sunt servanda* and the principles of customary international law
D. Neither *Pacta sunt servanda* nor principles of customary international law

95. Kelsen focuses on:
A. Primacy of *Pacta sunt servanda*
B. State behaviour being in conformity with customary international law
C. *Pacta sunt servanda* being responsible for the growth of customary international law
D. *Pacta sunt servanda* being independent of the principles of customary international law

Directions (Qs. No. 96-100): *Read the given passage carefully and answer the questions that follow:*

"In England justice goes to the people; in India the people had to come to justice (The litigant) had to find his way to this strange tribunal in an unknown land as best he could, in charge of the police, whose tender mercies he dreaded, or alone.

If he went alone, it was not for long. Around the Courts were swarms of petty lawyers who had their touts on the roads and in the villages. Longer he came within hail of the Court he had been fastened upon by several of these, and persuaded that his only chance of success was to put himself in their hands; say what they bade him; pay what, when, and to whom they told him; and above all, to beware of telling the truth; it would never be believed.

In those strange cases there was no common ground. What-ever one side asserted that other denied; all the witnesses were tutored: and whether true or not to begin with the case as presented on both sides was invariably concocted.

I for one came to the conclusion that nearly all, save a few of the graver cases, were episodes in some dispute not before the Court. The parties were not the real parties, but puppets of others, who remained in the back ground paying for and directing the proceedings. Most of the genuine disputes never reached our Courts at all, but were settled at some earlier stage in other ways.

While we dispensed justice as best as we could to those who came before us, we knew that an enormous number of injured persons never came to us at all. Many were deterred by difficulties in the way, many dared not come for fear of offending the local despot, who by threats of injuries – threats which he could carry out was able to prevent them from complaining and to stop the mouths of their witness".

96. What are the challenges for a litigant to seek justice in India and England? Choose the best option from the following:
A. There are no challenges. The passage is silent about this.
B. There are many challenges that are difficult to summarise.
C. In England, justice goes to the people. In India, the litigant faces many difficulties in approaching the strange tribunal to seek justice.
D. The way to the tribunal is easy and the litigant in India need nor dread at all.

97. What are the chances of success of any litigant? Choose the most appropriate answer:

A. The chance of success work only if he puts the hands of petty lawyers and touts
B. He need not beware of telling the truth
C. Cases on both sides were usually not concoted
D. There were no difficulties and the injured person could approach the court easily

98. Whether, in the strange cases, there were any common grounds?
A. There was no common ground
B. All grounds were common
C. Witnesses were not tutored
D. All witnesses were tutored

99. In the passage, it is said that all the genuine disputes never reached the courts.

Choose the correct answer:
A. Most of the genuine disputes never reached the courts
B. Parties to the cases were not the real parties in many cases
C. Many witnesses are not the real witnesses
D. Real parties were puppets of others and not the real parties

100. Many injured persons never came to the courts because of the following reason:
A. They were deterred by difficulties in the way
B. They had no interest
C. They were not sure to win
D. They could not arrange witnesses

ANSWERS

1	2	3	4	5	6	7	8	9	10
C	C	D	C	C	B	D	B	A	B
11	**12**	**13**	**14**	**15**	**16**	**17**	**18**	**19**	**20**
B	A	D	B	C	A	D	C	B	D
21	**22**	**23**	**24**	**25**	**26**	**27**	**28**	**29**	**30**
D	C	C	C	B	A	B	C	D	A, C
31	**32**	**33**	**34**	**35**	**36**	**37**	**38**	**39**	**40**
B	B	A	D	C	C	A	D	B	B
41	**42**	**43**	**44**	**45**	**46**	**47**	**48**	**49**	**50**
D	B	A	C	C	A	A	A	A	A
51	**52**	**53**	**54**	**55**	**56**	**57**	**58**	**59**	**60**
C	C	B	D	A	C	B	C	C	D
61	**62**	**63**	**64**	**65**	**66**	**67**	**68**	**69**	**70**
*	D	A	A	B	A	D	B	D	A
71	**72**	**73**	**74**	**75**	**76**	**77**	**78**	**79**	**80**
A	B	A	B	*	A	C	B	C	A
81	**82**	**83**	**84**	**85**	**86**	**87**	**88**	**89**	**90**
C	B	A	B	D	C	C	A	A	C
91	**92**	**93**	**94**	**95**	**96**	**97**	**98**	**99**	**100**
C	B	D	B	B	C	A	A	A	A

Previous Years' Paper (Solved)

National Testing Agency (NTA)

UGC-NET Junior Research Fellowship & Assistant Professor Eligibility Exam

Law, June-2021

(Online Exam held on 21-11-2021)

PAPER-II

1. According to Pound, law is:

A. The statement of circumstances in which the public force will be brought to bear upon men through courts

B. A social institution to satisfy social wants

C. Aggregate of rules set by men as politically superior or sovereign, to men as politically subject

D. A crystallized common sense of communities

2. Which of the following is not correct in relation to rights in its various forms and its correlatives?

A. Right (Strict sense) – Duty

B. Liberty – No right

C. Power – Liberty

D. Immunity – Disability

3. The main purpose of corporation sole is:

A. To protect the property of the Government

B. To make the property easily transferable

C. To make the property easily inheritable

D. To make continuity of an office

4. "Every man has a property in his own person, he has right to preserve his property, that is, his life, liberty and estate" .... is said by:

A. Bentham B. Henry Main

C. Locke D. Laski

5. Under the special powers of Rajya Sabha which of the following resolutions can originate only in Rajya Sabha.

(*a*) Resolution seeking removal of Vice President

(*b*) Any resolution seeking creation of one or more all India service

(*c*) Any resolution seeking legislation on state subject

(*d*) Introduction of money bills

Choose the correct answer from the options given below:

A. (*a*) and (*b*) only

B. (*a*) and (*c*) only

C. (*d*) and (*b*) only

D. (*a*), (*b*), (*c*) only

6. Vice President of India on expiry of his term:

A. Vacates his office

B. Gets a mandatory extension of 2 months

C. Continues to hold office until successor enters upon office

D. Elects his successor before relinquishing office

7. State Emergency or President Rule under Article 356 can be imposed in a State by the President for a maximum period of:

A. 3 years

B. 2 years extendable by 1 year

C. 6 months

D. 1 year

8. Besides providing for a functional government and consequential growth in the administrative process, the Constitution has provided elaborate control mechanism so that water may not over-run beyond banks. This has been ensured in which of the following articles of the Constitution?

A. Art 32, 226, 227
B. Art 14, 21 and 41
C. Art 15, 16 and 17
D. Art 246, 247, 248

9. Which of the following groups of Jurists who consider the law as a command of sovereign enforced by a superior political authority and accordingly subscribe to the view that International Law is not law as 'properly so called'?

A. Starke, Salmond, Holland
B. Hart, Starke, Oppenheim
C. Holland, Oppenheim, Hart
D. Hobbes, Pufendorf, Austin

10. Which one of the following Geneva conventions has the provisions on, "The protection of the victims of maritime warfare"?

A. The Second Geneva Convention, 1949
B. The Third Geneva Convention, 1949
C. The Fourth Geneva Convention, 1949
D. The First Geneva Convention, 1949

11. The World Court refused to give its Advisory opinion in which of the following case?

A. The Genocide Convention case
B. The legality of the use by a State of Nuclear weapons in Armed conflict
C. Interpretation of Peace Treaties case
D. Legality of the Threat or use of Nuclear weapons case

12. Which of the following is not the principal organ of the United Nations?

A. General Assembly
B. Economic and Social Council
C. International Court of Justice
D. International Human Rights Commission

13. The distinctive features of 'Rioting' are an activity which is accompanised by:

A. Use of force and violence
B. Causing alarm
C. Violence for a common purpose
D. Use of abusive language

14. Which among the following is the most serious offence, and thus severely punishable?

A. Unlawful Assembly
B. Rioting
C. Affray
D. Assault

15. 'Stalking' (following a women despite her disinterest, spying, etc) is an offence under:

A. Section 354 (1)(ii) IPC
B. Section 354 B IPC
C. Section 354 A (1) (iii)
D. Section 354 D IPC

16. In which of the following cases the supreme court observed. "There is a thin line between the preparation for and an attempt to commit an offence"?

A. State of Maharashtra V. Mohd. Yakul
B. Abhayanand Mishra V. State of Bihar
C. Malkiat Singh V. State of Punjab
D. Om Parkesh V. State of Punjab

17. Motor vehicle Amendment Act of 2019 refer to the earlier Motor vehicle Act of 1988 as:

A. Earlier Act
B. Old Act
C. Adapted Act
D. Principal Act

18. "The courts have created new torts by the gradual and sometimes almost imperceptible extension of old tort", who said the above statement?

A. Professor Good hart
B. Sir Frederick Pollock
C. Clerk and Lindsell
D. Salmond

19. Mental condition of a wrong doer at the time of wrong doing is:

A. Relevant in all torts
B. Relevant is torts based on fault
C. Relevant in tort based on strict liability
D. Not relevant at all

20. Section 53 of Consumer Protection Act of 2019 provides for establishment of National Consumer Disputes Redressal Commission. It is to be known as:

A. National Commission
B. National Council

C. National Dispute Redressal Commission
D. National Dispute Redressal Council

21. In a contract of Guarantee under the Indian Contract Act, 1872 there are:
A. Two parties and two contracts
B. Three parties and three contracts
C. Three parties and one contract
D. Two parties and one contract

22. In case of unascertained goods, the property in goods passes:
A. When goods are ascertained
B. When the parties intend the property in goods to pass
C. As soon as the contract of sale is signed
D. After the payment of goods is received by the seller

23. Where the money received from a third party by the firm, in ordinary course of business, is misapplied by one of the partners to his own use, then:
A. Defaulting partner alone is liable for the same
B. Third party has no remedy
C. Firm is liable for the same
D. Firm is not liable for the same

24. Who among the following can remove the name of company from Register of Companies on suo moto basis in terms of Section 248(1) of Companies Act, 2013?
A. Registrar of Companies
B. Securities and Exchange Board of India
C. National Company Law Tribunal
D. Ministry of Corporate Affair

25. Which one of the following is 'NOT' a primary source of Muslim Law?
A. Sunnat B. Ijma
C. Urf D. Qiyas

26. Originally under the Hindu Marriage Act, 1955, divorce was based on:
A. Consent Theory
B. Breakdown Theory
C. Fault Theory
D. Will Theory

27. Which of the following judgment does not deal with the need of enactment of 'Uniform Civil Code' in India?
A. Mohd. Ahmad Khan V. Shah Bano Begum
B. Ashok Hurra V. Rupa
C. Sarla Mudgal V. Union of India
D. John Vallamatton V. Union of India

28. Which of the following judgment do not deal with the matter of Live-in relationship?
A. Indra Sarma V. K.V. Sarma
B. Sharda V. Dharmpal
C. S. Khushboo V. Kanniammal
D. Chanmuniya V. Chanmuniya Kumar Singh

29. The Supreme Court of India recognised the significance of Inter-generational equity and held a government department's approval to establish forest based Industry to be invalid in one of the following case:
A. State of Himachal Pradesh V. Ganesh Wood products
B. Vellore citizen's forum V. Union of India
C. Dr. B.L. Wadehra V. Union of India
D. M.C, Metha V. Union of India

30. The preamble to both Environment (Protection) Act and Air (Prevention and Control of Pollution) Act were passed to implement the decision reached in one of the following:
A. San Francisco Conference, 1945
B. United Nations Conference on Environment and Development, 1992
C. United Nations Conference on the Human Environment, 1972
D. United Nations Conference on Environment, 1982

31. The Government of India's policy on abatement of pollution adopted certain guiding principles in the year 1992. Which of the following is not covered under the said guiding principles?
A. Prevention of pollution at source
B. Adoption of best available technology
C. Involvement of NGO's for all purposes
D. Public participation in decision making

32. Which one of the following is not the functions of Human Rights Council?

A. To promote Human Rights education and learning as well as advisory services

B. To decide issues without making any recommendations to the General Assembly

C. To work in close cooperation with the Government regional organisation, National Human rights institutions and civil society

D. To serve as forum for dialogue on thematic issues on all Human rights

33. 'Digital signature' is defined under which section of information technology Act, 2000?

A. Section 2 (p) B. Section 2 (q)
C. Section 2 (r) D. Section 2 (tb)

34. 'Cyber security' is defined under which section of information technology Act, 2000?

A. Section 2 (ua) B. Section 2 (za)
C. Section 2 (nb) D. Section 2 (tb)

35. The term private key refers to:

A. Authentication of any electronic record by a subscriber

B. Electronic signature certificate issued under section 35

C. Key pair in an asymmetric crypto system

D. Key of key pair used to create a digital signature

36. The validity of contracts formed through electronic means is contained under which section of Information Technology Act, 2000?

A. Section 3A B. Section 6A
C. Section 7A D. Section 10A

37. The right to information Act, 2005 explains the meaning of information under:

A. Section 2 (e) B. Section 2 (f)
C. Section 2 (g) D. Section 2 (h)

38. The Lokpal and Lokayukta Act 2013 came in to force in:

A. March 2013 B. February 2013
C. January 2013 D. August 2013

39. Which one of the following is related to Amendment of the U.S. constitution?

A. Article III B. Article IV
C. Article V D. Article VI

40. Section 8(1) of the RTI Act provides how many exemptions from the disclosure of information?

A. 7 B. 8
C. 9 D. 10

41. According to prof. Lon L Fullar:

(*a*) Law is the enterprise of subjecting human conduct to the governance of rules

(*b*) The morality of law has two aspects, external and internal

(*c*) External morality is the morality of aspiration, ideas from which it is possible to derive a procedural version of natural law

(*d*) Internal morality of law is a 'substantive version of natural law'

Choose the correct answer from the options given below:

A. (*a*) and (*b*) only
B. (*b*), (*c*) and (*d*) only
C. (*a*), (*c*) and (*d*) only
D. (*a*), (*b*) and (*c*) only

42. In which of the following cases the duties are not specifically enforced in respect of the act done?

(*a*) The liability of a borrower to repay a debt barred by statute of limitation

(*b*) The liability of a borrower to repay the money borrowed by him

(*c*) To refrain the wrong doer from publication when a libel has already been published

(*d*) To refrain the wrong doer to continue the commission of a nuisance

Choose the correct answer from the options given below:

A. (*a*) and (*b*) only B. (*a*) and (*c*) only
C. (*b*) and (*c*) only D. (*b*) and (*d*) only

43. Which of the following statements are correct?
(*a*) Global justice inquiries about what justice among human beings consists in.
(*b*) Global justice inquiries take individual human beings as of primary concern and seek to give an account of what fairness among such agents involves.
(*c*) In the domain of global justice, theorists seek primarily to define justice between states or nations.
(*d*) In international justice the nation or state is taken as the central entity of concern and justice among nations or states is the focus.

Choose the correct answer from the options given below:
A. (*a*), (*b*) and (*c*) only
B. (*a*), (*b*) and (*d*) only
C. (*a*), (*c*) and (*d*) only
D. (*b*), (*c*) and (*d*) only

44. Which of the following statements are correct?
(*a*) The Preamble contains in nutshell ideals and aspirations of the Constitution
(*b*) The Preamble is the key to open the minds of the Constitution makers
(*c*) The Preamble to the Constitution of India is solemnly resolved to secure to its citizens justice and equity
(*d*) The Preamble is not the part of the Constitution

Choose the correct answer from the options given below:
A. (*a*) and (*b*) only B. (*c*) and (*d*) only
C. (*a*) and (*c*) only D. (*a*) and (*b*) only

45. Which of the following statements are true under the Constitution of India?
(*a*) Article 61 deals with procedure for impeachment of the President
(*b*) Art 142 provides that law declared by the supreme court shall be biding on all courts
(*c*) Article 122 provides that courts shall not inquire into proceedings of Parliament
(*d*) Art 163 deals with the extent of executive power of State

Choose the correct answer from the options given below:
A. (*a*), (*b*) and (*c*) only
B. (*b*) and (*c*) only
C. (*a*) and (*c*) only
D. (*a*), (*c*) and (*d*) only

46. Which of the following statement/statements is/are correct?
(*a*) When a State is defeated or conquered, all the citizens acquire the Nationality of the conquering State. This is called 'cession' mode of gain of nationality.
(*b*) When a person gets Nationality of a State in place of the Nationality of another State. This is called 'substitution' mode of loss of nationality.
(*c*) The Public Trustee case is related to statelessness.
(*d*) The General Assembly decided to convene a conference to conclude, a convention on reduction of statelessness in 1961.

Choose the most appropriate answer from the options given below:
A. (*b*) and (*c*) only
B. (*a*), (*b*), (*c*) only
C. (*a*), (*c*), (*d*) only
D. (*a*), (*b*), (*c*) and (*d*)

47. Which of the following statement/statements, is/are correct?
(*a*) De Jure Recognition is final whereas De-facto Recognition is provisional
(*b*) De-Facto Recognition can be withdrawn but De-Jure Recognition is irrevocable
(*c*) De-Facto Recognition has retrospective operation as exactly as, in the case of De-Jure recognition
(*d*) There is no distinction between De-Jure and de Facto recognition for the purpose of giving effects to the internal acts of the recognised authority

Choose the most appropriate answer from the options given below:
A. (*a*), (*b*), (*d*) only
B. (*b*), (*c*), (*d*) only

C. (*a*), (*b*), (*c*) only
D. (*a*), (*b*), (*c*) and (*d*)

48. Which of the following statcment/statements is/are correct?
(*a*) On 16th June, 1987 the foreign secretaries of South Asian Regional Countries entered into agreement on Extradition
(*b*) Hongkong Pact on Extradition with India was entered in the middle of June 1980
(*c*) India and Germany signed an Extradition Treaty on 27 June, 2001
(*d*) India and France signed an Extradition Treaty on 24 June, 2002

Choose the most appropriate answer from the options given below:
A. (*a*), (*b*), (*d*) only
B. (*b*), (*c*), (*d*) only
C. (*a*), (*c*) only
D. (*a*), (*b*), (*c*) and (*d*)

49. Which of the following statement/statements is/are correct?
(*a*) The offence of abetment is defined under section 107 of IPC
(*b*) The essential ingredient of "the offence of conspiracy is the agreement to commit an offence"
(*c*) The punishment of criminal conspiracy is given under section 120 IPC
(*d*) State of Tamil Nadu through Superintendent of Police, CBI/SIT V. Nalini is a case related to offence of Abetment
(*e*) Abetment in India of offences committed outside of India is punishable under section 108A IPC

Choose the most appropriate answer from the options given below:
A. (*a*), (*b*), (*c*), (*d*) and (*e*)
B. (*b*), (*d*), (*e*) only
C. (*a*), (*b*), (*e*) only
D. (*b*), (*c*) only

50. Which of the following statement/statements are correct?
(*a*) 'Theft' is defined under section 378 IPC, as the dishonest removal of movable property out of the possession of any person without his consent
(*b*) In the offence of extortion punishment is upto 3 years under section 384 IPC
(*c*) The offence of 'Robbery' is defined under section 391 IPC
(*d*) Dacoity is Robbery committed by five or more persons
(*e*) The punishment for 'Dacoity' is prescribed under section 392 IPC

Choose the most appropriate answer from the options given below:
A. (*a*), (*b*), (*c*), (*d*) only
B. (*a*), (*b*), (*d*) only
C. (*d*), (*e*) only
D. (*a*), (*b*) only

51. Which of the following statement/statements is/are correct?
(*a*) The offence of 'sedition' is defined under section 124A of IPC
(*b*) The supreme court in Kedar Nath Singh V. State of Bihar held that section 124A IPC is not unconstitutional
(*c*) State (N.C.T. of Delhi) V. Navjot Sandhu Afsan Guru is a case related to sedition
(*d*) Mohd. Arif V State of NCT of Delhi is also known as Mumbai Terror Attack case
(*e*) Waging or attempt to wage war or abetting waging of war against the Government of India is an offence under section 121 IPC.

Choose the most appropriate answer from the options given below:
A. (*a*), (*b*), (*c*), (*d*) only
B. (*b*), (*c*), (*d*), (*e*) only
C. (*a*), (*b*), (*e*) only
D. (*d*), (*e*) only

52. In determining relevant geographic market, competition commission shall keep in mind which of the following factors?
(*a*) Regulatory trade barriers and natural procurement policies
(*b*) Language and local specification requirement

(*c*) Consumer preference and regular supply and after sale service
(*d*) Transport and distribution factors

Choose the most appropriate answer from the options given below:
A. (*a*), (*b*), (*c*) only B. (*a*), (*b*), (*d*) only
C. (*d*), (*c*), (*b*) only D. (*a*), (*b*), (*c*) and (*d*)

53. Consumer, Mediation Cell has to hold which of the following documents?
(*a*) List of empanelled mediators
(*b*) List of all cases handled by the cell
(*c*) Records of all proceedings
(*d*) Information specified by regulations

Choose the most appropriate answer from the options given below:
A. (*a*) and (*b*) only B. (*b*) and (*d*) only
C. (*c*) and (*d*) only D. (*a*), (*b*), (*c*) and (*d*)

54. Removal of members of Company Law Appellate Tribunal can be carried out in consultation by:
(*a*) Central Government
(*b*) Chief Justice
(*c*) Chairperson of Appellate Tribunal
(*d*) Auditor General

Choose the most appropriate answer from the options given below:
A. (*a*) and (*b*) only B. (*a*), (*b*), (*c*) only
C. (*c*) and (*b*) only D. (*a*), (*b*), (*c*) and (*d*)

55. Endorsement of Negotiable instrument followed by delivery
(*a*) Transfers the property in instrument to endorsee
(*b*) Transfers the right of further negotiation to the endorsee
(*c*) May exclude or restrict the right of further negotiation by endorsee
(*d*) May merely constitute the endorsee as an agent

Choose the most appropriate answer from the options given below:
A. (*a*) and (*b*) only B. (*c*) and (*d*) only
C. (*a*), (*b*), (*c*) only D. (*a*), (*b*), (*c*) and (*d*)

56. Under Muslim Law, divorce by common consent is known as:
(*a*) Talaq-e-Tafwid
(*b*) Khula
(*c*) Lian
(*d*) Mubarat

Choose the most appropriate answer from the options given below:
A. (*a*), (*b*) and (*d*) only
B. (*b*) and (*d*) only
C. (*c*) and (*d*) only
D. (*a*) and (*b*) only

57. Which of the following are fault grounds of divorce under the Hindu Marriage Act, 1955?
(*a*) Desertion
(*b*) Cruelty
(*c*) Consent obtained by force or fraud
(*d*) Conversion to non-Hindu religion

Choose the most appropriate answer from the options given below:
A. (*a*) and (*b*) only
B. (*b*), (*c*) and (*d*) only
C. (*a*) and (*c*) only
D. (*a*), (*b*) and (*d*) only

58. Under the provisions of the Hindu succession Act, 1956
(*a*) Son of a predeceased daughter is class I heir
(*b*) Widow of a predeceased son of a pre-deceased son is class II heir
(*c*) Mother's mother is class I heir
(*d*) Mother's father is class II heir

Choose the most appropriate answer from the options given below:
A. (*a*), (*b*) and (*c*) only
B. (*a*) and (*d*) only
C. (*b*) and (*d*) only
D. (*b*), (*c*) and (*d*) only

59. The National Commission for Women shall perform some of the following functions:
(*a*) Shall fund litigations involving issues affecting a large body of women
(*b*) Shall provide, financial assistance to all those who are self employed

(*c*) Shall call for specific studies or investigation in to specific problems
(*d*) Shall impose punishment to those found involved in discrimination of women
(*e*) Shall investigate and examine all matters relating to the safeguards provided for women under the Constitution and other laws

Choose the most appropriate answer from the options given below:
A. (*a*), (*c*), (*e*) only B. (*b*), (*d*), (*e*) only
C. (*a*), (*b*), (*d*) only D. (*e*), (*a*), (*b*) only

60. Examine the relevancy of class action suit and choose the correct answer:
(*a*) A class action would measurably assist in securing redress in Environmental cases
(*b*) Monetary recoveries from the tort feasors in environmental cases can only be obtained through a suit
(*c*) The writ procedure appears more suited than the class action procedure
(*d*) The most obvious use of class action is in the mass disasters of the sort that occurred in Bhopal

Choose the most appropriate answer from the options given below:
A. (*a*), (*b*), (*d*) only B. (*a*), (*c*), (*d*) only
C. (*b*), (*c*), (*d*) only D. (*a*), (*b*), (*c*) only

61. The geographical indications are distinctive signs or indications which identify any goods as:
(*a*) Act of unfair competition under Paris convention, 1967
(*b*) Originating in a specified territory
(*c*) Stipulate the misleading test guaranteeing a negative right
(*d*) Specific quality, reputation and characteristics
(*e*) Essentially attributable to origin

Choose the most appropriate answer from the options given below:
A. (*a*), (*b*), (*c*) only B. (*c*), (*d*), (*e*) only
C. (*a*), (*d*), (*b*) only D. (*b*), (*d*), (*e*) only

62. Nothing in TRIPS agreement, 1995 shall derogate from the existing obligations prescribed under:
(*a*) Paris Convention, 1967
(*b*) Rome Convention, 1961
(*c*) Berne Convention, 1971
(*d*) Biodiversity Convention, 1992
(*e*) Integrated Circuit Treaty, 1989

Choose the correct answer from the options given below:
A. (*a*), (*b*), (*c*), (*d*) only
B. (*b*), (*c*), (*d*), (*e*) only
C. (*a*), (*b*), (*c*), (*e*) only
D. (*e*), (*d*), (*c*), (*a*) only

63. 'Computer network' means the inter connection of one or more computers of computer systems or communication devices through:
(*a*) The use of satellite, microwave, terrestrial line, wire, wireless or other communication media
(*b*) A device or collection of devices including input and output support devices
(*c*) Any electronic, magnetic, optical and other high speed data processing device
(*d*) All input, out, processing, storage, computer software or communication facilities
(*e*) Terminal or a complex consisting of two or more interconnected computers or communication device

Choose the correct answer from the options given below:
A. (*b*) and (*c*) only B. (*d*) and (*c*) only
C. (*e*) and (*b*) only D. (*a*) and (*e*) only

64. Which of the following statements are correct?
(*a*) In Canada, the federation was not a voluntary union but was imposed by an Act
(*b*) In India, the Act of 1935 created autonomous units and forged them into a federation

(*c*) The American Union was formed by voluntary agreement among a number of sovereign states
(*d*) Indian constitution has been framed by the States and not by the people of India

Choose the most appropriate answer from the options given below:
A. (*a*), (*b*) and (*c*) only
B. (*a*), (*b*) and (*d*) only
C. (*a*), (*c*) and (*d*) only
D. (*b*), (*c*) and (*d*) only

65. Amendment in the American constitution may by proposed by:
(*a*) Congress with a 2/3 majority in both the Houses of Representatives and the Senate
(*b*) Congress with a 3/4 majority in both the Houses of Representatives and the Senate
(*c*) Constitutional convention called by two third of State Legislatures
(*d*) Constitutional convention called by three fourth of State Legislatures

Choose the most appropriate answer from the options given below:
A. (*a*) and (*c*) only B. (*b*) and (*c*) only
C. (*b*) and (*d*) only D. (*a*) and (*d*) only

66. Match List I with List II:

List-I (Books)	**List-II (Jurists)**
(*a*) The Growth of the Law	(*i*) H. Cairns
(*b*) The Theory of Legal Science	(*ii*) Cardozo
(*c*) An Introduction to the Principles of Morals and Legislation	(*iii*) John Rawls
(*d*) The Law of Peoples	(*iv*) Jeremy Bentham

Choose the correct answer from the options given below.

	(*a*)	(*b*)	(*c*)	(*d*)
A.	(*i*)	(*ii*)	(*iii*)	(*iv*)
B.	(*ii*)	(*i*)	(*iv*)	(*iii*)
C.	(*i*)	(*iii*)	(*iv*)	(*ii*)
D.	(*ii*)	(*iii*)	(*i*)	(*iv*)

67. Match List I with List II:

List-I	**List-II**
(*a*) Art 326 of the Constitution	(*i*) Chief Election Commissioner shall act as the chairman of the Election Commission
(*b*) Art 324 (3) of the Constitution	(*ii*) Ban to interference by courts in electoral matters
(*c*) Art 328 of the Constitution	(*iii*) Elections to be on the basis of adult suffrage
(*d*) Art 329 of the Constitution	(*iv*) Power of Legislature of a State to make provisions with respect to elections to such Legislature

Choose the correct answer from the options given below.

	(*a*)	(*b*)	(*c*)	(*d*)
A.	(*ii*)	(*iv*)	(*i*)	(*iii*)
B.	(*iii*)	(*iv*)	(*i*)	(*ii*)
C.	(*iii*)	(*i*)	(*iv*)	(*ii*)
D.	(*i*)	(*ii*)	(*iv*)	(*iii*)

68. Match List I with List II:

List-I (Conferences of W.T.O.)	**List-II (Places Where Held)**
(*a*) Third Ministerial Conference of WTO was held at	(*i*) Hong Kong (China)
(*b*) Sixth Ministerial Conference of WTO was held at	(*ii*) Seattle (US)
(*c*) Fourth Ministerial Conference of WTO was held at	(*iii*) Geneva (Switzerland)
(*d*) Seventh Ministerial Conference of WTO was held at	(*iv*) Doha (Qatar)

Choose the correct answer from the options given below.

	(a)	(b)	(c)	(d)
A.	(i)	(ii)	(iii)	(iv)
B.	(ii)	(i)	(iv)	(iii)
C.	(ii)	(iv)	(i)	(iii)
D.	(iv)	(iii)	(ii)	(i)

69. Match List I with List II:

List-I (Definitions of)	**List-II (Provisions of Indian Penal Code)**
(a) Solitary confinement	(i) Section 95 IPC
(b) Act of a child under seven years of age	(ii) Section 93 IPC
(c) Communication made in good faith	(iii) Section 73 IPC
(d) Act causing slight harm	(iv) Section 82 IPC

Choose the correct answer from the options given below.

	(a)	(b)	(c)	(d)
A.	(iii)	(iv)	(ii)	(i)
B.	(i)	(ii)	(iii)	(iv)
C.	(iv)	(ii)	(iii)	(i)
D.	(ii)	(iii)	(iv)	(i)

70. Match List I with List II:

List-I	**List-II**
(a) Negligence	(i) Ryland V Fletcher
(b) Strict liability	(ii) M.C. Mehta V Union of India
(c) Absolute liability	(iii) Glasgow corporation vs Muir
(d) Nervous shock	(iv) Bourhill V Young

Choose the correct answer from the options given below.

	(a)	(b)	(c)	(d)
A.	(ii)	(i)	(iii)	(iv)
B.	(i)	(iii)	(iv)	(ii)
C.	(iii)	(i)	(ii)	(iv)
D.	(iii)	(ii)	(i)	(iv)

71. Match List I with List II:

List-I	**List-II**
(a) Section 162 of the Indian Contract Act, 1872	(i) Pledge by Mercantile Agent
(b) Section 178 of the Indian Contract Act 1872	(ii) Bailor's duty to disclose faults in goods bailed
(c) Section 214 of the Indian Contract Act, 1872	(iii) Termination of gratuitous bailment by death
(d) Section 150 of the Indian Contract Act, 1872	(iv) Agent's duty to communicate with principal

Choose the correct answer from the options given below.

	(a)	(b)	(c)	(d)
A.	(i)	(iv)	(iii)	(ii)
B.	(ii)	(i)	(iv)	(iii)
C.	(iv)	(ii)	(i)	(iii)
D.	(iii)	(i)	(iv)	(ii)

72. Match List I with List II:

List-I	**List-II**
(a) Sec. 13 of C.P.C.	(i) Foreign court
(b) Sec. 2(5) of C.P.C.	(ii) Presumption as to foreign judgements
(c) Sec. 2(6) of C.P.C.	(iii) When foreign judgement not conclusive
(d) Sec. 14 of C.P.C.	(iv) Judgement of a foreign court

Choose the correct answer from the options given below.

	(a)	(b)	(c)	(d)
A.	(i)	(ii)	(iv)	(iii)
B.	(iii)	(i)	(iv)	(ii)
C.	(iii)	(i)	(ii)	(iv)
D.	(ii)	(iv)	(iii)	(i)

73. Match List I with List II:

List-I	**List-II**
(a) National Human Rights Commission	(i) Article 338

(*b*) National Commission for Backward Class	(*ii*) State to introduce regulatory regime in the National Interest
(*c*) National Commission for Minorities	(*iii*) Power to recommend payment of compensation
(*d*) National Commission for Scheduled Caste	(*iv*) Article 338-B

Choose the correct answer from the options given below.

	(*a*)	(*b*)	(*c*)	(*d*)
A.	(*i*)	(*ii*)	(*iii*)	(*iv*)
B.	(*iii*)	(*iv*)	(*ii*)	(*i*)
C.	(*iv*)	(*iii*)	(*ii*)	(*i*)
D.	(*iv*)	(*ii*)	(*i*)	(*iii*)

74. Match List I with List II:

List-I (Definitions of)	**List-II (Provisions under Information Technology Act 2000)**
(*a*) Computer	(*i*) Section 2 (g)
(*b*) Computer Network	(*ii*) Section 2 (k)
(*c*) Certifying Authority	(*iii*) Section 2 (j)
(*d*) Computer Resource	(*iv*) Section 2 (i)

Choose the correct answer from the options given below.

	(*a*)	(*b*)	(*c*)	(*d*)
A.	(*i*)	(*ii*)	(*iii*)	(*iv*)
B.	(*ii*)	(*i*)	(*iv*)	(*iii*)
C.	(*iv*)	(*iii*)	(*i*)	(*ii*)
D.	(*iii*)	(*iv*)	(*ii*)	(*i*)

75. Match List I with List II:

List-I	**List-II**
(*a*) Article-V	(*i*) Presidential Election Nov. 7, 2012
(*b*) Article-III	(*ii*) Congress on the eve of Presidential Election
(*c*) Chapter-V	(*iii*) The Judicial power in American Supreme Court
(*d*) Chapter-IV	(*iv*) Amendment of the Constitutions

Choose the correct answer from the options given below.

	(*a*)	(*b*)	(*c*)	(*d*)
A.	(*i*)	(*ii*)	(*iv*)	(*iii*)
B.	(*iii*)	(*i*)	(*iv*)	(*ii*)
C.	(*iv*)	(*iii*)	(*ii*)	(*i*)
D.	(*ii*)	(*iv*)	(*iii*)	(*i*)

76. Arrange in chronological order the publication of the books on Jurisprudence:

(*a*) A Practical Treatise of Architectural Jurisprudence by James Elmes

(*b*) The Spirit of Common Law by Roscoe Pound

(*c*) World Poverty and Human Rights by Thomas Pogge

(*d*) Taking Rights Seriously by Ronald Dworkin

(*e*) The Growth of the Law by Benjamin N. Cardozo

Choose the most appropriate answer from the options given below:

A. (*b*), (*a*), (*c*), (*e*), (*d*)
B. (*e*), (*b*), (*a*), (*c*), (*d*)
C. (*a*), (*b*), (*e*), (*d*), (*c*)
D. (*b*), (*a*), (*e*), (*c*), (*d*)

77. Chronologically arrange (Article wise) the following provisions of the Constitution of India:

(*a*) Special Provisions with respect to the State of Sikkim

(*b*) Special Provisions with respect to the State of Karnataka

(*c*) Special Provisions with respect to the State of Manipur

(*d*) Special Provisions with respect to the State of Nagaland

Choose the most appropriate answer from the options given below:

A. (*c*), (*d*), (*a*), (*b*) B. (*d*), (*c*), (*b*), (*a*)
C. (*d*), (*c*), (*a*), (*b*) D. (*c*), (*d*), (*b*), (*a*)

78. Indicate the correct chronological order of years the following cases they were decided:

(*a*) Case concerning the Temple of Preah Vihear

(*b*) Frontier Dispute (Burkina Faso V. Mali)
(*c*) The Caroline case
(*d*) R.V. Keyn
(*e*) Chorzow factory (Indemnity) case

Choose the most appropriate answer from the options given below:
A. (*a*), (*b*), (*c*), (*d*), (*e*)
B. (*e*), (*d*), (*c*), (*b*), (*a*)
C. (*c*), (*d*), (*e*), (*a*), (*b*)
D. (*b*), (*c*), (*d*), (*e*), (*a*)

79. Indicate the chronological order of the years of the following cases as decided by the Supreme Court:
(*a*) State of T.N. V. Balkrishna
(*b*) Mangesh V. State of Maharashtra
(*c*) Ram Kumar V. State of M.P.
(*d*) K.M. Nanavati V. State of Maharashtra
(*e*) Mahesh Chander V. State of Delhi

Choose the most appropriate answer from the options given below:
A. (*a*), (*b*), (*c*), (*d*), (*e*)
B. (*e*), (*c*), (*b*), (*d*), (*a*)
C. (*d*), (*a*), (*b*), (*c*), (*e*)
D. (*c*), (*d*), (*a*), (*b*), (*e*)

80. Arrange the correct sequence in which the liability for tort will arise for the following:
(*a*) Damages
(*b*) Breach of duty
(*c*) Duty to take care
(*d*) Causation

Choose the most appropriate answer from the options given below:
A. (*a*), (*b*), (*c*), (*d*) B. (*b*), (*c*), (*a*), (*d*)
C. (*c*), (*b*), (*d*), (*a*) D. (*c*), (*a*), (*b*), (*d*)

81. Arrange the provisions of the Indian Contract Act 1872 in chronological order (Section wise)
(*a*) Who are competent to contract
(*b*) Effect of mistakes as to law
(*c*) What agreements are contracts
(*d*) Agreement in restraint of marriage is void

Choose the most appropriate answer from the options given below:
A. (*c*), (*a*), (*d*), (*b*) B. (*a*), (*c*), (*b*), (*d*)
C. (*c*), (*a*), (*b*), (*d*) D. (*a*), (*c*), (*d*), (*b*)

82. Arrange in chronological order the following judgments on cruelty as a ground of divorce
(*a*) A. Jaya Chandra V. Aneel Kaur
(*b*) Naveen Kohli V. Neelu Kohli
(*c*) Dastane V. Dastane
(*d*) Bhagat V. Bhagat

Choose the most appropriate answer from the options given below:
A. (*c*), (*b*), (*d*), (*a*) B. (*a*), (*c*), (*b*), (*d*)
C. (*c*), (*d*), (*a*), (*b*) D. (*d*), (*c*), (*a*), (*b*)

83. Arrange the following in chronological order:
(*a*) United Nation Conference on the Human Environment
(*b*) United Nation Conference on Sustainable Development
(*c*) United Nations Conference on Environment and Development
(*d*) World Commission on Environment and Development
(*e*) United Nations Sustainable Development

Choose the most appropriate answer from the options given below:
A. (*a*), (*b*), (*c*), (*d*), (*e*)
B. (*b*), (*a*), (*d*), (*c*), (*e*)
C. (*a*), (*d*), (*c*), (*b*), (*e*)
D. (*e*), (*d*), (*b*), (*c*), (*a*)

84. Prof. William Fisher identified four analytical constructs of theories of intellectual property under which of the following sequence?
(*a*) Personality Theory
(*b*) Labour Theory
(*c*) Social Planning Theory
(*d*) Utilitarian Theory

Choose the most appropriate answer from the options given below:
A. (*b*), (*a*), (*d*), (*c*) B. (*c*), (*b*), (*a*), (*d*)
C. (*d*), (*b*), (*a*), (*c*) D. (*a*), (*d*), (*c*), (*b*)

85. The trend towards codification of the British constitution in whole or in part is a movement during the past decade from eminent quarters. Arrange them in chronological order:
(*a*) Northern Ireland Act
(*b*) Referendum Act
(*c*) Scotland Act
(*d*) European Communities Act

Choose the most appropriate answer from the options given below:

A. (*a*), (*d*), (*c*), (*b*) B. (*b*), (*c*), (*a*), (*d*)

C. (*d*), (*a*), (*b*), (*c*) D. (*c*), (*b*), (*d*), (*a*)

86. Given below are two statements:

Assertion A : The rule making power of the Supreme Court for regulating the practice and procedure of the court is not subject to any law made by the Parliament of India

Reason R : Only an impartial and independent judiciary can protect the right of individual without fear or favour

In the light of the above statements, choose the correct answer from the options given below:

A. Both A and R are true and R is the correct explanation of A

B. Both A and R are true and R is NOT the correct explanation of A

C. A is true, but R is false

D. A is false, but R is true

87. Given below are two statements: one is labelled as Assertion A and the other is labelled as Reason R.

Assertion A : The right of private defence of body extends to causing of death to the Assailant in case of assault of throwing or administering acid or an attempt to throw or administer acid which may reasonably cause the apprehension that grievous hurt will otherwise be the consequences of such Act.

Reason R : This provision was inserted under clause (7) of section 100 IPC by Act 13 of 2013 in view of increasing cases of acid throwing on the girls and women in India

In the light of the above statements, choose the correct answer from the options given below:

A. Both A and R are correct and R is the correct explanation of A

B. Both A and R are correct and R is NOT the correct explanation of A

C. A is correct, but R is not correct

D. A is not correct, but R is correct

88. Given below are two statements:

Statement I : Dominant position means position of strength enjoyed by an enterprise in relevant market in India which enables it to operate independently of operative forces and affects competitors and consumers in its favour.

Statement II : No enterprise shall abuse its dominant position.

In the light of the above statements, choose the correct answer from the options given below:

A. Both Statement I and Statement II are true.

B. Both Statement I and Statement II are false.

C. Statement I is true, but Statement II is false

D. Statement I is false, but Statement II is true

89. Given below are two statements: One is labelled Assertion A and the other is labelled as Reason R.

Assertion A : Under the companies Act of 2013 Central Government is authorised to implement a facility to file documents in electronic form.

Reason R : Central Government is authorised to make rules to implement this facility and section 398, 401 and 402 have been incorporated in the Act of 2013.

In the light of the above statements, choose the correct answer from the options given below:

A. Both A and R are true and R is the correct explanation of A

B. Both A and R are true and R is NOT the correct explanation of A

C. A is true, but R is false

D. A is false, but R is true

90. Given below are two statements:

Statement I : No person except the father or mother of a child shall have the capacity to give the child in adoption under the Hindu Adoptions and Maintenance Act 1956.

Statement II : Under the Hindu Adoptions and Maintenance Act 1956, the same child may not be adopted simultaneously by two or more persons.

In the light of the above statements, choose the most appropriate answer from the options given below:

A. Both Statement I and Statement II are correct.

B. Both Statement I and Statement II are incorrect.

C. Statement I is correct, but Statement II is incorrect

D. Statement I is incorrect, but Statement II is correct

Directions (Qs. No. 91-95): *Read the given passage and answer the questions that follow.*

Privacy of the individual is an essential aspect of dignity. Dignity has both an intrinsic and instrumental value. As an intrinsic value, human dignity is an entitlement or a constitutionally protected interest in itself. In its instrumental facet, dignity and freedom are inseperably inter-twined, each being a facilitative tool to achieve the other. The ability of the individual to protect a zone of privacy enables the realisation of the full value of life and liberty. Liberty has a broader meaning of which privacy is a subset. All liberties may not be exercised in privacy. Yet others can be fulfilled only within a private space. Privacy enables the individual to retain the autonomy of the body and mind. The autonomy of the individual is the ability to make decisions on vital matters of concern to life. Privacy has not been couched as an independent fundamental right. But that does not detract from the constitutional protection afforded to it, once the true nature of privacy and its relationship with those fundamental rights which are expressly protected is understood. Privacy lies across the spectrum of protected freedoms.

91. The referred paragraph is taken from the judgement of the Supreme Court in:

A. A.D.M. Jabalpur V. S. Shukla

B. Mohini Jain V. State of Karnataka

C. Maneka Gandhi V. Union of India

D. Justice K.S. Puttaswami (Retd.) and another V. Union of India and others

92. The referred paragraph is a part of the judgement delivered by:

A. Justice Chelameshwar

B. Justice D.Y. Chandrachud

C. Justice S.A. Bobde

D. Justice F.M. Nariman

93. In which of the following case it was held that right to privacy is not protected as a fundamental right under the Constitution?

A. M.P. Sharma V. Satish Chandra, District Magistrate, Delhi

B. Govind V. State of M.P.

C. R. Rajagopal V. State of Tamil Nadu

D. K.S. Puttaswami V. Union of India

94. In which of the following case it was held that the procedure established by law means the procedure must be just, fair and reasonable?

A. Kharak Singh V. State of U.P.

B. A.K. Gopalan V. Union of India

C. Maneka Gandhi V. Union of India

D. Govind V. State of M.P.

95. Which one of the following statement is correct?

A. Right to privacy is expressly provided as a fundamental right under the Constitution

B. Right to privacy is protected as a fundamental right under Article 21 of the constitution

C. Right to privacy is not protected as a fundamental right under Article 21 of the constitution

D. Article 21 of the constitution protects the life and personal liberty only from executive action

Directions (Qs. No. 96-100): *Read the passage carefully and answer the questions that follow.*

The acceptance of international law as law poses the problem of explaining its binding force, and this in turn raises questions as to the authority of all law. Some writers have sought to demonstrate the binding character of international law from its derivation from natural law. But we have seen that natural law is nothing more than morality and that the existence of moral rules is no guarantee of the existence of corresponding legal rules. Such an argument shows at most that the rules of international law are morally binding, not that they are legally binding. Moreover, many legal rules are morally indifferent; morality may demand the existence of some rule without specifying what that rule should be. Such is the case in municipal law with regard to the formalities required for wills, contracts and conveyances; and in international law with some of the rules regarding title to territory and the limits of jurisdiction. The binding force of such rules can hardly be attributed to any moral characteristic.

96. According to Austin, the positive law has following three attributes:
A. Command, Sovereign, Obedience
B. Command, Sovereign, Sanction
C. Command, Obedience, Sanction
D. Sovereign, Obedience, Sanction

97. Which one of the following statements is not correct?
A. Starke and Kelsen contend that there is both legislation and law enforcement in international law
B. According to Starke, legislation being provided by multilateral treaties in international law
C. According to Kelsen, sanctions are provided by the right of self-help and war in international law
D. Treaties and self-help can qualify as legislation and law-enforcement in a positivist sense

98. Who defines law 'as a body of rules for human conduct within a community, which by common consent of this community shall be enforced by external power?
A. Oppenheim B. Austin
C. Bentham D. Friedman

99. Which one of the following statements is not correct?
A. Hart's analysis of law suggests that international law consists of legal rules forming not a system but a set of rules.
B. The absence in international law of any basic rules of recognition prevents its being unified into a system
C. International law remains a mere set of separate rules
D. Many of the rules of international law rest on treaty, not on custom

100. The view that international law consisted of the precepts dictated to States by natural law was advanced by:
A. Kelsen B. Vattel
C. HLA Hart D. Salmond

ANSWERS

1	2	3	4	5	6	7	8	9	10
B	C	D	C	D	C	A	A	D	A
11	**12**	**13**	**14**	**15**	**16**	**17**	**18**	**19**	**20**
B	D	A	B	D	B	D	A	B	A
21	**22**	**23**	**24**	**25**	**26**	**27**	**28**	**29**	**30**
B	A	C	A	C	C	B	B	A	C

31	32	33	34	35	36	37	38	39	40
C	B	A	C	D	D	B	*	C	D
41	**42**	**43**	**44**	**45**	**46**	**47**	**48**	**49**	**50**
A	B	B	A, D	C	A	A	C	C	B
51	**52**	**53**	**54**	**55**	**56**	**57**	**58**	**59**	**60**
C	D	D	A	D	B	D	B	A	A
61	**62**	**63**	**64**	**65**	**66**	**67**	**68**	**69**	**70**
D	C	D	A	A	B	C	B	A	C
71	**72**	**73**	**74**	**75**	**76**	**77**	**78**	**79**	**80**
D	B	B	C	C	C	C	C	C	C
81	**82**	**83**	**84**	**85**	**86**	**87**	**88**	**89**	**90**
C	C	C	C	C	D	A	A	A	D
91	**92**	**93**	**94**	**95**	**96**	**97**	**98**	**99**	**100**
D	B	A	C	B	B	D	A	D	B

EXPLANATORY ANSWERS

1. According to Pound, "Law is social engineering which means a balance between the competing interests in society," in which applied science are used for resolving individual and social problems.

For the purpose of maintaining the legal framework and its proper functioning, certain interest needs to be considered like individual interests, public and social interests, a definition of limits within which such interests will be recognized and given effect to, and the securing of those interest within the limits as defined.

Social Interest: Social interests are the claim or demands or desires thought of in terms of social life and generalized as claims of social groups. Social interests are said to include :

- Social interest in general security—Social interest in the general security embraces those branches of the law which relate to:
  - ❑ General safety,
  - ❑ General health,
  - ❑ Peace and order,
  - ❑ Security of acquisitions, and
  - ❑ Security of transactions.
- Social interest in the security of social institutions—Social interest in the security of the social institutions include General security of domestic institutions, Religious institutions, Political institution and Economic institutions.
- Social interest in general morals—Social interest in general morals comprises of prevention and prohibition of prostitution, drunkenness, gambling, etc.
- Social interest in conservation of social resources—Social interests in the conservation of social resources covers conservation of social resources and protection and training of dependents and defectives, *i.e.*, conservation of human resources, protective and education of dependents and defectives, reformation of delinquents, protection of economically dependents.

- Social interest in general progress—Social interest in general progress has three aspects: Economic progress, political progress and cultural progress.

  Political progress covers free speech and free association, free opinion, free criticisms.

  Economic progress covers freedom of use and sale of property, free trade, free industry and encouragement of inventions by the grant of patents.

  Cultural progress covers free science, free letters, encouragements of arts and letters, encouragements of higher education an learning and aesthetics.

- Social interest in individual life—Meaning thereby each individual be able to live a human life according to the individual's Political life
  - ❑ Physical life
  - ❑ Cultural
  - ❑ Social and
  - ❑ Economic life

2. The term 'right' has been used in different ways. In its strict sense it has been used as correlative of legal duties. In legal terms a right is an interest recognised and protected by the State and enforceable through the court of law. A right is enforceable only to the extent it is protected by the state. Legal rights, in a wider sense of the term, do not necessarily correspond with duties. In this generic sense a legal right may be defined as any advantage or benefit conferred upon a person by a rule of law. Of rights in this sense there are four distinct kinds. These are: (1) Rights (in the strict sense), (2) Liberties, (3) Powers, and (4) Immunities. Since the rights cannot exist in vacuum, each of these has its correlative, namely—(1) Duties, (2) No rights, (3) Liabilities, and (4) Disabilities. The concept of right envisages the presence of two parties: one, who has the right and the accompanying capacity to get it enforced, and the other against whom the right has been conferred and can be enforced.

   Each of these kinds of rights has its correlative, namely, (1) duties, (2) no right, (3) liabilities, and (4) disabilities.

3. **Corporation Sole:** Is an incorporated series of successive persons. It consists of a single person who is personified and regarded by law as a legal person. In other words, a single person, who is in exercise of some office or function, deals in legal capacity and has legal rights and duties.

   A corporation sole is an individual person who represents an official position which has a single separate legal entity. The death of the individual will not affect the corporation as there is a right of succession. The Crown, bishops, deans, vicars and the Lord Mayor of London are examples of a corporation sole.

   The sole purpose of the corporation is to maintain the continuity of an office. Till it is in continuation its all others purposes like maximizing profit, increase in shareholders wealth can be achieved.

4. According to Locke: "Every man has a property in his person. Every individual has the right to preserve his property, that is, his life, liberty and estate."

   In a narrower sense, the property includes the proprietary rights of a person and not his rights. Proprietary rights constitute his estate or property, whereas, personal rights includes his status or personal condition. If viewed from the lens of a narrower sense, then only land, chattels, shares, and debts are personal property and not his life, liberty or reputation. This is the most commonly used interpretation of property in modern times.

5. **Legislative Functions of Rajya Sabha**

   What is a Bill

   A Bill is a draft statute which becomes law after it is passed by both the Houses of

Parliament and assented to by the President. All legislative proposals are brought before Parliament in the forms of Bills.

Types of Bills and their Specific Features:

- Bills may be broadly classified into Government Bills and Private Members' Bills depending upon their initiation in the House by a Minister or a Private Member.
- Content wise, Bills are further classified into:
  - ❑ Original Bills which embody new proposals, ideas or policies,
  - ❑ Amending Bills which seek to modify, amend or revise existing Acts,
  - ❑ Consolidating Bills which seek to consolidate existing law/enactments on a particular subject,
  - ❑ Expiring Laws (Continuance) Bills which seek to continue Acts which, otherwise, would expire on a specified date,
  - ❑ Repealing and amending Bill to cleanse the Statute Book,
  - ❑ Validating Acts to give validity to certain actions,
  - ❑ Bills to replace Ordinances,
  - ❑ Money and Financial Bills, and
  - ❑ Constitution Amendment Bills.
- However, procedurally, the Bills are classified as:
  - ❑ Ordinary Bills
  - ❑ Money Bills and Financial Bills
  - ❑ Ordinance Replacing Bills and
  - ❑ Constitution Amendment Bills.
- Money Bills are those Bills which contain only provisions dealing with all or any of the matters specified in sub-clauses (a) to (f) of clause (1) of article 110 of the Constitution. Financial Bills can be further classified as Financial Bills Categories A and B. Category A Bills contain provisions dealing with any of the matters specified in sub-clauses (a) to (f) of clause (1) of article 110 and other matters and Category B Bills involve expenditure from the Consolidated Fund of India.

  Except Money Bills and Financial Bills, Category A, which can be introduced only in the Lok Sabha, a Bill may originate in either House of Parliament. As per the provisions of article 109 of the Constitution, the Rajya Sabha has limited powers with respect to Money Bills. A Money Bill after having been passed by the Lok Sabha, and sent to Rajya Sabha for its recommendations, has to be returned to Lok Sabha by the Rajya Sabha, with in a period of fourteen days from the date of its receipt, with or without recommendations. It is open for the Lok Sabha, to either accept or reject all or any of the recommendations of the Rajya Sabha. If the Lok Sabha accepts any of the recommendations of the Rajya Sabha, the Money Bill is deemed to have been passed by both Houses with the amendments recommended by the Rajya Sabha and accepted by the Lok Sabha. If the Lok Sabha does not accept any of the recommendations of the Rajya Sabha, the Money Bill is deemed to have been passed by both Houses in the form in which it was passed by the Lok Sabha without any of the amendments recommended by the Rajya Sabha. In case a Money Bill is not returned by the Rajya Sabha to the Lok Sabha within a period of fourteen days from the date of its receipt, it is deemed to have been passed by both Houses in the form in which it was passed by the Lok Sabha after the expiry of said period.
- Financial Bill Category A can only be introduced in the Lok Sabha on the recommendation of the President. However, once it has been passed by the

Lok Sabha, it is like an ordinary Bill and there is no restriction on the powers of the Rajya Sabha on such Bills.

- Financial Bill Category B and Ordinary Bills can be introduced in either House of Parliament.
- Ordinance replacing Bills are brought before Parliament to replace an Ordinance, with or without modifications, promulgated by the President under article 123 of the Constitution of a subject. To provide continuity to the provisions of the Ordinance, such a Bill has to be passed by the Houses of Parliament and assented to by the President within six weeks of the reassembly of Parliament.
- As per the procedure laid down in the Constitution, Constitution Amendment Bills can be of three types viz.,
  - ❑ requiring simple majority for their passage in each House;
  - ❑ requiring special majority for their passage in each House i.e., a majority of the total membership of a House and by a majority of not less than two-thirds of the members of that House present and voting (article 368); and
  - ❑ requiring special majority for their passage and ratification by Legislatures of not less than one-half of the States by resolutions to that effect passed by those Legislatures (proviso to clause (2) of article 368). A Constitution Amendment Bill under article 368 can be introduced in either House of Parliament and has to be passed by each House by special majority.
- Under provisions of article 108 of the Constitution, if after a Bill passed by one House and transmitted to the other House:
  - ❑ is rejected by the other House; or
  - ❑ the Houses have finally disagreed as to the amendments to be made in the Bill; or
  - ❑ more than six months elapse from the date of its receipt by the other House without the Bill being passed by it, the President may, unless the Bill has elapsed by reason of a dissolution of the Lok Sabha, summon them to meet in a joint sitting for the purpose of deliberating and voting on the Bill. If at the joint sitting of the two Houses, the Bill, with such amendments, if any, as are agreed to in joint sitting, is passed by a majority of the total number of members of both Houses present and voting, it shall be deemed to have been passed by both Houses. However there is no provision of joint sittings on a Money Bill or a Constitution Amending Bill.
- After the dissolution of Lok Sabha all Bills except the Bills introduced in the Rajya Sabha and pending therein, lapse.

6. **Article 68:** An election to fill a vacancy created because of the completion of the term of office of Vice-President shall be completed before the expiry of the term. So that why he or she continues to hold office until successor enters upon office. The election to fill a vacancy created because of the death, resignation or removal of Vice-President shall be held as soon as possible.

7. **State emergency:** Article 356 Indian Constitution.

State Emergency

Article 355—It's the duty of the centre to protect state from this three things:

- External aggression
- Internal disturbance
- Respecting constitutional provisions.

Article 356: If any state's governor through report conveys the president that in his view the state is not governing properly or constitutionally.

If the president is satisfied that the states governor is not respecting the constitutional provision. At that point the president can proclaim the emergency in that state.

Now in respect of the state along with article 356 President has the power in Article 365— If state doesn't follow the directions of the centre in that situation president can say that this is the situation in which the state is not functioning according to the Constitution and can proclaim the emergency. President rule was imposed through validity of article 356 in case of SR Bommai v Union of India. The Supreme Court had said that the federal structure of India can't be compared with other country.

President satisfaction and the grounds which they are proclaiming emergency that is subject to judicial review.

What happens in a state emergency?

The declaration of a State of Emergency helps elected leaders achieve this mission. ... A State of Emergency, according to state law, can be declared during a situation or imminent threat of widespread or severe damage, injury or loss of life or property, resulting from a natural or man-made cause.

Approval and Duration. On the date from which the emergency is proclaimed from that to 2 months.

On the date when it is proclaim it will be send to parliament for the approval.

- Parliament (Rajya Sabha + Lok Sabha) = Simple majority *i.e.* Total memberships 50%. When parliament approves than the emergency period will be extended to 6 months and if parliament doesn't approve this than the emergency will over within 2 months.

State emergency can exits maximum upto 3 years but in every 6 months it have to take an approval from the Parliament. If the emergency exits for more than one year then two condition must fulfill-

A. A National Emergency is in operation.

B. Election commission certifies that the election to the state assembly cannot be held. If this two conditions are fulfilled than only the emergency can exits more than one year.

Revocation

If the president wants he can revoke the emergency without the permission of anybody at any time.

8. Judiciary plays a very important role in a democracy as it not only prevents the government authorities from using their powers arbitrarily but it also safeguards the rights of the citizens and the very Constitution of India. Thus, The Constitution of India envisages a strong, independent, and well-organised judiciary.

Article 32 and 226 empowers the Supreme Court and the High Courts respectively, with the power to initiate an action against government body in case of violation of rights and liberties of the citizen. This article describes the writ power that the Supreme Court and High Courts have under Article 32 and 226 and how these articles are different from each other.

Article 227 of the Constitution of India provides for the power of superintendence over all Courts and Tribunals throughout the territory by the High Courts. The nature of superintendence is administrative as well as judicial.

9. Through his positivist theory, John Austin hypothesized that international law is not true law. He took the stance that international law is not law as it has no sovereign. Austin stated that law is a subdivision of command. He characterized a command as: an insinuation or articulation of a wish to do or shun from accomplishing something, upheld by the ability to do damage to the actor on the off chance that he resists.

Further, he believed that 'the individual to whom the order is given is under an obligation to comply with it', and the threatened harm is characterized as a sanction. This position was intensely critiqued by H.L.A. Hart who was of the view that the possibility that law comprises simply of orders supported by threats is deficient to clarify present-day legal systems. This affirmation by Austin demonstrates that if a law does not come from the desire of a determinate sovereign then it isn't real law. The Hobbesian tradition, Vincent tells us, characterises international relations as such: 'International politics is a struggle for power; war is inevitable in the international anarchy; there is no right and wrong, only competing concepts of right; there is no society beyond the state; international law is an empty.

10. The 1949 Geneva Conventions

The first Geneva Convention protects wounded and sick soldiers on land during war: This Convention represents the fourth updated version of the Geneva Convention on the wounded and sick following those adopted in 1864, 1906 and 1929. It contains 64 articles. These provide protection for the wounded and sick, but also for medical and religious personnel, medical units and medical transports. The Convention also recognizes the distinctive emblems. It has two annexes containing a draft agreement relating to hospital zones and a model identity card for medical and religious personnel.

The second Geneva Convention protects wounded, sick and shipwrecked military personnel at sea during war. This Convention replaced Hague Convention of 1907 for the Adaptation to Maritime Warfare of the Principles of the Geneva Convention. It closely follows the provisions of the first Geneva Convention in structure and content. It has 63 articles specifically applicable to war at sea. For example, it protects hospital ships. It has one annex containing a model identity card for medical and religious personnel.

The third Geneva Convention applies to prisoners of war: This Convention replaced the Prisoners of War Convention of 1929. It contains 143 articles whereas the 1929 Convention had only 97. The categories of persons entitled to prisoner of war status were broadened in accordance with Conventions I and II. The conditions and places of captivity were more precisely defined, particularly with regard to the labour of prisoners of war, their financial resources, the relief they receive, and the judicial proceedings instituted against them. The Convention establishes the principle that prisoners of war shall be released and repatriated without delay after the cessation of active hostilities. The Convention has five annexes containing various model regulations and identity and other cards.

The fourth Geneva Convention affords protection to civilians, including in occupied territory: The Geneva Conventions, which were adopted before 1949, were concerned with combatants only, not with civilians. The events of World War II showed the disastrous consequences of the absence of a convention for the protection of civilians in wartime. The Convention adopted in 1949 takes account of the experiences of World War II. It is composed of 159 articles. It contains a short section concerning the general protection of populations against certain consequences of war, without addressing the conduct of hostilities, as such, which was later examined in the Additional Protocols of 1977. The bulk of the Convention deals with the status and treatment of protected persons, distinguishing between the situation of foreigners on the territory of one of the parties to the conflict and that of civilians in occupied territory. It spells out the obligations of the Occupying Power vis-à-vis the civilian population and contains detailed provisions on humanitarian relief for populations in occupied territory. It also contains a specific regime for the treatment of civilian internees. It has three annexes containing a model agreement on hospital and safety zones, model regulations on humanitarian relief and model cards.

11. By a letter dated 27 August 1993, filed in the Registry on 3 September 1993, the Director-General of the World Health Organization officially communicated to the Registrar a decision taken by the World Health Assembly to submit to the Court the following question, set forth in resolution WHA46.40 adopted on 14 May 1993. "In view of the health and environmental effects, would the use of nuclear weapons by a State in war or other armed conflict be a breach of its obligations under international law including the WHO Constitution?"

The Court decided that the WHO and the member States of that organization entitled to appear before the Court were likely to be able to furnish information on the question, in accordance with Article 66, paragraph 2, of the Statute. Written statements were filed by 35 States, and subsequently written observations on those written statements were presented by nine States. In the course of the oral proceedings, which took place in October and November 1995, the WHO and 20 States presented oral statements. On 8 July 1996, the Court found that it was not able to give the advisory opinion requested by the World Health Assembly.

It considered that three conditions had to be satisfied in order to found the jurisdiction of the Court when a request for advisory opinion was submitted to it by a specialized agency: the agency requesting the opinion had to be duly authorized, under the Charter, to request opinions of the Court ; the opinion requested had to be on a legal question; and that question had to be one arising within the scope of the activities of the requesting agency. The first two conditions had been met. With regard to the third, however, the Court found that although according to its Constitution the WHO is authorized to deal with the health effects of the use of nuclear weapons, or of any other hazardous activity, and to take preventive measures aimed at protecting the health of populations in the event of such weapons being used or such activities engaged in, the question put to the Court in the present case related not to the effects of the use of nuclear weapons on health, but to the legality of the use of such weapons in view of their health and environmental effects.

12. The United Nations (UN) has six main organs. Five of them - the General Assembly, the Security Council, the Economic and Social Council, the Trusteeship Council and the Secretariat - are based at UN Headquarters in New York. The sixth, the International Court of Justice, is located at The Hague in the Netherlands.

13. As provided under Section 146 of the Indian Penal Code, 1860, a riot is simply an unlawful assembly in a particular state of activity, that activity being accompanied by the use of force or violence. It is this use of force or violence that distinguishes rioting from an unlawful assembly.

The word 'Violence' in this context is not restricted to force used against persons only but it extends also in force used against inanimate objects. Thus, if an unlawful assembly came together to for the purpose of pulling down a house or a shop or destroying any other property, it would be enough to show that violence was used.

14. Unlawful Assembly Section 141 of the IPC, 1860 deals with the unlawful assembly. Article 19(1)(B) of the Indian Constitution, 1950 confers a fundamental right to assemble peacefully however this section seeks to criminalize an unlawful assembly.

Definition

Assembly of 5 or more people to commit an unlawful offence is called an unlawful assembly. An important aspect of an unlawful assembly is the presence of a common intention to disturb public peace and tranquillity. The mere presence of a person in an assembly without any motive to infringe the peace in the surrounding is not punishable. The common objective is to determine the aim and nature of the assembly. It is also possible that lawful assembly turns out to be an unlawful assembly.

Rioting Section 146 and 147 under IPC deal with rioting. It usually takes place as a way to dissent something or for a perceived threat or grievance.

When an offence is committed by a group of people or any person belonging to that group, is termed as rioting. For rioting the presence of at least 5 people is necessary. This offence is generally grounded in civil unrest and is usually sudden and provocative behaviour. It shows a herd-like mentality and this is the reason that in case if a person belonging to the guilty group has not committed a violent act, even then he/she will be liable for rioting.

One of the most important ingredients is to constitute rioting is a common intention and object of committing a crime. This very "common intention" makes all the people in the group liable to be punished even when they haven't even committed the crime themselves in rioting.

Historically rioting used to take place due to grievances against the government policies, outcome of a sporting event, frustration against any legal judgement, taxation, oppression, conflicts amongst races or was a way to channelise the suppression faced by the people to the government.

Punishment for rioting is present under section 148 of the IPC and is a description of a term of 3 years or fine or both. This offence is cognizable and could be tried by the first class magistrate.

15. Ins. by Act 13 of 2013, s. 7 (w.e.f. 3-2-2013). 354D. Stalking.

(1) Any man who-

- follows a woman and contacts, or attempts to contact such woman to foster personal interaction repeatedly despite a clear indication of disinterest by such woman; or
- monitors the use by a woman of the internet, email or any other form of electronic communication, commits the offence of stalking:

Provided that such conduct shall not amount to stalking if the man who pursued it proves that—

- it was pursued for the purpose of preventing or detecting crime and the man accused of stalking had been entrusted with the responsibility of prevention and detection of crime by the State; or
- it was pursued under any law or to comply with any condition or requirement imposed by any person under any law; or
- in the particular circumstances such conduct was reasonable and justified.

(2) Whoever commits the offence of stalking shall be punished on first conviction with imprisonment of either description for a term which may extend to three years, and shall also be liable to fine; and be punished on a second or subsequent conviction, with imprisonment of either description for a term which may extend to five years, and shall also be liable to fine.

16. Abhayanand Mishra vs State of Bihar

In this case, the court held that the attempt to commit an offence begins when all the preparations are complete and he takes a step towards the commission of the offence so there is a thin line between the preparation for and an attempt to commit offence.

17. Section 2 of Motor Vehicle (Amendment) Act, 2019 - In the Motor Vehicles Act, 1988 (hereinafter referred to as the principal Act).

19. Relevant is tort based on fault

In many of the branches of law of torts like assault, battery, fule imprisonment, deceit, malicious prosecution and conspiracy, the state of mind of a person is relevant to ascertain his liability. We may have to see whether a particular wrongful act was done intentionally or maliciously. Sometimes, we may compare the conduct of the defendant with that of a reasonable man and make him liable only if his conduct falls below the standard expected of a reasonable man. When the circumstances demand care and a person tails to erect thou Thedants perform the duty to take care, he is liable for the tort of negligence. On the other hand, if the defendant has taken such care as was expected from him he is not liable for the damage to the plaintiff. Mental element may become relevant in another way also. If the defendant's conduct is innocent insofar as the act done was due to an inevitable accident, he may be excused from liability. Thus, if I have no reason to believe that there are electric wires beneath my land and the same get damaged on my making the excavations there, I will not be liable for the damage to the wires. Similarly, if the defendant's horses, for no fault on his part, cause injury to somebody on a public highway, the defendant can take the defence of inevitable accident.

20. The Consumer Protection Act, 2019

Chapter-IV Consumer Disputer and Redressal Commission.

Section 53: Establishment of National Consumer Disputes Redressal Commission.

(1) The Central Government shall, by notification, establish a National Consumer Disputes, Redressal Commission, to be known as the National Commission.

(2) The National Commission shall ordinarily function at the National Capital Region and perform its functions at such other places as the Central Government may in consultation with the National Commission notify in the Official Gazette:

Provided that the Central Government may, by notification, establish regional Benches of the National Commission, at such places, as it deems fit.

21. In contract of guarantee there are 3 contracts, first is between principal debtor and creditor, second is between creditor and surety and third one is between surety and principal debtor.

Contract of guarantee

A contract of guarantee is precisely stated under Section 126 of the Indian Contract Act, 1872. According to this section, a contract of guarantee can be understood as a contract that requires an individual or a group of individuals to perform a promise made or to discharge their liability under the contract when the third party to the contract failed to fulfill their part of the promise. This guarantee can be oral or written.

A contract of guarantee requires three parties: the principal debtor, the creditor, and the surety. The individual on whose non-payment the guarantee has to be given is the principal debtor or the borrower, the creditor is the individual who is given the guarantee and the surety is the individual who gives the guarantee.

Surety makes a promise to the creditor that on the principal debtor's default, they will discharge the third party's liability or fulfill the promise which was made by the principal debtor. Therefore, the surety gives assurance to the creditor for the principal debtor's act.

It can be interpreted that the liability of the surety acts as collateral to the principal debtor's liability. In case the principal debtor defaults, the surety is bound by a conditional promise to be held liable.

Difference between contract of guarantee and contract of indemnity.

In contract of indemnity parties involved are 2 *i.e.*, indemnifier and indemnity holder whereas in contract of guarantee there are 3 parties involved *i.e.*, principal debtor, surety and creditor. In contract of guarantee there are 3 contracts, first is between principal debtor and creditor, second is between creditor and surety and third one is between surety and principal debtor.

However, there is no need to have three separate agreements between 3 parties. A single agreement can also make them parties to a contract of guarantee.

The nature of liability in the contract of indemnity is of the indemnifier i.e. The primary liability is of indemnifier. Whereas, the primary liability in a contract of guarantee is of the principal debtor and secondary liability is of surety.

22. Passing of Unascertained Goods

If there is a contract for the sale of unascertained goods, then the passing of the property of the goods to the buyer cannot happen unless the goods are ascertained. This is specified under Section 18 of The Sale of Goods Act, 1930.

Section 23

Further Section 23 lists two important rules for the passing of property of unascertained goods:

Sale of unascertained goods by description: Imagine a contract for the sale of unascertained or future goods by description. If any goods of that description are appropriated to the contract either by the buyer or the seller with the consent of the other party, then the property of the goods passes to the buyer. The consent can be express or implied and given before or after the appropriation is made.

Delivery to the carrier: If the seller delivers the goods to the buyer or a carrier or a bailee (whether named by the buyer or not) for the purpose of transmission to the buyer, but does not reserve the right of disposal, then he is deemed to have unconditionally appropriated the goods to the contract.

23. Section 27 in The Indian Partnership Act, 1932

Liability of firm for misapplication by partners. Where—

(a) a partner acting within his apparent authority receives money or property from a third party and misapplies it, or

(b) a firm in the course of its business receives money or property from a third party, and the money or property is misapplied by any of the partners while it is in the custody of the firm the firm is liable to make good the loss.

24. Strike-Off Suo Moto by the Registrar Of Companies [Section 248(1)]:

Suo Moto means 'on its own motion'. Therefore, if the ROC decides, by its own initiative, to strike-off a Company's name from its register, then it will be termed as Strike-Off Suo Moto by the ROC.

In this, the ROC shall notice to the Company and all the Directors of the Company. In this letter, the ROC will put forward his/her intention to remove the name of the Company from the register of companies.

After which, the ROC will request them to send their representations along with copies of the relevant documents, if any. The Company representatives will have a time of thirty days from the date of the notice to respond to the ROC's notice.

25. Sources of Muslim law is classify into two categories that is primary sources and secondary sources.

Primary Sources: Primary sources are those on which Muslim law relied on. These sources are the foundation of Muslim law. Primary sources of Muslim law are:

- Quran
- Sunnat
- Ijma
- Qiyas

Secondary Sources: These sources are not basic sources of Muslim law but the supplementary sources of Muslim law. The secondary sources of Muslim law are:

- Urf or Custom
- Judicial decision
- Legislation
- Equity, Justice & Good conscience

26. Ordinally, in Modern India Hindu Marriage Act, 1955, divorce was mainly based on fault theory. The theory of fault includes 9 grounds for divorce according to section 13(1), for both the husband and a wife to seek a divorce, and under section 13(2) two grounds of fault arise for women to seek divorce by themselves. They're also available other divorce ground such as Break down ground under section 13(1), viz clauses (viii) and (ix) which were renumbered as clause (i) and (ii) of section 13(1A), Divorce by mutual consent under section 13-B, and customary divorce and divorce under a special law.

28. Sharda vs Dharmpal on 28 March, 2003

JUDGMENT S.B. Sinha, J.

1. A matrimonial court has the power to order a person to undergo medical test.
2. Passing of such an order by the court would not be in violation of the right to personal liberty under Article 21 of the Indian Constitution.
3. However, the Court should exercise such a power if the applicant has a strong prima facie case and there is sufficient material before the Court. If despite the order of the court, the respondent refuses to submit himself to medical examination, the court will be entitled to draw an adverse inference against him.

30. The United Nations Conference on the Human Environment, having met at Stockholm from 5 to 16 June 1972, having considered the need for a common outlook and for common principles to inspire and guide the peoples of the world in the preservation and enhancement of the human environment.

31. The Policy Statement for Abatement of Pollution, adopted in 1992 lays emphasis on pollution prevention in place of the conventional end-of-the-pipe treatment also identified the adoption of best available and practicable technologies as the key element for pollution prevention. The focus of the programme is on such issues such as the promotion of clean and low waste technologies, wasteminimization, reuse or recycling, improvement of water quality, environment audit, natural resource accounting, development of mass-based standards, institutional and human resource development etc. The whole issue of pollution prevention and control is dealt with by a combination of command and control methods as well as voluntary regulations, fiscal measures, promotion of awareness etc.

32. The Human Rights Council is an inter-governmental body within the United Nations system responsible for strengthening the promotion and protection of human rights around the globe and for addressing situations of human rights violations and make recommendations on them.

33. Section 2(p): digital signature—means authentication of any electronic record by a subscriber by means of an electronic method or procedure in accordance with the provisions of section 3;

Section 2 (q): Digital Signature Certificate—means a Digital Signature Certificate issued under sub-section (4) of section 35;

Section 2 (r): electronic form—with reference to information, means any information generated, sent, received or stored in media, magnetic, optical, computer memory, micro film, computer generated micro fiche or similar device;

Section 2(tb): Electronic Signature Certificate —means an Electronic Signature Certificate issued under section 35 and includes Digital Signature Certificate.

34. Section 2(ua): Indian Computer Emergency Response Team—means an agency established under sub-section (1) of Section 70B.

Section 2(za): originator means a person who sends, generates, stores or transmits any electronic message or causes any electronic message to be sent, generated, stored or transmitted to any other person but does not include an intermediary Section 2(nb)—cyber security means protecting information, equipment, devices, computer, computer resource, communication device and information stored therein from unauthorised access, use, disclosure, disruption, modification or destruction;

Section 2(tb): Electronic Signature Certificate means an Electronic Signature Certificate issued under section 35 and includes Digital Signature Certificate.

35. Section 2(x): key pair, in an asymmetric crypto system, means a private key and its mathematically related public key, which are so related that the public key can verify a digital signature created by the private key;

Section 2(zc): private key means the key of a key pair used to create a digital signature;

Section 2(zd): public key means the key of a key pair used to verify a digital signature and listed in the Digital Signature Certificate.

36. Section 3A: Electronic signature. (1) Notwithstanding anything contained in section 3, but subject to the provisions of sub-section (2), a subscriber may authenticate any electronic record by such electronic signature or electronic authentication technique which-

(a) is considered reliable; and

(b) may be specified in the Second Schedule.

Section 6A: Delivery of services by service provider. (1) The appropriate Government may, for the purposes of this Chapter and for efficient delivery of services to the public through electronic means authorise, by order, any service provider to set up, maintain and upgrade the computerised facilities and perform such other services as it may specify, by notification in the Official Gazette.

Section 7A: Audit of documents, etc., maintained in electronic form.—Where in any law for the time being in force, there is a provision for audit of documents, records or information, that provision shall also be applicable for audit of documents, records or information processed and maintained in the electronic form.

Section 10A: Validity of contracts formed through electronic means.—Where in a contract formation, the communication of proposals, the acceptance of proposals, the revocation of proposals and acceptances, as the case may be, are expressed in electronic form or by means of an electronic records, such contract shall not be deemed to be unenforceable solely on the ground that such electronic form or means was used for that purpose.

37. Section 2 (e) "competent authority" means—

(*i*) the Speaker in the case of the House of the People or the Legislative Assembly of a State or a Union territory having such Assembly and the Chairman in the case of the Council of States or Legislative Council of a State;

(*ii*) the Chief Justice of India in the case of the Supreme Court;

(*iii*) the Chief Justice of the High Court in the case of a High Court;

(*iv*) the President or the Governor, as the case may be, in the case of other authorities established or constituted by or under the Constitution;

(*v*) the administrator appointed under article 239 of the Constitution;

Section 2(f) "information" means any material in any form, including records, documents, memos, e-mails, opinions, advices, press releases, circulars, orders, logbooks, contracts, reports, papers, samples, models, data material held in any electronic form and information relating to any private body which can be accessed by a public authority under any other law for the time being in force;

Section 2(g) "prescribed" means prescribed by rules made under this Act by the appropriate Government or the competent authority, as the case may be;

Section 2(h) "public authority" means any authority or body or institution of self-government established or constituted-

(a) by or under the Constitution;

(b) by any other law made by Parliament;

(c) by any other law made by State Legislature;

(d) by notification issued or order made by the appropriate Government, and includes any-

(i) body owned, controlled or substantially financed;

(ii) non-Government organisation substantially financed, directly or indirectly by funds provided by the appropriate Government.

39. Article V: The Congress, whenever two thirds of both houses shall deem it necessary, shall propose amendments to this Constitution, or, on the application of the legislatures of two thirds of the several states, shall call a convention for proposing amendments, which, in either case, shall be valid to all intents and purposes, as part of this Constitution, when ratified by the legislatures of three fourths of the several states, or by conventions in three fourths thereof, as the one or the other mode of ratification may be proposed by the Congress; provided that no amendment which may be made prior to the year one thousand eight hundred and eight shall in any manner affect the first and fourth clauses in the ninth section of the first article; and that no state, without its consent, shall be deprived of its equal suffrage in the Senate.

40. Section 8(1) Notwithstanding anything contained in this Act, there shall be no obligation to give any citizen,-

(a) information, disclosure of which would prejudicially affect the sovereignty and integrity of India, the security, strategic, scientific or economic interests of the State, relation with foreign State or lead to incitement of an offence;

(b) information which has been expressly forbidden to be published by any court of law or tribunal or the disclosure of which may constitute contempt of court;

(c) information, the disclosure of which would cause a breach of privilege of Parliament or the State Legislature;

(d) information including commercial confidence, trade secrets or intellectual property, the disclosure of which would harm the competitive position of a third party, unless the competent authority is satisfied that larger public interest warrants the disclosure of such information;

(e) information available to a person in his fiduciary relationship, unless the competent authority is satisfied that the larger public interest warrants the disclosure of such information;

(f) information received in confidence from foreign Government;

(g) information, the disclosure of which would endanger the life or physical safety of any person or identify the source of information or assistance given in confidence for law enforcement or security purposes;

(h) information which would impede the process of investigation or apprehension or prosecution of offenders;

(i) cabinet papers including records of deliberations of the Council of Ministers, Secretaries and other officers: Provided that the decisions of Council of Ministers, the reasons thereof, and the material on the basis of which the decisions were taken shall be made public after the decision has been taken, and the matter is complete, or over: Provided further that those matters which come under the exemptions specified in this section shall not be disclosed;

(j) information which relates to personal information the disclosure of which has no relationship to any public activity or interest, or which would cause unwarranted invasion of the privacy of the individual unless the Central Public Information Officer or the State Public Information Officer or the appellate authority, as the case may be, is satisfied that the larger public interest justifies the disclosure of such information: Provided that the information which cannot be denied to the Parliament or a State Legislature shall not be denied to any person.

41. Lon L. Fuller's book The Morality of Law. This imaginative, original, and thought-provoking book is richly stocked with a variety of themes, many of which deserve a much fuller treatment than this chapter accords to them. Its central theme is the unique virtue of conceiving of law and even of defining 'law' 'as the [purposive] enterprise of subjecting human conduct to the governance of rules'. The morality of duty and the morality of aspiration, and the inner and external moralities of law are described. In this book, Fuller considers the appropriateness to different types of issue of different decision-procedures, among them adjudication and majority vote.

44. Interpretation By The Supreme Court

Berubari Union case

In this case, it was held by the Supreme Court that the Preamble is the part of the Constitution. However, it recognised that the Preamble could be used as a guiding principle if a term in any article of the Constitution is ambiguous or has more than one meaning.

Keshvananda Bharti v. State of Kerala[7]

In this case, The Supreme Court overturned its earlier decision and held that the Preamble is a part of the Constitution and can be amended under Article 368 of the Constitution. Again, in LIC of India case, the Supreme Court held that the Preamble is a part of the Constitution.

45. Article 61. (1) When a President is to be impeached for violation of the Constitution, the charge shall be preferred by either House of Parliament.

Article 142. (1) The Supreme Court in the exercise of its jurisdiction may pass such decree or make such order as is necessary for doing complete justice in any cause or matter pending before it, and any decree so passed or order so made shall be enforceable throughout the territory of India in such manner as may be prescribed by or under any law made by Parliament and, until provision in that behalf is so made, in such manner as the President may by order prescribe.

Article 122. (1) The validity of any proceedings in Parliament shall not be called in question on the ground of any alleged irregularity of procedure.

(2) No officer or member of Parliament in whom powers are vested by or under this Constitution for regulating procedure or the conduct of business, or for maintaining order, in Parliament shall be subject to the jurisdiction of any court in respect of the exercise by him of those powers.

Article 163. (1) There shall be a Council of Ministers with the Chief Minister at the head to aid and advise the Governor in the exercise of his functions, except in so far as he is by or under this Constitution required to exercise his functions or any of them in his discretion.

46. Cession is an understanding under international law by which territory is transferred from one State to another with the consent of both States. By August 1958, the condition had been fulfilled and a United Nations Conference on the Elimination or Reduction of Future Statelessness was convened by the Secretary-General at the European Office of the United Nations, in Geneva, where it met from 24 March to 18 April 1959.

47. De Facto: Factual recognition is known as De Facto.

Membership to the United Nations is impossible once there is de facto recognition by the majority of states.

The State which has received De facto recognition would be having two rival governments.

The recognition that is conferred by De Facto is based on a factual situation and is not a process of law.

Diplomatic representatives are generally not sent to other states and neither are received in ones state in De Facto conditions.

State Succession rules are not applicable in De Facto recognition. This means the state cannot annex other states and impose succession laws in case its own recognition is De Facto. De Facto Government is in no position to recover a state asset or public debt De Facto recognition can be withdrawn at any time. For example: Learning Licence is De Facto in nature.

De Jure: Legal Recognition is called as De Jure.

Any state can get United Nations membership if majority of nations provide de jure recognition to them. The State that has received De Jure recognition has only one government De Jure is a recognition is given after following due procedure of law. Diplomatic representatives can be exchanged in De Jure conditions. Under De Jure conditions the rules of state succession are applicable and implemented in case of such a condition. A De Jure government has the position and power to recover state assets or public debt. De Jure recognition cannot be withdrawn at any stage.

Eg: Permanent licence is a De Jure recognition.

49. Section 120A: Definition of criminal conspiracy.-When two or more persons agree to do, or cause to be done,-

(1) an illegal act, or

(2) an act which is not illegal by illegal means, such an agreement is designated a criminal conspiracy: Provided that no agreement except an agreement to commit an offence shall amount to a criminal conspiracy unless some act

besides the agreement is done by one or more parties to such agreement in pursuance thereof. Explanation.—It is immaterial whether the illegal act is the ultimate object of such agreement, or is merely incidental to that object. Section 120B. Punishment of criminal conspiracy.

(1) Whoever is a party to a criminal conspiracy to commit an offence punishable with death, 1 [imprisonment for life] or rigorous imprisonment for a term of two years or upwards, shall, where no express provision is made in this Code for the punishment of such a conspiracy, be punished in the same manner as if he had abetted such offence.

(2) Whoever is a party to a criminal conspiracy other than a criminal conspiracy to commit an offence punishable as aforesaid shall be punished with imprisonment of either description for a term not exceeding six months, or with fine or with both.]

CBI / SIT V. Nalini is a case related to murder of Rajiv Gandhi; and thereby Nalini (A-1) to Ranganath (A-26) committed offences punishable under Section 120-B of IPC read with Sections 302 of IPC, 326 of IPC, 324 of IPC, 201 of IPC, 212 of IPC and 216 of IPC; Sections 3, 4 and 5 of Explosive Substances Act of 1908; Section 25 of Arms Act of 1959; Section 12 of Passport Act, 1967; Section 14 of the Foreigners Act, 1946; Section 6(1A) of the Wireless Telegraphy Act, 1933 and Sections 3, 4 and 5 of TADA of 1987.

50. **Section 390. Robbery:** In all robbery there is either theft or extortion.

When theft is robbery

Theft is "robbery" if, in order to the committing of the theft, or in committing the theft, or in carrying away or attempting to carry away property obtained by the theft, the offender, for that end voluntarily causes or attempts to cause to any person death or hurt or wrongful restraint, or fear of instant death or of instant hurt, or of instant wrongful restraint.

When extortion is robbery

Extortion is "robbery" if the offender, at the time of committing the extortion, is in the presence of the person put in fear, and commits the extortion by putting that person in fear of instant death, of instant hurt, or of instant wrongful restraint to that person or to some other person, and, by so putting in fear, induces the person so put in fear then and there to deliver up the thing extorted.

Section 391. Dacoity

When five or more persons conjointly commit or attempt to commit a robbery, or where the whole number of persons conjointly committing or attempting to commit a robbery, and persons present and aiding such commission or attempt, amount to five or more, every person so committing, attempting or aiding, is said to commit "dacoity".

Section 392. Punishment for robbery

Whoever commits robbery shall be punished with rigorous imprisonment for a term which may extend to ten years, and shall also be liable to fine; and, if the robbery be committed on the highway between sunset and sunrise, the imprisonment may be extended to fourteen years.

51. The three accused, namely, Mohd. Afzal, Shaukat Hussain Guru and S.A.R. Gilani were convicted for various offences under Sections 121, 121A, 122 read with Sections 302 & 307 of Indian Penal Code (IPC). Also Section 120B IPC and sub-sections (2), (3) and (5) of Section, sub-Sections (2), (3) & (5) of Section 3 of POTA and Section 4(b) of the same act and Sections 3 & 4 of Explosive Substances Act.

Mohd. V State of NCT of Delhi; The appellant (admittedly a Pakistani national) challenges his concurrent conviction by the trial Court and the High Court as also the death sentence awarded to him, in this appeal.

On 22.12.2000 at about 9 p.m. in the evening some intruders started indiscriminate firing and gunned down three army Jawans belonging to 7th Rajputana Rifles. This battalion was placed in Red Fort for its protection considering the importance of Red Fort in the history of India. There was a Quick Reaction Team of this battalion which returned the firing towards the intruders. However, no intruder was killed and the intruders were successful in escaping by scaling over the rear side boundary wall of the Red Fort. This attack rocked the whole nation generally and the city of Delhi in particular as Red Fort is very significant in the history which was taken over by British Army way back in 1857 and was retrieved back to India on 15.8.1947. It is also significant to note that the Prime Minister addresses the nation from this very Red Fort on every 15th of August.

53. Consumer Mediation Cell

The State Government shall establish, by notification, a consumer mediation cell to be attached to each of the District Commissions and the State Commissions of that State. The Central Government shall establish, by notification, a consumer mediation cell to be attached to the National Commission and each of the regional Benches. A consumer mediation cell shall consist of such persons as may be prescribed.

The Mediation Cell shall have such support staff as may be decided by the President of that Commission in consultation with the concerned Government and that Government shall provide all administrative assistance and infrastructure facilities required by the Commission.

54. Removal of Members

Section 417 provides that the Central Government may, after consultation with the Chief Justice of India, remove from office any member, who has been adjudged an insolvent; or has been convicted of an offence which, in the opinion of the Central Government, involves moral turpitude; or has become physically or mentally incapable of acting as such Member; or has acquired such financial or other interests as is likely to affect prejudicially his functions as member; or has so abused his position as to render his continuance in office prejudice to the public interest.

The member shall not be removed on any of the grounds specified in clauses (b) to (e) without giving him a reasonable opportunity of being heard.

56. Divorce by mutual agreement:

Khula and Mubarat: They are two forms of divorce by mutual consent but in either of them, the wife has to part with her dower or a part of some other property. A verse in the Holy Quran runs as: "And it not lawful for you that ye take from women out of that which ye have given them: except (in the case) when both fear that they may not be able to keep within the limits (imposed by Allah), in that case it is no sin for either of them if the woman ransom herself." The word khula, in its original sense means "to draw" or "dig up" or "to take off" such as taking off one's clothes or garments. It is said that the spouses are like clothes to each other and when they take khula each takes off his or her clothes, *i.e.*, they get rid of each other.

Talaaq-i-tafweez or delegated divorce is recognized among both, the Shias and the Sunnis. The Muslim husband is free to delegate his power of pronouncing divorce to his wife or any other person. He may delegate the power absolutely or conditionally, temporarily or permanently. A permanent delegation of power is revocable but a temporary delegation of power is not. This delegation must be made distinctly in favour of the person to whom the power is delegated, and the purpose of delegation must be clearly stated. The power of talaaq may be delegated to his wife and as Faizee observes, "this form of delegated divorce is perhaps the most potent weapon in the hands of a Muslim wife to obtain freedom without the intervention of any court and is now beginning to be fairly common in India".

Lian: If the husband levels false charges of unchastity or adultery against his wife then this amounts to character assassination and the wife has got the right to ask for divorce on these grounds. Such a mode of divorce is called Lian. However, it is only a voluntary and aggressive charge of adultery made by the husband which, if false, would entitle the wife to get the wife to get the decree of divorce on the ground of Lian. Where a wife hurts the feelings of her husband with her behaviour and the husband hits back an allegation of infidelity against her, then what the husband says in response to the bad behaviour of the wife, cannot be used by the wife as a false charge of adultery and no divorce is to be granted under Lian. This was held in the case of Nurjahan v. Kazim Ali by the Calcutta High Court.

57. Fault Ground: Under the Hindu Marriage Act 1955, section 13(1), lays down nine fault ground of divorce. Some of there are Adultery, Desertion, Cruelty, Insanity, Leporacy, Verenal Disease, while others such as Conversion, Or Renunciation of words are typically Hindu grounds.

58. [Section 8]

HEIRS IN CLASS I AND CLASS II

CLASS I

Son; daughter; widow; mother; son of a pre-deceased son; daughter of a pre-deceased son; son of a pre-deceased daughter; daughter of a pre-deceased daughter; widow of a pre-deceased son; son of a pre-deceased son of a pre-deceased son; daughter of a pre-deceased son of a pre-deceased son; widow of a pre-deceased son of a pre-deceased son.

CLASS II

I. Father.

II. (1) Son's daughter's son, (2) son's daughter's daughter, (3) brother, (4) sister.

III. (1) Daughter's son's son, (2) daughter's son's daughter, (3) daughter's daughter's son, (4) daughter's daughter's daughter.

IV. (1) Brother's son, (2) sister's son, (3) brother's daughter, (4) sister's daughter.

V. Father's father; father's mother.

VI. Father's widow; brother's widow.

VII. Father's brother; father's sister.

VIII. Mother's father; mother's mother.

IX. Mother's brother; mother's sister.

Explanation: In this Schedule, references to a brother or sister do not include references to a brother or sister by uterine blood.

59. SECTION 10

National Commission for Women Act, 1990 (Act No. 20 of 1990 of Govt. of India)

The commission shall perform all or any of the following functions, namely:

- investigate and examine all matters relating to the safeguards provided for women under the Constitution and other laws;
- present to the Central Government, annually and at such other times as the Commission may deem fit, reports upon the working of those safeguard;
- make in such reports recommendations for the effective implementation of those safeguards for the improving the conditions of women by the Union or any state;

- review, from time to time, the exiting provisions of the Constitution and other laws affecting women and recommend amendments thereto so as to suggest remedial legislative measures to meet any lacunae, inadequacies or shortcomings in such legislations;
- take up cases of violation of the provisions of the Constitution and of other laws relating to women with the appropriate authorities;
- look into complaints and take suomoto notice of matters relating to:
- deprivation of women's rights;
- non-implementation of laws enacted to provide protection to women and also to achieve the objective of equality and development;
- non-compliance of policy decisions, guidelines or instructions aimed at mitigating hardships and ensuring welfare and providing relief to women, and take up the issues arising out of such matters with appropriate authorities;
- call for special studies or investigations into specific problems or situations arising out of discrimination and atrocities against women and identify the constraints so as to recommend strategies for their removal;
- undertake promotional and educational research so as to suggest ways of ensuring due representation of women in all spheres and identify factors responsible for impeding their advancement, such as, lack of access to housing and basic services, inadequate support services and technologies for reducing drudgery and occupational health hazards and for increasing their productivity;
- participate and advice on the planning process of socio-economic development of women;
- evaluate the progress of the development of women under the Union and any State;
- inspect or cause to inspected a jail, remand home, women's institution or other place of custody where women are kept as prisoners or otherwise and take up with the concerned authorities for remedial action, if found necessary;
- fund litigation involving issues affecting a large body of women;
- make periodical reports to the Government on any matter pertaining to women and in particular various difficulties under which women toil;
- any other matter which may be referred to it by Central Government.

The Central Government shall cause all the reports referred to in clause (b) of sub-section (1) to be laid before each House of Parliament along with memorandum explaining the action taken or proposed to be taken on the recommendations relating to the Union and the reasons for the non-acceptance, if any, of any such recommendations.

Where any such report or any part thereof relates to any matter with which any State Government is concerned, the Commission shall forward an copy of such report or part to such State Government who shall cause it to be laid before the Legislature of the State along with a memorandum explaining the action taken or proposed to be taken on the recommendations relating to the State and the reasons for the non-acceptance, if any, of any such recommendations.

The Commission shall, while investigating any matter referred to in clause (a) or sub-clause (i) of clause (f) of sub-section (1), have all the powers of a civil court trying a suit and, in particular in respect of the following matters, namely:

- summoning and enforcing the attendance of any person from any part of India and examining him on oath;

- requiring the discovery and production of any document;
- receiving evidence on affidavits;
- requisitioning any public record or copy thereof from any court or office;
- issuing commissions for the examination of witnesses and documents; and any other matter which may be prescribed.

60. Class action lawsuits provide harmed people with many benefits, such as allowing large groups of similarly affected people to come together and file a lawsuit against the same company. This provides strength in numbers for all of the people harmed, typically by large corporations, or businesses that have a vast reach.

61. A geographical indication (GI) is a sign used on products that have a specific geographical origin and possess qualities or a reputation that are due to that origin. In order to function as a GI, a sign must identify a product as originating in a given place.

In addition, the qualities, characteristics or reputation of the product should be essentially due to the place of origin. Since the qualities depend on the geographical place of production, there is a clear link between the product and its original place of production.

A geographical indication right enables those who have the right to use the indication to prevent its use by a third party whose product does not conform to the applicable standards. For example, in the jurisdictions in which the Darjeeling geographical indication is protected, producers of Darjeeling tea can exclude use of the term "Darjeeling" for tea not grown in their tea gardens or not produced according to the standards set out in the code of practice for the geographical indication.

62. Article 2 of the TRIPS Agreement specifies that nothing in Parts I to IV of the agreement shall derogate from existing obligations that members may have to each other under the Paris Convention, the Berne Convention, the Rome Convention and the Treaty on Intellectual Property in respect of integrated circuits.

63. Section 2(1)(j) in The Information Technology Act, 2000

(j) "computer network" means the inter-connection of one or more computers or computer systems or communication device through:

(*i*) the use of satellite, microwave, terrestrial line, wire, wireless or other communication media; and

(*ii*) terminals or a complex consisting of two or more inter-connected computers or communication device whether or not the inter-connection is continuously maintained.

65. Article V of the Constitution provides two ways to propose amendments to the document. Amendments may be proposed either by the Congress, through a joint resolution passed by a two-thirds vote, or by a convention called by Congress in response to applications from two-thirds of the state legislatures.

69. Section 73: Solitary confinement.-Whenever any person is convicted of an offence for which under this Code the Court has power to sentence him to rigorous imprisonment, the Court may, by its sentence, order that the offender shall be kept in solitary confinement for any portion or portions of the imprisonment to which he is sentenced, not exceeding three months in the whole, according to the following scale, that is to say—a time not exceeding one month if the term of imprisonment shall not exceed six months; a time not exceeding two months if the term of imprisonment shall exceed six months and 1 [shall not exceed one] year a time not exceeding three months if the term of imprisonment shall exceed one year.

Section 82: Act of a child under seven years of age.—Nothing is an offence which is done by a child under seven years of age.

Section 93: Communication made in good faith.—No communication made in good faith is an offence by reason of any harm to the person to whom it is made, if it is made for the benefit of that person.

Section 95: Act causing slight harm.—Nothing is an offence by reason that it causes, or that it is intended to cause, or that it is known to be likely to cause, any harm, if that harm is so slight that no person of ordinary sense and temper would complain of such harm.

77. **Article 371A:** Special provision with respect to the state of Nagaland.

Article 371C: Special provision with respect to the State of Manipur.

Article 371F: Special provisions with respect to the State of Sikkim.

Article 371J: Special provisions with respect to State of Karnataka.

80. There are four essential elements of a tort:

The existence of a duty of reasonable care to be observed towards others.

The wrongful commission or omission of an act that is breach of duty.

Causation of actual damage or infringement of legal rights due to such wrongful commission or omission.

The remedy.

81. **Section 10:** What agreements are contracts.—All agreements are contracts if they are made by the free consent of parties competent to contract, for a lawful consideration and with a lawful object, and are not hereby expressly declared to be void.

Section 11: Who are competent to contract.—Every person is competent to contract who is of the age of majority according to the law to which he is subject, and who is of sound mind and is not disqualified from contracting by any law to which he is subject.

Section 21: Effect of mistakes as to law.—A contract is not voidable because it was caused by a mistake as to any law in force in 1 [India]; but a mistake as to a law not in force in [India] has the same effect as a mistake of fact.

Section 26: Agreement in restraint of marriage, void.—Every agreement in restraint of the marriage of any person, other than a minor, is void.

Previous Years' Paper (Solved)

National Testing Agency (NTA)

UGC-NET Junior Research Fellowship & Assistant Professor Eligibility Exam

Law, June-2020

(Online Exam held on 29-09-2020)

PAPER-II

1. "The movement of progressive societies has hitherto been a movement from status to contract". The statement has been made by:

A. Savigny B. Puchta

C. Maine D. Burke

2. Which of the following statements describes the relationship between law and morality among non-positive legal theorists?

A. Law is always in advance of moral ideas

B. Morality is generally in advance of the law

C. The law is inextricably bound up with morals

D. There is no relationship between law and morality

3. The main purpose of 'Corporation Sole' is to:

A. Make the property easily inheritable.

B. Make the property easily transferable.

C. Maintain continuity of an office.

D. Protect the property of state.

4. 'The real relation of Jurisprudence to Law depends not upon what law is treated, but how Law is treated,' is said by:

A. Gierke B. Gray

C. Rawls D. Duguit

5. In which case the Supreme Court held that the Preamble does form part of the Constitution?

A. Re Berubari Union and Exchange of Enclaves

B. Minerva Mills v. Union of India

C. Keshava Nand Bharti v. State of Kerala

D. S.R. Bommai v. Union of India

6. Under Article 14 of the Indian Constitution, the term 'Equal Protection of the Laws' has been taken from the:

A. American Constitution

B. British Constitution

C. Australian Constitution

D. Canadian Constitution

7. Article 72 of the Indian Constitution makes a provision for:

A. Discharge of the President's functions in other contingencies.

B. Power of President to grant pardons etc, and to suspend, remit or commute sentences in certain cases.

C. Extent of executive power of the Union

D. Council of Ministers to aid and advise the President

8. In which case, in respect of natural justice, Lord Denning said that "With a good man in the saddle, the unruly horse can be kept under control. It can jump over obstacles. It can leap fences put up by fictions and come down on the other side of justice"?

A. Enderby Town Football Club Ltd. v. Football Association Ltd.

B. Canara Bank v. Debasis Das

C. R.V. Hendon Rural District Council

D. American Cyanamide Co. v. Federal Trade Commission

9. The words 'International Law' were used for the first time by which one of the following eminent Jurists?

A. Oppenheim
B. W. Friedmann
C. Austin
D. Jermy Bentham

10. Which of the following chapters of the United Nations Charter deals with pacific settlement of disputes?

A. Chapter VI
B. Chapter VII
C. Chapter III
D. Chapter II

11. In which of the following cases, the rule, that "there is no distinction between *'de facto'* and *'de jure'* recognition for the purpose of giving effect to the internal acts of the recognised authority" was not applied?

A. Bank of Ethiopia v. National Bank of Egypt
B. Luther v. Sagor
C. Bank of China v. Wells Fargo Bank & Union Trust
D. The Arantzazu Mendi case

12. Which of the following provisions of the Statute of International Court of Justice lists "General Principles of Law Recognized by Civilised States" as the third source of International law?

A. Article 38 (a)
B. Para (1) (c) of Article 38
C. Article 38 (b)
D. Para (3) (c) of Article 38

13. 'A' an officer of a court of justice, being ordered by that court to arrest 'Y', and after due enquiry, believing 'Z' to be 'Y', arrests 'Z', 'A' has committed:

A. An offence of wrongful confinement
B. An offence of wrongful restraint
C. An offence of criminal trespass
D. No offence

14. Section 102 of the Indian Penal code deals with the provision relating to:

A. When the right of private defence of property extends to causing death.
B. Right of private defence against deadly assault when there is a risk of harm to an innocent person.
C. Commencement and continuance of a right of private defence of the body.
D. When the right of private defence of the body extends to causing death.

15. The provision regarding 'selling minors for purposes of prostitution etc' is given in Indian Penal code under:

A. Section 372
B. Section 373
C. Section 370 A
D. Section 371

16. Section 376 DB of Indian Penal Code provides for the:

A. Punishment for gang rape of a woman under sixteen years of age
B. Punishment of rape of woman under twelve years of age
C. Punishment for gang rape of a woman under twelve years of age
D. Punishment for causing death or resulting in a persistent vegetative state of the victim

17. According to whom is it 'Law of Tort and not Law of Torts?

A. Winfield
B. Pollock
C. Fraser
D. Salmond

18. "A tort is a civil wrong for which, the remedy is an action for damages and which is not exclusively breach of contract or breach of trust or breach of merely equitable obligation". The above definition was given by:

A. Salmond
B. Winfield
C. Fraser
D. Clerk and Lindsell

19. When two motorists coming from opposite directions in their cars collide with each other and in the process, they injure seriously a person who was standing on the roadside, the two motorists are:

A. Independent tortfeasors
B. Participate in contributory negligence
C. Two negligent persons
D. Joint tortfeasors

20. The maxim "Salus Populi Suprema Lex" means

A. Welfare of people is supreme law

B. Increasing population is the supreme cause of concern

C. No man is above law

D. Whatever the public collectively say, is the law

21. "Threatening to commit certain acts forbidden by Indian Penal Code" to induce a person to enter into a contract is associated with:

A. Undue influence

B. Coercion

C. Criminal intimidation

D. Threat

22. "An offer cannot be accepted unless it was brought to the knowledge of the person to whom it is made". This was laid down in the case of:

A. Lalman Shukla v. Gauri Dutt

B. Balfour v. Balfour

C. Mcgregor v. Mcgregor

D. Carlill v. Carbolic Smoke Ball Co.

23. Frustration of a contract occurs in two conditions. Firstly, where the contract has become physically impossible and secondly, where the object has failed. The above was laid down in the case of:

A. Krell vs Henry

B. Paradine vs Jane

C. Taylor vs Caldwell

D. Kamal Rani vs Chandram

24. A party who suffers loss as a result of a breach of contract can in the usual course claim.

A. Ordinary damages

B. Special damages

C. Exemplary damages

D. Penal damages

25. Which one of the following is not an 'Ancient Source' of Hindu Law?

A. Smriti B. Precedents

C. Digests D. Shruti

26. Which of the following is NOT a feature of 'Mitakshara Coparcenary'?

A. Unobstructed heritage

B. Obstructed heritage

C. Unpredictable and fluctuating interest

D. Community of interest and unity of possession

27. Rules relating to 'Sapinda Relationship' are based on the principle of:

A. Endogamy B. Polyandry

C. Polygyny D. Exogamy

28. A bigamous Hindu marriage is:

A. Void but not punishable

B. Void and punishable

C. Voidable

D. Valid

29. National Commission of Minorities was established under which of the following provisions?

A. Article 328 of the Constitution.

B. Article 328A of the Constitution.

C. Section 3 of National Commission of Minorities Act, 1992.

D. Article 280 of the Constitution of India

30. The Chairperson of National Human Rights Commission shall be:

A. Chief Justice of the Supreme Court

B. Chief Justice of a High Court

C. Judge of the Supreme Court

D. Chairpersons of National Commission of Women

31. The Commission on Sustainable Development was established in which year?

A. 1972 B. 1982

C. 1992 D. 2002

32. The legally binding limit to carbon emission was laid down in:

A. Kyoto Protocol on Global Warming, 1997

B. Copenhagen Summit on Climate Change, 2009

C. Durban Conference on Climate Change, 2009

D. Lima Conference on Climate Change

33. The provision relating to 'legal recognition of electronic signatures' is contained under which section of Information Technology Act, 2000?

A. Section 3 B. Section 3-A
C. Section 4 D. Section 5

34. What is a whistleblower?

A. A person who signals illegal or unethical practice to a prescribed body
B. Usually a disgruntled ex-employee
C. A subversive person spying on a company
D. An investigative journalist

35. When the biological resources are accessed for commercial utilization or the bio-survey and bio-utilization leads to commercial utilization, the applicant shall have the option to pay the benefit-sharing ranging from:

A. 0.1 to 0.2 B. 0.1 to 0.3
C. 0.1 to 0.4 D. 0.1 to 0.5

36. By which amendment, the third and fourth schedules of the IT Act were omitted?

A. Act 10 of 2009
B. Act 55 of 2002
C. Act 66 of 2009
D. Act 09 of 2009

37. In a parliamentary form of government, the British convention of 'Ministerial Responsibility' has been explicitly codified in the Indian Constitution under:

A. Article 74 (1) B. Article 74 (2)
C. Article 75 (2) D. Article 75 (3)

38. Which one of the following is the mandatory minimum requirement for a functional federation?

A. States should be represented in the Upper House of the National Legislature.
B. Judicial Review
C. Distribution of legislative and administrative powers between the two sets of Governments – National and State, so as to ensure the independence of the Government within their respective spheres.
D. Distribution of legislative and administrative powers between the two sets of Governments – National and State, so as to ensure the independent but coordinated exercise of powers of the Government.

39. In which case, the Supreme Court held that pardoning powers of the President under Article 72 and Governors under Article 161 is subject to the judicial review?

A. Satya Narain Sharma v. State of Rajasthan
B. Vineet Narain v. Union of India
C. Epuru Sudhakar v. State of Andhra Pradesh
D. Chhotey Lal v. State of U.P.

40. The provision regarding 'legislation for giving effect to international agreements' is given in the Indian Constitution under:

A. Article 253 B. Article 255
C. Article 251 D. Article 254

41. Which of the following duties have been included by Austin in the category of 'absolute duties'?

(*a*) Duties owed to persons indefinitely
(*b*) Self-regarding duties
(*c*) Duties owed to the sovereign
(*d*) Duties owed to parents

Choose the correct answer from the options given below:

A. (*a*), (*b*) and (*c*) only
B. (*b*), (*c*) and (*d*) only
C. (*a*), (*c*) and (*d*) only
D. (*a*), (*b*), (*c*) and (*d*) all

42. Which of the following conditions are essential for a custom to be valid?

(*a*) The custom had to possess a sufficient measure of antiquity
(*b*) The custom must have been enjoyed 'as a right'
(*c*) The custom need not be consistent with other customs in the same area
(*d*) The custom must be certain and precise

Choose the correct answer from the options given below:

A. (*a*) and (*b*) only
B. (*a*), (*b*), and (*c*) only
C. (*a*), (*b*), and (*d*) only
D. (*a*), (*b*), (*c*) and (*d*) all

43. Which of the following are the exceptions of the 'specific enforcement rule' of the Theory of Remedial Liability?

(*a*) Imperfect duties
(*b*) Duties that are impossible for specific performance
(*c*) Duties which are inexpedient to enforce specifically

Choose the correct answer from the options given below:

A. (*a*) and (*b*) only
B. (*a*) and (*c*) only
C. (*b*) and (*c*) only
D. (*a*), (*b*), and (*c*) all

44. The provisions given under Article 13 of the Indian Constitution are as follows:

(*a*) All laws in force in the territory of India immediately before the commencement of this Constitution will be void to the extent of the inconsistency.
(*b*) 'Laws in force' includes all laws passed or made by the legislature or other competent authority in the territory of India before the commencement of this constitution and not previously repeated.
(*c*) The state shall not make any law which takes or abridges right conferred by Part III and any law made in the contravention shall be void.
(*d*) 'Law' does not include any ordinance, order, bye-law, rule, regulation, notification, custom or usage etc.
(*e*) Article 13 shall apply to any amendment of the Constitution made under Article 368

Choose the correct answer from the options given below:

A. (*b*) and (*d*) only
B. (*d*) and (*e*) only
C. (*a*) and (*e*) only
D. (*a*), (*b*) and (*c*) only

45. Under Article 30 of the Indian Constitution, the right to minorities are guaranteed as under:

(*a*) The right is guaranteed to the religious minorities only.
(*b*) The right is guaranteed for linguistic and religious minorities.
(*c*) Right is given only to administer the educational institution
(*d*) Right is given to minorities to establish and administer the educational institution.
(*e*) The state is prohibited from making discrimination in the matter of grant of aid to any educational institution on the ground that it is managed by a religious minority or linguistic minority

Choose the correct answer from the options given below:

A. (*a*) and (*e*) only
B. (*b*) and (*c*) only
C. (*b*), (*d*) and (*e*) only
D. (*c*) and (*e*) only

46. Which of the following statements are NOT correct?

(*a*) In the Hague Conference of 1930, a convention on the conflict of Nationality law was signed and adopted
(*b*) Nottebohm case is related to "statelessness"
(*c*) On 7th November 1967, the General Assembly of the U.N. adopted the declaration on elimination of discrimination against women.
(*d*) The Convention on the Reduction of Statelessness, 1961 came into force on December 13, 1965.
(*e*) The Convention on the Status of Stateless Persons was adopted on 6th June 1960.

A. (*a*), (*c*), (*e*) only
B. (*b*), (*d*), (*e*) only
C. (*b*), (*c*), (*d*) only
D. (*a*), (*b*), (*c*) only

47. Which of the following statements are correct?

(*a*) The Dunkel Draft Text or Dunkel Package, or the Dunkel Draft Act embodying the results of Uruguay Round of Multilateral Trade Negotiation, was released on 20th December, 1995.

(*b*) The new World Trade Organisation (WTO) which came into effect on 1st January, 1995, replaced the General Agreement on Tariff and Trade (GATT).

(*c*) The functions of WTO are mentioned in Article III of the Agreement establishing WTO.

(*d*) The Sixth Ministerial Conference of WTO was held in Hongkong (China) from 13th to 18th December, 2008.

Choose the correct answer from the options given below:

A. (*b*), (*c*) only B. (*a*), (*c*), (*d*) only
C. (*a*), (*b*), (*c*) only D. (*a*), (*b*), (*c*), (*d*)

48. The provision regarding the offences against the Public Tranquility are as follows:

(*a*) Whoever, being aware of facts which render any assembly, an unlawful assembly, intentionally joins that assembly, or continues in it, is said to be a member of unlawful assembly.

(*b*) When two or more persons, by fighting in a public place, disturb the public peace, they are said to 'Commit an affray'.

(*c*) Whoever is a member of an unlawful assembly, shall be punished with imprisonment of either description for a term which may extend to one year.

(*d*) Whoever commits an affray, shall be punished with imprisonment of either description for a term which may extend to one month, or with fine which may extend to one hundred rupees, of with both.

(*e*) Whoever is guilty of rioting shall be punished with fine only.

A. (*b*) and (*c*) only
B. (*c*) and (*d*) only
C. (*a*), (*b*) and (*d*) only
D. (*a*) and (*c*) only

49. The quantum of punishments given under Indian Penal code are:

(*a*) Wnoever commits extortion shall be punished with imprisonment of either description for a term which may extend to three years or with fine or with both.

(*b*) Whoever commits criminal breach of trust shall be punished for a term which may extend to seven years.

(*c*) Whoever dishonestly misappropriates or converts to his own use any movable property, shall be punished with imprisonment of either description for a term which may extend to two years or with fine or with both.

(*d*) Whoever makes any preparation for committing dacoity shall be punished with fine only.

(*e*) If at the time of attempting to commit robbery or dacoity the offender is armed with deadly weapons, shall be punished for two years

Choose the correct answer from the options given below

A. (*b*) and (*c*) only
B. (*b*) and (*d*) only
C. (*a*), (*d*) and (*e*) only
D. (*a*) and (*c*) only

50. Under Section 361 of Indian Penal Code the "kidnapping from lawful guardianship" is:

(*a*) When someone takes or entices any minor without the consent of the guardian

(*b*) When someone takes or entices any person of unsound mind out of the keeping of lawful guardian without the consent of the guardian

(*c*) When someone entices or takes away any minor under 16 years of age if male and 18 years of age if female without consent of the guardian

Choose the correct answer from the options given below

A. (*a*) and (*b*) only
B. (*a*), (*b*) and (*c*) all
C. (*a*) and (*c*) only
D. (*b*) and (*c*) only

51. Where does vicarious liability generally arise from?

(*a*) A contract of service
(*b*) A contract for service
(*c*) A contract of service as well as a contract for service
(*d*) A wrongful act of servant

Choose the correct answer from the options given below:
A. (*a*) and (*d*) only
B. (*d*) only
C. (*a*), (*b*) and (*c*) all
D. (*b*) only

52. A person may be liable in respect of wrongful acts or omission of others in which of the following ways:
(*a*) As having ratified and authorised the particular act
(*b*) As standing towards the other person in a relation entailing responsibility for wrongs done by that person
(*c*) As having abetted the tortious acts committed by others

Choose the correct answer from the options given below:
A. (*a*) only B. (*b*) only
C. (*c*) only D. (*a*), (*b*), (*c*)

53. Any agreement in respect of production, supply, distribution, storage, acquisition, or control of goods or provision of service which causes or is likely to cause an appreciable adverse effect on competition in India is void. These agreements include:
(*a*) Tie in arrangement
(*b*) Exclusive supply agreement
(*c*) Exclusive distribution agreement
(*d*) Refusal to deal
(*e*) Resale price maintenance

Choose the correct answer from the options given below:
A. (*a*) and (*b*) only
B. (*c*), (*d*), (*e*) only
C. (*a*), (*b*), (*c*) only
D. (*a*), (*b*), (*c*), (*d*), (*e*) all

54. Which of the following are correct?
(*a*) The Doctrine of Priority of Consideration is applicable in India.
(*b*) The Doctrine of Priority of Consideration is not applicable in India.
(*c*) The Rule of Priority of Contract is applicable in India.
(*d*) The Rule of Priority of Contract is not applicable in India.

Choose the correct answer from the options given below:
A. (*a*) and (*c*) only
B. (*b*) and (*d*) only
C. (*b*) and (*c*) only
D. (*c*) only

55. Under Section 5 of the Sale of Goods Act, 1930, a contract for the sale of goods can be made:
(*a*) By writing and must be registered.
(*b*) By word of mouth.
(*c*) By partly in writing and partly word of mouth.
(*d*) By writing or partly in writing and partly by word of mouth.

Choose the correct answer from the options given below:
A. (*a*) and (*c*) only B. (*a*) and (*d*) only
C. (*a*) and (*b*) only D. (*b*) and (*d*) only

56. A company can convert into Limited Liability Partnership:
(*a*) By complying to requirements of the third schedule of Limited Liability Partnership Act, 2008.
(*b*) It can convert if there is no security interest in its assets subsisting at the time of application.
(*c*) Partners of Limited Liability Partnership are the erstwhile shareholders of the company and no one else.
(*d*) All the assets, interests, rights and privileges of the company are transferred to the firm.

Choose the correct answer from the options given below:
A. (*a*) only B. (*b*) only
C. (*c*) only D. (*a*), (*b*), (*c*), (*d*) all

57. Under the Muslim Women (Protection of Rights on Divorce) Act, 1986, a divorced woman shall be entitled to:

(*a*) A reasonable and fair provision and maintenance to be made and paid to her within the 'iddat' period by her former husband.

(*b*) Maintenance of children by her former husband for a period of three years.

(*c*) Get maintenance from her relatives even after her remarriage.

(*d*) All the properties given to her at any time only by her husband.

(*e*) An amount equal to the sum of 'Maher' or dower agreed to be paid to her at the time of marriage or at anytime thereafter according to Muslim Law.

Choose the correct answer from the options given below:

A. (*a*) and (*e*) only
B. (*a*), (*b*), and (*e*) only
C. (*b*), (*c*) and (*e*) only
D. (*a*) and (*b*) only

58. Which of the following is NOT a condition precedent for a valid adoption under the Hindu Adoptions and Maintenance Act, 1956?

(*a*) Adopter must have the capacity and right to take in adoption.

(*b*) The child must be eligible for adoption.

(*c*) The giver must have the capacity and right to give in adoption.

(*d*) Datta-homam is mandatory.

Choose the correct answer from the options given below:

A. (*a*) and (*b*) only
B. (*b*) and (*d*) only
C. (*c*) and (*d*) only
D. (*a*) and (*c*) only

59. The responsibilities of Economic and Social Council regarding improvement and protection of human rights is laid down under which Article of UN Charter?

(*a*) Article 62(2)
(*b*) Article 68
(*c*) Article 76(c)
(*d*) Article 96

Choose the correct answer from the options given below:

A. (*a*) only B. (*b*) only
C. (*c*) only D. (*d*) only

60. The provision relating to 'solid waste management' is contained under which Schedule of the Constitution of India?

(*a*) Schedule VII
(*b*) Schedule IX
(*c*) Schedule XI
(*d*) Schedule XII

Choose the correct answer from the options given below:

A. (*a*) only B. (*b*) only
C. (*c*) only D. (*d*) only

61. The provision relating to 'drinking water' is contained under which Schedule of the Constitution of India, 1950?

(*a*) Schedule VII
(*b*) Schedule IX
(*c*) Schedule XI
(*d*) Schedule XII

Choose the correct answer from the options given below:

A. (*a*) only B. (*b*) only
C. (*c*) only D. (*d*) only

62. In which of the following cases, the 'minimal creativity test' was laid down?

(*a*) Eastern Book Company v. D.B. Modak
(*b*) R.G. Anand v. Delux Films
(*c*) Amar Nath Sehgal v. Union of India
(*d*) University of London Press v. University Tutorial Press

Choose the correct answer from the options given below:

A. (*a*) only B. (*b*) only
C. (*c*) only D. (*d*) only

63. By which amendment of Information Technology Act, 2000 the third and fourth schedules were omitted?

(*a*) Act 10 of 2009
(*b*) Act 55 of 2009
(*c*) Act 66 of 2009
(*d*) Act 09 of 2009

Choose the correct answer from the options given below:

A. (*a*) only B. (*b*) only
C. (*c*) only D. (*d*) only

64. In the Presidential form of government:

(*a*) The chief executive is relatively free from sectional and party disputes.
(*b*) The chief executive is free to choose his team of ministers from the best talent available.
(*c*) The term of the chief executive is not fixed.
(*d*) It discourages the disease of defections.

Choose the correct answer from the options given below:

A. (*a*), (*b*) and (*c*) only
B. (*a*), (*b*) and (*d*) only
C. (*b*), (*c*) and (*d*) only
D. (*a*), (*b*) (*c*) and (*d*) all

65. Read the statements about 'rule of law':

(*a*) Rule of law is an important and fundamental pillar of a liberal and substantive democracy.
(*b*) The rule of law is not merely public order, the rule of law is social justice based on public order.
(*c*) The substantive 'rule of law' is the rule of proper law which balances the needs of the society and the individual.
(*d*) Substantive and liberal democracy is based solely on formal democracy.

Choose the correct answer from the options given below:

A. (*a*), (*b*) and (*c*) only
B. (*a*), (*c*) and (*d*) only
C. (*a*), (*b*) and (*d*) only
D. (*a*), (*b*), (*c*) and (*d*) all

66. Match List-I with List-II:

List-I	List-II
(*a*) Definition of Permanent Lok Adalat	(*i*) Section 22-B
(*b*) Establishment of Permanent Lok Adalat	(*ii*) Section 22-C
(*c*) Cognizance by Permanent Lok Adalat	(*iii*) Section 22-E
(*d*) Award of Permanent Lok Adalat	(*iv*) Section 22-A

Choose the correct answer from the options given below:

	(*a*)	(*b*)	(*c*)	(*d*)
A.	(*i*)	(*iv*)	(*iii*)	(*ii*)
B.	(*ii*)	(*iii*)	(*i*)	(*iv*)
C.	(*iii*)	(*ii*)	(*iv*)	(*i*)
D.	(*iv*)	(*i*)	(*ii*)	(*iii*)

67. Match List-I with List-II:

List-I Provision under the Constitution of India	List-II Article
(*a*) Special provisions with respect to the state of Manipur	(*i*) Article 371-F
(*b*) Special provisions with respect to the state of Karnataka	(*ii*) Article 371-G
(*c*) Special provisions with respect to the state of Sikkim	(*iii*) Article 371-C
(*d*) Special provisions with respect to the state of Mizoram	(*iv*) Article 371-J

Choose the correct answer from the options given below.

	(*a*)	(*b*)	(*c*)	(*d*)
A.	(*ii*)	(*i*)	(*iv*)	(*iii*)
B.	(*i*)	(*ii*)	(*iii*)	(*iv*)
C.	(*iv*)	(*iii*)	(*ii*)	(*i*)
D.	(*iii*)	(*iv*)	(*i*)	(*ii*)

68. Match List-I with List-II:

List-I (Provision)	List-II (Article of the statute of the International Court of Justice)
(*a*) Law applied by the International Court of Justice	(*i*) Article 36
(*b*) Courts power to allow a state to intervene in a case to which it is not a party	(*ii*) Article 38
(*c*) Jurisdiction of the International Court of Justice	(*iii*) Article 41
(*d*) Interim Measures or relief by the International Court of Justice.	(*iv*) Article 62

Choose the correct answer from the options given below.

	(*a*)	(*b*)	(*c*)	(*d*)
A.	(*i*)	(*ii*)	(*iii*)	(*iv*)
B.	(*ii*)	(*iv*)	(*i*)	(*iii*)
C.	(*ii*)	(*iii*)	(*i*)	(*iv*)
D.	(*iv*)	(*ii*)	(*iii*)	(*i*)

69. Match List-I with List-II:

List-I Provision under Indian Penal Code	List-II Section
(*a*) An act done in good faith for benefit of a person without consent.	(*i*) Section 423
(*b*) Dishonest or fraudulent execution of the deed of transfer containing false statement of consideration.	(*ii*) Section 381
(*c*) Voluntarily causing grievous hurt by use of acid etc.	(*iii*) Section 92
(*d*) Theft by clerk or servant of property in possession of master.	(*iv*) Section 326A

Choose the correct answer from the options given below:

	(*a*)	(*b*)	(*c*)	(*d*)
A.	(*iii*)	(*i*)	(*ii*)	(*iv*)
B.	(*iii*)	(*i*)	(*iv*)	(*ii*)
C.	(*i*)	(*ii*)	(*iii*)	(*iv*)
D.	(*iv*)	(*iii*)	(*ii*)	(*i*)

70. Match List-I with List-II:

List-I (Jurisdiction)	List-II (Section under Consumer Protection Act, 1986)
(*a*) Jurisdiction of District forum	(*i*) Section 11
(*b*) Jurisdiction of State Commission	(*ii*) Section 21
(*c*) Jurisdiction of National Commission	(*iii*) Section 22A
(*d*) Power to set aside *ex parte* orders	(*iv*) Section 17

Choose the correct answer from the options given below.

	(*a*)	(*b*)	(*c*)	(*d*)
A.	(*i*)	(*iv*)	(*ii*)	(*iii*)
B.	(*iii*)	(*ii*)	(*iv*)	(*i*)
C.	(*ii*)	(*iii*)	(*i*)	(*iv*)
D.	(*iv*)	(*i*)	(*iii*)	(*ii*)

71. Match List-I with List-II:

List-I (Terms)	List-II (Section of Companies Act, 2013)
(*a*) Abridged Prospectus	(*i*) Section 31
(*b*) Deemed Prospectus	(*ii*) Section 32
(*c*) Shelf Prospectus	(*iii*) Section 2(1)
(*d*) Red herring Prospectus	(*iv*) Section 25

Choose the correct answer from the options given below:

	(*a*)	(*b*)	(*c*)	(*d*)
A.	(*iii*)	(*iv*)	(*i*)	(*ii*)
B.	(*ii*)	(*iii*)	(*iv*)	(*i*)
C.	(*i*)	(*ii*)	(*iii*)	(*iv*)
D.	(*iv*)	(*i*)	(*ii*)	(*iii*)

72. Match List-I with List-II:

List-I (Provision)	List-II (Section under Muslim Woman Protection of Rights on Marriage Act, 2019)
(*a*) Punishment for pronouncing talaq	(*i*) Section 3
(*b*) Offences to be cognizable, compoundable etc.	(*ii*) Section 7
(*c*) Custody of minor children	(*iii*) Section 4
(*d*) Talaq to be void and illegal	(*iv*) Section 6

Choose the correct answer from the options given below:

	(*a*)	(*b*)	(*c*)	(*d*)
A.	(*i*)	(*ii*)	(*iii*)	(*iv*)
B.	(*iii*)	(*ii*)	(*iv*)	(*i*)
C.	(*ii*)	(*iv*)	(*iii*)	(*i*)
D.	(*iv*)	(*i*)	(*iii*)	(*ii*)

73. Match List-I with List-II:

List-I (Provision)	List-II (Section under National Green Tribunal Act, 2010)
(*a*) Hazardous Substance	(*i*) Section 2(a)
(*b*) Environment	(*ii*) Section 2(e)
(*c*) Handling	(*iii*) Section 2(f)
(*d*) Accident	(*iv*) Section 2(c)

Choose the correct answer from the options given below:

	(*a*)	(*b*)	(*c*)	(*d*)
A.	(*i*)	(*iii*)	(*iv*)	(*ii*)
B.	(*ii*)	(*i*)	(*iv*)	(*iii*)
C.	(*iii*)	(*iv*)	(*ii*)	(*i*)
D.	(*iv*)	(*iii*)	(*i*)	(*ii*)

74. Match List-I with List-II:

List-I (Provision)	List-II (Sections of Copyright Act, 1957)
(*a*) Performer	(*i*) Section 2(q)
(*b*) Performer's right	(*ii*) Section 38 B
(*c*) Performance	(*iii*) Section 38
(*d*) Moral Rights of Performer	(*iv*) Section 2(qq)

Choose the correct answer from the options given below:

	(*a*)	(*b*)	(*c*)	(*d*)
A.	(*i*)	(*iii*)	(*iv*)	(*ii*)
B.	(*ii*)	(*i*)	(*iv*)	(*iii*)
C.	(*iii*)	(*i*)	(*ii*)	(*iv*)
D.	(*iv*)	(*iii*)	(*i*)	(*ii*)

75. Match List-I with List-II:

List-I	List-II
(*a*) Murli S. Deora v. Union of India	(*i*) Protection against Inhuman treatment in Jail
(*b*) Sunil Batra v. Delhi Administration	(*ii*) Protection of Ecology and Environmental Pollution
(*c*) Hussainara Khatoon v. State of Bihar	(*iii*) Ban on smoking in public places
(*d*) Rural Litigation and Entitlement Kendra v. State of U.P	(*iv*) Speedy trial is an integral part of the fundamental right under Article 21 of the Indian constitution

Choose the correct answer from the options given below:

	(*a*)	(*b*)	(*c*)	(*d*)
A.	(*i*)	(*ii*)	(*iii*)	(*iv*)
B.	(*ii*)	(*i*)	(*iv*)	(*iii*)
C.	(*iii*)	(*i*)	(*iv*)	(*ii*)
D.	(*iv*)	(*iii*)	(*ii*)	(*i*)

76. Arrange in chronological order the publication of the books on Jurisprudence
(*a*) *Province of Jurisprudence Determined* by Austin
(*b*) *Concept of Law* by H.L.A. Hart
(*c*) *The Province and Function of Law* by Julius Stone
(*d*) *Nature of Judicial Process* by Benjamin N. Cardozo
(*e*) *Anatomy of Law* by Lon L Fuller

Choose the correct answer from the options given below:
A. (*a*), (*b*), (*c*), (*d*), (*e*)
B. (*a*), (*c*), (*b*), (*d*), (*e*)
C. (*a*), (*d*), (*b*), (*c*), (*e*)
D. (*a*), (*e*), (*b*), (*d*), (*c*)

77. Arrange chronologically the following cases decided by the Supreme Court year wise:
(*a*) Olga Tellis v. Bombay Municipal Corporation.
(*b*) Francis Coralie v. Union Territory of Delhi
(*c*) Satwant Singh v. Assistant Passport officer
(*d*) Kharak Singh v. the State of U.P.
(*e*) National Legal Services Authority v. Union of India

Choose the correct answer from the options given below:
A. (*c*), (*d*), (*a*), (*e*), (*b*)
B. (*a*), (*b*), (*c*), (*d*), (*e*)
C. (*b*), (*d*), (*a*), (*e*), (*c*)
D. (*d*), (*c*), (*b*), (*a*), (*e*)

78. Give the chronological order (year wise) of these cases decided by the courts:
(*a*) West Rand Central Gold Mining Company Ltd. V.R.
(*b*) Portugal v. India
(*c*) Burkina Faso v. Mali
(*d*) Mavrommatis Palestine Concessions case
(*e*) Chorzoo Factory (Indemnity) case.

Choose the correct answer from the options given below:
A. (*a*), (*c*), (*d*), (*b*), (*e*)
B. (*a*), (*b*), (*c*), (*d*), (*e*)
C. (*a*), (*e*), (*b*), (*c*), (*d*)
D. (*a*), (*e*), (*b*), (*d*), (*c*)

79. Arrange the provisions of Indian Penal Code in chronological order, section-wise:
(*a*) House-trespass in order to commit an offence punishable with imprisonment for life
(*b*) House-trespass in order to commit an offence punishable with death
(*c*) Lurking house-trespass or house-breaking in order to commit an offence punishable with imprisonment
(*d*) House-trespass in order to commit an offence punishable with imprisonment
(*e*) Lurking house-trespass or house-breaking by night in order to commit an offence punishable with imprisonment

Choose the correct answer from the options given below:
A. (*e*), (*a*), (*c*), (*b*), (*d*)
B. (*d*), (*a*), (*e*), (*c*), (*b*)
C. (*a*), (*b*), (*c*), (*d*), (*e*)
D. (*b*), (*a*), (*d*), (*c*), (*e*)

80. Arrange the following in chronological order (section wise) as stated in the Motor Vehicle Act, 1988.
(*a*) Procedure and Power of Claims Tribunal
(*b*) Award of Claim Tribunal
(*c*) Claim Tribunals
(*d*) Application for Compensation

Choose the correct answer from the options given below:
A. (*c*), (*d*), (*b*), (*a*)
B. (*a*), (*b*), (*c*), (*d*)
C. (*b*), (*c*), (*a*), (*d*)
D. (*c*), (*d*), (*a*), (*b*)

81. Arrange the provisions of the Indian Partnership Act, 1932 in chronological order (section wise)
(*a*) Partnership at will
(*b*) Mode of determining the existence of the partnership
(*c*) Property of a firm
(*d*) Duties of a partner

Choose the correct answer from the options given below:

A. (*b*), (*a*), (*d*), (*c*)
B. (*c*), (*b*), (*a*), (*d*)
C. (*a*), (*c*), (*b*), (*d*)
D. (*d*), (*a*), (*b*), (*c*)

82. Chronologically arrange the following Judgements of the Supreme Court of India on Uniform Civil Code:
(*a*) Daniel Latifi v/s Union of India
(*b*) John Vallamatton v/s Union of India
(*c*) Sarla Mudgal v/s Union of India
(*d*) Mohd. Ahmad Khan v/s Shah Bano Begum

Choose the correct answer from the options given below:
A. (*c*), (*b*), (*d*), (*a*)
B. (*d*), (*c*), (*b*), (*a*)
C. (*d*), (*c*), (*a*), (*b*)
D. (*a*), (*b*), (*c*), (*d*)

83. Arrange the initiatives on climate change in chronological order:
(*a*) Durban conference on climate change
(*b*) Montreal Protocol on climate change
(*c*) Vienna convention on climate change
(*d*) Copenhagen Summit on climate change
(*e*) Kyoto Protocol on climate change

Choose the correct answer from the options given below:
A. (*a*), (*b*), (*c*), (*d*), (*e*)
B. (*b*), (*c*), (*d*), (*e*), (*a*)
C. (*a*), (*d*), (*c*), (*b*), (*e*)
D. (*c*), (*b*), (*e*), (*d*), (*a*)

84. Arrange the theories of intellectual property in order of prominence and influence:
(*a*) Personality Theory
(*b*) Social Planning Theory
(*c*) Labour Theory
(*d*) Utilitarian Theory

Choose the correct answer from the options given below:
A. (*a*), (*d*), (*c*), (*b*)
B. (*b*), (*a*), (*c*), (*d*)
C. (*c*), (*b*), (*d*), (*a*)
D. (*d*), (*c*), (*a*), (*b*)

85. Arrange in chronological order, the cases relating to U.S. Constitutional Amendments:
(*a*) Plessy v. Ferguson
(*b*) Hawke v. Smith
(*c*) Laser v. Garnett
(*d*) U.S. v. Sprague

Choose the correct answer from the options given below:
A. (*a*), (*b*), (*c*), (*d*)
B. (*a*), (*c*), (*b*), (*d*)
C. (*b*), (*c*), (*d*), (*a*)
D. (*d*), (*b*), (*c*), (*a*)

86. Given below are two statements, one is labelled as Assertion (A) and the other is labelled as Reason (R):

Assertion (A): The Parliament has the power to make the laws for whole or any part of the territory of India and law made by the Parliament would be applicable beyond the territory of India also.

Reason (R): Article 245 Clause (1) of the Constitution of India empowers the Parliament to make the laws for the whole or any part of the territory of India and Article 245 Clause (2) says that no law made by Parliament shall be deemed to be invalid on the ground that it would have extra-territorial operation.

In light of the above statements, choose the correct answer from the options given below:
A. Both (A) and (R) are true and (R) is the correct explanation of (A).
B. Both (A) and (R) are true, but (R) is NOT the correct explanation of (A).
C. (A) is true, but (R) is false
D. (A) is false, but (R) is true

87. Given below are two statements, one is labelled as Assertion (A) and the other is labelled as Reason (R):

Assertion (A): According to Article 7 of the United Nations Charter, the International Court of Justice is one of the principal organs of the United Nations

Reason (R): The International Court of Justice consists of 15 judges who are elected by the Security Council.

In light of the above statements, choose the correct answer from the options given below:

A. Both (A) and (R) are true and (R) is the correct explanation of (A).
B. Both (A) and (R) are true, but (R) is NOT the correct explanation of (A).
C. (A) is true, but (R) is false
D. (A) is false, but (R) is true

88. Given below are two statements, one is labelled as Assertion (A) and the other is labelled as Reason (R):

Assertion (A): Whoever assaults or uses criminal force on any person, in attempting to commit theft on any property which that person is then wearing or carrying, shall be punished with imprisonment of either description for a term which may extend to two years, or with fine, or with both.

Reason (R): Section 356 of Indian Penal Code provides for the punishment of imprisonment of either description for a term which may extend to two years, or with fine, or with both if a person assaults or uses criminal force on any person in attempting to commit theft or any property which that person is then wearing or carrying.

In light of the above statements, choose the correct answer from the options given below:

A. Both (A) and (R) are true and (R) is the correct explanation of (A).
B. Both (A) and (R) are true, but (R) is NOT the correct explanation of (A).
C. (A) is true, but (R) is false
D. (A) is false, but (R) is true

89. Given below are two statements, one is labelled as Assertion (A) and the other is labelled as Reason (R):

Assertion (A): If the adoption is of a son, the adoptive Hindu father or mother by whom the adoption is made must not have a Hindu son, son's son or son's son's son (whether by legitimate blood relationship or by adoption) living at the time of adoption.

Reason (R): Section 11 (i) of the Hindu Adoptions and Maintenance Act, 1956, which deals with the right of adoptive parents 'under other conditions for a valid adoption' imposes this restriction.

In light of the above statements, choose the correct answer from the options given below:

A. Both (A) and (R) are true and (R) is the correct explanation of (A).
B. Both (A) and (R) are true, but (R) is NOT the correct explanation of (A).
C. (A) is true, but (R) is false
D. (A) is false, but (R) is true

90. Given below are two statements, one is labelled as Assertion (A) and the other is labelled as Reason (R):

Assertion (A): Once a performer consents to the incorporation of his performance in a cinematograph film by a written agreement, he/she will not object to the enjoyment of the performers' right by the producer in the same film.

Reason (R): The performer is entitled to royalties in case the producer of the film makes use of the performance for commercial use.

In light of the above statements, choose the correct answer from the options given below:

A. Both (A) and (R) are true and (R) is the correct explanation of (A).
B. Both (A) and (R) are true, but (R) is NOT the correct explanation of (A).
C. (A) is true, but (R) is false
D. (A) is false, but (R) is true

Directions (Qs. No. 91-95): *Read the passage carefully and answer the questions that follow.*

The right to live with dignity has been recognized as a human right on the international front and by the number of precedents of this Court and therefore, the Constitutional courts must strive to protect the dignity of every individual, for, without the right to dignity, every other right would be rendered meaningless. Dignity is an inseparable facet of every individual that invites reciprocative respect from others to every aspect of an individual which he/she perceives as an essential attribute of his/her individuality, be it an orientation or an optional expression of choice. The Constitution has ladened the judiciary with the very important duty to protect and ensure the right of every individual including the right to express and choose without any impediments so as to enable an individual to fully realize his/her fundamental right to live with dignity.

Sexual orientation is one of the many biological phenomena which is natural and inherent in an individual and is controlled by neurological and biological factors. The science of sexuality has theorized that an individual exerts little or no control over who he/she gets attracted to. Any discrimination on the basis of one's sexual orientation would entail a violation of the fundamental right of freedom of expression.

91. The above paragraph reflects the judgement in case of:
- A. Navtej Singh Johar v. Union of India
- B. Machi Singh v. State of Punjab
- C. Sate of U.P. v. Ram Swaroop
- D. Chairman Railway Board v. Chandrima Das

92. Discrimination on the basis of sexual orientation is violative of which of the following fundamental rights?
- A. Article 21 only
- B. Articles 14, 15 only
- C. Articles 15, 19 only
- D. Articles 14, 15, 19, 21

93. The consensual sexual act of an adult is criminalised under which of the following legislations?
- A. Indian Penal Code
- B. POCSO
- C. Criminal Law (Amendment) Act 2013
- D. Hindu Marriage Act, 1955

94. Which one of the following judges were part of the judgement referred to in the paragraph?
- A. J. Deepak Mishra
- B. J.R.F. Nariman
- C. Dr. D.Y. Chandrachud
- D. J. Indu Malhotra

95. The fundamental right of the freedom of expression is contained in the following articles of the Indian Constitution:
- A. Article 19 (1)(a)
- B. Article 19 (l)(f)
- C. Article 18(1)
- D. Article 21

Directions (Qs. No. 96-100): *Read the passage carefully and answer the questions that follow.*

The state of Uttar Pradesh and Uttarakhand have not cooperated with the central government to constitute a Ganga Management Board. The Uttarakhand High Court in the exercise of its *'parens patriae'* jurisdiction, ordered conversation of Ganga and Yamuna rivers as juristic/legal persons/living entities, hailing the status of a legal person. The rivers Ganga and Yamuna are thus legal persons with corresponding rights of a living person. The director NAMAMI Ganga, the Chief Secretary and Advocate General of Uttarakhand states were declared as persons in *'loco parentis'*.

The division bench of Uttarakhand High Court sharply berated the state terming their non-cooperation as the 'sign of non-governance'. The deterioration of Ganga and Yamuna is a classic case of 'desperate times, desperate measures', the court granted the juristic entity at par with Hindu idol. The Uttarakhand High Court in another case reiterated the constitution of the Ganga Management Board has become all the more necessary for the purpose of irrigation, water supply, hydropower generation, and navigation.

96. The term *'Parens Patriae'* refers to:
- A. Common Suit
- B. Descent from parent
- C. Parent of his/her own country/state
- D. Barred by res Judicata

97. The Uttarakhand High Court in another case reiterated 'the constitution...navigation' as quoted in the paragraph, refers to which one of the following cases?

A. Mohd. Salim v. State of Uttarakhand

B. Yogendra Nath v. Commissioner of Income Tax

C. Ram Jankijee v. State of Bihar

D. M.C. Mehta v. Kamal Nath

98. Hindu Idol is a juristic entity capable of holding property, was laid down in:

A. Bengal Immunity Co. Ltd. v. State of Bihar

B. Yogendra Nath Naskar v. Commissioner of Income tax

C. K.M. Basheer v. Lona Chakola

D. Nanak Chand v. State of U.P

99. 'The division bench of Uttarakhand High Court sharply berated... non-governance' was observed in which of the following cases?

A. Indian Council for Enviro-legal Action v. Union of India

B. Rural Litigation & Entitlement Kendra v. State of Uttarakhand

C. Divya Pharmacy v. Union of India

D. Lalit Miglani v. State of Uttarakhand

100. The term *'loco parentis'* refers to :

A. In equal fault B. In place of parent

C. Hizanat period D. Indigent suit

ANSWERS

1	**2**	**3**	**4**	**5**	**6**	**7**	**8**	**9**	**10**
C	B	C	B	C	A	B	A	D	A
11	**12**	**13**	**14**	**15**	**16**	**17**	**18**	**19**	**20**
C	B	D	C	A	C	A	A	A	A
21	**22**	**23**	**24**	**25**	**26**	**27**	**28**	**29**	**30**
B	A	A	A	B	B	D	B	C	A,C
31	**32**	**33**	**34**	**35**	**36**	**37**	**38**	**39**	**40**
C	A	D	A	D	A	D	C	C	A
41	**42**	**43**	**44**	**45**	**46**	**47**	**48**	**49**	**50**
A	C	D	D	C	B	A	C	D	D
51	**52**	**53**	**54**	**55**	**56**	**57**	**58**	**59**	**60**
A	D	D	*	D	D	A	C	B	D
61	**62**	**63**	**64**	**65**	**66**	**67**	**68**	**69**	**70**
C	A	A	B	A	D	D	B	B	A
71	**72**	**73**	**74**	**75**	**76**	**77**	**78**	**79**	**80**
A	B	C	D	C	C	D	*	D	A
81	**82**	**83**	**84**	**85**	**86**	**87**	**88**	**89**	**90**
A	C	D	D	A	A	C	A	A	B
91	**92**	**93**	**94**	**95**	**96**	**97**	**98**	**99**	**100**
A	D	A	A	A	C	A	B	D	B

EXPLANATORY ANSWERS

1. Sir. Henry Summer Maine is best known for the proposition advanced in Ancient Law that "the movement of the progressive societies has hitherto been a movement from status to contract." As he explained, the ancient law recognized and dealt with the relationships among extended families, not individuals. Individual members of a family were subject to the control of the family head. As he points out, under the Roman legal conception, *Pater Potestas*, the head of the family possessed virtually complete power, including those of life and death, over members of the family. Consequently, the laws did not recognize individuals qua individuals because they only had status within the realm of this patriarchal authority. The gradual erosion of the notion of *Pater Potestas* was marked by a movement to contract, wherein law recognized the capacity of individuals to assume powers, responsibilities, and authority. Progressive societies, as Maine shows, are those where this "emancipation" or "liberation" of the individual had taken place—"static" societies, those whose legal systems still adhere to "status."

3. Corporation sole is an incorporated series of successive persons. It consists of a single person who is personified and regarded by law as a legal person. In other words, a single person, who in exercise of some office or function, deals in the legal capacity and has rights and duties. A corporation sole is perpetual. The examples of corporation sole are Post-Master-General, Public Trustee, Comptroller & Auditor-General of India, the President of India, The Crown in England etc.

The sole purpose of the corporation is to maintain the continuity of an office. Till it is in continuation its all others purposes like maximizing profit, increase in shareholders wealth can be achieved.

4. The real relationship of jurisprudence to law depends not upon what law is treated but how law is created. John Chipman Gray- 1839-1915—stresses the fact that the statutes together with precedents, equity and custom are sources of law but the law itself is what the persons acting as judicial organs of the state laid down as rules of conduct. To determine, rights and duties, the judges settle what fact exists and also lay down rules according to which they deduce legal consequences from facts. Gray emphasizes the role which judges play in laying down the law because it is the judge who while interpreting the statute, custom or equity create law rather than discovering the law. The law as expressed in statutes or customs gets meaning or precision only after the judge expresses his opinion. The judge depend on the sources of the law such as statute, judicial precedent, opinion of experts, customs and public policies and principles of morality, the law becomes concrete and positive only in the pronouncements of the court. Judge made law is the final and authoritative form of law. He suggests that the judicial pronouncements of law are the true subject matter of jurisprudence for evaluations. Gray's contribution lies in the fact that judicial decisions often have been responsible for giving not only content but direction to political, social and economic thought.

The contribution of Gray in formulating the principle that the judges or the courts have the first and the final say as to what the law is and obviously the role of jurisprudence is to understand and evaluate the law made by judges is the realist approach to understanding law and legal institutions.

5. Kesavananda Bharati challenged the Constitution (29th Amendment) Act, 1972, questioning the Kerala government's attempts, under two-state land reform acts, to impose restrictions on the management of its (mutt) property. Bharati also challenged three Constitutional amendments - the 24th, 25th and 26th amendments - introduced by the Indira Gandhi government. The principal question that was raised in the case was about the power of Parliament to amend the Constitution in totality especially with respect to fundamental rights. To simply put, the basic question that the Supreme Court had to decide was whether Parliament could alter, amend, abrogate any part of the Constitution even to the extent of taking away all fundamental rights?

Senior lawyer Nani Palkhivala, Fali Nariman, and Soli Sorabjee fought the case for Kesavananda Bharati. A 13-judge bench was formed to preside over the case, heard over 68 days. In which, 11 different judgments were delivered in what is said to be a 7:6 majority. The Supreme Court then ruled that the 'basic structure' of the Constitution was inviolable, and could not be amended by Parliament. The 'basic structure' doctrine has since been regarded as a tenet of Indian constitutional law.

6. Equal protection of laws have been taken from the Constitution of America. The following provisions are given in it.

I. The similar application of the same laws to all persons who are similarly situated.

II. Equal treatment under equal circumstances, both in the privileges conferred and liabilities imposed by the laws.

III. All persons should be treated equally without any discrimination.

The Supreme Court believes that the rule of law written under Article 14 is the fundamental element of the Constitution. Therefore it cannot be abolished in any way even by amending the Constitution.

7. Article 72 empowers the President the power to grant pardons, reprieves, respites or remissions of punishment or to suspend, remit or commute the sentence of any person convicted of any offence. The meaning of these terms is as follows:

- **Pardon:** It removes both the sentence and the conviction and completely absolves the convict from all sentences, punishments, and disqualifications.
- **Commutation:** It denotes the substitution of one form of punishment with a lighter form of punishment. For example, a death sentence may be commuted to rigorous imprisonment.
- **Remission:** It implies reducing the period of the sentence without changing its character. For example, a sentence of rigorous imprisonment for five years may be remitted to rigorous imprisonment for one year.
- **Respite:** It denotes awarding a lesser sentence in place of one originally awarded due to some special fact, such as the physical disability of a convict or the pregnancy of a woman offender.
- **Reprieve:** It implies a stay of the execution of a sentence (especially that of death) for a temporary period. Its purpose is to enable the convict to have time to seek pardon or commutation from the President.

9. The words 'International Law' was coined for the first time by Jeremy Bentham in 1780. The term International Law is synonymous with the term law of nations. It is a body of rules and principles which regulate the conduct and relations of the members of the international community. International law is the set of rules generally regarded and accepted as binding in relations between states and nations. It serves as the indispensable framework for the practice of stable and organized international relations. International law differs from national legal systems in that it primarily concerns nations rather than private citizen.

10. United Nations Charter, Chapter VI : Pacific Settlement of Disputes

Article 33

1. The parties to any dispute, the continuance of which is likely to endanger the maintenance of international peace and security, shall, first of all, seek a solution by negotiation, enquiry, mediation, conciliation, arbitration, judicial settlement, resort to regional agencies or arrangements, or other peaceful means of their own choice.
2. The Security Council shall, when it deems necessary, call upon the parties to settle their dispute by such means.

Article 34

The Security Council may investigate any dispute, or any situation which might lead to international friction or give rise to a dispute, in order to determine whether the continuance of the dispute or situation is likely to endanger the maintenance of international peace and security.

Article 35

1. Any Member of the United Nations may bring any dispute, or any situation of the nature referred to in Article 34, to the attention of the Security Council or of the General Assembly.
2. A state which is not a Member of the United Nations may bring to the attention of the Security Council or of the General Assembly any dispute to which it is a party if it accepts in advance, for the purposes of the dispute, the obligations of pacific settlement provided in the present Charter.
3. The proceedings of the General Assembly in respect of matters brought to its attention under this Article will be subject to the provisions of Articles 11 and 12.

Article 36

1. The Security Council may, at any stage of a dispute of the nature referred to in Article 33 or of a situation of like nature, recommend appropriate procedures or methods of adjustment.
2. The Security Council should take into consideration any procedures for the settlement of the dispute which have already been adopted by the parties.
3. In making recommendations under this Article the Security Council should also take into consideration that legal disputes should as a general rule be referred by the parties to the International Court of Justice in accordance with the provisions of the Statute of the Court.

Article 37

1. Should the parties to a dispute of the nature referred to in Article 33 fail to settle it by the means indicated in that Article, they shall refer it to the Security Council.
2. If the Security Council deems that the continuance of the dispute is in fact likely to endanger the maintenance of international peace and security, it shall decide whether to take action under Article 36 or to recommend such terms of settlement as it may consider appropriate.

Article 38

Without prejudice to the provisions of Articles 33 to 37, the Security Council may, if all the parties to any dispute so request, make recommendations to the parties with a view to a pacific settlement of the dispute.

13. The Magistrate thought that the accused had deliberately made false statements, and that he did not act in good faith. He referred to the case of Dhania v. F.L. Clifford 13 B. 376 : 7 Ind. Dec. (N.S.) 250. But that case is not in point, as the accused there had not got the power of arresting a man as had the present accused. The Magistrate has not dealt specifically with the defence which was raised under Section 76, Indian Penal Code, by which nothing is an offence which is done by a person who is, or who by reason of a mistake of fact and not by reason of mistake of law in good faith believes himself to be bound by law to do it, and illust Ration (6) is as follows: A an officer of a Court of Justice, being ordered by that Court to arrest Y and, after due inquiry, believing Z to be Y, arrests Z, A has committed no offence.

14. Section 102 in The Indian Penal Code: Commencement and continuance of the right of private defence of the body. The right of private defence of the body commences as soon as a reasonable apprehension of danger to the body arises from an attempt or threat to commit the offence though the offence may not have been committed; and it continues as long as such apprehension of danger to the body continues.

15. Section 372 in The Indian Penal Code: Selling minor for purposes of prostitution, etc.- Whoever sells, lets to hire, or otherwise disposes of any [person under the age of eighteen years with intent that such person shall at any age be employed or used for the purpose of prostitution or illicit intercourse with any person or for any unlawful and immoral purpose, or knowing it to be likely that such person will at any age be] employed or used for any such purpose, shall be punished with imprisonment of either description for a term which may extend to ten years, and shall be liable to fine.

Explanation I: When a female under the age of eighteen years is sold, let for hire, or otherwise disposed of to a prostitute or to any person who keeps or manages a brothel, the person so disposing of such female shall, until the contrary is proved, be presumed to have disposed of her with the intent that she shall be used for the purpose of prostitution.

Explanation II: For the purposes of this section "illicit intercourse" means sexual intercourse between persons not united by marriage or by any union or tie which, though not amounting to a marriage, is recognised by the personal law or custom of the community to which they belong or, where they belong to different communities, of both such communities, as constituting between them a quasi-marital relation.

16. Section 376DB: Punishment for gang rape on woman under twelve years of age

Where a woman under twelve years of age is raped by one or more persons constituting a group or acting in furtherance of a common intention, each of those persons shall be deemed to have committed the offence of rape and shall be punished with imprisonment for life, which shall mean imprisonment for the remainder of that person's natural life, and with fine, or with death.

Provided that such fine shall be just and reasonable to meet the medical expenses and rehabilitation of the victim:

Provided further that any fine imposed under this section shall be paid to the victim.

17. Winfield is the chief supporter of Law of Tort and not Law of Torts theory. He says, all injuries done to another person are torts, unless there is some justification recognized by law. Thus according to this theory tort consists not merely of those torts which have acquired specific names but also included the wider principle that all unjustifiable harm is tortuous. This enables the courts to create new torts. Winfield while supporting this theory comes to the conclusion that law of tort is growing and from time to time courts have created new torts.

18. Salmond defined a tort is a civil wrong for which the remedy is common law action for unliquidated damages and which is not exclusively the breach of the contract or the breach of the trust or other merely equitable obligation".

According to section 2(m) of the Limitation Act 1963, 'Tort means a civil wrong which is not exclusively a breach of contract or breach of trust'. In the case of a civil wrong the injured party (Plaintiff) institutes, a civil proceeding against the wrongdoer (Defendant) and the main remedy is damages or compensation. In the case of a criminal wrong, the criminal proceedings against the accused are brought by the State and the victim is not compensated but the wrongdoer is punished.

19. When the acts of two or more persons, acting independently, concur to produce a single damage, they are known as independent tortfeasors. There is no concerted action on the part of independent tortfeasors. There is mere similarity of design on their part although they act quite independently of one another. For example, two motorists driving negligently and coming from the opposite direction collide and a pedestrian is crushed between the two cars, these motorists are independent tortfeasors.

20. Salus Populi Suprema Lex : This maxim means that the welfare of the people is the supreme law, enunciates the idea of law. This can be achieved only when justice is administered lawfully, judicially, without fear or favour and without being hampered and thwarted and this cannot be effective unless respect for it is fostered and maintained (Pritam Pal v. High Court of Madhya Pradesh AIR 1992 SC 904). The Andhra Pradesh High Court observed in Special Deputy Collector v. N. Vasudeva Rao [2003] 12 ILD 342 "The maxim 'salus populi suprema lex' *i.e.* 'the welfare of the people is the supreme law' adequately enunciates the idea of law. This can be achieved only when justice is administered lawfully, judicially, without fear or favour and without being hampered and thwarted, and this cannot be effective unless respect for it is fostered".

21. The term coercion has been defined in section 15 of the Act as "Coercion" is the committing or threatening to commit, any act forbidden by the Indian Penal Code (45 of 1860), or the unlawful detaining, or threatening to detain, any property, to the prejudice of any person whatever, with the intention of causing any person to enter into an agreement. **Explanation:** It is immaterial whether the Indian Penal Code (45 of 1860) is or is not in force in the place where the coercion is employed. From the above definition of coercion given in section 15, consent is said to be caused by coercion when it is obtained by any one of the following; (i) committing or threatening to commit any act forbidden by Indian Penal Code; (ii) unlawful detaining or threatening to detain the property of another person. Coercion may come from a person party to the contract or even third person not connected with the contract directly.

23. The well-known case of Krell v. Henry is the one which illustrates this. First: where the performance is physically cut off and second: where the object has failed. The Supreme Court of India has held that Section 56 will apply in both kinds of frustrations.

24. Ordinary Damages: On the breach of a contract, the suffering party may incur some damages arising naturally, in the usual course of events. Even if the suffering party knew about the likely damages if the contract was breached, he can claim compensation for such losses. For example,

Amar agrees to sell and deliver 10 bags of potatoes to Rohit for ₹ 5,000 after two months. On the date of delivery, the price of potatoes increases and Amar refuses to perform his promise. Rohit purchases 10 bags of potatoes for ₹ 5,500. He can receive ₹ 500 from Amar as ordinary damages arising directly from the breach.

25. Ancient Sources of Hindu Law:

(*i*) Shruti

(*ii*) Smriti

(*iii*) Digests and Commentaries and

(*iv*) Custom.

27. Sapindas is a term used in context of cousin marriages in Hinduism. The subject is to be counted as first generation, and the common ancestor defining Sapindas limit is to be within Sapindas limit. The theory of Sapinda marriage is based on exogamy. The Dharmashastra considered sex relationship with one's mother, or one's sister or one's daughter or with one's son's wife is highest sin in Hindu religion. In an ancient Hindu law, two theories of Sapinda relationship were take: (*a*) oblation theory and (*b*) particles of the same body theory. Hindu Marriage Act, 1955, section 3 on definition defines Sapindas in sub-section (f) as follows:

1. "Sapindas relationship with reference to any person extends as far as the third generation (inclusive) in the line of mother, and the fifth generation (inclusive) in the line of assent through the father, the line being traced upward in each case from the person concerned who is to be counted as the first generation.
2. Two persons are said to be "Sapindas" of each other if one is a lineal ascendant of the other within the limits of Sapindas relationship, or if they have common lineal ascendant who is within the limits of Sapindas relationship, or they have a common lineal ascendant who is within the limits of Sapindas relationship with reference to each of them.

28. Section 494 of the IPC provides about "Bigamy" as thus "Whoever, having a husband or wife living, marries again in any case in which such marriage is void by reason of its taking place during the life of such husband or wife shall be punished with imprisonment of either description for a term which may extend to seven years, and shall also be liable to fine". Bigamy has been made outlawed as it is a non-cognizable as well as a bailable crime in India.

The Indian Penal Code also recognizes also the fact that it is also a fraud on the part of the second wife/husband concerned to conceal the fact regarding the former marriage and doing such has been made punishable under section 495 of the IPC as such person committing such act shall be punishable with the imprisonment of either description for a term which may extend to maximum ten years and shall also be liable to fine.

29. The Government of India has also introduced the National Commission for Minorities (Repeal) Bill, 2004 in Lok Sabha on 23rd December, 2004. The Bill envisages dissolution of the existing Commission set up under Section 3 of the NCM Act, 1992. On dissolution of the Commission, the Members including Chairperson, Vice Chairperson and Members of the Commission shall vacate their offices. No compensation for pre-mature termination of the office is envisaged. It is envisaged to utilize the services of the Secretary and other officers and employees of the existing National Commission for Minorities for the proposed Commission. An amount of ₹ 303 lakhs has been provided for the National Commission for Minorities for the year 2004-05 (Non-Plan). The Repeal Bill will be effective after the Constitutional (One Hundred and Third Amendment) Bill, 2004 is enacted and come into force.

30. National Human Rights Commission is an independent body constituted by the Central Government and consists of highly knowledgeable team to work in the areas of human rights.

The composition of this Commission is:

- A Chairperson who is a retired Chief Justice of India
- One Member who is or has been a Judge of the Supreme Court
- One Member who is or has been the Chief Justice of a High Court
- Two persons having knowledge or practical experience in matters relating to Human Rights.

The President appoints the chairperson and the members of National Human Rights Commission, for which a committee nominates the names. This committee consists of Chairperson, the Prime Minister and the members including Home Minister, Leader of the Opposition in Lok Sabha, Leader of the Opposition in Rajya Sabha, Speaker and the Rajya Sabha Deputy Chairman.

31. The United Nations Commission on Sustainable Development (CSD) was established by the UN General Assembly in December 1992 to ensure effective follow-up of United Nations Conference on Environment and Development (UNCED), also known as the Earth Summit. From its inception, the CSD was highly participatory in structure and outlook, by engaging in its formal proceedings a wide range of official stakeholders and partners through innovative formulae.

At its eleventh session in 2003, the Commission decided on a multi-year work programme consisting of review and policy years. Since its establishment in 1992, the Commission has greatly advanced the sustainable development agenda within the international community.

At the United Nations Conference on Sustainable Development (Rio+20), Member States agreed to establish a high level political forum that will subsequently replace the Commission on Sustainable Development.

32. The Kyoto Protocol is an international agreement that aimed to reduce carbon dioxide (CO_2) emissions and the presence of greenhouse gases (GHG) in the atmosphere. The essential tenet of the Kyoto Protocol was that industrialized nations needed to lessen the amount of their CO_2 emissions.

The protocol was adopted in Kyoto, Japan in 1997, when greenhouse gases were rapidly threatening our climate, life on the earth, and the planet, itself.

33. Section 5 in The Information Technology Act, 2000: Legal recognition of [electronic signature]. Where any law provides that information or any other matter shall be authenticated by affixing the signature or any document shall be signed or bear the signature of any person, then, notwithstanding anything contained in such law, such requirement shall be deemed to have been satisfied, if such information or matter is authenticated by means of [electronic signature] affixed in such manner as may be prescribed by the Central Government.

Explanation: For the purposes of this section, "signed", with its grammatical variations and cognate expressions, shall, with reference to a person, mean affixing of his hand written signature or any mark on any document and the expression "signature" shall be construed accordingly.

34. A whistleblower is anyone who has and reports insider knowledge of illegal activities occurring in an organization. Whistleblowers can be employees, suppliers, contractors, clients, or any individual who becomes aware of illegal business activities. They are protected from retaliation under various programs created by the Occupational Safety and Health Administration (OSHA), Sarbanes Oxley Act, and the Securities and Exchange Commission (SEC). The protection of federal employees is under the Whistleblower Protection Act of 1989.

37. Article 75(3) provides for the Council of Ministers being Collectively Responsible to Lok Sabha. In the UK, the concept is that of Individual and Collective Responsibility of Ministers. Our Constitution, however, provides only for Collective Responsibility which means that there can be no no-confidence in a single Minister. The entire Council of Ministers is jointly responsible to Lok Sabha for all acts of Government. Therefore, it stands or falls together. If it loses the confidence of the House, the entire Council of Ministers must resign. Also, Collective Responsibility would mean that the Ministers must not speak in public in different voices.

39. In the Constitution of India, the power of Presidential Pardon is found in Article 72. It empowers the President to grant pardons, reprieves, respites or remissions of punishment in all cases where the punishment is for an offense against any law to which the executive power of the union extends. The same is also available against sentences of courts-martial and sentences of death. A parallel power is given to the Governor of a state under Article 161. A pardon may be absolute or conditional. It may be exercised at any time either before legal proceedings are taken or during their pendency or after conviction. The rejection of one clemency petition does not exhaust the pardoning power of the President.

In the judgment of Epuru Sudhakar v Government of Andhra Pradesh and Ors. The Court set aside a remission granted by the Governor of Andhra Pradesh on the ground that irrelevant and extraneous materials had entered into the decision making. The Report of the District Probation Officer which was one of the materials on which the decision was based, highlighted the fact that the prisoner was a 'Good Congress Worker' and that he had been defeated due to political conspiracy.

40. Article 253 of Constitution of India "Legislation for giving effect to international agreements".

Notwithstanding anything in the foregoing provisions of this Chapter, Parliament has power to make any law for the whole or any part of the territory of India for implementing any treaty, agreement or convention with any other country or countries or any decision made at any international conference, association or other body.

41. According to Austin, while every right is relative and has a correlative duty, every duty need not necessarily have a correlative right. In Austin's opinion some duties are absolute duties to which no corresponding rights are attached. According to Austin's analysis, there are four kinds of such duties:

1. duties not regarding persons (those owed to God and the lower animals),
2. duties owed to persons indefinitely (duties towards the community e.g. Duty not to commit nuisance), self regarding duties (duty owed to one self e.g. Duty not to commit suicide or duty not to become intoxicated.)
3. duty towards State.

As indicated above absolute duties are those which have no corresponding or correlative rights. Relative duties are those to which there is a corresponding right in some person or definite body of persons e.g., duty to pay one's debt to the creditor.

43. There are three exceptions to the general rule that a man is made to do so by the force of law what he is bound to do by a rule of law. They are as under:

1. Duties of imperfect obligation or imperfect duties:

The breach of an imperfect duly gives no cause of action. A time-barred debt, though a legal debt, cannot be enforced by law as the right to sue is destroyed.

2. Duties which cannot be specifically enforced after a breach has taken place: When once libel or defamation has been committed, its specific enforcement is not possible. The miscreant once he has published the libel cannot be made to undo that which he has already done.
3. Where the specific enforcement of the duty is inexpedient or inadvisable: The law, though capable of enforcing, refuses to enforce specific performance of a promise of marriage and instead allows damages.

44. Article 13 in The Constitution of India 1949 : Laws inconsistent with or in derogation of the fundamental rights:

1. All laws in force in the territory of India immediately before the commencement of this Constitution, in so far as they are inconsistent with the provisions of this Part, shall, to the extent of such inconsistency, be void
2. The State shall not make any law which takes away or abridges the rights conferred by this Part and any law made in contravention of this clause shall, to the extent of the contravention, be void.
3. In this article, unless the context otherwise requires law includes any Ordinance, order, bye law, rule, regulation, notification, custom or usages having in the territory of India the force of law; laws in force includes laws passed or made by Legislature or other competent authority in the territory of India before the commencement of this Constitution and not previously repealed, notwithstanding that any such law or any part thereof may not be then in operation either at all or in particular areas.
4. Nothing in this article shall apply to any amendment of this Constitution made under Article 368 Right of Equality

45. Article 30 in The Constitution of India 1949: Right of minorities to establish and administer educational institutions

1. All minorities, whether based on religion or language, shall have the right to establish and administer educational institutions of their choice.

1A. In making any law providing for the compulsory acquisition of any property of an educational institution established and administered by a minority, referred to in clause (1), the State shall ensure that the amount fixed by or determined under such law for the acquisition of such property is such as would not restrict or abrogate the right guaranteed under that clause.

2. The state shall not, in granting aid to educational institutions, discriminate against any educational institution on the ground that it is under the management of a minority, whether based on religion or language.

47. On 20 December 1991, Arthur Dunkel, the Director General of GATT, released the Draft Final Act embodying the results of the Uruguay Round of Multilateral Trade Negotiations which is known as the Dunkel Draft Text (DDT) or the Dunkel Package.

In 1993, the GATT was updated ('GATT 1994') to include new obligations upon its signatories. One of the most significant changes was the creation of the World Trade Organization (WTO). The 76 existing GATT members and the European Communities became the founding members of the WTO on 1 January 1995.

Article III: The WTO shall facilitate the implementation, administration and operation, and further the objectives, of this Agreement and of the Multilateral Trade Agreements, and shall also provide the framework for the implementation, administration and operation of the Plurilateral Trade Agreements.

The Sixth WTO Ministerial Conference was held in Hong Kong, China, 13-18 December 2005. In general, ministerial conferences are the WTO's highest decision-making body, meeting at least once every two years and providing political direction for the organization.

50. Under Section 361 in The Indian Penal Code the kidnapping from lawful guardianship. Whoever takes or entices any minor under 1[sixteen] years of age if a male, or under 2[eighteen] years of age if a female, or any person of unsound mind, out of the keeping of the lawful guardian of such minor or person of unsound mind, without the consent of such guardian, is said to kidnap such minor or person from lawful guardianship. *Explanation.* The words "lawful guardian" in this section include any person lawfully entrusted with the care or custody of such minor or other person.

Exception: This section does not extend to the act of any person who in good faith believes himself to be the father of an illegitimate child, or who in good faith believes himself to be entitled to lawful custody of such child, unless such act is committed for an immoral or unlawful purpose. STATE AMENDMENT

Manipur: In section 361 for the words 'eighteen' substitute the word 'fifteen'. [Vide Manipur Act 30 of 1950, sec. 3 (w.e.f. 16-4-1950), read with Act 81 of 1971, sec. 3 (w.e.f. 25-1-1972)]. COMMENTS—Inducement not immediate cause the accused was charged for kidnapping a minor girl, below 15 years of age from the lawful guardianship of her father. It was established that the accused had an earlier stage solicited or induced minor girl to leave her father's protection by conveying or indicating an encouraging suggestion, that he would give her shelter. Holding the accused liable for kidnapping under section 363, the Supreme Court said that the mere circumstances that his act was not the immediate cause of her leaving her parental home or guardian's custody would constitute no valid defence and would not absolve him from the offence of kidnapping.

51. Generally, a person is liable for his own wrongful acts and one does not incur any liability for the acts done by others. In certain cases, however, vicarious liability, that is the liability of one person for the act of another person, may arise. In order that the liability of A for the act done by B can arise, it is necessary that there should be certain kind of relationship between A and B, and the wrongful act should be, in certain way, connected with that relationship.

The common examples of such a liability are:

1. Liability of the principal for the tort of his agent;
2. Liability of partners of each other's tort;
3. Liability of the master for the tort of his servant.

So Vicarious Liability deals with cases where one person is liable for the acts of others. In the field of Torts it is considered to be an exception to the general rule that a person is liable for his own acts only. It is based on the principle of qui facit per se per alium facit per se, which means, "He who does an act through another is deemed in law to do it himself". So in a case of vicarious liability both the person at whose behest the act is done as well as the person who does the act are liable. Thus, Employers are vicariously liable for the torts of their employees that are committed during the course of employment.

Servant and Independent Contractor: A servant and independent contractor are both employed to do some work of the employer but there is a difference in the legal relationship which the employer has with them. A servant is engaged under a contract of services whereas an independent contractor is engaged under a contract for services. The liability of the employer for the wrongs committed by his servant is more onerous than his iiability in respect of wrongs committed by an independent contractor. If a servant does a wrongful act in the course of his employment, the master is liable for it. The servant, of course, is also liable. The wrongful act of the servant is deemed to be the act of the master as well. "The doctrine of liability of the master for act of his servant is based on the maxim respondeat superior, which means 'let the principal be liable' and it puts the master in the same position as he if had done the act himself. It also derives validity from the maxim qui facit per alium facit per se, which means 'he who does an act through another is deemed in law to do it himself'." Since for the wrong done by the servant, the master can also be made liable vicariously, the plaintiff has a choice to bring an action against either or both of them. Their liability is joint and several as they are considered to be joint tortfeasors. The reason for the maxim respondeat superior seems to be the better position of the master to meet the claim because of his larger pocket and also ability to pass on the burden of liability through insurance. The liability arises even though the servant acted against the express instruction, and for no benefit of his master.

53. Any agreement amongst enterprises or persons at different stages or levels of the production chain in different markets, in respect of production, supply, distribution, storage, sale or price of, or trade in goods or provision of services, including: (*a*) tie-in arrangement; (*b*) exclusive supply agreement; (*c*) exclusive distribution agreement; (*d*) refusal to deal; (*e*) resale price maintenance, shall be an agreement in contravention of sub-section (1) if such agreement causes or is likely to cause an appreciable adverse effect on competition in India. *Explanation.* For the purposes of this sub-section:

(*a*) "tie-in arrangement" includes any agreement requiring a purchaser of goods, as a condition of such purchase, to purchase some other goods;

(*b*) "exclusive supply agreement" includes any agreement restricting in any manner the purchaser in the course of his trade from acquiring or otherwise dealing in any goods other than those of the seller or any other person;

(*c*) "exclusive distribution agreement" includes any agreement to limit, restrict or withhold the output or supply of any goods or allocate any area or market for the disposal or sale of the goods;

(*d*) "refusal to deal" includes any agreement which restricts, or is likely to restrict, by any method the persons or classes of persons to whom goods are sold or from whom goods are bought;

(*e*) "resale price maintenance" includes any agreement to sell goods on condition that the prices to be charged on the resale by the purchaser shall be the prices stipulated by the seller unless it is clearly stated that prices lower than those prices may be charged.

55. Section 5 in The Sale of Goods Act, 1930:

(1) A contract of sale is made by an offer to buy or sell goods for a price and the acceptance of such offer. The contract may provide for the immediate delivery of the goods or immediate payment of the price or both, or for the delivery or payment by instalments, or that the delivery or payment or both shall be postponed.

(2) Subject to the provisions of any law for the time being in force, a contract of sale

may be made in writing or by word of mouth, or partly in writing and partly by word of mouth or may be implied from the conduct of the parties.

57. The Muslim Women (Protection of Rights on Divorce) Act, 1986

(1) Short title and extent:

(*a*) This Act may be called the Muslim Women (Protection of Rights on Divorce) Act, 1986.

(*b*) It extends to the whole of India except the State of Jammu and Kashmir.

In this Act, unless the context otherwise requires:

2(*a*). "divorced woman" means a Muslim woman who was married according to Muslim law, and has been divorced by, or has obtained divorce from, her husband in accordance with Muslim law;

2(*b*). "iddat period" means, in the case of a divorced woman,:

(*i*) three menstrual courses after the date of divorce, if she is subject to menstruation;

(*ii*) three lunar months after her divorce, if she is not subject to menstruation; and

(*iii*) if she is enceinte at the time of her divorce, the period between the divorce and the delivery of her child or the termination of her pregnancy, whichever is earlier;

2(*c*). "Magistrate" means a Magistrate of the First Class exercising jurisdiction under the Code of Criminal Procedure, 1973 (2 of 1974) in the area where the divorced woman resides.

2(*d*). "prescribed" means prescribed by rules made under this Act.

3. Maher or other properties of Muslim woman to be given to her at the time of divorce:

(1) Notwithstanding anything contained in any other law for the time being in force, a divorced woman shall be entitled to:

(*a*) a reasonable and fair provision and maintenance to be made and paid to her within the iddat period by her former husband;

(*b*) where she herself maintains the children born to her before or after her divorce, a reasonable and fair provision and maintenance to be made and paid by her former husband for a period of two years from the respective dates of birth of such children;

(*c*) an amount equal to the sum of mahr or dower agreed to be paid to her at the time of her marriage or at any time thereafter according to Muslim law; and

(*d*) all the properties given to her before or at the time of marriage or after the marriage by her relatives or friends or the husband or any relatives of the husband or his friends.

(2) Where a reasonable and fair provision and maintenance or the amount of mahr or dower due has not been made or paid or the properties referred to in clause (*d*) of sub-section (1) have not been delivered to a divorced woman on her divorce, she or any one duly authorised by her may, on her behalf, make an application to a Magistrate for an order for payment of such provision and maintenance, mahr or dower or the delivery of properties, as the case may be.

(3) Where an application has been made under sub-section (2) by a divorced woman, the Magistrate may, if he is satisfied that:

(*a*) her husband having sufficient means, has failed or neglected to make or pay her within the iddat period a reasonable and fair provision and maintenance for her and the children; or

(*b*) the amount equal to the sum of mahr or dower has not been paid or that the properties referred to in clause (*d*) of sub-section (1) have not been delivered to her make an order, within one month of the date of the filing of the application, directing her former husband to pay such reasonable and fair provision and maintenance to the divorced woman as he may determine as fit and proper having regard to the needs of the divorced woman, the standard of life enjoyed by her during her marriage and the means of her former husband or, as the case may be, for the payment of such mahr or dower or the delivery of such properties referred to in clause (d) of sub-section (1) to the divorced woman: Provided that if the Magistrate finds it impracticable to dispose of the application within the said period, he may, for reasons to be recorded by him, dispose of the application after the said period.

(4) If any person against whom an order has been made under sub-section (3) fails without sufficient cause to comply with the order, the Magistrate may issue a warrant for levying the amount of maintenance or maher or dower due in the manner provided for levying fines under the Code of Criminal Procedure, 1973 (2 of 1974) and may sentence such person, for the whole or part of any amount remaining unpaid after the execution of the warrant, to imprisonment for a term which may extend to one year or until payment if sooner made, subject to such person being heard in defence and the said sentence being imposed according to the provisions of the said Code.

59. The Econom:c and Social Council is one of the principal organs of the UN. It is responsible for the work of the Economic and Social for the work of the Economic and Social affairs of the bodies of the UN. It has 54 states as its members. They are elected by the General Assembly for three years term. The election of the States is based on geographical distribution of regions of the world. It meets once in a year. This is the main body mostly looks after the affairs of the Human Rights and recommends to the UN bodies. The responsibilities of Economic and Social Council regarding improvement and protection of human rights is laid down under Article 68 of UN Charter.

The Charter of United Nations lays down guiding principles with regard to the promotion of human rights and fundamental freedoms. The first step was towards the implementation of U.N. Charter provisions, under the authority of Article 68. Charter based bodies usually reach a final decision on a matter related to human rights through the mechanism of voting and generally pass resolutions documenting such decisions.

60. The provision relating to 'solid waste management' is contained under Schedule XII of the Constitution of India.

TWELFTH SCHEDULE (Article 243-W)

1. Urban planning including town planning.
2. Regulation of land use and construction of buildings.
3. Planning for economic and social development.
4. Roads and bridges.
5. Water supply for domestic, industrial and commercial purposes.
6. Public health, sanitation conservancy and solid waste management.
7. Fire services.

8. Urban forestry, protection of the environment and promotion of ecological aspects.
9. Safeguarding the interests of weaker sections of society, including the handicapped and mentally retarded.
10. Slum improvement and upgradation.
11. Urban poverty alleviation.
12. Provision of urban amenities and facilities such as parks, gardens, playgrounds.
13. Promotion of cultural, educational and aesthetic aspects.
14. Burials and burial grounds, cremations, cremation grounds and electric crematoriums.
15. Cattle ponds; prevention of cruelty to animals.
16. Vital statistics including registration of births and deaths.
17. Public amenities including street lighting, parking lots, bus stops and public conveniences.
18. Regulation of slaughterhouses and tanneries.

61. ELEVENTH SCHEDULE (Article 243G)

1. Agriculture, including agricultural extension.
2. Land improvement, implementation of land reforms, land consolidation and soil conservation.
3. Minor irrigation, water management and watershed development.
4. Animal husbandry, dairying and poultry.
5. Fisheries.
6. Social forestry and farm forestry.
7. Minor forest produce.
8. Small scale industries, including food processing industries.
9. Khadi, village and cottage industries.
10. Rural housing.
11. Drinking water.
12. Fuel and fodder.
13. Roads, culverts, bridges, ferries, waterways and other means of communication.
14. Rural electrification, including distribution of electricity.
15. Non-conventional energy sources.
16. Poverty alleviation programme.
17. Education, including primary and secondary schools.
18. Technical training and vocational education.
19. Adult and non-formal education.
20. Libraries.
21. Cultural activities
22. Markets and fairs.
23. Health and sanitation, including hospitals, primary health centres and dispensaries.
24. Family welfare.
25. Women and child development.
26. Social welfare, including welfare of the handicapped and mentally retarded.
27. Welfare of the weaker sections, and in particular, of the Scheduled Castes and the Scheduled Tribes.
28. Public distribution system.
29. Maintenance of community assets.

62. The most prominent case with respect to 'originality' under the Indian Copyright Law is the Eastern Book Company v DCB Modak. This judgment gave rise to two doctrines *i.e.* modicum of creativity and the skill and judgment test.

64. In a presidential system, the head of the government leads an executive, that is distinct from the legislature. Here, the head of the government and the head of the state are one and the same. Also, a key feature is that the executive is not responsible to the legislature.

Features of the Presidential System

1. The executive (President) can veto acts by the legislature.

2. The President has a fixed tenure and cannot be removed by a vote of no-confidence in the legislature.
3. Generally, the President has the power to pardon or commute judicial sentences awarded to criminals.
4. The President is elected directly by the people or by an electoral college.

67. **Article 371C :** Manipur special provision under Article 371C in the case of Manipur is similar to 371B for Assam. Here, too, the president may provide for the Constitution and functions of a committee of Legislative Assembly of the state, but consisting of members elected from the hill areas of Manipur.

Article 371J grants special status to six backward districts of Hyderabad-Karnataka region. The special provision requires that a separate development board be established for these regions (similar to Maharashtra and Gujarat) and also ensures local reservation in education and government jobs.

Article 371F was incorporated into the Constitution in 1975. It states that the Legislative Assembly shall consist of not less than 30 members. In order to protect the rights and interests of the different sections of the population in the state of Sikkim, seats in the assembly are provided to people of these different sections.

Article 371G : The Legislative Assembly of the state of Mizoram must consist of not less than 40 members. In addition, following the same provisions as Nagaland, an act of Parliament would not apply to Mizoram in matters relating to religious or social practices of Mizo, Mizo customary law and procedure, administration of civil or criminal justice involving decisions according to Mizo customary law, ownership and transfer of land and its resources.

68. **Article 38(1)** of the ICJ divides the sources of international law into those of a primary and secondary nature. The primary sources, which the Court will consider in its decisions, include conventions (or treaties), customary law, and general principles recognized by civilized nations.

Article 62 remained a dead letter for almost seventy years. The Chamber constituted to settle the frontier dispute between El Salvador and Honduras has changed this picture, and has allowed Nicaragua to intervene with respect to the legal régime of the Gulfof Fonseca. But it only accorded a non-party status to Nicaragua. However, the full Court had refused permission to intervene in two earlier cases with arguments that were based on the premiss of a party status for the intervening State. Only a future decision on a request for permission to intervene can tell whether the full Court will endorse the stances taken by the Chamber.

Article 36. 1: The jurisdiction of the Court comprises all cases which the parties refer to it and all matters specially provided for in the Charter of the United Nations or in treaties and conventions in force.

Article 41: ICJ may, without prejudice to the decision as to its jurisdiction in the case, where necessary, indicate interim measures for the protection of the rights of one of the parties.

69. **Section 92:** Act done in good faith for benefit of a person without consent—Nothing is an offence by reason of any harm which it may cause to a person for whose benefit it is done in good faith, even without that person's consent, if the circumstances are such that it is impossible for that person to signify consent, or if that person is incapable of giving consent, and has no guardian or other person in lawful charge of him from whom it is possible to obtain consent in time for the thing to be done with benefit.

Section 423: Dishonest or fraudulent execution of deed of transfer containing false statement of consideration.

Whoever dishonestly or fraudulently signs, executes or becomes a party to any deed or instrument which purports to transfer or subject to any charge any property, or any interest therein, and which contains any false statement relating to the consideration for such transfer or charge, or relating to the person or persons for whose use or benefit it is really intended to operate, shall be punished with imprisonment of either description for a term which may extend to two years, or with fine, or with both.

Section 326A: Voluntarily causing grievous hurt by use of acid, etc.: Whoever causes permanent or partial damage or deformity to, or bums or maims or disfigures or disables, any part or parts of the body of a person or causes grievous hurt by throwing acid on or by administering acid to that person, or by using any other means with the intention of causing or with the knowledge that he is likely to cause such injury or hurt, shall be punished with imprisonment of either description for a term which shall not be less than ten years but which may extend to imprisonment for life, and with fine.

Section 381: Theft by clerk or servant of property in possession of master: Whoever, being a clerk or servant, or being employed in the capacity of a clerk or servant, commits theft in respect of any property in the possession of his master or employer, shall be punished with imprisonment of either description for a term which may extend to seven years, and shall also be liable to fine.

70. Section 11 in the Consumer Protection Act, 1986

(1) Subject to the other provisions of this Act, the District Forum shall have jurisdiction to entertain complaints where the value of the goods or services and the compensation, if any, claimed 1 [does not exceed rupees twenty lakhs].

(2) A complaint shall be instituted in a District Forum within the local limits of whose jurisdiction.

Section 17: Jurisdiction of the State Commission

Subject to the other provisions of this Act, the State Commission shall have jurisdiction:

(*a*) to entertain

(*i*) complaints where the value of the goods or services and compensation, if any, claimed exceeds rupees [42 five lakhs but does not exceed rupees twenty lakhs 42]; and

(*ii*) appeals against the orders of any District Forum within the State; and

(*b*) to call for the records and pass appropriate orders in any consumer dispute which is pending before or has been decided by any District Forum within the State where it appears to the State Commission that such District Forum has exercised a jurisdiction not vested in it by law, or has failed to exercise a jurisdiction so vested or has acted in exercise of its jurisdiction illegally or with material irregularity.

Section 21 in the Consumer Protection Act, 1986—Subject to the other provisions of this Act, the National Commission shall have jurisdiction:

(*a*) to entertain

(*i*) complaints where the value of the goods or services and compensation, if any, claimed exceeds 1 [rupees one crore]; and

(*ii*) appeals against the orders of any State Commission; and

(*b*) to call for the records and pass appropriate orders in any consumer dispute which is pending before or has been decided by any State Commission where it appears to the National Commission that such State Commission has exercised a jurisdiction not vested in it by law, or has failed to exercise a jurisdiction so vested, or has acted in the exercise of its jurisdiction illegally or with material irregularity.

Section 22A: Power to set aside ex parte orders. Where an order is passed by the National Commission ex parte against the opposite party or a complainant, as the case may be, the aggrieved party may apply to the Commission to set aside the said order in the interest of justice.

71. **Abridged Prospectus** is the actual summary of a prospectus. According to section 2(1) of the Act "abridged prospectus" means a memorandum containing such salient features of a prospectus as may be specified by the Securities and Exchange Board by making regulations in this behalf.

A deemed prospectus has been stated under section 25(1) of the Companies Act, 2013. When any company to offer securities for sale to the public, allots or agrees to allot securities, the document will be considered as a deemed prospectus through which the offer is made to the public for sale.

Shelf prospectus is stated under section 31 of the Companies Act, 2013. Shelf prospectus is issued when a company or any public financial institution offers one or more securities to the public. A company shall provide a validity period of the prospectus, which should not be more than one year.

As per Section 32 of Companies Act, 2013, a company proposing to make an offer of securities may issue a red herring prospectus prior to the issue of a prospectus. It is basically a prospectus which is used in the public issue to attract different investors.

73. **"Hazardous substance"** means any substance or preparation which is defined as hazardous substance in the Environment (Protection) Act, 1986 (29 of 1986), and exceeding such quantity as specified or may be specified by the Central Government under the Public Liability Insurance Act, 1991 (6 of 1991)-Section 2(f) in The National Green Tribunal Act, 2010

- "Environment" includes water, air and land and the inter-relationship, which exists among and between water, air and land and human beings, other living creatures, plants, micro-organism and property)—Section 2(c) in The National Green Tribunal Act, 2010.
- "Handling", in relation to any hazardous substance, means the manufacture, processing, treatment, package, storage, transportation, use, collection, destruction, conversion, offering for sale, transfer or the like of such hazardous substance)—Section 2(e) in The National Green Tribunal Act, 2010.
- "Accident" means an accident involving a fortuitous or sudden or unintended occurrence while handling any hazardous substance or equipment, or plant, or vehicle resulting in continuous or intermittent or repeated exposure to death, of, or, injury to, any person or damage to any property or environment but does not include an accident by reason only of war or civil disturbance)—Section 2(a) in The National Green Tribunal Act, 2010.

75. **Murli S. Deora Vs. Union of India:** The instant case is a writ petition, filed in the Supreme Court of India under Article 32 of the Constitution of India by Murli S. Deora, regarding the prohibition of smoking in the public places. The two-judge bench comprising of M. B. Shah and R. P. Sethi heard the petition.

Sunil Batra v. Delhi Administration: The case of Sunil Batra v. Delhi Administration

& Others stands out in our legal history as a landmark judgment that helped secure the fundamental rights of prisoners. It was unique in a multitude of ways, one being that the petitioner in question was a convict on death row, something very much unheard of at that time. It brought to light a host of issues, including the clashes between various fundamental rights and the Prison Act of 1874.

Hussainara Khatoon v. State of Bihar: The present case is a landmark judgment on the speedy trial of cases that came to be recognized as a fundamental right of every accused person. It is a facet of the rightful administration of justice. The Constitutional obligation upon State to undertake the protection of rights of individuals under Article 21 is inclusive of the duty to ensure there is a speedy trial of cases. It also ensures the right to access free legal services to the poor as an essential part of Article 21 of the Constitution.

Rural Litigation and Entitlement Kendra v. State of Uttar Pradesh: The Supreme Court had received a writ petition from Rural Litigation and Entitlement Kendra regarding the unauthorised and illegal operation of lime-stone quarries in the Mussoorie Hill range, India. It was argued that the quarries caused a hazard to healthy environment and affected the perennial water springs.

The Court thereafter had appointed an expert committee for the purpose of inspecting the lime-stone quarries. They had divided the lime-stone quarries into three categories according to the grade of the adverse impact of the mining operations (category A had the least pronounced adverse impact, category B had a more pronounced adverse impact and category C had been directed to be closed down).

On a perusal of the previous order dated 12th March, 1985 the court was of the view that the said order had covered almost all the relevant aspects and had touched upon every issue germane to the matter. Besides that, it emphasized that preservation of the environment and keeping the ecological balance unaffected was a task which not only Governments but also every citizen had to undertake. It was a social obligation and every Indian citizen was reminded that it was his fundamental duty as enshrined in Article 51 A(g) of the Constitution.

77. Kharak Singh vs The State of U. P. & Others on 18 December, 1962.

Satwant Singh Sawhney vs D. Ramarathnam, Assistant Passport officer on 10 April, 1967.

Francis Coralie Mullin vs The Administrator, Union Territory of Delhi on 13 January, 1981.

Olga Tellis & Ors vs Bombay Municipal Corporation on 10 July, 1985.

National Legal Services Authority vs Union of India & Ors on 15 April, 2014.

79. **Section 449:** House-trespass in order to commit offence punishable with death.

Whoever commits house-trespass in order to the committing of any offence punishable with death, shall be punished, with imprisonment for life, or with rigorous imprisonment for a term not exceeding ten years, and shall also be liable to fine.

Section 450: House-trespass in order to commit offence punishable with imprisonment for life.

Whoever commits house-trespass in order to the committing of any offence punishable with imprisonment for life, shall be punished with imprisonment of either description for a term not exceeding ten years, and shall also be liable to fine.

Section 451: House-trespass in order to commit offence punishable with imprisonment

Whoever commits house-trespass in order to the committing of any offence punishable with imprisonment, shall be punished with imprisonment of either description for a term which may extend to two years, and shall also be liable to fine; and if the offence intended to be committed is theft, the term of the imprisonment may be extended to seven years.

Section 454: Lurking house-trespass or house-breaking in order to commit offence punishable with imprisonment.

Whoever commits lurking house-trespass or house-breaking, in order to the committing of any offence punishable with imprisonment, shall be punished with imprisonment of either description for a term which may extend to three years, and shall also be liable to fine; and if the offence intended to be committed is theft, the term of the imprisonment may be extended to ten years.

Section 457: Lurking house-trespass or house-breaking by night in order to commit offence punishable with imprisonment.

Whoever commits lurking house-trespass by night, or house-breaking by night in order to the committing of any offence punishable with imprisonment, shall be punished with imprisonment of either description for a term which may extend to five years, and shall also be liable to fine; and, if the offence intended to be committed is theft, the term of the imprisonment may be extended to fourteen years.

82. Mohd. Ahmed Khan vs Shah Bano Begum and Ors on 23 April, 1985

Smt. Sarla Mudgal vs Union of India & Ors on 10 May, 1995

Danial Latifi vs Union of India on 28 September, 2001

John Vallamattom vs Union of India on 21 July, 2003

83. The objective of the 1985 Vienna Convention is to preserve human health, and to protect the environment from any harmful effects of the depletion of the ozone layer.

The objective of the 1987 Montreal Protocol is to repair the ozone layer through the worldwide control, reduction and ultimately elimination of production and consumption of ozone depleting substances. The latest extension of the Montreal Protocol in 2016 —the Kigali Amendment — regulates hydrofluorocarbons as well. These chemicals are currently in use as a substitute for ozone-depleting substances, but are themselves potent greenhouse gases.

Kyoto Protocol, in full Kyoto Protocol to the United Nations Framework Convention on Climate Change, international treaty, named for the Japanese city in which it was adopted in December 1997, that aimed to reduce the emission of gases that contribute to global warming.

The Copenhagen Climate Change summit was a gathering of world leaders in the capital of Denmark over a two week period from 7th-18th December 2009. The aims of this meeting was to come up with a deal to replace the Kyoto protocol, a deal which is to expire in 2012.

The United Nations Climate Change Conference in Durban, South Africa, was held from 28 November - 11 December 2011. The conference involved a series of events, including the seventeenth session of the Conference of the Parties (COP 17) to the UN Framework Convention on Climate Change (UNFCCC) and the seventh meeting of the Conference of the Parties serving as the Meeting of Parties to the Kyoto Protocol (CMP 7).

86. Article 245 defines the ambit or territorial limits of legislative powers: Subject to the Constitutional provisions, Parliament may make laws for whole or any part of territory of India, and a State Legislature for the territory of that State.

No law made by Parliament shall be deemed to be invalid on the ground that it would have extra territorial operation.

87. The International Court of Justice shall be the principal judicial organ of the United Nations. It shall function in accordance with the annexed Statute, which is based upon the Statute of the Permanent Court of International Justice and forms an integral part of the present Charter.

The International Court of Justice is composed of 15 judges elected to nine-year terms of office by the United Nations General Assembly and the Security Council. The Court may not include more than one national of the same State.

88. Indian Penal Code (IPC) S. 356. Assault or criminal force in attempt to commit theft of property carried by a person:

Whoever assaults or uses criminal force to any person, in attempting to commit theft on any property which that person is then wearing or carrying, shall be punished with imprisonment of either description for a term which may extend to two years, or with fine, or with both.

89. Section 11 in The Hindu Adoptions and Maintenance Act, 1956

In every adoption, the following conditions must be complied with:

(*i*) if the adoption is of a son, the adoptive father or mother by whom the adoption is made must not have a Hindu son, son's son or son's son's son (whether by legitimate blood relationship or by adoption) living at the time of adoption;

(*ii*) if the adoption is of a daughter, the adoptive father or mother by whom the adoption is made must not have a Hindu daughter or son's daughter (whether by legitimate blood relationship or by adoption) living at the time of adoption;

(*iii*) if the adoption is by a male and the person to be adopted is a female, the adoptive father is at least twenty-one years older than the person to be adopted;

(*iv*) if the adoption is by a female and the person to be adopted is a male, the adoptive mother is at least twenty-one years older than the person to be adopted;

(*v*) the same child may not be adopted simultaneously by two or more persons;

(*vi*) the child to be adopted must be actually given and taken in adoption by the parents or guardian concerned or under their authority with intent to transfer the child from the family of its birth 1 [or in the case of an abandoned child or child whose parentage is not known, from the place or family where it has been brought up] to the family of its adoption.

Previous Years' Paper (Solved)

National Testing Agency (NTA)

UGC-NET Junior Research Fellowship & Assistant Professor Eligibility Exam

Law, December-2019*

PAPER-II

Note: *This paper contains* ***hundred (100)*** *objective type questions of* ***two (2)*** *marks each.* ***All questions*** *are* ***compulsory***.

1. Which of the following statements are correct?

(*a*) Article 353 of Constitution of India deals with effect of Proclamation of Emergency

(*b*) Article 354 of Constitution of India deals with income generating power of the Governor during Emergency

(*c*) Article 355 of the Constitution of India deals with duty of Union to protect states against External aggression and armed rebellion

(*d*) Article 356 of the Constitution of India deals with imposition of Emergency during Local disturbance by militants or terrorists

Choose the correct option:

A. (*a*) and (*b*) B. (*a*) and (*c*)
C. (*b*) and (*c*) D. (*c*) and (*d*)

2. 'A' in India, instigates 'B' a foreigner in Goa, to commit a murder in Goa. 'A' is guilty of:

A. Culpable homicide not amounting to murder
B. Committing the offence of murder
C. Criminal conspiracy
D. Abetting the murder

3. Consider the following statements and point out which statements are related to Positivism

(*a*) Laws are command

(*b*) Analysis of legal concept is distinct from Sociological and Historical analysis

(*c*) Decisions can be deducted logically with recourse to morality

(*d*) The 'Law as it is' has to be kept separate from 'Law ought to be'

Choose the correct option:

A. (a), (*b*) and (*c*) only
B. (*a*), (*b*) and (*d*) only
C. (*b*), (*c*) and (*d*) only
D. (*a*) and (*d*) only

4. Which sections of Hindu Marriage Act, 1955 deal with matrimonial remedy of divorce?

(*a*) Section 13 (*b*) Section 13 (1-A)
(*c*) Section 17 (*d*) Section 13-B

Choose the correct option:

A. (*a*), (*c*) and (*d*) only
B. (*b*), (*c*) and (*d*) only
C. (*a*), (*b*) and (*d*) only
D. (*a*), (*b*) and (*c*) only

5. Given below are two statements—one is labelled as Assertion (A) and the other is labelled as Reason (R).

Assertion (A) : Special provisions in Insurance law are required as to compensation in case of hit and run motor accidents.

Reason (R) : Section 161 of the Motor Vehicles Act, 1988, makes special provisions for payment or compensation in respect of the death of, or grevious hurt to, persons resulting from hit and run motor accidents.

**Online exam held on 03-12-2019.*

In the light of the above two statements choose the correct option.

A. Both (A) and (R) are true and (R) is not the correct explanation of (A)

B. Both (A) and (R) are true and (R) is the correct explanation of (A)

C. (A) is true, but (R) is false

D. (A) is false, but (R) is true

6. Which of the following is/are true about Bill of Exchange?

(*a*) A Bill of Exchange, requires in its inception of two parties

(*b*) A Bill of Exchange or draft is a written order by the drawer of drawee to pay money to the payee

(*c*) Bill of Exchange are primarily used in the International trade and are written orders by one person to his bank to pay the bearer a specific sum on a specific date

(*d*) Definition of Bill of Exchange is mentioned in the section 6 of the Negotiable Instrument Act

Choose the most appropriate option:

A. (*a*) and (*d*) B. (*a*), (*b*) and (*d*)
C. (*b*) and (*c*) D. (*c*) and (*d*)

7. Mention the following decisions in a chronological order on Extradition:

(*a*) Mubarak Ali Ahmed *vs* State of Bombay

(*b*) Hans Muller of Nurremberg *vs* Suptt. Presidency Jail Calcutta and Others

(*c*) Ram Babu Saxena *vs* State

(*d*) State of Madras *vs* C.G. Menon

Choose the correct option:

A. (*d*), (*c*), (*a*), (*b*) B. (*c*), (*d*), (*b*), (*a*)
C. (*b*), (*a*), (*d*), (*c*) D. (*d*), (*c*), (*b*), (*a*)

8. Arrange the provisions of Hindu Succession Act, 1956 in chronological order (Section wise):

(*a*) Presumption in case of simultaneous death

(*b*) Failure of heirs

(*c*) Act not to apply to certain properties

(*d*) Full blood preferred to half blood

Choose the correct option:

A. (*a*), (*b*), (*c*), (*d*) B. (*d*), (*c*), (*b*), (*a*)
C. (*c*), (*d*), (*a*), (*b*) D. (*d*), (*a*), (*c*), (*b*)

9. Arrange the following enactments in chronological order enacted to provide social justice:

(*a*) Equal Remuneration Act

(*b*) Immoral Traffic (Prevention) Act

(*c*) Medical Termination of Pregnancy Act

(*d*) Maternity Benefit Act

Choose the correct option:

A. (*a*), (*b*), (*c*), (*d*)

B. (*b*), (*c*), (*a*), (*d*)

C. (*b*), (*d*), (*c*), (*a*)

D. (*d*), (*c*), (*b*), (*a*)

10. Section 3(1) of the Trade Marks Act, 1999 deals with the provision relating to:

A. Refusal of registration

B. Application for registration

C. Appointment of Registrar of Trade Marks

D. Correction and amendment in the application

11. In which of the following cases our Supreme Court held that so far as the guarantee of equal protection in Article 14 is concerned, any State action—Executive, Legislative or Judicial, which contravenes Article 14 is void?

A. Amir Abbas *vs* State of M.B.

B. Naresh Mirajkar *vs* State of Bihar

C. Budhan *vs* State of Bihar

D. Himmatlal *vs* State of M.P.

12. Under Muslim Law, marriage with a woman, whose husband is alive, is:

A. Valid B. Sahih
C. Void D. Irregular

13. Arrange the provisions of Trade mark Act, 1999 in chronological order (section wise):

(*a*) classification of goods and services

(*b*) regulation in case of honest concurrent use etc

(*c*) limitation as to colour

(*d*) absolute grounds for refusal or registration

Choose the correct option:
A. (a), (b), (c), (d) B. (a), (c), (d), (b)
C. (a), (d), (c), (b) D. (b), (c), (d), (a)

14. Which of the following Section of the Patent Act, 1970 provides for the subject matters that are not invention under the Act?
A. Section 7 B. Section 3
B. Section 10 D. Section 11

15. Arrange the following judgements on Torts in Chronological order:
(a) Asbhy *vs* White
(b) MC Mehta *vs* Union of India
(c) Reyland *vs* Fletcher
(d) Donoghue *vs* Stevenson
Choose the correct option:
A. (b), (d), (c), (a) B. (a), (c), (d), (b)
C. (a), (c), (b), (d) D. (d), (b), (a), (c)

16. Mention the following cases in a chronological order on Election Commission:
(a) Kuldip Nayar *vs* Union of India
(b) T.N. Seshan *vs* Union of India
(c) People's Union for Civil Liberties *vs* Union of India
(d) S.S. Dhanoa *vs* Union of India
Choose the correct option:
A. (b), (c), (d), (a) B. (c), (d), (b), (a)
C. (a), (d), (b), (c) D. (d), (b), (a), (c)

17. Match the following:

List-I	List-II
(a) Exemplary damages	(i) MC Mehta *vs* Kamalnath
(b) Evaluation of cleanliness of various fuels	(ii) Sterilite Industries
(c) Public Trust Doctrine	(iii) Intergenerational equity
(d) Right of each generation to benefit from the past generation and to preserve such heritage for future	(iv) Bhurelal Committee

Choose correct option from those given below:

	(a)	(b)	(c)	(d)
A.	(i)	(ii)	(iii)	(iv)
B.	(ii)	(iv)	(i)	(iii)
C.	(iv)	(ii)	(i)	(iii)
D.	(iv)	(iii)	(i)	(ii)

18. Who among the following said that there is in essence, no difference between the legal personality of a company and that of an individual?
A. Maitland B. Dicey
C. Gierke D. Kelsen

19. "Human dignity is the Quintessence of Human Rights". This has been stated by:
A. Justice V.R. Krishna Iyer
B. Justice J.S. Verma
C. Justice Kuldeep Singh
D. Justice Ranganath Mishra

20. "In the British Constitution there is no such thing as the absolute seperarion of Legislative, Executive and Judicial powers. In practice it is inevitable that they overlap. In the Constitution of France and U.S.A. attempts to keep the organs of the government rigidly apart have been made but have proved unsuccessful". This position of doctrine of separation of powers has been summed-up by:
A. Prof. Ullman
B. Prof. K.T. Shah
C. Wade and Phillips
D. Donoghmore Committee

21. Which of the following statements are correct as per Article 111 of agreements establishing WTO? The main functions of the WTO are:
(a) To administer and promote agreements on individual and multinational agreements;
(b) To administer the rules and procedures governing the settlement of disputes;
(c) To administer the Trade Policy Review Mechanism (TPRM)

(*d*) To Coordinate IMF, TBRD and World Bank on regional economic policies.

Choose the correct option:

A. (*a*) and (*b*)
B. (*a*) and (*c*)
C. (*b*) and (*c*)
D. (*c*) and (*d*)

22. The expression "Minority" is a relative term and is referred to, to represent the linguistic or religious sections or groups forming less than 50% of the total population of the State, stated by the Supreme Court in the following case.

A. T.M.A. Pai Foundation *vs* State of Karnatka
B. P.A. Inamdar *vs* State of Maharashtra
C. Islamic Academy of Eduction *vs* State of Karnataka
D. Usha Mehta *vs* State of Maharashtra

23. Section 9 of the Geographical Indication of Goods (Registration and Protection) Act, 1999 provides for:

A. Prohibition of Registration of Certain geographical indications
B. Registration of Homonymous geographical indications
C. Geographical Indication Registry and Office thereof
D. Register of Geographical Indications

24. The Supreme Court in regard to Section 34 of Indian Penal Code observed that the existence of a common intention among the participants in a crime is the essential element for application of this section. It is not necessary that the act of the several persons charged with commission of an offence jointly must be the same or identically similar. In which of the following case the above observation was made by the Supreme Court?

A. Ashok Kumar *vs* State of Punjab
B. Shankar Narayan Bhadolkar *vs* State of Maharashtra
C. Gurubachan Singh *vs* State of Punjab
D. S.C. Bahri *vs* State of Bihar

25. Which of the following is not a valid defence in tort?

A. Private Defence
B. *Volenti non fit injuria*
C. *Vis major*
D. *Ex dolo malo non Oritur actio*

26. A valid contract can be entered into between parties under Indian Contract Act. Which of the following gives legal recognition to such contract.

(*a*) Section 10-A of Information Technology Act
(*b*) Section 65-B of Indian Evidence Act
(*c*) Section 1(4) of Information Technology Act
(*d*) Section 63 of Indian Evidence Act

Choose the correct option:

A. (*a*) and (*d*) B. (*a*) and (*b*)
C. (*a*) and (*c*) D. (*c*) and (*d*)

27. "The International Court of Justice is indeed a sine *qua* non for the establishment of Rule of Law in Inter state relations" is said by:

A. Justice Shigeru Oda
B. Justice Nagendra Singh
C. Justice Dalveer Bhandari
D. Justice R.S. Pathak

28. Frustation of contract implies:

A. Legal impediment to materialize the contract
B. Commercial hardship
C. Financial constraint to materialise the contract
D. Physical impossibility due to disappearance of the subject matter of contract or object has failed to materialise

29. The Maxim 'Damnum Sine injuria' means:

A. Infringement of Legal right with damage or loss
B. Damage or loss without infringement of legal right
C. Where there is a right, there is a remedy
D. Infringement of an absolute right without damage or loss

30. Various legislations relating to Human Rights in India are given below. Arrange them in chronological order since 1955:

A. (*a*) Bonded Labour system (Abolition) Act
(*b*) Protection of Civil Right Act
(*c*) Immoral Trafficking (Prevention) Act
(*d*) Child Labour (Prohibition and Regulation) Act

B. (*a*) Protection of Civil Rights Act
(*b*) Immoral Trafficking (Prevention) Act
(*c*) Bonded Labour System (Abolition) Act
(*d*) Child Labour (Prohibition and Regulation Act)

C. (*a*) Child labour (Prohibition and Regulation) Act
(*b*) Bonded Labour System (Abolition) Act
(*c*) Protection of Civil Rights Act
(*d*) Immoral Trafficking (Prevention) Act

D. (*a*) Bonded Labour System (Abolition) Act
(*b*) Immoral Trafficking (Prevention) Act
(*c*) Protection of Civil Right Act
(*d*) Child Labour Prohibition and Regulation) Act

31. Which of the following statements are correct?
(*a*) Chapter Vl of the UN Charter deals with the pacific settlement of disputes
(*b*) The purpose of United Nation Organisation is World Peace
(*c*) The Security Council comprises of 14 members
(*d*) The non-permanent member are elected by the General Assembly for a period of three years.

Choose the correct option:
A. (*a*) and (*b*) B. (*a*) and (*c*)
C. (*b*) and (*c*) D. (*b*) and (*d*)

32. Professor Dicey gave following three meanings of Rule of law:
(*a*) Absence of Arbitrary power or supremacy of the law
(*b*) Equality before law
(*c*) The constitution is the result of the ordinary law of land

Out of the above aspects which of the following apply to Indian system:
A. (*a*) and (*b*) only B. (*b*) and (*c*) only
C. (*a*) and (*c*) only D. all (*a*), (*b*) and (*c*)

33. Read the following statement in the light of Hindu Adoption and Maintenance Act, 1956
(*a*) Section 7 deals with capacity of a male Hindu to take in adoption
(*b*) Section 13 deals with valid adoption not to be cancelled
(*c*) Section 12 deals with effect of adoption
(*d*) Section 15 deals with right of adoptive parents to dispose off their properties

Choose the correct option:
A. (*a*) and (*c*) B. (*b*) and (*d*)
C. (*b*) and (*c*) D. (*a*) and (*d*)

34. "The provisions of the Constitution are not mathematical formulas having their essence in their form; they are organic living institutions transplanted from English soil. Their significance is vital not formal; it is to be gathered not simply by taking the words and a dictionary, but by considering their origin and the line of their growth".

The above observation is made by:
A. Schwartz B. Holmes, C.J.
C. S.A. de Smith D. Lord Russel

35. Which of the following statements is NOT correct in regard to distinction between Civil and Criminal liability?
A. Civil liability arises when a wrong is against a private individual but Criminal liability arises in case of offence which is a wrong against the society
B. Civil liability entails punishment whereas criminal liability results into damages
C. The procedure for determining Civil and Criminal liability is different
D. In Civil liability, it is the act and not the intention which is taken into consideration whereas in case of Criminal liability, *mens rea* is the determining factor

36. The Supreme Court or the High Court in exercise of the power of Judicial Review can declare a law passed by the Parliament or State Legislature as invalid on the ground that:

(*a*) It is not within the competence of the Legislature which passed the law

(*b*) It is in contravention of the fundamental rights stipulated in Part III of the Constitution or any other provision of the constitution

(*c*) The Legislature did not apply its mind or it was prompted by some improper motive or it was arbitrary or unreasonable

Choose the correct option:

A. (*a*) and (*c*) only
B. (*a*) and (*b*) only
C. (*b*) and (*c*) only
D. all (*a*), (*b*) and (*c*)

37. Which of the following is not correct under Section 8 of Hindu Succession Act, 1956? The property of a Hindu male dying intestate shall devolve:

A. Firstly upon class I heirs of the deceased
B. Secondly upon class II heirs of the deceased
C. Thirdly upon Agnates of all deceased
D. Fourthly upon the government

38. Legal sovereignty in India resides in the Constitution itself and not in 'We the People of India'. This idea was expressed in one of the following cases by the Supreme Court of India.

A. Kesavananda Bharti *vs* State of Kerala
B. Golaknath *vs* State of Punjab
C. State of West Bengal *vs* Union of India
D. Sajjah Singh *vs* State of Rajasthan

39. Following are good defences to an action in tort:

(*a*) Act of God
(*b*) *volenti non fit injuria*
(*c*) private defence
(*d*) *trustee do son tort*

Choose the correct option:

A. (*a*), (*b*) and (*d*) only
B. (*b*), (*c*) and (*d*) only
C. (*d*), (*a*) and (*c*) only
D. (*a*), (*b*) and (*c*) only

40. Match List-I with List-II:

List-I (Section of Hindu Marriage Act, 1955)	***List-II (Provision)***
(*a*) Section 5(i)	(*i*) Ceremonies of Hindu Marriage
(*b*) Section 7	(*ii*) Marriageable age
(*c*) Section 8	(*iii*) Monogamy
(*d*) Section 5(iii)	(*iv*) Registration of Marriage

Choose the correct option from those given below:

	(*a*)	(*b*)	(*c*)	(*d*)
A.	(*iv*)	(*iii*)	(*ii*)	(*i*)
B.	(*iii*)	(*i*)	(*iv*)	(*ii*)
C.	(*i*)	(*iv*)	(*iii*)	(*ii*)
D.	(*i*)	(*iv*)	(*ii*)	(*iii*)

41. Given below are two statements—One is labelled as Assertion (A) and the other is labelled as Reason (R):

Assertion (A) : Every Hindu is bound to maintain his or her legitimate or illegitimate minor Hindu children.

Reason (R) : Under section 20(2) of the Hindu Adoptions and Maintenance Act, 1956 a legitimate or illegitimate minor child may claim maintenance from his or her father or mother.

In the light of the above two statements choose the correct option:

A. (A) is true, but (R) is false
B. (A) is false, but (R) is true
C. Both (A) and (R) are true and (R) is the correct explanation of (A)
D. Both (A) and (R) are true and (R) is not the correct explanation of (A)

42. Arrange the following judgements of the Supreme Court on the issue of constitutionality of death penalty in chronological order:
(*a*) Rajendra Prasad *vs* State of UP
(*b*) Machhi Singh *vs* State of Rajasthan
(*c*) Jagmohan Singh *vs* State of UP
(*d*) Bachan Singh *vs* State of Punjab

Choose the correct option:
A. (*a*), (*b*), (*c*), (*d*)
B. (*c*), (*b*), (*a*), (*d*)
C. (*d*), (*c*), (*b*), (*a*)
D. (*c*), (*a*), (*d*), (*b*)

43. Given below are two statements—one is lebelled as Assertion (A) and other is labelled as Reason (R).

Assertion (A) : Whoever attempts to commit robbery shall be punished with rigorous imprisonment for a term which may extend to seven years and shall also be liable for fine.

Reason (R) : Section 393 of Indian Penal Code provides for rigorous imprisonment which may extends to seven years and fine for the offence of attempt to commit robbery.

In the light of the above two statements choose the correct option:
A. Both (A) and (R) are true and (R) is correct explanation of (A)
B. Both (A) and (R) are true and (R) is not the correct explanation of (A)
C. (A) is true, but (R) is false
D. (A) is false, but (R) is true

44. Which of the following is the composition of the International Bill of Human Rights?
(*a*) Universal Declaration of Human Rights
(*b*) International Covenant of Civil and Political Rights
(*c*) The International Covenant of Economic, Social and Cultural Rights
(*d*) The Optional Protocol to the International Covenant on Civil and Political Rights

Choose the most appropriate option:
A. (*a*), (*b*) and (*c*)
B. (*a*) and (*c*)
C. (*a*), (*b*), (*c*) and (*d*)
D. (*a*) and (*d*)

45. "The Law of nations is that collection of usages which civilized states have agreed to observe in their dealings with one another". This definition of International law is given by Lord Coleridge"—in:
A. Queen *vs* Keyn
B. West Rand Central Gold Mining Ltd Co. *vs* King
C. S.S. Lotus Case
D. A.M. Luther Co. *vs* Sugar and Co.

46. Match the following:

(*a*) Fisher *vs* Bell	(*i*) Privity of contract
(*b*) Harvey *vs* Facey	(*ii*) Minor contract is void
(*c*) Mohiri Bibi *vs* Dharodas Ghosh	(*iii*) Invitation to treat
(*d*) Dunlop Tyre *vs* Selfridge & Co.	(*iv*) Quotation of prices

Choose the correct option from those given below:

	(*a*)	(*b*)	(*c*)	(*d*)
A.	(*iii*)	(*iv*)	(*ii*)	(*i*)
B.	(*i*)	(*ii*)	(*iii*)	(*iv*)
C.	(*iv*)	(*ii*)	(*i*)	(*iii*)
D.	(*i*)	(*iii*)	(*iv*)	(*ii*)

47. Which one of the following can not be treated as delivery under the Sale of Goods Act, 1930?
A. Doing anything which has the effect of putting goods in possession of legal representatives of seller
B. Doing anything which has the effect of parting goods in possession of any person authorised by the buyer
C. Doing anything which has the effect of putting goods in possession of the buyer
D. Doing anything which the parties agree to be treated as delivery

48. In which of the following cases, the Supreme Court of India has specifically said that 'federal structure' is the basic feature of the Constitution?

A. A.K. Gopalan *vs* State of Madras
B. S.R. Bommai *vs* Union of India
C. Govind *vs* State of Madhya Pradesh
D. Maneka Gandhi *vs* Union of India

49. Starting from the earliest, arrange the following countries in chronological order where the Office of Ombudsman was created:

(*a*) Sweden
(*b*) United Kingdom
(*c*) New Zealand
(*d*) Finland

Choose the correct option:

A. (*a*), (*b*), (*c*), (*d*) B. (*a*), (*d*), (*c*), (*b*)
C. (*a*), (*c*), (*b*), (*d*) D. (*a*), (*b*), (*d*), (*c*)

50. Match the following sections of Indian Penal Code with provision given there under:

(*a*)	Section 80	(*i*)	Act done by person justified or by mistake of fact believing himself justified by law
(*b*)	Section 82	(*ii*)	Act of a child above seven and under twelve of immature understanding
(*c*)	Section 83	(*iii*)	Act of child under seven years of age
(*d*)	Section 79	(*iv*)	Accident in doing a lawful act

Choose the correct option from those given below:

	(*a*)	(*b*)	(*c*)	(*d*)
A.	(*iv*)	(*ii*)	(*iii*)	(*i*)
B.	(*ii*)	(*iv*)	(*i*)	(*iii*)
C.	(*iv*)	(*iii*)	(*ii*)	(*i*)
D.	(*iii*)	(*iv*)	(*ii*)	(*i*)

51. Which of the following factors are responsible for judicial activism in India?

(*a*) Denial of court access to the poor, down-trodden and underprivileged sections of the society who do not have sufficient means to approach the court
(*b*) Maladministration, misuse of public office and rampant corruption
(*c*) Increasing social problems as environmental pollution, child labour, smoking in public places, pitiable conditions of prisoners and exploitation of women etc.
(*d*) Gross violation of Human Rights

Choose the correct option:

A. only (*a*), (*b*) and (*c*)
B. only (*b*), (*c*) and (*d*)
C. only (*a*), (*c*) and (*d*)
D. all (*a*), (*b*), (*c*) and (*d*)

52. Which of the following provision was inserted by Act 22 of 2018 in Indian Penal Code?

A. Punishment for causing death or resulting persistent vegetative state of victim
B. Punishment for rape on women under Twelve Years of age
C. Sexual intercourse by husband upon his wife during seperation
D. Sexual intercourse by a person in authority

53. Match List-I with List-II:

(*a*)	Art 153	(*i*)	Appointment of Governor
(*b*)	Art 154	(*ii*)	Governor of States
(*c*)	Art 155	(*iii*)	Term of office of Governor
(*d*)	Art 156	(*iv*)	Executive power of state

Choose the correct option from those given below:

	(*a*)	(*b*)	(*c*)	(*d*)
A.	(*ii*)	(*i*)	(*iv*)	(*iii*)
B.	(*ii*)	(*iv*)	(*i*)	(*iii*)
C.	(*iii*)	(*iv*)	(*i*)	(*ii*)
D.	(*iv*)	(*iii*)	(*ii*)	(*i*)

54. In which of the following situations, the Quasi Contract Doctrine is not applied?

A. In disputes regarding payment for goods delivered or services rendered with a formal contract

B. Where no contract but fictional agreement arise
C. Where there is an unjust enrichment without a formal contract
D. Where there is a liability to pay gratuitous act

55. Choose the correct section of the Competition Act, 2002 which provides that 'No enterprise shall abuse its dominant position':
A. Section 4 B. Section 9
C. Section 8 D. Section 6

56. Salmond enumerates five characteristics of legal rights. Four such characteristics are:
(*a*) Subject of right
(*b*) Object of right
(*c*) Content of right
(*d*) Title of right

The fifth characteristic is:
A. Property in respect of which right is claimed
B. Act or omission required by the right
C. The legal reason for the existence of the right
D. The subject of the corresponding duty

57. Match the theories of Jurisprudence with the Jurists associated with it:

(*a*) Spirit of people	(*i*) Savigny
(*b*) Social Solidarity	(*ii*) Duguit
(*c*) Dictates of Reasoning	(*iii*) Thomas Acquinas
(*d*) Social Control	(*iv*) Ihering

Choose the correct option:

	(*a*)	(*b*)	(*c*)	(*d*)
A.	(*i*)	(*ii*)	(*iii*)	(*iv*)
B.	(*i*)	(*ii*)	(*iv*)	(*iii*)
C.	(*iv*)	(*iii*)	(*ii*)	(*i*)
D.	(*ii*)	(*iv*)	(*i*)	(*iii*)

58. Which one of the following is not within the scope of Implied Authority of a partner?
A. The act done for carrying on the business of the kind carried on by the firm
B. The act should be done in the usual way of business of the firm
C. The act of acquiring immovable property on behalf of the firm
D. The act must be done in the firm name or in any other manner expressing or implying an intention to bind the firm

59. Given below are two statements. One is labelled as Assertion (A) and the other is labelled as Reason (R):

Assertion (A) : The liability of the surety is co-executive and it can not go beyond the terms of guarantee.

Reason (R) : The rights and liabilities of a surety and borrower are different and distinct and everything depends upon its terms of guarantee.

In the light of the above two statements choose the correct option:
A. Both (A) and (R) are true and (R) is the correct explanation of (A)
B. Both (A) and (R) are true and (R) is not the correct explanation of (A)
C. (A) is true, but (R) is false
D. (A) is false, but (R) is true

60. Match the following sections of the Copyright Act, 1957 with provisions given there under:

(*a*) Section 2 (0)	(*i*) Performer Right
(*b*) Section 38	(*ii*) Meaning of Literary work
(*c*) Section 37	(*iii*) Meaning of sound recording
(*d*) Section 2 (XX)	(*iv*) Broadcast reproduction right

Choose the correct option from those given below:

	(*a*)	(*b*)	(*c*)	(*d*)
A.	(*ii*)	(*i*)	(*iv*)	(*iii*)
B.	(*iv*)	(*ii*)	(*iii*)	(*i*)
C.	(*ii*)	(*iii*)	(*i*)	(*iv*)
D.	(*i*)	(*iv*)	(*iii*)	(*ii*)

61. Match the following cases decided by the Supreme court with the subject given therein:

List-I	*List-II*
(*a*) Hussainara Khatom *vs* State of Bihar	(*i*) Ban on smoking in public places
(*b*) Murli S. Deora *vs* Union of India	(*ii*) Protection against inhuman treatment in jail
(*c*) Lakshmi Kant Pandey *vs* Union of India	(*iii*) Speedy Trial
(*d*) Sunil Batra *vs* Delhi Administration	(*iv*) Child welfare

Choose the correct option from those given below:

	(*a*)	(*b*)	(*c*)	(*d*)
A.	(*i*)	(*ii*)	(*iii*)	(*iv*)
B.	(*i*)	(*iii*)	(*iv*)	(*ii*)
C.	(*iii*)	(*i*)	(*iv*)	(*ii*)
D.	(*ii*)	(*iv*)	(*iii*)	(*i*)

62. The concept of Universalism is based on:
(*a*) Natural Theory
(*b*) Theory of Rationalism
(*c*) Theory of Positivism
(*d*) Theory of Cultural Relativism

Choose the most appropriate option:
A. (*a*) and (*b*)
B. (*a*), (*b*) and (*c*)
C. (*a*), (*b*), (*c*) and (*d*)
D. (*c*) and (*d*)

63. To constitute the offence of kidnapping from lawful guardianship under Section 361 of Indian Penal Code the age of the minor should be:
(*a*) Under eighteen years if male
(*b*) Under sixteen years if male
(*c*) Under eighteen years if female
(*d*) Under sixteen years if female

Choose the correct option:
A. (*a*) and (*b*) B. (*a*) and (*c*)
C. (*b*) and (*c*) D. (*a*) and (*d*)

64. Preamble of the National Green Tribunal Act; 2010 (NGT Act) does not mention about:
A. Johannesburg Conference
B. Rio Conference
C. Article 21 of the Constitution of India
D. The Stockholm Conference

65. 'Whoever by words, either spoken or written, or by signs, or by visible representation, or otherwise, brings or attempts to bring in hatred or contempt or excites or attempts to excite disaffection towards, the government established by law in India; amounts to the offence of:
A. Defamation
B. Sedition
C. Criminal Conspiracy
D. Assault

66. Section 49 of the Information Technology Act deals with the provision relating to:
A. Establishment of Cyber Appellate Tribunal
B. Qualification for appointment as Chair-person and member of Cyber Appellate Tribunal
C. Composition of Cyber Appellate Tribunal
D. Distribution of business among benches

67. The essential characteristics of Federation in USA are:
(*a*) Supremacy of the Constitution
(*b*) Distribution of powers amongst the various organs of the federation and of regional units of the federation by the provision of constitution
(*c*) Judicial review or enforcement of that supreme constitution as law
(*d*) The Rule of Law

Choose the correct option:
A. Only (*a*), (*b*) and (*c*)
B. Only (*a*), (*b*) and (*d*)
C. Only (*b*), (*c*) and (*d*)
D. All (*a*), (*b*), (*c*) and (*d*)

68. Which one of the following Jurists asserts that 'Law and morality are complementary and supplementary to each other'?

A. John Austin B. Hans Kelson
C. H.L.A. Hart D. Devlin

•. Under the Companies Act 2013, which of the following company is required to constitute a Corporate Social Responsibility Committee?

(*a*) company having networth of ₹ 500 crore or more

(*b*) company having turnover of ₹ 1000 crore or more

(*c*) company having net profit of ₹ 5 crore or more

(*d*) company having net profit of ₹ 2 crore or more during any financial year

Choose the most appropriate option:

A. (*a*), (*b*), (*c*) and (*d*)
B. (*a*) and (*d*)
C. (*a*), (*b*) and (*c*)
D. (*a*), (*c*) and (*d*)

0. Which of the following statement/statements are true?

A. In Nicaragua *vs* U.S.A.: the World Court by majority has taken the view that the sources of International Law are hierarchical

B. In Nicaragua *vs* U.S.A.: the World Court has taken unanimously the view that the sources of International Law are not hierarchical

C. In Nicaragua *vs* U.S.A.: the World Court by majority has taken the view that the sources of International Law are not hierarchical but are necessarily complimentry and inte-related

D. In Nicaragua *vs* U.S.A.: the World Court has taken unanimously the view that the sources of International Law are not hierarchical but are necessarily complimentary and inter-related.

1. To consitute the offence of Affray under Section 159 of the Indian Penal code there must be:

(*a*) Only one person

(*b*) Two or more persons

(*c*) Fighting in Public place to disturb public peace

(*d*) Fighting in private place

Choose the correct option:

A. (*a*) and (*c*)
B. (*b*) and (*c*)
C. (*b*) and (*d*)
D. (*a*) and (*d*)

72. Which of the following could be considered to be advantages of Legislation over Precedent?

(*a*) Abrogative capability

(*b*) Fore knowledge

(*c*) Prospective application

(*d*) Systematic arrangement

Choose the correction option:

A. (*a*), (*b*), (*d*) only
B. (*a*), (*b*), (*c*) only
C. (*a*), (*b*), (*c*) and (*d*)
D. (*a*) and (*c*) only

73. Given below are two statements—one is labelled as Assertion (A) and the other is labelled as Reason (R).

Assertion (A) : Subject to rules of Jus cogens local customary law can supplement or derogate from general custom.

Reason (R) : International law does not recognise the concept of local custom.

In the light of the above two statements choose the correct option.

A. Both (A) and (R) are true and (R) is the correct explanation cf (A)
B. Both (A) and (R) are true and (R) is not the correct explanation of (A)
C. (A) is true, but (R) is false
D. (A) is false, but (R) is true

74. Which of the following statements are correct?

(*a*) The Supreme Court of India has Original Jurisdiction in any dispute between the Government of India and one or more States.

(*b*) The Supreme Court of India has Original Jurisdiction in any dispute between Government of India and any State or States on one side and one or more States on other side.

(*c*) The Supreme Court of India has Original Jurisdiction in any dispute between Government of India and any individual on one side and State one or more on the other side.

(*d*) The Supreme Court of India has Original Jurisdiction in any dispute in India.

Choose the correct option:

A. (*a*) and (*b*) B. (*b*) and (*c*)

C. (*a*) and (*c*) D. (*a*) and (*d*)

75. Article 371-F, special provisions with respect to the state of Sikkim was inserted by:

A. The Constitution (Thirty Second Amendment) Act

B. The Constitution (Thirty Third Amendment) Act

C. The Constitution (Thirty Fifth Amendment) Act

D. The Constitution (Thirty Sixth Amendment) Act

76. Constitution of India requires the State to adopt the Protectionist Policy and Improvinistic Policy. Which one of the following Article declares the above:

A. Article of 51 A(g)

B. Article 38

C. Article 48 A

D. Article 37

77. The word "Tort" has been derived from the Latin Word:

A. Tortus B. Tortum

C. Torrent D. Torture

78. Which of the following is not correct under Muslim Law?

A. In a gift Transaction delivery of posses is necessary, in a Will it is not required

B. Doctrine of Mushaa is also applicable in case of disposition by Will

C. Right of Donor to a gift is unrestric but right of making a bequest is limi in two ways

D. After completion, a gift cannot be revo unless by a formal decree of a cour will may be revoked at any time a making of it

79. Which one of the following is not a 'Prim Source' of Muslim Law?

A. Qiyas

B. Quran

C. Takhleed

D. Sunnat

80. According to Art. 233 of the Constitution India, appointment of a District Judge sh be made by:

A. Collegium of the State High Co concerned

B. The Governor of the State concerned consultation with the Chief Justice India

C. The Governor of the State in Consultat with the High Court exercising Jurisc tion in relation to such State.

D. The President in consultation with Chief Justice of the High Court exercis Jurisdiction in relation to the St concerned

81. Right to Education Act seeks to provide f and compulsory education to all child between 6 and 14 years. But a modificat in Child Labour Act formalises employm of children 0 and 14 years in the fam enterprises. Therefore, which of the follow ILO Conventions is violated?

(*a*) Convention 138

(*b*) Convention 182

(*c*) Convention 126

(*d*) Convention 141

Choose the correct option:

A. (*a*) and (*b*)

B. (*c*) and (*d*)

C. (*a*) and (*d*)

D. (*b*) and (*c*)

82. In which of the following cases it was held that "there is no distinction between defacto and dejure recognition for the purpose of giving effect to the international acts of the recognised authority"?

A. Luther *vs* Sagar
B. U.S. *vs* Pink
C. Russian Socialist Federated Soviet Republic *vs* Cibrario
D. Guarantee Trust Co. of New York *vs* U.S.

83. The provision under Copyright Act is given as under:

(*a*) Section 52 B deals with provision relating to accounts and audit.
(*b*) Section 53 A deals with resale share rights in original copies.
(*c*) Section 52 deals with importation of infringing copies.
(*d*) Section 53 deals with certain acts not to be infringement of copyright.

Choose the correct option:

A. (*a*) and (*c*) B. (*b*) and (*d*)
C. (*a*) and (*d*) D. (*a*) and (*b*)

84. A malignant act likely to spread infection or disease dangerous to life and making atmosphere noxious to health are punishable offences for environment protection. But the punishment are meagre to meet objectives. Under which of the following law such meagre punishment is given:

A. Environment Protection Act, 1986
B. Indian Penal Code
C. The Air (Prevention and Control of Pollution) Act, 1981
D. The Water (Prevention and Control of Pollution) Act, 1974

85. Some of the notification under Environment Protection Act, 1986 is listed below:

Choose the correct option year wise:

A. Notification on:
(*a*) Coastal Regulation Zone
(*b*) Environmental Auditing
(*c*) Environmental Impact Assessment
(*d*) Dumping and Disposal of Fly Ash

B. Notification on:
(*a*) Dumping and Disposal of Fly Ash
(*b*) Coastal Regulation Zone
(*c*) Environmental Auditing
(*d*) Environmental Impact Assessment

C. Notification on:
(*a*) Coastal Regulation Zone
(*b*) Dumping and Disposal of Fly Ash
(*c*) Environmental Auditing
(*d*) Environmental Impact Assessment

D. Notification on:
(*a*) Environmental Impact Assessment
(*b*) Coastal Regulation Zone
(*c*) Environmental Auditing
(*d*) Dumping and Disposal of Fly Ash

86. Ownership can be:

(*a*) Legal and vested ownership
(*b*) Legal and equitable ownership
(*c*) Absolute and limited ownership
(*d*) Trust and beneficial ownership

Choose the correct option:

A. All (*a*), (*b*), (*c*) and (*d*)
B. Only (*b*), (*c*) and (*d*)
C. Only (*a*), (*b*) and (*c*)
D. Only (*a*), (*c*) and (*d*)

87. To constitute the offence of theft under Indian Penal code, there must be:

(*a*) taking away of the movable property
(*b*) without the consent of the person
(*c*) taking away of the immovable property
(*d*) with the consent of person

Choose the correct option:

A. (*b*) and (*c*) B. (*a*) and (*b*)
C. (*a*) and (*d*) D. (*b*) and (*d*)

88. Which of the following statement/statements are correct?

(*a*) Convention of Nationality was adopted in 1928.
(*b*) Convention of Nationality of married women was adopted in 1957.
(*c*) Convention on the Reduction of statelessness was adopted in 1961.
(d) Convention on the Nationality of newborn child was adopted in 1938.

Select the correct answer using the code given below:

A. (*a*) and (*b*) B. (*b*) and (*c*)
C. (*a*) and (*c*) D. (*b*) and (*d*)

89. Match List-I with List-II:

List-I	***List-II***
(*a*) United States of America *vs* Italy	(*i*) Legality of use of force
(*b*) El Salvador *vs* Honduras	(*ii*) Case concerning Elettronica Sicula S.pA (ELSI)
(*c*) Spain *vs* Canada	(*iii*) Land, Island and maritime dispute case
(*d*) Yugoslavia *vs* U.S.	(*iv*) Fisheries Jurisdiction

Choose the correct option from those given below:

	(*a*)	(*b*)	(*c*)	(*d*)
A.	(*ii*)	(*iii*)	(*iv*)	(*i*)
B.	(*iii*)	(*i*)	(*iv*)	(*ii*)
C.	(*ii*)	(*iv*)	(*i*)	(*iii*)
D.	(*iv*)	(*iii*)	(*ii*)	(*i*)

90. Match the following provisions with the Section under Consumer Protection Act, 1986:

(*a*) Jurisdiction of the District forum	(*i*) Section 17 B
(*b*) Composition of State Commission	(*ii*) Section 20
(*c*) Composition of National Commission	(*iii*) Section 16
(*d*) Circuit benches of State Commission	(*iv*) Section 11

Choose the correct option from those given below:

	(*a*)	(*b*)	(*c*)	(*d*)
A.	(*ii*)	(*iv*)	(*iii*)	(*i*)
B.	(*i*)	(*ii*)	(*iii*)	(*iv*)
C.	(*iii*)	(*ii*)	(*i*)	(*iv*)
D.	(*iv*)	(*iii*)	(*ii*)	(*i*)

Directions (Qs. No. 91-95): *Read the paragraph carefully and answer these questions.*

The Preamble of the Constitution is an integral part of the Constitution. Democratic form of government, federal structure, unity and integr of the nation, secularism, socialism, social just and judicial review are basic features of Constitution.

The Union of India shall protect the St Government and as corollary under Article 35(is enjoined that the government of every st should be carried on in accordance with provisions of the constitution. On receipt of a rep from the Governor or otherwise the Presid (Council of Ministers) on being satisfied tha situation has arisen in which the Government c State can not be carried on in accordance with provisions of the Constitution, is empowred to is Proclamation under Article 356(1) and imp president's rule in the state in a manner laid do in sub-clause (a) to (c) of Article 356(1) of constitution.

The exericse of the power under Article 35(an extraordinary one and needs to be used sparin when the situation contemplated by Article warrants to maintain democratic form of governm and to prevent paralysing of the political proc Single or individual act or acts of violation of constitution for good, bad or in differ administration does not necessarily constit failure of constitutional machinery or characteri that a situation has arisen in which the Governm of the State cannot be carried on in accorda with the provisions of the constitution. The exerc of power under Article 356 should under circumstances be for a political gain to the party power in the Union government. It should be u sparingly and with circumspection that government of the State functions w responsibility in accordance with the provisions the constitution.

Rule of law has been chosen as an instrum of social adjustment and resolution of conflict social problems to integrate diverse sections of society professing multi-religious faiths, creed, c or region fostering among them fraterni transcending social, religious, linguistic or regio barriers.

Citizen is either by birth or by domicile and not as a member of religion, caste, sect, region or language securalism has both positive and negative constants.

91. Article 356(1) (b) provides that:

A. Any proclamation under Article 356(1) may be revoked by a subsequent proclamation
B. Every proclamation under Article 356(1) shall be laid before each House of Parliament
C. A Proclamation under Article 356(l) shall cease to operate on the expiration of six months from the date of issue of proclamation
D. The President may by proclamation under Article 356(1) declare that the powers of the legislature of the state shall be exercisable by or under the authority of Parliament

92. Which one of the following provisions of the Constitution imposes an obligation on the Union to ensure that the Government of the State is carried on in accordance with the provisions of the constitution?

A. Article 352
B. Article 355
C. Article 356
D. Article 360

93. 'Rule of law' has been recognized by the constitution of India under:

A. Article 14
B. Article 19
C. Article 21
D. Article 22

94. In the light of the above, answer the following:

In which of the following cases, the supreme court held that the Preamble is the part of the Constitution

A. Buckingham and Carantic Co. Ltd *vs* Venkiah
B. Keshvanand Bharti Case
C. Golaknath *vs* State of Punjab
D. In re Berubari case

95. On which grounds of the following a restriction can be imposed on freedom of religion under article 25(1) of the constitution?

A. Public order, decency and morality
B. In the interest of general public
C. Public order, morality and health
D. In the interest of general public and for the protection of the interest or Scheduled

Directions (Qs. No. 96-100): *Read the paragraph carefully and answer these questions.*

Broadly speaking, legal theory involves a study of the characteristic features essential to law and common to legal systems and analysis of the basic elements of law which made it law and distinguish it from other forms of rules and standards, from systems which cannot be described as legal systems and from other social phenomena. In fact, it is not possible to reach our dogmatic answer to the question 'what is law' or provide exclusive answers to many questions which are asked about its essential nature.

The nature of legal theory lies in a study of the right which other theories may shed on distinctive attributes of law, by an examination of the relative merits and demerits of the principal—expositions of the subject. In the same strain legal theory is linked at one end, with philosophy and at other end, with political theory. Sometimes the starting point is philosophy and political ideology plays a secondary part.... sometimes the theory of knowledge and political ideology are welded into one coherent system, of course, it is true that some legal philosophies have been philosophizers first and foremost and juristic because they felt the need to express their political thought in legal form.... . In short, before the nineteenth century legal theory was essentially a by-product of philosophy, religion, ethics or politics.

The new era of legal philosophy arises mainly from the confrontation of professional lawyers, in his legal work, with problems of social justice. The modern jurists legal theory, no less than scholastic philosopher is based on ultimate beliefs whose inspiration comes from outside the law itself.

96. Law is always in a state of continual change. This is the basic tenet of:
A. Realist jurisprudence
B. Socialogical jurisprudence
C. Philosophical jurisprudence
D. Analytical jurisprudence

97. Law must remain free from social sciences, metaphysical, ethical and moral elements. This was propounded by:
A. Austin B. Pound
C. Kelson D. Salmond

98. Who defined jurisprudence as a formal science of positive law?
A. Austin B. H.L.A. Hart
C. Salmond D. Holland

99. In the right of above, answer the following. As the science of law or philosophy of law emerged, which of the following approach came into existence?
A. Analytical positivist approach
B. Socio-legal approach
C. Historical approach
D. Realist approach

100. Who, among the following jurists, says "legal theory is linked at one end with philosophy and, at other end, with political theory"?
A. John D. Finch
B. Friedman
C. Wayne Morrison
D. Jeremy Bentham

ANSWERS

1	2	3	4	5	6	7	8	9	10
B	D	B	C	B	C	B	C	C	C
11	**12**	**13**	**14**	**15**	**16**	**17**	**18**	**19**	**20**
C	C	C	B	B	D	B	D	B	D
21	**22**	**23**	**24**	**25**	**26**	**27**	**28**	**29**	**30**
C	A	A	A	D	B	B	D	B	B
31	**32**	**33**	**34**	**35**	**36**	**37**	**38**	**39**	**40**
A	A	A	B	B	B	D	A	D	B
41	**42**	**43**	**44**	**45**	**46**	**47**	**48**	**49**	**50**
C	D	A	C	A	A	A	B	B	C
51	**52**	**53**	**54**	**55**	**56**	**57**	**58**	**59**	**60**
D	B	B	A&D	A	D	A	C	A	A
61	**62**	**63**	**64**	**65**	**66**	**67**	**68**	**69**	**70**
C	B	C	A	B	C	A	C	C	C
71	**72**	**73**	**74**	**75**	**76**	**77**	**78**	**79**	**80**
B	C	C	A	D	C	B	B	C	C
81	**82**	**83**	**84**	**85**	**86**	**87**	**88**	**89**	**90**
A	A	D	B	A	B	B	B	A	D
91	**92**	**93**	**94**	**95**	**96**	**97**	**98**	**99**	**100**
D	B	A	B	C	A	C	D	B	B

EXPLANATORY ANSWERS

1. Article 353 in The Indian Constitution:

Effect of Proclamation of Emergency: While a Proclamation of Emergency is in operation, then—

(*a*) Notwithstanding anything in this Constitution, the executive power of the Union shall extend to the giving of directions to any State as to the manner in which the executive power thereof is to be exercised;

(*b*) The power of Parliament to make laws with respect to any matter shall include power to make laws conferring powers and imposing duties, or authorising the conferring of powers and the imposition of duties, upon the Union or officers and authorities of the Union as respects that matter, notwithstanding that is one which is not enumerated in the Union List; Provided that where a Proclamation of Emergency is in operation only in any part of the territory of India,

(*i*) The executive power of the Union to give directions under clause (*a*), and

(*ii*) The power of Parliament to make laws under clause (*b*), shall also extend to any State other than a State in which or in any part of which the Proclamation of Emergency is in operation if and in so far as the security of India or any part of the territory thereof is threatened by activities in or in relation to the part of the territory of India in which the Proclamation of Emergency is in operation.

Article 355 entrusts the duty upon Union to protect the states against "external aggression" and "internal disturbance" to ensure that the government of every State is carried on in accordance with the provisions of **Constitution**.

2. 'A' in India, instigates 'B' a foreigner in Goa, to commit a murder in Goa. A is **guilty of** abetting **murder**. Punishment of abetment if the act abetted is **committed** in consequence and where no express provision is made for its punishment.

4. There are basically three theories for divorce — fault theory, mutual consent theory and irretrievable breakdown of marriage theory. In modern Hindu law, all the three theories of divorce are recognised and divorce can be obtained on the basis of any one of them. The Hindu marriage Act, 1955 originally, based divorce on the fault theory, and enshrined nine fault grounds in Section 13(1) on which either the husband or wife could sue for divorce, and two fault grounds in Section 13(2) on which wife alone could seek the divorce.

In 1964, by an amendment, certain clauses of Section 13(1) were amended in the form of Section 13(1A), thus recognizing two grounds of the breakdown of the marriage. The 1976 amendment act inserted two additional fault grounds of divorce for wife and a new Section 13B for divorce by mutual consent.

6. A bill of exchange transaction can involve up to three parties. The drawee is the party that pays the sum specified by the bill of exchange. The payee is the one who receives that sum. The drawer is the party that obliges the drawee to pay the payee. The drawer and the payee are the same entity unless the drawer transfers the bill of exchange to a third-party payee.

A bill of exchange is a written order once used primarily in international trade that binds one party to pay a fixed sum of money to another party on demand or at a predetermined date. Bills of exchange are similar to checks and promissory notes—they can be drawn by individuals or banks and are generally transferable by endorsements.

7. Mubarak Ali Ahmed *vs* The State of Bombay on 6th September 1957.

Hans Muller of Nurrenberg *vs* Suptt. Presidency Jail Calcutta and Others on 23rd February, 1955.

Ram Babu Saxena *vs* State on 6th November, 1950.

State of Madras *vs* C.G. Menon on 19th May, 1954.

8. Presumption in cases of simultaneous death – Section 21.

Failure of heirs – Section 29.

Act not applied to certain properties – Section 5.

Full blood preferred to half blood – Section 18.

9. Immoral Traffic (Prevention) Act-1956/1986.

Maternity Benefit Act-1961/2017.

Medical Termination of Pregnancy Act-1971.

Equal Remuneration Act-1976.

11. In Budhan *vs* State of Bihar case our Supreme Court held that so far as the guarantee of equal protection in Article 14 is concerned, any State action—Executive, Legislative or Judicial, which contravenes Article 14 is void. The Supreme Court noted that judges at appeal first emphasised that the interpretation of Article 14 is well established and does not need to be re-addressed. The Article condemns both discrimination by law and by procedure, but the Constitution "does not assure unanimity of decisions or immunity from merely erroneous action" by courts or by bureaucracy. The judges quoted ample precedent to demonstrate that s. 30 of the Code of Criminal Procedure did not infringe the fundamental right guaranteed by Article 14 of the Constitution.

12. Under Muslim Law, marriage with a woman, whose husband is alive, is void. The Mohammedan law has made a departure from the usual classification of marriage into legal and illegal by introducing an intermediate kind of irregular marriages. Marriages are classified for purpose of validity into three classes, valid, irregular (or invalid) and void. According to the Mohammedan law there are some marriages which are not valid but which are not wholly void. Marriages of this kind are defective or irregular but are not entirely without any effect. There are important consequences resulting from an irregular marriage and such marriages may also in certain circumstances become valid marriages.

13. Classification of goods and services – Section 7.

Absolute grounds for refusal of registration – Section 9.

Limitation as to colour – Section 10.

Regulation in case of honest concurrent use etc – Section 12.

14. Section 3(j) of the Patents Act 1970 states that "plants and animals in whole or any part thereof other than micro-organisms but including seeds, varieties and species and essentially biological processes for production or propagation of plants and animals" are not inventions as per the act and hence not patentable.

Stem cells are considered to fall under the phrase "any part thereof" and hence are excluded from patentability. However, *in vitro* methods of differentiating, isolating/ purifying and culturing of stem cells may qualify as patentable subject matter, provided that the method is novel, involves an inventive step and has industrial applicability.

In addition, inventions pertaining to stem cells may also be opposed under Section 3(b) of the Act, which prohibits the grant of patent to:

An invention the primary or intended use or commercial exploitation of which could be contrary to public order or morality or which causes serious prejudice to human, animal or plant life or health or to the environment.

15. Ashby *vs* White on 1st January, 1703.

Reylands *vs* Fletcher on 17th July, 1868.

Donoghue *vs* Stevenson on 26th May, 1932.

M.C. Mehta *vs* Union of India on 30th December, 1996.

16. S.S. Dhanoa Vs Union of India – 1991.

T.N. Seshan Vs. Union of India – 1995.

People's Union of Civil Liberties *vs* Union of India – 2001.

Kuldip Nayar *vs* Union of India – 2006.

18. Kelsen's Theory of Legal Personality: He said that there is no difference between legal personality of a company and that of an individual. Personality in the legal sense is only a technical personification of a complex of norms and assigning complexes of rights and duties.

19. Human beings are rational beings. They by virtue of their being human possess certain basic and inalienable rights which are commonly known as human rights. Since these rights belong to them because of their very existence, they become operative with their birth. Human rights, being the birth right, are, therefore, inherent in all the individuals irrespective of their caste, creed, religion, sex and nationality.

These rights are essential for all the individuals as they are consonant with their freedom and dignity and are conducive to physical, moral, social and spiritual welfare. They are also necessary as they create an environment in which people can develop their full potential and lead productive and creative lives in accordance with their needs and provide suitable conditions for the material and moral uplift of the people. Because of their immense significance to human beings; human rights are also sometimes referred to as fundamental rights, basic rights, inherent rights, natural rights and birth rights.

Presently, the vast majority of legal scholars and philosophers agree that every human being is entitled to some rights. Thus, there is universal acceptance of human rights in principle in domestic and international plane. 'Human rights' is a generic term and it embraces civil rights, civil liberties and social, economic and cultural rights. It is therefore difficult to give a precise definition of the term "human rights". However, it can be said that the rights that all people have by virtue of their being human are human rights. These are the rights which no one can be deprived without a grave affront to justice. It is so because they may affect the human dignity. Thus, the idea of human rights is bound up with the idea of human dignity. Former CJI and NHRC chairman J.S. Verma has rightly stated that "human dignity is the quintessence of human rights."

20. In the report of the Donoughmore Committee it was stared that in the British constitution, there is no such thing as the absolute separation of legislative executive and judicial powers; in practice it is inevitable that they should overlap. In such constitutions as those of France and the USA, attempts to keep them rigidly apart have been made but have proved unsuccessful. The distinction is none the less real, and for our purposes important. So it could be seen in United Kingdom that there is no "Montesquieu's separation of powers". The government being made up of members of the legislatures means that minister have both legislative and executive functions and while parliament may dismiss a government through a vote of no confidence, one must remember that the government controls the legislative works of the parliament to a large extent.

21. The WTO's procedure for resolving trade conflicts under the Dispute Settlement Understanding is vital for enforcing the rules and therefore for ensuring that trade flows smoothly. Governments bring disputes to the WTO if they think their rights under the WTO agreements are being infringed. Judgements by specially appointed independent experts are based on interpretations of the agreements and individual members' commitments. The system encourages members to settle their differences through consultation with each other.

The WTO's Trade Policy Review Mechanism is designed to improve transparency, to create a greater understanding of the trade policies adopted by WTO members and to assess their impact. Many members see the reviews as constructive feedback on their policies. All WTO members must undergo periodic scrutiny, each review containing reports by the member concerned and the WTO Secretariat. In addition, the WTO undertakes regular monitoring of global trade measures. Initially launched in the wake of the financial crisis of 2008, this global trade monitoring exercise has become a regular function of the WTO, with the aim of highlighting WTO members' implementation of both trade-facilitating and trade-restricting measures.

22. In T.M.A. Pai Foundation *vs.* State of Karnataka, the Supreme Court held that the expression "Minority" is a relative term and is referred to, to represent the linguistic or religious sections or groups forming less than 50% of the total population of the State. The expression Minority is a relative term and its meaning should depend upon the territorial limits of its operation or the objective of a particular legislation. The problem of defining the term with exactness is however a very complex one and even the deliberations at the constituent Assembly reveal that the problem of defining the term arose there but the Assembly was unable to formulate any definition of Minority.

23. Section-9 of the Geographical Indication of Goods (Registration and Protection) Act, 1999 provides for prohibition of registration of certain geographical indications. The Geographical Indications of Goods (Registration and Protection) Act, 1999 (GI Act) is a sui generis Act of the parliament of India for protection of geographical indications in India. India, as a member of the WTO, enacted the Act to comply with the Agreement on Trade-Related Aspects of Intellectual Property Rights (TRIPs). The GI tag ensures that none other than those registered as authorised users (or at least those residing inside the geographic territory) are allowed to use the popular product name.

24. Section 34 has been enacted on the principle of joint liability in the doing of a criminal act. The Section is only a rule of evidence and does not create a substantive offence. The distinctive feature of the Section is the element of participation in action. The liability of one person for an offence committed by another in the course of criminal act perpetrated by several persons arises under Section 34 if such criminal act is done in furtherance of a common intention of the persons who join in committing the crime. Direct proof of common intention is seldom available and, therefore, such intention can only be inferred from the circumstances appearing from the proved facts of the case and the proved circumstances. In order to bring home the charge of common intention, the prosecution has to establish by evidence, whether direct or circumstantial, that there was plan or meeting of mind of all the accused persons to commit the offence for which they are charged with the aid of Section 34, be it pre-arranged or on the spur of moment; but it must necessarily be before the commission of the crime. The true contents of the Section is that if two or more persons intentionally do an act jointly, the position in law is just the same as if each of them has done it individually by himself. As observed in Ashok Kumar *vs.* State of Punjab (AIR 1977 SC 109), the existence of a common intention amongst the participants in a crime is the essential element for application of this Section. It is not necessary that the acts of the several persons charged with commission of an offence jointly must be the same or identically similar. The acts may be different in character, but must have been actuated by one and the same common intention in order to attract the provision.

27. Justice Nagendra Singh said, "The international court of justice is indeed a sine qua non for the establishment of Rule of Law in Inter State Relations."

28. Frustration of contract can be established upon the fulfillment of the following conditions:

- Existence of a valid contract between parties.
- The contract is **yet to be performed.**
- The performance of the contract becomes impossible or unlawful.
- The impossibility to perform is caused by an event which is beyond the control of both the parties.

Factors of Frustration of Contract:

1. Impossibility of Performance
2. Change of Circumstances
3. Loss of Object

29. Damnum Sine Injuria is a maxim, which refers to injury which is being suffered by the plaintiff but there is no violation of any legal right of a person. In such circumstances, where there is no violation of the legal right of but the injury, or damage is being suffered by the plaintiff, the plaintiff can't bring an action against the other for the same, as it is not actionable in law, unless there is some infringement of a legal right is present.

Damnum Sine Injuria, the literal meaning of the word refers to loss or damage in terms of money, property or any physical loss without the infringement of any legal right. It is not actionable in law even if the act so did was intentional and was done to cause injury to other but without infringing on the legal right of the person.

32. The Rule of Law was first originated by Sir Edward Coke, the Chief Justice in England at the time of King James I. Coke was the first person to criticise the maxims of Divine Concept. He strongly believed that the King should also be under the Rule of Law. The Rule of Law doctrine was later developed by A.V. Dicey in his book, "Introduction to the Law of Constitution (1885)." The Rule of Law according to Dicey means that no man is punishable or can be lawfully made to suffer in body or goods except for distinct breach of law and no man is above the law. The term Rule of Law thus, means the paramountcy of Law over Government.

Dicey's rule of law consists of following three meanings:

1. **Equality before the law:** Dicey says it emphasises the impartiality of law. It means that there shall be no distinction between the rich and the poor, officials and non-officials, majority and minority, no one can be degraded and no one can be upgraded. Law gives equal justice to all.

2. **Rule of Law alone:** The Rule of Law rejects all kinds of arbitrary and discretionary powers of the government or public officials. It implies that a man may be punished for a breach of law but he can't be punished for anything else. An alleged offence is required to be proved before the ordinary courts in accordance with the legal procedure.

3. **Constitutional Law stems from ordinary law:** It is generally presumed that the written constitution is the source of legal liberties of citizens. However, it is not true as Britain has an "unwritten Constitution." Legal spirit is the real source of law in England. The legal spirit is seen in its customs, conventions and judicial

decisions. Dicey opines that the individual rights and liberties are more safely protected in Britain than France.

The basic features of Rule of Law as per Dicey:

(*a*) Law does not recognise any special rights for any individual or group of individuals.

(*b*) Law does not recognise any distinction between one individual and the other on the basis of religion, race, sex, etc.

(*c*) None is punished without proper trial.

(*d*) All will be tried by the same court under the same law.

(*e*) The rule of law does not give scope to absolute and arbitrary powers to the executive.

33. The Hindu Adoptions and Maintenance Act, 1956:

Sec 7. Capacity of a male Hindu to take in adoption— Any male Hindu who is of sound mind and is not a minor has the capacity to take a son or a daughter in adoption.

Sec 12. Effect of adoptions—An adopted child shall be deemed to be the child of his or her adoptive father or mother for all purposes with effect from the date of the adoption and from such date all the ties of the child in the family of his or her birth shall be deemed to be severed and replaced by those created by the adoption in the adoptive family.

34. "The provisions of the Constitution are not mathematical formulas having their essence in their form; they are organic living institutions transplanted from English soil. Their significance is vital not formal; it is to be gathered not simply by taking the words and a dictionary, but by considering their origin and the line of their growth". The above statement is observed by Holmes, C.J. (Gompers *vs.* United States 1914).

36. The Supreme Court or the High Court in exercise of the power of Judicial Review can declare a law passed by the Parliament or State Legislature as invalid on the ground that:

It is not within the competence of the Legislature which passed the law.

It is in contravention of the fundamental rights stipulated in Part III of the Constitution or any other provision of the constitution.

Judicial Review in India is governed by the principle: 'Procedure Established by Law'. Under it the court conducts one test, *i.e.*, whether the law has been made in accordance with the powers granted by the Constitution to the law-making body and follows the prescribed procedure or not. It gets rejected when it is held to be violative of procedure established by law.

38. Legal sovereignty in India resides in the Constitution itself and not in 'We the People of India'. This idea was expressed in Kesavananda Bharti *vs* State of Kerala, 1973 by the Supreme Court of India. The above mentioned case is perhaps the most well-known constitutional decision of the Supreme Court of India.

39. When a plaintiff brings an action against the defendant for a tort committed by him, he will be held liable for it, if there exists all the essential ingredients which are required for that wrong. But there are some defences available to him using which he can absolve himself from the liability arising out of the wrong committed. These are known as '**General defences**' in the law of tort.

The defences available are given as follows:

- *Volenti non fit injuria or the defense of 'Consent'*
- The wrongdoer is the plaintiff
- Inevitable accident
- Act of God
- Private defense
- Mistake
- Necessity
- Statutory authority

41. Every Hindu is bound to maintain his or her legitimate or illegitimate minor Hindu children because under section 20(2) of the Hindu Adoptions and Maintenance Act, 1956 a legitimate or illegitimate minor child may claim maintenance from his or her father or mother. In this section "parent" includes a childless stepmother.

43. Section 393 of Indian Penal Code, 1860 prescribes punishment for the offence of attempt to commit robbery. It says that whoever attempts to commit robbery shall be punished with rigorous imprisonment for a term extending up to seven years, and shall also be liable to fine. Where the accused makes an effort to commit robbery and does all that he could do, or at least he has taken all the major steps towards its commission, but the result could not be achieved by him, he has made an attempt to commit robbery. It is important to note that simple imprisonment has not been provided as a penalty under this section. The offence under section 393 is cognizable, non-bailable and non-compoundable, and is triable by magistrate of the first class.

44. The International Bill of Human Rights is an informal name given to two international treaties and one General Assembly resolution established by the United Nations. It consists of the Universal Declaration of Human Rights (adopted in 1948), the International Covenant on Civil and Political Rights (1966) with its two Optional Protocols and the International Covenant on Economic, Social and Cultural Rights (1966). The two covenants entered into force in 1976, after a sufficient number of countries had ratified them.

45. In the Queen *vs.* Keyn (1876), LORD COLERIDGE, C.J., defined International law in the following words: "The law of nations is that collection of usages which civilized States have agreed to observe in their dealings with one another."

47. Doing anything which has the effect of putting goods in possession of legal representative of seller cannot be treated as delivery under the Sale of Goods Act. According to Section 2 (2) of the Sale of Goods Act, 1930, delivery means voluntary transfer of possession of goods from one person to another. Hence, if a person takes possession of goods by unfair means, then there is no delivery of goods.

48. In the historic case of S.R. Bommai *vs.* Union of India, the nine Judges' Bench had dealt with the importance of the concept of federalism in India. Justice Kuldip Singh J. observed that democracy and federalism are the essential features of the Indian Constitution and part of its Basic Structure. Justice Jeevan Reddy on the other hand pointed out that the Constitution of India has created a federation but with a bias in favour of the Centre and within the sphere allotted to the States, they are supreme. While endorsing the opinion of the brother Judges that federalism envisaged in the Constitution of India is a basic feature, Justice Ramasamy also observed that the objective of the founding fathers of the Constitution and the law of the land is to preserve the unity and territorial integrity of the nation and they have entrusted the common wheel to the Union while maintaining to preserve the federal character of the States, which are an integral part of the Union.

49. An **ombudsman** is an official who is charged with representing the interests of the public by investigating and addressing complaints of mal-administration or a violation of rights. Use of the term in its modern use began in Sweden, with the Swedish Parliamentary Ombudsman instituted by the Instrument of Government of 1809, to safeguard the rights of citizens by establishing a supervisory agency independent of the executive branch.

Chronological order:

1809 – Sweden

1920 – Finland
1962 – New Zealand
1967 – UK

51. As to its meaning, Judicial Activism is not a distinctly separate concept from usual judicial activities. The word 'activism' means "being active", 'doing things with decision' and activist is the 'one' who favours intensified activities. Justice Krishna Iyer observed 'every judge is an activist either on the forward gear or on the reverse'.

Judicial policy making can be either an activity in support of legislative and executive policy choices or in opposition to them. But the latter one is usually referred to as judicial activism. The essence of true judicial activism is the rendering of decision which is in tune with the temper and tempo of the times.

Activism in judicial policy making furthers the cause of social change or articulates concepts such as liberty, equality or justice. It has to be an arm of the social revolution. An activist judge activates the legal mechanism and makes it play a vital role in socio-economic process.

Causes of Judicial Activism: The following trends were the cause for the emergence of judicial activism — expansion of rights of hearing in the administrative process, excessive delegation without limitation, expansion of judicial review over administration, promotion of open government, indiscriminate exercise of contempt power, exercise of jurisdiction when non-exist; over extending the standard rules of interpretation in its search to achieve economic, social and educational objectives; and passing of orders which are unworkable.

52. A new Section 376 AB was inserted by Act 22 of 2018 in Indian Penal code, 1860. According to this section, "whoever, commits rape on a woman under 12 years of age shall be punished with rigorous imprisonment for a term which shall not be less than 20 years, but which may extend to imprisonment for life, which shall mean imprisonment for the remainder of that person's natural life, and with fine or with death:

Provided that such fine shall be just and reasonable to meet the Medical expenses and rehabilitation of the victim:

Provided further that any fine imposed under this section shall be paid to the victim".

53. ARTICLE 153: GOVERNORS OF STATES

There shall be a Governor for each State:

Provided that nothing in this article shall prevent the appointment of the same person as Governor for two or more States.

ARTICLE 154: EXECUTIVE POWER OF STATE

(1) The executive power of the State shall be vested in the Governor and shall be exercised by him either directly or through officers subordinate to him in accordance with this Constitution.

(2) Nothing in this article shall—

(*a*) be deemed to transfer to the Governor any functions conferred by any existing law on any other authority; or

(*b*) prevent Parliament or the Legislature of the State from conferring by law functions on any authority subordinate to the Governor.

ARTICLE 155: APPOINTMENT OF GOVERNOR

The Governor of a State shall be appointed by the President by warrant under his hand and seal.

ARTICLE 156: TERM OF OFFICE OF GOVERNOR

1. The Governor shall hold office during the pleasure of the President.
2. The Governor may, by writing under his hand addressed to the President, resign his office.

3. Subject to the foregoing provisions of this article, a Governor shall hold office for a term of five years from the date on which he enters upon his office:

Provided that a Governor shall, notwithstanding the expiration of his term, continue to hold office until his successor enters upon his office.

55. Section 4 of the Competition Act, 2002 prevents any enterprise or group from abusing its dominant position. The Act also provides circumstances under which there is abuse of dominant position. Section 4 (2) of the Act specifies the following practices by a dominant enterprises or group of enterprises as abuses:

(*i*) directly or indirectly imposing unfair or discriminatory condition in purchase or sale of goods or service; (*ii*) directly or indirectly imposing unfair or discriminatory price in purchase or sale (including predatory price) of goods or service; (*iii*) limiting or restricting production of goods or provision of services or market; (*iv*) limiting or restricting technical or scientific development relating to goods or services to the prejudice of consumers; (*v*) denying market access in any manner; (*vi*) making conclusion of contracts subject to acceptance by other parties of supplementary obligations which, by their nature or according to commercial usage, have no connection with the subject of such contracts; (*vii*) using its dominant position in one relevant market to enter into, or protect, other relevant market.

56. According to Salmond, every legal right has five Essential elements which are as follows:

The person of inheritance:

The first essential element of the legal right is that there must be a person who is the owner of the Right. He is the subject of the legal right. He is sometimes described as the person of inheritance. The owner of a right need not be a determinant or fixed person. If an individual owes a duty towards society at large, then an indeterminant body is the subject of inheritance.

Example: If 'X' purchased a car for ₹ 10 lakh from 'Y', then 'X' is called the subject of the right.

The person of incidence/Subject of the Duty:

A legal right occurs against another person or persons who are under a corresponding duty to respect that right. Such a person is called the person of incidence or the subject of the duty. If X has a particular right against Y, X is the person of inheritance and Y the subject of incidence.

Example: If 'X' purchased a car for ₹ 10 lakh from 'Y', then 'Y' is called the subject of the duty.

Subject matter or Contents of legal rights:

The content of the legal right deal with the subject matter of legal rights. It relates to some act to do or not to do any act or forbearance.

The object of legal rights:

The thing or an object over which the right is exercised is called 'Object of Right'.

Example: If 'X' purchased a car for ₹ 10 lakh, then the car is the object of right.

Title:

A title is nothing but the name given to the legal right. The title is a process, by which the right is vested/conferred. Purchase, gift, etc confer a title on a person.

From the above essentials of legal rights, we can conclude that every right involves a relationship between two or more legal persons, and only legal persons can be bound by duties or be the holders of legal rights. Similarly, rights and duties are correlated. We cannot have a right without a corresponding duty or a duty without corresponding right.

57. Jurisprudence is the branch of study of the philosophy of law. The modern jurisprudence began in the 18th century. One of the tasks of Jurisprudence is to construct and elucidate organizing concepts serving to render the complexities of law more manageable and more rational; and in this way theory can help to improve practice.

The four primary schools of thought in general jurisprudence are: Natural Law Theory, Legal Positivism, Legal Realism and Critical Legal Studies.

Correct match:

Spirit of People – Savigny

Social Solidarity – Duguit

Dictates of Reasoning – Thomas Acquinas

Social Control – Ihering

58. The act of acquiring immovable property on behalf of the firm does not come under the scope implied Authority of a Partner.

Section 19 in the Indian Partnership Act, 1932

Section 19: Implied authority of partner as agent of the firm—

1. Subject to the provisions of section 22, the act of a partner which is done to carry on, in the usual way, business of the kind carried on by the firm, binds the firm. The authority of a partner to bind the firm conferred by this section is called his implied authority.
2. In the absence of any usage or custom of trade to the contrary, the implied authority of a partner does not empower him to:

a. submit a dispute relating to the business of the firm to arbitration,

b. open a banking account on behalf of the firm in his own name,

c. compromise or relinquish any claim or portion of a claim by the firm,

d. withdraw a suit or proceeding filed on behalf of the firm,

e. admit any liability in a suit or proceedin against the firm,

f. acquire immovable property on behalf c the firm,

g. transfer immovable property belonging t the firm, or

h. enter into partnership on behalf of th firm

60. Sections of the Copyright Act, 1957 wit provisions:

Section 2(O) – Meaning of Literary work

Section 38 – Performer Right

Section 37 – Broadcast Reproduction Righ

Section 2(XX) – Meaning of Soun Recording

61. Correct matching:

Hussainara Khatom *vs.* State of Bihar – Speed Trial.

Murli S. Deora *vs.* Union of India – Ban o smoking in Public places.

Lakshmi Kant Pandey *vs.* Union of India - Child welfare.

Sunil Batra *vs.* Delhi Administration - Protection against inhuman treatment in jail

63. Section 361 of the Indian Penal code:

Kidnapping from lawful guardianship— Whoever takes or entices any minor unde (16) years of age if a male, or under (18 years of age if a female, or any person o unsound mind, without the consent of such guardian, is said to kidnap such minor o person from lawful guardianship.

Explanation — The word "lawful guardian" in this section include any person lawfully entrusted with the care or custody of such minor or other person.

Exception — This section does not extend to the act of any person who in good faith believes himself to be the father of an illegitimate child, or who in good faith believes himself to be entitled to lawful custody of such child, unless such act is committed for an immoral or unlawful purpose.

64. An Act to provide for the establishment of a National Green Tribunal for the effective and expeditious disposal of cases relating to environmental protection and conservation of forests and other natural resources including enforcement of any legal right relating to environment and giving relief and compensation for damages to persons and property and for matters connected therewith or incidental thereto.

And Whereas India is a party to the decisions taken at the United Nations Conference on the Human Environment held at Stockholm in June, 1972, in which India participated, calling upon the States to take appropriate steps for the protection and improvement of the human environment;

And Whereas decisions were taken at the United Nations Conference on Environment and Development held at *Rio de Janeiro* in June, 1992, in which India participated, calling upon the States to provide effective access to judicial and administrative proceedings, including redress and remedy and to develop national laws regarding liability and compensation for the victims of pollution and other environmental damage;

And Whereas in the judicial pronouncement in India, the right to healthy environment has been construed as a part of the right to life under article 21 of the Constitution;

And Whereas it is considered expedient to implement the decisions taken at the aforesaid conferences and to have a National Green Tribunal in view of the involvement of multi-disciplinary issues relating to the environment.

65. Section 124A of the Indian Penal Code; Sedition:

Whoever, by words, either spoken or written, or by signs, or by visible representation, or otherwise, brings or attempts to bring into hatred or contempt, or excites or attempts to excite disaffection towards, the Government established by law in India, shall be punished with imprisonment for life, to which fine may be added, or with imprisonment which may extend to three years, to which fine may be added, or with fine.

- **Explanation 1.** The expression "disaffection" includes disloyalty and all feelings of enmity.
- **Explanation 2.** Comments expressing disapprobation of the measures of the Government with a view to obtain their alteration by lawful means, without exciting or attempting to excite hatred, contempt or disaffection, do not constitute an offence under this section.
- **Explanation 3.** Comments expressing disapprobation of the administrative or other action of the Government without exciting or attempting to excite hatred, contempt or disaffection, do not constitute an offence under this section.

66. Section 49 in The Information Technology Act, 2000

1. The Cyber Appellate Tribunal shall consist of a Chairperson and such number of other Members, as the Central Government may, by notification in the Official Gazette, appoint: Provided that the person appointed as the Presiding Officer of the Cyber Appellate Tribunal under the provisions of this Act immediately before the commencement of the Information Technology (Amendment) Act, 2008 shall be deemed to have been appointed as the Chairperson of the said Cyber Appellate Tribunal under the provisions of this Act as amended by the Information Technology (Amendment) Act, 2008.
2. The selection of Chairperson and Members of the Cyber Appellate Tribunal shall be

made by the Central Government in consultation with the Chief Justice of India.

3. Subject to the provisions of this Act:
   (*a*) the jurisdiction, powers and authority of the Cyber Appellate Tribunal may be exercised by the Benches thereof;
   (*b*) a Bench may be constituted by the Chairperson of the Cyber Appellate Tribunal with one or two Members of such Tribunal as the Chairperson may deem fit;
   (*c*) the Benches of the Cyber Appellate Tribunal shall sit at New Delhi and at such other places as the Central Government may, in consultation with the Chairperson of the Cyber Appellate Tribunal, by notification in the Official Gazette, specify;
   (*d*) the Central Government shall, by notification in the Official Gazette, specify the areas in relation to which each Bench of the Cyber Appellate Tribunal may exercise its jurisdiction.
4. Notwithstanding anything contained in sub-section (3), the Chairperson of the Cyber Appellate Tribunal may transfer a Member of such Tribunal from one Bench to another Bench.
5. If at any stage of the hearing of any case or matter it appears to the Chairperson or a Member of the Cyber Appellate Tribunal that the case or matter is of such a nature that it ought to be heard by a Bench consisting of more Members, the case or matter may be transferred by the Chairperson to such Bench as the Chairperson may deem fit.

67. The essential Characteristics of Federation of USA are:

Supremacy of Constitution

Distribution of powers amongst the various organs of the federation and of regional units of the federation by the provision of constitution.

Judicial Review or enforcement of that supreme constitution as law

Essential Features of a Federation:

1. Division of Powers
2. Written Constitution
3. Rigid Constitution
4. Supremacy of the Constitution
5. Special Role of the Judiciary
6. Dual Administration
7. Dual Citizenship
8. Bicameral Legislature
9. Equality of all Federating States

68. Hart contends that it is necessary for law and morality to have certain element of natural law as a logical necessity. Thus morality is implicit in Hart's positive law which he describes as union of primary and secondary rules. As a member of society, individual feels morally bound to abide by these rules both as a matter of duty and obligation. Hart, therefore, asserts that law and morality are complementary and supplementary to each other. In his view, there are four attributes of morality, namely:

- Importance
- Immunity from deliberate change
- Voluntary character of moral offences
- Forms of moral pressure which separate it from etiquette, custom and other social rules

69. The **Companies Act, 2013** has formulated Section 135, **Companies (Corporate Social Responsibility) Rules, 2014** and Schedule VII which prescribes mandatory provisions for Companies to fulfill their CSR.

Applicability of CSR Provisions:

On every Company including its holding or subsidiary having:

- Net worth of ₹ 500 Crore or more, or
- Turnover of ₹ 1000 crore or more, or
- Net Profit of ₹ 5 crore or more

during the immediately preceding financial year

A foreign company having its branch office or project office in India, which fulfills the criteria specified above.

However, if a company ceases to meet the above criteria for 3 consecutive financial years then it is not required to comply with CSR Provisions till such time it meets the specified criteria.

CSR Committee:

Every Company on which CSR is applicable is required to constitute a CSR Committee of the Board:

- Consisting of 3 or more directors, out of which at least one director shall be an independent director. However, if a company is not required to appoint an independent director, then it shall have in 2 or more directors in the Committee.
- Consisting of 2 directors in case of a private company having only two directors on its Board.
- Consisting of at least 2 persons in case of a foreign Company of which one person shall be its authorised person resident in India and another nominated by the foreign company.

71. According to **Section 159 of the Indian Penal Code, Affray** is defined as "When two or more persons by fighting in a public place, disturb the public peace, they are said to commit an affray." The punishment for committing affray is imprisonment for up to one month or fine up to one hundred rupees or both (Section 160).

72. The chief advantages of legislation over precedent are the following:

1. **Abrogative Power:** Legislation is both constitutive and abrogative whereas precedent merely possesses constitutive efficacy. Legislation is not only a source of law, but it is equally effective in amending or annulling the existing law. Precedent, on the other hand, cannot abrogate the existing rule of law although it may produce very good law and in some respects better than legislation. What it does, it docs once for all. It cannot retrace its steps. Legislation as a destructive and reformative agent has no equal.

2. **Efficiency:** Legislation allows an advantageous division of labour by dividing the two functions of making the law and administering it. This results in increased efficiency. President, however, unites those two functions in the same hands.

3. **Declaration:** Justice demands that law should be known before they are applied and enforced by the law co[u]rts, but the ease law operates retrospectively, being applied to facts which are prior in date to the law itself. Statute law is seldom retrospective in its operation.

   Then legislation withstands the test of an interpretation of the statute by the courts of justice. If any alterations are proposed in the enacted law, they are published and opinions invited. Case law, on the contrary, is created and declared at one and the same time.

4. **Provision for future cases:** Legislation can make rules in anticipation for cases that have not as yet arisen, whereas precedent must wait for the occurrence of some dispute before the court can create any definite rule of law. Precedent is dependent on, and legislation is independent of, the accidental course of legislation.

   Legislation can till up vacancy or settle a doubt in legal system as soon as the defect is Drought to the notice of the legislature. This is not possible in the case of precedent. Case law, therefore, is incomplete, uncertain and unsystematic.

5. **Form:** Legislation is superior in form brief, clear, easily accessible and understandable, whilst valuable part of case law has to be extracted from a ton of dross. One has to wade through the whole judgement before the ratio decided can be found out or case law discovered. Figuratively, as Salmond observes, ease law is gold in mine a few grams of precious metal to the ton of useless material while statute law is coin of the realm, ready for immediate use.

73. In the *Asylum Case (Columbia* vs *Peru)* 1950 ICJ Rep 266, the Court recognised that Art. 38 of the Statute of the ICJ encompassed local custom as well as general Local customary law may exist where a practice has developed between two or more states, both or all of whom recognise the practice as binding. An example was Portugal's right of transit over Indian territory recognised in the *Rights of Passage Case* 1960 ICJ Rep 6. However, the state alleging the existence of local custom will be under a heavy burden to show that the practice was regarded as legally binding, rather than merely habitual or born of the desire for amicable relations. Subject to this, and to what will be said below about rules of *jus cogens,* local customary law can supplement or derogate from general custom. In practice, local or regional custom is most likely to develop between states sharing the same economic and political ideology (*e.g.* the EU), although, as the *Rights of Passage Case* shows, this is not essential.

74. In India, the Supreme Court has original, appellate and advisory jurisdiction. Its exclusive original jurisdiction extends to all **cases** between the Government of India and the States of India or between Government of India and states on one side and one or more states on other side or **cases** between different states.

75. Soon after the passage of the 36th constitutional amendment Act, the Governor was appointed under **Article 155** of the Indian Constitution, whereby its special role was fixed under clause (g) of **Article 371** (F) for ensuring the social and economic advancement of different sections of the population of Sikkim.

76. Article 48(A): "State shall endeavour to protect and improve the environment and to safeguard the forests and wildlife of the country."

Article 48(A) was added by the Constitution (42nd Amendment) Act, 1976. This article have to be considered in the light of Article 21 which secures right to life and personal liberty.

The Environment (Protection) Act, 1986 and the wildlife (Protection) Act, 1972, as amended by the Act of 1986, are among the steps taken to give effect to the mandate contained in Article 48(A). To enable effective steps being taken for the purpose, by both Centre and State Governments 'Wildlife' and 'forests' have now been placed in the concurrent list of the 7th Schedule by the Constitution (42nd Amendment) Act, 1976.

77. Tort comes from the Latin word *tortum,* meaning "wrong." When someone has done some wrong to you, you can seek justice (in the form of payment) by taking them to court.

79. The Muslim law has been derived from various primary as well as secondary sources. These are classified as:

A. Primary Sources
   1. Sunna or Ahadis
   2. Quran
   3. Ijma
   4. Qiyas

B. Secondary Sources
   1. Judicial Decision
   2. Custom
   3. Legislation
   4. Equity, Just & Good Conscience (Istihsn, Itislah & Istidal)

80. Article 233. Appointment of district judges

1. Appointments of persons to be, and the posting and promotion of, district judges in any State shall be made by the Governor of the State in consultation with the High Court exercising jurisdiction in relation to such State.
2. A person not already in the service of the Union or of the State shall only be eligible to be appointed a district judge if he has been for not less than seven years an advocate or a pleader and is recommended by the High Court for appointment.

81. India ratified ILO Conventions, 138 and 182, which says that the minimum age for employment should not be less than the age of completion of compulsory schooling (14 years of age in India's case) and calls for elimination of the worst forms of child labour, respectively.

82. In Luther *vs* Sagar case it was held that "there is no distinction between defacto and dejure recognition for the purpose of giving effect to the international acts of the recognised authority". In Luther *vs* Sagar , a case involving legislation of an unrecognised Soviet government, it was established that the courts must give effect only to legislation of a recognised state. While the case was in the lower courts (and the Soviet government at the time was unrecognised), the action was possible and indeed successful. The case could not, however, proceed once the Soviet government had been officially recognised.

84. Section 270, IPC, deals with a 'malignant act likely to spread infection of disease dangerous to life' and says: "Whoever malignantly does any act which is, and which he knows or has reason to believe to be, likely to spread the infection of any disease dangerous to life shall be punished with imprisonment or either description for a term which may extend to two years, or with fine, or with both."

85. The **coastal** areas of seas, bays, creeks, rivers, and backwaters which get influenced by tides up to 500 m from the high tide line (HTL) and the land between the low tide line (LTL) and the high tide line have been declared as **coastal regulation zone** (CRZ) in 1991.

In India, the process for environmental audit was first mentioned under the Environment Protection Act, 1986 by the Ministry of Environment of forests on 13th march, 1992. As per this act, every person owning an industry or performing an operation or process needs a legal consent and must submit an environmental report or statement.

Environmental Impact Assessment (EIA) is a process of evaluating the likely environmental impacts of a proposed project or development, taking into account inter-related socio-economic, cultural and human-health impacts, both beneficial and adverse.

After collecting the Fly Ash in ESP, it is then transported by trucks or conveyors at the sight and disposed of by constructing a dry embankment. In wet disposal system, the Fly Ash is mixed with water and transported as slurry through pipe and disposed of in ash ponds or dumping areas near the plants.

87. Section 378 in The Indian Penal Code – Theft

Whoever intending to take dishonestly any movable property out of the possession of any person without that person's consent, moves that property in order to such taking is said to commit theft.

Essential Ingredients:

1. There must be a dishonest intention of a person to take the property.
2. The property must be movable.
3. Such movable property must be taken away.
4. The property must be taken away from the possession of a person. In other words there must be a possession of that property.

5. Such property must be taken away without the consent of such person.

88. Convention on the Nationality of Married Women. The Convention on the Nationality of Married Women is an international convention passed by the United Nations General Assembly in 1957. It entered into force in 1958 and as of 2013 it has 74 state parties.

Convention on the Reduction of Statelessness. Adopted on 30 August, 1961 by a conference of plenipotentiaries which met in 1959 and reconvened in 1961 in pursuance of General Assembly resolution 896 (IX) of 4 December, 1954. Entry into force on 13 December 1975, in accordance with article 18.

89. On July 20, 1989, the International Court of Justice delivered its judgement in the case concerning Elettronica Sicula S.p.A. (ELSI) between the United States of America and Italy.

On 11 December, 1986, El Salvador and Honduras jointly notified the Court of a Special Agreement concluded between them on 24 May, 1986 whereby a dispute referred to as "Land, Island and Maritime Frontier Dispute" would be submitted for decision by a Chamber to be constituted according to Article 26 para.

Fisheries Jurisdiction case (Spain *vs.* Canada)... The Court concluded that the dispute submitted to it by Spain constituted a dispute "arising out of" and "concerning" "conservation and management measures taken by Canada with respect to vessels fishing in the NAFO Regulatory Area" and "the enforcement of such measures".

On 29 April 1999, the (former) Federal Republic of Yugoslavia (FRY) instituted proceedings before the International Court of Justice (ICJ) against the United States of America "for violation of the obligation not to use force", resulting from the bombing of Yugoslav territory by the United States and other Member States of NATO.

90. The Consumer Protection Act, 1986 seeks to provide for better protection of the interests of consumers and for the purpose, to make provision for the establishment of Consumer councils and other authorities for the settlement of consumer disputes and for matter connected therewith.

Correct match:

Jurisdiction of the District Forum – Section 11

Composition of State Commission – Section 16

Composition of National Commission – Section 20

Circuit benches of State commission – Section 17B

Previous Years' Paper (Solved)

National Testing Agency (NTA)

UGC-NET Junior Research Fellowship & Assistant Professor Eligibility Exam

Law, June-2019*

PAPER-II

Note: *This paper contains* ***hundred (100)*** *objective type questions of* ***two (2)*** *marks each.* ***All questions*** *are* ***compulsory.***

1. 'Test of control' deals with:

A. master and servant relationship
B. measures of damages
C. course of employment
D. implied authority

2. In which of the following cases the Supreme Court held that 'the audi alteram partem rule, in essence enforces the equality clause in Article 14 and it is applicable not only to quasi-judicial bodies but also to administrative order adversely affecting the party in question?"

A. U.P. Warehousing Corporation Vs. Vijay Narain
B. Delhi Transport Corporation Vs. DTC Majdoor Union
C. A.K. Gopalan Vs. State of Madras
D. Gullapalli Nageshwar Rao Vs. APSRTC

3. The inadequacy of consideration will be taken into account by a court of law:

A. when the promisor expresses his desire to get maximum return for his promise
B. when the promisor performs his promise
C. when fraud, coercion or undue influence in the formation of the contract is pleaded
D. always at the discretion of the court

4. The Sustainable Development Goals (SDGs) committed to provide:

(*a*) Universal access to affordable, reliable and modern energy services
(*b*) Improving the share of renewable energy
(*c*) Doubling of energy efficiency by 2030
(*d*) Protection of ocean and wetland

Select the correct answer using the options given below:

A. (*a*), (*b*) and (*c*) are true
B. (*a*), (*c*) and (*d*) are true
C. (*b*), (*c*) and (*d*) are true
D. (*a*), (*b*) and (*d*) are true

5. Which of the following statement/statements is/are NOT correct?

(*a*) The declaration of National Emergency on the ground of 'Armed Rebellion' was inserted by the Constitutional (42 Amendment) Act, 1976.
(*b*) President shall not issue a proclamation under Clause (1) Article 352 unless the decision of the Union Cabinet (the Prime Minister and his Council of Ministers) is communicated to him in writing.
(*c*) A resolution approving the proclamation of National Emergency must be passed by special majority.
(*d*) A proclamation of Emergency once approved by the Parliament shall remain in force until the emergency ceases.

Select the correct answers by using the codes given below:

A. Only (*a*)
B. (*a*) and (*d*) both
C. (*b*), (*c*) and (*d*)
D. (*a*), (*b*), (*c*) and (*d*)

*Online exam held on 21-06-2019.

6. Which of the following statement/statements is/are correct?

(*a*) If the other House does not pass an Ordinary Bill and more than six months have passed, the President may summon a Joint Session of both the Houses.

(*b*) At the Joint Session of two Houses, new amendment can be proposed in the Bill with the permission of the Presiding Officer (Speaker of the Lok Sabha).

(*c*) The Lower House has exclusive power over Money Bills.

(*d*) Money and Financial Bills can be only introduced in the Lok Sabha and with prior recommendations of the President.

Select the correct answer using the code given below:

A. Only (*a*) B. (*a*), (*b*) and (*c*)
C. (*a*), (*c*) and (*d*) D. (*a*), (*b*), (*c*) and (*d*)

7. 'Right to Environment' discourse includes:

(*a*) Right to Health
(*b*) Right to Sanitation
(*c*) Right to Clean Technology
(*d*) Right to Free Speech

Select the correct answer from the code given below:

A. (*a*), (*b*) and (*c*) are true
B. (*b*), (*c*) and (*d*) are true
C. (*a*), (*c*) and (*d*) are true
D. (*a*) and (*b*) are true whereas (*c*) and (*d*) are false

8. Every offence punishable under Section 147 of the Negotiable Instruments Act, 1881 is:

A. compoundable
B. non-compoundable
C. cognizable
D. Both (B) and (C) above

9. UN Commissioner for Human Rights is appointed by:

A. General Assembly
B. Security Council
C. Secretary General
D. Human Rights Council

10. Which of the following is correct?

A. Administrative Law is a branch of Public Law and is only a part of Constitutional Law. It cannot control the Constitutional Law
B. Administrative Law is a branch of Private Law
C. Administrative Law is independent to the Constitutional Law
D. Administrative Law is neither the branch of Public Law nor of Private Law but a part of Constitutional Law

11. Who among the following has defined jurisprudence as 'the knowledge of things divine and human, the science of right and wrong?'

A. Blackstone B. Hobbes
C. Salmond D. Ulpian

12. 'We have to evolve new principles and lay down new norms which will adequately deal with new problems which arise in a highly industrialised society' was laid down in:

A. Common Cause Vs. Union of India
B. M.C. Mehta Vs. Union of India
C. Invercargill City Council Vs. Hamlin
D. Union of India Vs. Sat Pal Dharam Vir

13. In which of the following case, it was held that if a person is not a citizen of any state, he will be called 'stateless'?

A. Nottebohm's Case
B. Whicker Vs. Hume
C. Winans Vs. A.G.
D. Stoeck Vs. The Public Trustee

14. The communication of an acceptance is complete as against the proposer:

A. when it is posted to him
B. when it comes to the knowledge of the proposer
C. when the letter containing acceptance is received by the proposer
D. when it is put in the course of transmission, so as to be out of the acceptor's power

15. The principle 'Restitution stops where repayment begins' can be applied against:

A. an alien enemy only
B. minors only
C. lunatics and idiots only
D. an incapable person

16. In which section of the Partnership Act it is laid down that there can be a partnership in a single or particular business venture?

A. Section 8 B. Section 9
C. Section 10 D. Section 11

17. Possession through an agent or servant is an example of:

A. corporeal possession
B. incorporeal possession
C. mediate possession
D. immediate possession

18. 'Cyber security' according to the IT Act, 2000 means:

A. a device and collection of devices, including input and output support devices and excluding calculations which are not programmable and capable of being used
B. any electronic, magnetic, optical or other high speed data processing device or system which performs logical, arithmetic and memory functions by manipulation of electronic, magnetic or optical impulse
C. protecting information, equipment, devices, computer, computer resource, communication device and information stored therein from unauthorised access, use, disclosure, disruption, modification or destruction
D. affixing with its grammatical variations and cognate expressions means adoption of any methodology or procedure by a person for the purpose of authenticating an electronic record

19. Match List-I with List-II:

List-I	List-II
(*a*) Date and year of establishment of United Nations	(*i*) 2 May, 1981
(*b*) The first Security Council came into being	(*ii*) 1 January, 1992
(*c*) Paris Declaration on Sanctions against South Africa	(*iii*) 12 January, 1946
(*d*) Mr. Boutros Boutras Ghali took over as Secretary General of the UN	(*iv*) 24 October, 1945

Choose the correct options from those given below:

	(*a*)	(*b*)	(*c*)	(*d*)
A.	(*i*)	(*ii*)	(*iii*)	(*iv*)
B.	(*iii*)	(*i*)	(*iv*)	(*ii*)
C.	(*iv*)	(*ii*)	(*iii*)	(*i*)
D.	(*iv*)	(*iii*)	(*i*)	(*ii*)

20. Which of the following is not the School of Muslim Law?

A. Hanafi
B. Maliki
C. Hanabali
D. Zaida

21. 'Public health, sanitation conservancy and solid waste management' is inserted to the Schedule of the Constitution by which of the following Constitutional Amendments?

A. 42nd Constitutional Amendment
B. 44th Constitutional Amendment
C. 73rd Constitutional Amendment
D. 74th Constitutional Amendment

22. In which of the cases did Supreme Court hold that a relationship in the nature of marriage under the Domestic Violence Act, 2005 must also fulfill some basic criteria, merely spending weekends together or one night would not make it a domestic relationship?

A. Payal Katara Vs. Supt. Nari Niketan and other
B. D. Velusamy Vs. D. Patchaiammal
C. Bharati Matha and others Vs. R. Vijaya Ranganathan and others
D. S. Khushboo Vs. Kanniammal and others

23. "Dower may be regarded as consideration for connubial intercourse by way of analogy to the contract for sale."

The above observation has been made is which of the following cases?

A. Abdul Kadir Vs. Salma
B. Zobair Ahmed Vs. Jainandan Prasad
C. Rahana Khattun Vs. Iqtidar-uddin
D. Hamidunissa Bibi Vs. Zaheer Sheik

24. The Doctrine of Separation of Powers in its strict and technical sense is applied in:

A. India B. U.K.
C. U.S.A. D. France

25. The Cyber Regulations Appellate Tribunal Rule, 2000 has been passed under which section of the IT Act, 2000?

A. Section 84 B. Section 85
C. Section 86 D. Section 87

26. Match List-I with List-II:

List-I	**List-II**
(*a*) Bentham	(*i*) Historical School
(*b*) Puchta	(*ii*) Sociological School
(*c*) Herbert Spencer	(*iii*) Analytical School
(*d*) Gray	(*iv*) The Realist School

Choose the correct options from those given below:

	(*a*)	(*b*)	(*c*)	(*d*)
A.	(*iii*)	(*i*)	(*ii*)	(*iv*)
B.	(*i*)	(*ii*)	(*iii*)	(*iv*)
C.	(*ii*)	(*iv*)	(*iii*)	(*i*)
D.	(*iv*)	(*iii*)	(*i*)	(*ii*)

27. In which of the following cases the Supreme Court said that Governor cannot exercise his power of suspension of the sentence under Article 213 of the Constitution of India, for the period when the Supreme Court is seized of the case. The order of the Governor could only operate until the matter became subjudice in the Supreme Court and it becomes so on the filing of the petition for special leave to appeal?

A. Satpal Dang Vs. State of Punjab
B. D.C. Wadhwa Vs. State of Bihar
C. K.M. Nanavati Vs. State of Bombay
D. A.K. Roy Vs. Union of India

28. Super Cassettes Industries Ltd. Vs. Myspace Inc. 2011 is a leading case on the Copyright Act, 1957 dealing with which section of the Act?

A. Section 14 B. Section 22
C. Section 30 D. Section 51

29. The remedies for the violation of Sections 3 and 4 of the Competition Act have been laid down under:

A. Section 26 B. Section 27
C. Section 42A D. Section 43A

30. The accused at the time of committing the act because of unsoundness of mind is incapable of knowing:

(*a*) the nature of the act
(*b*) that the act is wrong or contrary to law
(*c*) that the act is unethical and wrong
(*d*) that the act is morally wrong but not contrary to law

To claim the benefit of Sec. 84 of IPC which of the above needs to be proved?

Give the correct answer:

A. (*a*) and (*d*) B. (*a*) and (*b*)
C. (*b*) and (*c*) D. (*c*) and (*d*)

31. Which of the following is not a constituent of Tort?

A. Wrongful act B. Damage
C. Remedy D. Mens rea

32. X, with the intention to cause miscarriage administered a drug to a pregnant lady, Y. The child in the womb died. X is guilty of:

A. murder
B. culpable homicide not amounting to murder
C. no offence
D. causing miscarriage

33. Holback Hotel Ltd. Vs. Scarborough Borough Council is a leading case on:

A. negligence B. nuisance
C. trespass D. defamation

34. "Decision making process of those authorities besides being transparent must result in a reasoned conclusion which is reflective of a due application of mind to the diverse concerns arising from a project such as the present." This has been observed regarding Environment Impact Assessment Law in which of the following cases?

A. Utkarsh Mandal Vs. Union of India
B. Deepak Kumar Vs. State of Haryana
C. Gram Panchayat Navlakh Umbre Vs. Union of India
D. Tehri Bandh Virodhi Sangharsh Samiti Vs. State of UP

35. Match List-I with List-II:

List-I	List-II
(*a*) A right which although, recognised by law, is not enforceable	(*i*) Proprietory Right
(*b*) A person's right in relation to his property	(*ii*) Personal Right
(*c*) A person's right relating to status and that arising out of contract	(*iii*) Imperfect Right
(*d*) A right which does not create an immediate interest	(*iv*) Contingent Right

Choose the correct options from those given below:

	(*a*)	(*b*)	(*c*)	(*d*)
A.	(*i*)	(*ii*)	(*iii*)	(*iv*)
B.	(*iii*)	(*i*)	(*ii*)	(*iv*)
C.	(*ii*)	(*iii*)	(*iv*)	(*i*)
D.	(*iv*)	(*ii*)	(*i*)	(*iii*)

36. Which Article of the Indian Constitution states that 'the state shall endeavour to secure for the citizens a uniform civil code throughout the territory of India?'

A. Article 25 of the Constitution
B. Article 37 of the Constitution
C. Article 44 of the Constitution
D. Article 45 of the Constitution

37. Which of the following statement/statements is/are NOT correct?

(*a*) According to Article 16 of the Universal Declaration of Human Rights, 'Everyone has a right to seek and enjoy in other countries asylum from prosecution.'
(*b*) In 1967, United Nations Declaration on Territorial Asylum was unanimously adopted by the General Assembly.
(*c*) The Convention on the Status of Refugees, 1951 entered into force on April 24, 1956.
(*d*) In the Asylum Case (Colombia V. Peru) the International Court of Justice explained the distinction between territorial asylum and diplomatic asylum.

Select the correct answer using the code given below:

A. Only (*a*)
B. (*a*) and (*b*)
C. (*a*) and (*c*)
D. (*a*), (*b*), (*c*) and (*d*)

38. Which of the following statement/statements is/are correct?

(*a*) The operation of the doctrine of forum prorogation has not been envisaged under the UN Charter or the Statute of the International Court of Justice.
(*b*) The Doctrine of Forum Prorogatum may not operate where the court already has jurisdiction ratione personae.
(*c*) The Doctrine of the Forum Prorogatum affords an informal way for a state to express consent to the jurisdiction of the court.
(*d*) The principle underlying doctrine of forum prorogatum was enunciated by the Permanent Court of International Justice in the Island of Palm is Case (1928).

Select the correct answer from the code given below.

A. Only (*a*)
B. (*a*) and (*c*)
C. (*b*), (*c*) and (*d*)
D. (*a*), (*b*), (*c*) and (*d*)

39. 'A citizen has a fundamental right to use the best means of imparting and receiving information and as such to have an access to telecasting for the purpose' is the observation of the Supreme Court in:

A. Ministry of Information and Broadcasting, Government of India Vs. Cricket Association of Bengal (1995)
B. Prabhu Dutt Vs. Union of India (1982)
C. Dinesh Trivedi Vs. Union of India (1977)
D. Pramati Educational and Cultural Trust Vs. Union of India (2014)

40. "Nobody can be above the institution which he is supposed to serve. He is merely the creature of the institution, he can exist only if the institution exists. To protect the individual as mighter than the Constitution would be grave injustice."

In which of the following cases the Supreme Court, through Chief Justice Sikri has observed this?

A. S.S. Dhannoa Vs. Union of India
B. T.N. Seshan Vs. Union of India
C. In Presidential Reference, 2000
D. A.C. Jose Vs. Sivan Pillai

41. Under which of the following sections of Code of Civil Procedure (1908) did Indian courts recognise or derecognise the foreign decree of divorce?

A. Section 13 B. Section 12
C. Section 15 D. Section 16

42. Bayer Corporation Vs. Union of India, 2011 case is dealing on which subject matters?

A. Evergreening of patent
B. Grant and sealing of patent
C. Working of patenting process
D. Surrender and revocation of patent

43. Which one of the following is NOT a principle which is the very foundation of International Humanitarian Law and which must guide emergency humanitarian actions in armed conflicts?

A. Principle of Humanity
B. Principle of Impartiality
C. Principle of Neutrality
D. Principle of Self-determination

44. The institution of ombudsman was firstly initiated in the year 1809 by:

A. France B. USA
C. UK D. Sweden

45. Which of the following is a leading case on trespass ab initio?

A. Goldsmith Vs. Sperring Ltd.
B. Dumbell Vs. Roberts
C. Bird Vs. Jones
D. Six carpenters' case

46. 'A Statutory Board conducting examinations is not a service provider and does not offer services to candidates while conducting an examination' was held by the Supreme Court in:

A. Buddhist Mission Dental College and Hospital Vs. Bhupesh Khurana (2009)
B. Bihar School Examination Board Vs. Suresh Prasad Sinha (2009)
C. Madan Kumar Singh Vs. District Magistrate, Sultanpur (2009)
D. UT Chandigarh Administration Vs. Amarjeet Singh (2009)

47. How many core principles are laid down in United Nations Declaration of Permanent Sovereignty over Natural Resources?

A. Five core principles
B. Six core principles
C. Seven core principles
D. Eight core principles

48. "If one's artistic expressions are synonymous with one's personality, then they are deserving of protection just as much as the physical person."

The above observation is true about which theory of intellectual property?

A. Moral desert theory
B. Personality theory
C. Utilitarian theory
D. Libertian theory

49. Which of the following sections of the Hindu Adoption and Maintenance Act, 1956 deals with the 'rights of adoptive parents to dispose of their properties'?

A. Section 11 B. Section 12
C. Section 13 D. Section 14

50. In which one of the following cases it has been held that section 9 of Civil Procedure Code, 1973, which enables a civil court to try all suits of civil nature, impliedly confers jurisdiction to apply the law of torts as principles of justice, equity and good conscience?

A. Union Carbide Corporation Vs. Union of India
B. Gujarat State Road Transport Corporation Vs. Ramanbhai Prabhatbhai
C. Rohtas Industries Ltd. Vs. Rohtas Industries Staff Union
D. Waghela Rajsanji Vs. Shekh Masludin

51. Match List-I with List-II:

	List-I		**List-II**
(*a*)	Fighting by two or more persons in public place	(*i*)	Abetment
(*b*)	Intentional aiding in commission of an offence	(*ii*)	Sedition
(*c*)	Violence is caused by five or more persons	(*iii*)	Affray
(*d*)	Offence committed against state by words, signs or visible representation	(*iv*)	Riot

Choose the correct options from those given below:

	(*a*)	(*b*)	(*c*)	(*d*)
A.	(*iii*)	(*ii*)	(*iv*)	(*i*)
B.	(*iii*)	(*i*)	(*iv*)	(*ii*)
C.	(*iv*)	(*iii*)	(*ii*)	(*i*)
D.	(*i*)	(*iv*)	(*ii*)	(*iii*)

52. 'Uninsured vehicles are also within the scope of Section 165 of the Motor Vehicles Act' was held in:

A. LIC of India Vs. Raj Kumari Mittal (1985)
B. Kamal Kusha Vs. Kripal Singh (1988)
C. Permanand Thakur Vs. Commissioner, Coal Mines (1988)
D. New India Assurance Co. Ltd. Vs. Nakul Gurung (2010)

53. In which of the following cases the Supreme Court said that 'Fundamental Rights and Directive Principles' aim at the same goal of bringing about a social revolution and establishment of a Welfare State and they can be interpreted and applied together and they are supplementary and complementary to each other?

A. Maneka Gandhi Vs. Union of India
B. Re Kerala Education Bill
C. Minerva Mills Vs. Union of India
D. Kesvananda Bharati Vs. State of Kerala

54. Which one of the following is NOT correct?

A. Judicial review tends to elevate the judiciary to the rank of super legislature
B. The scope of judicial review is limited as it emphasises on the 'procedure established by law' rather than 'due procedure of law'
C. Judicial review is indispensable to a federal system of government
D. Judicial review does not include judicial competence to review executive enforcement of legislative enactments

55. Read both Assertion (A) and Reason (R) and give the correct answer by using the code given below:

Assertion (A): Article 38 of the statute of International Court of Justice lists International Conventions, whether general or particular, establishing rules expressly recognised by the contesting states as the first source of International Law.

Reason (R): In modern period, International Treaties are the most important source of International Law.

Select the correct answer.

A. Both (A) and (R) are correct and (R) is the correct explanation of (A)

B. Both (A) and (R) are correct, but (R) is not the correct explanation of (A)
C. (A) is correct, but (R) is wrong
D. (A) is wrong, but (R) is correct

56. Which of the following is an essential condition in Marz-ul-Maut?
A. A malady which makes it impossible for the patient to move
B. It must be continued for more than a year
C. There must be apprehension of death
D. A malady which causes problem with heart

57. Assertion (A): International Humanitarian Law (IHL) is the law that regulates the conduct of war (jus in bello). It is that branch of International Law which seeks, to limit the efforts of Armed Conflicts by protecting persons who are not participating in hostilities and by restricting and regulating the means and methods of warfare available to combatants.

Reason (R): International Humanitarian Law (IHL) is inspired by considerations of humanity and the mitigation of human sufferings.

Select the correct answer.
A. Both (A) and (R) are true and (R) is the correct explanation of (A)
B. Both (A) and (R) are true, but (R) is not the correct explanation of (A)
C. (A) is true, but (R) is false
D. (A) is false, but (R) is true

58. The Preamble to Agreement on Trade Related Aspects of Intellectual Property Rights (TRIPS) lays down:
(*a*) public policy objectives of national system
(*b*) special needs of the least developed countries
(*c*) resolving IP disputes through multilateral procedures
(*d*) establishing mutually supportive relationship between WTO and WIPO

Which of the following is/are true?
A. Only (*a*) is true
B. Only (*a*) and (*b*) are true
C. Only (*a*), (*b*) and (*c*) are true
D. (*a*), (*b*), (*c*) and (*d*) are true

59. The NGT Act, 2010 contains how many schedules?
A. One
B. Two
C. Three
D. Four

60. Macleods Pharmaceuticals Ltd. Vs. Tidal Laboratories Pvt. Ltd. (2011) is a case on which subject of intellectual property rights?
A. Patent
B. Trademark
C. Design
D. Geographical indications

61. 'A legal person is any subject matter other than a human being to which law attributes personality', is the statement of:
A. Blackstone
B. Salmond
C. Holland
D. Bentham

62. Regulation of Access to Biological Diversity is described under which one of the following Chapters of the Biological Diversity Act, 2002?
A. Chapter I
B. Chapter II
C. Chapter III
D. Chapter IV

63. In which one of the following cases the Supreme Court held that 'the federalism in India, is not a matter of administrative convenience, but one of principle?
A. S.R. Bommai Vs. Union of India (1994)
B. Raja Ram Pal Vs. Hon'ble Speaker, Lok Sabha (2007)
C. Madras Bar Association Vs. Union of India (2014)
D. State of West Bengal Vs. Committee for Protection of Democratic Rights, West Bengal (2010)

64. In which year the Commission on Status of Women was established by Economic and Social Council?
A. 1946
B. 1947
C. 1948
D. 1949

65. Chandra Vs. Suresh AIR 1971 Delhi 208 deals with:

A. maintenance
B. custody of children
C. Hindu undivided family
D. decree of judicial separation

66. A servant collected money from the debtor of his master as authorised by him. The servant retained the money because it was due to him as wages. He commits:

A. criminal breach of trust
B. theft
C. no offence
D. criminal misappropriation

67. In which of the following cases did the Supreme Court of India strike down Section 303 IPC as unconstitutional?

A. Machhi Singh Vs. State of Punjab
B. Bachan Singh Vs. State of Punjab
C. Gian Kaur Vs. State of Punjab
D. Mithu Kaur Vs. State of Punjab

68. "The law of every modern state shows as at a thousand points the influence of both the accepted social morality and wider moral ideals. These influences enter into law either abruptly and avowedly through legislation, or silently and piecemeal through the judicial process." Who said this?

A. Bentham B. Gray
C. Hart D. Karkunov

69. Which of the following statement/statements is/are correct?

(*a*) 'Hegel' is one of the chief exponents of the 'Constitutive Theory' of recognition.
(*b*) Civil Air Transport Incorporated Co. Vs. Central Air Transport Corporation is a leading case on the retrospective effect of recognition.
(*c*) De jure recognition is not final and can be withdrawn.
(*d*) In Luther Vs. Sagor it was held that there is distinction between de facto and de jure recognition for the purpose of giving effect to the internal acts of the recognised authority.

Select the correct answer using the code given below:

A. Only (*a*) is correct
B. (*a*), (*b*) and (*c*) are correct
C. (*a*), (*b*) and (*d*) are correct
D. (*a*), (*b*), (*c*) and (*d*) all are correct

70. A wife has an implied authority of the husband to buy articles of household necessity:

A. if the wife is living with her husband in a domestic establishment of their own
B. if the wife is living separately
C. if the wife is living with her husband not in a domestic establishment
D. if the wife is provided a reasonable allowance by the husband for the purchase of household needs

71. Sedition means:

A. expressing disapprobation of the measure of the government with a view to obtain their alteration
B. advocacy of boycott of foreign goods as a means of helping Indian industries
C. exciting or attempting to excite hatred towards the government through a writing which remains with the author unpublished
D. bringing or attempting to bring the government into hatred through words, signs or visible representation

72. Which one of the following is NOT an essential of parliamentary form of government?

A. The presence of a nominal executive head of the state who acts exclusively on the advice of cabinet
B. The cabinet, which is the real executive, consists of leaders of a party, who have the support of the majority in the legislature
C. The responsibility of the cabinet is collective
D. The President appoints ministers and assigns to them their offices

73. Which section of the Companies Act, 2013 deals with corporate social responsibility?
A. Section 133 B. Section 134
C. Section 135 D. Section 136

74. X with the intention to steal ornaments opened Y's box and found it empty. Which of the following statements is correct?
A. X is not liable for attempt to commit theft as the box being empty, commission of theft was impossible.
B. X is not liable for attempt to commit theft as he did not do the penultimate act towards commission of theft
C. X is not guilty of attempt to commit theft as the ornaments were not in the box.
D. X is guilty of attempt to commit theft as he had an intention to commit theft and did an act toward its commission.

75. The Constitution of India incorporates the 'Rule of Law' in:
A. Article 14 B. Article 19
C. Article 21 D. Article 32

76. Which Article of the UN Charter puts the promotion of respect for human rights on the same level as the maintenance of international peace and security as a purpose of the UN?
A. Article 1 B. Article 2
C. Article 3 D. Article 4

77. Which of the following Articles of Universal Declaration of Human Rights, 1948 deals with civil and political rights?
A. Articles 1 and 2
B. Articles 3 to 21
C. Articles 22 to 27
D. Articles 28 to 30

78. Read both Assertion (A) and Reason (R) and give the correct answer by using the code given below:
Assertion (A): Under the Indian Constitution, an Amendment Bill passed by both Houses of Parliament by required majority shall be presented to the President who shall give his assent and thereupon the Constitution shall stand amended.
Reason (R): The President is bound to give his assent to the Bill.
Codes:
A. Both (A) and (R) are right and (R) is the correct explanation of (A)
B. Both (A) and (R) are right, but (R) is not the correct explanation of (A)
C. (A) is right, but (R) is wrong
D. (A) is wrong, but (R) is right

79. Which of the following activities cannot be considered as relating to social responsibility under Section 135 of the Companies Act, 2013?
A. Amount spent on activities which only benefit the employees of the company
B. Amount spent to benefit people who are not economically backward
C. Amount spent on activities which only benefit the consumers of the organisation
D. Amount spent on activities which only benefit the suppliers of the organisation

80. Match List-I with List-II:

List-I (Provisions)	**List-II (Relevant Supreme Court Cases)**
(*a*) Appointment of judges of Supreme Court	(*i*) In Re: Vinay Chander Mishra
(*b*) Jurisdiction of Supreme Court as Court of Record	(*ii*) SC Advocates-on-Record Association Vs. Union of India
(*c*) Original jurisdiction of Supreme Court	(*iii*) A.R. Antulay Vs. R.S. Nayak
(*d*) Power of Supreme Court to withdraw and transfer of cases	(*iv*) State of Karnataka Vs. Union of India

Choose the correct option from those given below:

	(*a*)	(*b*)	(*c*)	(*d*)
A.	(*ii*)	(*i*)	(*iv*)	(*iii*)
B.	(*iv*)	(*iii*)	(*ii*)	(*i*)
C.	(*i*)	(*iv*)	(*iii*)	(*ii*)
D.	(*i*)	(*ii*)	(*iii*)	(*iv*)

81. The liability has been defined as 'the bond of necessity that exists between the wrongdoer and the remedy of the wrong' by:

A. Austin B. Bentham
C. Salmond D. Holland

82. Which of the following actions can be taken when an issue is made under the provisions of Section 42 of the Companies Act, 2013?

A. An advertisement can be issued in a local newspaper having city coverage
B. The money payable towards subscription can be received in cash
C. The share can be allotted within sixty days of the date of offer
D. The offer can be made to a maximum of fifty people

83. The Sapinda relationship on the line of ascent under the Hindu Law extends:

A. three degree through the father and two degree through the mother
B. four degree through the father and three degree through the mother
C. five degree through the father and three degree through the mother
D. seven degree through the father and five degree through the mother

84. Which of the following provisions of the Indian Constitution have been extended to Jammu and Kashmir state by Presidential Order?

(*a*) Provisions relating to freedom of trade, commerce and intercourse, services and citizenship.
(*b*) Provisions relating to Elections.
(*c*) Provision relating to Financial Emergency under Article 360 of the Constitution of India.
(*d*) Power of High Courts to issue writs for "Any other purpose."

Select the correct answer by using the codes given below:

A. Only (*a*) B. (*c*) and (*d*) both
C. (*a*) and (*b*) both D. (*a*), (*b*), (*c*) and (*d*)

85. The prohibition of registration of geographical indication under the GIG Act, 1999 contains as many as:

A. four grounds B. five grounds
C. six grounds D. seven grounds

86. Which of the following statements correctly reflects the cardinal principle, 'Actus Non Facit Reum Nisi Mens Sit Rea'?

A. Mens rea is an essential element of a crime and there cannot be a crime without mens rea.
B. Criminal liability under Indian law always implies mens rea.
C. To constitute a crime there must be actus reus and mens rea.
D. Actus reus is not always necessary to constitute a crime.

87. Which of the following statement/statements is/are correct?

(*a*) WTO was established as a result of the culmination of Uruguay Round of GATT.
(*b*) The new World Trade Organisation (WTO) came into effect on January 1, 1995.
(*c*) At the time of establishment WTO had 88 members.
(*d*) The 7th Ministerial Conference of WTO was held in Marrakesh (Morocco) from 30 November to December 2, 2008.

Select the correct answer from the code given below:

A. Only (*a*) B. (*b*) and (*c*)
C. (*a*) and (*b*) D. (*a*), (*b*), (*c*) and (*d*)

88. In India, 'the machinery of government is essentially British and the whole collection of British Constitutional Conventions has apparently been incorporated as conventions' is the observation of:

A. A.V. Dicey
B. Sir Ivor Jennings
C. S.A. de Smith
D. Wade and Phillips

89. Which of the following are the chief exponents of the 'Theory of Consent' regarding basis of International Law?

A. Anzilotti, Triepel, Oppenheim
B. Starke, Smith, Brierly
C. Fawett, Jellinck, Pollock
D. Kelson, Hart, Edward Collins

90. Which section of Indian Penal Code deals with solitary confinement?

A. Section 73 of IPC
B. Section 72 of IPC
C. Section 71 of IPC
D. Section 70 of IPC

91. Which of the following Articles provides coverage for the intervention in domestic jurisdiction for the enforcement of human right?

A. Article 2(5) of UN Charter
B. Article 2(6) of UN Charter
C. Article 2(7) of UN Charter
D. Article 2(8) of UN Charter

92. The absolute grounds for refusal of registration is contained under which section of the Trade Mark Act, 1999?

A. Section 7
B. Section 8
C. Section 9
D. Section 10

93. Which of the following is incorrect regarding meaning of 'Merchantable quality of goods'?

A. the goods are free from patent defects
B. the goods are free from latent defects
C. the goods can be used for the purpose for which they are bought
D. that the goods are marketable at their full value

94. Judicial Review of an administrative action means:

A. review by the Parliament
B. review by the Government
C. review by the Legislative Assembly
D. review by the Judiciary

95. Whoever counterfeits, or knowingly performs any part of the process of counterfeiting Indian coin under Section 232 by Indian Penal Code shall be punished with:

A. imprisonment which may extend to ten years and fine
B. imprisonment which may extend to seven years and fine
C. imprisonment which may extend to five years and fine
D. imprisonment which may extend to three years and fine

96. "Judges do not make law, but only declare what has always been law." This statement is of:

A. Salmond
B. Blackstone
C. Willis
D. Allen

97. A Hindu Contracting Second Marriage during pendancy of appeal against the decree of divorce is:

A. Valid
B. Invalid
C. Factum valid
D. Void

98. "I think adherence to precedent should be the rule and not the exception". This statement is of:

A. Keeton
B. Blackston
C. Cardozo
D. Paton

99. Which one of the following jurists is not related to Historical school?

A. Savigny
B. Ehrlich
C. Henry Main
D. Hegel

100. In which of the following case, the court held that, "Divorce is good in law through bad in Theology"?

A. Shah Bano case
B. Bai Tahira case
C. Shamim Ara case
D. Sarabai case

ANSWERS

1	2	3	4	5	6	7	8	9	10
A	B	C	A	B	C	A	A	C	A
11	**12**	**13**	**14**	**15**	**16**	**17**	**18**	**19**	**20**
D	B	D	D	B	A	C	C	D	D
21	**22**	**23**	**24**	**25**	**26**	**27**	**28**	**29**	**30**
D	B	A	C	D	A	C	D	B	B
31	**32**	**33**	**34**	**35**	**36**	**37**	**38**	**39**	**40**
D	D	B	C	B	C	A	B	A	*
41	**42**	**43**	**44**	**45**	**46**	**47**	**48**	**49**	**50**
A	C	D	D	D	B	D	B	C	A
51	**52**	**53**	**54**	**55**	**56**	**57**	**58**	**59**	**60**
B	C	D	D	A	C	A	D	C	B
61	**62**	**63**	**64**	**65**	**66**	**67**	**68**	**69**	**70**
B	B	A	A	D	D	D	C	C	A
71	**72**	**73**	**74**	**75**	**76**	**77**	**78**	**79**	**80**
D	D	C	D	A	A	B	A	*	A
81	**82**	**83**	**84**	**85**	**86**	**87**	**88**	**89**	**90**
C	D	C	C	D	C	C	B	A	A
91	**92**	**93**	**94**	**95**	**96**	**97**	**98**	**99**	**100**
C	C	*	D	A	B	D	C	B	D

EXPLANATORY ANSWERS

1. The control test is the oldest test for establishing employment status and it comes from a time when the only employment relationship that existed was that between the 'master' and 'servant'. It considers the degree of control and supervision that is exerted by the employer over their staff.

2. Article 14 of Constitution of India: Article 14 guarantees all citizens equality before law and equal protection of law. It hinders any form of discrimination and forbids both discriminatory laws and administrative action. Article 14 of Constitution of India, establishes to be safeguard against any arbitrary or discriminatory State action. The sphere of equality as embodied in Article 14 has been expanding as a result of the judicial decisions. This Article laid down a general preposition that all persons in similar circumstance shall be treated in a similar way both in privileges and liabilities imposed.

In Delhi Transport Corporation v. DTC Mazdoor Union, the Apex Court held that "the audi alteram parterm rule, in essence, enforce the equality clause in Article 14 of the Constitution, is applicable not only to quasi-judicial bodies but also to an administrative order adversely affecting the party unless the rule has been excluded by the Act in question."

Similarly in Maneka Gandhi v. Union of India the Supreme Court had opined that Article 14 is an authority for the proposition that the principles of natural justice are an integral part of the guarantee of equality assured by Article 14 an order depriving a person of his civil right passed without affording him an opportunity of being heard suffers from the vice of violation of natural justice.

3. According to Explanation 2 of Section 25 of the Indian Contract Act 1872, An agreement to which the consent of the promisor is freely given is not void merely because the consideration is inadequate, but the inadequacy of the consideration may be taken into account by the court in determining the question whether the consent of the promisor was freely given.

Section 13 of the Indian Contract Act states that, two or more person are said to consent when they agree upon the same thing in the same sense (consensus-ad-idem). Section 14 of the Indian Contract Act states that, Consent is said to be free when it is not caused by; coercion, undue influence, fraud, misrepresentation, mistake.

4. In 2015, all countries of the world agreed to adopt the 17 Sustainable Development'. Goals (SDGs) as a part of '2030 Agenda for Sustainable Development'. These goals came into force on 01 January, 2016 and are aimed towards ending poverty, protecting the planet and attaining prosperity for all. This was a unique achievement as these goals are applicable universally, and countries are making joint efforts to achieve them. These global goals which ecompass a broader sustainability agenda are expected to shape the global development policy wordwide till 2030. Although SDGs are not legally binding, countries are expected to take ownership and to voluntarily report the progress at the national level.

SDG 7—'Ensure access to affordable, reliable, sustainable and modern energy for all by 2030', is one of the SDGs which has been adopted. SDG 7 focuses on universal access to clean energy, increase in renewable energy share, improvement in energy efficiency, international cooperation, expanding infrastructure and upgrading technology.

5. Grounds of Imposition: If the President is satisfied that a grave emergency exists whereby the security of India or of any part of the territory thereof is threatened, whether by war or external aggression or armed rebellion he may, be Proclamation, make a declaration to that effect in respect of the whole of India or of such part of the territory thereof as may be specified in the Proclamation.

Originally the third ground of Proclamation of National Emergency was internal disturbance. But later it was substituted by armed rebellion by the 44th Constitutional Amendment Act 1978. The application of national emergency to in respect of the whole of India or of part of the territory was inserted by the 42nd Constitutional Amendment Act 1976.

A Proclamation of Emergency declaring that the security of India or any part of the territory thereof is threatened by war or by external aggression or by armed rebellion may be made before the actual occurrence of war or of any such aggression or rebellion, if the President is satisfied that there is imminent danger thereof. This provision was inserted by the 44th Constitutional Amendment Act 1978.

The President can vary previous Proclamation by subsequent Proclamation. This provision was inserted by the 44th Constitutional Amendment Act 1978.

Here President is empowered to issue different Proclamations on different grounds, being war or external aggression or armed rebellion or imminent danger of war, whether or not there is a Proclamation already issued by the President and such Proclamation is in operation. This provision was inserted by the 38th Constitutional Amendment 1975.

The President can declare such an emergency only on the basis of a written request by the Cabinet Ministers headed by the Prime Minister. This provision acts as a safeguard against the arbitrariness of the Prime Minister. This Provision has been introduced by the 44th Constitutional Amendment Act 1978 when in 1975 without consulting cabinet the Prime Minister Indira Gandhi advised the President to issue Proclamation of National Emergency. The cabinet came to know about Proclamation after applying it.

A Proclamation of national emergency comes under the purview of judicial review. A Proclamation of national emergency was kept out from the purview of Judicial Review by the 38th Constitutional Amendment Act 1975. But later it came under the purview of Judicial Review by the 44th Constitutional Amendment Act 1978. Further in the Minerva mills case the Supreme Court cleared that a Proclamation of National Emergency is challengeable in the court on malafide grounds or irrelevant facts.

Parliamentary Approval and Duration: Every Proclamation of National Emergency must be laid before each House of Parliament within month from the date of issue. Originally the time period for obtaining approval from Parliament was two months but later it was reduced by the 44th Constitutional Amendment Act 1978. Provided that if any such Proclamation (not being a Proclamation revoking a previous Proclamation) is issued at a time when the House of the People has been dissolved, or the dissolution of the House of the People takes place during the period of one month without giving approval to the Proclamation, then the Proclamation continues in force till 30 days from first sitting of the House of People after reconstitution of House of People. But in meantime the Council of States has approved it.

If resolution for Proclamation approved by both houses of Parliament, then the Proclamation continues in force for six months from the date of approval it. This proclamation can be extended for indefinite period by Parliamentary approval for every six months. The Provision for periodical parliamentary approval was inserted by the 44th Constitutional Amendment Act, 1978. Before the periodical Parliamentary approval once proclamation approved by Parliament, it could remain in force as long as executive desired. Provided further that if the dissolution of the House of the People takes place during any such period of six months without giving approval to the Proclamation, then the Proclamation continues in force till 30 days from first sitting of House of People after reconstitution of House of the People. But in meantime the Council of States has approved it.

Every resolution in respect of approving the national emergency or its continuance must be passed by either House of Parliament with special majority that is only by a majority of the total membership of that House and by a majority of not less than two-thirds of the Members of that House present and voting. This special majority provision was inserted by the 44th constitutional Amendment Act 1978. Earlier the constitution had simple majority provision for such resolution.

Procedure of Revocation: The President can revoke the Proclamation of National Emergency at any time by issuing subsequent proclamation. This proclamation does not need any Parliamentary approval.

The President shall revoke a Proclamation of National Emergency or a Proclamation varying such Proclamation if the House of the People passes a resolution disapproving, or disapproving the continuance in force of, such Proclamation. This provision has been inserted by the 44th Constitutional Amendment Act 1978. Before this amendment the President was empowered to revoke Proclamation on his own.

Section 147 of the Negotiable Instruments Act runs as, notwithstanding anything contained in the Code of Criminal Procedure, 1973 (2 of 1974), every offence punishable under this Act shall be compoundable. The section starts with a *non-obstante* clause, which will have the legal effect to prevail over any provisions in any other statutes, which are in vogue. By means of introduction of the said section, the legislature has enabled the parties to case under Section 138 of the Negotiable Instruments Act, to enter into a compromise.

The offence under Section 138 of the Act may be compounded at any stage of the case, even in its final stage.

Section 147 of the NI Act does not bar the parties from compounding an offence under Section 138 even at the appellate stage of the proceedings.

Therefore, there is no reason to reject an application under Section 147 of the NI Act even in a proceeding under Article 136 of the Constitution and where such a application is made the court is empowered under Article 142 of the Constitution to pass appropriate orders in line with Section 320(8) of Cr PC in order to do justice to the parties.

9. The Office of the United Nations High Commissioner for Human Rights (OHCHR) represents the world's commitment to the universal ideals of human dignity. With its headquarters in Geneva, Switzerland, OHCHR has a unique mandate from the international community to promote and protect all human rights. The High Commissioner for Human Rights is the principal human rights official of the United Nations.

The United Nations High Commissioner for Human Rights is accountable to the Secretary-General and is responsible for all the activities of OHCHR, as well as for its administration. The High Commissioner:

- Carries out the functions specifically assigned to him or her by the General Assembly in its resolution 48/141 of 20 December 1993 and subsequent resolutions of policy-making bodies;
- Advises the Secretary-General on the policies of the United Nations in the area of human rights;
- Ensures that substantive and administrative support is given to the projects, activities, organs and bodies of the human rights programme;
- Represents the Secretary-General at meetings of human rights organs and at other human rights events; and carries out special assignments as decided by the Secretary-General.

In accordance with General Assembly resolution 48/141, the United Nations High Commissioner for Human Rights is appointed by the Secretary-General of the United Nations and approved by the General Assembly, with due regard to geographical rotation for a fixed term of four years with a possibility of one renewal for another fixed term of four years.

10. Administrative law is a branch of public law. It deals with the relationship of individuals with the government. It determines the organisation and power structure of administrative and quasi-judicial authorities to enforce the law. It is primarily concerned with official actions and procedures and puts in place a control mechanism by which administrative agencies stay within bounds.

Difference between Administrative law and Constitutional law

There are significant differences between Administrative law and Constitutional law.

A Constitution is the supreme law of the land. No law is above the constitution and hence must satisfy its provisions and not be in its violation.

Administrative law hence is subordinate to constitutional law. In other words, while Constitution is the genus, administrative law is a species.

Constitution deals with the structure of the State and its various organs. Administrative law, on the other hand, deals only with the administration.

While Constitution touches all branches of law and deals with general principles relating to organisation and powers of the various organs of the State; administrative law deals only with the powers and functions of the administrative authorities.

Simply speaking the administrative authorities should first follow the Constitution and then work as per the administrative law.

11. The word Jurisprudence is made from two words or it is a combination of two latin words Juris and prudentia. Meaning of Juris is law and meaning of prudentia is knowledge. Clearly meaning of Jurisprudence is knowledge of law. The Study of Jurisprudence started among Romans at first.

Ulpian : Ulpian was a Roman Jurist, according to him Jurisprudence is the knowlege of things, divine and human, the science of right and wrong. This definition is similar to the definition of Dharma of Hindu philosophy. According to Jaimini Dharma is that which is signified by a command and leads to man's matarial and spiritual salvation.

Yajnavalkya has defined that "Vyavahara, means those rules which determine the Judicial Proceeding".

12. A writ petition was filed by M.C Mehta, a social activist lawyer, he sought closure for Shriram Industries as it was engaged in manufacturing of hazardous substances and located in a densely populated area of Kirti Nagar. While the petition was pending, on 4 and 6 December 1985, there was leakage of oleum gas from one of its units which caused the death of an advocate and affected the health of several others. The incident took place on December 4, 1985.

Just after one year from the Bhopal gas disaster a large number of persons—both amongst the workmen and public were affected. This incident also reminded of the Bhopal gas holocaust.

M.C Mehta filed a PIL under Articles 21 and 32 of the Constitution and sought closure and relocation of the Shriram Caustic Chlorine and Sulphuric Acid Plant which was located in a thickly populated area of Delhi. Factories were closed down immediately as Inspector of Factories and Commissioner (Factories) issued separate orders dated December 8 and 24, 1985. This incident took place only a few months before Environment (Protection) Act came into force, thus became a guiding force for having an effective law like this.

There are six reported orders in the Shriram Food and Fertilizer Industry case of the Supreme Court of India, out of these six, four orders were pronounced before Environment (Protection) Act, 1986 was passed and the date from which it came into force. Thus the reported orders are relevant and important as they shed new light on how highly toxic and hazardous substances industry should be dealt with and contained and controlled to minimize hazards to the workers and general public.

There are to date more than a dozen reported decisions of the Supreme Court under the name of *M.C. Mehta* v. *Union of India*. The petitioner in all these cases is a practising advocate of the Supreme Court. The first case, decided in February 1986, was a public interest writ petition filed before the Supreme Court under Article 32 of the Constitution. Orders were sought from the Court to restrain the re-opening of certain industrial plants of one Shriram Food and Fertiliser Corporation, which had been closed following a major leakage of oleum gas from one of its units in Delhi. The Court, after considering the reports of experts appointed by the government and by the Court, permitted the plants to be re-opened but only subject to the strict observation of conditions laid down by the Court.

In a separate order for compensation in the same case, the Court laid down new principles of absolute liability without exception. The rule laid down by the Court states that:

Where an enterprise is engaged in a hazardous or inherently dangerous activity and harm results to anyone on account of an accident in the operation of such hazardous or inherent activity resulting, for example, in escape of toxic gas, the enterprise is strictly and absolutely liable to compensate all those who are affected by the accident and such liability is not subject to any of the exceptions which operate vis-a-vis the tortious principle of strict liability under the rule in *Rylands* v. *Fletcher*.

The decision of the Indian Supreme Court in this case, laying down the new principle of absolute liability, is a significant departure from the established common law principle of strict liability. In laying down this rule, the then Chief Justice Bhagwati held:

We have to evolve new principles and lay down new norms which would adequately deal with the new problems which arise in a highly industrialised economy. We cannot allow our judicial thinking to be constricted by reference to the law as it prevails in England or for the matter for that in any other foreign country. We no longer need the crutches of a foreign legal order. We are certainly prepared to receive light from whatever source it comes but we have to build our own jurisprudence.

The judgement very clearly indicates the need to deviate from the common law tradition of the earlier legal order and at the same time shows the willingness to accommodate and accept what is found good in the earlier legal order or in other legal systems. This attitude of the Indian judges manifests the Indian legal culture of syncretism with its openness and readiness for legal osmosis.

On the question of compensating victims of industrial accidents and on the principles of liability of industries engaged in inherently dangerous and hazardous activities, the Court addressed the issues in a novel fashion. The new strategy was moulded under Article 32 of the Constitution to compensate those who were affected by violation of their fundamental rights guaranteed by the Constitution. The Court strengthened its power to grant remedial relief on the basis that it would otherwise rob Article 32 of its efficacy and render it impotent and futile. The Court felt that it would be gravely unjust to the person whose fundamental right was violated to require him to go to the civil court for claiming compensation. This shows that modern Indian environmental law developments are more than verbose exercises in philosophy. More recently, it has become obvious that the focus on implementation and on meaningful remedies has become a major element of the new rationale.

13. A person who is national of none of the states cannot enjoy the rights conferred upon him by the international law. Statelessness was defined in the holding of a case, 'Stoeck v. The Public Trustee'; "If a person is not a citizen of any state, he will be called stateless and this conditions is to be called 'statelessness'".

International Community where held a number of conventions to regulate nationality, also worked to discourage statelessness. 'Convention of Status of Refugees–1951 and Status of Stateless Persons–1954' are among the prominent endeavours made to check this practice. States have been asked to hesitate from depriving a person from his nationality and if deprived then the other states should liberally grant him nationality.

14. Communication of acceptance: Communication of an acceptance is complete in the following situations:

- As against the proposer, when it is put in course of transmission to him so as to be out of the power of the acceptor to withdraw the same.
- As against the acceptor, when it comes to the knowledge of the proposer.

When a proposal is accepted by a letter sent by the post, the communication of acceptance will be complete as against the proposer when the letter of acceptance is posted, and as against the acceptor when the letter reaches the proposer.

15. Doctrine of Restitution: In English law, if a minor fraudulently and unjustly enriched himself, equity demands that such enriched property or goods be restored.

In *Leslie (R) Ltd.* v. *Sheill,* (1914) 3 KB 607, court laid down three main propositions of doctrine of restitution, which are as follows:

(*i*) If the minor obtains property or goods by misrepresenting his age, he can be compelled to restore it, but only so long as the same is traceable in his possession.

(*ii*) Where the minor has sold the goods or converted them, he cannot be made to repay the value of the goods, because that would amount to enforcing a void contract.

(*iii*) The doctrine of restitution is not applied where the minor has obtained cash instead of goods, for 'restitution stops where repayment begins'.

In India, position is not the same. English doctrine of restitution is contained in Indian Law with some modification. In *Mohori Bibee* v *Dharm Das Ghose*, Privy Council held that restitution of money cannot be granted as a minor's agreement is absolutely void and not voidable. It was held that Sections 64 and 65 of Contract Act (restoration of benefit received under a voidable or void contract) starts from the basis of there being an agreement or contract between competent parties, whereas in minor's case there couldn't be any contract.

In *Khan Gul* v. *Lakha Singh*, AIR 1928 Lah 609, it was held that there is no difference between restoring the property and refunding the money, except that the property can be identifiable but cash cannot be traced .... It was held that doctrine of restitution would not be of any help unless it was extended to India to cover money cases also.

However in *Ajudhia Prasad* v. *Chandan Lal,* AIR 1937 All 610 Court refused the view of restitution made in *Khan Gul's* case. If follows the principle explained in *Leslie's* case.

Section 33 of Specific Relief Act, 1963 makes clear the doubt about principle of restitution. Principle contained in Section 33 is as follows:

(1) On adjudging the cancellation of an instrument, the Court may require the party to whom such relief is granted, to restore, so far as may be, any benefit which he may have received from the other party and to make any compensation to him which justice may require. (Where minor goes to court as plaintiff).

(2) Where a defendant successfully resists any suit on the ground (*a*)...(*b*)...that the agreement sought to be enforced against him in the suit is void by reason of his not having been competent to contract, under Section 11 of Contract Act, the Court may, if the defendant (minor) has

received any benefit under the agreement from the other party, require him to restore, so far as may be, such benefit to other party, to the extent to which he or his estate has benefited thereby.

(phrase 'estate has benefited' means some permanent benefit as opposed to a transient one.)

(3) Liability in Contract or in Tort arises out of contract: A minor is not liable for a tort, if arising out of contract. If he would made liable, then this would make indirect way of enforcing agreement. But where tort is independent of contract, he will be liable for such tort.

(4) Beneficial Contracts: Under English law contract of service and apprenticeship, which is for the benefit of minor could be enforced against the minor. But in India, position is different. Here contract of apprenticeship is valid but contract of service is void.

16. Section 8 of the Partnership Act, 1932 provides a partnership in a particular adventure or undertaking, for example, for construction of bridge or production of a film. It is not necessary there should be permanent bond between the partners. There can be as much a partnership in a single and brief business venture as in a business of particular adventure. In a partnership between two persons for entering into certain wagering transactions for particular season only. It was held to be a particular partnership. Partnership for a particular period of time is called fixed partnership. After the expiry of the period, the partnership comes to an end. When a partner in the firm includes only other person to share the benefits derived from the firm, such included person is called sub-partner. This partnership exists between the transferor partner and transferee person. Transferee is not a partner in the firm. Transferee is not entitled to take part in the management and conduct of the business of the firm.

17. Mediate and Immediate Possession: Possession over a thing may be mediate or immediate. A thing possessed by a person directly or personally is said to be in immediate possession while a thing possessed by a person through another man is said to be in mediate possession.

According to Salmond there are three kinds of Mediate Possessions:

1. The first mediate possession is acquired through servant or agent. Here agent or servant retains the possession on behalf of the principal. They don't have any personal interest in the thing possessed. The thing still carries in itself interest or claim of the owner.
2. Second kind of mediate possession is where an object is held by a person on his own behalf as well as on another behalf but recognises the superior right of the latter, who can obtain in whenever he choose to demand.
3. The third type of mediate possession is where the immediate possession of the object is with a person who claims over an object until some time has elapsed or some conditions have been fulfilled. The person in immediate possession acknowledges the title of the person for whom he holds the thing and is prepared to return it on the fulfilment of the condition.

20. There are four noted schools of law among the Sunnis Muslim namely, Hanafi, Maliki, Shafi and Hanbali schools of law. These schools, known as Madhbabs, earned wide recognition throughout the world of Islam. The founders of these schools were formidable scholars, especially in the field of Islamic law. They were very highly regarded for their piety and each one of them had great disciples who enriched further his school and spread the teachings of the master, usually referred to as the Imam. Many Muslims in succeeding generations followed one or the other of these schools.

21. In order to decentralize power, the Government of India took a historic decision as it legislated to confer constitutional authority to the ULBs through the 74th Constitutional Amendment Act (CAA) in 1992, making them pillars for tier-III governance, below the tier of centre and the states. It added Article 243 W (also known as the Twelfth Schedule) defining 18 functions that include urban planning, regulation of land use and construction of buildings, planning for economic and social development, water supply for domestic, industrial and commercial purposes, public health, sanitation conservancy and solid waste management, urban forestry; protection of the environment and promotion of ecological aspects, slum improvement and upgradation, urban poverty alleviation; parks, gardens, playgrounds; promotion of cultural, educational and aesthetic aspects; public amenities including street lighting, parking lots, bus stops and public conveniences and so on.

22. In *D. Veluswamy* v. *D. Patchaiammal,* the Supreme Court has examined the difference between the expression "relationship in the nature of marriage" which is included within the definition of "domestic relationship" but has not been defined in the Protection of Women from Domestic Violence Act, 2005 (2005 PWDV Act). The Court held that under the 2005 PWDV Act there is a distinction between the relationship of marriage and a relationship in the nature of marriage, and has provided that in either case the person who enters into either relationship is entitled to the benefit of the Act. The live-in relationship is still rare in our country, and is sometimes found in big urban cities in India, but it is very common in North America and Europe. The live-in relationship may be compared with the common law marriages which are recognised in some countries in the world. A common law marriage, sometimes called *de facto* marriage, or informal marriage is recognised in some countries as a marriage though no legally recognised marriage ceremony is performed or civil marriage contract is entered into or the marriage registered in a civil registry. According to common law marriage although spouses are not being formally married but: (*i*) they must hold themselves out to society as being akin to spouses, (*ii*) they must be of legal age to marry, (*iii*) they must be otherwise qualified to enter into a legal marriage, including being unmarried, (*iv*) they must have voluntarily cohabited and held themselves out to the world as being akin to spouses for a significant period of time. Referring the common law marriage the Supreme Court in *D. Veluswamy* case observed that a "relationship in the nature of marriage" under the 2005 PWDV Act must also fulfil the above requirements, and in addition the parties must have lived together in a "shared household" as defined in Section 2(s) of the Act.

23. The Islamic concept of dower is unfortunately one of the most misunderstood concepts of Mohammadan Law. Those who lean towards the contractual element of a Muslim marriage tend to equate it with consideration on the other hand, those more familiar with the Indian concept of dowry, confuse it with the same. The truth is that Mahar (dower) is neither consideration nor dowry; it is significant Institution in Islamic Law, occupying a unique position of its own. Mr. Justice Mahmood (in *Abdul Kadir* Vs. *Salima,* (1866) 8 All. 149) defined the term dower as under—

"Dower under the Mohammedan Law, is a sum of money or other property promised by the husband to be paid or delivered to the wife in consideration of the marriage, and even where no dower is expressly fixed or mentioned at the marriage ceremony, the law confers the right of dower upon the wife.

24. The doctrine of separation finds its home in U.S. It forms the basis of the American constitutional structure. Article I vests the legislative power in the Congress; Article II vests executive power in the President and Article III vests judicial power in the Supreme Court. The framers of the American constitution believed that the principle of separation of powers would help to prevent the rise of tyrannical government by making it impossible for a single group of persons to exercise too much power. Accordingly they intended that the balance of power should be attained by checks and balances between separate organs of the government. This alternative system existing with the separation doctrine prevents any organ to become supreme.

Despite of the express mention of this doctrine in the Constitution, U.S. incorporates certain exceptions to the principle of separation with a view to introduce system of checks and balances. For example, a bill passed by the Congress may be vetoed by the President in the exercise of his legislative power. Also treaty making power is with the President but it's not effective till approved by the Senate. It was the exercise of executive power of the senate due to which U.S. couldn't become a member to League of Nations. The Supreme Court has the power to declare the acts passed by the congress as unconstitutional. There are other functions of an organ also which are exercised by the other. India, too, followed U.S. in adoption of the checks and balances which make sure that the individual organs doesn't behold the powers absolutely.

30. When the accused appears to be of sound mind at the time of inquiry or trial, and the Magistrate is satisfied from the evidence given before him that there is reason to believe that the accused committed an act, which, if he had been of sound mind, would have been an offence, and that he was, at the time when the act was committed, by reason of unsoundness of mind, incapable of knowing the nature of the act or that it was wrong or contrary to law, the Magistrate shall proceed with the case, and, if the accused ought to be tried by the Court of Session, commit him for trial before the Court of Session.

31. The word *tort* is derived from the Latin term tortum, to twist, and implies conduct which is not justified by the law of the land. Sir F. Pollock, a well known authority on the law of tort, defines tort as "an act which causes harm to a determinate person, whether intentionally or not, not being a breach of a duty arising out of a personal relation or contract, and which is either contrary to law or an omission of a specific legal duty, or a violation of an absolute right". On the basis of the above definition, it is established that a tort is a civil wrong independent of contract for which the remedy is common law action for unliquidated damages. Unliquidated damages are those which the court has power to fix, exercisable in its discretion, as distinct from liquidated damages, which is a fixed amount claimed by the plaintiff.

Elements of Tort

To constitute a tort, three things must concur:

1. Some wrongful act or omission by the defendant: *i.e.* a person who is being sued for his alleged wrongful act.
2. Legal damage to the plaintiff; *i.e.* some of his legal right is violated like refusing him to vote without justified reasons.
3. The wrongful act must be of such a nature as to give rise to a legal remedy in the form of an action for damages.

The act or omission may or may not cause actual damage to the plaintiff. Certain civil wrongs are actionable even though no damage is suffered by the plaintiff (a person who brings the action in the court) *e.g.* trespass on land, and we have already mentioned that sometimes the same wrongful act may constitute tort and a crime, *e.g.* assault.

36. Uniform Civil Code generally refers to that part of law which deals with family affairs of an individual and denotes uniform law for all citizens, irrespective of his/her religion, caste or tribe. Article 44 of the Constitution says that there should be a Uniform Civil Code. According to this article, "The State shall endeavour to secure for the citizens a uniform civil code throughout the territory of India". Since the Directive Principles are only guidelines, it is not mandatory to use them. Uniform Civil Code was one of the key issues debated during the writing of the Constitution, with passionate arguments on both sides. However, unable to arrive at a solution, a directive principle was struck regarding this in the constitution.

- But, several members of the Constituent Assembly disagreed vehemently with the compromise and argued that one of the factors that have kept India back from advancing to nationhood has been the existence of personal laws based on religion which keep the nation divided into watertight compartments in many aspects of life.
- Though, after independence, few governments tried to have a UCC, religious conservative groups did not allow governments to proceed ahead in this regard.

37. Everyone has the right to seek and to enjoy in other countries asylum from persecution. This right may not be invoked in the case of prosecutions genuinely arising from non-political crimes or from acts contrary to the purposes and principles of the United Nations.

39. In its two separate Judgements, the Supreme Court in February 1995 said, "In the interest of ensuring plurality of opinions, the broadcasting media cannot be allowed to be under a monopoiy of anyone — be it the monopoly of Government or of an individual body or organisation. Government control, in effect, is not conducive to the free expression of contending viewpoints". Supreme Court judgement delivered by Justice P.B. Sawant and Justice S. Mohan on 9.2.1995 in the case between the Union of India & Cricket Association of Bengal said,

(*i*) The airwaves or frequencies are a public property. Their use has to be controlled and regulated by a public authority in the interests of the public and to prevent the invasion of their rights. Since, the electronic media involves the use of the airwaves, this factor creates an in-built restriction on its use as in the case of any other public property.

(*ii*) The right to impart and receive information is a species of the right to freedom of speech and expression guaranteed by Article 19 (1)(a) of the Constitution. A citizen has a fundamental right to use the best means of imparting and receiving information and as such to have an access to telecasting for the purposc. However, this right to have an access to telecasting has limitations on account of the use of the public property, viz., the airwaves, involved in the exercise of the right and can be controlled and regulated by the public authority. This limitation imposed by the nature of the public property involved in the use of the electronic media is in addition to the restriction imposed on the right to freedom of speech and expression under Article 19 (2) of the Constitution.

(*iii*) The Central Government shall take immediate steps to establish an independent autonomous public authority representatives of all sections and interests in the society to control and regulate the use of the airwaves.

Justice B. P. Jeevan Reddy while delivering judgement on 9.2.1995 in the case between the Union of India & Cricket Association of

Bengal said, "..... Airwaves constitute public property and must be utilised for advancing public good. No individual has a right to utilise them at his choice and pleasure and for purposes of his choice including profit. The right of free speech guaranteed by Article 19 (1) (a) does not include the right to use airwaves which are public property. The airwaves can be used by a citizen for the purpose of broadcasting only when allowed to do so by a statute and in accordance with such statute. Airwaves, being public property, it is the duty of the State to see that airwaves are so utilised as to advance the free speech right of the citizens which is served by ensuring plurality and diversity of views, opinions and ideas. This is imperative in every democracy where freedom of speech is assured. The free speech right guaranteed to every citizen of this country does not encompass the right to use these airwaves at his choosing. Conceding, such a right would be detrimental to the free speech rights of the body of citizens in as much as only the privileged few powerful economic, commercial and political interests—would come to dominate the media. By manipulating the news, views and information, by indulging in misinformation and dis-information, to suit their commercial or other interests, they would be harming—and not serving—the principle of plurality and diversity of views, news, ideas and opinions. This has been the experience of Italy, where a limited right, *i.e.* at the local level but not at the national level was recognised. It is also not possible to imply or infer a right from the guarantee of free speech which only a few can enjoy."

41. Foreign marriages and divorces are given recognition in India as long as they satisfy the provisions of section 13 of the Civil Procedure Code. Section 13 provides that a foreign judgement shall be conclusive as to any matter thereby directly adjudicated upon between the same parties or between parties under whom they or any of them claim litigating under the same title except:

- where it has not been pronounced by a court of competent jurisdiction;
- where it has not been given on the merits of the case;
- where it appears on the face of the proceedings to be founded on an incorrect view of international law or a refusal to recognise the law of India in cases in which such law is applicable;
- where the proceedings in which the judgement was obtained are opposed to natural justice;
- where it has been obtained by fraud;
- where it sustains a claim founded on a breach of any law in force in India.

The Supreme Court in *Y. Narasimha Rao* and *Ors.* v *Y. Venkata Lakshmi and Ors.* (1991) 3 SCC 451 held that Indian courts would not recognise a decree of divorce passed by courts of foreign countries if the petition of divorce is not based on the substantive and jurisdictional grounds provided for divorce under the Hindu Marriage Act, 1955 and the nine grounds of divorce which are required to be satisfied.

In *Smt. Satya* v *Teja Singh* (1975) 2 SCR 1971, the Supreme Court derecognised the decree of divorce of the foreign country on the ground that one party obtained the divorce decree by fraud in the foreign court upon representing incorrect jurisdictional facts. The Apex Court held that 'residence' does not mean a temporary residence for the purpose of obtaining a divorce, but habitual residence or residence which is intended to be permanent for future as well.

43. The humanity principle of alleviating life-threatening suffering wherever it may be found is the foundation of the Red Cross/Red Crescent movement and is broadly considered to form the core principle of humanitarian action. Together with the supporting principles of impartiality, neutrality and independence, it is the core principle of humanitarian aid.

There has been a long-term debate about whether humanitarian principles of impartiality, neutrality and independence are compatible with the human-rights approach used by many development organisations. Both approaches have a lot in common, because they are both grounded in international agreements (respectively international humanitarian law, and human rights) and they both have human dignity as their basis. Hence, the approaches are complementary. While humanitarian aid in the short-term aims to guard human dignity by providing direct aid, more rights-based approaches question the structural root causes and solutions to injustice, vulnerability and unrest.

Nevertheless, in practice both approaches can become conflictive. Selecting specific disadvantaged groups can (seem to) be contrary to the impartiality principle. Raising causes of conflict can be contrary to the principle of neutrality. Looking for structural solutions requires working with national and international governments, which can be contrary to the independence principle. The confused practice around principles can lead to problems in communication and images of humanitarian aid. The principles of impartiality, neutrality and independence are in the eye of the beholder. Even if organisations operate according to these principles, they can be seen by the population as partial. Suspected impartiality of humanitarian organisations can be dangerous and be one of the elements explaining increasing violence against aid workers in some crises areas.

44. The institution of Ombudsman was first created in Sweden in 1809. 'Ombud' is a Swedish term and refers to a person who acts as the representative or spokesman of another person. According to Donald C. Rowat, Ombudsman refers to "an officer appointed by the legislature to handle complaints against administrative and judicial action." The Swedish Ombudsman deals with the citizens' grievances in the following matters:

(*i*) Abuse of administrative discretion, that is, misuse of official power and authority.

(*ii*) Maladministration, that is, inefficiency in achieving the targets.

(*iii*) Administrative corruption, that is, demanding bribery for doing things.

(*iv*) Nepotism, that is, supporting one's own kith and kin in matters like providing employment and so on.

(*v*) Discourtesy, that is, misbehaviour of various kinds, for instance, use of abusive language.

The Swedish Ombudsman is appointed by the Parliament for a term of four years. He can be removed only by the Parliament on ground of its loss of confidence in him. He submits his annual report to the Parliament and hence, is also known as 'Parliamentary Ombudsman.' But, he is independent of the Parliament (legislature) as well as the executive and judiciary.

The Ombudsman is a constitutional authority and enjoys the powers to supervise the compliance of laws and regulations, by the public officials and see that they discharge their duties properly. In other words, he keeps a watch over all public officials—civil, judicial and military—so that they function impartially, objectively and legally, that is, in accordance with the law. However, he has no power to reverse or quash a decision and has no direct control over administration or the courts.

The Ombudsman can act either on the basis of a complaint received from the citizen against unfair administrative action or suo moto (*i.e.* on his own initiative). He can prosecute any erring official including the judges. However, he himself cannot inflict any punishment. He only reports the matter to the higher authorities for taking the necessary corrective action. In sum, the characteristics of the Swedish institution of Ombudsman are:

(*i*) Independence of action from the executive.

(*ii*) Impartial and objective investigation of complaints.

(*iii*) Suo moto power to start investigations.

(*iv*) Uninterrupted access to all the files of administration.

(*v*) Right to report to the Parliament as opposed to the executive. The institution of ombudsman is based on the doctrine of administrative accountability to legislature.

(*vi*) Wide publicity given to its working in press and others.

(*vii*) Direct, simple, informal, cheap and speedy method of handling the complaints.

From Sweden, the institution of Ombudsman spread to other Scandinavian countries—Finland (1919), Denmark (1955) and Norway (1962). New Zealand is the first Commonwealth country in the world to have adopted the Ombudsman system in the form of Parliamentary Commissioner for Investigation in 1962. The United Kingdom adopted the Ombudsman-like institution called Parliamentary Commissioner for Administration in 1967. Since then, more than 40 countries of the world have adopted the Ombudsman-like institutions with different nomenclature and functions. The Ombudsman in India is called as Lokpal/Lokayukta.

45. The old rule of trespass ***ab initio*** states that a person who enters land lawfully but subsequently abuses that right of entry will be liable for the entire transaction, not merely that portion of it which follows the abuse. The rule is illustrated by *The Six Carpenters' case (1610).*

The Six Carpenters' Case : Six carpenters entered a public house, the Queen's Head, Cripplegate, where they consumed a quart of wine worth 7d and bread worth 1d. They refused to pay. The issue was whether the refusal to pay made their entry into the public house tortious.

It was held that when a person has permission or authority to enter premises, he will be a trespasser *ab initio* if that purpose is abused, for example by a theft. The courts deem that the entry was in fact for that unlawful purpose and therefore a trespass. However, refusing to pay for wine and breed does not make the original entry tortious; it does not take away the entire reason for the entry.

47. Permanent Sovereignty Over Natural Resources: Confronted with the legacy of colonialism and continued foreign control over resources, throughout the 1950s developing states sought to affirm their economic independence. One avenue for the assertion of economic independence was through the United Nations General Assembly, which in 1952, passed the first of seven resolutions on Permanent Sovereignty Over Natural Resources. In the late 1950s the UN Commission on Permanent Sovereignty over Natural Resources was established to study the question of national control over resources. In 1962, the General Assembly passed Resolution 1803, which declares that the 'right of peoples and nations to permanent sovereignty over their natural wealth and resources must be exercised in the interest of their national development and of the well-being of the people of the State concerned.' The Resolution reaffirmed that the admission of foreign investment was subject to the authorization, restriction or prohibition of the state. Once admitted, however, foreign investment was to be treated in accordance with national and international law.

48. Personality Theory: According to Kant and Hegel, if one's artistic expressions are synonymous with one's personality, then they are deserving of protection just as much as the physical person is deserving of protection since in a sense they are a part of that physical person. However Palmer counters this by saying that if a work of art were part of an individual's personality then they would cease to exist after the person died.

49. Section 13 in the Hindu Adoptions and Maintenance Act, 1956: Right of adoptive parents to dispose of their properties—Subject to any agreement to the contrary, an adoption does not deprive the adoptive father or mother of the power to dispose of his or her property by transfer inter vivos or by will.

53. Kesvananda Bharti v State of Kerala: The Supreme Court has said that fundamental rights and directive principles aim at the same goal of bringing about a social revolution and establishment of welfare state and they can be interpreted and applied together. They are **supplementary and complementary** to each other. It can well be said that directive principles prescribed the goal to be attained and the fundamental rights lay down the means by which goal is to be achieved.

55. International Conventions: In the modern period, International treaties are the most important source of International Law. Article 38 of the statute of the International Court of Justice Lists "International Conventions whether general or particular, establishing rules expressly recognized by the contesting States. A convention may be general, either because of the number of parties to it, or because of the character of its contents, it may be particular because of the limited number of parties or because of the limited character of its subject-matter.

International treaties may be of two types:

(A) Law making treaties: These are directly the source of International law which are of two types:

(*a*) Treaties enunciating rules of Universal International Law.

(*b*) International Treaties which lay down general principles.

(B) Treaty Contracts.

56. The term *marz al-mawt (marz-ul-maut)* means 'the disease of death', or 'the disease which causes death'.

It is essential condition of *marz-ul-maut,* (*i.e.*, death illness) that the person suffering from the *marz* (malady) must be under an apprehension of *maut* (death).

According to Multa, a *marz-ul-maut* is a malady which induces an apprehension of death in the person suffering from it and which eventually results in death".

According to Baillie, "The most valid definition of death-illness is that it is one which will probably issue fatally".

According to Hedaya, "A malady is said to be of long continuance, if it has lasted a year, in which case it cannot be regarded as a *marz-ul-maut,* for the patient has become familiarized to the disease. This however, is not a hard and fast rule, and the question of apprehension of death must be determined by the court upon the evidence in each case."

In order to constitute *marz-ul-maut,* the following conditions are necessary:

(*i*) the illness must cause the death of the deceased;

(*ii*) the illness must cause apprehension of death in the mind of the deceased;

(*iii*) there must be some external indicia of a serious illness.

58. The WTO's Agreement on Trade-Related Aspects of Intellectual Property Rights came into effect in 1996. The TRIPS preamble also refers to the 'effective and adequate protection of intellectual property rights'. However, this agreement also explicitly recognises 'the underlying public policy objectives of national systems for the protection of intellectual property, including developmental and technological objectives' and 'the special needs of the least-developed country. Members in respect of maximum flexibility in the domestic implementation of laws and regulations in order to enable them to create a sound and viable technological base' (Preamble). The TRIPS agreement suggests that the public policy objectives of intellectual property are developmental and technological; development and technological objectives are met through intellectual property. It does not refer, as a public policy objective or in its own objectives, to balance between protection and access. However, it is notable that the agreement does recognise public policy objectives. As well, it does not, in its language, limit its recognition only to developmental and technological policy objectives; it merely 'includes' them—other policy objectives may also be recognised.

59. The National Green Tribunal (NGT) has been established under the NGT Act, 2010 on 18th October, 2010. The Tribunal has been established for the effective and expeditious disposal of cases relating to environmental protection and conservation of forests and other natural resources including enforcement of any legal right relating to environment and giving relief and compensation for damages to persons and property and for matters connected therewith or incidental thereto.

The Law Commission in its 186th Report recognised the inadequacies of the existing appellate authorities constituted under various environmental laws and reviewed their position with a view to bring uniformity in their constitution and the scope of their jurisdiction. The Law Commission undertook the study pursuant to the observations of the Supreme Court regarding the need for constitution of environmental courts. The Law Commission, in its said report, recommended for setting up of environmental courts in each State or for a group of States for exercising all powers of a civil court in its original jurisdiction and with appellate judicial powers against orders passed by the concerned authorities under the Water (Prevention and Control of Pollution) Act, 1974, the Air (Prevention and Control of Pollution) Act, 1981, the Environment (Protection) Act, 1986, the Public Liability Insurance Act, 1991.

The Law Commission's Report was considered in the Ministry. In view of the growing environmental challenges, it was decided to set up a green tribunal as a specialized body equipped with the necessary expertise to handle environmental disputes involving multi-disciplinary issues.

61. According to Salmond, a legal person is any subject mater other than a human being to which the law attributes personality.

62. The Biological Diversing Act, 2002, includes the following 12 chapters:

Chapter-I: Preliminary

Chapter-II: Regulation of Access to Biological Diversity

Chapter-III: National Biodiversity Authority

Chapter-IV: Functions and Powers of the National Biodiversity Authority

Chapter-V: Approval by the National Biodiversity Authority

Chapter-VI: State Biodiversity Board

Chapter-VII: Finance, Accounts and Audit of National Biodiversity Authority.

Chapter-VIII: Finance, Accounts and Audit of State Biodiversity Board

Chapter-IX: Duties of the Central and the State Governments

Chapter-X: Biodiversity Management Committees

Chapter-XI: Local, Biodiversity Fund

Chapter-XII: Miscellaneous

63. S.R. Bommai Vs Union of India was one of the most significant judgements given by the Supreme Court of India. The judgement discussed about the aspect of Federalism laid by the Indian Constitution at length. It particularly discussed about Article 365 of the Indian Constitution and various aspects related to it. The relations between the Central and the state government were dealt in this case. It was between 1988-91 when Article 365 was implemented in a few states of India based on the reports submitted by the respective state Governors.

64. Commission on the Status of Women (CSW): ECOSOC Resolution 11(II) (1946) established the Commission on the Status of Women. Unlike most of the international human rights machinery, the Commission on the Status of Women had its own secretariat, partially provided by the Division for the Advancement of Women (DAW). The functions of the Commission are governed by the powers granted to it in the enabling resolution (Economic and Social Council Resolution 11(II) of 21 June 1946). This was expanded in Resolution 1987/22.

66. Criminal misappropriation takes place when the possession has been innocently come by, but where, by a subsequent change of intention, or the knowledge of new fact with which the party was not previously acquainted, the retaining becomes wrongful and fraudulent. A person commits criminal misappropriation, if he:

1. Dishonestly misappropriates or converts any property into his own use,
2. Such property should be movable.

For Example : The retention of money by a servant authorized to collect it from a person may be criminal misappropriation even though he retains it on account of wages due to him.

Punishment: Whoever dishonestly misappropriates any movable property shall be punished with imprisonment, which may extend to two years or fine, or with both.

68. About the influence of morals on law: Hart says: "The law of every modern state shows at a thousand points the influence of both the accepted social morality and wider moral ideals. These influences enter into law either abruptly and avowedly through legislation, or silently and piecemeal through the judicial process. In some systems, as in the United States, the ultimate criteria of legal validity explicitly incorporate principles of justice or substantive moral values; in other systems as in England where there are no formal restrictions on the competency of the supreme legislature, its legislation may yet no less scrupulously conform to justice or morality. The further ways in which law mirrors morality which are myraid, and still insufficiently studied: statutes may be a mere legal shell and demand by their express terms to be filled out with the aid of moral principles; the range of enforceable contracts may be limited by reference to conceptions of morality and fairness; liability for both civil and criminal wrongs may be adjusted to prevailing views of moral responsibility. No positivist could deny that these are facts or that the stability of legal systems depends in part upon such types of correspondence with morals. If this is what is meant by the necessary connection of law and morals, its existence should be conceded."

70. The relationship between a husband and his wife is also that of a principal and the agent. The husband is treated as a principal and the wife as his agent. The agency relation between the husband and his wife may be discussed under the following two heads:

Wife Living with Her Husband

When the wife is living with her husband, she has implied an authority to buy the articles of household necessaries. The following conditions should be satisfied for treating the wife an an agent of the husband:

1. The husband and wife are living together in a domestic establishment of their own.

2. The wife should be in charge of the domestic establishment.
3. The wife must have purchased articles or goods suitable to the style in which the husband chooses to live.

However, the husband can escape his liability if he proves that:

1. He has forbidden his wife expressly to buy goods on credit. The tradesman is also expressly forbidden to supply goods on credit to his wife.
2. The wife was supplied with sufficient articles or goods.
3. The wife was supplied necessary funds to purchase the necessaries.
4. The goods purchased were not necessaries.

Wife Living Apart from Her Husband

Where the wife is living apart without any fault on her part then she is legally entitled to receive maintenance from her husband. If the husband does not provide her maintenance, the wife has implied an authority to purchase the necessaries of her life and the husband is bound to pay for the same.

71. Ingredients of sedition: Section 124A, I.P.C. defines the offence of sedition and prescribes punishment for sedition which may extend up to imprisonment for life, and fine, or imprisonment up to three years and fine.

The word sedition does not occur in the body of the section. It finds place only as a marginal note to the section which is not an operative part of the sedition, but simply states the name by which the offence defined in the section is known.

The following are the essential ingredients of the section, viz.,

(1) Bringing or attempting to bring into hatred; or

(2) Exciting or attempting to excite disaffection against the Government of India;

(3) Such act or attempt may be done (*a*) by words, either spoken or written, or (*b*) by signs, or (*c*) by visible representation; and

(4) The act must be intentional.

Explanation 1 to the section sets out the scope of disaffection and Explanations 2 and 3 state what is not considered seditious intention as indicated under English law. That is to say, criticism of Government measures and administrative and other actions of the Government, if done without exciting or attempting to excite hatred, contempt or disaffection towards the Government established by law, is not sedition.

The section places absolutely on the same footing the successful excitation of disaffection and the unsuccessful attempt to excitation. The offence consists in making use of any means for the purpose of bringing the Government into hatred or contempt.

73. Corporate Social Responsibility (CSR) is interchangeably used as Corporate Conscience, Corporate Citizenship, Social Performance or Sustainable Responsible Business/Responsible Business. The idea of CSR first came up in 1953 when it became an academic topic in HR Bowen's "Social Responsibilities of the Business". However, the term CSR gained popularity in 1990s when the German Betapham, a generic pharmaceutical company decided to implement CSR. Corporate social responsibility means the obligation, which a corporation owes to the society. World Bank Group defines CSR as "It is the commitment of businesses to contribute to sustainable economic development by working with employees, their families, the local community and society at large to improve their lives in ways that are good for business and for development". According to World Business Council for Sustainable Development, Corporate Social Responsibility is—"It is the continuing commitment by business to behave ethically and contribute to economic development while improving the quality of life of the workforce and their families as well as of the local community and society at large". The European Commission defines Corporate Social Responsibility as "The responsibility of enterprises for their impacts on society and outlines what an enterprise should do to meet that responsibility". CSR is generally understood as being the way through which a company achieves a balance of economic, environmental and social imperatives ("Triple-Bottom-Line-Approach"). Triple bottom line (TBL) incorporates the notion of sustainability into business decisions, coined by John Elkington in 1994. It is an accounting framework with 3 dimensions: social, environmental and financial. The TBL dimensions are also commonly called the 3 Ps: people, planet and profit and are referred to as the "three pillars of sustainability". CSR is the process of assessing an organization's impact on society and evaluating their responsibilities. CSR begins with an assessment of a business and their customers, suppliers, environment, communities and employees.

The section 135 of the Companies Act, 2013 deals with the Corporate Social Responsibility (CSR). In order to encourage more entities to participate in the process of development of the society through CSR, the Government of India has notified the rules for CSR spending u/s 135 of the New Companies Act 2013 along with Companies (Corporate Social Responsibility Policy) Rules, 2014 effective from 1st April 2014. India became the first country to mandate spend on CSR activities through a statutory provision.

74. Section 511 of the Indian Penal Code, 1860 explains about "attempts to commit offences". According to this Section, "attempt to commit offence is itself an offence." Whoever attempts to commit an offence punishable by this Code with imprisonment for life or imprisonment, or to cause such an offence to be committed, and in such attempt does any act towards the commission of the offence, shall, where no express provision is made by this Code for the punishment of such attempt, be punished with imprisonment of any description provided for the offence, for a term which may extend to one-half of the imprisonment for life or, as the case may be, one-half of the longest term of imprisonment provided for that offence, or with such fine as is provided for the offence, or with both.

Illustrations:

(*a*) A makes an attempt to steal some jewels by breaking open a box, and finds after so opening the box, that there is no jewel in it. He has done an act towards the commission of theft, and therefore is guilty under this Section.

(*b*) A makes attempt to pick the pocket of Z by thrusting his hand into Z's pocket. A fails in the attempt in consequence of Z's having nothing in his pocket. A is guilty under this Section.

75. The concept of Rule of Law is that the state is governed, not by the ruler or the nominated representatives of the people but by the law. A county that enshrines the rule of law would be one wherein the Grundnorm of the country, or the basic and core law from which all other law derives its authority is the supreme authority of the state. The monarch or the representatives of the republic are governed by the laws derived out of the Grundnorm and their powers are limited by the law. The King is not the law but the law is king.

This concept of the rule of law has been codified in the Indian Constitution under Article 14 and the Universal Declaration of Human Rights under the Preamble and Article 7.

76. The United Nations Charter refers to human rights in its Preamble and six other articles. In the Preamble to the Charter of the United

Nations, the People of the United Nations expressed their determination "to reaffirm faith in fundamental human rights, in the dignity, and worth of human person, in the equal rights of men and women and of nations large and small, and ...."

"to promote social progress and better standards of life in larger freedom."

Thus, the Preamble to the charter in most sonorous terms recognises the human rights and the dignity and worth of the human being, which were most flagrantly violated during the two World Wars. The Preamble of the United Nations begins with the words, "We the people of the United Nations". These words are neither superfluous nor have crept in the preamble incidently. They are very meaningful. They indicate the objectives which the framers of the Charter wanted to achieve.

The purposes of the United Nation's are proclaimed in article 1 of the Charter. Article 1(2) provides:

To develop *friendly relations* among nations *based on respect for the principle of equal rights and self-determination of peoples*, and to take other appropriate measures to strengthen universal (Emphasis added).

Article 1(3) further provides:

To achieve international co-operation in solving international problems of an economic, social, cultural, or humanitarian character, and in *promoting and encouraging respect for human rights and for fundamental freedoms for all without distinction as to race, sex, language, or religion.* (Emphasis added)

Thus, once again we find that the underlined purpose of the United Nations Charter is to promote and encourage human rights and fundamental freedoms.

The words "based on respect for the principle of equal rights and self determination of peoples" in article 1(2) and the words "in promoting and encouraging respect for human rights and for fundamental freedoms for all without distinction as to race, sex, language or religion" were not in the Dumbarton Oaks Proposals but were introduced in San Francisco. Article 1 puts the promotion of respect for human rights on the same level as the maintenance of international peace and security as a purpose of the United Nations. It is also a recognition of the reality that the entire mankind is after all one organic whole and that a denial of human dignity and liberty, anywhere is a threat to peace and security everywhere.

The basic obligations of the Organisation and its Member States in achieving these purposes are set out in articles 55 and 56 of the United Nations Charter.

77. The Universal Declaration of Human Rights contains thirty articles. Article 1 enunciates the basic principle of the Declaration: "All human beings are born free and equal in dignity and rights. They are endowed with reason and conscience and should act towards one another in a spirit of brotherhood." Article 2 sets out the principle of non-discrimination in the enjoyment of human rights. Articles 3-21 are devoted to civil and political rights such as the rights to life, liberty, and property, to freedom from torture or inhumane and degrading treatment, to freedom from arbitrary arrest, detention or exile, to a fair and public hearing by an independent and impartial tribunal, to freedom of thought and religion, to freedom of expression, to peaceful assembly and association, and to take part in the government of one's country. Articles 22-27 deal with economic and social rights: rights to social security, to work, to fair pay and fair conditions of work, to rest and leisure, to an adequate standard of living, to education, and to participate in the cultural life of the community. Articles 29-30 set out certain general limitations on the exercise of human rights requiring, for instance, that they be exercised with respect for the rights and freedoms of others.

78. **Article 368** in part XX of the constitution deals with the Power of Parliament to amend the constitution and its procedure. However, the Parliament cannot amend those provisions which form the "basic - structure" of the constitution. This was ruled by the supreme court in the Kesavananda a Bharti case (1973).

81. Liability or responsibility is the word or tie that comes into existence as a result of the wrongful act of an individual. This is called Vinculum juris by which a man who is under it, must do certain things. A man's liability consists in these things which he must suffer. It is the ultimatum of the law. It has its sources in the Supreme will of the State. According to Salmond, liability or responsibility is the bond of necessity that exists between the wrong doer, and the remedy. "He who commits a wrong is said to be liable or responsible for it".

Liability may be divided either as civil or criminal or as remedial or penal. In the case of civil or remedial liability, the object of the law is the enforcement of right, whereas in case of criminal or penal liability the purpose is the punishment of the wrong-doer. All criminal liability is penal. Civil liability on the other hand may be either penal or remedial.

82. Section 42 of the Companies Act, 2013 has specified certain conditions for 'private placement' of shares.

Some of the important conditions are given below:

(1) The offer of securities or invitation to subscribe securities, shall be made to such number of persons ***not exceeding fifty*** or such higher number as may be prescribed, excluding qualified institutional buyers and employees of the company being offered securities under a scheme of employees stock option.

(2) No fresh offer or invitation under this section shall be made unless the allotments with respect to any offer or invitation made earlier have been completed or that offer or invitation has been withdrawn or abandoned by the company.

(3) Any offer or invitation not in compliance with the provisions of this section shall be ***treated as a public offer*** and all provisions of this Act, and the Securities Contracts (Regulation) Act, 1956 and the Securities and Exchange Board of India Act, 1992 shall be required to be complied with.

(4) All monies payable towards subscription of securities under this section shall be paid through cheque or demand draft or other banking channels but not by cash.

83. The sapinda-relationship refers to blood relationship. It indicates that the person belongs to a common ancestor and have community of blood particles in him. This relationship of a Hindu arise out of birth in the family. The relationship becomes closer or remoter with the common ancestor according to the number of blood particles present in him or her. Accordingly sapinda relationship arises between two persons on account of their being connected by particles of one body. Sapinda relationship is based on two theories:

(*a*) oblation theory and

(*b*) particles of the same body theory.

Sapinda relationship has been defined in Section 3 (f) of the Hindu Marriage Act, 1955. According to this Section:

(*i*) 'sapinda relationship' with reference to any person extends as far as the third generation (inclusive) in the line of ascent through the mother, and the fifth (inclusive) in the line of ascent through the father, the line being traced upwards in each case from the person concerned who is to be counted as the first generation;

(*ii*) two persons are said to be 'sapindas' of each other if one is a lineal ascendant of the other within the limits of sapinda relationship, or if they have a common lineal ascendant who is within the limits of sapinda relationship with reference to each of them."

Thus in the modern Hindu law the sapinda relationship extends upto five degrees on the paternal side and three degrees on the maternal side.

85. India has enacted the Geographical indications of Goods (Registration and Protection) Act, 1999 (the GIG Act). The GIG Act provides for registration and better protection of geographical indications relating to goods to help identify the place of origin of goods quality, reputation and other distinctive characteristics of these goods. The GIG Act now helps in protecting unique.

Indian products linked to some geographical region of India, such as Basmati Rice, Darjeeling Tea, Alphonso Mangoes, Malabar Pepper, Cardamom and Hyderabad Grapes, which are all well known in the international market. For many years, these products have been exported on a regular basis, demonstrating India's reputation of high quality of these products and, therefore, require such protection. Under the GIG Act, assignment of geographical indications is prohibited, being public property. The GIG Act also lays down provisions for infringement actions. The GIG Act helps prevent geographical indications of goods becoming generic which may otherwise lead to a loss of distinctiveness and consequently loss of protection.

86. For all crimes, except crimes of strict liability there are two elements which must be proved by the prosecution as shown in Figure. These are:

- *actus reus*
- *mens rea*

These terms come from a latin maxim, actus non facit reum nisi mens sit rea, which means 'the act itself does not constitute guilt unless done with a guilty mind'. Both an act (or omission) and a guilty mind must be proved for most criminal offences.

ACTUS REUS	+	MENS REA	=	OFFENCE

Fig: Elements of an offence

Actus reus has a wider meaning than an 'act', as it can cover omissions or a state of affairs. The term has been criticised as misleading. Lord Diplock in *Miller* (1983) 1 All ER 978 preferred the term 'prohibited conduct', while the Law Commission in the Draft Criminal Code (1989) used the term 'external element'.

Mens rea translates as 'guilty mind', but this also is misleading. The Law Commission in the Draft Criminal Code (1989) used the term 'fault element'. The levels of 'guilty mind' required for different offences vary from the highest level, which is specific intention for some crimes, to much lower levels such as negligence or knowledge of a certain fact for less serious offences.

The *actus* reus and *mens rea* will be different for different crimes. For example, in murder the *actus reus* is the killing of a human being and the *mens rea* is causing the death with 'malice aforethought'. For theft the *actus reus* is the appropriation of property belonging to another, while the *mens rea* is doing this dishonestly and with the intention permanently to deprive the other of the property. The *actus reus* and the *mens rea* must be present together, but if there is an ongoing act, then the existence of the necessary *mens rea* at any point during that act is sufficient.

88. In fact, many of the mandatory provisions of our Constitution are Conventions of the British Constitution. Dr. B. R. Ambedkar had consistently emphasised on the fact that we had chosen the British Model of Government and called for adherence to Westminster system. Ivor Jennings stated that "the machinery of Government in India is essentially British and the whole collection of British Conventions has apparently been incorporated as Conventions".

89. Theory of Consent: According to the supporters of this theory - consent of States is the basis of the International Law. States observed rules of International Law because they have given their consent for it. The chief exponents of this theory are Anzilotti, Triepel, Oppenheim etc.

90. Solitary Confinements (Section 73): Whenever any person is convicted of an offence for which under this Code the Court has power to sentence him to rigorous imprisonment, the Court may order for solitary confinement.

Time period: Maximum three month, that is to say.

a time not exceeding one month if the term of imprisonment shall not exceed six months.

a time not exceeding two months if the term of imprisonment shall not exceed one year.

a time not exceeding three months if the terms of imprisonment shall exceed one year.

Limit of Solitary Confinement (Section 74)

If total punishment is not more than three months: Confinement shall be in no case exceed fourteen days at a time, with intervals between the periods of solitary confinement of not less duration than such periods.

When imprisonment shall exceed three months: Solitary confinement shall not exceed seven days in any one month of the whole imprisonment awarded with intervals between the periods of solitary confinement of not less duration than such periods.

94. Judicial review, the power of courts to review statutes and the governmental action to determine whether they confirm to rules & principles laid down in constitution. Judicial review is based on the idea that a constitution which dictates the nature, functions and limits of a government — is the supreme law. Consequently, any action by a government that violates the principles of its constitution is invalid. The system of judicial review of administrative action has been inherited from Britain. It is on this foundation that the Indian Courts have built a superstructure of control mechanism. The whole law of judicial review of administrative action has been developed by judges on case to case basis. Consequently, a thicket of technicalities and inconsistencies surrounds it.

Judicial review means review by courts of administrative actions with a view to ensure their legality. Review is different from appeal. In appeal the appellate authority can go into the merits of the decisions of the authority appealed against. In judicial review, the court does not go into the merits of the administrative action; court's function is restricted to ensuring that such authority does not act in excess of its power. The court is not supposed to substitute its decision for that of the administrative authority. In Judicial review of administrative action, the courts merely enquire whether the administrative authority has acted according to the law. Judicial Review of administrative action, according to de Smith, is 'inevitably sporadic and peripheral'. It undertakes scrutiny of administrative action on the touchstone of the Doctrine of *ultravires.* The administrative authorities are given powers by the statutes and such powers have to be exercised within the limits drawn upon them by the statutes. As long as an authority acts within the ambit of the power given to it, no court should interfere. It is in this sense that such an authority is said to have the liberty to act rightly as well as wrongly. It has been held that a court exercising judicial review should not act as a court of appeal over a tribunal as an administrative authority whose decision comes before it for review. The Supreme Court reiterated this principle of judicial review in *State of M.P.* v. *M.V. Vyavasaya Co. Ltd.*

96. The eighteenth-century legal commentator, William Blackstone, introduced the declaratory theory of law, stating that judges do not make law, but merely, by the rules of precedent, discover and declare the law that has always been: '[the judge] being sworn to determine, not according to his private sentiments ... not according to his own private judgement, but according to the known laws and customs of the land: not delegated to pronounce a new law, but to maintain and expound the old one'. Blackstone does not accept that precedent ever offers a choice between two or more interpretations of the law: where a bad decision is made, he states, the new one that reverses or overrules it is not a new law, nor a statement that the old decision was bad law, but a declaration that the previous decision was 'not law', in other words that it was the wrong answer. His view presupposes that there is always one right answer, to be deduced from an objective study of precedent.

98. In his famous work 'The Nature of the Judicial Process' Cardozo J said: I think adherence to precedent should be the rule and nor the exception ... the labour of judges would be increased almost to the breaking point if every past decision could be reopened in every case, and one could not lay one's own course of bricks on the secure foundation of the courses laid by others who had gone before him ... [W]e have had ten judges, of whom only seven sit at a time. It happens again and again, where the question is a close one, that a case which one week is decided one way might be decided another way the next if it were then heard for the first time. The situation would, however, be intolerable if the weekly changes in the composition of the court were accompanied by changes in its rulings. In such circumstances there is nothing to do except to stand by the errors of our brethren of the week before, whether we relish them or not. But I am ready to concede that the rule of adherence to precedent, though it ought not to be abandoned, ought to be in some degree relaxed ... when a rule, after it has been duly tested by experience, has been found to be inconsistent with the sense of justice or with the social welfare, there should be less hesitation in frank avowal and full abandonment.

Previous Paper (Solved)

UGC-NET-Junior Research Fellowship & Assistant Professor Exam

LAW, July-2018*

PAPER-II

Note: *This paper contains* **hundred (100)** *objective type questions of* **two (2)** *marks each.* ***All*** *questions are* ***compulsory.***

1. Which of the following is not included in the definition of law under Article 13 of the Constitution of India?

A. Legislation
B. Customs
C. Usage having no force of law
D. Ordinance

2. Which of the following Article of the Constitution uses the term 'martial law'?

A. Article 33 B. Article 34
C. Article 352 D. Article 353

3. Read Assertion (A) and Reason (R) and give correct answer by using the code given below:

Assertion (A): A person shall be disqualified for being chosen as, and for being, a member of either House of Parliament if he holds any office of profit under the Government.

Reason (R): If 'pecuniary gain' is receivable in connection with the office. Then it shall not become an office of profit, irrespective of whether such gains are actually promised or not.

Codes:

A. Both (A) and (R) are correct and (R) is the correct explanation of (A)
B. Both (A) and (R) are correct, but (R) is not the correct explanation of (A)
C. (A) is correct and (R) is incorrect
D. (A) is incorrect, but (R) is correct

4. Which of the following statement/statements is/are incorrect? Give answer by using the code given below:

(*a*) The election of the President shall be held in accordance with the system of proportional representation by means of single non-transferable vote.
(*b*) The President may resign, by writing under his hand addressed to the Chief Justice of India.
(*c*) No resolution to remove the Vice-President of India from his office, shall be moved unless at least thirty days notice has been given to him.
(*d*) Vice-President shall, not with standing the expiration of his term, continue to hold office until his successor enters upon his office.

Codes:

A. (*a*), (*b*), (*c*) and (*d*) are incorrect
B. (*a*), (*b*) and (*c*) are incorrect
C. Only (*a*) and (*b*) are incorrect
D. Only (*a*) is incorrect

5. Match List-I (name of the case) with List-II (related subject) and give correct answer by using the code below:

List-I	List-II
(*a*) K.M. Nanawati Vs. State of Bombay	(*i*) Right to life
(*b*) Ram Prasad Vs. State of U.P.	(*ii*) Power to pardon
(*c*) Lily Thomas Vs. Union of India	(*iii*) Fundamental Duties
(*d*) Dr. P. Naller Thampy Terah Vs. Union of India	(*iv*) Disqualification of members

* Exam held on 08 July, 2018.

Codes:

	(a)	(b)	(c)	(d)
A.	(ii)	(iii)	(iv)	(i)
B.	(i)	(ii)	(iii)	(iv)
C.	(iii)	(iv)	(i)	(ii)
D.	(iv)	(i)	(ii)	(iii)

6. Which of the following case is not related to 'Theory of basic structure' under Article 368 of the Constitution?
A. Minerva Mills Vs. Union of India
B. Waman Rao Vs. Union of India
C. L. Chandra Kumar Vs. Union of India
D. T.K. Rangarajan Vs. Government of Tamil Nadu

7. Which of the following is incorrect in relation to the declaration of financial emergency by the President under Article 360 of the constitution?
A. It shall cease to operate at the expiration of one month unless approved by both Houses of Parliament
B. Salary and allowances of persons serving in connection with affairs of state may be reduced
C. It may be revoked or varied by a subsequent proclamation by President
D. Salary and allowances of the Judges of Supreme Court and High Courts may be reduced

8. Which of the following statement/statements is/are correct? Give correct answer by using the code given below:
(a) An ordinary Bill can only originate in council of states
(b) A Bill pending in House of people shall not lapse by reason of the prorogation of the House
(c) A Bill pending in the council of state which has not been passed by the House of people shall not lapse on a dissolution of the House of the people
(d) A Bill pending in the House of people shall not lapse by reason of the dissolution of the House

Codes:
A. (a) and (b) are correct
B. (b) and (c) are correct
C. (a) and (d) are correct
D. (b) and (d) are correct

9. In which of the following case the Parliament has no power to legislate on the state list?
A. Consent of two states
B. Implementing international agreements
C. Emergency is in operation
D. In the Public interest if so declared by council of states

10. Match List-I (name of case) with List-II (related subject) and give correct answer by using the code below:

List-I	List-II
(a) Union of India Vs. Sankalchand Seth	(i) Power to do complete justice
(b) Leila David Vs. State of Maharashtra	(ii) Foreign Precedent
(c) B.S.E.S. Ltd. Vs. Fenner India Ltd.	(iii) Power to punish for contempt
(d) Darsan Gupta Vs. Radhika Gupta	(iv) Appointment/ Transfer of Judges

Codes:

	(a)	(b)	(c)	(d)
A.	(iv)	(iii)	(ii)	(i)
B.	(i)	(ii)	(iii)	(iv)
C.	(ii)	(i)	(iv)	(iii)
D.	(iii)	(iv)	(i)	(ii)

11. Which of the following case is not related to the Parliamentary previleges?
A. M.S.M. Sharma Vs. Sri Krishna Sinha
B. State of Karnataka Vs. Union of India
C. Jatish Chandra Ghose Vs. Harisadhan Mukherjee
D. State of Tamil Nadu Vs. K. Shyam Sunder

12. Which of the following statement/statements is/are correct? Answer by using code given below:
(a) It shall be the duty of every citizen to respect the country and abide by the constitution.

(*b*) All minorities, whether based on religion or language, shall have the right to establish and administer educational institutions of their choice.

(*c*) The state shall in particular, take steps for preserving and improving the breeds, and prohibiting the slaughter of cows and calves and other milch and draught cattle.

(*d*) No law here after enacted by the legislature of Jammu and Kashmir shall be void on the ground that it is inconsistent with any rights conferred on other citizens of India by any provision of part-III of the Constitution.

Codes:

A. Only (*a*) and (*b*) are correct
B. Only (*c*) and (*d*) are correct
C. (*a*), (*b*) and (*c*) are correct
D. (*a*), (*b*), (*c*) and (*d*) are correct

13. Which one of the following Jurists distinguished between 'expositorial' jurisprudence (What the law is) and 'Censorial' jurisprudence (What the law ought to be)?

A. John Austin
B. Hans Kelsen
C. Jeremy Benthem
D. H.L.A. Hart

14. 'Now, natural law is not considered as absolute but as relative. It is natural law with variable contents.' This observation specifically relates to:

A. Dabin B. Stammler
C. Finnis D. Acquinas

15. According to Professor Hart the meaning of the term 'Positivism' includes:

(*a*) Laws are commands.
(*b*) The analysis of legal concepts is distinct from sociological and historical inquiries.
(*c*) Moral judgments cannot be established or defended by rational argument, evidence or proof.
(*d*) The law as it is actually laid down, has to be kept separate from the law that ought to be.

Codes:

A. Only (*a*) and (*c*) are correct
B. Only (*a*), (*b*) and (*d*) are correct
C. Only (*a*), (*c*) and (*d*) are correct
D. (*a*), (*b*), (*c*) and (*d*) all are correct

16. Match List-I with List-II and give the correct answer by using the code given below:

List-I (Theory)	List-II (Jurist)
(*a*) Theory of social solidarity	(*i*) Ehrlich
(*b*) Theory of categorical Imperative	(*ii*) Duguit
(*c*) Imperative Theory of Law	(*iii*) John Austin
(*d*) Theory of Living Law	(*iv*) Emanual Kant

Codes:

	(*a*)	(*b*)	(*c*)	(*d*)
A.	(*iv*)	(*i*)	(*iii*)	(*ii*)
B.	(*ii*)	(*iv*)	(*i*)	(*iii*)
C.	(*ii*)	(*iv*)	(*iii*)	(*i*)
D.	(*i*)	(*ii*)	(*iv*)	(*iii*)

17. Match List-I with List-II and give the correct answer by using the code given below:

List-I (Book)	List-II (Author)
(*a*) The Growth of the Law	(*i*) Gray
(*b*) Foundations of Jurisprudence	(*ii*) R. Dworkin
(*c*) The Nature and Sources of Law	(*iii*) Cardozo
(*d*) Taking Rights Seriously	(*iv*) Jerome Hall

Codes:

	(*a*)	(*b*)	(*c*)	(*d*)
A.	(*i*)	(*ii*)	(*iii*)	(*iv*)
B.	(*iii*)	(*iv*)	(*i*)	(*ii*)
C.	(*ii*)	(*iii*)	(*i*)	(*iv*)
D.	(*iv*)	(*i*)	(*ii*)	(*iii*)

18. Which one of the following are the two main theories of legal right?

A. Interest Theory and Fiction Theory
B. Realist Theory and Will Theory
C. Bracket Theory and Interest Theory
D. Interest Theory and Will Theory

19. Which of the following is not a theory relating to corporate personality?

A. Fiction Theory
B. Realistic Theory
C. Purpose Theory
D. Functional Theory

20. Match List-I with List-II and give the Jural correlatives by using the code given below:

List-I	List-II
(*a*) Claim	(*i*) No claim
(*b*) Liberty	(*ii*) Disability
(*c*) Power	(*iii*) Duty
(*d*) Immunity	(*iv*) Liability

Codes:

	(*a*)	(*b*)	(*c*)	(*d*)
A.	(*ii*)	(*iii*)	(*i*)	(*iv*)
B.	(*iii*)	(*i*)	(*iv*)	(*ii*)
C.	(*iv*)	(*iii*)	(*ii*)	(*i*)
D.	(*i*)	(*ii*)	(*iii*)	(*iv*)

21. 'X', a servant, finds a bag at the basement of the shop. He hands it over to 'Y', the owner of the shop, who asks him to place it in the almirah. Now, the bag is in possession of :

A. 'X', because he was the finder
B. 'Y', because he was the owner of the shop
C. 'Y', because in him there was corpus and animus
D. 'X', because he kept it in the almirah

22. Read Assertion (A) and Reason (R) and give the correct answer by using the code given below:

Assertion (A): Laws are valid only if they are just.

Reason (R): The aim of law is to secure justice.

Codes:

A. Both (A) and (R) are true, and (R) is the correct explanation of (A)
B. Both (A) and (R) are true, but (R) is not the correct explanation of (A)
C. (A) is true, but (R) is false
D. (A) is false, but (R) is true

23. Read Assertion (A) and Reason (R) and give the correct answer by using the code given below:

Assertion (A): Judges must follow authoritative precedents.

Reason (R): Authoritative precedents derive their authority from basic postulates of the legal system itself.

Codes:

A. Both (A) and (R) are true, and (R) is the correct explanation of (A)
B. Both (A) and (R) are true, but (R) is not the correct explanation of (A)
C. (A) is true, but (R) is false
D. (A) is false, but (R) is true

24. Which of the following statement/statements is/are correct?

(*a*) Hobbes, Austin and Pufendorf subscribe to the view that law "Properly so called" in command of the sovereign and enforced by a superior political authority and hence deny legal character of International law.
(*b*) Oppenheim has remarked that International law is the vanishing point of Jurisprudence.
(*c*) Holland subscribes to the view that International law is really law.
(*d*) Starke has expressed the view that International law is a "Weak law".

Codes:

A. Only (*a*) is correct
B. (*a*) and (*d*) both are correct
C. (*a*), (*b*), (*c*) are correct
D. (*a*), (*b*), (*c*) and (*d*) all correct

25. 'Triepel' and 'Anzilloti' are the exponents of which of the following theory of Relationship between International law and Municipal law?

A. Monism
B. Dualism
C. Specific Adoption Theory
D. Delegation Theory

26. Which one of the following is one of the Chief Exponents of 'Constitutive Theory' of Recognition?

A. Pit corbett
B. Kelson
C. Hegel
D. Hall

27. Which of the following statement/statements is/are not correct?

(*a*) In accordance with the provisions of Article 7 of the United Nations Charter, the Security Council is one of the Principal organs of the United Nations.

(*b*) The First Security Council came into being on 12th January, 1946.

(*c*) At Dumharton proposals, it was finally decided to establish such as an organ in the form of the Security Council

(*d*) Ten non-permanent members of the Security Council are elected by the General Assembly for 5 years.

Codes:

A. Only (*c*) is not correct
B. (*c*) and (*d*) are not correct
C. (*a*), (*b*), (*c*) are not correct
D. (*a*), (*b*), (*c*) and (*d*) all are not correct

28. Match List-I with List-II and give the correct answer by using the code given below:

List-I (Provisions)	**List-II (Articles of statute of court of International Justice)**
(*a*) Law applied by the International Court of Justice	(*i*) Article 41
(*b*) Binding force of the decision of International Court of Justice	(*ii*) Article 62
(*c*) Interim Measures or Relief	(*iii*) Article 38
(*d*) International court's power to allow a state to intervene, in case to which it is not a party	(*iv*) Article 59

Codes:

	(*a*)	(*b*)	(*c*)	(*d*)
A.	(*iii*)	(*iv*)	(*i*)	(*ii*)
B.	(*i*)	(*ii*)	(*iii*)	(*iv*)
C.	(*ii*)	(*iii*)	(*iv*)	(*i*)
D.	(*iv*)	(*i*)	(*ii*)	(*iii*)

29. Match List-I with List-II and give the correct answer by using the code given below:

List-I (Modes)	**List-II (Provision)**
(*a*) Cession	(*i*) Acquisition of Nationality
(*b*) Reprisal	(*ii*) Loss of Nationality
(*c*) Good offices	(*iii*) Pacific means of settlement of International Disputes
(*d*) Substitution	(*iv*) Coercive means of settlement of International Disputes

Codes:

	(*a*)	(*b*)	(*c*)	(*d*)
A.	(*i*)	(*iv*)	(*iii*)	(*ii*)
B.	(*ii*)	(*iii*)	(*iv*)	(*i*)
C.	(*iii*)	(*ii*)	(*i*)	(*iv*)
D.	(*iv*)	(*i*)	(*ii*)	(*iii*)

30. Read Assertion (A) and Reason (R) both and give the correct answer by using the code given below:

Assertion (A): Article 10 of the U.N. charter confers upon the General Assembly very wide deliberative functions except in respect of those matters which are being considered by the Security Council.

Reason (R): The Resolutions or declarations of the General Assembly are not binding upon the states. They are merely recommendations.

Codes:

A. Both (A) and (R) are correct and (R) is the correct explanation of (A)
B. Both (A) and (R) are correct, but (R) is not the correct explanation of (A)
C. (A) is correct, but (R) is wrong
D. (A) is wrong, but (R) is correct

31. Which of the following statement/statements is/are correct?

(*a*) All members of the United Nations are ipso facto the members of the statute of the International court of justice.

(*b*) The International court of justice consists of 25 judges. Which are elected by the General Assembly.

(*c*) The judges of the International court of justice are elected for a term of 5 years.

(*d*) All the decisions of the International court of justice are on the basis of the majority of judges.

Codes:

A. Only (*a*) is correct

B. (*a*) and (*b*) are correct

C. (*a*) and (*d*) are only correct

D. (*a*), (*b*), (*c*) and (*d*) all are correct

32. Read both Assertion (A) and Reason (R) and give the correct answer by using the code given below:

Assertion (A): When a state behaves in discourteous manner with another state, International law confers right upon the state affected to resort to 'retorsion' which means retaliation.

Reason (R): If the International disputes are not resolved through 'peaceful', means then the states resort to compulsive or coercive means.

Codes:

A. Both (A) and (R) are correct and (R) is correct explanation of (A)

B. Both (A) and (R) are correct, but (R) is not correct explanation of (A)

C. (A) is correct, but (R) is wrong

D. (A) is wrong, but (R) is correct

33. The 'U.N. Commission on Human Rights' was established in 1946 by:

A. General Assembly

B. Security Council

C. Economic and Social Council

D. International Court of Justice

34. Under Hindu law, the persons descended from a common ancestor but by different wives, are known as:

A. Full blood Relations

B. Half Blood Relations

C. Uterine Blood Relations

D. No Blood Relations

35. Match List-I with List-II and give the correc answer by using the code given below:

List-I	List-II
(*a*) Agnate	(*i*) What was heard
(*b*) Shruti	(*ii*) Related wholly through males
(*c*) Cognate	(*iii*) What has been remembered
(*d*) Smriti	(*iv*) Related not wholly through males

Codes:

	(*a*)	(*b*)	(*c*)	(*d*)
A.	(*i*)	(*iv*)	(*ii*)	(*iii*)
B.	(*ii*)	(*i*)	(*iv*)	(*iii*)
C.	(*ii*)	(*iv*)	(*iii*)	(*i*)
D.	(*iii*)	(*iv*)	(*i*)	(*ii*)

36. If the condition laid down under section 5(iii) of the Hindu Marriage Act, 1955 is violated, such marriage under the Act is:

A. Void but not punishable

B. Valid and not punishable

C. Void and Punishable

D. Valid but Punishable

37. Under sec. 2 of the Dissolution of Muslim Marriages Act 1939, the following grounds of divorce are available to a wife:

(*a*) Where abouts of the husband have not been known for a period of four years.

(*b*) Four years imprisonment of the husband.

(*c*) Husband has treated her with cruelty.

(*d*) The husband has neglected her or has failed to pay her maintenance for a period of two years.

Codes:

A. (*a*), (*c*) and (*d*)

B. (*b*), (*d*), (*c*) and (*a*)

C. (*d*), (*c*), (*b*) and (*a*)

D. (*a*), (*d*), (*b*) and (*c*)

38. Read both Assertion (A) and Reason (R) and answer by using the code given below:

Assertion (A): No person except the father or mother or guardian of a Hindu child has the capacity to give such child in adoption.

Reason (R): No re-adoption may take place under the Hindu Adoptions and maintenance Act, 1956.

Codes:

A. (A) is correct, but (R) is false
B. (A) is false, but (R) is correct
C. Both (A) and (R) are correct
D. Both (A) and (R) are false

39. Match List-I with List-II in the light of the Hindu Adoptions and Maintenance Act, 1956 and give correct answer by using the code given below:

List-I (Section)	List-II (Provision)
(*a*) Sec. 18	(*i*) Maintenance of dependants
(*b*) Sec. 19	(*ii*) Amount of maintenance
(*c*) Sec. 22	(*iii*) Maintenance of wife
(*d*) Sec. 23	(*iv*) Maintenance of widowed daughter-in law

Codes:

	(*a*)	(*b*)	(*c*)	(*d*)
A.	(*iii*)	(*iv*)	(*ii*)	(*i*)
B.	(*iii*)	(*iv*)	(*i*)	(*ii*)
C.	(*i*)	(*iii*)	(*ii*)	(*iv*)
D.	(*iv*)	(*iii*)	(*i*)	(*ii*)

40. "Marriages of all persons who are citizens of India belonging to various religions should be made compulsorily registrable in their respective states where the marriage is solemnized". This was ruled by the supreme court in which of the following case:

A. Sarla Mudgil v/s Union of India
B. Gurupad v/s Hirabai
C. Shastri v/s Muldass
D. Seema v/s Ashwani Kumar

41. Give the correct answer with the help of code given below:

A 'Muta' marriage is:

(*a*) A temporary marriage
(*b*) Recognized under sunni law
(*c*) Recognized under shia law
(*d*) A marriage for a fixed period

Codes:

A. (*d*), (*b*), (*a*) and (*c*)
B. (*b*), (*c*) and (*d*)
C. (*a*), (*c*) and (*d*)
D. (*a*), (*b*) and (*d*)

42. Match List-I with List-II in the light of the Hindu Marriage Act, 1955, and give correct answer with the help of code given below:

List-I (Section)	List-II (Provision)
(*a*) Section 14	(*i*) Alternative Relief in divorce proceedings
(*b*) Section 13-A	(*ii*) Restitution of conjugal Rights
(*c*) Section 9	(*iii*) Judicial separation
(*d*) Section 10	(*iv*) No petition for divorce within one year of marriage

Codes:

	(*a*)	(*b*)	(*c*)	(*d*)
A.	(*iv*)	(*i*)	(*ii*)	(*iii*)
B.	(*i*)	(*iv*)	(*iii*)	(*ii*)
C.	(*iv*)	(*iii*)	(*ii*)	(*i*)
D.	(*ii*)	(*iii*)	(*i*)	(*iv*)

43. Read Assertion (A) and Reason (R) and give the correct answer by using the code given below:

Assertion (A): A proposal may be revoked at any time before the communication of its acceptance is complete as against the proposer, but not afterwards.

Reason (R): Section 5 of the Indian contract Act 1872, deals with the revocation of proposals and acceptances.

Codes:

A. Both (A) and (R) are correct, but (R) is not related to (A)
B. (A) is correct, but (R) is wrong
C. (A) is wrong, but (R) is correct
D. Both (A) and (R) are correct, and (R) is the correct explanation of (A)

44. Which of the following statement/s is/are correct?

Consideration is:

(*a*) a price for any promise
(*b*) only a moral obligation
(*c*) a motive for any promise
(*d*) something of value in the eye of law

Codes:

A. (*a*) and (*c*) are correct
B. (*a*) and (*d*) are correct
C. (*b*), (*c*) and (*d*) are correct
D. (*c*) and (*d*) are correct

45. Consider the following statements and give correct answer with the help of code given below:

The case of Mohori Bibee Vs Dharmodas Ghose:

(*a*) has laid down that a minor's contract becomes valid when he attains majority.
(*b*) is the decision of the Supreme Court of India regarding minor's contract.
(*c*) is the decision of Privy Council regarding voidness of minor's contract.
(*d*) has laid down that contract without consideration is void.

Codes:

A. (*c*) and (*d*) are correct, but (*a*) and (*b*) are incorrect.
B. (*a*) and (*b*) are correct, but (*c*) and (*d*) are incorrect.
C. (*c*) is correct, but (*a*), (*b*) and (*d*) are incorrect.
D. (*b*) and (*d*) are correct, but (*a*) and (*c*) are incorrect.

46. Read Assertion (A) and Reason (R) and give the correct answer with the help of codes given below:

Assertion (A): Acceptance is to offer what a lighted match is to a train of gunpowder.

Reason (R): Acceptance cannot be separated from offer.

Codes:

A. (A) is true, but (R) is false.
B. (A) is false, but (R) is true.
C. Both (A) and (R) are true, and (R) is the correct explanation of (A).
D. Both (A) and (R) are true, but (R) is not the correct explanation of (A)

47. The defence of 'non est factum' is available to the contracting party who has committed mistake as to the:

A. Identity of the other contracting party
B. Nature of contract
C. Quality of the subject matter of the contract
D. Quality of the promise made by the other party

48. Under the Indian Contract Act 1872 Which one of the following does not fall in the meaning of fraud?

A. Active concealment of a fact.
B. Suggestion, as a fact, of that which is not true, by one who does not believe it to be true.
C. Positive assertion of unwarranted statements.
D. A promise made without any intention of performing it.

49. Special damages will be awarded in case of a breach of contract:

A. Only when the contracting parties express the same specifically as the terms of the contract.
B. Always in the special circumstances leading to the formation of the contract.
C. Only when the court of law thinks fit in the special circumstances of the case.
D. Only when the special circumstances causing loss of profit resulting from the breach of contract were brought to the notice of the party committing breach at the time of formation of the contract.

50. Which of the following statement/statements is/are correct? Give correct answer by using the code given below:

(*a*) Tort is a civil wrong for which remedy is a common law action.

(*b*) Tort is exclusively a breach of contract or breach of trust.

(*c*) Tort is an infringement of a right in rein of a private individual.

(*d*) Tort is violation of a legal duty owed to people generally for maintenance of law and order.

Codes:

A. Only (*b*) and (*d*) are correct

B. Only (*b*) and (*c*) are correct

C. Only (*a*) and (*c*) are correct

D. Only (*a*) and (*d*) are correct

51. Match List-I (name of case) with List-II (name of defense) and give the correct answer by using the code given below:

List-I	List-II
(*a*) Samira Kohli Vs Prabha Manchanda	(*i*) Plaintiff a wrong-doer
(*b*) Sodan Singh Vs New Delhi Municipal Committee	(*ii*) Leave and licence
(*c*) Bird Vs Holbrook	(*iii*) Act of God
(*d*) Kallulal Vs Hemchand	(*iv*) Necessity

Codes:

	(*a*)	(*b*)	(*c*)	(*d*)
A.	(*ii*)	(*iv*)	(*i*)	(*iii*)
B.	(*i*)	(*ii*)	(*iv*)	(*iii*)
C.	(*ii*)	(*i*)	(*iii*)	(*iv*)
D.	(*iii*)	(*i*)	(*ii*)	(*iv*)

52. Which of the following is correctly matched in relation to the defences of tort of defamation?

A. Fair comment – An expression of statement of fact rather than expression of opinion

B. Absolute previlege – Statements made by the members of either House of Parliament in the House or outside the House

C. Justification by truth – It is enough if the statement is substantially true and may not be mathematically accurate

D. Consent – Plaintiff has not consented to the publication of defamatory words by the defendant

53. Which of the following case is **not** related to 'Remoteness of Damage'?

A. Scott Vs Shepherd

B. In re an Arbitration between Polemis and Furness, Withy and Co.

C. Sirros Vs. Moore

D. Overseas Tankship Ltd. Vs Morts Dock and Engineering Co.

54. Which of the following tort is **not** related to nuisance based on 'Physical discomfort' or interference with another's health and safety?

A. Obstruction of light

B. Injury to property

C. Noise pollution

D. Pollution of water and air

55. Match List-I (name of case) with List-II (capacity to sue) and give the correct answer by using the code given below:

List-I	List-II
(*a*) State of Saurashtra Vs Memon Haji Ismail	(*i*) No right to Sue as an un-incorporated association
(*b*) Delhi Transport Corporation Vs Kumari Lalita	(*ii*) Municipal law does not apply
(*c*) Brown Vs Lewis	(*iii*) Suit against corporation
(*d*) Campbell Vs Paddington	(*iv*) Suit by minor

Codes:

	(*a*)	(*b*)	(*c*)	(*d*)
A.	(*ii*)	(*iv*)	(*i*)	(*iii*)
B.	(*i*)	(*ii*)	(*iv*)	(*iii*)
C.	(*iii*)	(*i*)	(*ii*)	(*iv*)
D.	(*iv*)	(*iii*)	(*i*)	(*ii*)

56. Read Assertion (A) and Reason (R) and answer by using the code given below:

Assertion (A): Negligence means a conduct which creates a risk of causing damage, rather than a state of mind.

Reason (R): It is safe to start a bus before passengers completely get into it.

Codes:

A. Both (A) and (R) are correct, and (R) is the correct explanation of (A)
B. Both (A) and (R) are correct, but (R) is not the correct explanation of (A)
C. (A) is incorrect and (R) is correct
D. (A) is correct and (R) is incorrect

57. Which of the following statement is correct in relation to Consumer Courts?

A. National Commission has power to transfer a pending complaint from a District Forum to another in the same State
B. State Commission has power to transfer a pending complaint from a District Forum to another in the same State
C. National Commission can not have circuit benches except the permanent bench at New Delhi
D. State Commission can not have circuit benches but can have two State Commissions

58. Point out the correct statement:

A. Crime is necessarily an immoral act
B. Crime is necessarily an anti-social act
C. Crime is necessarily an anti-communal act
D. Crime is necessarily an anti-religious act

59. Four accused with common intention to kill, shot one B in the bona fide belief that B was A. In this case:

A. None of them is liable for the offence of murder
B. All accused are guilty of causing death
C. Section 34 of Indian Penal Code does not apply
D. All accused are guilty of causing death without invoking Section 34

60. Under Section 65 of Indian Penal Code, 1860, sentence of imprisonment for non-payment of fine shall be limited to:

A. One-half of the maximum term of imprisonment fixed for the offence
B. One-third of the maximum term of imprisonment fixed for the offence
C. One-fourth of the maximum term of imprisonment fixed for the offence
D. One-fifth of the maximum term of imprisonment fixed for the offence

61. Under which of the following sections of the Indian Penal Code, 1860, promoting enmity between different groups on grounds of religion, race, place of birth, residence, language etc. and doing acts prejudicial to maintenance of harmony is dealt with?

A. Section 153
B. Section 153-A
C. Section 153-AA
D. Section 153-B

62. A instigates B to murder D. B in pursuance of the instigation stabs D. D recovers from the wound. Here A is guilty of:

A. Instigating B to commit murder
B. Instigating B to commit attempt to murder
C. Instigating B to commit grievous hurt
D. No offence

63. Under which of the following provisions of the Indian Penal Code, 1860, an assault or criminal force used in attempting to commit theft of property is punishable?

A. Section 356　　B. Section 378
C. Section 379　　D. Section 384

64. 'X' gives grave and sudden provocation to 'Y'. 'Y' on this provocation, fires a pistol at 'X', neither intending nor knowing himself to be likely to kill 'Z', who is near him, but out of sight. 'Y' kills 'Z'. Here 'Y' has committed:

A. Death by negligence
B. Murder
C. Culpable homicide not amounting to murder
D. No offence

65. Match List-I with List-II and give the correct answer by using the code given below:

List-I	List-II
(*a*) Dishonest taking of property	(*i*) Criminal breach of Trust

(*b*) Dishonestly inducing any person to deliver property	(*ii*) Extortion
(*c*) Entrustment of property	(*iii*) Criminal Misapprociation
(*d*) Conversion of property	(*iv*) Theft

Codes:

	(*a*)	(*b*)	(*c*)	(*d*)
A.	(*i*)	(*ii*)	(*iii*)	(*iv*)
B.	(*iv*)	(*ii*)	(*i*)	(*iii*)
C.	(*iii*)	(*iv*)	(*ii*)	(*i*)
D.	(*ii*)	(*iii*)	(*i*)	(*iv*)

66. Read Assertion (A) and Reason (R) and give the correct answer by using the code given below:

Assertion (A): Nothing is an offence which is done by a person who, at the time of doing it, by reason of unsoundness of mind, is incapable of knowing the exact nature of the act.

Reason (R): Mistake of fact is a good defence and mistake of law is no defence.

Codes:

A. Both (A) and (R) are true, and (R) is the correct explanation of (A)
B. Both (A) and (R) are true, but (R) is not the correct explanation of (A)
C. (A) is true, but (R) is false
D. (A) is false, but (R) is true

67. Match List-I with List-II and give the correct answer by using the code given below:

List-I	List-II
(*a*) Mehboob Shah Vs. Emperor	(*i*) Mens rea
(*b*) State of Maharashtra Vs. M.H. George	(*ii*) Intoxication
(*c*) Director of Public Prosecutions Vs. Beard	(*iii*) Common Intention
(*d*) R.V. Dudley Vs. Stephens	(*iv*) Necessity

Codes:

	(*a*)	(*b*)	(*c*)	(*d*)
A.	(*i*)	(*ii*)	(*iii*)	(*iv*)
B.	(*ii*)	(*iv*)	(*i*)	(*iii*)
C.	(*iii*)	(*i*)	(*ii*)	(*iv*)
D.	(*iv*)	(*ii*)	(*iii*)	(*i*)

68. Match List-I with List-II and give the correct answer by using the code given below:

List-I (Provision for)	List-II (Sections of I.P.C.)
(*a*) Punishment for causing death or resulting in persistent vegetative state of victim	(*i*) Section 376-D
(*b*) Sexual intercourse by husband upon his wife during separation	(*ii*) Section 376-B
(*c*) Sexual intercourse by a person in authority	(*iii*) Section 376-A
(*d*) Gang rape	(*iv*) Section 376-C

Codes:

	(*a*)	(*b*)	(*c*)	(*d*)
A.	(*i*)	(*ii*)	(*iii*)	(*iv*)
B.	(*ii*)	(*iv*)	(*i*)	(*iii*)
C.	(*iii*)	(*ii*)	(*iv*)	(*i*)
D.	(*iv*)	(*i*)	(*iii*)	(*ii*)

69. Give the correct answer by using the code given below:

(*a*) The workman has a right to approach the Labour court directly without waiting for the conciliation proceedings and government reference.

(*b*) The appropriate government in respect of Corporations and Public Sector undertakings owned or controlled by the central government will be the central government.

(*c*) Every industry employing 20 or more workmen is under legal obligation to Constitute and have a Grievances Redressal Committee.

(*d*) The award passed by the Labour Court can be transmitted to a Civil Court for the effective enforcement of the award.

Codes:

A. Only (*a*) and (*b*) are correct
B. Only (*c*) and (*d*) are correct
C. Only (*a*), (*b*) and (*c*) are correct
D. (*a*), (*b*), (*c*) and (*d*) all are correct

70. Read Assertion (A) and Reason (R) and give the correct answer with the help of codes given below:

Assertion (A): The strike or lockout as the weapon has to be used sparingly for redressal of urgent and pressing grievances when no means are available or when available means have failed to resolve it.

Reason (R): The employment that workmen get and the profit the employer earns are both generated by utilisation of the resources of the society in one form or other and they are to act as Trustees of the said resources.

Codes:

A. (A) and (R) are true, and (R) is the correct explanation of (A)
B. (A) and (R) are true, but (R) is not the correct explanation of (A)
C. (A) is false, but (R) is true
D. (A) is true, but (R) is false

71. Match List-I with List-II and select the correct answer by using the code given below:

List-I	List-II
(*a*) A strike could be legal or illegal and illegal strike could be justified one	(*i*) Award
(*b*) Right of the Workmen to approach the Labour Court directly within a period of three years	(*ii*) Bharat Singh Vs Management of New Delhi Tuberculosis Centre
(*c*) Right of the workmen to payment of full wages pending proceedings in the High Courts	(*iii*) Justice V.R. Krishna Iyer
(*d*) An interim or a final determination of any Industrial Dispute	(*iv*) Section 2-A(2) Industrial Dispute (Amendment) Act 2010

Codes:

	(*a*)	(*b*)	(*c*)	(*d*)
A.	(*iii*)	(*iv*)	(*ii*)	(*i*)
B.	(*i*)	(*ii*)	(*iii*)	(*iv*)
C.	(*ii*)	(*iii*)	(*iv*)	(*i*)
D.	(*iv*)	(*ii*)	(*i*)	(*iii*)

72. "Although the Judicial interpretation given to the expression "Industry" by Supreme Court in Bangalore Water Supply Case was intended to settle the test to determine its scope judicial trends point out that it has done more damage than good, not merely to organisations but also to employees by curtailment of employment opportunities" The above trend is reflected through one of the following case:

A. Corporation of city of Nagpur Vs Employees
B. State of Bombay Vs Hospital Mazdoor Sabha
C. Coir Board, Ernakulam, Cochin and another Vs Indira Devi P.S. and other
D. Madras Gymkhana Club Employees Union Vs Gymkhana Club

73. Answer the following using the code given below:

The condition precedent to the order of Reference under section 10(1) of the Industrial Disputes Act is the satisfactions of the appropriate government to the following

(*a*) Existence of Industrial Dispute
(*b*) Apprehension of Industrial Dispute

Codes:

A. Both (*a*) and (*b*) are correct
B. (*a*) alone is correct
C. (*b*) alone is correct
D. Both (*a*) and (*b*) are wrong

74. Read Assertion (A) and Reason (R) and give the correct answer with the help of code given below:

Assertion (A): (*a*) The unrecognised union has right to meet and discuss with the employer the grievances of Individual workman with the employer and

(*b*) to appeal and participate in a Domestic Departmental Enquiry in which its member is involved.

Reason (R): This is a statutory recognition of a unrecognised Union.

Codes:

A. (A) and (R) are true and (R) is the correct explanation of (A)

B. (A) and (R) are true, but (R) is not the correct explanation of (A)

C. (A) is false, but (R) is True

D. (A) is true, but (R) is False

75. Answer the following using the code given below:

The following are the pre-condition for acquiring Jurisdiction by the National Tribunal Under the Industrial Disputes Act:

(*a*) Industrial Dispute must involve question of National importance in the opinion of the Central Government

OR

(*b*) Industrial Dispute must involve question of State importance in the opinion of the State Government

OR

(*c*) Industrial Disputes must be of such a nature that Industries situated in more than one State and are likely to be interested in or affected by such disputes

OR

(*d*) Industrial Disputes must be of such a nature that Industries situated in more than five States and are likely to be interested in or affected by such disputes.

Codes:

A. (*a*) and (*d*) are correct

B. (*a*) and (*c*) are correct

C. (*b*) and (*d*) are correct

D. (*d*) alone is correct

76. Read Assertion (A) and Reason (R) and give correct answer by using code below:

Assertion (A): Administrative law is a branch of public law in contradiction to Private law.

Reason (R): Administrative law primarily deals with the relationship of individuals *inter se.*

Codes:

A. Both (A) and (R) are correct and (R) is the correct explanation of (A)

B. Both (A) and (R) are correct, but (R) is not the correct explanation of (A)

C. (A) is correct, but (R) is incorrect

D. (A) is incorrect, but (R) is correct

77. Match List-I (name of case) with List-II (principle of natural justice) and give correct answer by using the code below:

List-I	List-II
(*a*) Hira Nath Mishra Vs Rajindra Medical College	(*i*) Right to notice or requirement of notice
(*b*) Union of India Vs Mohd. Ramzan Khan	(*ii*) No evidence should be taken at back of the other party
(*c*) Maneka Gandhi Vs Union of India	(*iii*) Report of the enquiry to be shown to the other party
(*d*) Union of India Vs Narendra Singh	(*iv*) Reasoned decision or speaking orders

Codes:

	(*a*)	(*b*)	(*c*)	(*d*)
A.	(*iii*)	(*iv*)	(*i*)	(*ii*)
B.	(*iv*)	(*iii*)	(*ii*)	(*i*)
C.	(*i*)	(*ii*)	(*iii*)	(*iv*)
D.	(*ii*)	(*iii*)	(*iv*)	(*i*)

78. Match List - I (name of case) with List - II (name of writ) and give correct answer by using code given below:

List-I	List-II
(*a*) Sunil Batra Vs Delhi Administration	(*i*) Quo Warranto
(*b*) U.N.R. Rao Vs Indira Gandhi	(*ii*) Habeas Corpus
(*c*) Gujrat State Financial Corporation Vs Lotus Hotels	(*iii*) Certiorari
(*d*) Nalini Ranjan Vs Annada Shankar	(*iv*) Mandamus

Codes:

	(*a*)	(*b*)	(*c*)	(*d*)
A.	(*iii*)	(*iv*)	(*i*)	(*ii*)
B.	(*iv*)	(*iii*)	(*ii*)	(*i*)
C.	(*ii*)	(*i*)	(*iv*)	(*iii*)
D.	(*i*)	(*ii*)	(*iii*)	(*iv*)

79. In which of the following case the Supreme Court of India ruled that when the selection process consists of only a viva-voce test without any written examination no limit need to be imposed on prescribing marks for the interview.

A. A.K. Roy Vs Union of India
B. A.P. State Financial Corporation Vs C.M. Ashok Raju
C. Sambhu Nath Sarkar Vs State of W.B.
D. P. Lakhanpal Vs Union of India

80. Which of the following statement/statements is/are correct? Give correct answer by using the code given below:

(*a*) Absolute discretion is a ruthless master.
(*b*) Where reasonable conduct of government official is expected, the criterion of reasonableness is subjective and not objective
(*c*) Every action of the executive government must be informed with excuse and should be arbitrary.
(*d*) Exercise of discretion is an inseparable part of sound administration.

Codes:

A. Only (*a*) and (*b*) are correct
B. Only (*c*) and (*d*) are correct
C. Only (*b*) and (*d*) are correct
D. Only (*a*) and (*d*) are correct

81. Which of the following Acts shall be amended as per Section 58 of the Lokpal and Lokayukta Act, 2013? Give correct answer by using the code given below:

(*a*) Commission of Inquiry Act
(*b*) Central Vigilance Commission Act
(*c*) Code of Civil Procedure
(*d*) Central Bureau of Investigation Act

Codes:

A. (*a*) and (*b*) are correct
B. (*c*) and (*d*) are correct
C. (*a*) and (*d*) are correct
D. (*b*) and (*c*) are correct

82. Which one of the following is incorrect?

A. Montreal protocol is related to Hazardous Waste.
B. The Precautionary Principle and Polluter Pays Principle are essential features of the principles of sustainable development
C. The Stockholm Declaration of 1972 has been described as the Magna Carta of our environment
D. No state has a right to use or permit the use of its territory so as to cause injury by fumes in the territory of another

83. "The State is the trustee of all natural resources which are by nature meant for public use and enjoyment and that Indian legal system includes the Public Trust Doctrine as a part of its jurisprudence"

The Supreme Court of India has observed the above in one of the following case:

A. T.N. Godavarman Thirumulpad Vs Union of India
B. Indian Council for Enviro-Legal Action Vs Union of India
C. M.C. Mehtha Vs Union of India
D. Shri Sachidananda Pandey Vs State of West Bengal

84. Match List - I with List - II and give correct answer by using the code given below:

List-I	List-II
(*a*) No state has a right to use or permit the use of its territory so as to cause injury by fumes in the territory of another	(*i*) Basel Convention
(*b*) The Economic Benefit must substantially exceed its Environmental Cost	(*ii*) Trial Smelter Case
(*c*) The present generation has no right to deplete all the existing forest and leave nothing for the next and future generation	(*iii*) Environment Impact Assessment
(*d*) Transboundary Movements of Hazardous Wastes and their Disposal	(*iv*) Inter Generational Equity

Codes:

	(*a*)	(*b*)	(*c*)	(*d*)
A.	(*i*)	(*iii*)	(*iv*)	(*ii*)
B.	(*iii*)	(*ii*)	(*iv*)	(*i*)
C.	(*ii*)	(*iii*)	(*iv*)	(*i*)
D.	(*i*)	(*ii*)	(*iii*)	(*iv*)

85. Read both Assertion (A) and Reason (R) and give the correct answer by using the code given below:

Assertion (A): It is the duty of the state to devise and implement a coherent and co-ordinated programme to meet its obligation of Sustainable Development.

Reason (R): Adherence to the principle of Sustainable Development is now a Constitutional requirement.

Codes:

A. Both (A) and (R) are correct and (R) is the correct explanation of (A)

B. Both (A) and (R) are correct, but (R) is not the correct explanation of (A)

C. (A) is correct, but (R) is wrong

D. (A) is wrong, but (R) is correct

86. Which of the following do not come under the powers and functions of the Central Board as provided Under the Air (Prevention and Control of Pollution) Act, 1981?

A. Planning and execution of National programme for prevention, control and abatement of Air Pollution

B. Co-ordinating activities of State Boards and resolving disputes among them.

C. Fixing standards of Quality of Air.

D. Making recommendations to the State government for removal of State Board which is defaulter in discharging its duties under the Act.

87. In which one of the following case the Supreme Court of India held that right to access to drinking water is fundamental to life and it is the duty of the State under Act 21 to provide clean drinking water to its citizens?

A. Vellore Citizens Welfare forum Vs Union of India

B. A.P. Pollution Control Board Vs M.V. Nayadu

C. M.C. Mehtha Vs Union of India

D. Karnataka Industrial Area Development Board Vs Shri C. Kenchappa

88. Read both Assertion (A) and Reason (R) and give the correct answer by using the code given below:

Assertion (A): The provisions concerning Human Rights run throughout the U.N. Charter 'like a golden thread'.

Reason (R): Much of the credit for this goes to the determined lobbying by non-governmental organisations at San Francisco Conference.

Codes:

A. Both (A) and (R) are correct and (R) is the correct explanation of (A)

B. Both (A) and (R) are correct, but (R) is not the correct explanation of (A)

C. (A) is correct, but (R) is wrong

D. (A) is wrong, but (R) is correct

89. Which of the following statement/statements is/are correct?

Under its terms of reference, the UN Commission on Human Rights was directed to prepare recommendations and reports on:

(*a*) An International Bill on Human Rights.

(*b*) International Conventions or declarations on civil liberties; the status of woman, freedom of information and similar other matters.

(*c*) The protection of Minorities.

(*d*) The prevention of discrimination on the basis of race, sex, language or religion and other matters concerning Human Rights.

Codes:

A. Only (*a*) is correct

B. Only (*b*) and (*c*) are correct

C. Only (*a*), (*b*) and (*c*) are correct

D. (*a*), (*b*), (*c*) and (*d*) all are correct

90. Match List-I with List-II and give the correct answer by using the code given below:

List-I	List-II
(*a*) Human Rights Council	(*i*) 1993
(*b*) The Universal Declaration of Human Rights	(*ii*) 2006
(*c*) The International Covenant on Civil and Political Rights	(*iii*) 1948
(*d*) World Conference on Human Rights, Vienna	(*iv*) 1966

Codes:

	(*a*)	(*b*)	(*c*)	(*d*)
A.	(*i*)	(*ii*)	(*iii*)	(*iv*)
B.	(*iv*)	(*iii*)	(*ii*)	(*i*)
C.	(*ii*)	(*iii*)	(*iv*)	(*i*)
D.	(*iii*)	(*i*)	(*ii*)	(*iv*)

91. Which of the following statement/statements is/are **not** correct?

(*a*) The position of U.N. High Commissioner for Human Rights was created by the Economic and Social Council.

(*b*) The High Commissioner was to be appointed by the Secretary. General subject to approval by the General Assembly.

(*c*) The term of office of High Commissioner was five years.

(*d*) The High Commissioner's principal location would be in New York.

Codes:

A. Only (*d*) is not correct

B. (*a*), (*c*) and (*d*) all are not correct

C. (*a*), (*b*) and (*c*) are not correct

D. (*a*), (*b*), (*c*) and (*d*) all are not correct

92. Which of the following statement/statements are correct?

(*a*) The Chairperson of the National Human Rights Commission shall be who has been the Chief Justice of Supreme Court.

(*b*) The Chairperson and the other Members of National Human Rights Commission are appointed by the President of India after consultation with Prime Minister.

(*c*) Chairperson and other Members of National Human Rights Commission are eligible for re-appointment.

(*d*) The Chairperson and the other Members of the Commission can be removed on the Recommendation of the Law Minister of India.

Codes:

A. Only (*a*) is correct

B. (*a*) and (*c*) are correct

C. (*a*), (*b*) and (*c*) are correct

D. (*a*), (*b*), (*c*) and (*d*) all are correct

93. Match List-I with List-II and give the correct answer by using the code given below:

List-I (Provisions)	List-II (Sections of the Protection of Human Rights Act, 1993)
(*a*) Constitution of National Human Rights Commission	(*i*) Section 10
(*b*) Constitution of State Human Rights Commission	(*ii*) Section 12

(*c*) Functions of the National Human Rights Commission	(*iii*) Section 3
(*d*) Procedure of the Commission	(*iv*) Section 21

Codes:

	(*a*)	(*b*)	(*c*)	(*d*)
A.	(*i*)	(*ii*)	(*iii*)	(*iv*)
B.	(*ii*)	(*iii*)	(*iv*)	(*i*)
C.	(*iv*)	(*i*)	(*ii*)	(*iii*)
D.	(*iii*)	(*iv*)	(*ii*)	(*i*)

94. Which one of the following is incorrect?

Under the Partnership Act, a minor who has been admitted to partnership when attains majority should adhere to the following:

A. Issue a public notice that he has elected to become or that he has elected not to become a partner

B. Option must be exercised within 2 months on attaining majority

C. When the minor opted to become a partner his rights and liabilities as a minor continue upto the date on which he becomes a partner

D. When the minor opted not to become a partner his rights and liabilities shall continue upto the date on which he gives a public notice

95. Match List-I with List-II and select the correct answer using the code given below:

List-I	List-II
(*a*) Mutual Rights and Liabilities of Partners	(*i*) Section 34 of Partnership Act
(*b*) Dissolution of Partnership	(*ii*) Section 13 of Partnership Act
(*c*) Retirement of a Partner	(*iii*) Section 39 of Partnership Act
(*d*) Insolvency of a Partner	(*iv*) Section 32 of Partnership Act

Codes:

	(*a*)	(*b*)	(*c*)	(*d*)
A.	(*i*)	(*ii*)	(*iv*)	(*iii*)
B.	(*ii*)	(*iii*)	(*iv*)	(*i*)
C.	(*iii*)	(*ii*)	(*i*)	(*iv*)
D.	(*i*)	(*ii*)	(*iii*)	(*iv*)

96. Read Assertion (A) and Reason (R) and give the correct answer with the help of code given below:

Assertion (A): The surety has no right to restrain execution against him until the creditor exhausted all his remedies against the Principal Debtor.

Reason (R): The Liability of the surety is co-extensive with that of the Principal Debtor, unless it is otherwise provided by contract.

Codes:

A. (A) and (R) are true and (R) is the correct explanation of (A).

B. (A) and (R) are true, but (R) is not the correct explanation of (A)

C. (A) is false, but (R) is true

D. (A) is true, but (R) is false

97. Which one of the following is incorrect?

Under the Sale of Goods Act, to make the buyer liable for neglecting or refusing delivery of goods the following conditions must be fulfilled:

A. The seller was ready and willing to deliver the goods

B. The seller requested the buyer to take delivery

C. The seller informed the buyer to ignore the delay and take delivery

D. The buyer did not, within a reasonable time after such request take delivery of the goods

98. Read Assertion (A) and Reason (R) and answer by using code given below:

Assertion (A): Under the Company Law, though any outsider is presumed to be aware of the documents which are publicly accessable, but not the internal proceedings of which he can not reasonably aware of, because those are not accessible to the public.

Reason (R): The Doctrine of indoor management evolved as a partial exception to the Doctrine of Constructive Notice and the rule was laid down in Royal British Bank Vs Turquand.

Codes:

A. Both (A) and (R) are correct and (R) is the correct explanation of (A)

B. Both (A) and (R) are correct, but (R) is not the correct explanation of (A)

C. (A) is true, but (R) is false

D. (A) is false, but (R) is true

99. Which one of the following is incorrect? Any mis-statement made in the Prospectus would attract the liability of the following persons under the Companies Act:

A. Every person who is a director of the company at the time of the issue of the prospectus

B. Every person who has authorised himself to be named and is named in the prospectus either as director or as having agreed to become a director either immediately or after an interval of time

C. Every person who is a promotor of the company

D. An Expert, whose consent has not been endorsed to the registration and liable in respect of every content in the prospectus

100. Which one of the following is not the essential requirement to fulfil an instrument intended to be a Promissory Note?

A. The instrument must contain a promise to pay

B. A mere acknowledgement of indebtedness is sufficient

C. The sum of money to be paid must be certain

D. Promise to pay must be unconditional

ANSWERS

1	2	3	4	5	6	7	8	9	10
C	B	C	B	A	D	A	B	D	A
11	**12**	**13**	**14**	**15**	**16**	**17**	**18**	**19**	**20**
D	D	C	B	D	C	B	D	D	B
21	**22**	**23**	**24**	**25**	**26**	**27**	**28**	**29**	**30**
C	D	A	B	B	C	B	A	A	B
31	**32**	**33**	**34**	**35**	**36**	**37**	**38**	**39**	**40**
C	A	C	B	B	D	A	C	B	D
41	**42**	**43**	**44**	**45**	**46**	**47**	**48**	**49**	**50**
C	A	D	B	C	A	B	C	D	C
51	**52**	**53**	**54**	**55**	**56**	**57**	**58**	**59**	**60**
A	C	C	B	A	D	B	B	B	C
61	**62**	**63**	**64**	**65**	**66**	**67**	**68**	**69**	**70**
B	A	A	C	B	B	C	C	D	A
71	**72**	**73**	**74**	**75**	**76**	**77**	**78**	**79**	**80**
A	C	A	A	B	C	D	C	B	D
81	**82**	**83**	**84**	**85**	**86**	**87**	**88**	**89**	**90**
A	A	A	C	A	D	B	A	D	C
91	**92**	**93**	**94**	**95**	**96**	**97**	**98**	**99**	**100**
B	A	D	B	B	A	C	A	D	B

EXPLANATORY ANSWERS

1. **Article 13**
   - It expressively provides for judicial review.
   - All Laws that are inconsistent with or in derogation of any fundamental rights shall be void.
   - Supreme Court and High Court can declare the law unconstitutional/invalid on the above ground.
   - Now there is some information about Article 13 as everyone is not aware about it so it may help them out.

2. **Martial law** is the imposition of the highest-ranking military officer as the military governor or as the head of the government, thus removing all power from the previous executive, legislative, and judicial branches of government. It is usually imposed temporarily when the government or civilian authorities fail to function effectively (*e.g.*, maintain order and security, or provide essential services).

   Article 34 in The Constitution of India: Restriction on rights conferred by this Part while martial law is in force in any area notwithstanding anything in the foregoing provisions of this Part, Parliament may by law indemnify any person in the service of the Union or of a State or any other person in respect of any act done by him in connection with the maintenance or restoration of order in any area within the territory of India where martial law was in force or validate any sentence passed, punishment inflicted, forfeiture ordered or other act done under martial law in such area.

6. **T.K. Rangarajan vs Govt. of Tamil Nadu and Ors. on 24 July, 2003:** Article 368 (1) of the Constitution of India grants constituent power to make formal amendments and empowers Parliament to amend the Constitution by way of addition, variation or repeal of any provision according to the procedure laid down therein, which is different from the procedure for ordinary legislation. Article 368 has been amended by the 24th and 42nd Amendments in 1971 and 1976 respectively. The following is the full text of Article 368 of the Constitution, which governs constitutional amendments.

7. **Article 360 in The Constitution of India:** Provisions as to financial emergency, If the President is satisfied that a situation has arisen whereby the financial stability or credit of India or of any part of the territory thereof is threatened, he may by a Proclamation make a declaration to that effect.

9. There are five conditions under which parliament can make laws on state list.
   1. If Rajya Sabha approves a resolution with special majority and declares that a subject is of **national interest.** (under Article-249).
   2. During times of **National Emergency (under Article 250).**
   3. If the legislature of two or more state **request** parliament to make law for an item in state list. For example Kerala and Tamilnadu can ask for water disputes. (under Article 252).
   4. The parliament has the power to make laws for the whole or any part of India for implementing any treaty, agreement or convention with any other country or any decision made at any international conference. (Under Article 253).

11. The term parliamentary privileges is used in constitutional writings to denote both these types of rights and immunities. Sir Thomas Erskine May has defined the expression parliamentary privileges as follows. The sum of the peculiar rights enjoyed by each house collectively is a constituent part of the High court of parliament , and by members of each house of parliament individually, without which they cannot discharge their functions, and which exceed those possessed by other bodies or inviduals.

Important cases related to Parliamentary Privileges are as under:

1. Sir Thomas Erskine May: Parliamentary Practice.
2. Tej Kiran Jain v. N. Sanjeeva Reddy, (1970).
3. Pandit M.S.M. Sharma v. Sri Krishna Sinha.
4. P.V. Narsimha Rao v. State (1998).
5. Jatish Chandra Ghosh v. Harisadhan Mukharjee.
6. Powers, Privileges and Immunities of the State Legislature, Re, AIR 1965 SC 745: (1965) 1 SCR 413
7. Ansumali Majumdar v. State of W.B. AIR 1952.
8. State of Karnataka v. Union of India (1977) 4 SCC 608, 654.
9. Indira Nehru Gandhi v. Raj Narain 1975.
10. In case of Parliament, Articles 118 and 120.

13. The history of the concept of law states that jurisprudence began in the 21st century modern jurisprudence from the Greek era, with its various changes in its nature at different stages of its development. Jurisprudence is a concept for the theory and to bring life into meditation. It is related to the fundamental principles on which the superstructure of law has been upheld. The concept of jurisprudence basically helps in developing your thoughts in relation to a particular theory. Whose knowledge base and the foundation of the whole legal study. Jurisprudence is a name given for a certain type of investigation in the law, where we are concerned about the nature of legal rules and the underlying meaning of legal concepts and the necessary characteristics of the legal system.

14. Stammler was professor of Roman law in various universities of Germany. He succeded Prof KOHLER as professor of law in the university of Berlin. He defined law as, "species of will, other-regarding, self-authoritative and iviolable". For him, a just law was the highest expression of man's social life and aims at preservation of freedom of individuals. According to him, the two fundamental principles necessary for a just law were:

1. Principles ofrespect, and
2. The principle ofimmunity participation.

With a view to distinguishing the new revived natural law from the older one, he called the former as "natural law with variable content". According to him, law of nature means "fust law" which harmonizes the purposes in the society. The purpose of law is not to protect the will of one but to unify the purposes of all.

15. Herbert Lionel Adolf's Hart considers the law as a social phenomenon: it can only be understood and understood in terms of the actual social practices of the community. Why? It is a fact that in order to survive a human society as a collective force or group, some rules should be present. Otherwise all of us members are "suicidal clubs." They are the result of our human limitations such as human vulnerability, estimated similarity, limited altruism, limited resources and limited understanding and the power of desire.

Therefore, rules are required to protect individuals, property and ensure that the promises are maintained.

18. Theories of Legal Rights—There are following three main theories of legal rights:

1. **Protection Theory of Rights:** It is to be noted that the source of all legal right is Law. It is a fact that it is only law which creates, protects and recognises the rights so created. Thus, one of the characteristic feature of a legal right is its recognition. It is recognised by a legal system and is enforced by a legal process.
2. **Will Theory of Right:** Will theory is upheld by many on the ground that the very purpose of the law is to grant the widest possible means of self-expression-the maximum of individual self-assertion. To the advocates of this theory, "rights, therefore, are inherent attribute of human will." The right to self-expression and self-

assertion is a part of individual's freedom which is inseparable of man and his individuality.

3. **Interest Theory of Right:** There are some jurists who say, that fundamental basis of right is an "interest" and not They argue, that a person may not have a will but still he has rights. Thus, "a baby of one day old, and irrational idiot, a corporation or a foundation" cannot be said to have a will, but in law they have right. What a right protects is not a will or choice, but some interest for the benefit of the person who holds the right.

9. **Theories of Corporate Personalities:** Corporate sole and corporate aggregate are treated as persons by law. There are various theories which are developed to show the nature of personality. These theories could be either political which talks about the relationship between the state and group residing within the state or it could be a philosophical explanation which is pertaining to existence of those persons which are created by law. But the courts have not uniformly followed any of these particular theories to deal with any problem or issue which is pertaining to corporation but on the other hand they are also guided by the practical considerations. So, here are some of the theories as follows:
1. The Fiction Theory
2. The Realistic Theory
3. The Concession Theory
4. The Organism Theory
5. The Ownership Theory
6. The Symbolist Theory aka The Bracket Theory

9. **Article-10:** The General Assembly may discuss any questions or any matters within the scope of the present Charter or relating to the powers and functions of any organs provided for in the present Charter, and, except as provided in Article 12, may make recommendations to the Members of the United Nations or to the Security Council or to both on any such questions or matters.

33. **The United Nations Commission on Human Rights (UNCHR):** The Commission on Human Rights was intended to examine, monitor and publicly report on human rights situations in specific countries or territories (known as country mechanisms or mandates) as well as on major phenomena of human rights violations worldwide (known as thematic mechanisms or mandates). The Human Rights division of the U.N. is also expected to uphold and protect the Universal Declaration of human rights.

34. **Section 3 in the Hindu Marriage Act, 1955**
Full blood and half blood - two persons are said to be related to each other by full blood when they are descended from a common ancestor by the same wife and by half blood when they are descended from a common ancestor but by different wives.

36. **Section 5 in the Hindu Marriage Act, 1955**
Conditions for a Hindu marriage—
A. A marriage may be solemnized between any two Hindus, if the following conditions are fulfilled, namely
   1. neither party has a spouse living at the time of the marriage;
   2. at the time of the marriage, neither party
   3. is incapable of giving a valid consent to it in consequence of unsoundness of mind;
B. Though capable of giving a valid consent, has been suffering from mental disorder of such a kind or to such an extent as to be unfit for marriage and the procreation of children; or
C. Has been subject to recurrent attacks of insanity.

37. **Section 2 in the Dissolution of Muslim Marriages Act, 1939**
A woman married under Muslim law shall be entitled to obtain a decree for the dissolution of her marriage on any one or more of the following grounds, namely:
(*i*) that the whereabouts of the husband have not been known for a period of four years;

(*ii*) that the husband has neglected or has failed to provide for her maintenance for a period of two years;

(*iii*) that the husband has been sentenced to imprisonment for a period of seven years or upwards;

(*iv*) that the husband has failed to perform, without reasonable cause, his marital obligations for a period of three years;

(*v*) that the husband was impotent at the time of the marriage and continues to be so;

(*vi*) that the husband has been insane for a period of two years or is suffering from leprosy or a virulent venereal disease;

(*vii*) that she, having been given in marriage by her father or other guardian before she attained the age of fifteen years, repudiated the marriage before attaining the age of eighteen years.

39. Section 18 in The Hindu Adoptions and Maintenance Act, 1956. (1) Subject to the provisions of this section, a Hindu wife, whether married before or after the commencement of this Act, shall be entitled to be maintained by her husband during her life time.

Section 19 in the Hindu Adoptions and Maintenance Act, 1956. (1) A Hindu wife, whether married before or after the commencement of this Act, shall be entitled to be maintained after the death of her husband by her father-in-law: Provided and to the extent that she is unable to maintain herself out of her own earnings or other property or, where she has no property of her own, is unable to obtain maintenance-

(*a*) from the estate of her husband or her father or mother, or

(*b*) from her son or daughter, if any, or his or her estate.

Section 22 in The Hindu Adoptions and Maintenance Act, 1956

Maintenance of dependants:

1. Subject to the provisions of sub-section (2) the heirs of a deceased Hindu are bound to maintain the dependants of the decea out of the estate inherited by them fr the deceased.
2. Where a dependant has not obtained, testamentary or intestate-succession, share in the estate of a Hindu dying a the commencement of this Act, dependant shall be entitled, subject to provisions of this Act, to maintenance fr those who take the estate.
3. The liability of each of the persons w takes the estate shall be in proportion the value of the share or part of the est taken by him or her.
4. Notwithstanding anything contained sub-section (2) or sub-section (3), no per who is himself or herself a dependant sh be liable to contribute to the maintena of others, if he or she has obtained a sh or part, the value of which is, or would the liability to contribute were enforc become less than what would be awar to him or her by way of maintenance un this Act.

Section 23 in The Hindu Adoptions a Maintenance Act, 1956: Amount maintenance: (1) It shall be in the discret of the Court to determine whether any, an so what, maintenance shall be awarded un the provisions of this Act, and in doing the Court shall have due regard to considerations set out in sub-section (2), sub-section (3), as the case may be, so fa they are applicable.

41. *Muta* is a distinct kind of marriage recogni only by the Ithna Asharia Shias. Muta m be defined as a temporary union of male a female for specified duration, on payment some consideration. As against the perman or a regular marriage (Nikah), the Muta m be regarded as a temporary marriage. Lite meaning of the Arabic word 'Muta' 'enjoyment'; therefore, it may also be regar as 'marriage for pleasure'. In order to av the development of prostitution in the soci and to confer legitimacy upon children of such unions, temporary marriage was recognised and permitted by the Prophet for some time. But later on, when he felt that this concession was being exploited, he prohibited it absolutely.

Since then, the Muta form of marriage has not been in practice under any school of Muslim law except the Ithna Asharia Shia law. Accordingly, the Muta form of marriage is now not recognised under any school of Muslim law except the Ithna Asharia. However, the practice of Muta is not very common in India.

45. Mohori Bibee *v.* Dharmodas Ghose

Definition of Proposal (Offer): According to Section 2(A) of the Indian Contracts Act, 1872, when one person signifies to another his willingness to do or to abstain from doing anything, with a view to obtaining the assent of that other to such act or abstinence, he is said to make a proposal.

Hence, proposal is synonymous to offer. So, we can say that the above definition of proposal is also valid for offer.

46. Acceptance is to offer what a lighted match is to train of gunpowder. The position is related to revocation of proposal or acceptance has been describe by Anson in the following words: This statement primarily good under the English low. Here gunpowder offer and lighted match stick = acceptance. When a lighted match is to train of gunpowder, It explode and something happen, which cannot be undone, similarly an offer once accepted cannot be revoked. But so long a lighted match is to shown the gunpowder remain insert and can be removed, similarly an offer can remove before its acceptance. But in Indian Contract act, acceptance can be revoked by resorting to quicker means of communication, So that offer or learn about before its acceptance. Thus, the above statement doesn't hold in relation to revocation of acceptance under Indian Law. The above statement is basically an analogy *i.e.*, it is a comparison of two different phenomenon's that are similar in some way. The two important or main phenomenon in this statement are "offer" and "acceptance". To understand the meaning of this analogy it is important to know what an offer and acceptance is. They are briefly defined under the Contract Act.

47. Every contract springs from a legally enforceable agreement between the parties reflecting the identity or meeting of minds, generally referred by the Latin phrase, consensus ad idem. If either or both the parties to the contract err in the understanding of any essential term of the contract, apparently, there would not be any consensus ad idem. To have a blanket rule categorically rendering such agreements unenforceable, may actually trigger more problems than it may aim to solve by the blatant abuse of the rule with impunity. To prevent such abuse of the legal provisions, the common law has evolved some sophisticated set of rules dealing with mistake.

The "more-than-a-century-old" doctrine was applied to circumstances when people were illiterate and therefore could not read what they were signing. The doctrine provided a remedy when a document had been forged, when it was quite "literally" true to say that "it was not my deed".

But the doctrine also applied to situations where someone had signed due to fraudulent representations or had not an inkling of an idea as to what she was signing.

48. "Fraud" means and includes any of the following acts committed by a party to a contract, or with his connivance, or by his agents, with intent to deceive another party thereto or his agent, or to induce him to enter into the contract:

1. The suggestion as a fact, of that which is not true, by one who does not believe it to be true;
2. The active concealment of a fact by one having knowledge or belief of the fact;

3. A promise made without any intention of performing it;
4. Any other act fitted to deceive;
5. Any such act or omission as the law specially declares to be fraudulent.

Explanation: Mere silence as to facts likely to affect the willingness of a person to enter into a contract is not fraud, unless the circumstances of the case are such that, regard being had to them, it is the duty of the person keeping silence to speak, or unless his silence is, in itself, equivalent to speech.

49. Special damages are a specific type of damage available for breach of contract. When a contract is breached, special damages may be awarded to reimburse the non-breaching party for damages that result indirectly from, or that "flow from" the breach. Special damages awards cover losses besides the contractual losses; this may include a broad range of losses such as loss of profits or damage to business reputation.

Special damages are often requested in addition to general damages. General damages in a breach of contract claim cover contractual losses, such as the difference between market prices and contract prices, or losses due to money being withheld. Both general and specific damages fall under the category of "compensatory damages".

50. According to legal scholar John William Salmond, 'A tort is a civil wrong for which the remedy is action in common law for unliquidated damages and which is not exclusively a breach of contract or breach of trust or other equitable obligation.'

Tortious liability arises from the breach of duty primarily affixed by law. The duty is towards persons in general and its breach is redressable by an action for unliquidated damages.

In other words, it can be said that tort in an infringement of a right in rem of a private individual giving a right of compensation at the suit of the injured party.

Thus, it can be seen that tort is an act while the law of tort is the branch of law that provides relief to the person who has been injured due to a tortious act. From the above definitions, it is clear that the nature of a tort is that it is a civil wrong. However, not all civil wrongs are torts.

53. **Remoteness of damage** relates to the requirement that the damage must be of a foreseeable type. In negligence claims, once the claimant has established that the defendant owes them a duty of care and is in breach of that duty which has caused damage, they must also demonstrate that the damage was not too remote. Remoteness of damage must also be applied to claims under the Occupiers Liability Acts and also to nuisance claims.

59. **Section 34 in The Indian Penal Code:** Acts done by several persons in furtherance of common intention.-When a criminal act is done by several persons in furtherance of the common intention of all, each of such persons is liable for that act in the same manner as if it were done by him alone.

60. **Legal Provisions of Section 65 of Indian Penal Code, 1860.**

Limit to imprisonment for non-payment of fine, when imprisonment and fine awardable: The use of the words 'imprisonment as well as fine' indicates that the section is applicable where an offence is punishable with imprisonment and fine and also where the offence is punishable with imprisonment or fine, but not both. The section does not apply to such cases which are covered under section 67 of the Code where the only punishment is fine. The section makes it clear that in such cases the imprisonment in default of payment of fine can in no case exceed one-fourth of the term which is the maximum provided for the offence.

61. Promoting enmity between different groups on grounds of religion, race, place of birth, residence, etc. and doing acts prejudicial to maintenance of harmony:

This section was first added in the Code by the Indian Penal Code (Amendment) Act, 1898 with a view to deal with certain other matters relating to breach of public tranquillity which were not covered in the original Indian Penal Code. In the year 1969 sections 153-A and 505 were extensively amended, on the recommendations of the National Integration Council, by Act XXV of 1969 to widen the scope of the two sections to deal with cases of communal and class tensions more effectively.

62. Section 108 in The Indian Penal Code

108 Abettor.-A person abets an offence, who abets either the commission of an offence, or the commission of an act which would be an offence, if committed by a person capable by law of committing an offence with the same intention or knowledge as that of the abettor.

Explanation 1. The abetment of the illegal omission of an act may amount to an offence although the abettor may not himself be bound to do that act.

Explanation 2. To constitute the offence of abetment it is not necessary that the act abetted should be committed, or that the effect requisite to constitute the offence should be caused. Illustrations

(*a*) A instigates B to murder C. B refuses to do so. A is guilty of abetting B to commit murder.

(*b*) A instigates B to murder D. B in pursuance of the instigation stabs D. D recovers from the wound. A is guilty of instigating B to commit murder.

Explanation 3. It is not necessary that the person abetted should be capable by law of committing an offence, or that he should have the same guilty intention or knowledge as that of the abettor, or any guilty intention or knowledge.

63. Legal Provisions of Section 356 of Indian Penal Code, 1860.

Assault or criminal force in attempt to commit theft of property carried by a person: This section punishes assault or use of criminal force in attempt to commit theft of property wore or carried by a person. The section says that whoever assaults or uses criminal force to any person, in his attempt to commit theft of any such property which that person is then wearing or carrying, shall be punished with simple or rigorous imprisonment for a term extending up to two years, or with fine, or with both.

64. All murders are Culpable Homicides but not all culpable homicides are murder.

Culpable Homicide under section 299: Whoever causes death by doing an act with the intention of causing death, or with the intention of causing such bodily injury as is likely to cause death, or with the knowledge that he is likely by such act to cause death, commits the offence of culpable homicide.

Ingredients-

1. Intention of causing death.
2. Intention of causing such bodily injury as is likely to cause death.
3. Knowledge that the act done is likely to cause death.

66. Criminal Defenses of Mistakes of Fact and Mistakes of Law

The Criminal Defense of Mistake: In many situations, a criminal defendant may wish to argue that he or she never intended to commit a crime and that the criminal act that occurred was a result of a mistake of facts regarding the circumstances of the crime or a misunderstanding concerning the law at the time. Such mistakes of fact can be applied to a variety of criminal activities, but mistakes of law are only rarely allowed as full defenses to criminal conduct.

Mistakes of Fact: Mistakes of fact arise when a criminal defendant misunderstood some fact that negates an element of the crime. For instance, if an individual is charged with larceny but believed that the property he took was rightfully his, this misunderstanding negates any intent to deprive another of the property. One important qualification, however, is that this mistake of fact must be honest and reasonable. Thus, a defendant cannot later claim that he or she was mistaken when he or she actually knew the situation. Likewise, the mistake must be one that would appear reasonable to a judge or jury. If the same individual was repeatedly told that the property was not his, and he could not take it, it would no longer be reasonable for him to mistakenly have believed that he could rightfully take the property.

Mistakes of fact may apply to a variety of crimes. Some crimes may set forth that mistake of fact is a defense. Otherwise, if the criminal defendant can prove that the mistake reasonably negated an element of the crime, the defense will usually be held to apply and absolve the defendant of liability.

70. Every right comes with its own duties. Most powerful rights have more duties attached to them. Today, in each country of globe whether it is democratic, capitalist, socialist, give right to strike to the workers. But this right must be the weapon of last resort because if this right is misused, it will create a problem in the production and financial profit of the industry. This would ultimately affect the economy of the country.

Today, most of the countries, especially India, are dependent upon foreign investment and under these circumstances it is necessary that countries who seeks foreign investment must keep some safeguard in there respective industrial laws so that there will be no misuse of right of strike.

In India, right to protest is a fundamental right under Article 19 of the Constitution of India. But right to strike is not a fundamental right but a legal right and with this right statutory restriction is attached in the industrial dispute Act, 19.

72. Coir Board, Ernakulum, cochin and another vs Indian Devi P.S. and other

In these appeals from a judgment of the Full Bench of the Kerala High Court, we have to examine whether the appellant-Coir Board is an industry as defined in the Industrial Disputes Act. 1947. The appellant-Coir Board, Ernakulam, Cochin, had been set up under the Choir Industry Act, 1953. In the Statement of Objects and Reasons for the Act, it is scatted, The Choir Industry has definite role to play in our national economy. It is of very great economic importance to Travancore Cochin where it is concentrated and also, from the point of view of earning foreign exchange, of importance to the whole country.

It has, however, been passing through acute depression since the middle of 1952 as a result of the marked decline in experts. With a view to controlling production, improving its quality, weeding out the undesirable elements in the export trade and developing the internal marked so as to reduce the industry's dependence on exports, it is considered necessary to establish a Statutory Board on the lines of Boards set up for other plantation industries.

75. Where the Central Government is of opinion that any industrial dispute exists or is apprehended and the dispute involves any question of national importance or is of such a nature that industrial establishments situated in more than one State are likely to be interested in, or affected by, such dispute and that the dispute should be adjudicated by a National Tribunal, then, the Central Government may, whether or not it is the appropriate Government in relation to that dispute, at any time, by order in writing, refer the dispute or any matter appearing to be connected with, or relevant to, the dispute, whether it relates to any matter specified in the Second Schedule or the Third Schedule, to a National Tribunal for adjudication.

86. Subject to the provisions of this Act, and without prejudice to the performance of its functions under the Water (Prevention and Control of Pollution) Act, 1974 (6 of 1974), the main functions of the Central Board shall be to improve the quality of air and to prevent, control or abate air pollution in the country.

In particular and without prejudice to the generality of the foregoing functions, the Central Board may:

(*a*) advise the Central Government on any matter concerning the improvement of the quality of air and the prevention, control or abatement of air pollution;

(*b*) plan and cause to be executed a nation-wide programme for the prevention, control or abatement of air pollution;

(*c*) co-ordinate the activities of the State Boards and resolve disputes among them;

(*d*) provide technical assistance and guidance to the State Boards, carry out and sponsor investigations and research relating to problems of air-pollution and prevention, control or abatement of air pollution;

(*dd*) perform such of the functions of any State Board as may be specified in an order made under sub-section (2) of Section 18;

(*e*) plan and organize the training of persons engaged or to be engaged in programmes for the prevention, control or abatement of air pollution on such terms and conditions as the Central Board may specify;

(*f*) organize through mass media a comprehensive programme regarding the prevention, control or abatement of air pollution;

(*g*) collect, compile and publish technical and statistical data relating to air pollution and the measures devised for its effective prevention, control or abatement and prepare manuals, codes or guides relating to prevention, control or abatement of air pollution;

(*h*) lay down standards for the quality of air;

(*i*) collect and disseminate information in respect of matters relating to air pollution;

(*j*) perform such other functions as may be prescribed.

88. The concept of human rights is as old as human history and as broad as 'social life'. Although the same is developed on the principles of inalienable rights of natural law, the term human rights has its origin in international law. The concept took centre stage in the post World War era, especially when the Western States started recognizing the status of the individual as part of the international legal order. Same was the case with India. Though the concept of human rights gained legitimacy with the adoption of written constitution in 1950, its substance and spirit have come a long way through the historical path. In short, the history of human rights in India is as old as the history of human rights in rest of the world.

89. The International Bill of Human Rights consists of the Universal Declaration of Human Rights, the International Covenant on Economic, Social and Cultural Rights, and the International Covenant on Civil and Political Rights and its two Optional Protocols.

Human rights had already found expression in the Covenant of the League of Nations, which led, inter alia, to the creation of the International Lab our Organization. At the 1945 San Francisco Conference, held to draft the Charter of the United Nations, a proposal to embody a "Declaration on the Essential Rights of Man" was put forward but was not examined because it required more detailed consideration than was possible at the time. The Charter clearly speaks of "promoting and encouraging respect for human rights and for fundamental freedoms for all without distinction as to race, sex, language or religion".

92. "Human Rights" means the rights related to life, liberty, equality and dignity of the individual guaranteed by the constitution or embodied in the International covenants and enforceable by courts in India. "Commission" means the National Human Rights

Commission constituted under section of All human beings are born free and equal in dignity and rights known as Human rights, as commonly understood, are the rights that every human being is entitled to enjoy freely irrespective of his religion, race, caste, sex and nationality, etc. (Jagdish chand, 2007) In Declaration of Independence acknowledged the fundamental human rights. Human right means different thing to different people. Human Rights are not static, but are rather dynamic in nature.

New rights are recognized and enforced from time to time. Only persons fully conversant with the latest development about the expanding horizons of Human Rights can promote their awareness better other.

94. Section 63 of Indian Partnership Act, 1932- when a change in the constitution of a registered firm any incoming, continuing or outgoing partner, and when a registered firm is dissolved any person who was a partner immediately before the dissolution, or the agent of any such partner or person specially authorized in this behalf, may give notice to the registrar of such change or dissolution, specifying the date therefore, and the registrar shall make a record of the notice in the entry relating to the firm in the register of firms, and shall file the notice along with the statement relating to the firm filed under section 59.

96. Section 128 of the Contract Act is related to the liability of a surety *viz - a viz* the Principal debtor and not with regard to the liability of a director/promoter of a company viz-a-viz the principal debtor where such debtor is the company. In the case of Industrial investment Bank of india vs Biswanath Jhunjhunwala Industrial Investment (supra) referred to by IDBI Bank, the question that arose for determination was whether or not a guarantor can be proceeded against without the principal debtor being proceeded against. This is not the case in the present application.

97. Definition sale of goods: A contract of sa is a legal contract an exchange of good services or property to be exchanged fro seller to buyer for an agreed upon value money paid or the promise to pay same. It a specific type of legal contract.

Meaning of Goods: In Section 61, goc includes all personal chattels but exclude all the services or chooses in action or mone Products of the soil are generally sold with view to severance and though they ma sometimes be of the nature of land for th purpose of the Law of Property (Miscellaneou Provisions) Act 1989, they are usually good within the meaning of the Act of 1979. No would crops sold with the land on whic they are growing because they are not in suc a case to be 'severed before sale or under th contract of sale' as section 61 requires.

98. Doctrine of constructive notice: Th company is given the status of an artifici person. The memorandum and articles c association, of a company, contemplates th documents, which sets out the objects an powers of a company. These documents ar accessible to the people either without an costs or on payment of a nominal amoun Therefore, any person who enters into contract with the company is thus presume to have inspected such documents and thu to be aware of the powers that are bein delegated to the directors. In other words every person dealing with the company i presumed to have read these documents an understood them in their true perspective.

100. Promissory note: A promissory note is a instrument in writing (not being a bank not or a currency note) containing a unconditional undertaking signed by th maker, to pay a certain sum of money onl to, or to order of a certain person, or to th bearer of the instrument." The person wh makes the promise to pay is called the Maker He is the debtor and must sign the instrument The person who will get the money (th creditor) is called Payee.

Previous Paper (Solved)

UGC-NET-JRF & Assistant Professor Exam Law, November-2017*

PAPER-II

Note: *This paper contains* ***fifty (50)*** *objective type questions of* ***two (2)*** *marks each.* ***All questions are compulsory.***

1. Read Assertion (A) and Reason (R) and answer using the code given below:

Assertion (A): The preamble to the constitution of India clearly indicates the ideals set before the Nation.

Reason (R): The ideals set before the Nation are Justice, Equity, Fraternity of the individual and unity and integrity of the Nation.

Codes:

A. Both (A) and (R) are true and (R) is the correct explanation of (A)
B. Both (A) and (R) are true, but (R) is not the correct explanation of (A)
C. (A) is true, but (R) is false
D. (A) is false, but (R) is true

2. Arrange the following leading cases in order, pronounced by the Supreme Court by using the code given below:

(*a*) Selvi v. State of Karnataka
(*b*) Official Liquidator v. Dayananda
(*c*) I.R. Coelho v. State of Tamil Nadu
(*d*) P.A. Inamdar v. State of Maharastra

Codes:

A. (*d*), (*a*), (*c*), (*b*)
B. (*d*), (*c*), (*b*), (*a*)
C. (*c*), (*b*), (*d*), (*a*)
D. (*b*), (*c*), (*d*), (*a*)

3. Which of the following statement is correct?

A. The Fundamental Duties are mandatory on all the persons
B. The Fundamental Duties have always been a part of the Constitution of India
C. The Fundamental Duties have been added through an amendment to the Constitution of India
D. The Fundamental Duties can be enforced by Writs

4. Read Assertion (A) and Reason (R) and answer using the code given below:

Assertion (A): No person is eligible for appointment as Governor unless he is a citizen of India and has completed the age of Thirty Five Years.

Reason (R): He is debarred from holding any other office of profit during his term of office.

Codes:

A. Both (A) and (R) are true and (R) is the correct explanation of (A).
B. Both (A) and (R) are true, but (R) is not the correct explanation of (A).
C. (A) is true, but (R) is false.
D. (A) is false, but (R) is true.

5. Which one of the following pairs is correctly matched with regard to the provisions of the Constitution of India?

A. Art 352.... Effect of proclamation of Emergency
B. Art 353....Application of provisions relating to distribution of revenues while a proclamation is in operation
C. Art 354.... Determination of executive powers of the Union, during emergency
D. Art 355.... Duty of the Union to protect States against external aggression and internal disturbance

* Exam held on 05 November 2017.

6. Which one of the following pairs is not correctly matched with regard to constitutional amendment?

A. The Constitution (Seventh Amendment) Act ......1956.

B. The Constitution (Fourteenth Amendment) Act......1962.

C. The Constitution (Thirty First Amendment) Act.....1973.

D. The Constitution (Forty Second Amendment) Act.....1975.

7. Match List-I with List-II and give the correct answer by using the code given below the lists:

List-I	List-II
(*a*) The principles of constructive resjudicata are also applicable to writ petition	(*i*) Woman's Education Trust V. State of Haryana
(*b*) Writ petition dismissed for want of prosecution can be restored	(*ii*) M. Nagabhushana V. State of Karnataka
(*c*) Direction given by the High Court under Article 226 cannot be altered by the State Government	(*iii*) Ratan Singh V. State of Rajasthan
(*d*) The disposal of several writ petitions in a batch by a single order would be permissible if facts of all cases are similar or almost similar	(*iv*) V. Porukutty Mannadissior V. State of Kerala

Codes:

	(*a*)	(*b*)	(*c*)	(*d*)
A.	(*ii*)	(*iii*)	(*iv*)	(*i*)
B.	(*iii*)	(*iv*)	(*i*)	(*ii*)
C.	(*ii*)	(*i*)	(*iv*)	(*iii*)
D.	(*iv*)	(*iii*)	(*i*)	(*ii*)

8. "Judges do not make law, but only declare what has always been law." This statement is of:

A. Salmond B. Blackstone

C. Willis D. Allen

9. Which of the following statements is/are correct in regard to a valid custom?

(*a*) The custom has to possess a sufficient measure of antiquity.

(*b*) The custom must have been enjoyed 'as of right'.

(*c*) The custom need not to be consistent with other custom in the same area.

(*d*) The custom must be certain and precise.

Codes:

A. Only (*a*) and (*b*) are correct.

B. Only (*a*), (*b*) and (*c*) are correct.

C. Only (*a*), (*b*) and (*d*) are correct.

D. (*a*), (*b*), (*c*) and (*d*) all are correct.

10. Match List-I with List-II and select the correct answer using the code given below:

List-I (Theory)	List-II (Jurist)
(*a*) Scientific Positivism	(*i*) Herbert Spencer
(*b*) Social Solidarity	(*ii*) Gierke
(*c*) Organic Theory of Society	(*iii*) Auguste Compte
(*d*) Theory of reality of group personality	(*iv*) Duguit

Codes:

	(*a*)	(*b*)	(*c*)	(*d*)
A.	(*i*)	(*iv*)	(*ii*)	(*iii*)
B.	(*iii*)	(*iv*)	(*i*)	(*ii*)
C.	(*ii*)	(*iv*)	(*iii*)	(*i*)
D.	(*iv*)	(*ii*)	(*i*)	(*iii*)

11. Match List-I with List-II and select the correct answer using the code given below:

List-I	List-II (Jural correlatives)
(*a*) Right	(*i*) Liability
(*b*) Privilege	(*ii*) Disability
(*c*) Power	(*iii*) Duty
(*d*) Immunity	(*iv*) No-right

Codes:

	(*a*)	(*b*)	(*c*)	(*d*)
A.	(*i*)	(*ii*)	(*iii*)	(*iv*)
B.	(*iii*)	(*iv*)	(*i*)	(*ii*)
C.	(*iii*)	(*ii*)	(*iv*)	(*i*)
D.	(*iv*)	(*i*)	(*iii*)	(*ii*)

12. "Ownership denotes the relation between a person and an object forming the subject-matter of his ownership." This observation was made by:

A. Salmond B. Pound
C. Holland D. Savigny

13. Read the following statements and give the correct answer by using the code given below:

Assertion (A): A perfect duty is one which a person not merely ought to perform, but may be justly compelled to perform.

Reason (R): A perfect duty is one which is not merely recognised by law but enforceable.

Codes:

A. (A) and (R) both are correct and (R) is the correct explanation of (A).
B. (A) and (R) both are correct and (R) is not the correct explanation of (A).
C. (A) is correct, but (R) is wrong.
D. (A) is wrong, but (R) is correct.

14. In which of the following cases Judge Alvarez has aptly remarked, "The fundamental principles of international law are passing through a serious crisis and this necessitates its reconstruction. A new international law is developing which embodies not only this reconstruction but also some entirely new elements"?

A. Anglo - Norwegian Fisheries Case
B. Aegean Sea Continental Shelf Case
C. Conditions of admission of a State to the United States
D. International Status of South West Africa

15. Which of the following statement/statements is/are not correct?

(*a*) The words 'International Law' were used for the first time by eminent British Jurist, Jermy Bentham in 1780.
(*b*) J.S. Starke has remarked that international law is a "living and expanding code."
(*c*) Prof. Oppenheim has remarked that international law is the vanishing point of jurisprudence.
(*d*) Holland has viewed that International law is mere a positive morality.

Codes:

A. Only (*c*) is incorrect.
B. (*a*) and (*d*) both are incorrect.
C. (*b*), (*c*) and (*d*) are only incorrect.
D. (*a*), (*b*), (*c*) and (*d*) all are incorrect.

16. Which of the following is **not** a theory of relationship between international law and municipal law?

A. Specific Adoption Theory
B. Delegation Theory
C. Declaratory Theory
D. Monism

17. Match List-I with List-II and give the correct answer by using the code given below the lists:

List-I	List-II
(*a*) Decision given by the Permanent Court of Arbitration	(*i*) The Right of Minorities in the upper Silesia (Minority schools)
(*b*) The principle/ doctrine of Forum Prorogatum was enunciated in the case	(*ii*) Pious Fund case
(*c*) A leading case on "reprisal" is :	(*iii*) The Asylum (Colombia v. Peru) case
(*d*) Case decided by International Court of Justice under 'Contentious Jurisdiction'	(*iv*) Naulilaa Incident

Codes:

	(*a*)	(*b*)	(*c*)	(*d*)
A.	(*ii*)	(*i*)	(*iv*)	(*iii*)
B.	(*i*)	(*ii*)	(*iii*)	(*iv*)
C.	(*iii*)	(*iv*)	(*i*)	(*ii*)
D.	(*iv*)	(*iii*)	(*ii*)	(*i*)

18. Which of the following cases are **not** related to "recognition"?

(*a*) Civil Air Transport Incorporated Co. v. Central Air Transport Corporation
(*b*) The Azantzazu Mendi case
(*c*) Barcelona Traction case
(*d*) United States v. Schooner

Codes:

A. Only (*d*)
B. (*a*), (*b*) and (*c*) only
C. (*c*) and (*d*) both
D. (*a*), (*b*), (*c*) and (*d*) all

19. Which of the following statement/statements is/are correct?

(*a*) The most important purpose of the United Nations is to maintain international peace and security.
(*b*) The principles of the United Nations are provided under Article 2 of the U. N. Charter.
(*c*) Section 6 of the U. N. Charter provides for provisions to withdraw of a Member-Slate from the United Nations.
(*d*) There are five (5) principal organs of the United Nations.

Codes:

A. Only (*a*) is correct.
B. (*a*), (*b*) and (*c*) are correct.
C. (*a*), (*b*), (*c*) and (*d*) all are correct.
D. Only (*a*) and (*b*) are correct.

20. In which of the following cases the Supreme Court held that "it is now well established that in the absence of any rule of Hindu Law, the court have authority to decide cases on the principle of justice, equity and good conscience"?

A. Gurunath v. Kamlabai
B. Lohar Amrit v. Doshi Janti Lal
C. Sarastivali v. Jagadammbai
D. Munna Lal v. Rajkumar

21. Match List-I with List-II and indicate the correct answer using the code given below:

List-I	List-II
(*a*) Vishwanath Agrawal vs Sarla Agrawal	(*i*) Divorce by mutual consent
(*b*) Geeta Maugalani v Jagdesh Maugalani	(*ii*) Saptapadi
(*c*) Manish Goel v Rohni Goel	(*iii*) Cruelty
(*d*) Vishnu Prakash v Sheela Devi	(*iv*) Desertion

Codes:

	(*a*)	(*b*)	(*c*)	(*d*)
A.	(*ii*)	(*iv*)	(*iii*)	(*i*)
B.	(*i*)	(*iii*)	(*iv*)	(*ii*)
C.	(*iii*)	(*iv*)	(*i*)	(*ii*)
D.	(*i*)	(*iv*)	(*iii*)	(*ii*)

22. A Hindu Contracting Second Marriage during pendancy of appeal against the decree of divorce is:

A. Valid
B. Invalid
C. Factum valid
D. Void

23. A Married Hindu Contracting Second Marriage after professing Islam, would be guilty of offence punishable under:

A. Section 17 HM Act 1955 only
B. Section 494 IPC only
C. Section 17 HM Act read with S.494 IPC
D. Neither S.17 nor S.494.IPC

24. Which is not the modern source of Hindu Law?

A. Precedent
B. Legislation
C. Dharamshastra
D. Justice, equity and good conscience

25. In which of the following case, the Supreme court held that "Triple Talaq" would be treated as a "Single Talaq" and not a valid talaq?

A. Bai Tahira Case
B. Fazlunbi Case
C. Mohd Ahmad Khan Case
D. Shamim Ara Case

26. Read Assertion (A) and Reason (R) and answer by using code given below:

Assertion (A): An agreement would be void if both the parties to the agreement were under a mistake as to a matter of fact not essential to the agreement.

Reason (R): Because Section 20 of the Indian Contract Act so provides.

Codes:

A. (R) is correct, but (A) is incorrect.
B. (A) is correct, but (R) is incorrect.

C. Both (A) and (R) are correct.
D. Both (A) and (R) are incorrect.

27. Match List-I with List-II and select the correct answer using the code given below:

List-I	List-II
(*a*) Lapse of offer	(*i*) Week v. Tybald
(*b*) General offers	(*ii*) Henthon v. Fraser
(*c*) Communication of proposal	(*iii*) Coffee Board v. CCT
(*d*) Implied proposal	(*iv*) Lalman Shukla v. Gauri Datt

Codes:

	(*a*)	(*b*)	(*c*)	(*d*)
A.	(*iv*)	(*iii*)	(*i*)	(*ii*)
B.	(*ii*)	(*i*)	(*iii*)	(*iv*)
C.	(*ii*)	(*i*)	(*iv*)	(*iii*)
D.	(*i*)	(*ii*)	(*iv*)	(*iii*)

28. "Consideration is the recompense given by the party contracting to the other": Above definition is attributed to ....
A. Pollock
B. Justice Patterson
C. Cheshire and Fifoot
D. Blackstone

29. Which of the following statement is correct?
A. Acceptance may be made in the manner prescribed or indicated by the offerer.
B. Acceptance has to be made in the manner prescribed or indicated by the offeree.
C. Acceptance has to be made in the manner prescribed or indicated by the offerer.
D. Acceptance need not be made in the manner prescribed or indicated by the offerer.

30. In which of the following cases law of frustration was applied? Answer using code given below:
(*a*) Paradine v. Jane
(*b*) Taylor v. Caldwell
(*c*) Krell v. Henry
(*d*) Cricklewood Property and Investment Trust Ltd. v. Leighton's Investment Trust Ltd.

Codes:
A. (*a*) only
B. (*a*) and (*b*) only
C. (*a*), (*b*) and (*c*) only
D. (*a*), (*b*), (*c*) and (*d*)

31. Which one of the following cases enshrine the present position of the doctrine of public policy in India?
A. Ramchand Hirachand v. Askar Nawaz Jung
B. Gherulal Parakh v. Mahadeodas
C. Muniammal v. Raja
D. Geeta Satish Gokarna v. Satish Shankarrao Gokarna

32. Read Assertion (A) and Reason (R) and answer using code given below:

Assertion (A) : A contract is a property in the nature of a promise supported by some consideration upon which either the remedy of specific performance or that of damages is available.

Reason (R): Above principle is laid down in Sunrise Associates v. Govt. of NCT of Delhi.

Codes:
A. Both (A) and (R) are correct.
B. Both (A) and (R) are incorrect.
C. (A) is correct, but (R) is incorrect.
D. (R) is correct, but (A) is incorrect.

33. Which of the following statement/s is/are correct? Answer by using the code below:
(*a*) In tort duty is imposed by law and is owed to the community at large.
(*b*) A tort is founded upon consent of parties.
(*c*) A tort is civil wrong for which the remedy is a common law action for liquidated damages.
(*d*) In tort 'motive' for the violation of right is immaterial.

Codes:
A. Only (*a*) is correct.
B. (*a*) and (*b*) are correct.
C. (*a*), (*b*) and (*c*) are correct.
D. (*a*), (*b*), (*c*) and (*d*) are correct.

34. Match List-I (Name of defence) with List-II (Related case) and give the answer by using the code given below:

List-I	List-II
(*a*) Plaintiff a wrongdoer	(*i*) Nichols v. Marsland
(*b*) Act of God	(*ii*) Bird v. Holbrook

(*c*) Inevitable accident (*iii*) Consolidated Co. v. Curtis

(*d*) Mistake (*iv*) Stanley v. Powell

Codes:

	(*a*)	(*b*)	(*c*)	(*d*)
A.	(*iv*)	(*iii*)	(*ii*)	(*i*)
B.	(*iii*)	(*iv*)	(*i*)	(*ii*)
C.	(*ii*)	(*i*)	(*iv*)	(*iii*)
D.	(*i*)	(*ii*)	(*iii*)	(*iv*)

35. Read Assertion (A) and Reason (R) and give correct answer with the help of code given below:

Assertion (A): The relations of partners inter se is that of principal and agent.

Reason (R): The rules of the law of agency does not apply in case of their liability.

Codes:

A. Both (A) and (R) are true and (R) is the correct explanation of (A)
B. Both (A) and (R) are true, but (R) is not the correct explanation of (A)
C. (A) is right, but (R) is wrong
D. (A) is wrong, but (R) is right

36. A servant is engaged by the master under ....

A. Contract of service
B. Contract for services
C. Contract from services
D. Contract in services

37. Match List-I (Name of Rule) with List-II (Related case) and give correct answer by using code given below:

List-I	**List-II**
(*a*) Last opportunity	(*i*) Bernina Mills v. Armstrong
(*b*) Apportionment of damages	(*ii*) Davies v. Mann
(*c*) Alternative danger	(*iii*) Shyam sunder v. State of Rajasthan
(*d*) Identification	(*iv*) Vidya Devi v. M.P. Road Transport Corporation

Codes:

	(*a*)	(*b*)	(*c*)	(*d*)
A.	(*ii*)	(*iv*)	(*iii*)	(*i*)
B.	(*i*)	(*iii*)	(*ii*)	(*iv*)
C.	(*iii*)	(*ii*)	(*i*)	(*iv*)
D.	(*iv*)	(*i*)	(*ii*)	(*iii*)

38. Which of the following is an exception to the rule of strict liability?

A. Defendant's own fault
B. Statutory authority
C. Consent of third party
D. Act of defendant

39. Match the appropriate statements with that of its authors:

Statement	**Author**
(*a*) The behaviour as criminal is part of the political process	(*i*) Klare H. J.
(*b*) Disobedience of law may be termed as a crime	(*ii*) Huda
(*c*) Crime is not absolute like sin	(*iii*) Terence Morris
(*d*) Crime is an act committed or omitted in violation of a public law	(*iv*) Blackstone

Codes:

	(*a*)	(*b*)	(*c*)	(*d*)
A.	(*iv*)	(*iii*)	(*ii*)	(*i*)
B.	(*ii*)	(*iii*)	(*i*)	(*iv*)
C.	(*i*)	(*iv*)	(*ii*)	(*iii*)
D.	(*i*)	(*ii*)	(*iii*)	(*iv*)

40. In the absence of any evidence as to the mens rea, in which of the cases the criminal liability can be fixed upon a person?

A. Where the consequences are not so harmful to the society.
B. Where there is no violent presumption.
C. The intended consequence is not injurious but conjointly injurious on other facts.
D. Where an act is not performed wantonly.

41. In the application of the principle 'Nemo debet proeadem causa bis vexari', what enquiries are relevant?

A. Whether the accused is not in jeopardy on the first indictment?

B. Whether there was final verdict?

C. Whether the previous charge was not the same as that of the present one?

D. Whether the statute directs not to have a second trial?

42. Read the following statements and state where the principles of joint liability is applied instantly flowing from mens rea?

A. When he himself commits a crime.

B. When he shares in the commission of crime.

C. When he, with a view to the commission of crime, sets some third agency to work.

D. When he helps the offender after commission of the crime in screening the offence.

43. Acts done in moments of delusion are protected because:

A. By virtue of absence of free will.

B. Lack of intelligence to distinguish between good and evil.

C. Expediency grounds says so.

D. Circumstances are such that they are incompatible to the existence of Mens rea.

44. Which of the factors are essential for fixing criminal liability on importing girls from different territory other than India for seduction?

A. That girl must be below the age of 21 years.

B. That imported girl must be from Indian origin irrespective of age.

C. That girl must be from Jammu and Kashmir or any other UN recognised country and is brought forcefully to render domestic help.

D. That girl is on a tourist Visa and above 21 years and is likely that she will be forced to illicit intercourse.

45. Read Assertion (A) and Reason (R) and answer using the code given below:

Assertion (A): There is a more continuous and systematic surveillance over industrial disputes on the part of the government by resorting to compulsory adjudications as the tradition of free collective bargaining has always been weak in India.

Reason (R): With respect to the merits and demerits of collective bargaining Vis-a-Vis compulsory adjudications there is a serious conflict and over lapping of views.

Codes:

A. Both (A) and (R) are true and (R) is the correct explanation of (A).

B. Both (A) and (R) are true and (R) is not the correct explanation of (A).

C. (A) is true, but (R) is false.

D. (A) is false, but (R) is true.

46. Match List-I with List-II and select the correct answer using the code given below the list:

List-I	List-II
(*a*) Food corporation of India staff union v. Food corporation of India and others	(*i*) Settlements are the "live wires" of the Act for ensuring industrial peace and prosperity.
(*b*) Virudhachalam v. Management of Lotus Mills	(*ii*) An unregistered trade union or trade union whose registration has been cancelled has no right.
(*c*) B. Srinivasa Reddy v. Karnataka water Supply and Drainage Board Employees Association	(*iii*) Reflection of recent judicial trends on the interpretation of definition of industry.
(*d*) Coir Board, Ernakulam, Cochin and another v. Indira Devi P.S. and others	(*iv*) Norms and procedure to be followed for assessing the representative character of Trade Union by a secret ballot system.

Codes:

	(a)	*(b)*	*(c)*	*(d)*
A.	*(iv)*	*(i)*	*(ii)*	*(iii)*
B.	*(i)*	*(ii)*	*(iii)*	*(iv)*
C.	*(iii)*	*(ii)*	*(i)*	*(iv)*
D.	*(ii)*	*(i)*	*(iv)*	*(iii)*

47. Which one of the following is wrong?

A. The right to strike or declare lock-out may be controlled or restricted by appropriate industrial legislation.

B. The conciliation officers under the industrial disputes Act are charged with the duty of adjudication of disputes.

C. An interim award is like a preliminary decree within the meaning of Section 2 (2) of Code of Civil Procedure.

D. The Works Committee is not authorised to consider real or substantial changes in the conditions of service.

48. The Fifth Schedule, under the Industrial Disputes Act contains several unfair labour practices. In which of the conditions of category I, it is required to establish that Employer Sponsored Trade Union of workmen is said to be Unfair Labour Practice?

A. Employees or their Trade Union

B. Employee only

C. Employers or their Trade Union

D. Employer and Employee Collectively

49. When a party to dispute under the Industrial Disputes Act is prevented from appearing at the hearing, due to sufficient cause and is faced with exparte award, the Industrial Tribunal has:

A. no power to set aside the exparte award.

B. only duty to set aside the exparte award.

C. both power and duty to set aside the exparte award which is based on the rule of statutory construction.

D. express provision in the Act or rules giving the tribunal the jurisdiction to set aside the award.

50. "The concept of compulsory adjudication of industrial disputes was statutorily ushered with a view to providing a forum and compelling the parties to resort to the forum for arbitration, so as to avoid confrontation and dislocation in industry."

The above observation was made by one of the justice in a case decided by the Supreme Court:

A. Justice V.R. Krishna Iyer

B. Justice O. Chinnappa Reddy

C. Justice Desai

D. Justice Gajendragadkar

ANSWERS

1 C	**2** B	**3** C	**4** B	**5** D	**6** D	**7** B	**8** B	**9** C	**10** B
11 B	**12** A	**13** A	**14** C	**15** C	**16** C	**17** A	**18** C	**19** D	**20** A
21 C	**22** D	**23** C	**24** C	**25** D	**26** D	**27** C	**28** D	**29** C	**30** D
31 B	**32** B	**33** A	**34** C	**35** C	**36** A	**37** A	**38** B	**39** A	**40** C
41 B	**42** B	**43** D	**44** A	**45** A	**46** A	**47** B	**48** C	**49** C	**50** C

EXPLANATORY ANSWERS

1. The Preamble to India's constitution reads WE, THE PEOPLE OF INDIA, having solemnly resolved to constitute India into a SOVEREIGN SOCIALIST SECULAR DEMOCRATIC REPUBLIC and to secure to all its citizens:

JUSTICE, social, economic and political;

LIBERTY of thought, expression, belief, faith and worship;

EQUALITY of status and of opportunity; and to promote among them all

FRATERNITY assuring the dignity of the individual and the unity and integrity of the Nation;

IN OUR CONSTITUENT ASSEMBLY this 26th day of November, 1949, do HEREBY ADOPT, ENACT AND GIVE TO OURSELVES THIS CONSTITUTION.

Hence, according to the preamble, the ideals set are—Justice, liberty, equality and fraternity assuring the dignity of the individual and the unity and integrity of the Nation. Hence (A) is correct, but (R) is false as the terms equality and liberty have not been mentioned therein.

2. The correct chronological order is

- P.A. Inamdar v. State of Maharashtra (2005) 6 SCC 537
- I.R. Coelho v. State of Tamil Nadu (2007) 2 SCC 1
- Official Liquidator v. Dayanand (2008) 10 SCC 1
- Selvi v. State of Karnataka (2010) 7 (SCC) 263.

3. Fundamental duties were not incorporated in the initial constitution. Part IVA of the constitution dealing with fundamental duties was inserted for the first time in 1976 by 42nd Constitutional Amendment. Initially there were 10 fundamental duties, later in 2002 by the 86th Constitutional Amendment clause (k) has been inserted as 11th fundamental duty. Citizens are morally obligated by the Constitution to perform these duties. However, just like the Directive Principles, these are non-justiciable.

- To abide by the Constitution and respect its ideals and institutions, the National Flag and the National Anthem;
- To cherish and follow the noble ideals which inspired our national struggle for freedom;
- To uphold and protect the sovereignty, unity and integrity of India;
- To defend the country and render national service when called upon to do so;
- To promote harmony and the spirit of common brotherhood amongst all the people of India transcending religious, linguistic and regional or sectional diversities; to renounce practices derogatory to the dignity of women;
- To value and preserve the rich heritage of our composite culture;
- To protect and improve the natural environment including forests, lakes, rivers, wildlife and to have compassion for living creatures;
- To develop the scientific temper, humanism and the spirit of inquiry and reform;
- To safeguard public property and to abjure violence;
- To strive towards excellence in all spheres of individual and collective activity, so that the nation constantly rises to higher levels of endeavour and achievement;

- Who is a parent or guardian, to provide opportunities for education to his child, or as the case may be, ward between the age of six to fourteen years.

4. Article 157 of The Constitution states Qualifications for appointment as Governor:

- No person shall be eligible for appointment as Governor unless he is a citizen of India and has completed the age of thirty-five years.

Article 158 lays down the conditions for Governor's office. Here Article 158 (2) of The Constitution states

- The Governor shall not hold any other office of profit.

Hence, both (A) and (R) are true, but (R) is not the correct explanation of (A).

5. The correct content of the mentioned Articles of the Constitution are as under:

- Article 352—Proclamation of Emergency
- Article 353—Effect of Proclamation of Emergency
- Article 354—Application of provisions relating to distribution of revenues while a Proclamation of Emergency is in operation
- Article 355—Duty of the Union to protect States against external aggression and internal disturbance

Hence only (D) is correctly matched

6. 42nd Amendment Act came into force on 2nd November 1976. Remaining options are correctly matched.

8. William Blackstone was an English jurist who attained eminence in the early eighteenth century. His Commentaries on the Laws of England is a considered to be the most influential treatise on common law till date.

9. The essentials of a valid custom are

- **Antiquity:** A custom must be in existence from time immemorial. English law fixed the year 1189 to test the antiquity of a custom.
- **Continuous Observation:** Uninterrupted and continuous practice is an essential feature of the custom. If a custom becomes legally unenforceable even for a short time it would not the recognized as a valid custom.
- **Peaceable enjoyment:** It is essential that custom must have been enjoyed peacefully by the concerned people.
- **Matter of right:** A valid custom must result in creating obligatory force *i.e.*, it should create corresponding rights and duties for people concerned. If a practice is observed as a courtesy and not as a matter of right then it cannot be termed to be a "custom" in legal parlance.
- **Certainty:** A legal obligation such as Custom must be certain to be enforceable. If the nature and content of the obligation is vague and ambiguous then it cannot be enforced.
- **Consistency:** A custom must not be in conflict with other prevailing customs or statutes. A custom in conflict with a prevailing statute loses its validity.

13. A perfect duty is the one in which has a corresponding right in some entity to compel performance. For example, an adult male's duty to maintain his old parents unable to maintain their selves. This is a perfect duty as under section 125 CrPC, this duty is enforceable against the son. However, the fundamental duties appearing in part IVA of the constitution, are imperfect duties as there is no correlative right in any entity to compel their performance.

15. Statement (*a*) is correct.

Statement (*b*) is incorrect. The remark that International Law is a "living and expanding Code" was made by Lord Chancellor Sankey in the case *Re Piracy Jure Gentium* (1934) A.C 586.

Statement (*c*) is incorrect. The statement that "International Law is the vanishing point of jurisprudence" is attributed to Holland.

Statement (*d*) is incorrect. The view that international law is merely positive, international morality is attributed to Austin.

16. Declaratory theory deals with recognition of new states and authority of governments representing them. According to this theory existence of statehood is independent of recognition and recognition is merely an acknowledgement of certain facts which already exist.

Remaining theories deal with relationship of international law with municipal law.

18. Barcelona Traction case deals with concept of corporate personality and use of this principle of procedure as a 'General Principle' recognized by all civilized states as a source of law.

United States v Schooner case deals with treaty law.

Remaining cases are related to recognition.

19. Statement (*a*) is correct.

Statement (*b*) is correct.

Statement (*c*) is incorrect. Article 2 of the UN Charter lists the principles in accordance of which all its members should act. Article 6 states the ground of expulsion of a member from UN membership.

Statement (*d*) is incorrect. UN has six principal organs—General Assembly, Security Council, Economic and Social Council, Secretariat, International Court of Justice and Trusteeship Council.

22. Section 15 of the Hindu Marriage Act, 1955 states

Divorced persons when may marry again: When a marriage has been dissolved by a decree of divorce and either there is no right of appeal against the decree or, if there is such a right of appeal, the time for appealing has expired without an appeal having been presented, or an appeal has been presented but has been dismissed, it shall be lawful for either party to the marriage to marry again.

23. A married Hindu male cannot escape liability under section 17 HMA and section 494 IPC merely by professing Islam at a later date. In the Sarla Mudgal case (1995 SC) it was held by the apex court that a Hindu husband cannot marry a second time simply by embracing Islam without lawfully dissolving the first marriage.

24. Dharmashastra's are ancient sources of Hindu law and not modern sources. This means that a judge while deciding a dispute under Hindu Law is not to consult or make an inquiry into the Dharmshastra's to know what is the governing law in the present dispute. Judges only need to conform to modern sources of law *i.e.*, legislation, precedent and justice, equity and good conscience.

26. According to section 20 of The Indian Contract Act, where both the parties to an agreement are under a mistake as to a matter of fact essential to the agreement the agreement is void.

Hence, both (A) and (R) are incorrect.

29. **According to section 7 of the Indian Contract Act:** Acceptance must be absolute—In order to convert a proposal into a promise the acceptance must—In order to convert a proposal into a promise the acceptance must—(1) be absolute and unqualified; (2) be expressed in some usual and reasonable manner, unless the proposal prescribes the manner in which it is to be accepted. If the proposal prescribes a manner in which it is to be accepted, and the acceptance is not made in such manner, the proposer may, within a reasonable time after the acceptance is communicated to him, insist that his proposal shall be accepted in the prescribed manner, and not otherwise; but, if he fails to do so, he accepts the acceptance.

31. In Gherulal Parekh v Mahadeodas (1959 SC), there was a Partnership agreement with object of entering into wagering transactions. When plaintiff sued for certain money payable under the partnership contract the defendant alleged that the agreement made between them was illegal and unenforceable on account of S.23. In this case the court has held that object of entering into wagering transactions is not against public policy.

32. A contract is not a property. It is only a promise supported by some consideration upon which either the remedy of specific performance or that of damage is available.

36. Contract of service denotes a master-servant relationship in which the master not only controls 'what' is to be done but also 'how' it is to be done. In contrast, a contract for services denotes a client-independent contractor relationship, in which the degree of command and supervision exercised by the client is much less than a 'contract of service' and the client dictates only 'what' is to be done and not 'how' it is to be done.

41. The maxim *Nemo debet proeadem causa bis vexari* means that no individual should be used more than once for the same cause.

44. Section 366B of the Indian Penal Code stat deals with the offence of Importation of gi from foreign country and states that—Whoev imports into India from any country outsi India or from the State of Jammu and Kashm any girl under the age of twenty-one yea with intent that she may be, or knowing it be likely that she will be, forced or seduc to illicit intercourse with another person, sha be punishable with imprisonment which ma extend to ten years and shall also be liable fine.

47. Statement (B) is incorrect. The conciliati officers are tasked to bring about resoluti of industrial disputes by means of conciliati and not through any adjudication of th dispute. Remaining statements are correct.

48. There are two parts to the 5th Schedule Industrial Disputes Act, 1948 r/w section 2(ra Part I deals with those unfair trade practic which may be committed on the part employers and trade unions of employe while Part II deals with those unfair tra practices which may be practiced on the pa of workmen and trade unions of workmen

PAPER-III

ote: *This paper contains* ***seventy five (75)*** *objective pe questions of* ***two (2)*** *marks each.* ***All*** *questions* ***re compulsory.***

1. Answer the following by using code given below. 'Economic Justice' is one of the objectives of the Constitution of India. It has been provided in

(*a*) Preamble
(*b*) Fundamental Rights
(*c*) Directive Principles of State Policy
(*d*) Fundamental Duties

Codes:

A. (*a*) and (*b*) are correct
B. (*a*) and (*c*) are correct
C. (*b*) and (*c*) are correct
D. (*b*), (*c*) and (*d*) are correct

2. Arrange the following decided cases in a chronological order and answer by using the code given below:

(*a*) Union of India v. N.S. Rathnam and others
(*b*) Basawaraj v. Special Land Acqisition Officer
(*c*) Usha Mehta v. Government of A.P
(*d*) City Industrial Development v. Platinum Entertainment

Codes:

A. (*c*), (*b*), (*d*), (*a*) B. (*b*), (*c*), (*d*), (*a*)
C. (*d*), (*b*), (*c*), (*a*) D. (*b*), (*c*), (*a*), (*d*)

3. Read Assertion (A) and Reason (R) and answer using the code given below:

Assertion (A): The Constitution of India under Article 40 states that The State shall take steps to organise village panchayats and endow them with such powers and authority as may be necessary to enable them to function as units of self government.

Reason (R): This directive gives an assurance that every village where maximum people live, has to be made an autonomous republic, self-sufficient, self-sustaining and capable of managing its own affairs.

Codes:

A. Both (A) and (R) are correct and (R) is the correct explanation of (A)
B. Both (A) and (R) are correct and (R) is not the correct explanation of (A)
C. (A) is true, but (R) is false
D. (A) is false, but (R) is true

4. Which of the following statements are correct? Answer by using the code given below.

(*a*) Persons in Govt/Judicial service need not resign to participate in District Judge selection process held in "Vijay Kumar Misra and another v. High court of Judicature at Patna" by the Supreme Court of India
(*b*) The Supreme Court of India held in S. Kazi v. Muslim education society that All Tribunals are not necessary parties to the proceedings where legality of its orders challenged
(*c*) The Supreme Court of India observed in Cardamom Marketing Corporation and others v. State of Kerala and others that Social Security to the legal profession becomes an essential part of legal system
(*d*) The Supreme Court of India held in 'Union of India v. Rajasthan High Court and others that High Court Judges are exempted from Airport frisking.

Codes:

A. Only (*b*) is correct
B. (*a*), (*b*) and (*c*) are correct
C. (*b*), (*c*) and (*d*) are correct
D. (*a*), (*b*) and (*d*) are correct

5. Which one of the following pairs is correctly matched with regard to the provisions of the Constitution of India?

A. Art 118 .... Duration of parliament
B. Art 119 .... Restriction on discussion in Parliament
C. Art 120 .... Language to be used in Parliament

D. Art 121 .... courts not to inquire into the Proceedings of Parliament

6. Match List-I with List-II and select the correct answer using the code given below:

List-I (Constitutional Provision)	List-II (Subject)
(*a*) Article 249	(*i*) Power of Parliament to legislate for two or more States by consent and adoption of such legislation by any other State
(*b*) Article 250	(*ii*) Power of Parliament to legislate with respect to any matter in the State List if a Proclamation of Emergency is in operation
(*c*) Article 252	(*iii*) Legislation for giving effect to international agreements
(*d*) Article 253	(*iv*) Power of Parliament to legislate with respect to a matter in the State List in the national interest

Codes:

	(*a*)	(*b*)	(*c*)	(*d*)
A.	(*i*)	(*ii*)	(*iii*)	(*iv*)
B.	(*iv*)	(*ii*)	(*i*)	(*iii*)
C.	(*iii*)	(*ii*)	(*iv*)	(*i*)
D.	(*ii*)	(*iii*)	(*i*)	(*iv*)

7. Which of the following statements is/are correct regarding Constitutional Amendment Bill? Give correct answer by using the code given below:

(*a*) Prior permission of President is required before introducing the constitutional Amendment Bill in Parliament

(*b*) Constitutional Amendment Bill can be introduced in either House of Parliament.

(*c*) President is bound to give his assent to the Bill if duly passed by both Houses of Parliament and ratified, if required, by the Legislatures of not less than one - half of the States

(*d*) President may return the Bill to th Houses for reconsideration

Codes:

A. Only (*a*), (*b*) and (*c*) are correct

B. Only (*b*) and (*c*) are correct

C. Only (*b*), (*c*) and (*d*) are correct

D. (*a*), (*b*), (*c*) and (*d*) all are correct

8. Match List-I with List-II and select the corre answer using the code given below:

List-I	List-II
(*a*) Article 324(1)	(*i*) Composition c Election Commissic
(*b*) Article 324(2)	(*ii*) Appointment c Regional Comm ssioners
(*c*) Article 324(4)	(*iii*) Powers vested in th Election Commissic
(*d*) Article 324(5)	(*iv*) Conditions of servic and tenure of offic of Election Comm ssion

Codes:

	(*a*)	(*b*)	(*c*)	(*d*)
A.	(*iii*)	(*i*)	(*ii*)	(*iv*)
B.	(*i*)	(*ii*)	(*iii*)	(*iv*)
C.	(*ii*)	(*iv*)	(*i*)	(*iii*)
D.	(*iv*)	(*ii*)	(*iii*)	(*i*)

9. Administrative Law as a separate branch legal discipline, especially in India, came be recognised in the middle of:

A. 17th century B. 18th century

C. 19th century D. 20th century

10. Read Assertion (A) and Reason (R) and answ using code given below:

Assertion (A): Natural justice is justice of th nature where the lion devours the lamb ar the tiger feeds upon the antilope

Reason (R): Above statement is taken fro Union of India V. Tulsiram Patel

Codes:

A. Both (A) and (R) are correct

B. (A) is correct, but (R) is incorrect

C. (R) is correct, but (A) is incorrect

D. Both (A) and (R) are incorrect

11. In which of the following cases, underwritten quotation is taken from? "Principles of natural justice must be read into the provision of law".

A. State of U.P. v. Vijay Kumar Tripathi
B. P. Satyanarayana v. Land Reforms Tribunal
C. I.T.C. v. State of Madras
D. Manjula Manjari Devi v. Director of Public Instruction

12. Match List-I (Name of Principle) with List-II (Related Case) and answer by using the code below:

List-I	List-II
(*a*) Res judicata	(*i*) S.P. Gupta v. Union of India
(*b*) Legitimate expectation	(*ii*) Motilal Padampat Sugar Mills v. State of Uttar Pradesh
(*c*) Promissory estoppel	(*iii*) Daryao v. State of Uttar Pradesh
(*d*) Locus standi	(*iv*) Monnet Ispat and Energy Ltd. v. Union of India

Codes:

	(*a*)	(*b*)	(*c*)	(*d*)
A.	(*ii*)	(*iv*)	(*iii*)	(*i*)
B.	(*iii*)	(*iv*)	(*ii*)	(*i*)
C.	(*i*)	(*iii*)	(*iv*)	(*ii*)
D.	(*iv*)	(*iii*)	(*ii*)	(*i*)

13. Which of the following is a ground for judicially attacking the exercise of administrative discretion? Answer by using code below:

(*a*) Ultra vires the law
(*b*) Mala fide intent
(*c*) Arbitrariness
(*d*) Irrelevant considerations

Codes:

A. (*a*) and (*b*) are correct
B. (*b*) and (*c*) are correct
C. (*a*), (*b*) and (*c*) are correct
D. (*a*), (*b*), (*c*) and (*d*) are correct

14. "Writ of certiorari can be issued to quash actions which are administrative in nature". Above principle was laid down in:

A. Indian Rly. Construction Co. Ltd v. Ajay Kumar
B. A.K. Kraipak v. Union of India
C. Union of India v. Bashyan
D. Rajesh Kumar v. C.I.T.

15. Which is the qualification of a judicial member of Lokpal?

A. A member of Parliament
B. A member of State Legislature
C. A retired High Court judge
D. A retired Chief Justice of a High Court

16. "I think adherence to precedent should be the rule and not the exception". This statement is of:

A. Keeton B. Blackston
C. Cardozo D. Paton

17. Which one of the following jurists was hostile to the natural law school?

A. Emmanuel Kant B. John Rawls
C. Jeremy Benthem D. Stammeler

18. Match List-I with List-II and select the correct answer using the code given below:

List-I	List-II
(*a*) Utilitarian Individualism	(*i*) Pound
(*b*) Social Utilitarian	(*ii*) Bentham
(*c*) Scientific Positivism	(*iii*) Ihering
(*d*) Social Engineering	(*iv*) Compte

Codes:

	(*a*)	(*b*)	(*c*)	(*d*)
A.	(*i*)	(*ii*)	(*iii*)	(*iv*)
B.	(*ii*)	(*iii*)	(*iv*)	(*i*)
C.	(*iii*)	(*ii*)	(*iv*)	(*i*)
D.	(*ii*)	(*iv*)	(*iii*)	(*i*)

19. Which one of the following sources of law has the basis under Article 141 of the Constitution of India?

A. Supreme legislation
B. Subordinate legislation
C. Colonial legislation
D. Precedent

20. Which one of the following jurists is not related to Historical school?

A. Savigny B. Ehrlich
C. Henry Main D. Hegel

21. Read Assertion (A) and Reason (R) and give the correct answer using code given below:

Assertion (A): A legal right is a legally protected interest

Reason (R): An element of advantage is essential to constitute right

Codes:

A. Both (A) and (R) are right and (R) is the correct explanation of (A)
B. Both (A) and (R) are right and (R) is not the correct explanation of (A)
C. (A) is right, but (R) is wrong
D. (R) is right, but (A) is wrong

22. Match List-I with List-II and select the correct answer by using the code given below:

List-I	List-II
(*a*) Inner morality of Law	(*i*) Maine
(*b*) Minimum content of law	(*ii*) Stammler
(*c*) Law with a variable Content	(*iii*) Fuller
(*d*) 'Status to contract' Theory	(*iv*) Hart

Codes:

	(*a*)	(*b*)	(*c*)	(*d*)
A.	(*i*)	(*ii*)	(*iii*)	(*iv*)
B.	(*iii*)	(*iv*)	(*ii*)	(*i*)
C.	(*i*)	(*iv*)	(*ii*)	(*iii*)
D.	(*iii*)	(*ii*)	(*iv*)	(*i*)

23. Match List-I with List-II and select the correct answer using the code given below:

List-I (Theory)	List-II (Subject)
(*a*) Will Theory	(*i*) Legal Person
(*b*) Concession Theory	(*ii*) Analytical School
(*c*) Declaratory Theory	(*iii*) Legal Right
(*d*) Command Theory	(*iv*) Precedent

Codes:

	(*a*)	(*b*)	(*c*)	(*d*)
A.	(*iii*)	(*i*)	(*ii*)	(*iv*)
B.	(*i*)	(*iii*)	(*ii*)	(*iv*)
C.	(*iii*)	(*i*)	(*iv*)	(*ii*)
D.	(*i*)	(*ii*)	(*iii*)	(*iv*)

24. The Self evident principle of criminal justice is based on:

A. *Nullum crimen sine lege, nulla poena sine lege*
B. Perils of his life and liberty on refusal of bail
C. Simple Principles based on corrective law
D. To avoid purposeless cruelty

25. What is the basic justification on the law of conspiracy?

A. It does not allow a preventive action because an act of conspiracy is derived when the crime results
B. It dispenses the difficult requirement of proximity in attempt
C. The momentum justifies punishment
D. The object is simply to make of a crime

26. Which one of the expressive factors does not constitute sedition?

A. Disapprobation of the government
B. Excite disrespect against government
C. Commenting on administrative actions of the government
D. Attempting to excite disaffection against government

27. The right to private defence against an act done by a public servant is not available:

A. When it is discharged in good faith
B. When it is attempted to be done by him
C. When it was done while he was not in his office
D. When it is strictly to be justifiable by law

28. Which of the conditions are essential for enhanced punishment to an offender with previous conviction?

A. The previous conviction must have been for not less than 3 years of imprisonment
B. The subsequent offence is not punishable with imprisonment for more than 3 years
C. The offence must be an offence relating to property or coin or government stamp
D. The previous conviction was not in India

29. *Non - Compos mentis* denotes:

A. Every person is considered to be sane unless contrary is proved
B. When a criminal act is performed during derrangement

C. When the cognitive facilities are such that he does not know what he has done
D. Non - serene memory not from birth

30. In which of the conditions the act will not be wrongful confinement?
A. Circumscribing limits
B. Malice
C. Moral force
D. Mistaken exercise of power

31. Which of the following statement is correct?
A. A publisher is responsible for publishing a defamatory statement for first time only and not for repeating it
B. Only editor and not printer and publisher are responsible for that defamatory statement in the newspaper
C. Defamatory imputation concerning any person may be conveyed obliquely or indirectly, or by way of question, conjecture, exclamation or by irony
D. The court does not distinguish between "character" and "reputation" for fixing liability against defamation

32. Read Assertion (A) and Reason (R) and answer using the code given below:

Assertion (A): Redemption of the damaged environment is a part of the process of sustainable development and as such polluter in liable to pay the cost of the individual sufferers as well as the cost of reversing the damaged ecology

Reason (R): "Polluter pays principle" is part of the environmental jurisprudence of this country

Codes:

A. Both (A) and (R) are correct and (R) is the correct explanation of (A)
B. Both (A) and (R) are correct and (R) is not the correct explanation of (A)
C. (A) is true, but (R) is false
D. (A) is false, but (R) is true

33. Which one of the following principle is associated with "Trial Smelter" case?
A. Principle of sustainable development
B. No state has a right to use or permit the use of its territory so as to cause injury by fumes in the territory of another
C. Redemption of the damaged environment is a part of the process of sustainable development
D. Placing a duty on the State to hold environmental resources in trust for the benefit of public

34. Match List-I with List-II and give the correct answer by using the code given below:

List-I	List-II
(*a*) National Environ-mental Tribunal	(*i*) Basel Convention, 1989
(*b*) "Doctrine of *Sic utere tuo ut alienum non leadas*"	(*ii*) Rio Declaration
(*c*) To stop and prevent the international traffic in dumping and resultant accumulation of toxic and dangerous products and wastes	(*iii*) Kyoto Protocol, 1997
(*d*) Convention or climate change strengthened	(*iv*) Principle 21 and 22 of Stockhalm Declarations

Codes:

	(*a*)	(*b*)	(*c*)	(*d*)
A.	(*i*)	(*iii*)	(*iv*)	(*ii*)
B.	(*iv*)	(*ii*)	(*i*)	(*iii*)
C.	(*ii*)	(*iv*)	(*i*)	(*iii*)
D.	(*iii*)	(*ii*)	(*i*)	(*iv*)

35. Which one of the following statement is wrong?
A. Every person enjoys the right to a wholesome environment which is a facet of the right to life guaranteed under Art 21 of the Constitution of India
B. The power confered under an Environmental Statute may be exercised only to advance Environment Protection and not for a purpose that would defeat the object of the law

C. Financial constraints of the government may be a reasonable factor to exonorate the Government/Municipal bodies from performing its statutory liability

D. Precautionary principle imposes the onus of proof on the developer to show his or her action is environmentally benign

36. The Supreme Court in which one of the following cases observed that, "the issue of pollution should not be resolved at the cost of the poor people's livelihood"?

A. Indian Council for Enviro Legal Action v. Union of India

B. Municipal Council, Ratlam v. Vardichand

C. M.C. Metha v. Union of India

D. T.N. Godavarman Thimmulpaad v. Union of India

37. Under the Wild Life Protection Act, the boundaries of a National Park shall be made in one of the following way:

A. By passing a resolution in the Parliament

B. By passing a resolution in the Legislature of a State

C. By passing a resolution both in the Parliament and State Legislature

D. By passing a resolution in the Municipal Body and State Legislature

38. 'Basel Convention' is associated with one of the following conventions on:

A. International Trade in Endangered Species of Wild Fauna and Flora

B. The control of transboundary movements of Hazardous Wastes and their disposal

C. Climate Change

D. Protection of the ozone layer

39. Which of the following jurists deny legal character of international law?

(*a*) Habbes (*b*) Pufendorf

(*c*) Oppenheim (*d*) Starke

Codes:

A. Only (*a*)

B. Both (*a*) and (*b*)

C. (*a*), (*b*) and (*c*)

D. (*a*), (*b*), (*c*) and (*d*) all

40. In which of the following cases the world court by majority has taken the view that the sources of law are not hierarchal but are necessarily complimentary and inter related?

A. Nicaragua v. U.S.A

B. Frontier Dispute (Burkina Faso v. Mali)

C. Portugal v. India

D. Case concerning the Temple of Preah Vihear

41. Who of the following has viewed that there is legal duty on the part of the existing states to recognise any community that has in fact acquired the characteristics of Statehood?

A. Oppenheim B. Lauterpacht

C. Philip C. Jessup D. Anzilloti

42. Which of the following statement/statements is/are correct?

(*a*) In Nottelohm's case the International Court of Justice held that in respect of grant of nationality there is no obligation of the states if that man has no relationship with the State of Naturalisation

(*b*) In famous Re lynch case it was held that if a person is not a citizen of any state he will be called Stateless

(*c*) Nationality is the principal link between an individual and international law

(*d*) The Convention on the Reduction of Statelessness was adopted in 1959 by the General Assembly

Codes:

A. Only (*a*) is correct

B. (*a*), (*b*) and (*c*) are correct

C. (*b*), (*c*) and (*d*) are correct

D. (*a*) and (*c*) both are correct

43. Read both Assertion (A) and Reason (R) and give the correct answer by using the code given below:

Assertion (A): It is a very important principle of International Law that extradition for political crimes is not allowed.

Reason (R): Stoeck v. The Public Trustee is a leading case relating to non - extradition of political criminals.

Codes:

A. Both (A) and (R) are correct and (R) is the correct explanation of (A)

B. Both (A) and (R) are correct, but (R) is not the correct explanation of (A)

C. (A) is correct, but (R) is wrong

D. (A) is wrong, but (R) is correct

44. Which of the following statement/statements is/are not correct?

(*a*) United Nations Declaration on Territorial Asylum was unanimously adopted in 1977 by the General Assembly

(*b*) Article 14 of the 1948 Universal Declaration of Human Rights makes obligatory by states to grant Asylum

(*c*) The international court of justice explained the distinction between 'Territorial asylum' and 'diplomatic asylum' in the Colombia v. Perus

(*d*) The Convention on the status of Refugees, 1951 entered into force on April 22, 1954

Codes:

A. Only (*a*) is not correct

B. (*a*) and (*d*) are not correct

C. (*a*), (*b*) and (*c*) all are not correct

D. (*a*), (*b*), (*c*) and (*d*) all are not correct

45. Which of the following statement/statements is/are correct?

(*a*) The General Assembly consists of all the members of the United Nations. Each member may not have not more than five representatives in the General Assembly

(*b*) China, Russia, America, Britain and Italy are the permanent members of the security Council

(*c*) The members of the Economic and Social Council are elected by the security council, one - third of its members are elected every year by the security council for a term of five years

(*d*) All members of the United Nations are *ipso facto* the members of the Statute of International Court of Justice

Codes:

A. Only (*a*) and (*d*) are correct

B. (*a*), (*b*) and (*c*) are correct

C. (*b*), (*c*) and (*d*) are correct

D. (*a*), (*b*), (*c*) and (*d*) all are correct

46. Advisory opinion can be given by the International Court of Justice on legal question:

A. On the request of Security Council only

B. On the request of the General Assembly only

C. On the request of General Assembly or the Security Council both

D. On the request of the Economic and Social Council if authorised by the Security Council

47. Read both Assertion (A) and Reason (R) and answer using the code given below:

Assertion (A): In Mithila, a widow cannot adopt at all, not even if she has the express authority of her husband.

Reason (R) : A widow may adopt under the authority from her husband.

Codes:

A. Both (A) and (R) are correct and (R) is the correct explanation of (A)

B. Both (A) and (R) are correct and (R) is not correct explanation of (A)

C (A) is correct, but (R) is false

D. (A) is false, but (R) is correct

48. In which of the following cases, the Supreme Court held that "We are not prepared to express any definite opinion on the question whether there can be two Karta of a Joint Hindu Family".

A. Moraka Properties v. Biharilal Moraka

B. Union of India v. Sree Ram Bohra

C. Nopany Investment v. Santosh Singh

D. Commissioner of Income Tax v. Govindram Sugar Mills

49. In which of the following case, the court held that, "Divorce is good in law through bad in Theology"?

A. Shah Bano case B. Bai Tahira case

C. Shamim Ara case D. Sarabai case

50. In Muslim law "Hizanat" related to:
A. Father's custody of child
B. Brother's custody of child
C. Mother's custody of child
D. Sister's custody of child

51. Match the List-I with List-II and indicate the correct answer using the code given below:

List-I	List-II
(*a*) Nijhawan v Nijhawan	(*i*) Dowry
(*b*) Daniel Latifi v Union of India	(*ii*) Uniform civil code
(*c*) Husain Ara v Zubaida Begum	(*iii*) Cruelty
(*d*) Gujarat Woman Workers Association Case	(*iv*) Maintenance

Codes:

	(*a*)	(*b*)	(*c*)	(*d*)
A.	(*iii*)	(*iv*)	(*i*)	(*ii*)
B.	(*i*)	(*iii*)	(*ii*)	(*iv*)
C.	(*iii*)	(*ii*)	(*i*)	(*iv*)
D.	(*ii*)	(*iv*)	(*iii*)	(*i*)

52. Read Assertion (A) and Reason (R) and answer using the code given below:

Assertion (A): 'Option of Puberty' is an easy process to repudiate the marriage under Hindu Law.

Reason (R): "Option of Puberty" is not an easy process to repudiate the marriage under Muslim Law.

Codes:
A. Both (A) and (R) are correct and (R) is the correct explanation of (A)
B. Both (A) and (R) are correct and (R) is not the correct explanation of (A)
C. (A) is correct (R) is false
D. (A) is false (R) is correct

53. The Dissolution of Muslim Marriages Act, 1939 brought various grounds for dissolution of marriage based on the principles of:
A. Shia Schools
B. Hanafi School
C. Shafai School
D. Maliki School

54. A muslim husband has E-mailed Talaq letter writing "I divorce you, I divorce you, I divorce you," without the signature of witnesses, Talaq will be:
A. Valid
B. Voidable
C. Void
D. Neither valid nor void or no talaq

55. Sec 2(*d*) of 'The protection of Human Rights Act, 1993 defines ,"human rights" means the rights relating to .... of the individual guaranteed by the Constitution or embodied in the International Covenants and enforceable by courts in India. Fill in the blank.
A. Life, Liberty, Equality and Dignity
B. Life, Equality, Liberty and Dignity
C. Life, Equality, Dignity and Liberty
D. Life, Liberty, Dignity and Equality

56. Which one of the following pairs is correctly matched with regard to National Human Rights Commission of India, under the Protection of Human Rights Act, 1993?
A. Sec 3 ...... Appointment of chairperson and other members
B. Sec 4 ...... Removal of a member of the commission
C. Sec 5 ...... Member to act as chairperson in certain times
D. Sec 6 ...... Term of office of members

57. Which one of the following pairs is not correctly matched with regard to the duration of the position of the members/chairpersons of N.H.R.C of India?
A. Justice S. Rajendra Babu – 02.04.2007 to 31.05.2009
B. Justice K.G. Bala Krishnan – 07.06.2010 to 11.05.2015
C. Justice Ms. M. Fathima Beevi – 03.11.1993 to 24.01.1997
D. Justice V.S. Malimat – 05.08.1994 to 12.10.1998

58. Match List-I with List-II and give the correct answer by using the code given below:

List-I

(*a*) Optional Protocol to the Convention on the Elimination of All Forms of Discrimination against Women

(*b*) Declaration on the Elimination of violence against women

(*c*) Convention on the Elimination of All forms of Discrimination against Women

(*d*) Declaration on the protection of women and children in Emergency and Armed conflict

List-II

(*i*) Proclaimed by the U.N. General Assembly resolution 3318 (XXIX) of 14 December, 1974

(*ii*) Adopted and opened for signature, ratification and accession by the U.N. General Assembly resolution 34/180 of 18 December, 1979

(*iii*) Proclaimed by the U.N. General Assembly resolution 48/104 of 20 December, 1993

(*iv*) Adopted by the U.N. General Assembly Resolution 54/4 of 6 October, 1999 and opened for signature, ratification and accession on 10 December, 1999

Codes:

	(*a*)	(*b*)	(*c*)	(*d*)
A.	(*iv*)	(*iii*)	(*ii*)	(*i*)
B.	(*iv*)	(*i*)	(*ii*)	(*iii*)
C.	(*ii*)	(*iv*)	(*i*)	(*iii*)
D.	(*iii*)	(*iv*)	(*i*)	(*ii*)

59. Which of the following statement/statements is/are incorrect?

(*a*) Optional Protocol to the Convention on the Rights of the Child on the involvement of Children in Armed Conflict was adopted and opened for signature, ratification and accession by the United Nations General Assembly resolution 54/263 of 25 May, 2000

(*b*) Worst forms of Child Labour Convention, 1999 (No.182) was adopted on 15 June, 1999 by the General Conference of the International Labour Organisation at its eighty - seventh session

(*c*) Minimum Age Convention, 1973 (No. 138) was adopted on 26 August, 1973 by the General Conference of the International Labour Organisation at its Fifty Eighth session

(*d*) Convention on the Rights of the Child was adopted and opened for signature, ratification and accession by the United Nations General Council Resolution 44/25 of 20 November, 1989

Codes:

A. (*a*), (*b*) and (*c*) are incorrect

B. (*b*), (*c*) and (*d*) are incorrect

C. (*a*) and (*b*) are incorrect

D. (*a*), (*b*), (*c*) and (*d*) all are incorrect

60. The division of Human Rights into three generations was initially proposed in 1979 by one of the following Czech Jurist at the International Institute of Human Rights in Strasbourg?

A. Karel Vasak B. Charles O. Lee

C. Maurice Cranston D. Frederic Bastial

61. Arrange the following decided cases on the right to health in a chronological order and choose the answer by using the code given below:

(*a*) Paschim Banga Khet Mazdoor Samiti v. State of West Bengal

(*b*) Paramananda Katara v. Union of India

(*c*) Social Jurists v. Govt. of NCT of Delhi

(*d*) Sahara House v. Union of India

Codes:

A. (*b*), (*a*), (*c*), (*d*)

B. (*d*), (*a*), (*b*), (*c*)

C. (*b*), (*d*), (*c*), (*a*)

D. (*c*), (*d*), (*a*), (*b*)

62. Which of the following statement(s) is/are correct with regard to 'absolute liability' principle laid down in M.C. Mehta v. Union of India. Answer by using the code below:

(*a*) The principle was approved except as to quantum of damages in Charan Lal Sahu v. Union of India (*b*) The principle in determining compensation was applied in Union Carbide Corporation v. Union of India

(*c*) The compensation to be awarded must have some broad correlation not only with magnitude and capacity of the enterprise but also with the harm caused by it was held in Deepak Nitrite v. State of Gujrat.

(*d*) The principle is not followed in India because Parliament could not pass yet Public Liability Insurance Bill, 1991

Codes:

A. Only (*a*) is correct
B. (*a*) and (*b*) are correct
C. (*a*), (*b*) and (*c*) are correct
D. (*a*), (*b*), (*c*) and (*d*) are correct

63. Which of the following pair is correctly matched?

A. Defamation published in permanent form – Slander
B. Libel is recognized as offence – England
C. Truth of defamatory matter is no defence – Civil law
D. Action lies for defamatory statement – Absolute Privilege

64. Read Assertion (A) and Reason (R) and answer by using the code below:

Assertion (A): The existence of a duty to take care is essential before a person can be held liable in negligence.

Reason (R): The standard of care required is not a matter of law and does vary according to the individuals although it does not vary according to the circumstances.

Codes:

A. Both (A) and (R) are true and (R) is the correct explanation of (A)
B. Both (A) and (R) are true and (R) is not the correct explanation of (A)
C. (A) is right, but (R) is wrong
D. (A) is wrong, but (R) is right

65. Match List-I with List-II with regard to tort of nuisance and answer by using code below:

List-I	**List-II**
(*a*) Burden of proof, once nuisance is proved	(*i*) Prescription
(*b*) Remedy for the private nuisance	(*ii*) Occupier
(*c*) Right to action for nuisance of a temporary nature	(*iii*) Abatement
(*d*) Right to commit a private nuisance may be acquired	(*iv*) Defendant

Codes:

	(*a*)	(*b*)	(*c*)	(*d*)
A.	(*iii*)	(*ii*)	(*iv*)	(*i*)
B.	(*ii*)	(*iv*)	(*iii*)	(*i*)
C.	(*i*)	(*ii*)	(*iii*)	(*iv*)
D.	(*iv*)	(*iii*)	(*ii*)	(*i*)

66. Read Assertion (A) and Reason (R) and answer by using code below:

Assertion (A): According to the 'law of tort' every wrongful act for which there is no justification or excuse to be treated as a tort.

Reason (R): Theory of 'pigeon - hole' was propounded by Salmond.

Codes:

A. Both (A) and (R) are true and (R) is the correct explanation of (A)
B. Both (A) and (R) are true and (R) is not the correct explanation of (A)
C. (A) is right, but (R) is wrong
D. (A) is wrong, but (R) is right

67. The provisions of the Consumer Protection Act shall be:

A. Only in derogation of other law
B. No addition to other law
C. Not in addition and in derogation of other law
D. In addition to and not in derogation of other law

68. Section 19 - A of the Consumer Protection Act provides that State and National Commissions shall hear as expeditiously as possible and an endeavour shall be made to finally dispose of the appeal within ninety days from the date of its admission. The Section further empowers the Commissions to make following orders; answer by using code below:

(*a*) Ordinarily grant no adjournment unless sufficient cause

(*b*) To impose costs occasioned by adjournment

(*c*) Record the reason for delay while disposing of the appeal

(*d*) Dispose of the appeal ex *parte*

Codes:

A. (*a*) and (*b*) are correct

B. (*a*), (*b*) and (*c*) are correct

C. (*a*), (*b*) and (*d*) are correct

D. (*b*), (*c*) and (*d*) are correct

69. Read Assertion (A) and Reason (R) and answer using code below:

Assertion (A): Where a bill is unintentionally cancelled by the holder or his agent and the cancellation is not apparent thereon, the bill is discharged.

Reason (R): Above principle is laid down in Section 82 of the Negotiable Instruments Act.

Codes:

A. Both (A) and (R) are wrong

B. Both (A) and (R) are right

C. (A) is right, but (R) is wrong

D. (A) is wrong, but (R) is right

70. Match List-I with List-II and select the correct answer using the code given below:

List-I	**List-II**
(*a*) Partnership not created by status	(*i*) CST v. K. Kelukutty
(*b*) Essentials of partnership	(*ii*) Kshetra Mohan v. Commr. of Excess Profit Tax
(*c*) Joint Hindu Family and partnership	(*iii*) Rakesh Kumar Dinesh Kumar v. U.G. Hotels and Resorts Ltd.
(*d*) Partnership between outsiders and joint family	(*iv*) Ganpat v. Annaji

Codes:

	(*a*)	(*b*)	(*c*)	(*d*)
A.	(*iii*)	(*i*)	(*iv*)	(*ii*)
B.	(*i*)	(*iii*)	(*iv*)	(*ii*)
C.	(*iii*)	(*i*)	(*ii*)	(*iv*)
D.	(*iv*)	(*ii*)	(*i*)	(*iii*)

71. Match List-I with List-II and select the correct answer using the code given below:

List-I (Duties of partners)	**List-II (Relevant section under the Indian Partnership Act)**
(*a*) Duty of absolute good faith	(*i*) Section 16 (*b*)
(*b*) Duty not to compete	(*ii*) Sections 12 (*b*) and 13 (f)
(*c*) Duty of due deligence	(*iii*) Section 10
(*d*) Duty to indemnify for fraud	(*iv*) Section 9

Codes:

	(*a*)	(*b*)	(*c*)	(*d*)
A.	(*i*)	(*iv*)	(*ii*)	(*iii*)
B.	(*iv*)	(*i*)	(*ii*)	(*iii*)
C.	(*iv*)	(*i*)	(*iii*)	(*ii*)
D.	(*ii*)	(*iii*)	(*i*)	(*iv*)

72. Read Assertion (A) and Reason (R) and answer using code given below:

Assertion (A): "Goods" means every kind of movable property including actionable claims and money and excludes stock and shares, growing crops, grass and things attached to or forming part of the land which are agreed to be severed before sale or under the contract of sale.

Reason (R): Above principle is laid down in Section 2 (7) of the Sale of Goods Act.

Codes:

A. Both (A) and (R) are right

B. Both (A) and (R) are wrong

C. (A) is wrong, but (R) is right

D. (A) is right, but (R) is wrong

of a public as opposed to a purely private or domestic character has to determine matters affecting subjects provided always that it has a duty to act judicially."

15. According to Sec 3(3)(a) of Lokpal and Lokayukta Act, 2013—A person shall be eligible to be appointed as a Judicial Member if he is or has been a Judge of the Supreme Court or is or has been a Chief Justice of a High Court.

17. Jeremy Bentham was a positivist while the rest belong to the naturalist school of Jurisprudence.

19. Article 141 of the Indian Constitution states—The law declared by the Supreme Court shall be binding on all courts within the territory of India.

24. Nullum crimen sine lege, nulla poena sine lege means that crimes and corresponding penalties should be declared in unambiguous statutory text before the commission of the offence. According to this principle a person cannot or should not face criminal punishment except for an act that was criminalized by law before he/she performed the act.

26. According to section 124A of the Indian Penal Code: Whoever, by words, either spoken or written, or by signs, or by visible representation, or otherwise, brings or attempts to bring into hatred or contempt, or excites or attempts to excite disaffection towards the Government established by law in India shall be punished with imprisonment for life, to which fine may be added, or with imprisonment which may extend to three years, to which fine may be added, or with fine.

Explanation 1: The expression "disaffection" includes disloyalty and all feelings of enmity.

Explanation 2: Comments expressing disapprobation of the measures of the Government with a view to obtain their alteration by lawful means, without exciting or attempting to excite hatred, contempt or disaffection, do not constitute an offence under this section.

Explanation 3: Comments expressing disapprobation of the administrative or other action of the Government without exciting or attempting to excite hatred, contempt or disaffection, do not constitute an offence under this section.

27. According to Section 99 of the Indian Penal Code: There is no right of private defence against an act which does not reasonable cause the apprehension of death or of grievous hurt, if done, or attempted to be done, by a public servant acting in good faith under colour of his office, though that act, may not be strictly justifiable by law.

Further, the explanations appended to this section provide that

- A person is not deprived of the right of private defence against an act done, or attempted to be done, by a public servant, as such, unless he knows or has reason to believe, that the person doing the act is such public servant.
- A person is not deprived of the right of private defence against an act done, or attempted to be done, by the direction of a public servant, unless he knows, or has reason to believe, that the person doing the act is acting by such direction, or unless such person states the authority under which he acts, or if he has authority in writing, unless he produces such authority, if demanded.

28. According to section 75 of Indian Penal Code: Whoever, having been convicted, by a Court in India, of an offence punishable under Chapter XII or Chapter XVII of this Code with imprisonment of either description for a term of three years or upwards, shall be guilty of any offence punishable under either of those Chapters with like imprisonment for the like term, shall be subject for every such subsequent offence to imprisonment for life, or to imprisonment of either description for a term which may extend to ten years.

33. Trail Smelter Arbitration was a trans-boundary environmental damages case between US and Canada in 1941. A trail smelter being owned and operated by a Canadian corporation was causing environmental damage in Washington City of USA. In the arbitration in which USA demanded injunction on operation of the trail smelter and damages for the environmental damage already sustained it was held that it is the responsibility of the state in whose jurisdiction the corporation is situate to protect other states from environmental hazards (air pollution in this case) arising out of such activity.

37. Section 35(5) of the Wildlife Protection Act states—No alteration of the boundaries of a National Park shall be made except on a resolution passed by the Legislature of the State.

40. In Nicaragua v. USA (1985) the ICJ was confronted with the issue whether USA violated the principles of non-intervention and prohibition of use of force against Nicaragua. On the issue whether certain sources of international law override other sources the court observed that the sources of international law are complimentary to each other and not set out in any hierarchical order. This is especially true in the case of treaties and customs.

41. Sir Hersch Lauterpacht is one of the most distinguished and eminent international law jurist of the 20th century. He held the view that states are under a duty to recognize new states once the essentials of statehood are met. However, this view is not supported by state practice as recognition is generally treated to be a political act and states frequently delay or grant recognition promptly because of political considerations.

42. Statement (*a*) is correct.

Statement (*b*) is incorrect. In Re Lynch case it was held that statelessness shall not be imposed as a penalty for a crime.

Statement (*c*) is correct.

Statement (*d*) is incorrect. The convention on the Reduction of Statelessness was adopted in the year 1961.

43. Stoeck v Public Trustee is a landmark case on nationality of a person and the concept of statelessness.

44. Statement (*a*) is incorrect. UN Declaration on Territorial Asylum was adopted on 14 December 1967.

Statement (*b*) is incorrect. Article 14 of the UDHR simply gives everyone a right "to seek and to enjoy asylum" but does not make it obligatory upon the states to grant asylum.

Statement (*c*) is incorrect. In Asylum Case (Columbia v Peru 1950) the ICJ discussed whether there exist any local custom in Latin American countries to grant asylum in embassies.

Statement (*d*) is correct.

45. Statement (*a*) is correct.

Statement (*b*) is incorrect. Permanent members of Security council are UK, USA, Russia, China & France.

Statement (*c*) is incorrect. The Council's members are elected by the General Assembly for overlapping three-year terms.

Statement (*d*) is correct.

46. Only states may be parties before the ICJ. However for certain international organizations a special advisory procedure is available. This procedure is available to five United Nations organs, fifteen specialized agencies and one related organization.

47. In Mithila school consent of husband is sine qua non for adoption. Since after death this consent cannot be obtained so effectively widows cannot adopt under mithila school.

50. Hizanat means right to custody of a child. In Muslim law, the right to custody of a child primarily belongs to the mother as this is believed to be in the best interest of the child. Mother cannot be denied this right until and unless she is not disqualified or found guilty of misconduct. In different schools this right to custody shifts in favour of father after the child completes a certain age or gains puberty.

55. According to Section 2(d) of Human Rights Act, 1993 defines human rights to mean the rights relating to life, liberty, equality and dignity of the individual guaranteed by the Constitution or embodied in the International Covenants and enforceable by courts in India.

59. Statement (*a*) is correct.

Statement (*b*) is incorrect. Worst forms of Child Labour Convention was signed on 17 June, 1999.

Statement (*c*) is incorrect. Minimum Age Convention was adopted on 26th June, 1973.

Statement (*d*) is incorrect. Convention on the Rights of the Child was opened for signing on 28th February, 2012.

60. Karel Vasak was a Czech jurist who proposed classification of human rights into three generations. He classified human rights into First Generation human rights, Second Generation human rights and Third Generation human rights.

62. Statement (*d*) is incorrect. Public Liability Insurance Act, 1991 came into force on 1st April, 1991. Remaining statements are correct.

67. Section 3 of the Consumer Protection Act provides that—The provisions of this Act shall be in addition to and not in derogation of the provisions of any other law for the time being in force.

68. There is no provision to dispose of the appeal ex parte in Section 19.

69. According to section 82 of Negotiable Instruments Act, the maker, acceptor or indorser respectively of a negotiable instrument is discharged from liability thereon—

(*a*) by cancellation—to a holder thereof who cancels such acceptor's or indorser's name with intent to discharge him, and to all parties claiming under such holder;

(*b*) by release—to a holder thereof who otherwise discharges such maker, acceptor or indorser, and to all parties deriving title under such holder after notice of such discharge;

(*c*) by payment—to all parties thereto, if the instrument is payable to bearer, or has been indorsed in blank, and such maker, acceptor or indorser makes payment in due course of the amount due thereon.

75. In Attorney General v Great Eastern Railway, the doctrine of ultravires was given a liberal and reasonable interpretation. A parliamentary act authorized a company to construct railways. This company entered into a contract with other companies to provide certain rolling stocks. The validity of this contract was assailed on the ground of it being ultravires the incorporating documents of the railway company. Held, that such a power though not expressly stated but was warranted by the statutory purpose for which the company was brought into existence—'whatever may fairly be regarded as incidental to, or consequential upon, those things which the Legislature has authorized, ought not (unless expressly prohibited) to be held, by judicial construction, to be ultravires.'

Previous Paper (Solved)

UGC-NET-JRF & Assistant Professor Exam Law, January-2017*

PAPER-II

Note: *This paper contains fifty (50) objective type questions of two (2) marks each. All questions are compulsory.*

1. The Preamble to the Constitution of India proclaims that, 'we, the people of India,' have established:

A. A Sovereign, Socialist, Democratic, Republic only
B. A Sovereign, Secular, Democratic, Republic only
C. A Secular, Socialist, Democratic, Republic only
D. A Sovereign, Socialist, Secular, Democratic Republic

2. Match List-I with List-II and give the correct answer using the codes given below:

List-I	List-II
(*a*) Article 16(3) Amended by	(*i*) 1st Amendment
(*b*) Article 19(5) Amended by	(*ii*) 17th Amendment
(*c*) Article 19(6) Amended by	(*iii*) 7th Amendment
(*d*) Article 31A(2)(*a*) Amended by	(*iv*) 44th Amendment

Codes:

	(*a*)	(*b*)	(*c*)	(*d*)
A.	(*iii*)	(*iv*)	(*i*)	(*ii*)
B.	(*iii*)	(*i*)	(*ii*)	(*iv*)
C.	(*i*)	(*ii*)	(*iv*)	(*iii*)
D.	(*ii*)	(*iii*)	(*i*)	(*iv*)

3. Read Assertion (A) and Reason (R) and give the correct answer with the help of codes given below:

Assertion (A): Under Art. 226 of the Constitution of India the High Court has discretionary remedy to issue writs.

Reason (R): If the High Court is satisfied that the aggrieved party can have an adequate remedy elsewhere it can refuse to grant writ.

Codes:

A. (A) and (R) are true and (R) is the correct explanation of (A).
B. (A) and (R) are true, but (R) is not the correct explanation of (A).
C. (A) is true, but (R) is false.
D. (A) is false, but (R) is true.

4. Match List-I with List-II and select the correct answer using the codes given below:

List-I (Cases)	List-II (Principles)
(*a*) Indira Nehru Gandhi v/s. Raj Narain	(*i*) Departmental bias
(*b*) Gullapalli Nageswara Rao v/s. A.P.S.R.T.C.	(*ii*) Preventive detention
(*c*) Fagu Shaw v/s. State of W.B.	(*iii*) Rights of inmates of protective homes
(*d*) Upendra Baxi v/s. State of U.P.	(*iv*) Rule of law

Codes:

	(*a*)	(*b*)	(*c*)	(*d*)
A.	(*iv*)	(*i*)	(*ii*)	(*iii*)
B.	(*i*)	(*iv*)	(*ii*)	(*iii*)
C.	(*iv*)	(*i*)	(*iii*)	(*ii*)
D.	(*ii*)	(*iii*)	(*i*)	(*iv*)

* Exam held on 22 January 2017.

5. "The Fundamental Duties incorporated in Article 51A of the Constitution of India are mere reminder to the citizens, with no enforceability, to ensure their compliance" was said by:

A. Justice J.S. Verma
B. Justice O. Chinnapa Reddy
C. Justice Y.V. Chandrachud
D. Justice P.N. Bhagwati

6. Justice Mukherjee C.J., speaking for the court, stated "that though the executive power is vested in the president, the president is only a formal or constitutional head of the executive. The real power is vested in the Council of Ministers on whose aid and advice the president acts in the exercise of his functions," in the following case:

A. U.N.R. Rao v/s. Indira Gandhi
B. Ram Jawaya Kapur v/s. State of Punjab
C. Jayantilal Amratlal Shodan v/s. F.N. Rao
D. Sardarilal v/s. Union of India

7. The right of a person to be appointed as a guardian of his minor children under the personal law is not a fundamental right was decided by the Supreme Court in one of the following cases:

A. Mohd-Aslam v/s. Union of India
B. Sahifzada Saiyed Muhammed Amirabbas Abbasi v/s. State of Madyabharat
C. Khatri v/s. State of Bihar
D. Mohd. Faruk v/s. State of M.P.

8. According to Austin the positive law has following three attributes:

A. command, sovereign, obedience
B. command, sovereign, sanction
C. command, obedience, sanction
D. sovereign, obedience, sanction

9. "The movement of progressive societies has hitherto been a movement from status to contract." This statement is of:

A. Hegel B. Savigny
C. Henry Main D. Puchta

10. Match List-I with List-II and give the correct answer using the codes given below:

List-I	List-II
(*a*) The Concept of Law	(*i*) Austin
(*b*) The Province of Jurisprudence Determined	(*ii*) Bentham
(*c*) Some Reflections on Jurisprudence	(*iii*) Hart
(*d*) Limits of Jurisprudence Defined	(*iv*) Buckland

Codes:

	(*a*)	(*b*)	(*c*)	(*d*)
A.	(*iii*)	(*ii*)	(*i*)	(*iv*)
B.	(*iii*)	(*i*)	(*iv*)	(*ii*)
C.	(*i*)	(*ii*)	(*iii*)	(*iv*)
D.	(*iv*)	(*i*)	(*ii*)	(*iii*)

11. Which one of the following is not a theory of corporate personality?

A. Fiction Theory B. Interest Theory
C. Bracket Theory D. Will Theory

12. 'A' has a house and nobody should interfere with the enjoyment of proprietary right over the house. This right is called:

A. Personal right B. Imperfect right
C. Right in rem D. Right in personam

13. Match List-I with List-II and give the correct answer using the codes given below:

List-I	List-II
(*a*) Theory of Volksgeist	(*i*) Bentham
(*b*) Theory of Social Interest	(*ii*) Ihering
(*c*) Theory of Utilitarian Individualism	(*iii*) Burke
(*d*) Gradual and organic process theory	(*iv*) Savigny

Codes:

	(*a*)	(*b*)	(*c*)	(*d*)
A.	(*i*)	(*ii*)	(*iii*)	(*iv*)
B.	(*iv*)	(*ii*)	(*iii*)	(*i*)
C.	(*iv*)	(*ii*)	(*i*)	(*iii*)
D.	(*iii*)	(*i*)	(*iv*)	(*ii*)

14. Who has remarked that "It is both practically inconvenient and also contrary to the best juristic thought to deny its (International law) legal character"?

A. H.L.A. Hart B. J.G. Starke

C. Edward Collins D. J.L. Brierly

15. Read both Assertion (A) and Reason (R) and give the correct answer using the codes given below:

Assertion (A): 'Res Judicata', 'estoppel', etc., are examples of the General Principles of Law recognised by the civilised states.

Reason (R): In the case of diversion of water from Muese, the Permanent Court of International Justice applied 'Res Judicata' and 'Estoppel'.

Codes:

A. Both (A) and (R) are correct and (R) is correct explanation of (A).

B. Both (A) and (R) are correct, but (R) is not correct explanation of (A).

C. (A) is correct, but (R) is wrong.

D. (A) is wrong, but (R) is correct.

16. Which of the following is not a "theory" propounded to explain the relationship between International Law and Municipal Law?

A. Transformation Theory

B. Delegation Theory

C. Fiction Theory

D. Specific Adoption Theory

17. Which of the following statement/s is/are correct? Answer using the codes below:

(*a*) The Charter of the United Nations came into force on October 24, 1945.

(*b*) The purposes of the United Nations are enshrined in Article 2 of the Charter.

(*c*) The seventh and the last principle of the United Nations states that nothing contained in present Charter shall authorise the United Nations to intervene in matters which are essentially within domestic jurisdiction of any state.

(*d*) The provision relating to suspension of a Member finds mention in Article 3 of the charter.

Codes:

A. Only (*a*) and (*c*) are correct.

B. (*a*), (*b*) and (*c*) are correct.

C. (*b*), (*c*) and (*d*) are correct.

D. (*a*), (*b*), (*c*) and (*d*) all are correct.

18. Which of the following statement/s is/are correct? Answer using the codes below:

(*a*) "Mediation" is not "pacific means" of settlement of International Disputes.

(*b*) "Pious Fund Case" is an important decision given by the Permanent Court of Arbitration.

(*c*) "Retorsion" is a compulsive or 'coercive' means of settlement of International Disputes.

(*d*) A leading case on "Reprisal" is the "Naulilaa Incident".

Codes:

A. Only (*b*) is correct.

B. (*a*), (*b*) and (*c*) are correct.

C. Only (*b*), (*c*) and (*d*) are correct.

D. (*a*), (*b*), (*c*) and (*d*) all are correct.

19. Which of the following statement/s is/are incorrect? Answer using the codes below:

(*a*) The Commission on Human Rights was established by the Economic and Social Council in February, 1946.

(*b*) The General Assembly decided to replace U.N. Human Rights Commission by Human Rights Council Vide Resolution 60/251 of 15 March, 2006.

(*c*) The Human Rights Council concluded its first session at Hague on 30 June, 2007.

(*d*) The Universal Declaration of Human Rights was adopted by the General Assembly by a vote of 48 to nil with eight abstentions.

Codes:

A. Only (*c*) is incorrect.

B. (*a*), (*b*) and (*c*) are incorrect.

C. (*b*), (*c*) and (*d*) are incorrect.
D. (*a*), (*b*), (*c*) and (*d*) are incorrect.

20. Read the following statements and answer with the help of codes given below:

(*a*) Two persons are said to be related to each other by full blood when they are descended from a common ancestor by the same wife.

(*b*) Two persons are said to be related to each other by uterine blood when they are descended from a common ancestress but by different husbands.

(*c*) Two persons are said to be related to each other by half blood when they are descended from a common ancestor by the same wife.

(*d*) Two persons are said to be related to each other by half blood when they are descended from a common ancestor but by different wives.

Codes:

A. (*a*) and (*b*) are correct, but (*c*) and (*d*) are incorrect.
B. (*a*), (*b*) and (*d*) are correct, but (*c*) is incorrect.
C. (*d*) and (*b*) are correct, but (*c*) and (*a*) are incorrect.
D. (*b*) and (*c*) are correct, but (*a*) and (*d*) are incorrect.

21. A person shall not be treated as Buddhist under sec. 2(1) of the Hindu Marriage Act, 1955, if:

A. Both of his parents were Buddhists.
B. His father was a Christian, mother was a Buddhist and he was brought up as a Buddhist child.
C. His father was a Christian, mother was a Buddhist and he was brought up as a Christian child.
D. He was a Muslim and has converted to Buddhist religion.

22. Ancient sources of Hindu law are:

A. Custom, Sruti, Precedent
B. Sruti, Vedas, Custom, Legislation
C. Smritis, Custom, Precedent
D. Sruti, Smritis, Custom, Digests etc.

23. The Muslim Personal Law (Shariat) Application Act, 1937 is applicable to all kinds of property except:

A. Agricultural land, testamentary succession and Charities other than wakfs.
B. Testamentary succession and charities other than wakfs only.
C. Agricultural land and testamentary succession only.
D. Agricultural land and charities other than wakfs only.

24. Match List-I with List-II under the Hindu Marriage Act, 1955 and give the correct answer using the codes given below:

List-I	List-II
(*a*) Age of marriage	(*i*) Section 13(1-A)
(*b*) Breakdown grounds of marriage	(*ii*) Section 8
(*c*) Overriding effect of Act	(*iii*) Section 5(iii)
(*d*) Registration of Marriage	(*iv*) Section 4

Codes:

	(*a*)	(*b*)	(*c*)	(*d*)
A.	(*i*)	(*iii*)	(*ii*)	(*iv*)
B.	(*iii*)	(*i*)	(*iv*)	(*ii*)
C.	(*ii*)	(*iii*)	(*iv*)	(*i*)
D.	(*iv*)	(*iii*)	(*i*)	(*ii*)

25. Presently the Hindu Marriage Act, 1955 recognizes the following theories of divorce:

A. Fault and Mutual Consent
B. Mutual Consent and Breakdown of Marriage
C. Fault, Breakdown of Marriage, Mutual Consent and Customary
D. Fault, Irretrievable Breakdown of Marriage and Mutual Consent

26. Talaq ahsan is:

A. Irrevocable

B. Revocable during the tuhr in which it has been pronounced
C. Revocable until the next successive tuhr
D. Revocable during the period of iddat

27. Match List-I with List-II and select the correct answer using the codes given below:

List-I	List-II
(*a*) Proposal	(*i*) Grainger & Son v. Gough
(*b*) Invitation to make an offer	(*ii*) Maharashtra Rajya Sahakari Kappas Utpadak Panan Mahasabha Ltd. v. Manga Bhaga Chaudhary
(*c*) Communication of acceptance of offer by acceptor himself	(*iii*) Henthorn v. Fraser
(*d*) Revocation of offer	(*iv*) Powell v. Lee

Codes:

	(*a*)	(*b*)	(*c*)	(*d*)
A.	(*ii*)	(*i*)	(*iv*)	(*iii*)
B.	(*i*)	(*ii*)	(*iv*)	(*iii*)
C.	(*ii*)	(*i*)	(*iii*)	(*iv*)
D.	(*iv*)	(*iii*)	(*i*)	(*ii*)

28. Read Assertion (A) and Reason (R) and answer using codes given below:

Assertion (A): An agreement made with consideration is void unless it is in writing and registered.

Reason (R): Because Section 25(1) of the Indian Contract Act stipulates so.

Codes:

A. Both (A) and (R) are right and (R) is correct reason for (A).
B. Both (A) and (R) are wrong.
C. (A) is right, but (R) is wrong.
D. (R) is right, but (A) is wrong.

29. In which one of the following cases doctrine of frustration was laid down?

A. BOI Finance Ltd. v. Custodian
B. Orissa Textile Mills Ltd. v. Ganesh Das
C. Sachidananda Patnaik v. G.P. & Co.
D. Taylor v. Caldwell

30. Which of the following statements is correct?

A. A person who wrongfully rescinds a contract is entitled to compensation for any damage which he has sustained through the non-fulfilment of the contract.
B. A person who rightfully rescinds a contract is not entitled to compensation for any damage which he has sustained through the non-fulfilment of the contract.
C. A person who rightfully rescinds a contract is entitled to compensation for any damage which he has sustained through the non-fulfilment of the contract.
D. A person who rightfully rescinds a contract is entitled to compensation for any damage which he has not sustained through the non-fulfilment of the contract.

31. Every person is competent to contract:

A. who is of the age of minority according to law to which he is subject, and who is of sound mind, and is not disqualified from contracting by any law to which he is subject.
B. who is of the age of majority according to law to which he is not subject, and who is of sound mind, and is not disqualified from contracting by any law to which he is subject.
C. who is of the age of majority according to law to which he is subject, and who is of sound mind, and is not qualified from contracting by any law to which he is subject.
D. who is of the age of majority according to law to which he is subject, and who is of sound mind, and is not disqualified from contracting by any law to which he is subject.

32. Match List-I with List-II and select the correct answer using the codes given below:

List-I (Types of Vitiating elements of a contract)	List-II (Relevant case-law)
(a) Undue influence	(i) Nursey Spg. and Wvg. Co. Ltd., Re
(b) Misrepresentation	(ii) Jaggan Nath v. Secy of State for India
(c) Fraud	(iii) Lancashire Loans v. Black
(d) Mistake	(iv) Derry v. Peek

Codes:

	(a)	(b)	(c)	(d)
A.	(ii)	(iv)	(iii)	(i)
B.	(i)	(iii)	(iv)	(ii)
C.	(iii)	(i)	(iv)	(ii)
D.	(iii)	(i)	(ii)	(iv)

33. Read Assertion (A) and Reason (R) and answer using codes given below:

Assertion (A): Compensation is recoverable for any loss or damage which the parties knew at the time of the contract as unlikely to result from the breach of the contract.

Reason (R): Because above rule is laid down in Hadley v. Baxendale case.

Codes:

A. Both (A) and (R) are correct and (R) is correct reason for (A).

B. Both (A) and (R) are wrong.

C. (A) is right, but (R) is wrong.

D. (R) is right, but (A) is wrong.

34. Match List-I (Name of case) with List-II (Decision of case) using codes below:

List-I (Name of case)	List-II (Decision of case)
(a) Manju Bhatia v. New Delhi Municipal Corporation	(i) Liability of owner of tree for an injury caused by its falling
(b) Municipal Corporation Delhi v. Sushila Devi	(ii) Legal duty of Railway to assure reasonable safety at railway level crossing
(c) Union of India v. Lalman	(iii) Teacher's duty of case towards children when they are taken out on a picnic for fun and swim
(d) M.S. Grewal v. Deepchand Sood	(iv) Liability of builder towards purchasers of flats

Codes:

	(a)	(b)	(c)	(d)
A.	(ii)	(i)	(iii)	(iv)
B.	(i)	(ii)	(iv)	(iii)
C.	(iii)	(iv)	(i)	(ii)
D.	(iv)	(i)	(ii)	(iii)

35. Read Assertion (A) and Reason (R) and answer using codes given below:

Assertion (A): Acts of state are directed against another sovereign state or its sovereign personally or its subjects.

Reason (R): Acts of executive Government in the name of President in normal course of administration are acts of state and are not open to judicial scrutiny.

Codes:

A. Both (A) and (R) are correct and (R) is correct reason of (A).

B. Both (A) and (R) are correct, but (R) is not correct reason of (A).

C. (A) is right, but (R) is wrong.

D. (R) is right, but (A) is wrong.

36. Which of the following is correct? Answer using the codes below:

(a) Corporation is vicariously liable for acts done by its employees.

(b) Minor is liable for the torts committed by him.

(c) Wife is liable under law of torts to her husband if she negligently fractures his legs.

(d) Tort committed by any partner in the ordinary course of business of firm all other partners are liable.

Codes:

A. (*a*), (*b*), (*c*) and (*d*)

B. (*a*), (*b*) and (*c*)

C. (*a*), (*b*) and (*d*)

D. (*a*) and (*d*)

37. In which case the principle 'ubi jin ibi remedium' was recognized?

A. Rylands v. Flecher

B. Asbhy v. White

C. Ashdown v. Samuel Williams

D. Pema Chibber v. Union of India

38. State Government may notify that State Commission may perform its function at other places other than state capital. Who needs to be consulted by the State Government for such notification under Consumer Protection Act?

A. Central Government

B. National Commission

C. State Commission

D. State Commission and High Court

39. Who among the following cannot file a complaint before the District Forum under Section 12 of the Consumer Protection Act?

A. One consumer and not more than one consumer

B. Any recognized consumer association

C. Central and State Government

D. One or more consumers

40. 'The degree of cogence need not reach certainty but it must carry a high degree of probability.'

As per the statement answer using codes as to in which of the situations, in sequential order the principle of natural justice is applied:

Codes:

(*a*) Alibi

(*b*) Self-incrimination

(*c*) Presumption of innocence

(*d*) Strict liability

Sequence of order:

A. (*a*), (*b*), (*c*), (*d*) B. (*d*), (*c*), (*a*), (*b*)

C. (*c*), (*b*), (*a*), (*d*) D. (*b*), (*c*), (*d*), (*a*)

41. The principle of 'Quod necessitas non habet leegen' is applied in circumstances of:

A. an act done in order to avoid consequence

B. in a little harm that resulted in the consequence

C. a harm resulted in order to do another evil

D. self-preservation

42. Aggravated abetment can be found within the public:

A. when the act was done by any one of the ten or more members present.

B. when the act was done by one of the seven members while collecting funds from other public.

C. while a person affixing a poster on the wall specially called attention of an assembly of five persons to protest against police excesses.

D. when an un-named member of a fluctuating population incites others to undertake a strike to stop train movement.

43. In which of the matters it was held that disclosure of identity of victim either by printing or publishing will not amount to penal liability?

A. In a judgement given by the Session's Judge on the ground of social victimisation.

B. In a judgement given by the High Court on the ground of Ostracism.

C. In a judgement given either by High Court or Supreme Court on the ground of preventing social victimisation or contracism.

D. In a judgement given by the Supreme Court on the ground of prevention from social victimisation.

44. Read Assertion (A) and Reason (R) and answer the reasonableness using the 'code' given below:

Assertion (A): Section 304-A is directed at offences outside the range of Sections 299 and 300.

Reason (R): It contemplates those acts into which neither intention nor knowledge enters.

Codes:

A. Both (A) and (R) are correct as the act results from rash and negligence act.

B. (A) is correct as certain acts are unjustifiable while (R) is not the correct reason as it falls short of culpable homicide.

C. (R) is correct while (A) is an incorrect application to the rule of culpable homicide to cause murder.

D. Both (A) and (R) are incorrect statements as to impose penalty.

45. Read Assertion (A) and Reason (R) and answer using codes given below:

Assertion (A): Multiple Trade Unions in industries and the consequential necessity for selecting one as the recognised union by the management devising a method on democratic principles is necessary.

Reason (R): The Union which represents the largest number of workmen working in the undertaking must acquire the status as that would be in tune with the concept of Industrial democracy.

Codes:

A. (A) and (R) are correct and (R) is the correct explanation of (A).

B. (A) and (R) are correct, but (R) is not the correct explanation of (A).

C. (A) is correct, but (R) is wrong.

D. (A) is wrong, but (R) is correct.

46. "The working class unfamiliar with the sophistications of definitions and shower of decisions, unable to secure expert legal opinion, what with poverty pricing them out of justice market and denying them the staying power to withstand the multi-decked litigative process, defacto is denied social justice if legal drafting is vagarious, definitions indefinite and court rulings contradictory."

The above remarks were made in support of an expensive definition of "Industry" by one of the following justices:

A. Justice O. Chinnappa Reddy

B. Justice V.R. Krishna Iyer

C. Justice Gajendragadkar

D. S.P. Bharucha

47. Which one of the following is incorrect?

A. Workman whose name is borne on the muster rolls of an industrial establishment and who has completed one year of continuous service under an employer is laid off, whether continuously or intermittently shall be paid by the employer for all days during which he is so laid off except for such weekly holidays.

B. Termination on the ground of misconduct or continued ill health of a workman is not a retrenchment.

C. Lock-out means the permanent closing of a place of employment, or the total suspension or the refusal by an employer to continue to employ any number of persons employed.

D. The right to close down the business, trade or undertaking is subject to payment of compensation to the workers engaged in the business immediately before the closure.

48. Match List-I with List-II and select the correct answer using the codes given below:

List-I	List-II
(*a*) Kalinga Tubes Ltd. v. Their workmen	(*i*) Deduction of wages for the period of strike
(*b*) Bank of India v. T.S. Kelawala and others	(*ii*) Closure has to be genuine and bonafide
(*c*) Bombay Union of Journalist v. State of Bombay	(*iii*) Definition of Industry
(*d*) Coir Board v. Indira Devi P.S. and others	(*iv*) Condition precedent to retrenchment of workman

Codes:

	(a)	(b)	(c)	(d)
A.	(iii)	(ii)	(i)	(iv)
B.	(ii)	(i)	(iv)	(iii)
C.	(i)	(ii)	(iv)	(iii)
D.	(iv)	(ii)	(iii)	(i)

49. Reference of an Industrial Dispute, the subject matter of which is covered by a settlement as defined in Section 2(P) of the Act would be:

A. valid during the operation of such settlement

B. invalid during the operation of such settlement

C. valid and subject to the importance of Industrial Dispute

D. voidable at the option of the parties to the dispute during the operation of such settlement

50. Read Assertion (A) and Reason (R) and answer using codes given below:

Assertion (A): The retention of Industrial Adjudication is necessary till all Trade Unions attain sufficient strength to bargain with employers, from a position of equality.

Reason (R): Collective Bargaining presently provides only lip services, whereas in practice it has perpetuated Adjudication.

Codes:

A. (A) and (R) are correct and (R) is the correct explanation of (A).

B. (A) and (R) are correct, but (R) is not the correct explanation of (A).

C. (A) is correct, but (R) is wrong.

D. (A) is wrong, but (R) is right.

ANSWERS

1	2	3	4	5	6	7	8	9	10
D	A	A	A	A	B	B	B	C	B
11	**12**	**13**	**14**	**15**	**16**	**17**	**18**	**19**	**20**
D	C	C	D	A	C	A	C	A	B
21	**22**	**23**	**24**	**25**	**26**	**27**	**28**	**29**	**30**
C	D	A	B	C	D	A	B	D	C
31	**32**	**33**	**34**	**35**	**36**	**37**	**38**	**39**	**40**
D	C	B	D	C	C	B	C	A	B
41	**42**	**43**	**44**	**45**	**46**	**47**	**48**	**49**	**50**
D	A	C	A	A	B	C	B	B	A

EXPLANATORY ANSWERS

1. The Preamble to the Constitution reads, "WE, THE PEOPLE OF INDIA, having solemnly resolved to constitute India into a **SOVEREIGN SOCIALIST SECULAR DEMOCRATIC REPUBLIC...**" The words 'Socialist Secular' were not a part of the original Constitution and were incorporated by the Constitution (Forty-second Amendment) Act, 1976 w.e.f 03-01-1977. Till date the Preamble has been amended only once.

2. Article 16 of the Indian constitution has been amended on four occasions. **First in 1956 vide Constitution (Seventh Amendment) Act, 1956 which amended Art 16(3),** Second in

1995 vide the Constitution (Seventy-seventh) Amendment Act, 1995 which inserted clause (4A) in Article 16 enabling the state to make provisions in matters of promotion in favour of SCs and STs, third in the year 2000 vide the Constitution (Eighty-First) Amendment Act, 2000 which inserted clause (4B) enabling the state to carry forward unfilled vacancies for reserved categories over and above the 50% ceiling limit. Last amendment of Article 16 was done in 2001 which amended the newly inserted Clause (4A) which accorded 'consequential seniority' to candidates promoted under the clause. The preceding amendment was made vide the Constitution (Eighty-Fifth) Amendment Act, 2001, however, it was made retrospectively effective from 17.06.1995.

Article 19 has been amended a total four times vide

First Amendment Act, 1951: Amended Art 19(2) relating to reasonable restrictions on freedom of speech & **Art 19(6) relating with reasonable restrictions on the right to practise any profession and the right to carry on any occupation, trade or business.**

Sixteenth Amendment Act, 1963: Inserted the words [Sovereignty and Integrity of India] in Article 19(2) & 19(3) as grounds for imposing reasonable restrictions on freedom of speech and freedom to assemble peaceably and without arms respectively.

Forty-Fourth Amendment Act, 1978: Amendment of Article 19(1)(e) to omit sub clause 19(1)(f) and consequently **amended Art 19(5) to drop reference to 19(1)(f).**

Ninety-Seventh Amendment Act, 2011: Added the words [or cooperative societies] to Art. 19(1)(c).

3. The writ jurisdiction of High Courts is discretionary and the rule of exhaustion of remedies, *i.e.*, requiring the petitioner to exhaust all available, ordinary and efficacious legal remedies before reaching the High Court is a rule of policy, convenience and discretion rather than a rule of law. The State of Uttar Pradesh vs Mohammad Nooh 1958 AIR 86.

7. The alleged right of the first petitioner to guardianship of his minor children under the Personal Law is not one of the fundamental rights guaranteed to him by the Constitution; 'nor by appointing respondent No. 2 as the guardian of the minors under the Guardian and Wards Act is discrimination practised against the minors. The second respondent was appointed guardian of the minors by order of a competent court and denial of equality before the law or the equal protection of the laws can be claimed against executive action or legislative process but not against the decision of a competent tribunal. The remedy of a person aggrieved by the decision of a competent judicial tribunal is to approach for redress a superior tribunal if there be one.

8. John Austin (1790–1859) was an English jurist most famous for his contribution to legal positivism and remembered for his. "Command Theory" of law. According to Austin a Sovereign is "A Determinate rational being or body that the other rational beings are in the habit of obeying." According to Command Theory, Law is nothing but commands flowing from the Sovereign to those under his habitual obedience and failure to comply with the commands leads to imposition of sanction. Command, sovereignty and sanctions are the three most important attributes of law according to Austin.

11. (There appears to be some mistake in the question as both Option 2 and Option 4 are correct choices).

Fiction theory and Bracket theory are theories on corporate personality.

Interest theory and Will theory are theories on legal rights.

12. Right in rem is a right against the world or public at large. Whereas right in personam is a right against a particular person, for example, a right arising out of a contract or fiduciary relationship. A right in personam is also called a personal right.

An imperfect right is a right correlative to which there is no duty present in any determinate person or where duty is present it cannot legally be enforced under law, for example, a time barred debt. An imperfect right is an exception to the rule of *ubi jus ibi remedium* or where there is a right there is a remedy.

17. Statement (*a*) is correct

Statement (*b*) is incorrect. The purposes of the United Nations are enshrined in Article 1

Statement (*c*) is correct.

Statement (*d*) is incorrect. The provision relating to suspension of a member finds mention in Article 5 of the charter.

18. Statement (*a*) is incorrect. Mediation is a pacific means of settlement of International disputes.

Statement (*b*) is correct.

Statement (*c*) is correct.

Statement (*d*) is correct

19. Statement (*c*) is incorrect. The United Nations Human Rights Council is an intergovernmental body formed in the year 2006 to prevent and promote Human Rights across the world. It has 47 members which are elected from the UN General Assembly for a three-year term. Its first session was concluded through June 16-30, 2006.

20. Statement (*c*) is incorrect. Two persons are said to be related with each other by half blood when they are descended from the same ancestor but different wives.

21. The explanation appended to section 2(1) of Hindu Marriage Act, 1955 reads

Explanation: The following persons are Hindus, Buddhists, Jainas or Sikhs by religion, as the case may be: (*a*) any child, legitimate or illegitimate, both of whose parents are Hindus, Buddhists, Jainas or Sikhs by religion; (*b*) any child, legitimate or illegitimate, one of whose parents is a Hindu, Buddhist Jaina or Sikh by religion and **who is brought up as a member of tribe, community, group or family to which such parents belong or belonged.**

Since, in the present statement one of the parents of the child is Christian and the child has been brought up as a Christian, the child would be treated as a Christian as far as HMA 1955 is concerned.

22. (*i*) **Shruti:** The shrutis are considered to be the authorless texts contained in the Vedas which were heard from the Rishis of the Vedic age. They are the primary source of Hindu Law.

(*ii*) **Smritis:** Smritis are also derived from shrutis but they are based on memory of later sages who forgot their original form and wrote it down in their own language. Hence unlike shrutis, smritis are often attributed to authors. Dharmasutras and Dharmashastras are types of smritis.

(*iii*) **Digests and Commentaries:** From 7th century onwards various digests and commentaries on the smritis and shrutis were compiled which helped in elaborating and explaining the law contained in them. The Dayabhaga and Mitakshara schools of Hindu law are also based on two different interpretations of the Hindu Law, one by Jimutavahana, who authored Dayabhaga and one by Mitakshara which is based on commentaries by Vijnaneswar.

(*iv*) **Custom:** One of the requirements for a custom to take force of law in Hindu Law is that it should be ancient apart from being certain, uninterrupted and not opposed to public policy.

23. Section 2 of Muslim Personal Law (Shariat) Application Act, 1937 reads

Notwithstanding any custom or usage to the contrary, in all questions (save questions relating to agricultural land) regarding intestate succession, special property of females, including personal property inherited or obtained under contract or gift or any other provision of Personal Law, marriage, dissolution of marriage, including talaq, ila, zihar, lian, khula and mubaraat, maintenance, dower, guardianship, gifts, trusts and trust properties, and waqfs (other than charities and charitable institutions and charitable and religious endowments) the rule of decision in cases where the parties are Muslims shall be the Muslim Personal Law (Shariat).

25. Fault Theory: Also known as guilt theory recognizes that one of the parties in a marriage must be at fault for the marriage to dissolve, *i.e.*, a marriage cannot be dissolved until and unless the guilt or fault of one party is conclusively established.

Breakdown of Marriage: This is a fairly recent concept which has been accepted by courts. Unlike the fault theory, in breakdown theory the court may dissolve the marriage even if the guilt of one party has not been conclusively established if in the opinion of the court the conditions are such that the marriage has irretrievably broken down and in the interests of justice it is desirable that such marriage be dissolved.

Mutual Consent: The parties are free to take divorce by mutual consent after exhausting all avenues of reconciliation. This is contained in section 13-B of HMA 1955.

Customary: Customary divorce deed is also permissible in the Hindu Law. After entering into legally enforceable customary divorce deed the parties may file a declaratory suit in a court of law declaring that the divorce deed is legal and enforceable and the parties had ceased to be husband and wife from the date of execution of the deed.

26. Talaq Ahsan: It is the most proper and approved form of Talaq. Pronouncement of Talaq is done in a single sentence when the wife is in a state of purity or *tuhr*. The Talaq is revocable during the period of *iddat* at the lapse of which it becomes irrevocable.

28. An agreement with consideration be made orally and it will result into a valid contract. Also, Section 25(1) of Indian Contract Act, 1872 reads "An agreement made without consideration is void, unless it is expressed in writing and registered under the law for the time being in force for the registration of documents, and is made on account of natural love and affection between parties standing in a near relation to each other".

29. In Taylor v Caldwell, the defendants agreed to rent out their music concert hall to the plaintiff. A night before the concert the hall was burnt to ground and the defendants failed to comply with the contract. In this case, the court recognized the doctrine of frustration of contract on the grounds of impossibility arising out of situations outside the scope of defendants.

30. Section 30 of Specific Relief Act reads, "On adjudging the rescission of a contract, the court may require the party to whom such relief is granted to restore, so far as may be, any benefit which he may have received from the other party and to make any compensation to him which justice may require".

31. Section 11 of Indian Contract Act 1872 reads, "Every person is competent to contract who is of the age of majority according to the law to which he is subject, and who is of sound mind and is not disqualified from contracting by any law to which he is subject".

33. In Hadley v Baxendale, Baxendale failed to ship a broken crankshaft to engineers appointed by Hadley to fix it on a date fixed under the contract. This led Hadley to suffer huge losses as he lost business. Baxendale had no knowledge that Hadley may suffer exceptional losses if delivery was not made in time. Question arose what shall be the extent of damages payable by Baxendale. It was held that Baxendale was liable only to the extent of foreseeable damages based on the information available to him.

Hence, both assertion and reason are wrong.

35. Assertion (A) is true. However, in India judicial review of executive action is permissible. Hence, Reason (R) is not true.

36. Statement (*c*) is incorrect. There is no tortuous liability upon the wife towards her husband if she fractures her legs.

37. Ashby v White is a landmark common law judgement delivered on 1st January, 1703 by Court of King's bench, UK. In this case, one Mr. Ashby was wrongfully prevented from casting his vote by a public officer Mr. White. Although Mr. Ashby's candidate won the election and Mr. Ashby suffered no damage yet it was held that Mr. Ashby did suffer from a legal injury as his right to cast vote was infringed. The court allowed damages on this account. This case is an illustrative example of the maxims *ubi jus ibi remedium* and *injuria sine damno*.

38. Section 17B of Consumer Protection Act, 1986 which talks about Circuit Benches, reads "The State Commission shall ordinarily function in the State Capital but may perform its functions at such other place as the State Government may, in consultation with the State Commission, notify in the Official Gazette, from time to time."

39. A single consumer or more than one consumers jointly are fully capable of filing a complaint before the District Consumer Forum. Section 12 of the Consumer Protection Act 1986 reads as following:

Manner in which complaint shall be made:

(1) A complaint in relation to any goods sold or delivered or agreed to be sold or delivered or any service provided or agreed to be provided may be filed with a District Forum by:

(*a*) the consumer to whom such goods are sold or delivered or agreed to be sold or delivered or such service provided or agreed to be provided;

(*b*) any recognised consumer association whether the consumer to whom the goods sold or delivered or agreed to be sold or delivered or service provided or agreed to be provided is a member of such association or not;

(*c*) one or more consumers, where there are numerous consumers having the same interest, with the permission of the District Forum, on behalf of, or for the benefit of, all consumers so interested; or

(*d*) the Central Government or the State Government, as the case may be, either in its individual capacity or as a representative of interests of the consumers in general.

Also, explanation appended to this section clarifies that "For the purpose of this section "recognised consumer association" means any voluntary consumer association registered under the Companies Act, 1956 or any other law for the time being in force".

41. The maxim *Quod necessitas non habet leegen* means that necessity knows no law. Hence, in a situation when a person is faced with self-preservation or breaking the law he may break the law in view of his dire need.

42. The offence mentioned under Section 117 of the Indian Penal Code is a form of aggravated abetment and it reads

Abetting commission of offence by the public or by more than ten persons (S. 117 IPC). Whoever abets the commission of an offence by the public generally or by any number or class of persons exceeding ten, shall be punished with imprisonment of either description for a term which may extend to three years, or with fine, or with both.

Illustration: A affixes in a public place a placard instigating a sect consisting of more than ten members to meet at a certain time and place, for the purpose of attacking the members of an adverse sect, while engaged in a procession. A has committed the offence defined in this section.

43. Section 228A(1) of IPC reads "Whoever prints or publishes the name or any matter which may make known the identity of any person against whom an offence under Section 376, Section 376A, Section 376B, Section 376C or Section 376D is alleged or found to have been committed (hereafter in this section referred to as the victim) shall be punished with imprisonment of either description for a term which may extend to two years and shall also be liable to fine." However, the explanation appended to this section clarifies that, "the printing or publication of the judgement of any High Court or the Supreme Court does not amount to an offence within the meaning of this section".

Also, in Bhupinder Sharma v. State of Himachal Pradesh 2003 Supp(4) SCR 792, it was laid down by Arijit Pasayat J. that— "We do not propose of mention name of the victim. Section 228-A of the Indian Penal Code, 1860 (in short the 'IPC') makes disclosure of identity of victim of certain offences punishable. Printing or publishing name of any matter which may make known the identity of any person against whom an offence under Sections 376, 376-A, 376-B, 376-C or 376-D is alleged or found to have been committed can be punished. True it is, the restriction does not relate to printing or publication of judgement by High Court or Supreme Court. But keeping in view the social object of presenting social victimization or ostracisms of the victim of a sexual offence for which Section 228-A has been enacted, it would be appropriate that in the judgements, be it of High Court or lower Court, the name of the victim should not be indicated. We have chosen to describe her as 'victim' in the judgement."

44. Section 304A of Indian Penal Code deals with causing death by negligence and reads as "Whoever causes the death of any person by doing any rash or negligent act not amounting to culpable homicide, shall be punished with imprisonment of either description for a term which may extend to two years, or with fine, or with both."

47. Section 2(l) of Industrial Disputes Act, 1947 defines a lock-out as "the temporary closing of a place of employment or the suspension of work, or the refusal by an employer to continue to employ any number of persons employed by him".

49. According to Section 2(p) of ID Act, "settlement" means a settlement arrived at in the course of conciliation proceeding and includes a written agreement between the employer and the workmen arrived at otherwise than in the course of conciliation proceeding where such agreement has been signed by the parties thereto in such manner as may be prescribed and a copy.

According to Section 19(2) of ID Act "Such settlement shall be binding for such period as is agreed upon by the parties, and if no such period is agreed upon, for a period of six months 2 [from the date on which the memorandum of settlement is signed by the parties to the dispute], and shall continue to be binding on the parties after the expiry of the period aforesaid, until the expiry of two months from the date on which a notice in writing of an intention to terminate the settlement is given by one of the parties to the other party or parties to the settlement."

PAPER-III

Note: *This paper contains* ***seventy five (75)*** *objective type questions of* ***two (2)*** *marks each.* ***All questions are compulsory.***

1. Match List-I with List-II and give the correct answer using codes given below the lists:

List-I	List-II
(*a*) Kesavananda Bharati v. State of Kerala	(*i*) Basic structure doctrine new dimensions added
(*b*) Indira Nehru Gandhi v. Raj Narain	(*ii*) Basic structure doctrine created
(*c*) Minerva Mills v. Union of India	(*iii*) Basic structure doctrine strengthened
(*d*) I.R. Coelho v. State of Tamil Nadu	(*iv*) Basic structure doctrine crystallised

Codes:

	(*a*)	(*b*)	(*c*)	(*d*)
A.	(*ii*)	(*iii*)	(*iv*)	(*i*)
B.	(*ii*)	(*iv*)	(*i*)	(*iii*)
C.	(*iv*)	(*i*)	(*ii*)	(*iii*)
D.	(*iii*)	(*iv*)	(*ii*)	(*i*)

2. Read Assertion (A) and Reason (R) and give the correct answer with the help of codes given below:

Assertion (A): A State made law on any matter of Concurrent List prevails notwithstanding any repugnancy with an earlier law made by the Parliament.

Reason (R): The Parliament can make a law, on any matter in the Concurrent List that prevails over any repugnant state law.

Codes:

A. (A) and (R) are true and (R) is the correct explanation of (A).

B. (A) and (R) are true, but (R) is not the correct explanation of (A).

C. (A) is false, but (R) is true.

D. (A) is true, but (R) is false.

3. Read Assertion (A) and Reason (R) and give the correct answer with the help of codes given below:

Assertion (A): The President of India has a right to seek advisory opinion of the Supreme Court of India on a question of law or fact has arisen or likely to arise, which is of such nature and of such public importance.

Reason (R): The Constitution of India makes it obligatory for the President to accept the advice rendered the Supreme Court of India.

Codes:

A. (A) and (R) are true and (R) is the correct explanation of (A).

B. (A) and (R) are true, but (R) is not the correct explanation of (A).

C. (A) is true, but (R) is false.

D. (A) is false, but (R) is true.

4. Match List-I with List-II and give the correct answer using codes given below the lists:

List-I	List-II
(*a*) Art 136	(*i*) Appellate jurisdiction of Supreme Court in regard to criminal matters.
(*b*) Art 134	(*ii*) Seat of Supreme Court
(*c*) Art 131	(*iii*) Special leave to appeal jurisdiction of the Supreme court over any court or administrative tribunal.
(*d*) Art 130	(*iv*) Original jurisdiction of the Supreme Court.

Codes:

	(*a*)	(*b*)	(*c*)	(*d*)
A.	(*iv*)	(*i*)	(*iii*)	(*ii*)
B.	(*i*)	(*iii*)	(*iv*)	(*ii*)
C.	(*ii*)	(*iv*)	(*i*)	(*iii*)
D.	(*iii*)	(*i*)	(*iv*)	(*ii*)

5. Match List-I with List-II and give the correct answer using codes given below the lists:

List-I	List-II
(*a*) Art 221	(*i*) Transfer of a Judge from one High Court to another
(*b*) Art 222	(*ii*) Appointment of acting Chief Justice of a High Court
(*c*) Art 223	(*iii*) Appointment of additional and acting Judges of the High Court
(*d*) Art 224	(*iv*) Salaries, etc., of High Court Judges

Codes:

	(*a*)	(*b*)	(*c*)	(*d*)
A.	(*iv*)	(*i*)	(*ii*)	(*iii*)
B.	(*ii*)	(*iv*)	(*i*)	(*iii*)
C.	(*iii*)	(*iv*)	(*ii*)	(*i*)
D.	(*iii*)	(*i*)	(*iv*)	(*ii*)

6. Read Assertion (A) and Reason (R) and give the correct answer with the help of codes given below:

Assertion (A): An accused person is guaranteed under the Constitution of India the right to be informed of the nature and cause of his accusation.

Reason (R): The accused person has to be produced before the nearest District Judge within twenty four hours.

Codes:

A. (A) and (R) are true and (R) is the correct explanation of (A).
B. (A) and (R) are true, but (R) is not the correct explanation of (A).
C. (A) is false, but (R) is true.
D. (A) is true, but (R) is false.

7. Read Assertion (A) and Reason (R) and give the correct answer with the help of codes given below:

Assertion (A): Subject to anything in this Constitution, Parliament may in exercise of its constituent power amend by way of addition, variation or repeal any provision of this Constitution in accordance with the procedure laid down in this article.

Reason (R): Above statement is Article 368(1) of the Indian Constitution.

Codes:

A. Both (A) and (R) are correct and (R) is the correct reason of (A).
B. Both (A) and (R) are wrong.
C. (A) is wrong, but (R) is right.
D. (R) is wrong, but (A) is right.

8. Read Assertion (A) and Reason (R) and give the correct answer with the help of codes given below:

Assertion (A): No person to be eligible for election in, or to claim to be included in a special electoral roll on grounds of religion, race, caste or sex.

Reason (R): Above statement is title of Article 325 of the Indian Constitution.

Codes:

A. Both (A) and (R) are correct and (R) is the correct reason for (A).
B. Both (A) and (R) are wrong.
C. (A) is wrong, but (R) is right.
D. (R) is wrong, but (A) is right.

9. Discretion, when applied to a court of justice, means sound discretion guided by law. It must be governed by rule, not by humour; it must not be arbitrary, vague and fanciful but legal and regular. This observation was made in:

A. Union of India v. Kuldeep Singh
B. Reliance Airport Developers (P) Ltd. v. Airports Authority of India.
C. Maneka Gandhi v. Union of India
D. National Insurance Co. Ltd v. Keshav Bahadur

10. Under which of the following condition(s) a writ of mandamus can be granted? Give correct answer using the codes:

(*a*) There must be a public duty.

(*b*) There must be a specific demand and refusal.
(*c*) There must be a clear right to enforce the duty.
(*d*) The right must be subsisting on the date of the petition.

Codes:

A. All (*a*), (*b*), (*c*) and (*d*) are correct.
B. Only (*a*), (*b*) and (*c*) are correct.
C. Only (*a*) and (*c*) are correct.
D. Only (*a*) and (*b*) are correct.

11. In which one of the following cases, the Supreme Court made it explicit that 'even when the authority has statutory power to take action without hearing, it would be arbitrary to take action without hearing and, thus, violative of Article 14 of the Constitution'?

A. A.K. Kraipak v. Union of India
B. Union of India v. Satish Chandra
C. A.K. Roy v. State of Punjab
D. H.L. Trehan v. Union of India

12. Match List-I with List-II and select the correct answer using the codes given below:

List-I	List-II
(*a*) Personal bias	(*i*) Jeejeebhoy v. Collector
(*b*) Pecuniary bias	(*ii*) Krishna Bus Service (P) Ltd. v. State of Haryana
(*c*) Subject-matter bias	(*iii*) Manak Lal v. Dr. Prem Chand
(*d*) Departmental bias	(*iv*) G. Nageswara Rao v. A.P.S.R.T.C.

Codes:

	(*a*)	(*b*)	(*c*)	(*d*)
A.	(*i*)	(*ii*)	(*iii*)	(*iv*)
B.	(*iii*)	(*i*)	(*iv*)	(*ii*)
C.	(*iii*)	(*ii*)	(*iv*)	(*i*)
D.	(*iv*)	(*i*)	(*ii*)	(*iii*)

13. Read the Assertion (A) and Reason (R) and give the correct answer with the help of codes given below:

Assertion (A): A writ of prohibition can be issued on the same grounds on which the writ of certiorari can be issued except in case of an error of law apparent on the face of the record.

Reason (R): A writ of certiorari is issued at a stage when proceedings are in progress, to forbid the authority from continuing the proceedings whereas a writ of prohibition is issued at a stage when the authority has given a final decision, to quash the decision.

Codes:

A. Both (A) and (R) are true and (R) is the correct explanation of (A).
B. Both (A) and (R) are true, but (R) is not the correct explanation of (A).
C. (A) is correct, but (R) is false.
D. (A) is false, but (R) is correct.

14. Match List-I with List-II and select the correct answer using the codes given below:

List-I (*Subject*)	List-II (*Provision of the Lokpal and Lokayuktas Act, 2013*)
(*a*) The composition of Lokpal	(*i*) Section 3(2)
(*b*) Establishment of Lokayukta	(*ii*) Section 6
(*c*) Term of office of Chairperson and Members of Lokpal	(*iii*) Section 37
(*d*) Removal of Chairperson and Members of Lokpal	(*iv*) Section 63

Codes:

	(*a*)	(*b*)	(*c*)	(*d*)
A.	(*i*)	(*ii*)	(*iii*)	(*iv*)
B.	(*i*)	(*iv*)	(*ii*)	(*iii*)
C.	(*ii*)	(*iii*)	(*i*)	(*iv*)
D.	(*i*)	(*ii*)	(*iv*)	(*iii*)

15. The appointment of Chairperson of Lokpal shall be made by the President after obtaining the recommendation of a selection committee consisting of:

A. The Prime Minister; The Speaker of the House of the People and the Chief Justice of India.

B. The Prime Minister; The Speaker of the House of the People; The leader of opposition in the House of the people.

C. The Prime Minister; The Leader of opposition in the House of the People and one eminent jurist to be nominated by the President.

D. The Prime Minister; The Speaker of the House of the People, The Leader of opposition in the House of the People, The Chief Justice of India or a Judge of the Supreme Court nominated by him and one eminent jurist to be nominated by the President.

16. "Law is not only a set of rules but is a method or technique for harmonizing conflicting interests." This statement is of:

A. Auguste Comte B. Herbert Spencer

C. Roscoe Pound D. Leon Duguit

17. Match List-I with List-II and give the correct answer using the codes given below:

List-I *(Meaning)*	List-II *(Jurists associated with)*
(*a*) Jurisprudence is a science of just and unjust.	(*i*) Salmond
(*b*) Jurisprudence is the science of the first principle of civil law.	(*ii*) Gray
(*c*) Jurisprudence is the philosophical aspect of knowledge of law.	(*iii*) Ulpian
(*d*) Jurisprudence is in truth no more a formal science than physiology.	(*iv*) Cicero

Codes:

	(*a*)	(*b*)	(*c*)	(*d*)
A.	(*i*)	(*ii*)	(*iii*)	(*iv*)
B.	(*iii*)	(*i*)	(*iv*)	(*ii*)
C.	(*ii*)	(*iii*)	(*i*)	(*iv*)
D.	(*iii*)	(*iv*)	(*ii*)	(*i*)

18. Which one of the following requisites is not necessary to be fulfilled for a custom to be valid and operative as a source of law?

A. Reasonableness

B. Conformity with statute law

C. Immemorial antiquity

D. May not have been practised continuously

19. Match List-I with List-II and give the correct answer using the codes given below:

List-I *(Theory)*	List-II *(Jurist Associated with)*
(*a*) Inner Morality	(*i*) Compte
(*b*) Concept of living law	(*ii*) Fuller
(*c*) Organic concept of society	(*iii*) Burke
(*d*) Gradual and organic process	(*iv*) Ehrlich

Codes:

	(*a*)	(*b*)	(*c*)	(*d*)
A.	(*ii*)	(*iv*)	(*i*)	(*iii*)
B.	(*iii*)	(*iv*)	(*i*)	(*ii*)
C.	(*ii*)	(*iii*)	(*iv*)	(*i*)
D.	(*i*)	(*ii*)	(*iii*)	(*iv*)

20. If 'A' leaves his car with the driver, the driver's possession will be:

A. Immediate whereas that of 'A' would be mediate.

B. Mediate whereas that of 'A' would be immediate.

C. Incorporeal whereas that of 'A' would be corporeal.

D. Corporeal whereas that of 'A' would be incorporeal.

21. Read Assertion (A) and Reason (R) and answer using the codes given below:

Assertion (A): The legislature can forge a sledge-hammer capable of cracking open the corporate shell.

Reason (R): Corporate personality cannot be used as a shield to harm national interest.

Codes:

A. Both (A) and (R) are true and (R) is the correct explanation of (A).

B. Both (A) and (R) are true, but (R) is not the correct explanation of (A).

C. (A) is true, but (R) is false.

D. (A) is false, but (R) is true.

22. Read Assertion (A) and Reason (R) and answer using the codes given below:

Assertion (A): The most important power of an owner is the right to exclude others.

Reason (R): The owner may grant to another many of his rights and yet remain owner.

Codes:

A. Both (A) and (R) are true and (R) is the correct explanation of (A).

B. Both (A) and (R) are true, but (R) is not the correct explanation of (A).

C. (A) is true, but (R) is false.

D. (A) is false, but (R) is true.

23. "Law is a social engineering to remove the existing imbalance and to further the progress, serving the needs of the Socialist Democratic Bharat under the rule of Law." This was the observation of Justice K. Ramaswami in:

A. Delhi Transport Corp. v. D.T.C. Mazdoor Congress

B. Indra Sawhney v. Union of India

C. State of Karnataka v. Appa Balu Ingale

D. Parmanand Kataria v. Union of India

24. In which of the crimes retributive theory strikes the moral blameworthiness of the offender to punish him?

A. Clamping prohibitory orders

B. Sexual harassment at workplace

C. Wilful attempt to defame

D. Common intention to commit riot

25. In which of the circumstances the defense of necessity involves a collusion of interest and the consequential judgement of values?

A. Stealing to avert hungers

B. Absolute necessity for self-preservation

C. Private homicide for keeping up the honour

D. Acts done against anarchy

26. Read Assertion (A) and Reason (R) and using the codes given below choose the appropriate answer:

Assertion (A): The apprehension of use of criminal force must emanate from the gesture of a person to attract punishment.

Reason (R): Mere advancing with a threatening attitude will not amount to criminal force.

Codes:

A. Both (A) and (R) are contradictory to each other.

B. (A) is correct while (R) is not the cause of it.

C. (A) is incorrect while (R) is appropriate.

D. (A) is correct while (R) is the cause of it.

27. Read Assertion (A) and Reason (R) and using the codes given below write the correct answer.

Assertion (A): In a case of attempt to rape there must be an indecent assault or action with any resistance from the victim.

Reason (R): There was some action which shows that he was going to have sexual connection with her.

Codes:

A. (R) is the correct explanation of (A) and both (A) and (R) are complementary to each other.

B. (A) is correct, but (R) is not complementary to (A).

C. (A) and (R) have no legal standing in view of change of burden of proof.
D. (R) is essential to formulate (A) otherwise there may not be a crime.

28. Which of the factors fall under the limits within which the right of private defense should be exercised?
A. Where there is time to have recourse to the protection of the public authorities.
B. When a public servant performs an act in good faith.
C. An act committed strictly in conformity with law.
D. Where the act was irregular and outside the scope of power.

29. Dacoity with murder creates co-extensive responsibility of each participant because:
A. Collective liability is the core-essence whether it was culminated suddenly or not.
B. Mere non-participation in dacoity will not exempt from criminal liability since there was pre-concert.
C. Planning was to commit only dacoity, but another person, for earlier enmity, abetted to commit murder while there was no common object.
D. There must be one or more participants for the constructive action by each member.

30. What offence, if any, has been committed by a married woman giving free consent to her own abduction?
A. Abetting her own abduction
B. Criminal conspiracy for abduction
C. No criminal liability against her as the act was not committed in deceitful manner.
D. Attempt to abduction when there was failure to obtain clear consent.

31. A young man waves a currency note of rupees one thousand in front of a woman as if he offers the money for an indecent favour from the woman, he may be criminally booked under:
A. Section 506 of IPC
B. Section 507 of IPC
C. Section 508 of IPC
D. Section 509 of IPC

32. One of the following International Conventions is not related to wild life conservation. Give the correct answer:
A. Convention on International Trade in Endangered Species of Wild Fauna and Flora.
B. Convention on Environmental Impact Assessment in Transboundary Context.
C. Convention on Migratory Species of Wild Animals.
D. Convention on International Union for Conservation of Nature and Natural Resources.

33. The Montreal Protocol is related to:
A. Transboundary Air pollution
B. Ozone Layer
C. Climate change
D. Hazardous waste

34. Read both Assertion (A) and Reason (R) and give the correct answer using the codes given below:

Assertion (A): Over 200 central and state statutes which have atleast some concern with environmental protection, either directly or indirectly have unfortunately not resulted in preventing environmental degradation, on the contrary has increased over the years.

Reason (R): Unless the Government policy is backed by adequate budgetary allocation, changes to the statutory regime and a bureaucratic will, the government's intention is apt to remain on paper.

Codes:
A. Both (A) and (R) are correct and (R) is the correct explanation of (A).
B. Both (A) and (R) are correct, but (R) is not the correct explanation of (A).

C. (A) is correct, but (R) is wrong.
D. (A) is wrong, but (R) is correct.

35. Match List-I and List-II and find correct answer using codes given below:

List-I	List-II
(*a*) Public Liability	(*i*) State of Bihar v. Murad Ali Khan
(*b*) Sustainable Development	(*ii*) M.C. Metha and Another v. Union of India and Others
(*c*) Wild life protection	(*iii*) Research Foundation for Science v. Union of India and Others
(*d*) Hazardous waste material	(*iv*) Narmada Bachao Andolan v. Union of India

Codes:

	(*a*)	(*b*)	(*c*)	(*d*)
A.	(*i*)	(*iii*)	(*iv*)	(*ii*)
B.	(*ii*)	(*iv*)	(*i*)	(*iii*)
C.	(*ii*)	(*iii*)	(*iv*)	(*i*)
D.	(*iv*)	(*ii*)	(*iii*)	(*i*)

36. Give correct answer using codes given below:

The Environmental approach has led the Supreme Court to derive, adopt and apply a range of principles to guide the development of environmental jurisprudence. Notable amongst the fundamental norms recognised by the court are:

(*a*) Every person enjoys the right to a wholesome environment, which is a facet of the right to life guaranteed under Art. 21 of the Constitution.

(*b*) Enforcement agencies are under an obligation to strictly enforce environmental laws.

(*c*) Government agencies may not plead non-availability of funds, inadequacy of staff or other insufficiencies to justify the non-performance of their obligations under environmental laws.

(*d*) Stringent action ought to be taken against contumacious defaulters and persons who carry on industrial or development activity for profit without regard to environmental laws.

Codes:

A. Only (*a*) and (*b*)
B. Only (*a*), (*b*) and (*c*)
C. (*a*), (*b*), (*c*) and (*d*)
D. Only (*a*)

37. In which of the following cases the Supreme Court after referring to International Covenant of Civil and Political Rights and Universal Declaration of Human Rights observed that, "It is almost an accepted proposition of law that rule of customary international law which is not contrary to the Municipal Law shall be deemed to be incorporated in the domestic law"?

A. M.C. Mehta v. Union of India
B. Rural Litigation and Entitlement Kendra v. State of U.P.
C. P.U.C.L. v. Union of India
D. Church of God (Full Gospels) in India v. K.K.R. Majestic Colony Welfare Association

38. Which one of the following is correct?

The Air (Prevention and Control of Pollution) Act of 1981 was enacted:

A. by the Parliament under Art 252(1) of the Constitution after securing enabling resolution from the States.
B. by the Parliament invoking the power under Art 253 to make laws implementing decisions taken at International Conferences.
C. by the states, as the executive functions under the Air Act are carried out by the State Pollution Control Board.
D. by the Parliament based on the directions given by the Supreme Court.

39. Which of the following pair/pairs is/are correctly matched ? Give correct answer using the codes given below:

(*a*) J.G. Starke – An Introduction to International Law

(*b*) Hackworth – Digest of International Law
(*c*) J.L. Brierly – The Changing Structure of International Law.
(*d*) W. Friedman – The Basis of Obligation in International Law.

Codes:

A. Only (*b*) B. Both (*a*) and (*b*)
C. (*a*), (*b*) and (*c*) D. (*a*), (*b*), (*c*) and (*d*)

40. In which of the following cases the International Court of Justice pointed out that when in regard to any matter or practice, two states follow it repeatedly for a long time, it becomes a binding customary rule?

A. West Rand Central Gold Mining Company Ltd., v. R. Case
B. South West Africa Case
C. Right of Passage over Indian Territory Case (Portugal v. India)
D. North Sea Continental Shelf Case

41. In International law a good example of the application of the principle sovereignty is the "Theory of Auto Limitation". According to this theory, states follow International law because they have by their consent reduced their powers. This principle is based on the principle of state sovereignty. The chief exponent of this principle was:

A. Only Anzilotti
B. Both Anzilotti and Triepel
C. Salmond
D. Max Huber

42. Which of the following statement/statements is/are incorrect ? Give correct answer using the codes given below:

I. "Subjugation" is a mode of 'acquisition' of Nationality under the International Law.
II. Stock v. The Public Trustee is a case related to Double Nationality.
III. Articles 3 to 6 of the Hague Convention of 1930 provide the provisions for solving the problem of Double Nationality of married women.
IV. "Cession" is a mode of 'Loss' of Nationality under the International Law.

Codes:

A. Only II is incorrect.
B. I, II and III are incorrect.
C. II, III and IV are incorrect.
D. I, II, III and IV all are incorrect.

43. Read both Assertion (A) and Reason (R) and give the correct answer using the codes given below:

Assertion (A): The General Assembly is one of the principal organs of the United Nations which consists of all the members of United Nations.

Reason (R): The Resolutions or Declaration of the General Assembly are not binding upon the States. They are merely recommendations.

Codes:

A. Both (A) and (R) are correct and (R) is the correct explanation of (A).
B. Both (A) and (R) are correct individually, but (R) is not the correct explanation of (A).
C. (A) is correct, but (R) is wrong.
D. (A) is wrong, but (R) is correct.

44. Match List-I with List-II and give the correct answer using the codes given below the Lists:

List-I ***(Jurisdiction of the International Court of Justice)***	**List-II** ***(Cases decided)***
(*a*) Case decided under contentious jurisdiction	(*i*) Nicaragua v. United States of America
(*b*) Under Advisory Jurisdiction	(*ii*) North Sea Continental Shelf Case
(*c*) Courts' competence in respect of determination of its own jurisdiction	(*iii*) Western Sahara Case
(*d*) Transferred Jurisdiction	(*iv*) Anglo-Iranian Oil Company Case

Codes:

	(a)	(b)	(c)	(d)
A.	(iv)	(i)	(ii)	(iii)
B.	(i)	(ii)	(iii)	(iv)
C.	(ii)	(iii)	(iv)	(i)
D.	(iii)	(iv)	(i)	(ii)

45. Which of the following pair/pairs is/are not correctly matched? Give correct answer using the codes given below:

(a) Composition of the Security Council of U.N. – Article 23 of the U.N. Charter
(b) Composition of the Economic and Social Council – Article 61 of the U.N. Charter
(c) Composition of the General Assembly of the United Nations – Article 86 of the U.N. Charter
(d) Composition of Trusteeship Council – Article 28 of the U.N. Charter

Codes:

A. Only (d)
B. (c) and (d) both
C. (a), (b) and (c)
D. (a), (b), (c) and (d) all

46. Match List-I and List-II and find correct answer using the codes given below:

List-I (Case Law)	List-II (Decision)
(a) Saroj Rani v. Sudarshan Kumar	(i) Uniform Civil Code
(b) Jorden Diengdeh v. S.S. Chopra	(ii) Meaning of Hindu
(c) Russel v. Russel	(iii) Constitutionality of Section 9 of Hindu Marriage Act, 1955
(d) Shastri V/s. Muldas	(iv) Meaning of Cruelty

Codes:

	(a)	(b)	(c)	(d)
A.	(ii)	(iii)	(i)	(iv)
B.	(iv)	(ii)	(iii)	(i)
C.	(iii)	(i)	(iv)	(ii)
D.	(i)	(iv)	(iii)	(ii)

47. A marriage solemnized between any two Hindus who are Sapindas of each other shall be:

A. Valid, if the custom or usage governing any of them permits a marriage between the two.
B. Valid, if the custom or usage governing each of them permits a marriage between the two.
C. Voidable, if the custom or usage governing each of them permits a marriage between the two.
D. Void, if the custom or usage governing each of them permits a marriage between the two.

48. Read the following and give correct answer with the help of codes given below:

A married Hindu female can adopt a child:

(a) Only with the consent of her husband.
(b) In case of void marriage, consent of husband is necessary.
(c) In case of voidable marriage, consent of husband is not necessary.
(d) If husband has converted to Muslim religion, his consent is not necessary.

Codes:

A. (a) and (d) are correct, but (b) and (c) are incorrect.
B. (a), (c) and (d) are correct, but (b) is incorrect.
C. (b) and (d) are correct, but (a) and (c) are incorrect.
D. (d) and (b) are correct, but (c) and (a) are incorrect.

49. Which of the following is not a ground of divorce available to wife under Section 13(2) of the Hindu Marriage Act, 1955?

A. Pre-Act bigamy of the husband
B. Repudiation of marriage
C. Cruelty by the husband
D. Husband is guilty of rape, sodomy and bestiality

50. Read the following statements and give correct answer with the help of codes given below:

(*a*) A Muslim woman can marry a Kitabi.
(*b*) A Shia male can contract 'Muta' with a fire worshipper.
(*c*) Marriage of a Muslim woman with a Hindu would be irregular.
(*d*) A Muslim man cannot marry his niece.

Codes:

A. (*a*) and (*b*) are correct, but (*c*) and (*d*) are incorrect.
B. (*b*) and (*c*) are correct, but (*a*) and (*d*) are incorrect.
C. (*c*) and (*d*) are correct, but (*a*) and (*b*) are incorrect.
D. (*b*) and (*d*) are correct, but (*a*) and (*c*) are incorrect.

51. Read the following statements in the light of Hindu Adoptions and Maintenance Act, 1956 and give correct answer with the help of codes given below:

(*a*) The obligation of husband to maintain his wife is co-extensive with his property.
(*b*) Sec. 18(2) provides for maintenance and separate residence of wife in some conditions.
(*c*) Father-in-law's obligation to maintain widowed daughter-in-law is a personal obligation.
(*d*) An unchaste and non-Hindu wife is not entitled to maintenance.

Codes:

A. (*a*) and (*d*) are correct, but (*b*) and (*c*) are incorrect.
B. (*b*) and (*d*) are correct, but (*a*) and (*c*) are incorrect.
C. (*c*) and (*d*) are correct, but (*a*) and (*b*) are incorrect.
D. (*a*) and (*c*) are correct, but (*b*) and (*d*) are incorrect.

52. Which of the following is not a ground of divorce under section 2 of the Dissolution of Muslim Marriage Act, 1939?

A. 7 years imprisonment to the husband
B. Failure of the husband to pay maintenance for the last two years.
C. Whereabouts of the husband have not been known for a period of three years.
D. Failure of the husband to perform, without reasonable cause, his marital obligations for a period of three years.

53. Which of the following are not available to a Hindu husband as grounds of Judicial Separation?

Answer with the help of codes given below:

(*a*) Extra marital sex by wife
(*b*) Conversion of wife to a non-Hindu religion
(*c*) Wife's pre-marriage pregnancy
(*d*) Non consummation of marriage owing to impotence of wife.

Codes:

A. (*a*) and (*b*) only B. (*b*) and (*c*) only
C. (*d*) and (*a*) only D. (*c*) and (*d*) only

54. Which Article of the U.N. Charter charges the U.N. to promote "Universal respect for, and observance of, human rights and fundamental freedoms for all without distinction as to sex, race, language or religion"?

A. Article 56 B. Article 55(*c*)
C. Article 62 D. Article 76(*c*)

55. Match List-I and List-II and give the correct answer using the codes given below:

List-I	List-II
(*a*) The Commission on Human Rights was established by the Economic and Social Council on	(*i*) December 15, 1989
(*b*) The General Assembly created the position of U.N. High Commissioner for Human Rights on	(*ii*) 20 December, 1993

(*c*) The General Assembly adopted Second Optional Protocol to the International Co-venant on Civil and Political Rights on — (*iii*) February, 1946

(*d*) The Optional Protocol to the International Law on Civil and Political Rights, 1966 came into force on — (*iv*) March 23, 1976

Codes:

	(*a*)	(*b*)	(*c*)	(*d*)
A.	(*iii*)	(*ii*)	(*i*)	(*iv*)
B.	(*iv*)	(*iii*)	(*ii*)	(*i*)
C.	(*iii*)	(*iv*)	(*ii*)	(*i*)
D.	(*ii*)	(*i*)	(*iv*)	(*iii*)

56. Which of the following pair/pairs is/are not correctly matched? Give the correct answer using the codes given below:

(*a*) The World Conference on Human Rights was held in Vienna – Year 1993

(*b*) International Conference on Human Rights in Tehran was held – Year 1958

(*c*) First World Conference on Women was held in Beijing in – 1985

(*d*) International Convention on Elimination of all forms of Racial Discrimination – 1973

Codes:

A. Only (*b*) B. (*a*) and (*b*)

C. (*b*), (*c*) and (*d*) D. (*a*), (*b*), (*c*) and (*d*)

57. Which of the following has commented on the legal significance of the Universal Declaration of Human Rights thus, "The declaration is merely a statement of principles, not a legally binding instrument; but it has become one of the best known international documents, and it has been often referred to in resolutions of the U.N., the Specialised Agencies, regional arrangements and other International Organisations, and in national constitutions; legislation and court decision. It is a beacon light for all mankind even though it has been honoured more often in the breach than in the observance"?

A. Starke B. H. Lauterpacht

C. Oppenheim D. Palmer and Perkins

58. Read both Assertion (A) and Reason (R) and give the correct answer using the codes given below:

Assertion (A): The Universal Declaration of Human Rights does not define the term 'Human Rights'. It refers them as "the equal and inalienable rights of all members of the Humanity".

Reason (R): The framers of the Indian Constitution were influenced by the concept of Human Rights and guaranteed most of the Human Rights contained in the Universal Declaration of Human Rights.

Codes:

A. Both (A) and (R) are correct and (R) is the correct explanation of (A).

B. Both (A) and (R) are correct, but (R) is not the correct explanation of (A).

C. (A) is correct, but (R) is wrong.

D. (A) is wrong, but (R) is true.

59. To which of the following International Conventions on Human Rights, India has become party to such conventions? Give correct answer with the help of codes given below:

(*a*) Convention on the Political Rights of Women.

(*b*) Convention on the Right of the Child.

(*c*) Convention for the Suppression of the Traffic in Person and of exploitation of the prostitution of others.

(*d*) Convention on International Recovery of Child Support and Other Forms of Family Maintenance.

Codes:

A. Only (*a*)
B. (*a*) and (*d*) only
C. (*a*), (*b*) and (*c*)
D. (*a*), (*b*), (*c*) and (*d*) all

60. Match List-I and List-II and give the correct answer using the codes given below:

List-I (*Provisions of Protection of Human Rights Act, 1993*)	List-II (*Relevant Sections*)
(*a*) Removal of a Member of the Commission	(*i*) Section 12
(*b*) Functions of the Commission	(*ii*) Section 4
(*c*) Procedure with respect to Armed Forces	(*iii*) Section 5
(*d*) Appointment of Chairperson and other Members	(*iv*) Section 19

Codes:

	(*a*)	(*b*)	(*c*)	(*d*)
A.	(*ii*)	(*iv*)	(*i*)	(*iii*)
B.	(*i*)	(*ii*)	(*iii*)	(*iv*)
C.	(*iii*)	(*i*)	(*ii*)	(*iv*)
D.	(*iv*)	(*iii*)	(*i*)	(*ii*)

61. In which among the following cases malice becomes relevant to determine a person's liability in law of torts. Answer using codes below:

(*a*) Malice may result in aggravation of damages.
(*b*) In torts of deceit and conspiracy one of the essential is malice.
(*c*) When act is lawful, intention can be gathered from past circumstances.
(*d*) Causing of personal comfort by lawful means may turn lawful act into a tort.

Codes:

A. (*a*) and (*b*) B. (*a*) and (*c*)
C. (*a*), (*b*) and (*c*) D. (*a*), (*b*), (*c*) and (*d*)

62. Match List-I (Maxims) with List-II (Cases) and give correct answer using codes given below:

List-I (*Maxims*)	List-II (*Cases*)
(*a*) Damnum sine injuria	(*i*) Padmavati v. Dugganika
(*b*) Injuria sine damno	(*ii*) Vishnu Datt v. Board of Higher Secondary and Intermediate Education, U.P.
(*c*) Volenti non fit injuria	(*iii*) Bindra Devi Chauhan v. State of H.P.
(*d*) Res ipsa loquitor	(*iv*) Bhim Singh v. State of Jammu and Kashmir

Codes :

	(*a*)	(*b*)	(*c*)	(*d*)
A.	(*ii*)	(*iv*)	(*iii*)	(*i*)
B.	(*ii*)	(*iii*)	(*i*)	(*iv*)
C.	(*ii*)	(*iv*)	(*i*)	(*iii*)
D.	(*i*)	(*ii*)	(*iv*)	(*iii*)

63. In which of the following cases originator of defamatory statement will be liable for the damage resulting from repetitive publication by third persons? Answer using codes below:

(*a*) He himself authorized repetition.
(*b*) Repetition was the natural and probable consequence of his act.
(*c*) There was immoral obligation on the person in whose presence the slander was made to repeat it.
(*d*) There was moral obligation on the person in whose absence the slander was made to repeat it.

Codes:

A. (*a*) and (*b*) B. (*a*) and (*c*)
C. (*a*) and (*d*) D. (*b*) and (*d*)

64. Which of the following is true in relation to nuisance?

A. An action for nuisance is actionable per se and no special damage need to be proved.

B. It can be committed through the medium of intangible objects.
C. It is a direct interference with the possession of plaintiff.
D. There is no interference with plaintiff's use or enjoyment of land.

65. Read Assertion (A) and Reason (R) and answer using codes below:

Assertion (A): The law takes no cognizance of carelessness in the abstract.

Reason (R): Cause of action for negligence accrues when damage that is real damage is suffered.

Codes:

A. Both (A) and (R) are true and (R) is right explanation of (A).
B. Both (A) and (R) are true, but (R) is not the right explanation of (A).
C. (A) is right, but (R) is wrong.
D. (A) is wrong, but (R) is right.

66. Which of the following is not correct in relation to the Consumer Protection Act?

A. It extends to whole of India except the State of Jammu and Kashmir.
B. It shall come into force on such date as the Central Government may by notification appoint.
C. This Act shall be in addition to and not in derogation of provisions of any other law for the time being in force.
D. This Act shall overside the provisions of Sale of Goods Act.

67. What is the period of limitation to file a complaint before the Consumer Dispute Redressal Agencies?

A. Within one year from the date of cause of action.
B. Within two years from the date of cause of action.
C. Within three years from the date of cause of action.
D. No limitation period to file a complaint.

68. Read Assertion (A) and Reason (R) and answer using codes below:

Assertion (A): Salary drawn by a partner from the firm for his services rendered to it has been treated different from his right to get an additional amount in the form of salary as his share of the firm's profit.

Reason (R): Because R.M. Chidambaram Pillai v. Commissioner of Income Tax case laid down above principle.

Codes:

A. Both (A) and (R) are correct and (R) is the correct reason for (A).
B. Both (A) and (R) are wrong.
C. (A) is right, but (R) is wrong.
D. (R) is right, but (A) is wrong.

69. Match List-I with List-II and select the correct answer using the codes given below:

List-I *(Principles of mutual rights and liabilities of partners)*	List-II *(Relevant case-law)*
(*a*) Remuneration to a partner in the absence of an agreement on this matter.	(*i*) Md. Abdul Sattar v. State of Andhra Pradesh
(*b*) Fixation of remuneration by agreement in respect of a partner does not alter his status as a partner	(*ii*) Ghisulal v. Ghumbirmal
(*c*) Interest on the capital of a partner	(*iii*) Shelat Brothers v. Nanalal Harilal Shelat
(*d*) Action against a partner for balance due to another	(*iv*) Bhagchand v. Kaluram alias Moolchand and others

Codes:

	(*a*)	(*b*)	(*c*)	(*d*)
A.	(*iv*)	(*ii*)	(*i*)	(*iii*)
B.	(*iii*)	(*i*)	(*ii*)	(*iv*)
C.	(*i*)	(*iii*)	(*iv*)	(*ii*)
D.	(*iii*)	(*i*)	(*iv*)	(*ii*)

70. Read Assertion (A) and Reason (R) and answer using codes given below:

Assertion (A): Partner of an erstwhile unregistered partnership firm can bring a suit to enforce a right arising out of a contract falling within the ambit of section 69 of the Indian Partnership Act.

Reason (R): Because Judgement in case of Loonkaran Sethia v. Ivan E. John laid down above judicial principle.

Codes:

A. Both (A) and (R) are correct and (R) is the correct reason for (A).
B. Both (A) and (R) are wrong.
C. (A) is right, but (R) is wrong.
D. (A) is wrong, but (R) is right.

71. Which of the following statements is correct according to Section 2(9) of the Sale of Goods Act?

"Mercantile Agent" means a mercantile agent

A. having in the usual course of business as such seller authority either to sell goods, or to consign goods for the purpose of sale, or to buy goods, or to distribute money for security of goods.
B. having in the customary business as such agent power either to sell goods, or to mortgage goods for purpose of sale.
C. having in the customary course of business as such agent authority to sell goods.
D. having in the normal course of business as such agent authority to confine goods or to raise goods for purpose of the security of money.

72. Which of the following statements is/are correct? Answer using the codes given below:

(*a*) Ascertainment of goods for sale is done by the buyer.
(*b*) Appropriation of goods for sale is done by the seller.
(*c*) Distinction between ascertainment of goods and appropriation of goods that former involves "the element of common intention between buyer and seller", whereas later can be a unilateral act by the buyer.
(*d*) Property in goods does not pass to buyer till appropriation.

Codes:

A. Only (*a*), (*c*) and (*d*) are correct.
B. Only (*b*) is correct.
C. Only (*d*) is correct.
D. Only (*c*) is correct.

73. Which of the following are presumptions as to a negotiable instrument under Section 118 of the Negotiable Instruments Act? Answer using codes given below:

(*a*) Presumption of contractual capacity
(*b*) Presumption of consideration
(*c*) Presumption of maturity of instrument
(*d*) Presumption of date

Codes:

A. Only (*a*) and (*c*) B. Only (*b*) and (*d*)
C. Only (*a*) and (*d*) D. Only (*a*) and (*b*)

74. Which of the following statements is correct? Answer using codes given below:

(*a*) Doctrine of indoor management applies in case of knowledge of irregularity in company.
(*b*) Doctrine of indoor management does not apply in case of suspicion of irregularity.
(*c*) Doctrine of indoor management applies in case of forgery.
(*d*) Doctrine of indoor management does not apply if the act of an officer of a company is one which would ordinarily be beyond the powers of such an officer.

Codes:

A. Only (*a*) is correct B. Only (*b*) is correct
C. Only (*c*) is correct D. Only (*d*) is correct

75. Find answer using codes given below:

Director may be removed by

(*a*) Other Directors
(*b*) Creditors
(*c*) Central Government
(*d*) Shareholders in a general meeting

Codes:

A. Only (*a*) and (*b*) are correct.
B. Only (*b*) and (*c*) are correct.
C. Only (*c*) and (*d*) are correct.
D. Only (*d*) and (*a*) are correct.

ANSWERS

1	2	3	4	5	6	7	8	9	10
A	A	C	D	A	D	B	B	B	A
11	**12**	**13**	**14**	**15**	**16**	**17**	**18**	**19**	**20**
D	B	C	B	D	C	B	D	A	A
21	**22**	**23**	**24**	**25**	**26**	**27**	**28**	**29**	**30**
A	B	A	B	D	B	A	C	A	C
31	**32**	**33**	**34**	**35**	**36**	**37**	**38**	**39**	**40**
D	B	B	A	B	C	C	B	B	C
41	**42**	**43**	**44**	**45**	**46**	**47**	**48**	**49**	**50**
B	C	B	A	B	C	B	A	C	D
51	**52**	**53**	**54**	**55**	**56**	**57**	**58**	**59**	**60**
B	C	D	B	A	C	D	B	C	A
61	**62**	**63**	**64**	**65**	**66**	**67**	**68**	**69**	**70**
A	C	A	B	A	D	B	B	D	B
71	**72**	**73**	**74**	**75**					
C	C	B	D	C					

EXPLANATORY ANSWERS

2. Article 254(2) of the Constitution reads, "Where a law made by the Legislature of a State with respect to one of the matters enumerated in the concurrent List contains any provision repugnant to the provisions of an earlier law made by Parliament or an existing law with respect to that matter, then, the law so made by the Legislature of such State shall, if it has been reserved for the consideration of the President and has received his assent, prevail in that State: Provided that nothing in this clause shall prevent Parliament from enacting at any time any law with respect to the same matter including a law adding to, amending, varying or repealing the law so made by the Legislature of the State".

3. The Indian Constitution confers upon the Supreme Court advisory jurisdiction on certain matters upon the President's reference. According to Article 143 of the Constitution the President may seek the opinion of the Supreme Court on any question of law or fact of public importance on which he thinks it expedient to obtain such an opinion. On receiving such reference the Supreme Court, after giving it such hearing as it deems fit, may report to the President its opinion. The opinion is only advisory and is not binding upon the President.

6. Clause (1) and (2) of Article 22 of the Constitution of India that deals with Protection against arrest and detention in certain cases provide that:

(1) No person who is arrested shall be detained in custody without being informed, as soon as may be, of the grounds for such arrest nor shall he be

denied the right to consult, and to be defended by a legal practitioner of his choice.

(2) Every person who is arrested and detained in custody shall be produced before the **nearest magistrate** within a period of twenty four hours of such arrest excluding the time necessary for the journey from the place of arrest to the court of the magistrate and no such person shall be detained in custody beyond the said period without the authority of **a magistrate**.

7. Article 368(1) that deals with the Power of Parliament to amend the Constitution and procedure therefore provides that "Notwithstanding anything in this Constitution, Parliament may in exercise of its constituent power amend by way of addition, variation or repeal any provision of this Constitution in accordance with the procedure laid down in this article".

Assertion (A) states that such power is subject to anything contained in the constitution, this is an incorrect reading of Article 368.

8. Article 325 provides that "No person to be ineligible for inclusion in, or to claim to be included in a special, electoral roll on grounds of religion, race, caste or sex. There shall be one general electoral roll for every territorial constituency for election to either House of Parliament or to the House or either House of the Legislature of a State and no person shall be ineligible for inclusion in any such roll or claim to be included in any special electoral roll for any such constituency on grounds only of religion, race, caste, sex or any of them".

10. The writ of mandamus is a writ compelling performance of a specific legal duty by a lower court or a government officer/department by the High Court or the Supreme Court under their writ jurisdiction in Article 226 or Article 32 respectively. Statements (*a*) to (*d*) mention attributes necessary for the grant of writ flowing from diverse judgements.

11. The Supreme Court in **H.L.Trehan v. Union of India 1989 AIR 568** observed: "in our opinion, the post-decisional opportunity of hearing does not sub-serve the rules of natural justice. The authority which embarks upon a post-decisional hearing will normally proceed with a closed mind and there is hardly any chance of getting a proper consideration of the representation at such a post-decisional opportunity."

13. The writ of prohibition is used as a prevention while the writ of certiorari is used as a cure. Certiorari is exercised when a lower judicial or quasi judicial authority has exercised its jurisdiction and given a decision on merits of the proceedings. In such a scenario the High Court or the Supreme Court as the case may be, issues a writ of certiorari and calls the records of the case for final disposition. However, prohibition is a writ which is issued while the proceedings are in progress and no final decision has been made. In such a scenario a writ of prohibition will put a stay on the court from continuing with the proceedings.

15. Section 4 of the Lokpal and Lokayuktas Act, 2013 provides for the selection committee for the appointment of Chairperson of Lokpal comprising:

(*a*) the Prime Minister–Chairperson;

(*b*) the Speaker of the House of the People–Member;

(*c*) the Leader of Opposition in the House of the People–Member;

(*d*) the Chief Justice of India or a Judge of the Supreme Court nominated by him–Member;

(*e*) one eminent jurist, as recommended by the Chairperson and Members referred to in clauses (*a*) to (*d*) above, to be nominated by the President–Member.

16. Roscoe Pound is one of the most influential exponents of the Sociological School of Jurisprudence. According to him law is a means of "social engineering", *i.e.*, minimizing conflict and optimizing the benefit of society.

18. When people habitually and voluntarily practise a certain conduct for their own benefit or to regulate their affairs among each other, such practice or conduct over a long period of time acquires the sanctity of a custom. For a custom to have the force of law it shall have the following ingredients:

(*i*) Custom shall be certain and not ambiguous.

(*ii*) Custom shall be uniformly and universally applicable within the local area or the local community which claims its application.

(*iii*) It shall be ancient or observed since immemorial antiquity.

(*iv*) Its observance shall be continuous and uninterrupted.

(*v*) It shall be in conformity with prevailing public policy or the statute law.

20. Mediate Possession is when a person who is legally entitled to hold/possess it through somebody else. Immediate possession is the person who holds a thing on behalf of someone else. The person in immediate possession of a thing has a better title to possess a thing than everybody else except the person in whom the mediate possession for the thing resides.

22. Ownership in a thing gives many rights to the person owning. One of the important rights is the right to exclude others from its use. However, in many cases the owner maybe able to grant many of his rights and yet remain owner. For example, a house given on rent, the owner leases his right to exclude others from its use, possession of the property, etc., at the time of entering the lease.

26. Section 350 of IPC defines Criminal force as —Whoever intentionally uses force to any person, without that person's consent, in order to the committing of any offence, or intending by the use of such force to cause, or knowing it to be likely that by the use of such force he will cause injury, fear or annoyance to the person to whom the force is used, is said to use criminal force to that other.

28. According to Section 9 of IPC, there is no right of private defence against an act which does not reasonably cause the apprehension of death or of grievous hurt, if done, or attempted to be done, by a public servant acting in good faith under colour of his office, though that act, may not be strictly justifiable by law. There is no right of private defence against an act which does not reasonably cause the apprehension of death or of grievous hurt, if done, or attempted to be done, by the direction of a public servant acting in good faith under colour of his office, though that direction may not be strictly justifiable by law. There is no right of private defence in cases in which there is time to have recourse to the protection of the public authorities.

29. Section 396 of Indian Penal Code provides an aggravated form of dacoity in which murder has also been caused. The section reads as "If anyone of five or more persons, who are conjointly committing dacoity, commits **murder** in so committing dacoity, every one of those persons shall be punished with death, or imprisonment for life, or rigorous imprisonment for a term which may extend to ten years, and shall also be liable to fine".

30. Since, there was no dishonest intention on part of the woman no criminal liability can be fastened upon her.

31. Section 509 IPC makes punishable ***any*** word, gesture or act intended to insult the modesty of a woman. The section reads "If anyone of five or more persons, who are conjointly committing dacoity, commits **murder** in so committing dacoity, every one of those persons shall be punished with death, or [imprisonment for life], or rigorous imprisonment for a term which may extend to ten years, and shall also be liable to fine". Since the action of the young man falls in the category of a 'gesture' intended to insult the woman, he is liable under section 509.

32. Convention on Environmental Impact Assesment in Transboundary Context, also known as the Espoo Convention is a UN Convention that deals with early stage environmental impact assessment for certain activites. Other conventions are targeted at wildlife conversation.

33. Montreal Protocol was signed through 14-16 September 1987 and is effective since 1st January 1989. It is a protocol targeted to reduce emissions of CFCs and other harmful gases that adversely affect the ozone layer.

38. The Preamble to Air (Prevention and Control of Pollution) Act of 1981 states that this law is enacted to implement the Stockholm Convention 1972. Article 253 empowers Parliament to make laws for implementing any treaty, agreement or convention with any other country/countries or for implementing any decision made at any international conference, association or other body. This Article, along with Article 51(c) which castes an obligation on the State that it shall endeavour to foster respect for international law and treaty obligations, enable the Parliament to enact laws on any entries contained in List II of the constitution, *i.e.*, the state list.

40. The right of passage (Portugal v India) is a landmark judgement on recognition of customs in International Law. In this case there was a more than century old custom between India and Portugal which allowed the Portuguese ships the right for passage to and fro its enclaves in India. The International Court held that regional customs if proved are legally valid and binding between the parties.

42. Statement II is incorrect. Stock v Public Trustee is a case on absent nationality. Statement III is incorrect.

Article 3 to Article 6 of Hague Convention 1930 read as following:

Article 3: Subject to the provisions of the present Convention, a person having two or more nationalities may be regarded as its national by each of the States whose nationality he possesses.

Article 4: A State may not afford diplomatic protection to one of its nationals against a State whose nationality such person also possesses.

Article 5: Within a third State, a person having more than one nationality shall be treated as if he had only one. Without prejudice to the application of its law in matters of personal status and of any conventions in force, a third State shall, of the nationalities which any such person possesses, recognise exclusively in its territory either the nationality of the country in which he is habitually and principally resident, or the nationality of the country with which in the circumstances he appears to be in fact most closely connected.

Article 6: Without prejudice to the liberty of a State to accord wider rights to renounce its nationality, a person possessing two nationalities acquired without any voluntary act on his part may renounce one of them with the authorisation of the State whose nationality he desires to surrender. This authorisation may not be refused in the case of a person who has his habitual and principal residence abroad, if the conditions laid down in the law of the State whose nationality he desires to surrender are satisfied.

Statement IV is incorrect. "Cession" is a mode of assignment of property (*e.g.*, Land) to another entity.

45. Composition of General Assembly is provided for in Article 9 of UN Charter. Composition of Trusteeship Council is provided for in Article 86 of UN Charter.

48. Statement (*b*) is incorrect: In case of a void marriage there is no legal marriage subsisting hence, the lady needs no consent from the man.

Statement (*c*) is incorrect: A voidable marriage is a valid marriage until a decree of annulment is not obtained from the court of law. Till the time a valid marriage is subsisting the wife needs consent of husband.

49. Under Section 13(2) wife has four additional grounds available for divorce. These are:

(*i*) in the case of any marriage solemnised before the commencement of this Act, that the husband had married again before such commencement or that any other wife of the husband married before such commencement was alive at the time of the solemnisation of the marriage of the petitioner: Provided that in either case the other wife is alive at the time of the presentation of the petition; or

(*ii*) that the husband has, since the solemnisation of the marriage, been guilty of rape, sodomy or bestiality or

(*iii*) that in a suit under Section 18 of the Hindu Adoptions and Maintenance Act, 1956 (78 of 1956), or in a proceeding under Section 125 of the Code of Criminal Procedure, 1973 (2 of 1974) [or under the corresponding Section 488 of the Code of Criminal Procedure, 1898 (5 of 1898)], a decree or order, as the case may be, has been passed against the husband awarding maintenance to the wife notwithstanding that she was living apart and that since the passing of such decree or order, cohabitation between the parties has not been resumed for one year or upwards; or

(*iv*) that her marriage (whether consummated or not) was solemnised before she attained the age of fifteen years and she has repudiated the marriage after attaining that age but before attaining the age of eighteen years.

The ground of cruelty is not contained in 13(2) but it is contained in 13(1) and is common to both husband and wife.

50. Statement (*a*) is incorrect: Under Muslim Law, a muslim male may marry a Kitabia (*e.g.*, a Christian) but a Muslim woman cannot marry a Kitabia and such marriage will be invalid and void.

Statement (*c*) is incorrect: An irregular marriage is one which can be validated by some post act of the parties. However, a Muslim woman's marriage to a fire worshipper (*e.g.*, a Hindu) is invalid and it cannot be regularized.

51. Statement (*a*) is incorrect: The obligation of husband to maintain his wife is not subject or co-extensive to his property.

Statement (*c*) is incorrect: According to Section 19(2) the obligation of a father-in-law to maintain his daughter-in-law is not his personal obligation and he is not liable to maintain her if he has not the means to do so from any coparcenary property in his possession out of which the daughter-in-law has not obtained any share, and any such obligation shall cease on the remarriage of the daughter-in-law.

52. The grounds available to a Muslim woman for obtaining divorce under Section 2 of Muslim Marriage Act, 1939 are:

(*i*) that the whereabouts of the husband have not been known for a period of four years;

(*ii*) that the husband has neglected or has failed to provide for her maintenance for a period of two years;

(*iii*) that the husband has been sentenced to imprisonment for a period of seven years or upwards;

(*iv*) that the husband has failed to perform, without reasonable cause, his marital obligations for a period of three years;

(*v*) that the husband was impotent at the time of the marriage and continues to be so;

(*vi*) that the husband has been insane for a period of two years or is suffering from leprosy or a virulent venereal disease;

(*vii*) that she, having been given in marriage by her father or other guardian before she attained the age of fifteen years, repudiated the marriage before attaining the age of eighteen years.

53. The grounds for judicial separation available to the husband are same as the grounds available for divorce under Section 13(1). According to Section 13(1) any marriage solemnised, whether before or after the commencement of this Act, may, on a petition presented by either the husband or the wife, be dissolved by a decree of divorce on the ground that the other party—

(*i*) has, after the solemnisation of the marriage, had voluntary sexual intercourse with any person other than his or her spouse; or

(*a*) has, after the solemnisation of the marriage, treated the petitioner with cruelty; or

(*b*) has deserted the petitioner for a continuous period of not less than two years immediately preceding the presentation of the petition; or

(*ii*) has ceased to be a Hindu by conversion to another religion; or

(*iii*) has been incurably of unsound mind, or has been suffering continuously or intermittently from mental disorder of such a kind and to such an extent that the petitioner cannot reasonably be expected to live with the respondent.

(*iv*) has been suffering from a virulent and incurable form of leprosy; or

(*v*) has been suffering from venereal disease in a communicable form; or

(*vi*) has renounced the world by entering any religious order; or

(*vi*) has not been heard of as being alive for a period of seven years or more by those persons who would naturally have heard of it, had that party been alive.

54. Article 55: With a view to the creation of conditions of stability and well-being which are necessary for peaceful and friendly relations among nations based on respect for the principle of equal rights and self-determination of people, the United Nations shall promote:

(*a*) higher standards of living, full employment, and conditions of economic and social progress and development;

(*b*) solutions to international economic, social, health, and related problems; and international cultural and educational cooperation; and

(*c*) universal respect for, and observance of, human rights and fundamental freedoms for all without distinction as to race, sex, language, or religion.

Article 56: All members pledge themselves to take joint and separate action in co-operation with the Organization for the achievement of the purposes set forth in Article 55.

Article 62 deals with the powers and functions of ECOSOC.

Article 76 deals with the basic objectives of the trusteeship system.

64. Nuisance is derived from the word *nuire* or 'to annoy'. Annoyance can be from a variety of intangible things such as sight, smell, noise etc.

66. Section 3 of the Consumer Protection Act 1986 specifically provides that the Act is not in derogation of any other law. The said section reads as "The provisions of this Act shall be in addition to and not in derogation of the provisions of any other law for the time being in force." This means that it does not override any other act including the sale of goods act and is only in addition to it.

67. Section 24A(1) of Consumer Protection Act 1986 reads as "The District Forum, the State Commission or the National Commission shall not admit a complaint unless it is filed within two years from the date on which the cause of action has arisen."

74. The doctrine of indoor management acts for the benefit of the outsiders dealing with the company and is opposite to the rule of constructive notice. According to this doctrine, if the transaction is valid and proper as far as the memorandum and articles of association of a company are concerned then the outsiders are not in an obligation to inquire about the internal functioning of the company. The doctrine raises a presumption that all internal proceedings of the company are as per the Memorandum and Articles and the company is carrying out its work in a manner prescribed by law. However, this doctrine has certain exceptions.

1. **Knowledge:** If the outsider has knowledge of the irregularity being committed by the company then he cannot raise the presumption of innocence. Even in cases where there are reasonable grounds of suspicion and the outsider has not acted diligently even then he cannot take the benefit of this doctrine.
2. **Forgery:** A company cannot be held to be bound by any forgery committed by any of its officers. For such an act the offenders shall be personally liable.
3. **Act beyond the scope of powers:** If an outsider is dealing with such an officer of the company who in ordinary course is evident that is not vested by such powers to enter into a transaction on behalf of the company then also the benefit of this doctrine cannot be availed.

75. The right to remove a Director is a legal right of the shareholders under Section 169 of Companies Act 2013. Section 169(1) of the Companies Act provides that "A company may, by ordinary resolution, remove a director, not being a director appointed by the Tribunal under Section 242, before the expiry of the period of his office after giving him a reasonable opportunity of being heard".

Previous Paper (Solved)

UGC-NET-JRF & Assistant Professor Exam

Law, July-2016

PAPER-II

Note: *This paper contains **fifty (50)** objective type questions of **two (2)** marks each. **All** questions are compulsory.*

1. In Golaknath Vs State of Punjab Justice K. Subba Rao observed:

A. The Preamble contains in a nutshell ideals and aspirations of the Constitution.

B. The Preamble is the key to open the minds of the Constitution makers.

C. The Preamble is enforceable by the Judiciary.

D. The Preamble of our Constitution is of great importance and it should be implemented.

2. The Five Judges Constitution Bench held that 'Imparting Education cannot be treated as a Trade or Business' in which of the following cases?

A. Unnikrishanan Case

B. Mohini Jain Case

C. Dinesh Kumar Case

D. P.A. Inamdar Case

3. As per the Constitution of India, which of the following statement(s) is/are correct?

(*a*) The state may make provision for securing just and humane conditions of work.

(*b*) The state shall endeavour to provide early childhood care and education for all the children until they complete the age of six years.

(*c*) The state shall not endeavour to secure for the citizens a uniform civil code in the territory of India.

(*d*) The state shall endeavour to protect and improve the environment and to safeguard the forests and wildlife of the country.

Codes:

A. (*a*), (*b*) and (*c*) B. (*b*), (*c*) and (*d*)

C. (*b*) and (*d*) D. (*c*) and (*d*)

4. Read Assertion (A) and Reason (R) and answer using the codes given below:

Assertion (A): No minimum age is prescribed for appointment as a Judge of the Supreme Court of India nor is there any fixed period of office.

Reason (R): The original jurisdiction of the Supreme Court is dealt within Article-132 of the Constitution of India.

Codes:

A. (A) and (R) are right and (R) is the correct explanation of (A).

B. (A) and (R) are right, but (R) is not the right explanation of (A).

C. (A) is right, but (R) is wrong.

D. Both (A) and (R) are wrong.

5. In which one of the following cases the Supreme Court of India had invalidated a Constitutional Amendment for non compliance with the procedure contained in the proviso to clause (2) of Article-368?

A. Kihoto Hollohan Vs. Zachilhu and others

B. Keshavanand Bharati Vs. State of Kerala

C. Golaknath Vs. State of Punjab

D. State of West Bengal Vs. Union of India

* Exam held on 10/07/2016.

6. If the President of India is satisfied that a grave emergency exists whereby the security of India or any part of the territory thereof is threatened whether by war or external aggression or armed rebellion he may by proclamation make a declaration to that effect. Here the 'satisfaction' of the President of India means:

A. The personal satisfaction of the President of India.

B. The personal satisfaction of the Prime Minister and all the Council of Ministers and informing to the President of India.

C. The decision of the Union Cabinet that such a proclamation may be issued, has been communicated to him in writing.

D. The decision of the Union Cabinet, that such a proclamation may be issued, has been communicated to him in writing along with 2/3rd Parliament Member's signature.

7. Match the List-I with List-II and select the correct answer using the codes given below:

List-I	List-II
(*a*) Hari Krishna Bhargav Vs Union of India	(*i*) Conditional Legislation
(*b*) Godfrey Philips India Ltd. Vs State of UP	(*iii*) Principles of Interpretation to avoid over lapping
(*c*) K.C. Gajapati Narayan Deo Vs State of Orissa	(*ii*) Power of Parliament to levy taxes on income other than Agricultural Income
(*d*) In re : The Delhi Laws Act	(*ii*) Colourable Legislation

Codes:

	(*a*)	(*b*)	(*c*)	(*d*)
A.	(*iii*)	(*ii*)	(*iv*)	(*i*)
B.	(*ii*)	(*iii*)	(*i*)	(*iv*)
C.	(*iii*)	(*iv*)	(*ii*)	(*i*)
D.	(*ii*)	(*iii*)	(*iv*)	(*i*)

8. "The task of social engineering is to build as efficient structure of the society as possible with minimum friction and waste."

This statement is of:

A. Kelsen

B. Roscoe Pound

C. Savigny

D. Karl Marx

9. Ratio decidendi may be defined as:

A. Statement of law applied to the legal problems disclosed by facts.

B. Finding of material facts, direct and inferential, based on earlier case law.

C. The rule of law which others regard as being of binding authority.

D. All of the above

10. Which one of the following groups indicate the four sanctions as enumerated by Bentham for various kinds of pleasure and pain?

A. Physical, Moral, Ethical and Political

B. Physical, Political, Moral and Religious

C. Moral, Social, Legal and Political

D. Legal, Ethical, Moral and Social

11. The three defects in the simple social structure of primary rules as enunciated by Hart are:

A. Their inadequacy, immobility and efficiency

B. Their uncertainty, static and inefficiency

C. Their mobility, easiness and simplicity

D. Their abnormality, violability and unsoundness

12. Match the List-I with List-II and select the correct answer using the codes given below:

List-I (Book)	List-II (Author)
(*a*) The Concept of Law	(*i*) Gray
(*b*) The Nature and Sources of the Law	(*ii*) Julius Stone
(*c*) Some Reflections on Jurisprudence	(*iii*) Buckland
(*d*) The Province and Function of Law	(*iv*) H.L.A. Hart

Codes:

	(a)	(b)	(c)	(d)
A.	(iv)	(i)	(iii)	(ii)
B.	(iv)	(ii)	(i)	(iii)
C.	(iv)	(i)	(ii)	(iii)
D.	(i)	(iii)	(iv)	(ii)

13. Which one of the following is not a theory of the nature of 'Legal Persons'?

A. Purpose Theory B. Fiction Theory
C. Interest Theory D. Bracket Theory

14. "International law must be continuously developed by revision in content, expansion of scope and improvement of the means of securing compliance, so that it is kept in accordance with the changing needs of the international community."

This statement is made by:

A. Starke B. Edward Collins
C. L. Oppenheim D. W. Friedman

15. Which of the following statement(s) is/are not correct?

(*a*) Decisions or determinations of the organs of International Institution does not find mention in Article-38 of the Statute of the International Court of Justice.

(*b*) *West Rand Central Gold Mining Company Ltd.* Vs. *R* is related to general principles of law recognised by civilized states.

(*c*) *Frontier Dispute (Barkina Faso Vs Mali)* is a case related to International customs as a source of law.

(*d*) The importance of the works of the jurists has been stressed by Justice Gray in *Barcelona Traction Case.*

Codes:

A. Only (*a*), (*b*) and (*c*) are not correct.
B. Only (*b*), (*c*) and (*d*) are not correct.
C. Only (*c*) and (*d*) are not correct.
D. (*a*), (*b*), (*c*) and (*d*) all are not correct.

16. Read the following statements and give the correct answer by using the codes given below:

Assertion (A): According to the exponents of Monism Theory, law is a Unified branch of knowledge, no matter whether it applies on persons or other entities.

Reason (R): In view of the Monistic writers in the ultimate analysis of the law we find that man is at the root to all laws.

Codes:

A. (A) and (R) both are correct and (R) is the correct explanation of (A).
B. (A) and (R) both are correct, but (R) is not the correct explanation of (A).
C. (A) is correct, (R) is wrong.
D. (A) is wrong, (R) is correct.

17. Which of the following statement(s) is/are correct?

(*a*) According to the constitutive theory of recognition, statehood or the authority of the new government exists as such prior to and independently of recognition.

(*b*) De Jure recognition is by nature provisional and may be made dependent on conditions with which the new entity has to comply.

(*c*) The principle that there is no distinction between de facto and de jure recognition for the purpose of giving effect to the internal acts of the recognised authority was laid down in *Luther* Vs. *Sagar.*

(*d*) De jure recognition is final and once given cannot be withdrawn.

Codes:

A. Only (*b*) is correct.
B. Only (*a*), (*b*) and (*c*) are correct.
C. Only (*b*), (*c*) and (*d*) are correct.
D. (*a*), (*b*), (*c*) and (*d*) all are correct.

18. The principle of self-determination has been incorporated in the Charter of United Nations under:

A. Article 2(7)
B. Article 5
C. Article 6
D. Articles 1(2), 55 and 56

19. The Commission on Human Rights was replaced by Human Rights Council by the General Assembly vide its Resolution:

A. 60/251 of 15 March, 2006
B. 61/260 of 15 March, 2008
C. 60/251 of 20 March, 2006
D. 60/251 of 30 March, 2006

20. 'Sapinda Relationship', which prohibits marriage among Hindus with near relatives on paternal and maternal sides, is based on the principle of

A. Monogamy B. Endogamy
C. Exogamy D. Polygamy

21. Match List-I with List-II under the Hindu Marriage Act, 1955 and give the correct answer with the help of codes given below:

List-I	List-II
(*a*) Ceremonies for a Hindu marriage	(*i*) Sec. 15
(*b*) Restitution of Conjugal Rights	(*ii*) Sec. 7
(*c*) Remarriage of divorced persons	(*iii*) Sec. 16
(*d*) Legitimacy of Children	(*iv*) Sec. 9

Codes:

	(*a*)	(*b*)	(*c*)	(*d*)
A.	(*i*)	(*iii*)	(*ii*)	(*iv*)
B.	(*ii*)	(*iv*)	(*i*)	(*iii*)
C.	(*iv*)	(*ii*)	(*iii*)	(*i*)
D.	(*iii*)	(*iv*)	(*ii*)	(*i*)

22. Read the following statement and answer with the help of the codes given below:

The guilt theory of divorce, on the one hand, implies a guilty party and on the other, it implies that the other party is innocent. In view of this which of the following is/are correct?

(*a*) If cruelty is provoked, divorce will be refused.
(*b*) If innocent party condones the acts of the guilty party, no divorce can be granted.
(*c*) If both parties were guilty, divorce would not be granted to either.
(*d*) Unreasonable delay in filing petition is no bar for the relief of divorce.

Codes:

A. Only (*a*) and (*c*) are correct.
B. Only (*b*) and (*c*) are correct.
C. Only (*a*), (*b*) and (*c*) are correct.
D. Only (*c*) and (*d*) are correct.

23. Match List-I with List-II and select the correct answer using the codes given below:

List-I (Veda)	List-II (Deals with)
(*a*) Yajurveda	(*i*) Praise of forces of nature
(*b*) Samveda	(*ii*) Magic, Spell and Incantation
(*c*) Atharvaveda	(*iii*) Rituals
(*d*) Rigveda	(*iv*) Dance

Codes:

	(*a*)	(*b*)	(*c*)	(*d*)
A.	(*i*)	(*ii*)	(*iv*)	(*iii*)
B.	(*ii*)	(*iv*)	(*i*)	(*iii*)
C.	(*iv*)	(*ii*)	(*iii*)	(*i*)
D.	(*iii*)	(*iv*)	(*ii*)	(*i*)

24. Which of the following statement(s) is/are correct in relation to 'muta' marriage?

(*a*) It is a temporary marriage.
(*b*) It is recognised under Sunni law.
(*c*) It is recognised under Shia law.
(*d*) It is a marriage for a fixed period.

Codes:

A. Only (*a*), (*c*) and (*d*) are correct.
B. Only (*b*), (*c*) and (*d*) are correct.
C. Only (*b*) is correct.
D. (*a*), (*b*), (*c*) and (*d*) all are correct.

25. Read Assertion (A) and Reason (R) and answer using the codes given below:

Assertion (A): The Shariat Act, 1937 makes Muslim law applicable expressly to all Muslims.

Reason (R): The Act has abrogated almost all the customs (except relating to agricultural land) applicable to Muslims.

Codes:

A. (A) is right, but (R) is wrong.
B. Both (A) and (R) are wrong.

C. (R) is right, but (A) is wrong.
D. Both (A) and (R) are right and (R) is the correct reason of (A).

26. The remedy of Restitution of Conjugal Rights has its roots in

A. Jewish Law
B. French Law
C. English Law
D. Indian Law

27. Read Assertion (A) and Reason (R) and answer using the codes given below:

Assertion (A): A juvenile delinquent may have physical capacity to commit crime, while he has no contractual capacity to do so.

Reason (R): According to Section-11 of the Indian Contract Act, a juvenile has no contractual capacity to commit crime.

Codes:

A. Both (A) and (R) are right and (R) is correct answer for (A).
B. Both (A) and (R) are wrong.
C. (A) is wrong, but (R) is right.
D. Both (A) and (R) are right, but (R) is not correct answer for (A).

28. "Consideration means a reasonable, equivalent or other valuable benefit passed on by the transferor to the transferee. Similarly, when the word 'consideration' was qualified by the word 'adequate' it makes the consideration stronger so as to make it sufficient and valuable having regard to the facts, circumstances and necessities of the case."

Above Principle was laid down in

A. Sonia Bhatia Vs State of U.P.
B. LIC of India Vs Pushpa P. Mansukhani
C. Dipraich Sugar Mills Ltd. Vs Mazdur Union
D. A.B.C. Laminart Pvt. Ltd. Vs A.P. Agencies, Salem

29. Which of the following statements is right?

A. An agreement not to do an impossible act in itself is void.
B. An agreement to do a possible act is void.
C. An agreement to do an act impossible in itself is void.
D. A contract to do an act, which after the contract is made, becomes impossible, or, by reason of some event which the promisor could not prevent to be unlawful, becomes valid, when the act becomes impossible or unlawful.

30. Match List-I with List-II and select the correct answer using the codes given below:

List-I	List-II
(*a*) Remoteness of damage	(*i*) Chief Secretary, State of Gujarat Vs Kothari and Associates
(*b*) Proof of loss to be given to claim special damages	(*ii*) Madras Railways Co. Vs Govind Rau
(*c*) Loss of profit is special loss	(*iii*) Karsandas H. Thacker Vs Saran Engg. Co. Ltd.
(*d*) Consequences of delays in transit	(*iv*) Union of India Vs Steel Stock Holders

Codes:

	(*a*)	(*b*)	(*c*)	(*d*)
A.	(*i*)	(*ii*)	(*iv*)	(*iii*)
B.	(*ii*)	(*i*)	(*iii*)	(*iv*)
C.	(*ii*)	(*iii*)	(*i*)	(*iv*)
D.	(*iv*)	(*i*)	(*iii*)	(*ii*)

31. Which of the following aspects are the parts of undue influence? Answer using codes given below:

(*a*) Inability to dominate will of other.
(*b*) A party unduly influencing and another party being unduly influenced are on equal footing.
(*c*) A relationship involving trust and confidence.
(*d*) In a relationship, one party is a person in mental distress.

Codes:

A. (*a*) and (*b*) only
B. (*b*) and (*c*) only
C. (*c*) and (*d*) only
D. (*a*) and (*d*) only

32. Which of the following statements are wrong? Answer using the codes given blow:

(*a*) Fraud renders a contract void.

(*b*) Misrepresentation renders a contract voidable.

(*c*) Misrepresentation is more or less an intentional wrong, whereas fraud may be quite innocent.

(*d*) Damages for loss caused by innocent misrepresentation are assessed on the same principles as in the case of a deliberate fraud.

Codes:

A. (*a*) and (*c*) only B. (*b*) and (*d*) only

C. (*a*) and (*d*) only D. (*a*) and (*b*) only

33. Which one of the following statements is correct in relation to the law of torts in India?

A. It is based on morality that no one has a right to injure or harm other intentionally or even innocently.

B. It is a civil wrong for which remedy is a common law action for liquidated damages.

C. It is based on law which in the constitutional context means judicially developed equity, covers everything which is covered by a statute.

D. It is an act and not omission suffered by a determinate person.

34. Match List-I with List-II and select the correct answer using the codes given below:

List-I (Defences in Tort)	List-II (Related cases)
(*a*) Volenti non fit injuria	(*i*) Olga Tellis Vs Municipal Corporation, Bombay
(*b*) Judicial acts	(*ii*) Samira Kohli Vs Prabha Manchanda
(*c*) Acts of State	(*iii*) Anwar Hussain Vs Ajoy Kumar
(*d*) Necessity	(*iv*) Vinod Kumar Shantilal Gosalia Vs Gangadhar Narsinghadas Agarwal

Codes:

	(*a*)	(*b*)	(*c*)	(*d*)
A.	(*ii*)	(*iii*)	(*iv*)	(*i*)
B.	(*ii*)	(*i*)	(*iv*)	(*iii*)
C.	(*iv*)	(*iii*)	(*i*)	(*ii*)
D.	(*i*)	(*ii*)	(*iii*)	(*iv*)

35. The police officers failed to observe the provisions of U.P. Police Regulations in taking care of the gold seized. The injury had been committed by the employees of the state during the course of its employment, but the employment was in special category of sovereign power, so the claim was not sustainable. It was held by the Supreme Court in

A. Mohammad Murad Vs Govt. of U.P.

B. Kasturilal Ralia Ram Jain Vs State of U.P.

C. State of U.P. Vs Hindustan Lever Ltd.

D. State of U.P. Vs Tulsiram

36. In which of the following cases the Supreme Court of India applied the principle of absolute liability? Give answer by using codes below:

(*a*) M.C. Mehta Vs Union of India

(*b*) Charan Lal Sahu Vs Union of India

(*c*) Indian Council for Enviro Legal Action Vs Union of India

(*d*) M.C. Mehta Vs State of MP

Codes:

A. (*a*), (*b*), (*c*) and (*d*)

B. (*b*), (*c*) and (*d*) only

C. (*c*) and (*d*) only

D. (*a*), (*b*) and (*c*) only

37. What remoteness of damage mean in relation to liability of defendant?

A. The defendant is not liable for all direct consequences of the tortuous acts if he could foresee them.

B. Forseeability is no test of remoteness of damages.

C. Liable in Law only for consequences which are not remote.

D. Directness of the consequences is the only test for the remoteness of the damages.

38. Andhra Pradesh State Road Transport Corporation Vs K. Hemlatha and Municipal Corporation Greater Bombay Vs Laxman Iyer are important cases decided by the Supreme Court on the rule of:
A. Act of God
B. Contributory Negligence
C. Nuisance
D. Trespass

39. Read the following Principle :
"There is always an imposed duty on a person to act on moral necessity to preserve one's life, yet there may be justifiable occasions of causing harm on innocent persons."

In the light of the above, in which of the following circumstances the accused can claim doctrine of self-preservation under the provisions of Sec. 81 of IPC?
A. When necessity is pleaded as a means of defence under sections 96 to 106.
B. Self-preservation is not an absolute necessity, so killing the weaker is justifiable by the stronger.
C. Arresting a drunken person moving in great danger at a public place.
D. When there is no choice of evil affecting the accused.

40. In the absence of any cogent definition of unsoundness of mind, the worldwide acceptance of its equivalent to insanity was propounded by:
A. Stephan B. Harris
C. Kenny D. Davis

41. The underlying principle covering the law on 'consent' is based on absolute and unconditional prohibition on the gravity of the offence relating to:
A. Simple hurt
B. Death
C. Theft from an unlocked house
D. Submission for detaining indecent liberties

42. The right of private defence is not allowed in which of the facts leading to:
A. The death was consequence of the assault.
B. More harm was done than necessary.
C. When the fact is clearly based on conjectures.
D. When the fact reveals about imminent danger to self or property.

43. When a person tries to escape from lawful custody while being taken to a Magistrate to furnish security for good behaviour could be punished under the provision of:
A. Section 224 of IPC
B. Section 225 of IPC
C. Section 225A of IPC
D. Section 225B of IPC

44. The distinction between intentional killing in hot blood and intentional killing when the blood was cool may be inferred through:
A. Provocation B. Self-control
C. Passion D. Resentment

45. Read Assertion (A) and Reason (R) and answer using the codes given below:

Assertion (A): In an illegal termination of workman the reinstatement of workman in service does not appear to be an acceptable option in all cases. The monetary compensation may sufficiently meet the ends of justice.

Reason (R): The compensation in lieu of reinstatement is the normal rule.

Codes:
A. Both (A) and (R) are true and (R) is the correct explanation of (A).
B. (A) and (R) are true, but (R) is not the correct explanation of (A).
C. (A) is true, but (R) is false.
D. (A) is false, but (R) is true.

46. An arbitration award is binding on:
A. All parties to the dispute.
B. All the workmen employed on the date of dispute and subsequent to the dispute.
C. The parties to the arbitration agreement.
D. All parties summoned to appear as parties to the dispute.

47. The Supreme Court referred the ILO instruments to reiterate the workers participation in the industrial process as enshrined in the constitution and other labour legislations in one of the following case:

A. Chandra Bhavan Boarding & Lodging, Bangalore Vs State of Mysore
B. Monogram Mills Ltd. Vs State of Gujarat
C. University of Delhi Vs Ramnath
D. K.V.S. Ravi Vs Bangalore Metropolitan Transport Corporation

48. Where an undertaking is closed for any reason whatsoever, every workman is entitled to compensation if such workman has been in the continuous service

A. for not less than 90 days
B. for not less than 6 months
C. for not less than one year
D. for not less than two years

49. "A strike could be legal or illegal and an illegal strike could be a justified one" was opined by Justice V.R. Krishna Iyer in one of the following case.

A. Bharat Kumar K. Palicha Vs State of Kerala
B. Gujarat Steel Tubes Vs Its Majdoor Sabha
C. Monogram Mills Ltd. Vs State of Gujarat
D. University of Delhi Vs Ramnath

50. A Seven Judges Bench of the Supreme Court exhaustively considered the scope of the definition 'Industry' and laid down the 'Triple test' in one of the following case:

A. State of Bombay Vs Hospital Mazdoor Sabha
B. University of Delhi Vs Ramnath
C. Management of Safdurjung Hospital, Delhi Vs Kuldip Singh
D. Bangalore Water Supply Vs A. Rayappa

ANSWERS

1	2	3	4	5	6	7	8	9	10
A	A	C	C	A	C	A	B	D	B
11	**12**	**13**	**14**	**15**	**16**	**17**	**18**	**19**	**20**
B	A	C	B	B	A	C	D	A	C
21	**22**	**23**	**24**	**25**	**26**	**27**	**28**	**29**	**30**
B	C	D	A	D	A	B	A	C	B
31	**32**	**33**	**34**	**35**	**36**	**37**	**38**	**39**	**40**
C	A	A	A	B	D	C	B	C	A
41	**42**	**43**	**44**	**45**	**46**	**47**	**48**	**49**	**50**
B	B	D	A	A	C	B	C	B	D

EXPLANATORY ANSWERS

1. The Golaknath case is a landmark judgement famous for holding that parliament has no power to amend the fundamental rights and recognising for the first time, the doctrine of prospective overruling.

Justice K Subba Rao was the ninth Chief Justice of India (30 June 1966–11 April 1967). He observed in Golaknath Judgement "it (preamble) contains in a nutshell, its ideals and its aspirations. The preamble is not a platitude but the, mode of its realisation is worked out in detail in the Constitution."

2. In J.P. Unnikrishnan Vs. the State of Andhra Pradesh case (A.I.R. 1993 SC 2178) it was held that children under the age of 14 have the fundamental right to free education. The

SC applied the principle of harmonious construction with respect to Art. 45 (Directive Principle) and Art. 21 (Fundamental Right) holding that access to education is an essential feature of right to life. Also, on the issue whether education is a trade or business the apex court observed, "We are, therefore, of the opinion, adopting the line of reasoning in State of Bombay Vs. R.M.D.C, 1957 S.C.R. 874, that imparting education cannot be treated as a trade or business. Education cannot be allowed to be converted into commerce nor can the petitioners seek to obtain the said result by relying upon the wider meaning of 'occupation'."

Prior to Unnikrishnan's case, right to education was held to be inherent in the right to life guaranteed by the constitution in Mohini Jain Vs. State of Karnataka and Ors 1992 SCR(3) 658 and excessive capitation fee being charged by medical and technical institutes in the country was struck down as violative of Art. 14 and Art. 21. This case was also challenged in the Unnikrishnan case. In P.A. Inamdar & Ors. Vs. State of Maharashtra it was held that the State can't impose its reservation policy on minority and non-minority unaided private colleges, including professional colleges.

4. Original Jurisdiction of Supreme Court is dealt within Article 131. Article 132 deals with appellate jurisdiction of the Supreme Court in appeals from High Courts in certain cases.

5. In Kihoto Hollohan Vs. Zachilhu and others, the amendment relating to the 10th schedule of the constitution (anti-defection law) was challenged. Paragraph 7 of the Tenth Schedule to the Constitution in terms and in effect excluded the jurisdiction of all Courts including the Supreme Court and High courts. It was argued that this brought about a change in the operation and effect of Articles 136, 226 and 227 of the constitution and therefore, the amendment would require ratification from at least half of the legislatures of state in accordance with the proviso to Article 368(2).

Thus, para 7 of the Tenth Schedule was invalidated for non-compliance with the procedure contained in proviso to Article 368(2) and doctrine of severability was applied to hold the remaining provisions constitutionally valid.

6. Article 352(3) of Indian Constitution says, "The President shall not issue a Proclamation under clause (1) or a Proclamation varying such Proclamation unless the decision of the Union Cabinet (that is to say, the Council consisting of the Prime Minister and other Ministers of Cabinet rank appointed under article 75) that such a Proclamation may be issued has been communicated to him in writing."

8. American jurist Roscoe Pound is considered as the father of 'Sociological School' of jurisprudence and is credited with the theory of 'Social Engineering' as a purpose of law.

10. Bentham in his book, *'An Introduction to the Principles of Morals and Legislation'* cites the four sources from which pleasure and pain usually flows as—Physical, Political, Moral and Religious.

11. According to HLA Hart, a society which consists of only primary rules will suffer from a variety of defects like, uncertainty, static character and inefficiency. This is because while primary rule governs conduct of individuals in a society it is the secondary rules that allow for their creation, alteration, interpretation or extinction. Hence, in absence of a systematic method of rule creation (secondary rule), there would always be uncertainty as to what the primary rules are in the first place. Further, changes in primary rules would be brought out organically thus making the system very static. Also, in absence of secondary rules the application of the rules in case of disputes will always be problematic hence introducing inefficiencies.

13. Interest Theory is a theory of function of legal rights. According to this, the function of a legal right is to further the right-holders' interests. Major exponents of interest theory of legal rights are—Bentham, Ihering, Austin, Lyons, MacCormick, Raz and Kramer. The remaining are theories concerning with 'Legal Persons'.

Fiction theory: Only humans are capable of legal personality corporations and institutions are imputed legal personality by fiction. Main exponents : Savigny, Salmond, Coke, Blackstone and Holland.

Purpose theory: Juristic or artificial persons merely function as a legal device for protecting or giving effect to some real purpose. Major exponents: Becker & Brinz.

Bracket theory: A bracket is put around the members of the corporation to indicate that they are to be treated as one single unit when they form themselves into a corporation. Major exponent: Ihering.

14. This statement has been made by Edward Collins in his book, 'International Law in a changing world: Cases, documents and readings'.

15. Statement (a): Article 38 of the statute of ICJ concerns with sources of International law. These are—International conventions, international customs, general principles of law recognised by civilised nations and judicial decisions and the teachings of the most highly qualified publicists of the various nations, as subsidiary means for the determination of rules of law. Hence, there is no mention of decisions of international institutions.

Statement (b): In West Rand case, an English Company had brought a suit against British govt. regarding the value of gold seized from it by the Republic of South Africa before it was conquered by the British Government. This case was decided on the principles of state succession as observed in customary international law (and not general principles of law recognised by civilised nations). The claim of the company was defeated as according to customary international law a conquering state does not become liable to discharge the financial obligations of the conquered state unless the conquering state has agreed expressly to do so.

Statement (c): In the Frontier Dispute case the ICJ settled the border dispute between Burkina Faso and Mali relying on resolution by Organisation for African Unity (International convention) and the principle of uti posseditis juris *i.e.*, respect for intangibility of frontiers (general rule of international law relating to state of succession)

Statement (d): The Barcelona Tractions case concerned with action brought against Spain by Belgium for alleged financial injury to Belgian shareholders in Barcelona Tractions (a company incorporated in Canada carrying out its business in Spain). The claim was eventually defeated on account of Belgium not having sufficient *jus standi*.

Hence, only statement (a) is correct rest are incorrect.

17. Statement (a): There are two competing theories of state recognition, Constitutive theory and declaratory theory. The Constitutive theory holds that states come into existence in the legal sense only when they are recognised as such by other states *i.e.*, recognition is not automatic. Whereas, the declaratory theory holds that recognition is irrelevant and statehood is based on fact and not on discretion to recognise exercised by other states.

Statement (b) & (d): Sometimes de facto recognition precedes de jure recognition. The former is a provisional recognition and is liable to be withdrawn if the state fails to gather sufficient stability whereas the latter is legal recognition and not liable to be withdrawn unless under exceptional change of circumstances. Hence, these statements are correct.

Statement (c): It is correct.

18. Article 1(2): To develop friendly relations among nations based on respect for the principle of equal rights and self-determination of peoples, and to take other appropriate measures to strengthen universal peace.

Article 55: With a view to the creation of conditions of stability and well-being which are necessary for peaceful and friendly relations among nations based on respect for the principle of equal rights and self-determination of peoples, the United Nations shall promote:

(*a*) higher standards of living, full employment, and conditions of economic and social progress and development;

(*b*) solutions of international economic, social, health, and related problems; and international cultural and educational cooperation; and

(*c*) universal respect for, and observance of, human rights and fundamental freedoms for all without distinction as to race, sex, language, or religion.

Article 56: All Members pledge themselves to take joint and separate action in co-operation with the Organization for the achievement of the purposes set forth in Article 55.

20. Exogamy means marrying outside one's community/family. Under Hindu law, Sapinda relationship extends to 5 generations on the line of ascent of father's side and 3 generations on the line of ascent of mother's side. Marrying within the Sapinda relationship is prohibited thus promoting exogamy.

22. Statement (a): It is a settled principle that a party shall not be allowed to take benefit from its own wrong. Hence, if cruelty is provoked then it is not a ground of divorce for the party alleging cruelty.

Statement (b): According to guilt theory of divorce, condonation acts as a bar for granting the relief of divorce.

Statement (c): Guilt theory requires existence of one guilty party and one innocent party, if both parties are guilty then according to this theory none is entitled for the relief of divorce. However, by employing the concept of 'comparative rectitude' the court may grant divorce to the party who is least at fault.

Statement (d): According to section 23(d) of Hindu Marriage Act, 1955 every petitioner has to prove that there has not been any unnecessary or improper delay in instituting the proceeding.

Hence, according to the given options, (C) is the most appropriate answer.

27. Section 11 of The Indian Contract Act deals with a minor's capacity to contract. It does not deal with the capacity to commit crime.

32. Statement (a) & (b): When consent to an agreement is caused by coercion, fraud or misrepresentation, the agreement is a contract voidable at the option of the party whose consent was so caused. (Section 19, Indian Contract Act, 1872)

Statement (c): Misrepresentation is caused innocently whereas Fraud is committed with intent to deceive. (Refer section 17 & 18, Indian Contract Act, 1872)

Statement (d): It is correct.

Hence, (A) is the most appropriate answer.

33. Statement (A) is correct.

Statement (B): In Indian law the remedy is a civil law action for unliquidated damages.

Statement (C): Law of torts generally covers all those civil wrongs which are not covered by any statute for the time being.

Statement (D): It can be an act as well as omission.

34. Volenti Non Fit Injuria: Samira Kohli Vs Prabha Manchanda is a case that deals with consent for a surgery removing reproductive organs from a female. It was held that consent obtained from the appellant's mother was not a valid consent because the appellant was neither a minor, nor mentally challenged, nor incapacitated. When a patient is a competent adult, there is no question of someone else giving consent on their behalf. There was no medical emergency during surgery. The appellant was only temporarily unconscious, undergoing only a diagnostic procedure. The respondent ought to have waited till the appellant regained consciousness, discussed the result of the laparoscopic examination and then taken her consent for the surgery. Hence, this case deals with the maxim *volenti non fit injuria*.

Judicial Acts: In Anwar Hussain Vs Ajoy Kumar an SDM was fined ₹5000 for acting maliciously in arresting the petitioner. The protection extended to judicial officers against civil and criminal liabilities for acts done in bonafide exercise of powers was held to be non applicable in this case as there was evidence to suggest that the officer had acted recklessly and with malafide intention.

Acts of State: In Vinod Kumar Shantilal Gosalia Vs Gangadhar Narsinghdas Agarwal it was held that all mining manifests issued by the Portuguese government in Goa were lapsed after the liberation of Goa and take over by Government of India.

Necessity: Olga Tellis Vs Municipal Corporation, Bombay, the case dealt with rights of pavement dwellers being summarily displaced by the state government. It was observed that poor people live on pavements because of job opportunities in towns. It is out of sheer necessity for a bare existence that the petitioners are driven to occupy the pavements and slums. The Supreme Court subsequently held that right of livelihood is part of fundamental right to life.

36. The rule of absolute liability in Indian context was first laid out in MC Mehta Vs Union of India. The same rule was approved by the Apex Court in Charan Lal Sahu Vs Union of India while upholding the validity of the Bhopal Act, 1985. Later, in Indian Council for Enviro-Legal Action Vs Union of India also this principle was applied.

37. Tortuous liability exists for all direct and reasonably foreseeable consequences of tortuous acts.

39. The defence of necessity is based on the principle that the accused had no legal alternative to violating the law as they were confronted by two or more evils and had to choose the lesser of the evil. Section 81 of IPC reads as "Nothing is an offence merely by reason of its being done with the knowledge that it is likely to cause harm, if it be done without any criminal intention to cause harm, and in good faith for the purpose of preventing or avoiding other harm to person or property." In the instant question, a drunken person moving in great danger in public place is likely to cause harm to himself or to others, hence, arresting such a person to prevent any such harm entails protection of section 81 of IPC.

44. Only grave and sudden provocation capable of depriving power of self-control is a defence under section 300. Cold-blooded killing signifies that the provocation is no longer sudden and that the offender has had sufficient opportunity to regain his self-control.

50. Section 2(j) of Industrial Disputes Act, 1947 gives the definition of industry, which was elaborated upon by the Supreme Court in the Bangalore Water Supply case. In this case the term industry has been given a wide scope and the according to it any activity will be industry if it satisfies the 'triple test':

1. Systematic and organized activity.
2. Carried out with the cooperation between Employers and employees.
3. For the production and distribution of goods and services whether or not involving investment of capital.

(*c*) A.K. Roy Vs. Union of India	(*iii*) No deprivation of existing right enjoyed by government servant without giving him opportunity of being heard.
(*d*) H.L. Trehan Vs. Union of India	(*iv*) Principles of natural justice are not rigid norms of unchanging context, they have to be tailored to suit the nature of the proceeding.

Codes:

	(*a*)	(*b*)	(*c*)	(*d*)
A.	(*ii*)	(*i*)	(*iv*)	(*iii*)
B.	(*i*)	(*ii*)	(*iii*)	(*iv*)
C.	(*iv*)	(*iii*)	(*ii*)	(*i*)
D.	(*ii*)	(*i*)	(*iii*)	(*iv*)

12. A statute confers discretionary powers on an official for his use, by denoting expressions like:

(*a*) Reasonable (*b*) Appropriate
(*c*) Equitable (*d*) Sufficient

Codes:

A. Only (*a*) is correct
B. Only (*a*) and (*b*) are correct
C. Only (*a*), (*b*) and (*c*) are correct
D. (*a*), (*b*), (*c*) and (*d*) are correct

13. Read the Assertion (A) and Reason (R) and answer by using the codes given below:

Assertion (A): The court can direct competent authority to exercise discretion in accordance with law but court cannot direct to exercise the discretion in a particular manner.

Reason (R): The Supreme Court strikes down a decision of competent authority on ground of 'extraneous consideration' and 'improper purpose'.

Codes:

A. Both (A) and (R) are true and (R) is the correct explanation of (A).
B. Both (A) and (R) are true, but (R) is not the correct explanation of (A).
C. (A) is true, but (R) is false.
D. (A) is false, but (R) is true.

14. What is the objective of the Lokpal and Lokayukta Act, 2013?

A. To investigate the charges of corruption against public and private companies.
B. To substitute the Central Vigilance Commission by the institution of Lokpal.
C. To repeal the Lokayukta and establish Lokpal.
D. To inquire into allegations of corruption against public functionaries.

15. Which of the following declarations relating to assets and liabilities by a public servant are to be made under the Lokpal and Lokayukta Act, 2013? Answer by using the codes given below:

(*a*) Assets of which he, his spouse and his dependent children are jointly or severally, owner or beneficiary.
(*b*) Assets of which he, his parents and children are owner or beneficiary.
(*c*) His liabilities and that of his spouse and his dependent children.
(*d*) His liabilities and that of his spouse, parents and children.

Codes:

A. (*a*) and (*b*) B. (*c*) and (*d*)
C. (*a*) and (*c*) D. (*b*) and (*d*)

16. Which one of the following statements is incorrect?

A. In Jurisprudence we are concerned to derive rules from authority and apply them to problems.
B. In Jurisprudence we are concerned to reflect on the nature of legal rules.
C. In Jurisprudence we are concerned on the underlying meaning of legal concepts.
D. In Jurisprudence we are concerned on the essential features of legal systems.

17. Which of the following requisites are necessary to be fulfilled for a custom to be valid source of law?

(*a*) Reasonableness, antiquity and conformity with statute law.
(*b*) Immemorial antiquity, conformity with statute law and observance as of right.
(*c*) Specificity, efficacy and reasonableness.

Codes:

A. (*a*) and (*c*) only B. (*a*), (*b*) and (*c*) all
C. (*b*) and (*c*) only D. (*a*) and (*b*) only

3. Read the Assertion (A) and Reason (R) and give the correct answer with the help of codes given below:

Assertion (A): Judges must follow authoritative precedents.

Reason (R): Authoritative precedents derive their authority from basic postulate of the legal system itself.

Codes:

A. Both (A) and (R) are true and (R) is the correct explanation of (A).
B. Both (A) and (R) are true, but (R) is not the correct explanation of (A).
C. (A) is true, but (R) is false.
D. (A) is false, but (R) is true.

. Read the Assertion (A) and Reason (R) and give the correct answer using the codes given below:

Assertion (A): A person in possession of a thing is deemed to be the owner of the thing possessed.

Reason (R): Possession is as good as ownership.

Codes:

A. Both (A) and (R) are true and (R) is the correct explanation of (A).
B. Both (A) and (R) are true, but (R) is not the correct explanation of (A).
C. (A) is true, but (R) is false.
D. (A) is false, but (R) is true.

. Read the Assertion (A) and Reason (R) and give the correct answer with the help of codes given below:

Assertion (A): A claim to recover a debt barred by lapse of time is an imperfect right.

Reason (R): The statute of limitations does not provide that after a certain time a debt shall become extinct.

Codes:

A. Both (A) and (R) are true and (R) is the correct explanation of (A).
B. Both (A) and (R) are true, but (R) is not the correct explanation of (A).
C. (A) is true, but (R) is false.
D. (A) is false, but (R) is true.

21. The fundamental principle of legal positivism is to draw a clearcut demarcation between law and morals, between law as it is and law as ought to be wherein the former is essential in the nature of 'command' and latter being merely:

A. routine and normal
B. persuasive and non-obligatory
C. non-persuasive and obligatory
D. directive and non-persuasive

22. Which one of the following is not a theory of corporate personality?

A. Fiction theory B. Will theory
C. Realist theory D. Bracket theory

23. Match List-I with List-II and give the correct answer by using the codes given below the lists:

List-I (Theory)	**List-II (Jurist associated with)**
(*a*) Interest theory of legal rights	(*i*) Duguit
(*b*) Realist theory of corporate personality	(*ii*) Ihering
(*c*) Doctrine of social solidarity	(*iii*) Gierke
(*d*) Doctrine of social engineering	(*iv*) Pound

Codes:

	(*a*)	(*b*)	(*c*)	(*d*)
A.	(*iii*)	(*ii*)	(*i*)	(*iv*)
B.	(*ii*)	(*iii*)	(*i*)	(*iv*)
C.	(*iv*)	(*i*)	(*iii*)	(*ii*)
D.	(*iii*)	(*i*)	(*ii*)	(*iv*)

C. T.N. Godavarman Thirulmulpad Vs. Union of India
D. A.P. Pollution Control Board Vs. Prof. M.V. Nayudu

39. Who has remarked that International Law is the vanishing point of Jurisprudence because in his view, rules of International Law are followed by courtesy and hence they should not be kept in the category of law?
A. Prof. H.L.A. Hart B. J.G. Starke
C. Louis Henkin D. Holland

40. In which of the following cases the World Court by majority has taken the view that the sources of international law are not hierarchical but are necessarily complimentary and inter-related?
A. Nicaragua V. U.S.A.
B. In North Sea Continental Shelf case
C. In the Barcelona Traction case
D. Frontier dispute (Burkina Faso Vs. Mali)

41. Who has remarked that the wide acceptance of declaratory theory is due to the reaction against the traditional conception of recognition as a political act purely and simply. There is a legal duty on the part of the state to recognise any community that has in fact acquired the characteristics of statehood?
A. L. Oppenheim B. Hans Kelson
C. Lauterpacht D. Anzilloti

42. In which of the following cases the Supreme Court clarified the distinction between 'expulsion' and 'extradition' following international norms?
A. Mobarak Ali Ahmad Vs. State of Bombay
B. Hans Muller of Nurenburg Vs. Supdt, Presidency Jail, Calcutta and Others
C. Dharam Teja's case
D. Ram Babu Saxena Vs. State

43. Which of the following statement/statements is/are correct?
(*a*) By asylum we mean shelter and active protection extended to a political refugee from another state which admits him on his request.
(*b*) Under Article 14 of the Univers Declaration of Human Rights, Right asylum is recognised.
(*c*) International Court of Justice explain the distinction between territorial a extraterritorial asylum in the *Asylu Case* (*Colombia Vs. Perus*).
(*d*) In 1966, the United Nations declarati on territorial asylum was unanimous adopted by the General Assembly.

Codes:
A. Only (*a*) is correct.
B. Only (*a*), (*b*) and (*c*) are correct.
C. Only (*c*) and (*d*) both are correct.
D. (*a*), (*b*), (*c*) and (*d*) all are correct.

44. Which of the following statement/stateme is/are not correct in reference to the Econon and Social Council (ECOSOC)?
(*a*) The Economic and Social Coun (ECOSOC) consists of 54 members whi are elected by General Assembly.
(*b*) Half of its members are elected each ye for a term of two years.
(*c*) India is one of the members of t council.
(*d*) President of ECOSOC is elected for t year term.

Codes:
A. only (*d*) is not correct.
B. (*b*) and (*d*) both are not correct.
C. only (*a*), (*b*) and (*c*) are not correct.
D. (*a*), (*b*), (*c*) and (*d*) all are not correct.

45. Under which Article of the United Natic Charter, the Security Council is empower to implement the judgements of the Wo Court in case one of the parties fails implement it and other party to the dispu brings the matter to the Security Council
A. Article 94 B. Article 96
C. Article 62 D. Article 36(5)

46. Read the following propositions and gi correct answer with the help of codes giv below:

Propositions are:
(*i*) A voidable Hindu marriage is regarded a valid marriage until a decree annulli it has been passed by a competent co

(*ii*) A void Hindu marriage is never a valid marriage and there is no necessity of any decree annulling it.

(*iii*) A void Hindu marriage remains valid until a decree annulling it has been passed by a competent court.

(*iv*) Children of void and voidable Hindu marriages are legitimate.

Codes:

A. Only (*i*) and (*iii*) are correct, but (*iv*) is incorrect.

B. (*i*), (*ii*) and (*iv*) are correct, but (*iii*) is incorrect.

C. (*i*), (*ii*), (*iii*) and (*iv*) are correct.

D. (*i*) and (*iv*) are correct, but (*ii*) and (*iii*) are incorrect.

47. Match List-I and List-II and find correct answer by using codes given below:

List-I (Case Law)	List-II (Decision)
(*a*) Seema V/s Ashwani	(*i*) Cruelty as a ground of divorce
(*b*) Githa Hariharan V/s Reserve Bank of India	(*ii*) Maintenance of Muslim wife
(*c*) V. Bhagat V/s D. Bhagat	(*iii*) Compulsory registration of marriages
(*d*) Mohd. Ahmad Khan V/s Shah Bano	(*iv*) Mother as natural guardian

Codes:

	(*a*)	(*b*)	(*c*)	(*d*)
A.	(*ii*)	(*i*)	(*iii*)	(*iv*)
B.	(*i*)	(*iii*)	(*iv*)	(*ii*)
C.	(*iii*)	(*iv*)	(*i*)	(*ii*)
D.	(*iv*)	(*ii*)	(*i*)	(*iii*)

48. Which of the following is not a condition for a marriage under Section 5 of the Hindu Marriage Act, 1955?

A. No Sapinda and prohibited degree relationship

B. Mental capacity

C. Monogamy

D. Free consent of the parties

49. Read the following and answer with the help of codes given below:

A married Hindu male can adopt a child :

(*i*) Only with his wife's consent.

(*ii*) If he has more than one wife, consent of all the wives is necessary.

(*iii*) In case of void marriage, consent of wife is necessary.

(*iv*) In case of voidable marriage, the wife's consent is necessary.

Codes:

A. (*i*), (*ii*) and (*iv*) are correct, but (*iii*) is incorrect.

B. Only (*i*) and (*ii*) are correct.

C. (*ii*), (*iii*) and (*iv*) are correct, but (*i*) is incorrect.

D. (*i*), (*iii*) and (*iv*) are correct, but (*ii*) is incorrect.

50. The most proper or approved form of divorce among Muslims is

A. Triple talak | B. Ahsan talak
C. Hasan talak | D. Talak-al-biddat

51. Which of the following is not a ground of divorce under the Hindu Marriage Act, 1955?

A. Leprosy | B. Insanity
C. Epilepsy | D. Veneral disease

52. In default of the mother and female relatives, the following persons are entitled to the custody of a Muslim child:

(*i*) Nearest paternal grandfather

(*ii*) Father

(*iii*) Full brother

(*iv*) Consanguine brother etc.

Among the aforesaid the correct order of priority is:

Codes:

A. (*i*), (*ii*), (*iii*), (*iv*) | B. (*ii*), (*i*), (*iii*), (*iv*)
C. (*iv*), (*i*), (*ii*), (*iii*) | D. (*iii*), (*ii*), (*i*), (*iv*)

53. Under the Muslim Women (Protection of Rights on Divorce) Act, 1986, besides the former-husband of Muslim woman, the following relatives etc. are also liable to pay maintenance to her:

(*i*) Children
(*ii*) Other relatives
(*iii*) State Wakf Board
(*iv*) Parents

Give the correct order of liability of the above with the help of codes given below:

Codes:

A. (*iv*), (*ii*), (*iii*), (*i*) B. (*i*), (*iii*), (*ii*), (*iv*)
C. (*i*), (*ii*), (*iv*), (*iii*) D. (*i*), (*iv*), (*ii*), (*iii*)

54. The Vienna Declaration and Programme of Action on Human Rights was adopted by the World Conference on

A. 25th June, 1993 B. 10th June, 1994
C. 15th June, 1995 D. 25th June, 1996

55. Which one of the following slogan was adopted for the Fiftieth Anniversary of UDHR?

A. 'All Human Rights for All'
B. 'Save the Child'
C. "Women Empowerment"
D. "Clean Environment For All"

56. Which one of the following countries originally suggested the idea of an International Treaty on the Rights of the Child?

A. United States of America
B. China
C. Poland
D. India

57. 'It is my aspiration that health will finally be seen not as a blessing to be wished for, but as a Human Right to be fought for'. It was said by

A. Dr. Lee Jong-Wook
B. Dr. Boutros Boutros Ghali
C. Barack Obama
D. Kofi Annan

58. Match List-I with List-II and select the correct answer using the codes given below:

List-I	List-II
(*a*) Convention relating to the status of Refugees	(*i*) 1948
(*b*) American Convention on Human Rights	(*ii*) 1963
(*c*) American Declaration of the Rights and Duties of Man	(*iii*) 1950
(*d*) International Convention on the Elimination of All Forms of Racial Discrimination	(*iv*) 1969

Codes:

	(*a*)	(*b*)	(*c*)	(*d*)
A.	(*iii*)	(*iv*)	(*i*)	(*ii*)
B.	(*ii*)	(*iii*)	(*iv*)	(*i*)
C.	(*i*)	(*iii*)	(*ii*)	(*iv*)
D.	(*iv*)	(*ii*)	(*iii*)	(*i*)

59. The General Assembly of the United Nations created the office of UN High Commissioner for Human Rights in the year:

A. 1993 B. 1994
C. 1995 D. 1996

60. Under Section 3(2) of the Protection of Human Rights Act, 1993 the Chairperson shall be

A. one who has been a Chief Justice of the Supreme Court.
B. one who has been a Chairperson of a National Tribunal or Commission.
C. an Eminent jurist in the field of Human Rights.
D. a judge of the Supreme Court who served not less than five years.

61. Match List-I with List-II and select the correct answer using the codes given below:

List-I (Case)	List-II (Maxim)
(*a*) Bhim Singh Vs. State of J & K	(*i*) Damnum sine injuria
(*b*) Municipal Corporation of Delhi Vs. Subhagwanti	(*ii*) Injuria sine damnum
(*c*) Nichols Vs. Marsland	(*iii*) Res ipsa loquitur
(*d*) Mogul Steamship Co. Vs. McGregor Gow and Co.	(*iv*) Vis major

Codes:

	(*a*)	(*b*)	(*c*)	(*d*)
A.	(*i*)	(*ii*)	(*iii*)	(*iv*)
B.	(*iv*)	(*iii*)	(*ii*)	(*i*)
C.	(*ii*)	(*iii*)	(*iv*)	(*i*)
D.	(*ii*)	(*i*)	(*iv*)	(*iii*)

62. Read Assertion (A) and Reason (R) and answer using codes given below:

Assertion (A): Making statement of fact on matters of public interest is a defence to an action for defamation.

Reason (R): If defendant in a newspaper publishes a statement of facts making serious allegations of dishonesty against the plaintiff, and subsequently could not prove the truth, the plea of fair comment shall fail as based on untrue facts.

Codes:

A. Both (A) and (R) are right and (R) is the correct explanation of (A).
B. Both (A) and (R) are right, but (R) is not correct explanation of (A).
C. (A) is right, but (R) is wrong.
D. (A) is wrong, but (R) is right.

63. The prescriptive right of easement of access and use of light and air can be acquired if it has been:

(*a*) Enjoyed with interruption
(*b*) As a matter of concession
(*c*) Enjoyed without interruption as right
(*d*) For twenty years

Codes:

A. (*a*) and (*b*) are incorrect and (*c*) and (*d*) are correct.
B. (*a*) and (*d*) are incorrect and (*b*) and (*c*) are correct.
C. (*a*) and (*c*) are correct and (*b*) and (*d*) are incorrect.
D. (*b*) and (*a*) are correct and (*d*) and (*c*) are incorrect.

64. Which of the following is not true about the slander form of defamation?

A. Statement is made in some transient form.
B. It is addressed to ear.
C. Slander is always a criminal offence.
D. It is not actionable in absence of proof of actual damage.

65. Arrange the following cases in the chronological order by using codes:

(*a*) Municipal Corporation of Delhi Vs. Sushila Devi
(*b*) Shyam Sunder Vs. State of Rajasthan
(*c*) Pushpabai Vs. Ranjit Ginning and Pressing Co.
(*d*) Syad Akbar Vs. State of Karnataka

Codes:

A. (*d*), (*a*), (*b*) and (*c*)
B. (*b*), (*c*), (*d*) and (*a*)
C. (*b*), (*a*), (*c*) and (*d*)
D. (*a*), (*b*), (*c*) and (*d*)

66. What are the rights of consumers which are to be protected and promoted by Consumer Councils under the Consumer Protection Act? Answer by using codes below:

(*a*) Protection against marketing of goods and services which are hazardous to life and property.
(*b*) Information about quality, quantity and price of goods and services.
(*c*) Access to a variety of goods and services at competitive prices.
(*d*) Consumer education.

Codes:

A. Only (*a*) is correct.
B. Only (*b*) and (*c*) are correct.
C. Only (*a*), (*b*) and (*c*) are correct.
D. (*a*), (*b*), (*c*) and (*d*) are correct.

67. If a complaint is found frivolous or vexatious under the Consumer Protection Act, complainant shall pay to opposite party the cost:

(*a*) As specified by orders of the court.
(*b*) Dismissal of complaint without any cost.
(*c*) Not exceeding ten thousand rupees.
(*d*) One-tenth of the amount claimed as relief.

Codes:

A. Only (*a*) and (*c*) are correct.
B. Only (*c*) and (*d*) are correct.
C. Only (*b*) and (*d*) are correct.
D. Only (*a*) and (*b*) are correct.

68. Read Assertion (A) and Reason (R) and answer using codes given below:

Assertion (A): It shall not be a defence in a prosecution for an offence under Section 138 of the Negotiable Instrument Act that the drawer had no reason to believe when he issued the cheque that the cheque may be dishonoured on presentment for the reason stated in that Section.

Reason (R): Above assertion is laid down in Section 140 of the Negotiable Instrument Act.

Codes:

A. Both (A) and (R) are wrong.

B. Both (A) and (R) are right and (R) is correct explanation of (A).

C. (A) is right, but (R) is wrong.

D. (R) is right, but (A) is wrong.

69. Match List-I with List-II and select the correct answer using the codes given below:

List-I (Consequences of ultra vires transaction)	List-II (Judgement)
(*a*) Right of a member of company to get injunction against ultra vires transaction	(*i*) Jehangir R. Modi Vs. Shamji Ladha
(*b*) Personal liability of directors	(*ii*) Attorney General Vs. Great Eastern Railway Company
(*c*) Breach of warranty of authority to induce a third party to enter into ultra vires transaction with company	(*iii*) Coltman Vs. Coltman
(*d*) Ultra vires acquired property	(*iv*) Weeks Vs. Propert

Codes:

	(*a*)	(*b*)	(*c*)	(*d*)
A.	(*ii*)	(*i*)	(*iv*)	(*iii*)
B.	(*i*)	(*ii*)	(*iv*)	(*iii*)
C.	(*ii*)	(*i*)	(*iii*)	(*iv*)
D.	(*iv*)	(*iii*)	(*i*)	(*ii*)

70. Match List-I with List-II and select the correct answer using codes given below

List-I (Exceptions to doctrine of indoor management)	List-II (Judgement)
(*a*) Knowledge of irregularity	(*i*) T.R. Pratt Ltd. Vs. M.T. Ltd.
(*b*) Suspicion of irregularity	(*ii*) Ruben Vs. Great Fingall Consolidated
(*c*) Forgery	(*iii*) Anand Behari Ltd. Vs. Dinshaw & Co.
(d) Acts outside apparent authority	(*iv*) Morris Vs. Kanssen

Codes:

	(*a*)	(*b*)	(*c*)	(*d*)
A.	(*ii*)	(*iii*)	(*i*)	(*iv*)
B.	(*iv*)	(*i*)	(*iii*)	(*ii*)
C.	(*i*)	(*iv*)	(*ii*)	(*iii*)
D.	(*iv*)	(*i*)	(*ii*)	(*iii*)

71. Read Assertion (A) and Reason (R) and answer using codes given below:

Assertion (A): Payer alone, whether a corporeal person or incorporeal person, shall be competent in case of dishonour of cheque.

Reason (R): Because Section 138 of Negotiable Instrument Act mandates so.

Codes:

A. Both (A) and (R) are right and (R) is correct explanation of (A).

B. Both (A) and (R) are wrong.

C. (A) is wrong, but (R) is right.

D. (A) is right, but (R) is wrong.

72. Which of the following statement is correct?

A. A condition is a stipulation essential to any purpose of the contract.

B. A warranty is a stipulation collateral to any purpose of the contract.

C. When a buyer waives a warranty, it becomes a condition.

D. Where a contract of sale is not severable and the buyer has accepted the goods or part thereof, the breach of any condition to be fulfilled by the seller can only be treated as a breach of warranty and not as a ground for rejecting the goods and treating the contract as repudiated, unless there is a term of the contract, express or implied to that effect.

73. Match List-I with List-II and select the correct answer using codes given below:

List-I	List-II
(a) Goods in sale of goods	*(i)* Bhopal Sugar Industries Ltd. Vs. STO
(b) Consideration for a sale of goods	*(ii)* Instalment Supply Ltd. Vs. STO
(c) Sale and agreement to sale	*(iii)* R.D. Goyal Vs. Reliance Industries Ltd.
(d) Difference between contract of sale and contract of agency	*(iv)* Aldridge Vs. Johnson

Codes:

	(a)	*(b)*	*(c)*	*(d)*
A.	*(iii)*	*(iv)*	*(ii)*	*(i)*
B.	*(iv)*	*(iii)*	*(ii)*	*(i)*
C.	*(iii)*	*(iv)*	*(i)*	*(ii)*
D.	*(ii)*	*(i)*	*(iv)*	*(iii)*

74. Which of the following partnerships are legal? Answer using the codes given below:

(a) Twelve members forming a banking firm.

(b) A partnership to create a monopoly.

(c) Twenty members forming a firm for tea trade on a railway platform.

(d) Trustees carry on business of a firm in their own name.

Codes:

A. *(a)*, *(b)*, *(c)* and *(d)*

B. *(b)*, *(c)* and *(d)* only

C. *(b)* and *(c)* only

D. *(c)* and *(d)* only

75. Read Assertion (A) and Reason (R) and answer using codes given below:

Assertion (A): Notwithstanding a contract between the partners, a partner shall not indemnify the firm for any loss caused to it by his wilful neglect in the conduct of the business of the firm.

Reason (R): Because Section 13(f) of Indian Partnership Act stipulates so.

Codes:

A. Both (A) and (R) are right and (R) is correct explanation of (A).

B. Both (A) and (R) are wrong.

C. (A) is right, but (R) is wrong.

D. (R) is right, but (A) is wrong.

ANSWERS

1	**2**	**3**	**4**	**5**	**6**	**7**	**8**	**9**	**10**
D	D	D	D	B	C	B	D	D	C
11	**12**	**13**	**14**	**15**	**16**	**17**	**18**	**19**	**20**
A	D	A	D	C	A	D	A	C	A
21	**22**	**23**	**24**	**25**	**26**	**27**	**28**	**29**	**30**
B	B	B	B	A	D	A	B	A	C
31	**32**	**33**	**34**	**35**	**36**	**37**	**38**	**39**	**40**
B	B	B	C	A	D	A	B	D	A
41	**42**	**43**	**44**	**45**	**46**	**47**	**48**	**49**	**50**
C	B	B	B	A	B	C	D	A	B
51	**52**	**53**	**54**	**55**	**56**	**57**	**58**	**59**	**60**
C	B	D	A	A	C	D	A	A	A
61	**62**	**63**	**64**	**65**	**66**	**67**	**68**	**69**	**70**
C	D	A	C	B	D	A	B	A	D
71	**72**	**73**	**74**	**75**					
B	D	A	D	B					

EXPLANATORY ANSWERS

4. Public Accounts Committee is a parliamentary committee set up annually for auditing of the revenue and the expenditure of the Government of India. It consists of a maximum of 22 members, 15 from the Lok Sabha and 7 from the Rajya Sabha.

6. Statement (i): the words 'and the states' do not appear in the fundamental duties as enshrined in the Indian Constitution.

9. The system of Droit Administratif is the system of administrative law prevalent in France. It is based on strict separation of powers between the administration and courts.

10. *Audi Alteram Partem* or the principle that no one shall be condemned unheard requires that the reasoned decision must be based on the satisfaction of the concerned authority.

12. All these words whenever they appear in a statute give scope to the official/authority to exercise discretion.

14. According to the Lokpal and Lokayukta Act, 2013, the objective of the act is stated to be: An Act to provide for the establishment of a body of Lokpal for the Union and Lokayukta for States to inquire into allegations of corruption against certain public functionaries and for matters connected therewith or incidental thereto.

16. Jurisprudence is concerned with understanding principles behind law that make that law. It is not concerned with deriving rules and applying them to problems.

17. For a custom to take the force of law, it must have the following ingredients:

(*a*) **Antiquity:** The custom must be ancient. According to Blackstone "A custom, in order that it may be legal and binding must have been used so long that the memory of man runs not to the contrary, so that, if any one can show the beginning of it, it is no good custom".

(b) **Certainty:** If a custom is vague and ambiguous, so much so that no uniform observance of it exists, it is not a valid custom.

(c) **Reasonableness:** A custom is treated to be unreasonable if it is opposed to the principles of justice, equity and good conscience and hence invalid.

(d) **Compulsory observance:** A custom is not a valid custom. If those who observe it treat it as a mere obligation and are free to deviate from it at will. For a custom to take the force of law it must enjoy compulsory observance in the region and community it is observed.

(e) **Conformity with statute law:** Those customs that are opposed to public policy or are entirely opposed to statute law are not valid customs.

Hence, out of all the given options (D) is the most appropriate.

18. Authoritative precedents are those which must be followed by subordinate courts compulsorily. For example, the decisions of the High Court are authoritative precedents for the subordinate Courts and the decisions of the Supreme Court are authoritative precedents for the High Courts and all other subordinate Courts. In contrast to authoritative precedents, Persuasive precedents are those which the Courts are at liberty to follow or not. Thus, judgement by one high court has a merely persuasive force on the other high court.

19. Possession and ownership are two entirely different concepts in legal theory. A person in possession of a thing is deemed to be owner of the thing. However, this is a rebuttable presumption of law. According to *Ihering*, "Possession is the objective realization of ownership." It is the external realization of ownership but it is not ownership *per se*. At best, it is an important piece of evidence to show the existence of ownership. It is in fact what ownership is in right. It is the de facto exercise of a claim while ownership is the de jure recognition of that claim. For example, a tenant is though in possession of a house but is not the owner of it. Similar is the relationship between a bailor and bailee.

20. Law of limitation only bars the remedy and not the right. Hence, a claim to recover a debt barred by lapse of time is an imperfect right in the sense that a suit for recovery might fail due to expiry of limitation period. However, if the debtor still pays the time barred debt to the creditor he cannot claim it back on the plea that it was time barred. Also, under Sec. 25(3) of the Contract Act, 1872, an agreement in writing to pay a time barred debt is valid and binding. A barred debt can constitute a valid consideration for a new contract. Only, in very special cases, as dealt with in section 27 of limitation act does the right as well as the remedy both get extinguished. Section 27 of the Limitation Act provides that when the period limited to a person for instituting a suit for possession of any property has expired, his right to such property is extinguished. Hence, section 27 deals with only title over a property and not time barred debt.

22. Will Theory is a theory of function of legal rights. According to this, the function of a legal right is to give its holder control over another's duty. For example, If a person A has a right (say ownership) over the house he has given to person B on rent. Then, person A has control over the duties person B has towards A in relation to his use of A's house. Hart is one of the most prominent will theorist. The remaining theories are concerned with 'Corporate Personality'.

24. A person is considered to be Doli Capax if he is beyond such tender age as to have sufficient capacity to form an intention to commit a tort or a crime.

26. According to Section 351 of the Indian Penal Code, "Whoever makes any gesture, or any preparation intending or knowing it to be likely that such gesture or preparation will cause any person present to apprehend that he who makes that gesture or preparation is about to use criminal force to that person, is said to commit an assault." Hence, if from the person making the gesture no apprehension of the use of criminal force is arising then such a person has committed no offence as per this section.

27. According to section 304B of Indian penal code, when the death of a woman is caused by any burns or bodily injury or occurs otherwise than under normal circumstances within seven years of her marriage and it is shown that soon before her death she was subjected to cruelty or harassment by her husband or any relative of her husband for, or in connection with, any demand for dowry, such death shall be called "dowry death". Hence, it is essential that the death is not caused under any normal circumstances.

29. In the instant case, the intention to cause death cannot be imputed to the snatcher. Neither can it be said that the intention of cutting nostrils was an intention to cause such bodily injury as is likely to cause death, or with the knowledge that he is likely by such act to cause death. Hence, since none of the ingredients of Section 299 are satisfied the snatcher has not committed the offence of culpable homicide or murder. However, cutting of nostrils does fall under clause sixthly of section 320 *i.e.*, causing grievous hurt by permanent disfiguration of the head or face. Hence, according to the given options (A) is the most appropriate.

32. Article 48A has been added in the directive principles of state policy and Article 51A(g) has been added in the list of fundamental duties in our constitution.

Article 48A: Protection and improvement of environment and safeguarding of forests and wild life. The State shall endeavour to protect and improve the environment and to safeguard the forests and wild life of the country.

Article 51A(g): To protect and improve the natural environment including forests, lakes, rivers and wild life, and to have compassion for living creatures.

33. In Narmada Bachao Andolan Vs Union of India it was held that precautionary principle can only be applied in those cases where the loss to environment is unpredictable and non-negligible. In case of building a dam, environmental impact can be carefully assessed and mitigated; hence it will not attract the precautionary principle.

34. The first international conference on environment and development was held at Stockholm on 5 June 1972 in which 107 nations participated. 26 principles on environment protection were propounded during this conference which is widely considered as magna-Carta on human environment.

36. It was during the course of MC Mehta Vs Union of India that the **Bhure Lal Committee** was established under Section 3 of the Environment (Protection) Act, 1986. It was based on recommendations of this committee that a time-frame for switching over to CNG fuel for Government and Public transport was fixed.

37. The public trust doctrine has its origins in the Roman law. In Indian context, the doctrine was first applied in **M.C. Mehta** Vs. **Kamal Nath** and others. In this case, owners of a motel tried to divert the natural flow of a river to save their motel from floods in future. The Supreme Court held that the State is the trustee of all natural resources, which are by nature meant for public use and enjoyment. Public at large is the beneficiary of the seashore, running waters, airs, forests and ecologically fragile lands. The State as a trustee is under a legal duty to protect the natural resources. These natural resources are meant for public use and cannot be converted into objects of private ownership.

39. According to Holland, International Law is the vanishing point of jurisprudence. In his view, rules of international law are followed by courtesy and hence they should not be kept in the category of law. Absence of a sovereign who could declare laws and sanctions which can enforce obedience are one the primary reasons for Holland to hold this view. Also, Holland considered that International Law is followed merely as an act of courtesy by civilised nations and no authoritative judge or arbiter exists to settle disputes between them.

42. In Hans Muller of Nurenburg Vs Supdt, Presidency Jail, Calcutta and others, a West German citizen was detained by Govt. of West Bengal for his expulsion from India consequent to appropriate orders made in that regard by the Central Government. The distinction between extradition and expulsion was clarified in this case. Extradition requires a requisition from a foreign state whereas expulsion does not require any such request. A sovereign state can expel a foreigner *suo motu* according to the laws framed by it in this regard.

43. **Statement (*d*):** In 1967, the UN General Assembly adopted a Declaration on Territorial Asylum. The Declaration reiterated that granting asylum is a peaceful and humanitarian act which cannot be regarded as unfriendly or hostile by any other State. The declaration also observed that it is the responsibility of the country providing asylum to evaluate a person's claim.

Other statements are correct. Hence, the most appropriate option is (B).

44. Statement (*b*): The ECOSOC's 54 members are elected by the General Assembly for overlapping three-year terms. Seats are allotted based on geographical representation with fourteen allocated to African States, eleven to Asian States, six to Eastern European States, ten to Latin American and Caribbean States, and thirteen to Western European and other States.

Statement (*d*): The President of the ECOSOC is selected for a one-year term.

Statement (*a*) & (*c*) are correct. Hence, the most appropriate option is (B)

45. Article 94 of the UN Charter reads as follows:

1. Each Member of the United Nations undertakes to comply with the decision of the International Court of Justice in any case to which it is a party.
2. If any party to a case fails to perform the obligations incumbent upon it under a judgement rendered by the Court, the other party may have recourse to the Security Council, which may, if it deems necessary, make recommendations or decide upon measures to be taken to give effect to the judgement.

46. A void marriage is void *ab initio* and no decree annulling it is required.

48. According to Section 5 of Hindu Marriage Act two Hindus may marry each other if neither party has a spouse living at the time of marriage (monogamy), the parties are not sapindas to each other and neither party is incapable of giving a valid consent due to unsoundness of mind. This means that according to Hindu marriage act valid consent and not free consent is a condition for marriage. Hence, option (D) is the correct choice.

49. Statement (*i*) & (*ii*): According to section 7, of Hindu Adoptions and Maintenance Act, any male Hindu who is of sound mind and is not a minor has the capacity to take a son or a daughter in adoption. Provided that, if he has a wife living, he shall not adopt except with the consent of his wife unless the wife has completely and finally renounced the world or has ceased to be a Hindu or has been declared by a court of competent jurisdiction to be of unsound mind. Explanation appended to this section reads—If a person has more than one wife living at the time of adoption, the consent of all the wives is necessary unless the consent of any one of them is unnecessary for any of the reasons specified in the preceding proviso.

Statement (*iii*): A void marriage is void *ab initio i.e.*, it is not recognised as a marriage in the eyes of the law and parties to such a marriage have no legal relation as husband and wife. Hence, in case of such a marriage no consent of wife is required for a valid adoption.

Statement (*iv*): A voidable marriage is a perfectly valid marriage until and unless a decree annulling the marriage is passed by a competent court. Hence, parties to such a marriage are legally husband and wife to each other and section 7 of Hindu Adoptions and maintenance Act will apply to them.

Hence, out of all the given options, option (A) is the most appropriate.

50. *Ahsan Talaq* is considered to be the most approved form of divorce among muslims because of two reasons—single pronouncement of *talaq* and revocability. In Muslim theology, *talaq* is considered an evil word. In *Ahsan Talaq*, the husband is required to pronounce *talaq* only once during the period of *tuhr* (purity) of wife and then abstain from revocation, whether express or implied for the entire period *iddat*. *Hasan Talaq* is also revocable but in this form of divorce, *talaq* needs to be pronounced thrice in three successive *tuhrs*.

51. Epilepsy was earlier a ground for annulment of marriage but it was omitted by Marriage Laws (Amendment) Act, 1999, w.e.f. 29-12-1999.

52. Under Muslim law, right to custody of child is called Hizanat and it primarily belongs to the mother. Mother, if not disqualified by misconduct or some other disability cannot surrender this right in favour of any one including her husband. Father's right of Hizanat commences upon the expiry of this right in favour of the mother, either by disqualification or when the child reaches the age up to which his/her mother is entitled custody. Apart from father, certain other male relations are also entitled to custody in a hierarchical order:

1. Nearest paternal grandfather
2. Full brother
3. Consanguine brother
4. Full brother's son
5. Consanguine brother's father
6. Full brother of the father
7. Consanguine brother of the father
8. Father's full brother's son
9. Father's consanguine brother's son

54. This was the first conference on human rights after the end of cold war. The Vienna Declaration and Programme for Action on Human Rights saw the creation of the office of UN High Commissioner for Human Rights.

55. 'All human rights for all' this slogan was adopted to celebrate the 50th anniversary of the Universal Declaration of Human Rights in 1998.

56. On November 20th, 1989, the General Assembly of the United Nations adopted the Convention on the Rights of the Child as part of Resolution 44/25. However, the process had begun more than ten years back in 1978 when Poland first proposed the idea of such a convention to be legally binding on all the member states of United Nations.

59. The Vienna Declaration and Programme for Action on Human Rights was adopted on 25th June 1993. This declaration created the office of UN High Commissioner for Human Rights.

62. Merely making statement of facts on public interest is not a defence to an action of defamation. Statement of facts should also be true. A publisher cannot put up the defence that he published defamatory material against plaintiff believing the material to be true and that he had no intention to defame. The act of defamation is complete the moment untrue information capable of prejudicing plaintiff's reputation in the minds of right thinking members of the society is published.

63. According to Section 15 of Indian Easements Act, 15, where the access and use of light or air and for any building have been peaceably enjoyed therewith, as an easement, without interruption, and for twenty years. The right, to such access and use of light or air, support, or other easement, shall be absolute. Hence, (A) is the most appropriate option.

64. Slander is a species of defamation. In India defamation can be both a civil and a criminal wrong depending upon the action brought by plaintiff. It is incorrect to hold that slander is always a criminal offence.

65. The cases in chronological order are:

Shyam Sunder and Others Vs. *The State of Rajasthan* on 12 March, 1974

Pushpabai Purshottam Udeshi & Ors Vs. Ranjit Ginning & Pressing Co. on 25 March, 1977

Syad Akbar Vs. State of Karnataka on 25 July, 1979

The Municipal Corporation of Delhi Vs. Smt. Sushila Devi & Ors on 7 May, 1999.

66. According to Section 6 of Consumer Protection Act, 1986, the consumers have various rights such as

(a) The right to be protected against the marketing of goods and services which are hazardous to life and property;

(b) The right to be informed about the quality, quantity, potency, purity, standard and price of goods or services, as the case may be so as to protect the consumer against unfair trade practices;

(c) The right to be assured, wherever possible, access to a variety of goods and services at competitive prices;

(d) The right to be heard and to be assured that consumer's interests will receive due consideration at appropriate forums;

(e) The right to seek redressal against unfair trade practices or restrictive trade practices or unscrupulous exploitation of consumers; and

(f) The right to consumer education.

71. According to section 138 of Negotiable Instruments Act, payee or the holder in due course both are competent to sue the drawer of the cheque in case of dishonour of cheque.

74. According to Companies Act 1956, the maximum number of partners in a banking business could be 10 and for other businesses this number was 20. However, under the new Companies Act, 2013 this distinction has been eliminated and now maximum no. of members in a partnership firm can be 100. Creating a monopoly is against the prevailing competition policy of the country and are as such illegal. Since, any contract entered into with an illegal object is void *ab initio* a partnership to create a monopoly is not valid in the eyes of law. Also, as per the Indian Partnership Act there is no bar on the trustees in carrying a business in their own name. Hence, out of the given options, (D) is the most appropriate.

75. According to section 13(f) of Indian Partnership Act, 1932, subject to a contract to the contrary a partner shall indemnify the firm for any loss caused to it by his willful neglect in the conduct of the business of the firm.

Previous Paper (Solved)

UGC-NET-JRF & Assistant Professor Exam Law, December-2015

PAPER-II

Note: *This paper contains fifty (50) objective type questions of two (2) marks each. All questions are compulsory.*

1. Read **Assertion (A)** and **Reason (R)** and answer using the codes given below:

Assertion (A): The preamble of the Constitution of India defines the ideal philosophy of Indian democracy and its key-concepts are laid down as Justice, Liberty, Equality and Fraternity.

Reason (R): A democracy to be real must be characterised by two features.

Codes:

A. Both (A) and (R) are true and (R) is the correct explanation of (A).
B. Both (A) and (R) are true, but (R) is not the correct explanation of (A).
C. (A) is true, but (R) is false.
D. (A) is false, but (R) is true.

2. Which of the following statements is **wrong** to issue Writ of Quo warranto?

A. The office in question should be a public office
B. The office should be held by an usurper without legal authority
C. The petition is barred by res-judicata
D. It is necessary for the petitioner to show that he himself suffered a personal injury nor it is necessary to show that he is seeking redress of a personal grievance

3. Match **List-I** with **List-II** and select the **correct** answer using the codes given below the lists:

List-I	List-II
(a) S.R. Chaudhuri *vs.* State of Punjab	*(i)* Ban on smoking at public places
(b) Murali S. Deora *vs.* Union of India	*(ii)* Two extra increments to the existing employees on earning Higher Qualification
(c) Food Corporation of India *vs.* Bharatiya Khadya Nigam Karmachari Sangh	*(iii)* Classifications based on the number of children for elected post in Panchayat
(d) Javed *vs.* State of Haryana	*(iv)* Non-member cannot be re-appointed as minister if he fails to get elected within six months

Codes:

	(a)	*(b)*	*(c)*	*(d)*
A.	*(iv)*	*(i)*	*(ii)*	*(iii)*
B.	*(iv)*	*(ii)*	*(i)*	*(iii)*
C.	*(ii)*	*(iii)*	*(i)*	*(iv)*
D.	*(iii)*	*(ii)*	*(iv)*	*(i)*

4. Which of the following statements are **correct**; use the codes and answer?

Freedom of press includes:

(a) Right to print and publish news
(b) Distribution of printed matter
(c) Criticism of public affairs
(d) Pre-censorship

Codes:

A. *(a)*, *(b)*, *(c)* and *(d)* B. *(a)*, *(b)* and *(c)*
C. *(a)*, *(c)* and *(d)* D. *(b)*, *(c)* and *(d)*

5. During a Financial Emergency, the executive authority of the union exercises control over state finances through the following measures:

(*a*) It can issue directions to states to observe certain cannons of financial propriety

(*b*) It can ask the states to reserve their money bills for the consideration of the President

(*c*) It can direct the states to reduce the salaries and allowances of all the persons serving in connection with the affairs of the states, including the judges of the Supreme Court and High Courts.

Codes:

A. (*a*) and (*b*) B. (*a*) and (*c*)

C. (*b*) and (*c*) D. (*a*), (*b*) and (*c*)

6. Justice Pasayat held that 'pardon obtained on the basis of manifest mistake or fraud can be rescinded or cancelled' in the following case:

A. G. Krishta Goud *vs.* State of A.P.

B. Maru Ram *vs.* Union of India

C. Epuru Sudhakar *vs.* Govt. of A.P.

D. Kehar Singh *vs.* Union of India

7. Read **Assertion (A)** and **Reason (R)** and answer using the codes given below :

Assertion (A): The administrative control over the Subordinate Judiciary in the State lies with the Governor.

Reason (R): The High Court has a power of Superintendence over all courts and tribunals throughout the territory in relation to which it exercises jurisdiction, except military tribunals.

Codes:

A. Both (A) and (R) are true and (R) is the correct explanation of (A)

B. Both (A) and (R) are true, but (R) is not the correct explanation of (A)

C. (A) is true, but (R) is false

D. (A) is false, but (R) is true

8. Who has described Jurisprudence as "The lawyer's extraversion. It is lawyer's examination of the precepts, ideals, and techniques of the law in the light derived from present knowledge in disciplines other than the law"?

A. Paton B. Holland

C. Austin D. Julius Stone

9. Who may be regarded as the leading contemporary representative of British Positivism?

A. Holland B. Salmond

C. Hart D. Hohfeld

10. Match **List-I** with **List-II** and give the **correct** answer by using the codes given below:

List-I	List-II
(*a*) Justice is realised only through good law	(*i*) Jerome Hall
(*b*) Moral value needs to be included in a definition of positive law	(*ii*) John Finnis
(*c*) Natural law with a variable content	(*iii*) Morris
(*d*) A sophisticated version of Natural Law has been put forward in the tradition of Aristotle and Aquinas	(*iv*) Stammler

Codes:

	(*a*)	(*b*)	(*c*)	(*d*)
A.	(*ii*)	(*iv*)	(*i*)	(*iii*)
B.	(*i*)	(*ii*)	(*iii*)	(*iv*)
C.	(*iii*)	(*i*)	(*iv*)	(*ii*)
D.	(*iv*)	(*iii*)	(*ii*)	(*i*)

11. According to whom, whenever a person looked like an owner in relation to a thing, he had possession of it, unless possession was denied him by special rules based on practical convenience. The 'Animus' element was simply an intelligent awareness of the situation?

A. Salmond B. Pollock

C. Ihering D. Savigny

12. Match **List-I** with **List-II** and give the **correct** answer by using the codes given below:

List-I	List-II
(*a*) Social Solidarity	(*i*) Roscoe Pound
(*b*) Social Utilitarian	(*ii*) Grotius
(*c*) Social Engineering	(*iii*) Duguit
(*d*) Social Contract	(*iv*) Ihering

Codes:

	(a)	(b)	(c)	(d)
A.	(i)	(ii)	(iii)	(iv)
B.	(ii)	(iii)	(iv)	(i)
C.	(iv)	(i)	(ii)	(iii)
D.	(iii)	(iv)	(i)	(ii)

13. Match **List-I** with **List-II** and give the **correct** answer by using the codes given below:

List-I	List-II
(a) No one has any other 'right' than always to do his duty.	(i) Gray
(b) 'Right' is power over an object which by means of this right he subjected to will of the person enjoying the right.	(ii) Holland
(c) Legal right means, "A capacity residing in one man of controlling with the assent and assistance of the state, the acts of the other".	(iii) Duguit
(d) 'Right' is not the interest by itself but it is a mean by which enjoyment of interest is secured.	(iv) Pachta

Codes:

	(a)	(b)	(c)	(d)
A.	(iv)	(iii)	(i)	(ii)
B.	(i)	(ii)	(iii)	(iv)
C.	(iii)	(i)	(ii)	(iv)
D.	(ii)	(iv)	(i)	(iii)

14. Who has stated that "As a matter of fact International law is neither a myth on the one hand nor a panacea on the other, but just one institution among others which we can use for the building of a better international order"?

A. Prof. Louis Henkin
B. J.L. Brierly
C. J.G. Starke
D. Oppenheim

15. Which one of the following sources of International Law does not find or mention in Article 38 of the statute of the International Court of Justice but it has now become a well recognised source?

A. International conventions
B. General Principles of Law Recognised by Civilized Nations
C. Decisions of Judicial or Arbitral Tribunals and Juristic Works
D. Decisions or Determinations of the Organs of International Institutions

16. Which of the following statement/statements is/are **correct**?

(a) Custom is the oldest and the original source of International as well as of law in general.
(b) In Barcelona Traction case, the International Court applied the general rule of subrogation.
(c) In Chorzow factory (Indemnity) case the Permanent Court of Justice ruled that the International law is based on justice, equity and good conscience.
(d) In Nicaragua vs. U.S.A. The World Court has taken the view that the sources of International law are not hierarchial but are necessarily complimentary and inter related.

Codes:

A. Only (a) is correct
B. (a), (b), (c) are correct
C. (a) and (d) are both correct
D. (a), (b), (c) and (d) all are correct

17. Which of the following statement/statements is/are **incorrect**?

(a) There are five prominent theories of relationship between International law and Municipal law
(b) According to Dualism Theory law is a unified branch of knowledge
(c) 'Monism' and 'Dualism' are diametrically opposed to each other
(d) Wright, Kelson and Duguit are prominent exponents of Dualism Theory

Codes:

A. (b) and (d) are incorrect
B. (a), (b) and (d) are incorrect

C. Only (*d*) is incorrect

D. (*a*), (*b*), (*c*) and (*d*) all are incorrect

18. Match **List-I** with **List-II** and give the **correct** answer by using the codes given below the lists:

List-I (Provisions)	**List-II (Articles of Statute of International Court)**
(*a*) Law applied by the International Court of Justice	(*i*) Article 62
(*b*) Transferred Jurisdiction	(*ii*) Article 59
(*c*) Court power to allow a state to intervene in case to which it is not a party	(*iii*) Article 38
(*d*) Binding Force of the decisions of the International Court of Justice	(*iv*) Article 36 (5)

Codes:

	(*a*)	(*b*)	(*c*)	(*d*)
A.	(*i*)	(*ii*)	(*iii*)	(*iv*)
B.	(*iv*)	(*iii*)	(*ii*)	(*i*)
C.	(*iii*)	(*iv*)	(*i*)	(*ii*)
D.	(*ii*)	(*i*)	(*iv*)	(*iii*)

19. Assertion (A): When a state wants to delay the de jure recognition of any state, it may, in the first stage grant de-facto recognition.

Reason (R): There is no distinction between 'de facto' and 'de jure' recognition for the purpose of giving effect to the Internal Acts of the Recognised Authority.

Use the codes below and give the **correct** answer.

Codes:

A. Both (A) and (R) are correct and (R) is the correct explanation of (A)

B. Both (A) and (R) are correct, but (R) is not the correct explanation of (A)

C. (A) is correct, (R) is wrong

D. (A) is wrong, (R) is correct

20. Two persons are said to be related to each other by uterine blood when they are descended from:

A. a common ancestor by the same wife

B. a common ancestor but by different wives

C. a common ancestress by the same husband

D. a common ancestress but by different husbands

21. Match **List-I** with **List-II** under the Hindu Marriage Act, 1955 and give the **correct** answer with the help of codes given below:

List-I	**List-II**
(*a*) Restitution of Conjugal Rights	(*i*) Section-5
(*b*) Marriageable Age	(*ii*) Section 29 (2)
(*c*) Customary Divorce	(*iii*) Section-9
(*d*) Ceremonies of Marriage	(*iv*) Section-7

Codes:

	(*a*)	(*b*)	(*c*)	(*d*)
A.	(*iv*)	(*i*)	(*ii*)	(*iii*)
B.	(*iii*)	(*ii*)	(*i*)	(*iv*)
C.	(*iii*)	(*i*)	(*ii*)	(*iv*)
D.	(*i*)	(*ii*)	(*iii*)	(*iv*)

22. In which of the following cases, a child could be a Hindu? Answer with the help of codes:

(*a*) Only one parent is a Hindu and the child was brought up as a Hindu

(*b*) Only one parent is a Hindu and the child was not brought up as a Hindu

(*c*) If after the birth of child, father converts to non-Hindu religion

(*d*) Both the parents are Hindu

Codes:

A. (*a*), (*c*) and (*d*) only

B. (*b*), (*c*) and (*d*) only

C. (*a*) and (*d*) only

D. (*c*) and (*d*) only

23. Under the provisions of the Hindu Marriage Act, 1955 the decree of Judicial Separation:

(*a*) dissolve the marriage

(*b*) does not dissolve the marriage bond but only suspends marital rights and obligations during the subsistence of the decree.

(*c*) the parties continue to be husband and wife but not obligated to live together and neither party is free to marry.

(*d*) if after a decree of judicial separation the parties have not resumed cohabitation for a period of one year, either party may seek divorce.

Codes:

A. (*a*), (*b*) and (*c*) B. (*b*), (*a*) and (*d*)

C. (*b*), (*c*) and (*d*) D. (*a*), (*b*), (*c*) and (*d*)

24. Read **Assertion (A)** and **Reason (R)** and give the **correct** answer with the help of codes given below:

Assertion (A): The Muslim Personal Law (Shariat) Application Act, 1937 makes Muslim Law applicable expressly to all Muslims.

Reason (R): The Muslim Personal Law (Shariat) Application Act, 1937 has abrogated the customs and restored to Muslims their own personal law in almost all cases.

Codes:

A. (A) and (R) are true and (R) is the correct explanation of (A)

B. (A) is true, but (R) is false

C. (A) is false, but (R) is true

D. Both (A) and (R) are false

25. Observance of 'Iddat' is necessary:

A. Where Cohabitation is lawful *i.e.* consummation of marriage

B. Where Cohabitation is unlawful *i.e.* illicit intercourse and the pregnancy follows the illicit intercourse

C. In both A and B

D. Only in A and not in B

26. Modern sources of Hindu law are:

A. Legislation, Precedents and Digests

B. Legislation, Precedents, Equity etc.

C. Precedents, Smritis, Legislation

D. Legislation, Customs, Precedents and Commentaries

27. Match **List-I** with **List-II** and select the **correct** answer using the codes given below:

List-I (Heads of Public Policy)	List-II (Case - Law)
(*a*) Trading with enemy	(*i*) Girdhari Singh *vs.* Neeladhar Singh
(*b*) Trafficking in public offices	(*ii*) Espostiv *vs.* Bowden
(*c*) Interference with administration of justice	(*iii*) Shivsaran Lal *vs.* Keshav Prasad
(*d*) Marriage brokage contracts	(*iv*) Nand Kishor *vs.* Kunj Behari Lal

Codes :

	(*a*)	(*b*)	(*c*)	(*d*)
A.	(*i*)	(*iv*)	(*ii*)	(*iii*)
B.	(*iv*)	(*i*)	(*ii*)	(*iii*)
C.	(*iv*)	(*i*)	(*iii*)	(*ii*)
D.	(*ii*)	(*iii*)	(*i*)	(*iv*)

28. Read **Assertion (A)** and **Reason (R)** and answer using codes given below:

Assertion (A): Compensation is recoverable for any loss or damage arising unnaturally in the unusual course of things from breach of contract, or which the parties did not know at the time of the contract as likely to result from the breach.

Reason (R): Because Section-73 of the Indian Contract Act stipulates so.

Codes:

A. Both (A) and (R) are right and (R) is correct reason for (A)

B. Both (A) and (R) are wrong

C. (A) is right, but (R) is wrong

D. (R) is right, but (A) is wrong

29. Doctrine of frustration was laid down for the first time in:

A. Krell *vs.* Henry

B. Taylor *vs.* Caldwell

C. Paradine *vs.* Jane

D. Cricklewood Property and Investment Trust Ltd. *vs.* Leighton's Investment Trust Ltd.

30. Which of the following statements is **correct**?

A. A contract is voidable because it was caused by a mistake as to any law in force in India.

B. A mistake as to law not in force in India has the same effect as a mistake of fact.
C. A contract is voidable merely because it was caused by one of the parties to it being under a mistake as to a matter of fact.
D. Where both the parties to an agreement are under a mistake as to a matter of fact essential to the agreement, the agreement is not void.

31. An agreement without consideration is valid, unless :
A. It is in writing and registered
B. Is a promise to compensate for something done
C. It is made by two minors
D. Is a promise to pay a debt barred by limitation law

32. A proposal is revoked:
A. By the notice of revocation of the proposal
B. By the lapse of a reasonable time if the time is prescribed in the proposal
C. By acceptance of a condition precedent to acceptance
D. By the death or insanity of the proposer, if the fact of his death or insanity comes to the knowledge of the acceptor before acceptance

33. In order to bring an action for tort, the plaintiff has to prove that:
A. There has been a legal damage caused to him
B. Violation of a legal right not vested in him
C. There has been no legal damage caused to him
D. Violation of no legal right and has not resulted in harm to him

34. In which case it was held by the Supreme Court that state was **not** liable on the ground that police were acting in discharge of statutory powers and power of the police in keeping the property in the police *Malkhana* was a sovereign power?
A. Ramawati Kaur *vs.* State of Bihar
B. Radha Aggarwal *vs.* State of U.P.
C. Kasturi Lal *vs.* State of U.P.
D. State of Bihar *vs.* Rameshwar Prasad

35. Match **List-I** with **List-II** and give the **correct** answer by using the codes given below:

List-I (Name of defence)	**List-II (Name of Case - Law)**
(*a*) Act of State	(*i*) Buron *vs.* Denman
(*b*) Consent	(*ii*) Hall *vs.* Brookland and Auto Racing Club
(*c*) Act of God	(*iii*) Metropolitan Asylum Board *vs.* Hills
(*d*) Statutory authority	(*iv*) Nicholas *vs.* Marsland

Codes:

	(*a*)	(*b*)	(*c*)	(*d*)
A.	(*iii*)	(*ii*)	(*i*)	(*iv*)
B.	(*i*)	(*ii*)	(*iv*)	(*iii*)
C.	(*iii*)	(*i*)	(*ii*)	(*iv*)
D.	(*iv*)	(*i*)	(*iii*)	(*ii*)

36. In which of the following cases, is the occupier of a house liable for 'negligence'?
A. Keeping a dog, which may bite trespassers
B. Fixing broken glass pieces on the top of a wall to prevent trespassers
C. Setting spring guns in the premises to prevent trespassers
D. Constructing a compound wall to prevent trespassers

37. Read **Assertion (A) and Reason (R)** and give the **correct** answer with the help of codes given below:

Assertion (A): Mental element is an essential element in most of the torts.

Reason (R): State of mind of the defendant is not relevant to ascertain his liability in all branches of law of torts.

Codes:
A. Both (A) and (R) are true and (R) is the correct explanation of (A)
B. Both (A) and (R) are true, but (R) is not the correct explanation of (A)

C. Both (A) and (R) are true
D. Both (A) and (R) are wrong

38. Which one of the following is **not** an exception to the rule of *volenti non fit injuria*?
A. Surgeon amputates a limb of a patient to save his life
B. Injury is caused while play-fighting with naked swords at a religion function
C. Injury is caused while doing lawful acts under contract
D. Injury is caused to a player in football match

39. Which of the facts do not include within the principle of joint liability?
A. The actuated act need not be a crime or when it was foisted.
B. An act done in a pre-arranged plan between more than one person.
C. Mere participation in some manner in the act constituting the offence.
D. An act done in furtherance of an intention to cause harm.

40. 'Imposing punishment implies that some one should be legally authorised to impose it upon the offender'. In which of the following cases a private person can impose such punishment?
A. Where the law recognises moral blame worthiness.
B. Where there is justification for punishing any person provided the offender had broken a law.
C. Where one can establish the connection between punishment and crime.
D. Where the act falls within a retroactive penal legislation.

41. The Apex court has shown as to how compromise is not a free choice of the rape survivor but a hidden secret of law where justice is reduced to a bargain between the victim's kin, state authorities and the accused. Identify the case law:
A. Ravindra *vs.* State of M.P.
B. Shreya Singhal *vs.* Union of India
C. Sanskar Marathe *vs.* State of Maharashtra
D. Khursheed Ahmed Khan *vs.* State of U.P.

42. There is a specific provision that the intention to screen the offender must be primary and the role object of the accused. This provision is provided in ....
A. Section 202 B. Section 201
C. Section 199 D. Section 203

43. Which of the following offences fall under causing hurt as well as assault?
A. Digging a pit in the public path
B. Flinging boiling water over a person
C. Mixing deleterious poison in a liquid and placing the same on another table
D. Pulling hair of a woman

44. There must be dishonest intention which should co-exist while taking a thing for an offence of theft. In which of the following situations it will **not** amount to theft?
A. Taking a stick from the person to beat him
B. Taking a sugar packet from another person in good faith while his own packet was at the shop
C. A senior student snatching some books from a junior student with promise to return on the next day
D. Not finding the helmet hanged on a bike, a person takes away a similar helmet from the adjacent bike, but afterwords repenting on his fault returns the same to the owner

45. The Constitution of Works Committee under the Industrial Disputes Act is to:
A. Remove causes of friction between the employer and workmen in the day to day waking of the establishment
B. Remove causes of friction between the employer and workmen relating to wage settlement
C. Remove causes of friction between the employer and workmen relating to standing orders
D. Remove causes of friction between the employer and workmen relating to implementation of award

46. Under the Industrial Disputes Act, a reference to an Industrial tribunal will be:

A. Only where both the parties to an Industrial Dispute apply for such reference

B. Only where the appropriate government considers it expedient to do so

C. Only where both the parties to an Industrial Dispute apply for such reference and also where the appropriate government considers it expedient to do so

D. Only where the affected party to the dispute apply for such reference

47. To which settlement machinery can the central government refer the dispute under Rule 81-A?

A. Conciliation B. Arbitration

C. Adjudication D. Supreme Court

48. A settlement under the Industrial Disputes Act arrived at in the course of conciliation proceding, between the employer and a recognised majority union will be binding on:

A. parties to the settlement

B. all workmen of the establishment

C. all workmen of a recognised majority union

D. all workmen of a registered Trade Union

49. The permission applied for by the government shall be deemed to have been granted if the appropriate government does not communicate the order under I.D. Act, granting or refusing to grant permission within a period of:

A. 15 days B. 30 days

C. 60 days D. 90 days

50. "The right to strike may be controlled or restricted by appropriate industrial legislation and the validity of such legislation would have to be tested not with reference to the criteria laid down in clause (4) of Article 19 but by totally different considerations", was observed by the Supreme Court in:

A. Syndicate Bank *vs.* Umesh Nayak

B. All India Bank Employees Association *vs.* I.T.

C. Management of Churakulam Tea Estate (P) Ltd *vs.* The workmen and another

D. Ramnagar cane and sugar Co. *vs.* Jatin Chalin

ANSWERS

1	2	3	4	5	6	7	8	9	10
C	C	A	B	D	C	D	D	C	A
11	**12**	**13**	**14**	**15**	**16**	**17**	**18**	**19**	**20**
C	D	A	B	D	C	A	C	B	D
21	**22**	**23**	**24**	**25**	**26**	**27**	**28**	**29**	**30**
C	A	C	A	C	B	B	B	B	B
31	**32**	**33**	**34**	**35**	**36**	**37**	**38**	**39**	**40**
C	D	A	C	B	C	D	D	A	B
41	**42**	**43**	**44**	**45**	**46**	**47**	**48**	**49**	**50**
A	B	B	A	A	C	C	B	B	B

SOME SELECTED EXPLANATORY ANSWERS

1. The 'Preamble' of the Constitution of India is a brief introductory statement that sets out the guiding purpose and principles of the document, and it indicates the source from which the document which derives its authority, meaning, the people. It may be considered as the soul of Constitution. The preamble can highlights the essence of the entire Constitution. So, **Assertion (A)** is true as it is mentioned that the preamble of the Constitution of India defines the ideal philosophy of Indian democracy and its key-concepts are laid down as Justice, Liberty, Equality and Fraternity.

   In most common way, Democracy can be defined as the Government of the people, by the people and for the people. In such government, the supreme power is vested in the people and exercised by them directly or indirectly through a system of representation usually involving periodically held free elections. These principles are reflected in all eligible citizens being equal before the law and having equal access to legislative processes. Thus, as given in **Reason (R)** it will be false to say that a democracy to be real must be characterised by two features.

2. *Res judicata* or *res iudicata*, also known as claim preclusion, is the Latin term for "a matter [already] judged", and refers to either of two concepts: in both civil law and common law legal systems.

   In the case of *res judicata*, the matter cannot be raised again, either in the same court or in a different court. A court will use *res judicata* to deny reconsideration of a matter. The legal concept of *res judicata* arose as a method of preventing injustice to the parties of a case supposedly finished, but perhaps mostly to avoid unnecessary waste of resources in the court system. *Res judicata* does not merely prevent future judgments from contradicting earlier ones, but also prevents litigants from multiplying judgments, and confusion. So it will be wrong to issue Writ of quo warranto if the petition is barred by res-judicata.

3. (*a*) Article 164(4) contemplates appointment of a Minister who is not a Member of the Legislature of a State and also continuation in the office of a person as Minister after he ceases to be a member of a State Legislature. In both cases, the Minister can hold office only for a period of six consecutive months. A three-Judge Bench of the Supreme Court in *S.R. Chaudhuri* v. *State of Punjab* case held that a Minister who is appointed under Article 164(4) does not enjoy the privileges under Article 194(2).

   (*b*) Murali S. Deora *vs.* Union of India was a case to ban on smoking at public places. Initiating through Litigation Supreme Court Orders in Murli S. Deora *vs.* Union of India case in the Supreme Court of India Civil Original Jurisdiction Writ Petition (Civil) No. 316 of 1999 Murli S. Deora ... Petitioner Versus Union of India and Others ... Respondents Order Heard the learned counsel for the parties. Fundamental right guaranteed under Article 21 of Constitution of India inter alia, provides that none shall be deprived of his life without due process of law. Then why a non-smoker should be afflicted by various diseases including lung cancer or of heart, only because he is required to go to public places? In any case, there is no reason to compel non-smokers to be helpless victims of air pollution.

   (*c*) In the Supreme Court of India Civil Appellate Jurisdiction, Food Corporation of India & Ors. Appealed (Civil Appeal

No. 7268 of 2002) for two extra increments to the existing employees on earning Higher Qualification. Earlier the petition was made to High Court of Jammu & Kashmir but verdict was impugned to the appellant. However, in the Supreme Court verdict, some courses of study were approved for grant of the two increments.

(*d*) Javed *vs.* State of Haryana was a case of Classifications based on the number of children for elected post in Panchayat. Petition was given against the provision made by Haryana that those having more than two children cannot fight for gram panchayat elections. The verdict considered that the provision is arbitrary and hence violative of Article 14 of the Constitution; that the disqualification does not serve the purpose sought to be achieved by the legislation.

4. In a series of decisions from 1950 onwards the Supreme Court has ruled that Freedom of the Press is implicit in the guarantee of freedom of speech and expression guaranteed by Article 19(1) (a) of the Constitution [5]. Thus, freedom of the press by judicial interpretation has been accorded constitutional status even if there is no specific provision in the Constitution ensuring freedom of press as such. Thus, in India, freedom of the press is implied from the freedom of speech and expression guaranteed by Article 19(1) (a).

5. If the President is satisfied that there is an economic imbalance in which the financial stability or credit of India is threatened, he or she can declare financial emergency under Article 360. Such an emergency must be approved by the Parliament within two months.

In case of a financial emergency, the President can reduce the salaries of all government officials, including judges of the Supreme Court and High Courts. All money bills passed by the State legislatures are submitted to the President for his approval. He can direct the state to observe certain principles (economy measures) relating to financial matters; but fundamental rights cannot be suspended.

6. In *Epuru Sudhakar vs. Govt. of A.P. & Ors.* Air 2006 SC 3385, the Court held that reasons had to be indicated while exercising power under Articles 72/161. It was further observed (per Kapadia, J) in his concurring opinion: "Pardons, reprieves and remissions are manifestation of the exercise of prerogative power. These are not acts of grace. They are a part of Constitutional scheme. When a pardon is granted, it is the determination of the ultimate authority that public welfare will be better served by inflicting less than what the judgment has fixed... Exercise of Executive clemency is a matter of discretion and yet subject to certain standards. It is not a matter of privilege. It is a matter of performance of official duty. It is vested in the President or the Governor, as the case may be, not for the benefit of the convict only, but for the welfare of the people who may insist on the performance of the duty..... Granting of pardon is in no sense an overturning of a judgment of conviction, but rather it is an Executive action that mitigates or sets aside the punishment for a crime.

7. Assertion (A) is false, as the administrative control over the Subordinate judiciary in the State does not lie with the Governor; rather it lies with a District and Sessions Judge. The usual designations on the civil side are District Judge, Additional District Judge, and Civil Judge. On the criminal side, we have Sessions Judge, Additional Sessions Judge, Chief Judicial Magistrate, Judicial Magistrate etc.

Reason (R) is true, as it is truly said that the High Court has a power of Superintendence over all courts and tribunals throughout the territory in relation to which it exercises jurisdiction, except military tribunals. The

High Court is the supreme judicial tribunal of the State, having both Original and Appellate jurisdiction.

8. Julius Stone (7 July 1907 – 1985) was Challis Professor of Jurisprudence and International Law at the University of Sydney from 1942 to 1972, and thereafter a visiting Professor of Law at the University of New South Wales and concurrently Distinguished Professor of Jurisprudence and International Law at the Hastings College of Law, University of California. He is the author of 27 books on jurisprudence and international law, and is hailed by his official biography at the Julius Stone Institute of Jurisprudence as one of the premier legal theorists. It was Julius Stone described Jurisprudence as "The lawyer's extraversion. It is lawyer's examination of the precepts, ideals, and techniques of the law in the light derived from present knowledge in disciplines other than the law".

9. Professor Herbert Lionel Adophus Hart (H.L.A. Hart) is an influential legal professor, who revolutionised the methods of jurisprudence and the philosophy of law. He authored *The Concept of Law* and made major contributions to political philosophy. He is regarded as the leading contemporary representative of British positivism. From his book, it shows that he is a linguistic, philosopher, barrister and a jurist. To Hart, law is a system of rules.

11. The given quotation is of Rudolf von Jhering, Jhering also spelled Ihering (born August 22, 1818, Aurich, Hanover [Germany]—died September 17, 1892, Göttingen, Germany), German legal scholar, sometimes called the father of sociological jurisprudence. He developed a philosophy of social utilitarianism that, in emphasising the needs of society, differed from the individualist approach of the English utilitarian philosopher Jeremy Bentham.

Ihering taught Roman law at Giessen (1852–68), at Göttingen (from 1872), and at four other universities for briefer periods. In his most ambitious work, *Geist des römischen Rechts*, 4 vol. (1852–65; "The Spirit of the Roman Law"), he elaborated the relation of law to social change. Even more influential in the 20th century was his *Law As a Means to an End*, 2 vol. (1877–83; originally in German), which maintained that the purpose of law was the protection of individual and societal interests by coordinating them and thus minimising occasions for conflict.

12. (*a*) **Duguit:** 1859-1928 and his theory of social solidarity Duguit made a distinction between the kinds of need of men in society firstly there are common needs of individuals which are satisfied by mutual assistance and secondly there are diverse need of individuals which are satisfied by the exchange of service; therefore the division of labour is the most important fact of social cohesion. He named it social solidarity. Interdependence of men in the society Duguit built his theory on social solidarity. He insisted on the necessity of viewing social life as it is actually lived. The most important fact of the society is the interdependence of men. The end of all human activities and organisation should be to ensure the inter dependence of men. This is called Duguit's theory of social solidarity.

(*b*) Rudolf von Ihering, German legal scholar, is sometimes called the father of sociological jurisprudence. He developed a philosophy of social utilitarianism that, in emphasising the needs of society, differed from the individualist approach of the English utilitarian philosopher Jeremy Bentham.

(*c*) Nathan Roscoe Pound (October 27, 1870 – June 30, 1964) was a distinguished American legal scholar and educator. He was Dean of Harvard Law School from 1916 to 1936. *The Journal of Legal Studies* has identified Pound as one of the most cited legal scholars of the 20th century. Roscoe Pound also made a significant contribution to jurisprudence in the tradition of sociological jurisprudence, which emphasised on the importance of social relationships in the development of law and vice versa. His best-known theory consists of conceptualising law as social engineering. According to Pound, a lawmaker acts as a social engineer by attempting to solve problems in society using law as a tool.

(*d*) Hugo Grotius (10 April 1583 – 28 August 1645), also known as Huig de Groot or Hugo de Groot, was a Dutch jurist. Along with the earlier works of Francisco de Vitoria and Alberico Gentili, Grotius laid the foundations for international law, based on natural law. A teenage intellectual prodigy, for his involvement in the intra-Calvinist disputes of the Dutch Republic, he was imprisoned and then escaped hidden appropriately in a chest of books. He wrote most of his major works in exile in France. Hugo Grotius is one of the most prominent of 17th- and 18th-century theorists of social contract and natural rights. He solved the problem of political authority in a different way.

14. The quoted statement about International law is made by James Leslie Brierly, CBE (9 September 1881 – 20 December 1955), a British lawyer and professor in the field of international law. During his time as Chichele professor, he wrote *The Law of Nations* which is his most famous work. In 1948, he was one of the founding members in the International Law Commission selected and worked 1949-1950 as its reporter on issues of international treaty law. In 1951, he took over for a year the Commission Presidency. Besides, he made many accomplishments in the faculty of law.

15. The decisions and determination of the organs of International institutions such as the General Assembly, Security Council, the International Court of Justice etc. of the United Nations Organization and other such major international organs can become a source of International Law. The organs frame rules and regulations that are binding on all member countries and hence will have international acceptance.

16. Both (a) and (d) are correct.

(*a*) Custom is the oldest and the original source of International as well as of law in general. Though Customary law is not a written source, it's a rule of customary law, *e.g.*, requiring States to grant immunity to a visiting Head of State.

(*d*) *The Republic of Nicaragua v. The United States of America* (1986) ICJ 1 is a public international law case decided by the International Court of Justice (ICJ). The ICJ ruled in favor of Nicaragua and against the United States and awarded reparations to Nicaragua. The ICJ held that the U.S. had violated international law by supporting the Contras in their rebellion against the Nicaraguan government and by mining Nicaragua's harbours.

The Court had 16 final decisions upon which it voted. In Statement 9, the Court stated that while the U.S. encouraged human rights violations by the Contras by the manual entitled *Psychological Operations in Guerrilla Warfare*, this did not, however, make such acts attributable to the U.S.

17. (b) It will be incorrect to say that according to Dualism Theory, law is a unified branch of knowledge, as the terms monism and dualism are used to describe two different theories of the relationship between international law and national law. Many states, perhaps most, are partly monist and partly dualist in their actual application of international law in their national systems.

(d) The three philosophers namely – Wright, Kelson and Duguit were not the exponents of Dualism Theory. Hence, associating their names to Dualism Theory, as its prominent exponents, is incorrect.

20. Uterine siblings are those who take birth or get delivered from the same uterus, meaning from the same mother or one mother. For example, X is the son of his mother W and father V. Soon V dies or divorces W. In between, W marries another man named, M. Then W gets pregnant by M and she gives birth to Y. Thus, X and Y have different fathers namely V and M, but both have one/same mother that is W. So in such case X and Y are uterine brothers. In this way, if it is claimed that two persons are said to be related to each other by uterine blood when they are descended from a common ancestress but by different husbands.

21. (*a*) Section 9 of Hindu Marriage Act, 1955 grants Restitution of Conjugal Rights. If your spouse has left you without giving any reasonable ground, the Hindu Marriage Act 1955 gives you remedy in the form of Section 9 under the restitution of conjugal rights. The section 9 of the HMA reads that when either the husband or the wife has, without reasonable excuse, withdrawn from the society of the other, the aggrieved party may apply for restitution of conjugal rights. What the aggrieved party needs to do is file a petition to the district court and on being satisfied of the truth of the statements made in such petition and that there is no legal ground why the application should not be granted, the judge may decree restitution of conjugal rights in his favour.

(*b*) Among the 5 conditions necessary for solemnisation of marriage as per Section 5 (iii) of Hindu Marriage Act, 1955, is Marriageable Age. The bridegroom must have completed the age of twenty-one years and the bride must have completed the age of eighteen years at the time of their marriage.

(*c*) Section 29 (2) in The Hindu Marriage Act, 1955 is about Customary Divorce. Nothing contained in this Act shall be deemed to affect any right recognised by custom or conferred by any special enactment to obtain the dissolution of a Hindu marriage, whether solemnised before or after the commencement of this Act.

(*d*) Section 7 of the Hindu Marriage Act 1955 recognises the ceremonies and customs of marriage. Hindu marriage may be solemnised in accordance with the customary rites and ceremonies of either party. Such rites and rituals include the Saptapadi—the taking of seven steps by the bridegroom and the bride jointly before the sacred fire. The marriage becomes complete and binding when the seventh step is taken.

22. A child will be regarded as a Hindu in the following cases (given as per codes of the question paper and answer sheet):

(*a*) If only one parent is a Hindu and the child was brought up as a Hindu. It means even if one parent – either father or mother follows the religion other than Hinduism but the child follows Hindu religion or has been brought under the influence of Hindu rituals, he/she will be recognised as a Hindu by law.

(*c*) If after the birth of child, father converts to non-Hindu religion. It may be exemplified well as thus: Suppose X was born to a Hindu father and Hindu mother. But later on, father becomes a Muslim, Christian or Buddhist etc. In such case the child X continues to be a Hindu.

(*d*) Both the parents are Hindu. It's so simple and natural that if both father and mother of a child are Hindu, then naturally the child will be a Hindu until the child attains the age of adulthood and then converts to other religion.

23. Section 10 of Hindu Marriage Act deals with the judicial separation for married Hindu couples. Law allows an opportunity to both the husband and the wife to think about the continuance of their relationship while at the same time directing them to live separate, thus allowing them the much needed space and independence to choose their path.

In this question, the answer from the options (given codes) (b), (c) and (d) makes the matter more clear and comprehensive.

24. **Assertion (A):** The Muslim Personal Law (Shariat) Application Act, 1937 makes Muslim Law applicable expressly to all Muslims, is true because a couple can only become husband and wife if both of them get their marriage solemnised by the ritual of Nikah as elaborated in their Shariah law.

Reason (R) is true and correct explanation of (A), as their Shariat law Application Act, 1937, has abrogated the unnecessary customs practised during marriage ceremony, and rather restored to them their own personal law in almost all cases.

25. In Islam, *iddah* or *iddat* (*period of waiting*) is the period a woman must observe after the death of her spouse or after a divorce, during which she may not marry another man. Its purpose is to ensure that the male parent of any offspring produced after the cessation of a *nikah* (solemnisation of marriage) would be known. The length of *iddah* varies according to a number of circumstances.

The *iddah* of a woman divorced by her husband is three monthly periods, unless she is pregnant in which case the '*iddah* lasts until she gives birth, or unless the marriage was not consummated in which case there is no *iddah*, or unless she does not menstruate, in which case "the scholars say that she should observe an '*iddah* of a full year, nine months for pregnancy and three months for *iddah*."

For a woman whose husband has died, the *iddah* is four lunar months and ten days after the death of their husbands, whether or not the marriage was consummated. The period, four months and ten days after the death of a spouse, is calculated on the number of menses that a woman has.

Islamic scholars consider this directive to be a balance between mourning of husband's death and protecting the widow from criticism that she might be subjected to from remarrying too quickly after her husband's death. This is also to ascertain whether a woman is pregnant or not, since four and a half months is half the length of a normal pregnancy.

Husbands should make a will in favour of their wives for the provision of one year's residence and maintenance, unless the wives themselves leave the house or take any other similar step.

However, as given in the question, the answer option on the answer sheet will be (3) that makes clear as to where the observance of *Iddat* is mandatory.

26. Modern sources of Hindu law are based on the following:

(i) Justice, Equity and Good Conscience

The courts cannot refuse to settle the dispute in the absence of law and they are under an obligation to decide such a case also. For determining such cases, the courts rely upon the basic values, norms and standards of fair play and propriety. In terminology, this is known as principles of justice, equity and good conscience. They may also be termed as Natural law. This principle in our country has enjoyed the status of a source of law since the 18th century when the British administration made it clear that in the absence of a rule, the above principle shall be applied.

(ii) Legislation

Legislations are Acts of Parliament, which have been playing a paramount role in the formation of Hindu law. After India's independence, some important aspects of Hindu Law have been codified.

After codification, any point dealt with by the codified law is final. If matters not specifically covered by the codified law, the old textual law contains to have applications.

(iii) Precedents

After the establishment of British rule in India, the hierarchy of courts was established. The doctrine of precedent based on the principle of treating like cases alike was established. Today, the decisions of Privy Council are binding on all the lower courts in India except where they have been modified or altered by the Supreme Court whose decisions are binding on all the courts except for itself.

28. Section 73 of Indian Contract Act, 1872 deals with Compensation for loss or damage caused by breach of contract. As define in the Section, it is also to be born in mind that in estimating the loss or damage arising from a breach of contract, the means, which existed of remedying the inconvenience caused by non-performance of the contract must be taken into account.

Thus, both **Assertion (A)** and **Reason (R)** are right and **(R)** is the correct reason for **(A)**.

29. Doctrine of frustration was laid down for the first time in ***Taylor v. Caldwell*** case in the UK in 1863, a brief detail of which is given below:

Facts: Caldwell (D) contracted to permit Taylor (P) the use of the Musical Hall at Newington. Caldwell was to retain possession of the hall and Taylor merely had the use of it for four days to present four concerts in exchange for 100 pounds per day. The contract stated that the Hall must be fit for a concert but there was no express stipulation regarding disasters.

The Hall was destroyed by fire before the first concert was to be held and neither party was at fault. The concerts could not be performed at any other location and Taylor sued for breach and sought reimbursement for costs in preparing for the concerts.

Issue: May contract performance be excused for impossibility of performance if performance depends on the continued existence of a person or thing, and that person or thing ceases to exist?

Holding and Rule (Blackburn): Yes. If contract performance depends on the continued existence of a person or thing, and that person or thing ceases to exist, performance may be excused for impossibility of performance.

If the nature of the contract is such that the parties must have known at the time of contracting that it could not be fulfilled unless some specified thing continued to exist, it is not a positive contract, and there is an implied condition that the parties will be excused from performance if that thing ceases to exist without fault of the parties. However, if a party gives an express or implied warranty that that thing will continue to exist, that party is liable for breach if it ceases to exist.

When there is a positive contract to do a thing the contractor must perform it or pay damages, although in consequence of unforeseen accidents, the performance of his contract has become unexpectedly burdensome or even impossible. But this rule is only applicable when the contract is positive and absolute and not subject to any condition either express or implied.

Regarding contracts for the services of a specific person, the executors are not liable if that person dies, even though the contract by its terms will have been broken.

Disposition: Judgment for D.

Notes: This is an example of objective impossibility; it is impossible for either party to perform. If the parties in such an arrangement do not allocate the risk at the time of contract, the court will let the loss lie where it falls. In this example, Taylor suffered the loss of resources invested in preparing for the concerts, and Caldwell suffered the loss of the destroyed hall. This rule only applies if neither party is at fault in the destruction of the person or thing.

30. In contract law, a mistake is an erroneous belief, *at contracting*, that certain facts are true. It can be argued as a defence, and if raised successfully can lead to the agreement in question being found void *ab initio* or voidable, or alternatively an equitable remedy may be provided by the courts.

Mistake of Fact: Where both the parties enter into an agreement are under a mistake as to a matter of fact essential to the agreement, the agreement is void.

31. An agreement without consideration is valid, unless it is made by two minors. As per law, a person who is yet to complete his or her 18 years of age signifies as minor. Law acts as the guardian of minors and protects their rights, because their mental faculties are not mature; they do not possess the capacity of judgement what is good and what is bad for them. Accordingly, where is a minor charged with obligations and the other contracting party seeks to enforce those obligations against the minor, the agreement is deemed as void. A person who does not possess a sound mind or whose mental powers are not arranged or whose mental condition is not under his or her own control. Any agreement by person of unsound mind is absolutely void because he has no capacity to judge, what is good and what is bad for him.

32. As per Section 6 of the Indian Contract Act, 1872, a proposal will be revoked by the death or insanity of the proposer, if the fact of his death or insanity comes to the knowledge of the acceptor before acceptance.

33. A tort is a civil breach committed against another in which the injured party can sue for damages. In personal injury cases, the injured party will attempt to receive compensation with the representation of a personal injury lawyer in order to recover from damages incurred. Tort law decides whether a person should be held legally responsible for injury against another, and what type of compensation the injured party is entitled to. There are four elements to tort law: duty, breach of duty, causation, and injury. In order to claim damages, there must be a breach in the duty of the defendant towards the plaintiff, which results in an injury. The three main types of torts are negligence, strict liability (product liability), and intentional torts.

However, in order to bring an action for tort, the plaintiff has to prove that there has been a legal damage caused to him/her. The necessity for a negligence case to be tried in a court of law is essential and evident. Tort law, like any other law, is tough to decide upon when an enforcement or violation issue arises, and is furthermore tedious. In negligence cases, a court appoints a jury to make a decision upon a case based on the direct or circumstantial evidence that is available to them. The burden of proof a plaintiff faces in a case, relates to four elements of proof that must exist in order for them to be able to prove that a negligent act not only existed, but the fact that the act by a defendant, led to the injury sustained by the plaintiff.

35. (*a*) The term "Act of State" has various distinct meanings this article is, however, concerned with it solely in the narrow sense of an act done on behalf of the Crown in respect of which no action will lie, although, if done by anyone else, it would have been tortious. The present law has as its basis a well-known trilogy of cases, Buron *v*. Denman, 2 Walker *v*. Baird and Johnstone *v*. Pedlar, 'the effect of which may be stated as follows: an act done against a person not within Her Majesty's allegiance or against such person's property either with the prior authorisation of the Crown or its subsequent ratification is an act of state, which fact, if pleaded, will oust the jurisdiction of any of Her Majesty's courts.

(*b*) It's a case of consent in 1933. This case was not about the procurement of buses – of which there are well-known cases in EU procurement law. Rather, it is about the abstract nature of the many guises of the bonus pater familias, the 'fair and reasonable man, an intellectual (legal) tradition of defining a legal standard by reference to a hypothetical person, stretching back to Roman law. In English law, Greer LJ launched the concept in *Hall v. Brooklands Auto-Racing Club*, to determine the standard of care required to avoid being found negligent.

(*c*) *Nichols v. Marsland* (1876) 2 ExD 1: The defendant diverted a natural stream on his land to create ornamental lakes. Exceptionally heavy rain caused the artificial lakes and waterways to be flooded and damage adjoining land. The defendant was held not liable under Rylands *v.* Fletcher as the cause of the flood was an act of God.

Mellish LJ: "Now the jury have distinctly found, not only that there was no negligence in the construction or the maintenance of the reservoirs, but that the flood was so great that it could not reasonably have been anticipated, although, if it were anticipated, the effect might have been prevented; and this seems to us in substance a finding that the escape of the water was owing to the act of God. However, great the flood had been, if it had not been greater than floods that had happened before and might be expected to occur again, the defendant might not have made out that she was free from fault; but we think she ought not be held liable because she did not prevent the effect of an extraordinary act of nature, which she could not anticipate."

(*d*) It's the case of *Metropolitan District Asylum Board vs. Hills* in 1881 that pertained to Statutory authority. A hospital authority (appellants) was empowered by statute to build a hospital for contagious diseases. Thus, the hospital was built in a residential district, causing danger of infection to people living in the vicinity. The Court said that the building of the hospital was nuisance. Though the statute gave the hospital authority to build such hospitals, it did not sanction the erection in places where this would constitute danger. So injunction was granted the statutory authority was conditional.

36. The primary issue presented here is whether an owner may protect personal property in an unoccupied boarded-up farmhouse against trespassers and thieves by a spring gun capable of inflicting death or serious injury. The concern not about a man's right to protect his home and members of his family. Defendants' home is several miles from the scene of the incident to which it is referred infra.

37. Torts is a broad area of law in the USA in which the plaintiff sues a defendant for a personal injury or damage to property by negligence or wrongful conduct of the defendant.

There are four essential elements in most of the torts and those are: (1) Duty, (2) Breach of Duty, (3) Causation, and (4) Damages. Thus, as mentioned in **Assertion (A)** that mental element is an essential element in most of the torts, is wrong. The statement is given in **Reason (R)** is also wrong.

38. *Volenti non fit injuria* (or *injuria*) (Latin: "to a willing person, injury is not done") is a common law doctrine which states that if someone willingly places themselves in a position where harm might result, knowing that some degree of harm might result, they are not able to bring a claim against the other party in tort or delict. *Volenti* only applies to the risk, which a reasonable person would consider them as having assumed by their actions. In other words, *Volenti non fit* *injuria* is a defence in tort that means where a person engages in an event accepting and aware of the risks inherent in that event, then they cannot later complain of, or seek compensation for an injury suffered during the event. This is used often to defend against tort actions as a result of a sports injury. Thus, if injury is caused to a player in a football match, it would be exemplified as a case of *Volenti non fit injuria* because the player cannot sue a case against the other player from whom the injury is inadvertently caused to him, as the player took risk; he was well-aware that if he played football, he may sustain injury while playing.

39. When two or more parties are *jointly and severally liable* for a tortuous act, each party is independently liable for the full extent of the injuries stemming from the tortuous act. Thus, if a plaintiff wins a money judgment against the parties collectively, the plaintiff may collect the full value of the judgment from any one of them. That party may then seek contribution from the other wrongdoers.

Legally, 'actuated' means to put any act (an offence) into action.

40. Imposing punishment implies that some one should be legally authorised to impose it upon the offender. A private person can impose such punishment where there is justification for punishing any person provided the offender had broken a law. There are certain limits and situations within which a private person can proceed to punish someone for committing an offence. For example, parents can punish their children morally for any wrong done by them but they cannot do so upon their neighbours' children.

42. Section 201 in IPC has the following details: Causing disappearance of evidence of offence, or giving false information to screen offender.—Whoever, knowing or having reason to believe that an offence has been committed, causes any evidence of the commission of that offence to disappear, with the intention of screening the offender from legal punishment, or with that intention gives any information respecting the offence which he knows or believes to be false; if a capital offence—shall, if the offence which he knows or believes to have been committed is punishable with death, be punished with imprisonment of either description for a term which may extend to seven years, and shall also be liable to fine; if punishable with imprisonment for life — and if the offence is punishable with [imprisonment for life], or with imprisonment which may extend to ten years, shall be punished with imprisonment of either description for a term which may extend to three years, and shall also be liable to fine; if punishable with less than ten years' imprisonment—and if the offence is punishable with imprisonment for any term not extending to ten years, shall be punished with imprisonment of the description provided for the offence, for a term which may extend to one-fourth part of the longest term of the imprisonment provided for the offence, or with fine, or with both. Illustration A, knowing that B has murdered Z, assists B to hide the body with the intention of screening B from punishment. A is liable to imprisonment of either description for seven years, and also to fine.

43. Flinging boiling water over a person is an offence that falls under causing hurt as well as assault *i.e.*, physical injury. Take the example of such case in Baltimore, USA. A Baltimore man convicted of throwing boiling water on his roommate after a dispute over breakfast sausages, has been sentenced to 25 years in prison.

44. In this question, it has been tried to explain that though something is taken or snatched from someone else expressing that it would be returned to him after using it. For example, if someone takes a stick from the person to beat him, it will not amount to theft.

45. The Industrial Disputes Act 1947 extends to the whole of India and regulates Indian labour law so far as that concerns trade unions. It came into force on April 1, 1947. The objective of the Industrial Disputes Act is to secure industrial peace and harmony by providing machinery and procedure for the investigation and settlement of industrial disputes by negotiations. The laws apply only to the organised sector.

46. Under Section 10 in The Industrial Disputes Act, 1947, a reference to an Industrial tribunal will be only where both the parties to an Industrial Dispute apply for such reference and also where the appropriate government considers it expedient to do so. Thus, here the dispute is to be resolved subject to the condition if both the parties apply for such reference.

47. The Act for the settlement of an industrial dispute, either by reference to a Board of Conciliation or to a Court of Inquiry, conclusive and binding on the parties to the dispute, this defect was overcome during the war by empowering under Rule 81-A of th Defence of India Rules the Centra Government to refer industrial disputes t adjudicator and to enforce their awards. Rul 81-A, which was to lapse on the 1st October 1946, is being kept in force by the Emergenc Powers (Continuance) Ordinance, 1946, for further period of six months; and as industria unrest in checking which this rule has prove useful, is gaining momentum due to the stres of post industrial re-adjustment, the need o permanent legislation in replacement of thi rule is self-evident.

50. Having Equivalent citations: 1962 AIR 171 1962 SCR (3) 269, All India Bank Employee Association *vs.* National Industrial Tribuna & Others was a case in Supreme Court o India, in which the Petitioner was All Indi Bank Employees' Association who pu petition on 28 August 1961 while th Respondent was National Industrial Tribuna & Others. It was the case in which the criteri laid down in clause (4) of Article 19 wer observed by the Supreme Court.

PAPER-III

Note: *This paper contains* ***seventy five*** *(75) objective type questions of* ***two*** *(2) marks each.* ***All*** *questions are* ***compulsory***.

1. Match **List-I** and **List-II** and find **correct** answer by using codes given below:

List-I	List-II
(*a*) To renounce practices derogatory to the dignity of women	(*i*) Surya Narain Choudhary *vs.* Union of India
(*b*) Mandamus cannot be sought against an individual who does not observe a fundamental duty	(*ii*) Union of India *vs.* Naveen Jindal
(*c*) Respect to National Anthem	(*iii*) Bijoe Emmanuel *vs.* State of Kerala
(*d*) Respect and dignity to National Flag	(*iv*) Union of India *vs.* Naveen Jindal

Codes:

	(*a*)	(*b*)	(*c*)	(*d*)
A.	(*i*)	(*ii*)	(*iii*)	(*iv*)
B.	(*ii*)	(*i*)	(*iii*)	(*iv*)
C.	(*ii*)	(*i*)	(*iv*)	(*iii*)
D.	(*iii*)	(*iv*)	(*i*)	(*ii*)

2. Match **List-I** with **List-II** according to th provisions of the Constitution of India. Giv **correct** answer by using the codes give below:

List-I (Provisions)	List-II (Articles)
(*a*) Power of Parliament to legislate with respect to a matter in the state list in the national interest	(*i*) Article 253
(*b*) Legislation for giving effect to international agreements	(*ii*) Article 247

(*c*) Power of Parliament to provide for the establishment of certain additional courts — (*iii*) Article 252

(*d*) Power of Parliament to legislate for two or more states by consent — (*iv*) Article 249

Codes:

	(*a*)	(*b*)	(*c*)	(*d*)
A.	(*iv*)	(*i*)	(*ii*)	(*iii*)
B.	(*i*)	(*ii*)	(*iii*)	(*iv*)
C.	(*iv*)	(*iii*)	(*i*)	(*ii*)
D.	(*i*)	(*ii*)	(*iv*)	(*iii*)

3. Read **Assertion (A)** and **Reason (R)** and answer using the codes given below:

Assertion (A): The rule making power of the Supreme Court of India is not subject to any law made by the Parliament.

Reason (R): Only an impartial and independent judiciary can protect the rights of Individual without fear or favour.

Codes:

A. Both (A) and (R) are correct and (R) is correct explanation of (A)
B. Both (A) and (R) are correct, but (R) is not the correct explanation of (A)
C. (A) is false, but (R) is true
D. (A) is true, but (R) is false

4. Who among the following shall be disqualified as a member of either House of Parliament?

Give answer by selecting codes given below:

(*a*) Who is not a citizen of India.
(*b*) Who has acquired the citizenship of a foreign state.
(*c*) Who is under any acknowledgement to a foreign state.
(*d*) Who is under acknowledgement of adherence to a foreign state.

Codes:

A. Only (*a*) B. Only (*a*) and (*b*)
C. (*a*), (*b*) and (*c*) D. (*a*), (*b*), (*c*) and (*d*)

5. Under Article 324 of the Constitution the Election Commission of India shall be responsible to conduct elections to:

Give answers by using the codes given below:

(*a*) Parliament and State Legislature
(*b*) President and Vice-President
(*c*) Zilla Parishad and Panchayats
(*d*) Municipal Corporations and Municipal Committees

Codes:

A. (*a*), (*b*), (*c*) and (*d*)
B. (*a*) and (*b*) only
C. (*a*), (*b*) and (*c*)
D. (*a*), (*c*) and (*d*)

6. Who among the following can establish additional court for better administration of any existing law with respect to a matter concerned in union list?

A. Chief Justice of India
B. Parliament
C. The Concerned State Legislature
D. High Court of the State Concerned

7. Which one of the following statements is **correct**?

Article 368 of the Constitution of India lays down:

A. Procedure for amendment of the Constitution only
B. Power of Parliament to amend the Constitution only
C. Power of Parliament to amend the Constitution and procedure therefore
D. Limitation on the power of the Parliament to amend the Constitution

8. In which one of the following cases the Supreme Court held that, 'No election can be challenged on the ground of defect in electoral rolls'?

A. Inderjit Barua *vs.* Election Commission of India
B. N.P. Ponnuswami *vs.* Returning Officer
C. Kalyan Lal Omar *vs.* R.K. Trivedi
D. Mohinder Singh Gill *vs.* Chief Election Commissioner

9. Who defined administrative law as; "Law relating to the Administration. It determines the organisation, powers and duties of administrative authorities"?

A. Sir Ivor Jennings
B. A.V. Dicey
C. Kenneth Culp Davis
D. Griffith and Strut

10. What was specifically declared by the Supreme Court in the Delhi Laws Act case?

Answer using codes given below:

(*a*) Legislature should not delegate its essential function.

(*b*) Excessive delegation of powers can be struck down by courts.

(*c*) Extension of laws with certain modification and by changing the underlying policy of legislation is allowed.

(*d*) Legislature should itself lay down standard in the delegating Act learning the delegate with the power to make rules to execute the policy laid down in the Legislation

Codes:

A. (*c*), (*a*), (*d*) B. (*b*), (*d*), (*a*)
C. (*d*), (*c*), (*b*) D. (*a*), (*b*), (*d*)

11. Which of the following is **not** true regarding the application of 'doctrine of promissory estoppel'?

A. The court may refuse to apply promissory estoppel against the government if the 'public interest' suffers in fulfilling the promise.
B. The government cannot be compelled to carry out a promise which falls outside its power and contrary to law.
C. The promise in question may be tentative or uncertain and it need not to be unambiguous and unequivocal.
D. There can be no promissory estoppel against the Legislature in the exercise of its legislative functions.

12. Match **List-I** with **List-II** in the light of cases decided by the Supreme Court:

List-I (Case Law)	**List-II (Principles)**
(*a*) Canara Bank *vs.* V.K. Awasthy (2005)	(*i*) Duty to act fairl - in administrativ functions as we
(*b*) Gullapalli Nageswara Rao *vs.* A.P. State Road Transport Corporation, 1959	(*ii*) Post decisional hearing
(*c*) Swadeshi Cotton Mills *vs.* Union of India (1981)	(*iii*) Exclusion of ru of hearing
(*d*) A.K. Kraipak *vs.* Union of India (1970)	(*iv*) One who decide must hear

Codes:

	(*a*)	(*b*)	(*c*)	(*d*)
A.	(*i*)	(*ii*)	(*iii*)	(*iv*)
B.	(*iv*)	(*iii*)	(*i*)	(*ii*)
C.	(*ii*)	(*iv*)	(*iii*)	(*i*)
D.	(*iii*)	(*iv*)	(*ii*)	(*i*)

13. Read **Assertion (A)** and **Reason (R)** an answer using codes given below:

Assertion (A): A High Court may decline t exercise its extra-ordinary jurisdiction unde Article 226 and dismiss the writ summarily c *in limine.*

Reason (R): It would be proper for the Hig Court to dispose of the petition summarily c *in limine,* when no important question of la are raised in a writ petition.

Codes:

A. Both (A) and (R) are right and (R) is corre reason of (A)
B. Both (A) and (R) are right, but (R) is n correct reason of (A)
C. (A) is right, but (R) is wrong
D. (A) is wrong, but (R) is right

14. When a writ is issued to a public authority i respect of any type of administrativ legislative, Quasi-judicial or judicial function it is called a writ of:

A. Mandamus B. Quo-warranto
C. Certiorari D. Prohibition

15. Read **Assertion (A)** and **Reason (R)** and answer using codes given below:

Assertion (A): In judicial review of administrative actions, generally the court would not interfere with the merits of the case by embarking upon inquiry into the facts.

Reason (R): Courts can review the procedure through which a decision has been taken by the administrative authority but courts cannot supplement its own decision and act as appellate court over the administrative authority.

Codes:

A. Both (A) and (R) are correct and (R) is the correct explanation of (A)
B. Both (A) and (R) are correct, but (R) is not correct explanation of (A)
C. (A) is right, but (R) is wrong
D. (A) is wrong, but (R) is right

16. "The polemical version of legal realism has wielded enormous influence on the entire judicial system". Who propounded such philosophy?

A. Gray B. Holmes
C. Salmond D. Waismann

17. The *liberum arbitrium* of the courts depends upon what is right, justice, equitable or reasonable and is dependent upon:

A. Evidence and demonstration of public
B. Arguments submitted with reason
C. Discovering the right or justice of the matter
D. Pure intellectual process

18. *Obiter dicta* has no binding authority but it helps to:

A. Rationalise legal sanctions
B. Encourages providing solution to future litigations
C. It allows greater prestige to the judge
D. It makes the acceptability of precedents more flexible

19. The statement "equitable ownership of a legal right is different from the ownership of an equitable right" shows that law and equity differ with regard to:

A. Only the existence of right
B. Only the ownership of rights
C. Both existence and ownership of rights
D. The existence of a right but not regarding the consistency of a right

20. Read **Assertion (A)** and **Reason (R)** and give **correct** answer using codes given below:

Assertion (A): The relation of morality to a concept of law cannot be stated simply in the form of a stark alternative that the former is either externally or internally related to the later.

Reason (R): It is depending upon time-frame of reference.

Codes:

A. Both (A) and (R) are wrong
B. Both (A) and (R) are right and (R) is correct reason of (A)
C. (A) is wrong, but (R) is right
D. (A) is right, but (R) is wrong

21. The House of Lords upheld the Attorney General's political discretion in refusing to invoke the law in face of a threatened criminal offence in deliberate defiance of an Act of Parliament, in the case of:

A. Gouriet *vs.* Union of Post Office Workers
B. Francome *vs.* Mirror Group Newspaper Ltd.
C. R. *vs.* Bourne
D. Johnson *vs.* Phillips

22. Modern doctrine of bindingness of precedents was first laid down in:

A. London Transways Co. *vs.* LCC
B. Young *vs.* Bristol Aeroplane Co. Ltd.
C. Mirehouse *vs.* Rennel
D. Sirros *vs.* Moore

23. Read **Assertion (A)** and **Reason (R)** and answer using the codes given below:

Assertion (A): Shareholders are not, in the eye of law, part owners of a company. The company is something different from the totality of the shareholders.

Reason (R): Shareholders are collective owners of the company.

Codes:

A. Both (R) and (A) are right and (R) is correct reason of (A)

B. Both (A) and (R) are wrong

C. (A) is right, but (R) is wrong

D. (R) is right, but (A) is wrong

24. An idea of inducement by exciting hope or desire on the other is known as ....

A. Seduction B. Enticing

C. Inciting D. Abduction

25. A takes his own suit from the tailor without his knowledge but had the intention of returning it to the tailor later. What offence, if any has been committed by A?

A. Stealing B. Dishonest taking

C. Theft D. Unlawful retention

26. Read **Assertion (A)** and **Reason (R)** and answer using codes given below:

Assertion (A): That the act is imminently dangerous or that in all probability it will cause death.

Reason (R): Such specific principle apply to punish a person although there is no intention to cause death.

Codes:

A. Both (A) and (R) are concurrent as per Sec. 299(c) and 300(4) respectively

B. Both (A) and (R) are intravivos as per Sec. 300 and Sec. 302

C. Both (A) and (R) are dependant upon facts based as per Sec. 299(b) and Sec. 302

D. Both (A) and (R) must co-exist as per Sec. 300(2) and Sec. 301

27. The aggravated form of perjury is known from:

A. False statement on oath

B. False evidence in a judicial proceeding

C. Administering oath to speak truth

D. False affidavit before honorary Magistrate

28. Which of the following is **not** a crime in order to provide protection to currency?

A. A war medal

B. Gold Mohur

C. Current Coin

D. Genuine specimen of antique coin

29. Which of the following cases does **not** amount to robbery?

A. Taking away ornaments from the body of a lady while she was in coma.

B. Removal of ornaments after death of a lady.

C. Voluntary disposition of valuables.

D. While theft is committed along with assault.

30. Criminal liability for abandonment of a child is based on the principle of *loco-parentis*. Who else could be responsible for that offence?

A. Adoptive father before the completion of formalities of adoption

B. When a mother leaves the house for her husband's ill-treatment and abandons the children to the care of husband

C. When the school master who has been teaching infants placed under him for education

D. A mother leaves a blind child on a foot path promising to return after fetching food but never returned

31. Which of the following **do not** constitute an offence of forgery?

A. The intention to induce a belief that the document was duly signed.

B. The intention to induce a belief that the document was duly sealed.

C. The intention to induce a belief that the document was executed by the authority of a person.

D. Knowingly makes false entries initially in the public record on his own authority by a public officer.

32. "Where directive principles have found statutory expression in do's and dont's the court will not sit idle and allow government to become a statutory mockery for protection of environment. The law will relentlessly be enforced and the plea of poor finance will be poor alibi when people in misery cry for justice." The above was observed in Municipal Council of Ratlam *vs.* Vardhichand by:

A. Justice Chinnappa Reddy
B. Justice V.R. Krishna Iyyer
C. Justice P.N. Bhagavati
D. Justice Ranganath Misra

33. Protection and Improvement of Environment and safeguarding forest and wildlife is:
A. A Fundamental Right
B. One of the Directive Principles of State Policy
C. One of the Fundamental Duties
D. Both Directive Principles of State Policy and Fundamental Duty

34. In which of the following cases, the Supreme Court directed closing down and demolition of shrimp Industries in coastal regulation zone and implement the "Precautionary principle" and "the pollůter pays principle" and held them liable for payment of compensation for reversing the ecology and compensate the individual for loss suffered?
A. M.C. Mehta *vs.* Union of India
B. S. Jaganath *vs.* Union of India
C. Church of God (Full Gospels) in India *vs.* K.K.R. Majestic Colony Welfare Association
D. Vellore Citizen's Welfare Forum *vs.* Union of India

35. Read **Assertion (A)** and **Reason (R)** and give the answer by using the codes given below:

Assertion (A): The right to clean drinking water and right to pollution free air to breath are attributes of "Right to Life".

Reason (R): Because they are the basic elements which sustain life.

Codes:
A. Both (A) and (R) are true. (R) is good explanation of (A)
B. Both (A) and (R) are true, but (R) is not a good explanation of (A)
C. (A) is true, but (R) is false
D. (A) is false, but (R) is true

36. In which of the following cases the Supreme Court applied the doctrine of public trust that the state as a trustee of all natural resources is under a legal duty to protect the natural resources. These natural resources are meant for public use and cannot be converted into private ownership?
A. M.C. Mehta *vs.* Union of India (Ganga Water Pollution Case)
B. M.C. Mehta *vs.* Kamalnath and others
C. M.C. Mehta *vs.* Union of India (Replacing diesel vehicles by CNG vehicles)
D. Rural Litigation and Entitlement Kendra *vs.* State of U.P.

37. What is the main objective of the Prohibition of Employment as Manual Scavengers and their Rehabilitation Act, 2013? Give answer by using codes below:
(*a*) To prohibit employment of manual scavengers
(*b*) To rehabilitate manual scavengers
(*c*) To rehabilitate manual scavengers and their families
(*d*) To rehabilitate manual scavengers only and not their families

Codes:

A. Only (*a*)	B. Only (*a*) and (*b*)
C. (*a*), (*b*) and (*c*)	D. (*a*), (*b*), (*c*) and (*d*)

38. Which one of the following is the main objective of the Wild Life (Protection) Act, 1972 as amended upto 2003?
A. To check on poaching and illegal trade in domestic and wild animals.
B. To check on poaching and on illegal trade in ivory.
C. To check on poaching and legal trade in dog.
D. To check on hunting and legal trade in elephant.

39. Whose observations are these on the point that whether International law is a mere positive Morality?

"If International Law were only a kind of morality, the framers of State papers concerning foreign policy would throw all their weight on moral arguments. But, as a matter of fact, this is not what they do. They appeal not to the general feeling of moral rightness, but to precedents. to treaties and to opinion of specialists."

A. H.L.A. Hart B. Oppenheim
C. Edward Collins D. Frederick Pollock

40. Which of the following statement/Statements is/are **not correct**?

(*a*) Principle of law which is recognised by domestic law of a large number of states does not automatically become a 'Principle' of International Law.

(*b*) Para (1) (G) of Article 38 of the Statute of International Court of justice lists "General Principles of Law Recognised by Civilized States" as the Second Source of International Law.

(*c*) General Principles of law recognised by civilized states include only substantive principles provided they have received general recognition of Civilized States.

(*d*) The development of general principles of law recognised by civilized states as an important source of law, has given a death-knell to the positivism.

Codes:

A. Only (*b*) is incorrect
B. Both (*b*) and (*c*) are incorrect
C. (*a*), (*b*) and (*c*) are incorrect
D. All (*a*), (*b*), (*c*) and (*d*) are incorrect

41. Which one of the following cases is not a case on the point that there is no distinction between 'De Facto' and 'De - Jure' recognition for the purpose of giving effect to the internal acts of the recognized authority?

A. Bank of Ethopia *vs*. National Bank of Egypt and Liquori
B. Luther *vs*. Sagor
C. Civil Air Transport Incorporated Co. *vs*. Central Air Transport Corporation
D. The Arantzazu Mendi Case

42. In which one of the following cases the International Court of Justice has held that in respect of grant of nationality there is no obligation of the states if a man has no relationship with the state of Naturalisation and the court has applied the 'Principle of effective nationality'?

A. Re Lynch Case
B. Stoeck *vs*. The Public Trustee
C. Nottebohm's Case
D. Paneyezys Soldutisk

43. Which one of the following institution is **not** authorised for requesting for 'Advisory Opinion' of the International Court of Justice?

A. Economic and Social Council
B. The Trusteeship Council
C. The International Atomic Energy Agency
D. Secretariat

44. Read both **Assertion (A)** and **Reason (R)** and give the **correct** answer by using the codes given below:

Assertion (A): International Law is not potent enough to restrain a powerful state which has no respect for public opinion.

Reason (R): Sanctions behind International Law are weak.

Codes:

A. Both (A) and (R) are correct and (R) is the correct explanation of (A)
B. Both (A) and (R) are correct, but (R) is not the correct explanation of (A)
C. (A) is true, but (R) is false
D. (A) is false, but (R) is true

45. Consider the following:

The Recommendation of the Security Council made to the Member under Article 42 of U.N. Charter becomes an obligation for them which none can shirk?

(*a*) If the Security Council decides to take action no time is given for further declarations by the General Assembly.

(*b*) When the Security Council decides for taking enforcement measures, it also determines the part to be played by each member state.

(*c*) All or only some members may be requested to participate but every member is to join in mutual assistance.

(*d*) The legal requirements for military action are still not satisfied even after the council has acted.

Which of the above statement/statements is/are **correct**?

A. (*a*), (*b*), (*d*) are correct
B. (*b*), (*c*) and (*d*) are correct
C. (*a*), (*b*) and (*c*) are correct
D. (*c*), (*d*) and (*a*) are correct

46. Match **List-I** with **List-II** and give the **correct** answer by using the codes given below:

List-I (Provisions)	List-II (Article of UN Charter)
(*a*) Voting procedure of the General Assembly	(*i*) Article 23
(*b*) Composition of Security Council	(*ii*) Article 96
(*c*) Composition of Trusteeship Council	(*iii*) Article 4
(*d*) Provisions regarding Membership in the United Nations	(*iv*) Article 18

Codes:

	(*a*)	(*b*)	(*c*)	(*d*)
A.	(*ii*)	(*iii*)	(*iv*)	(*i*)
B.	(*i*)	(*ii*)	(*iii*)	(*iv*)
C.	(*iii*)	(*i*)	(*ii*)	(*iv*)
D.	(*iv*)	(*ii*)	(*i*)	(*iii*)

47. Which of the following is **not** a ground of Judicial Separation under the Hindu Marriage Act, 1955?

A. Renunciation of the world
B. Seven years absence
C. Conversion to Non-Hindu religion
D. Desertion for one year

48. Grounds of divorce meant exclusively for wife under section 13(2) of the Hindu Marriage Act, 1955 are:

(*a*) Pre-Act bigamy by Husband.
(*b*) Husband is guilty of rape, sodomy and bestiality.
(*c*) Non-payment of maintenance and no cohabitation for one year or upwards.
(*d*) Repudiation of marriage by wife.

Codes:

A. (*a*), (*c*) and (*d*) B. (*c*), (*d*), (*a*) and (*b*)
C. (*b*), (*c*) and (*d*) D. (*a*), (*b*) and (*c*)

49. Under the provisions of the Hindu Adoptions and Maintenance Act, 1956 an adopted child:

(*a*) Can be given in adoption generally
(*b*) Cannot be given in adoption
(*c*) Can be given in adoption with the consent of natural parents
(*d*) Can be given in adoption only with the prior permission of the court

Codes:

A. (*b*) and (*d*) are correct, but (*a*) and (*c*) are incorrect
B. (*d*) is correct but (*a*), (*b*) and (*c*) are incorrect
C. (*b*) is correct but (*a*), (*c*) and (*d*) are incorrect
D. (*a*) and (*b*) are correct but (*c*) and (*d*) are incorrect

50. Match **List-I** with **List-II** in relation to the Hindu Adoptions and Maintenance Act, 1956 and give the **correct** answer by using the codes given below the lists:

List-I	List-II
(*a*) Maintenance of wife	(*i*) Sec. 19
(*b*) Maintenance of widowed daughter-in-law	(*ii*) Sec. 22
(*c*) Maintenance of parents and children	(*iii*) Sec. 18
(*d*) Maintenance of dependants	(*iv*) Sec. 20

Codes:

	(*a*)	(*b*)	(*c*)	(*d*)
A.	(*iii*)	(*i*)	(*iv*)	(*ii*)
B.	(*i*)	(*iii*)	(*ii*)	(*iv*)
C.	(*iv*)	(*ii*)	(*i*)	(*iii*)
D.	(*ii*)	(*i*)	(*iv*)	(*iii*)

51. After the petition is presented under Section 13-B of Hindu Marriage Act, 1955, the parties have to wait for a minimum period of:

A. One year B. Eighteen months
C. Two years D. Six months

52. Talaq 'ahsan' is:

A. Revocable during the tuhr in which it has been pronounced
B. Revocable until the next successive tuhr
C. Revocable during the period of iddat
D. Irrevocable

53. Match **List-I** with **List-II** in the light of the Dissolution of Muslim Marriage Act, 1939 and give the **correct** answer by using the codes given below:

List-I (Provision)	**List-II (Section)**
(*a*) Notice to heirs of the husband when his whereabouts are not known	(*i*) Sec. 4
(*b*) Effect of conversion to another faith	(*ii*) Sec. 3
(*c*) Rights to dower not to be affected	(*iii*) Sec. 2(v)
(*d*) Impotence of the husband as a ground of divorce	(*iv*) Sec. 5

Codes:

	(*a*)	(*b*)	(*c*)	(*d*)
A.	(*i*)	(*iii*)	(*ii*)	(*iv*)
B.	(*ii*)	(*i*)	(*iv*)	(*iii*)
C.	(*iv*)	(*ii*)	(*i*)	(*iii*)
D.	(*iii*)	(*i*)	(*iv*)	(*ii*)

54. Match **List-I** with **List-II** under the Hindu Minority and Guardianship Act 1956 and give the **correct** answer with the help of the codes given below:

List-I (Provision)	**List-II (Section)**
(*a*) Testamentary guardian and their powers	(*i*) Sec. 6
(*b*) Natural guardians of a Hindu Minor	(*ii*) Sec. 9
(*c*) Welfare of minor to be paramount consideration	(*iii*) Sec. 11
(*d*) De facto guardian not to deal with minor's property	(*iv*) Sec. 13

Codes:

	(*a*)	(*b*)	(*c*)	(*d*)
A.	(*ii*)	(*i*)	(*iv*)	(*iii*)
B.	(*i*)	(*iv*)	(*iii*)	(*ii*)
C.	(*iv*)	(*ii*)	(*i*)	(*iii*)
D.	(*iii*)	(*i*)	(*iv*)	(*ii*)

55. Read both statements **(A)** and **(R)** and give the **correct** answer by using the codes given below:

Assertion (A): The member state of United Nations Organisation have committed to promote and the respect for observance of Human Rights.

Reason (R): The Human Rights are Inalienable, Natural, Interdependent and Indivisible. They are means to achieve human dignity.

Codes:

A. Both (A) and (R) are true and (R) is not the correct explanation of (A)

B. Both (A) and (R) are true and (R) is the correct explanation of (A)

C. (A) is false, but (R) is true

D. (A) is true, but (R) is false

56. The International covenant on Economic, Social and Cultural Rights came into force on:

A. January 3, 1976 B. January 13, 1976

C. June 30, 1977 D. June 13, 1977

57. UNICEF was created by the UN General Assembly to help:

A. Children after World War I

B. Children after World War II in Europe

C. Children of third world countries

D. Children of suffering from malnutrition

58. Match **List-I** with **List-II** and select the **correct** answer using the codes given below:

List-I	**List-II**
(*a*) Mr. Jose Ayala Lasso	(*i*) President International Court of Justice
(*b*) Justice Nagendra Singh	(*ii*) Secretary General U.N.O.
(*c*) Kofi Annan	(*iii*) Chairperson Commission on Human Rights
(*d*) Mrs. F.D. Roosevelt	(*iv*) U.N. High Commissioner for Human Rights

Codes:

	(*a*)	(*b*)	(*c*)	(*d*)
A.	(*iv*)	(*i*)	(*ii*)	(*iii*)
B.	(*ii*)	(*iv*)	(*iii*)	(*i*)
C.	(*iii*)	(*ii*)	(*i*)	(*iv*)
D.	(*iii*)	(*ii*)	(*iv*)	(*i*)

59. The Universal Declaration of Human Rights 1948 contains provisions relating to:

A. Operationalization of Human Rights

B. Establishment of Human Rights Institutions

C. Establishment of Human Rights Committee
D. Conceptualization of Human Rights

60. Which of the following statement is **correct**?
A. The U.N. Convention on Elimination of all Forms of Discrimination Against Women (CEDAW) was adapted by the General Assembly in 1979, but India ratified it in June 1993.
B. The U.N. Convention on Elimination of all Forms of Discrimination Against Women (CEDAW) was adapted by the General Assembly in 1979, but India ratified it in December 1997.
C. The U.N. Convention on Elimination of all Forms of Discrimination Against Women (CEDAW) was adapted by the General Assembly in 1981, but India ratified it in June 1993.
D. The U.N. Convention on Elimination of all Forms of Discrimination Against Women (CEDAW) was adapted by the General Assembly in 1981, but India ratified it in December 1997.

61. The correct chronological order of the following Human Rights documents be choosen using the codes given below:
(*a*) International Covenant on Civil and Political Rights.
(*b*) Convention on the Elimination of all Forms of Discrimination Against Women.
(*c*) Universal Declaration of Human Rights.
(*d*) Convention on the Rights of the Child.
Codes:
A. (*c*), (*b*), (*a*), (*d*) B. (*c*), (*a*), (*b*), (*d*)
C. (*d*), (*c*), (*a*), (*b*) D. (*c*), (*d*), (*b*), (*a*)

62. Who defined law of tort as "tortious liability arises from the breach of a duty primarily fixed by the law : this duty is towards persons generally and its breach is redressible by an action for unliquidated damages"?
A. Salmand B. Lord Denning
C. Fraser D. Winfield

63. Which of the following is **not** a form of *damnum sine injuria*? Choose the **correct** answer from the codes below:
(*a*) There is no right of action for damages for contempt of court.
(*b*) Loss inflicted on individual traders by competition.
(*c*) Damage is done by a man acting under necessity to prevent a greater evil.
(*d*) Damage caused by defamatory statements made on any occasion.
Codes:
A. (*a*), (*b*), (*c*) and (*d*)
B. (*a*) and (*b*)
C. (*b*) and (*d*)
D. None of the above

64 Facts: "The defendant was a plaintiff's landlord and was living in the same building on the floor above him. Some rats damaged a rain water box maintained by the defendant for the benefit both of himself and plaintiff and the water running through injured plaintiff's goods below." What action can be taken on the above mentioned facts in view of the exceptions to the theory of 'strict liability'?
A. No action lie because of plaintiff's own fault
B. Action lie because it is not act of God
C. No action lie because of the consent of plaintiff
D. Action lie because it is not an act of stranger

65. Read **Assertion (A)** and **Reason (R)** and give the correct answer with the help of codes given below:

Assertion (A): A master is liable for the torts committed by his servant while not acting in the course of his employment.

Reason (R): Liability of the master for the act of his servant is based on the maxim *respondent superior.*
Codes:
A. Both (A) and (R) are true and the (R) is the correct explanation of (A)
B. Both (A) and (R) are true, but (R) is not the correct explanation of (A)
C. (A) is right, but (R) is wrong
D. (A) is wrong, but (R) is right

66 Match **List-I** with **List-II** and give the **correct** answer by using the codes given below:

List-I (Case Laws)	**List-II (Principles)**
(*a*) Re Polemis and Furness, Withy and Co. Ltd.	(*i*) Vicariom liability of the state
(*b*) Saheli *vs.* Commissioner of Police, Delhi	(*ii*) Remoteness of damages
(*c*) Municipal Corporation of Delhi *vs.* Subhagwanti	(*iii*) Duty of case to plaintiff
(*d*) South Wales Miners Federation *vs.* Glamorgan Coal Company	(*iv*) Malice in fact

Codes:

	(*a*)	(*b*)	(*c*)	(*d*)
A.	(*ii*)	(*i*)	(*iii*)	(*iv*)
B.	(*i*)	(*ii*)	(*iv*)	(*iii*)
C.	(*i*)	(*ii*)	(*iii*)	(*iv*)
D.	(*ii*)	(*iii*)	(*i*)	(*iv*)

67. What is the period of limitation under Section 24 A of the Consumer Protection Act, 1986 (as amended w.e.f 18.6.1993) for filing a complaint from the date of the cause of action?

A. No period of limitation
B. Three years
C. Two years
D. One year

68. Match the **List-I** with **List-II** and give answer by using the codes below: (Re : Tort of Defamation)

List-I (Name of Case Law)	**List-II (Principle)**
(*a*) Tolley *vs.* J.S. Fry and Sons Ltd.	(*i*) Publication of statement
(*b*) Williamson *vs.* Frier	(*ii*) Innuendo
(*c*) Alexander *vs.* North Eastern Railway	(*iii*) Fair comment
(*d*) Merivale *vs.* Carson	(*iv*) Defence of truth

Codes:

	(*a*)	(*b*)	(*c*)	(*d*)
A.	(*ii*)	(*i*)	(*iv*)	(*iii*)
B.	(*i*)	(*ii*)	(*iii*)	(*iv*)
C.	(*iv*)	(*i*)	(*ii*)	(*iii*)
D.	(*iii*)	(*ii*)	(*i*)	(*iv*)

69. Match **List-I** with **List-II** and select the **correct** answer using the codes given below:

List-I	**List-II**
(*a*) Kundan Lal Rallaram *vs.* Custodian	(*i*) Presumption under section 118 of the Negotiable Instrument Act arises only if the execution of the document is proved as true
(*b*) C.T. Joseph *vs.* I.V. Phillip	(*ii*) Burden of proof of failure of consideration for a negotiable instrument
(*c*) A.V. Murthy *vs.* B.S. Nagabasavanna	(*iii*) A negotiable instrument is presumed to be drawn for consideration
(*d*) Beni Madhavnath *vs.* Jugandra Nath Balwan	(*iv*) The statutory presumption envisaged under section 118(a) of the Negotiable Instrument Act is rebuttable.

Codes:

	(*a*)	(*b*)	(*c*)	(*d*)
A.	(*ii*)	(*i*)	(*iii*)	(*iv*)
B.	(*i*)	(*ii*)	(*iii*)	(*iv*)
C.	(*ii*)	(*iv*)	(*i*)	(*iii*)
D.	(*iii*)	(*i*)	(*iv*)	(*ii*)

70. Which of the following statement is **incorrect**?

A. A cheque is a bill of exchange, but every bill of exchange is not a cheque.
B. A cheque is always payable on demand.
C. A cheque is a conditional order from the drawer of a cheque to the drawee bank to make payment of money only.
D. A post dated cheque cannot be considered as a valid cheque till the date of maturity.

71. Which of the following cases is about doctrine of indoor management?

A. Ashbury Railway Carriage and Iron Co. Ltd. *vs.* Riche
B. Rama Corpn. *vs.* Proved tin and General Investment Co.
C. London Country Council *vs.* Attorney-General
D. A. Lakshmana Swamy Mudaliar *vs.* L.I.C.

72. Read **Assertion (A)** and **Reason (R)** and answer using codes given below:

Assertion (A): For the proper exercise of the functions of a director, it is essential that he be disinterested, that is, be free from any conflicting interest.

Reason (R): Conflict is injurious to mental and physical health.

Codes:

A. Both (A) and (R) are correct, and (R) is correct reason of (A).
B. (A) is correct, but (R) is wrong.
C. Both (A) and (R) are incorrect.
D. Both (A) and (R) are correct, but (R) is not correct legal reason of (A).

73. Which are essentials of a partnership? Answer using codes given below:

(*a*) A contract of two or more competent persons
(*b*) Agreement to share profits
(*c*) Mutual agency
(*d*) Lawful business

Codes:

A. Only (*a*), (*b*), (*c*)
B. Only (*a*), (*b*), (*d*)
C. Only (*b*), (*c*), (*d*)
D. (*a*), (*b*), (*c*), (*d*)

74. Match **List-I** with **List-II** and select the **correct** answer using the codes given below:

	List-I		**List-II**
(*a*)	Section 54 of the Sale of Goods Act	(*i*)	Risk where goods are delivered at distant place
(*b*)	Section 40 of the Sale of Goods Act	(*ii*)	Delivery of wrong quantity
(*c*)	Section 37 of the Sale of Goods Act	(*iii*)	Sale by description
(*d*)	Section 15 of the Sale of Goods Act	(*iv*)	Rights of unpaid seller against the goods

Codes:

	(*a*)	(*b*)	(*c*)	(*d*)
A.	(*i*)	(*iv*)	(*ii*)	(*iii*)
B.	(*iv*)	(*i*)	(*ii*)	(*iii*)
C.	(*iv*)	(*i*)	(*iii*)	(*ii*)
D.	(*ii*)	(*iii*)	(*i*)	(*iv*)

75. Which of the following cases is about performance of contract?

A. Maruti Udyog Ltd. *vs.* Susheel Kumar Gabgetra
B. Great Northern Railway Co. *vs.* Harrison
C. Joyce *vs.* Swann
D. Behn *vs.* Burness

ANSWERS

1	2	3	4	5	6	7	8	9	10
B	A	C	D	B	B	D	A	A	D
11	**12**	**13**	**14**	**15**	**16**	**17**	**18**	**19**	**20**
C	C	A	A	A	B	B	A	C	B
21	**22**	**23**	**24**	**25**	**26**	**27**	**28**	**29**	**30**
A	C	C	B	C	A	C	C	B	C
31	**32**	**33**	**34**	**35**	**36**	**37**	**38**	**39**	**40**
D	B	D	B	A	B	C	B	D	B

41	42	43	44	45	46	47	48	49	50
C	C	D	A	C	A	D	B	C	A
51	**52**	**53**	**54**	**55**	**56**	**57**	**58**	**59**	**60**
D	C	B	A	B	A	B	C	A	A
61	**62**	**63**	**64**	**65**	**66**	**67**	**68**	**69**	**70**
B	D	C	C	D	A	C	A	A	C
71	**72**	**73**	**74**	**75**					
B	D	D	B	B					

SOME SELECTED EXPLANATORY ANSWERS

3. The statement in **Assertion (A)** is false; as the fact is that the Supreme Court of India is subject to any law made by the Parliament. It is Parliament where the law is legislated, not Supreme Court. Of course, cases are heard and verdicts are given by the Supreme Court of India in the light of the laws legislated by the Parliament of India.

Reason (R) is true because it is only an impartial and independent judiciary, which can protect the rights of individual without fear or favour.

4. The Constitution makes it absolutely clear that the Parliament has to make one law for a person to be disqualified for being elected and for being a Member of either House of Parliament or Legislative Assembly or Legislative Council of any state. Under Articles 102(1)(e) and 191(1)(e) of the Constitution of India, the Parliament does not have the power to make different laws for a person to be disqualified for being chosen as a member and for a person to be disqualified for continuing as a member of Parliament or the state legislature.

It is clearly mentioned that a person shall be disqualified as Member of Legislative Assembly (MLA) or Member of Legislative Council (MLC) if he holds any office of profit under the Government of India or a state or an office declared by a law of the state. However, many states have passed such laws declaring certain offices, holding of which will not disqualify a person for being an MLA. However, all the four options given here in the question with their codes (a), (b), (c) and (d) – are correct, as the members of either of the House can be disqualified on the grounds given here.

5. Under Article 324 of the Constitution, the Election Commission of India shall be responsible to conduct elections to (a) Parliament and State Legislature, and (b) President and Vice-President only. The first clause of the said Article reads as thus: Superintendence, direction and control of elections to be vested in an Election Commission (1) The superintendence, direction and control of the preparation of the electoral rolls for, and the conduct of, all elections to Parliament and to the Legislature of every State and of elections to the offices of President and Vice President held under this Constitution shall be vested in a Commission (referred to in this Constitution as the Election Commission).

6. Parliament of India has been conferred with some specific powers to use in accordance with the prevailing situations, and those powers are mentioned in different Articles of the Constitution, which are meant for different objectives.

Article 247 of Constitution provides power to Parliament to provide for the establishment of certain additional courts. As mentioned, notwithstanding anything in this Chapter, Parliament may by law provide for the establishment of any additional courts for the better administration of laws made by Parliament or of any existing law with respect to a matter enumerated in the Union List.

7. Article 368 of the Constitution of India lays down Limitation on the power of the Parliament to amend the Constitution, and the pertinent details are as thus:

1. Notwithstanding anything in this Constitution, Parliament may in exercise of its constituent power amend by way of addition, variation or repeal any provision of this Constitution in accordance with the procedure laid down in this article.
2. An amendment of this Constitution may be initiated only by the introduction of a Bill for the purpose in either House of Parliament, and when the Bill is passed in each House by a majority of the total membership of that House and by a majority of not less than two-thirds of the members of that House present and voting, it shall be presented to the President who shall give his assent to the Bill and thereupon the Constitution shall stand amended in accordance with the terms of the Bill: Provided that if such amendment seeks to make any change in –
    1. article 54, article 55, article 73, article 162 or article 241, or
    2. Chapter IV of Part V, Chapter V of Part VI, or Chapter I of Part XI, or
    3. any of the Lists in the Seventh Schedule, or
    4. the representation of States in Parliament, or
    5. the provisions of this article, the amendment shall also require to be ratified by the Legislatures of not less than one-half of the States by resolutions to that effect passed by those Legislatures before the Bill making provision for such amendment is presented to the President for assent.
3. Nothing in article 13 shall apply to any amendment made under this article.
4. {No amendment of this Constitution (including the provisions of Part III) made or purporting to have been made under this article whether before or after the commencement of Section 55 of the Constitution (Forty-second Amendment) Act, 1976 shall be called in question in any court on any ground.} Invalidated by the Sup. Court ruling on *Minerva Mills Ltd. and Others* vs. *Union of India*.
5. {For the removal of doubts, it is hereby declared that there shall be no limitation whatever on the constituent power of Parliament to amend by way of addition, variation or repeal the provisions of this Constitution under this article.} Invalidated by the Sup. Court ruling on *Minerva Mills Ltd. and Others* vs. *Union of India*.

8. Inderjit Barua & Ors *vs.* Election Commission of India is a case of 1984, whose judgment was given on 28 September 1984. The petition of the case was made by Inderjit Barua & Ors. while Election Commission of India was respondent in this case.

The brief details of the case are as thus:

1. Transferred Writ Petitions 365 to 382 of 1984 challenge the validity of the elections to the Assam Legislative Assembly held in February 1983. The principal ground on which the validity of the elections has been challenged is that the electoral rolls were not revised before the elections in contravention of the provisions of Section 21 sub-section (2)(a) of the Representation of People Act, 1950 and the elections were held on the basis of the electoral rolls of 1979. Now it is undoubtedly true that the electoral rolls were not revised before the impugned elections were held but the

Election Commission dispensed with the revision of the electoral rolls by an order dated January 7, 1983 made under the opening part of Section 21 sub-section (2) and this order has not been challenged in any of the writ petitions. Hence, the impugned elections cannot be challenged on the ground that they were held on the basis of the electoral rolls of 1979 without revision of the electoral rolls.

2. In the first place, Article 329(b) of the Constitution bars any challenge to the impugned elections by a writ petition under Article 226 as also on the ground that the electoral rolls on the basis of which the impugned elections were held were invalid.

9. "Law relating to the Administration determines the organisation, powers and duties of administrative authorities" is defined by Sir William Ivor Jennings, KBE, QC (16 May 1903 – 19 December 1965), who was a British lawyer and academic. He was an authority on constitutional law and is author of a definitive book on the workings of the then British constitution.

11. First, there is a need to understand what is promissory estoppel. The doctrine of promissory estoppel is that the party relying on the doctrine must establish that the other party has, by words or conduct, made a promise or assurance, which was intended to affect their legal relationship and to be acted on.

Hence, it will not be true to say that the promise in question may be tentative or uncertain and it need not to be unambiguous and unequivocal.

12. (*a*) It's a Post-decisional hearing case of 2005 between Canara Bank and V.K. Awasthy in which Canara Bank was petitioner while V.K. Awasthy was respondent and the judgment came out on 31 March 2005.

Challenge in this Appeal is to correctness of the judgment rendered by a Division Bench of the Kerala High Court holding that the order directing respondent's dismissal from service was in violation of the principles of natural justice. Therefore, it was held that the order was passed without proper application of mind regarding the findings recorded by the Disciplinary Authority on the basis of report of the enquiry officer, and relating to imposition of punishment. However, High Court permitted the respondent – writ petitioner to make a detailed representation to the Disciplinary Authority in respect of the enquiry proceedings and findings, within a stipulated time and direction was given to the Disciplinary Authority to consider the submission and pass a fresh order. High Court further directed that the period during which respondent was out of service was to be treated as period under suspension, and the employee was to be paid subsistence allowance. It would be relevant to note that the respondent filed a Writ Petition questioning the order directing his dismissal from service. Learned Single Judge came to hold that the quantum of punishment *i.e.* dismissal from service was disproportionate to the misconduct proved. It was however, held that no prejudice was caused to the writ petitioner and there was no violation of principles of natural justice. Both the writ petitioner and the present appellant had preferred writ appeals before the High Court, which were heard and disposed of by the impugned common judgment.

(*b*) It's a 1959 case of one who decides must hear. In Gullapalli Nageswara Rao Etc. *vs.* The State of Andhra Pradesh case, Petitioner was Gullapalli Nageswara Rao Etc. while the Respondent was the State of Andhra Pradesh & Others, and the judgment was given on 21 August 1959.

The short details of the case are as thus:

The appellants were carrying on motor transport business in Krishna District in Andhra Pradesh. The General Manager of the State Transport Undertaking published a scheme for nationalisation of motor transport and objections to the said scheme were invited. The appellants, among others, filed their objections. The Secretary in-charge of the Transport department gave personal hearing to the objectors and heard the representation made on behalf of the State Transport Undertaking. The Chief Minister, who was in charge of transport, passed the order approving the scheme. The appellants moved this Court under Art. 32 of the Constitution for quashing the said scheme and this Court in Gullapalli Nageswara Rao *vs.* Andhra Pradesh Road Transport Corporation, previously decided, held that the Secretary-in-charge of the Transport Department was incompetent to hear the objections on the around that no party could be a judge in his own cause and quashed the order approving the scheme. Thereafter, the Government issued the notices to the objectors. The Chief Minister himself heard the representatives of the objectors and the Road Transport Corporation and passed the order approving the scheme as originally published. The appellants moved the High Court under Article 226 of the Constitution for writs of certiorari quashing the order passed by the Government confirming the scheme and subsequent orders made by the Regional Transport Authority cancelling their stage carriage permits. The High Court rejected the petitions and the appellants appealed. It was contended, *inter alia*, on their behalf that the same infirmity which attached to the Secretary in-charge of the Transport Department on the previous occasion, attached to the Chief Minister, who was in charge of transport, and rendered him incompetent to hear the objections.

(*c*) It's a 1979 case of Exclusion of rule of hearing. Appellant No. 1 in Civil Appeal 1629 of 1979 is Swadeshi Cotton Mills Co. Ltd. (hereinafter referred to as the Company). It was incorporated as a private company with an authorised capital of ₹ 30 lakhs in 1921 by the Horseman family by converting their partnership business into a Private Joint Stock Company. Its capital was raised in 1923 to ₹ 32 lakhs and thereafter in 1945 to ₹ 52.50 lakhs by issue of bonus shares. In 1946, the Jaipuria family acquired substantial holding in the company. Jaipuria family is the present management. By issue of further bonus shares in 1946, the capital of the company was increased to ₹ 122.50 lakhs. In 1948, the paid-up capital of the company was raised to ₹ 210 lakhs by the issue of further bonus shares. The subscribed and issued capital consisting mainly of the bonus shares has since remained constant at ₹ 210 lakhs.

In the year 1946, the company had only one undertaking, a textile unit at Kanpur, known as "The Swadeshi Cotton Mills, Kanpur". Between 1956 and 1973, the Company set up and/or acquired five further textile units in Pondicherry, Naini, Udaipur, Maunath Bhanjan and Rae Bareilly. Each of these six units or undertakings of the Company was separately registered in accordance with the provisions of Section 10 of the Industries (Development and Regulation) Act, 1951 (hereinafter called the IDR Act).

13. Assertion (A) is right as a High Court may decline to exercise its extraordinary jurisdiction under Article 226 and dismiss the writ summarily or *in limine*. Article 226 in this regard contains the following:

1. Notwithstanding anything in article 32, every High Court shall have power,

throughout the territories in relation to which it exercises jurisdiction, to issue to any person or authority, including in appropriate cases, any Government, within those territories directions, orders or writs, including writs in the nature of habeas corpus, mandamus, prohibition, quo warranto and certiorari, or any of them, for the enforcement of any of the rights conferred by Part III and for any other purpose.

2. The power conferred by clause (1) to issue directions, orders or writs to any Government, authority or person may also be exercised by any High Court exercising jurisdiction in relation to the territories within which the cause of action, wholly or in part, arises for the exercise of such power, notwithstanding that the seat of such Government or authority or the residence of such person is not within those territories.

3. Where any party against whom an interim order, whether by way of injunction or stay or in any other manner, is made on, or in any proceedings relating to, a petition under clause (1), without –

(*a*) furnishing to such party copies of such petition and all documents in support of the plea for such interim order; and

(*b*) giving such party an opportunity of being heard, makes an application to the High Court for the vacation of such order and furnishes a copy of such application to the party in whose favour such order has been made or the counsel of such party, the High Court shall dispose of the application within a period of two weeks from the date on which it is received or from the date on which the copy of such application is so furnished, whichever is later, or where the High Court is closed on the last day of that period, before the expiry of the next day afterwards on which the High Court is open; and if the application is not so disposed of, the interim order shall, on the expiry of that period, or, as the case may be, the expiry of the said next day, stand vacated.

4. The power conferred on a High Court by this article shall not be in derogation of the power conferred on the Supreme Court by clause (2) of article 32.

Reason (R) is right and correct reason of **(A)**, as it correctly says that it would be proper for the High Court to dispose of the petition summarily or *in limine*, when no important question of law is raised in a writ petition.

14. Mandamus is a writ or order issued from a court of superior jurisdiction that commands an inferior or lower tribunal, corporation, Municipal corporation, or individual to perform, or refrain from performing, a particular act, the performance or omission of which is required by law as an obligation. It may be issued by a court at any time when it is appropriate, but it is usually issued in a case that has already begun.

16. Among the many justices who have sat on the United States Supreme Court, Oliver Wendell Holmes stands out for his enduring influence on the Court's jurisprudence. Among his many accomplishments as a member of the Court was to help eradicate judicial reasoning based on principles of natural law or natural right.

Holmes's understanding of legal realism shows his relationship to the natural law and natural rights traditions. For Holmes, law and society are always in flux, and courts adjudicate with an eye to law's practical effects. Morality has nothing to do with law. Holmes thus raises squarely a fundamental question: if the Constitution does not dictate anything that is not time-bound, is there any ground for faith in the Constitution, or liberal constitutionalism? The latter would seem to require an understanding that only promulgated and known laws whose meaning is stable over time can bind citizens, yet Holmesian legal realism denies the very possibility of such laws. In short, the polemical version of legal realism as propounded by Holmes has wielded great influence on the entire judicial system.

17. The *liberum arbitrium* means free will to choose between different possible courses of action and in the courts it depends upon what is right, justice, equitable or reasonable and is dependent upon arguments submitted with reason. The courts assess the arguments submitted whether they are found to be reasonable and rational, and then only the courts give verdict in a case accordingly.

18. The Latin word, *Orbiter dicta* is the plural form of *Obiter dictum.* More usually, it is used in the plural for a word said "by the way", that is, a remark in a judgment that is "said in passing". It is a concept derived from English common law, whereby a judgment comprises only two elements: *ratio decidendi* and *obiter dicta.* For the purposes of judicial precedent, *ratio decidendi* is binding, whereas *obiter dicta* are persuasive only. Though *Obiter dicta* has no binding authority, it helps rationalise legal sanctions.

20. In the modern world, morality and law are almost universally held to be unrelated fields and, where the term "legal ethics" is used, it is taken to refer to the professional honesty of lawyers or judges, but has nothing to do with the possible "rightness" or "wrongness" of particular laws themselves. Hence, as given in **Assertion (A)**, that the relation of morality to a concept of law cannot be stated simply in the form of a stark alternative that the former is either externally or internally related to the later, is right. And as given in **Reason (R)** that it is depending upon timeframe of reference, is also correct.

21. Major John Prendergast Gouriet (1 June 1935 – 4 September 2010) was a British Army officer, company director and political activist. He was best known as a founder of the National Association for Freedom (now The Freedom Association), and for pioneering the use of legal action to oppose actions of trade unions and campaigning groups which he believed interfered with personal liberty, during three years as the Association's director.

The case of *Gouriet* V. *Union of Post Office Workers* mirrors some rare legal aspect. The principle of the Rule of Law required not only that the law should apply to everyone—citizen and state, rich and poor, powerful and weak—but also that there should be effective legal remedies for use of where there is the breach of the law. The Rule of Law does not cease to operate merely because the law is broken—crime exists in all societies—but it is violated if someone breaks the law openly and with impunity because legal remedies do not exist or because he is too powerful for them to be applied to him. The case of *Gouriet V. Union of Post Office Workers* raised the question of how far the Rule of Law operates in contemporary Britain.

22. Different Justices have given their own remarks on *Mirehouse* v. *Rennel* case. A very significant remark is given by Justice Park on this case. Regarding this case, he said, "Our common law system consists in the applying to new combinations of circumstances those rules of law which we derive from legal principles and judicial precedents; and for the sake of attaining uniformity, consistency and certainty, we must apply those rules, where they are not plainly unreasonable and inconvenient, to all cases which arise; and we are not at liberty to reject them, and to abandon all analogy to them, in those to which they have not yet been judicially applied, because we think that the rules are not as convenient and reasonable as we ourselves could have devised. It appears to me to be of great importance to keep this principle of decision steadily in view, not merely for the determination of the particular case, but for the interests of law as a science." Here the emphasis is laid on uniformity and consistency.

23. A shareholder or stockholder is an individual or institution (including a corporation) that legally owns a share of stock in a public or private corporation. Shareholders are the owners of a limited company. Unlike the owners of sole proprietorships or partnerships, corporate shareholders are not personally liable for the company's debts and other obligations. Also, corporate shareholders do not play a major role in running the company. They are not, in the eye of law, part owners of a company. Hence, the statement given in **Assertion (A)** is right but as given in **Reason (R)**, it will be wrong to say that shareholders are collective owners of the company.

24. In legal perspective, the act of enticing is to wrongly indulge someone in committing wrongful act by persuading, procuring unwanted things that in the beginning or ultimately harms him/her. Thus, an idea of inducement exciting hope or desire on the other is known as enticing in legal perspective.

25. The act committed by A will be called Theft, because when A had taken his own suit from the tailor without tailor's knowledge (or without informing him), he did not have the intent to return it. He cherished the intent of returning it later.

26. The **Assertion (A)** indicates the case that comes under Section 299(c) of IPC. This particular section can be defined as thus:

A, by shooting at a fowl with intent to kill and steal it, kills B who is behind a bush; A not knowing that he was there. Here, although A was doing an unlawful act, he was not guilty of culpable homicide, as he did not intend to kill B, or to cause death by doing an act that he knew was likely to cause death. Explanation 1.—A person who causes bodily injury to another who is labouring under a disorder, disease or bodily infirmity, and thereby accelerates the death of that other, shall be deemed to have caused his death. Explanation 2.—Where death is caused by bodily injury, the person who causes such bodily injury shall be deemed to have caused the death.

Such specific principle as given in **Reason (R)** is a case of 300(4). The Exception 4 in Section 300 says as thus,—Culpable homicide is not murder if it is committed without premeditation in a sudden fight in the heat of passion upon a sudden quarrel and without the offender having taken undue advantage or acted in a cruel or unusual manner.

Hence, both **(A)** and **(R)** are concurrent as per Sections 299(c) and 300(4) respectively.

27. Perjury is a crime that occurs when anyone wilfully makes a false statement during a judicial proceeding, after he or she has taken an oath to speak nothing except the truth. The common law crime of perjury is now government by both state and federal laws. In addition, the Model Penal code, which has been adopted in some from by many states and promulgated by the Commission on Uniform State Laws, also sets forth the following basic elements for the crime of perjury: (1) a false statement is made under oath or equivalent affirmation during a judicial proceedings; (2) the statement must be material or relevant to the proceeding; and (3) the witness must have the Specific Intent to deceive.

29. Removal of ornaments after death of a lady does not amount to robbery because after her death those valuables may be collected by the next of kin of the deceased or those become the family asset. Her ornaments cannot be put on the pyre of her body in case she is a Hindu and similarly, the ornaments cannot be buried in the grave along with her body if the lady is a Muslim or a Christian. So in such case, removal of these valuables cannot be considered a crime in the eyes of law.

30. The term *in loco-parentis*, Latin for "in the place of a parent" refers to the legal responsibility of a person or organisation to take on some of the functions and responsibilities of a parent. Originally derived from English common law, it is applied in the following two separate areas of the law: First, it allows institutions such as colleges and schools to act in the best interests of the students as they see fit, although not allowing what would be considered violations of the students' civil liberties.

Second, this doctrine can provide a non-biological parent to be given the legal rights and responsibilities of a biological parent if they have held themselves out as the parent.

32. Justice V.R. Krishna Iyer (15 November 1915 – 4 December 2014) was an Indian judge and minister who reformed the Indian criminal justice system, stood up for the poor and the underprivileged. He was conferred with the Padma Vibhushan in 1999. It was Justice Iyer who observed the case of Municipal Council of Ratlam *vs.* Vardhichand minutely.

Perhaps the most influential decision made by Krishna Iyer in the context of environmental justice, at least from the perspective of distributive justice, is that of *Ratlam Municipal Council v Shri Vardhichand & Ors (Ratlam)*. 9 Residents of a locality within the municipality of Ratlam were tormented by a public nuisance caused by inadequate public drains, human excrement deposited on roads by slum dwellers for want of public toilets, and the discharge of malodorous effluent from a nearby alcohol plant into the roads. The Magistrate ordered the Council to draft a plan for removing the public nuisance within six months. On appeal, the Magistrate's order was reversed by the Sessions Court but it was subsequently upheld by the High Court, and on further appeal, by the Supreme Court. Krishna Iyer, in delivering the judgement of the Supreme Court (Krishna Iyer and Chinnapa Reddy JJ), held that the citizens could bring suit before a magistrate to force the Council, under the Criminal Procedure Code 1974, to abate a public nuisance.

33. The Directive Principles of State Policy are guidelines or principles given to the central and state governments of India, to be kept in mind while framing laws and policies. These provisions, contained in Part IV of the Constitution of India, are not enforceable by any court, but the principles laid down therein are considered fundamental in the governance of the country, making it the duty of the State to apply these principles in making laws to establish a just and healthy society in the country.

Therefore, when the issue of protecting and improving the Environment and safeguarding forests and wildlife arises, both Directive Principles of State Policy and Fundamental duty must be brought into practice.

34. When the lower courts fail to do the needful in regard of safeguarding the environment, it is the Supreme Court that comes into action and *S. Jagannath* vs. *Union of India* in which Jagannath was the petitioner and Union of India the respondent. It is a glaring example of such case. The Supreme Court of India analysed many national and international studies on the ecological and social implications of commercial shrimp farming that took into account the issues of loss of agricultural land and mangroves, obstruction of natural drains, salinisation, destruction of natural seed resources, use of drugs and chemicals, extraction of groundwater and loss of biodiversity, among others. The court emphasised that the new trend of more intensified shrimp farming – without much control of feeds, seeds, and other inputs and water management practices – had brought to the fore a serious threat to the environment and ecology. The industry had to develop under the unified motto of environment and development. There had to be an environmental impact assessment also taking into account the social impact on different population strata in the area before permission was granted to install commercial shrimp farms. It also had to take into consideration the inter-generational equity and the compensation for those who were affected and prejudiced. The court, therefore, directed, *inter alia*, that the Central Government had to constitute an authority with all the powers necessary to protect the ecologically fragile coastal areas.

35. The right to consume clean drinking water and right to breathe pollution-free air are attributes of "Right to Life". Every individual has the fundamental right to have access to these boons of nature because these are the basic elements to sustain life on this earth. Therefore, both **Assertion (A)** and **Reason (R)** are true and **(R)** is the correct explanation of **(A)**.

36. *M.C. Mehta* v. *Kamal Nath* was a landmark case in Indian environmental law, in which, the Supreme Court of India held that the public trust doctrine applied in India.

Fact of the case: The *Indian Express* published an article reporting that Span Motels Private Limited, which owns Span Resorts, had floated another ambitious venture, Span Club. The family of Indian politician Kamal Nath has direct links with this company. The club was built by encroaching upon 27.12 bighas of land, including a substantial forestland, in 1990. The land was later regularised and leased out to the company on 11 April 1994.

The regularisation was done when Nath was Minister of Environment & Forests. This encroachment led to the swelling of the Beas River that changed its course and engulfed the Span Club and the adjoining lawns, washing it away. Almost after five months, the Span Resorts management moved bulldozers and earth movers to turn the course of the Beas for a second time.

A worrying thought was that of the river eating into the mountains, leading to landslides, which were an occasional occurrence in that area. In September, these caused floods in the Beas and property estimated to be worth ₹ 105 crore met its destruction. The Government of India, Ministry of Environment & Forests by the letter dated 24.11.1993, addressed to the Secretary, Forest, Government of Himachal Pradesh, Shimla conveyed its prior approval in terms of Section 2 of the Forest (Conservation) Act, 1980 for leasing to the Motel 27 bighas and 12 biswas of forest land adjoining to the land already on lease with the Motel. An expert committee formed to assess the situation of the area arrived at the following conclusion:

The river is presently in a highly unstable regime after the extraordinary floods of 1995, and it is difficult to predict its behaviour in case of another high flood occurred in the near future. A long-term planning for flood control in the Kullu Valley needs to be taken up immediately with the advice of an organisation having expertise in the field, and permanent measures shall be taken to protect the area so that recurrence of such a heavy flood is mitigated permanently.

Judgement of the Court: The forestlands, which have been given on lease to the Motel by the State Government are situated at the bank of the river Beas, which is a young and dynamic river. The river is fast-flowing, carrying large boulders, at the time of flood. When water's velocity is not sufficient to carry the boulders, those are deposited in the channel often blocking the flow of water. Under such circumstances the river stream changes its course, remaining within the valley but swinging from one bank to the other. The right bank of the river Beas where the motel is located mostly comes under forest, the left bank consists of plateaus, having steep-bank facing the river, where fruit orchards and cereal cultivation are predominant. The area being ecologically fragile and full of scenic beauty should not have been permitted to be converted into private ownership and for commercial gains.

Orders of the Court: The public trust doctrine, as discussed by the Court in this judgment was a part of the law of the land. The prior approval granted by the Government of India, Ministry of Environment & Forest and the lease-deed dated 11.04.1994 in favour of the Motel were quashed. The lease granted to the Motel by the said lease-deed in respect of 27 bighas and 12 biswas of area, is cancelled and set aside. The Himachal Pradesh Government shall take over the area and restore it to its original-natural conditions. The Motel shall pay compensation by way of cost for the restitution of the environment and ecology of the area. The pollution caused by various constitutions made by the Motel in the riverbed and the banks on the river Beas have to be removed and reversed.

38. The Wildlife Protection Act, 1972 is an Act of the Parliament of India enacted for protection of plants and animal species. However, the main objective of the Act, as amended up to 2003, is to check on poaching and on illegal trade in ivory.

It extends to the whole of India, except the State of Jammu and Kashmir, which has its own wildlife Act.

40. The statements given in codes, (b) and (c) are incorrect. First, there is no (G) in Para (1) of Article 38 of the Statute of International Court of Justice. Moreover, the given matter is also different. The matter given in code (c) is also incorrect.

42. *Nottebohm Case (Liechtenstein* v. *Guatemala)* [1955] ICJ 1 is the proper name for the 1955 contentious case adjudicated by the International Court of Justice (ICJ). Liechtenstein sought a ruling to force Guatemalan recognition of Friedrich Nottebohm as a Liechtenstein national.

Nottebohm, born on 16 September 1881, in Hamburg, Germany, possessed German citizenship. Despite living in Guatemala from 1905 until 1943, he could never obtain the citizenship of Guatemala. On 9 October 1939, Nottebohm applied to become a naturalised citizen of Liechtenstein. The application was approved and he became a citizen of Liechtenstein. He then returned to Guatemala on his Liechtenstein passport and informed the local government of his change of nationality. When he tried to return to Guatemala once again in 1943, he was refused entry as an enemy alien since the Guatemalan authorities did not recognise his naturalisation and regarded him as still German. It has been suggested that the timing of the event was due to the recent entry of the United States and Guatemala into the Second World War.

He was later extradited to the United States, where he was held at an internment camp until the end of the war. All his possessions in Guatemala were confiscated. After his release, he lived out the rest of his life in Liechtenstein.

The Government of Liechtenstein granted Nottebohm protection against unjust treatment by the government of Guatemala and petitioned the International Court of Justice. However, the government of Guatemala argued that Nottebohm did not gain Liechtenstein citizenship for the purposes of international law. The court agreed and thus stopped the case from continuing.

Although the Court stated that it is the sovereign right of all states to determine its own citizens and criteria for becoming one in municipal law, such a process would have to be scrutinised on the international plane where the question is of diplomatic protection. The Court upheld the principle of effective nationality, (the *Nottebohm* principle) where the national must prove a meaningful connection to the state in question. This principle was previously applied only in cases of dual nationality to determine which nationality should be used in a given case. However, Nottebohm had forfeited his German nationality and thus only had the nationality of Liechtenstein. The Nottebohm case was subsequently cited in many definitions of nationality.

43. Five UN organs and sixteen agencies of the UN family are authorised to request advisory opinions but Secretariat is not included among them. The UN General Assembly and Security Council have inherited with respect to the ICJ a power, which the Covenant of the League of Nations previously conferred on the Assembly and Council of the League with respect to the PCIJ. The UN General Assembly and the Security Council may request an advisory opinion "on any legal question".

44. The existence of law, however, does not mean that conflict is any easier to resolve. Instead, as law becomes more elaborate and constraining, it becomes increasingly contentious. The powerful countries do not wish to be constrained in their ability to respond to threats. At the same time, developing countries see much of international law as being crafted largely without their input, primarily due to the so-called democratic deficit in intergovernmental organisations (IGOs), which now are typically the negotiating venues for the creation of new law. There are examples of some powerful countries, which have violated the International law so brazenly, and no legal action is taken against them, because of they have power. Moreover, sanctions behind International Law are also weak. So both **Assertion (A)** and **Reason (R)** are correct and **(R)** is the correct explanation of **(A)**.

46. (*a*) Article 96 of UN Charter has the following provision: (1) The General Assembly or the Security council may request the International Court of Justice to give an advisory opinion on any legal question. (2) Other organs of the United Nations and specialised agencies, which may at any time be so authorised by the General Assembly, may also request advisory opinions of the Court on legal questions arising within the scope of their activities.

(*b*) Article 4 of UN Charter has the following provision: (1) Membership in the United Nations is open to other peace-loving states which accept the obligations contained in the present Charter and, in the judgement of the Organisation, are able and willing to carry out these obligations. (2) The admission of any such state to membership in the Nations will be effected by a decision of the General Assembly upon the recommendation of the Security Council.

(*c*) Article 18 of UN Charter has the following provision: (1) Each member of the general Assembly shall have one vote. (2) Decisions of the General Assembly on important questions shall be made by a two-thirds majority of the members present and voting. These questions shall include: recommendations with respect to the maintenance of international peace and security, the election of the non-permanent members of the Security council, the election of the members of the Economic and Social Council, the election of members of the Trusteeship Council in accordance with paragraph 1 of Article 86, the admission of new Members to the United Nations, the suspension of the rights and privileges of membership, the expulsion of Members, questions relating to the operation of the trusteeship system, and budgetary questions. (3) Decisions on other questions, including the determination of additional categories of questions to be decided by a two-third majority, shall be made by a majority of the members present and voting.

(*d*) Article 23 of UN Charter has the following provision: (1) The Security Council shall consist of fifteen Members of the United Nations. The Republic of China, France, the Union of Soviet Socialist, the United Kingdom of Great Britain and Northern Ireland, and the United States of America shall be permanent members of the Security Council. The General Assembly shall elect ten other Members of the United Nations to be non-permanent members of the Security Council, due regard being specially paid, in the first in-stance to the contribution of Members of the United Nations to the maintenance of international peace and security and to the other purposes of the Organisation, and also to equitable geographical distribution. (2) The non-permanent members of the Security Council shall be elected for a term of two years. A retiring member shall not be eligible for immediate re-election. (3) Each member of the Security Council shall have one representative.

47. Section 10 of the Hindu Marriage Act, 1955, provides for Judicial Separation. According to Section 10 of the Act, either party to a marriage, whether solemnised before or after the commencement of this Act, may present a petition praying for a decree for judicial separation on any of the grounds specified in sub-section (1) of Section 13, and in the case of a wife also on any of the grounds might have been presented.

Among a few certain grounds, deserting for a continuous period of not less than two years by husband or wife legally enables her/him to obtain a decree of Judicial Separation. Thus, desertion for one year will not be a ground of Judicial Separation under the Hindu Marriage Act, 1955 because this period is less than the stipulated period of two years.

48. As per Hindu Marriage Act 1955, a wife under Section 13(2) of this Act may seek and get divorce from her husband on the following grounds:

Non-payment of maintenance and no cohabitation for one year or upwards: As the case may be, if a decree or order has been passed against the husband awarding maintenance to the wife notwithstanding that she was living apart and that since the passing of such decree or order, cohabitation between the both has not been resumed for one year or upwards.

Repudiation of marriage by wife: If her marriage (whether consumated or not) was solemnised before attaining the age of fifteen years and she repudiates the marriage after attaining that age but before attaining the age of eighteen years.

Pre-Act bigamy by husband: If the husband has already one wife and then marries another lady without having divorced to his first wife. In such case, the second wife may seek divorce from her husband on the ground of pre-act bigamy.

Husband is guilty or rape, sodomy and bestiality: A wife can seek divorce from her husband if any competent court declares him the guilty of such crime as rape, sodomy and bestiality. If he commits rape or sodomy (having anal sex) or bestiality (having sex with animal), he is an offender and his wife has full right to take divorce from him.

49. The Hindu Adoptions and Maintenance Act of 1956 deals specifically with the legal process of adopting children by a Hindu adult. From the date of the adoption, the child remains under the legal guardianship of the new adopted parent(s) and thus should enjoy all the benefits from those family ties. This also means that this child, therefore, is cut off from all legal benefits (property, inheritance, etc.) from the family who had given him or her up for adoption. So as per the said Act, once a child is adopted, he/she cannot be given in adoption. Thus, the matter given in only code (b) is correct; rest all are incorrect.

51. Section 13-B of Hindu Marriage Act, 1955 pertains to Divorce by mutual consent:

1. Subject to the provisions of this Act a petition for dissolution of marriage by a decree of divorce may be presented to the district court by both the parties to a marriage together, whether such marriage was solemnised before or after the commencement of the Marriage Laws (Amendment) Act, 1976 (68 of 1976), on the ground that they have been living separately for a period of one year or more, that they have not been able to live together and that they have mutually agreed that the marriage should be dissolved.

2. On the motion of both the parties made not earlier than six months after the date of the presentation of the petition referred to in sub-section (1) and not later than eighteen months after the said date, if the petition is not withdrawn in the meantime, the court shall, on being satisfied, after hearing the parties and after making such inquiry as it thinks fit, that a marriage has been solemnised and that the averments in the petition are true, pass a decree of divorce declaring the marriage to be dissolved with effect from the date of the decree.

52. Talaq 'ahsan' or the most laudable divorce is where the husband repudiates his wife by making one pronouncement within the term of *Tahr* (purity, when the woman is not passing through the period of menses) during which he has not had sexual intercourse with her, and she is left to observe her 'Iddat'. In this case, the Iddat is a period during which Talaq 'ahsan' is revocable.

53. (*a*) Section 3 of Muslim Marriage Act, 1939 deals with the Notice to be served on heirs of the husband when the husband's whereabouts are not known.

In a suit to which clause (i) of section 2 applies:

(*a*) the names and addresses of the persons who would have been heirs of the husband under Muslim Law if he had died on the date of the filing of the plaint shall be stated in the plaint.

(*b*) notice of the suit shall be served on such persons, and

(*c*) such persons shall have the right to be heard in the suit:

Provided that paternal-uncle and brother of the husband, if any, shall be cited as party even if he or they are not heirs.

(*b*) Section 4 deals with Effect of conversion to another faith.

The renunciation of Islam by a married Muslim woman or her conversion to a faith other than Islam shall not by itself operate to dissolve her marriage:

Provided that after such renunciation, or conversion, the woman shall be entitled to obtain a decree for the dissolution of her marriage on any of the grounds mentioned in section 2;

Provided further that the provisions of this section shall not apply to a woman converted to Islam from some other faith who re-embraces her former faith.

(*c*) Section 5 deals with right to dower not be affected.

Nothing contained in this Act shall affect any right, which a married woman may have under Muslim law to her dower or any part thereof on the dissolution of her marriage.

(*d*) Section 2(v) deals with Impotence of the husband as a ground of divorce.

It means the husband was impotent at the time of the marriage and continues to be so.

54. (*a*) Section 9 of Hindu Minority and Guardianship Act, 1956 pertains to

Testamentary guardians and their powers:

1. A Hindu father entitled to act as the natural guardian of his minor legitimate children, may, by will, appoint a guardian for any of them in respect of the minor's person or in respect of the minor's property (other than the undivided interest referred in section 12) or in respect of both.
2. An appointment made under sub-section (1) shall have no effect if the father predeceases the mother, but shall revive if the mother dies without appointing by will, any person as guardian.
3. A Hindu widow entitled to act as the natural guardian of her minor legitimate children, and a Hindu mother entitled to act as the natural guardian of her minor legitimate children by reason of the fact that the father has become disentitled to act as such, may, by will, appoint a guardian for any of them in respect of the minor's person or in respect of the minor's property (other than the undivided interest referred to in section 12) or in respect of both.
4. A Hindu mother entitled to act as the natural guardian of her minor legitimate children may, by will, appoint a guardian for any of them in respect of the minor's person or in respect of the minor's property or in respect of both.
5. The guardian so appointed by will has the right to act as the minor's guardian after the death of the minor's father or mother, as the case may be, and to exercise all the rights of a natural guardian under this Act to such extent and subject to such restrictions, if any, as are specified in this Act and in the will.
6. The right of the guardian so appointed by will shall, where the minor is a girl, cease on her marriage.

(*b*) Section 6 pertains to Natural guardians of a Hindu minor:

The natural guardians of a Hindu, minor, in respect of the minor's person as well as in respect of the minor's property (excluding his or her undivided interest in joint family property), are:

(*a*) in the case of a boy or an unmarried girl— the father, and after him, the mother: provided that the custody of a minor who has not completed the age of five years shall ordinarily be with the mother;

(*b*) in the case of an illegitimate boy or an illegitimate unmarried girl – the mother, and after her, the father;

(*c*) in the case of a married girl – the husband;

Provided that no person shall be entitled to act as the natural guardian of a minor under the provisions of this section—

(*a*) if he has ceased to be a Hindu, or

(*b*) if he has completely and finally renounced the world by becoming a hermit (vanaprastha) or an ascetic (yati or sanyasi)

Explanation: In this section, the expressions 'father' and 'mother' do not include a step-father and a step-mother.

(*c*) Section 13 pertains to Welfare of minor to be paramount consideration:

1. In the appointment of declaration of any person as guardian of a Hindu minor by a court, the welfare of the minor shall be the paramount consideration.
2. No person shall be entitled to the guardianship by virtue of the provisions of this Act or of any law relating to guardianship in marriage among Hindus, if the court is of opinion that his or her guardianship will not be for the welfare of the minor.

(*d*) Section 11 pertains to De facto guardian not to deal with minors property:

After the commencement of this Act, no person shall be entitled to dispose of, or deal with, the property of a Hindu minor merely on the ground of his or her being the de facto guardian of the minor.

56. The International Covenant on Economic, Social and Cultural Rights (ICESCR) is a multilateral treaty adopted by the United Nations General Assembly on 16 December 1966, and in force from 3 January 1976. It commits its parties to work toward the granting of economic, social and cultural rights (ESCR) to the Non-Self-Governing and Trust Territories and individuals, including labour rights and the right to health, the right to education, and the right to an adequate standard of living. As of 2015, the Covenant has 164 parties. A further six countries, including the United States, have signed but not ratified the Covenant.

The ICESCR is part of the International Bill of Human Rights, along with the Universal Declaration of Human Rights (UDHR) and the International Covenant on Civil and Political Rights (ICCPR), including the latter's first and second Optional Protocols. The Covenant is monitored by the UN Committee on Economic, Social and Cultural Rights.

57. UNICEF was created by the United Nations General Assembly on December 11, 1946, to provide emergency food and healthcare to children in countries, especially the European countries that had been devastated by World War II. Maurice Pate, American humanitarian and businessman, co-founded the UNICEF with Herbert Hoover in 1947. Pate served as its first executive director from 1947 until his death in 1965. In 1953, UNICEF became a permanent part of the United Nations System and its name was shortened from the original United Nations International Children's Emergency Fund but it has continued to be known by the popular acronym based on this previous title.

58. (*a*) Jose Ayala Lasso (born in Quito on 29 January 1932) is a retired Ecuadorian lawyer and diplomat, currently residing in Quito. He served as Foreign Minister of Ecuador on three occasions. Pursuant to United Nations General Assembly Resolution A/RES/48/141 of 20 December 1993 Dr. Ayala Lasso was appointed first United Nations High Commissioner for Human Rights and started his four-year mandate on 5 April 1994. His first important challenge was to give contours to his mandate and establish the credibility of the Office. His years as High Commissioner were marked by a continuous effort to give greater visibility to the United Nations human rights programme.

(*b*) Maharaj Sri Nagendra Singh (Dungarpur, 18 March 1914 – The Hague, 11 December 1988) was an Indian lawyer and administrator who served as President of the International Court of Justice from 1985 to 1988. He was one of the three judges from India to have been on the International Court of Justice in The Hague.

(*c*) Born on 8 April 1938, Kofi Atta Annan was a Ghanaian diplomat and President International Court of Justice. He served as the seventh Secretary-General of the United Nations from January 1997 to December 2006. Annan and the United Nations were the co-recipients of the 2001 Nobel Peace Prize "for their work for a better organised and more peaceful world."

From 23 February until 31 August 2012, Annan was the UN-Arab League Joint Special Representative for Syria, to help find a resolution to ongoing conflict there. Annan quit after becoming frustrated with the UN's lack of progress with regard to conflict resolution.

(*d*) Anna Eleanor Roosevelt (11 October 1884 – 7 November 1962), who after marrying the US President Franklin D. Roosevelt, became Mrs. F.D. Roosevelt, was an American politician, diplomat, and activist. She was the longest-serving First Lady of the United States, holding the post from March 1933 to April 1945 during her husband's Presidency for four terms, and served as United States Delegate to the United Nations General Assembly from 1945 to 1952 and U.N. High Commissioner for Human Rights. President Harry S. Truman later called her the "First Lady of the World" in tribute to her human rights achievements.

59. The Universal Declaration of Human Rights (UDHR) is a declaration adopted by the United Nations General Assembly on 10 December 1948 at the Palais de Chaillot, Paris. The Declaration, which contains provisions relating to operationalisation of Human Rights, arose directly from the experience of the Second World War and represents the first global expression of rights to which all human beings are inherently entitled.

61. Following are Human Rights documents which have been placed according to correct chronological order:

(*a*) The International Covenant on Civil and Political Rights (ICCPR) is a multilateral treaty adopted by the United Nations General Assembly on **16 December 1966**, and in force from 23 March 1976. It commits its parties to respect the civil and political rights of individuals, including the right to life, freedom of religion, freedom of speech, freedom of assembly, electoral rights and rights to due process and a fair trial.

(*b*) The Convention on the Elimination of All Forms of Discrimination against Women (CEDAW), adopted in **1979** by the UN General Assembly, is often described as an international bill of rights for women. Consisting of a preamble and 30 articles, it defines what constitutes discrimination against women and sets up an agenda for national action to end such discrimination.

(*c*) The Universal Declaration of Human Rights (UDHR) is a declaration adopted by the United Nations General Assembly on **10 December 1948** at the Palais de Chaillot, Paris. The Declaration arose directly from the experience of the Second World War and represents the first global expression of rights to which all human beings are inherently entitled.

(*d*) The United Nations Convention on the Rights of the Child (commonly abbreviated as the CRC, CROC, or UNCRC) is a human rights treaty, which sets out the civil, political, economic, social, health and cultural rights of children. The Convention defines a child as any human being under the age of eighteen, unless the age of majority is attained earlier under a state's own domestic legislation. The UN General Assembly adopted the Convention and opened it for signature on **20 November 1989** (the 30th anniversary of its Declaration of the Rights of the Child). It came into force on 2 September 1990, after it was ratified by the required number of nations.

62. Sir Percy Henry Winfield (16 September 1878–7 July 1953) FBA was Rouse Ball Professor of English Law between 1928 and 1943. It was Winfield who defined law of tort as, "tortuous liability arises from the breach of a duty primarily fixed by the law: this duty is towards persons generally and its breach is redressible by an action for unliquidated damages?"

63. Latin term, *Damnum sine injuria* literally means condemnation without injury. Simply translated, the term would mean "injury with no damages." *Damnum sine injuria* refers to a legal situation in which plaintiff's right is not respected by another but where the breach of plaintiff's right does not cause damage, or at least not a calculable or admissible damage. A finding of *damnum sine injuria* can be the basis for a finding of nominal damages. Thus in cases of *damnum sine injuria,* the injury is *de minimis, i.e.* too small to be remedied practically at the law. In such cases, the plaintiff will have a satisfaction remedy of nominal damages – which are also called symbolic damages. So, in the light of this, the cases as defined in codes (b) and (d) will not be a form of *damnum sine injuria*.

64. It is not the case of volunteer damage caused to the plaintiff. The damage and subsequent inconvenience are caused by none other than rats. Moreover, the rainwater box maintained by the defender was for the benefit of both – the defender and plaintiff and, it was continued to be so with the consent of the plaintiff. Therefore, no action lies because of the consent of the plaintiff.

65. A tort, in common law jurisdictions, is a civil wrong that unfairly causes someone else to suffer loss or harm resulting in legal liability for the person who commits the tortuous act, called a tortfeasor. Although crimes may be torts, the cause of legal action is not necessarily a crime, as the harm may be due to negligence, which does not amount to criminal negligence. The victims of the harm can recover their loss as damages in a lawsuit. In order to prevail, the plaintiff in the lawsuit, commonly referred to as the injured party, must show that the actions or lack of action was the legally recognisable cause of the harm. The equivalent of tort in civil law jurisdictions is delict. So as given in **Assertion (A)**, that a master is liable for the torts committed by his servant while not acting in the course of his employment will be a wrong assertion.

Respondeat superior (Latin: "let the master answer"; plural: *respondeant superiores*) is a legal doctrine which states that, in many circumstances, an employer is responsible for the actions of employees performed within the course of their employment. This rule is also called the master-servant rule, recognised in both common law and civil law jurisdictions. In a broader scope, *respondeat superior* is based upon the concept of vicarious liability. Thus, **Reason (R)** containing the assertion that Liability of the master for the act of his servant is based on the maxim *respondeat superior* is right.

67. Under Section 24A in the Consumer Protection Act, 1986, the District Forum, the State Commission or the National Commission shall not admit a complaint unless it is filed within two years from the date on which the cause of action has arisen.

70. A cheque (or check in American English) is a document that orders a bank to pay a specific amount of money from a person's account to the person in whose name the cheque is issued. The person writing the cheque, the *drawer*, has a transaction banking account (often called a current, cheque, chequing or checking account) where their money is held. The drawer writes the various details including the monetary amount, date, and a payee on the cheque, and signs it, ordering their bank, known as the *drawee*, to pay that person or company the amount of money stated.

Cheques are a type of bill of exchange and were developed as a way to make payments without the need to carry large amounts of money. Paper money evolved from promissory notes, another form of negotiable instrument similar to cheques in that they were originally a written order to pay the given amount to whomever had it in their possession (the "bearer").

Technically, a cheque is a negotiable instrument instructing a financial institution to pay a specific amount of a specific currency from a specified transactional account held in the drawer's name with that institution. Both the drawer and payee may be natural persons or legal entities.

Therefore, it will be incorrect to say that a cheque is a conditional order from the drawer of a cheque to the drawee bank to make payment of money only.

71. The doctrine of indoor management lays down that persons dealing with a company having satisfied themselves that the proposed transaction is not in its nature inconsistent with the memorandum and articles, are not bound to inquire the regularity of any internal proceeding. In other words, while persons contracting with a company are presumed to know the provisions of the contents of the memorandum and articles, they are entitled to assume that the provisions of the articles, they are entitled to assume that the officers of the company have observed the provisions of the articles.

Rama Corporation vs. *Proved Tin and General Investment Co.* where one T was the active director of the defendant company. He, purporting to act on behalf of his company, entered into a contract with the plaintiff company under which he took a cheque from the plaintiffs. The company's article contained a clause providing that "the directors may delegate any of their powers, other than the power to borrow and make calls to committees, consisting of such members of their body as they think fit". The board had not in fact delegated any of their powers to T and the plaintiffs had not inspected the defendants' articles and, therefore, did not know of the existence of power to delegate.

It was held that the defendant company was not bound by the agreement. Slade J', was of the opinion that knowledge of articles was essential. "A person who at the time of entering into a contract with a company has no knowledge of the company's articles of association, cannot rely on those articles as conferring ostensible or apparent authority on the agent of the company with whom he dealt." He could have relied on the power of delegation only if he knew that it existed and had acted on the belief that it must have been duly exercised.

72. As said in **Assertion (A)**, it is correct that for the proper exercise of the functions of a director, it is essential that he be disinterested, that is, be free from any conflicting interest. When a director befalls himself into the tangle of any conflict, he cannot discharge his duties properly as a director, because that conflict may eat into his potentialities of all kinds.

Conflict is injurious to mental and physical health, as given in **Reason (R)** is also correct because conflict always remains to be a factor behind deterioration of mental and physical health. However, **(R)** is not the correct legal reason of **(A)** as it has no relevance with what is said in **(A)**.

73. Following are the essentials of a partnership:

(*a*) A contract is made between two or more competent persons to place their money, effects, labour, and skill, or some or all of them, in lawful commerce or business, with the understanding that there shall be a proportional sharing of the profits and losses between/among them.

(*b*) An agreement to share profits must also be signed to prevent any sort of controversy and discordance in sharing the dividends and losses.

(*c*) Mutual agency is one of the essentials of partnership business that means rights of all partners in a partnership to act as agents for the normal business operations of the partnership, and their responsibility for their partners' business related (but not personal) actions.

(*d*) A lawful business is legally authorised, sanctioned, or allowed by law. A business against the law may face fear and failure and there may cause conflict among the partners in absence of law in the business.

Previous Paper (Solved)

UGC-NET-JRF & Assistant Professor Exam Law, June-2015

PAPER-II

Note: *This paper contains fifty* **(50)** *objective type questions of* **two (2)** *marks each.* **All** *questions are compulsory.*

1. Which of the following statement(s) is/are **incorrect**?

(*a*) In Keshavananda Bharati case, the Supreme Court has said that the Preamble to the constitution is a key to open the mind of the makers.

(*b*) "Socialist and Secular" words were added to the Preamble by 44th Amendment of the Constitution.

(*c*) Preamble can only be amended if it violates the Basic Structure of the Constitution.

(*d*) Since Preamble is not Articled so it is not the part of the Constitution.

Codes:

A. only (*b*)

B. (*c*) and (*d*)

C. (*a*), (*b*) and (*c*)

D. (*a*), (*b*), (*c*) and (*d*) all are incorrect

2. Match **List-I** with **List-II** and give the correct answer by using the codes given below the Lists:

List-I	**List-II**
(*a*) Article 329	(*i*) Golak Nath Vs. State of Punjab
(*b*) 10th Schedule Part-7	(*ii*) Keshavananda Bharati Vs. State of Kerala
(*c*) Article 31-C	(*iii*) Indira Nehru Gandhi Vs. Raj Narain
(*d*) Article 13(2)	(*iv*) Kihota Vs. Zachilhu

Codes:

	(*a*)	(*b*)	(*c*)	(*d*)
A.	(*ii*)	(*i*)	(*iii*)	(*iv*)
B.	(*iii*)	(*iv*)	(*ii*)	(*i*)
C.	(*iv*)	(*iii*)	(*i*)	(*ii*)
D.	(*i*)	(*ii*)	(*iv*)	(*iii*)

3. "If I was asked to name any particular Article in this Constitution as the most important an Article without which this constitution would be a nullity I could not refer to any other Article except this one (Article 32) .... It is the soul of the Constitution and the very heart of it".

Whose observations are these?

A. Justice P.N. Bhagwati

B. Dr. B.R. Ambedkar

C. Justice V.R. Krishna Iyer

D. Pundit Jawahar Lal Nehru

4. Which of the following statement(s) is/are **incorrect**?

(*a*) Chapter III on Fundamental Rights of the Constitution is based upon Bill of Rights of the U.S.A.

(*b*) 'Right to die' is a Fundamental Right Under Article 21 of the Constitution.

(*c*) Indian Constitution is a Complete Federal Constitution.

(*d*) Fundamental Rights can be waived under the Indian Constitution.

Codes:

A. only (*b*) B. (*c*) and (*d*) only

C. (*b*) and (*c*) only D. (*b*), (*c*) and (*d*)

5. Match **List-I** with **List-II** and give the correct answer by using the codes given below the Lists:

List-I (Principles)	List-II (Case Law)
(*a*) Equal work for Equal pay	(*i*) R.D. Shetty Vs. The International Airport Authority of India
(*b*) "Agencies or Instrumentalition" of the State are covered under the definition of State Under Article 12 of the Constitution	(*ii*) Rudal Sah Vs. State of Bihar
(*c*) Fundamental Rights and Directive Principles of state policy are supplementary and complimentary to each other	(*iii*) Randhir Singh Vs. Union of India
(*d*) Damages can be awarded for violation of Fundamental Rights Under Article 21 of the Constitution	(*iv*) Unikrishnan Vs. State of A.P.

Codes:

	(*a*)	(*b*)	(*c*)	(*d*)
A.	(*iii*)	(*i*)	(*iv*)	(*ii*)
B.	(*i*)	(*ii*)	(*iii*)	(*iv*)
C.	(*iv*)	(*iii*)	(*i*)	(*ii*)
D.	(*ii*)	(*iv*)	(*iii*)	(*i*)

6. Match **List-I** with **List-II** and give the correct answer by using the codes given under the Lists:

List-I (Added/Amended Provisions)	List-II (Amendment)
(*a*) Article 15 clause (4) providing for special provisions for socially and educationally backward classes.	(*i*) 25th Amendment Act, 1971
(*b*) Article 13 clause (4) providing for nothing shall apply to any constitutional amendment.	(*ii*) Constitution (85th Amendment) Act, 2001
(*c*) Article 16 clause (4 A) providing for consequential seniority with promotion to SC/ST.	(*iii*) Constitution (86th Amendment) Act, 2002
(*d*) Article 21 A providing for Right to Education as Fundamental Right.	(*iv*) Constitution (1st Amendment) Act, 1951

Codes:

	(*a*)	(*b*)	(*c*)	(*d*)
A.	(*i*)	(*ii*)	(*iii*)	(*iv*)
B.	(*iv*)	(*i*)	(*ii*)	(*iii*)
C.	(*iii*)	(*iv*)	(*i*)	(*ii*)
D.	(*ii*)	(*iii*)	(*iv*)	(*i*)

7. Assertion (A): Powers and functions are distributed between the two tiers of government under the written Constitution in India.

Reason (R): Union and the States are completely independent of each other under the Indian Constitution.

Codes:

A. (A) is correct and (R) is the correct explanation of (A).

B. (A) is correct, but (R) is not the correct explanation of (A).

C. (A) is correct, but (R) is wrong.

D. (A) is wrong, but (R) is correct.

8. Which of the following school in jurisprudence encompasses the 'functional approach'?

A. Philosophical school

B. Natural school

C. Sociological school

D. Historical school

9. A legal system which works to ensure a fair division of social benefits and burdens among the members of a community. It serves to secure a balance and equilibrium among the members of the society. What is the name of this legal system?
A. Distributive justice
B. Corrective justice
C. Remedial justice
D. Adversarial justice

10. Which of the following is **not correct** regarding Legislation and Precedent?
A. Legislation reflects the formal will of the state and precedent has its source in judgement of court
B. Legislation is the formal expression of new laws by legislature and precedent is the creation of law by recognition
C. Legislation is general declaration of law in abstract form and precedent is the manifestation of law in action
D. Legislations are based on the minority opinion and precedents are created or based for future decisions

11. Read **Assertion (A)** and **Reason (R)** and give the correct answer with the help of codes given below:

Assertion (A) : A person in possession of a thing is deemed to be the owner of the thing possessed.

Reason (R): Possession is as good as ownership.

Codes:
A. (A) and (R) are true, and (R) is the correct explanation of (A)
B. (A) and (R) are true, but (R) is not the correct explanation of (A)
C. (A) is true, but (R) is false
D. (A) is false, but (R) is true

12. Which of the following is not a 'kind of possession'?
A. *De facto* and *De jure*
B. Concurrent and duplicate
C. Corporeal and Immediate
D. Infinity and Antequity

13. Which of the following are elements of legal right?
A. Responsibility, Liability and Power
B. Subject, Object and Title
C. Liability, Title and Accountability
D. Accountability, Responsibility and Impartiality

14. "International Law or the Law of Nations is the name of body of rules which according to the usual definitions regulate the conduct of the states in their intercourse with one another". Who has given this definition?
A. Hack Warth
B. Charles G. Fenwick
C. Gray
D. Whiteman

15. In which of the following cases the Permanent Court of International Justice applied the general principle of Subrogation?
A. Chorzow Factory (indemnity case)
B. Case Concerning the Temple of Preah Vihear
C. Bracelona Traction Case
D. Mavrommatis Palestine Concessions Case

16. In which of the following cases Justice Gray remarked : "International law is a part of our law and must be ascertained and administered by the courts of justice of appropriate jurisdiction as often as questions of rights depending on it are duly presented for administration."
A. Nicaragua Vs. U.S.
B. Paquete Habana case
C. U.S. Vs. Schooner
D. U.S. Vs. Canada

17. Match **List-I** with **List-II** and give the correct answer by using the codes given below the Lists:

List-I (Charter of the United Nations) Titles	**List-II (Number of the Chapter)**
(*a*) Membership	(*i*) Chapter XIV
(*b*) The Security Council	(*ii*) Chapter II

(c) The International Court of justice	(iii) Chapter V
(d) The General Assembly	(iv) Chapter IV

Codes:

	(a)	(b)	(c)	(d)
A.	(i)	(ii)	(iii)	(iv)
B.	(ii)	(iii)	(iv)	(i)
C.	(ii)	(iii)	(i)	(iv)
D.	(iv)	(i)	(ii)	(iii)

18. Who has observed, "*De Facto* recognition is by nature provisional and may be made dependent upon conditions which the new entity has to comply. It differs from *De Jure* recognition, in that there is not yet a formal exchange of diplomatic representatives. *De Jure* recognition .... is complete, implying, full and normal diplomatic relations".

A. Lauterpacht
B. Philip C. Jessup
C. Oppenheim
D. Schwarzenberger

19. Assertion (A): International customs used to be the most important source of International Law in the past.

Reason (R): The development of custom is very slow and as compared to it rapid changes made through Treaties.

Codes:

A. Both (A) and (R) are correct and (R) is the correct explanation of (A)
B. Both (A) and (R) are correct, but (R) is not the correct explanation of (A)
C. (A) is correct, but (R) is false
D. (A) is false, but (R) is correct

20. Marriage under the Hindu Marriage Act, 1955 is:

A. Purely contractual
B. Purely sacramental
C. Semblance of contract and sacrament
D. Neither contractual nor sacramental

21. Match the **List-I** with **List-II** under the Hindu Marriage Act, 1955 and give the correct answer with the help of codes given below:

List-I	List-II
(a) Monogamy	(i) Section 10
(b) Judicial separation	(ii) Section 5
(c) Void Marriage	(iii) Section 11
(d) Divorce by Mutual Consent	(iv) Section 13-B

Codes:

	(a)	(b)	(c)	(d)
A.	(ii)	(i)	(iii)	(iv)
B.	(i)	(iii)	(iv)	(ii)
C.	(ii)	(iii)	(iv)	(i)
D.	(iv)	(iii)	(i)	(ii)

22. Which of the following are fault grounds of divorce under the Hindu Marriage Act, 1955?

(a) Extra marital sex
(b) Consent obtained by force or fraud
(c) Desertion
(d) Conversion to non Hindu religion

Codes:

A. (a), (b) and (c) B. (b), (c) and (d)
C. (b), (a) and (d) D. (a), (c) and (d)

23. A Muslim male is prohibited from marrying the following relations:

(a) Mother, Grand-mother (how high so ever)
(b) Daughter, Grand-daughter (how low so ever)
(c) Aunt, Great-aunt (how high so ever, whether paternal or maternal)
(d) Niece, Grand-niece (how low so ever)

Codes:

A. (a), (c) and (d) B. (d), (b) and (a)
C. (b), (c), (d) and (a) D. (c), (b) and (d)

24. The Dissolution of Muslim Marriage Act, 1939 makes available the following grounds of divorce to a Muslim woman married under Muslim Law:

(a) Seven years imprisonment of the husband.
(b) No maintenance by husband for 2 years.
(c) Whereabouts of the husband are not known for a period of 4 years.
(d) Failure of husband to perform marital obligation for a period of 3 years.

Codes :

A. (c), (b) and (d) B. (a), (b), (c) and (d)
C. (b), (c) and (a) D. (a), (b) and (d)

25. The ancient sources of Hindu Law include:
(*a*) Shruti
(*b*) Smriti
(*c*) Customs
(*d*) Digests and Commentaries
Codes :
A. (*b*), (*c*) and (*d*) B. (*d*), (*a*) and (*b*)
C. (*a*), (*b*) and (*c*) D. (*d*), (*c*), (*b*) and (*a*)

26. Originally under the Hindu Marriage Act, 1955, divorce was based on:
A. Fault theory only
B. Breakdown theory
C. Consent theory
D. Fault and consent theories

27. "A grocer supplied goods worth ₹ 6,000 on credit to A. In addition the grocer solicited a donation of ₹ 2,000 for his sons education to which A consented. Later A refused to pay both sums as he lost money on stock transaction". Which one of the following is correct while deciding the liability of A?
(*a*) A has already availed of the benefits in terms of goods supplied, hence consideration between the two binds A to pay.
(*b*) A is not bound to pay ₹ 2,000 as it a gift which is not enforceable in Law.
(*c*) A is liable to pay both sums as it is a promise between A and grocer.
(*d*) A is not liable to pay either of the sums as both of them are joint and not separate.
Codes:
A. (*a*) and (*b*) B. (*a*) and (*c*)
C. (*b*) and (*d*) D. (*c*) and (*d*)

28. "X makes an offer to Y. X dies the next day, but Y does not know of the death. Y sends a communication to the address of X accepting the offer". Is the agreement formed between the parties? Choose the correct answer.
(*a*) Requirements of offer followed by acceptance are met.
(*b*) Absence of knowledge of death will not invalidate the agreement.
(*c*) No meeting of minds which does not render it to agreement.
(*d*) Death of the offerer reduces it to nullity.
Codes:
A. (*a*) and (*c*) B. (*a*) and (*b*)
C. (*c*) and (*d*) D. (*b*) and (*d*)

29. Match items of **Group-A** with those of **Group-B** and choose the correct answer using codes:

Group-A	**Group-B**
(*a*) Food Corporation of India Vs. Ram Keshav Yadav	(*i*) Impossibility of performance
(*b*) Kedar Nath Bhattacharji Vs. Gori Mohammed	(*ii*) Capacity of minor to enter into contract
(*c*) K. Balakrishnan Vs. K. Kamalam	(*iii*) Offer and acceptance
(*d*) Satyabrata Goshe Vs. Mugneeram Bangar and Co.	(*iv*) Consideration

Codes:

	(*a*)	(*b*)	(*c*)	(*d*)
A.	(*iv*)	(*ii*)	(*iii*)	(*i*)
B.	(*iv*)	(*iii*)	(*ii*)	(*i*)
C.	(*iii*)	(*iv*)	(*ii*)	(*i*)
D.	(*i*)	(*ii*)	(*iii*)	(*iv*)

30. Agreement without consideration is valid under Indian Law. Among the following statements choose the one which is against this rule:
A. When agreements written exist on account of natural love and affection.
B. When the consideration is too inadequate.
C. Where the consideration is past one.
D. Where the consideration is from third party.

31. Choose the **incorrect** combination:
A. Proposal + Acceptance = Promise
B. Promise + Consideration = Agreement
C. Agreement + Enforceability = Contract
D. Proposal + Consideration = Acknowledgment

32. Match items of **Group-A** with **Group-B** and answer the correct one given in the code:

Group-A	**Group-B**
(*a*) Doctrine of unjust enrichment	(*i*) Section 11 of Contract Act
(*b*) Doctrine of absolute contract	(*ii*) Section 56

(*c*) Doctrine of Estoppel (*iii*) Section 72
(*d*) Doctrine of Pari Delicto (*iv*) Section 23

Codes:

	(*a*)	(*b*)	(*c*)	(*d*)
A.	(*i*)	(*iii*)	(*ii*)	(*iv*)
B.	(*ii*)	(*iii*)	(*i*)	(*iv*)
C.	(*iii*)	(*ii*)	(*i*)	(*iv*)
D.	(*iv*)	(*ii*)	(*iii*)	(*i*)

33. "Just as the criminal law consists of a body of rules establishing specific offence, so the law of torts consists of a body of rules establishing specific injuries". Who stated this?

A. Austin B. Salmond
C. Winfield D. Pollock

34. Consider the following elements:
(*a*) Infringement of a legal right
(*b*) Any damage
(*c*) Existence of a legal right
(*d*) Legal damages

Right to claim damages in tort would arise only if:

Codes:
A. (*d*), (*b*) and (*a*) are present
B. (*b*) and (*d*) are present
C. (*a*), (*c*) and (*d*) are present
D. (*b*), (*c*) and (*a*) are present

35. Assertion (A) : X opens a food court in front of Y's 'food joint'. All the customers of Y patronise X. Y cannot claim damages from X.

Reason (R): There is a Latin maxim '*damnum sine injuria*'.

Give the answer using the following Codes:

Codes:
A. (A) is true but (R) is false
B. (A) is false but (R) is true
C. Both (A) and (R) are true but (R) is not the correct explanation of (A)
D. Both (A) and (R) are true and (R) is the correct explanation of (A)

36. In contributory negligence:
A. Only one party is negligent and other has not taken due care.
B. Both parties have contributed to negligence equally.
C. Lack of care is equal on both sides.
D. One party is negligent resulting in injury while the other has taken due care.

37. Match **List-I** with **List-II** and select the correct answer using the codes given below:

List-I (Principle)	**List-II (Associated Case)**
(*a*) Absolute Liability	(*i*) Gloucester Grammar School
(*b*) *Damnum sine injuria*	(*ii*) Ashby *vs.* White
(*c*) *Injuria sine damnum*	(*iii*) Stanley *vs.* Powel
(*d*) Inevitable accident	(*iv*) Ryland *vs.* Fletcher

Codes:

	(*a*)	(*b*)	(*c*)	(*d*)
A.	(*i*)	(*ii*)	(*iii*)	(*iv*)
B.	(*ii*)	(*iii*)	(*iv*)	(*i*)
C.	(*iv*)	(*ii*)	(*i*)	(*iii*)
D.	(*iii*)	(*i*)	(*ii*)	(*iv*)

38. Which one of the following is not a valid defence in tort?
A. Vis major
B. Volenti non fit injuria
C. Inevitable accident
D. *Scienti not fit injuria*

39. Fill in the gap:
The *actus reus* of omission commands ....
A. There must be moral duty.
B. There should be legal duty to act.
C. The state has option to fix criminal liability.
D. The act performed is due to unavoidable accident.

40. Several persons can be vicariously liable for the Criminal act of another provided there is prior meeting of mind between the persons. Which of the objectives of Criminal Law is applied in such a Case?
A. A pre-arranged plan with intention of performing the act.
B. A pre-arranged plan for causing injury.

C. A pre-arranged plan to kill the deceased whether fatal blow was given by that accused or not.

D. The pre-arranged plan must be incompatible with the innocence of the accused.

41. The applicability of the principle on common object has two essential features. One purpose is that the object must import a high degree of probability; while the other purpose is:

A. An act committed immediately connected to the common object of the assembly.

B. The member must have prior knowledge that there is possibility of the happening of the act.

C. The Co-accused knows that he will be responsible for offence that is likely to be committed.

D. The object was to cause simple injury but a fatal injury resulted.

42. In which of the cases the measures of self-defence is considered to be proportionate to the quantum of force by the person accused for an offence?

A. Aggression

B. Accident

C. Apprehension

D. Assault of harmless nature

43. Ignorance of law does not permit acquittal as it is built against justification of a Crime while in extreme cases it allows:

A. Pardon

B. Suspended sentence

C. Deferred sentence

D. Paper sentence

44. In which of the circumstances an inchoate instigation to Commit a Crime is said to be incomplete?

A. Withdrew from the act after instigation.

B. The letter posted could not reach the person so sent.

C. When the purported crime is different from that of instigation.

D. When the crime results through the conspiracy of another person.

45. Read Assertion (A) and Reason (R) and answer using codes given below:

Assertion (A): Managers collectively bargain with labourers to get cheapest labour rates and derive maximum benefit from labourers.

Reason (R): Management must manage to maximise profits for company and give maximum dividend to shareholders. Management must be economically sound.

Codes:

A. Both (A) and (R) are correct and (R) is correct reason of (A).

B. (A) is right, but (R) is wrong.

C. (A) is wrong, but (R) is right.

D. Both (A) and (R) are correct, but (R) is not the correct answer for (A).

46. An Independent Industrial Relation Commission to provide labour welfare in India was recommended by:

A. Ramanujam Committee

B. Madhavan Committee

C. Vasudevan Committee

D. Santhanam Committee

47. Match **List-I** with **List-II**, using codes given below. Answer in context of rights and liabilities of trade unions:

List-I	**List-II**
(*a*) Convey *vs*. Wade	(*i*) Role and right of minority trade unions
(*b*) Rohtas Industries Staff Union *vs*. Bihar	(*ii*) Inducement to break a contract without violence is permissible
(*c*) Chairman, S.B.I. *vs*. Orissa Bank Association	(*iii*) Amplification of scope of immunity provisions for striking employees
(*d*) Food Corporation of India Staff Union *vs*. F.C.I.	(*iv*) Secret ballot is valid as a credible system for determining the representative character of a trade union in a multi union establishment

Codes:

	(a)	(b)	(c)	(d)
A.	(iii)	(ii)	(i)	(iv)
B.	(ii)	(iii)	(i)	(iv)
C.	(iii)	(ii)	(iv)	(i)
D.	(i)	(iv)	(ii)	(iii)

48. Read Assertion (A) and Reason (R) and answer using codes given below:

Assertion (A) : Civil servants are engaged in the task of sovereign and regal task of the Government and as such they can be included with the definition of 'workman' in an 'industry' as contemplated in Section 2(s) and 2(j) of the Industrial Disputes Act.

Reason (R): Because Tamil Nadu, N.G.O. Union Vs. Registrar of Trade Unions decided so.

Codes:

A. (A) and (R) are correct, and (R) is the correct reason of (A)

B. (A) and (R) are correct, but (R) is not the correct reason of (A)

C. (A) is correct, but (R) is wrong

D. Both (A) and (R) are incorrect

49. Which of the following statements, is **correct**?

A. A Trade Union cannot constitute a separate or political fund under Section 6(1) of the Trade Union Act.

B. The general fund of a trade union cannot be utilised for the purpose stipulated in Section 15 of Trade Union Act.

C. Trade Unions are not immune from civil and criminal liability.

D. Certain officers of trade union, who are styled as protected workmen, are given certain safeguards in the matter of alteration of service conditions and termination of service during the pendency of any proceeding in respect of an industrial dispute.

50. Which of the following is **incorrect**?

A. An Employee having less than one year of continuous service will not be retrenched.

B. One months notice with reasons and one months wages in lieu of such notice is necessary.

C. Employee is entitled to compensation equivalent to 15 days average pay for every completed one year.

D. Serving of notice to appropriate Government or any such authority is not mandatory

ANSWERS

1	2	3	4	5	6	7	8	9	10
D	B	B	D	A	B	C	C	A	D
11	**12**	**13**	**14**	**15**	**16**	**17**	**18**	**19**	**20**
C	D	B	C	D	B	C	D	B	C
21	**22**	**23**	**24**	**25**	**26**	**27**	**28**	**29**	**30**
A	D	C	B	D	A	A	B	B	B
31	**32**	**33**	**34**	**35**	**36**	**37**	**38**	**39**	**40**
D	C	B	C	D	A	D	D	B	C
41	**42**	**43**	**44**	**45**	**46**	**47**	**48**	**49**	**50**
A	C	A	C	C	A	B	D	D	D

SOME SELECTED EXPLANATORY ANSWERS

1. (*a*) Kesavananda Bharati Sripadagalvaru and Ors. *vs*. State of Kerala and Anr. (case citation: (1973)4 SCC 225) is a landmark decision of the Supreme Court of India that outlined the Basic Structure doctrine of the Constitution. Through this doctrine, Justice Hans Raj Khanna asserted that the Constitution possesses a basic structure of constitutional principles and values.

(*b*) The words "Socialist and Secular" were added to the Preamble by 42nd Amendment of the Constitution. The Preamble changed through 42nd Amendment in 1976, reads "We, the people of India, having solemnly resolved to constitute India into a Sovereign Socialist Secular Democratic Republic..."

(*c*) Adopted on 26 November 1949 by the Constituent Assembly and brought into effect from 26 January 1950, Preamble to the Constitution of India is a brief introductory statement that sets out the guiding purpose and principles of the document. The Preamble can be referred to as the preface, which highlights the essence of the entire Constitution.

(*d*) In Beru Bari case, the Supreme Court of India had declared that the Preamble is not an integral part of the Indian Constitution, and therefore it is not enforceable in a court of law. However, in the Kesavananda case, the Supreme Court of India overruled its earlier decisions and recognised that the Preamble may be used to interpret ambiguous areas of the Constitution where differing interpretations present themselves. In the 1995 case of Union Government *vs* LIC of India also, the Supreme Court has once again held that Preamble is the integral part of the Constitution.

2. (*a*) The Parliament passed the 39th Constitutional Amendment, which introduced and added a new Article 329A to the Constitution of India as a repercussion of Indira Nehru Gandhi Vs. Raj Narain case when Raj Narain had filed a case in Allahabad High Court against Indira Gandhi for her winning the election by malpractice. Article 392A stated that the election of the Prime Minister and the Speaker cannot be challenged in any court in the country. It can be rather challenged before a committee formed by the Parliament itself. Despite validating the election of Indira Gandhi, the Supreme Court declared the 39th Amendment to be unconstitutional as it violated the basic structure of the Constitution. The 39th Amendment was made to validate with retrospective effect the election of the then Prime Minister which was set aside by the Allahabad High Court.

(*b*) Commonly known as the Anti-Defection Law, the Tenth Schedule to the Constitution of India contains provisions as to disqualification of a Member of Parliament or a State Legislature on the ground of defection. The Tenth Schedule has 6 paragraphs in effect. Paragraph 7 was declared invalid for want of ratification in accordance with the proviso to clause (2) of article 368 by the Supreme Court in *Kihoto Hollohon v. Zachilhu* and others (1992) 1 SCC 309. Paragraph 3 was repealed by the 91st Amendment in 2004.

(*c*) Article 31-C was inserted by the 25th Constitutional Amendment to get over the difficulties placed by judicial decisions in the way of giving effect to the Directive Principles in Part IV. It provided immunity from any challenge on the grounds of violation of Article 14, 19 and 31 any law enacted for implementing the directives in clause (*b*) and (*c*) of Article 39. In

Keshavananda Bharati case, the issue was whether the Article 31-C survived after the judgment struck down a part of this Article in 1973, as it originally stood. However, in the Keshavananda Bharati case (1973), the Supreme Court held the provision in bold and italics to be valid.

(*d*) Golaknath *vs*. State of Punjab (1967 AIR 1643, 1967 SCR (2) 762), or simply the Golaknath case, was a 1967 Indian Supreme Court case, in which the Court ruled that Parliament could not curtail any of the Fundamental Rights in the Constitution.

3. Article 32 is referred to as the "Constitutional Remedy" for enforcement of Fundamental Rights. Dr. B.R. Ambedkar described this Article as the most important one, without which the Constitution would be reduced to nullity. It is also referred to as the heart and soul of the Constitution. By including Article 32 in the Fundamental Rights, the Supreme Court has been made the protector and guarantor of these Rights.

4. (*b*) Article 21 of the Constitution of India 1949 provides the provision of protection of life and personal liberty. No person shall be deprived of his life or personal liberty except according to procedure established by law.

(*c*) Though up to a certain extent the Constitution of India is federal in nature, it is unitary in spirit. The common features of a federation such as written Constitution, supremacy of Constitution, rigidity of Constitution, two governments, division of powers bicameralism and independent judiciary as well as unitary features like single Constitution, single citizenship, integrated judiciary, flexible Constitution, a strong Centre, appointment of state governor by the Centre, All-India Services, Emergency Provisions etc can be seen in Indian Constitution. This unique combination makes it Quasi-Federal but not Complete Federal.

(*d*) As far as waiving of rights or privileges is concerned, the doctrine of waiver explains clearly that a person, along with the entitlement to a right or privilege, has the freedom to waive that right or privilege. It is voluntary abandonment of a known existing legal right or privilege. Waiver is certain agreement between the parties and only a party fully knowing of his right agrees not to assert a right for a consideration. Once a person has so waived his right, he would not be allowed to claim it later on but this is not true when it comes the case of the fundamental rights because in any case they cannot be waived.

6. (*a*) Article 15 clause (4) providing for special provisions for socially and educationally backward classes is the result of the First Amendment of the Constitution of India, officially known as The Constitution (First Amendment) Act, 1951 that made several changes to the Fundamental Rights provisions of the Constitution. Thus, nothing in clause 4 of Article 15 or in clause 2 of Article 29 shall prevent the State from making any special provision for the advancement of any socially and educationally backward classes of citizens or for the Scheduled Castes and the Scheduled Tribes.

(*b*) Clause 4 of Article 13 providing nothing shall apply to any amendment of the Constitution made under article 368, is the result of the 25th Amendment of the Constitution of India officially known as The Constitution (Twenty-fifth Amendment) Act, 1971. This Amendment curtailed the right to property, and permitted the acquisition of private property by the government for public use, on the payment of compensation that would be determined by the Parliament and not the courts.

(*c*) Clause 4 A of Article 16 is the result of the 85th Amendment of the Constitution of India, officially known as The

Constitution (Eighty-fifth Amendment) Act, 2001. It enables the State to make any provision for reservation in favour of the ST and SC, giving them the benefit of consequential seniority in matters of promotion to any class or classes of posts in the services under the State, if they are not adequately represented.

(*d*) Article 21 A is the result of 86th Amendment of the Constitution of India, officially known as The Constitution (Eighty-sixth Amendment) Act, 2002. It made the Right to Education a Fundamental Right, by providing the right to free and compulsory education to all children between the ages of six and fourteen years. It also altered a Directive Principle of the Constitution for the Constitution to provide for the "early childhood care and education for all children until they complete the age of six years".

7. The government of India is based on a tiered system, in which the Constitution of India delineates the subjects on which each tier of government has executive powers. The Constitution originally provided for a two-tier system of government, the Union government (also known as the Central Government), representing the Union of India, and the State governments. Later, a third tier was added in the form of Panchayats and Municipalities.

India is a federal union of states comprising twenty-nine states and seven union territories. The Constitution of India distributes the sovereign powers exercisable with respect to the territory of any state between the Union and that State. Both Union Government and the State governments are given certain power to exercise as per Constitution of India and they depend upon each other on many matters. Thus, it will be wrong to say that Union and the States are completely independent of each other under the Indian Constitution.

8. Structural functionalism, or simply functionalism, is a framework for building theory that sees society as a complex system whose parts work together to promote solidarity and stability. This approach looks at society through a macro-level orientation, which is a broad focus on the social structures that shape society as a whole, and believes that society has evolved like organisms. This approach looks at both social structure and social functions. Functionalism addresses society as a whole in terms of the function of its constituent elements; namely norms, customs, traditions, and institutions. Thus, each social structure has social functions, or consequences for the operation of society as a whole.

9. Distributive justice is such legal system that concerns the nature of a socially just allocation of goods in a society. A society in which incidental inequalities in outcome do not arise would be considered a society guided by the principles of distributive justice. The concept includes the available quantities of goods, the process by which goods are to be distributed, and the resulting allocation of the goods to the members of the society.

10. Legislations are not based on the minority opinion. Legislation means to making law, and laws can be made by a collective legislature or by a single legislator, resulting in statutes, by executive through decrees and regulations, or by judges through binding precedent, normally in common law jurisdictions. Precedent is one of the sources of law and it is not created or based for future decisions. The judgements passed by some of the learned jurists become another significant source of law. When there is no legislature on a particular point, which arises in changing conditions, the judges depend on their own sense of right and wrong and decide the disputes. Such decisions become authority or guide for subsequent cases of a similar nature and they are called precedents.

11. A person in possession of anything or any property is deemed to be the owner of the thing or property possessed but legally he cannot be the full-fledged owner, because a property may be given to someone on lease or rent. Thus, the person possessing that thing or property on lease or rent may be regarded as the possessor as he is possessing for his use but he cannot be the ultimate owner of that property just by possession. Thus, possession does not always imply ownership. Like ownership, the possession of things is commonly regulated by states under property law.

12. Infinity and Antiquity cannot be a kind of possession because they are different possessive aspects. Infinity means something infinite or countless while antiquity alludes to something antique or the practice of very old things.

13. Legally, the discussion of property depends on identifying the objects (things) and subjects (persons and groups). In property law, a title is a bundle of rights in a piece of property in which a party may own either a legal interest or equitable interest. The rights in the bundle may be separated and held by different parties. It may also refer to a formal document, such as a deed, that serves as evidence of ownership. Thus, subject, object and title are elements of legal right.

14. Sir Gerald Gray Fitzmaurice GCMG QC (24 October 1901 – 1982), a British barrister and judge, was a member of the Permanent Court of Arbitration between 1964 and 1973. He continued to be a Senior Judge of the International Court of Justice from 1967 to 1973, before becoming a Judge of the European Court of Human Rights at Strasbourg in 1974.

15. From 30 August 1924, Mavrommatis Palestine Concessions is known as a decision of the Permanent Court of International Justice. In 1914, the authorities of the Ottoman Empire had with the Greek entrepreneurs Mavrommatis, a concession agreement on the construction of a tram and the expansion of the water and electricity supply in Jerusalem closed. Due to the First World War, the work was delayed, after the end of which was Palestine under the administration of Great Britain. The British government refused to uphold the contract with Mavrommatis and awarded the concession to a British entrepreneur. Article nine of XII Additional Protocol to the Treaty of Lausanne, however, stipulated that until 1914 award concessions on the part of the successor states (in this case, Palestine and its government mandate) were observed. After it came between Greece and the United Kingdom through negotiations, no agreement is reached, Greece rose to safeguard the rights of its nationals Mavrommatis' action before the International Court of Justice.

16. Paquete Habana; The Lola, 175 U.S. 677 (1900), was a landmark case in United States Supreme Court that reversed an earlier court decision allowing the capture of fishing vessels under Prize. Its importance rests on the fact that it integrated Customary international law with American law, perhaps the quintessential position of those who hold a monist perspective of international law.

17. (*a*) Chapter II of the United Nations Charter deals with membership of the UN organisation. Membership is open to the original signatories and "all other peace-loving states which accept the obligations contained in the present Charter and, in the judgement of the Organisation, are able and willing to carry out these obligations."

(*b*) Chapter V of the United Nations Charter contains provisions establishing the United Nations Security Council that is established with the composition of 5 permanent members and 10 non-permanent members. The 10 non-permanent members are elected for a term of 2 years by the General Assembly.

(*c*) Chapter XIV of the United Nations Charter deals with the International Court of Justice. Most provisions related to the World Court are contained in the Statute of the International Court of Justice, which is annexed to the Charter. Chapter XIV is analogous to Article 14 (and to some extent, Article 13) of the Covenant of the League of Nations.

(*d*) Chapter IV of the United Nations Charter contains the Charter's provisions dealing with the UN General Assembly, specifically its composition, functions, powers, voting and procedures. The chapter on the UN General Assembly appears in the Charter before the chapters on the other five principal organs (UN Security Council, UN Economic and Social council, Trusteeship Council, International Court of Justice, and UN Secretariat).

18. Though born in Heilbronn, Germany in 1908, George Schwarzenberger became a British national. He was a distinguished scholar of law. But after his migration from Germany to England, he changed his scholarly area from international law to international relations.

19. Sources of International Law include treaties, international customs, general principles of law as recognised around the world, the decisions of national and lower courts, and scholarly writings. Some treaties are the result of codifying existing customary law, such as laws governing th global commons, and *jus ad bellum*. While the purpose is to establish a code of general application, its effectiveness depends upon the number of states that ratify or accede to the particular convention. Thus, when a customary rule remains in the process of development, its incorporation in a multilateral treaty may have the effect of consolidating or crystallising the law in the form of the rule.

20. Of course, marriage under the Hindu Marriage Act, 1955 is semblance of contract and sacrament but the Hindu marriage contemplated by the Act hardly remains sacramental. The Act has brought in some changes of far reaching consequences, which have undermined the sacramental nature of marriage and rendered it contractual in nature to a great extent. A Hindu marriage is now not so much concerned with religion. It is more a result of mutual consent than sacramental [Sections 5(ii), (iii), 11 to 13 and 7].

21. (*a*) Section 5(i) of The Hindu Marriage Act, 1955 elucidates that a marriage may be solemnised between any two Hindus, if neither party has a spouse living at the time of the marriage. Thus, this section allows monogamy at a time.

(*b*) Section 10(i) in The Hindu Marriage Act, 1955 elucidates that either party to a marriage, whether solemnised before or after the commencement of this Act, may present a petition praying for a decree for judicial separation on any of the grounds specified in sub-section (i) of section 13, and in the case of a wife also on any of the grounds specified in sub-section (ii) thereof, as grounds on which a petition for divorce might have been presented.

(*c*) Section 11 of Hindu Marriage Act, 1955 deals with nullity of marriage and divorce – Void marriages, *i.e.* any marriage solemnised after the commencement of this Act shall be null and void and may, on a petition presented by either party thereto, against the other party by so declared by a decree of nullity if it contravenes any one of the conditions specified in clauses (i), (iv) and (v).

(*d*) Section 13-B of the Hindu Marriage Act, 1955 provides for the couple seeking divorce through mutual consent to wait for a period of six months after making first joint application for divorce. It is only after the expiry of the six months that the couple can move second application for the dissolution of their marriage.

23. As per Muslim personal law, a Muslim male is allowed to marry only those females who are *ghair-mehram* to him. He cannot marry a *mehram* female. *Mehram* refers to all those females whom a Muslim male cannot marry at any time in his life whatsoever. For a Muslim male, the relations like mother, grandmother, daughter, granddaughter, aunt, great-aunt, niece, grandniece – all come in the category of *mehram*.

24. The Dissolution of Muslim Marriage Act, 1939 extends to the whole of India except the State of Jammu and Kashmir. A woman married under Muslim personal law shall be entitled to obtain a decree for the dissolution of her marriage on any of nine grounds, four of which are given here in the answers (*a*), (*b*), (*c*) and (*d*).

25. Hindu law is a set of personal laws governing the social conditions of Hindus (such as marriage and divorce, adoption, inheritance, minority and guardianship, family matters, etc.). Following are the ancient sources of Hindu Law:

Shruti: Literally, Shruti means whatever is heard. The word is derived from the root "shru" meaning 'to hear'. In theory, it is the primary and the most vital source of Hindu law and is believed to be the language of the divine revelation through the sages.

Smritis: Smriti is derived from the root word "smri" which means 'to remember'. Traditionally, Smritis contain those portions of the Shrutis, which the sages forgot in their original form and the notion whereby they wrote in their own language with the help of their memory. Thus, the basis of the Smritis is Shrutis but they are human works.

Digests and Commentaries: After Shrutis, there came the era of commentators and digests. Commentaries (Tika or Bhashya) and Digests (Nibandhs) covered a period of more than thousands years from 7th century to 1800 AD. In the first part of the period, most of the commentaries were written on the Smritis but in the later period of the works were in the nature of digests containing a synthesis of the various Smritis and explaining and reconciling the various contradictions.

Custom: Custom is regarded as the third source of Hindu law. From the earliest period, custom (achara) is regarded as the highest 'dharma'. As defined by the Judicial Committee, custom signifies a rule, which in a particular family or in a particular class or district has from long usage, obtained the force of law. Custom is a principle source and its position is next to the Shrutis and Smritis but usage of custom prevails over the Smritis. It is superior to written law. However, there are certain characteristics, which need to be fulfilled to declare the validation of custom.

26. Before the commencement of the Hindu Marriage Act, 1955, there were Acts in some of the States providing for divorce in certain circumstances, viz., the Bombay Hindu Divorce Act (22 of 1947), the Madras Hindu (Bigamy, Prevention and Divorce) Act (6 of 1949), and the Saurashtra Hindu Divorce Act (30 of 1952). These Acts were repealed by Section 30 of the Hindu Marriage Act 1955. Under the Hindu Marriage Act 1955, initially, adultery, cruelty, and desertion were not made ground of divorce but of judicial separation. These grounds were based on the fault theory of divorce.

29. (*a*) It is a case between Food Corporation of India (FCI) and its employee Ram Keshav Yadav. The Appellant – FCI introduced a scheme for granting compassionate appointment to dependants of departmental workers, who died while in service or who were retired by FCI on medical grounds Vide Circular dated 2.2.1977. By a subsequent circular dated 3.7.1996, the said benefit of compassionate appointment was extended to dependants of departmental workers who sought voluntary retirement on medical grounds at their own request, subject to the conditions stipulated in the said circular. So Sri Ram Keshav Yadav appealed in consideration of his retirement on medical ground that since his health did not allow him to continue his service of such a hard work, his son may please be provided with an employment in his place. Actually, it was the case of consideration and that's why Sri Ram Keshav Yadav appealed for consideration of his case on medical ground.

(*b*) Kedarnath Bhattacharya (alias Kumar Shanu) Vs Gori Mohammed was the case in which the defendant had agreed to subscribe Rs. 100 towards the construction of a Town Hall at Howrah in West Bengal. The Secretary, on the faith of the promise, called for plans and entrusted the work to contractors and undertook liability to pay them. The Defendant refused to pay the promised amount.

(*c*) The only substantial question of law involved in this appeal is whether the appellant, who was minor on the date of execution of the gift-deed dated 24.9.1945, can be held to have legally accepted the property in suit gifted to him and the said gift-deed was irrevocable. So the appellant shall hereinafter be described as 'the donee' and his deceased mother as the 'doner'.

(*d*) In Satyabrata Ghosh Vs. Mugneeram Bangar and Co. case, Section 56 occurs in Chapter IV of the Indian Contract Act, which relates to performance of contracts and it purports to deal with one circumstance under which performance of a contract is excused or dispensed with on the ground of the contract being void. A contract to do an act which after the contract is made, becomes impossible, or, by reason of some event which the promise maker could not prevent, unlawful, becomes void when the act becomes impossible or unlawful.

30. Agreement without consideration is invalid unless it is in writing and registered or is a promise to compensate for something done or is a promise to pay a debt barred by limitation law. If the consideration is too inadequate, it will be considered against this rule.

31. When the person to whom the proposal is made signifies his assent thereto, the proposal is said to be accepted. A proposal, when accepted, becomes a promise, which justifies the combination of Proposal + Acceptance = Promise. Every promise and every set of promises, forming the consideration for each other, is an agreement that justifies the combination of Promise + Consideration = Agreement. Similarly, an agreement enforceable by law becomes a contract, which justifies the combination of Agreement + Enforceability = Contract. However, when the combination Proposal + Consideration = Acknowledgement is brought into this purview, it is found to be incorrect.

33. Alexander Elliot Anderson Salmond (born 31 December 1954) is a Scottish politician who served as the fourth First Minister of Scotland from 2007 to 2014. Currently, he is a member of both the Scottish and United Kingdom parliaments.

34. A tort is a civil breach committed against another in which the injured party can sue for damages. In personal injury cases, the injured party will attempt to receive compensation with the representation of a personal injury lawyer in order to recover from the damages incurred. Tort law decides whether a person should be held legally responsible for injury against another, and what type of compensation the injured party is entitled to. Thus, right to claim damages in tort would arise only if infringement of a legal right; existence of a legal right or legal damages, not in case of any sort of damages.

35. In this case, Y cannot claim the damages caused by X because it is a case of *damnum sine injuria*. The term 'damnum sine injuria' means, "there may be an injury inflicted without any act of injustice." There is another term for such case that is *damnum absque injuria*, which means damage or harm without an injury in the legal sense. In other words, a loss or injury to someone which does not give that person a legal right to sue the person causing the loss.

36. In legal definition, Contributory Negligence means that if a person was injured in part due to his/her own negligence (his/her negligence "contributed" to the accident), the injured party would not be entitled to collect any damages (money) from another party who supposedly caused the accident. Under this rule, a badly injured person who was only slightly negligent could not win in court against a very negligent defendant.

37. (*i*) Gloucester Grammar School case is a *Damnum sine injuria* as two masters of the said school brought an action of trespass against another master. They stated they were appointed to have the government of the scholars of the school, and to teach children and others there. But the defendant set up another school in the midst of the town, and thereby the plaintiffs who had been used to obtain either forty pence of two shillings for the quarter's schooling of the pupil could now obtain only twelve pence. Hence, no action lays.

(*ii*) *Injuria sine damno* is used in law of torts and is related to damages. The meaning of this adage is infringement of an absolute private right without any actual loss or damage. Here the actual damage means physical loss in terms of money, comfort, health etc. In the case of Ashby Vs. White, the defendant, the returning officer, wrongfully refused to register a duly tendered vote of plaintiff, a legally qualified voter, at a parliamentary election and the candidate for whom the vote was tendered was elected, and no loss was suffered by the rejection of the vote. Here the defendant spitefully refused to register the vote of plaintiff. This is considered as legal damage caused to plaintiff, as it is infringement of fundamental rights of a person who has the right to vote and is unconstitutional.

(*iii*) Absolute liability is a standard of legal liability found in tort and criminal law of various legal jurisdictions. In a crime of absolute liability or strict liability, an accused could be guilty even if there was no intention to commit a crime. Powell was originally charged with conspiring with Judd Powell, Jr., his brother, and Mark Stanley to possess with intent to distribute marijuana, in violation of 21 U.S.C. §§ 841(a)(1) and 846. A second count alleged possession of 3,575 pounds of marijuana with intent to distribute, in violation of 21 U.S.C. § 841(a)(1). Judd Powell and Stanley were also indicted on this count. After a jury trial, Powell was convicted on the conspiracy charge and acquitted on the possession charge. He appealed and this court reversed his conspiracy conviction because of prejudicial errors concerning the admission of evidence and the denial of a continuance.

(*iv*) Rylands *vs* Fletcher [1868] UKHL 1 was a decision by the House of Lords which established a new area of English tort law. Rylands employed contractors to build a reservoir, playing no active role in its construction. When the contractors discovered a series of old coal shafts improperly filled with debris, they chose to continue work rather than properly blocking them up. The result was that on 11 December 1860, shortly after being filled for the first time, Rylands's reservoir burst and flooded a neighbouring mine, run by Fletcher, causing £937 worth of damage. Fletcher brought a claim under negligence, through which the case eventually went to the Exchequer of Pleas. The majority ruled in favour of Rylands; however, Bramwell B, dissenting, argued that the claimant had the right to enjoy his land free of interference from water, and that as a result the defendant was guilty of trespass and the commissioning of a nuisance. Bramwell's argument was affirmed, both by the Court of Exchequer Chamber and the House of Lords, leading to the development of the "Rule in *Rylands v Fletcher*"; that "the person who for his own purposes brings on his lands and collects and keeps there anything likely to do mischief if it escapes, must keep it in at his peril, and, if he does not do so, is *prima facie* answerable for all the damage which is the natural consequence of its escape".

39. The terms *actus reus* and *mens rea* developed in English Law are derived from the principle stated by Edward Coke, namely, *actus non facit reum nisi mens sit rea*, which means "an act that does not make a person guilt unless his/her mind is also guilty." Hence, th general test of guilt is one that requires proo of fault, culpability or blameworthiness bot in thought and in action. *Actus reus* omissio involves a failure to engage in a necessar bodily movement resulting in injury.

42. An apprehension of attack is an element o the defence or self-defence that can be usec in a criminal prosecution for assault anc battery, manslaughter, or murder. A individual who acts under apprehension o attack does not have to fear injury. It i sufficient that there is a likelihood of actua injury to justify the person's taking steps tc protect himself or herself.

43. *Ignorantia juris non excusat* or *ignorantic legis neminem excusat* (Latin for "ignorance o the law excuses not" and "ignorance of law excuses no one" respectively) is a lega principle holding that a person who is unaware of a law may not escape liability for violating that law merely because he or she was unaware of its content. However, in extreme cases in which the court finds that, the accused deserve acquittal, then he/she may be pardoned.

PAPER-III

Note: ***This paper contains seventy five (75) objective type questions of two (2) marks each. All questions are compulsory.***

1. Through 42nd Amendment to the constitution which of the following 'Expressions' were added to the Preamble?

(*a*) Sovereign (*b*) Socialist
(*c*) Secular (*d*) Integrity

Codes:

A. Only (*a*), (*b*) and (*c*)
B. Only (*b*), (*c*) and (*d*)
C. Only (*a*), (*c*) and (*d*)
D. (*a*), (*b*), (*c*) and (*d*)

2. Match **List-I** with **List-II** and give the correct answer by using the codes given below the lists:

List-I	**List-II**
(*a*) Compensation to persons killed in "Fake Encounter"	(*i*) Delhi Domestic working women's forum *vs.* Union of India
(*b*) Compensation to Rape Victims	(*ii*) Bodhisathwa Gautam *vs.* Shubhra Chakraborty
(*c*) Interim Compensation to Rape Victims	(*iii*) People's Union for Civil liberties *vs.* Union of India
(*d*) Protection against illegal arrest, detentions and custodial deaths.	(*iv*) Joginder Kumar *vs.* State of U.P.

Codes:

	(a)	(b)	(c)	(d)
A.	(iv)	(iii)	(ii)	(i)
B.	(iii)	(i)	(ii)	(iv)
C.	(ii)	(iv)	(i)	(iii)
D.	(i)	(ii)	(iii)	(iv)

3. Match **List-I** with **List-II** and give the correct answer by using the codes given below the Lists:

List-I	List-II
(a) Right to speak includes Right not to speak	(i) R. Rajagopal *vs.* State of T.N.
(b) Government has no monopoly on electronic media	(ii) Tata Press Ltd. *vs.* Mahanagar Telephone Nigam Ltd.
(c) Commercial Advertisement is part of Freedom of Speech and Expression	(iii) Secretary, Ministry I and B *vs.* Cricket Association of Bengal (W.B.)
(d) Government cannot impose prior restraint on publication of defamatory material against its officials	(iv) Bijoe Emmanuel *vs.* State of Kerala

Codes:

	(a)	(b)	(c)	(d)
A.	(iv)	(iii)	(ii)	(i)
B.	(iii)	(ii)	(i)	(iv)
C.	(i)	(iv)	(iii)	(ii)
D.	(ii)	(i)	(iv)	(iii)

4. Which of the following statement/statements is/are correct?

(a) Fundamental Rights are not absolute. They are subject to reasonable restrictions.

(b) Freedom of Press is implict in Article 19 of the Constitution

(c) Socially and economically backward classes of persons are entitled to get benefit under clause (4) of Article 15 of the Constitution

(d) 'Equal protection of laws' under Article 14 of the constitution is based upon English law

Codes:

A. Only (a) and (b) are correct

B. (a), (b) and (c) are correct

C. (c) and (d) are correct

D. (a), (b), (c), (d) all are correct

5. Match **List-I** with **List-II** and give the correct answer by using the codes given below the lists:

List-I	List-II
(a) Parliamentary Form of Government	(i) The U.S.A. Constitution
(b) Directive Principles of State Policy	(ii) German Constitution
(c) Fundamental Rights	(iii) United Kingdom Constitution
(d) Emergency Provisions	(iv) Constitution of Ireland

Codes:

	(a)	(b)	(c)	(d)
A.	(iv)	(iii)	(i)	(ii)
B.	(iii)	(iv)	(i)	(ii)
C.	(i)	(ii)	(iii)	(iv)
D.	(ii)	(i)	(iv)	(iii)

6. In which of the following cases the Supreme Court held that Art. 31-C was beyond the amending power of the parliament and was void since it destroyed the basic features of the constitution. The court observed that the constitution is founded on the bedrock of the balance between Part III and Part IV. To give absolute primary to one over the other is to disturb the harmony of the constitution which is essential feature of the Basic Structure.

A. Minerva Mills *vs.* Union of India

B. In Re Kerala Education Bill Case

C. Keshavananda Bharati *vs.* State of Kerala

D. Sarla Mudgal *vs.* Union of India

7. Match **List-I** with **List-II** and give the correct answer by using the codes given below the lists:

List-I	List-II
(a) Original Jurisdiction of the Supreme Court	(i) Article 143
(b) Advisory Jurisdiction	(ii) Article 136
(c) Appeal by Special leave	(iii) Article 132
(d) Appellate Jurisdiction	(iv) Article 131

Codes:

	(a)	(b)	(c)	(d)
A.	(ii)	(iii)	(iv)	(i)
B.	(i)	(ii)	(iii)	(iv)
C.	(iv)	(i)	(ii)	(iii)
D.	(iii)	(iv)	(i)	(ii)

8. Which of the following statement/statements is/are correct?

(*a*) Predominance is given to the Union List Under Article 246 (1) of the Constitution

(*b*) Residuary powers are given to states under the Indian Constitution

(*c*) "Pith and Substance" means "the true object of the legislation or a statute"

(*d*) "Colourable Legislation" means "what you can do directly you can also do indirectly"

Codes:

A. Only (*a*) and (*c*) are correct

B. (*a*), (*b*) and (*c*) are correct

C. (*b*), (*c*) and (*d*) are correct

D. (*a*), (*b*), (*c*) and (*d*) all are correct

9. Administrative law primarily does **not** concern itself with which of the official functions?

A. Rule - making

B. Rule - application

C. Quasi - judicial action

D. Private law

10. Which of the following is **not** an exception to the principles of natural justice?

A. Impracticability

B. Legislative action

C. Rule against dictation

D. Statutory necessity

11. Match the **List-I** with **List-II** using codes given below:

List-I	List-II
(*a*) Ram Jawaya Kapur *vs.* State of Punjab	(*i*) Doctrine of post decisional hearing
(*b*) Maneka Gandhi *vs.* Union of India	(*ii*) Doctrine of public accountability
(*c*) Vineet Narain *vs.* Union of India	(*iii*) Doctrine of separation of powers
(*d*) Union of India *vs.* Hindustan Development Corporation	(*iv*) Doctrine of legitimate expectation

Codes:

	(a)	(b)	(c)	(d)
A.	(iii)	(i)	(ii)	(iv)
B.	(iv)	(ii)	(i)	(iii)
C.	(i)	(iv)	(iii)	(ii)
D.	(i)	(ii)	(iii)	(iv)

12. Read Assertion (A) and Reason (R) and answer using the codes given below:

Assertion (A): It is true that in any intensive form of government, the government cannot function without the exercise of some discretion by its official.

Reason (R): Giving discretion to government officials is necessary for the welfare of people.

Codes:

A. (A) and (R) are right and (R) is the right reason for (A)

B. (A) and (R) are right, but (R) is not the correct explanation of (A)

C. (A) is right, but (R) is wrong

D. Both (A) and (R) are wrong

13. Which of the following is correct in relation to the functioning of the institution of *Lokayukta* in Indian States?

A. Provided with independent investigating agency

B. They have not been given constitutional status

C. Prosecution and final punishment power vested with them

D. Their decisions are final and not recommendentory in nature

14. Which of the following is not considered 'irrational', basing upon the *Wednesbury* principles laid down in *Associated Provincial Picture House* Ltd. V. *Wednesbury Corporation*, 1948 (KB)?

A. Without the authority of law

B. Based on no evidence

C. It has sanction of law

D. It is unreasonable

15. On which of the following ground writ of *certiorari* cannot be issued?

A. Abuse of jurisdiction

B. Exercise of jurisdiction
C. Violation of principles of natural justice
D. Error of law apparent on the face of the record

16. Which of the following is not a jural postulate of the legal system of a society as propounded by Roscoe Pound. So in a civilized society men must be able to assume:
A. That these will be no intentional aggression
B. That members of society will act in good faith
C. That people will control for their beneficial use, what they have created
D. That people will cause injury to others during their course of work

17. Who said that customs are superior to the legislation. Therefore legislations should not abrogate the customs rather synthesize them with the common consciousness of the people and society?
A. Henry Maine B. H.L.A. Hart
C. Savigny D. Hans Kelson

18. Who among the following is **not** the exponent of Philosophical school?
A. Hegel B. Kant
C. Puchta D. Holland

19. According to Hohfeld, table of jural relations the jural correlative of right is duty. What are the jural correlatives of Liberty, Power and Immunity respectively?
A. No claim, Liability and Power
B. No claim, Responsibility and Liability
C. No claim, Duty and Liberty
D. No claim, Liability and Disability

20. 'The Limits of Jurisprudence Defined' was published in 1945. It was written in 1782 by ....
A. Bentham B. Blackstone
C. Hobbes D. Locke

21. Who among the following has not associated his theory of the state with 'Social Contract'?
A. Hobbes B. Locke
C. Henry Maine D. Rousseau

22. Read Assertion (A) and Reason (R) and give the correct answer with the help of codes given below:

Assertion (A): Criminal is a victim of circumstances, he is sick so he requires treatment.

Reason (R): Prison reforms and juvenile schools are established to reform the criminals.

Codes:
A. (A) and (R) are true and (R) is the correct explanation of (A).
B. (A) and (R) are true, but (R) is not the correct explanation of (A).
C. (A) is true, but (R) is false.
D. (A) is false, but (R) is true.

23. Match **List-I** with **List-II** using the codes below:

List-I	**List-II**
(*a*) Right of a person not to be assaulted	(*i*) Right in re-propria
(*b*) Right of a person in his own property	(*ii*) Right in rem
(*c*) Right of a person to enjoy his premises	(*iii*) Right in personam
(*d*) Right of a person in the property of someone else	(*iv*) Right in re-aliena

Codes:

	(*a*)	(*b*)	(*c*)	(*d*)
A.	(*ii*)	(*i*)	(*iii*)	(*iv*)
B.	(*iv*)	(*iii*)	(*i*)	(*ii*)
C.	(*i*)	(*ii*)	(*iv*)	(*iii*)
D.	(*iii*)	(*iv*)	(*ii*)	(*i*)

24. Read the following situations and state which combination is correct to claim benefit under the broad concept of unsoundness of mind:
(*a*) Extreme Anger (*b*) Somnambulism
(*c*) Irresistible impulse (*d*) Hallucination

Codes:
A. (*a*) and (*b*) both B. (*a*) and (*c*) both
C. (*b*) and (*c*) both D. (*b*) and (*d*) both

25. Read the following situations and choose the correct one, where right of private defence is available:

A. Against an act done or attempted to be done by a public servant
B. Where there is time available to have recourse to state authorities
C. Where there is a reasonable apprehension of causing injury to third person
D. Where harm caused in no case should exceed the quantum of harm

26. Match cases from **Group-A** with relevant legal provisions from **Group-B** and find the correct answer:

Group-A	Group-B
(*a*) K.N. Mehra *vs.* State of Rajasthan	(*i*) Section 300
(*b*) Aruna Ramchandra Shanbaugh *vs.* Union of India	(*ii*) Section 120-A
(*c*) State (NCT of Delhi) *vs.* Navjot Sandhu aka Afsana Guru	(*iii*) Section 309
(*d*) Virsa Singh *vs.* State of Punjab	(*iv*) Section 378

Codes:

	(*a*)	(*b*)	(*c*)	(*d*)
A.	(*i*)	(*iii*)	(*iv*)	(*ii*)
B.	(*i*)	(*iii*)	(*ii*)	(*iv*)
C.	(*iv*)	(*iii*)	(*ii*)	(*i*)
D.	(*iii*)	(*iv*)	(*ii*)	(*i*)

27. Criminal Law (Amendment) Act 2013, seems to have determined quantum of punishment proportionate to the severity of offence. Following are two sets of offences and punishment. Match the correct ones and give appropriate answer using the code.

Offences	Maximum Punishment
(*a*) Voluntarily causing grevious hurt by acid attack	(*i*) Life imprisonment (Remainder of the period of life)
(*b*) Stalking	(*ii*) 3 years
(*c*) Gang rape	(*iii*) Life imprisonment and fine
(*d*) Sexual intercourse by husband upon his wife during separation	(*iv*) 7 years and fine

Codes:

	(*a*)	(*b*)	(*c*)	(*d*)
A.	(*ii*)	(*iii*)	(*i*)	(*iv*)
B.	(*iii*)	(*ii*)	(*i*)	(*iv*)
C.	(*i*)	(*ii*)	(*iii*)	(*iv*)
D.	(*i*)	(*iii*)	(*ii*)	(*iv*)

28. X a servant committed theft of Mobile ph of his master M and ran away from ho While travelling the said mobile phone taken away by Y a co-traveller without knowledge of X. Decide the liability of choose correct one among the following
A. Criminal misappropriation as the ph was lying on the seat of X.
B. Criminal Breach of Trust–as they w co-travellers
C. Theft–as property in possession of X taken without his consent
D. Cheating as the method adopted dubious

29. Certain factors are essential to get Extor converted to Robbery. Following are a given factors, choose the one which is required for the said conversion:
A. Dishonesty
B. Removal of property from the possess of another, by putting him in fear
C. It is immaterial whether the person putt another in fear must be in the immedi presence or far away
D. Such fear should result in the delivery property

30. "There are two facets to the definition dishonesty and it is sufficient to establish existence of any one of them. There is requirement in Law to establish both"

Choose the correct case among the follow in which the above statement of Supre Court has been laid down as ratio.
A. Tulsi Ram *vs.* State of Uttar Pradesh
B. Hari Sao *vs.* State of Bihar
C. Gurdatta Mal *vs.* State of Uttar Prades
D. State of Bihar *vs.* Nathu Pandey

31. Following are given some Provisions of L (IPC). Choose the odd one out.

A. Section 149 B. Section 141
C. Section 34 D. Section 147

32. Which one of the following institutions gave suggestion for imposing environmental tax?
A. Amnesty International
B. World Water Institute
C. UNESCO
D. United Nations

33. Under the Environment (Protection) Act, the term 'environment' does **not** include:
A. Water, air and land
B. Inter-relationship which exists between water, air and land, and human beings
C. Inter-relationship which exists between water, air and land, and plants
D. Environment at workplace

34. Match **List-I** with **List-II** and select the correct answer using the codes given below:

List-I	**List-II**
(*a*) Power of Central Government to take measures to protect and improve environment	(*i*) Section 6 of Environment (Protection) Act
(*b*) Constitution of Central Pollution Control Board	(*ii*) Section 3 of Environment (Protection) Act
(*c*) Power of Central Government to make rules to regulate environmental pollution	(*iii*) Section 6 of the Water (Prevention and Control of Pollution) Act
(*d*) Gaseous or liquid pollutants in the atmosphere injurious to human beings	(*iv*) Section 2(*a*) of the Air (Prevention and Control of Pollution) Act

Codes:

	(*a*)	(*b*)	(*c*)	(*d*)
A.	(*i*)	(*iii*)	(*iv*)	(*ii*)
B.	(*ii*)	(*iv*)	(*i*)	(*iii*)
C.	(*ii*)	(*iii*)	(*i*)	(*iv*)
D.	(*iii*)	(*iv*)	(*ii*)	(*i*)

35. Match **List-I** with **List-II** and select the correct answer using the codes given below:

List-I	**List-II**
(*a*) Rylands *vs.* Fletcher	(*i*) Principle of public trust for ecological protection
(*b*) Indian Council for Environment Legal Action *vs.* Union of India	(*ii*) Precautionary Principle
(*c*) Vellore Citizens Welfare Forum *vs.* Union of India	(*iii*) Principle of Polluter pays
(*d*) M.C. Mehta *vs.* Kamal Nath	(*iv*) Principle of Strict liability

Codes:

	(*a*)	(*b*)	(*c*)	(*d*)
A.	(*iv*)	(*iii*)	(*ii*)	(*i*)
B.	(*i*)	(*ii*)	(*iv*)	(*iii*)
C.	(*ii*)	(*iv*)	(*iii*)	(*i*)
D.	(*i*)	(*ii*)	(*iii*)	(*iv*)

36. Which one of the following statements is **incorrect**?
A. The Public Liability Insurance Act was enacted to provide immediate relief to the victims of an accident involving a hazardous substance
B. The Public Liability Insurance Act imposes 'no fault' liability upon the owner of the hazardous substance and requires the owner to compensate the victims irrespective of any neglect or default on his part.
C. The Public Liability Insurance Act, does not provide for maximum compensation for injury or death of the victims
D. The Public Liability Insurance Act obligates every owner to take out an insurance policy covering potential liability from an accident

37. Read Assertion (A) and Reason (R) and answer using codes given below:

Assertion (A): Polluter pays principle means polluters should internalise the costs of their pollution, control it at its source, and pay for its effects, including remedial or cleanup costs, rather than forcing other states or future generations to bear such costs.

Reasons (R): Vellore citizen's welfare forum *vs.* Union of India decided so.

Codes:

A. (A) is right, but (R) is wrong
B. Both (A) and (R) are right and (R) is the correct reason of (A)
C. Both (A) and (R) are wrong
D. Both (A) and (R) are right, but (R) is not the correct reason of (A)

38. Match **List-I** with **List-II** and select the correct answer using the codes given below:

List-I	List-II
(*a*) Rural Litigation and Entitlement Kendra, Dehradun *vs.* State of Uttar Pradesh	(*i*) Grant of a lease of land or its renewal without the approval of the central government is void
(*b*) Samatha *vs.* State of Andhra Pradesh	(*ii*) Balancing environmental and ecological integrity against industrial demands on forest resources.
(*c*) K.V. Shanmugam *vs.* State of Tamil Nadu	(*iii*) Renewal of lease on forest land is not a vested right
(*d*) State of Himachal Pradesh *vs.* Ganesh Wood Products	(*iv*) Forest-based industries do not have an absolute or an unrestricted right to operate their units where forest resources are scarce.

Codes:

	(*a*)	(*b*)	(*c*)	(*d*)
A.	(*ii*)	(*iii*)	(*i*)	(*iv*)
B.	(*i*)	(*iv*)	(*ii*)	(*iii*)
C.	(*ii*)	(*iii*)	(*iv*)	(*i*)
D.	(*i*)	(*ii*)	(*iii*)	(*iv*)

39. Who of the following has remarked th International law is a "Living and Expandir Code"?

A. Judge Alvarez
B. Lord Chancellor Sankey
C. J.G. Starke
D. Prof. Lissitzyn

40. Which of the following statement/statemen is/are **incorrect**?

(*a*) Long duration is an essential element fc International Custom
(*b*) The custom should be completely uniforr and consistent to be an Internationa custom
(*c*) In an International custom, universality c practice is not necessary, the practic should have been generally observed o repeated by numerous states.
(*d*) *Opinio Juris* is present, that is to say customary pratice to be a Internationa Custom, must be recognised as being required by International law.

Codes:

A. Only (*a*) is incorrect
B. Only (*a*) and (*b*) are incorrect
C. (*b*), (*c*) and (*d*) are incorrect
D. (*a*), (*b*), (*c*), (*d*) all are incorrect

41. Match **List-I** with **List-II** and give the correct answer by using the codes given below the lists:

List-I (Topics)	List-II (Related Cases)
(*a*) Sources of International law	(*i*) Haya Dela Torra Case
(*b*) Recognition	(*ii*) Re Castioni Case
(*c*) Extradition	(*iii*) The Arantzazu Mendi Case
(*d*) Asylum	(*iv*) United States *vs.* Schooner

Codes:

	(*a*)	(*b*)	(*c*)	(*d*)
A.	(*iv*)	(*iii*)	(*ii*)	(*i*)
B.	(*iii*)	(*ii*)	(*iv*)	(*i*)
C.	(*iv*)	(*iii*)	(*i*)	(*ii*)
D.	(*ii*)	(*iv*)	(*iii*)	(*i*)

42. Which one of the following cases is not a case decided by permanent court of International Justice?

A. Movrommatis Palestine Concessions Case
B. S.S. Wimbledon Case
C. Anglo Norwegian Fisheries Case
D. Chorzow Factory (Indemnity) Case

43. Read both statements (A) and (R) and give the correct answer by using the codes given below:

Assertion (A): By the term 'Asylum' we generally mean the shelter and active protection which is extended to a political refugee from another state, by a state which admits him on his request.

Reason (R): Everyone has a right to seek and enjoy in other countries, an asylum from prosecution.

Codes:

A. Both (A) and (R) are correct and (R) is the correct explanation of (A)
B. Both (A) and (R) are correct, but (R) is not correct explanation of (A)
C. (A) is correct, but (R) is wrong
D. (A) is wrong, but (R) is correct

44. Which of the following is the only Principal organ of the UNO which consists of all the Members of United Nations?

A. Security Council
B. General Assembly
C. The Economic and Social Council
D. Trusteeship Council

45. Match **List-I** with **List-II** and give the correct answer by using the codes given below:

List-I (Provisions)	**List-II (Articles of U.N. Charter)**
(*a*) Suspension of Members	(*i*) Article 5
(*b*) Veto Power	(*ii*) Article 97
(*c*) Appointment of Secretary General	(*iii*) Article 27
(*d*) Composition of Trusteeship Council	(*iv*) Article 86

Codes:

	(*a*)	(*b*)	(*c*)	(*d*)
A.	(*i*)	(*iii*)	(*ii*)	(*iv*)
B.	(*iv*)	(*iii*)	(*ii*)	(*i*)
C.	(*iii*)	(*ii*)	(*iv*)	(*i*)
D.	(*ii*)	(*i*)	(*iii*)	(*iv*)

46. Which is not the official language of the United Nations?

A. Russian B. Japanese
C. Spanish D. Arabic

47. The offence of bigamy is not committed under the Hindu Marriage Act, 1955 if a person marries during lifetime of his or her spouse provided:

(*a*) The first marriage is null and void
(*b*) The first marriage was performed without ceremonies
(*c*) The first marriage is voidable and decree annulling it has not been passed
(*d*) The first marriage is valid

Codes:

A. (*a*) and (*c*) B. (*a*) and (*b*)
C. (*b*) and (*c*) D. (*b*) and (*d*)

48. A marriage under the Hindu Marriage Act 1955, must be solemnised in accordance with the customary rites and ceremonies of:

A. The bridegroom
B. The bride
C. Either bride or bridegroom
D. Both bride and bridegroom

49. The absence of witnesses make a Muslim marriage:

A. Irregular under Sunni law, but void under Shia law.
B. Irregular under Sunni and Shia Law.
C. Valid under Sunni law but irregular under Shia law.
D. Valid under Shia law, but irregular undei Sunni law.

50. Section 14 of the Hindu Marriage Act, 1955 enacts a 'fair trial' rule, according to which a person:

A. Can petition for divorce within one year of marriage

B. Cannot petition for divorce within one year of marriage except in exceptional cases
C. Cannot petition for judicial separation within one year of marriage
D. Can petition for restitution of Conjugal Rights within one year of marriage

51. With the help of codes given below mark the incorrect statement in the light of the Hindu Adoptions and Maintenance Act, 1956:
(*a*) Permission of the court is not necessary except when guardian gives the child in adoption.
(*b*) An adoption once made is revocable by natural parents only.
(*c*) Mother may give the child in adoption with the consent of father.
(*d*) Performance of 'datta homam' ceremony is essential for a valid adoption.

Codes:
A. (*c*) and (*d*) B. (*d*) and (*b*)
C. (*b*) and (*c*) D. (*a*) and (*d*)

52. Abstinence from sexual intercourse for a period of not less than four months persuant to a vow is called:
A. Divorce in hasan form
B. Divorce in ahsan form
C. Divorce by Zihar
D. Divorce of Ila

53. In which of the following cases the Supreme Court of India has **not** addressed the issue of Uniform Civil Code:
A. Sarla Mudgal *vs.* Union of India
B. John Vallamattom *vs.* Union of India
C. Ramesh Chander *vs.* Savitri
D. John Deingdeh *vs.* S.S. Chopra

54. Answer using the following codes:
A Hindu wife is entitled to claim maintenance from her husband under the provisions of the Hindu Adoption and Maintenance Act, 1956 if:
(*a*) She is unchaste but living with her husband
(*b*) She is unchaste but not living with her husband
(*c*) She is living separate on any ground mentioned under section 18(2) of the Act.
(*d*) She has converted to Muslim religion

Codes:
A. (*a*) and (*c*) B. (*a*) and (*b*)
C. (*b*) and (*c*) D. (*c*) and (*d*)

55. Which of the following statement is wrong? Answer using codes given below:
(*a*) Human Rights are essentially a product of bureaucracy.
(*b*) Human Rights are a reaction to tyranny
(*c*) Primitive man could move all over world, without any restriction
(*d*) All women are born free, but everywhere they are in chains.

Codes:
A. (*a*) B. (*b*)
C. (*c*) D. (*d*)

56. Read Assertion (A) and Reason (R) and answer using codes given below:
Assertion (A): In the exercise of his rights and freedoms, no one shall be subjected only for such limitations as are determined by law solely for the purpose of securing due recognition and respect for the rights and freedoms of others, and of meeting the just requirements of morality, public order, and the general welfare in a democratic society.
Reason (R): Because Article 29(2) of the Universal Declaration of Human Rights states so.

Codes:
A. Both (A) and (R) are right and (R) is correct reason of (A)
B. (A) is right, but (R) is wrong
C. (A) is wrong, but (R) is right
D. Both (A) and (R) are wrong

57. Section 3 of the protection of Civil Rights Act, 1955 prescribes punishment for:
A. Enforcing economic disabilities
B. Civil disobedience
C. Enforcing religions disabilities
D. Enforcing political disabilities

58. Article 6 of the Universal Declaration of Human Rights provides for:

A. Right to life
B. Prohibition of slavery
C. Right to be recognised as a person before law
D. Equality before law

59. Match **List-I** with **List-II** in the light of Geneva Convention Relating to the Treatment of Prisoners of War, using codes given below:

List-I	List-II
(*a*) Categories of Prisoners to be treated as prisoner of war	(*i*) Article 13
(*b*) Prisoners of war to be humanly treated	(*ii*) Article 91
(*c*) No physical or mental torture	(*iii*) Article 4
(*d*) Escape of prisoner of war	(*iv*) Article 17

Codes:

	(*a*)	(*b*)	(*c*)	(*d*)
A.	(*i*)	(*iii*)	(*ii*)	(*iv*)
B.	(*i*)	(*iii*)	(*iv*)	(*ii*)
C.	(*iii*)	(*i*)	(*ii*)	(*iv*)
D.	(*iii*)	(*i*)	(*iv*)	(*ii*)

60. Match **List-I** with **List-II** in the light of Human Rights under the Constitution of India.

List-I Case Law	List-II Principles
(*a*) East Coast Railway *vs.* Madhav Appa Rao	(*i*) Freedom of expression
(*b*) L.I.C. *vs.* Professor Manubhai D. Shah	(*ii*) Equality
(*c*) Vakil Prasad Singh *vs.* State of Bihar	(*iii*) Religious instructions
(*d*) Aruna Roy *vs.* Union of India	(*iv*) Speedy trial

Codes:

	(*a*)	(*b*)	(*c*)	(*d*)
A.	(*ii*)	(*i*)	(*iv*)	(*iii*)
B.	(*i*)	(*ii*)	(*iv*)	(*iii*)
C.	(*i*)	(*ii*)	(*iii*)	(*iv*)
D.	(*ii*)	(*i*)	(*iii*)	(*iv*)

61. State of Kerala *vs.* N.M. Thomas is about:
A. Religious minorities
B. Linguistic minorities
C. Areawise reservation
D. Backward class

62. The main aims of law of tort are:
(*a*) Punishment
(*b*) Deterrence to wrong doers
(*c*) Restoration of original position
(*d*) Damages to victims

Codes:
A. (*a*) and (*c*) B. (*c*) and (*b*)
C. (*b*) and (*d*) D. (*c*) and (*d*)

63. The 'Absolute Liability' theory on the basis of pollution causing industrial injuries was propounded by:
A. V.R. Krishna Iyer, J.
B. P.N. Bhagwati, C.J.
C. Kuldip Singh, J.
D. M.N. Venkatachaliah, C.J.

64. Defence of absolute privilege in case of defamation is available in which of the following cases:
(*a*) Parliamentary Proceedings
(*b*) Publication of matters of Public interest
(*c*) State of Communications
(*d*) Judicial Proceedings

Codes:
A. (*a*), (*b*) and (*c*) B. (*b*), (*c*) and (*d*)
C (*a*), (*b*) and (*d*) D. (*d*), (*c*) and (*a*)

65. The essential ingredients of the tort of negligence are:
(*a*) One owes a duty of care towards the other
(*b*) One commits a breach of that duty
(*c*) The other person suffers damage as a consequence thereof.

Choose your correct answer with the help of codes given below:

Codes:
A. Only the first is an essential ingredient
B. None of them is an essential ingredient
C. All of them are essential ingredients
D. Even if the first is absent the tort of negligence is committed

66. Negligence is failure in duty of taking due care. The expression 'duty' means:
A. A legal duty

B. A legal as well as moral duty
C. A legal as well as social duty
D. A specific legal duty

67. There is no qualitative difference between a medical practitioner and an advocate, ... from the point of view of his status, duties and regulatory control by a statutory body. Hence there is no reason why the legal practitioner should be excluded from the purview of Consumer Protection Act.

From the following choose the correct decision in which it has been held:
A. K. Vishnu *vs.* National Consumer Dispute Redressal Commission and others
B. Joshi *vs.* Motor Industries Co.
C. Charan Sing *vs.* Healing touch Hospital
D. Arvind Mills Ltd *vs.* Associated Roadways

68. Read Assertion (A) and Reason (R) and answer using codes below:
Assertion (A): Consumer Act is made to simplify the procedure and avoid the complexity so that an ordinary citizen can file a complaint without a difficulty.
Reason (R): It intends to protect a large body of consumers from exploitation.
Codes:
A. (A) and (R) are right and (R) is the right reason for (A)
B. Both (A) and (R) are wrong
C. (A) is right and (R) is wrong
D. (R) is right and (A) is wrong

69. Which are essentials of sale of goods? Answer using codes given below:
(*a*) Contractual capacity
(*b*) Bilateral contract
(*c*) Profit for seller
(*d*) Mutual and free consent of parties to the contract of sale of goods
Codes:
A. (*a*), (*b*), (*c*) B. (*a*), (*b*), (*d*)
C. (*b*), (*c*), (*d*) D. (*a*), (*c*), (*d*)

70. Read Assertion (A) and Reason (R) and answer using codes given below:
Assertion (A): Every partner is an agent of the other partner.
Reason (R): Partnership is agency
Codes:
A. Both (A) and (R) are wrong
B. (A) is right, but (R) is wrong
C. (A) is wrong, but (R) is right
D. Both (A) and (R) are right and (R) is correct reason of (A)

71. Match **List-I** with **List-II** and select the correct answer using the code given below:

List-I	List-II
(*a*) Instalment Supply Ltd. *vs.* STO	(*i*) Conditions applied by trade usage
(*b*) Gardiner *vs.* Gray	(*ii*) *Nemo dat quo non habet*
(*c*) Peter Darlington Partners Ltd. *vs.* Gesho Co. Ltd.	(*iii*) Sale by description
(*d*) Farquharson Bros *vs.* King and Co.	(*iv*) Difference between sale and agreement to sale

Codes:

	(*a*)	(*b*)	(*c*)	(*d*)
A.	(*iii*)	(*iv*)	(*ii*)	(*i*)
B.	(*iii*)	(*iv*)	(*i*)	(*ii*)
C.	(*iv*)	(*iii*)	(*i*)	(*ii*)
D.	(*iv*)	(*iii*)	(*ii*)	(*i*)

72. Which one statement is **correct** from the following statements?
A. A director of a company as a director is a servant of the company
B. A director is an agent of his company
C. A director is not a fiduciary person of his company
D. A director is master of his company

73. Match **List-I** with **List-II** and select the correct answer using codes given below:
Answer in context of the Negotiable Instruments Act.

List-I	List-II
(*a*) Time and place for presentment	(*i*) Section 19
(*b*) Cheques are payable in demand	(*ii*) Section 8
(*c*) Holder of a negotiable instrument	(*iii*) Section 61
(*d*) Fictitious drawer or payee	(*iv*) Section 42

Codes:

	(a)	(b)	(c)	(d)
A.	(i)	(iv)	(ii)	(iii)
B.	(iii)	(ii)	(iv)	(i)
C.	(ii)	(iii)	(iv)	(i)
D.	(ii)	(iii)	(i)	(iv)

74. Which of the following statement is **correct**?
A. Open cheques are those which cannot be directly presented to the drawee bank for payment across the counter
B. A 16 year old girl can draw a cheque
C. Indorsement is written on front of a cheque
D. Indorsement cannot be made by the holder of a negotiable instrument

75. Which of the following statement (s) is/are incorrect? Answer using codes given below:
(a) In Attorney General *vs.* Great Eastern Railway Co. the House of Lords observed that the doctrine of *ultra vires* as it was explained in the *Ashbury* case, should not be maintained.
(b) Section 13 (i) (c) of the Companies Act provides incidental objects which need not be stated in the memorandum.
(c) If incidental objects are not stated in the memorandum, they would not be allowed by the principle of reasonable construction
(d) The doctrine of indoor management operates to protect insiders against the company

Codes:
A. Only (a) and (b)
B. Only (b) and (c)
C. Only (a), (b) and (c)
D. (a), (b), (c) and (d)

ANSWERS

1	2	3	4	5	6	7	8	9	10
B	B	A	A	B	A	C	A	D	C
11	**12**	**13**	**14**	**15**	**16**	**17**	**18**	**19**	**20**
A	A	B	C	B	D	C	D	D	A
21	**22**	**23**	**24**	**25**	**26**	**27**	**28**	**29**	**30**
C	B	A	D	C	C	B	C	C	A
31	**32**	**33**	**34**	**35**	**36**	**37**	**38**	**39**	**40**
C	B	D	C	A	C	B	A	B	B
41	**42**	**43**	**44**	**45**	**46**	**47**	**48**	**49**	**50**
A	C	A	B	A	B	B	C	D	B
51	**52**	**53**	**54**	**55**	**56**	**57**	**58**	**59**	**60**
B	D	C	A	A	D	C	C	D	A
61	**62**	**63**	**64**	**65**	**66**	**67**	**68**	**69**	**70**
D	C	B	D	C	D	A	A	B	D
71	**72**	**73**	**74**	**75**					
C	B	*	B	D					

SOME SELECTED EXPLANATORY ANSWERS

1. Officially known as The Constitution (Forty-second amendment) Act, 1976, it was enacted during the Emergency (25 June 1975 – 21 March 1977) by the Indian National Congress government headed by Indira Gandhi. The amendment brought about the most widespread changes to the Constitution in its history. With the addition of such expressions

Supreme Court that ruled that the MTNL has no right to hold back Tata Press Ltd. from publishing Tata Yellow Pages.

(*d*) Government cannot impose prior restraint on publication of defamatory material against its officials, as after reviewing a range of comparative law material, the Court found that the State and its officials have no authority in law to do so. In a historic judgement in R. Rajagopal *vs.* State of Tamil Nadu, the Supreme Court has held that the government has no authority in law to impose a prior restrain upon publication of defamatory material against its officials.

4. (*a*) The Fundamental Rights guaranteed by the Constitution of India are not absolute. There are certain restrictions, which can be imposed by the state according to the procedure established by law. However, these restrictions must be reasonable and not arbitrary. Article 19 covers these fundamental freedoms as well as the restrictions, which can be imposed on these rights.

(*b*) The Constitution of India provides the right to freedom, given in articles 19, 20, 21 and 22, with the view of guaranteeing the citizens that were considered vital by the framers of the Constitution. Article 19 pertains to guaranteeing the Freedom of speech and expression, as one of its six freedoms. Like individual, Press or Media also have the right to express themselves by broadcasting news and views that is implicit in Article 19 of the Constitution.

5. (*a*) Parliamentary Form of Government is a system of democratic governance of a state in which the executive branch derives its democratic legitimacy from, and is held accountable to, the legislature (parliament); the executive and legislative branches are thus inter-connected. The Constitution of the United Kingdom is based on constitutional monarchy, where a monarch is the ceremonial head of state while the head of government is regularly from the legislature.

(*b*) The Directive Principles of State Policy are guidelines or principles given to the central and state governments in countries like Ireland and India. Though these principles are non-justifiable, they are fundamental in the governance of the country.

(*c*) In American Constitutional Law, fundamental rights have special significance under the U.S. Constitution. Those rights enumerated in the U.S. Constitution are recognised as "fundamental" by the U.S. Supreme Court. According to the Supreme Court, enumerated rights that are incorporated are so fundamental that any law restricting such a right must both serve a compelling state purpose and be narrowly tailored to that compelling purpose.

(*d*) The German Emergency Acts (*Notstandsgesetze*) were passed on 30 May 1968 at the time of the *First Grand Coalition* between the Social Democratic Party of Germany and the Christian Democratic Union of Germany. The Emergency Acts faced opposition from outside the German parliament. It was the 17th constitutional amendment to the *Grundgesetz*, adding emergency clauses to ensure the federal government's ability to act in crises such as natural disasters, uprisings or war.

6. Minerva Mills Ltd. and Ors. *vs.* Union of India and Ors. (case citation: AIR 1980 SC 1789) is a landmark decision of the Supreme Court of India that applied and evolved the basic structure doctrine of the Constitution of India. In this case, the Supreme Court provided key clarifications on the interpretation of the basic structure doctrine. The court unanimously ruled that the power of the Parliament of India to amend the constitution is limited by the Constitution. Hence, the Parliament cannot exercise this limited power to grant itself an unlimited power. Moreover, a majority of the court also held that the Parliament's power to amend is not a power to destroy. Hence, the parliament cannot emasculate the fundamental rights of individuals, including the right to liberty and equality.

(*a*) Article 131 in the Constitution of India 1949; the original jurisdiction of the Supreme Court subject to the provisions of this Constitution, shall, to the exclusion of any other court, have original jurisdiction in any dispute (*i*) between the Government of India and one or more states; or (*ii*) between the Government of India and one or more states; or (*iii*) between two or more states, if and in so far as the dispute involves any question (whether of law or fact) on which the existence or extent of a legal right depends....

(*b*) In India, the President of India can request the Supreme Court of India to provide its advice on certain matters. This procedure is called "Presidential Reference". As per Article 143 of the Constitution of India, the President of India may refer to the Supreme Court of India, a question of law or fact, which he thinks, is of public importance. However, it is not binding on the Supreme Court to answer questions raised in the reference.

(*c*) The Constitution of India under Article 136 vests the Supreme Court of India with a special power to grant special leave to appeal against any judgement or order or decree in any matter or cause passed or made any Court/tribunal in the territory of India. This special power bestowed upon the Supreme Court of India, which is the Apex Court of the country to grant leave to appeal against any judgement in case any substantial constitutional question of law is involved or gross injustice has been done. Special Leave Petition (SLP) holds a prime position in the Indian judicial system that the aggrieved party a special permission to be heard in Apex Court in appeal against any judgement or order of Court/tribunal in the territory of India.

(*d*) The Appellate Jurisdiction of the Supreme Court of India can be invoked by a certificate granted by the High Court concerned under Article 132(1), 133(1) or 134 of the Constitution in respect of any judgement, decree or final order of a High Court in both civil and criminal cases, involving substantial questions of law as to the interpretation of the Constitution.

8. (*a*) The legislative field of the Parliament and the State Legislatures has been specified in Article 246 of the Constitution. Article 246 (1) states that, the Parliament has exclusive power to make laws with respect to any of the matters enumerated in List I or the Union List in the Seventh Schedule.

(*c*) Pith and Substance is essentially a Canadian Doctrine, now firmly entrenched in the Indian Constitutional Jurisprudence. This legal doctrine is used in determining under which head of power a given piece of legislation falls. This doctrine is primarily used when a law is challenged on the basis that one level of government (be it provincial or federal) has encroached upon the exclusive jurisdiction of another level of government. It is essentially a matter of interpretation. The court looks at the words used in the impugned legislation as well as the background and circumstances surrounding its enactment. In conducting this analysis, the court should not be concerned with the efficacy of the law or whether it achieves the legislature's goals.

9. In immensely concise definition, Private Law pertains to governing relationships between individuals, such as the Law of Contracts and the Law of Torts whereas the Administrative Law or Public Law is the relationship between individuals and the state. Administrative Law primarily does not concern itself with Private Law because Administrative Law refers to the body of law, which regulates bureaucratic managerial procedures and defines the powers of administrative agencies.

10. There are several well-established limitations on Principles of Natural Justice. Existence of certain circumstances deprives the individual from availing the benefit of principles of natural justices, authors in this research work undertake to cover the circumstances in which judiciary admitted the exceptions to the observance of Principles of Natural Justice. Authors are of the conclusion that the Courts both in India and England in relation to administrative proceedings created various exceptions to the requirement of Natural Justice Principles and procedure there off. However, these exceptions are all circumstantial and not conclusive. As far as the Rule against dictation is concerned, it is not an exception to the principles of natural justice.

11. (*a*) Doctrine of separation of power is meant for removing the amount of power from any group's hands, making it more difficult to abuse. However, in India, we follow a separation of functions rather than of powers. The case of Ram Jawaya Kapur *vs.* State of Punjab, AIR 1955 S.C. 549 is related to it.

(*b*) Post decisional hearing is a hearing, which takes place after a provisional decision is reached. This principle was laid down in Maneka Gandhi *vs.* Union of India. There is a nexus between pre-decisional and post-decisional hearings. The logic behind introducing the post-decisional hearing is to increase and maintain administrative fairness.

(*c*) Vineet Narain *vs.* Union of India, A.I. 1996 S.C. 3386, is a case of Publ accountability. In this case, the Cou developed the procedure of "continui mandamus," making the princip investigating body in India accountab to it. Later, noting the detriment consequences of vehicular pollution the population's general health, the Co restricted the use of commercial vehicl including the conversion of the city b fleet in New Delhi to a single mode compressed natural gas and t introduction of certain European vehicu pollution norms known as Euro-I a Euro-II.

(*d*) Union of India *vs.* Hindustan Developm Corporation is a case of legitim expectation. The doctrine of 'legitim expectation' imposes in essence a duty public authority to act fairly by tak into consideration all relevant fact relating to such legitimate expectati

12. In most administrative actions, the powe act or not to act in one way or other is ca Discretionary power. 'Discretion' is the po to decide or act according to one's judgem It is true that in any intensive form government, the government cannot func without exercising some discretion by officials as that can be the source of wel of the people.

13. The Lokayukta is an anti-corruption auth constituted at the state level, w investigates allegations of corruption and administration against public servants a tasked with speedy redressal of pu grievances. The Administrative Refo Commission (1966-70), had recommende creation of the Lokpal at the Centre Lokayukta in the states. Maharashtra wa first state to introduce the institutio Lokayukta through The Lokayukta and Lokayuktas Act in 1971. It was followe similar acts being enacted by states of O

Rajasthan, Bihar, Uttar Pradesh, Karnataka, Madhya Pradesh, Andhra Pradesh, Gujarat and Delhi. However, they are yet to have constitutional status.

14. "It has sanction of law" is considered reasonable (rational) as per the principles of the Wednesbury as laid down in Associated Provincial Picture House Ltd. *vs.* Wednesbury Corporation, (1948) 1 KB 223). It is an English law case that sets out the standard of unreasonableness of public-body decisions that would make them liable to be quashed on judicial review, known as *Wednesbury* unreasonableness. A reasoning of decision is Wednesbury unreasonable (or irrational) if it is so unreasonable that no reasonable person acting reasonably could have made it (*Associated Provincial Picture Houses Ltd v Wednesbury Corporation (1948) 1 KB 223*). The court in this respect, gave three conditions on which it would intervene to correct a bad administrative decision, including on grounds of its unreasonableness in the special sense later articulated in Council of Civil Service Unions *vs* Minister for the Civil Service by Lord Diplock.

15. *Certiorari* is a writ issued from a superior court calling up the record of a proceeding in an inferior court for review. Review on a writ of *certiorari* is not a matter of right, but of judicial discretion. A petition for a writ of *certiorari* will be granted only for compelling grounds; it cannot be issued on such ground as Exercise of jurisdiction.

16. The jural postulates by Roscoe Pound are working hypotheses, which explain most adequately human claims, demands or interests. They are formulated as a result of observing social phenomena and are hence always subject to further inquiry. Pound did not regard the jural postulates as absolutes. New facts could render them inapplicable. Until obsolete however, they are useful for bringing society's legal institutions into harmony with the jural postulates, and thereby harmonising them with the actual demands of men in the society. Thus, according to Roscoe Pound, to say that people will cause injury to others during their course of work is not a jural postulate of the legal system of a society.

17. Friedrich Karl Von Savigny, a German jurist and legal scholar, was one of the founders of the dominant "historical school" of jurisprudence. He says that customs are superior to the legislation. He propounds that the proper form of law is custom (*Gewohnheit*). He speaks of law generally, although his focus is on private law, which he assumes (as in Roman law) to be fundamental. According to Savigny, custom is a safeguard against *Willkür* (arbitrariness or despotic caprice) and of course, people are against that.

18. Holland Virginia Taylor (born on 14 January 1943) is an American film, stage and television actress and also a playwright. She is not an exponent of Philosophical school whereas Hegel, Kant and Puchta are Germans and they all are exponent of Philosophical school.

19. Wesley Newcomb Hohfeld, late professor of law in Yale University, was widely known among his professional colleagues as a successful teacher and a keen analyst of legal problems. The jural correlatives of Liberty, Power and Immunity according to the Hohfeld System of fundamental Legal Concepts, is set as No claim (Right), Liability and Disability. It was the first attempt at a complete systematic arrangement of jural relations. No writer in any country, prior to Hohfeld, had sought to give a systematic account, with suitable terminology, of the passive side of jural relations.

20. Jeremy Bentham, an author of *The Limits of Jurisprudence Defined*, was a British philosopher, jurist, and social reformer. He is regarded as the founder of modern utilitarianism. Written in 1782 and published by Columbia University Press in 1945, *The Limits of Jurisprudence Defined* that deals mainly with penal law was edited and co-authored by Charles Warren Everett.

21. The social contract theory sheds light on the origin of the society. As per this theory, all men are born free and equal. Society came into existence by virtue of the agreement entered into by the individuals. The classical representatives of this school of thought are Thomas Hobbes, John Locke and Rousseau but Sir Henry James Sumner Maine does not associate his theory of the state with 'Social Contract', as in his book *Ancient Law*, Maine says, "the movement of progressive societies has hitherto been a movement from status to contract".

24. (*b*) Somnambulism is sleep walking that makes a person claim benefit under the broad concept of unsoundness of mind. In 1925, Isom Bradley Rose late at night in his Texas home, apparently due to a lucid dream that an intruder was present, and fired several shots; when he woke up, he found he'd shot his girlfriend. With a similar, medically-vague sleepwalking defence, Bradley was exonerated by the court, which set the following precedent: "Somnambulist does not enjoy the free and rational exercise of his understanding and is more or less unconscious of his outward relations; none of his acts can rightfully be imputed to him as crimes."

(*d*) Hallucinations can cause one to detach from reality and to see or hear things that do not exist. There are five types of hallucination. In order to qualify for benefits, one must be suffering from a condition that is listed by the Social Security Administration (SSA) as one of the conditions that qualify for benefits. To qualify for benefits, the claimant will have to prove that he/she suffers from severe hallucinations or conditions that result in hallucinations, such as schizophrenia. The claimant of benefits must be able to prove that the hallucinations are severe enough to prevent him/her from engaging in any meaningful or income-generating work.

25. The right of self-defence is the right of a civilian to justifiably engage in violent actions for the sake of defending one's self, one's property or the lives of others. Self-defence can be asserted as an affirmative defence to criminal charges for an act of violence, providing justification for the violent actions and absolving the accused of any criminal liability. In essence, acting out of self-defence can negate the requisite *mens rea* required to assert criminal liability in many circumstances. Hence, the right of private defence is available where there is a reasonable apprehension of causing injury to third person.

26. (*a*) It was a May 1952 case of theft of an Air Force aircraft that took off from Jodhpur air base and force-landed at a field in the territory of Pakistan in which K.N. Mehra and Phillip were made accused as per Section 378 of the Indian Penal Code. Section 378 is laid down as: "Whoever, intending to take dishonestly any movable property out of the possession of any person without that person's consent, moves that property in order to such taking, is said to commit theft".

(*b*) Aruna Ramchandra Shanbaugh *vs.* Union of India & Ors. Writ Petition (Criminal) No. 115 of 2009, was decided on 7 March 2011. Shanbaugh (1 June 1948 – 18 May 2015), a nurse in King Edward Memorial Hospital, Mumbai, was sexually assaulted by a ward boy, Sohanlal Bhartha Walmiki in 1973. She was sodomised and assaulted so brutally that caused damage to her brain and that resulted in spending her whole life in vegetative state like a live skeleton. Plea for her euthanasia (mercy killing) was put before the court by the victim's friend, journalist Pinki Virani but the petition was rejected on 7 March 2011 as Section 309 of IPC lays down the punishment (the maximum punishment which can be awarded is imprisonment for a term of 1 year) for attempted suicide. However, the Supreme Court of India finally responded to the plea for euthanasia. In its landmark opinion, it allowed passive euthanasia in India but before that Aruna Shanbaugh died from pneumonia on 18 May 2015.

(*c*) The genesis of this case lies in the incident of macabre Parliament firing by the terrorists on 13 December 2001 killing 14 people and injuring 22. The attack triggered extensive investigations which revealed possible involvement of four accused namely, Afzal Guru (already hanged), Shaukat Hussain, S.A.R. Gilani and Navjot Sandhu aka Afsana. Charges were framed under various sections of IPC. Afzal Guru, Shaukat Hussain and SAR Gilani were convicted for the offences under Sections 121, 121A, 122, Section 120B read with Sections 302 & 307 read with Section 120B IPC, sub-Sections (2), (3) & (5) of Section 3 and Section 4(b) of POTA and Sections 3 & 4 of Explosive Substances Act. The accused 1 and 2 were also convicted under Section 3(4) of POTA. However, accused No.4 namely, Navjot Sandhu aka Afsana was acquitted of all the charges except the one under Section 123 IPC for which she was convicted and sentenced to undergo Rigorous imprisonment for five years and to pay a fine.

(*d*) It was the case of murder of Khem Singh by the hands of Virsa Singh who attacked the deceased with a spear to cause grievous injury to him. It was impossible for the accused Virsa Singh to escape the law because bodily injury that was sufficient to cause death in the ordinary course of nature as Section 300 of IPC third clause states, "If it is done with the intention of causing bodily injury to any person and the bodily injury intended to be inflicted is sufficient in the ordinary course of nature to cause death". Thus, on 11 March 1958, the judgement of the Punjab High Court was delivered by J. Bose in which the appellant Virsa Singh was sentenced to imprisonment for life under Section 302 of the IPC for the murder of Khem Singh.

27. (*a*) The Section 326A in the Indian Penal Code lays down certain punishment for acid throwing. The minimum punishment for voluntarily causing grievous hurt by acid attack is 10 years imprisonment. It can extend up to life imprisonment with fine.

(*b*) In legal definition, Stalking means, "to follow a woman and contact, or attempt to contact such woman to foster personal interaction repeatedly despite a clear indication of disinterest by such woman; or monitor the use by a woman of the internet, email or any other form of electronic communication. There are exceptions to this section which include such act being in course of preventing or detecting a crime authorised by State or in compliance of certain law or was reasonable and justified". As per Section 354D of IPC, the punishment for stalking is imprisonment not less than one year but which may extend to three years, and shall also be liable to fine.

(*c*) Section 376 D of IPC is applied on rape cases in India. Gang rape is a heinous crime where a woman is raped by one or more persons constituting a group or acting in furtherance of a common intention, each of those persons shall be deemed to have committed the offence of rape and shall be punished with rigorous imprisonment for a term which shall not be less than twenty years, but which may extend to life which shall mean imprisonment for the remainder of that person's nature life, and with fine; provided that such fine shall be just and reasonable to meet the medical expenses and rehabilitation of the victim; provided further that any fine imposed under this section shall be paid to the victim.

(*d*) Having sex by husband with his wife during separation without wife's consent leads up to seven years of imprisonment, according to the proposed ordinance on anti-rape law approved by the Union Cabinet. Justice J S Verma Committee recommended deletion of IPC's Section 376A (Intercourse by a man with his wife during separation) under which currently maximum punishment is two years. Implied in that was the view that marital rape should also be brought under the definition of rape. However, the government has decided to retain it but enhanced the punishment for the crime from two years to maximum seven years of imprisonment.

28. Theft—as property in possession of X was taken without his consent. In such case, like X, the co-traveller Y has also brought the phone in his possession not only without the consent of its real owner but also without his knowledge. If Y has found the phone incidentally and taken into his possession, he is supposed to submit it to the nearest police station or any such competent government authority with its detail so that the lost/stolen phone can reach its real owner.

29. The difference between robbery and extortion is that in robbery there is immediate threat to the victim whereas, in extortion the victim often willingly hands over money or property or valuables to avoid future violence or damage. Therefore, if extortion needs to be converted to robbery, the factor not required for this conversion will be that it is immaterial whether the person putting another in fear must be in the immediate presence or far away.

30. In the case of Tulsi Ram *vs.* State of Uttar Pradesh on 27 September 1962, the appellants were tried and convicted for conspiracy to cheat certain banks. The prosecution had put on record a letter from the undersecretary to Government, which stated that the Governor had been pleased to grant sanction for the prosecution of the appellants. Finally, the case reached the Supreme Court of India, which states that wrongful gain and wrongful loss are two facets of the definition of dishonesty and it was enough to establish the existence of one of them. In this case, the appellants had made wrongful gain to themselves by obtaining credits by unlawful means and even if no wrongful loss was caused to the banks, the appellants were guilty of cheating.

31. Why Section 34 is considered odd out of other such sections of IPC as Section 149; Section 141 and Section 147, because in Section 34 in the IPC if a criminal act is committed by several persons in furtherance of the common intention of all, each of such persons will be liable for that act in the same manner as if it were done by him alone. However, in other given sections, if any one person from the unlawful assembly or gathering commits a crime, the whole lot will be penalised for that offence/crime.

32. The World Water Institute imparts education on our contributions to understanding of watershed health and all pertaining to utilisation and preservation of water besides doing research to help address critical water management issues related to flood damage reduction and natural resource enhancement. The Institute suggested for imposing environment tax. As a general matter, this tax measures either imposing a tax cost on some product or activity that is environmentally damaging, or they give a tax benefit to some product or activity that is environmentally beneficial. For example, the federal government imposes a significant excise tax on ozone-depleting chemicals, and it offers a tax credit to people who buy electric vehicles. In both instances, the tax code has altered the "price" of the commodity, injecting an important signal into the economic calculations that affect behaviour.

33. The Environment (Protection) Act, 1986 is an Act to provide for the protection and improvement of environment and for matters connected therewith. Under this Act, the term 'environment' does not include the environment at workplace, as environment at workplace pertains to one's behaviour within a workplace that creates an environment that may be either good or bad for another person to work in; it does not pertain to ecosystem.

34. (*a*) Power of Central Government to take measures to protect and improve environment comes under Section 3 of Environment (Protection) Act. Section 3 has 3 clauses and the 2nd clause of this Section has 14 sub-clauses – all speak about the different matters related to powers, prerogatives and other roles of Central Government.

(*b*) Established in 1974, Central Pollution Control Board (CPCB) of India is a statutory organisation under Water (Prevention and Control of Pollution) Act, 1974. CPCB is entrusted with the powers and functions under the Air (Prevention and Control of Pollution) Act, 1981. It serves as a field formation and also provides technical services to the Ministry of Environment and Forests of the provisions of the Environment (Protection) Act, 1986.

(*c*) Power of Central Government to make rules to regulate environmental pollution comes under Section 6 of Environment (Protection) Act, 1986. Section 6 has 2 clauses and its second clause has 6 sub-clauses, all laying down the matters relating to rules to regulate the environmental pollution.

(*d*) Gaseous or liquid pollutants in the atmosphere injurious to human beings fall under Section 2(a) of the Air (Prevention and Control of Pollution) Act. This Section states, "Air pollution means any solid, liquid or gaseous substance (including noise) present in the atmosphere in such concentration as may be or tend to be injurious to human beings or other living creatures or plants or property or environment.

36. The Public Liability Insurance Act, 1991 is an Act to provide for public liability – insurance for the purpose of providing immediate relief to the persons affected by accident occurring while handling any hazardous substance and for matters connected therewith or incidental thereto. Therefore, it would be wrong to say that this Act does not provide for maximum compensation for injury or death of the victims.

37. The given Assertion (A) is true, as Polluter pays principle means polluters should internalise the costs of their pollution, control it at its source, and pay for its effects, including remedial or cleanup costs, rather than forcing other states or future generations to bear such cost. It has been well exemplified by the case of Vellore Citizen's Welfare Forum *vs.* Union of India when the polluting industries had to pay the fine of ₹ 10,000 each as compensation of spoiling the environment to the affected people.

39. John Sankey, 1st Viscount Sankey, GBE, KSTJ, PC, KC (26 October 1866 – 6 February 1948) was a British lawyer, judge, Labour politician and Lord Chancellor of Great Britain. He is famous for many of his judgements in the House of Lords. He gave his name to Sankey Declaration of the Rights of Man (1940). His remark that International law is a "Living and Expanding Code" added to his eminence in the faculty of law.

42. Also known as *Anglo Norwegian Fisheries Case*, the United Kingdom *vs*. Norway [1951] ICJ 3 was the culmination of a dispute, originating in 1933, over how large an area of water surrounding Norway was Norwegian waters (that Norway thus had exclusive fishing rights to) and how much was 'high seas' (that the UK could thus fish). The UK on 24 September 1949, made a plea that the International Court of Justice determine how far Norway's territorial claim extended to sea, and to award the UK damages in compensation for Norwegian interference with UK fishing vessels in the disputed waters, claiming that Norway's claim to such an extent of waters was against international law. The judgement came on 18 December 1951, as the ICJ decided that Norway's claims to the waters were not inconsistent with international laws concerning the ownership of local sea-space.

43. Article 14 of the Universal Declaration of Human Rights states that, "Everyone has the right to seek and to enjoy in other countries asylum from persecution." The United Nations 1951 Convention Relating to the Status of Refugees and the 1967 Protocol Relating to the Status of Refugees guides national legislation concerning political asylum.

44. The United Nations General Assembly is one of the six principal organs of the United Nations and the only one in which all member nations have equal representation. Its powers are to oversee the budget of the United Nations, appoint the non-permanent members to the Security Council, receive reports from other parts of the United Nations and make recommendations in the form of General Assembly Resolutions. It has also established a large number of subsidiary organs.

45. (*a*) Article 5 of United Nations Charter deals with the suspension of members. A member of the United Nations against which preventive or enforcement action has been taken by the Security Council may be suspended from the exercise of the righ and privileges of membership by t General Assembly upon the recommendati of the Security Council. The exercise these rights and privileges may be restor by the Security Council.

(*b*) Article 27 of UN Charter pertains to Ve Power. As per Article 27, (i) Each memb of the Security Council shall have o vote. (ii) Decisions of the Security Coun on procedural matters shall be made an affirmative vote of nine members. (Decisions of the Security Council on other matters shall be made by affirmative vote of nine membe including the concurring votes of permanent members; provided that, decisions under Chapter VI, and un paragraph 3 of Article 52, a party to dispute shall abstain from voting.

(*c*) Article 97 of UN Charter concerns w appointment of Secretary General. T Secretariat shall comprise a Secreta General and such staff as the Organisat may require. The Secretary-General sh be appointed by the General Assem upon the recommendation of the Secu Council. He shall be the chief administra officer of the Organisation.

(*d*) Article 86 of UN Charter is applied Composition of Trusteeship Council. Trusteeship Council shall consist of those members of the United Nati which are administering trust territor (ii) such of those members mentioned name in Article 23 as are not administe trust territories; and (iii) as many o members elected for three-year terms the General Assembly as may be neces to ensure that the total number of mem of the Trusteeship Council is equ divided between those members of United Nations which administer t territories and those which do not.

Each member of the Trusteeship Council shall designate one specially qualified person to represent it therein.

46. There are six official languages of the United Nations. These are Arabic, Chinese, English, French, Russian and Spanish. The correct interpretation and translation of these languages, in both spoken and written form, merits vital importance for the work of the Organisation, as this enables clear and concise communication on issues of global importance. Though Japan has a distinguished position in the world map, Japanese is still not included in the official language of United Nations.

47. The case of bigamy is dealt in Sections 5, 11 and 17 of the Hindu Marriage Act, 1955. Section 5(i) prohibits bigamy or polygamy. Section 11 makes a bigamous marriage void and Section 17 makes it a penal offence for both Hindu males and females under Section 494 and 495 of IPC. The offence of bigamy is committed only if the required ceremonies of marriage are performed. The second marriage cannot be taken to be proved by the mere admission of the parties; essential ceremonies and rites must be proved to have taken place. In the case of a bigamous marriage, the "second wife" has no status of wife.

48. Marriage among Hindus being a religious and sacred tie, performance of certain ceremonies is necessary for a valid marriage. There were three important stages wherein certain ceremonies were to be performed: (1) Betrothal or Sagai (2) Kanyadan (3) Saptapadi. Saptapadi that consisted in performing a ceremony of taking seven steps before the sacred fire by the bride and groom marked the completion of a marriage. As per Section 7, a marriage is a ceremonial affair. Customary ceremonies may not include any one of the Shastric ceremonies including Saptapadi. It may be totally non-religious ceremony or it may be quite a simple ceremony as well. For instance, among Santhals smearing of vermilion by bridegroom on the bride's forehead is the only essential ceremony. However, necessary ceremonies, Shastric or customary, whichever are prevalent on the side of either bride or bridegroom, must be performed, otherwise marriage will not be valid.

49. Marriage/*Nikah* as per Muslim Law is a contract underlying a permanent relationship based on mutual consent. There are certain preconditions for solemnisation of marriage of a Muslim couple. Besides other preconditions, there is also a condition of witnesses. Under the Sunni Law, the proposal and acceptance (in Nikah) must be made in presence of two males or one male and two female witnesses who should be sane, adult and Muslim. On the contrary, under Shia Law, witnesses are not necessary at the time of marriage. They are required at the time of dissolution of marriage.

50. Section 14 of the Hindu Marriage Act, 1955 enacts a 'fair trial' rule, according to which a person cannot petition for divorce within one year of marriage except in exceptional cases. Such exceptions may consist of exceptional hardship to the petitioner (for divorce) or of exceptional depravity on the part of the respondent.

51. Section 15 of the Hindu Adoptions and Maintenance Act, 1956 elucidates, "Valid adoption not to be cancelled. No adoption which has been validly made can be cancelled by the adoptive father or mother or any other person, nor can the adopted child renounce his/her status as such and return to the family of his/her birth." Thus, it becomes clear that an adoption once made is irrevocable by natural parents. *Datta homam* ceremony is essential for a valid adoption. *Homam* or *homa* is a Sanskrit word, which refers to another Sanskrit word *havan* that is a ritual in which making offerings into a consecrated fire is the primary action.

52. Apart from talaaq, a Muslim husband can repudiate his marriage by two other modes, that are, Ila and Zihar. They are called constructive divorce. In Ila, the husband takes an oath not to have sexual intercourse with his wife. Followed by this oath, there is no consummation for a period of four months. After the expiry of the fourth month, the marriage dissolves irrevocably. But if the husband resumes cohabitation within four months, Ila is cancelled and the marriage does not dissolve. Under Ithna Asharia (Shia) School, Ila does not operate as divorce without order of the court of law. After the expiry of the fourth month, the wife is simply entitled for a judicial divorce. If there is no cohabitation, even after expiry of four months, the wife may file a suit for restitution of conjugal rights against the husband.

53. Ramesh Chander *vs.* Savitri is the case in which the Supreme Court of India has not addressed the issue of Uniform Civil Code. In this case, Supreme Court without going into the merits of the case, cut short the matter on the basis that, "the marriage is dead emotionally and practically. Continuance of marital alliance for name sake is prolonging the agony and affection .... the marriage being dead the continuance of it would be cruelty and in exercise of the power under Article 142 of the Constitution of India the court dissolves the marriage".

54. Under Hindu Law, the wife has an absolute right to claim maintenance from her husband. But she loses her right if she deviates from the path of chastity. Her right to maintenance is codified in the Hindu Adoptions and Maintenance Act, 1956 (78 of 1956). In assessing the amount of maintenance, the court takes into account various factors like position and liabilities of the husband. It also judges whether the wife is justified in living apart from husband. Justifiable reasons are spelt out in the Act.

If a Hindu wife is living separately, she is also entitled to claim her maintenance from her husband if any of the following sub-clauses of Section 18(2) of Hindu Adoption and Maintenance Act, 1956 falls under her case:

(*a*) if her husband is guilty of desertion, that is to say, of abandoning her without reasonable cause and without her consent or against her wish, or wilfully neglecting her;

(*b*) if he has treated her with such cruelty as to cause a reasonable apprehension in her mind that it will be harmful or injurious to live with her husband;

(*c*) if he is suffering from a virulent form of leprosy;

(*d*) if he has any other wife living;

(*e*) if he keeps a concubine in the same house in which his wife is living or habitually resides with a concubine elsewhere;

(*c*) if he has ceased to be a Hindu by conversion to another religion;

(*g*) if there is any other cause justifying living separately.

55. The concept of human rights is a product of modern history with its roots in a number of religious, philosophical and political theories that developed mainly in eighteenth- and nineteenth-century Europe. Thus, it will be wrong to say that human rights are essentially a product of bureaucracy.

56. None of the clauses of Article 29 of the Universal Declaration of Human rights states so as mentioned in Assertion (A). On the contrary, this Article correctly states, "Everyone has duties to the community in which alone the free and full development of his personality is possible. In the exercise of his rights and freedoms, everyone shall be subject only to such limitations as are determined by law solely for the purpose of securing due recognition and respect for the

rights and freedoms of others and of meeting the just requirements of morality, public order and the general welfare in a democratic society. These rights and freedoms may in no case be exercised contrary to the purposes and principles of the United Nations."

57. Whosoever on the ground of "untouchability" prevents any person from entering any place of public worship which is open to other persons professing the same religion or any section thereof as such person; or from worshipping or offering prayers or performing any religious service in any place of public worship, or bathing in, or using the waters of any sacred tank, well, spring or water-course, river or lake or bathing at any that of such tank, water course river or lake in the same manner and to the same extent as is permissible to the other person professing the same religion or any section thereof, as such person; then according to Section 3 of the Protection of Civil Rights Act, 1955, he shall be punishable with imprisonment for a term of not less than one month and not more than six months and also with fine which shall be not less than one hundred rupees and not more than five hundred rupees.

58. The Universal Declaration of Human Rights (UDHR) is a declaration adopted by the United Nations General Assembly on 10 December 1948 at the Palais de Chaillot, Paris. The Declaration arose directly from the experience of the Second World War and represents the first global expression of rights to which all human beings are inherently entitled. Article 6 of UDHR is Right to recognition as a person before the law that means everyone has the right to recognition everywhere as a person before the law.

59. (*a*) Article 4 of The Third Geneva Convention relates to the treatment of prisoners of war. It is one of the four treaties of the Geneva Conventions. The Geneva Convention relative to the Treatment of Prisoners of War was first adopted in 1929, but significantly revised and replaced by the Third Geneva Convention of 1949. It defines humanitarian protections for prisoners of war.

(*b*) Articles 13 to 16 of Geneva Convention state that prisoners of war must be treated humanely without any adverse discrimination and that their medical needs must be met.

(*c*) Articles 17 to 20 dictate what information a prisoner must give and interrogation methods that the detaining power may use: "No physical or mental torture, nor any other form of coercion".

(*d*) Article 91 that pertains to the escape of a prisoner of war shall be deemed to have succeeded when (i) he has joined the armed forces of the Power on which he depends, or those of an allied Power; (ii) he has left the territory under the control of the Detaining Power, or of an ally of the said Power; (iii) he has joined a ship flying the flag of the Power on which he depends, or of an allied Power, in the territorial waters of the Detaining Power, the said ship not being under the control of the last named Power. Prisoners of war who have made good their escape in the sense of this Article and who are recaptured, shall not be liable to any punishment in respect of their previous escape.

61. The case of State of Kerala & Anr Vs. N.M. Thomas & Ors on 19 September 1975 is about whether the State Government can grant exemption for specified period to employees belonging only to the scheduled castes or scheduled tribes from passing departmental test for the purpose of promotion under clause (1) of Article 16 of the Constitution. It is an important question, which arises for determination in this appeal filed on certificate by the State of Kerala and the Inspector General of Registration against the judgement of the Kerala High Court. The

High Court answered the question in the negative in a petition filed by N.M. Thomas, a lower divisional clerk of the Registration Department of the Kerala State, respondent No.1, under Article 226 of the Constitution.

62. Among the aims of law of tort, the two main of them include Deterrence to wrongdoers and Damages to victims. Deterrence is often used in relation to criminal law; the basic theory of deterrence is aimed at deterring the criminal from repeating his offences or deterring from repeating the same act. Damages to victims concerns with justice, which has two aspects: one is for the victim and other is for the wrongdoer, which are compensation to the victim and retribution against the defendant.

63. Prafullachandra Natwarlal Bhagwati (born 21 December 1921) was the 17th Chief Justice of India, serving from 12 July 1985 until his retirement on 20 December 1986. He is well known for introducing the concepts of Public Interest Litigation and Absolute liability in India.

64. Certain types of communications are absolutely privileged. Absolute privilege means that the person making the statement has the absolute right to make that statement at that time, even if it is defamatory. In other words, the person making the defamatory statement is immune from a defamation lawsuit. Generally, absolute privilege exempts persons from liability for potentially defamatory statements made. Defence of absolute privilege in case of defamation is available in such cases as Judicial Proceedings, State of Communications, and Parliamentary Proceedings.

65. Generally known as *negligence*, the area of tort law involves harm caused by *carelessness*, not intentional harm, as Jay M. Feinman of the Rutgers University School of Law, remarks, "The core idea of negligence is that people should exercise reasonable care when they act by taking account of the potential harm that they might foreseeably cause to other people". Duty of care towards the other is a moral duty of each individual. One should always be caring about his neighbours and those around him rather than being negligent in any manner, which may cause harm to them in different forms. If one commits a breach of that duty, it will be an essential ingredient of the tort of negligence. Similarly, if others suffer damage as a consequence of negligence by someone, it will also be counted among the sheer negligence according to tort law.

66. The expression 'duty' in tort law means a duty of care that is a legal obligation (duty), which is imposed on an individual requiring adherence to a standard of reasonable care while performing any acts that could foreseeably harm others. It is the first element that must be established to proceed with an action in negligence. The claimant must be able to show a duty of care imposed by law, which the defendant has breached.

68. Consumer Protection Act is an Act of the Parliament of India enacted in 1986 to protect the interests of consumers in India. It makes provision for the establishment of consumer councils and other authorities for the settlement of consumers' disputes and for matters connected therewith, as this Act intends to protect a large body of consumers from exploitation.

69. Contractual capacity refers to the ability of a contracting party to enter into legally binding relations. If a party does not have the capacity to do so, then subsequent contracts may be invalid; however, in the interests of certainty, there is a prima facie presumption that both parties hold the capacity to contract.

A bilateral contract is the type of agreement most people regard a traditional contract as a mutual exchange of promises among the parties. In a bilateral contract, each party may be considered as both making a promise, and being the beneficiary of a promise.

Mutual and free consent of parties to the contract of sale of goods means a legally enforceable agreement between two or more parties with mutual obligations. Mutually agreed contract needs to obtain consent of each party involved in the sale and purchase of the goods.

70. The legal definition of a partnership is generally stated as "an association of two or more persons to carry on as co-owners of a business for profit" (Revised Uniform Partnership Act § 101 [1994]). Partnership is an agency. When a partner has the apparent or actual authority and acts on behalf of the business, the partner binds the partnership and each of the partners for the resulting obligations. Similarly, a partner's admission concerning the partnership's affairs is considered an admission of the partnership.

72. A director is an agent of his company. He can bind the company with valid contracts entered into with third parties such as buyers, lenders, and suppliers.

74. Though children and teenagers below the age of 18 years are considered minors under current rules, a 16-year old girl can draw a cheque. To boost financial inclusion, the Reserve Bank of India (RBI) has said that banks are at liberty to allow minors above 10 years to independently open and operate savings bank accounts. So, once they are allowed to open and operate bank accounts independently, naturally drawing a cheque and all transactions pertaining to bank account are also allowed to them.

Previous Paper (Solved)

UGC-NET/JRF & Assistant Professor Exam Law, December-2014

PAPER-II

Note : *This paper contains **fifty (50)** objective type questions of **two (2)** marks each. **All** questions are compulsory.*

1. Which of the following statements is right?

A. Law consist of rules in accordance with reason and nature has formed the basis of imperative law

B. Natural law is a type of command

C. Law, according to positivist, is made through medium of courts

D. Hart talks in terms of conduct supplemented by an attitude of mind to the effect that the conduct in question is obligatory because it is required by rule

2. Right *in re aliena* means a right over

A. his own property

B. a property of someone else

C. property situated in a foreign country

D. property situated in one's own country

3. Assertion (A) : A perfect duty is one which a man not merely ought to perform, but may be justly compelled to perform.

Reason (R) : A perfect duty is one which is not merely recognised by law but enforced.

1. (A) is true, but (R) is false.
2. (A) is false, but (R) is true.
3. Both (A) and (R) are true.
4. Both (A) and (R) are false.

A. 1 and 2 B. 2 and 3

C. 3 alone D. 4 alone

4. Possession is prima facie evidence of title of ownership. Hence :

A. long adverse possession confers title even to a property which originally belonged to another

B. in all cases possession leads to ownership

C. transfer of possession is not a mode of transferring ownership

D. long possession do not confer title to the property which originally belonged to government

5. Who among the following said that there is in essence no difference between the legal personality of a company and that of an individual?

A. Maitland B. Dicey

C. Gierke D. Kelson

6. Ownership of Goodwill of a business is

A. Limited ownership

B. Corporeal ownership

C. Incorporeal ownership

D. Beneficial ownership

7. It was remarked in 'Golaknath *vs.* State of Punjab' that our 'Preamble to the Constitution contains in a nutshell its ideals and aspirations' by one of the judges?

A. Justice V.R. Krishna Iyer

B. Justice K. Subba Rao

C. Justice A.N. Ray

D. Justice H.R. Khanna

8. Right of eligible employees to be considered for promotion is virtually a part of Fundamental Right of employees, was decided by the Supreme Court in:

A. Union of India *vs.* Hemraj Singh Chauhan

B. Supreme Court Employees Association *vs.* Union of India

C. John Vallamattam *vs.* Union of India

D. St. Stephens College *vs.* University of Delhi

9. In Vishram Singh Raghubanshi *vs.* State of Uttar Pradesh (AIR2011 SC2275) the court held that:

A. It is the duty of Superior Courts to protect the reputation of judicial officers of subordinate courts

B. Procedure laid down in the appointment of officers of subordinate courts

C. Procedure laid down in the salaries and service conditions of the judicial officers of the lower judiciary

D. Transfer of the Judges of the High Court

10. In which of these cases, Fundamental Duties are judicially invoked? Answer using codes given below:

(*i*) Prem Prakash *vs.* Punjab University

(*ii*) Suresh Koshy George *vs.* University of Kerala

(*iii*) Rural Litigation and Entitlement Kendra *vs.* State of Uttar Pradesh

(*iv*) Shri Sachidanand Pandey *vs.* State of West Bengal

Codes:

A. (*i*) and (*ii*) are correct

B. (*ii*) and (*iii*) are correct

C. (*iii*) and (*iv*) are correct

D. (*i*), (*ii*), (*iii*) and (*iv*) are correct

11. Match List-I with List-II using codes given below:

List-I

(*i*) Executive power must be exercised in accordance with the Constitution.

(*ii*) Executive power is the residue of functions of Government, which are not legislative or judicial.

(*iii*) Executive power may be exercised without prior legislative support.

(*iv*) The President is not bound to hear a petitioner for mercy before he rejects the petition.

List-II

(*a*) H.H. Maharajadhiraja Madhav Rao Jivaji Rao Scindia Bahadur *vs.* Union of India

(*b*) Maganbhai Ishwarbhai Patel *vs.* Union of India

(*c*) Kehar Singh *vs.* Union of India

(*d*) A. Sanjeevi Naidu *vs.* State of Madras

Codes :

	(*i*)	(*ii*)	(*iii*)	(*iv*)
A.	(*d*)	(*a*)	(*b*)	(*c*)
B.	(*a*)	(*d*)	(*b*)	(*c*)
C.	(*d*)	(*a*)	(*c*)	(*b*)
D.	(*b*)	(*c*)	(*a*)	(*d*)

12. The Supreme Court has laid down guidelines for imposing emergency under Art. 356 in one of the following cases:

A. A.K. Roy *vs.* Union of India

B. S.R. Bommai *vs.* Union of India

C. State of Rajasthan *vs.* Union of India

D. Rameśwar Prasad *vs.* Union of India

13. By which constitutional amendment "The total number of ministers, including the Prime Minister, in the Council of Ministers shall not exceed fifteen per cent of the total number of members of the House of the people"?

A. Ninety First B. Ninety Second

C. Ninety Third D. Ninety Fifth

14. Match List-I with List-II and give correct answers by using the codes given below:

List-I

(Principles applied by the Courts)

1. Law must be based on justice, equity and good conscience
2. Subrogation
3. Res-Judicata
4. Estoppel

List-II (Cases)

(*a*) R.V. Keyn

(*b*) Chorzaw Factory (Indemnity) Case

(*c*) Mavrommatis Palestine Concessions Case

(*d*) Barcelona Traction Case

Codes :

	(*a*)	(*b*)	(*c*)	(*d*)
A.	3	2	4	1
B.	1	3	2	4
C.	2	4	3	1
D.	1	2	3	4

15. Who is not the Exponent of the Constitutive Theory of 'Recognition'?

A. Hegel B. Oppenheim
C. Hall D. Anzilloti

16. Match List-I with List-II and select the correct answer using the codes given below :

List-I
(Sources of Public International Law)

1. General principles of law recognised by the civilized countries
2. Juristic Work
3. International Customs
4. Justice and Equity

List-II (Case-related)

(*a*) North Continental Self case
(*b*) Burkina Faso *vs.* Mali
(*c*) Portugal *vs.* India
(*d*) Paquete Habaana case

Codes :

	(*a*)	(*b*)	(*c*)	(*d*)
A.	1	2	3	4
B.	2	3	4	1
C.	3	4	1	2
D.	4	1	3	2

17. Statement-I : Subject to Rules of Jus Cogens, local customary law can supplement or derogate from general custom.

Statement-II : International law does not recognise the concept of local custom.

Using the codes given below give the correct answer:

A. Both the Statements are individually true and Statement-II is the correct explanation of statement-I.
B. Both the Statements are individually true but Statement-II is not the correct explanation of Statement-I.
C. Statement-I is true, but Statement-II is false.
D. Statement-I is false, but Statement-II is true.

18. Using the codes given below indicate the chronological sequence in which the following judgements were delivered by the International Court of Justice:

1. Right of passage over Indian Territory case.
2. South-West Africa case.
3. Frontier Dispute.
4. Temple of Preah Vihear

Codes:

A. 1, 2, 3, 4 B. 2, 4, 1, 3
C. 1, 4, 2, 3 D. 3, 2, 4, 1

19. Match List-I with List-II and give the correct answer by using the codes given below:

List-I
(Provisions under Statute of International Court of Justice)

1. Binding force of decrees of International Court of Justice
2. Methods of conferring Jurisdiction upon the court.
3. Advisory Jurisdiction of the Court.
4. Courts power to allow a state to intervene in case to which it is not a party

List-II (Related Articles)

(*a*) Article 65
(*b*) Article 62
(*c*) Article 59
(*d*) Article 36

Codes :

	(*a*)	(*b*)	(*c*)	(*d*)
A.	3	4	1	2
B.	2	3	4	1
C.	4	2	3	1
D.	1	2	3	4

20. In which of the following cases, a child could not be a 'Hindu' under the Hindu Marriage Act, 1955?

I. Only one parent is a Hindu and the child was brought up as a Hindu.
II. If after the birth of a child both the parents convert to Buddhism.
III. Only one parent is Jain and the child was not brought up as a Jain.
IV. If after the birth of a child both the parents convert to Muslim religion and in the exercise of parental right the child is also converted to Muslim religion.

Codes:

A. I, II and IV B. III and IV
C. II and I D. I, II and III

21. When two Hindus are descendants of a common ancestress but by different husbands, they are said to be related to each other by

A. Uterine Blood B. Half Blood
C. Full Blood D. Fosterage

22. A 'Muta' marriage is:

I. A temporary marriage.
II. Recognized under Sunni law.
III. Recognized under Shia law.
IV. For a fixed period.

Codes:

A. II and IV only B. I, II, III and IV
C. I, III and IV D. II and III

23. A decree of judicial separation:

I. dissolve the matrimonial bond.
II. does not dissolve the matrimonial bond but merely suspends marital rights and obligations during the subsistence of the decree.
III. mandates that the parties still continue to be husband and wife but not obliged to live together.
IV. provides that if the parties have not resumed cohabitation for a period of one year either party may seek divorce.

Codes:

A. I, II and IV B. I, II, III and IV
C. I and IV D. II, III and IV

24. Match List-I with List-II and select the correct answer with the help of codes given below:

List-I	**List-II**
(*i*) Ijma	(*a*) Cancellation of marriage
(*ii*) Faskh	(*b*) Opinion of one individual only
(*iii*) Mahr-ul-misl	(*c*) Collective opinion of commentators
(*iv*) Qiyas	(*d*) Customary dower

Codes :

	(*i*)	(*ii*)	(*iii*)	(*iv*)
A.	(*c*)	(*a*)	(*d*)	(*b*)
B.	(*a*)	(*b*)	(*c*)	(*d*)
C.	(*c*)	(*d*)	(*b*)	(*a*)
D.	(*d*)	(*b*)	(*a*)	(*c*)

25. Rules relating to spinda relationship are based on the principle of

A. Polygyny B. Endogamy
C. Exogamy D. Polyandry

26. Divorce by Zihar is a species of

A. actual divorce
B. inchoate divorce
C. khula divorce
D. constructive divorce

27. For a valid contract acceptance should be

A. absolute and qualified
B. partial but unqualified
C. absolute and unqualified
D. absolutely qualified

28. According to Explanation 2 to Section 25 of the Indian Contract Act, which of the following statements are correct?

I. An agreement to which the consent of the promisor is not freely given is valid because consideration is adequate.
II. An agreement to which the consent of promisor is freely given is valid even if consideration is inadequate.
III. Consideration must be legal.
IV. Consideration can be illegal.

Codes:

A. I and II are correct
B. II and III are correct
C. III and IV are correct
D. I and IV are correct

29. In Jyotindra Bhattacharjee *vs.* Mrs. Sona Balon Bora, it was held that

A. the onus of proving soundness of mind of a person always rests upon a person who alleges such state of mind of another person.
B. the onus of proving unsoundness of mind of a person always rests upon a person who alleges such state of mind of another person.
C. the onus of proving unsoundness of mind rests upon person of unsound mind.
D. the onus of proving unsoundness of mind is on the judge deciding the case involving person of unsound mind.

30. Read Assertion (A) and Reason (R) and give the correct explanation with the help of codes given below:

Assertion (A) : Agreement is void when both parties are under mistake as to the matter of law.

Reason (R) : Parties entering into a contract are legally obliged to know the law relating to the contract.

Codes:

A. (A) and (R) are correct and (R) is correct reason for (A).
B. (A) is correct, but (R) is wrong.
C. (R) is correct, but (A) is wrong.
D. Both (A) and (R) are wrong.

31. Where, a law promulgated after the contract is made, makes the performance of the agreement impossible, the agreement becomes

A. Voidable B. Valid
C. Void D. Absolutely binding

32. Match List-I with List-II and select the correct answer using the codes given below:

List-I

(*i*) Damages arising in the usual course of things
(*ii*) Compensation for mental anguish
(*iii*) Measure of damages
(*iv*) Compensation for breach of contract where penalty is stipulated for

List-II

(*a*) Ghaziabad Dev. Authority *vs.* Union of India
(*b*) Hadley *vs.* Baxendale
(*c*) M/s. Ganga Maruthi *vs.* Nagaraj
(*d*) Jamal *vs.* Moolla Dawood

Codes :

	(*i*)	(*ii*)	(*iii*)	(*iv*)
A.	(*b*)	(*a*)	(*d*)	(*c*)
B.	(*a*)	(*b*)	(*d*)	(*c*)
C.	(*b*)	(*a*)	(*c*)	(*d*)
D.	(*d*)	(*c*)	(*a*)	(*b*)

33. Who is the propounder of 'Pigeon hole' theory?

A. Winfield B. Salmond
C. Flemming D. Paton

34. The owner of the bus instructed the driver not to race and compete with other omnibuses on a particular route. Driver still tried to obstruct a rival omnibus and caused an accident. What shall be the nature of liability?

A. The driver shall be liable for the accident because he did not follow the instructions of his owner.
B. It shall be the liability of the owner of bus because he has no authority to give instruction to his driver and his act was totally wrong.
C. The owner of the bus shall be vicariously liable for the accident committed by his driver during the course of employment.
D. Neither owner nor driver shall be liable.

35. Which of the following is NOT a sovereign function of the State?

A. Construction of military road
B. Injury to the plaintiff during the lathi-charge by the police to disperse the unlawful crowd
C. A government jeep being taken from the workshop to the collector's bungalow fo[r] his use
D. Distribution of meals to army personnel

36. **Assertion (A) :** A wooden chair while bein[g] used by a guest, caused an injury to him du[e] to defective manufacture. The guest is entitle[d] to claim damages from the manufacturer.

Reason (R) : The manufacturer owes a dut[y] to take care only towards the lawful buye[r] under the Consumer Protection Act.

Codes:

A. Both (A) and (R) are true and (R) is th[e] correct explanation of (A).
B. Both (A) and (R) are true, but (R) is n[ot] the correct explanation of (A).
C. (A) is true, but (R) is false.
D. (A) is false, but (R) is true.

37. If a journalist publishes an article in a leadi[ng] newspaper that all lawyers were thieves, [no] particular lawyer could sue him unless the[re] is something to point to the particul[ar] individual. It refers to

A. Defamation of a company
B. Innuendo
C. Defamation of public figures
D. Defamation of class of persons

38. Match the List-I with List-II and select the correct answer using the codes given below:

List-I (Name of Case)
1. Municipal Corporation *vs.* Subhagwanti
2. Roop Lal *vs.* Union of India
3. State *vs.* Chironji Lal
4. Rural Transport Service *vs.* Bezlum Bibi

List-II (Name of Court)
(*a*) High Court of Madhya Pradesh
(*b*) High Court of Jammu & Kashmir
(*c*) High Court of Calcutta
(*d*) Supreme Court

Codes :

	1	2	3	4
A.	(*d*)	(*b*)	(*a*)	(*c*)
B.	(*b*)	(*a*)	(*d*)	(*c*)
C.	(*c*)	(*d*)	(*b*)	(*a*)
D.	(*d*)	(*a*)	(*c*)	(*b*)

39. The Revenue Inspector knowingly disobeys the direction to conduct enquiry at a place for demarcation, what offence, if any, has been caused by him under IPC?
A. An offence as per Sec. 166-A
B. For continuing to remain in an unlawful assembly as per Sec. 145
C. For touching any point material as per Sec. 199
D. For giving false information as per Sec. 201

40. A man has committed physical contact involving unwelcome sexual overture against a female. What offence has been caused by him under IPC?
A. Requesting for sexual favour as per Sec. 354-A(1)(ii)
B. Sexual harassment as per Sec. 354(1)(i)
C. Out-raging of modesty as per Sec. 354
D. Attempt to rape as per Sec. 370(A)

41. Read the Assertion (A) and the Reason (R) given below to answer the correct explanation using the codes:

Assertion (A) : The legal right involves freedom from penalty.

Reason (R) : A legal right is one which is either enforceable or recognised.

Codes :
A. Both (A) and (R) are correct, but (R) is not the correct explanation of (A).
B. Both (A) and (R) are true and (R) is the correct explanation of (A).
C. Assertion (A) is correct, but Reason (R) is wrong.
D. Assertion (A) is incorrect because Reason (R) fixes liability when not enforceable or derecognised.

42. The maxim 'ream linguam non facit nisi mens rea' is propounded by
A. Coke B. Lord Kenyon
C. Augustine D. Lord Arbinger

43. Fill in the gap:
Disobedience of law is not ordinarily a crime unless that act is declared as crime by some ....
A. law B. method
C. society D. All the above

44. The Indian Penal Code prohibits fixing of liability on a person so long he is authorised or gives assent to it. But there is an exceptional situation arising out of:
A. Libel
B. Public nuisance
C. Contempt of Court
D. All of them

45. Who among the following moved a resolution in the Central Legislative Assembly recommending that the Government should introduce a legislation for registration and protection of Trade Union in the year 1921?
A. B.P. Wadia B. M.N. Joshi
C. N.M. Lokhanddey D. V.V. Giri

46. "Works Committee under the Industrial Disputes Act should be substituted by an 'Industrial Relations Committee' to promote in-house dispute settlement." This recommendation was made by

A. Royal Commission on Labour
B. National Commission on Labour 1969
C. National Commission on Labour 2002
D. National Commission for enterprises in the Unorganised Sector

47. Who is a protected workman under the Industrial Disputes Act? Answer from the codes given below:
1. A workman who is a member of a registered Trade Union.
2. Recognised by the Registrar of the Trade Union as protected workman.
3. A workman who is a member of the Executive or other office bearer of a registered Trade Union connected with the establishment.
4. Recognised as protected workman under the rules applicable to the establishment.

Codes:
A. 1 and 2 B. 2 and 4
C. 3 and 4 D. 1 and 3

48. Failure of the conciliation proceedings under the Industrial Disputes Act leads to refer the matter to adjudication by
A. the conciliation officer
B. both employer and employee
C. the employer
D. the appropriate government

49. The power of the Government to refer a Dispute under the Industrial Disputes Act is
A. Mandatory
B. Discretionary
C. Recommendatory
D. Either mandatory or discretionary

50. Read the Assertion (A) and Reason (R). Write the correct answer using the codes given below:

Assertion (A) : The conciliation officer has no power under the Industrial Disputes Act when neither industrial disputes exists or apprehended.

Reason (R) : Conciliation officer only investigates the Industrial disputes which exists or apprehended.

Codes:
A. Both (A) and (R) are wrong.
B. Both (A) and (R) are correct.
C. (A) is correct and (R) is wrong.
D. (A) is wrong and (R) is correct.

ANSWERS

1	2	3	4	5	6	7	8	9	10
D	B	C	A	D	C	D	A	D	C
11	**12**	**13**	**14**	**15**	**16**	**17**	**18**	**19**	**20**
A	B	A	B	C	D	C	C	A	B
21	**22**	**23**	**24**	**25**	**26**	**27**	**28**	**29**	**30**
A	C	D	A	C	B	C	B	B	D
31	**32**	**33**	**34**	**35**	**36**	**37**	**38**	**39**	**40**
C	A	B	C	C	C	D	A	A	B
41	**42**	**43**	**44**	**45**	**46**	**47**	**48**	**49**	**50**
B	C	A	D	B	C	C	D	B	B

SOME SELECTED EXPLANATORY ANSWERS

1. Justice H.R. Khanna had remarked in 'Golaknath *vs.* State of Punjab' that our 'Preamble to the Constitution contains in a nutshell its ideals and aspirations'. In Golaknath *vs.* State of Punjab, the constitutional validity of the Seventeenth

Amendment Act (1964) which inserted certain state acts in the Ninth Schedule was challenged. The Supreme Court ruled that the Fundamental Rights are given a 'transcendental and immutable' position and hence the Parliament cannot abridge or take away any of these Rights. A constitutional amendment act is also a law within the meaning of Article 13 and hence would be void for violating any of the Fundamental Rights.

10. Fundamental Duties were judicially invoked in Rural Litigation and Entitlement Kendra *vs.* State of Uttar Pradesh and in Shri Sachidanand Pandey *vs.* State of West Bengal. The Fundamental Duties in the Indian Constitution are inspired by the Constitution of erstwhile USSR. In 1976, the Congress Party set up the Sardar Swaran Singh Committee to make recommendations about fundamental duties. The committee recommended the inclusion of a separate chapter on fundamental duties in the constitution. The congress government at centre accepted these recommendations and enacted the 42nd Constitutional Amendment Act in 1976.

12. In S.R. Bommai *vs.* Union of India (1994), the following propositions have been laid down by the Supreme Court on imposition of President's rule in a state under Article 356:

1. The presidential proclamation imposing President's Rule is subject to judicial review.
2. The satisfaction of the President must be based on relevant material. The action of the President can be struck down by the court if it is based on irrelevant or extraneous grounds or if it was found to be malafide or perverse.
3. Burden lies on the centre to prove that relevant material exist to justify the imposition of the President's rule.
4. The court cannot go into the correctness of the material or its adequacy but it can see whether it is relevant to the action.
5. If the court holds the presidential proclamation to be unconstitutional and invalid, it has power to restore the dismissed state government and revive the state legislative assembly if it was suspended or dissolved.
6. The state legislative assembly should be dissolved only after the Parliament has approved the presidential proclamation. Until such approval is given, the president can only suspend the assembly. In case the Parliament fails to approve the proclamation, the assembly would get reactivated.
7. Secularism is one of the 'basic features' of the constitution. Hence a state government pursuing anti-secular politics is liable to action under Article 356.
8. The power under Article 356 is an exceptional power and should be used only occasionally to meet the requirements of special situations.

15. Hegel, Anzilloti and Oppenheim have advocated the constitutive theory. According to this theory, an entity does not become a state by possessing essential attributes of statehood, it becomes so when it recognised by other states. It implies that other states constitute the personality of a state by granting recognition. Thus a new entity cannot become a state ipso facto, it has to be recognized by other states so as to become an international person (and thus acquire rights and duties under international law).

18. The correct chronological sequence in which the following judgements were delivered by the International Court of Justice:

(*a*) Rights of passage over Indian Territory case – 1960

(*b*) Temple of Preah Vihear – 1962

(*c*) South-West Africa case – 1966

(*d*) Frontier Dispute – 1986

22. Muta is a distinct kind of marriage recognised only by the Shias, Muta may be defined as a temporary union of male and female for specified duration, on payment of some consideration. As against the permanent or a regular marriage (Nikah), the Muta may be regarded as a temporary marriage. Literal meaning of the Arabic word 'Muta' is 'enjoyment'; therefore it may also be regarded as 'marriage for pleasure'.

27. According to section 2(b) of the Indian Contract Act, 1872—"when the person to whom the proposal is made signifies his assent thereto, the proposal is said to be accepted". Acceptance must be absolute and unqualified. For example, A says to B "I offer to sell my car for ₹ 50,000." B replies "I will purchase it for ₹ 45,000." This is not acceptance and hence it amounts to a counter offer.

33. Salmond propounded the concept of 'Pigeon hole theory'. According to this theory, the 'law of torts' consists of a neat/clear set of pigeon-holes each containing a labelled/specific tort like assault, battery, false imprisonment, slander etc. If the defendant's wrong will not fit any of these pigeon-holes he has committed no tort.

34. Generally speaking a person is liable for his own acts, but in many cases he may be held responsible for the torts committed by others. This is known as the 'vicarious liability' i.e. liability incurred for, or instead of, another. A master is liable for the torts committed by his servant while acting in the course of his employment. The servant is also liable. They are considered to be joint tort-feasors and their liability is joint and several.

34. The master's liability arises when the following essentials are present:
(*a*) The tort was committed by his servant;
(*b*) The servant committed the tort while acting in the course of the employment.

35. As regards immunity from tortuous liability, an important issue that has to be considered, relates to position of the government. The doctrine of 'sovereign immunity' implies that a state can claim immunity from law just because it is sovereign. In P & O, Steam Navigation Co. *vs.* Secretary of State, India (1861) 5 Bom. H.C.R. App. 1, it was held that if the act was done in the exercise of sovereign functions the East India Company would not have been liable, but if the function was a non-sovereign one it would have been liable. In the above case, maintenance of the dockyard was considered to be a non-sovereign function and therefore, for the negligence of its employees the government was held liable.

37. A group or class of people cannot sue for defamation. However, if a defamatory statement is made about a group or class of people and the group is small enough or the state or the statement is presented in such a way that it is understood to refer to an individual or individuals who are members of the group or class, the individuals may have a claim.

45. N.M. Joshi moved a resolution in the Central Legislative Assembly recommending that the government should introduce a legislation for registration and protection of Trade Union in the year 1921.

46. The National Commission on Labour 2002 recommended that "works committee under the Industrial Disputes Act should be substituted by an Industrial Relations Committee to provide in-house dispute settlement.

47. Section 33(3) of the Industrial Disputes Act 1947 provides that a workman means (*a*) A workman who is a member of the Executive or other officer bearer of a registered Trade Union connected with the establishment and (*b*) Recognized as a protected workman under the rules applicable to the establishment.

48. Under section 10 of the Industrial Disputes Act, 1947—where the appropriate government is of the opinion that any industrial dispute exists or is apprehended, it may refer the dispute for adjudication.

49. Under section 10 of the Industrial Disputes Act, 1947, the appropriate government has the discretionary power to refer the dispute for arbitration.

PAPER-III

Note : *This paper contains **seventy five** (75) objective type questions of **two** (2) marks each. **All** questions are compulsory.*

1. Read Assertion (A) and Reason (R) and answer using the codes given below:

Assertion (A) : The writ of Habeas Corpus can be granted to enable the detainee to argue his case in person.

Reason (R) : Because R *vs.* Secretary of State for Home Department ex parte Wynne (1992) decided so.

Codes:

A. (A) and (R) are right and (R) is right reason for (A).
B. (A) is right, but (R) is wrong.
C. (A) is wrong, but (R) is right.
D. Both (A) and (R) are wrong.

2. Which of the following are matched incorrectly?

(*i*) Habeas Corpus – 'To produce the body'
(*ii*) Quo warranto – 'Issued to a lower court to stop proceedings in a case'.
(*iii*) Prohibition – 'Issued to a lower court quashing a decision or order'
(*iv*) Mandamus – 'Commands a person to perform a public duty'.

A. (*i*), (*ii*) and (*iii*) B. (*ii*) and (*iii*)
C. (*ii*), (*iii*) and (*iv*) D. (*ii*) and (*iv*)

3. Article 51 A of the Constitution of India is confined to

A. All citizens of India
B. All persons of India
C. All Non-Residents of India
D. All students of India

4. Read Assertion (A) and Reason (R) and answer using codes given below:

Assertion (A) : Code of conduct has statutory force.

Reason (R) : Because Article 102 of the Constitution says so.

Codes:

A. (A) and (R) are right and (R) is right reason for (A).
B. Both (A) and (R) are wrong.
C. (A) is right, but (R) is wrong.
D. (R) is right, but (A) is wrong.

5. Read Assertion (A) and Reason (R) to answer using codes given below:

Assertion (A) : One of the two Acts enacted under List I Entry 66 and the other under List III Entry 25 can be repugnant to each other.

Reason (R) : Because in Annamalai University *vs.* Secretary of Inf. and Tourism Department decided so.

Codes:

A. (A) and (R) are right and (R) is right reason for (A).
B. (A) is right, but (R) is wrong.
C. (A) is wrong, but (R) is right.
D. Both (A) and (R) are wrong.

6. If the Government is defeated on the floor of Rajya Sabha, what is the consequence?

A. Parliament is dissolved.
B. Prime Minister has to submit his resignation.
C. President's rule is imposed immediately.
D. Nothing happens.

7. Read Assertion (A) and Reason (R) and answer using the codes given below:

Assertion (A) : The power under 368 of the Constitution is a constituent power subject to the constitutional scheme as to distribution of legislative power according to entries in the Seventh Schedule.

Reason (R) : Because Sasanka Sekhar Maity *vs.* Union of India decided so.

Codes :

A. Both (A) and (R) are wrong.
B. Both (A) and (R) are right, but (R) is not right reason for (A).
C. (A) is right and (R) is wrong.
D. (A) is wrong and (R) is right.

8. Using codes given below, find out correct answers:

Administrative law deals with

(*i*) the powers of constitutional authorities

(*ii*) the powers of judicial authorities

(*iii*) the powers of the administrative authorities

(*iv*) the powers of the legislative authorities.

Codes :

A. Only (*i*) and (*ii*) are correct.

B. Only (*ii*) is correct.

C. Only (*iii*) is correct.

D. (*i*), (*ii*), (*iii*) and (*iv*) are correct.

9. Match List-I with List-II using codes given below :

List-I

(*i*) There is no rigid formula for principles of natural justice.

(*ii*) Choice of application of rules of natural justice.

(*iii*) Justice should not only be done, but manifestly and undoubtedly be seen to be done.

(*iv*) Meaning of bias

List-II

(*a*) R.S. Dass *vs.* Union of India

(*b*) R. *vs.* Sussex Justices

(*c*) Union of India *vs.* P.K. Roy

(*d*) Secy. to Govt. Transport Dept. *vs.* Munuswamy

Codes :

	(*i*)	(*ii*)	(*iii*)	(*iv*)
A.	(*b*)	(*d*)	(*a*)	(*c*)
B.	(*c*)	(*a*)	(*d*)	(*b*)
C.	(*a*)	(*c*)	(*b*)	(*d*)
D.	(*c*)	(*a*)	(*b*)	(*d*)

10. Read Assertion (A) and Reason (R) and find out correct answer using codes given below:

Assertion (A) : Legitimate expectation does not grant an absolute right to a claimant.

Reason (R) : Legitimate expectation protects the right of fair hearing before a decision which results in negating a promise or withdrawing an undertaking is taken.

Codes :

A. (A) and (R) are true and (R) is correct explanation of (A).

B. (A) and (R) are true, but (R) is not correc explanation of (A).

C. (A) is true and (R) is false.

D. (A) is false and (R) is true.

11. Which of the following statement is correct

A. Gullappalli Nageswara Rao *vs.* State o AP, is about bias.

B. K.L. Tripathi *vs.* State Bank of India, i about right of cross examination.

C. General Medical Council *vs.* Speakmen is about irrelevance of principles of natura justice; if in reaching a decision, th principles make no difference.

D. N. Kalindi *vs.* Tata Locomotives, is abou the right of representation by a lawye being considered to be a part of natura justice and it can be claimed as of righ

12. Which one of the following is the correc statement?

A. While certiorari can be issued again judicial or quasi-judicial authoritie mandamus can be issued again administrative authorities also.

B. Mandamus can be issued for a declaratio that an Act is ultra vires the Constitutio and certiorari can also be issued fo correcting that defect.

C. Certiorari can be issued against a quas judicial authority to prevent it fro exercising jurisdiction not vested in i Mandamus cannot be issued for th purpose.

D. Certiorari cannot be issued again usurping a public officer, but Mandam can be issued for that purpose.

13. Abuse of discretion can be inferred from th following circumstances. Find out the answ from the codes given below:

(*i*) Non-application of mind.

(*ii*) Colourable exercise of power.

(*iii*) Non-observance of audi alteram parten

(*iv*) Irrelevant considerations.

Codes :

A. Only (*i*) is correct.

B. Only (*i*) and (*ii*) are correct.

C. Only (*ii*) and (*iii*) are correct.

D. Only (*ii*), (*iii*) and (*iv*) are correct.

14. What was the principle laid down by the Supreme Court in A.K. Kraipak *vs.* Union of India? Find correct answer from the following statements:

A. Rule of law is embedded in Article 14 of the Constitution of India.

B. Judicial review is a part of basic structure of the Constitution.

C. Principles of natural justice are applicable to administrative proceedings.

D. Post-decisional hearing would be sufficient for the observance of principles of natural justice.

15. Find correct answer from the following statement:

A. A quasi-judicial body may never review its own decision unless authorised by the statute.

B. A quasi-judicial body may review its own decision if there is grave error of law in it.

C. A quasi-judicial body may review its own decision if there is violation of natural justice.

D. All tribunals may review their decisions.

16. Select the correct answer using the code given below on the following decided cases about possession:

1. Cartwright *vs.* Green
2. R. *vs.* Hudson
3. Daimler Co. *vs.* Continental Tyre and Rubber Co.

Codes:

A. 3 only B. 2 and 3

C. 1 and 3 D. 1 and 2

17. Austin described ownership as a right over determinate thing with reference to one of the following. Specify the correct answer.

A. Restricted in point of disposition

B. Indefinite in point of user

C. Unlimited in point of duration

D. Unlimited in point of space

18. Consider the following statements regarding vested and contingent rights:

1. A vested right creates an immediate interest and is transferable and heritable.
2. A contingent right creates an immediate interest and is defeated when the required facts have not occurred.

Which of the Statement given above is/are correct?

A. 1 only B. 2 only

C. Both 1 and 2 D. Neither 1 nor 2

19. There is a clear cut division between the spheres of legislature and judiciary. The former makes the laws and the latter applies them. Which of the school propounds this doctrine?

A. Analytical jurisprudence

B. Historical jurisprudence

C. Sociological jurisprudence

D. Philosophical jurisprudence

20. In which one of the following cases was it observed by the Supreme court that precedent should not be petrified nor judicial dicta divorced from the socio-economic mores of the age?

A. Mamleshwar *vs.* Kanahaiya Lal

B. Bengal Immunity Company Ltd. *vs.* State of Bihar

C. State of West Bengal *vs.* Corporation of Calcutta

D. K.C. Dora *vs.* G Annamanaidu

21. Who among the following divided the sources of Law into formal sources and material sources?

A. Gray B. Keaton

C. Allen D. Salmond

22. According to Professor Goodhart a *ratio decidendi* of a case is

A. the principle of law laid down in a decision which is the decisive element

B. the conclusion reached by the judge on the basis of the material facts of the case

C. the reason given by the court for its decision

D. any opinion of the court on a question of law

23. Read Assertion (A) and Reason (R) and with the help of codes given below find the correct explanation:

Assertion (A) : *Nullum Crimen* is an injunction to the legislature not to implicate all the suspected persons to be prosecuted.

Reason (R) : To avoid impossibility and to settle the question, the legislature must have to use administrative ruling.

Codes:

A. Both (A) and (R) are true and (R) is the correct explanation of (A).

B. Both (A) and (R) are true, but (R) is not the correct explanation of (A).

C. (A) is correct, but (R) is false.

D. (A) is false, but (R) is true.

24. Read Assertion (A) and Reason (R) and with the help of codes given below find the correct explanation:

Assertion (A) : Participation in some manner in the act constituting the offence of common intention by all the persons to be prosecuted is necessary.

Reason (R) : Physical presence at the time of commission of crimes is not mandatory in all cases.

Codes :

A. Both (A) and (R) are true, but (R) is not the correct explanation of (A).

B. Both (A) and (R) are true and (R) is the correct explanation of (A).

C. (A) is correct, but (R) is false.

D. (A) is false, but (R) is true.

25. Which of the mitigating factors do not justify the award of death penalty?

A. Where the murder has been previously planned.

B. Such murder involves exceptional depravity.

C. When such murder was against a public servant while on duty.

D. When the offence was committeed by the accused under the influence of extreme mental disturbance.

26. Read Assertion (A) and Reason (R) and with the help of codes given below find the correct explanation:

Assertion (A) : The gist of conspiracy lies in forming the scheme between two or more persons to perform the overt act.

Reason (R) : The alleged agreement must provide circumstantial evidence about the participation by all to establish conspiracy.

Codes:

A. Both (A) and (R) are true and (R) is the correct explanation of (A).

B. Both (A) and (R) are true, but (R) is not the correct explanation of (A).

C. (A) is correct, but (R) is false.

D. (A) is false, but (R) is true.

27. Which of these facts do not constitute the degree of knowledge for holding a person to be criminally liable for adducing false evidence?

A. A statement known to be false.

B. A statement believed to be false.

C. A statement not believed to be true.

D. An offence committed but not affirmed.

28. What offence, if any, has been caused by the accused 'X' in the following facts:

'X' had some verbal wrangle with his wife 'Y' and incourse of that he gave her a blow with great force and after an interval for two hours 'Y' died. Medical evidence provided the causative factor as rapture in the spleen."

A. Culpable homicide not amounting to murder

B. Grievous hurt

C. Homicide

D. Simple hurt

29. Which of the following properties could not be held to be an offence of theft, when committed/taken by a person?

A. Durga Idol

B. Cooking Gas

C. Running Electricity

D. Forgotten Umbrella

30. Read Assertion (A) and Reason (R) and using codes given below, answer:

Assertion (A) : In criminal breach of trust, there is conversion of property held by a person in a fiduciary capacity.

Reason (R) : A person has a right to convert property held by him in a fiduciary capacity.

Codes:

A. Both (A) and (R) are right and (R) is correct reason for (A).

B. (A) is right, but (R) is wrong.

C. (A) is wrong, but (R) is right.

D. Both (A) and (R) are wrong.

31. The main objective of the Air (Prevention and Control of Pollution) Act is:

A. To provide for the prevention, control and abatement of air pollution.

B. To provide for ensuring standards for emission from automobiles.

C. To put restrictions on the establishment of certain industrial plants.

D. To establish air laboratory for air quality standards.

32. The definition of 'environmental pollution' under the Environment (Protection Act) is:

A. Any pollution of air, water and soil.

B. The presence of any solid, liquid or gaseous substance in the environment that causes injuries to man

C. The presence in the environment of any environmental pollutant

D. Any pollution in land, sea and air

33. Assertion (A) : A company was unlawfully polluting streams and rivers by discharging trade effluents which raised pollution level beyond permissible limits.

Reason (R) : The court decided that the company could not be held liable under Water Act, 1974.

Codes:

A. Both (A) and (R) are true and (R) is the correct explanation of (A).

B. Both (A) and (R) are true, but (R) is not the correct explanation of (A).

C. (A) is true, but (R) is false.

D. (A) is false, but (R) is true.

34. The National Environment Tribunal Act provides for compensation on the basis of no fault liability in the cases of

(*i*) Death of any person

(*ii*) Injury to any person

(*iii*) Death and injury to workman

(*iv*) Damage to any property

Codes :

A. (*i*) and (*ii*) are correct

B. (*ii*) and (*iii*) are correct

C. Only (*iv*) is correct

D. (*i*), (*ii*) and (*iv*) are correct

35. Arrange the following cases in the chronological order on the basis of the year in which they have been decided by the Supreme Court on Public Trust doctrine under Environment law. Use the code given below:

(*i*) M.C. Mehta *vs.* Kamal Nath

(*ii*) M.I. Builders Pvt. Ltd. *vs.* Radhey Shyam Sahu

(*iii*) Hinch Lal Tiwari *vs.* Kamala Devi

(*iv*) Intellectual Forum, Thirupathi *vs.* State of Andhra Pradesh

Codes :

A. (*iv*), (*iii*), (*i*), (*ii*)

B. (*iii*), (*ii*), (*iv*), (*i*)

C. (*iii*), (*i*), (*iv*), (*ii*)

D. (*i*), (*ii*), (*iii*), (*iv*)

36. Match items in List-I with items in List-II using codes given below:

List-I

(*i*) Intergenerational Equity

(*ii*) Sustainable Development

(*iii*) Precautionary Principle

(*iv*) Polluter Pays Principle

List-II

(*a*) Earth Summit, 1992, Principle 15

(*b*) Rio Declaration, 1992, Principle 16

(*c*) Stockholm Declaration 1972, Principles 1 & 2

(*d*) Rio Declaration, 1992, Principle 3

Codes :

	(*i*)	(*ii*)	(*iii*)	(*iv*)
A.	(*d*)	(*c*)	(*a*)	(*b*)
B.	(*a*)	(*c*)	(*b*)	(*d*)
C.	(*b*)	(*d*)	(*a*)	(*c*)
D.	(*c*)	(*d*)	(*a*)	(*b*)

37. For which special purpose a conditional permit for hunting any wild animal, cannot be granted under the Wild Life (Protection) Act?

A. Preparation of snake venom for manufacturing of life saving drugs.

B. Collection of specimen for zoos and museums.

C. Scientific research.

D. Research in traditional and established Universities.

38. Under whose specification the recycling of plastic is undertaken as per the Plastic Manufacture, Sales and Usage Rules, 1999?
A. Indian Standard Institution
B. Bureau of Indian Standards
C. Indian Standard Organisation
D. Indian Plastic Bureau

39. "International law may be defined in broad terms as the body of general principles and specific rules which are binding upon the members of the International Community in their mutual relations". Who has given this definition of Public International Law?
A. J.G. Starke
B. Charles G. Fenwick
C. Whiteman
D. Torsten Gihl

40. Match List-I with List-II and give the correct answer by using the codes given below:

List-I
(Name of Cases)
(*i*) Portugal *vs.* India
(*ii*) Burkina Faso *vs.* Mali
(*iii*) Spain *vs.* Canada
(*iv*) Columbia *vs.* Peru

List-II (Popular Names)
(*a*) The Asylum Case
(*b*) Fisheries Jurisdiction Case
(*c*) Frontier Dispute Case
(*d*) Right of Passage over Indian Territory Case

Codes :

	(*i*)	(*ii*)	(*iii*)	(*iv*)
A.	(*a*)	(*b*)	(*c*)	(*d*)
B.	(*d*)	(*c*)	(*b*)	(*a*)
C.	(*b*)	(*d*)	(*a*)	(*c*)
D.	(*c*)	(*a*)	(*d*)	(*b*)

41. Match List-I with List-II and give the correct answer by using the codes given below:

List-I
(*i*) Recognition clothes the recognized State with rights and duties under International law.
(*ii*) Recognition is merely a formal acknowledgement through which established facts are accepted
(*iii*) State recognized possesses the essential elements of statehood and fit to be subject of International law.
(*iv*) Recognition is final and once granted cannot be withdrawn

List-II
(*a*) De Facto Recognition
(*b*) Constitutive Theory of Recognition
(*c*) De-Jure Recognition
(*d*) Declaratory Theory of Recognition

Codes :

	(*i*)	(*ii*)	(*iii*)	(*iv*)
A.	(*b*)	(*d*)	(*a*)	(*c*)
B.	(*a*)	(*b*)	(*c*)	(*d*)
C.	(*c*)	(*d*)	(*b*)	(*a*)
D.	(*d*)	(*c*)	(*a*)	(*b*)

42. The Estrada Doctrine was propounded by
A. The Home Minister of Mexico
B. The Foreign Minister of Mexico
C. The External Secretary of U.S.A.
D. The Prime Minister of U.K.

43. Provision, "that the U.N.O. has no competence to intervene in matters which are essentially within the domestic jurisdiction of any State", has been provided under which Article of U.N. Charter?
A. Article 1(7) B. Article 2(7)
C. Article 7(2) D. Article 98(7)

44. Match List-I with List-II and give the correct answer by using the codes given below:

List-I (Name of Cases)	**List-II (Year of decision)**
(*i*) Lether *vs.* Sagor	(*a*) 1939
(*ii*) Bank of Ethiopia *vs.* National Bank of Egypt	(*b*) 1942
(*iii*) Arantzazu Mendi Case	(*c*) 1937
(*iv*) U.S. *vs.* Pink	(*d*) 1921

Codes :

	(*i*)	(*ii*)	(*iii*)	(*iv*)
A.	(*a*)	(*b*)	(*c*)	(*d*)
B.	(*c*)	(*d*)	(*b*)	(*a*)
C.	(*b*)	(*a*)	(*d*)	(*c*)
D.	(*d*)	(*c*)	(*a*)	(*b*)

45. Give the chronological order of the following in which they came into existence:
1. Charter of United Nations.
2. Universal Declaration of Human Rights.
3. International Covenant on Civil and Political Rights.
4. International Covenant on Economic, Social and Cultural Rights.

Codes:

A. 1 3 2 4
B. 4 2 1 3
C. 1 2 4 3
D. 3 4 2 1

46. Propositions are:

(*i*) A void marriage remains valid until a decree annulling it has been passed by a competent court.

(*ii*) A void marriage is never a valid marriage and there is no necessity of any decree annulling it.

(*iii*) A voidable marriage is a valid subsisting marriage until a decree annulling it has been passed by a court of competent jurisdiction.

In respect of the aforesaid propositions which is correct?

A. (*i*) and (*iii*) are correct, but (*ii*) is incorrect.
B. (*ii*) and (*iii*) are correct, but (*i*) is incorrect.
C. (*i*) and (*iii*) are incorrect, but (*ii*) is correct.
D. (*i*) and (*ii*) are incorrect, but (*iii*) is correct.

47. A per Section 5 of the Hindu Marriage Act, 1955 the essential conditions of a Hindu marriage are:

(*i*) Monogamy
(*ii*) Mental capacity
(*iii*) The bridegroom has completed the age of 21 years and the bride of 18 years
(*iv*) No prohibited degree and sapinda relationship unless saved by custom.

Codes :

A. (*i*), (*ii*) and (*iv*)
B. (*ii*), (*iii*) and (*iv*)
C. (*i*), (*ii*) and (*iii*)
D. (*i*), (*ii*), (*iii*) and (*iv*)

48. Section 9 of the Hindu Marriage Act, 1955 was held to be 'intra-vires' the Constitution by the Supreme Court in the case of

A. T. Sareetha *vs.* T.V. Subbhiah
B. Saroj Rani *vs.* Sudarshan
C. Harvinder Kaur *vs.* Harmandar Singh
D. Sarla Mudgil *vs.* Union of India

49. A Muslim has given Triple Talaaq to his wife and now wants to marry her again. He can do so

A. without any restriction
B. only on request of such wife
C. cannot marry her
D. only if such woman marry another man, the marriage is consummated and he has [second Husband] divorced her

50. In giving a child in adoption by the Hindu father, the requirement of the consent of the mother, can be dispensed with if

(*i*) She has been declared to be of unsound mind by the Court of Competent jurisdiction.
(*ii*) She has finally and completely renounced the world.
(*iii*) She has ceased to be a Hindu.
(*iv*) Her age is less than 18 years.

Codes :

A. (*ii*), (*iii*) and (*iv*)
B. (*i*), (*ii*), (*iii*) and (*iv*)
C. (*i*), (*ii*) and (*iii*)
D. (*i*), (*iii*) and (*iv*)

51. "A Hindu mother can be natural guardian of her minor child during the life of father of the child if he is not taking due care of the child." This was held by the Supreme Court of India in case of

A. M.M. Ganguli *vs.* Jayanti Ganguli
B. Jijabai *vs.* Pathan Khan
C. Sarla Mudgil *vs.* Union of India
D. Githa Hariharan *vs.* Reserve Bank of India

52. Match List-I with List-II in the light of Section 2 of the Dissolution of Muslim Marriage Act, 1939 and select the correct answer using the codes given below:

List-I	List-II
(*a*) Imprisonment of Husband	(*i*) Sec. 2(vii)
(*b*) Option of puberty	(*ii*) Sec. 2(iii)
(*c*) Husband missing	(*iii*) Sec. 2(v)
(*d*) Impotency of husband	(*iv*) Sec. 2(i)

Codes :

	(*a*)	(*b*)	(*c*)	(*d*)
A.	(*ii*)	(*i*)	(*iv*)	(*iii*)
B.	(*i*)	(*ii*)	(*iii*)	(*iv*)
C.	(*iv*)	(*ii*)	(*i*)	(*iii*)
D.	(*iii*)	(*i*)	(*ii*)	(*iv*)

53. Which of the following has not yet been statutorily recognized as a theory of divorce under the Hindu Marriage Act, 1955?

A. Fault Theory
B. Will Theory
C. Breakdown Theory
D. Mutual Consent Theory

54. Read Assertion (A) and Reason (R) and answer using codes given below:

Assertion (A) : Human Rights are regarded as those fundamental but alienable rights which are preferred for life as human being.

Reason (R) : Change is general rule of life. Therefore legislatures are free to change human rights according to changing needs and circumstances.

Codes :

A. Both (A) and (R) are right and (R) is correct reason for (A).
B. Both (A) and (R) are right, but (R) is not correct reason for (A).
C. Both (A) and (R) are wrong.
D. (A) is wrong and (R) is right.

55. Which of the following statements are wrong? Answer using codes:

(*i*) Human rights are created by legislation.
(*ii*) Legal duty to protect human rights is not duty to respect them.
(*iii*) International concern with human rights as enshrined in the United Nations Charter is a modern innovation.
(*iv*) A human right violation is now conceived as violation of those personally and directly aggrieved, but not of everyone.

Codes :

A. (*i*), (*ii*) B. (*ii*), (*iii*)
C. (*iii*), (*iv*) D. (*i*), (*ii*), (*iii*) & (*iv*)

56. Read Assertion (A) and Reason (R) and answer using codes given below:

Assertion (A) : The purpose of the United Nation is to maintain national security and peace.

Reason (R) : Because Article–I of the Charter of the United Nations says so.

Codes:

A. Both (A) and (R) are right and (R) is right reason for (A)
B. Both (A) and (R) are wrong.
C. (A) is right and (R) is wrong.
D. (A) is wrong and (R) is right.

57. Right to nationality, right to marry and to found a family are the rights under

(*i*) Only women rights
(*ii*) Social and cultural rights
(*iii*) Civil and political rights
(*iv*) Inherent rights

Codes :

A. (*i*), (*ii*) and (*iv*) B. (*ii*), (*iii*) and (*iv*)
C. (*ii*) and (*iii*) D. (*iii*)

58. Which of the following court normally is/are notified by the State Governments to act as Human Rights Court for speedy trial of offences violating Human Rights?

(*i*) Munsiff Courts
(*ii*) Lok Adalats
(*iii*) Senior Civil Judge Court
(*iv*) Sessions Court

Codes :

A. (*i*) and (*iv*) B. (*i*), (*iii*) and (*iv*)
C. (*ii*) and (*iv*) D. (*iv*)

59. The power of 'enquiry and investigation' was given to Human Rights Commission under the following sections of the protection of Human Rights Act 1993.

(*i*) Sec. 13 (*ii*) Sec. 14
(*iii*) Sec. 9 (*iv*) Sec. 10

Codes :

A. (*i*) and (*ii*) B. (*i*) and (*iii*)
C. (*ii*) and (*iii*) D. (*iii*) and (*iv*)

60. Read Assertion (A) and Reason (R) and answer using codes given below:

Assertion (A) : A refugee means any person who, owing to well-founded fear of being prosecuted for reason of race, religion, nationality, membership of a particular social group or political opinion, is outside the country of his nationality.

Reason (R) : Because the United Nations Convention on the Refugees 1951 in its Article 1A says so.

Codes :

A. Both (A) and (R) are right and (R) is right reason of (A).
B. (A) is wrong and (R) is right.
C. (A) is right and (R) is wrong.
D. Both (R) and (A) are wrong.

61. Match the List-I ***(Name of Maxim)*** with List-II ***(Meaning of Maxim)*** by using the codes given below:

List-I

(*a*) Scienti non fit injuria
(*b*) Qui facit per alium facit per se
(*c*) Ubi jus ibi remedium
(*d*) Ubi remedium ibi jus

List-II

(*i*) Where there is remedy there is a right
(*ii*) He who does an act through another is deemed in law to do it himself.
(*iii*) No injury is done to one who knowingly does an act
(*iv*) Where there is wrong there is remedy

Codes :

	(*a*)	(*b*)	(*c*)	(*d*)
A.	(*iii*)	(*iv*)	(*i*)	(*ii*)
B.	(*iv*)	(*iii*)	(*ii*)	(*i*)
C.	(*iii*)	(*ii*)	(*iv*)	(*i*)
D.	(*i*)	(*ii*)	(*iii*)	(*iv*)

62. Which of the following is an effective defence in the *tort* of nuisance?

(*i*) Public good
(*ii*) Prescription
(*iii*) Statutory authority
(*iv*) Reasonable care

Codes :

A. (*i*) and (*iii*) are correct
B. (*ii*) and (*iv*) are correct
C. (*ii*) and (*iii*) are correct
D. (*i*) and (*iv*) are correct

63. Assertion (A) : Negligence as a ***tort*** is the breach of legal duty to take care which results in damage.

Reason (R) : In the ***tort*** of negligence law takes cognizance of carelessness only if it is supported by the legal duty to care.

Codes:

A. Both (A) and (R) are true and (R) is the correct explanation of (A).
B. Both (A) and (R) are true, but (R) is not the correct explanation of (A).
C. (A) is true, but (R) is false.
D. (A) is false, but (R) is true.

64. In the ***tort*** of slander it is essential that some special damage has been resulted from the use of word by the defendant. In which of the following case an action of slander may be maintained, without proof of special damage? Answer using the codes:

(*i*) Words imputing criminal offence to the plaintiff.
(*ii*) Words imputing to the plaintiff that he has an infectious disease.
(*iii*) Words prejudice the plaintiff in his office, profession etc.
(*iv*) Words imputing unchastity to a woman.

Codes :

A. (*i*) and (*ii*) are correct
B. (*i*), (*ii*) and (*iii*) are correct
C. (*i*), (*ii*) and (*iv*) are correct
D. (*i*), (*ii*), (*iii*) and (*iv*) are correct

65. Which of the following is not an exception to the strict liability principle laid down in Rylands *vs.* Flecher?

A. Independent contractor
B. Statutory authority
C. Act of God
D. Consent of the plaintiff

66. Which of the following is the right of the consumer under Consumer Protection Act, 1986?

(*i*) Right to consumer education
(*ii*) Right to seek redressal

(*iii*) Access to a variety of goods and services at competitive prices

(*iv*) Take goods and services free of cost

Codes :

A. (*i*) and (*iii*) are correct

B. (*i*), (*ii*) and (*iii*) are correct

C. (*i*) and (*ii*) are correct

D. (*i*), (*ii*), (*iii*) and (*iv*) are correct

67. What is the pecuniary jurisdiction of the State Commission under the Consumer Protection Act?

A. Exceeds rupees fifty lakhs but does not exceed rupees one crore.

B. Exceeds rupees twenty lakhs but does not exceed rupees one crore.

C. Exceeds rupees ten lakhs but does not exceed rupees one crore.

D. Exceeds rupees one crore.

68. According to Section 12 of the Partnership Act, any difference arising as to ordinary matters connected with the business of partnership may be decided by

A. the seniormost partner

B. an arbitrator

C. a majority of partners

D. a judge

69. Which are essentials of a contract of sale of goods? Answer using codes given below:

(*i*) Offer

(*ii*) Acceptance of offer

(*iii*) Exchange of goods for money

(*iv*) Transfer of property in goods from seller to buyer

Codes :

A. Only (*i*) and (*ii*)

B. Only (*iii*) and (*iv*)

C. Only (*ii*) and (*iii*)

D. (*i*), (*ii*), (*iii*) and (*iv*)

70. Read Assertion (A) and Reason (R) and answer using the codes below:

Assertion (A) : Where under a contract of sale the property in the goods has passed to the buyer and the buyer wrongfully neglects to pay for the goods according to the terms of the contract, the buyer may sue the seller for the price of the goods.

Reason (R) : The seller is entitled to get the contractual price.

Codes :

A. Both (A) and (R) are correct, and (R) is correct reason for (A).

B. Both (A) and (R) are wrong.

C. (A) is wrong, but (R) is right.

D. (R) is wrong, but (A) is right.

71. Match List-I with List-II and select the correct answer using the codes given below:

List-I

(*i*) Intention of parties to pass property in goods

(*ii*) Ascertainment of intention to pass property in goods

(*iii*) Passing of property in goods

(*iv*) Specific goods in deliverable State

List-II

(*a*) Ghasiram *vs.* State

(*b*) Badriprasad *vs.* State of Madhya Pradesh

(*c*) United Breweries Ltd. *vs.* State of Andhra Pradesh

(*d*) Usha Beltron Ltd. *vs.* State of Punjab

Codes :

	(*i*)	(*ii*)	(*iii*)	(*iv*)
A.	(*b*)	(*d*)	(*a*)	(*c*)
B.	(*c*)	(*a*)	(*b*)	(*d*)
C.	(*a*)	(*c*)	(*d*)	(*b*)
D.	(*c*)	(*a*)	(*d*)	(*b*)

72. Which one statement is correct from the following statements:

A. If the contract is inconsistent with the public documents, the person contracting will not be prejudiced by irregularities that may be set the outdoor working of the company.

B. If the contract is consistent with the public documents, the person contracting will not be prejudiced by irregularities that may be set the indoor working of the company.

C. The doctrine of indoor management seeks to protect the company against the outsider.

D. The doctrine of ultra vires seeks to protect the outsider against internal irregularities of the company.

73. Match List-I with List-II and select the correct answer using the codes given below:

List-I

(*i*) Directors with unlimited liability

(*ii*) Prevention of management of a company by undesirable persons.

(*iii*) A director cannot assign his office in favour of any one else.

(*iv*) Appointment to a place of profit under the company.

List-II

(*a*) Section 202 and 203 of the Companies Act

(*b*) Section 312 of the Companies Act.

(*c*) Section 322 and 323 of the Companies Act.

(*d*) Section 314 of the Companies Act

Codes :

	(*i*)	(*ii*)	(*iii*)	(*iv*)
A.	(*a*)	(*c*)	(*b*)	(*d*)
B.	(*c*)	(*a*)	(*b*)	(*d*)
C.	(*c*)	(*a*)	(*d*)	(*b*)
D.	(*b*)	(*d*)	(*a*)	(*c*)

74. Match List-I with List-II and select the correct answer using the codes given below:

List-I

(*i*) Inchoate stamped instrument

(*ii*) Liability of acceptor of a negotiable instrument

(*iii*) Liability of an endorser

(*iv*) Liability of the drawee of a cheque

List-II

(*a*) Union Bank of India *vs.* Ankur Corp.

(*b*) Section 31 of the Negotiable Instrument Act

(*c*) Section 35 of the Negotiable Instrument Act

(*d*) Section 20 of the Negotiable Instrument Act

Codes :

	(*i*)	(*ii*)	(*iii*)	(*iv*)
A.	(*a*)	(*d*)	(*c*)	(*b*)
B.	(*d*)	(*a*)	(*c*)	(*b*)
C.	(*d*)	(*a*)	(*b*)	(*c*)
D.	(*c*)	(*b*)	(*a*)	(*d*)

75. Which of the following statements are correct? Answer using codes given below:

In order that a person can be called a holder in due course, he must show:

(*i*) that he is the drawer of the negotiable instrument.

(*ii*) that he has obtained it without consideration.

(*iii*) that he has obtained it before the maturity of the negotiable instrument.

(*iv*) that he has obtained the negotiable instrument in good faith.

Codes :

A. (*i*) and (*ii*) are correct

B. (*ii*) and (*iii*) are correct

C. (*iii*) and (*iv*) are correct

D. (*i*) and (*iv*) are correct

ANSWERS

1	2	3	4	5	6	7	8	9	10
D	B	A	B	D	D	A	C	D	A
11	**12**	**13**	**14**	**15**	**16**	**17**	**18**	**19**	**20**
B	A	D	C	A	D	B	A	A	B
21	**22**	**23**	**24**	**25**	**26**	**27**	**28**	**29**	**30**
D	B	A	B	D	A	D	B	C	B
31	**32**	**33**	**34**	**35**	**36**	**37**	**38**	**39**	**40**
A	C	C	D	D	D	D	D	B	B
41	**42**	**43**	**44**	**45**	**46**	**47**	**48**	**49**	**50**
A	B	B	D	C	B	D	B	D	C
51	**52**	**53**	**54**	**55**	**56**	**57**	**58**	**59**	**60**
D	A	B	C	D	B	D	D	A	D
61	**62**	**63**	**64**	**65**	**66**	**67**	**68**	**69**	**70**
C	C	A	D	A	B	B	C	D	C
71	**72**	**73**	**74**	**75**					
D	B	B	B	C					

SOME SELECTED EXPLANATORY ANSWERS

3. In 1976, the Congress Party set up the Sardar Swaran Singh Committee to make recommendations about fundamental duties. The committee recommended the inclusion of a separate chapter on fundamental duties in the constitution. The 42nd Amendment Act, 1976 added a new part i.e. part IVA to the Constitution. This new part consists of only one Article, that is Article 51A.

According to Article 51A, it shall be the duty of every citizen of India:

(*a*) to abide by the Consitition and respect its ideals and institutions, the National Flag and the National Anthem;

(*b*) to herish and follow the noble ideals that inspired the national struggle for freedom;

(*c*) to uphold and protect the sovereignty, unity and integrity of India;

(*d*) to defend the country and render national service when called upon to do so.

(*e*) to promote harmony and the spirit of common brotherhood amongst all the people of India transcending religious, linguistic and regional or sectional diversities and to renounce pratices derogatory to the dignity of women.

(*f*) to value and preserve the rich heritage of the country's composite culture;

(*g*) to protect and improve the natural environment including forests, lakes, rivers and wildlife and to have compassion for living creatures;

(*h*) to develop scientific temper, humanism and the spirit of;

(*i*) to safeguard public property and to abjure violence;

(*j*) to strive towards excellent in all spheres of individual and collective activity so that the nation constantly rises to higher levels of endeavour and achievement, and

(*k*) to provide opportunities for education to his child or ward between the age of six and fourteen years. This duty was added by the 86th Constitutional Amendment Act, 2002.

8. Administrative law is the body of law that governs the activities of administrative agencies of government, government agency action can include rule making, adjudication or the enforcement of a specific regulatory agenda. Administrative law is considered a branch of public law. As a body of law, administrative law deals with the decision-making of administrative units of government. Administrative law expanded greatly during the twentieth century, as legislative bodies worldwide created more government agencies to regulate the increasingly complex social, economic and political spheres of human interaction.

12. **Mandamus** is an order issued by the court against a tribunal, public body or official requiring it to perform a duty that it has failed to perform. For example an official might be required to consider an application for a license that it had refused to consider. Certiorari is an order setting aside a decision. An order for certiorari would be sought where a decision has been made. An order for certiorari would be issued against judicial or quasi-judicial authorities. A writ of certiorari is a writ from a higher court to a lower court whereby the higher court reviews the decisions of the lower court.

15. A **quasi-judicial body** is an entity such as an arbitrator or tribunal board, generally of a public administrative agency, which has powers and procedures resembling those of a court of law and which is obliged to objectively determine facts and draw conclusions from them so as to provide the basis of an official action. A quasi-judicial body may never review its decision unless authorised by the statute.

19. **Analytical jurisprudence** is a legal theory that draws on the resources of modern analytical philosophy to try to understand the nature of law. H.L.A. Hart was probably the most influential writer in the modern school of analytical jurisprudence. This theory stated that there is a clear cut division between the spheres of legislature and judiciary. The former makes the laws and the latter applies them.

22. *Ratio decidendi* is a Latin phrase meaning "the reason" or "the rationale for the decision". The *ratio decidendi* is "the point in a case which determines the judgement" or "the principle which the case establishes". In other words, *ratio decidendi* is a legal rule derived from, and consistent with, those parts of legal reasoning within a judgement on which the outcome of the case depends.

31. The Air (Prevention and Control of Pollution) Act, 1981 was enacted to provide for the prevention, control and abatement of air pollution. By this Act, air pollution means the presence in the atmosphere of any air and air pollutant means any solid, liquid or gaseous substance (including noise) present in the atmosphere and in such concentration as may be or tend to be injurious to human beings or other living creatures or plants or property or environment.

32. The Environment (Protection) Act, 1986 provides for the protection and improvement of environment and for matters connected therewith. Under this act "environment" includes water, air and land and the interrelationship which exists among and between water, air and land and human beings, other living creatures, plants, micro-organisms and property. By this act, "environmental pollutant" means any solid, liquid or gaseous substances present in such concentration as may be, or tend to be, injurious to environment. According to this act "environment pollution" means the presence in the environment of an environmental pollution.

34. The National Environmental Tribunal Act provides for compensation on the basis of no liability in the cases of (*a*) Death of any person; (*b*) Injury to any person; (*c*) Damage to any property.

35. The correct chronological order of these cases decided by the Supreme Court are:
- M.C. Mehta *vs.* Kamal Nath (1997), SCC 388
- M.I. Builders Pvt. Ltd. *vs.* Radhey Shyam Sahu, AIR 1999 SC 2468
- Hinch Lal Tiwari *vs.* Kamal Devi 2001
- Intellectuals Forum, Thirupathi *vs.* State of A.P. & Ors 2006.

In all these cases, public trust doctrine was propounded. The public trust doctrine "is based on the notion that the public holds inviolable rights in certain land and resources and that regardless of title ownership" and that "the state retains certain rights in such lands and resources in trust for the public.

41. There are two theories of Recognition– Constitutive and Declaratory theory. According to Constitutive theory, an entity does not become a state by possessing essential attributes of statehood, it becomes so, when it is recognized by other states. It implies that other states constitute the personality of a state by granting recognition. Declaratory theory states that statehood or the authority of the new government exists as such prior to and independently of recognition. Recognition is merely a formal acknowledgement through which established facts are accepted. The act of recognition is merely declaratory or evidence of an existing fact that a particular state or government possesses the essential attributes as required under international law.

Recognition may be of two kinds: de facto recognition and de jure recognition.

(*a*) ***De facto recognition:*** When an existing state considers that the new state has not acquired sufficient stability, it may grant recognition to the latter provisionally which is termed de facto recognition. It is granted normally when the recognizing state considers that the new state although has a legitimate government, its effectiveness and continuance to govern the territory is doubtful.

(b) ***De jure recognition:*** When an existing state considers that the new state is capable of possessing all the essential attributes of statehood with stability and permanency, the recognition granted is known as de jure recognition.

42. The ***Estrada doctrine*** is generally understood to mean that recognition of government is unnecessary once the state has been recognized. This doctrine was propounded by Mr. Estrada, the Foreign Minister of Mexico. He stated that his government would no longer issue declarations in the sense of grants of recognition inasmuch as such a course is an insulting practice. He declared that regarding the establishment of diplomatic relations with other states, Mexico government considers itself free to determine it in accordance with the facts and circumstances of each case.

45. The Charter of the United Nations came into existence in 1945. The Universal Declaration of Human Rights came into existence in 1948. The International Covenant on Civil and Political Rights (ICCPR) is a multilateral treaty adopted by the United Nations General Assembly on 16 December 1966 and in force from 23rd March 1976. It commits its parties to respect the civil and political rights of individuals. The International Covenant on Economic, Social and Cultural Rights (ICESCR) is a multilateral treaty adopted by the UN General Assembly on 16 December 1976 and in force from 3rd January 1976. It commits its parties to work towards the granting of economic, social and cultural right of its members.

47. According to section 5 of the Hindu Marriage Act, 1955, the essential conditions of a Hindu Marriage are: (*a*) Monogamy; (*b*) Mental capacity; (*c*) The bridegroom has completed the age of 21 years and the bride of 18 years; (*d*) If two persons are in prohibited degrees of their relationship or sapindas of each other, then they cannot be allowed to marry, until and unless customs of both persons are allowed.

48. In Saroj Rani *vs.* Sudarshan, the Supreme Court held section 9 of the Hindu Marriage Act as intra vires of the Constitution–Section 9 of the Hindu Marriage Act (HMA) provides for restitution of conjugal rights. The three essential conditions of HMA are: (*a*) Firstly one party must have withdrawn from the society of the other; (*b*) secondly the withdrawal must be without any reasonable reason, and (*c*) thirdly, the aggrieved party applies for the restitution of conjugal rights.

50. In giving a child in adoption by the Hindu Father, the requirement of the consent of the mother, can be dispensed with if (*a*) she has been declared to be of unsound mind by the Court of competent jurisdiction; (*b*) she has finally and completely renounced the world; (*c*) she has ceased to be a Hindu.

62. Prescription and statutory authority are effective defences in the tort of Nuisance.

Prescription: A right to do an act, which would otherwise be a private nuisance, may be acquired by prescription (*i.e.* by elapse of certain number of years). A right to commit a private nuisance may be acquired as an easement if the same has been peacefully and openly enjoyed as an easement and of right for a period of 20 years.

Statutory authority: An act done under the authority of a statute is a complete defence. Thus, a railway company authorised to run railway trains is not liable if, in spite of due care, the sparks from the engine set fire in the adjoining property.

63. Actionable negligence consists in the neglect of the use of ordinary care or skill towards a person to whom the defendant owes the duty of observing ordinary care or skill, by which neglect the plaintiff has suffered injury, to his person or property.

'Duty of care' means a legal duty rather than mere moral, religious or social duty. In the absence of such legal duty, negligence in the popular sense has no legal consciousness. It is not sufficient to show that the defendant

was careless; the plaintiff has to establish that the defendant owed to the plaintiff a specific legal duty to take care.

64. In the following cases, however, slander is actionable per se *i.e.* special damage to the plaintiff need not be proved:

(*a*) Accusation of criminal offence
(*b*) Accusation of virulent disease
(*c*) Imputation against office, profession or trade
(*d*) Unchastity in woman or girl

65. Simply stated the rule of strict liability makes the defendant liable for accidental harms caused without any intention and negligence on his part. In other words, sometimes the law recognizes 'no fault' liability. The undertakers of hazardous or dangerous activities have to compensate for the damage caused irrespective of any carelessness on their part. The rule laid down in Rylands *vs.* Fletcher is called the rule of strict liability.

The following are the exceptions to the Rylands vs. Fletcher rule:

(*a*) **Plaintiff's own default:** No action can be maintained for any injury which has been brought by the wilful and the intentional act of the party complaining. In Ponting *vs.* Moakes (1894) 2QB281, the plaintiff's horse nibbed the poisonous leaves on the boundary of the defendant and died. The defendant was held not liable because damage would not have occurred but for the horse's own intrusion into the defendant's land.

(*b*) **Act of God:** If the escape has been unforeseen and because of supernatural forces without any human intervention the defence of act of God can be pleaded. Thus, storm, tempest, lightning, extraordinary rainfall etc fall under the category of act of God.

(*c*) **Act of third party/stranger:** If the harm has been caused due to the wrongful or malicious act of a stranger, who is neither defendant's servant or agent nor the defendant has any control over him, the defendant will not be liable under this rule.

(*d*) **Consent of the plaintiff:** In cases of volenti non fit injuria, i.e. where the plaintiff has consented to the accumulation of the dangerous things on the defendant's land the liability under the Rylands rule does not arise.

(*e*) **Statutory authority:** No action will lie for doing that which the legislature has authorized, if it were done without negligence.

67. The pecuniary jurisdiction of the State Commission under the Consumer Protection Act is more than twenty lakh rupees, but less than one crore rupees.

69. The essentials of a contract of sale of goods are (*i*) Offer; (*ii*) Acceptance of offer; (*iii*) Exchange of goods for money's (*iv*) Transfer of property in goods from seller to buyer.

73. Section 322 and 323 of the Companies Act deals with directors with unlimited liability. Section 202 and 203 of the Companies Act deals with prevention of management of a company by undesirable persons. Section 312 of the Companies Act deals with—A director cannot assign his office in favour of anyone else. Section 314 of the Companies Act deals with appointment to a place of profit under the company.

75. The definition of holder in due course in section 9 of the Negotiable Instruments Act, 1881 means that any person who for the consideration paid becomes the possessor of a negotiable instruments, before its maturity, in good faith and without any sufficient reason to believe that any defect existed in the title of the person from whom he obtained it. In order that a person can be called a holder in due course, he must show:

(*a*) He must be a holder in due course.
(*b*) He must be a holder of valuable consideration.
(*c*) He must become a holder of the negotiable instrument before the date of maturity.
(*d*) He must become a holder of the negotiable instrument in good faith.

Previous Paper (Solved)

UGC-NET/JRF & Assistant Professor Exam
Law, June-2014

PAPER-II

Note : *This paper contains fifty (50) objective type questions of two (2) marks each. All questions are compulsory.*

1. In which of the following cases, the Supreme Court held that 'the preamble is the part of the constitution'?

A. Berubari union and Exchage of enclave
B. Golaknath *Vs.* State of Punjab
C. Kesavananda Bharati *Vs.* State of Kerala
D. None of the above

2. Clause(5) of article-15 has been added to the constitution by :

A. Constitution (First Amendment) Act
B. Constitution (Seventh Amendment) Act
C. Constitution (Forty-second Amendment) Act
D. Constitution (Ninety-third Amendment) Act

3. Match List-I with List-II and select the correct answer using the codes given below:

List-I	List-II
(*i*) Equal justice and free legal aid	(*a*) Article-44
(*ii*) Uniform civil code for citizens	(*b*) Article-48A
(*iii*) Protection and improvement of environment and safeguarding of forests and wild life.	(*c*) Article-39A
(*iv*) Promotion of international peace and security	(*d*) Article-51

Codes :

	(*i*)	(*ii*)	(*iii*)	(*iv*)
A.	(*c*)	(*b*)	(*d*)	(*a*)
B.	(*c*)	(*a*)	(*b*)	(*d*)
C.	(*a*)	(*b*)	(*c*)	(*d*)
D.	(*d*)	(*a*)	(*b*)	(*c*)

4. Rights of a citizen under Article-19 are automatically suspended during the period of emergency, if emergency under Article-352 is declared on the grounds of :

A. war, external aggression or armed rebellion
B. war or armed rebellion
C. external aggression or armed rebellion
D. war or external aggression

5. In which of the following cases the supreme court has held that the word 'law' in Article-21 does not mean merely an enacted piece of law but must be just, fair and reasonable law?

A. A.K. Gopalan *Vs.* State of Madras
B. Maneka Gandhi *Vs.* Union of India
C. Both A and B
D. None of the above

6. A distinguished jurist can be appointed as a judge of the :

A. High Court only
B. Supreme Court only
C. Both (A) and (B)
D. None of the above

7. 'Which cannot be done directly, cannot be done indirectly.' – This statement epitomises the doctrine of :

A. colourable legislation
B. pith and substance
C. harmonious construction
D. eclipse

8. Match List-I with List-II by using the codes given below :
Possession must be protected because :

List-I	List-II
1. Kent	(*a*) Man by taking possession has brought the object within his sphere of will.
2. Hegal	(*b*) In possession there is manifestation of individual's will.
3. Hollard	(*c*) Every act of violence is unlawful.
4. Savigny	(*d*) It is essential for preservation of peace.

Codes :

	1	2	3	4
A.	(*c*)	(*b*)	(*d*)	(*a*)
B.	(*a*)	(*d*)	(*b*)	(*c*)
C.	(*b*)	(*d*)	(*c*)	(*a*)
D.	(*a*)	(*b*)	(*c*)	(*d*)

9. Which one of the following statements is not correct?
A. Austin and Kelson did much to rescue jurisprudence from the so-called confusion of social sciences.
B. Historical school of jurisprudence was a reaction against a prior methods of reasoning of eighteen century natural law.
C. Cujas and Hugo also applied the historical approach in the study of law.
D. Savigny did not discard the principle of natural law.

10. Match List-I with List-II and select the correct answer:

List-I (Name of Books)	List-II (Writers)
(*a*) Pure theory of law	1. Hans Kelson
(*b*) Three lectures on Vedanta philosophy	2. Max Muller
(*c*) Judiciary attacks and survivals	3. Justice V.D. Tulzapurkar
(*d*) The growth of law	4. Justice Cardozo

Codes :

	(*a*)	(*b*)	(*c*)	(*d*)
A.	1	2	3	4
B.	4	3	2	1
C.	3	1	4	2
D.	2	4	1	3

11. The term 'Legal Theory' has been first time coined by :
A. Hans Kelson
B. W. Friedman
C. Salmond
D. Ronald Dworkin

12. Which of the following statement is not true about the conformity of custom?
A. It should be in conformity with public policy.
B. It should be in conformity with statutory law.
C. In England, custom will be recognised even if it is in conflict with some fundamental principles of law.
D. The custom must not be in conflict with tradition.

13. "No one has any other right than always to do his duty." It was stated by :
A. Kelsen
B. Prof. Duguit
C. Holland
D. Salmond

14. **Assertion (A) :** Custom is per se law, independent of its prior recognition by the sovereign or the judge.
Reason (R) : Custom is a source of law.
Codes :
A. Both (A) and (R) are true, but (R) is the correct explanation of (A).
B. Both (A) and (R) are true, but (R) is not a correct explanation of (A).
C. (A) is true but (R) is false.
D. (A) is false but (R) is true.

15. **Assertion (A) :** According to John Austin, international law is true law and not negative international morality.
Reason (R) : Three elements in Austin's definition of law, namely command of the

sovereign, duty of inferiors and sanction incase inferior who commit breach of the command are absent in international law.

Codes :

A. Both (A) and (R) are true and (R) is the correct explanation of (A).

B. Both (A) and (R) are true but (R) is not a correct explanation of (A).

C. (A) is true, but (R) is false.

D. (A) is false, but (R) is true.

16. "International law is international morality or ethics, international courtesy or convention in the social sense of the word, comity as distinguished from rule of law."

Above statement is attributed to :

A. Hobbes B. Pufendorf

C. Bentham D. Kelsen

17. Match List-I with List-II and select the correct answer using the codes given below :

List-I	List-II
(*i*) International custom	(*a*) Peace keeping
(*ii*) United Nations	(*b*) Source of international law
(*iii*) Enforcing judgement of international court of justice	(*c*) Entry 14, list I read with Article-73.
(*iv*) Nirmal bose *Vs.* Union of India, AIR Calcutta, p.506	(*d*) Political mechanism

Codes :

	(*i*)	(*ii*)	(*iii*)	(*iv*)
A.	(*b*)	(*a*)	(*d*)	(*c*)
B.	(*a*)	(*b*)	(*d*)	(*c*)
C.	(*a*)	(*b*)	(*c*)	(*d*)
D.	(*d*)	(*b*)	(*a*)	(*c*)

18. Estrada doctrine relates to

A. Necessity of recognition

B. Form of recognition

C. No necessity of recognition

D. Recognition is superficial

19. Principle of United Nation is

A. Some sovereigns are more equal than others.

B. Member nations have rights but no obligations.

C. All members shall settle their international disputes by peaceful means.

D. All members shall settle their national disputes by peaceful means.

20. Doctrine of forum prorogatum means

A. Jurisdiction cannot be conferred upon an existing tribunal not otherwise competent by the litigants during the proceedings.

B. Jurisdiction can be conferred upon an existing tribunal not otherwise competent by the litigants during the proceedings.

C. Jurisdiction can be conferred upon an existing tribunal not otherwise competent by the litigants after the proceedings.

D. None of the above

21. Assertion (A) : Nikah is a regular and permanent form of marriage among Muslims.

Reason (R) : Muta is contractual form of marriage and is most uncommon in India.

Codes :

A. Both (A) and (R) are correct.

B. (A) is correct but (R) is false.

C. (R) is correct but (A) is false.

D. Neither (A) is correct nor (R) is correct.

22. Where a Hindu male and Hindu female contract their marriage under the special Marriage Act, 1954, Hindu personal law :

A. Applies to such marriage

B. Does not apply

C. Applies with some modifications

D. Applies with Indian Contract Act

23. When two persons are descendants of a common ancestor but by different wives, they are said to be related to each other by :

A. Full Blood B. Uterine Blood

C. Half-Blood D. None of the above

24. The term "Hindu" denotes the persons :

(*i*) professing Hindu religion

(*ii*) professing Buddh, Jain or Sikh religion

(*iii*) who are not professing Muslims, Christian, Parsi or Jain religion.

In respect of the aforesaid propositions which is correct?

A. (*i*) and (*ii*) are correct and (*iii*) is incorrect.
B. (*ii*) and (*iii*) are correct and (*i*) is incorrect.
C. (*i*) and (*iii*) are incorrect but (*ii*) is correct.
D. (*i*), (*ii*) and (*iii*) all are correct.

25. **Assertion (A) :** A having a wife alive, marries another wife. The marriage is void.

Reason (R) : Monogamy is the Law.

Codes :

A. Both (A) and (R) are true.
B. Both (A) and (R) are false.
C. (A) is true but (R) is false.
D. (A) is false but (R) is true.

26. A marriage under Muslim law between persons with fosterage relationship is :

A. Sahih B. Batil
C. Fasid D. None of the above

27. Under the Indian Contract Act, acceptance of proposal should be

A. Conditional or Unconditional
B. Conditional but not absolute
C. Unconditional and absolute
D. Unconditional but not absolute

28. In Indian Contract Act, the term voidable contract has been defined under :

A. Section 2(e) B. Section 2(h)
C. Section 2(i) D. Section 2(g)

29. Contractual liability arises, where

A. there is offer and acceptance only
B. there is intention to create legal relation
C. there is loss to one party
D. the loss of one party is the gain of other party

30. There may be a contract without consideration, if

A. agreement is in writing and registered.
B. parties to the agreement are in near relationship.
C. agreement is made due to natural love and affection.
D. All the above elements are present.

31. An agreement of trade combination to regulate legal trade in organised way is

A. Void B. Voidable
C. Legal D. Illegal

32. Which one of the following statements is true?

A. Intimation of minimum price is proposal.
B. An agreement against public policy is voidable.
C. An agreement, the meaning of which is not certain is void.
D. Contingent contracts are illegal.

33. Which one of the following is correct?

A. Damages can be dispensed with in tort
B. Damages cannot be awarded in tort when other remedies are provided by a statute
C. A remedy by way of damages is essential ingredient of tort
D. Damages can be awarded only if there is a physical injury

34. After considering the following, choose the right choice :

1. infringement of a legal right
2. legal damage
3. any damage
4. existence of a legal right

Right to claim damages in tort would arise only if :

A. 1, 2 and 3 are present.
B. 1, 2 and 4 are present.
C. 1, 3 and 4 are present.
D. All 1, 2, 3, 4 are present.

35. Mental condition of the wrong doer is

A. relevant in all torts
B. not relevant in tortious liability
C. relevant in case of strict liability
D. relevant in torts based on fault

36. P voluntarily accepted lift from D who was drunk and driving the car. D was affected by the drink and this was known to P. D caused the accident in which P suffered injury. Here,

A. D can escape the liability because P was aware of risk.
B. D is liable because P did not agree to suffer the harm.

C. D is not liable because he gave free lift to P.

D. D is liable because the degree of intoxication was not to such an extent that it can be assumed that there was voluntary assumption of risk by P.

37. A rickshaw was being pulled by the rickshaw puller with three passengers on board, which was against law. A bus was being driven rashly and negligently by its driver. The bus collides with rickshaw resulting into damage to rickshaw and injury to rickshaw passengers. Here

A. passengers cannot claim compensation from bus operator for the injury as they themselves were not acting according to law.

B. passengers cannot claim compensation from bus operator as there was contributory negligence on their part.

C. passengers can claim full compensation from bus operator as their negligence has not contributed to their injury.

D. passengers are entitled for compensation which shall be proportionally reduced taking into account their illegal act.

38. Consider the following and then select the right code :

1. Absolute liability implies liability without fault.
2. In case of absolute liability defendant is liable for the injury if his act is the direct and proximate cause of plaintiff's injury.
3. Absolute liability is the liability of the defendant without any defence.
4. In absolute liability, defendant can escape the liability if he can prove that the damage was the result of an act of stranger.

Codes :

A. 1, 2 and 4 are correct.

B. 2 and 3 are correct.

C. 1, 2 and 3 are correct.

D. 1 and 4 are correct.

39. Causing one thing to resemble another thing is known as :

A. Counterfeit B. Deception

C. Cheating D. All of them

40. A private libel is not considered as strict liability because :

A. There is no common injury or danger inferred from the facts

B. It was the result of bonafide belief

C. It is not a statutory offence

D. The principles of Rayland *Vs.* Fletcher is not applicable

41. Assertion (A) : The principle of common intention applies when a criminal act is done by several persons in furtherance of that intention.

Reason (R) : A intentional cooperation for committing an offence culminated from several acts.

Codes :

A. (A) is true but (R) is not the reason.

B. Both (A) and (R) are true and (R) is the reasonable explanation of (A).

C. Both are distinctive offences and (A) is not dependent on (R).

D. (A) is false but (R) is true.

42. Assertion (A) : The right of private defence does not depend upon the actual criminality of the aggressor but on the wrongful character of the act attempted.

Reason (R) : Even if an act is treated as offence the right of private defence arises against the author despite his personal incapacity.

Codes :

A. (A) is correct principle because (R) is the right reason.

B. (A) is untenable under law while (R) is the justifiable cause.

C. (A) is the law on an unlawful act while (R) results without mens rea.

D. (A) is not true while (R) is false.

43. The maxim "De Minimis non curat" relates to _______.

A. Slight harm

B. Trifles

C. Exhibition of disrespect

D. Annoyance

44. Instigating or .engaging in a conspiracy or intentionally aiding a person to commit an offence is better known as _____.

A. Principal Crime

B. Second Degree Crime

C. Wilful mis-representation

D. Abetment

45. The First Come Last Go, and the Last Come First Go rule is associated with

A. Strike

B. Lockout

C. Retrenchment

D. Closure

46. One of the following is not the duty of works committee under the Industrial Disputes Act.

A. To promote measures for securing and preserving amity and good relations between the employees and workmen.

B. To form groups among workmen and strengthen mediation between employer and employee.

C. To achieve the object, it is their duty to comment upon matter of common interest or concern of employers and workmen.

D. To endeavour to compose any material difference of opinion in respect of matters of common interest or concern between employers and workmen.

47. An unregistered trade union has one of the following disadvantage :

A. It can acquire and hold both movable and immovable property.

B. It has no corporate existence.

C. It can contract through agents.

D. It is a legal entity.

48. In order to entitle the workmen to wages for the period of strike, the strike should be legal as well as justified. The above principle was laid down in one of the following case by the apex court :

A. Crompton Greaves *Vs.* The workmen AIR 1978 SC.

B. Ballarpur collieries *Vs.* C.G.I.T Dhanbad AIR 1972 SC.

C. Management of India Radiatiors Ltd and another *Vs.* presiding officer and another AIR 2003 II LLJ (Mad)

D. Workmen of Motor Industries Co. Ltd *Vs.* Management of Motor Industires Co Ltd AIR 1969 SC.

49. In one of the following case the Supreme Court held that when retrenchment of a workmen is invalid reinstatement can be ordered :

A. Harindara Singh *Vs.* Punjab State warehousing Corporation 2010 II LLJ SC

B. Surendara Kumar Verma *Vs.* Central Govt. Indl. Tribunal 1981 ILLJ SC

C. Management W.B. India Ltd *Vs.* Jagannath AIR 1974 SC

D. Pioneer Ltd *Vs.* Tajdar Hussain AIR 1974 SC

50. In which of the following, the members of the registered trade union can claim immunity in criminal cases?

A. The combination of two or more members of a registered trade union act in furtherance of a trade dispute.

B. The combination of two or more members of a registered trade union act with an intention to create loss or damage to the properties of the employer.

C. The trade union leaders in exercise of the managerial powers direct the workers from abstaining to do the work.

D. The members of a trade union act in combination with an intention to coerce the employer to acced to their demands.

ANSWERS

1	2	3	4	5	6	7	8	9	10
C	D	B	D	B	B	A	B	D	A
11	12	13	14	15	16	17	18	19	20
D	C	B	A	C	C	A	C	C	B
21	22	23	24	25	26	27	28	29	30
A	A	C	D	A	B	C	C	B	D
31	32	33	34	35	36	37	38	39	40
C	C	C	B	D	D	C	C	C	A
41	42	43	44	45	46	47	48	49	50
C	A	A	D	C	B	B	A	B	A

SOME SELECTED EXPLANATORY ANSWERS

1. Preamble limits the power of the Amendment the objectives specified in the Preamble contain the basic structure of our Constitution. It was argued in the famous Keshvananda Bharti case that by virtue of the amending power of Article 368 even the Preamble can be amended as it is a part of the Constitution. However, it was stated that the Preamble contains the basic elements or the fundamental features of our Constitution. Consequently, amending power cannot be used so as to destroy or damage these basic features mentioned in the Preamble. The Preamble declares that the people of India resolved to constitute their country into Sovereign Democratic and Republic. The amending power cannot change the Constitution in such a way that it ceased to be a 'Sovereign Democratic and Republic'.

2. Ninety Third (Amendment) Act, 2005—This amendment has added a new Clause (5) to Article 15 of the Constitution. Clause (5) provides that nothing in Article 15 or in sub-clause (g) of Clause (1) of Article 19 prevent the State in making any special provision, by law, for the advancement of socially and educationally backward classes of citizens or for the Scheduled Castes or Scheduled Tribes in so far as sc such special provision relate to admission to educational institutions, including private educational institutions, whether aided or un-aided by the State, other than minority educational institutions referred to in Clause (1) of Article 30.

3. Article 44 provides that the State shall endeavour to secure for the citizens a uniform civil code throughout the territory of India.

Article 39A: To promote equal justice and to provide free legal aid to the poor.

Article 48A: To protect and improve the environment and to safeguard forests and wild life.

Article 51: Promotion of international peace and security. The State shall endeavour to:

(*a*) promote international peace and security;

(*b*) maintain just and honourable relations between nations;

(*c*) foster respect for international law and treaty obligations in the dealings of organized peoples with one another; and

(*d*) encourage settlement of international disputes by arbitration.

4. According to Article 352, 'If at any time the President of India is satisfied that there has arisen a grave emergency created by war or armed rebellion which threatens the security of India or any part of its territory, he can by declaration:

(*a*) give directions to the directions to the constituent states as to how their authority is to be exercised, and

(*b*) suspend from operation several Articles (268 to 280) of the Constitution under which it is obligatory on the union government to make certain contributions to the state.

Such proclamation of Emergency suspends automatically the Fundamental Rights guaranteed under Article 19. But the citizens right to move the court to enforce Fundamental Rights can be suspended only by a separate proclamation.

11. Ronald Dworkin, who had died aged 81, was widely respected as the most original and powerful philosopher of law in the English-speaking world. The word "Legal Theory" was first coined by Him. Legal theory has been an attempt to identify the functions of the positive law in supporting an otherwise unproblematic society.

13. According to Duguit, there is no such concept as 'legal right'. He says that 'no one has any other right than always to do his duty'. According to him, the basis of law is the objective fact of 'social solidarity'. It is social law of social solidarity (mutual interdependence) which alone satisfies individual needs through exchange and division of labour on the basis which each perform their mutual duty in society.

16. International law—to use Bentham's innovation of 1789, which has found favor with the public, instead of the older, more expressive term, law of nations—has been variously denounced and praised as international morality or ethics; international courtesy or convention in the social sense of the word; comity as distinguished from rule of law; or merely and finally as the foreign policy, such as the Monroe Doctrine.

19. All Members shall settle their international disputes by peaceful means in such a manner that international peace and security, and justice, are not endangered. Whereas the function of the Organisation refers to adjustment and settlement of international disputes or situations, the obligation of the Members refers only to the settlement of international disputes. Whereas the Organisation's function is to bring about adjustment or settlement of international disputes or situations 'which might lead to a breach of the peace,' the Members are obliged to settle all their international disputes. Whereas the Organisation shall bring about adjustment or settlement of disputes or situations 'by peaceful means, and in conformity with the principles of justice and international law, the Members are obliged to settle their disputes 'by peaceful means in such a manner that international peace and security, and justice, are not endangered.'

20. The principle that jurisdiction can be conferred on an existing tribunal, not otherwise competent, by the litigants during the proceedings (known as prorogated jurisdiction), is an institution found in Roman law.

22. The Special Marriage Act, 1954 has been passed to solemnise the inter religion marriage. However, in 1954 Act, there were hindrances to such marriages due to the provisions of Sec. 19, which provided that the marriage solemnised under this Act of any member of any undivided family who professes the Hindu, Budhists, Sikhs or Jain religion shall be deemed to effect his severance from such family. Now, Section 21 inserted by 1976 Amendment Act had done away with this hindrance.

23. Two persons are related to each other by full blood when they are descended from a common ancestor by the same wife and by half blood when they are descended from a common ancestor but by different wives.

Two persons are said to be related to each other by uterine blood when they are descended from a common ancestress but by different husbands. In more simple word it is defined as:

(*a*) Where two persons share both parents, mother as well as father, their relationship is by full blood.

(*b*) Where two persons share only the male parent, their relationship is of half blood. The blood is said to be half when they are descended from a common ancestor but by different wives. *i.e.*, womb is not the same but is different one.

26. Relationship: *Consanguinity (Batil)* in Muslim law. If a person contracts marriage with—

(*a*) his mother or grand-mother, how high-so-ever;

(*b*) his daughter or grand-daughter, how low-so-ever;

(*c*) his sister full consanguine; or

(*d*) his niece or great niece how low-so-ever;

(*e*) his aunt or great-aunt (it includes aunt from father's side or mother's side as well), the marriage is void on the ground of consanguinity.

28. Voidable Contract: According to Section 2(i), "an agreement which is enforceable by law at the option of one or more of the parties thereto, but not at the option of the other or others, is a voidable contract." Thus, a voidable contract is one which is enforceable by law at the option of one of the parties. Until it is avoided or rescinded by the party entitled to do so by exercising his option in that behalf, it is a valid contract.

Usually a contract becomes voidable when the consent of one of the parties to the contract is obtained by coercion, undue influence, misrepresentation or fraud. Such a contract is voidable at the option of the aggrieved party *i.e.*, the party whose consent was so caused (Secs. 19 and 19A). But the aggrieved party must exercise his option of rejecting the contract (*i*) within a reasonable time, and (*ii*) before the rights of third parties intervene, otherwise the contract cannot be repudiated.

30. Agreement Made without Consideration:

An agreement made without consideration is void, unless

(*a*) It is expressed in writing and registered under the law for the time being enforce for the registration of (documents), and is made on account of natural love and affection between parties standing in a near relation to each other; or unless.

(*b*) It is a promise to compensate, wholly or in part, a person who has already voluntarily done something for the promisor, or something which the promissory was legally compellable to do, or unless.

(*c*) It is a promise, made in writing and signed by the person to be charged therewith, or by his agent generally or specially authorized in the behalf, to pay wholly or in part a debt of which the creditor might have enforced payment but for the law for the limitation of suits.

In any of these cases, such an agreement is a contract.

32. Agreements, the meaning of which is not certain, or capable of being made certain, are void.

35. The mental element is "irrelevant" in the law of tort. The term "irrelevant" denotes that presence or absence of mental element shall not negative the liability of the wrong doer. Torts can be intentional as well as unintentional. In case of the former the presence of mental element is required to determine tortious liability (for example in assault, battery, false imprisonment), while in latter, the mental element is insignificant in determination of tortious liability (negligence). The underlying principle is that a wrong doer cannot escape liability under the law of tort, simply on the ground that he had no intention to cause harm. However, a wrong doer may not be held liable in certain exceptional cases.

43. The maxim *de minimis non curat lex* is related to Section 95. According to section 95, nothing is an offence by reason that it causes, or that is intended to cause or it is known to be likely to cause, any harm, if that harm is so slight that no person of ordinary sense and temper would complain of such harm.

For Example—

(*a*) Use the ink pot of other.

(*b*) Use the Match Box of other person.

(*c*) A person takes pods almost valueless from a tree on the Government waste land.

44. The abet means to instigate, to help, to encourage, Abetment consists of three acts. It may be:

(*a*) By instigate a person to commit an offence.

(*b*) By encourage in a conspiracy to commit it.

(*c*) By intentionally aiding a person to commit it.

All the parties stand in the mutual relation of principals and agent, the agents being urgent forward by a person who does not act himself, but procures or instigate another to put in execution his criminal intention.

46. Duty of works committee Under Industrial Disputes Act.

(*a*) The promotion of measures for securring and preserving amity and good relations between employers and workmen.

(*b*) To achieve the object, it is their duty to comment upon matter of common interest or concern of employers and workmen.

(*c*) To endeavour to compose any material difference of option in respect of matters of common interest or concern between employers and workmen.

(*d*) The prevention of illegal strikes and lock-outs.

(*e*) Relief to workmen in the matter of lay-off, retrenchment and closure of an undertaking.

(*f*) Collective bargaining.

PAPER-III

Note : *This paper contains* ***seventy five*** *(75) objective type questions of* ***two*** *(2) marks each.* ***All*** *questions are compulsory.*

1. 'The constitution establishes a system of government which is almost quasi-federal .... a unitary state with subsidiary federal features rather than a federal state with subsidiary unitary features.' This is the opinion of :

A. K.C. Wheare

B. Jennings

C. A.V. Dicey

D. None of the above

2. Match List-I with List-II and select the correct answer using the codes given below :

List-I	List-II
(*i*) Appointment of Judges	(*a*) Article-124
(*ii*) A Court of Record	(*b*) Article-129
(*iii*) Appeal in civil cases	(*c*) Article-133
(*iv*) Certificate for appeal to Supreme Court	(*d*) Article-134A

Codes :

	(*i*)	(*ii*)	(*iii*)	(*iv*)
A.	(*a*)	(*b*)	(*c*)	(*d*)
B.	(*a*)	(*c*)	(*b*)	(*d*)
C.	(*a*)	(*b*)	(*d*)	(*c*)
D.	(*b*)	(*a*)	(*d*)	(*c*)

3. The constitution of Election Commission is provided in the constitution under :

A. Article-323 B. Article-324

C. Article-327 D. Article-329

4. Match List-I with List-II and select the correct answer using the codes given below :

List-I	List-II
(*i*) Doctrine of Eclipse	(*a*) RMDC *Vs.* Union of India
(*ii*) Doctrine of severability	(*b*) State of Bombay *Vs.* F.N. Balsara
(*iii*) Doctrine of Waiver	(*c*) Bhikaji *Vs.* State of M.P.
(*iv*) Doctrine of pith and substance	(*d*) Bashesher Nath *Vs.* Income Tax Commissioner

Codes :

	(*i*)	(*ii*)	(*iii*)	(*iv*)
A.	(*c*)	(*b*)	(*d*)	(*a*)
B.	(*b*)	(*c*)	(*a*)	(*d*)
C.	(*c*)	(*a*)	(*d*)	(*b*)
D.	(*d*)	(*b*)	(*c*)	(*a*)

5. Incase there is any inconsistency between the laws made by parliament and the laws made by the state legislature, which one of the following shall prevail?

A. The law made by parliament only if it is passed before the law made by state legislature.

B. The law made by parliament only if it is passed after the law made by state legislature.

C. The law made by parliament whether it is passed before or after the law made by state legislature.

D. The law made by state if it is passed after the law made by parliament.

6. Which of the following statements is true?

A. All self incriminatory statements are valid.

B. All self-incriminatory statements are violative of article-20(3).

C. Self incriminatory statements furnished under compulsion are violative of article-20(3).

D. None of the above.

7. Assertion (A) : Under Article-368, the parliament can amend any part of the constitution of India.

Reason (R) : The parliament is supreme legislative body elected by people of India.

Codes :

A. Both (A) and (R) are true and (R) is the correct explanation of (A).

B. Both (A) and (R) are true but (R) is not the correct explanation of (A).

C. (A) is true, but (R) is false.

D. (A) is false, but (R) is true.

8. Match List-I with List-II and select the correct answer using the codes given below :

List-I	List-II
(*i*) Separation of judiciary from executive	(*a*) Article-51
(*ii*) Promotion of international peace and security	(*b*) Article-48A
(*iii*) Organisation of village panchayats	(*c*) Article-50
(*iv*) Protection and improvement of forests and wild life	(*d*) Article-40

Codes :

	(*i*)	(*ii*)	(*iii*)	(*iv*)
A.	(*a*)	(*b*)	(*c*)	(*d*)
B.	(*c*)	(*a*)	(*d*)	(*b*)
C.	(*c*)	(*b*)	(*d*)	(*a*)
D.	(*b*)	(*a*)	(*c*)	(*d*)

9. Lokpal or Lokayukta is competent to

A. Discharge the functions of administrative officer.

B. Investigate complaints involving grievances in respect of administrative actions.

C. Conduct inquiry against administrative officer for disciplinary action.

D. Give observations and recommendations in respect of administrative actions to the government.

10. Assertion (A) : Indian Constitution has not recognized the doctrine of separation of power in its absolute rigidity.

Reason (R) : Doctrine of separation of power accommodates a system of checks and balances.

Codes :

A. Both (A) and (R) are true and (R) is the correct explanation of (A).

B. Both (A) and (R) are true but (R) is not the correct explanation of (A).

C. (A) is true, but (R) is false.

D. (R) is true, but (A) is false.

11. Administrative law is concerned with the operation and control of the powers of administrative authorities with emphasis on functions rather than on structure. This definition was given by

A. K.C. Davis B. Jennings

C. A.V. Dicey D. Wade

12. Which one of the following is not basic source of administrative law ?

A. Custom

B. Delegated legislation

C. Ordinance promulgated by Governor

D. Reports of the committees and commission

13. Doctrine of pleasure is related to

A. Fundamental duties

B. Fundamental rights

C. Directive principles of state policy

D. None of the above

14. Which of the following statements is true ?

A. Mandamus lies against quasi-judicial order.

B. Mandamus is issued where inferior court declined jurisdiction.

C. Mandamus may be issued, even if alternate remedy is available.

D. Mandamus may be issued even no legal right of petitioner subsists.

15. The rule of 'Audi alteram partem' requires reasonable opportunity of hearing. Hearing may be

A. only in writing

B. only orally

C. written or oral

D. written and oral both

16. The high court can exercise the supervisory jurisdiction over the courts and tribunals subordinate to it under

A. Article-32 B. Article-226

C. Article-227 D. Article-141

17. Fiction theory is related to which one of the following concepts?

A. Ownership B. Justice

C. Legal personality D. None of the above

18. "We must admit openly that precedent makes law as well as declare it …….. . Original precedents are the outcome of the international exercise by the courts of their privileges of developing the law at the same time that they administer it." Who said it?

A. Salmond B. Redcliffe

C. Lord Denning D. Starke

19. Prof. Holland distinguishes a legal right from:

A. Moral and Natural rights

B. External and Internal rights

C. Might and Moral rights

D. Sight and Moral rights

20. Match List-I with List-II and select the correct answer using the codes given below :

List-I (Concepts)	List-II (Jurists)
(*i*) Minimum content of law	(*a*) Fuller
(*ii*) Inner morality of law	(*b*) Hart
(*iii*) Law with a variable content	(*c*) Kohler
(*iv*) Law as a phenomenon of civilization	(*d*) Stammler

Codes :

	(i)	(ii)	(iii)	(iv)
A.	(c)	(a)	(b)	(d)
B.	(b)	(c)	(d)	(a)
C.	(b)	(a)	(d)	(c)
D.	(a)	(b)	(c)	(d)

21. The 'Bracket Theory' contemplates :

A. The members of the corporation are the only persons who have rights and duties.
B. Law puts a bracket around the persons, by organising juristic personality.
C. Only human beings can have personality.
D. Group has a real will, read mind and real power of action.

22. Consider the following statements and give the correct answer by using the codes given below:

I. Equitable ownership always presupposes the existence of a legal ownership.
II. Where property is given by A to B for the benefit of C. B becomes the legal owner and C the equitable owner.
III. In many cases, equity recognises ownership whereas law does not recognise ownership owing to some flaw or defect.
IV. Contingent ownership is spes successions.

Codes :

A. I, II and III are correct.
B. II and III are correct.
C. I and II are correct.
D. II and IV are correct.

23. Who defined possession as "to gain possession a man must stand in a certain physical relation to the object and to the rest of world and must have a certain intent"?

A. Holmes B. Salmond
C. Pollock D. Savigny

24. Statement I : Person of inheritance is the owner of the right.

Statement II : Inheritance is a means to ownership.

Codes :

A. Both Statement I and II are individually true statements and Statement II is the correct explanation of Statement I.
B. Both Statements I and II are individually true, but Statement II is not the correct explanation of Statement I.
C. Statement I is true, but Statement II is false.
D. Statement I is false, but Statement II is true.

25. Malum Prohibitum means :

A. Intrinsically wrong
B. Course of law has made it otherwise
C. Innocent but made punishable by statute.
D. All of them.

26. Demolishing a private structure standing encroached on a public street amounts to :

A. Gain by unlawful means.
B. Wrongful gain for public purpose.
C. Wrongful loss by mischief.
D. None of above.

27. Assertion (A) : When an act is done dishonestly it does not require deception or concealment as its ingredient.

Reason (R) : Dishonesty requires an intention to cause wrongful loss or gain of property.

Codes :

A. (A) is true, but (R) is not the reason.
B. Both (A) and (R) are true because (R) is the right reason of (A).
C. Both (A) and (R) are distinctive offences.
D. (A) is false, while (R) is true.

28. Assertion (A) : Harbouring includes supplying a person with shelter, food, money or conveyance.

Reason (R) : The supply must relate to evading apprehension.

Codes :

A. (A) is correct clarification, but (R) is not the correct reason.
B. (A) is not true while (R) is the correct explanation.
C. Both (A) and (R) are correct proposition.
D. Only in exceptional situation (R) is the reason of (A).

29. The real and abiding concern for the dignity of human life was decided in the case of :

A. Rajendra Prasad *Vs.* State of U.P.

B. Mohindra Singh *Vs.* Delhi Administration
C. Javed Ahmed *Vs.* State of Maharashtra.
D. Bachan Singh *Vs.* State of Punjab.

30. An unlawful assembly is a particular state of activity accompanied by the use of force or violence is riot, but it does not include :
A. There must be five or more persons
B. There must be animation by a common object
C. Persons assembled for lawful purpose but started quarrelling without any previous intention.
D. All of them.

31. Which of the following statements are not false evidence in discharge of public justice?
A. A false statement given under instigation.
B. A statement known to be false.
C. A statement not believed to be true.
D. None of above.

32. A ceremonial pollution is an act relating to unclean worship and is known as the offence of ______.
A. Insult to religion
B. Defilement
C. Anti secularism
D. Religious hatredness

33. One of the following case is popularly known as "Doon Valley case":
A. Pathumna *Vs.* State of Kerala AIR 1978, 2 SCC.
B. M.C. Metha *Vs.* Union of India AIR 1987 SC.
C. Unni Krishnan *Vs.* State of A.P. AIR 1993, 1 SCC.
D. R.L. & E. Kendra *Vs.* State of UP AIR 1985 SC.

34. The polluter pays principle has been incorporated in
A. Principle 15 of the Rio Declaration on Environment and Development
B. Principle 27 of the Rio Declaration on Environment and Development
C. Principle 8 of the Rio Declaration on Environment and Development
D. Principle 16 of the Rio Declaration on Environment and Development

35. Protection and Improvement of environment and safeguarding forests and wild life is
A. One of the Directive Principles of state policy
B. A fundamental right
C. Fundamental duty
D. Both directive principles of state policy and fundamental duties

36. Two important Amendments were brought in the year 1976. One with reference to directive principles of state policy making the state responsible to protect and improve the environment and safeguard the forests and wild life of the country. The other under fundamental duties making every citizen to protect and improve the natural environment including forests, lakes, rivers and wild life and to have compassion for living creatures.

The relevant amendment is
A. 49th Amendment
B. 45th Amendment
C. 43rd Amendment
D. 42nd Amendment

37. Section 19 of the Environment (Protection) Act 1986 enables a person to file a complaint in a criminal court after giving a notice to the Pollution Control Board. Once a complaint has been made, the board is bound to make available to the complaint all relevant reports to him on demand. The board may also refuse to disclose on public interest.

Similar provisions are also available under
A. Section 49 of the Water Act 1974 and Section 43 of the Air Act 1981
B. Section 43 of the Water Act 1974 and Section 49 of the Air Act 1981
C. Section 42 of the Water Act 1974 and Section 46 of the Air Act 1981
D. Section 41 of the Water Act 1974 and Section 42 of the Air Act 1981

38. The Supreme Court of India ordered conversion from fuel to CNG on July 28,

1998. It also set up a committee to evaluate the cleanliness of various fuels on April 27, 2001. The name of the committee is

A. Bhurelal Committee

B. Santhanam Committee

C. Mallimath Committee

D. Madanlal Committee

39. "The public trust doctrine primarily rests on the principle that certain resources like air, sea, water and the forests have such a great importance to the people as a whole that it would be wholly injustified to make them a subject of private ownership."

The above Doctrine was discussed in detail in one of the following case :

A. M.C. Metha *Vs.* Kamalnath 1997 1 SCC.

B. Rural litigation and Environment Kendra *Vs.* Union of India AIR.1985 SC.

C. Vellore Citizen's welfare Forum *Vs.* Union of India 1996, 5 SCC.

D. M.C. Metha *Vs.* Union of India AIR. 1987 SC.

40. "Form of rules accepted by civilized states as determining their conduct towards each other and each other's subject, is defined as international law."

Above statement is attributed to :

A. S.S. Lotus case

B. West Rand Central Gold Mining Ltd. Co. *Vs.* King

C. Queen *Vs.* Keyn

D. L. Oppenheim

41. Assertion (A) : International convention is the most important source of law.

Reason (R) : International convention has generic wisdom.

Codes :

A. Both (A) and (R) are true and (R) is the correct explanation of (A).

B. Both (A) and (R) are true but (R) is not the correct explanation of (A).

C. (A) is true, but (R) is false.

D. (A) is false, but (R) is true.

42. Which of the following statement is true?

A. The community to be recognized as an international person should be organised one.

B. Control of the community over definite territory is desirable.

C. The control over the territory may be permanent.

D. The community must be independent.

43. Which of the following statement is correct?

A. Primary responsibility of international peacekeeping and security is on the General Assembly.

B. The Security Council is a deliberative organ.

C. Members may not accept and carry out the advice of the security council.

D. Social and economic council is to discharge the responsibility of the states enshrined in Chapter-IX from Articles 55-60. This council operates under the authority and supervision of general assembly.

44. Match List-I with List-II and select the correct answer using the codes given below :

List-I	List-II
(*i*) Doctrine of forum prorogatum	(*a*) Certain expenses case, ICJ Rep. 1962, p. 151
(*ii*) Condition of reciprocity	(*b*) Nicaragua v. US, ICJ Rep. 1984, pp. 392, 421-26
(*iii*) Advisory jurisdiction	(*c*) Interhandel case, ICJ Rep. 1959, p.6
(*iv*) Reservations	(*d*) Corfu channel case, (Preliminary objection), ICJ Rep. 1948, p.28

Codes :

	(*i*)	(*ii*)	(*iii*)	(*iv*)
A.	(*c*)	(*d*)	(*a*)	(*b*)
B.	(*d*)	(*c*)	(*a*)	(*b*)
C.	(*d*)	(*c*)	(*b*)	(*a*)
D.	(*a*)	(*b*)	(*d*)	(*c*)

45. Which of the following statement is true ?

A. Mere counting of heads is enough to assess the degree of authority and credibility of a resolution of General Assembly.

B. Mere counting of heads is not enough to assess the degree of authority and credibility of a resolution of General Assembly.

C. Mere counting of heads is enough to assess integrity of General Assembly.

D. None of the above

46. Assertion (A) : Recognition of a state is not the same as recognition of its government.

Reason (R) : Within existing states, governments come and go and normally the changes raise no question of recognition.

Codes :

A. Both (A) and (R) are correct and (R) is the correct explanation of (A).

B. Both (A) and (R) are correct but (R) is not the correct explanation of (A).

C. (A) is true, but (R) is false.

D. (A) is false, but (R) is true.

47. A Muslim wife may sue for divorce under the Dissolution of Muslim Marriage Act, 1939 if the husband has been insane for a period of:

A. 1 year B. 2 years

C. 3 years D. 5 years

48. Which of the following is not essential for divorce by mutual consent?

A. They have been living separately for one year.

B. They have not been able to live together.

C. The wife has not received any maintenance.

D. They have mutually agreed that the marriage should be dissolved.

49. That the respondent was, at the time of the marriage, pregnant by some person other than the petitioner, is a ground for voidable marriages under

A. Section-12(1)(*a*) B. Section-12(1)(*b*)

C. Section-12(1)(*c*) D. Section-12(1)(*d*)

50. A petition for the dissolution of the marriage by a decree of divorce may be presented, if cohabitation as between the parties to the marriage, after the passing of a decree of judicial separation, is not resumed for a period of :

A. One year or upwards

B. Two years or upwards

C. Six months or upwards

D. None of the above

51. Match List-I with List-II and select the correct answer using the codes given below :

List-I	List-II
(*a*) Marriage during Iddat period is	(*i*) Void
(*b*) Marriage with an impotent person is	(*ii*) Irregular
(*c*) Marriage below the age of 18 years is	(*iii*) Voidable
(*d*) Inter-caste marriage	(*iv*) Valid

Codes :

	(*a*)	(*b*)	(*c*)	(*d*)
A.	(*i*)	(*ii*)	(*iii*)	(*iv*)
B.	(*ii*)	(*i*)	(*iv*)	(*iii*)
C.	(*iii*)	(*ii*)	(*i*)	(*iv*)
D.	(*ii*)	(*iii*)	(*i*)	(*iv*)

52. Where the marriage has not been consummated, Iddat has to be observed in case of :

A. Death of husband

B. Divorce

C. Both death and divorce

D. Neither death nor divorce

53. Match List-I with List-II and select the correct answer using the codes given below :

List-I (Cases)	List-II (Grounds)
(*a*) Ram Narayan *Vs.* Rameshwari	(*i*) Insanity
(*b*) Lachman *Vs.* Meena	(*ii*) Cruelty
(*c*) Dastane *Vs.* Dastane	(*iii*) Desertion
(*d*) Mr. X *Vs.* Hospital Z	(*iv*) Venereal Diseases

Codes :

	(a)	(b)	(c)	(d)
A.	(iii)	(i)	(iv)	(ii)
B.	(ii)	(iv)	(iii)	(i)
C.	(i)	(iii)	(ii)	(iv)
D.	(iv)	(ii)	(i)	(iii)

54. Under the Shia school, what is the cronical order of persons entitled to the 'Hizanat' of a minor child?

(a) Father (b) Mother
(c) Grandfather (d) Grandmother

A. (b), (a), (c), (d)
B. (b), (a), (d), (c)
C. (c), (b), (a), (d)
D. (d), (c), (b), (a)

55. The solidarity rights, more commonly known as 'Third Generation Human Rights' is based on :

A. Independent needs of people
B. Concept of universalism
C. Right to self-determination
D. Common heritage of mankind

56. "Human rights have two main dimensions. One of them can be called negative freedom in the sense that it is less important, it is negative because such freedom is based on a bedrock of what cannot be done, rather than what can be done."

The above is from the thoughts of

A. Kofi Annan
B. P.N. Bhagwati
C. Amartya Sen
D. M.N. Venkatachaliah

57. Match List-I containing Human rights and List-II containing related Articles of Universal Declaration of Human Rights, using the codes given below :

List-I	List-II
(i) Rights to own property	(a) Article-18
(ii) Freedom of religion	(b) Article-9
(iii) Right to liberty and security of person	(c) Article-12
(iv) Right to privacy	(d) Article-17

Codes :

	(i)	(ii)	(iii)	(iv)
A.	(a)	(c)	(d)	(b)
B.	(a)	(d)	(c)	(b)
C.	(a)	(d)	(b)	(c)
D.	(d)	(a)	(b)	(c)

58. Human rights are inscribed in the hearts of the people ; they were there long before law makers drafted their first proclamation. This statement was made by :

A. Kofi Annan B. Krishna Iyer, J.
C. Mary Robinson D. None of the above

59. Human Rights Council has taken the place of:

A. Human Right Committee
B. International Human Rights Institute
C. Centre for Human Rights
D. Human Right Commission

60. Select the best answer using the codes given below :

The national Human Rights commission can:

1. itself take action and punish those who violate human rights.
2. recommend the government to take action.
3. initiate proceedings in the court.
4. join as a party to a case in the court involving violation of human rights.

Codes :

A. 1 and 2 are correct.
B. 2, 3 and 4 are correct.
C. 1, 2 and 3 are correct.
D. 3 and 4 are correct.

61. Some of the human rights are contained in the Indian Constitution under :

A. Part III and Part IV-A
B. Part III and Part IV
C. Part IV and Part IV-A
D. Part II and Part IV-A

62. Tort is defined as "an infringement of a right in rem of a private individual giving a right of compensation of the suit of the injured party" by

A. Salmond B. Franger
C. Winfield D. Flemmings

63. Which of the following correctly represent the position under the law of torts ?

Select from the code given below : A person is responsible for

1. all the consequences of his wrongful act.
2. consequences which directly flow from his wrongful act.
3. consequences which are not too remote.
4. all the consequences which are reasonably foreseable.

Codes :

A. 1 and 2 are correct.
B. 1, 2 and 3 are correct.
C. 2 and 3 are correct.
D. 2, 3 and 4 are correct.

64. Which of the following is not necessary in tort of defamation?

A. The statement is defamatory.
B. There is intention to refer to the plaintiff.
C. The right thinking members in the society infer that the statement refers to plaintiff.
D. The statement is made known to other members of society.

65. A film critic in his review of a film comments adversely on the cinematic values and quality of the film. The director of the film sues the film critic for defamation. Which of the following is correct, use the code given below:

1. The film critic is not liable as he can raise the defence of justification.
2. The critic is not liable because it was a fair and bonafide comment in public interest.
3. It was an expression of opinion and not assertion of facts.
4. It was a fair criticism of a film meant for public entertainment.

Codes :

A. 1 and 4 are correct.
B. 1 and 2 are correct.
C. 2, 3 and 4 are correct.
D. 1 and 3 are correct.

66. The 'standard of care' generally used in care of negligence is

A. the care taken by an intelligent and prudent man.
B. the skill and care taken by a qualified and competent person.
C. the foresight of an adult person.
D. the care and skill of a prudent and careful man belonging to defendant's calling or business or skill.

67. Which one of the following is a good defence for the tort of private nuisance?

A. Plaintiff has come to the place of nuisance.
B. Reasonable care was taken to prevent nuisance.
C. The activity is for the public benefit.
D. The activity is continuing for the past 20 years.

68. Who is a consumer under the Consumer Protect Act, 1986?

A. A person who gives his pants for stitching to a tailor.
B. A person who purchases goods for sale in his shop.
C. A person who purchases a car for being used as a taxi in his taxi service.
D. A person who avails of medical services free of cost.

69. Partnership is

A. Trust
B. Company
C. Mutual agency
D. Mutual fund

70. Assertion (A) : When something of valuable nature is acquired by a partner in breach of his duty in good faith, it is taken to be acquired for the benefit of all the partners and has to be accounted for to the firm.

Reason (R) : Partnership is a trust.

Codes :

A. Both (A) and (R) are true and (R) is the correct explanation of (A).
B. Both (A) and (R) are true but (R) is not the correct explanation of (A).
C. (A) is true, but (R) is false.
D. (A) is false, but (R) is true.

71. Arrange the following concepts in which sequence they appeared, using the codes given below :

(*i*) Damage

(*ii*) Breach of terms of agreement of partnership

(*iii*) Damaged

(*iv*) Agreement to share profits from business of firm

Codes :

A. (*i*), (*ii*), (*iv*), (*iii*)

B. (*iv*), (*ii*), (*i*), (*iii*)

C. (*ii*), (*iv*), (*i*), (*iii*)

D. (*iii*), (*i*), (*ii*), (*iv*)

72. Match items in List-I with items in List-II using the codes given below :

List-I	List-II
(*i*) Liability for misappropriation by a partner	(*a*) Section-26
(*ii*) Liability of a partner for torts	(*b*) Section-27
(*iii*) Liability of a partner for holding out	(*c*) Section-28
(*iv*) Doctrine of implied authority of a partner	(*d*) Sections-18 and 19

Codes :

	(*i*)	(*ii*)	(*iii*)	(*iv*)
A.	(*c*)	(*d*)	(*a*)	(*b*)
B.	(*b*)	(*a*)	(*d*)	(*c*)
C.	(*a*)	(*b*)	(*c*)	(*d*)
D.	(*b*)	(*a*)	(*c*)	(*d*)

73. Which one of the following pairs does match?

A. Definition and essentials of sale – E. & S 5 : 02 PM Ruben Ltd. *Vs.* Faire Bros. (1949)1 KB 254

B. Formalities of sale – Drummond & Sons *Vs.* Van Ingen, (1887) 12 App. Cases 284

C. Conditions implied by trade and usage – Peter Darlington Partners Ltd. *Vs.* Gosho Co. Ltd., (1964) 1 Lloyds Rep. 149

D. Sale by sample – Rowland *Vs.* Divall (1923) 2 KB 500, CA.

74. Which one of the following statements is true?

A. The order contained in the bill of exchange may be conditional.

B. A bill of exchange must contain a request to pay.

C. Every bill of exchange is a promissory note.

D. The payee must be certain.

75. Haward *Vs.* Patent Ivory Manufacturing Co., (1888) 38 Ch.D. 156 is a case about

A. Doctrine of ultra vires

B. Doctrine of indoor management

C. Doctrine of public notice

D. Doctrine of social responsibility

ANSWERS

1	**2**	**3**	**4**	**5**	**6**	**7**	**8**	**9**	**10**
A	A	B	C	C	C	D	B	B	A
11	**12**	**13**	**14**	**15**	**16**	**17**	**18**	**19**	**20**
D	A	D	B	C	C	C	A	C	C
21	**22**	**23**	**24**	**25**	**26**	**27**	**28**	**29**	**30**
B	A	A	A	C	C	B	C	D	C
31	**32**	**33**	**34**	**35**	**36**	**37**	**38**	**39**	**40**
A	B	D	D	D	D	A	A	A	B
41	**42**	**43**	**44**	**45**	**46**	**47**	**48**	**49**	**50**
B	D	D	B	B	A	B	C	D	A

51	52	53	54	55	56	57	58	59	60
D	B	C	A	B	C	D	C	B	B
61	62	63	64	65	66	67	68	69	70
B	B	D	B	C	D	D	A	C	C
71	72	73	74	75					
B	D	C	D	B					

SOME SELECTED EXPLANATORY ANSWERS

1. Some scholars hesitate to characterise the Indian Constitution as truly federal because according to them in certain circumstances the Constitution empowers the Centre to interfere in the State matters and thus places the States in the subordinate position, which violates the federal principle. They, therefore, use such expressions for it as 'quasi-federal', 'unitary with federal features' or 'federal with unitary features'.

   Prof. Wheare opines 'The Constitution establishes a system of Government which is almost quasi-federal, a unitary state with subsidiary federal features rather than a federal state with subsidiary unitary features.

2. The Supreme Court consists of Chief Justice of India and 30 other judges. The Chief Justice and other judges are appointed by the President of India and they hold office upto the age of 65 years. [Article 124(1) and (2)].

   A Supreme Court is the court of record and has power to punish for its own contempt. (Article 129).

   An appeal shall also lie to the Supreme Court from any judgement, decree or final order in a civil proceeding of a High Court, if the case involves a substantial question of law. (Article 133).

   An appeal shall also lie to the Supreme Court from any judgement, final order or sentence in a criminal proceeding of a High Court. (Article 134)

3. According to Article 324 (1), the superintendence, direction and control of the preparation of the electoral rolls for, and the conduct of all elections to the Parliament and to the Legislature of every state and of elections of the offices of the President and the Vice-President held under the Constitution, shall be vested in the Election Commission.

   - The Commission shall consist of one Chief Election Commissioner and such number of other Election Commissioners as the President may from time to time fix [Article 324(2)]. The appointment of the Chief Election Commissioner and other Election Commissioners shall be made by the President subject to the provisions of any law made in this regard by Parliament. When any other Election Commissioner is so appointed, the Chief Election Commissioner shall act as the chairman of the Election Commission.
   - The President may also appoint, after consultation with the Election Commission, such regional Commissioners as he may consider necessary to assist the Election Commission in the performance of its functions [Article 324(4)].
   - The conditions of service and tenure of office of the Election Commissioners and the regional Commissioners shall be such as the President may by rule determine. The conditions of service of the Chief Election Commissioner shall not be varied to his disadvantage after his appointment.

- He can be removed from office in the same way as a judge of the Supreme Court can be removed. Any other Election Commissioner or a regional Commissioner shall not be removed from office, except on the recommendation of the Chief Election Commissioner [Article 324(5)].
- The President, or the Governor of a State shall, when so requested by the Election Commission, make available to the Election Commission or to a regional Commissioner such staff as may be necessary for the discharge of its functions [Article 324(6)].

5. Under Article 251, the Constitution provides that in case inconsistencies arise between the laws made by Parliament under Articles 249 and 250, and laws made by State Legislatures on the same subject either before or after, laws made by Parliament prevail while the Emergency is in operation. Parliament also has overriding legislative powers in case proclamation of Emergency under Article 356 is in operation. Article 254 provides that in case of inconsistencies between the laws made by Parliament on any matter on which it is competent to make laws or on any matter enumerated in the Concurrent List, the law made by Parliament, whether passed before or after, shall prevail over the laws made by State Legislatures on the same subject.

8. Encourage settlement of international disputes by arbitration (Article 51).

The State shall, through 42nd Amendment (1976), endeavour to protect and improve the environment and safeguard forests and wildlife of country (Article 48A).

The State shall take steps to organize village panchayats and endow them with such powers and authority as may be necessary to enable them to function as units of self-government (Article 40).

The State shall take steps to separate judiciary from executive (Article 50). Through various laws, steps have been taken to separate judiciary and executives.

11. H. W. R. Wade in his book "Administrative Law," eighth edition, argued that administrative law is concerned with the operation and control of the power of administrative authorities with emphasis on functions rather than structure. He went further, stating that: "Administrative law is the law relating to the control of governmental powers."

13. **Doctrine of Pleasure:** The doctrine of pleasure is a British concept where all the government officials serve during the pleasure of the Crown. This doctrine is also practiced in India (Article 311) but the Indian doctrine is a modified version and the pleasure of the President is not unguided, whimsical or based on fantasy. In India, the doctrine is subject to constitutional safeguards and theory of natural justice.

14. *Certiorari* and *Prohibition* are instruments to control an inferior tribunal which has exceeded its jurisdiction or wrongly exercised its jurisdiction. *Mandamus* is issued against an inferior tribunal which has declined to exercise its jurisdiction.

16. Every High Court has power of superintendence over all courts and tribunals throughout its territories of that State., (Article 227).

17. **Fiction Theory:** The followers of this theory are Savigny, Salmond and Dicey. According to this theory only human beings are actually persons and by fiction of law some other can be supposed as legal personality.

21. The bracket theory of the personality of the corporation maintains that the members of a corporation have their rights and liabilities referred to the corporation itself, simply from the point of view of convenience. To determine, however, the real nature of the corporation and its state of affairs, the brackets have to be removed, for the names of the members of the corporation are kept in brackets. If and when the brackets are removed, one would be able to see what the corporation is, what its true nature is, and how its members are revealed through the removal of brackets.

23. The permutations of the facts might be capable of infinite variation, but in essence they were facts of control, comprising physical and mental elements. So Holmes declared confidently that:

To gain possession ... a man must stand in a certain physical relation to the object and to the rest of world, and must have a certain intent.

25. It is no defense to a prosecution for an offense malum prohibitum unless the wording of the particular statute has imposed a requirement, by providing a penalty for such an act only if "knowingly" committed.

28. A real and abiding concern for the dignity of human life postulates resistance to taking a life through law's instrumentality, that ought not to be done save in the rarest of rare cases when the alternative option is unquestionably foreclosed arret *Bachan Singh vs State of Punjab.*

32. Section 295, I.P.C. punishes damaging or defiling any place of worship or object held sacred by any class of persons. The word object under the section refers only to inanimate objects and does not include animate objects. The defilement of the place of worship does not mean making a sacred place dirty, it means only ceremonial pollution. The most important ingredient for punishing a person under this section is that the person who destroyed, or defiled the place should have the intention or knowledge that his act will insult the religion of others.

Section 297 extends the principle laid down in section 295 to places which are treated as sacred. This section deals more especially with trespass on a place of sopulture and place set apart for the performance of funeral rites and as depositories for the remains of the dead. Intention or knowledge is the essence of the offence under both sections.

33. In India, the first break through of importance in this regard came in the case of Rural Litigation And Entitlement Kendra vs. State of UP AIR 1985 SC 652, popularly known as Doon Valley Case. The Dehradun Valley in India is surrounded in one side by the Himalayan range and the Ganges and Yamuna rivers in the other, has been an exquisite region but because of uncontrolled quarrying of limestone, its landscape lost its former beauty. In this case a letter received from the Rural Litigation and Entitlement Kendra, Dehradun, was treated as writ petition and the Supreme Court by its Judgment and Order dated 12th March, 1985, AIR SC 652, directed closing down the mines of 'A' category located within the municipal limits of Mussoorie.

35. Environmental Protection, was introduced into the Constitution in the following manner:

In part IV, relating to Directive Principles of State Policy, an Article 48A was inserted which provides: "The State shall endeavour to protect and improve the environment and to safeguard the forests and wildlife of the country".

38. The Supreme Court ordered conversion to CNG on July 28, 1998. It set up the Bhure Lal Committee to evaluate "cleanliness" of various fuels...on April 27, 2001. It gave four weeks to the Committee to collect and assess mountains of literature on pros and cons of various fuels.

45. As Judge Dillard observed in the Fisheries case, the mere counting of heads is not enough to assess the degree of authority and credibility of a resolution of General assembly.

47. The Dissolution of Muslim Marriages Act (VIII) of 1939 provides the women grounds for dissolving the marriage at the instance of the court. The grounds are:

1. Whereabouts of the husband not known for four years;
2. Husband neglected or failed to provide maintenance for a period of two years;
3. He is sentenced to imprisonment for seven years or upwards;
4. He failed to perform without reasonable cause his marital obligations for three years;
5. Is impotent;
6. Is insane for two years or suffers from leprosy or virulent venereal disease;
7. She has exercised her option of puberty before the age of eighteen years;
8. The husband assaults her or makes her life miserable by cruelty of conduct,
9. Associates with women of evil repute, forces her to lead immoral life;
10. Disposes her property or prevents her to exercise her rights over the same;
11. Obstructs her to observe her religious profession;
12. In case of more wives than one is not equal in treatment.

49. Under Section 12(1)(d) of the Hindu Marriage Act which provide any marriage solemnized, whether before or after the commencement of this Act, shall be voidable and may be annulled by a decree of nullity on the grounds, namely: that the respondent was at the time of the marriage pregnant by some person other than the petitioner.

52. Period of *Iddat*: The period of *Iddat* depends upon the manner in which the marriage is dissolved. Marriage may be dissolved, by death or divorce. So the period of *Iddat* will be observed in the following manner:

In the case of dissolution of marriage by Death:

(*a*) If the marriage is valid (whether it was consummated or not) and is dissolved by death of the husband, the wife is to observe the period of 4 lunar months and 10 days and if pregnant, the period of *Iddat* will extend up to the death or delivery or whichever period is longer.

(*b*) If the marriage is irregular, and is dissolved by death of the husband, the wife shall observe the prescribed period of *Iddat* only if the marriage was consummated.

(*c*) The period of *Iddat,* in case of death of the husband commences from the date of death.

55. The protracted debate in around the classification of human rights into three 'generations'. French jurist Karel Vasak first identified these 'three generations of human rights'. The first generation consists of civil and political rights. The second generation consists of economic, social and cultural rights and the third generation consists of the so-called solidarity rights. During the era of Cold War hostilities between the West and East blocs human rights discourse was trapped in the debate about categories and cultural relativism.

58. Human rights are inscribed in the hearts of people; they were there long before lawmakers drafted their first proclamation. Mary Robinson, former UN High Commissioner for Human Rights.

59. Having regard to Resolution (78) 41 of the Committee of Ministers which recommended that universities and other competent authorities adopt various measures to encourage study of the international and national protection of human rights.

Considering that in 1969 the late Rene Cassin, a President of the European Court of Human Rights and of the United Nations Commission on Human Rights as well as a winner of the Nobel Peace Prize, founded the International Institute of Human Rights, which will be celebrating its fifteenth anniversary in December 1984.

Considering that one of the principal aims of the International Institute of Human Rights is to foster the protection and development of fundamental rights throughout the world and to train university teachers in the subject.

61. The Indian Constitution guarantees essential human rights in the form of fundamental rights under Part III and also directive principles of State Policy in Part IV which are fundamental to the governance of the country. Freedoms granted under Part III have been liberally construed by various pronouncements of the Supreme Court in last half a century in favour of the subjects also, keeping in view the international covenants.

67. It is possible for a person to obtain a prescriptive rights to carry on an activity that in the eyes of some amounts to a private nuisance. The activity complained of must have been continuously carried on for at least 20 years. Throughout that time it must have been actionable as a private nuisance but nobody has in fact taken action.

69. Mutual Agency—There must exist a mutual agency relationship among the partners. 'Mutual Agency' relationship means that each partner is both an agent and a principal. Each partner is an agent in the sense that he has the capacity to bind other partners by his acts done. Each partner is a principal in the sense that he is bound by the acts of other partners.

The mutual relationship of agency is emphasized in Section 18 of the Indian Partnership Act, which reads as under.

"Subject to the provision of this Act, a partner is the agent of the firm for the business of the firm."

74. The payee must be certain: As in the case of maker, the payee of a note must also be certain on the face of the instrument. A note is valid even in conditions wherein the payee is misnamed or indicated by the official designation. A promissory note may be payable to two or more payees jointly. Further, alternative payees are permissible and it may be made payable to one of two, or one or some of several payees. A note made payable to bearer, or in favour of a fictitious person, is illegal and void. A promissory note made payable to the maker himself is also considered a nullity, as the same person is both the promisor and the promise.

Previous Paper (Solved)

UGC-NET LAW, DECEMBER 2013

PAPER-II

Note : *This paper contains fifty (50) objective type questions, each question carrying two (2) marks each.* ***All questions are compulsory.***

1. Social, economic and political Justice is
A. an idea enshrined in the Preamble to the Constitution of India
B. guaranteed by Fundamental Rights in the Constitution of India
C. a Directive Principle of State Policy taken into consideration while making enactments
D. guaranteed to the people by the writs issued by the High Courts and Supreme Court

2. Without paying proper remuneration, labour taken from the prisoners is 'forced labour' and violation of
A. Art. 20 of the Constitution of India
B. Art. 21 of the Constitution of India
C. Art. 22 of the Constitution of India
D. Art. 23 of the Constitution of India

3. Art. 51A of the Constitution of India provides for the Fundamental Duties of
A. Citizens of India
B. Public Servants
C. All those who run public and private sectors
D. Prime Minister and his Council of Ministers

4. The appropriate writ issued by Supreme Court to quash the appointment of a person to a public office is
A. Certiorari B. Mandamus
C. Prohibition D. Quo-Warranto

5. The power of the President of India to issue an ordinance is a
A. Legislative power
B. Executive power
C. Quasi-judicial power
D. Judicial power

6. The jurisdiction of Supreme Court of India may be enlarged by
A. The President of India
B. The Parliament by resolution
C. The Parliament by Law
D. The President in consultation with the Chief Justice of India

7. At the first instance, the President can issue a proclamation of financial emergency for a period of
A. Fifteen days B. Two months
C. One month D. Six months

8. Legal Theory is based on
A. a systematic study of positive laws
B. purely logical and empirical study
C. concepts like morality, justice and ethics
D. total exclusion of customary practices, morality and social vagaries

9. Who separated jurisprudence from religion?
A. Kant B. Hugo Grotius
C. Salmond D. Jethro Brown

10. Under how many categories the five theories of punishment can be divided?
A. 2 B. 4
C. 5 D. 3

11. On which one of the following one can have corporeal ownership ?
A. A right B. Trademark
C. Movable property D. A debt

12. "Sovereignty must be determinate, it is essential, is indivisible and is unlimited and illimitable." Who conceived this about the sovereignty?
A. Hobbes B. Austin
C. Jean Bodin D. Plato

13. Consider the following statements:

1. Statements, which are not partaking of the character of ratio decidendi can be ignored while deciding the latter case.
2. The ratio decidendi is not the reason of decision.
3. Only that part of the judgement in an earlier decision is binding which constitutes the ratio decidendi of that case.
4. A judicial decision has a binding force for subsequent cases but the whole judgement is not binding, only a part of it is biding.

Which of the above statement(s) is/are correct?

A. 1, 3, 4 B. 1, 2, 3
C. 2, 3, 4 D. 1, 2, 4

14. "Case law is gold in the mine, a few grains of the precious metal to the tons of useless matter, while statute law is coin of the realm ready for immediate use." Who said these words?

A. Ihering B. Austin
C. Kelson D. Salmond

15. Which of the following statements are true?

1. There is no rule to determine when usage shall give rise to a custom.
2. Customary rules of International law are diminishing and are being replaced by Treaties and Conventions.
3. Treaty contracts are not direct source of International law.
4. International law is a positive morality.

Codes:

A. 1, 2, 3 and 4 B. 2, 3 and 4
C. 1, 2 and 3 D. 1 and 2

16. "The law of National or International law may be defined as the body of rules and principles of actions which are binding upon civilized states in their relations with one-another." This definition of International law was given by

A. J.L. Brierly B. Torsten Vitel
C. Hackworth D. None of the above

17. Match the following :

List-I	*List-II*
(*a*) Recognition only and exclusively bestows a State with rights and duties under International Law.	(*i*) De-facto recognition
(*b*) It is a first step towards final recognition.	(*ii*) De-Jure recognition
(*c*) It is a final recognition by a State.	(*iii*) Declaratory Theory
(*d*) International personality of a State does not depend upon recognition.	(*iv*) Constitutive Theory

Codes:

	(*a*)	(*b*)	(*c*)	(*d*)
A.	(*iv*)	(*i*)	(*ii*)	(*iii*)
B.	(*i*)	(*ii*)	(*iii*)	(*iv*)
C.	(*iv*)	(*iii*)	(*ii*)	(*i*)
D.	(*iii*)	(*ii*)	(*i*)	(*iv*)

18. The Charter of the United Nations can be amended by

A. Five-third of the members of General Assembly.
B. The Security Council only.
C. Two-third of the members of the U.N. including all permanent members of the Security Council after recommendations by a two-thirds vote of a conference convened for the purpose, is received.
D. Two-thirds of the members of the Security Council including five permanent members.

19. In which of the following case, International Court of Justice denied existence of customary rule?

A. North Sea Continental Shelf case.
B. The Lotus case.
C. Both of the above.
D. None of the above.

20. Which organ of the United Nations has been given responsibility of promoting international co-operation in the realisation of human rights?

A. General Assembly
B. Security Council
C. Both of the above
D. None of the above

21. In which of the following case the Supreme Court held that even the wife of a void marriage is entitled to maintenance?

A. Amarjeet Kaur Vs. Harbhajan Singh (2003) 10 SCC 228.
B. Chand Dhawan Vs. Jawaharlal Dhawan (1993) 3 SCC 406.
C. Nirmala Devi Vs. Ram Dass (2001) 2 SCC 4
D. Ramesh Chandra Vs. Veena Kausal AIR 1978 SC 1807

22. In which of the following case, the court held that "Dower is a sale price of woman"?

A. Maina Bibi case
B. Humara Bibi case
C. Subrunnisan case
D. Abdul Kadir case

23. Read Assertion (A) and Reason (R). Find correct answer using codes given below:

Assertion (A): "Option of Puberty" is an easy process to repudiate the marriage under Hindu Law.

Reason (R): "Option of Puberty" is not an easy process to repudiate the marriage under Muslim Law.

Codes:

A. (A) is correct, but (R) is incorrect.
B. (A) and (R) both are correct.
C. (R) is correct, but (A) is incorrect.
D. (A) and (R) both are incorrect.

24. 'Tuhr' means

A. Period of menstruation
B. Period of iddat
C. Period between menstruation
D. None of the above

25. Match an item in List-I with correct answer in List-II using the codes given below:

List-I	***List-II***
(*a*) Gujarat Women's Workers Association Vs. Union of India	(*i*) Dower
(*b*) Humara Bibi Vs. Zubaida Bibi	(*ii*) Triple Divorce
(*c*) Anwari Begum Vs. Ziauddin	(*iii*) Uniform Civil Code
(*d*) Bai Tahira Vs. Ali Hussain Fissalli	(*iv*) Maintenance

Codes:

	(*a*)	(*b*)	(*c*)	(*d*)
A.	(*i*)	(*iv*)	(*ii*)	(*iii*)
B.	(*i*)	(*ii*)	(*iii*)	(*iv*)
C.	(*iii*)	(*i*)	(*ii*)	(*iv*)
D.	(*ii*)	(*iii*)	(*iv*)	(*i*)

26. Which form of talaq is revocable during period of 'iddat' ?

A. Talaq-i-Ahsan
B. Talaq-i-Hasan
C. Triple Talaq
D. None of the above

27. Essentials of valid contract is

A. Meeting of minds
B. Meeting of parties
C. Meeting to discuss consideration
D. Meeting to discuss proposal and acceptance

28. Read Assertion (A) and Reason (R) and with help of codes given below, point out the correct explanation.

Assertion (A): A proposal, when accepted, results in an agreement.

Reason (R): It is only after the acceptance of the proposal that a contract between the two parties can arise.

Codes:

A. Both (A) and (R) are true and (R) is good explanation of (A).
B. Both (A) and (R) are true, but (R) is not a correct explanation of (A).
C. (A) is true, but (R) is false.
D. (A) is false, but (R) is true.

A minor is son of a beggar. He is told by a law professor that he would not be liable for any goods he purchases. The minor purchases a car and a bread loaf. Decide liability for payment of car and bread loaf, using codes given below.

A. The minor is liable to pay price of car and bread loaf.
B. The minor is liable to pay reasonable compensation for car.
C. The minor is liable to pay price of bread.
D. The minor's parent/guardian is liable to pay reasonable compensation for bread loaf.

Arrange following concepts in sequence in which they occur, using codes given below:

(*i*) Offer
(*ii*) Acceptance
(*iii*) Damage
(*iv*) Damages

Codes:

A. (*iv*), (*iii*), (*ii*), (*i*) B. (*i*), (*ii*), (*iv*), (*iii*)
C. (*i*), (*iv*), (*ii*), (*iii*) D. (*i*), (*ii*), (*iii*), (*iv*)

A contract may be vitiated by :

(*i*) Fraud
(*ii*) Mistake
(*iii*) Frustration
(*iv*) Undue influence

Find correct answer, using codes :

Codes:

A. Only (*i*) is correct.
B. Only (*i*) and (*ii*) are correct.
C. Only (*i*), (*ii*) and (*iii*) are correct.
D. All are correct.

Match items in Table-A with items in Table-B, using codes given below:

Table-A	***Table-B***
(*a*) Promise	(*i*) Section 56
(*b*) Frustration	(*ii*) Section 2(d)
(*c*) Effect of refusal to accept offer of performance	(*iii*) Section 26
(*d*) Agreement in restraint of marriage	(*iv*) Section 38

Codes:

	(*i*)	(*ii*)	(*iii*)	(*iv*)
A.	(*b*)	(*d*)	(*a*)	(*c*)
B.	(*b*)	(*a*)	(*d*)	(*c*)
C.	(*a*)	(*b*)	(*d*)	(*c*)
D.	(*a*)	(*b*)	(*c*)	(*d*)

33. P, owner of a car, asked his friend Q to drive the car to Bombay where he would join him. As the car was about five kilometres from Bombay, it hit a pedestrian R, on account of Q's negligent driving and injured him seriously. R sued P for damages. In this case:

A. P is not liable.
B. The liability is solely of Q, as P was not accompanying him.
C. Since Q was driving P's car was under his authority, P is liable.
D. P has the defence of inevitable accident.

34. "If it was lawful act, however ill the motive might be, the defendant had a right to do it." This observation was made by the court in one of the following cases:

A. Mayor of Bradford Corporation Vs. Pickles
B. Ashby Vs. White
C. Christie Vs. Davey
D. Hollywood Silver Fox Farm Ltd. Vs. Emmet

35. P and Q, unknown to R, sought and got a lift in R's car, but on account of some mechanical defect in the car, of which R was not aware, one of the front wheels of the car got detached and flew away, and the car toppled. P and Q got serious injuries and later on, P died of his injuries. Q and P's next kin sued R for damages for negligent driving. What defence R has?

A Volenti non fit injuria
B. No responsibility towards P and Q who got a free lift
C. Inevitable accidert
D. No defence

36. In contributory negligence :

A. Both parties have contributed to the negligence equally.
B. Only one party is negligent and other has not taken due care.
C. One party is negligent resulting in injury while the other has taken due care.
D. When lack of care is equal on both sides.

37. P shoot at Q with the view to kill him. When Q was being taken to hospital, a tree fell upon Q on the way and Q died in the hospital a few days later. If it was proved that the falling of the tree caused Q's death, then

A. P shall be responsible for the death of Q.
B. Falling of tree has broken the chain of causation.
C. P is not liable to pay compensation to the dependents of Q.
D. P is responsible for the death of Q as Q's death was the direct consequence of P's act.

38. Which one of the following has been laid down as basis of responsibility by the rule in Rylands Vs. Fletcher?

A. Fault liability
B. Conditional liability
C. Strict liability
D. Insurance liability

39. Read Assertion–I and Reason–II and with the help of codes given below decide what offence if any was committed?

Assertion–I: A and Z agree to fence with each other for a game. But because of foul, despite playing fairly, Z was injured.

Reason–II:

(*a*) No offence by virtue of consent between A and Z.
(*b*) Consent was obtained in good faith to gain prize, so no offence by A.
(*c*) A is criminally liable because he had knowledge about the likelihood of injury.
(*d*) Despite implied consent the intention was bad so A is liable.

Codes:

A. Reason (*a*) is true when (*b*), (*c*) and (*d*) are not asserted.
B. Reason (*b*) is true when (*a*), (*c*) and (*d*) are not asserted.
C. Reason (*c*) is true when (*a*), (*b*) and (*d*) are not asserted.
D. Reason (*d*) is true when (*a*), (*b*) and (*c*) are not asserted.

40. Read Assertion–I and Reason–II and with the help of codes given below select the correct answer:

Assertion–I: Common intention is assert

Reason–II:

(*a*) A period which is anterior in time am the offenders.
(*b*) From the facts of pre-arranged plan.
(*c*) From the act of conduct resulting fr prior concert.
(*d*) From the totality of circumstances in wh the act was committed.

Codes:

A. (*a*) is false because (*b*), (*c*) and (*d*) do support it.
B. (*d*) is true as (*a*), (*b*) and (*c*) support
C. (*c*) is true irrespective of support of (*a*), and (*d*).
D. (*b*) is true being supported by (*a*), (*c*) (*d*).

41. Select the statement that is most suitabl law:

Culpable homicide is not murder when or deprived of the power of self-control resul from:

A. Grave and sudden provocation
B. When death results by volunt provocation.
C. Where death results in course of obedi of law.
D. When death results by mistake.

42. B a married man commits sex with C a child of 16 years with her consent. V offence B has committed?

A. Adultery B. Rape
C. No offence D. Sexual outrag

43. Fill in the blank :

Extortion is ________, when it is comm under fear of instant hurt.

A. Theft
B. Attempt to steal property
C. Robbery
D. Wrongful restraint

44. Find answer of the following question:

What is the distinctive feature between information and false charging?

A. Using lawful power to cause annoy so as to institute a criminal proceed

B. To omit act which ought not to be done.
C. A case for false information can only be started by a complaint while false charge can be initiated by police.
D. There is no real distinction.

45. Collective bargaining serves purposes:
A. Regulating wages and conditions of service
B. Regulating labour management relations.
C. Both (A) and (B).
D. None of the above.

46. In which country where statutes make it obligatory to negotiate non-performance of the obligation invites penalty, failure to carry obligation is treated as unfair labour practice?
A. U.K. B. U.S.A.
C. France D. India

47. In which of the following case, the Supreme Court held that "there was no rule of thumb that in every case of termination of workman's service in violation of Section 25F of ID Act relief of re-instatement should be granted?
A. Talwara Co-operative Credit & Service Society Ltd. Vs. Sushil Kumar (2009) I LLJ 326 S.C.
B. Gujarat Steel Tubes Ltd. Vs. G.S.T. Mazdoor Sabha (1980) I LLJ 137 (S.C.)
C. Mavji C. Lakum Vs. Central Bank of India -(2008) III LLJ.1.(SC)
D. None of the above

48. The Registrar to Pensions Appeal Tribunal was appointed as presiding officer of a Labour Court. The appointment is
A. Valid B. Void
C. Void ab-initio D. None of the above

49. Match List-I with List-II and select the correct answer using the codes given below:

List-I (Subject)	***List-II (Provisions of ID Act)***
(*a*) Tribunal	(*i*) Section 2(ra)
(*b*) Wages	(*ii*) Section 2(r)
(*c*) Unfair Labour Practices	(*iii*) Section 2 (rb)
(*d*) Village Industries	(*iv*) Section 2 (rr)

Codes:

	(*a*)	(*b*)	(*c*)	(*d*)
A.	(*i*)	(*iv*)	(*iii*)	(*ii*)
B.	(*ii*)	(*iii*)	(*i*)	(*iv*)
C.	(*ii*)	(*iv*)	(*i*)	(*iii*)
D.	(*i*)	(*iii*)	(*ii*)	(*iv*)

50. Read Assertion (A) and Reason (R), using codes given below, select correct answer :
Assertion (A): Strike is individual stoppage of work to press management to get more pay.
Reason (R): Individual has fundamental right of strike.
Codes:
A. (A) and (R) are true and (R) is correct explanation of (A).
B. (A) and (R) are true, but (R) is not correct explanation of (A).
C. (A) and (R) are false.
D. (A) is true, but (R) is false.

ANSWERS

1	2	3	4	5	6	7	8	9	10
A	D	A	D	A	C	B	C	B	D
11	**12**	**13**	**14**	**15**	**16**	**17**	**18**	**19**	**20**
C	B	A	D	C	A	A	D	C	C
21	**22**	**23**	**24**	**25**	**26**	**27**	**28**	**29**	**30**
B	C	B	C	C	A	A	A	D	D
31	**32**	**33**	**34**	**35**	**36**	**37**	**38**	**39**	**40**
D	B	C	A	C	B	B	C	A	B
41	**42**	**43**	**44**	**45**	**46**	**47**	**48**	**49**	**50**
A	C	C	B	C	B	A	C	C	C

SOME SELECTED EXPLANATORY ANSWERS

1. According to the Preamble of the Indian constitution, some of the important objectives which the Preamble secures to every citizen are: Justice-social, economic and political; Liberty of thought, expression, belief, faith and worship; Equality of status and of opportunity and to promote among them all; Fraternity—Assuring the dignity of the individual and the unity and integrity of the Nation.

2. Article 23 of the Indian Constitution deals with Prohibition of Traffic in Human Beings and Forced Labour and begar and other similar forms of forced labour. 'Traffic in human beings' means selling and buying men and women like goods and includes immoral traffic in women and children for immoral or other purposes. Article 23 protects the individual not only against the state but also private citizens. It imposes a positive obligation on the state to take steps to abolish evils of traffic in human beings, and begar and other similar forms of forced labour wherever they are found. Article 23 prohibits the system of bonded labour because it is a form of forced labour within the meaning of this Article.

3. Article 51-A was added to the Constitution by the 42nd Amendment, 1976. This Article for the first time specifies a code of 11 fundamental duties for citizens of India. Article 51-A, says that it shall be the duty of every citizen of India: to abide by constitution and respect its ideal and institutions, the National Flag and National Anthem; to cherish and follow the noble ideals which inspired our national struggle for freedom; to uphold and protect the sovereignty, unity, integrity of India; to defend the country and render national service are some of the important Fundamental duties.

4. Quo-warranto is a question asking 'with what authority or warrant'. The writ may be sought to clarity in public interest the legal position in regard to claim of a person to hold a public office. An application seeking such a writ may be made by any person provided th office in question is a substantive publi office of a permanent nature created by th constitution or law and a person has bee appointed to it without a legal title and i contravention of the constitution or the laws So, the appropriate writ issued by suprem court to quash the appointment of a person t a public office is Quo-warranto.

5. The most important legislative power of th President is his Ordinance making power. at any time, when both Houses of th Parliament are not in session and the Preside is satisfied that circumstances exist whic render it necessary for him to take immedia action, he may issue such ordinance as th circumstances appear to him to require. Th ordinance issued by him shall have the san force as an Act of Parliament. Such ordinance however, must be laid before both Houses Parliament and shall cease to operate, at th expiry of six weeks from the date of r assembly of Parliament, unless a resoluti disapproving it is passed by both Hous before the expiration of six weeks. A ordinance promulgated under Article 123 a law having the same force and effect as Act of Parliament. The ordinance maki power has been vested in the President deal with unforeseen or urgent matters.

7. The President is authorized by Article 360 declare by a proclamation financial emergen if he is satisfied that the financial stability credit of India or any part of its territory threatened. It has to be laid before both Hous of Parliament and ceases to operate at t expiration of two months unless meanwh approved by the resolutions of the two Hous Once approved by Parliament unli proclamations under Article 352, it m continue indefinitely until revoked or vari During the operation of financial emergen the executive authority of the Union exte to the giving of directions to any state

observe certain specified canons or financial propriety and such other direction that the President may find necessary or adequate. The President may also direct reduction in salaries etc., of all those serving in connection with the affairs of Union including Judges of the Supreme court and the High Courts.

22. Dower is a sale price of woman, it was held in Subrunnisan case. Dower or Mohr is a peculiar Muslim law concept. It is a sum of money/other property promised by the husband to be paid or delivered to the wife in the consideration of the marriage, and even where no dower is expressly fixed or mentioned at the marriage ceremony, the law confers the right of dower upon the wife. However, non-specification of dower does not render a Muslim marriage void. Dower is an invaluable right of a Muslim wife. Probably, it is also used as a deterrent to Muslim husband's absolute power to pronouncing divorce on his wife. It is an integral part of marriage and may be fixed before, at or after the marriage; in case, not fixed by the parties, it is implied in every marriage, and is usually fixed by the courts. No school of Muslim law fixes the maximum amount of dower, and a Muslim couple may fix any amount of dower—even an amount which is evidently much beyond the means of the husband.

27. According to Section 13 of the Indian Contract Act, 1872, one of the essentials of a valid contract is 'Consensus-ad-idem' *i.e.*, meeting of minds. Section 13 defines consent as, when Two or more persons are said to consent when they agree upon the same thing in the same sense.

31. A contract may be vitiated by Fraud according to Section 17 of the Indian Contract Act, 1872, by Mistake under Section 20, by Frustration under Section 56 and by undue influence under Section 16 of the Indian Contract Act, 1872.

35. In the given scenario, R can avail the defence of Inevitable accident. It means an unexpected injury, which could not have been, avoided inspite of a reasonable care on the part of the defendant. It is important to note that this defence is available only if the accident occurs during the prosecution of a lawful act and not when the act done is unlawful.

36. In certain circumstances a person who has suffered an injury will not be able to get damages from another for the reason that his own negligence has contributed to his injury; every person is expected to take reasonable care of himself. According to John. G. Fleming, "Negligence is conduct that fails to confirm to the standards required by law for safeguarding others (actionable negligence) or oneself (contributory negligence) against unreasonable risk of injury". Thus when the plaintiff by his own want of care contributes to the damage caused by negligence or wrongful conduct of the defendant, he is considered to be guilty of contributory negligence.

38. Simply stated the rule of strict liability makes the defendant liable for accidental harms caused without any intention and negligence on his part. In other words, sometimes the law recognizes 'no fault' liability. The undertakers of hazardous or dangerous activities have to compensate for the damage caused irrespective of any carelessness on their part. The basis of liability is the foreseeable risk inherent in the very nature of the activities. In this respect, principle of strict liability resembles negligence, but differs, as here the defendant would be liable even if he could not by reasonable care have avoided the damage. The rule laid down in Rylands Vs. Fletcher is called the rule of strict liability.

43. According Section 390 of the Indian Penal Code, 1860, Extortion is robbery if the offender at the time of committing the extortion, is in the presence of the person put in fear, and commits the extortion by putting that person in fear of instant death or of instant hurt, or of instant wrongful restraint to that person, or to some other person, and, by so putting in fear, induces the person so put in fear then and there to deliver up the thing extorted.

PAPER-III

Note : *This paper contains **seventy five (75)** objective type questions of **two (2)** marks each. **All** questions are compulsory.*

1. Who among the following expressed the view that the Indian Constitution is Federal as much as it establishes what may be called a dual polity?

A. Dr. B.R. Ambedkar
B. Sir Ivor Jennings
C. Prof. K.C. Wheare
D. Sir B.N. Rau

2. In which of the following amendment the words 'Nothing in Article 13 shali apply to any amendment made under Article 368' were inserted?

A. 22nd Amendment
B. 24th Amendment
C. 42nd Amendment
D. 44th Amendment

3. The Supreme Court of India held in which of the following case that the views expressed by it in exercise of its advisory jurisdiction are binding on all courts within the territory of India?

A. In Re-Berubari case
B. In Re-Cauvery Water Disputes Tribunal case
C. In Re-Kerala Education Bill
D. In Re-Special Courts Bill

4. In which one of the following case has the Supreme Court upheld the Constitutional validity of the Constitution (93rd Amendment) introducing Article 15(5)?

A. TMA Pai Foundation Vs. State of Karnataka
B. Indra Sawhney Vs. Union of India
C. M. Nagaraj Vs. Union of India
D. Ashok Kumar Thakur Vs. Union of India

5. Match List-A with List-B and select the correct answer using the codes given below:

List-A	*List-B*
(*a*) Independence of the Judiciary	(*i*) Administrative adjudication
(*b*) Executive Legislation	(*ii*) Parliamentary form of Government
(*c*) Quasi-Judicial function	(*iii*) Appointment of Judges
(*d*) Collective responsibility	(*iv*) Ordinance

Codes:

	(*a*)	(*b*)	(*c*)	(*d*)
A.	(*ii*)	(*i*)	(*iv*)	(*iii*)
B.	(*iii*)	(*iv*)	(*i*)	(*ii*)
C.	(*ii*)	(*iv*)	(*i*)	(*iii*)
D.	(*iii*)	(*i*)	(*iv*)	(*ii*)

6. Read Assertion (A) and Reason (R) and find correct answer using codes given below:

Assertion (A): The Council of Ministers is the hub of the Parliamentary form of Government.

Reason (R): The Government is formed from the majority party.

Codes:

A. Both (A) and (R) are true, but (R) is not the correct explanation of (A).
B. Both (A) and (R) are true and (R) is the correct explanation of (A).
C. (A) is true, (R) is false.
D. (A) is false, but (R) is true.

7. The jurisdiction of the Supreme Court of India may be enlarged by

A. The President of India
B. The President of India in consultation with the Prime Minister and Chief Justice of India
C. The Parliament by resolution
D. The Parliament by law.

8. What are exceptions to the rule of natural justice? Answer using codes given below:

(*i*) Exclusion by statutory provisions.
(*ii*) Exclusion by Constitutional provision
(*iii*) Exclusion in case of legislative act.
(*iv*) Exclusion in public interest.

Codes:

A. Only (*i*) is correct.
B. Only (*i*) and (*ii*) are correct.
C. Only (*i*), (*ii*) and (*iii*) are correct.
D. All of above are correct.

. Read Assertion (A) and Reason (R) and find correct answer using codes given below:

Assertion (A): In India the order passed in violation of the principles of natural justice is void.

Reason (R): In India there is void in the area of principles of justice by nature.

Codes:

A. (A) and (R) are true and (R) is correct explanation of (A).
B. (A) and (R) are true, but (R) is not correct explanation of (A).
C. (A) is true, but (R) is false.
D. (A) is false, but (R) is true.

In which of the following conditions, the abuse of discretionary power is inferred?

(*i*) Use for improper purpose
(*ii*) Mala fide
(*iii*) Relevant consideration
(*iv*) Leaving out irrelevant consideration

Answer using codes given below:

Codes:

A. Only (*i*) is correct.
B. Only (*i*) and (*ii*) are correct.
C. Only (*i*), (*ii*) and (*iii*) are correct.
D. All of above are correct.

Read Assertion (A) and Reason (R) and find correct answer using codes given below:

Assertion (A): Equality is antithetic to arbitrariness.

Reason (R): Article 14 of the Indian Constitution prevents arbitrary discretion being vested in the executive.

Codes:

A. Both (A) and (R) are true and (R) is correct explanation of (A).
B. Both (A) and (R) are true, but (R) is not correct explanation of (A).
C. (A) is true, but (R) is false.
D. (A) is false, but (R) is true.

12. The writ of habeas corpus will be issued if

A. Detention is legal.
B. Detention is prima facie legal.
C. Detention is prima facie illegal.
D. Detention is primarily illegal.

13. Reading Assertion (A) and Reason (R), select correct answer using codes given below:

Assertion (A): Lokpal is the demand of time.

Reason (R): Lokpal is a time saving institution.

Codes:

A. Both (A) and (R) are true, and (R) is correct explanation of (A).
B. Both (A) and (R) are true, but (R) is not correct explanation of (A).
C. (A) is true, but (R) is false.
D. (A) is false, but (R) is true.

14. "Administrative Law is the law concerning the powers and procedures of administrative agencies, including especially the law governing judicial review of administrative action." This definition of Administrative Law is given by:

A. Ivor Jenning B. Garner
C. K.C. Davis D. Wade

15. In which of the following grounds, a writ of certiorari may be issued ?

A. Error of jurisdiction
B. Error apparent on face of record
C. Violation of natural justice
D. All of the above

16. Who propounded the Doctrine of 'Moral Reasoning' ?

A. Kohler B. Pound
C. H.L.A. Hart D. Kant

17. Which of the following avoid any dogmatic formulation and concentrate on the decisions given by law courts?

A. Realist school
B. Analytical school
C. Philosophical school
D. Sociological school

18. 'Jus civile', 'Jus gentium' and 'Jus naturale' are found in

A. American Law B. Greek Law
C. Roman Law D. French Law

19. Match the following:

(*a*) Ancient theories		(*i*) Grotius, Hobbes and Locke	
(*b*) Modern theories		(*ii*) Thomas Acquinas	
(*c*) Renaissance theories		(*iii*) Stamler and Kohler	
(*d*) Medieval theories		(*iv*) Socrates, Aristotle and Plato	

Codes:

	(*a*)	(*b*)	(*c*)	(*d*)
A.	(*iii*)	(*iv*)	(*ii*)	(*i*)
B.	(*i*)	(*ii*)	(*iii*)	(*iv*)
C.	(*ii*)	(*iii*)	(*iv*)	(*i*)
D.	(*iv*)	(*iii*)	(*i*)	(*ii*)

20. "Law is without doubt a remedy for greater evil, yet it brings with it evils of its own." Who said it?
A. Blackstone B. Friedman
C. Salmond D. Hobbes

21. According to Salmond, every right involves a three fold relation.
I. It is a right against some person or persons.
II. It is a right to some act or omission of such person or persons.
III. It is a right over or to something to which that act or omission relates.

Codes:
A. I and II are false.
B. I, II and III are true.
C. II and III are false.
D. Only I is true.

22. Assertion (A): Srutis and Smritis form the greatest treasure house of Hinduism.

Reason (R): Srutis and Smritis are considered immemorial, timeless and eternal.

Examine the above statement (A) and Reason (R) and select whether the reason is a correct explanation of the assertion, using the codes given below:

Codes:
A. Both (A) and (R) are true, but (R) is not the correct explanation of (A).
B. Both (A) and (R) are true and (R) is t correct explanation of (A).
C. (A) is true, but (R) is false.
D. (A) is false, but (R) is true.

23. Personality is a very vague and wide te and it has a variety of meanings. It is deriv from the word persona which is a
A. Latin word B. French word
C. German word D. Greek word

24. Fill in the blank with appropriate offence
Extortion is ______, when it is commit under fear of instant hurt.
A. Theft B. Attempt to murc
C. Robbery D. Wrongful restra

25. Fill in the blank with suitable statement:
Z dies in possession of gold ring, gold ch and a gold wrist watch during the course an accident. A, before anyone entitled to su possession, dishonestly misappropriates same causing ______.
A. An aggravated form of misappropriat as per Section 404 of IPC.
B. A type of possession by some process per Section 405 of IPC.
C. No offence because the property question was entrusted to A before death of Z.
D. No offence because the property question was possessed by some casua

26. Fill in the blank with correct proposition law:
The malicious injury to property as maxim *Sic Utre tuo ut allenum non lea* (to use your own property so as not to inj your neighbour's property) as provi in______.
A. Damage of property as per Section IPC.
B. Mischief as per Section 425 IPC.
C. Mischief to cause wrongful restrain per Section 440 IPC.
D. Destruction of landmark as per Sec 433 IPC.

27. Read Assertion I and Reason II and with the help of codes given below write the appropriate answer:

I. Assertion: The distinctive feature between preparation and attempt must be based on.

II. Reason: Preparation consists in devising means necessary for the commission of offence while attempt is the direct movement towords commission.

Codes :

A. Both I and II are true, but II is not correct explanation of I.
B. Both I and II are true while II is the correct explanation of I.
C. I is true, but II is false.
D. II is true, but I is only a stage of crime.

28. The accused caused bodily pain, disease or infirmity. But it is cognizable, bailable or compoundable. What offence, if any, has been committed by the accused?

A. Voluntary causing grievous hurt as per Section 322 IPC.
B. Voluntary causing serious hurt as per Section 325 IPC.
C. Voluntary causing grievous hurt by dangerous weapon as per Section 324 IPC.
D. Voluntary causing grievous hurt by dangerous weapon as per Section 326 IPC.

29. An individual's act of abridgement of another's right to movement could be an offence of:

A. wrongful confinement as per Section 340 IPC.
B. an act of abridgement of right to movement was done in good faith and hence no offence.
C. the movement route being diverted so assault results.
D. wrongful restraint as per Section 329 IPC.

30. Match the statement that *mens rea* is a loose term of elastic significance with that of the meaning in sequential order.

(*a*) Foresight of the consequences of the act.
(*b*) Criminal intention of deepest dye.
(*c*) An act which is visible.
(*d*) It depends upon knowledge and belief.

Matching probabilities :

A. It is the bare capacity to know in the sequence of (*a*), (*b*), (*c*) and (*d*).
B. It is essential ingredient of criminal offence in the sequence of (*d*), (*c*), (*b*) and (*a*).
C. It is a presumption to fix criminal liability in the sequence of (*c*), (*b*), (*a*) and (*d*).
D. Applicability of the principle becomes essential by the sequence of (*b*), (*a*), (*d*) and (*c*).

31. Read Assertion I and Reason II and with the help of codes given below point out the correct explanation.

I. **Assertion:** Generally a master is not criminally liable merely because his servant has committed a negligent act.

II. **Reason:** In ordinary course of employment a master may be criminally liable against the negligent acts of the servant.

Codes:

A. Both I and II are true, but II is not the correct explanation of I.
B. I is true and II is the genuine reason of I.
C. II is true, but I is not absolutely correct.
D. II is false, but I is only an assertion.

32. On which date and place the Earth Summit was held at?

A. 6th June, 1997 at Geneva.
B. 20th June, 1997 at London.
C. 21st June, 1992 at Rio.
D. 27th June, 1992 at Rio.

33. "In case of violation of Article 21 by disturbing the environment, the court could award damages not only for the restoration of the ecological balance but also for the victim who have suffered due to that disturbance."

In which case the Supreme Court of India has made above observations?

A. M.C. Mehta Vs. Union of India, AIR 1997 SC 734
B. M.C. Mehta Vs. Kamal Nath, (1997) 1 SCC 388

C. M.C. Mehta Vs. Kamal Nath AIR 2000 SC 1997

D. M.C. Mehta Vs. Kamal Nath 2000 (2) SCALE 654

34. In which of the following case the constitutionality, legal validity, propriety and fairness of the settlement of the claims of the victims in a mass tort action relating to Bhopal Gas Leak Disaster has been challenged in Supreme Court of India?

A. Union Carbide Corp. Vs. Union of India, AIR 1990 SC 273

B. M.C. Mehta Vs. Union of India, AIR 1987 SC 1086

C. Union Carbide Corp. Vs. Union of India, AIR 1992 SC 248

D. Charanlal Sahu Vs. Union of India, AIR 1990 SC 1480

35. Under which Article of the Constitution Environment (Protection) Act, 1986 was enacted?

A. Article 253 B. Article 258

C. Article 255 D. Article 254

36. The problem of the pollution of river Ganga by the inaction of the municipalities was brought to light in which of the following case?

A. Indian Council for Enviro-Legal Action Vs. Union of India, AIR 1996 SC 1446

B. A.P. Pollution Control Board Vs. M.V. Nayudu, AIR 1999 SC 812

C. S. Jagannath Vs. Union of India, AIR 1997 SC 811

D. M.C. Mehta Vs. Union of India, AIR 1988 SC 1115

37. Which one of the following cases relates to Sariska Tiger Park?

A. Tarun Bharat Sangh Vs. Union of India, AIR 1992 SC 514

B. Consumer Education and Research Society Vs. Union of India, AIR 2000 SC 975

C. Pradeep Krishen Vs. Union of India, AIR 1997 SC 2040

D. Animal and Environmental Legal Defence Fund case, AIR 1997 SC 1070

38. Which of the following case relates to transfer of Tribal lands by Government to Non-tribal people?

A. Shri Manchegowda Vs. State of Karnataka, AIR 1984 SC 1151

B. Samatha Vs. State of Andhra Pradesh, AIR 1997 SC 3297

C. Suresh Lohiya Vs. State of Maharashtra, (1996) 10 SCC 397

D. Fatesang Gimba Vasava Vs. State of Gujarat, AIR 1987 Guj. 09

39. Match List-I with List-II and select the correct answer:

	List-I		***List-II***
(*a*)	Suspension of Members	(*i*)	Article 5
(*b*)	Veto power	(*ii*)	Article 6
(*c*)	Appointment of Secretary-General	(*iii*)	Article 27
(*d*)	Objective of the Trusteeship System	(*iv*)	Article 76
		(*v*)	Article 97

Codes:

	(*a*)	(*b*)	(*c*)	(*d*)
A.	(*i*)	(*ii*)	(*iii*)	(*iv*)
B.	(*i*)	(*iii*)	(*iv*)	(*v*)
C.	(*i*)	(*iii*)	(*v*)	(*iv*)
D.	(*iii*)	(*ii*)	(*v*)	(*i*)

40. Which of the following Jurist regard the controversy "whether international law is a law, a dispute about words and not things"?

A. Lawrence B. Austin

C. Hobbes D. Hart

41. What should be the order of the use of material source of International law ?

1. Treaties and Conventions.
2. Customs
3. General principles of law recognised by civilised States.
4. Judicial decisions and juristic opinion as subsidiary means for the determination of law.

A. 4, 3, 2, 1 B. 2, 3, 1, 4

C. 4, 2, 1, 3 D. 1, 2, 3, 4

42. Which of the Article of the Statute of International Court of Justice makes it clear that the decision of the court will have no binding force except between the parties and in respect of that particular case only?

A. Article 60 B. Article 59
C. Article 68 D. Article 38(1)

43. Which of the following functions are performed by Economic and Social Council?

1. It may make or initiate studies with respect to international economic, social, cultural, educational, health and related matters.
2. It may make recommendations for the purpose of promoting respect for and observance of human rights.
3. It may make recommendations to promote friendly relations and understanding amongst member States.
4. It may prepare draft conventions for submission to the General Assembly on any of the subjects falling within its competence.

Select the correct answer using the codes given below:

Codes:

A. 1, 2, 3, 4 B. 1, 3, 4
C. 1, 2, 4 D. 2, 3, 4

44. Match List–I with List–II and select the correct answer :

List-I	*List-II*
(*a*) The Covenant on Civil and Political Rights	(*i*) 16th Dec. 1966
(*b*) The Declaration on Human Rights	(*ii*) 1948
(*c*) Convention on the Rights of Child	(*iii*) 1990
(*d*) American Convention on Human Rights	(*iv*) 1969

Codes:

	(*a*)	(*b*)	(*c*)	(*d*)
A.	(*iv*)	(*iii*)	(*ii*)	(*i*)
B.	(*ii*)	(*iii*)	(*iv*)	(*i*)
C.	(*i*)	(*ii*)	(*iii*)	(*iv*)
D.	(*iv*)	(*ii*)	(*iii*)	(*i*)

45. Assertion (A): International law is not a law.

Reason (R): It lacks determinate superior political authority to enforce its rules.

Using the codes given below give the correct answer.

Codes:

A. Both (A) and (R) are true and (R) is the correct explanation of (A).
B. Both (A) and (R) are true, but (R) is not the correct explanation of (A).
C. (A) is true, but (R) is false.
D. (A) is false, but (R) is true.

46. The junior widow has adopted a child without the consent of senior widow. Decide the adoption.

A. Valid B. Void
C. Voidable D. None of the above

47. In which State, where a widow may adopt a child without an express authority from her husband, before the HA and M Act, 1956?

A. Bihar and M.P.
B. U.P. and Haryana
C. Chennai and Mumbai
D. Odisha and Andhra Pradesh

48. In ancient Hindu Marriage, which one is not approved form of Marriage?

A. Brahma B. Davia
C. Prajapatya D. Asura

49. Read Assertion (A) and Reason (R) and with the help of codes given below select the correct explanation.

Assertion (A): The Muslim Women (Protection of Divorce Rights) Act, 1986 brought changes like limit the period of maintenance to Muslim divorcee till 'iddat' period and in case of no relatives the liability on Wakf Boards.

Reason (R): The changes were brought under Muslim's pressure.

Codes:

A. Both (A) and (R) are true and (R) is correct explanation of (A).
B. Both (A) and (R) are true, but (R) is not correct explanation of (A).

C. (A) is correct, but (R) is false.
D. (A) is false, but (R) is true.

50. Read Assertion (A) and Reason (R) and with the help of codes given below select the correct explanation.

Assertion (A): The Dissolution of Muslim Marriages Act, 1939 brought different grounds for dissolution of marriage and based on Maliki schools.

Reason (R): The DMM Act, 1939 is brought on the opinion of Ulema (Ijma).

Codes:

A. (A) and (R) are true, (R) is correct explanation of (A).
B. (A) and (R) are true, but (R) is not correct explanation of (A).
C. (A) is correct, but (R) is false.
D. (A) is false, but (R) is true.

51. A Muslim husband has failed to have 'sexual intercourse' continuously for four months with wife. It could be a form of divorce and is called

A. Illa B. Mubarrah
C. Zihar D. Khula

52. Match List-I with List-II and select correct answer from the codes :

List-I	***List-II***
(*a*) Judicial separation	(*i*) Section 9
(*b*) Divorce	(*ii*) Section 10
(*c*) Voidable Marriages	(*iii*) Section 13
(*d*) Restitution of Conjugal Rights	(*iv*) Section 12

Codes:

	(*a*)	(*b*)	(*c*)	(*d*)
A.	(*i*)	(*iii*)	(*ii*)	(*iv*)
B.	(*ii*)	(*iv*)	(*iii*)	(*i*)
C.	(*i*)	(*ii*)	(*iv*)	(*iii*)
D.	(*ii*)	(*iii*)	(*iv*)	(*i*)

53. Match List-I with List-II and select correct answer from the codes :

List-I	***List-II***
(*a*) Impotency of Husband	(*i*) Divorce
(*b*) Marriage within Sapinda Relationship	(*ii*) Voidable Marriage
(*c*) Pre-marriage Pregnancy	(*iii*) Nullity of Marriage
(*d*) Option of Puberty	(*iv*) Void Marriage

Codes:

	(*a*)	(*b*)	(*c*)	(*d*)
A.	(*iv*)	(*iii*)	(*i*)	(*ii*)
B.	(*iii*)	(*iv*)	(*ii*)	(*i*)
C.	(*i*)	(*iii*)	(*iv*)	(*ii*)
D.	(*ii*)	(*iv*)	(*i*)	(*iii*)

54. The Human Rights has been classified into three categories, viz

(a) The Human Rights of first generation
(b) The Human Rights of Second generation and
(c) The Human Rights of third generation, by

A. Louis B. Sohan
B. Theodoor C. Bowen
C. R. Dworkin
D. Bernard Mayo

55. "Everyone has the right to recognition everywhere as a person before the law". This has been stated in which of the following Article of Universal Declaration of Human Rights?

A. Article 6 B. Article 7
C. Article 8 D. Article 9

56. The United Nations High Commission for Refugees was established in which of the following year by the General Assembly?

A. 1951 B. 1953
C. 1955 D. 1957

57. "The most glaring instance of violation of Human Rights is the continuing poverty among masses in the country." Said by

A. Justice A.S. Anand
B. Justice N. Venkatachalaiah
C. Justice P.N. Bhagwati
D. Justice Koka Subba Rao

58. Match List-I with List-II and select the correct answer:

List-I	***List-II***
(*a*) The Magna Carta	(*i*) 1628
(*b*) The Petition of Rights	(*ii*) 1789
(*c*) The English Bill of Rights	(*iii*) 1215
(*d*) The U.N. Bill of Rights	(*iv*) 1689

Codes:

	(a)	(b)	(c)	(d)
A.	(iii)	(i)	(iv)	(ii)
B.	(i)	(iii)	(iv)	(ii)
C.	(iii)	(ii)	(iv)	(i)
D.	(iii)	(i)	(ii)	(iv)

59. Gurupadaswamy Committee, 1979 was constituted to look into the working conditions of:

A. Minorities B. Women

C. Children D. N.G.Os.

60. Using codes, arrange following instruments according to sequence of their enactment starting from past towards present:

(i) The Convention on the Political Rights of Women.

(ii) The Declaration on the elimination of discrimination against women.

(iii) The Convention on consent to marriage, minimum age for marriage and registration of marriage.

(iv) The Convention on the nationality of married women.

Codes:

A.	(i)	(iv)	(iii)	(ii)
B.	(iv)	(iii)	(ii)	(i)
C.	(iii)	(ii)	(i)	(iv)
D.	(ii)	(i)	(iv)	(iii)

61. Which one of the following statements is not correct?

A. In tort, there is a breach of duty which is primarily fixed by law.

B. In tort, there is a violation of a right in rem.

C. In tort, the motive for breach of duty is immaterial.

D. In tort, the damages are fixed according to the terms and conditions.

62. Assertion (A): A wooden chair while being used by a guest caused injury to him due to defective manufacture. The guest is entitled to claim damages from the maker.

Reason (R): Manufacturer owes a duty of care to the ultimate user.

Select the correct answer using the codes below:

Codes:

A. Both (A) and (R) are true and (R) is the correct explanation of (A).

B. Both (A) and (R) are true, but (R) is not the correct explanation of (A).

C. (A) is true, but (R) is false.

D. (A) is false, but (R) is true.

63. In which of the following situations is slander actionable per se in India?

A. An imputation that a certain female player is of unchaste character.

B. An imputation that a certain person is a habitual smuggler.

C. An imputation that a certain person is liar.

D. An imputation that the wrestler is womanizer.

64. Match List-I with List-II and indicate the correct answer using the codes given below:

List-I	***List-II***
(a) A patient is a consumer	(i) Vasantha P. Nair Vs. Smt. V.P. Nair
(b) Doctor's duty to maintain secrecy	(ii) K. Rangaswami Vs. Jaya Vital & others
(c) Free service	(iii) Indian Medical Association Vs. V.P. Shantha
(d) Contract of personal service	(iv) Dr. Tokugha Vs. Apollo Hospital Enterprises Ltd.

Codes:

	(a)	(b)	(c)	(d)
A.	(i)	(ii)	(iii)	(iv)
B.	(iv)	(ii)	(i)	(iii)
C.	(i)	(iv)	(iii)	(ii)
D.	(iii)	(ii)	(i)	(iv)

65. State in which of the following cases, it amounts to nuisance?

A. Planting of trees on another's land.

B. When branches of trees project on the land of their neighbour.

C. Construction of a pond on the land of another.

D. All of the above

66. In which of the following cases, the rule of absolute liability laid down by the Supreme Court of India was followed?

A. Indian Council for Enviro-Legal Action Vs. Union of India, A.I.R. 1996 SC 1446

B. Klaus Mittelbachert Vs. East India Hotels Ltd., A.I.R. 1997 Del.201

C. Both (A) and (B) above.

D. None of the above.

67. Match List-I with List-II and indicate the correct answer using the codes given below:

List-I	List-II
(*a*) The Wagon Mound case	(*i*) Remote but proximate
(*b*) Re Polemis and Furness Withy & Co. Ltd.	(*ii*) The test of reasonable foresight
(*c*) Scott Vs. Shepherd	(*iii*) The test of directness
(*d*) Fardon Vs. Harcourt Rivington	(*iv*) Reasonable foreseeability

Codes:

	(*a*)	(*b*)	(*c*)	(*d*)
A.	(*i*)	(*ii*)	(*iii*)	(*iv*)
B.	(*ii*)	(*iii*)	(*i*)	(*iv*)
C.	(*i*)	(*iv*)	(*iii*)	(*ii*)
D.	(*ii*)	(*i*)	(*iv*)	(*iii*)

68. Find right answer from following statements:

A. Every partnership is based on mutual agency.

B. Every agency is based on mutual partnership.

C. Every agent is a partner.

D. Every partner is a sleeping partner.

69. Which statements are correct, answer using codes given below :

(*i*) Directors are trustees of company.

(*ii*) Directors are mentors of company.

(*iii*) Directors are agents of company.

(*iv*) Director are agents of shareholders.

Codes:

A. (*i*) and (*ii*) are correct.

B. (*i*) and (*iii*) are correct.

C. (*i*) and (*iv*) are correct.

D. (*ii*) and (*iv*) are correct.

70. Read Assertion (A) and Reason (R) and with help of codes given below, point out the correct explanation:

Assertion (A): The doctrine of indoor management seeks to protect the company against the outsider.

Reason (R): The company has right to privacy.

Codes:

A. Both (A) and (R) are true and (R) is correct explanation of (A).

B. Both (A) and (R) are true, but (R) is not correct explanation of (A).

C. (A) is true, but (R) is false.

D. (A) is false, but (R) is true.

71. Match items in Table-A with items in Table-B, using codes given below:

Table-A	Table-B
(*a*) Essentials of partnership	(*i*) Section 41
(*b*) Partnership at will	(*ii*) Section 4
(*c*) Effect of nonregistration of firm	(*iii*) Section 7
(*d*) Compulsory dissolution of firm	(*iv*) Section 69

Codes:

	(*a*)	(*b*)	(*c*)	(*d*)
A.	(*i*)	(*ii*)	(*iv*)	(*iii*)
B.	(*ii*)	(*iii*)	(*iv*)	(*i*)
C.	(*iii*)	(*iv*)	(*i*)	(*ii*)
D.	(*i*)	(*ii*)	(*iii*)	(*iv*)

72. Find correct answer, using codes given below:

(*i*) Bulk shall correspond with sample, is an implied condition.

(*ii*) Buyer shall have a reasonable opportunity of comparing bulk with sample, is an implied condition.

(*iii*) Goods should be free from any defect rendering them unmerchantable, is an implied condition.

(*iv*) There is an implied condition that the buyer shall have and enjoy possession of the goods.

Codes:

A. (*i*) only is correct.
B. (*i*) and (*ii*) only are correct.
C. (*i*), (*ii*) and (*iii*) only are correct.
D. All of above are correct.

73. Choose correct statement from following:

A. Right against the goods can be exercised only by a paid seller.
B. Right against the goods can be exercised only by an unpaid seller.
C. Right against the goods can be exercised only by a paid buyer.
D. Right against the goods can be exercised only by an unpaid buyer.

74. Match items in Table A with items in Table B, using codes given below:

Table A	*Table B*
(*a*) Prabhu Dayal Vs. Jwala Bank, ILR 1938 All. 634	(*i*) Section 100
(*b*) Discharge from liability by cancellation	(*ii*) Section 10
(*c*) Payment in due course	(*iii*) Forgery of signature
(*d*) Protest	(*iv*) Section 82

Codes:

	(*a*)	(*b*)	(*c*)	(*d*)
A.	(*i*)	(*iii*)	(*ii*)	(*iv*)
B.	(*iii*)	(*iv*)	(*ii*)	(*i*)
C.	(*iv*)	(*iii*)	(*ii*)	(*i*)
D.	(*ii*)	(*i*)	(*iii*)	(*iv*)

75. Find correct legal principle from following statements:

A. While collecting a cheque for a banker, the customer is under an obligation to present it promptly so as to avoid any loss due to change of circumstances.
B. While collecting a cheque for a customer, the banker is under an obligation to present it properly so as to avoid any loss due to change of circumstances.
C. While collecting a cheque for a customer, the banker is under no obligation to present it properly so as to avoid any loss due to change of circumstances.
D. While collecting a cheque for a banker, the customer is under no obligation to present it promptly so as to avoid any loss due to change of circumstances.

ANSWERS

1	2	3	4	5	6	7	8	9	10
A	B	D	C	B	A	D	D	C	B
11	**12**	**13**	**14**	**15**	**16**	**17**	**18**	**19**	**20**
A	C	B	C	D	A	A	C	D	C
21	**22**	**23**	**24**	**25**	**26**	**27**	**28**	**29**	**30**
B	B	D	C	A	B	B	C	D	D
31	**32**	**33**	**34**	**35**	**36**	**37**	**38**	**39**	**40**
B	C	D	C	A	D	A	B	C	A
41	**42**	**43**	**44**	**45**	**46**	**47**	**48**	**49**	**50**
D	A	A	C	B	C	C	D	A	A
51	**52**	**53**	**54**	**55**	**56**	**57**	**58**	**59**	**60**
A	D	B	A	A	A	A	A	C	A
61	**62**	**63**	**64**	**65**	**66**	**67**	**68**	**69**	**70**
D	A	A	C	D	C	B	A	B	C
71	**72**	**73**	**74**	**75**					
B	C	B	B	B					

SOME SELECTED EXPLANATORY ANSWERS

2. In order to remove difficulties created by the decision in Golaknath's case, Parliament enacted 24th Amendment Act, 1971. It not only restored the amending power of Parliament but also extended its scope by adding the words in Article 368, "to amend by way of the addition or variation or repeal any provision of this constitution in accordance with the procedure laid down in this Article". A new clause added to Article 13 which provides that "nothing in this Article shall apply to any amendment of this constitution made under Article 368". Thus, the validity of a constitutional Amendment Act shall not be open to question on the ground that it takes away or affects a fundamental right. The 24th Amendment has been held to be valid in Keshavanand's case.

3. The Supreme Court is not bound to answer a reference made to it by President. Thus, it has a discretion in the matter and for good reason to refuse to express any opinion on the question submitted to it. The advisory opinion of the court, though entitled to great respect, is not binding on all courts because it is not a law, within the meaning of Article 141. But in Re-special courts Bill case, the court made it clear that the views of it under Article 143 are binding on all courts. The court, however, suggested that the reference should not be vague and general but must be made an specific questions, otherwise the courts would not be bound to answer. The advisory opinion of the Supreme Court has been taken on such important issues as cauvery dispute, Ayodhya dispute, Appointment and Transfer of Judges etc.

12. Habeas Corpus, literally means 'a demand to produce the body (whether dead or alive)'. The issuance of the writ means an order to the detaining authority or person to physically present before the court the detained person and show the cause of detention so that the court can determine its legality or otherwise. If the detention is found to be illegal, the detained person is set free forth with. Its purpose is not to punish the Wrongdoer but merely to secure the release of the person illegally detained. The supreme court can issue the writ of habeas corpus only against the state in cases of violation of fundamental rights, the High court can issue it also against private individuals illegally or arbitrarily detaining any other person.

15. 'Certiorari' is a Latin word meaning 'to inform'. It was essentially a royal demand for information. The king wishing to be certified of some matter, ordered that the necessary information be provided for him. Certiorari, may be defined as a Judicial order operating in personam and made in the original legal proceedings, directed to any constitutional, statutory or non-statutory body or person, requiring the records of any action to be certified by the court and dealt with according to law. It can be issued against constitutional bodies like legislature, executive and Judiciary, statutory bodies like corporations, non-statutory bodies like companies and cooperative societies and private bodies and persons. Certiorari can be issued to quash Judicial, quasi-judicial as well as administrative actions.

24. According to Section 390 of Indian Penal Code, 1860, Extortion is robbery if the offender at the time of committing the extortion by putting that person in fear of instant death, or of instant hurt, or of instant wrongful restraint to that person, or to some other person, and by so putting in fear, induces the person so put in fear then and there to deliver up the thing extorted.

26. According to Section 425 of the Indian Penal Code, 1860, whoever, with the intent to cause, or knowing that he is likely to cause, wrongful loss or damage to the public or to any person, causes the destruction of any property, or any such change in any property or in the situation thereof as destroys or diminishes its value or utility, or affects it injuriously, commits "mischief".

28. According to Section 324 of the Indian Penal Code, 1860, whoever, except in the case provided for by Section 334, voluntarily causes hurt by means of any instrument for shooting, stabbing or cutting, or any instrument which, used as a weapon of offence, is likely to cause death, or by means of fire of any heated substance, or by means of any poison or any corrosive substance, or by means of any explosive substance, or by means of any substance which it is deleterious to the human body to inhale, to swallow, or to receive into the blood, or by means of any animal, shall be punished with imprisonment of either description for a term which may extend to 3 years or with fine, or with both.

29. According to Section 339 of the Indian Penal Code, 1860, whoever, voluntarily obstructs any person so as to prevent that person from proceeding in any direction in which that person has a right to proceed, is said wrongfully to restrain that person. The obstruction of a private way over land or water which a person in good faith believes himself to have a lawful right to obstruct, is not an offence within the meaning of this section. **Illustration:** A obstructs a path along which Z has a right to pass, A not believing in good faith that he has a right to stop the path, Z is thereby prevented from passing. A wrongfully restrains Z.

32. The Earth Summit was held on 21st June, 1992 at Rio. Government officials from 178 countries and between 20,000 and 30,000 individuals from governments, NGOs and the media participated in this event to discuss solutions for global problems such as poverty, war or the growing gap between industrialised and developing countries. In the centre was also the question of how to relieve the global environmental system through the introduction to the paradigm of sustainable development. It emphasises that economic and social progress depends critically on the preservation of the natural resource base with effective measures to prevent environmental degradation. The UN Summit focused on three broad concepts : An 'Earth Charter", covering a number of principles aiming at development and the protection of the environment, was the first focus for discussion. Secondly, "Agenda 21" was intended to be a global action plan for sustainable development, thirdly, developing countries demanded a substantial increase in new funding from developed countries to contribute to sustainable development in the South.

35. Most of the environment related laws enacted by the Parliament have been an Article 253 of the Constitution. For instance, Environment (Protection) Act 1986, The Water (Prevention and Control of Pollution) Act, 1974. The Air (Prevention and Control of Pollution) Act, 1981 was promulgated under Article 253 of the constitution, which authorises the Parliament to enact legislation on such matter as necessary for compliance of international agreement to which India has been a party.

51. Besides talaq, a Muslim husband can repudiate his marriage by two other modes, that are Ila and Zihar. They are called constructive divorce. In Ila, the husband takes an oath not to have sexual intercourse with his wife. Followed by this oath, there is no consummation for a period of four months. After the expiry of the fourth month, the marriage dissolves irrevocably. But if the husband resumes cohabitation within four months, Ila is cancelled and the marriage does not dissolve. Under Ithana Asharia (Shia) School, Ila, does not operate as divorce without order of the court of law. After the expiry of the fourth month, the wife is simply entitled for a Judicial divorce. If there is no cohabitation, even after the expiry of four months, the wife may file asuit for restitution of conjugal rights against the husband.

Previous Paper (Solved)

UGC-NET LAW, JUNE 2013

PAPER-II

Note : *This paper contains fifty (50) objective type questions, each carrying two (2) marks each. All questions are compulsory.*

1. "It is likely that free India may be federal India, though in any event there would be a great deal of Unitary Control." This statement was made by

A. Sir Alladi Krishna Swami Iyyer

B. Dr. B.R. Ambedkar

C. Pt. Jawahar Lal Nehru

D. Sardar Vallabh Bhai Patel

2. Judicial Review in the Constitution of India is based on

A. Precedents and conventions

B. Rule of law

C. Due process of law

D. Procedure established by law

3. The Constitution of India embodies the parliamentary form of government because :

A. The Council of Ministers is collectively responsible to the Lok Sabha.

B. The Council of Ministers is responsible to Lok Sabha and Rajya Sabha.

C. The President, the head of the executive, is answerable to Parliament.

D. The Prime Minister, the Head of the Cabinet, is accountable to Parliament.

4. The Supreme Court held that Election Commissioners cannot be placed on par with the Chief Election Commissioner in terms of power and authority in the following case :

A. S.S. Dhannoa Vs Union of India

B. T.N. Seshan Vs Union of India

C. A.C. Jose Vs Sivan Pillai

D. Venkatachalam Vs A. Swamickan

5. The maximum interval between the tw sessions of each House of Parliament is

A. Three months B. Four months

C. Five months D. Six months

6. The Supreme Court observed that "Parli mentary proceedings are not subject Fundamental Rights" in the following cas

A. Keshav Singh Vs Speaker, U.P. Assembl

B. Gunapati Vs Habibul Hasan

C. M.S.M. Sharma Vs Srikrishna Sinha

D. State of Punjab Vs Satpal Dang

7. For the purpose of creating a new State i India an amendment to the Constitution c India must be passed by

A. 2/3rd majority of the members of bot Houses of Parliament present and voting

B. 2/3rd majority of the members of bot Houses of Parliament and ratification b not less than 2/3rd majority of the States

C. A simple majority in Parliament an ratification by not less than half of th States.

D. A simple majority by the Parliament.

8. Match the following :

(a) Perfect right (i) Which has corre lative positive duty

(b) Negative right (ii) Which has a corre lative duty that ca be legally enforced.

(c) Imperfect right (iii) A has a right to receive damages.

(d) Positive right (iv) That right whicl although recognisec by State but no enforceable.

Codes :

	(a)	(b)	(c)	(d)
A.	(iii)	(iv)	(i)	(ii)
B.	(ii)	(iii)	(iv)	(i)
C.	(iv)	(iii)	(ii)	(i)
D.	(i)	(ii)	(iii)	(iv)

9. According to which school, "the purpose of jurisprudence is to analyse and dissect the law of the land as it exists today"?

A. Analytical Jurisprudence
B. Historical Jurisprudence
C. Sociological Jurisprudence
D. Philosophical Jurisprudence

10. "The one who holds the property is the owner."

Give your correct response from following on the basis of above statement :

A. The holder of property may be mere possessor or bailee.
B. The holder of property need not be the owner.
C. This statement is not correct.
D. This statement is correct.

11. The sources of law have been divided into two classes. These are

A. Divine sources and human sources
B. Formal sources and material sources
C. Natural sources and universal sources
D. (A) and (B) both of the above

12. According to whose theory, "Law is not universal in its nature; like language it varies with people and age"?

A. Bentham's theory
B. Austin's theory
C. Savigny's theory
D. Montesquieu's theory

13. Which one of the following pairs is not correctly matched?

A. Law properly so-called (in regard to notion of law)	:	Which is distinct from morals.
B. Law improperly so-called (in regard to notion of law)	:	Other laws.
C. Audi alteram partem	:	Rule of natural justice.
D. Conspectus of justice	:	Justice denied.

14. Assertion (A) : The Maneka Gandhi's case is a landmark decision from the point of human rights and remedial jurisprudence.

Reason (R) : From the positivist point of view, equality is antithetic to arbitrariness.

Examine the above statements (A) and (R) and select whether the Reason is a correct explanation of the Assertion using the codes given below :

Codes :

A. Both (A) and (R) are true and (R) is the correct explanation of (A).
B. Both (A) and (R) are true, but (R) is not the correct explanation of (A).
C. (A) is true, but (R) is false.
D. (A) is false, but (R) is true.

15. Who among the following said that the law of nation is "the body of legal rules which apply between states and such entities as have been granted international personality"?

A. Fenwick B. Oppeheim
C. Schwarzenberger D. Verdoss

16. The main difference between Defacto and De-jure recognition is

1. De-facto recognition may be withdrawn while De-jure recognition is full and final.
2. Only De-jure recognised states can represent the old states, for the purpose of state succession.
3. In De-jure recognition, formal diplomatic relations are established while in case of Defacto they may not be entered into.
4. Former is legal and the latter is a factual recognition.

A. 1, 2 & 3 B. 2, 3 & 4
C. 2 & 3 D. 1 & 2

17. A member of the United Nations can be suspended from the exercise of rights and privileges of membership by the

A. General Assembly
B. Security Council
C. General Assembly on the recommendations of the Security Council
D. Secretary General on the recommendations of the Security Council

18. Read Assertion (A) and Reason (R) and with the help of codes given below select the correct answer.

Assertion (A) : International Law consists for the most part of customary rules.

Reason (R): Customary rules are the original and oldest source of International Law.

Codes :

A. Both (A) and (R) are true, and (R) is the correct explanation of (A).
B. Both (A) and (R) are true, but (R) is not the correct explanation of (A).
C. (A) is true, but (R) is false.
D. (A) is false and (R) is true.

19. Universal Declaration of Human Rights was adopted on

A. December 10, 1948
B. November 10, 1948
C. October 20, 1948
D. January 21, 1948

20. Read Assertion (A) and Reason (R) and with the help of codes given below select the correct answer.

Assertion (A) : Human Rights occupy a significant place in the UN Charter.

Reason (R) : Members of the UN have committed themselves to promote respect for and observance of human rights and fundamental rights.

Codes :

A. Both (A) and (R) are individually true and (R) is the correct explanation of (A).
B. Both (A) and (R) are individually true, but (R) is not the correct explanation of (A).
C. (A) is true, but (R) is false.
D. (A) is false, but (R) is true.

21. Adultery by a Hindu husband is

A. Ground of divorce only
B. Not a ground of divorce
C. Ground of judicial separation
D. None of the above

22. 'A' marries 'B', the widow of the elder brother. The marriage is

A. Valid
B. Void
C. Voidable
D. None of the above

23. Marriage with an impotent and has not been consummated.
The marriage is

A. Valid B. Void
C. Nullity D. Irregular

24. 'Khula' is a form of divorce by

A. Sale B. Purchase
C. Agreement D. Coercion

25. Muta marriage could not be dissolved

A. Ipso facto by the efflux of the period
B. By death
C. By divorce
D. By Hiba-i-Mudat

26. By which of the following way a Muslim marriage can be dissolved by a Muslim husband?

A. Talaq B. Illa
C. Zihar D. Above all

27. When a person making a false statement believes the statement to be true and does not intend to mislead to the other party to the contract, it is known as

A. Mistake B. Fraud
C. Misrepresentation D. Undue influence

28. Read Assertion (A) and Reason (R) and with help of codes given below, point out the correct explanation.

Assertion (A) : An agreement not enforceable by law is said to be void.

Reason (R) : Law has no force.

Codes :

A. Both (A) and (R) are true and (R) is good explanation of (A).
B. Both (A) and (R) are true, but (R) is not correct explanation of (A).

C. (A) is true, but (R) is false.
D. (A) is false, but (R) is true.

29. A and B are friends. A told to B to show him a new movie in a posh theatre, upon which A promised to offer him lunch in a 5 star hotel. B showed him a movie in a posh theatre, but A gave lunch to B in a road side dhaba. Decide A's liability using codes given below :

Codes :

A. A is liable because there was intention to create legal relation between A and B.
B. A is not liable because there was no intention to crate legal relation between A and B.
C. B was mistaken.
D. A was mistaken.

30. Arrange the following concepts in sequence in which they occur, using codes given below:
(i) Offer is communicated.
(ii) Counter offer is made.
(iii) Offer is rejected.
(iv) Counter offer is accepted.

Codes :

A. (i), (ii), (iii), (iv)
B. (i), (iii), (ii), (iv)
C. (i), (iv), (ii), (iii)
D. (ii), (i), (iii), (iv)

31. Following are essentials of valid contract :
(i) Parties to contract should have capacity to contract.
(ii) Parties to contract should have legal mind.
(iii) Parties to contract should be intelligent.
(iv) Invitation to offer should be accepted.

Find correct answer, using codes :

A. Only (i) is correct.
B. Only (i) and (iv) are correct.
C. All of above are correct.
D. Only (ii) is correct.

32. Match items in Table-A with items in Table-B, using codes given below :

Table-A	Table-B
(a) Ambiguous and uncertain agreements	(i) Section 15
(b) Coercion	(ii) Section 25(2)
(c) Past consideration	(iii) Section 73
(d) Remoteness of damage	(iv) Section 29

Codes :

	(i)	(ii)	(iii)	(iv)
A.	(b)	(c)	(d)	(a)
B.	(c)	(b)	(d)	(a)
C.	(c)	(b)	(a)	(d)
D.	(a)	(d)	(c)	(b)

33. Which one of the following statements is incorrect ?

A. Tort is a civil wrong in which claim for unliquidated damages is made.
B. In tort, action lies against the wrong-doer in a civil court.
C. For a tortious liability, a jail term can also be awarded.
D. In some torts an injunction can also be issued against the wrong-doer

34. Which one of the following defences is not available in Law of Tort?

A. Volenti non-fit injuria
B. Act of God
C. Contributory negligence
D. Inevitable accident

35. 'Sometimes it happens that the legal right of a person is violated but he does not suffer any harm.' From which one of the following maxim we can attribute it ?

A. Damnum sine injuria
B. Injuria sine damno
C. Volenti non-fit injuria
D. Res ipsa loquitur

36. The rule of 'absolute liability' was laid down by the Supreme Court of India in the following case :

A. Rylands Vs Fletcher
B. M.C. Mehta (Sriram Food and Fertilizer Co.) Vs Union of India
C. M.C. Mehta (C.N.G. Fuel case) Vs Union of India
D. None of the above

37. In which of the following cases did the Supreme Court of India gave the ruling that sovereign immunity of the State is subject to the Fundamental Rights?

A. Kasturilal Ralia Ram Jain Vs State of U.P.

B. State of Rajasthan Vs Vidhyawati

C. People's Union for Democratic Rights Vs State of Bihar

D. Shyam Sundar Vs State of Rajasthan

38. The rule laid down in Re Polemis case is that the defendant shall be liable for all

A. direct consequences of his act.

B. direct consequences of his act, if he could foresee some damage to the plaintiff from his act.

C. direct consequences of his act, only if he could foresee the kind of damage which has actually occurred.

D. foreseeable damage.

39. Match List-I (Jurists) with List-II (Assumptions) and select the correct answer using the codes given below :

List-I	List-II
(a) Lord T.B. Macauley	(i) Preparation of Penal Code of India
(b) Jermy Bentham	(ii) Un written jurisprudence on Penal principles
(c) Kelson	(iii) Substantive law on crimes
(d) Sir Barnes Peacock	(iv) Revision of Penal law

Codes :

	(a)	(b)	(c)	(d)
A.	(i)	(ii)	(iii)	(iv)
B.	(ii)	(i)	(iv)	(iii)
C.	(iii)	(iv)	(i)	(ii)
D.	(iv)	(i)	(ii)	(iii)

40. Match List-I (Objectives) with List-II (Propositions) and select the correct answer using the codes given below :

List-I	List-II
(a) Inchoate crime	(i) 'Whaton' says it is the beginning but not complete.
(b) Attempt	(ii) It does not act towards the commission of offence.
(c) Preparation	(iii) Culprit commences to do something.
(d) Intention	(iv) When preparation merges itself with attempt.

Codes :

	(a)	(b)	(c)	(d)
A.	(ii)	(iii)	(iv)	(i)
B.	(i)	(ii)	(iii)	(iv)
C.	(iii)	(iv)	(i)	(ii)
D.	(iv)	(i)	(ii)	(iii)

41. Fill in the blank using appropriate statement.

Non Compos Mentis means ______

A. Not of sound mind.

B. Who lacks the requisite mens rea.

C. Unable to know that the act is either wrong or contrary to law.

D. A concussion of brain.

42. Fill in the blank using appropriate reason.

Right to private defence by a friend is generally not available because ______

A. There was no specified circumstances.

B. Explanation II of Section 300 IPC is a bar for it.

C. The act was not with an intention to protect the friend.

D. The offending party was an aggressor.

43. Read Assertion (I) and Reason (II) and with the help of codes given below select the correct explanation.

Assertion (I) : Section 95 of IPC is intended to prevent penalisation of negligible wrongs of trivial character because :

Reasons (II) :

(a) The injury is negligible.

(b) The victim and the wrongdoer were related to each other.

(c) The injured and the offender were not related by circumstances.

(d) The nature of injury was very minor.

Codes :

A. (a) is true and (d) is the reason while (b) and (c) are not true.

B. (b) is true and (c) is the reason while (a) and (d) are false.

C. (c) is true and (d) is the reason while (a) and (b) are not true.

D. (d) is the only reason while all others (a), (b) and (c) are false.

44. Fill in the blank :

Deceiving dishonestly by inducing a person to retain the property is known as ______ offence.

A. Concealment

B. Deception by false pretention

C. Cheating

D. Fraud

45. Which of the following amount to Industrial Dispute?

A. Any dispute between Employers and Employees.

B. Between Employers and Workmen.

C. Between Workmen and Workmen.

D. All these.

46. In which of the following case, the Supreme Court held that "the benefit of running allowance had to be taken into consideration for computing pension only once, at the time of retirement of the employee, not for any future calculation"?

A. U.O.I. Vs Dhingara and others (2008) I LLJ 867(SC)

B. Bennet Coleman & Co. Vs Punya Priyadas AIR 1970 SC 426

C. State Bank of Patiala Vs Phoolpati (2005) II LLJ 473 (SC)

D. Pearlite Lines Pvt. Ltd. Vs Manorama Sirse (2004) I LLJ 1041 (SC)

47. Which rights remain unaffected, during the pendency of a proceeding before a court of inquiry under Sections 22, 23 and 33 of the I.D. Act, 1947?

A. Workmen to go on strike.

B. The rights of Employer to dismiss or to punish the workmen.

C. Employer to lock-out his business.

D. All the above.

48. Read Assertion (A) and Reason (R), using codes given below, select the correct answer.

Assertion (A) : Termination of service does not amount to retrenchment.

Reason (R) : Amount of loss of retrenchment is more than amount of termination.

Codes :

A. (A) and (R) are true, and (R) is correct explanation of (A).

B. (A) and (R) are true, but (R) is not correct explanation of (A).

C. (A) is true, but (R) is false.

D. (A) is false, but (R) is true.

49. Read Assertion (A) and Reason (R) and using codes given below choose correct answer.

Assertion (A) : Strike is stoppage of work by a body of persons employed in any service acting in combination.

Reason (R) : Combined work is service oriented.

Codes :

A. (A) and (R) are true, and (R) is correct explanation of (A).

B. (A) and (R) are true, but (R) is not correct explanation of (A).

C. (A) and (R) are false.

D. (A) is true, (R) is false.

50. Trade unionism to be fully effective demands

A. Union of trade

B. Trade of union

C. Democratic spirit and education

D. Soul-elevating and democratic spirits

ANSWERS

1	2	3	4	5	6	7	8	9	10
C	D	A	A	D	C	D	B	A	B
11	**12**	**13**	**14**	**15**	**16**	**17**	**18**	**19**	**20**
A	C	D	B	C	A	C	B	A	B
21	**22**	**23**	**24**	**25**	**26**	**27**	**28**	**29**	**30**
D	B	C	B	C	D	C	C	B	B
31	**32**	**33**	**34**	**35**	**36**	**37**	**38**	**39**	**40**
A	A	C	C	B	B	C	B	A	B
41	**42**	**43**	**44**	**45**	**46**	**47**	**48**	**49**	**50**
A	B	A	C	D	A	D	C	C	C

SOME SELECTED EXPLANATORY ANSWERS

2. Judicial review in the Constitution of India is based on Procedure established by law. Judicial review means that Judiciary can declare a law or legislation as unconstitutional if it is beyond the competence of legislature according to the distribution of powers, or it is in contravention of fundamental rights or any of the mandatory provisions of the constitution. The supreme court under our constitution is the final interpreter and guardian of constitution, which keeps the democratic structure intact. Philosophy of Judicial review is rooted in the principle that constitution is the fundamental law, all governmental organs must not do anything which is inconsistent with the provisions of the constitution. Thus, Judicial review makes constitution legalistic.

3. The constitution of India embodies the parliamentary form of government because according to the provisions of Article 75(3) the council of ministers shall be collectively responsible to the House of the People, *i.e.*, the Lok Sabha.

5. According to Article 85(1) of the Indian Constitution, The President shall from time-to-time summon each House of Parliament to meet at such time and place as he thinks fit, but six months shall not intervene between its last sitting in one session and the date appointed for its first sitting in the next session.

7. According to Article 368 of the Indian Constitution, for the purposes of amendment the provisions of constitution fall under 3 categories. Amendment by simple majority—of each House of Parliament. It is like an ordinary Bill. Formation of new states, creation or abolition of legislative councils is made by such procedure. Thus, amendment at the instance of the states or amendment by state legislatures, is included in such category. Amendments under this category are expressly excluded from the purview of Art. 368.

19. The Universal Declaration of Human Rights (UDHR) is a declaration adopted by the United Nations General Assembly on 10 December, 1948 at the Palais de Chaillot, Paris. The Declaration arose directly from the experience of the Second World War and represents the first global expression of rights to which all human beings are inherently entitled. The Declaration consist of thirty articles which have been elaborated in subsequent international treaties etc. In 1966 the General Assembly adopted the two detailed covenants, which complete the

International Bill of Human Rights; and in 1976, after the covenants had been ratified by a sufficient number of individual nations, the Bill took on the force of international law.

21. According to the Section 497 of Indian Penal Code, 1860, Adultery is "whoever has sexual intercourse with a person who is and whom he knows or has reason to believe to be the wife of another man, without the consent or connivance of that man, such sexual intercourse not amounting to the offence of rape, is guilty of the offence of audltery, and shall be punished with imprisonment of either description for a term which may extend to five years, or with fine, or with both."

24. The words 'Khula' means "to put off". It is the laying down by a husband of his right and authority over his wife for an exchange. A divorce by Khula is a divorce with the consent, and at the instance of the wife, in which she gives or agrees to give a consideration, to the husband for her release from the marriage tie ('divorce by purchase'). Failure on the part of the wife to pay the consideration for the divorce does not invalidate the divorce, though the husband may sue the wife for it. Many authors view Khula as a divorce by mutual consent. Since in the Khula the desire to separate originates from the wife, and she has to make her husband agree to it by giving consideration, it would be proper to call it divorce at the instance of the wife, when she feels that she cannot continue to live in matrimony.

25. The Shia law (Ithana Ashari School) recognizes two kinds of marriage, namely permanent and muta (literally means enjoyment or use) or temporary. The fundamental difference between the two is that in former the term is not specified, while in the latter it is. Sunnis do not recognize such marriage. Muta marriage is an ancient Arabian custom. According to the Muslim Law, Muta marriage cannot be dissolved by divorce.

31. Section 10 of the Indian Contract Act, 1872 states that, all agreements are contracts if they are made by the free consent of parties competent to contract, for a lawful consideration and with a lawful object. Section 11 defines who are competent to contract; "Every person is competent to contract who is of the age of majority according to the law to which he is subject, and who is of sound mind, and is not disqualified from contracting by any law to which he is subject." So here option (A) is the most appropriate answer according to which, Parties to contract should have capacity to contract.

34. In an action for a tort, the defendant may avoid his liability by taking the plea of some defence. There are some general defences, which may be taken against action for a number of wrongs, which as follows—Volenti non-fit injuria, Plaintiff is the wrong doer, Inevitable Accident, Act of God, Mistake, Necessity etc, but contributory negligence is not a defence in Law of Torts.

35. This maxim "Injuria Sine damnum", means violation of a legal right without causing any harm, loss or damage to the plaintiff. Thus, it is the behaviour, which is actionable as a tort. It is always actionable as legal wrongs entail a remedy. Every injury imports damage. Generally the courtawards nominal damages. Torts are of two kinds—namely, those, which are actionable perse, and those, which are actionable only on proof of actual damage resulting from them. In Ashby Vs. White, the plaintiff was a qualified voter at a parliamentary election, but the defendant, a returning officer, wrongfully refused to take plaintiff's vote. No loss was suffered by such refusal because the candidate for whom he wanted to vote won inspite of that. The defendant was held liable.

36. In M.C. Mehta Vs. Union of India, the supreme court evolved the rule of absolute liability as part of Indian Law in preference to the rule of strict liability laid down in Rylands Vs. Fletcher. It expressly declared that the new rule was not subject to any of the exceptions under the Rylands rule. Because those who had established hazardous industries in and around thickly populated areas could escape the liability for the havoc caused thereby pleading some exception to the Rylands rule. The court observed: "This rule (Rylands Vs. Fletcher) evolved in the 19th century at a time when all these developments of science and technology had not taken place. We have to evolve new principles and lay down new norms which would adequately deal with the new problems which arise in a highly industrialized economy". The supreme court also laid down that the measure of compensation should be correlated to the magnitude and capacity of the enterprise, so that the compensation can have the deterrent effect.

44. According to Section 415 of the Indian Penal Code, 1860, whoever by deceiving any person, fraudulently or dishonestly induces the person so deceived to deliver any property, to any person or to consent that any person shall retain any property, or intentionally induces the person so deceived to do or omit to do anything which he would not do or omit if he were not so deceived and which act or omission causes or is likely to cause damage or harm to that person in body, reputation or property, is said to commit the offence of cheating.

PAPER-III

Note : *This paper contains seventy five (75) objective type questions of two (2) marks each. All questions are compulsory.*

1. In E.P. Royappa case which of the Supreme Court Judge propounded the new concept of Equality as "Equality is a dynamic concept with many aspects and dimensions and it cannot be 'crippled, combined and confined' within traditional and doctrinaire limits"?

A. Justice Y.V. Chandrachud
B. Justice P.N. Bhagawati
C. Justice V.R. Krishna Iyer
D. Justice O.P. Chinnapa Reddy

2. The State shall make provisions for securing just and humane conditions of work and for maternity relief is found

A. As a part of the Preamble to the Constitution of India.
B. As a Fundamental Right under Art. 21 of the Constitution of India.
C. As a Directive Principle of the State Policy.
D. As a Fundamental Duty of the State.

3. Fundamental duties under Part IVA was inserted in the Constitution by

A. 17th Amendment B. 25th Amendment
C. 42nd Amendment D. 44th Amendment

4. The powers of the President of India are

A. Supra-Constitutional
B. Beyond the Constitution
C. In accordance with the Parliament of India
D. In accordance with the Constitution of India

5. Which one of the following has been considered as authority of power?

A. The Constitution of India
B. The President of India
C. The Parliament of India
D. The Supreme Court of India

6. In which of the following judgements it was held that according to Art. 226, Courts are flooded with large number of PIL, so it is desirable for Courts to filter out frivolous petitions and dismiss them with costs ?

A. Deepak Sharma Vs Vineeta Sharma
B. Dharampal Vs State of Uttar Pradesh
C. Holicow Pictures Pvt. Ltd. Vs Premchandra Mishra
D. M.C. Mehta Vs Union of India

7. A resolution for the revocation of the proclamation of National Emergency may be moved by

A. Ten members of Lok Sabha
B. One-fifth of the total membership of the Lok Sabha.
C. One-tenth of the total membership of the Lok Sabha.
D. One-fifteenth of the total membership of the Lok Sabha.

8. Answer the following using the codes given below:

Administrative Law deals with :

(i) Composition, powers and functions of the administrative authorities.
(ii) Procedures to be followed by the administrative authorities in the exercise of their powers and functions.
(iii) Methods of control of powers of the administrative authorities.
(iv) Remedies available to a person in case of violation of his rights by the administrative authorities.

Codes :

A. Only (i) is correct.
B. Only (i) and (ii) are correct.
C. Only (i), (ii) and (iii) are correct.
D. All of the above are correct.

9. Read Assertion (A) and Reason (R) and with the help of codes given below, point out the correct explanation :

Assertion (A) : One of the principles of natural justice is, 'No man shall be judge in his own cause'.

Reason (R) : Principles of natural justice require fair play in action.

Codes :

A. (A) and (R) are true and (R) is the correct explanation of (A).
B. (A) and (R) are true, but (R) is not the correct explanation of (A).
C. (A) is true and (R) is false.
D. (A) is false and (R) is true.

10. Match List-I with List-II and indicate the correct answer using the codes given below:

List-I	List-II
(a) A.K. Kraipak Vs. Union of India	(i) Postdecisional hearing
(b) Manak Lal Vs. Dr. Prem Chand	(ii) Personal bias
(c) Maneka Gandhi Vs. Union of India	(iii) Pecuniary bias
(d) Olga Tellis Vs. Bombay Municipal Corporation	(iv) Reasonable opportunity of hearing

Codes :

	(a)	(b)	(c)	(d)
A.	(i)	(ii)	(iii)	(iv)
B.	(i)	(iii)	(iv)	(ii)
C.	(ii)	(iii)	(i)	(iv)
D.	(iii)	(ii)	(iv)	(i)

11. Answer the following using the codes given below :

Which of the following doctrines were developed by the Court to control the administrative actions?

(i) Doctrine of Promissory Estoppel.
(ii) Doctrine of Legitimate Expectations.
(iii) Doctrine of Separation of Power and Rule of Law.
(iv) Judicial Activism.

Codes :

A. Only (i), (ii) and (iii) are correct.
B. Only (ii) and (iv) are correct.
C. Only (i) and (iii) are correct.
D. All of the above are correct.

12. Answer the following using the codes given below :

In which of the following grounds the judicial review of an administrative action be made?

(i) Abuse of discretion
(ii) Mala fide or Bad faith
(iii) Irrelevant consideration
(iv) Unreasonableness

Codes :

A. Only (i), (ii) and (iii) are correct.
B. Only (i) and (ii) are correct.
C. Only (ii) and (iii) are correct.
D. All (i), (ii), (iii) and (iv) are correct.

13. A writ of mandamus will not lie against

A. President of India
B. Parliament
C. Local authorities
D. Courts and Tribunals

14. Match List-I with List-II and indicate the correct answer using the codes given below:

List-I	List-II
(a) Bring the body before the Court	(i) Writ of Mandamus
(b) Petitioner's legal right to compel the performance of public duty	(ii) Writ of Mandamus
(c) By what authority a person is holding the public post	(iii) Writ of Habeas Corpus
(d) Action of subordinate Court in violation of the principles of natural justice	(iv) Writ of Quowarranto

Codes :

	(a)	(b)	(c)	(d)
A.	(i)	(ii)	(iii)	(iv)
B.	(iii)	(i)	(iv)	(ii)
C.	(iii)	(ii)	(i)	(iv)
D.	(iii)	(iv)	(ii)	(i)

15. Which one of the following States has not yet established the institution of Lokayukta?

A. Uttar Pradesh B. Karnataka
C. Uttarakhand D. None of the above

16. "A legal person is any subject matter other than a human being to which law attributes personality." Who said these words ?

A. Savigny B. Bentham
C. Austin D. Salmond

17. "Pure theory of Law is an exercise in logic and not life." This observation was made by

A. Pound B. Savigny
C. Maine D. Harold Laski

18. "Law is derived from social facts and not dependent on State authority but on social compulsion." Who said this?

A. Putchta B. Ehrlich
C. Friedman D. Pound

19. Which one of the following pairs is not correctly matched?

A. Sie utere tero out alierum non laedas : To use your own property as not to injure your neighbour's right

B. Re Legitima Portis : A person cannot dispose of his entire property

C. Jus turtii : To set up title of a third person other than himself or the plaintiff

D. Nec vi nec calur precario : Possession must show to the competitor

20. Assertion (A) : In India the distinction between legal and equitable ownership is not recognised.

Reason (R) : The trustees are, subject to the law relating to trust and trustees, bound to carry out the trust according to the dictates of the maker of the trust.

Examine the above statements (A) and Reason (R) and select whether the reason is a correct explanation of the assertion using the codes given below :

Codes :

A. Both (A) and (R) are true and (R) is the correct explanation of (A).
B. Both (A) and (R) are true, but (R) is not the correct explanation of (A).
C. (A) is true, but (R) is false.
D. (A) is false, but (R) is true.

21. The purpose theory is based on the assumption that "person is applicable only to human beings; they alone can be the subjects of rural relations".

Who developed this theory of Brinz in England?

A. Barker B. Duguit
C. Salmond D. Hoffman

22. "Ownership in its comprehensive signification, denotes the relation between a person and any right that is vested in him. That which a man owns in this sense is in all cases a right."

Who is the exponent of this theory ?

A. Miss Tay B. Maitland
C. Salmond D. Fuller

23. "Legal rights are institutional rights to decisions in Courts. Institutions about justice presuppose a fundamental right, namely, the right to equality, which I call the right to equal concern and respect."

Who propounded this theory in relation to natural rights?

A. Dworkin B. Fuller
C. Jerome Hall D. Professor Hart

24. Fill in the gap that is most appropriate.

Who ever entices a girl child of less than 16 years has said to have caused kidnapping out of the keeping of the lawful ______.

A. Parents B. Foster parents
C. Adopted parents D. Guardians

25. Fill in the gap with the offence that the accused has committed.

Who ever dishonestly uses any moveable property to his own advantage has committed the offence of ______.

A. Breach of trust B. Wrongful gain
C. Misappropriation D. None of the above

26. Read Assertion I and Reason II and with the help of codes given below point out the correct explanation.

Assertion I : Moral derangement is a state of will and turns to be the vehicle of vicious actions.

Reason II : Crime is committed under the influence of instructive and irresistible impulse.

Codes :

A. Moral insanity or imbecility are not exempted from criminal liability as per Section 53 of IPC.
B. Both I and II are correct statements to attract criminal liability as per Section 53 IPC as both are diabolical criminal conduct.
C. Only by II criminal responsibility can be fixed but not with the help of I.
D. McNaghten's Rule can be applied in I but not in II.

27. Read Assertion I and Reason II and with the help of given codes point out the correct explanation.

Assertion I : Consent of husband or wife of the victim does not grant immunity from the offence of bigamy.

Reason II : Sexual offence with the consent of one spouse does not fix liability for adultery.

Codes :

A. I is correct, but not with the reason of II.
B. I is correct, but with the support of II.
C. II is only the correct proposition while I is void.
D. II is valid when I is not admissible.

28. Read Assertion I and Reason II and with the help of codes given below point out the correct explanation.

Assertion I : To establish a charge of conspiracy, knowledge about indulgence in an illegal act by certain legal means, is necessary.

Reason II : The normal rule is that when a particular unlawful use being intended has to be inferred from the chain of actions.

Codes :

A. I is the judicious cause of conspiracy, because II is the correct explanation.
B. II is more appropriate explanation than merely fixing charge as per I.
C. I is the correct proposition as II optional.
D. I is not correct because as per II there must be pre-meditation.

29. Read Assertion I and Reason II and with the help of codes given below point out the correct explanation.

Assertion I : Publishing a report of proceedings of a Court will not amount to defamation.

Reason II : It is an exception to the principle of defamation.

Codes :

A. I is true, because II is the specific objective.
B. I is true, but II is not the correct proposition.
C. II is always true, because I is not dependent.
D. II is false, because I is always independent of criminal liability.

30. Read Assertion I and Reason II and with the help of codes given below point out the correct explanation.

Assertion I : Independently putting a person in fear of injury to another is extortion.

Reason II : It is an exception to the rule of delivering the valuable security.

Codes :

A. I is true, but II is not the correct statement.
B. I is true, because II is the correct proposition.
C. Both I and II are independent of proof.
D. Both I and II are false.

31. Read Assertion I and Reason II and with the help of codes given below find out the correct explanation.

Assertion I : Disorder of mind which impairs the mental faculties is known as unsoundness of mind as such it acts as defence to a criminal charge.

Reason II : Insanity is the mental abnormality and when it impairs the cognitive faculty and if an act results during that period criminal liability could be exempted.

Codes :

A. By I there is transgression of harmful acts while II refers to established rules of society for which no prosecution stands.
B. Both I and II are correct explanations as per Section 84 of IPC.
C. II is more precise while I is only a supportive factor.
D. The true test of I and II is to apply Mc Naghten's Rule.

32. The Air (Prevention and Control of Pollution) Act, 1981, and the Environment (Protection) Act, 1986, were passed by the Parliament under :

A. Article 252 of the Constitution of India.
B. Article 253 of the Constitution of India.
C. Article 250 of the Constitution of India.
D. None of the above.

33. Which of the following Judges of the Supreme Court is famously known as the "Green Judge"?

A. Justice V.R. Krishna Iyyar
B. Justice P.N. Bhagwati
C. Justice Kuldip Singh
D. Justice B.N. Kirpal

34. Which of the following Articles of the Constitution of India have been mostly used by the Supreme Court to protect environment?

A. Article 32
B. Article 21
C. Both Articles 21 and 32
D. None of the above

35. What is the period of notice required to be served upon the Central Government for filing a criminal complaint by any person, under the provisions of Environment (Protection) Act, 1986?

A. Not less than 30 days
B. Not less than 60 days
C. Not less than 90 days
D. None of the above

36. Which one of the following cases is considered as "High Water-mark case in Forest Protection" decided by the Supreme Court ?

A. Salebhai Mulla Mohmadali Vs. State of Gujarat.
B. T.N. Godavarman Tirumulkpad Vs. Union of India.
C. Narmada Bachao Andolan Vs. Union of India.
D. Samatha Vs. State of Andhra Pradesh.

37. The Parliament enacted the Water (Prevention and Control of Pollution) Act, 1974 for the control of water pollution :

A. On the request from States.
B. Of his own.
C. On the direction of United Nations.
D. On the direction of Supreme Court.

38. Under which of the following Article of the Constitution of India, the provisions regarding duty of the State "to protect and improvement of environment and safeguard the forest and wildlife", exist ?

A. Article 51(g)
B. Article 47
C. Article 48-A
D. None of the above

39. Read Assertion (A) and Reason (R) and with the help of codes given below write the correct answer.

Assertion (A): Under International law extradition is mostly a matter of bilateral treaties.

Reason (R) : There is no general duty of States in respect of extradition of criminals.

Codes :

A. Both (A) and (R) are individually true and (R) is the correct explanation of (A).

B. Both (A) and (R) are individually true, but (R) is not the correct explanation of (A).

C. (A) is true, but (R) is false.

D. (A) is false, but (R) is true.

40. Which of the following case does not concern with the judgement that a non-recognised State cannot sue in the courts of the State which was not recognised?

A. Russian Socialist Federated Soviet Republic Vs. Cibraria.

B. Guarantee Trust Company of New York Vs. United States.

C. U.S. Vs. Pink.

D. Bank of Ethopia Vs. National Bank of Egypt and Liquori.

41. Match List-I with List-II and select the correct answer :

List-I (Name of the Case)	List-II (Principle Propounded)
(a) The Caroline case	(i) Self-Defence
(b) The Nottebohm case	(ii) Effective Rouscher
(c) Re Castioni case	(iii) Non-Extradition of Political Criminals
(d) U.S. Vs. Rouscher	(iv) Rule of Speciality

Codes :

	(a)	(b)	(c)	(d)
A.	(i)	(ii)	(iii)	(iv)
B.	(iv)	(iii)	(ii)	(i)
C.	(iii)	(iv)	(i)	(ii)
D.	(ii)	(i)	(iv)	(iii)

42. Match List-I with List-II and select the correct answer :

List-I	List-II
(a) Australia and Prussia exercised joint sovereignty over	(i) New Helarides
(b) Great Britain and France exercised joint sovereignty over	(ii) Schleswig Holstein Anenburg
(c) Great Britain exercised sovereignty over	(iii) Germany
(d) In 1898 China leased the district of Kiaochow to	(iv) Turkish Island

Codes :

	(a)	(b)	(c)	(d)
A.	(ii)	(i)	(iv)	(iii)
B.	(i)	(ii)	(iii)	(iv)
C.	(iv)	(iii)	(ii)	(i)
D.	(iii)	(iv)	(i)	(ii)

43. Which of the following statements is correct?

A de-facto government is government :

A. Whose origin and existence is contrary to the Constitutional law of the State concerned and legality is challenged in International law.

B. Whose origin and existence is in conformity with the Constitutional law of the State represented and whose legality is uncontested in International law.

C. Which exercise control over a Foreign State.

D. Which has been forced to leave the territory of its State due to enemy occupation or civil war.

44. Under which of the following Article of the U.N. Charter there is an obligation to inform the Security Council if the regional arrangements take any enforcement action for maintenance of peace and security?

A. Article 51 B. Article 54

C. Article 107 D. Article 108

45. In which one of the following cases the permanent court of International justice held, "it is a generally acceptable principle of international law that in relations, between powers, who are contracting parties to a treaty, the provisions of the municipal law cannot prevail over the treaty"?

A. Navlilaa Incident Case
B. Greco, Bulgarian Communities Case.
C. Panevezys Saldutiskis Railway Case
D. Polish Postal Service Case

46. The wife's sister's daughter's son can be adopted. The adoption is

A. void B. valid
C. voidable D. none of the above

47. Kritrima Adoption is prevalent in which areas of India?

A. Madras B. Banaras
C. Avadh D. Mithila

48. In which case the Supreme Court held that "Cohabitation leads to presumption that person are living as husband and wife"?

A. Balasubramaniyam Vs Suruttayan AIR 1992 SC 756
B. Seema Vs Ashwin Kumar AIR 2006 SC 1158
C. Vishnu Prakash Vs Sheela Devi (2001) 4 SCC 729
D. None of the above.

49. In which of the case, the Supreme Court held that it is desirable that "all marriages should be Compulsorily Registered in the State, where they are solemnized"?

A. S. Nagalingam Vs. Sivagani AIR (2001) SC 3576
B. Shanti Dev Berma Vs K.P. Devi AIR (1991) SC 816
C. Seema Vs Ashwin Kumar AIR 2006 SC 1158
D. None of the above

50. Rules relating to prohibited degrees are based on the principle of

A. Monogamy B. Polygamy
C. Exogamy D. Endogamy

51. In Islamic Law, marriage is both 'Ibadt' and 'Mammulat'. Who said this?

A. Amir Ali Justice B. Dr. Fayzee
C. Abdur-Rahim D. Mahmood Justice

52. A Muslim husband can delegate his right of Talaq to

A. Any other person
B. Wife only
C. Both (A) and (B)
D. None of the above

53. A Muslim minor wife can cease her right to repudiate the marriage in case :

A. when she attained the age of puberty.
B. when the marriage was consummated before attaining the age of puberty.
C. when she is less than 18 years of age.
D. none of the above.

54. Find correct answer using codes given below:

Following are main approaches to explain nature and meaning of human rights :

(i) The scientific right theory
(ii) The moral right theory
(iii) The natural right theory
(iv) The legal right theory

Codes :

A. (i) and (ii) are correct.
B. (ii) and (iii) are correct.
C. (iii) and (iv) are correct.
D. (iv) and (i) are correct.

55. Read Assertion (A) and Reason (R).

Find correct answer using codes given below:

Assertion (A) : The purpose of Human Rights is to provide protection against the abuse of power committed by the organs of State.

Reason (R) : Due to absence of Lok Pal the misuse of power by the State cannot be effectively checked.

Codes :

A. (A) and (R) are correct and (R) is correct explanation of (A).
B. (A) and (R) are correct, but (R) is not correct explanation of (A).
C. (A) is true and (R) is false.
D. (A) is false and (R) is true.

56. Match item in Table-A with items in Table-B using codes given below :

Table-A	Table-B
(a) The first generation of Human Rights	(i) Idealistic Theory of Law
(b) The second generation of Human Rights	(ii) Collective Rights
(c) The third generation of Human Rights	(iii) Civil and Political Rights
(d) Theoretical approach to Human Rights	(iv) Economic, Social and Cultural Rights

Codes :

	(a)	(b)	(c)	(d)
A.	(i)	(iii)	(ii)	(iv)
B.	(iii)	(iv)	(ii)	(i)
C.	(iv)	(iii)	(ii)	(i)
D.	(iii)	(iv)	(i)	(ii)

57. In Indian Constitution, Civil and Political Rights given in its

A. Part II
B. Part III
C. Part IV
D. Part IX

58. "No one shall be subjected to arbitrary arrest, detention or exile."

Above law is in

A. Article 21 of the Indian Constitution
B. Criminal Procedure Code
C. Civil Procedure Code
D. Article 9 of the Universal Declaration of Human Rights

59. Read Assertion (A) and Reason (R) and find correct answer using codes given below :

Assertion (A) : Advancement of rights of women has been the concern of world community since the end of Second World War.

Reason (R) : In Second World War, population of men was significantly decreased.

Codes :

A. (A) and (R) are true and (R) is correct explanation of (A).
B. (A) and (R) are true, but (R) is not correct explanation of (A).
C. (A) is true and (R) is false.
D. (A) is false, but (R) is true.

60. Read Assertion (A) and Reason (R) and find correct answer using codes given below :

Assertion (A) : The child must be given the means requisite for his normal development, both materially and spiritually.

Reason (R) : Spirituality is material and material is spiritual.

Codes :

A. (A) and (R) are true and (R) is correct explanation of (A).
B. (A) and (R) are true, but (R) is not correct explanation of (A).
C. (A) is true, but (R) is false.
D. (A) is false, but (R) is true.

61. State which of the following statements is incorrect?

A. Liability in tort arises from breach of duty primarily fixed by law.
B. The duty, breach of which results in tortious liability, is towards the public generally.
C. The duty, breach of which results in liability in tort, is towards some person in particular.
D. The breach of duty, which results in liability in tort, is redressable by an action for unliquidated damages.

62. The plaintiff was watching a cricket match at a stadium organized by the Cricket Club of India. He was seriously injured by a mighty hit from the batsman. In this case, who is liable to pay the damages to the plaintiff ?

A. The Batsman
B. The Cricket Club of India
C. Both (A) and (B) above
D. None of the above

63. Which one of the following sets correctly identifies the specific defence available in an action for defamation?

A. Privilege, Truth, Fair comment.
B. Privilege, Mistake, Fair comment.
C. Truth, Mistake, Fair comment.
D. Truth, Privilege, Mistake.

64. Read Assertion (A) and Reason (R) and with the help of codes given below, point out the correct explanation.

Assertion (A) : Pleading lack of intention to defame someone does not absolve one from liability for defamation.

Reason (R) : The essence of defamation lies in the lowering a person in the estimation of the right thinking members of the society, even without intention.

Codes :

A. Both (A) and (R) are true and (R) is the correct explanation of (A).

B. Both (A) and (R) are true and (R) is not the correct explanation of (A).

C. (A) is true, but (R) is false.

D. (A) is false, but (R) is true.

65. Assertion (A) : In India, defendants collecting water in reservoirs have not been held liable for damage caused due to the escape of water from these reservoirs in absence of negligence.

Reason (R) : The rule of strict liability laid down in Rylands Vs Fletcher case has been held to be not applicable in India.

Select the correct answer using the codes given below ;

Codes :

A. Both (A) and (R) are true and (R) is the correct explanation of (A).

B. Both (A) and (R) are true, but (R) is not the correct explanation of (A).

C. (A) is true, but (R) is false.

D. (A) is false, but (R) is true.

66. Assertion (A) : In tort of nuisance, interference by the defendant may cause damage to the plaintiff's property or personal discomfort in the enjoyment of property.

Reason (R) : Every interference in the use of property is a nuisance.

Select the correct answer using the codes given below :

Codes :

A. Both (A) and (R) are individually true and (R) is the correct explanation of (A).

B. Both (A) and (R) are individually true, but (R) is not the correct explanation of (A).

C. (A) is true, but (R) is false.

D. (A) is false, but (R) is true.

67. Match List-I with List-II and indicate the correct answer using the codes given below:

List-I	List-II
(a) Composition of the District Forum	(i) Section 10, C.P. Act
(b) Complaint to be accompanied by court fee	(ii) Section 17, C.P. Act
(c) Jurisdiction of the State Commission	(iii) Section 23, C.P. Act
(d) Appeals from National Commission to the Supreme Court	(iv) Section 12(2) C.P. Act

Codes :

	(a)	(b)	(c)	(d)
A.	(i)	(ii)	(iii)	(iv)
B.	(i)	(iv)	(ii)	(iii)
C.	(ii)	(iv)	(i)	(iii)
D.	(iv)	(iii)	(ii)	(i)

68. Find correct legal principle from following statements:

A. A company may do an act which is necessary for or incidental to the attainment of its objects or which is otherwise not authorized by the Act.

B. A company may not do an act which is necessary for or incidental to the attainment of its objects which is otherwise not authorized by the Act.

C. A company may do an act which is necessary for or incidental to the attainment of its objects or which is otherwise authorized by the Act.

D. A company may do an act which is unnecessary for or not incidental to attainment of its goals or which is otherwise barred by the Act.

). Match items from Table-A with items in Table-B, using codes given below:

Table-A	Table-B
(a) Lakshmi Ratan Cotton Mills Vs. J.K. Jute Mills Co., AIR1957 All 311	(i) Director's duty of care, diligence and skill
(b) Automatic Self-cleansing Filter Syndicate Co. Ltd. Vs. Cuninghame, (1906) 2 Ch.34	(ii) Statutory protection to Directors against liability
(c) G. Ramesh Vs. ROC, (2007) 135 Comp Cas 655.	(iii) Powers of Directors
(d) City Equitable Fire Insurance Company, Re, (1924) All E Rep 485	(iv) Scope of authority of Directors

Codes :

	(a)	(b)	(c)	(d)
A.	(iv)	(iii)	(ii)	(i)
B.	(iii)	(ii)	(i)	(iv)
C.	(ii)	(i)	(iv)	(iii)
D.	(i)	(iv)	(iii)	(ii)

. Read Assertion (A) and Reason (R) and with help of codes given below, point out the correct explanation.

Assertion (A) : A contract of sale may be absolute or conditional.

Reason (R) : There is no absolute condition for a contract of sale.

Codes :

A. Both (A) and (R) are true and (R) is correct explanation of (A).

B. Both (A) and (R) are true, but (R) is not correct explanation of (A).

C. (A) is true, but (R) is false.

D. (A) is false, but (R) is true.

"Where under a contract of sale the property in the goods is transferred from the seller to the buyer, the contract is called a sale, but where the transfer of the property in the goods is to take place at a future time or subject to some condition thereafter to be fulfilled, the contract is called an agreement to sell."

Read above statement and find correct answer, using codes given below :

Codes :

A. Contract of sale is conditional.

B. Contract of agreement to sell is conditional.

C. There is no difference between sale and agreement to sell, as both are contracts.

D. Sale is a contract, agreement to sell is not a contract.

72. Essential feature of a partnership is

(i) Agreement

(ii) Object to carry on a business

(iii) To share profits

(iv) Business is to be carried by all or any of them acting for all.

Codes :

A. Only (i) is correct.

B. Only (i) and (ii) are correct.

C. Only (i), (ii) and (iii) are correct.

D. All of above are correct

73. Find the correct legal statement from following statements :

A. Every partner is liable, severally with all the other partners and jointly for all acts of the firm done while he is a partner.

B. Every partner is liable, jointly with all the other partners and severally for all acts of the firm done while he is a partner.

C. Every partner is liable only for acts done by him as acts of the firm done while he is a partner.

D. Sleeping partner is not liable for acts done by him as acts of the firm done while he is a partner.

74. Read Assertion (A) and Reason (R) and with help of codes given below, point out the correct explanation.

Assertion (A) : It is the duty of the banker to be acquainted with the customer□fs handwriting.

Reason (R) : A banker must be hand writing expert.

Codes :

A. Both (A) and (R) are true and (R) is correct explanation of (A).

B. Both (A) and (R) are true, but (R) is not correct explanation of (A).

C. (A) is true, but (R) is false.

D. (A) is false, but (R) is true.

75. When a negotiable instrument is dishonoure the party liable to pay, becomes bound pay compensation to

A. The bank

B. The endorser

C. Holder or endorsee

D. The Court

ANSWERS

1	2	3	4	5	6	7	8	9	10
B	C	C	D	A	C	C	D	A	C
11	**12**	**13**	**14**	**15**	**16**	**17**	**18**	**19**	**20**
D	D	A	B	D	D	D	B	D	B
21	**22**	**23**	**24**	**25**	**26**	**27**	**28**	**29**	**30**
A	C	A	D	C	B	A	A	A	B
31	**32**	**33**	**34**	**35**	**36**	**37**	**38**	**39**	**40**
B	B	C	C	B	B	A	C	B	D
41	**42**	**43**	**44**	**45**	**46**	**47**	**48**	**49**	**50**
A	A	A	B	B	B	D	A	C	C
51	**52**	**53**	**54**	**55**	**56**	**57**	**58**	**59**	**60**
C	C	B	C	B	B	B	D	B	C
61	**62**	**63**	**64**	**65**	**66**	**67**	**68**	**69**	**70**
D	D	A	D	A	C	B	C	A	C
71	**72**	**73**	**74**	**75**					
B	D	B	C	C					

SOME SELECTED EXPLANATORY ANSWERS

2. Article 42 of the Indian Constitution, states that there should be provision for just and humane conditions of work and maternity relief. The state shall make provision for securing there relief. These provisions are provided in the constitution as a Directive Principle of the State Policy.

3. Fundamental duties under Part IV A was inserted in the constitution by the 42nd Amendment Act, 1976. Fundamental duties are provided under Article 51-A of the Constitution. In all there are eleven fundamental duties. It shall be the duty of eve citizen of India—

(*a*) to abide by the constitution and respe its ideals, the National Flag and t National Anthems;

(*b*) to cherish and follow the noble idea which inspired our national struggle f freedom;

(*c*) to uphold and protect the sovereignt unity and integrity of India;

(*d*) to defend the country and render nation service when called upon;

(*e*) to promote harmony and the spirit of common brotherhood amongst all the people of India;

(*f*) to value and preserve the rich heritage of our composite culture;

(*g*) to protect and improve natural environment;

(*h*) to develop the scientific temper, humanism and the spirit of inquiry and reform;

(*i*) to safeguard public property and to abjure violence;

(*j*) to strive towards excellence in all spheres of individual and collective activity and

(*k*) who are parents as Guardian for provisions the opportunity of education to their children, as the case, be shall be Guardian of children of 6 years to 14 years of age.

. According to Article 53 of the Indian Constitution, the executive power of the Union shall be vested in the President and shall be exercised by him either directly or through officers subordinate to him in accordance with this constitution.

. Article 352(8) of the Indian Constitution states that; where a notice in writing signed by not less than one-tenth of the total number of members of the House of the People has been given, of their intention to move a resolution for disapproving, or, as the case may be, for disapproving the continuance in force of, a Proclamation issued under clause (1) or a Proclamation varying such Proclamation—to the speaker, if the House is in session; or to be President, if the House is not in session.

. A writ of Mandamus will not lie against President of India. Mandamus is a command to act lawfully and to desist from perpetrating an unlawful act. Mandamus may lie against any authority, officers, government or even judicial bodies that fail to or refuse to perform a public duty and discharge a legal obligation. Mandamus is a judicial remedy in the form of an order to do or to forbear from doing some specific act which that agency is obliged to do or to refrain from doing under the law and which is in the nature of a public duty or a statutory duty. It is considered as a residuary remedy of the public law. It is a general remedy whenever justice has been denied to any person.

24. Section 361 of the Indian Penal Code, 1860, states that, whoever takes or entices any minor under sixteen years of age if a male or under eighteen years of age if a female or any person of unsound mind, out of the keeping of the lawful guardian of such minor or person of unsound mind, without the consent of such guardian, is said to kidnap such minor or person from lawful guardianship. The words "lawful guardian", in this section include any person lawfully entrusted with the care or custody of such minor or other person.

25. Section 403 of the Indian Penal Code, 1860, deals with Dishonest misappropriation of property. This section states that, whoever dishonestly misappropriates or converts to his own use any movable property, shall be punished with imprisonment of either description for a term which may extend to two years or with fine or with both. **Example:** 'A' finds a better on the road, containing a bank note. From the direction and contents of the letter he learns to whom the note belongs. He appropriates the note. He is guilty of an offence under this section.

38. Article 48-A of the Indian Constitution is one of the Directive Principles of State Policy. This article deals with the Protection and Improvement of Environment and Safeguarding of Forests and Wildlife. This article provides that, the state shall endeavour to protect and improve the environment and to safeguard the forests and wildlife of the country.

Previous Paper (Solved)

UGC-NET LAW, DECEMBER 2012

PAPER-II

Note : *This paper contains* ***fifty (50)*** *objective type questions, each question carrying* ***two (2)*** *marks each.* ***All*** *questions are compulsory.*

1. Clause (4) of Article 15 has been added to the Constitution by
A. The Constitution First Amendment Act.
B. The Constitution Second Amendment Act
C. The Constitution Fourth Amendment Act.
D. The Constitution Sixth Amendment Act.

2. The State shall endeavour to secure for the citizens a Uniform Civil Code throughout the territory of India as per
A. Article 40 B. Article 43
C. Article 44 D. Article 48

3. In India sovereignty lies with
A. The Constitution
B. The Supreme Court
C. The Parliament
D. The People

4. The Supreme Court of India formulated the doctrine of eclipse in
A. Bhikaji Narain Dhakras Vs State of M.P.
B. Bashesharnath Vs Income Tax Commissioner.
C. State of W.B. Vs Anwar Ali Sarkar
D. Maneka Gandhi Vs Union of India

5. The satisfaction of the President means the satisfaction of the Council of Ministers and not his personal satisfaction, held in
A. Samsher Singh Vs State of Punjab
B. U.N. Rao Vs Indira Gandhi
C. Ram Jawaya Kapoor Vs State of Punjab
D. Sardar Lal Vs Union Government

6. The Concurrent List was described as a 'Twilight Zone', as it were for both the Union and the States are competent to legislate in this field without coming in to conflict" stated by
A. Basu, D.D. B. Dicey, A.V.
C. Pyle, M.V. D. Ambedkar, B.

7. Article 360 has been invoked
A. only one time.
B. two times.
C. three times.
D. never invoked

8. "Jurisprudence is concerned primarily w the effects of law upon society and only to lesser extent with questions about the soc determination of law." Who said it ?
A. Roscoe Pound B. Eugen Ehrlich
C. Emile Durkheim D. Max Weber

9. "True law is that which has right reason agreement with nature" was propagated b
A. Cicero B. Hart
C. Grotius D. Salmond

10. Match List-I with List-II and select the corr answer using the codes given below the lis

List-I	List-II
I. Privilege	(*a*) Gives content to t claim of a person
II. Duty	(*b*) Freedom from claim another
III. Power	(*c*) Have no correlative cla according to Austin
IV. Absolute	(*d*) Ability of a Duty pers to change legal relatio

Codes :
A. I-a II-b III-d IV-c
B. I-b II-a III-d IV-c
C. I-a II-b III-c IV-d
D. I-b II-a III-c IV-d

11. 'X' a servant finds a bag at the basement of the shop. He hands it over to 'Y' the owner of the shop, who asks him to place it in the almirah. Now, the bag is in possession of
A. 'X' because he was the finder.
B. 'Y' because he was the owner of the shop.
C. 'X' because he has kept it in the almirah.
D. 'Y' because in him there was union of corpus and animus.

12. Which one of the following jurists emphasised that "We cannot understand what a thing is unless we study what it does"?
A. Salmond B. Roscoe Pound
C. Kelsen D. Austin

13. Who defines "ownership as planary control over an object"?
A. Austin B. Salmond
C. Holland D. Savigny

14. Assertion (A) : A legal right is a legally protected interest.
Reason (R) : An element of advantage is essential to constitute right.
Codes :
A. Both (A) and (R) are true, and (R) is the correct explanation of (A).
B. Both (A) and (R) are true, but (R) is not correct explanation of (A).
C. (A) is true, but (R) is false.
D. (A) is false, but (R) is true.

15. Assertion (A) : International Law Commission has initiated studies and prepared draft codes on diverse fields in international law.
Reason (R) : International Law Commission was established under General Assembly Resolution No. 174 (11) adopted on 21 November 1947 with an object to promote, progressively develop and codify international law.
Codes :
A. Both (A) and (R) are true.
B. (A) is true but (R) is false.
C. (R) is true but (A) is false.
D. Both (A) and (R) are false.

16. Match List-I with List-II.

	List-I **Declaration/ Treaty/Convention**	**List-II** **Year of Adoption**
(*a*)	Universal Declaration of Human Rights	(i) 1948
(*b*)	International Convention on Civil and Political Rights	(ii) 1966
(*c*)	Convention on the Rights of the Child	(iii) 2006
(*d*)	Convention on the Rights of Persons with Disabilities	(iv) 1999

Codes :

	(*a*)	(*b*)	(*c*)	(*d*)
A.	i	ii	iv	iii
B.	ii	i	iv	iii
C.	iv	iii	ii	i
D.	iii	ii	iv	i

17. Jus Cogens means
A. Peremptory norm of international law.
B. Norm of international law.
C. Peremptory norm which does not permit derogation.
D. None of the above.

18. Which one of the following is primary source of international law?
A. Decisions of International Court of Justice.
B. Resolutions of U.N. General Assembly.
C. General Principles of law recognized by Civilized Nations.
D. None of the above

19. Which one of the following is not a permanent member of the U.N. Security Council?
A. U.K. B. U.S.A.
C. Japan D. China

20. "Recognition operates retroactively not to invalidate the acts of a former government, but to validate the acts of a de facto government which has become the new de jure government" has been held by the court in the case of :

B. An act done by me against my will is not my act.

C. Neither I nor my person can be held liable for an act done under compulsion.

D. All of them.

40. The general principles as to protection of an accused is based on :

(i) Autrefois acquit and Autrefois convict.

(ii) Reasonable doubt as to presumption of innocence.

(iii) Natural Justice.

(iv) Conviction can not be based without proving the guilt even if it was admitted.

Which statement is correct ?

A. (i) is correct.

B. (i) and (ii) are correct.

C. (i), (ii) and (iii) are correct.

D. (i), (ii), (iii) and (iv) are correct.

41. Fill in the blanks with appropriate words : The distinctive features of riot and unlawful assembly are an activity which is accompanied by ____

A. use of force and violence.

B. causing alarm.

C. violence on a common purpose.

D. all of them.

42. The offence of __________ homicide supposes knowledge of likelihood of causing death.

A. unlawful B. abnormal

C. culpable D. all types of

43. The expression 'Seduced' used in Section 366 A of Indian Penal Code means to ________ a woman to submit to illicit intercourse at any time.

A. use of force by stress

B. deceitfully induce

C. willfully influence

D. none of them

44. Preparation consists in devising or arranging means necessary for the commission of the offence. Such attempt is not punishable because

(i) the motive was harmless.

(ii) impossibility to reach wrongful end.

(iii) does not affect the security of any person.

(iv) it remained without culmination.

The reasoned answer is

A. Only (i) is correct.

B. The most probability is (i) and (ii).

C. There is quite likelihood of (i) and (iii).

D. All the reasons (i), (ii), (iii) and (iv) have to be examined.

45. No person employed in a public utility service shall go on strike

(I) without giving notice of strike to employer.

(II) within 14 days of giving such notice.

(III) after expiry of date specified in notice for strike.

(IV) within 7 days of conclusion of conciliation proceeding.

Codes :

A. I and IV B. I and III

C. I and II D. II and III

46. There can be lay-off for

A. One day

B. More than one day

C. Maximum seven days

D. Any period, even less than one day

47. In which of the following cases the court reiterated the well-known legal position that even a temporary worker can claim retrenchment compensation, if he is covered by the provisions of Section 25 F of the Industrial Disputes Act, 1947?

A. Tatanagar Foundary Co. Vs Their Workmen.

B. Management of Willcox Buckwell (India) Ltd. Vs Jagannath.

C. Barsi Light Railway Co. Ltd. Vs Joglekar.

D. Modern Stores Vs Krishandas.

48. Which one of the following statement is true?

A. All Government departments are industries.

B. No Government department can be industry.

C. Government department carrying on business or trade may be industry.

D. Government department carrying on only sovereign function may be industry.

49. According to Section 9 A of the Trade Union Act, 1926 minimum requirement about membership of a trade union is
A. Seven
B. Ten percent or one hundred of the workmen.
C. Ten percent or one hundred of the workmen, whichever is less.
D. Ten percent or one hundred of the workmen, whichever is less, subject to minimum seven.

50. To be a member of trade union, a person must attain the age of
A. 18 years B. 16 years
C. 15 years D. 21 years

ANSWERS

1	2	3	4	5	6	7	8	9	10
A	C	D	A	A	C	D	A	C	B
11	12	13	14	15	16	17	18	19	20
D	A	C	C	A	A	C	C	C	B
21	22	23	24	25	26	27	28	29	30
B	A	C	B	D	A	C	C	B	A
31	32	33	34	35	36	37	38	39	40
D	B	D	A	A	A	B	B	B	D
41	42	43	44	45	46	47	48	49	50
D	C	B	D	C	D	B	C	D	A

SOME SELECTED EXPLANATORY ANSWERS

1. Clause (4) of the Article 15, was added by the Constitution First Amendment Act, 1951, according to which nothing in this article or in Clause (2) of Article 29 shall prevent the state from making any special provision for the advancement of any socially and educationally backward classes of citizens or for the Scheduled Castes and the Scheduled Tribes.

2. Article 44 of the Indian Constitution provides for the provision of Uniform Civil Code for the citizens, according to this article the state shall make efforts to secure for the citizens a uniform civil code throughout the territory of India.

7. Article 360 of the Indian Constitution has never been invoked till date. This article provides for the provisions as to financial emergency, if the president is satisfied that a situation has arisen whereby the financial stability or credit of India or of any part of the territory thereof is threatened, he may by a Proclamation make a declaration to that effect.

11. According the principles of the Criminal Law in order to prove the possession and ownership, both *Animus corpus* and *Animus intendi* should be present. In the given scenario, bag is in the possession of Y, because in him there was union of corpus and animus.

21. Principle of Exogamy, governs the rules relating to sapinda relationship. All systems prohibit marriage among near relations. According to the rule of exogamy, a person is not permitted to marry within the same tribe. The shastric prohibition of marrying within the same gotra and pravara or sapinda falls under this head. However, today, sagotra or sapravara marriages are valid.

23. Brakdown Theory of divorce is reflected in

Section 13(IA) of the Hindu Marriage Act, 1955. This theory represents the modern theory of divorce. A fundamental shift in the policy was discernible from the judicial recognition of the view that the purpose of divorce law was not to punish the guilty but to protect the innocent spouse. The breakdown of marriage is defined as, such failure in the matrimonial relationship or such circumstances adverse to that relation that no reasonable probability remains for the spouses again living together as husband and wife.

26. According to Section 13(B) of the Hindu Marriage Act, 1955, a petition for dissolution of marriage by mutual consent may be presented on the ground that the spouses have been living separately for a period of one year or more, that they have not been able to live together and that they have mutually agreed that the marriage should be dissolved.

32. Section 29 of the Indian Contract Act, 1872, deals with, Agreements which are void because of uncertainty, so in the given question option (B) is incorrect. Section 28 of the Indian Contract Act, 1872 deals with Agreements which are void due to restraint of Legal proceedings.

33. According to the Law of Torts, a person is liable for his own acts, but in many cases he may be held responsible for the torts committed by others. This is known as vicarious liability, *i.e.,* liability incurred for, or instead of, another. Vicarious liability is a kind of strict liability, however, in vicarious liability the liability arises because of the relationship between the principal and the wrongdoer. The common examples of such a liability are: Liability of the principal for the tort of his agent, Liability of partners for each other's tort and Liability of the master for the tort of his servant.

35. The rule of Absolute Liability was propounded by Justice P.N. Bhagwati in M.C. Mehta Vs. Union of India (AIR 1987). The supreme court evolved the rule of absolute liability as part of Indian Law in preference to the rule of strict liability laid down in Rylands Vs. Fletcher. It expressly declared that the new rule was not subject to any of the exceptions under the Rylands rule.

36. According to the Law of Torts, the defence to strict Liability is based on the maxim, volenti non fit injuria *i.e.,* leave and licence. Everyone is the best judge of his interest and therefore the one who voluntarily agrees to suffer harm is not allowed to complain for that and one's consent is a good defence against oneself. This is so because the harm voluntarily suffered does not constitute the legal injury. No man can enforce a right, which he has voluntarily waived or abandoned. Consent to suffer the harm may be express or implied.

38. According to the maxim "Injuria Sine Damnum", in the Law of Torts, both the statements 3 and 4 are correct. This maxim means violation of a legal right without causing any harm, loss or damage to the plaintiff. Thus, it is the behaviour, which is actionable as a tort. It is always actionable as legal wrongs entail a remedy.

39. According Section 94 of the Indian Penal Code, 1860, nothing is an offence which is done by a person who is compelled to do it by threats, which, at the time of doing it, reasonably cause the apprehension that instant death to that person will otherwise be the consequence. This section recognises the principle that offences committed out of compulsion is a defence to criminal liability. Compulsion is a restraint upon the will of a person.

41. According to Section 141 of the Indian Penal Code, 1860, An unlawful assembly is an assembly of five or more persons is designated an unlawful assembly, if the common object of persons composing that assembly is—to overawe by criminal force. Section 146 of the Indian Penal Code defines Rioting as, whenever force or violence is used by an unlawful assembly or by any member thereof, in prosecution of the common object of such assembly, every member of such assembly is guilty of the offence of rioting. So option (D) is the most appropriate choice.

42. According to Section 299 of the Indian Penal Code, 1860, whoever causes death by doing an act with the intention of causing death or with the intention of causing such bodily injury as is likely to cause death or with the knowledge, that he is likely by such act to cause death, commits the offence of culpable homicide. So option (C) is the most appropriate choice.

46. According to Section 2(KKK) of the Industrial Disputes Act, 1947, lay-off, means the failure, refusal or inability of an employer on account of shortage of coal, power or raw materials or the accumulation of stocks or the breakdown of machinery or natural calamity or for any other connected reason to give employment to a workman whose name is borne on the muster rolls of his industrial establishment and who has not been retrenched. Lay-off can be for any period.

PAPER-III

Note : *This paper contains* ***seventy five (75)*** *objective type questions of* ***two (2)*** *marks each.* ***All questions*** *are compulsory.*

1. Democracy and Federalism are essential features of our Constitution and basic feature of its structure. This observation was made in S.R. Bommai Vs. Union of India by the Judge.

A. Justice P.B. Sawant
B. Justice S.R. Pandyan
C. Justice J.S. Verma
D. Justice A.M. Ahmadi

2. According to A.V. Dicey in India the 'Rule of Law' is embodied in

A. Article 12 of the Constitution of India
B. Article 13 of the Constitution of India
C. Article 14 of the Constitution of India
D. Article 21 of the Constitution of India

3. When the court declare that certain provisions of the Act as invalid, it does not affect the validity of the Act and it remains as it is. The principle is known as :

A. Doctrine of prospective over ruling.
B. Doctrine of severability.
C. Doctrine of pleasure.
D. Doctrine of Eclipse.

4. **Assertion (A) :** A Bill which contains a taxation clause besides clauses dealing with other matters may also be a Money Bill.
Reason (R) : All Bills dealing with taxes are Money Bills.

Codes :

A. Both (A) and (R) are true, but (R) is not the correct explanation of (A).
B. Both (A) and (R) are true and (R) is the correct explanation of (A).
C. (A) is false, but (R) is true.
D. (A) is true, but (R) is false.

5. Article 40 of the Constitution of India deals with

A. Provision for Just and humane conditions of work and maternity relief.
B. Living wages etc. for workers.
C. Duty of the State to raise the level of nutrition.
D. Organisation of Village Panchayats.

6. Article 20 and Article 21 has been taken from the purview of Article 359 of the Constitution of India by

A. 42nd Amendment B. 43rd Amendment
C. 44th Amendment D. 59th Amendment

7. The Chairperson of Delimitation Commission

A. Justice Kuldeep Singh
B. Justice R.S. Sarkaria
C. Justice R.S. Pathak
D. Justice S.N. Phukan

8. Representation of House of People is based on

A. Literacy of State B. Area of the State
C. Population D. Community

9. Find correct answer :
Administrative law is the law relating to the powers and procedures of
A. The Parliament
B. The Legislature
C. The Administrative Authorities
D. Judiciary

10. Find the correct answer :
The principles of natural justice are :
(i) No person can be judge in his own case.
(ii) No person shall be condemned unheard.
Codes :
A. only (i) is correct.
B. only (ii) is correct.
C. (i) and (ii) are correct.
D. None of the above are correct.

11. Find correct answer :
Administrative Tribunals exercises :
A. Purely Administrative functions
B. Purely Judicial functions
C. Purely Legislative functions
D. Quasi Judicial functions

12. What is the effect of violation of the rule : "Audi Alteram Partem" on an administrative action?
A. Mere irregularity B. Null and void
C. An illegality D. Voidable

13. In which of the following cases, the Supreme Court held that the principles of natural justice are applicable to administrative proceedings?
A. M.C. Mehta Vs. Union of India.
B. Maneka Gandhi Vs. Union of India.
C. A.K. Kraipak Vs. Union of India.
D. Smt. Indira Nehru Gandhi Vs. Raj Narain.

14. Find correct answer :
The writ of prohibition may be issued, when there is
A. an absence of jurisdiction or abuse of jurisdiction.
B. violation of principles of natural justice and fraud.
C. any kind of contravention of the law of the land.
D. all of the above.

15. Find correct answer :
The writ of certiorari necessarily implies that
A. An error of fact, cannot corrected.
B. An error of law apparent on the face of the record, can be corrected.
C. Violation of natural justice.
D. None of the above.

16. "Common law is essentially a Judge made law".
This opinion was expressed by
A. Pollock B. Austin
C. Paton D. Salmond

17. Match the following :

List-I	**List-II**
a. Enacted law	1. Legislation
b. Case law	2. Agreement
c. Customary law	3. Precedent
d. Conventional law	4. Custom

Codes :

	(*a*)	(*b*)	(*c*)	(*d*)
A.	1	2	4	3
B.	1	2	3	4
C.	1	3	4	2
D.	3	1	4	2

18. State the legal status of Hindu Joint family.
A. Hindu Joint family is a legal person.
B. Hindu Joint family is a natural person.
C. Hindu Joint family is both a legal and natural person.
D. None of the above.

19. "Case-law is gold in the mine-a few grains of precious metal to the tons of useless matter, while the statute law is coin of the state which ready for immediate use".
Who gave this statement ?
A. Bentham B. Salmond
C. Kelsen D. Holland

20. "Law is the guarantee of the conditions of life of society, assured by the States" "power of constraint" who said it ?
A. Dvguit B. Ihering
C. Savigny D. Ehrlich

21. Match List-I (Legal Right) with List-II (Nature of Legal Right) and select the correct answer by using the codes given below the lists:

List-I	List-II
(*a*) Time barred debt	1. Personal Right
(*b*) Right to reputation	2. Right in Personam
(*c*) Right to physical integrity	3. Imperfect Right
(*d*) Right arising out of a contract	4. Right in Rem

Codes :

	(*a*)	(*b*)	(*c*)	(*d*)
A.	3	4	2	1
B.	3	2	1	4
C.	2	3	1	4
D.	3	4	1	2

22. Right in re aliena means a right over
A. his own property.
B. a property of someone else.
C. a property situated in a foreign country.
D. a property situated in one's own country.

23. The birth and death of legal person is determined by
A. Nature
B. Custom
C. Law
D. Precedent

24. Read the following passage and match the column :

The social tolerance towards crime establishes the concept of crime. No longer people accept that crime is related to sin by which people feel remorse and undergo penance to seek exoneration from punishment. But there is a general opinion that crime is relatively connected to individual behaviour, which very often changes. To resolve the conflict, the general view is that, anything which is injurious to public welfare is a crime.

Column 'P'		**Column 'Q'**
(i) Russell	—	Crime is not absolute as it depends upon social tolerance.
(ii) Black Stone	—	Changing concept of crime as it is related to sin.
(iii) H.J. Klare	—	Crime is known through attributes as it is related to behavior.
(iv) G.W. Patton	—	Act which does not attract law is not a crime.

Correct answer is
A. (i) B. (ii)
C. (iii) D. (iv)

25. Fill in the gap.
Contributory negligence is ______ defense to a criminal charge.
A. genuine B. accurate
C. sharp D. no

26. The accused fired two shots with a revolver at point blank range at the Acting Governor but the bullets failed to produce the desired result because of some defect in the ammunition or intervention of leather wallet. What offence is caused ?
A. Culpable Homicide
B. Attempt to Murder
C. Attempt to harm
D. None of them

27. In a case where a minor girl was in the custody of her mother. Later the mother obtained divorce from her husband and thereafter the father forcefully removed the daughter from the school. What offence is created by the father?
A. Abduction
B. Kidnapping
C. Confinement
D. Custody

28. Can a woman be prosecuted for gang rape?
A. Occasionally
B. As the case demands
C. Not at all
D. When she is a party to it

29. Criminal breach of trust is an offence which signifies :
A. Entrustment
B. Demand
C. Refusal
D. Wrongful intention

30. 'X' a Police Officer while executing a warrant of arrest against 'Y' asks 'Z' to identify 'Y'. 'Z' knowingly tells that 'M' is 'Y' and consequently 'M' is arrested. What offence is committed by 'Z'?
A. Abetment by Instigation
B. Abetment by Aiding
C. Abetment by False representation
D. Abetment by Mischief

31. A married man commits adultery if he commits sexual intercourse with
A. A teen aged girl.
B. An unmarried woman.
C. Any woman who is not his wife.
D. Married woman.

32. In which of the following cases, the Supreme Court applied the doctrine of public trust that the State as a trustee of all natural resources is under a legal duty to protect the natural resources. These natural resources are meant for public use and cannot be converted into private ownership ?
A. M.C. Mehta Vs. Kamalnath and Others.
B. M.C. Mehta Vs. Union of India (Ganga Water Pollution case)
C. M.C. Mehta Vs. Union of India (Replacing diesel vehicles by CNG vehicles)
D. Church of God (Full Gospel) in India Vs. KKR Majestic Colony Welfare Association.

33. In which of the following cases, the Supreme Court discussed the development of the precautionary principle?
A. A.P. Pollution Control Board Vs. M.V. Nayudu.
B. Rural Litigation and Entitlement Kendra Vs. State of U.P.
C. M.C. Mehta Vs. Union of India (Ganga Water Pollution case)
D. Olga Tellis (1986) case

34. The term "environment" under Section 2(a of the Environment (Protection) Act, 198 means
A. Air, Water and Land only.
B. Water, Air, Land and interrelationshi between air, water, and land only.
C. Water, Air, Land, and the interrelationshi between water, air and land and huma beings, other living creatures, plants, micr organism and property.
D. None of the above.

35. Assertion (A) : The right to clean drinking water and right to free air to breath are attributes of the right to life.

Reason (R) : Because they are the basic elements which sustain life.

Codes :
A. (A) and (R) are true. (R) is good explanation of (A).
B. Both (A) and (R) are true. But (R) is not a good explanation of (A).
C. (A) is true, (R) is false.
D. (A) is false, (R) is true.

36. In which of the following cases, the Supreme Court observed that, 'When there is a state of uncertainty due to the lack of data or material about the extent of damage or pollution likely to be caused, then in order to maintain the ecological balance, the burden of proof that the said balance will be maintained must necessarily be on the industry or the unit which is likely to cause pollution'?
A. M.C. Mehta Vs. Union of India.
B. Olga Tellis Vs. Bombay Municipal Corporation.
C. Taj Trapezium case.
D. None of the above.

37. In which of the following cases, the Supreme Court directed closing down and demolition of shrimp industries in coastal regulation zone and implement the "precautionary principle" and "the polluter pays principle" and held them liable for payment of compensation for reversing the ecology and compensate the individual for loss suffered ?

A. S. Jagannath Vs. Union of India.
B. Vellore Citizens Welfare Forum Vs. Union of India.
C. M.C. Mehta Vs. Union of India.
D. Church of God (Full Gospels) in India Vs. KKR Majestic Colony Welfare Association.

3. In which of the following cases, the Supreme Court upheld the governmental direction to close down the lime-stone mining operations and quarrying permanently, holding it the duty of the lessee to protest and safeguard the right of the people to live in a healthy environment with minimal disturbance of ecological balance?
A. All India Council for Enviro Legal Action Vs. Union of India.
B. Rural Litigation and Entitlement Kendra Vs. State of Uttar Pradesh.
C. Vellore Citizens Welfare Forum Vs. Union of India.
D. M.C. Mehta Vs. Union of India.

. Match the correct answer from List-B to the item in List-A.

List-A	List-B
a. The polluter pays principle	A. Each generation should be obligated to conserve the diversity of natural and cultural resources base so that it does not restrict options of the future generations.
	B. Affirmative State Action for efficient management of resources and empowers the citizens to question ineffective management of natural resources.
	C. The pollutant not only has an obligation to make good the loss to the victims but has to bear the costs of restoring the environment to its original state.
	D. State's obligation to devise and implement a cohesive and coordinated programme to meet its obligation to sustainable development.

40. "If International Law were only a kind of morality, the framers of state papers concerning foreign policy would throw all strength on moral argument. But as a matter of fact, this is not what they do. They appeal not to the general feeling of moral rightness, but to precedents, to treaties, and to opinions of specialists. They assume the existence among statesmen and publicists of a series of legal as distinguished from moral obligations in the affairs of nations."
This observation is made by
A. Frederick Pollock B. L. Oppenheim
C. Hans Kelsen D. P.C. Corbett

41. What are essential tests for the existence of International Custom?
A. Uniform practice of States and longevity of time period.
B. Uniform practice of States and opino juris sine necessitatis.
C. Uniform practice of States, longevity of time period and opino juris sine necessitatis.
D. None of the above.

42. In which of the following cases, Judge Alvarez evolved a doctrine that General Assembly resolutions are virtually binding upon States in a legislative sense?
A. South West Africa Voting Procedure case, ICJ Reports, 1975, p.12
B. Western Sahara case, ICJ Reports, 1975, p.12
C. Anglo-Norwegian Fisheries case, ICJ Reports, 1951, p. 152
D. South West Africa Voting Procedure case, ICJ Reports, 1955, p.67

43. Which of the following cases relates to nationality of an individual which is an evidence of the link of an individual with the State?

Codes :

	(a)	(b)	(c)	(d)
A.	1	2	4	3
B.	2	1	4	3
C.	2	1	3	4
D.	3	4	2	1

64. Nuisance is a form of Tort

A. Which is actionable per-se.

B. Which is not actionable per-se.

C. Actionable per-se if plaintiff suffers pecuniary loss.

D. None of the above

65. Assertion (A) : Services rendered to a patient by a Medical Practitioner, by way of consultation, diagnosis and treatment would fall within the ambit of 'services' as defined, in Section 2(1) (O) of the Consumer Protection Act.

Reason (R) : Like other professions, Medical Practitioner should also conduct himself by using of reasonable skill and care.

Find correct answer using codes given below:

Codes :

A. (A) is true and (R) is false.

B. (R) is true, but (A) is false.

C. (A) and (R), both are true, but (R) is not correct explanation of (A).

D. (A) and (R) both are true and (R) is correct explanation of (A).

66. Which of the following is an essential constituent of negligence?

1. Defendant was under a legal duty to exercise due care.
2. This duty was owed to plaintiff.
3. Defendant committed breach of such duty.
4. That the breach of such duty was the direct and proximate cause of the damage alleged.

A. 1, 2 and 3 are correct.

B. 1, 2, 3 and 4 are correct.

C. 2, 3 and 4 are correct.

D. 1, 2 and 4 are correct.

67. The Rule of 'Absolute Liability' was laid down in the case

A. M.C. Mehta Vs. Union of India

B. Madras Railways Co. Vs. Zamidar

C. K. Nagireddi Vs. State of A.P.

D. Minu B. Mehta Vs. Balakrishna

68. Consider the following elements :

1. Infringement of a legal right
2. Legal damage
3. Any damage
4. Existence of legal right

Right to claim damages in Tort would arise only if :

A. 1 and 2 are present.

B. 1, 2 and 4 are present.

C. 1, 3 and 4 are present.

D. 3 and 4 are present.

69. Which statements are correct ?

Directors are

(i) Trustees of Company

(ii) Managers of Company

(iii) Agents of Company

(iv) Owners of Company

Codes :

A. (i) and (ii) are correct.

B. (ii) and (iii) are correct.

C. (iii) and (iv) are correct.

D. (i) and (iii) are correct.

70. Which one of the following is correct statement?

A. Every agency is partnership.

B. Every partnership is agency.

C. Every partnership is limited company.

D. Every private limited company is partnership.

71. Read the following passage and match the column.

No suit to enforce a right arising from a contract shall be initiated in any court by any person suing as a partner in a non-registered firm. Registration of firms is not compulsory. There is no penalty for non-registration. An unregistered firm cannot sue any third person for the enforcement of any right arising from contract.

Column-P	**Column-Q**
a. Registration	1. No penalty
b. Non-registration	2. Optional
c. Partner of a registered firm	3. Unenforceability of his rights
d. Partner of a non-registered firm	4. Can sue

Codes :

	(*a*)	(*b*)	(*c*)	(*d*)
A.	1	2	3	4
B.	2	1	4	3
C.	2	1	3	4
D.	1	3	2	4

72. Assertion (A) : Doctrine of Indoor Management protects an outsider dealing with a company from irregularities inside a company.

Reason (R) : Doctrine of ultra vires protects an outsider dealing with a company for corporate capacity not mentioned in the objects clause.

Choose correct answer from below :

Codes :

A. (A) is true, but (R) is false.
B. (A) is false, but (R) is true.
C. (A) and (R) are true, but (R) is not an explanation of (A).
D. (A) and (R) are true, and (R) is an explanation of (A).

73. Match items in Column-P with items in Column-Q, according to provisions of the Negotiable Instrument Act.

Column-P	**Column-Q**
(*a*) Definition of promissory note	1. Section 30
(*b*) Drawer of cheque	2. Section 45-A
(*c*) Holder's right to duplicate	3. Section 135
(*d*) Dishonour	4. Section 4

Codes :

	(*a*)	(*b*)	(*c*)	(*d*)
A.	2	4	1	3
B.	4	2	3	1
C.	4	1	3	2
D.	4	1	2	3

74. Which statements are correct ?

(i) Partners have right to profit.
(ii) Partners have right to attend general meeting.
(iii) Partners have right to interest.
(iv) Partners have right to appoint proxy.

Codes :

A. (i) and (ii) are correct.
B. (ii) and (iii) are correct.
C. (iii) and (iv) are correct.
D. (i) and (iii) are correct.

75. Match an item in List-P with an item in List-Q.

List-P	**List-Q**
(*a*) Prohibition of assignment of office by Director.	1. Section 267
(*b*) Appointment of alternate Director.	2. Section 312
(*c*) Disqualifications to be a Director.	3. Section 5
(*d*) Officer who is in default.	4. Section 313

Codes :

	(*a*)	(*b*)	(*c*)	(*d*)
A.	4	2	1	3
B.	2	4	1	3
C.	2	4	3	1
D.	2	3	1	4

ANSWERS

1	2	3	4	5	6	7	8	9	10
A	C	B	A	D	C	A	C	C	C
11	12	13	14	15	16	17	18	19	20
D	B	C	A	B	D	C	A	B	B
21	22	23	24	25	26	27	28	29	30
D	B	C	A	D	B	B	C	A	C
31	32	33	34	35	36	37	38	39	40
D	A	A	C	A	D	A	B	C	A
41	42	43	44	45	46	47	48	49	50
C	C	A	D	B	A	A	C	B	B
51	52	53	54	55	56	57	58	59	60
C	D	D	D	D	B	A	D	B	A
61	62	63	64	65	66	67	68	69	70
D	B	B	A	C	B	A	B	D	B
71	72	73	74	75					
B	C	D	D	B					

SOME SELECTED EXPLANATORY ANSWERS

2. The concept of Rule of Law is embodied in Article 14 of the Indian Constitution. The guarantee of equality before the law is an aspect of what Dicey calls the rule of Law in England. It means that no person is above the law and that every person is subject to the jurisdiction of ordinary courts. Professor dicey gave three meanings of the Rule of law thus—(1) Absence of Arbitrary power or supremacy of the law. (2) Equality before the law. (3) The constitution is the result of the ordinary law of the land. According to Article 14, the state shall not deny to any person equality before the law or the equal protection of the laws within the territory of India.

3. Doctrine of Severability or Separability, states that when apart of the statute is declared unconstitutional, then the unconstitutional part is to be removed and the remaining valid portion will continue to be valid. The idea is to retain the Act or legislation in force by discarding/deleting only the void portion and retaining the rest. Article 13 of the Indian constitution provides for the Doctrine of Severability which states that; all laws in force in India before the commencement of constitution shall be void in so far they are inconsistent with the Provisions of the Constitution.

5. Article 40 of the Indian constitution which enshrines one of the Directive Principles of state policy lays down that the state shall take steps to organise village panchayats and endow them with such powers and authority as may be necessary to enable them to function as units of self government. In the light of the experience in the last forty years and in view of the short-comings which have been observed, it is considered that there is an imperative need to enshrine in the constitution certain basic and essential features of Panchayati Raj institutions to impart certainty, continuity and strength to them.

8. The Lok Sabha or House of people is a popular House. Its members are directly elected by the people. Article 81 of the Indian constitution provides the composition of the

House of People. The maximum strength of the House envisaged by the constitution of India is 552, which is made up by election of up to 530 members from the states, upto 20 members from the Union Territories and not more than two members of the Anglo-Indian community to be nominated by the President of India.

12. Audi alteram partem, is a latin maxim which means that "hear the other side too", or hear the alternative party too. It is most often used to refer to the principle that no person should be judged without a fair hearing in which each party is given the opportunity to respond to the evidence against them. Audi alteram partem, is considered a principle of fundamental justice or equity in most legal systems. The principle includes the rights of a party to confront the witnesses against him, to have a fair opportunity to challenge the evidence presented by the other party, to summon one's own witnesses and to present evidence, and to have counsel, if necessary at public expense, in order to make one's case properly. So it can be concluded that the effect of violation of the rule "Audi alteram patrem" on an administrative action, makes it Null and void.

4. Writs are issued by Supreme Court (U/Article 32) and High Courts (U/Article 226), in case of any violation of the fundamental rights. The writ of prohibition is a judicial order to the agencies from continuing their proceedings in excess or abuse of their jurisdiction or in violation of the principles of natural justice or in contravention of the law of the land.

5. 'Certiorari' is a Latin word meaning 'to inform'. Certiorari may be defined as a Judicial order operating in personam and made in the original legal proceedings. The writ is corrective in nature, thus its scope of operation is quite large. The purpose of Certiorari is not only negative but it contains affirmative or positive action also. Writ of certiorari necessarily implies that an error of law apparent on the face of the record, can be corrected. Grounds for the issue of certiorari are: (1) Lack of jurisdiction (2) Excess of Jurisdiction (3) Abuse of Jurisdiction (4) Violation of the principles of natural justice (5) Error of law apparent on the face of the record.

26. Section 307 of the Indian Penal Code, 1860 provides that the definition as to what amounts to an attempt to commit murder. In order to constitute an offence under this section, two elements are essential. First, the intention or knowledge to commit murder. Second, the actual act of trying to commit the murder. Thus, it must have both the necessary *mens rea* and *actus rea*. In the given scenario, both the elements are present as the accused fired two shots from point blank range which proves both knowledge or intention and the actual act of trying to kill the governor.

27. According to Section 361 of the Indian Penal Code, 1860, in the given scenario, the father has committed the offence of kidnapping from the lawful guardianship, because the two essential elements of this section are present here, firstly the girl is a minor, secondly the father forcefully removed the daughter from the school, without the consent of guardian *i.e.*, the mother. Section 361, states that whoever takes or entice any minor under sixteen years of age if a male or under eighteen years of age if a female, out of the keeping of the lawful guardian of such minor, without the consent of such guardian, is said to kidnap such minor or person from lawful guardian.

28. A woman cannot be prosecuted for gang rape, because Rape is a crime committed by a male against the female. According to Section 375 of the Indian Penal Code, 1860, A man is said to commit rape, who except in the cases hereinafter excepted, has sexual intercourse with a woman under circumstances falling under any of the six following descriptions namely: (1) Against her will, (2) Without her consent, (3) With her consent, where it has been obtained by putting her or any person in whom she is interested in fear of death or of hurt, (4) With her consent, when the man knows that he is not her husband, (5) With her consent, when, at the time of giving such consent, by reason of unsoundness of mind or intoxication is unable to understand the nature and consequences, (6) With or without her consent, when she is under 16 years of age. So it is crystal clear from the above section the female or woman can never be prosecuted for gang rape, as it is a crime against women.

29. According to Section 405 of the Indian Penal Code, 1860, criminal breach of trust is an offence which signifies Entrustment. This section states that, whoever, being in any manner entrusted with property or with any dominion over property, dishonestly misappropriates or converts to his own use that property or dishonestly uses or disposes of that property in violation of any direction of law prescribing the mode in which such trust is to be discharged, commits "criminal breach of trust".

30. According to Section 107, Explanation 1 of the Indian Penal Code, 1860, in the given scenario, 'Z' has committed the offence of Abetment by False representation or by wilful misrepresentation. Section 107 states that; A person abets the doing of a thing who—(1) Instigates any person to do that thing (2) Engages with one or more persons in any conspiracy for the doing of that thing (3) Intentionally aids, by any act or illegal omission, the doing of that thing (4) A person who, by wilful misrepresentation or by wilful concealment of a material fact, which he is bound to disclose, voluntarily causes or procures, or attempts to cause or procure, a thing to be done, is said to instigate the doing of that thing.

31. According to Section 497 of the Indian Pe Code, 1860, a married man commits adulte if he commits sexual intercourse with married woman. This section defines, Adulte as, whoever has sexual intercourse with person who is and whom he knows or l reason to believe to be wife of another m without the consent or connivance of t man, such sexual intercourse not amounti to the offence of rape, is guilty of the offer of adultery, and shall be punished w imprisonment of either description for a te which may extend to five years. In such c the wife shall not be punishable as an abett

49. Section 13 (ib) of the Hindu Marriage A 1955, states that, any marriage Solemnis whether before or after the commencement this Act, may, on a petition presented either husband or the wife, be dissolved b decree of divorce on the ground that the ot party—has deserted the petitioner fo continuous period of not less than two ye immediately preceding the presentation the petition.

50. The breakdown of marriage is defined "such failure in the matrimonial relations or such circumstances adverse to that relat that no reasonable probability remains the spouses again living together as husb and wife." If a marriage has broken do beyond all possibilities of repair, than should be brought to an end, without look into the causes of breakdown and with fixing any responsibility on either party. S marriage should be dissolved even if one the parties to the marriage does not desire This ground was recommended as additional ground of Divorce, by the L Commission of India, in its 71st Report.

51. Section 7 of the Hindu Marriage Act, 19 provides for the ceremonies for a Hi Marriage. According to Section 7(2), s rites and ceremonies include the saptap (that is, the taking of seven steps by bridegroom and the bride jointly before sacred fire), the marriage becomes complete and binding when the seventh step is taken.

53. Dower (Mehar) is a sale price of woman, was upheld in Abdul Kadir case. Dower of Mehar is a peculiar muslim law concept. It is a sum of money promised by the husband to be paid or delivered to the wife in the consideration of the marriage, and even where no dower is expressly fixed or mentioned at the marriage ceremony, the law confers the right of dower upon the wife. It is an obligation imposed upon the husband as a mark of respect for the wife.

54. Iddat is a period during which it is incumbent upon a woman, whose marriage has been dissolved by divorce or death to remain in seclusion, and to abstain from marrying another man. The abstinence is imposed to ascertain whether she is pregnant by the husband, so as to avoid confusion of the parentage. Not merely the woman is prohibited from marrying during the Iddat period, even the husband of the woman can't remarry during the period she is undergoing Iddat. The husband to provide maintenance to her during the period of Iddat.

64. According to the Law of Torts, Nuisance is a form of Tort, which is actionable per-se. The term nuisance has exhaustive and diverse definitions. The word nuisance is derived from the French word 'nuire', to hurt, or to annoy. In Durga Prasad Vs. State, it was observed that nuisance ordinarily means anything, which annoys, hurts or that which is offensive. Nuisance is of two kinds *i.e.*, Public or Common nuisance and Private nuisance.

66. Generally speaking one is responsible for the direct consequences of his negligent acts where he is placed in such a position with regard to another that it is obvious that if he does not use due care in his own conduct he will cause injury to another. Actionable negligence consists in the neglect of the use of ordinary care or skill towards a person to whom the defendant owes the duty of observing ordinary care or skill, by which neglect the plaintiff has suffered injury, to his person or property. In an action for negligence, the plaintiff has to prove the following essentials: (1) That the defendant owed duty of care to the plaintiff. (2) The defendant made a breach of the duty *i.e.*, he failed to exercise due care and skill. (3) Plaintiff suffered damage as a consequence thereof.

67. The Supreme Court of India evolved the 'rule of Absolute liability' in M.C. Mehta Vs. Union of India (AIR 1987), as part of Indian Law in preference to the rule of strict liability laid down in Rylands Vs. Fletcher. It expressly declares that the new rule was not subject to any of the exceptions under the Rylands rule. The court observed: 'This rule (Rylands Vs Fletcher) evolved in the 19th century at a time when all these developments of science and technology had not taken place. We have to evolve new principles and lay down new norms which would adequately deal with the new problems which arise in a highly industrialized economy.

Previous Paper (Solved)

UGC-NET LAW, June 2012

PAPER-II

Note : *This paper contains fifty (50) objective type questions, each question carrying two (2) marks each. **All** questions are compulsory.*

1. The Supreme Court held in which of the following cases that preamble is not the part of the Constitution of India

A. Berubari case

B. A. K. Gopalan case

C. Balaji Case

D. Minerva Mill's case

2. Article 16(4A) which gives power to the State to make laws regarding reservation in favour of Scheduled Castes and Scheduled Tribes was added by the

A. 75th Amendment to the Constitution of India.

B. 76th Amendment to the Constitution of India.

C. 77th Amendment to the Constitution of India.

D. 78th Amendment to the Constitution of India.

3. The protection and improvement of environment including forests and wild life of the country is

A. Directive Principle of State Policy

B. Fundamental National Policy

C. Fundamental Duty of a Citizen

D. Both Directive Principle of State Policy and Fundamental Duty of a Citizen

4. Originally the Supreme Court consisted of a Chief Justice and

A. Seven other judges

B. Twelve other judges

C. Thirteen other judges

D. Fifteen other judges

5. A resolution passed under Clause (1) of Article 249 shall remain in force for such period not exceeding

A. Three months B. Six months

C. Nine months D. Twelve months

6. The President's rule under Article 356 of the Constitution of India remains valid in the State for maximum period of

A. One month B. Three months

C. Six months D. One year

7. The power of the Parliament to amend the Constitution of India is a constituent power laid down in Article 368 by

A. Twenty Fourth Amendment Act

B. Twenty Sixth Amendment Act

C. Forty Second Amendment Act

D. Forty Fourth Amendment Act

8. 'Jurisprudence is as big as law and bigger'. Who said this?

A. Austin B. Lloyds

C. Lewellyn D. Holland

9. "Rousseau is a Janus like figure in the history of national law" – who said this?

A. Hobbes B. J. S. Mill

C. Locke D. Barker

10. Match List-I (Jurist) with List-II (Assumption) and select the correct answer using the codes given below the lists:

List-I	List-II
I. Acquinars	(a) Jural postulates
II. Pound	(b) Spirit of people
III. Kelsen	(c) Ground norm
IV. Savigny	(d) Reason and will in law

Codes:

	I	II	III	IV
A.	(b)	(d)	(c)	(a)
B.	(d)	(b)	(c)	(a)
C.	(b)	(d)	(a)	(c)
D.	(d)	(b)	(a)	(c)

11. Match List-I with List-II and select the correct answer using the codes given below the lists

List-I	List-II
I. Law in a changing society	(a) Fuller
II. Human Law and Human Justice	(b) Friedmann
III. The morality of law	(c) Stone
IV. Ancient law	(d) Main

Codes:

	I	II	III	IV
A.	(a)	(c)	(b)	(d)
B.	(c)	(a)	(b)	(d)
C.	(b)	(a)	(d)	(c)
D.	(a)	(b)	(d)	(c)

12. Which one of the following schools of Jurisprudence considers that "a reasoned scale of values can be discovered as a basis for legal development"?

A. Sociological B. Historical
C. Analytical D. Philosophical

13. According to Salmond, the correlative of liberty is

A. Duty B. No rights
C. Subjection D. Disabilities

14. **Assertion (A) :** Customs to have the force of law must be immemorial.

Reason (R) : Custom represents common consciousness of people.

Codes:

A. Both (A) and (R) are true and (R) is the correct explanation of (A).
B. Both (A) and (R) are true and (R) is not a correct explanation of (A).
C. (A) is true, but (R) is false.
D. (A) is false, but (R) is true.

15. **Assertion (A) :** International Court of Justice has power to decide cases on the basis of equity.

Reason (R) : Equity is one of the General Principles of Law recognized by Civilized Nations.

Codes:

A. Both (A) and (R) are true and (R) is correct explanation of (A).
B. Both (A) and (R) are true, but (R) is not a correct explanation of (A).
C. (A) is true, but (R) is false.
D. (A) is false, but (R) is true.

16. Match List-I with List-II:

List-I (Subject Matter)	List-II (Cases)
(a) International Custom	(i) S. S. Lotus (France v. Turkey) PCIJ, Series A, No. 10
(b) Res Judicata	(ii) U. N. Administrative Tribunal case, International Law Reports, 1954, P. 310
(c) Legal status of General Assembly Resolutions on decolonization and self determination	(iii) Western Sahara Case, Advisory Opinion, ICJ Rep., 1975, P. 12
(d) Human Rights	(iv) Lawless Case, American Journal of International Law, Vol. 56, 1962, P. 187

Codes:

	(a)	(b)	(c)	(d)
A.	(i)	(ii)	(iii)	(iv)
B.	(ii)	(i)	(iii)	(iv)
C.	(iii)	(ii)	(i)	(iv)
D.	(iv)	(ii)	(iii)	(i)

17. U. N. Commission on Human Rights has been discarded and replaced by

A. Economic, Social and Cultural Rights Committee
B. Amnesty International
C. Human Rights Committee
D. Human Rights Council

18. Which of the following is not a primary source of International Law?

A. International Treaty
B. Decision of International Court of Justice
C. International Custom
D. General Principle of Law recognized by Civilized Nations

19. Which of the following cases relates to retroactive nature of the act of recognition of government?

A. Aksionairnoye Obschestro A.M. Luthar Vs. James Sagor & Co., (1921) 3 K.B. P. 532

B. Trendtex Trading Corporation Vs. Central Bank of Nigeria, (1977) B. P. 529
C. Central Air Transport Inc. Vs. Central Air Transport Corporation, (1953) A. C. P. 70
D. Nicaragua Vs. U.S.A., ICJ Rep., 1984, P. 169.

20. In a case concerning the legality of the Threat or use of Nuclear Weapons, the International Court of Justice gave advisory opinion at the request of:
A. U.N. Security Council
B. U. N. General Assembly
C. World Health Organization
D. United Nations Educational and Cultural Organization

21. Which is not the modern source of Hindu Law?
A. Equity, Justice and Good Conscience
B. Precedent
C. Sruti
D. Legislation

22. Consider the following propositions and give the correct answer
I. A void marriage remains valid until a decree annulling it has been passed by a competent court.
II. A void marriage is never a valid marriage and there is no necessity of any decree annulling it.
III. A voidable marriage is regarded as a valid marriage until a decree annulling it has been passed by a competent court.

Codes:
A. I, II and III are correct
B. I and II are correct
C. II and III are correct
D. I and III are correct

23. Assertion (A) : Break down of marriage as such is not a ground for Divorce.

Reason (R) : It may result into an easy way of dissolution of marriage and shall result into instability in the society.

Codes:
A. Both (A) and (R) are correct.
B. (A) is correct, but (R) is incorrect.
C. Both (A) and (R) are wrong.
D. (R) is correct, but (A) is wrong.

24. Dastane Vs. Dastane is a case decided by the Supreme Court relating to:
A. Adultery B. Dessertion
C. Cruelty D. None of the above

25. Marriages of all persons who are citizens of India belonging to various religions should by made compulsory registrable in their respective States where the marriage is solemnised. This was held by the Supreme Court in the case of:
A. Githa Hariharn Vs. RBI
B. Seema Vs. Ashwani Kumar
C. John Vallamathom Vs. Union of India
D. None of the above

26. Assertion (A) : The Hindu Marriage Act, 1955 brought changes like prohibition of polygamy and prigamy and permission for inter-caste marriages.

Reason (R) : The changes were brought under social pressure.

Codes:
A. Both (A) and (R) are true and (R) is correct explanation of (A).
B. Both (A) and (R) are true but (R) is not the correct explanation of (A).
C. (A) is correct but (R) is false.
D. (A) is false but (R) is true.

27. An agreement made by mistake is
A. Void B. Voidable
C. Illegal D. Immoral

28. Which of the following statements are true?
(i) Minor's contract can be ratified on attaining majority.
(ii) Minor's contract cannot be ratified on attaining majority.
(iii) Minor's contract can be ratified jointly by both the parties to the contract.
(iv) Minor is not liable under minor's contract.

Codes:
A. (i) and (iii) B. (ii) and (iv)
C. (i) and (ii) D. (ii) and (iii)

29. Assertion (A) : Damages must be related to damage.

Reason (R) : Damage is damaging and damages are compensating.

Codes:

A. Both (A) and (R) are true, but (R) is not correct explanation of (A).

B. Both (A) and (R) are true, and (R) is correct explanation of (A).

C. (A) is true, but (R) is false.

D. (A) is false, but (R) is true.

30. Arrange the following concepts in sequence in which they appeared. Use the codes given below:

(i) Offer by x to y

(ii) Undue influence of x over y

(iii) Demand of damages by y from x

(iv) Acceptance of the offer by y.

Codes:

A. (i), (ii), (iii), (iv) B. (i), (iv), (iii), (ii)

C. (ii), (i), (iv), (iii) D. (ii), (iv), (i), (iii)

31. Which one of the following pairs is correctly matched?

A. In India, consideration must follow........ from promisee only.

B. In India, consideration must follow.......... from only promisor or only promisee.

C. In India, consideration must follow......... from promisor or any other person.

D. In India, consideration must follow........... promisee or any other person.

32. Assertion (A) : Collateral transactions to wagering agreements are valid.

Reason (R) : Only wagering agreements are declared void under Section 30 of the Indian Contract Act.

Codes:

A. (A) is true, but (R) is false.

B. (A) is false, but (R) is true.

C. Both (A) and (R) are true, but (R) is not correct explanation of (A).

D. Both (A) and (R) are true and (R) is correct explanation of (A).

33. Liability in torts depends on

A. quantum of damages suffered

B. involvement of intention

C. infringement of legal right

D. effect of public interest

34. Which of the following ingredients are essential to make master liable for the acts of the servant?

(1) Tort was committed by the servant.

(2) Tort was committed in the course of employment.

(3) Express authority was given by master.

(4) Master has knowledge of all constituent offers of tort.

Codes:

A. 1, 2, 3 B. 1, 2, 4

C. 3, 4 D. 1, 2

35. Which of the following is an essential constituent of negligence?

(1) Defendant was under or legal duty to exercise due care

(2) This duty was owed to plantiff

(3) Defendant committed breach of such duty

(4) That the breach of such duty was the direct and proximate cause of the damage alleged.

Codes:

A. 1, 2 and 3 B. 1, 2, 3 and 4

C. 2, 3 and 4 D. 1, 2 and 4

36. Which one of the following is not a good defence in suits for damages or negligence?

A. Contributory Negligence

B. Express contract with plantiff

C. Express contract where statute prohibits

D. Voluntary assumptions of risk

37. Match List-I with List-II and select the correct answer using the codes given below the lists

List-I	List-II
(a) Rayland Vs Fletcher	1. Compensation for pain and suffering
(b) Donoghue Vs. Stevenson	2. Loss caused by Competition in business
(c) Gludster Grammer School Case	3. Strict liability
(d) Rose Vs. Ford	4. Liability of minor for tests
	5. Liability for negligence

Codes:

	(a)	(b)	(c)	(d)
A.	1	2	3	4
B.	2	3	4	5
C.	3	5	2	1
D.	3	4	2	1

38. Assertion (A) : Tort is a civil wrong redressible by an action for unliquidated damages only.

Reason (R) : Law does not provide compensation in the nature of liquidated damages.

Codes:

A. Both (A) and (R) are true and (R) is correct explanation of (A).

B. Both (A) and (R) are true but (R) is not the correct explanation of (A).

C. (A) is true but (R) is false.

D. (A) is false but (R) is true.

39. 'Z' while walking along a deserted road at night during winter saw a just born baby abandoned on a side. For a moment he realized that he could save the baby without appreciable trouble, expense or loss of his time and also felt that if the baby is left over unprotected, it might die. But he did nothing and went away.

'P' another person also passed through that road and saw the baby and acted just like 'Z' and went away. Next morning the infant baby died of exposure.

Decide who is responsible?

A. Only 'Z' who saw first

B. 'P' for omitting to be compassionate

C. Both 'Z' and 'P' for negligence

D. Neither 'Z' nor 'P' is responsible

40. Decide on whom criminal liability can be fixed on the following :

The accused 'P' caught hold of the victim and exhorted on the main accused 'L' to strike the victim; upon which he inflicted a kirpan wound and consequently the victim died.

Assertions :

(i) 'P' is liable for punishment.

(ii) 'P' and 'L' are both liable for common intention.

(iii) 'P' and 'L' are both responsible for victims death for having common object.

(iv) 'P' is not liable for any offence.

Reasons:

A. (i) is quite possible

B. (ii) is reasonable

C. (iii) is as occasion demands

D. (iv) is most accurate

41. 'M' a quack, an uneducated in matters of surgery, had performed an operation on a man for internal piles with the help of ordinary knife, unlike previous occasions, for which the man died due to haemorrhage. Decide on 'M''s liability.

(i) 'M' is a recognised quack and hence not liable.

(ii) 'M''s profession is not legally acceptable hence liable.

(iii) 'M' is not liable because the man consented for such operation.

(iv) 'M' is not liable because it was a post-operational syndrome

The probable answer is :

A. Statement (i) is correct

B. Statement (ii) is correct

C. Statement (iii) is correct

D. Statement (iii) and (iv) are correct

42. Fill in the gap:

'P' in support of a just claim of 'Q' has stated against 'Z', for a sum of Rupees one thousand and falsely sweared on a trial that he heard 'Z' admitted as to the just claim of 'Q'. The court decides that it was an affirmation of ________.

A. Statement of truth

B. False evidence

C. Making a declaration

D. None of them

43. One of the essentials of holding a person responsible for dowry death is

A. subjected to harassment by peer groups.

B. subjected to harassment for dowry

C. subjected to harassment under suspicious circumstances

D. All of them

44. Fill in the gap:

An act of grievous hurt is always inferred through enormity to _______ and not merely a slight more than a frolic.

A. Murder B. Bodily injury

C. Amputation D. All of them

45. Assertion (A) : Before Bangalore Water Supply case educational institutions were excluded from the definition of an industry.

Reason (R) : Main purpose of such institutions is to impart education, and not to run business or trade.

Codes:

A. Both (A) and (R) are true and (R) is the correct explanation.

B. Both (A) and (R) are true but (R) is not the correct explanation.

C. (A) is true but (R) is false.

D. (A) is false but (R) is true.

46. An individual dispute becomes industrial dispute when it is taken up by

A. Union only.

B. Union or substantial number of workmen.

C. Continuous support of union.

D. Subsequent support of union.

47. Which of the following statements are true?

I. All employees are workmen.

II. All employees are not workmen.

III. All workmen are employees.

IV. All managerial staff are workmen.

Codes:

A. I and II B. II and III

C. III and IV D. I and III

48. In which of the following cases the Supreme Court held that medical representative is not workman?

A. Standard Vacuum Oil Company Vs. Commissioner of Labour

B. Anand Bazar Patrika Vs. Its Workmen

C. Workmen Vs. Greaves Cotton & Co.

D. J & J Dechane Vs. State of Kerala

49. Which one of the following statement is true?

A. The general funds of a registered trade union shall not be spent on the payment of salaries.

B. A registered Trade union may constitute a separate fund for the promotion of the civic and political interests.

C. No appeal lies against the order of refusal of the Registrar to register a Trade union.

D. Every registered Trade Union shall not be a body corporate.

50. Match List-I with List-II and select the correct answer using the codes given below:

List-I (Subject)	List-II (Provisions of Trade Union Act, 1926)
(i) Appointment of Registrar	1. Section 24
(ii) Appeal	2. Section 10
(iii) Amalgamation of Trade Unions	3. Section 3
(iv) Cancellation of registration	4. Section 11

Codes:

	(i)	(ii)	(iii)	(iv)
A.	2	4	1	3
B.	4	1	3	2
C.	3	4	1	2
D.	1	3	2	1

ANSWERS

1	2	3	4	5	6	7	8	9	10
A	C	D	A	D	C	A	C	D	A
11	**12**	**13**	**14**	**15**	**16**	**17**	**18**	**19**	**20**
B	D	B	D	A	A	D	B	C	B
21	**22**	**23**	**24**	**25**	**26**	**27**	**28**	**29**	**30**
C	C	A	C	B	C	A	B	A	C
31	**32**	**33**	**34**	**35**	**36**	**37**	**38**	**39**	**40**
D	D	C	D	B	C	C	C	D	B
41	**42**	**43**	**44**	**45**	**46**	**47**	**48**	**49**	**50**
B	B	B	A	A	B	B	D	B	C

PAPER-III

Note : *This paper contains* ***seventy five (75)*** *objective type questions of* ***two (2)*** *marks each.* ***All*** *questions are compulsory.*

1. "The new Constitution establishes, indeed a system of Government which is at the most quasi-federal, almost devolutionary in character, a unitary state with subsidiary federal features rather than the federal state with unitary features" said by

A. Dr. K.C. Wheare
B. Dr. Rajendra Prasad
C. Dr. B.R. Ambedkar
D. Pandit Jawaharlal Nehru

2. In which of the following case it was held that 'Right to Life does not include Right to Die'?

A. Gian Kaur Vs. State of Punjab
B. Chenna Jagdeshwar Vs. State of A.P.
C. State of U.P. Vs. Sanjay Kumar Bhatia
D. Deena Vs. Union Bank of India

3. **Assertion (A) :** An accused person cannot be compelled to give his signature or thumb impression.

Reason (R) : An accused person cannot be compelled to be a witness against himself.

Codes:

A. (A) is true but (R) is false.
B. (A) is false but (R) is true.
C. Both (A) and (R) are true.
D. Both (A) and (R) are false.

4. After a Money Bill has been passed by the House of the People, within how many days it is transmitted to the Council of States for its recommendations?

A. Thirty days B. Twenty four days
C. Sixty days D. Fourteen days

5. **Assertion (A) :** Directive Principles are not enforceable by any Court.

Reason (R) : Directive Principles are more or less fundamental in the governance of the country.

Codes:

A. Both (A) and (R) are true but (R) is not the correct explanation of (A).
B. Both (A) and (R) are true and (R) is the correct explanation of (A).
C. (A) is false but (R) is true.
D. (A) is true but (R) is false.

6. The Supreme Court does not have original jurisdiction regarding a dispute between

A. a citizen and a State
B. the Government of India and one State
C. two States
D. the Government of India and one State on one side and one State on the other side

7. In the Constitution of India, provision relating to the formation of new States can be amended by

A. A Parliamentary resolution which should be ratified by majority of State Legislatures.
B. A simple majority in each House of Parliament.
C. 3/4th majority in the Parliament
D. 2/3rd majority in the each House of Parliament provided they also constitute the majority of total members of each House.

8. Holding of periodic, free and fair elections by the Election Commission is part of the basic structure of the Constitution as per the following:

A. Election Commission of India Vs. AIADMK
B. S.S. Dhanoa Vs. Union of India
C. In Gujarat Assembly Election matter
D. Sadiq Ali Vs. Election Commission of India

9. Writ of *Mandamus* cannot be issued, where a fundamental right is infringed by

A. A Statute
B. A Statutory Order
C. An Executive Order
D. Private Body

10. **Assertion (A) :** The principles of natural justice ensures fair hearing.

Reason (R) : It requires unbiased judge to decide after hearing all parties.

Codes:

A. Both (A) and (R) are true and (R) is good explanation of (A).

B. Both (A) and (R) are true and (R) is not a good explanation of (A).

C. (A) is true, but (R) is false.

D. (A) is false, but (R) is true.

11. Prerogative writs to review an administrative action are:

A. Two : Writ of Habeas Corpus and Writ of Mandamus.

B. Three : Writ of Habeas Corpus and Writ of Mandamus and Writ of Prohibition.

C. Four : Writ of Habeas Corpus and Writ of Mandamus and Writ of Prohibition and Writ of Certiorari and Writ of Quo Warranto.

D. Five : Writ of Habeas Corpus, Writ of Mandamus, Writ of Quo warranto, Writ of Certiorari and Writ of Prohibition.

12. A mandatory procedural requirement for an administrative tribunal must be

A. Legal representation

B. Cross examination

C. Reasoned decision

D. All of the above

13. Judicial review of an administrative action means

A. Review by the Parliament

B. Review by the Government

C. Review by the Legislative Assembly

D. Review by the Judiciary

14. Match an item in List-I with correct answer in List-II.

List-I	List-II
Institution of Lokpal and Lokayukta	A. Law should be able to control the numerous wide discretionary powers
	B. Ensure fair hearing
	C. Evaporate maladministration and corruption to bring good governance
	D. Check and control abuse of power and executive excesses

15. Find correct answer:

A. Administrative law is a branch of public law and is only a part of Constitutional law. It cannot control the Constitutional law.

B. Administrative law is a branch of private law.

C. Administrative law is independent to Constitutional law.

D. Administrative law is neither the branch of public law nor of private law, but a part of Constitutional law.

16. Bentham's definition of law is imperative in nature because

A. law is an assembling of signs.

B. law is declaration of volition conceived or adopted by sovereign in a State.

C. because it is adopted by non-sovereign State.

D. (A) & (B) both

17. The term 'Legal theory' has been first time used by

A. Llewlyne B. Ihring

C. Salmond D. W. Friedman

18. Bracket theory of corporate personality is also known as

A. Concession theory B. Symbolist theory

C. Fiction theory D. Will theory

19. 'A' says to 'B' that he will give a sum of rupees five thousand if 'B' marries his daughter, this is

A. Vested Right B. Contingent Right

C. Primary Right D. Secondary Right

20. Assertion (A) : Kelsen follows Kant in distinguishing between 'is' and 'ought'.

Reason (R) : Kelsen is a forerunner of philosophical school.

Codes:

A. Both (A) and (R) are true, and (R) is the correct explanation of (A).

B. Both (A) and (R) are true but (R) is not a correct explanation of (A).

C. (A) is true, but (R) is false.

D. (A) is false, but (R) is true.

21. The possession is the

A. five point in ownership

B. seven point in ownership

C. nine point in ownership
D. ten point in ownership

22. Which of the following duties have been included by Austin in the category of 'absolute duties'?
I. Duties owed to persons indefinitely
II. Self regarding duties
III. Duties owed to the sovereign
IV. Duties owed to the parents
Select the correct answer using the codes
Codes:
A. I, III and IV B. II, III and IV
C. I, II and IV D. I, II and III

23. Which one of the following get along correctly?
A. Trust and co-ownership
B. Legal and contingent ownership
C. Sole and limited ownership
D. Legal and equitable ownership

24. A person who causes bodily injury to another who is labouring under a disorder, disease or bodily infirmity and thereby accelerates the death of the person. Under which it shall be deemed to have caused his death?
A. Explanation I to Section 299
B. Explanation I to Section 300
C. Explanation II to Section 299
D. Explanation II to Section 300

25. In which provision of Indian Penal Code the definition of 'valuable security' is explained?
A. Section 29 B. Section 30
C. Section 31 D. Section 13

26. State the age limit prescribed under Section 82 of Indian Penal Code in which if a child commits an overt act is not considered as an offence?
A. Under the age of 12 years.
B. Under the age of 7 years.
C. Under the age of 16 years.
D. Under the age of 18 years.

27. When the injury is intentional and sufficient to cause death in the ordinary course of nature and death follows. The offence is of the category:
A. Attempt to murder
B. Culpable homicide not amounting to murder
C. Murder
D. Attempt to suicide

28. **Principle** : Theft + Violence or Threat to violence = Robbery.
Facts : M meets B and her child on a river bridge. M takes the child and threatens to fling it down to the river unless B delivers her purse. B in consequence delivers her purse.
What offence 'M' has committed?
A. M is liable for theft.
B. M is liable for coercion.
C. M is liable for robbery.
D. M is liable for extortion.

29. Fill in the gap:
A disability for ________ days constitutes grievous hurt.
A. A week
B. A fortnight
C. A month
D. A minimum of twenty days

30. Fill in the gap with appropriate word : Wrongful restraint means keeping a person from out of his ________ of his residence.
A. House B. Place
C. Hotel D. Guest House

31. Fill in the gap which is more appropriate.
Inducing a girl under 18 years of age to go away with him from ________ is an offence of
A. Normal home B. Place of work
C. Domestic area D. Any place

32. Find the correct answer :
The principle of intergenerational equity envisages:
A. Conservation of options
B. Conservation of quality
C. Conservation of access
D. All the above

33. Find the correct answer:
The Supreme Court allowed compensation of ₹ 23.84 lakhs and later allowed additional compensation of ₹ 47 lakhs to the farmers whose crops got damaged, being irrigated by subsoil water drawn from a stream which was polluted from untreated effluents of 22 industries. It was decided in the case of

A. Vellore Citizens Welfare Forum vs. Union of India
B. Indian Council For Environment Action vs. Union of India
C. S. Jagannath vs. Union of India
D. Narmada Bachao Andolan vs. Union of India

34. The concept of sustainable development contains which of the following essentials?
A. The precautionary principle
B. The polluter pays principle
C. The doctrine of public trust
D. All above

35. **Assertion (A) :** The Supreme Court in *Banwasi Seva Ashram vs. State of Uttar Pradesh*, permitted the government agency to acquire the forest land, ousting certain tribal dwellers to implement a power project only after they agreed to provide certain facilities approved by the Court.
Reason (R) : Because the governmental action had an environmental impact that threatened to dislocate poor forest dwellers and disrupt their life-style infringing their fundamental right to life, which include the right to livelihood.
Codes:
A. (A) is true and (R) is false.
B. (A) and (R) both are true, but (R) is not a correct explanation of (A).
C. (A) is false and (R) is true.
D. Both (A) and (R) are true and (R) is good explanation of (A).

36. The Supreme Court observed that noise pollution cannot be tolerated, even if such noise was a direct result of and was connected with religious activities in the case of
A. A.P. Pollution Control Board vs. Prof M.V. Naidu
B. Church of God (Full Gospel) in India vs. KKR Majestic Colony Welfare Association.
C. K.M. Chinappa vs. Union of India
D. Narmada Bachao Andolan vs. Union of India

37. **Assertion (A) :** Nobody can claim a fundamental right to create noise pollution by amplifying the sound of his speech with the help of loudspeaker.
Reason (R) : While one has a right to speech, others have a right to listen or decline to listen. Anyone who wishes to live in peace, comfort and quiet within his house has a fundamental right to prevent the noise as pollutantion reaching him.
Codes:
A. (A) is true, but (R) is false.
B. (A) is false, but (R) is true.
C. Both (A) and (R) are true, but (R) is not a correct explanation.
D. Both (A) and (R) are true and (R) is good explanation of (A)

38. In which of the following cases it was held that there is no reason to compel non-smokers to be helpless victims of air pollution?
A. Samantha Vs. State of A.P.
B. M.C. Mehta Vs. Union of India
C. Murli Deora Vs. Union of India
D. Sheela Barse Vs. Union of India

39. Protection and improvement of environment and safeguarding forests and wildlife is
A. A fundamental right
B. One of the Directive Principles of State Policy.
C. One of the Fundamental Duties
D. Both one of the Directive Principles of State Policy and one of the Fundamental Duties

40. Who stated that international law is not true law but 'positive international morality' only, analogous to the rules binding a club or society?
A. Oscar Schachter B. John Austin
C. Louis Flenkin D. Hans Kelson

41. *Opino juris sive necessitatis means*
A. Opinions of jurists is necessary evidence for determining rules of international custom
B. Opinions of jurists is not necessary for ascertaining the rules of international law
C. The feeling on the part of States that in acting as they do they are fulfilling a legal obligation
D. None of the above

42. Which of the following cases supports constitutive theory of recognition, namely, the act of recognition alone confers international personality on an entity purporting to be a state or clothes new government with an authority to enter into international relations?

A. The Arantzazu Mendi, (1939) A.C. P 256

B. A.M. Luther Vs. James Sagor & Co, (1921) 3 K.B. P.532

C. Tinoco Concessions, (1923) 1 United Nations Reports of International Arbitral Awards P 369

D. None of the above

43. Which of the following statements is true?

A. Nationality is the evidence of the link or relations of an individual with the State whereas domicile denotes *de facto* residence of an individual in a State with an intention to permanently settle there.

B. Nationality is an evidence of residence of an individual with an intention to permanently settle there.

C. Domicile denotes the link or relations of an individual with the State.

D. None of the above

44. The Charter of the Untied Nations came into force on

A. 26 June 1945 B. 10 December 1945

C. 24 October 1945 D. 1 November 1945

45. A member of the United Nations which has persistently violated the principles contained in the Charter may be expelled from the United Nations by the

A. Security Council

B. General Assembly

C. General Assembly upon the recommendation of the Security Council

D. Security Council upon the recommendation of the General Assembly

46. The Judges of the International Court of Justice are elected by the

A. General Assembly

B. Security Council

C. General Assembly upon recommendation of the Security Council

D. General Assembly and the Security Council independently of one another

47. Under Section 6 of the Hindu Minority and Guardianship Act, 1956 the natural guardian of a minor child is

A. Mother

B. Father

C. Both Mother and Father

D. Either Mother or Father

48. A Muslim wife can relinquish her Mahr

A. When she is minor

B. When she has attained the age of puberty

C. When she is not less than 18 years of age

D. When she is not less than 21 years of age.

49. In Islamic Law "Faskh" means

A. Restitution of conjugal rights

B. Judicial separation

C. Dissolution or rescission of the contract of marriage by judicial decree at the instance of the husband.

D. Dissolution on rescission of the contract of marriage by judicial decree at the instance of the wife.

50. Muta marriage is recognised by

A. Hanafi School B. Maliki School

C. Ithna Ashari School D. Hanbali School

51. The term 'Hindu' denotes the person

(i) Professing Hindu Religion

(ii) Professing Buddh, Jain or Sikh Religion

(iii) Who are not professing Muslim, Christian, Parsi or Jew Religion.

In respect of the aforesaid propositions which is correct?

A. (i) and (ii) are correct but (iii) is incorrect.

B. (ii) and (iii) are correct and (i) is incorrect.

C. (i) and (iii) are correct and (ii) is incorrect.

D. (i), (ii) and (iii) are all correct.

52. Match the List-I with List-II using the codes given below :

List-I	List-II
(a) Void Marriages	(i) Section 9
(b) Voidable marriages	(ii) Section 11
(c) Divorce	(iii) Section 13
(d) Restitution of Conjugal Rights	(iv) Section 12

Codes:

	(a)	(b)	(c)	(d)
A.	(ii)	(iv)	(iii)	(i)
B.	(iv)	(iii)	(ii)	(i)
C.	(iii)	(i)	(ii)	(iv)
D.	(i)	(ii)	(iii)	(iv)

53. In which of the following case the Court held that Section 9 of the Hindu Marriage Act was Constitutionally violative of right to Human dignity and privacy?
A. Bipin Chandra Vs. Prabhavati
B. T. Sareetha Vs. T. Venkatasubah
C. Lachman Vs. Meena
D. None of the above

54. Match the List-I with List-II and indicate the correct answer using the codes given below:

List-I	List-II
(a) Pre-Marriage Pregnancy	(i) Divorce
(b) Marriage within Prohibited Degree Relationship	(ii) Voidable Marriage
(c) Cruelty	(iii) Void Marriage
(d) When any spouse without reasonable excuse withdraws from the society of the other	(iv) Restitution of Conjugal Rights

Codes:

	(a)	(b)	(c)	(d)
A.	(ii)	(iv)	(i)	(iii)
B.	(ii)	(iii)	(i)	(iv)
C.	(iv)	(ii)	(iii)	(i)
D.	(i)	(ii)	(iii)	(iv)

55. International Women's Day is celebrated every year on
A. 2nd March B. 4th March
C. 6th March D. 8th March

56. Which one of the following is correct according to Art I of the Universal Declaration of Human Rights, 1948?
A. All human beings are born free and equal in rights.
B. All human beings are born free, equal and dignity
C. All human beings are equal in dignity and rights.
D. All human beings are born free and equal in rights and dignity.

57. Regional Human Rights Court does not exist in
A. Africa B. Europe
C. America D. Asia

58. Which protocol to the European Convention on Human Rights has abolished European Commission of Human Rights?
A. Protocol 1 B. Protocol 2
C. Protocol 3 D. Protocol 11

59. Which one of the following convention has neither interstate communication procedure nor individual communication procedure?
A. International Convention on Civil and Political Rights
B. International Convention on Economic, Social and Cultural Rights
C. Convention on the Rights of Child.
D. Convention on the Rights of persons with Disabilities.

60. The term of the office of the Chairperson and Members of the NHRC under Protection of Human Rights Act, 1993 is
A. 5 years from the date on which he enters the office or until he attains the age of 70 years whichever is earlier.
B. 4 years from the date on which he enters the office or until he attains the age of 70 years whichever is earlier.
C. 3 years from the date on which he enters the office or until he attains the age of 68 years whichever is earlier.
D. 5 years from the date on which he enters the office or until he attains the age of 68 years whichever is earlier.

61. The Chairperson of National Commission on Minorities shall be deemed member of
A. Human Rights Council
B. Law Commission of India
C. National Human Rights Commission
D. International Law Commission

62. Which one of the following is an 'actionable' wrong?
A. Injuria sine damnum
B. Damnum sine injuria
C. Both of the above
D. None of the above

63. Which of the following is the gist of tortious liability?
A. Legal damages
B. Violation of legal right
C. Availability of legal duty
D. None of the above

64. The Rule of Absolute Liability is subject to
A. All the exceptions mentioned in the rule of *Rylands* Vs. *Fletcher*
B. Half of the exceptions mentioned in the rule of *Rylands* Vs. *Fletcher*
C. None of the exceptions mentioned in the rule of *Rylands* Vs. *Fletcher*
D. All the exceptions mentioned in rule of *M.C. Mehta* Vs. *Union of* India

65. Assertion (A) : If a person speaks ill of the business which X is doing, it amounts to defamation.

Reason (R) : Slander is actionable *per se.*

Codes:
A. Both (A) and (R) are true and (R) is the correct explanation of (A).
B. Both (A) and (R) are true but (R) is not the correct explanation of (A).
C. (A) is true but (R) is false.
D. (A) is false but (R) is true.

66. In *res Ipsa Loquitor* :
(1) Presumption of negligence is there.
(2) Plaintiff has to bring direct evidence.
(3) Plaintiff is discharged from the duty of proving negligence on the part of the defendant.
(4) Court does not give chance to defendant to avoid his liability.

Codes:
A. (1) and (2) are correct.
B. (1), (2) and (4) are correct.
C. (1), (2) and (3) are correct.
D. (1) and (3) are correct.

67. Which one of the following statements is true?
A. Both public as well as private nuisance are punishable under criminal law.
B. Only private nuisance is punishable under criminal law, while there is no punishment for general nuisance.
C. Public nuisance is punishable under criminal law while private nuisance is a moral wrong only.
D. Public nuisance is punishable under criminal law, while private nuisance under civil law.

68. For constituting tort of nuisance, there should be
A. Unreasonable interference
B. Interference should be with the use of enjoyment of land.
C. Damage
D. All of the above

69. Partnership is based on
A. Mutual trust B. Mutual benefit
C. Mutual interest D. Mutual agency

70. Which statements are correct?
(i) An undisclosed principal can intervene against express terms.
(ii) An undisclosed principal cannot intervene against express terms.
(iii) An undisclosed principal cannot intervene when he knows that the other party would not have dealt with him.
(iv) An undisclosed principal can intervene when he knows that the other party would not have dealt with him.

Codes:
A. (i) and (ii) are correct.
B. (ii) and (iii) are correct.
C. (iii) and (iv) are correct.
D. (iv) and (i) are correct.

71. Read the following passage, and match the column:

A negotiable instrument contains a contract and therefore must be supported by consideration. In order to be a holder in due course, the holder must have obtained the instrument before its maturity. An instrument payable on demand is current at least as long as no demand for payment is made. To make a holder in due course, the instrument must be complete and regular. A postdated cheque may not be complete and regular.

Column-P	Column-Q
(a) Negotiable instrument	(i) Before maturity
(b) Holder in due course	(ii) Demand for payment
(c) Currency of instrument	(iii) Post dated cheque
(d) Complete and regular	(iv) Consideration

Codes:

	(a)	(b)	(c)	(d)
A.	(i)	(iv)	(ii)	(iii)
B.	(ii)	(iii)	(i)	(iv)

C. (iv) (i) (ii) (iii)
D. (iv) (iii) (i) (ii)

72. **Assertion (A) :** Every public company shall have at least three and every private company at least two Directors.

Reason (R) : Directors are trustees for the company and not for individual shareholders.

Codes:

A. (A) and (R) are true, but (R) is not an explanation for (A).
B. (A) and (R) are true and (R) is an explanation for (A).
C. (A) is true, but (R) is false.
D. (R) is true, but (A) is false.

73. Arrange the following concepts in a sequence in which they appeared. Use the code given below:

(i) Right of an unpaid seller to stop goods in transit.
(ii) Agreement to sell goods.
(iii) Damages for breach of contract of sale of goods.
(iv) Conditions and warranties.

Codes:

A. (ii), (iv), (iii), (i)
B. (iv), (ii), (i), (iii)
C. (ii), (i), (iv), (iii)
D. (i), (ii), (iv), (iii)

74. Which statements are correct?

(i) Partner has a duty of good faith.
(ii) Partner has duty not to compete.
(iii) Partner has duty of due diligence.
(iv) Partner has duty to indemnify for fraud.

Codes:

A. Only (i) is correct.
B. Only (i) and (ii) are correct.
C. Only (i), (ii) and (iii) are correct.
D. (i), (ii), (iii) and (iv) are correct.

75. Match an item in List P with an item in List Q :

List-P	List-Q
(a) Removal of Directors by Company Law Board	(i) Section 318
(b) Duty of Directors to disclose interest	(ii) Sections 299-300
(c) Compensation for loss of office of Director	(iii) Section 402
(d) Director with unlimited liability	(iv) Sections 322-323

Codes :

	(a)	(b)	(c)	(d)
A.	(iii)	(ii)	(i)	(iv)
B.	(ii)	(iii)	(i)	(iv)
C.	(ii)	(iii)	(iv)	(i)
D.	(ii)	(i)	(iii)	(iv)

ANSWERS

1	2	3	4	5	6	7	8	9	10
A	A	B	D	A	A	B	C	D	A
11	**12**	**13**	**14**	**15**	**16**	**17**	**18**	**19**	**20**
D	D	D	C	A	D	D	B	B	A
21	**22**	**23**	**24**	**25**	**26**	**27**	**28**	**29**	**30**
C	D	D	A	B	B	C	C	D	B
31	**32**	**33**	**34**	**35**	**36**	**37**	**38**	**39**	**40**
D	D	B	D	D	B	D	C	D	B
41	**42**	**43**	**44**	**45**	**46**	**47**	**48**	**49**	**50**
C	D	A	C	C	D	B	C	C	C
51	**52**	**53**	**54**	**55**	**56**	**57**	**58**	**59**	**60**
D	A	B	B	D	D	D	D	C	A
61	**62**	**63**	**64**	**65**	**66**	**67**	**68**	**69**	**70**
C	A	B	C	C	D	D	D	B	B
71	**72**	**73**	**74**	**75**					
C	A	B	D	A					

YOUR SPACE